WRITERS' & ARTISTS'
YEARBOOK 1992

CW01394371

Writers' & Artists' Yearbook 1992

EIGHTY-FIFTH YEAR OF ISSUE

*A directory for writers, artists, playwrights,
writers for film, radio and television,
photographers and composers*

A & C BLACK · LONDON

© 1992 A & C BLACK (PUBLISHERS) LIMITED
35 BEDFORD ROW, LONDON WC1R 4JH

Apart from any fair dealing for the purposes of research or private study,
or criticism or review, as permitted under the Copyright, Designs and
Patents Act, 1988, this publication may be reproduced, stored or
transmitted, in any form or by any means, only with the prior permission
in writing of the publishers, or in the case of reprographic reproduction in
accordance with the terms of licences issued by the Copyright Licensing
Agency. Inquiries concerning reproduction outside those terms should be
sent to the publishers at the above named address.

The publishers make no representation,
express or implied, with regard to the
accuracy of the information contained
in this book and cannot accept any
legal responsibility for any errors
or omissions that may take place.

A CIP catalogue record for this book
is available from the British Library.

ISBN 0-7136-3486-3

Typeset by Page Bros., Norwich, England
Printed and bound in Great Britain by
BPCC Hazell Books
Aylesbury, Bucks, England

Contents

PART ONE: Markets

Articles, reports, short stories

Books

Illustration and design

Photography

Picture research

Music

Agents

See also SCRIPTS FOR THEATRE,
RADIO, TELEVISION AND FILM section

PART TWO: General Information

Finance

Law and regulations

Publishing practice

Preparation of materials, resources

Societies and prizes

Preface

Writers' & Artists' Yearbook is arranged to form two main parts with fourteen clearly defined sections.

The *first part* provides *Markets* for articles, books, scripts, poetry, illustrations, photographs, picture research and music.

The *second part* offers *General information*, with articles on many practical and legal matters of importance to writers and artists, together with lists of resources and useful addresses. This part also provides details of societies, associations and clubs, as well as a list of literary prizes and awards.

This 85th annual edition of *Writers' & Artists' Yearbook* has been completely revised. Each directory entry is checked and up-dated by its subject so that all addresses, requirements, rates of payment and other details are correct at the time of going to press. All the other sections of the book are carefully revised by reference to the original source.

This 1992 edition includes much new and additional information. Specially commissioned are new articles on *Word Processing*, *Desktop Publishing* and *Picture Research*. *Poetry Publishing Today* has been considerably expanded. A new topic is featured this year, *Pictures into Print*, a practical guide for authors wishing to provide their own illustrations. A detailed index makes for easy and rapid reference.

Vanity publishing Every edition of the *Yearbook* in recent years has contained a strong warning that authors who pay for the publication of their work are almost invariably making an expensive mistake. It has been suggested that several distinguished poets have found it necessary to underwrite their first books in order to establish themselves, and in this respect the cautionary note on 'vanity publishing' on page 230 has been mildly modified; but unhappily there still is ample evidence that an emphatic general warning is necessary.

It should be repeated, too, that the publishers of the *Yearbook* cannot provide an advisory service, and that to rely on an out-of-date edition is to invite inevitable difficulties and disappointments.

PART ONE

Markets

Articles, reports and short stories

SUBMITTING MATERIAL

More than seven hundred titles are included in the United Kingdom newspapers and magazines section of the *Yearbook*, almost all of them offering opportunities to the writer. Some 200 leading Commonwealth and South African titles are also included, and while some of these have little space for freelance contributions, many of them will always consider outstanding work. Many do not appear in our lists because the market they offer for the freelance writer is either too small or too specialised, or both. It is impossible to include all such publications in the *Yearbook*, for the benefit of only a small proportion of its purchasers, without substantially increasing its price. Those who wish to offer contributions to technical, specialist or local journals are likely to know their names and can ascertain their addresses; before submitting a manuscript to any such periodical they are advised to write a preliminary letter to its editor.

Magazine editors frequently complain to us about the unsuitability of many manuscripts submitted to them. Not only are the manuscripts unsuitable, but no postage is sent for their return. In their own interests, writers and others are advised to *enclose postage for the return of unsuitable material*.

Before submitting manuscripts, writers should study carefully the editorial requirements of a magazine; not only for the subjects dealt with, but for the approach, treatment, style and length. Obvious though these comments may be to the practised writer, the beginner would be spared much disappointment by studying the markets more carefully (but should not expect editors to send free specimen copies of their magazines). An article or short story suitable for *Woman's Realm* is unlikely to appeal to the readers of the *Spectator*. The importance of studying the market cannot be over-emphasised. It is an editor's job to know what readers want, and to see that they get it. Thus freelance contributions must be tailored to fit a specific market; subject, theme, treatment, length, etc., must meet the editor's requirements.

Writers and artists, and others, are advised not to accept from editors less than a fair price for their work, and to ascertain exactly what rights they are being asked to dispose of when an offer is made.

It has always been our aim to obtain and publish the rates of payment offered for contributions by newspapers and magazines. Certain journals of the highest standard and reputation are reluctant, for reasons that are understandable, to state a standard rate of payment, since the value of a contribution may be dependent not upon length but upon the standing of the writer or of the information given. Many periodicals when giving a rate of payment indicate that it is the 'minimum rate'; others, in spite of efforts to extract more precise information from them, prefer to state 'by negotiation' or 'by arrangement'.

A number of magazines and newspapers will accept and pay for letters to the editor, paragraphs for gossip columns and brief filler paragraphs. For a list of these see the **Classified Index** at the end of this section. This index provides only a rough guide to markets and must be used with discrimination. For lists of recent mergers, changes of title, and terminations, also see end of this section.

A list of British magazine publishers, with their addresses, follows the Classified Index.

Writing for the UK market Many editors nowadays prefer a preliminary, written query for feature articles. A query should give the title of the proposed article, the first two or three paragraphs, and an indication of the points to be covered, plus a note of any special qualifications and photocopies of previously published work. An sae should be sent with all submissions – both queries and finished articles. Copies should be kept of all material and correspondence, together with a note of telephone conversations.

When a query proposal is accepted – a decision may take up to three months, less for topical material – the following should be confirmed in writing: rate of payment, probable date of publication, rights being offered (usually First British Serial Rights only, see below). Most magazines pay on publication; if the material is not used, full or part payment should be made, provided the writer has fulfilled his/her contract.

Most editors will seek only First British Serial Rights, but it is advisable always to retain ownership of the copyright, to take full advantage of any syndication rights, i.e. further use made of the article, both home and overseas.

Potential contributors living outside the UK should always enclose return postage in the form of International Reply Coupons when submitting queries or MSS. They might also consider approaching an agent to syndicate their material. Most agents operate on an international basis and are more aware of current market requirements. Again, return postage should always be included.

See also *Typescripts* under **Preparation of Materials**, **Resources**, and **Syndicates, News and Press Agencies**.

Writing for EC markets See article on page 102.

Writing for other markets outside the UK The lists of overseas newspapers and magazines contain only a selection of those journals which offer some market for the freelance. To print, and to keep up to date, a complete list for each English-speaking country would increase the extent and cost of the *Yearbook* quite disproportionately to the value of such enlargement. The overseas market for stories and articles is small and editors often prefer their fiction to have a local setting.

The larger newspapers and magazines buy many of their stories, as the smaller papers buy general articles, through one or other of the well-known syndicates, and a writer may be well advised to send printed copies of stories he/she has had published at home to an agent for syndication overseas.

Most of the big newspapers depend for news on their own staffs and the press agencies. The most important papers have permanent representatives in Britain who keep them supplied, not only with news of especial interest to the country concerned, but also with regular summaries of British news and with articles on events of particular importance. While many overseas newspapers and magazines have a London office, it is usual for MSS from freelance contributors to be submitted to the headquarters' editorial office overseas.

When sending MSS abroad it is important to remember to enclose International Reply Coupons; these can be exchanged in any foreign country for stamps representing the minimum postage payable on a letter sent from that country to this country.

List of Newspapers and Magazines

UNITED KINGDOM

(For Northern Ireland publications, see under Irish listings, page 93.)

Aberdeen Evening Express, R.J. Williamson, Lang Stracht, Aberdeen AB9 8AF *tel* (0224) 690222 *telex* 73133 Jnlsab G *fax* (0224) 699575.
22p. D. Lively evening paper reading. *Illustrations:* mainly half-tone, some colour. *Payment:* by arrangement.

Accountancy (1889), Brian Singleton-Green, 40 Bernard Street, London WC1N 1LD *tel* 071-833 3291 *fax* 071-833 2085.
£2.85. M. Articles on accounting, taxation, financial, legal and other subjects likely to be of professional interest to accountants in practice or industry, and to top management generally. *Illustrations:* cartoons. *Payment:* £100 per page; £40.

Accountancy Age (1969), Peter Williams, VNU Business Publications, VNU House, 32-34 Broadwick Street, London W1A 2HG *tel* 071-439 4242 *telex* 23918 VNU G *fax* 071-437 7001.
£1.50. W. Articles of accounting, financial and business interest. *Illustrations:* colour and b&w photos; freelance assignments commissioned. *Payment:* by arrangement; NUJ rates.

Accounting World (1920), Garry Carter, The Publishing Dimension Ltd, 13 High Street, Windsor, Berks. SL4 1LD *tel* (0753) 830909 *fax* (0753) 830034. Journal of The Institute of Financial Accountants and The International Association of Book-keepers, Burford House, 44 London Road, Sevenoaks, Kent TN13 1AS *tel* (0732) 458080.
£18.00 p.a. M. Articles on accounting, management, company law, data processing, information technology, pensions, factoring, investment, insurance, fraud prevention and general business administration. *Length:* 1000-2000 words. *Illustrations:* offset litho (mono or colour). *Payment:* by arrangement.

Achievement, World Trade House, 145 High Street, Sevenoaks, Kent TN13 1XJ *tel* (0732) 458144.
£1.50. Q. Lively articles relating to British business achievements in international project management. *Illustrations:* first-class photos. *Payment:* by arrangement.

Acumen (1985), Patricia Oxley, 6 The Mount, Higher Furzeham, Brixham, South Devon TQ5 8QY *tel* (08045) 51098.
£5.00 p.a. Bi-annual (Apr/Oct). Poetry, literary articles, interviews with poets on poetry. Send sae with submissions. *Illustrations:* line drawings. *Payment:* by negotiation.

Administrator (1971), 16 Park Crescent, London W1N 4AH *tel* 071-580 4741 *fax* 071-323 1132.
£2.50. M. (£32.00 p.a. post free) Official journal of The Institute of Chartered Secretaries and Administrators. Practical and topical articles 750-1600 words on law, finance and development affecting company secretaries and other senior administrators in business, nationalised industries, local and central government and other institutions in Britain and overseas. Most articles commissioned from leading administrators. *Illustrations:* line, half-tone. *Payment:* by arrangement.

Aeromodeller (1935), Geoff Clarke, Argus Specialist Publications, Argus House, Boundary Way, Hemel Hempstead, Herts. HP2 7ST   *tel* (0442) 66551   *fax* (0442) 66998.
£1.95. M. Articles and news concerning model aircraft and radio control of model aircraft. Suitable articles and first-class photos by outside contributors are always considered. *Length:* 750-2000 words, or by arrangement. *Illustrations:* photos and line drawings to scale.

Aeroplane Monthly (1973), Richard R. Riding, Prospect Magazines, IPC Magazines, Prospect House, 9-13 Ewell Road, Cheam, Surrey SM1 4QQ   *tel* 081-661 6854   *telex* 892084   *fax* 081-642 6562.
£2.00. M. Articles relating to historical aviation. *Length:* up to 2500 words. *Illustrations:* line, half-tone, colour. *Payment:* £35 per 1000 words; photos £10; colour £40 minimum.

African Business (1978), Linda Van Buren, PO Box 261, Carlton House, 69 Great Queen Street, London WC2B 5BN   *tel* 071-404 4333   *telex* 8811757 Araby G   *fax* 071-404 5336.
£1.50. M. Articles on business, economic and financial topics of interest to businessmen, ministers, officials concerned with African affairs. *Length:* 400-750 words; shorter coverage 100-400 words. *Illustrations:* line, half-tone. *Payment:* £70 per 1000 words; £1 per column cm.

Agenda, William Cookson and Peter Dale, 5 Cranbourne Court, Albert Bridge Road, London SW11 4PE   *tel* 071-228 0700.
£16.00 p.a. Q. (libraries, institutions and overseas: rates on application) Poetry and criticism. Contributors should study the journal before submitting MSS with an sae. *Illustrations:* half-tone. *Payment:* £12 per poem or per page of poetry, £8 per page for reviews and criticism; illustrations £35.

Air Pictorial, HPC Publishing, Drury Lane, Hastings, East Sussex TN34 1XW   *tel* (0424) 720477   *fax* (0424) 443693/434086. Editor: Ian Hawkins *tel* (0621) 856990   *fax* (0621) 852310.
£1.50. M. Covers all aspects of aviation. Many articles commissioned, and the editor is glad to consider competent articles exploring fresh ground or presenting an individual point of view on technical matters. *Illustrations:* line, half-tone; new photos of unusual or rare aircraft considered. *Payment:* £18 per 1000 words; £2.50 minimum.

Amateur Gardening (1884), G. Clarke, Westover House, West Quay Road, Poole, Dorset BH15 1JG   *tel* (0202) 680586   *fax* (0202) 674335.
35p. W. Articles up to 700 words about any aspect of gardening. *Payment:* by arrangement. *Illustrations:* colour.

Amateur Photographer (1884), Keith Wilson, IPC Magazines Ltd, King's Reach Tower, Stamford Street, London SE1 9LS   *tel* 071-261 5000.
£1.10. W. Original articles of pictorial or technical interest, preferably illustrated with either photos or diagrams. Good instructional features especially sought. *Length preferred:* (unillustrated) 400-800 words: articles up to 1500 words; (illustrated) 2 to 4 pages. *Payment:* monthly, at rates according to usage. *Illustrations* unaccompanied by text will be considered for covers or feature illustrations; please indicate if we can hold on file.

Amateur Stage (1946), Charles Vance, 83 George Street, London W1H 5PL   *tel* 071-486 1732/7930   *fax* 071-224 2215.
£1.50. M. Articles on all aspects of the amateur theatre, preferably practical and factual. *Length:* 600-2000 words. *Illustrations:* photos and line drawings. *Payment:* none.

Ambit (1959), Dr Martin Bax, 17 Priory Gardens, Highgate, London N6 5QY *tel* 081-340 3566.
£5.00. Q. Poems, short stories, criticism. *Payment:* by arrangement. *Illustrations:* line, half-tone.

Angler's Mail, Roy Westwood, IPC Magazines Ltd, King's Reach Tower, Stamford Street, London SE1 9LS *tel* 071-261 5778.
60p. W. Features and news items about sea, coarse and game fishing. *Length:* 650-800 words. *Payment:* by arrangement. *Illustrations:* half-tone, colour, line and wash drawings (Web offset litho printing).

Angling Times (1953), Neil Pope, EMAP Pursuit Publishing Ltd, Bretton Court, Bretton, Peterborough PE3 8DZ *tel* (0733) 266222/264666 *fax* (0733) 265515.
55p. W. Articles, pictures, news stories, on all forms of angling. *Illustrations:* line, half-tone, colour. *Payment:* by arrangement.

Animal World, Michaela Miller, RSPCA, Causeway, Horsham, West Sussex RH12 1HG *tel* (0403) 64181.
50p. 6 p.a. RSPCA magazine for junior members aged 17 and under. News stories and features about animal welfare and RSPCA activities. Unsolicited material from contributors other than junior members rarely published.

Annabel, D.C. Thomson & Co. Ltd, 80 Kingsway East, Dundee DD4 8SL, and 185 Fleet Street, London EC4A 2HS.
85p. M. Colour gravure monthly for the modern woman with wide interests. Biographical stories of well-known personalities, family and parenthood topics, fashion, cookery, knitting, fiction. Art *illustrations* and photos in full colour and b&w. *Payment:* on acceptance.

The Antique Collector (1930), David Coombs, Eagle House, 50 Marshall Street, London W1V 1LR *tel* 071-439 5000 *fax* 071-439 5177.
£3.00. M. Authoritative, topical and fully illustrated information for those interested in extending their knowledge and enjoyment of all aspects of antiques and art. *Illustrations:* fine b&w and colour photos. *Payment:* £150 per feature; at cost.

The Antique Dealer & Collectors Guide, Philip Bartlam, PO Box 85, Greenwich, London SE10 8TD *tel* 081-691 4820.
£2.25. M. Articles on antique collecting and art. *Length:* 1500-2000 words. *Payment:* £76 per 1000 words. *Illustrations:* half-tone, colour.

Antiques Folio (incorporating **Antiques**) (1963), Maria Rayska, Old Rectory, Hopton Castle, Craven Arms, Shropshire SY7 0QJ *tel* (05474) 464.
50p. Q. Articles on antiques and of interest to antique dealers and serious collectors. *Length:* 300-600 words. *Payment:* on merit. *Illustrations:* line, half-tone.

Apollo (1925), Robin Simon, 3 St James's Place, London SW1A 1NP *tel* 071-629 4331 *fax* 071-491 1682.
£4.50. M. Knowledgeable articles of about 2500 words on art, ceramics, furniture, armour, glass, sculpture, and any subject connected with art and collecting. *Payment:* by arrangement. *Illustrations:* half-tone, colour.

The Aquarist and Pondkeeper (1924), John Dawes, Dog World Ltd, 9 Tufton Street, Ashford, Kent TN23 1QN *tel* (0233) 621877 *fax* (0233) 645669.
£1.40. M. Illustrated authoritative articles by professional and amateur biologists, naturalists and aquarium hobbyists on all matters concerning life in and near water, conservation and herpetology. *Length:* about 1500 words. *Illustrations:* line, half-tone, colour. *Payment:* by arrangement.

The Architects' Journal (1895), 33-35 Bowling Green Lane, London EC1R 0DA   *tel* 071-837 1212   *fax* 071-833 3073.
£1.25. W. Articles (mainly technical) on architecture, planning and building accepted only with prior agreement of synopsis. *Illustrations:* photos and drawings. *Payment:* by arrangement.

Architectural Design (1930), Dr Andreas C. Papadakis, Academy Group Ltd, 42 Leinster Gardens, London W2 3AN   *tel* 071-402 2141   *telex* 896928 Academy G   *fax* 071-723 9540.
£49.50 p.a. 6 double issues. International magazine comprising an extensively illustrated thematic profile presenting architecture and critical interpretations of architectural history, theory and practice. Uncommissioned articles not accepted. *Illustrations:* drawings and photos, colour, half-tone, line (colour preferred). *Payment:* by arrangement.

Architectural Review (1896), Peter Davey, 33-35 Bowling Green Lane, London EC1R 0DA   *tel* 071-837 1212   *telex* 299049 Mbcbgl G   *fax* 071-278 4003.
£4.75. M. Articles on architecture and the allied arts. Writers must be thoroughly qualified. *Length:* up to 3000 words. *Payment:* by arrangement. *Illustrations:* photos, drawings, etc.

Arena (1986), The Old Laundry, Ossington Buildings, London W1M 3HY   *tel* 071-935 8232   *fax* 071-935 2237.
£2.00. Bi-M. Profiles, articles on a wide range of subjects intelligently treated; art, architecture, politics, sport, business, music, film, design, media, fashion. *Length:* up to 3000 words. *Payment:* £130 per 1000 words. *Illustrations:* b&w and colour photos.

Army Quarterly & Defence Journal (1829), Editor: T.D. Bridge, Research Director: Major-General H.M. Tillotson, 1 West Street, Tavistock, Devon PL19 8DS   *tel* (0822) 613577/612785   *fax* (0822) 612785.
£40.00 p.a. Q. (£105.00 3-yr saver contract) Articles on a wide range of British and international defence issues, historical and current, and UN forces; also Quarterly Diary, Defence Contracts, International Defence Review, book reviews. *Length:* 1000-6000 words. *Preliminary letter preferred. Illustrations:* b&w photos, line drawings, maps. *Payment:* by arrangement.

Art & Craft (1946), Eileen Lowcock, Scholastic Publications (Magazines) Ltd, Villiers House, Clavendon Avenue, Leamington Spa, Warks. CV32 5PR   *tel* (0926) 887799   *fax* (0926) 883331.
£1.50. M. Articles offering fresh, creative ideas of a practical nature, based on sound art practice, for the infant/junior school teacher. Articles by experts on traditional crafts. *Illustrations:* colour and b&w line drawings. *Payment:* by arrangement.

Art & Design (1985), Dr Andreas C. Papadakis, Academy Group Ltd, 42 Leinster Gardens, London W2 3AN   *tel* 071-402 2141   *telex* 896928 Academ G   *fax* 071-723 9540.
£39.50 p.a. 6 double issues. International magazine covering the whole spectrum of the arts, with particular emphasis on New Art. Each issue comprises extensively illustrated thematic features together with critical articles from well-known writers. Feature articles, exhibition reviews/previews, book reviews. Uncommissioned articles not accepted. *Illustrations:* line, half-tone, colour (colour preferred). *Payment:* by arrangement.

Art Business Today (1991; formerly **The Fine Art Trade Guild Journal**), The Fine Art Trade Guild, 16-18 Empress Place, London SW6 1TT   *tel* 071-381 6616   *fax* 071-381 2596.

£2.50. Q. Distributed to the fine art and framing industry. Covers essential information on new products and technology, market trends and business analysis. *Length:* 2000-3000 words wi*+*h clear *illustrations.* *Payment:* NUJ rates.

The Artist (1931), Sally Bulgin, Caxton House, 63-65 High Street, Tenterden, Kent TN30 6BD *tel* (05806) 3673.
£1.50. M. Practical and appreciative articles on all aspects of the visual arts. *Payment:* by arrangement. *Illustrations:* line, half-tone, colour.

The Artist's & Illustrator's Magazine (1986), Meryl Ryan, 4th Floor, 4 Brandon Road, London N7 9TP *tel* 071-609 2177 *telex* 299656 Cii G *fax* 071-700 4985.
£1.85. M. Mainly technical and practical articles on all the artistic media. *Length:* 1500-2000 words. *Payment:* £80 per 1000 words. *Illustrations:* colour transparencies.

Artrage, Black Arts Quarterly (1982), Jacob Ross, 28 Shacklewell Lane, London E8 2EZ *tel* 071-254 7275.
£2.00. Q. Black literature, performing arts and media arts, including arts reviews, interviews, poetry. *Length/payment:* 500-1000 words, £30; 1000-1800 words, £50-£80. *Illustrations:* line, half-tone.

Arts Review (1949), Starcity Ltd, 69 Faroe Road, London W14 0EL *tel* 071-603 7530/8533.
£2.20. F. (£49.00 p.a.) Art criticism and reviews. Commissioned work only. *Payment:* modest. *Illustrations:* line, half-tone, colour.

Asian Times (1982), Arif Ali, Hansib Publishing Ltd, Tower House, 139/149 Fonthill Road, London N4 3HF *tel* 071-281 1191 *fax* 071-263 9656.
40p. W. News stories, articles and features of interest to Asian readers. *Illustrations:* line, half-tone. *Payment:* by negotiation; £10 minimum.

The Author (1890), Derek Parker, 84 Drayton Gardens, London SW10 9SB *tel* 071-373 6642.
£4.50. Q. Organ of The Society of Authors. Commissioned articles from 1000-2000 words on any subject connected with the legal, commercial or technical side of authorship. Little scope for the freelance writer: *preliminary letter* advisable. *Payment:* by arrangement.

Auto Express (1988), Andrew Bordiss, United Consumer Magazines Ltd, Ludgate House, 245 Blackfriars Road, London SE1 9UZ *tel* 071-921 5900 *fax* 071-928 9847.
90p. W. News stories, and general interest features about drivers as well as cars. *Illustrations:* colour photos. *Payment:* features £150 per 1000 words; photos, varies.

Autocar & Motor (1895), Bob Murray, Haymarket Publishing Ltd, 38-42 Hampton Road, Teddington, Middlesex TW11 0JE *tel* 081-943 5013 *telex* 8952440 *fax* 081-943 5653.
£1.10. W. Articles on all aspects of cars, motoring and motor industries: general, practical, competition and technical. *Payment:* varies; mid-month following publication. *Illustrations:* tone, line (litho) and colour. Press day news: Friday.

Back Street Heroes (1983), Steven Myatt, PO Box 28, Altrincham, Cheshire WA15 8SH *tel* 061-928 3480 *fax* 061-941 6897.
£1.60. M. Custom motorcycle features plus informed life style pieces. Biker fiction. *Payment:* by arrangement. *Illustrations:* half-tone, colour, cartoons.

Balance (1935), Lesley Hallett, The British Diabetic Association, 10 Queen Anne Street, London W1M 0BD   *tel* 071-323 1531   *fax* 071-637 3644.
£1.00. Bi-M. Articles on diabetes or related topics. *Length:* 1000-2000 words. *Payment:* £75 per 1000 words. *Illustrations:* line, half-tone, colour.

Ballroom Dancing Times (1956), Executive Editor: Mary Clarke, Clerkenwell House, 45-47 Clerkenwell Green, London EC1R 0BE   *tel* 071-250 3006.
65p. M. Ballroom dancing from every aspect, but chiefly from the serious competitive, teaching and medal test angles. Well-informed freelance articles are occasionally used, but only after preliminary arrangements. *Payment:* by arrangement. *Illustrations:* web offset; action photos preferred.

The Banker (1926), Gavin Shreeve, 102-8 Clerkenwell Road, London EC1M 5SA   *tel* 071-251 9321   *telex* 23700 Finbi G   *fax* 071-251 4686.
£3.50. M. Articles on capital markets, trade finance, bank analysis and top 1000 listings. *Illustrations:* half-tones of people, charts, tables. *Payment:* by negotiation.

Banking World (1983), Garth Hewitt, 3rd Floor, Greater London House, Hampstead Road, London NW1 7QQ   *tel* 071-822 3630   *telex* 922488 Bureau G ref HWY   *fax* 071-383 7570.
£2.50. M. Commissioned articles on developments in retail banking world-wide. *Length:* 200-2000 words. *Illustrations:* line, half-tone. *Payment:* by arrangement.

Baptist Times (1855), John Capon, PO Box 54, Didcot, Oxon OX11 8XB   *tel* (0235) 512012   *fax* (0235) 512013.
28p. W. Religious or social affairs material, up to 800 words. *Payment:* by arrangement. *Illustrations:* half-tone.

BBC Wildlife Magazine, Rosamund Kidman Cox, Broadcasting House, White-ladies Road, Bristol BS8 2LR   *tel* (0272) 732211   *fax* (0272) 467075.
£1.60. M. Popular but scientifically accurate articles about wildlife and conservation (national and international), some linked by subject to BBC TV and radio programmes. Two news sections for short, topical biological and environmental stories. *Length:* 1000-2000 words. *Illustrations:* top-quality colour and b&w photos. *Payment:* £200-£350 per article; according to reproduction size, £35-£140.

The Beano, D.C. Thomson & Co. Ltd, Courier Place, Dundee DD1 9QJ   *tel* (0382) 23131   *fax* (0382) 22214; and 185 Fleet Street, London EC4A 2HS   *tel* 071-242 5086   *fax* 071-404 5694.
26p. W. Comic strips for children. Series, 11-22 pictures. *Payment:* on acceptance.

Beano Library, D.C. Thomson & Co. Ltd, Courier Place, Dundee DD1 9QJ   *tel* (0382) 23131   *fax* (0382) 22214; and 185 Fleet Street, London EC4A 2HS   *tel* 071-242 5086   *fax* 071-404 5694.
35p. 2 p.m. Extra-long comic adventure stories featuring well-known characters from the weekly Beano publication.

Beano Puzzle Library, D.C. Thomson & Co. Ltd, Courier Place, Dundee DD1 9QJ   *tel* (0382) 23131   *fax* (0382) 22214; and 185 Fleet Street, London EC4A 2HS   *tel* 071-242 5086   *fax* 071-404 5694.
35p. M. 64 pages of puzzles, word-games and teasers featuring the well-known characters from the weekly Beano, Dandy and Beezer-Topper publications.

Bedfordshire Magazine (1947), Betty Chambers, 50 Shefford Road, Mepper-shall, Shefford SG17 5LL   *tel* Hitchin (0462) 813363.

£1.25. Q. Articles of Bedfordshire interest, especially history and biography. *Length:* up to 1500 words. *Illustrations:* line, half-tone. *Payment:* £1.05 per 1000 words; by agreement.

Beezer-Topper, D.C. Thomson & Co. Ltd, Courier Place, Dundee DD1 9QJ *tel* (0382) 23131 *fax* (0382) 22214; and 185 Fleet Street, London EC4A 2HS *tel* 071-242 5086 *fax* 071-404 5694.
35p. W. Comic strips for boys and girls. Approx. 10 pictures per single page story and 18 pictures per double page story. Promising artists encouraged. *Payment:* on acceptance.

Bella (1987), Editor-in-Chief: Sharon Brown, Shirley House, 25 Camden Road, London NW1 9LL *tel* 071-284 0909.
40p. W. General interest magazine for women. Practical articles on fashion and beauty, health, cooking, home, travel. Short stories up to 2000 words. *Payment:* by arrangement. *Illustrations:* half-tone, line including cartoons, colour.

Best (1987), Caroline Richards, 10th Floor, Portland House, Stag Place, London SW1E 5AU *tel* 071-245 8700 *fax* 071-245 8825.
48p. W. Short stories (accepted Apr and Oct *only*), articles, celebrity interviews, features. *Length:* from small columns to 1500-word features. *Illustrations:* line, half-tone, colour, cartoons. *Payment:* by agreement.

Bicycle Action (1984), Karin Zeitvogel, Stonehart Leisure Magazines, 67-71 Goswell Road, London EC1V 7EN *tel* 071-250 1881 *fax* 071-410 9440.
£1.75. M. Racing, touring, mountain bikes, fitness, technical. Emphasis on sports and active cycling. *Payment:* by arrangement.

Birmingham Evening Mail (1870), I. Dowell, Colmore Circus, Birmingham B4 6AX *tel* 021-236 3366 *telex* 337552. London Office: 19-21 Tudor Street, EC4Y 0AL *tel* 071-353 0811.
22p. D. Ind. Features of topical Midland interest considered. *Length:* 400-800 words.

The Birmingham Post, V. Kelly, PO Box 18, 28 Colmore Circus, Birmingham B4 6AX *tel* 021-236 3366 *telex* 337552. London Office: 19-21 Tudor Street, EC4Y 0LA *tel* 071-353 0811.
22p. D. Authoritative and well-written articles of industrial, political or general interest are considered, especially if they have relevance to the Midlands. *Length:* up to 1000 words. *Payment:* by arrangement.

Blue Jeans Photo Novels, D.C. Thomson & Co. Ltd, Courier Place, Dundee DD1 9QJ *tel* (0382) 23131 *fax* (0382) 22214; and 185 Fleet Street, London EC4A 2HS *tel* 071-242 5086 *fax* 071-404 5694.
35p. 4 p.m. Teenage stories in photo story form, approx. 120 frames. Scripts required. *Payment:* on acceptance.

Boards (1982), Jeremy Evans, 196 Eastern Esplanade, Southend-on-Sea, Essex SS1 3AB *tel* (0702) 582245 *fax* (0702) 588434.
£1.70. 9 p.a. (M. during summer, Bi-M. during winter) Articles, photos and reports on all aspects of windsurfing and boardsailing. *Payment:* by arrangement. *Illustrations:* line, half-tone, colour.

Bolton Evening News (1867), Chris Walder, Newspaper House, Churchgate, Bolton, Lancs. BL1 1DE *tel* (0204) 22345 *telegraphic address* Newspapers, Bolton.
22p. D. Articles, particularly those with South Lancashire appeal. *Length:* up to 700 words. *Illustrations:* photos; considered at usual rates. *Payment:* on 15th of month following date of publication.

The Book Collector (1952) (incorporating **Bibliographical Notes and Queries**), Editorial Board: Nicolas Barker (Editor), A. Bell, J. Commander, J. Fergusson, T. Hofmann, D. McKitterick, The Collector Ltd, 68 Neal Street, London WC2H 9PA   *tel* 071-379 5416   *fax* 071-379 0132.
£25.00 p.a. ($45.00), postage extra. Q. Articles, biographical and bibliographical, on the collection and study of printed books and MSS. *Payment:* for reviews only.

Book News From Wales—see **Llais Llyfrau**.

Books Magazine (1987), Rodney Burbeck, 43 Museum Street, London WC1A 1LY   *tel* 071-404 0304   *fax* 071-242 0762.
£1.20. Bi-M. Reviews, features, interviews with authors. *Payment:* negotiable.

The Bookseller (1858), Louis Baum, J. Whitaker and Sons Ltd, 12 Dyott Street, London WC1A 1DF   *tel* 071-836 8911   *fax* 071-836 6381.
£74.00 p.a. W. Journal of the publishing and bookselling trades. While outside contributions are always welcomed, most of the journal's contents are commissioned. *Length:* about 1000-1500 words. *Payment:* by arrangement.

Bowls International (1981), Chris Mills, Key Publishing Ltd, PO Box 100, Stamford, Lincs. PE9 1XQ   *tel* (0780) 55131   *telex* 265871 Monref G Attn YQQ332   *fax* (0780) 57261.
£1.30. M. Sport and news items and features; occasional, bowls-oriented short stories. *Illustrations:* colour transparencies, b&w photos, occasional line. *Payment:* sport/news approx. 10p per line, features approx. £25 per page; colour £20-£25, b&w £8-£10.

Brewing & Distilling International (1865), Bruce Stevens, 52 Glenhouse Road, Eltham, London SE9 1JQ   *tel* 01-859 4300   *fax* 01-859 5813.
Controlled circulation. M. Journal for brewers, maltsters, hop merchants, distillers, soft drinks manufacturers, bottlers and allied traders, circulating in over 80 countries. Technical and marketing articles (average 1000 words) accepted, by prior arrangement, from authors with specialist knowledge. *Illustrations:* line drawings, photos. *Payment:* by prior agreement with editor.

Bridge (formerly **Bridge International**) (1926), Paul Lamford, Pergamon Bridge, Railway Road, Sutton Coldfield, West Midlands B73 6AZ   *tel* 021-354 2536/7   *fax* 021-355 0655.
£21.95 p.a. M. Articles on bidding and play; instruction, competitions, tournament reports and humour. *Payment:* by arrangement. *Illustrations:* line, half-tone.

Bristol Evening Post (1932), A. King, Temple Way, Bristol BS99 7HD   *tel* (0272) 260080.
22p. D.

La Brita Esperantisto (1905), W. Auld, 140 Holland Park Avenue, London W11 4UF   *tel* 071-727 7821.
£2.20. M. (£12.00 p.a.) Journal of the Esperanto Association de Britujo. Articles in Esperanto, by arrangement, on the applications of the International Language, Esperanto, to education, commerce, travel, international affairs, scouting, radio, television, literature, linguistics, etc. *Illustrations:* photos by arrangement. *Payment:* by arrangement.

British Birds (1907), Dr J.T.R. Sharrock, Fountains, Park Lane, Blunham, Bedford MK44 3NJ   *tel* (0767) 40025.
£38.40 p.a. M. Original observations relating to birds on the West Palearctic list. *Illustrations:* line, half-tone, colour. *Payment:* none.

British Book News (1940), Jennifer Creswick, The British Council, 65 Davies Street, London W1Y 2AA   *tel* 071-930 8466   *telex* 8952201 Bricon G   *fax* 071-493 5035. Subscriptions: Journal Dept, Basil Blackwell, 108 Cowley Road, Oxford OX4 1JF.
£33.50 p.a. M. (£46.00 p.a. institutions; overseas rates on application) High quality articles on the book trade, book surveys, company profiles and reviews of new journals. *Length:* up to 2000 words. *Payment:* by arrangement.

British Chess Magazine (1881), B. Cafferty, 9 Market Street, St Leonards-on-Sea, East Sussex TN38 0DQ   *tel* (0424) 424009   *fax* (0424) 435439.
£1.95. M. (£22.20 p.a. post free) Articles, 800-2500 words, on historical and cultural aspects of chess. *Payment:* by arrangement.

The British Deaf News (1955), Mrs Irene Hall, The British Deaf Association, 38 Victoria Place, Carlisle CA1 1HU   *tel* (0228) 48844 (Voice), (0228) 28719 (DCT)   *fax* (0228) 41420.
50p. M. (£9.50 p.a.) Articles, news items, letters dealing with deafness. *Payment:* by arrangement. *Illustrations:* line, half-tone.

British Journal of General Practice (formerly **Journal of the Royal College of General Practitioners**), Dr A.F. Wright, FRCGP, 12 Queen Street, Edinburgh EH2 1JE   *tel* 031-225 7629   *fax* 031-220 6750.
£90.00 p.a. M. (£100 overseas, £110 by airmail). Articles relevant to general medical practice. *Payment:* none. *Illustrations:* half-tone, colour.

The British Journal of Photography (1854), Chris Dickie, Henry Greenwood & Co. Ltd, 58 Fleet Street (entrance 3 Pleydell Street), London EC4Y 1JU   *tel* 071-583 0175   *fax* 071-583 5183.
£1.00. W. Articles on professional, commercial and press photography, and on the more advanced aspects of amateur, technical, industrial, medical, scientific and colour photography. *Payment:* by arrangement. *Illustrations:* line, half-tone, colour.

British Journal of Special Education, Margaret Peter, 12 Hollycroft Avenue, London NW3 7QL   *tel* 071-794 7109.
£20.00 p.a. Q. (£40.00 p.a. UK institutions) Official Journal of the National Council for Special Education. Articles by specialists on the education of the physically, mentally and emotionally handicapped, including the medical, therapeutic and sociological aspects of special education. *Length:* about 2000-3000 words. *Payment:* by arrangement. *Illustrations:* line, half-tone.

British Journalism Review (1989), Geoffrey Goodman, BJR Publishing Ltd, 27 Meadowbrook, Old Oxted, Surrey RH8 9LT   *tel* (0883) 715242   *fax* (0883) 730803.
£5.00. Q. Comment/criticism/review of matters published by, or of interest to, the media. *Length:* 1000-3000 words. *Illustrations:* b&w photos. *Payment:* £100 per 1000 words; £25.

British Medical Journal (1840), Richard Smith, BSc, MB, ChBEd, British Medical Association House, Tavistock Square, London WC1H 9JR   *tel* 071-387 4499.
£3.50. W. Medical and related articles.

British Printer (1888), Sian Griffiths, Maclean Hunter House, Chalk Lane, Cockfosters Road, Barnet, Herts. EN4 0BU   *tel* 081-975 9759.
£35.00 p.a. M. Articles on technical and aesthetic aspects of printing processes and graphic reproduction. *Payment:* by arrangement. *Illustrations:* offset litho from photos, line drawings and diagrams.

British-Soviet Friendship (formerly **Russia To-day**) (1927), 36 St John's Square, London EC1V 4JH   *tel* 071-253 4161.

80p. M. Illustrated magazine on British-Soviet relations. Good photos and well-informed news items and articles up to 900 words (on Soviet Union and British-Soviet relations). *Payment:* for articles and photos only by special arrangement.

Broadcast, Marta Wohrle, 7 Swallow Place, London W1R 7AA   *tel* 071-491 9484   *telex* 299973 Itp Lng   *fax* 071-355 3177.
£1.40. W. (£75.00 p.a.) News and authoritative articles designed for all concerned with the British broadcast and non-broadcast industries, and with programmes and advertising on television, radio, video, cable, satellite, business. *Payment:* by arrangement.

Brownie, Lynn Hurdwell, 17-19 Buckingham Palace Road, London SW1W 0PT   *tel* 071-834 6242.
85p. M. Official Magazine of The Girl Guides Association. Short articles for Brownies (girls 7-10 years); serials with Brownie background (500-800 words per instalment); puzzles; 'things to make', etc. *Illustrations:* line, colour. *Payment:* £40 per 1000 words; varies.

Budgerigar World (1982), The County Press, Bala, Gwynedd LL23 7PG   *tel* (0678) 520262.
£1.60. M. (£20.00 p.a.) Articles about exhibition budgerigars. *Payment:* by arrangement. *Illustrations:* half-tone, colour.

Building (1842), Peter Bill, Builder House, 1 Millharbour, London E14 9RA   *tel* 071-537 2222   *fax* 071-537 2007.
£1.50. W. Covers the entire professional, industrial and manufacturing aspects of the building industry. Articles on architecture and techniques at home and abroad considered, also news and photos. *Payment:* by arrangement.

Built Environment, Professor Peter Hall, Alexandrine Press, PO Box 15, 51 Cornmarket Street, Oxford OX1 3EB   *tel* (0865) 724627   *fax* (0865) 792309.
£37.50 p.a. M. Articles about architecture, planning and the environment. *Length:* 1000-5000 words. *Preliminary letter* advisable. *Payment:* by arrangement. *Illustrations:* photos and line.

Bulletin of Hispanic Studies (1923), D.S. Severin and A.L. Mackenzie, Department of Hispanic Studies, The University, PO Box 147, Liverpool L69 3BX   *tel* 051-794 2775/2774. Published by the Liverpool University Press, PO Box 147, Liverpool L69 3BX.
£18.50 p.a. Q. (£47.00 p.a. institutions, £10.00 p.a. students) Specialist articles on the languages and literatures of Spain, Portugal and Latin America, written in English, Spanish, Portuguese, Catalan or French. *Payment:* none.

Bunty, D.C. Thomson & Co. Ltd, Courier Place, Dundee DD1 9QJ   *tel* (0382) 23131   *fax* (0382) 22214; and 185 Fleet Street, London EC4A 2HS   *tel* 071-242 5086   *fax* 071-404 5694.
33p. W. Vividly told picture-story serials for young girls of school age: 16-18 frames in each 2-page instalment; 23-24 frames in each 3-page instalment. Comic strips and features. Special encouragement to promising scriptwriters and artists. *Payment:* on acceptance.

Bunty Library, D.C. Thomson & Co. Ltd, Courier Place, Dundee DD1 9QJ   *tel* (0382) 23131   *fax* (0382) 22214; and 185 Fleet Street, London EC4A 2HS   *tel* 071-242 5086   *fax* 071-404 5694.
35p. M. Picture-stories for schoolgirls, 64 pages (about 140 line drawings): ballet, school, adventure, theatre, sport. Scripts considered; promising artists and scriptwriters encouraged. *Payment:* on acceptance.

Burlington Magazine (1903), Caroline Elam, 6 Bloomsbury Square, London WC1A 2LP   *tel* 071-430 0481   *fax* 071-242 1205.

£8.25. M. Deals with the history and criticism of art. Average *length* of article, 500-3000 words. The editor can use only articles by those who have special knowledge of the subjects treated and cannot accept MSS compiled from works of reference. Book and exhibition reviews and an illustrated monthly Calendar section. No verse. *Payment:* up to £100. *Illustrations:* almost invariably made from photos.

Buses (1949), Stephen Morris, Terminal House, Station Approach, Shepperton, Middlesex TW17 8AS *tel* (0932) 228950 *fax* (0932) 232366.
£1.45. M. Articles of interest to both road passenger transport operators and bus enthusiasts. *Preliminary enquiry* essential. *Illustrations:* colour transparencies, half-tone, line maps. *Payment:* on application.

Business (1986), Christopher Parkes, 234 King's Road, London SW3 5UA *tel* 071-351 7351 *telex* 914549 Intmag G *fax* 071-351 2794.
£2.00. M. Business and finance articles. *Illustrations:* photos, graphics, colour. *Payment:* by arrangement. Ceased publication.

Business Scotland (1947), Graham Lironi, Peebles Publishing Group, Bergius House, Clifton Street, Glasgow G3 7LA *tel* 041-331 1022 *fax* 041-331 1395.
Controlled circulation. M. Features, profiles and news items of interest to business and finance in Scotland. *Payment:* by arrangement.

Buster (1960), Greater London House, Hampstead Road, London NW1 7QQ *tel* 071-383 7156.
40p. W. Juvenile comic. Comedy characters in picture strips, for children aged 6 to 12. Full colour, 2 colour and b&w.

Cage and Aviary Birds (1902), Brian Byles, Prospect House, 9-13 Ewell Road, Cheam, Sutton, Surrey SM1 4QQ *tel* 081-661 4491 *fax* 081-661 0887.
70p. W. Practical articles on aviculture. First-hand knowledge only. *Illustrations:* line, half-tone, colour. *Payment:* by arrangement.

Campaign, Dominic Mills, 22 Lancaster Gate, London W2 3LY *tel* 071-402 4200 *fax* 071-402 7885.
£1.30. W. News and articles covering the whole of the mass communications field, particularly advertising in all its forms, marketing and the media. Features should not exceed 2000 words. News items also welcome. Press day, Wednesday. *Payment:* by arrangement.

Camping & Walking (1961), Philip Pond, Link House, Dingwall Avenue, Croydon CR9 2TA *tel* 081-686 2599 *telex* 947709 Linkho G *fax* 081-760 0973.
£1.60. M. Articles based on real family camping experiences and walks, all aspects, illustrated with photos; also camp site reports. *Length:* 600-1500 words average. *Illustrations:* line, half-tone, colour. *Payment:* by arrangement.

Car (1962), Gavin Green, 97 Earls Court Road, London W8 6QH *tel* 071-370 0333 *fax* 071-244 8692.
£2.00. M. Top-grade journalistic features on car driving, car people and cars. *Length:* 1000-2500 words. *Payment:* minimum £150 per 1000 words. *Illustrations:* b&w and colour photos to professional standards.

Car Mechanics, Graham Steed, EMAP National Publications Ltd, Bushfield House, Orton Centre, Peterborough PE2 0UW *tel* (0733) 237111 *fax* (0733) 231137.
£1.50. M. Practical articles on car maintenance and repair for the technical motorist with limited facilities. *Preliminary letter* outlining the article necessary. *Length:* average 1500 words of hard fact. *Payment:* by arrangement. *Illustrations:* line and half-tone.

Caravan Magazine (1933), Barry Williams, Link House, Dingwall Avenue, Croydon CR9 2TA *tel* 081-686 2599 *fax* 081-760 0973.
£1.70. M. Lively articles based on real experience of touring caravanning, especially if well illustrated by photos. General countryside or motoring material not wanted. *Payment:* by arrangement.

Caribbean Times (1981), Arif Ali, Hansib Publishing Ltd, Tower House, 139/149 Fonthill Road, London N4 3HF *tel* 071-281 1191 *fax* 071-263 9656.
35p. W. News stories, articles and features of interest to black readers. *Illustrations:* half-tone, line. *Payment:* by negotiation; £10 minimum.

Caring (1982), Charles Lloyd, Stanley House, 9 West Street, Epsom, Surrey KT18 7RL *tel* (0372) 741411.
£1.00. M. Factual and informative articles aimed at the disabled, carers and the elderly. *Length:* up to 1200 words. *Illustrations:* line, half-tone. *Payment:* by arrangement; £20 colour, £5 b&w.

Cat World (1981), Joan Moore, 10 Western Road, Shoreham-by-Sea, West Sussex BN43 5WD *tel* (0273) 462000 *fax* (0273) 455994.
£1.20. M. Bright, lively articles on any aspect of cat ownership. Articles on breeds of cats and veterinary articles by acknowledged experts only. No unsolicited fiction. *Illustrations:* b&w and colour photos. *Payment:* by arrangement; £7.50 each.

Catch, D.C. Thomson & Co. Ltd, Courier Place, Dundee DD1 9QJ *tel* (0382) 23131 *fax* (0382) 22214; and 185 Fleet Street, London EC4A 2HS *tel* 071-242 5086 *fax* 071-404 5694.
95p. M. 100-page gravure monthly for 18-22-year-old women. Fiction (up to 1800 words), fashion, beauty, features. *Illustrations:* art illustrations in full colour, colour photos. *Payment:* on acceptance.

Caterer & Hotelkeeper (1893), Clare Walker, Reed Business Publishing Group, Room 1504, Quadrant House, The Quadrant, Sutton, Surrey SM2 5AS *tel* 081-661 3500 *telex* 892084 Reedbp G *fax* 081-661 8973.
£1.15. W. Articles on all aspects of the hotel and catering industries. *Length:* up to 1500 words. *Illustrations:* line, half-tone, colour. *Payment:* £80 per 1000 words; NUJ rates.

Catholic Gazette (1910), Fr. Martin Hayes, 114 West Heath Road, London NW3 7TX *tel* 081-458 3316 *fax* 081-905 5780.
80p. M. Articles on evangelisation and the Christian life. *Length:* up to 1500 words. *Illustrations:* b&w photos, line, cartoons. *Payment:* by arrangement.

The Catholic Herald, Peter Stanford, Herald House, Lambs Passage, Bunhill Row, London EC1Y 8TQ *tel* 071-588 3101 *fax* 071-256 9728.
35p. W. An independent newspaper covering national and international affairs from a Catholic Christian viewpoint as well as Church news. *Length:* articles 600-1100 words. *Illustrations:* photos of Catholic and Christian interest. *Payment:* by arrangement.

Catholic Pictorial (1961), Brian P. Martin, Media House, Mann Island, Pier Head, Liverpool L3 1DQ *tel* 051-236 2191 *fax* 051-236 2216.
35p. W. News and photo features (maximum 1000 words plus illustration) *strictly* of Lancashire Catholic interest only. Has a strongly social editorial and is a trenchant tabloid. *Payment:* £1 per 100 words. News: on merit.

Cencrastus: Scottish & International Literature, Arts and Affairs (1979), Raymond Ross, Unit One, Abbeymount Techbase, Abbeymount, Edinburgh EH8 8EJ *tel* 031-661 5687.
£1.50. Q. Articles, short stories, poetry. *Payment:* by arrangement. *Illustrations:* line, half-tone.

Certified Accountant, Dominic Mitchell, Accountancy Publishing Group, Carew House, Railway Approach, Wallington, Surrey SM6 0DX *tel* 081-661 4714 *fax* 081-661 4748.
£1.75. M. Articles of accounting and financial interest. *Payment:* £75 per 1000 words.

Chapman (1969), Joy Hendry, 4 Broughton Place, Edinburgh EH1 3RX *tel* 031-557 2207.
£2.20. Q. (£9.50 p.a.) Poetry, short stories, reviews, articles on Scottish culture. *Illustrations:* line, half-tone. *Payment:* £8.50 per page; £10 or by negotiation.

Chat (1986), Terry Tavner, IPC Magazines Ltd, King's Reach Tower, Stamford Street, London SE1 9LS *tel* 071-261 6565 *fax* 071-261 6534.
38p. W. Tabloid weekly for women; fiction. *Length:* up to 500 words. *Illustrations:* half-tone, colour. *Payment:* by arrangement.

Cheshire Life (1934), Patrick O'Neill, Town & County Magazines, 70 Watergate Street, Chester CH1 2LA *tel* (0244) 345226 *fax* (0244) 348430.
£1.50. M. Articles of county interest only. No fiction. *Length:* 800-1500 words. *Illustrations:* line and half-tone, 4-colour positives. Photos of definite Cheshire interest. *Payment:* £50 per 800 words minimum; from £35.

Child Education (1924), Gill Moore, Scholastic Publications Ltd, Villiers House, Clavendon Avenue, Leamington Spa, Warks. CV32 5PR *tel* (0926) 887799 *fax* (0926) 883331.
£1.50. M. For teachers, pre-school staff, nursery nurses and parents concerned with children aged 3-8. Articles by specialists on practical teaching ideas and methods, child development, education news. *Length:* 1000-2000 words. *Payment:* by arrangement. Profusely illustrated with photos and line drawings; also large pictures in full colour. Also **Infant Projects** (formerly Child Education Special) (1978). Margot O'Keeffe. £1.50. Bi-M.

The China Quarterly, Brian Hook, School of Oriental and African Studies, Thornhaugh Street, Russell Square, London WC1H 0XG *tel* 071-637 2388 *telex* 291829 Soasp *fax* 071-436 3844.
£6.00. Q. (£24.00 p.a.) Articles on contemporary China. *Length:* 8000 words approx. *Payment:* on specially commissioned articles only.

Choice (1974), Wendy James, 3rd Floor, 2 St Johns Place, St Johns Square, London EC1M 4DE *tel* 071-490 7070 *fax* 071-253 9393. Published by EMAP in conjunction with Bayard Presse of France.
£1.65. M. Life style magazine for the 50+ market. Editor insists that writers should read and digest magazine before making contact with her. Travel and news/features ideas with colour photos can be commissioned. *Payment:* by agreement.

Christian Herald (1866), 96 Dominion Road, Worthing, West Sussex BN14 8JP *tel* (0903) 821082 *fax* (0903) 821081.
38p. W. Conservative, evangelical paper aimed at families. News, well-illustrated 'it really happened' and short filler items. *No* short stories. *Payment:* none, or modest.

Christian Week (Interdenominational Weekly) (1969), Christian Weekly Newspapers, 5th Floor, 77-79 Farringdon Road, London EC1M 3JY *tel* 071-430 2572 *fax* 071-430 9986.
30p. W. Emphasis on news features for Evangelical Free Church market. Feature articles mostly commissioned. *Length:* up to 1000 words. *Payment:* c. £25 per 1000 words. *Illustrations:* photos and line drawings.

Church of England Newspaper (1828), Christian Weekly Newspapers, 5th Floor, 77-79 Farringdon Road, London EC1M 3JY   *tel* 071-430 2572   *fax* 071-430 9986.
30p. W. Anglican news and articles relating the Christian faith to everyday life. Evangelical basis; mostly commissioned articles. Study of paper desirable. *Length:* up to 1000 words. *Illustrations:* photos, line drawings. *Payment:* c. £25 per 1000 words; photos £15, line by arrangement.

Church Times (1863), John Whale, 33 Upper Street, London N1 6PN   *tel* 071-359 4570   *fax* 071-226 3073.
35p. W. Articles on religious topics are considered. No verse or fiction. *Length:* up to 800 words. *Illustrations:* news photos. *Payment:* £80 per 1000 words; Periodical Publishers' Association negotiated rates.

Classic Cars Tony Dron, Prospect House, 9-13 Ewell Road, Cheam, Surrey SM1 4QQ   *tel* 081-661 6711   *telex* 892084 Bisprs G   *fax* 081-770 7091.
£2.00. M. Specialist articles on older cars. *Length:* from 1000-4000 words (subject to prior contract). *Illustrations:* half-tone, colour. *Payment:* by negotiation.

Classical Music (1976), Graeme Kay, 241 Shaftesbury Avenue, London WC2H 8EH   *tel* 071-836 2383   *fax* 071-528 7991.
£1.80. F. News, opinion, features on classical music and general arts. All material commissioned. *Illustrations:* b&w photos and line; colour covers. *Payment:* minimum £65 per 1000 words; from £35.

Climber and Hill Walker (1962), Peter Evans, The Plaza Tower, The Plaza, East Kilbride, Glasgow G74 1LW   *tel* (03552) 46444.
£1.60. M. Articles on all aspects of mountaineering and hill walking in Great Britain and abroad, and on related subjects. *Length:* 1500-2000 words, preferably illustrated. *Study of magazine* essential. *Illustrations:* line, half-tone, colour. *Payment:* according to merit.

Clocks (1978), Argus Specialist Publications. Editorial address: 38 Rosslyn Crescent, Edinburgh EH6 5AX   *tel* 031-554 5660   *fax* 031-554 5665.
£2.25. M. Well-researched articles on antique clocks and their makers, clock repair and restoration, and in general anything of interest to knowledgeable horologists. Sundials, barometers and associated scientific instruments are minority interests of Antique Clocks readers. *Length:* 1500-3000 words. *Illustrations:* line, half-tone, colour. No cartoons. *Payment:* £30 per 1000 words, £5 per b&w photo, £8 per colour print/transparency.

Club Secretary (1953), Elaine Cavanagh, MBC Retail Publications, Warwick House, Swanley, Kent BR8 8JF   *tel* (0322) 669411   *fax* (0322) 614474.
£28.00 p.a. M. Features, news, drink news, catering news, legal and financial advice as a guide to the successful management of clubs. *Payment:* by arrangement. *Illustrations:* line and half-tone.

Coin Monthly (1966), Marion Hornett, Sovereign House, Brentwood, Essex CM14 4SE   *tel* (0277) 219876.
£2.95. M. Articles on all aspects of numismatics, including tokens, medals, banknotes. *Length:* 1500-2000 words. *Illustrations:* half-tone. *Payment:* £17.50 per 1000 words; varies.

Coin News (1964), John W. Mussell, Token Publishing Ltd, 84 High Street, Honiton, Devon EX14 8JW   *tel* (0404) 45414   *fax* (0404) 45313.
£1.65. M. Articles of high standard on coins, tokens, paper money. *Length:* up to 2000 words. *Payment:* by arrangement.

Commando, D.C. Thomson & Co. Ltd, Albert Square, Dundee DD1 9QJ   *tel* (0382) 23131   *fax* (0382) 22214; and 185 Fleet Street, London EC4A 2HS   *tel* 071-242 5086   *fax* 071-404 5694..
35p. 8 p.m. Fictional war stories of World War II told in pictures. Scripts should be of about 135 pictures. Synopsis required as an opener. New writers encouraged; send for details. *Payment:* on acceptance.

Commercial Motor (1905), Brian Weatherley, Reed Business Publishing Group, Quadrant House, The Quadrant, Sutton, Surrey SM2 5AS   *tel* 081-661 3302/3303   *fax* 081-661 8969.
£1.00. W. Technical and road transport articles only. *Length:* up to 2000 words. *Payment:* varies. *Illustrations:* drawings and photos.

Community Care (1974), Terry Philpot, Carew House, Wallington, Surrey SM6 0DX   *tel* 081-661 4861.
£1.20. W. Articles of professional interest to local authority and voluntary body social workers, managers, teachers and students. *Preliminary letter* advisable. *Length:* 800-1500 words. *Payment:* at current rates. *Illustrations:* line, half-tone.

Company (1978), Mandi Norwood, National Magazine House, 72 Broadwick Street, London W1V 2BP   *tel* 071-439 5000.
£1.30. M. Articles on a wide variety of subjects, relevant to young, independent women. Most articles commissioned. *Payment:* usual magazine rate. *Illustrated*.

Computer Weekly (1966), John Lamb, Reed Business Publishing Group, Quadrant House, The Quadrant, Sutton, Surrey SM2 5AS   *tel* 081-661 3122   *telex* 892084 Reedbp G   *fax* 081-661 8979.
£1.50. W. Feature articles on computer-related topics for business/industry users. *Length:* 1200 words. *Illustrations:* b&w photos, line, cartoons. *Payment:* £150 per feature; negotiable.

Computing (1973), Sarah Underwood, 32-34 Broadwick Street, London W1A 2HG   *tel* 071-439 4242   *fax* 071-437 3516.
£70.00 p.a. W. Features and news items on the computer industry and on applications and implications of computers and microelectronics. *Length:* up to 1800 words. *Payment:* £130 per 1000 words. *Illustrations:* line, half-tone.

Construction Weekly (incorporating **Construction Plant & Equipment** and **Civil Engineering**), Richard Northcote, Morgan-Grampian (Construction Press) Ltd, 30 Calderwood Street, London SE18 6QH   *tel* 081-855 7777   *telex* 896238   *fax* 081-854 8058.
Controlled circulation. W. Contains news of construction matters, in-depth technical articles of current interest to civil engineers, contractors and manufacturers of plant and equipment. *Preliminary letter* essential. *Length:* 1000-2000 words. *Illustrations:* line drawings, charts, graphs and colour pictures relating to articles. *Payment:* by arrangement.

Contemporary Review (incorporating the **Fortnightly**) (1866), Betty Abel, 61 Carey Street, London WC2A 2JG   *tel* 071-831 7791.
£1.50. M. Independent, slightly left of centre review dealing with questions of the day, chiefly politics, theology, history, literature, travel, poetry, the arts. Mostly commissioned, but there is scope for freelance specialists. Articles should be typewritten, about 2000-3000 words. If refused, articles are returned, *if sae is enclosed*. Intending contributors should *study journal* before submitting MSS. *Payment:* £5 per page (500 words), 2 complimentary copies.

Control & Instrumentation (1958), Brian J. Tinham, BSc. CEng. MInstMC, Morgan-Grampian (Process Press) Ltd, 30 Calderwood Street, Woolwich, London SE18 6QH   *tel* 081-855 7777.

£48.00 p.a. M. Authoritative main feature articles on measurement, automation, control systems, instrumentation and data processing. Also export, business and engineering news. *Length of articles:* 750 words for highly technical pieces, 1000-2500 words main features. *Payment:* according to value. *Illustrations:* photos and drawings of equipment using automatic techniques, control engineering personalities.

Cosmetic World News (1949), M.A. Murray-Pearce, Caroline Marcuse, 130 Wigmore Street, London W1H 0AT   *tel* 071-486 6757/8   *fax* 071-487 5436. £84.00 p.a. M. International news magazine of perfumery, cosmetics and toiletries industry. World-wide reports, photo-news stories, articles (500-1000 words) on essential oils and new cosmetic raw materials, and exclusive information on industry's companies and personalities welcomed. *Payment:* by arrangement, minimum 10p per word. *Illustrations:* b&w and colour photos or colour separations.

Cosmopolitan (1972), Marcelle D'Argy Smith, National Magazine House, 72 Broadwick Street, London W1V 2BP   *tel* 071-439 5000   *fax* 071-439 5016. £1.50. M. Short stories, articles. Commissioned material only. *Payment:* by arrangement. *Illustrated.*

Country (1901), Tom Quinn, Keymark Communications, 19 Featherstone Street, London EC1Y 8SL   *tel* 071-490 3131 £1.70. M. The Magazine of the Country Gentlemen's Association. Authoritative articles on wildlife, countryside and general interest. Gardening, cookery, fashion, travel. *Length:* 500-1000 words. *Payment:* by arrangement.

Country Homes & Interiors (1986), Vanessa Berridge, IPC Magazines Ltd, King's Reach Tower, Stamford Street, London SE1 9LS   *tel* 071-261 6434   *fax* 071-261 6895. £1.95. M. Articles on property, country homes, interior designs. *Illustrations:* half-tone, colour. *Payment:* £150 per 1000 words; £75 minimum.

Country Life (1897), Jenny Greene, IPC Magazines Ltd, King's Reach Tower, Stamford Street, London SE1 9LS   *tel* 071-261 7058   *fax* 071-261 5139. £1.50. W. Illustrated journal chiefly concerned with British country life, social history, architecture and the fine arts, natural history, agriculture, gardening and sport. *Length of articles:* about 700, 1000 or 1300 words. *Illustrations:* mainly photos. *Payment:* according to merit; £30 per b&w photo.

Country Living (1985), Francine Lawrence, 72 Broadwick Street, London W1V 2BP   *tel* 071-439 5000   *fax* 071-437 6886. £1.60. M. Well-written features or news items on all aspects of country living. *Do not* send valuable transparencies; magazine cannot accept responsibility for loss of unsolicited material. *Illustrations:* line, half-tone, colour. *Payment:* by arrangement.

Country Quest, Ray Bower, North Wales Newspapers, Business Park, Mold, Clwyd   *tel* (0352) 700022. 90p. M. Illustrated articles on matters relating to countryside of Wales and border counties. No fiction. Illustrated work preferred. *Length:* 500-1500 words. *Illustrations:* line, half-tone. *Payment:* by arrangement.

The Countryman (1927), Christopher Hall, Sheep Street, Burford, Oxford OX8 4LH   *tel* (099 382) 2258. £1.80. Bi-M. Every department of rural life and progress except field sports. Party politics and sentimentalising about the country barred. Copy must be trustworthy, well-written, brisk, cogent and light in hand. Articles up to 1500 words. Good paragraphs and notes, first-class poetry and skilful sketches of life and character from personal knowledge and experience. Dependable natural history based on writer's own observation. Really good matter from old unpublished letters and MSS. *Illustrations:* b&w photos and drawings, but all must be exclusive and out of the ordinary, and bear close scrutiny. Humour welcomed if genuine. *Payment:* from £40 per 1000 words, according to merit; illustrations from £10, according to merit.

Country-Side (1905), Dr David Applin, PO Box 87, Cambridge CB1 3UP.
£10.00 p.a. Q. Official organ of the British Naturalists' Association (BNA), the national body for naturalists. Original observations on wildlife and its protection, and on natural history generally, but not on killing for sport. *Preliminary letter* or study of magazine advisable. *Payment:* 1400 words plus pictures £30, shorter articles pro-rata. *Illustrations:* photos, drawings.

The Courier and Advertiser (1816 and 1801), D.C. Thomson & Co. Ltd, 7 Bank Street, Dundee DD1 9HU *tel* (0382) 23131 *telex* DCThom 76380 *fax* (0382) 27159; and 185 Fleet Street, London EC4A 2HS *tel* 071-242 5086.
24p. D. Ind.

Coventry Evening Telegraph, Chazy Dowaliby, Corporation Street, Coventry CV1 1FP *tel* (0203) 633633 *fax* (0203) 550869.
22p. D. Topical, illustrated articles, those with a Warwickshire interest particularly acceptable. *Length:* up to 600 words.

Creative Camera (1968), Peter Turner, CC Publishing, Battersea Arts Centre, Old Town Hall, Lavender Hill, London SW11 5TF *tel* 071-924 3017.
£3.50. Bi-M. Illustrated articles and pictures dealing with creative photography, sociology of, history of and criticism of photos. Book and Exhibition reviews. Arts Council supported. *Payment:* by arrangement. *Illustrations:* b&w, colour.

The Cricketer International (1921), Peter Perchard, Third Street, Langton Green, Tunbridge Wells, Kent TN3 0EN *tel* (0892) 862551 *fax* (0892) 863755.
£1.85. M. Articles on cricket at any level. *Illustrations:* line, half-tone, colour. *Payment:* £50 per 1000 words; minimum £15.

The Criminologist (1966), East Row, Little London, Chichester, West Sussex PO19 1PG *tel* (0243) 775552 *fax* (0243) 779278.
£32.00 p.a. post free. Q. Specialised material designed for an expert and professional readership. Covers both nationally and internationally criminology, the police, forensic science, the law, penology, sociology and law enforcement. Articles are welcomed, up to 4000 words, from those familiar with the journal's style and requirements. *A preliminary letter* with a brief résumé is requested. *Payment:* according to merit. *Illustrations:* line and photos.

Crisis (1988), Michael W. Bennent, Fleetway Publications, Greater London House, Hampstead Road, London NW1 7QQ *tel* 071-383 7156 *fax* 071-383 7485.
£1.75. M. Comic for 15-25 year olds. Serious/adult illustrated features and strip art scripts. *Length:* 2000-3000 words. *Illustrations:* colour strip art, cartoons. *Payment:* negotiable – scripts £35 per page; strip art £180 per page colour, £110 b&w.

Critical Quarterly (1959), Editorial Board: C.B. Cox, Kate Pahl, Colin MacCabe, Bryan Loughrey. The Secretary, Drama Dept, Roehampton Institute, Digby Stuart College, Roehampton Lane, London SW15 5HS.
£16.50 p.a. Q. (£24.00 p.a. institutions) Fiction, poems, literary criticism. *Length:* 2000-5000 words. Interested contributors should *study magazine* before submitting MSS. *Payment:* by arrangement.

CTN (Confectioner, Tobacconist, Newsagent), Peter Arnott-Job, International Thomson Business Publishing, Greater London House, Hampstead Road, London NW1 7QZ   *tel* 071-387 6611.
70p. W. (£40.00 p.a.) Trade news and brief articles illustrated when possible with photos or line drawings. Must be of current interest to retail confectioner-tobacconists and newsagents. *Length:* Articles 600-800 words. *Payment:* news lineage rates, minimum of £6.50 per 100 words; articles at negotiated rates.

Cumbria (1951), Hilary Gray, Dalesman Publishing Company Ltd, Clapham, via Lancaster LA2 8EB   *tel* (046 85) 225   *fax* (046 85) 708.
60p. M. Articles of genuine rural interest concerning Lakeland. Short *length* preferred. *Illustrations:* line drawings and first-class photos. *Payment:* according to merit.

Custom Car (1970), Link House, Dingwall Avenue, Croydon CR9 2TA   *tel* 081-686 2599   *telex* 947709 Linkho G.
£1.60. *Length:* by arrangement. *Payment:* by arrangement.

Cycling (1891), Andrew Sutcliffe, Prospect House, 9-13 Ewell Road, Cheam, Surrey SM1 4QQ   *tel* 081-661 6651   *fax* 081-642 6006.
£1.00. W. Racing and technical articles not exceeding 1500 words. Topical photos with a cycling interest also considered. *Payment:* by arrangement.

Daily Express, Nicholas Lloyd, Ludgate House, 245 Blackfriars Road, London SE1 9UX   *tel* 071-928 8000   *cables* Lon Express   *telex* 21841/21842   *fax* 071-633 0244; Great Ancoats Street, Manchester M60 4HB   *tel* 061-236 2112.
28p. D. Exclusive news: striking photos. Leader page articles, 600 words; facts preferred to opinions. *Payment:* according to value.

Daily Mail (1896) (now incorporating **News Chronicle** and **Daily Sketch**), Sir David English, Northcliffe House, 2 Derry Street, London W8 5TT   *tel* 071-938 6000   *fax* 071-937 3251.
28p. D. Highest *payment* for good, exclusive news. Ideas welcomed for leader page articles, 500-800 words average. Exclusive news photos always wanted.

Daily Mirror (1903), Richard Stott, Holborn Circus, London EC1P 1DQ   *tel* 071-353 0246.
25p. D. Top *payment* for exclusive news and news pictures. Few articles from freelances used, but ideas bought: send synopsis only. 'Unusual' pictures and those giving a new angle on the news are welcomed.

Daily Post (1855), Keith Ely, PO Box 48, Old Hall Street, Liverpool L69 3EB   *tel* 051-227 2000.
24p. D. Ind. Articles of general interest and topical features of special interest to North West England and North Wales. No verse or fiction. *Payment:* according to value. News and feature photos used.

Daily Record, Editor-in-Chief: E.J. Laird, Anderston Quay, Glasgow G3 8DA   *tel* 041-248 7000   *telex* 778277; London Office: 33 Holborn, EC1P 1DQ   *tel* 071-353 0246.
24p. D. Web offset with full colour facilities. Topical articles of from 300-700 words. Exclusive stories of Scottish interest and exclusive photos.

Daily Star (1978), Brian Hitchen, cbe, Ludgate House, 245 Blackfriars Road, London SE1 9UX   *tel* 071-928 8000   *cables* Lon Express   *telex* 21841/21842   *fax* 071-620 1641.
25p. D. Hard news exclusives, commanding substantial payment. Major interviews with big-star personalities; short features; series based on people rather than things; picture features. *Payment:* short features £75-£100; full page £250-£300; double page £400-£600, otherwise by negotiation. *Illustrations:* line, half-tone, cartoons.

The Daily Telegraph (1855), Editor-in-Chief: Max Hastings, Peterborough Court at South Quay, 181 Marsh Wall, London E14 9SR *tel* 071-538 5000 *telex* 22874/5/6 *fax* 071-538 3810.
40p. D. 45p. Sat. Ind. Articles on a wide range of subjects of topical interest considered. *Preliminary letter* and synopsis required. *Length:* 700-1000 words. *Payment:* by arrangement.

Dairy Farmer, David Shead, Wharfedale Road, Ipswich IP1 4LG *tel* (0473) 241122 *fax* (0473) 240501.
Controlled circulation. M. Authoritative articles dealing in practical, lively style with dairy farming. Topical controversial articles invited. Well-written, illustrated accounts of new ideas being tried on dairy farms are especially wanted. *Length:* normally up to 1500 words. *Payment:* by arrangement. *Illustrations:* line, half-tone, colour.

Dairy Industries International (1936), Sarah Cunningham, Maxwell Business Communications, Wilmington House, Church Hill, Wilmington, Dartford, Kent DA2 7EF *tel* (0322) 277788 *fax* (0322) 276474.
£50.00 post free (UK). M. Covers the entire field of milk processing, the manufacture of products from liquid milk, and ice cream. Articles relating to dairy plant, butter and cheese making, ice cream making, new product developments and marketing, etc. *Payment:* by arrangement. *Illustrations:* glossy prints and Indian ink diagrams.

The Dalesman (1939), David Joy, Dalesman Publishing Company Ltd, Clapham, via Lancaster LA2 8EB *tel* (046 85) 225 *fax* (046 85) 708.
65p. M. Articles and stories of genuine rural interest concerning Yorkshire; but no fiction. Short *length* preferred. *Payment:* according to merit. *Illustrations:* line drawings and first-class photos preferably featuring people.

Dance & Dancers (1950), John Percival, 214 Panther House, 38 Mount Pleasant, London WC1X 0AP *tel/fax* 071-837 2711.
£1.75. M. Specialist features, reviews on modern/classical dance, dancers. *Length:* by prior arrangement. *Payment:* by arrangement. *Illustrations:* line, half-tone; colour covers.

Dancing Times (1910), Editor: Mary Clarke, Editorial Adviser: Ivor Guest, Clerkenwell House, 45-47 Clerkenwell Green, London EC1R 0BE *tel* 071-250 3006.
£1.30. M. Ballet and stage dancing, both from general, historical, critical and technical angles. Well-informed freelance articles are occasionally used, but only after preliminary arrangements. *Payment:* by arrangement. *Illustrations:* web offset, occasional line, action photos always preferred.

The Dandy, D.C. Thomson & Co. Ltd, Courier Place, Dundee DD1 9QJ *tel* (0382) 23131 *fax* (0382) 22214; and 185 Fleet Street, London EC4A 2HS *tel* 071-242 5086 *fax* 071-404 5694.
26p. W. Comic strips for children. 10-12 pictures per single page story, 18-20 pictures per 2-page story. Promising artists encouraged. *Payment:* on acceptance.

Dandy Cartoon Library, D.C. Thomson & Co. Ltd, Courier Place, Dundee DD1 9QJ *tel* (0382) 23131 *fax* (0382) 22214; and 185 Fleet Street, London EC4A 2HS *tel* 071-242 5086 *fax* 071-404 5694.
35p. M. 64 pages of jokes and gags in cartoon form featuring the well-known characters from the weekly Beano, Dandy and Beezer-Topper publications.

Dandy Library, D.C. Thomson & Co. Ltd, Courier Place, Dundee DD1 9QJ *tel* (0382) 23131 *fax* (0382) 22214; and 185 Fleet Street, London EC4A 2HS *tel* 071-242 5086 *fax* 071-404 5694.

35p. 2 p.m. Extra-long comic adventure stories featuring the well-known characters from the weekly Dandy publication. 'Guest appearances' by characters from weekly Beezer-Topper publication.

Darts World (1972), Tony Wood, World Magazines Limited, 2 Park Lane, Croydon, Surrey CR9 1HA　*tel* 081-681 2837　*fax* 081-688 5159.
£1.10. M. Articles and stories with darts theme. *Illustrations:* half-tone, cartoons. *Payment:* £40-£50 per 1000 words; by arrangement.

Day by Day (1963), Patrick Richards, Woolacombe House, 141 Woolacombe Road, Blackheath, London SE3 8QP　*tel* 081-856 6249. Published by The Loverseed Press.
65p. M. Articles and news on non-violence and social justice. Reviews of art, books, films, plays, musicals and opera. Cricket reports. Occasional poems and very occasional short stories in keeping with editorial viewpoint. *Payment:* £2 per 1000 words. No *illustrations* required.

Debbie Library, D.C. Thomson & Co. Ltd, Courier Place, Dundee DD1 9QJ　*tel* (0382) 23131　*fax* (0382) 22214; and 185 Fleet Street, London EC4A 2HS　*tel* 071-242 5086　*fax* 071-404 5694.
35p. M. 64-page picture-stories for schoolgirls (about 140 line drawings). Adventure, animal, mystery, school, sport. Scripts considered; promising scriptwriters and artists encouraged. *Payment:* on acceptance.

Dental Update (1973), Andrew Baxter, Reed Healthcare Communications, Friary Court, 13-21 High Street, Guildford, Surrey GU1 3DX　*tel* (0483) 502125　*telex* 859500 Ref S/054　*fax* (0483) 301441.
£32.00 p.a. 10 p.a. (£17.00 p.a. students) Clinical articles, clinical quizzes. *Illustrations:* line, colour. *Payment:* £50-£100 per 1000 words; £50 cover photos only.

Derbyshire Life and Countryside (1931), Lodge Lane, Derby DE1 3HE　*tel* (0332) 47087/8/9　*fax* (0332) 290688.
85p. M. Articles, preferably illustrated, about Derbyshire life, people and history. *Length:* 800-1000 words. Some short stories set in Derbyshire accepted, but verse not used. *Payment:* according to nature and quality of contribution. *Illustrations:* photos of Derbyshire subjects.

Design (1949), Marion Hancock, Design Council, 28 Haymarket, London SW1Y 4SU　*tel* 071-839 8000.
£3.95. M. Articles on industrial, graphic and interior design, and design management. International coverage. *Payment:* by arrangement. *Illustrations:* commissioned; £200 per day plus expenses for photography, approx. £350 per illustration.

Designers' Journal (1985), Aidan Walker, 33–39 Bowling Green Lane, London EC1R 0DA　*tel* 071-837 1212　*fax* 071-833 3073.
£2.00. M. Articles on new developments in interior design, new products, technical innovation and practice guidance. *Payment:* by arrangement. *Illustrations:* photos, drawings.

Devon Life (1965), Neville Hutchinson, 48 Queen Street, Exeter, Devon EX4 3SR　*tel* (0392) 216766　*fax* (0392) 71050.
£1.00. M. Articles and stories about nature, people, life in Devon. *Length:* 1000 words. *Illustrations:* line, photos. *Payment:* by arrangement.

The Dickensian, Dickens House, 48 Doughty Street, London WC1N 2LF.
£9.00 p.a. 3 p.a. (£11.00 p.a. institutions; overseas rates on application) Published by The Dickens Fellowship. Welcomes articles on all aspects of Dickens' life, works and character. *Payment:* none. Contributions and editorial

correspondence to the editor: Dr Malcolm Andrews, Eliot College, University of Kent, Canterbury, Kent CT2 7NS.

Digests with one or two exceptions are not included since they seldom use original material, but reprint articles previously published elsewhere and extracts from books. But see **The Reader's Digest**.

Director (1947), Stuart Rock, Mountbarrow House, 6-20 Elizabeth Street, London SW1W 9RB *tel* 071-730 6060 *telex* 918802 DP G *fax* 071-235 5627.
£2.00. M. Authoritative business-related articles. Send synopsis of proposed article and examples of printed work. *Length:* 1000-3000 words. *Payment:* by arrangement. *Illustrated* mainly in colour.

Dirt Bike Rider (1981), Peter Donaldson, PO Box 100, Stamford, Lincs. PE9 1XQ *tel* (0780) 55131 *fax* (0780) 57261.
£1.30. M. Features, track tests, coverage on all aspects of off road motor-cycling. *Length:* up to 1000 words. *Payment:* £80 per 1000 words. *Illustrations:* half-tone, colour.

Disability Now (1957), Mary Wilkinson, The Spastics Society, 12 Park Crescent, Lor.don W1N 4EQ *tel* 071-636 5020 *fax* 071-436 2601.
£10.00 p.a. M. (£15.00 for organisations/overseas) Topical, authoritative articles of interest to people with a wide range of disabilities, carers and professionals; also arts and book reviews. Contributions from people with disabilities particularly welcome. *Preliminary letter or phone call desirable. Length:* up to 1000 words. *Illustrations:* b&w news photos, cartoons. *Payment:* £60 per 1000 words; by arrangement.

Diver (1953), Bernard Eaton, 55 High Street, Teddington, Middlesex TW11 8HA *tel* 081-943 4288 *fax* 081-943 4312.
£1.80. M. Articles on sub aqua diving and underwater developments. *Length:* 1500-2000 words. *Illustrations:* line, half-tone, colour. *Payment:* by arrange-ment.

Do It Yourself (1957), John McGowan, Link House, Dingwall Avenue, Croydon CR9 2TA *tel* 081-686 2599 *fax* 081-760 0973.
£1.40. M. Authoritative articles on every aspect of DIY in the house, garden, workshop and garage. Press 3 months ahead. Leaflet describing style require-ments available on request. *Length:* up to 1000 words unless negotiated. *Illustrations:* line drawings and photos. *Payment:* by arrangement.

Doctor (1971), Helena Sturridge, Reed Healthcare Communications Ltd, Friary Court, 13-21 High Street, Guildford, Surrey GU1 3DX *tel* (0483) 502125 *telegraphic address* Same, Guildford *telex* 859500 5/054 *fax* (0483) 301441.
£2.00. W. Commissioned articles and features of interest to GPs. *Length:* various. *Illustrations:* colour photos – news, features, clinical; some line. *Payment:* NUJ rates.

Dorset County Magazine (1967), John Newth, Trinity Lane, Wareham, Dorset BH20 4LN *tel* (0929) 551264.
£1.15. M. Articles (500-1500 words), photos (colour or b&w) and line drawings with a *specifically* Dorset theme. *Payment:* by arrangement.

The Downside Review, Dom Daniel Rees, Downside Abbey, Stratton-on-the-Fosse, Nr Bath, Somerset BA3 4RH *tel* Stratton-on-the-Fosse (0761) 232 295.

£5.00. Q. (£20.00 p.a.) Articles and book reviews on theology, metaphysics, mysticism and modernism, and monastic and church history. *Payment:* not usual.

DR The Fashion Business (formerly **Drapers Record**) (1887), Sally Bain, Greater London House, Hampstead Road, London NW1 *tel* 071-387 6611 *fax* 071-383 3128.
£1.10. W. Editorial aimed at fashion retailers, large and small. No unsolicited material. *Payment:* by negotiation. *Illustrations:* colour and b&w: photos, drawings and cartoons.

Dundee Evening Telegraph and Post, D.C. Thomson & Co. Ltd, Bank Street, Dundee DD1 9HU *tel* (0382) 23131 *telex* DCThom 76380 *fax* (0382) 27159; and 185 Fleet Street, London EC4A 2HS *tel* 071-242 5086 *fax* 071-404 5694.
22p. D.

Early Music (1973), Nicholas Kenyon, Oxford University Press, 7-8 Hatherley Street, London SW1P 2QT *tel* 071-233 5466 *fax* 071-233 6638.
£7.50. Q. (£29.00 p.a., institutions £34.00 p.a.) Lively, informative and scholarly articles on aspects of medieval, renaissance, baroque and classical music. *Payment:* £20 per 1000 words. *Illustrations:* colour, line, half-tone.

Early Times (1988), Alison Haymonds, 12 Skerne Road, Kingston upon Thames, Surrey KT2 5AF *tel* 081-546 2261 *fax* 081-541 3743.
50p. W. Serious weekly newspaper for children. News and features of interest to 7-15-year-olds. *Payment:* by arrangement. *Illustrations:* line, half-tone.

East Lothian Life (1989), Pauline Jaffray, 7 West Port, Dunbar, East Lothian EH42 1BT *tel* (0368) 63593.
£2.00. Q. Articles and features with an East Lothian slant. *Length:* up to 1000 words. *Illustrations:* b&w photos, line. *Payment:* negotiable.

Eastern Daily Press (1870), L. Sear, Prospect House, Rouen Road, Norwich NR1 1RE *tel* (0603) 628311 *telex* 975276 Ecnnch G *fax* (0603) 612930. London Office: 242 Vauxhall Bridge Road, SW1V 1AU *tel* 071-828 7141.
30p. D. Ind. Limited market for articles of East Anglian interest not exceeding 900 words.

Eastern Evening News (1882), Tim Bishop, Prospect House, Rouen Road, Norwich NR1 1RE *tel* (0603) 628311 *telex* 975276 Ecnnch G *fax* (0603) 612930. London Office: 242 Vauxhall Bridge Road, SW1V 1AU *tel* 071-828 7141.
24p. D. Ind. Interested in news-based features, material for advert features and cartoons. *Length:* up to 500 words. *Payment:* NUJ or agreed rates.

The Ecologist, Edward Goldsmith, First Floor, Corner House, Station Road, Sturminster Newton, Dorset *tel* (0258) 73476.
£3.00. 6 p.a. Fully-referenced articles on economic, social and environmental affairs from an ecological standpoint. *Study* magazine for level and approach. *Length:* 1000-5000 words. *Illustrations:* line, half-tone. *Payment:* by arrangement; not usually.

Economic Journal (1891), John D. Hey, Department of Economics, University of York, York YO1 5DD *tel* (0904) 433575 *fax* (0904) 433433.
Free to members. Bi-M. (£78.00 p.a.) Organ of the Royal Economic Society. Economic theory, applied economics and the development of economic thinking in relation to current problems. Statistical and economic diagrams. Reviews of new books, software and other publications. *Payment:* none.

Economica (1921. New Series, 1934), Editors: Dr F.A. Cowell, Dr M. Schankerman, Dr D.C. Webb, London School of Economics and Political Science, Houghton Street, London WC2A 2AE *tel* 071-405 7686, ext. 3087 *fax* 071-242 0392.
£7.50. Q. (subscription rates on application) Learned journal covering the fields of economics, economic history and statistics.

The Economist (1843), 25 St James's Street, London SW1A 1HG *tel* 071-839 7000.
£1.60. W. Articles staff-written.

Edinburgh Evening News, Terry Quinn, 20 North Bridge, Edinburgh EH1 1YT *tel* 031-225 2468 *fax* 031-225 7302.
20p. D. Independent. Features on current affairs, preferably in relation to our circulation area. Women's talking points, local historical articles; subjects of general interest.

Edinburgh Review (1969), Murdo Macdonald, 22 George Square, Edinburgh EH8 9LF *tel* 031-650 4215 *fax* 031-662 0053.
£4.95. Q. (£16.00 p.a.) Fiction, clearly written articles on Scottish and international cultural and philosophical ideas. *Payment:* by arrangement.

Education (1903), George Low, 21-27 Lamb's Conduit Street, London WC1N 3NJ *tel* 071-242 2548 *fax* 071-831 2855.
£1.30. W. Specialist articles on educational administration, all branches of education; technical education; universities; school building; playing fields; environmental studies; physical education; school equipment; school meals and health; teaching aids. *Length:* 1000-1200 words. *Illustrations:* photos and drawings. *Payment:* by arrangement.

Electrical Review (1872), T.C.J. Cogle, BSc (Eng). MICE, FICE, Reed Business Publishing, Quadrant House, The Quadrant, Sutton, Surrey SM2 5AS *tel* 081-661 3113 *telex* 892084 Reedbp G.
£2.50. F. Technical and business articles on electrical and control engineering; outside contributions considered. Electrical news welcomed. *Illustrations:* photos and drawings. *Payment:* according to merit.

The Electrical Times (1891), W. Evett, Reed Business Publishing, Quadrant House, The Quadrant, Sutton, Surrey SM2 5AS *tel* 081-661 3115 *telex* 892084 Reedbp G *fax* 081-661 8972.
£2.25. M. Business, technical articles of interest to electric installers, with illustrations as necessary. *Length:* 750 words. *Payment:* £100 per article. *Illustrations:* line, half-tone.

Elle (UK) (1985), Maggie Alderson, Rex House, 4-12 Lower Regent Street, London SW1Y 4PE *tel* 071-930 9050.
£1.60. M. Commissioned material only. *Payment:* by arrangement. *Illustrations:* colour.

Embroidery, The Embroiderers' Guild, PO Box 42b, East Molesey, Surrey KT8 9BB *tel* 081-943 1229.
£2.00. Q. (£10.00 p.a.) Articles on historical and contemporary embroidery by curators and artists. Exhibition and book reviews. Saleroom report. Diary of events. *Illustrations:* line, half-tone, colour. *Payment:* by arrangement; none.

Empire (1989), Barry McIlheney, 42-48 Great Portland Street, London W1N 5AH *tel* 071-436 5430 *fax* 071-631 0781.
£1.85. M. Monthly guide to film and video, network and satellite TV – articles, features, news. *Length:* various. *Illustrations:* colour and b&w photos. *Payment:* approx. £100 per 1000 words; varies.

The Engineer (1856), Chris Barrie, 30 Calderwood Street, London SE18 6QH *tel* 081-855 7777.
£3.00. W. (£75.00 p.a.) Covers the business and technology of the engineering industry. Outside contributions paid for if accepted.

Engineering (1866), Richard Wood, Design Council, 28 Haymarket, London SW1Y 4SU   *tel* 071-839 8000   *fax* 071-925 2130.
£3.25. M. Contributions considered on all aspects of engineering, particularly design. *Payment:* by arrangement. *Illustrations:* photos and drawings.

English Historical Review (1886), Dr R.J.W. Evans, Dr J.R. Maddicott, Academic Dept, Longman Group UK Ltd, Burnt Mill, Harlow, Essex CM20 2JE   *tel* (0279) 26721.
£52.00 p.a. Q. High-class scholarly articles, documents, and reviews or short notices of books. Contributions are not accepted unless they supply original information and should be sent direct to Dr R.J.W. Evans, Editor, E.H.R., Brasenose College, Oxford OX1 4AJ. Books for review should be sent to Dr J.R. Maddicott, Editor, E.H.R., Exeter College, Oxford OX1 3DP. *Payment:* none.

Entomologist's Monthly Magazine (1864), K.G.V. Smith, Gem Publishing Co., Brightwood, Bell Lane, Brightwell cum Sotwell, Wallingford, Oxon OX10 0QD   *tel* (0491) 33882   *fax* (0491) 25161.
£24.00 p.a. 3 p.a. Articles on all orders of insects and terrestrial arthropods, foreign and British. *Payment:* none.

Envoi (1957), Anne Lewis-Smith, Pen Ffordd, Newport, Dyfed SA42 0QT   *tel* (0239) 820285.
£6.00 p.a. 3 p.a. New poetry and reviews. Poetry Competitions. Editorial panel of 30 who criticise subscribers' poems (with sae) at no charge. *Payment:* 2 complimentary copies.

ES Magazine (1987), Michael Watts, Northcliffe House, 2 Derry Street, London W8 5EE   *tel* 071-938 6000.
Free with the Evening Standard. M. Feature ideas, not exclusively about London. *Payment:* by negotiation. *Illustrations:* all types.

Esquire (1991), Alex Finer, National Magazine House, 72 Broadwick Street, London W1V 2BP   *tel* 071-439 5000   *telegraphic address* Shanmag, London W1   *telex* 263879 Natmag G   *fax* 071-439 5067.
£2.00. M. Quality men's interests magazine – articles, features, short stories. *Length:* various. *Illustrations:* colour and b&w photos, line. *Payment:* by arrangement.

Essentials (1988), Gilly Cubitt, GE Magazines Ltd, Garden House, 57-59 Long Acre, London WC2E 9JL   *tel* 071-836 0519   *telex* 929414 Gepub   *fax* 071-836 0280.
£1.10. M. Features, plus fashion, health and beauty, cookery; also short stories, 2000-3000 words. *Illustrations:* colour. *Payment:* by negotiation.

Essex Countryside (1952), Meg Davis-Berry, Essex Countryside Ltd, Wenden Court, Wendens Ambo, Saffron Walden, Essex CB11 4LB   *tel* (0799) 41675   *fax* (0799) 41682.
95p. M. Articles of county interest. *Length:* approximately 1000 words. *Illustrations:* line, half-tone, colour.

EuroBusiness (1988), 21 Gold Street, Saffron Walden, Essex CB10 1EJ   *tel* (0799) 21150   *telex* 817197   *fax* (0799) 24805.
£1.50. M. Features and news stories of interest to European-oriented businesses. *Length:* features up to 2000 words, news stories up to 700 words. *Payment:* up to £200 per 1000 words. *Illustrated.*

Euromoney (1969), Garry Evans, Nestor House, Playhouse Yard, London EC4V 5EX   *tel* 071-236 3288   *telex* 928726/7 (editorial/research), 914553/4/5 (adv./survey/prod.)   *fax* 071-236 6970.
£110.00 p.a. M. Articles of general interest on finance, banking and capital markets. *Length:* up to 6000 words. *Illustrations:* colour photos, cartoons. *Payment:* £250 per 1000 words; £50.

The European (1990), John Bryant, 5 New Fetter Lane, London EC4A 1AP   *tel* 071-822 2002   *telex* 94015046   *fax* 071-377 4891.
50p. Fri. News reports, analytical articles and features on subjects of interest and importance to Europe as a whole, including business affairs, sport, arts, literature, leisure, fashion. *Illustrations:* line, half-tone, colour transparencies. *Payment:* by arrangement.

European Plastics News (1929), Kevin O'Toole, Reed Business Publishing, Quadrant House, The Quadrant, Sutton, Surrey SM2 5AS   *tel* 081-661 3292   *telex* 892084   *fax* 081-661 8924.
£10.00. M. (£75.00 p.a.) Technical articles dealing with plastics and allied subjects. *Length:* depending on subject. *Illustrations:* b&w or colour photos/diagrams. *Payment:* by arrangement; none.

Evangelical Quarterly (1929), Prof. I.H. Marshall, Department of New Testament, King's College, Aberdeen AB9 2UB. Published from Paternoster House, 3 Mount Radford Crescent, Exeter, Devon EX2 4JW   *tel* (0392) 50631.
£2.90. Q. International review of Bible and theology in defence of the historic Christian faith. Articles on the defence or exposition of biblical theology as exhibited in the great Reformed Confessions. *Payment:* none.

Evening Chronicle, Graeme Stanton, Newcastle Chronicle and Journal Ltd, Thomson House, Groat Market, Newcastle upon Tyne NE1 1ED   *tel* 091-232 7500   *fax* 091-232 2256.
22p. D. News, photos and features covering almost every subject of interest to readers in Tyne and Wear, Northumberland and Durham. *Payment:* according to value.

Evening Post, 395 High Street, Chatham, Kent ME4 4PG   *tel* Medway (0634) 830999   *fax* (0634) 829479.
18p. M.-F. Local news covering the Medway towns, Gravesend, Dartford, Swale and Maidstone. Also national news. Paper with emphasis on news and sport, plus regular feature pages. *Illustrations:* line, half-tone.

Evening Post (1965), Ranald Allan, 8 Tessa Road, Reading RG1 8NS   *tel* (0734) 575833   *fax* (0734) 599363.
20p. D. Topical articles based on current news. *Length:* 800-1200 words. *Payment:* based on lineage rates. *Illustrations:* half-tone.

Evening Standard (1827), Paul Dacre, Northcliffe House, 2 Derry Street, London W8 5EE   *tel* 071-938 6000.
25p. D. Ind. Articles of general interest considered, 1500 words or shorter; also news, pictures and ideas.

Everyday Electronics (1971), Mike Kenward, Wimborne Publishing Ltd, 6 Church Street, Wimborne, Dorset BH21 1JH   *tel* (0202) 881749   *fax* (0202) 841692.
£1.50. M. Constructional and theoretical articles aimed at the student and hobbyist. *Length:* 1000-5500 words. *Payment:* £55-£90 per 1000 words depending on type of article. *Illustrations:* line, half-tone.

Everywoman (1985), Barbara Rogers, 34 Islington Green, London N1 8DU   *tel* 071-359 5496.

£1.40. M. Features, especially news features; short stories (up to 2500 words). *Study* of this feminist magazine essential; covering note should state which section a piece is for. *Illustrations:* line, half-tone, cartoons. *Payment:* for commissions, by arrangement; £20.

Exchange and Mart (1868), Link House, 25 West Street, Poole, Dorset BH15 1LL *tel* (0202) 671171 *telex* 417109.
95p. W. No editorial matter used.

Express and Star (1874), Keith Parker, Queen Street, Wolverhampton WV1 3BU *tel* (0902) 313131. London Office: Hamilton House, 1 Temple Avenue, Victoria Embankment, EC4Y 0HA.
22p. D. Will consider topical contributions up to 750 words with or without illustrations. *Payment:* by arrangement.

The Face (1980), Sheryl Garratt, The Old Laundry, Ossington Buildings, Moxon Street, London W1M 3HY *tel* 071-935 8232.
£1.50. M. Articles on music, fashion, films, popular youth culture. *Illustrations:* half-tone, colour. *Payment:* £110 per 1000 words; approx. £110 per page.

Faith and Freedom: A Journal of Progressive Religion (1947), Manchester College, Oxford. Editor: Peter B. Godfrey, BA, 41 Bradford Drive, Ewell, Epsom, Surrey KT19 0AQ *tel* 081-393 9122.
£10.00 p.a., 2 p.a. (Apr, Oct) Articles on philosophy and religion from free, non-dogmatic point of view. *Length:* 3000-5000 words. *Payment:* none.

Family Circle, IPC Magazines Ltd, King's Reach Tower, Stamford Street, London SE1 9LS *tel* 071-261 5000 *fax* 071-261 5929.
90p. 13 p.a. Practical, medical human interest material; short stories. *Length:* 650-11,500 words. *Illustrated. Payment:* NUJ rates or above.

Family Law (1971), Elizabeth Walsh, Miles McColl, 21 St Thomas Street, Bristol BS1 6JS *tel* (0272) 230600 *telex* 449119 *fax* (0272) 230063 *DX* 78161 Bristol.
£65.00 p.a. M. Articles dealing with all aspects of the law as it affects the family, written from a legal or socio-legal point of view. *Length:* from 1000 words. *Payment:* £15 per 1000 words, or by arrangement. No *illustrations*.

Family Tree Magazine (1984), John Michael and Mary Armstrong, 15/16 High-lode, Stocking Fen Road, Ramsey, Huntingdon, Cambs. PE17 1AB *tel* (0487) 814050.
£1.50. M. (£18.00 p.a.) Articles on any genealogically related topics. *Illustrations:* half-tone, line, cartoons. *Payment:* £18.00 per 1000 words; by arrangement.

Fantasy Tales (1977), Stephen Jones and David A. Sutton, Robinson Publishing, 11 Shepherd House, Shepherd Street, London W1Y 7LD *tel* 071-493 1064 *telex* 262433 Monref G ref 778 *fax* 071-409 7226.
£2.99. Bi-annual (Spr/Aut). All types of fantasy and horror short stories. *Payment:* by negotiation. *Illustrations:* line drawings – commissioned only, but examples of artwork welcomed. *Sae* essential. MSS submissions to: David A. Sutton, 194 Station Road, Kings Heath, Birmingham B14 7TE; artwork submissions to: Stephen Jones, 130 Park View, Wembley, Middlesex HA9 6JU.

Farmers Weekly (incorporating **Power Farming**) (1934), Ted Fellows, Reed Business Publishing, Greenfield House, 69-73 Manor Road, Wallington, Surrey SM6 0DE *tel* 081-661 4910.
60p. W. Articles on agriculture from freelance contributors will be accepted subject to negotiation.

Farming News (1983), Marcus Oliver, Morgan-Grampian Farming Press, 30 Calderwood Street, London SE18 6QH   *tel* 081-855 7777   *telex* 896238   *fax* 081-854 6795.
60p. W. (£45.00 p.a.) News, business, technical, leisure articles; crosswords, features. *Payment:* NUJ freelance rates. *Illustrations:* half-tone, colour, cartoons.

Fashion Forecast International (1946), Managing Editor: Nina Hirst, 33 Bedford Place, London WC1B 5JX   *tel* 071-637 2211   *telex* 8954884   *fax* 071-637 2248.
£22.00 p.a. UK/Europe, £32.00 p.a. outside Europe. 2 p.a. (Feb, Aug) **Hosiery Forecast** and **Lingerie Forecast** are included in each issue. Factual articles on fashions and accessories with forecast trends. *Length:* 800-1000 words. *Illustrations:* line, half-tone. *Payment:* by arrangement.

Fashion Weekly (1959), Karen Falconer, Ground Floor, Greater London House, Hampstead Road, London NW1 7QZ   *tel* 071-387 6611.
£1.05 W. (£51.00 p.a.) Fashion business newspaper primarily for retailers and wholesalers. *Payment:* by arrangement. *Illustrations:* line, half-tone, colour.

Fear (1988), Newsfield, Ludlow, Shropshire SY8 1QS   *tel* (0584) 87 5851   *fax* (0584) 87 6044.
£1.95. M. (USA $4.95) Fantasy, horror and science fiction short stories; also interviews, articles, news items, book, film and video reviews. *Length:* 1500-4000 words. *Illustrations:* line, half-tone, colour. *Payment:* at Newsfield's current rates; by negotiation.

The Field (1853) (incorporating **Land and Water, The Country Gentleman** and **Country Times and Landscape**), Jonathan Young, 10 Sheet Street, Windsor, Berks. SL4 1BG   *tel* (0753) 856061   *fax* (0753) 831086.
£2.25. M. Specific, topical and informed features on the British countryside and country pursuits, including natural history, field sports, gardening and farming. Overseas subjects considered but opportunities for such articles are limited. No fiction or children's material. Articles, *length* 800-2000 words, by outside contributors considered. *Illustrations:* colour photos of a high standard. *Payment:* on merit.

Film Monthly, Ken Ferguson, Argus Specialist Publications, Argus House, Boundary Way, Hemel Hempstead, Herts. HP2 7ST   *tel* (0442) 66551   *telex* 827797   *fax* (0442) 66998.
£1.50. M. Features on the film, video and TV scene. Sae to be enclosed for return of MS, if not suitable. *Payment:* by arrangement.

Filtration & Separation (1964), Simon Atkinson, Mayfield House, 256 Banbury Road, Oxford OX2 7DH   *tel* (0865) 512242.
£6.50. Bi-M. Articles on the design, contruction and application of filtration and separation equipment and dust control and air cleaning equipment for all industrial purposes; articles on filtration and separation and dust control and air cleaning operations and techniques in all industries. *Payment:* by arrangement. *Illustrations:* line, half-tone.

Financial Adviser (1987), Ceri Jones, Boundary House, 91-3 Charterhouse Street, London EC1M 6HR   *tel* 071-608 3471   *fax* 071-250 0004.
Free to SRO members. W. (£52.00 p.a.) Topical personal finance news and features. *Length:* variable. *Payment:* by arrangement.

Financial Director (1984), Jane Simms, VNU Business Publications, VNU House, 32-34 Broadwick Street, London W1A 2HG   *tel* 071-439 4242   *telex* 23918 VNU G   *fax* 071-437 7001.
£2.00 (free to finance directors). M. Features on financial and strategic

management issues. *Length:* 1500-2000 words. *Illustrations:* colour and b&w photos, line drawings. *Payment:* £120-£150 per 1000 words; photos, variable; line, £250-£300.

Financial Times (1888), Richard Lambert, Number One, Southwark Bridge, London SE1 9HL   *tel* 071-873 3000.
55p. D. Articles of financial, commercial, industrial and economic interest. *Length:* 800-1000 words. *Payment:* by arrangement.

Flight International (1909), A. Winn, Reed Business Publishing, Quadrant House, The Quadrant, Sutton, Surrey SM2 5AS   *tel* 081-661 3883   *telex* 892084 Reedbp G   *fax* 081-661 3840.
£1.75. W. Deals with all branches of aviation: operational and technical articles, illustrated by photos, engineering cutaway drawings; also news, paragraphs, reports of lectures, etc. News press days: Thu, Fri. *Illustrations:* tone, line, 2- and 4-colour. *Payment:* varies; by agreement.

Fly-Fishing & Fly-Tying (1990), Mark Bowler, The Lodge, Meridian House, Bakewell Road, Orton Southgate, Peterborough PE2 0XU   *tel* (0733) 371937   *fax* (0733) 361056.
£1.80. Bi-M. Fishing and fly-tying articles, fishery features, short stories. *Length:* 800-1500 words. *Illustrations:* colour and b&w photos. *Payment:* by arrangement.

Football Picture Story Library, D.C. Thomson & Co. Ltd, Courier Place, Dundee DD1 9QJ   *tel* (0382) 23131   *fax* (0382) 22214; and 185 Fleet Street, London EC4A 2HS   *tel* 071-242 5086   *fax* 071-404 5694.
35p. 2 p.m. Football stories for boys told in pictures.

For Him (1987), Geoffrey Aquilina-Ross, 9-11 Curtain Road, London EC2A 3LT   *tel* 071-247 5447   *fax* 071-247 5892.
£2.00. 10 p.a. Features, fashion, grooming, travel (adventure) and men's interests. *Length:* 2000-3000 words. *Illustrations:* colour photos. *Payment:* £150 per 1000 words; by negotiation.

Forensic Photography, incorporating **Medico-Legal Photography** (1972), 87 London Street, Chertsey, Surrey KT16 8AN   *tel* (0932) 562933.
£15.00 p.a. Q. Though this journal goes only to subscribers and is not sold through retail channels, the editor is always interested in articles (illustrated or not) concerned with photographic techniques slanted to the professional and concerned with any aspect of the journal's title. *Payment:* by arrangement. *Illustrations:* line, half-tone.

Freelance Market News—see **Freelance Press Services** in **Editorial, Literary and Production Services.**

Freelance Writing & Photography (1965), John T. Wilson, Weavers Press Publishing, Tregeraint House, Zennor, St Ives, Cornwall TR26 3DB   *tel/fax* (0736) 797061.
£2.50. Q. (£11.50 p.a.) Articles, features, reviews, interviews, market news, competitions, tips and hints for the freelance writer and photographer. *No work will be considered* unless accompanied by an sae. Letter of enquiry or outline preferred in first instance. *Length:* 250-1000 words. *Illustrations:* line, half-tone. *Payment:* £20 per 1000 words on acceptance; £5 per photo/illustration.

Fresh Produce Journal (1895), Andrew Clayton, 430 Market Towers, New Covent Garden, Nine Elms Lane, London SW8 5NN   *tel* 071-622 6677   *telex* 915149 Fpjjnl G   *fax* 071-720 2047.
£1.00. W. Articles dealing with above trades on the marketing aspects of production but particularly importing, distribution and post-harvest handling;

articles should average 500-700 words. *Payment:* by arrangement. *Illustrations:* half-tone.

The Friend (1843), Sally Juniper, Drayton House, 30 Gordon Street, London WC1H 0BQ   *tel* 071-387 7549. Publishing: Headley Brothers Ltd, Ashford, Kent.
60p. W. Quaker weekly paper. Material of interest to the Society of Friends, devotional or general, considered from outside contributors. No fiction. *Length:* up to 1200 words. *Illustrations:* b&w or colour prints for cover: seasons, children, Third World, minorities. *Payment:* none.

Garden News (1958), Mike Wyatt, EMAP National Publications Ltd, Apex House, Oundle Road, Peterborough PE2 9NP   *tel* (0733) 898100   *fax* (0733) 898418.
53p. W. Gardening news and features on gardeners and their methods of success. *Payment:* £25 per 1000 words; higher rate for good short pieces and suited to our style. *Illustrations:* line, half-tone, colour.

Gas World (1884), Alan Bakalor, Benn Industrial Publications Ltd, Sovereign Way, Tonbridge, Kent TN9 1RW   *tel* (0732) 364422   *telex* 95162 Benton G   *fax* (0732) 361534.
£5.00. M. (£52.00 p.a.) Full news coverage and technical articles on all aspects of engineering and management in the gas industry. *Length:* up to 1800 words. Pictures and news items of topical interest accepted. *Payment:* by arrangement.

Gay Times (1982), John Marshall, 283 Camden High Street, London NW1 7BX   *tel* 071-482 2576   *fax* 071-284 0329.
£1.50. M. Full news and review coverage of all aspects of homosexual life. Short stories and feature articles. *Length:* up to 2000 words. *Illustrations:* line and half-tone, cartoons. *Payment:* by arrangement.

Gemmological Newsletter (1969), Michael O'Donoghue, 7 Hillingdon Avenue, Sevenoaks, Kent TN13 3RB   *tel* (0732) 453503.
£6.50 p.a. 30 p.a. (Oct-Jul) Articles about minerals, gemstones, man-made crystals and lapidary. *Length:* up to 800-1000 words. *Payment:* by arrangement. *Illustrated.*

Geographical Journal (1893), Dr R.A.M. Gardner, Royal Geographical Society, Kensington Gore, London SW7 2AR   *tel* 071-589 5466   *telex* 933669   *fax* 071-581 9918.
£14.00 (post free). 3 p.a. (£37.50 p.a.) Papers on all aspects of geography, including some read before the Royal Geographical Society. *Length:* up to 4500 words. *Payment:* for reviews. *Illustrations:* photos, maps and diagrams.

Geographical Magazine (1935), Mark Ausenda, World Publications Ltd (BBC Magazines), under licence from the Royal Geographical Society, Hyde Park House, Manfred Road, London SW15 2RS   *tel* 081-877 1080   *fax* 081-874 1845.
£1.50. M. Topical geography in a broad sense. *Length:* 2000 words. *Illustrations:* colour slides, b&w prints or vintage material; maps and graphs always needed. *Payment:* £100 per 1000 words; from £25.

Geological Magazine (1864), Dr C.P. Hughes, Professor I.N. McCave, Dr N.H. Woodcock, Dr M.J. Bickle, Cambridge University Press, The Edinburgh Building, Shaftesbury Road, Cambridge CB2 2RU   *tel* (0223) 312393.
£103.00 p.a. Bi-M. (£109.00 p.a. overseas) Original articles on all earth science topics containing the results of independent research by experts and amateurs. Also reviews and notices of current geological literature, correspondence on geological subjects – illustrated. *Length:* variable. *Payment:* none.

Gifts International, Vhairi Cotter, Benn Business Magazines Ltd, Bullen Lane, East Peckham, Tonbridge, Kent TN12 5LP   *tel* (0622) 872972   *fax* (0622) 872346.
£38.00 p.a. M. (£48.00 p.a. overseas) News of gift industry – products, trends, shops. *Articles:* retailing, exporting, importing, manufacturing, crafts (UK and abroad). *Payment:* by agreement. *Illustrations:* products, news, personal photos.

Girl About Town Magazine (1973), Claire Gillman, 141-3 Drury Lane, Covent Garden, London WC2B 5TS   *tel* 071-836 4433   *fax* 071-836 2618.
Free. W. Articles of general interest to London women. *Length:* about 1000 words. *Illustrations:* line, half-tone, colour. *Payment:* by arrangement.

Glasgow Evening Times (1876), George McKechnie, 195 Albion Street, Glasgow G1 1QP   *tel* 041-552 6255; London Office: 1 Jerome Street, E1 6NJ   *tel* 071-377 0890   *telex* 779818   *fax* 041-553 1355.
25p. D.

Glasgow Herald (1783), Arnold Kemp, 195 Albion Street, Glasgow G1 1QP   *tel* 041-552 6255   *fax* 041-552 2288; London Office: Chelsea Bridge House, Queenstown Road, SW8 4NN   *tel* 071-739 8159.
35p. D. Ind. Articles up to 1000 words.

Gloucestershire Life, Group Editor: Bill Charlton, County Life Magazines, The Old Bank House, 7a Gosditch Street, Cirencester, Glos. GL7 2AG   *tel* (0285) 652122.
£1.00. M. Articles of interest to the county dealing with people in the news, personalities who live in the area; projects concerning individuals and communities; historical articles. *Length:* 800-1000 words. *Illustrations:* preference given to articles accompanied by good photos. *Payment:* by arrangement.

Golf Illustrated Weekly, Neil Elsey, Advance House, 37 Millharbour, Isle of Dogs, London E14 9TX   *tel* 071-538 1031   *fax* 071-537 2053.
£1.00. W. News, tournament reports and articles on golf and of interest to golfers. *Payment:* by arrangement. *Illustrations:* photos of golfers and golf courses.

Golf Monthly (1911), Colin Callander, King's Reach Tower, Stamford Street, London SE1 9LS   *tel* 071-261 7237   *fax* 071-261 7240.
£2.20. M. Original articles on golf considered (not reports), golf clinics, handy hints. *Payment:* by arrangement. *Illustrations:* half-tone, colour.

Golf World (1962), Robert Green, Advance House, 37 Millharbour, Isle of Dogs, London E14 9TX   *tel* 071-538 1031   *fax* 071-538 4106.
£1.75. M. Expert golf instructional articles, 500-3000 words; general interest articles, personality features 500-3000 words. Little fiction. *Payment:* by negotiation. *Illustrations:* line, half-tone, colour.

Good Housekeeping (1922), Noëlle Walsh, National Magazine House, 72 Broadwick Street, London W1V 2BP   *tel* 071-439 5000.
£1.40. M. Articles of 1000-2500 words from qualified writers are invited on topics of interest to intelligent women. Domestic subjects covered by staff writers. Short stories and humorous articles occasionally used. *Payment:* good magazine standards. *Illustrations:* mainly commissioned.

The Good Ski Guide A-Z, John Hill, 1-2 Dawes Court, 93 High Street, Esher, Surrey KT10 9QD   *tel* (0372) 469799   *fax* (0372) 466365.
£3.50. Q. Factual articles on all aspects of skiing. *Illustrations:* colour slides/prints. *Payment:* £100 per 1000 words; £200 for cover; £50 inside page.

GQ (1988), Alexandra Shulman, Vogue House, Hanover Square, London W1R 0AD   *tel* 071-499 9080   *telex* 27338 Volon G   *fax* 071-493 1345.
£2.00. M. Articles relating to the life style of the successful, stylish man. *Illustrations:* b&w and colour photos, line drawings, cartoons. *Payment:* by arrangement.

Gramophone, Christopher Pollard, 177-179 Kenton Road, Harrow, Middlesex HA3 0HA   *tel* 081-907 4476.
£1.95. M. Outside contributions are occasionally used. Features on recording artists, technical articles, and articles about gramophone needs. *Length:* 1000-1500 words preferred. *Payment:* by arrangement. *Illustrations:* line, half-tone.

Granta (1889; new series 1979), Editor: Bill Buford, Managing Director: Derek Johns, 2/3 Hanover Yard, Noel Road, Islington, London N1 8BE   *tel* 071-704 9776   *fax* 071-704 0474. Published in association with Penguin Books UK Ltd.
£6.99. Q. Original fiction and cultural journalism. *Length:* determined by content. *Illustrations:* photos. *Payment:* by arrangement.

The Great Outdoors (1978), Cameron McNeish, The Plaza Tower, The Plaza, East Kilbride, Glasgow G74 1LW   *tel* (03552) 46444.
£1.60. M. (£20.00 p.a.) Articles on walking or camping in specific areas, preferably illustrated. *Length:* 1500-2000 words. *Payment:* by arrangement. *Illustrations:* line, half-tone, colour.

Green Magazine (1989), Alister Townley, The Northern & Shell Building, PO Box 381, Millharbour, London E14 9TW   *tel* 071-987 5090   *telex* 24676 Norshl G   *fax* 071-538 3690.
£1.95. M. Feature articles and topical news items covering all aspects of the environment. No fiction. *Length:* features 1000-2500 words. *Illustrations:* colour and b&w photos and line. *Payment:* £120 per 1000 words; by arrangement.

The Grocer (1861), A. de Angeli, William Reed, Broadfield Park, Crawley, West Sussex RH11 9RJ   *tel* (0293) 613400   *fax* (0293) 515174.
25p. W. Journal devoted entirely to the trade: accepts articles or news or illustrations of general interest to the grocery and provision trades. *Payment:* by arrangement.

The Grower (1923), Peter Rogers, 50 Doughty Street, London WC1N 2LS   *tel* 071-405 0364.
85p. W. News and practical articles on commercial horticulture, preferably illustrated. *Illustrations:* photos, line drawings. *Payment:* by arrangement.

The Guardian (1821), Peter Preston, 119 Farringdon Road, London EC1R 3ER   *tel* 071-278 2332   *telex* 8811746/7/8 Guardn G; 164 Deansgate, Manchester M60 2RR   *tel* 061-832 7200.
40p. D. Ind. The paper takes few articles from outside contributors except on its specialist pages. Articles should not normally exceed 1200 words in *length. Payment:* from £142.60 per 1000 words. *Illustrations:* news and features photos.

Guiding, Nora Warner, 17-19 Buckingham Palace Road, London SW1W 0PT   *tel* 071-834 6242.
£1.00. M. Official Organ of the Girl Guides Association. Articles of interest to women of all ages, with special emphasis on youth work and the Guide Movement. *Length:* 500-1500 words. *Illustrations:* line, half-tone. *Payment:* £50 per 1000 words; £100 full colour page, £60 b&w – negotiable.

The Haiku Quarterly (1990), Kevin Bailey, 39 Exmouth Street, Kingshill, Swindon, Wilts. SN1 3PU   *tel* (0793) 523927.

£1.80. Q. (£6.00 p.a.) Short poems – from Haiku and Tanka to Welsh englyn and Gaelic epigrams; also Imagistic/Minimalistic poetry of less than about 14 lines. Book and magazine reviews. *Payment:* small. Commissioned *illustrations.*

Hampshire—The County Magazine, Dennis Stevens, 74 Bedford Place, Southampton SO1 2DF   *tel* (0703) 223591/333457.
£1.00. M. Factual articles concerning all aspects of Hampshire and Hampshire life, past and present. *Length:* 500-1500 words. *Payment:* £10 per 1000 words. *Illustrations:* photos and line drawings.

Harpers & Queen (1929), Vicki Woods, National Magazine House, 72 Broadwick Street, London W1V 2BP   *tel* 071-439 5000   *fax* 071-439 5506.
£2.50. M. Features, fashion, beauty, art, theatre, films, travel, interior decoration, mainly commissioned. *Illustrations:* line, wash, full colour and two- and three-colour, and photos.

Health & Efficiency International (1900), Jane Hendy-Smith, 28 Charles Square, Pitfield Street, London N1 6HT   *tel* 071-253 4037   *fax* 071-253 0539.
£1.70. M. (also publishes separate Q. and Bi-A. editions) Articles on naturist and human relationship matters. Naturist travel features; some health and humour. *Length:* 750-1500 words. *Illustrations:* line, half-tone, colour transparencies, colour prints, cartoons. *Payment:* £40 per 1000 words; varies.

Health & Fitness (1984), Sharon Walker, 40 Bowling Green Lane, London EC1R 0NE   *tel* 071-278 0333   *fax* 071-837 7612.
£1.50. M. Articles on all aspects of health and fitness. *Illustrations:* line, half-tone, colour, cartoons. *Payment:* by arrangement; varies.

Heredity: An International Journal of Genetics (1947), J.S. Parker, School of Biological Sciences, Queen Mary & Westfield College, University of London, Mile End Road, London E1 4NS.
£112.50 (UK), overseas rates on application (two volumes each of three parts yearly) Research and review articles in genetics of 1000-15,000 words with summary and bibliography. Book reviews and abstracts of conferences. *Illustrations:* line, half-tone. *Payment:* none.

Here's Health, Emap Élan, Victory House, Leicester Place, London WC2H 7BP   *tel* 071-437 9011   *telex* 266400   *fax* 071-434 0656.
£1.20. M. Articles on nutrition, alternative medicine, environment and health, natural treatment success stories. *Preliminary letter* essential. *Length:* 750-1800 words. *Payment:* on publication. *Illustrated.*

Hertfordshire Countryside (1946), Ken Washbrook, Beaumonde Publications Ltd, 4 Mill Bridge, Hertford, Herts. SG14 1PY   *tel* (0992) 553571   *fax* (0992) 587713.
£1.00. M. Articles of county interest, 1000 words. *Payment:* £25 per 1000 words. *Illustrations:* line, half-tone.

The Heythrop Journal (1960), Dr T.J. Deidun, Heythrop College, University of London, 11 Cavendish Square, London W1M 0AN   *tel* 071-580 6941.
£4.00 inc. postage. Q. (£13.50 p.a.; USA $35.00; institutions £20.00 p.a.; USA $48.00) Accept articles on philosophy, theology – speculative and positive, scripture, canon law, church relations, moral and pastoral psychology, of general interest but of technical merit. *Length:* 5000-8000 words. *Payment:* authors receive 24 offprints.

Hi!, D.C. Thomson & Co. Ltd, 2 Albert Square, Dundee DD1 9QJ   *tel* (0382) 23131   *fax* (0382) 22214; and 185 Fleet Street, London EC4A 2HS   *tel* 071-242 5086/8   *fax* 071-404 5694.

38p. W. 32 pages of features, photo stories and picture stories, with 75% colour. Aimed at trendy 10-14 year olds. *Payment:* on acceptance.

Hi-Fi News & Record Review (1956), Steve Harris, Link House, Dingwall Avenue, Croydon CR9 2TA   *tel* 081-686 2599   *fax* 081-760 0973.
£1.95. M. Articles on all aspects of high quality sound recording and reproduction; also extensive record review section and supporting musical feature articles. Audio matter is essentially technical, but should be presented in a manner suitable for music lovers interested in the nature of sound. *Length:* 2000-3000 words. *Illustrations:* line and/or half-tone, cartoons. *Payment:* by arrangement.

High Fidelity (incorporating **New Hi-Fi Sound**) (1990), Elizabeth Hughes, Haymarket Publishing Ltd, 38-42 Hampton Road, Teddington, Middlesex TW11 0JE   *tel* 081-943 5000.
£1.80. M. Articles by professional contributors on audio equipment and related subjects by arrangement with editor. *Preliminary letter* essential. *Payment:* by arrangement. *Illustrated.*

Higher Education Quarterly (1946), Michael Shattock, University of Warwick, Coventry CV4 7AL   *tel* (0203) 523523.
£20.50 p.a. Q. (£48.50 p.a. institutions) (subscriptions from Basil Blackwell Ltd, 108 Cowley Road, Oxford OX4 1JF) Articles on national and international higher education policy. *Length:* 2000-6000 words. *Payment:* 6 copies of issue.

History (1916), Professor W.A. Speck, MA, DPhil. Editorial: School of History, The University of Leeds, Leeds LS2 9JT   *tel* (0532) 333587. Published by the Historical Association, 59A Kennington Park Road, London SE11 4JH   *tel* 071-735 3901.
£9.50 for Historical Ass. members; £29.00 p.a. non-members. 3 p.a. Historical articles and reviews by experts. *Length:* usually up to 8000 words. *Illustrations:* only exceptionally. *Payment:* none.

History Today (1951), Gordon Marsden, 83-84 Berwick Street, London W1V 3PJ   *tel* 071-439 8315.
£2.25. M. History in the widest sense – political, economic, social, biography, relating past to present; world history as well as British. *Length:* articles 3500 words; shorter news/views pieces 600-1200 words. *Illustrations:* from prints and original photos. Please do not send original material until publication is agreed. *Payment:* by arrangement.

Home and Country (1919), Penny Kitchen, 104 New King's Road, London SW6 4LY   *tel* 071-371 9300   *fax* 071-736 4061.
45p. M. Official Journal of the National Federation of Women's Institutes for England and Wales. Publishes material related to the Federation's activities; also considers articles of general interest to women, particularly country women, of 800-1200 words. *Illustrations:* photos and drawings. *Payment:* by arrangement; varies.

Home and Family (1954), Margaret Duggan, The Mothers' Union, The Mary Sumner House, 24 Tufton Street, London SW1P 3RB   *tel* 071-222 5533.
30p. Q. Short articles related to Christian family life. *Payment:* approx. £20-£35 per 1000 words. *Illustrations:* line and half-tone, usually commissioned.

Home Words (1870), PO Box 44, Guildford, Surrey GU1 1XL   *tel* (0483) 33944.
M. Illustrated C of E magazine insert. Articles of popular Christian interest (400-800 words) with relevant photos. *Payment:* by arrangement.

Homes and Gardens (1919), Amanda Evans, IPC Magazines Ltd, King's Reach Tower, Stamford Street, London SE1 9LS   *tel* 071-261 5000   *fax* 071-261 6247.
£1.60. M. Articles on home interest or design. *Length:* articles, 900-1000 words. *Illustrations:* all types. *Payment:* generous, but exceptional work required; varies.

Horse and Hound, M.A. Clayton, IPC Magazines Ltd, King's Reach Tower, Stamford Street, London SE1 9LS   *tel* 071-261 6315.
£1.00. W. Special articles, news items, photos, on all matters appertaining to horses, hunting. *Payment:* by negotiation.

Horse & Pony (1980), Sarah Haw, EMAP Pursuit Publishing Ltd, Bretton Court, Bretton, Peterborough PE3 8DZ   *tel* (0733) 264666   *fax* (0733) 265515.
80p. F. All material relevant to young people with equestrian interests. *Payment:* on value to publication rather than length. *Illustrations:* colour, b&w, with a strong story line.

Horse and Rider (1959), Managing Editor: Kate Austin, Editor: Alison Bridge, 296 Ewell Road, Surbiton, Surrey KT6 7AQ   *tel* 081-390 8547   *fax* 081-390 8696.
£1.20. M. Sophisticated magazine covering all forms of equestrian activity at home and abroad. Good writing and technical accuracy essential. *Length:* 1000-1600 words. *Illustrations:* photos and drawings, the latter usually commissioned. *Payment:* by arrangement; £15.

Horticulture Week, J. Aspinall, 38-42 Hampton Road, Teddington, Middlesex TW11 0JE   *tel* 081-943 5023.
90p. W. (£50.00 p.a.) Practical horticultural journal for the nursery and garden centre trade, landscape industry and public parks and sports ground staff. Outside contributions considered and, if accepted, paid for. No fiction. *Length:* 500-1500 words. *Illustrations:* line, half-tone, colour. *Payment:* by arrangement.

Hortus (1987), David Wheeler, The Neuadd, Rhayader, Powys LD6 5HH   *tel* (0597) 810227.
£24.00 p.a. Q. Articles on decorative horticulture: plants, gardens, history, design, literature, people. Book reviews. *Length:* 1500-5000 words, longer by arrangement. *Payment:* by arrangement. *Illustrations:* line, half-tone and wood-engravings.

Hospitality (1980), Consultant Editor: Alan Sutton, 58 Collingdon Street, Luton, Beds. LU1 1RX   *tel* (0582) 480065   *fax* (0582) 33531.
£2.00. M. Official magazine of the Hotel Catering & Institutional Management Association. Articles for a management readership on food, accommodation services and related topics in hotels, restaurants, tourism, educational establishments, the health service, industrial situations, educational and other institutions. *Illustrations:* photos, line. *Payment:* by arrangement.

House & Garden, Robert Harling, Vogue House, Hanover Square, London W1R 0AD   *tel* 071-499 9080   *telex* 27338 Volon G   *fax* 071-493 1345.
£2.00. M. Articles (always commissioned), on subjects relating to domestic architecture, interior decorating, furnishing, gardening, household equipment.

House Beautiful (1989), Pat Roberts, National Magazine House, 72 Broadwick Street, London W1V 2BP   *tel* 071-439 5500   *fax* 071-437 6886.
£1.00. M. Specialist 'home' features for the homes of today. *Preliminary study* of magazine advisable. *Payment:* according to merit. *Illustrated.*

House Builder, Phillip Cooke, 82 New Cavendish Street, London W1M 8AD   *tel* 071-580 5588.

£6.00. M. Official Journal of the House-Builders Federation and National House-Building Council. Technical articles on design, construction and equipment of dwellings, estate planning and development, and technical aspects of house-building, aimed at those engaged in house and flat construction and the development of housing estates. *Preliminary letter* advisable. *Length:* articles from 500 words, preferably with illustrations. *Payment:* by arrangement. *Illustrations:* photos, plans, construction details.

i-D Magazine (1980), Matthew Collin, Third Floor, 134/146 Curtain Road, London EC2A 3AR   *tel* 071-729 7305   *fax* 071-729 7266.
£1.80. M. (£20.00 p.a.) Youth and general interest magazine: i-Deas, fashion, clubs, music, people. Will consider unsolicited material. *Illustrations:* colour and b&w photos. *Payment:* £80 per 1000 words; £45 per page.

Ideal Home (1920), Terence Whelan, IPC Magazines Ltd, King's Reach Tower, Stamford Street, London SE1 9LS   *tel* 071-261 6474.
£1.30. M. Specialised home subjects magazine, and articles usually commissioned. Contributors advised to *study editorial content* before submitting material. *Payment:* according to material. *Illustrations:* usually commissioned.

The Illustrated London News (1842), James Bishop, 20 Upper Ground, London SE1 9PF   *tel* 071-928 2111   *fax* 071-620 1594.
£2.00. 6 p.a. Magazine dealing chiefly with London and the UK, travel, environment and the quality of life. Interesting articles accepted; but most material commissioned. *Payment:* usual rates; special rates for exclusive material.

Impact of Science on Society (1950), Howard Moore, Unesco, 31 rue François-Bonvin, Paris 75015, France   *tel* 33(1) 45 68 41 44/49   *telegraphic address* Unesco, Paris   *telex* 204461 Paris   *fax* 33(1) 43 06 11 22.
96p. Q. Articles and original studies on the social, economic and cultural effects of new developments in science and technology. Intending contributors are advised to study the magazine; *preliminary letter* to the editor is requested. *Length:* 4500 words. *Illustrations:* photos, tables, graphs and drawings. *Payment:* up to £150 on acceptance; none.

In Britain (1930), Sandra Harris, Headway Publications, Greater London House, Hampstead Road, London NW1 7QQ   *tel* 071-377 4633   *fax* 071-383 7570.
£1.25. M. (£17.50 p.a.) Upmarket features magazine about places and people in Britain. Some freelance material accepted. *Illustrated. Payment:* by arrangement.

Incentive Today (1982), Charles Ford, Langfords Publications Ltd, Ridgeland House, 165 Dyke Road, Hove, East Sussex BN3 1TL   *tel* (0273) 206722   *fax* (0273) 736250.
£2.50. M. Articles on sales promotion, marketing, motivation and travel. *Illustrations:* line, half-tone, colour. *Payment:* by negotiation.

The Independent (1986), Andreas Whittam Smith, 40 City Road, London EC1Y 2DB   *tel* 071-253 1222.
40p. D. 45p. Sat. Occasional freelance contributions; *preliminary letter* advisable. *Payment:* by arrangement.

The Independent Magazine (1988), Alexander Chancellor, 40 City Road, London EC1Y 2DB   *tel* 071-253 1222   *fax* 071-962 0016.
Free with newspaper. W. Profiles and illustrated articles of topical interest; *all material commissioned. Preliminary study* of the magazine essential. *Length:* 500-3000 words. *Illustrations:* cartoons; commissioned colour and b&w photos. *Payment:* by arrangement.

The Independent on Sunday (1990), Ian Jack, 40 City Road, London EC1Y 2DB *tel* 071-253 1222 *telex* 9419611 *fax* 071-415 1333.
60p. W. News, features and articles. *Illustrated. Payment:* approx. £150 per 1000 words; by negotiation.

Index on Censorship (1972), Andrew Graham-Yooll, 39c Highbury Place, London N5 1QP *tel* 071-359 0161 *fax* 071-226 8666.
£2.10. 10 p.a. (£21.00 p.a.) Articles up to 5000 words dealing with political censorship, book reviews 750-1500 words. *Payment:* articles £50 per 1000 words, book reviews £25.

The Indexer (1958), Hazel Bell, 139 The Ryde, Hatfield, Herts. AL9 5DP *tel* (0707) 265201.
Free to members. 2 p.a. (subscription £20.00 p.a. from Journal Subscriptions Officer, 16 Coleridge Close, Hitchin, Herts. SG4 0QX). Journal of the Society of Indexers, American Society of Indexers, Australian Society of Indexers, and Indexing & Abstracting Society of Canada. Articles of interest to professional indexers, authors, publishers, documentalists. *Payment:* none.

An Indian Bookworm's Journal (1987), Shreeram Vidyarthi, Institute of India Studies, 45 Museum Street, London WC1A 1LR *tel* 071-405 7226/3784 *fax* 071-831 4517.
£1.35. Q. (£2.00 overseas) Articles and news pieces about books with specific interest for the Indian subcontinent. *Preliminary letter* preferred. *Payment:* by arrangement. *Illustrations:* line, including cartoons; half-tone.

Information and Software Technology (1959), Butterworth-Heinemann Ltd, Linacre House, Jordan Hill, Oxford OX2 8DP *tel* (0865) 310366 *fax* (0865) 310898.
£137.00 p.a. 11 p.a. (£147.00 p.a. Europe, £157.00 p.a. elsewhere) Papers on software design and development and the application of information processing in large organisations, especially multinationals. *Length:* 5000 words. *Illustrations:* line, half-tone. *Payment:* commissioned material only by arrangement; none.

The Inquirer (1842), Keith Gilley, 1-6 Essex Street, London WC2R 2HY *tel* 071-240 2384.
30p. F. Journal of news and comment for Unitarians and religious liberals. Articles up to 750 words of general religious, social, cultural and international interest. Articles should be liberal and progressive in tone. *Payment:* none.

Insurance Brokers' Monthly (1950), Brian Susman, 7 Stourbridge Road, Lye, Stourbridge, West Midlands DY9 7DG *tel* Lye (0384) 895228.
£2.00. M. Articles of technical and non-technical interest to insurance brokers and others engaged in the insurance industry. Occasional articles of general interest to the City, on finance, etc. *Length:* 1000-1500 words. *Payment:* from £18.50 per 1000 words on last day of month following publication. Authoritative material written under true name and qualification receives highest payment. *Illustrations:* line and half-tone, 100-120 screen.

InterMedia (1970), Rex Malik, International Institute of Communications, Tavistock House South, Tavistock Square, London WC1H 9LF *tel* 071-388 0671 *telex* 24578 IIC LDN *fax* 071-380 0623.
£35.00 p.a. 5 p.a. (£55.00 p.a. institutions) International journal concerned with policies, events, trends and research in the field of communications and broadcasting. *Preliminary letter* essential. *Illustrations:* b&w line. *Payment:* by arrangement.

International Affairs (1922), Royal Institute of International Affairs, Chatham House, 10 St James's Square, London SW1Y 4LE *tel* 071-930 2233 *fax* 071-839 3593.
£11.00. Q. (£27.00 p.a., institutions £34.00 p.a., overseas £37.00 p.a.) Serious long-term articles on international affairs and reviews of books. *Preliminary letter* advisable. *Length:* average 7000 words. *Illustrations:* none. *Payment:* by arrangement.

International Broadcast Engineer, David Kirk, Argus Business Publications Ltd, Queensway House, 2 Queensway, Redhill, Surrey RH1 1QS *tel* (0737) 768611 *telex* 948669 Topjnl G *fax* (0737) 760564.
£55.00 p.a. Bi-M. Independent journal devoted to the structure and operation of professional television and radio broadcast equipment. Circulates to over 144 countries and technical aspect is emphasised. *Preliminary letter* essential. *Illustrations:* line, half-tone. *Payment:* by arrangement.

International Construction, A.J. Peterson, Maclean Hunter Ltd, Maclean Hunter House, Chalk Lane, Cockfosters Road, Barnet, Herts. EN4 0BU *tel* 081-975 9759 *telex* 299072 Machun G *fax* 081-975 9760.
Controlled circulation. M. Articles dealing with new techniques of construction, applications of construction equipment and use of construction materials in any part of the world. *Length:* maximum 1500 words plus illustrations. *Payment:* from £100 per 1000 words minimum, plus illustrations. *Illustrations:* line, half-tone, colour. Some two-colour line illustrations can be used.

Interzone (1982), David Pringle, 124 Osborne Road, Brighton, East Sussex BN1 6LU *tel* (0273) 504710.
£2.25. M. (£26.00 p.a.) Science fiction and fantasy short stories, articles, interviews and reviews. *Please read magazine* before submitting. *Length:* 2000-6000 words. *Illustrations:* line, half-tone, colour. *Payment:* by arrangement.

Inverness Courier (1817), Alex Main, PO Box 13, 9-11 Bank Lane, Inverness IV1 1QW *tel* (0463) 233059.
25p. Bi-W. Short articles (no stories or verses) of Highland interest only. Unsolicited material *not* accepted. Preliminary letter of enquiry essential. *Payment:* by arrangement. No *illustrations*.

Investors Chronicle, Gillian O'Connor, Greystoke Place, Fetter Lane, London EC4A 1ND *tel* 071-405 6969 *fax* 071-405 5276.
£1.40. W. Journal covering investment and personal finance. Occasional outside contributions for surveys are accepted. *Payment:* by negotiation.

Involvement & Participation (1884), Anthony Barry, 87-95 Tooley Street, London SE1 2RA *tel* 071-403 6018.
£23.00 p.a. UK, £33.00 p.a. overseas, post free. Q. Journal of the Involvement & Participation Association. Articles on participation and involvement in industry, employee shareholding, joint consultation, the sharing of information, labour-management relations, workers participation, and kindred industrial subjects from the operational angle, with emphasis on the practice of particular enterprises, usually written by a member of the team involved, whether manager or workers, and with a strong factual background. *Length:* up to 3000 words. *Payment:* £80 per 1000 words.

Iron (1973), Peter Mortimer, 5 Marden Terrace, Cullercoats, North Shields, Tyne and Wear NE30 4PD *tel* Tyneside (091) 2531901.
£2.40, inc. postage. 3 p.a. Poems; short stories up to 6000 words. *Illustrations:* line, half-tone. *Payment:* £10 per page; £5.

IS (formerly **Industrial Society**) (1918), Anna Smith, The Industrial Society, Robert Hyde House, 48 Bryanston Square, London W1H 7LN   *tel* 071-262 2401   *fax* 071-706 1096.

£19.50 p.a. Q. (overseas £24.90 p.a.) Articles, news items, photos on people management in industry and commerce in five inter-related areas: effective leadership, productive management-union relations and participation, practical communication, relevant conditions of employment and working environment and the development of young employees. *Length:* 1000-2000 words. *Illustrations:* half-tones and line drawings. *Payment:* by arrangement.

Jackie, D.C. Thomson & Co. Ltd, Courier Place, Dundee DD1 9QJ   *tel* (0382) 23131   *fax* (0382) 22214; and 185 Fleet Street, London EC4A 2HS   *tel* 071-242 5086   *fax* 071-404 5694.

40p. W. Colour gravure magazine for teenage girls. Complete photo love stories. Type stories up to 1500 words dealing with young romance. Pop features and pin-ups. General features of teen interest – emotional, astrological, humorous. Fashion and beauty advice. *Illustrations:* transparencies, colour illustrations for type stories. *Payment:* on acceptance.

Jane's Defence Weekly (1984), Peter Howard, Sentinel House, 163 Brighton Road, Coulsdon, Surrey CR5 2NH   *tel* 081-763 1030   *telex* 916907 Janes G   *fax* 081-763 1007.

£95.00 p.a. W. Defence news, military, political, industrial; analysis or briefing articles. *Length:* up to 1250 words. *Payment:* minimum £100 per 1000 words used. *Illustrations:* line, half-tone, colour.

Jazz Journal International (1948), Publisher and Editor-in-Chief: Eddie Cook, Jazz Journal Ltd, 113-117 Farringon Road, London EC1R 3BT   *tel* 071-278 0631/0637   *fax* 071-833 5720.

£2.00. M. Articles on jazz, record reviews. Prospective contributors are advised to call or write before submitting material. *Payment:* by arrangement. *Illustrations:* photos.

Jewish Chronicle (1841), Edward J. Temko, 25 Furnival Street, London EC4A 1JT   *tel* 071-405 9252.

35p. W. Authentic and exclusive news stories and articles of Jewish interest from 500-1500 words are considered. There are weekly children's, women's and teenage sections. *Payment:* by arrangement. *Illustrations:* of Jewish interest, either topical or feature.

Jewish Quarterly (1953), Colin Shindler, PO Box 1148, London NW5 2AZ   *tel* 071-485 4062.

£2.95. Q. (£10.00 p.a., £15.00 p.a. overseas) Articles of Jewish interest, literature, history, music, politics, poetry, book reviews, fiction. *Length:* 2000-3000 words. *Illustrations:* half-tone.

Jewish Telegraph (1950), Paul Harris, Telegraph House, 11 Park Hill, Bury Old Road, Prestwich, Manchester M25 8HH   *tel* 061-740 9321   *fax* 061-740 9325; 4A Roman View, Leeds LS8 2LW   *tel* (0532) 695044; Harold House, Dunbabin Road, Liverpool L15 6XL   *tel* 051-722 3999.

16p. W. Non-fiction articles of Jewish interest, especially humour. Exclusive Jewish news stories and pictures, international, national and local. *Length:* 1000-1500 words. *Payment:* by arrangement. *Illustrations:* line, half-tone.

The Journal, Christopher Cox, Thomson House, Groat Market, Newcastle upon Tyne NE1 1ED   *tel* Tyneside (091) 232 7500   *fax* Tyneside (091) 232 2256; London Office: Pemberton House, 3rd Floor, East Harding Street, EC4A 3AS   *tel* 071-353 9131.

22p. D. Ind. **Northern Business,** full colour business magazine, distributed free with paper third Thursday each month.

Journal of Alternative and Complementary Medicine (1983), Leon Chaitow, Mariner House, 53A High Street, Bagshot, Surrey GU19 5AH   *tel* (0276) 51522   *fax* (0276) 51557.
£1.95. M. (£25.00 p.a.) Feature articles (*length:* up to 2000 words) and news stories (*length:* up to 250 words). Unsolicited material seldom used. *Illustrations:* line, half-tone, colour. *Payment:* £100 per 1000 words; by negotiation.

Journalist, Tim Gopsill, NUJ, Acorn House, 314 Gray's Inn Road, London WC1X 8DP   *tel* 071-278 7916   *telex* 892384   *fax* 071-837 8143.
45p. M. (£9.50 p.a., £13.00 p.a. overseas) Newspaper of the National Union of Journalists. Relating to journalism, trade unionism and general conditions in the newspaper industry. Mainly contributed by members, and outside written contributions not paid.

Judy, D.C. Thomson & Co. Ltd, Courier Place, Dundee DD1 9QJ   *tel* (0382) 23131   *fax* (0382) 22214; and 185 Fleet Street, London EC4A 2HS   *tel* 071-242 5086   *fax* 071-404 5694. Merged with **Mandy,** *q.v.*
30p. W. Picture-story paper for schoolgirls. Stories (mainly line drawings) as serials or series, 8-9 frames per page. Encouragement to young artists and writers of promise. *Payment:* on acceptance.

Judy Library, D.C. Thomson & Co. Ltd, Courier Place, Dundee DD1 9QJ   *tel* (0382) 23131   *fax* (0382) 22214; and 185 Fleet Street, London EC4A 2HS   *tel* 071-242 5086   *fax* 071-404 5694.
35p. M. 64-page (about 140 line drawings) picture-stories for schoolgirls: ballet, school, adventure, theatre, sport. Scripts considered; promising artists and scriptwriters encouraged. *Payment:* on acceptance.

Junior Bookshelf, Marsh Hall, Thurstonland, Huddersfield HD4 6XB   *tel* (0484) 661811.
£1.75. 6 p.a. (£8.50 p.a., overseas £10.50 p.a.) Articles on children's books and authors. *Length:* about 1200-1500 words.

Junior Education (1977), Mrs Terry Saunders, Scholastic Publications Ltd, Villiers House, Clavendon Avenue, Leamington Spa, Warks. CV32 5PR   *tel* (0926) 887799   *fax* (0926) 883331.
£1.50. M. For teachers, educationalists and students concerned with children aged 7-12. Articles by specialists on practical teaching ideas and methods, plus in-depth coverage and debate on current issues in education. *Length:* 800-1200 words. *Payment:* by arrangement. *Illustrated* with b&w photos and line drawings; includes colour poster. **Junior Projects** (1982), Margot O'Keeffe, £1.50. Bi-M. Project-based magazine for teachers of 7-12 year olds. Includes 12 pages of project notes on a different theme each issue. Photocopiable material and posters form an integral part of the practical cross-curricular activities outlined.

Just Seventeen (1983), Morag Prunty, EMAP Metro Publications Ltd, 5th Floor, Mappin House, 4 Winsley Street, London W1N 7AR   *tel* 071-437 8050   *fax* 071-494 0851 (ext. 2738, after 6 p.m.).
55p. W. Articles of interest to girls aged between 12 and 18. Fashion, beauty, pop, and various features. Short stories up to 1500 words. Quizzes. *Payment:* £110 per 1000 words. *Illustrations:* line, half-tone, colour, cartoons.

Justice of the Peace (1837), F.W. Davies, Little London, Chichester, West Sussex PO19 1PG   *tel* (0243) 775552.
£106.50 p.a., inc. postage. W. Articles on magisterial law and associated subjects including children and young persons, criminology, medico-legal

matters, penology, police, probation (length preferred, under 1400 words). Short reports of conferences, meetings, etc. *Preliminary letter* welcomed although not essential. *Payment:* articles minimum £7.50 per column except when otherwise commissioned.

Kent, Clifford W. Russell, FRSA, 193 White Horse Hill, Chislehurst, Kent BR7 6DH   *tel* 081-857 7509.
Free to members. Q. Journal of the Men of Kent and Kentish Men. Articles referring to County of Kent or former Kent people of interest. *Length:* maximum 500-600 words. *Payment:* modest, by arrangement. *Illustrations:* photos and line.

Kent Messenger, 6 and 7 Middle Row, Maidstone, Kent ME14 1TG   *tel* (0622) 695666; London Office: Suite 511 International Press Centre, 76 Shoe Lane, EC4A 3JB.
35p. Fri. Articles of special interest to Kent particularly Maidstone and Mid-Kent areas. *Payment:* state price. *Illustrations:* any format.

The Lady (1885), Joan L. Grahame, 39-40 Bedford Street, Strand, London WC2E 9ER   *tel* 071-379 4717.
55p. W. British and foreign travel, countryside, human-interest, animals, cookery, historic-interest and commemorative articles (*preliminary letter* advisable for articles dealing with anniversaries). *Length:* 800-1400 words; Viewpoint: 600 words. *Payment:* by arrangement, averaging £55 per 1000 words for first British Serial Rights only, plus varying *payments* for *illustrations* (drawings, b&w photos).

Lancashire Evening Post, C.S. Kendall, Oliver's Place, Fulwood, Preston PR2 4ZA   *tel* (0772) 54841   *fax* (0772) 563288/204939.
19p. D. Topical articles on all subjects. Area of interest Wigan to Lake District and coast. *Length:* 600-900 words. *Payment:* by arrangement. *Illustrations:* half-tones and line blocks.

Lancashire Evening Telegraph (1886), Peter Butterfield, Telegraph House, High Street, Blackburn, Lancs. BB1 1HT   *tel* (0254) 63588.
22p. D. Will consider general interest articles, such as holidays, property, motoring, finance, etc.

Lancashire Life, Brian Hargreaves, Town & County Magazines, Oyston Mill, Strand Road, Preston PR1 8UR   *tel* (0772) 722022   *fax* (0772) 736496.
£1.50. M. Quality features and photographic material of regional interest. *Payment:* by negotiation.

Lancashire Magazine (1977), Winston Halstead, Barclays Bank Chambers, Sowerby Bridge, West Yorkshire HX6 2DX   *tel/fax* Halifax (0422) 885678.
80p. Bi-M. Articles about people, life and character of all parts of Lancashire. *Length:* 1500 words. *Payment:* £25-£30 approx. per published page. *Illustrations:* line, half-tone, colour.

Lancet (1823), Robin Fox, FRCPE, 42 Bedford Square, London WC1B 3SL   *tel* 071-436 4981   *telex* 291785   *fax* 071-436 7550.
£2.75. W. Mainly for medical profession and medical scientists.

Land & Liberty (1894), Fred Harrison, 177 Vauxhall Bridge Road, London SW1V 1EU   *tel* 071-834 4266.
£1.25. Bi-M. (£7.50 p.a.) Articles on land economics, land taxation, land prices, land speculation as they relate to housing, the economy, production, politics. *Study of journal* essential. *Length:* up to 3000 words. *Payment:* by arrangement. *Illustrations:* half-tone.

Learned Publishing (1988) (successor to **ALPSP Bulletin**), Hazel K. Bell, 139 The Ryde, Hatfield, Herts. AL9 5DP   *tel* (0707) 265201.
Free to members. Q. (£50.00 p.a.) Articles, reports and book reviews on publishing and learned societies: editorial, production, marketing and distribution, copyright. *Length:* 1000-1500 words. *Illustrations:* line, half-tone. *Payment:* none.

Leisure Management (1981), Liz Terry, Dicestar Ltd, 40 Bancroft, Hitchin, Herts. SG5 1LA   *tel* (0462) 431385   *fax* (0462) 433909.
£30.00 p.a. (on subscription). M. Articles on the development of leisure, recreation, tourism, entertainment, sports, hotels, heritage and countryside matters. Unsolicited manuscripts, cartoons, news and ideas welcomed. *Length:* up to 1000 words. *Illustrations:* colour and b&w photos, cartoons. *Payment:* not usually.

The Leisure Manager (1985), Judy Richardson, Victoria House, 25 High Street, Over, Cambs. CB4 5NB   *tel* (0954) 30940   *fax* (0954) 31886.
£35.00 p.a. M. Official Journal of The Institute of Leisure and Amenity Management. Articles on amenity, leisure, parks, entertainment, recreation and sports management. *Payment:* by arrangement. *Illustrations:* line, half-tone.

Leisure Painter (1966), Irene Briers, 63-65 High Street, Tenterden, Kent TN30 6BD   *tel* (05806) 3315.
£1.45. M. Instructional articles on painting and fine arts. *Payment:* £50 per 1000 words. *Illustrations:* line, half-tone, colour, original artwork.

Liberal Democrats News, Mike Harskin, 4 Cowley Street, London SW1P 3NB   *tel* 071-222 7999   *fax* 071-222 7904.
60p. W. (£25.00 p.a.) Official newspaper of the Liberal Democrats. News, political and social features. *Payment:* none.

The Library (1889), M.J. Jannetta, British Library, Humanities & Social Sciences, Collection Development, Great Russell Street, London WC1B 3DG *tel* 071-323 7605. Oxford University Press for the Bibliographical Society.
£10.00. Q. (£32.00 p.a.) Articles up to 15,000 words as well as shorter Notes, embodying original research on subjects connected with bibliography. *Illustrations:* line, half-tone. *Payment:* none.

Life and Work: Record of the Church of Scotland, 121 George Street, Edinburgh EH2 4YN   *tel* 031-225 5722   *fax* 031-220 3113.
35p. M. Articles not exceeding 1200 words and news. Seldom uses poems or stories. *Study* the magazine. *Payment:* up to £35 per 1000 words, or by arrangement. *Illustrations:* photos and line.

Lines Review (1952), Tessa Ransford, Edgefield Road, Loanhead, Edinburgh, Midlothian EH20 9SY   *tel* 031-440 0246   *fax* 031-440 0315.
£1.50. Q. (£7.00 p.a.) Poetry, essays, criticism, reviews. *Illustrations:* line/half-tone for frontispiece only. *Payment:* £20 per 1000 words; £10.

The Linguist, Dr J.L. Kettle-Williams, The Institute of Linguists, 24A Highbury Grove, London N5 2EA   *tel* 071-359 7445   *fax* 071-354 0202.
£3.50. Bi-M. (£17.00 p.a.) Articles of interest to professional linguists in translating, interpreting and teaching fields. Articles usually contributed, but *payment* by arrangement. All contributors have special knowledge of the subjects with which they deal. *Length:* 2000-3000 words. *Illustrations:* line.

The Literary Review (1979), Auberon Waugh, 51 Beak Street, London W1R 3LF   *tel* 071-437 9392.
£1.65. M. (£18.00 p.a.) Reviews, articles of cultural interest, interviews, profiles, short stories. Material mostly commissioned. *Length:* stories 2000

words maximum, articles and reviews 800-1500 words. *Payment:* £25 per article. *Illustrations:* line.

Liverpool Echo, John Griffith, PO Box 48, Old Hall Street, Liverpool L69 3EB   *tel* 051-227 2000.
22p. D. Ind. Articles of up to 600-800 words of local or topical interest. *Payment:* according to merit; special rates for exceptional material. This newspaper is connected with, but independent of, the Liverpool **Daily Post.** Articles not interchangeable.

Living (1967), Olwen Rice, IPC Magazines Ltd, King's Reach Tower, Stamford Street, London SE1 9LS   *tel* 071-261 5000.
£1.00. M. General interest and human interest features; law, money, health, leisure, home, food, fashion and beauty. *Payment:* by arrangement. *Illustrated.*

Llais Llyfrau/Book News From Wales (1964), John Rhys, Welsh Books Council, Castell Brychan, Aberystwyth, Dyfed SY23 2JB   *tel* (0970) 624151   *fax* (0970) 625385.
£4.00 p.a. Q. Articles in Welsh and English on authors and their books, Welsh publishing; reviews and book lists. Mainly commissioned. *Payment:* by arrangement.

Local Council Review, Valerie Shepard, BA, MAIE, 51 Stephens Road, Tadley, Basingstoke, Hampshire RG26 6RS   *tel* (0734) 815682   *fax* (0734) 816392.
£4.15 p.a. post free. Q. Official Journal of the National Association of Local Councils. Local government in relation to parish, town and community councils in England and Wales.

Local Government Chronicle (1855), Paul Keenan, 122 Minories, London EC3N 1NT   *tel* 071-623 2530   *fax* 071-481 0636.
£1.10. W. Articles relating to financial, political, legal and administrative work of the local government manager. *Payment:* by arrangement. *Illustrations:* half-tone, cartoons.

Local Government Review (until 1971, part of **Justice of the Peace,** 1837), Ian McLeod, Little London, Chichester, West Sussex PO19 1PG   *tel* (0243) 775552.
£132.75 p.a. inc. postage. W. Articles on local government law and practice, including administration, finance, environmental health, town and country planning, rating and valuation (*length* preferred, 1200-1400 words). Short reports of Conferences, Meetings, etc. *Preliminary letter* welcomed although not essential. *Payment:* articles minimum £4.50 per column except where otherwise commissioned.

The Local Historian (formerly **The Amateur Historian**) (1952), Dr Philip Morgan, Department of Adult & Continuing Education, The University, Keele ST5 5BG   *tel* (0782) 621111. British Association for Local History, Shopwyke Hall, Chichester, West Sussex PO20 6BQ   *tel* (0243) 787639.
£3.50. Q. (£12.00 p.a. post free). Articles, popular in style but based on knowledge of research, covering methods of research, sources and background material helpful to regional, local and family historians – histories of particular places, people or incidents *not* wanted. *Length:* maximum 4000 words. *Illustrations:* line and photos. *Payment:* none.

London Magazine: A Review of the Arts (1954), Alan Ross, 30 Thurloe Place, London SW7 2HQ   *tel* 071-589 0618.
£4.75. M. (£28.50 p.a.) Poems, stories, literary memoirs, critical articles, features on art, photography, sport, theatre, cinema, music, architecture, events, reports from abroad, drawings. Sae necessary. *Payment:* by arrangement.

London Review of Books (1979), Karl Miller, Mary-Kay Wilmers, Tavistock House South, Tavistock Square, London WC1H 9JZ *tel* 071-388 6751 *fax* 071-383 4792.

£1.50. Bi-M. Features, essays, short stories, poems. *Payment:* by arrangement. *Illustrations:* line, half-tone.

Love Story (1987), Group Editor: Ann Jaloba, Argus Consumer Publications, 2-4 Leigham Court Road, Streatham, London SW16 2PD *tel* 081-677 7538.

95p. M. First-person romantic stories, 4500-7000 words. But currently all material is anglicised from American magazines so *no freelance fiction can be considered.*

Loving (1970), Lorna Read, IPC Magazines Ltd, King's Reach Tower, Stamford Street, London SE1 9LS *tel* 071-261 5000.

85p. M. General romantic fiction stories. Can be first or third person, male or female viewpoint, for 18-30 market. Do not accept uncommissioned features material, but unsolicited stories welcome. Send sae for authors' guidelines. *Length:* 1000-5000 words. *Payment:* by arrangement.

Mail on Sunday (1982), Stewart Steven, Northcliffe House, 2 Derry Street, London W8 5TT *tel* 071-938 6000.

55p. W. Articles. *Payment:* by arrangement. *Illustrations:* line, half-tone. Includes colour supplement – **You,** *q.v.*

Making Music (1986), Paul Colbert, 20 Bowling Green Lane, London EC1R 0BD *tel* 071-251 1900 *telex* 299049 Utpres G *fax* 071-278 4003.

£12.00 p.a. M. Technical, musicianly and instrumental features. *Length:* 500-1000 words. *Payment:* £75 per 1000 words. *Illustrations:* colour; b&w cartoons.

Management Today (1966), Philip Beresford, 32 Lancaster Gate, London W2 3LP *tel* 071-413 4566 *fax* 071-413 4138.

£2.10. M. Easy-to-read analysis – columns from 1000 words, features up to 3000 words. *Payment:* £200 per 1000 words. *Illustrations:* colour transparencies, usually commissioned.

Manchester Evening News, Michael Unger, 164 Deansgate, Manchester M60 2RD *tel* 061-832 7200.

25p. D. Feature articles of up to 1000 words, topical or general interest and illustrated where appropriate, should be addressed to the Features Editor. *Payment:* on acceptance.

Mandy/Judy, D.C. Thomson & Co. Ltd, Courier Place, Dundee DD1 9QJ *tel* (0382) 23131 *fax* (0382) 22214; and 185 Fleet Street, London EC4A 2HS *tel* 071-242 5086 *fax* 071-404 5694.

30p. W. Picture-story paper for schoolgirls. Serials and series in line drawings: 2 and 3 page instalments, 8-9 frames per page. Editorial co-operation offered to promising scriptwriters. *Payment:* on acceptance.

Mandy Library, D.C. Thomson & Co. Ltd, Courier Place, Dundee DD1 9QJ *tel* (0382) 23131 *fax* (0382) 22214; and 185 Fleet Street, London EC4A 2HS *tel* 071-242 5086 *fax* 071-404 5694.

35p. M. 64-page (about 140 line drawings) picture-stories for schoolgirls: adventure, animal, mystery, school, sport. Scripts considered; promising scriptwriters and artists encouraged. *Payment:* on acceptance.

Manx Life (1971), Ian Faulds, Trafalgar Press Ltd, 14 Douglas Street, Peel, Isle of Man *tel* (0624) 842160.

75p. M. Factual articles on historical or topical aspects of the social, commercial, agricultural or cultural activities and interests of the Isle of Man. *Payment:* £20 per 1000 words on publication or by arrangement. *Illustrations:* line, half-tone.

Marie Claire (1988), Glenda Bailey, European Magazines Ltd, Mercury House, 195 Knightsbridge, London SW7 1RE *tel* 071-261 5240 *fax* 071-261 5277. £1.60. M. Feature articles of interest to today's woman; plus beauty, health, food, drink and travel. *Commissioned material* only. *Payment:* by negotiation. *Illustrated* in colour.

Market Newsletter (1965), John Tracy, Focus House, 497 Green Lanes, London N13 4BP *tel* 081-882 3315/6.
Private circulation. M. Published by the Bureau of Freelance Photographers. Current information on markets and editorial requirements of interest to writers and photographers.

Masonic Square (1975), B.P. Hutton, Terminal House, Shepperton, Middlesex TW17 8AS *tel* Walton-on-Thames (0932) 228950/222211.
£1.75. Q. (£8.00 p.a.) Biographies, history, symbolism, news items – all relevant to Freemasonry or affiliated subjects. *Length:* 1000-1500 words. *Illustrations:* line, half-tone.

Mayfair (1966), Stephen Bleach, 2 Archer Street, London W1V 7HE *tel* 071-734 9191 *fax* 071-734 0614.
£1.75. M. Masculine interest, well-researched features of 2000-3000 words. Short humorous articles, sport, music, motoring. Up-beat, pacey reader-identifying short stories. *Payment:* by arrangement. *Illustrations:* colour transparencies to illustrate highly visual feature ideas.

Me (1989), Kay Goddard, G E Magazines Ltd, Garden House, 57-59 Long Acre, London WC2E 9JL *tel* 071-836 0519 *fax* 071-497 2364.
48p. W. Features include: celebrities, reviews, women and home. *Commissioned material* only. *Payment:* by negotiation. *Illustrated* in colour.

Medal News (1989), Diana Birch, Token Publishing Ltd, 84 High Street, Honiton, Devon EX14 8JW *tel* (0404) 45414 *fax* (0404) 45313.
£1.50. 10 p.a. Well-researched articles on military history with a bias towards medals. *Length:* up to 2000 words. *Illustrations:* b&w preferred. *Payment:* £20 per 1000 words; none.

Media Week (1985), Liz Roberts, City Cloisters, 188-196 Old Street, London EC1V 9BP *tel* 071-490 5500 *fax* 071-490 0957.
£1.20. W. News and analysis of UK and international advertising media. *Illustrations:* half-tone, colour.

Melody Maker, Allan Jones, IPC Magazines Ltd, King's Reach Tower, Stamford Street, London SE1 9LS *tel* 071-261 6229 *fax* 071-261 6706.
60p. W. Technical, entertaining and informative articles on rock and pop music. *Payment:* by arrangement. *Illustrations:* line, half-tone.

Men Only (published by Paul Raymond: 1971), Nevile Player, 2 Archer Street, London W1V 7HE *tel* 071-734 9191 *fax* 071-734 5030.
£1.75. M. Erotic fiction; humour; glamour photography. *Payment:* by arrangement.

Methodist Recorder (1861), Michael Taylor, 122 Golden Lane, London EC1Y 0TL *tel* 071-251 8414.
35p. W. Methodist and Free Church newspaper; ecumenically involved. Limited opportunities for freelance contributors. *Preliminary letter* is advised.

Metropolitan Home (1990), Dee Nolan, 141-143 Drury Lane, London WC2B 5TB *tel* 071-497 1199 *fax* 071-497 1919.
£2.00. Bi-M. International style magazine. Features and profiles on people and interiors. *Length:* various. *Illustrations:* colour and b&w photos, line. *Payment:* by arrangement.

Military Modelling, Kenneth M. Jones, Argus Specialist Publications, Argus House, Boundary Way, Hemel Hempstead, Herts. HP2 7ST *tel* (0442) 66551 *fax* (0442) 66998.
£1.65. M. Articles on military modelling. *Length:* up to 2000 words. *Payment:* by arrangement. *Illustrations:* line, half-tone, colour.

Millennium—Journal of International Studies (1971), Marjorie Martin, Evan Potter, London School of Economics and Political Science, Houghton Street London WC2A 2AE *tel* 071-405 7686 ext. 2407-8.
£5.00. 3 p.a. (£14.00 p.a.) Serious articles on International Studies; original research work published, as well as topical articles on all aspects of international affairs. *Length:* 4500-8000 words (in triplicate with abstract). *Payment:* none. No *illustrations.*

Mind (1876), Professor Mark Sainsbury, Oxford University Press, Pinkhill House, Southfield Road, Eynsham, Oxford OX8 1JJ.
£25.00 p.a. Q. Review of philosophy intended for those who have studied and thought on this subject. Articles from about 5000 words; shorter discussion notes; critical notices and reviews. *Payment:* none.

Mobile & Holiday Homes (1960), Anne Webb, Link House, Dingwall Avenue, Croydon CR9 2TA *tel* 081-686 2599 *telex* 947709 Linkho G *fax* 081-760 0973.
£1.60. M. Informative articles on residential mobile homes (park homes) and holiday static caravans – personal experience articles, site features, news items. No preliminary letter. *Payment:* by arrangement. *Illustrations:* photos, half-tone, colour transparencies and line.

Model Boats (1964), John L. Cundell, Argus Specialist Publications, Argus House, Boundary Way, Hemel Hempstead, Herts. HP2 7ST *tel* (0442) 66551 *fax* (0442) 66998.
£1.65. M. Articles, drawings, plans, sketches of model boats. *Payment:* £25 per page; plans £80. *Illustrations:* line, half-tone.

Model Engineer (1898), Ted Jolliffe, Argus Specialist Publications, Argus House, Boundary Way, Hemel Hempstead, Herts. HP2 7ST *tel* (0442) 66551 *fax* (0442) 66998.
£1.40. 2 p.m. Detailed description of the construction of models, small workshop equipment, machine tools and small electrical and mechanical devices; articles on small power engineering, mechanics, electricity, workshop methods, clocks and experiments. *Payment:* up to £35 per page. *Illustrations:* line, half-tone, colour.

Model Railways (1971), Dave Lowery, Argus Specialist Publications, Argus House, Boundary Way, Hemel Hempstead, Herts. HP2 7ST *tel* (0442) 66551 *fax* (0442) 66998.
£1.60. M. Descriptive articles on model railways and prototype railways suitable for modelling. Articles covering all aspects of construction, planning, electrical wiring, experimental model railway engineering, and operation of model layouts. *Payment:* by arrangement. *Illustrations:* photos, line.

Modern Churchman (1911), The Modern Churchpeople's Union, The School House, Leysters, Leominster, Hereford HR6 0HS *tel* (056 887) 271.
£1.30. Q. Covers contemporary and pastoral theology, ethics, politics, current affairs. *Length:* 1500-3500 words. Contributions voluntary.

Modern Language Review (1905), Modern Humanities Research Association, King's College, Strand, London WC2R 2LS.

£47.00 p.a. Q. (£56.00 overseas, $112.00 USA) Articles and reviews of a scholarly or specialist character on English, Romance, Germanic and Slavonic languages and literatures. *Payment:* none, but offprints are given.

Modus, Geoffrey Thompson, Hamilton House, Mabledon Place, London WC1H 9BJ *tel* 071-387 1441 *fax* 071-383 7230.
£2.45. 8 p.a. (£19.50 p.a.) Official Journal of the National Association of Teachers of Home Economics: aimed at teachers and educationists. Articles on the teaching of home economics and technology, including textiles, nutrition, and social and technical background information for teachers. *Length:* up to 1500 words. *Payment:* by arrangement. *Illustrations:* line and half-tone.

Money Week (1987), Nick Morgan, EMAP Business Information Ltd, 67 Clerkenwell Road, London EC1R 5BH *tel* 071-251 6222 *fax* 071-430 2505.
Free. W. Any articles of interest to independent financial advisers, e.g. Financial Services Act, life insurance, pensions. *Length:* up to 1000 words. *Payment:* £150 per 1000 words. *Illustrations:* half-tone.

MoneyMarketing (1985), Tim Potter, St Giles House, 50 Poland Street, London W1V 4AX *tel* 071-287 5678 *fax* 071-734 9379.
£1.00. W. News, features, surveys, viewpoints; cartoons. *Length:* features – from 900 words. *Illustrations:* b&w photos, colour and b&w line. *Payment:* £100 per 1000 words; cartoons £60, colour line £150, b&w line £100, b&w photos £80.

The Month (1864), John McDade, sj, 114 Mount Street, London W1Y 6AH *tel* 071-491 7596 *fax* 071-495 1673.
£1.10. M. Review of Christian thought, and world affairs, with arts and literary sections, edited by the Jesuit Fathers. *Preliminary letter* desirable. *Length:* up to 3000 words. *Payment:* by arrangement. *Illustrations:* b&w photos.

Morning Star (formerly **Daily Worker,** 1930), Tony Chater, The Morning Star Co-operative Society Ltd, 1-3 Ardleigh Road, London N1 4HS *tel* 071-254 0033 *telegraphic address* Morsta Telex, London *telex* 916463 *fax* 071-254 5950.
30p. Daily newspaper for the Labour movement. Articles of general interest. *Illustrations:* photos, cartoons and drawings.

Mortgage Finance Gazette (1869), Neil Madden, Franey & Co. Ltd, South Quay Plaza, 183 Marsh Wall, London E14 9FS *tel* 071-538 5386.
£2.75. M. (£35.75 p.a. pre-paid) Articles on all aspects of building society management, mortgage finance, retail financial services. *Length:* up to 2000 words. *Average payment:* £135 per 1000 words. *Illustrations:* line, half-tone.

Mother & Baby (1956), Stephanie Neuman, Emap Élan, Victory House, Leicester Place, Leicester Square, London WC2H 7BP *tel* 071-437 9011 *telex* 266400 *fax* 071-434 0656.
£1.10. M. Features and practical articles. *Length:* 1200-2800 words. *Payment:* by negotiation. *Illustrated.*

Motor Boat and Yachting (1904), Alan Harper, IPC Magazines Ltd, King's Reach Tower, Stamford Street, London SE1 9LS *tel* 071-261 5000.
£2.10. M. General interest as well as specialist motor boating material welcomed. Features up to 2000 words considered on all aspects, sea-going and on inland waterways. *Payment:* varies. *Illustrations:* photos (mostly colour and transparencies preferred) and line.

Motor Caravan Magazine (1985), Paul Carter, Link House Magazines Ltd, Link House, Dingwall Avenue, Croydon CR9 2TA *tel* 081-686 2599 *fax* 081-760 0973.

£1.60. M. Practical features, touring features (home and abroad). *Length:* up to 1500 words. *Payment:* £35-£40 per page. *Illustrations:* line, half-tone, colour.

Motor Cycle News (1955), Peter Bolt, EMAP National Publications Ltd, Bushfield House, Orton Centre, Peterborough PE2 0UW *tel* (0733) 237111 *telex* 32157 *fax* (0733) 231137.
68p. W. Features (up to 1000 words), photos and news stories of interest to motor cyclists.

Motorcaravan and Motorhome Monthly (1966 as Motor Caravan and Camping), Penny Smith, 8 Swan Meadow, Pewsey, Wilts. SN9 5HW *tel* (0980) 630349 *fax* (0980) 630770.
£1.50. M. Articles including motorcaravan travel in the UK and DIY. *Payment:* from £10 per printed page. *Illustrations:* line, half-tone, colourprint.

Museums Journal (1901), The Museums Association, 34 Bloomsbury Way, London WC1A 2SF *tel* 071-404 4767 *fax* 071-430 0167.
£5.00. M. (Free to members; £30.00 p.a. individuals; £48.00 p.a. institutions.) Articles and news items on museum and art gallery policy, administration, research, architecture and display, notes on technical developments, book reviews. *Length:* 100-2500 words. *Payment:* by negotiation. *Illustrations:* line, half-tone, colour.

Music and Letters (1920), Editorial: Dr Nigel Fortune, Dr John Whenham, Department of Music, Barber Institute of Fine Arts, University of Birmingham, Birmingham B15 2TS *tel* 021-414 3726. For other matters: Journals Production, Oxford University Press, Pinkhill House, Southfield Road, Eynsham, Oxford OX8 1JJ.
£9.00. Q. Scholarly articles, up to 10,000 words, on musical subjects, neither merely topical nor purely descriptive. Technical, historical and research matter preferred. *Illustrations:* music quotations and plates. *Payment:* none.

The Music Review (1940), A.F. Leighton Thomas, Glyneithin, Burry Port, Dyfed SA16 0TA. Other matters: Black Bear Press, King's Hedges Road, Cambridge CB4 2PQ.
£12.50. Q. (£42.50 p.a.) Articles from 1500-8000 words dealing with any aspect of standard or classical music (no jazz). *Payment:* small, by arrangement.

Music Teacher (1908), Tim Homfray, Rhinegold Publishing Ltd, 241 Shaftesbury Avenue, London WC2H 8EH *tel* 071-836 2384 *fax* 071-528 7991.
£1.80. M. Provides information and articles for both school and private music teachers. Articles and illustrations must have a teacher, as well as a musical, interest. *Length:* articles 1000-1500 words. *Payment:* by arrangement.

Music Week (1959), Steve Redmond, 23-27 Tudor Street, London EC4Y 0HR *tel* 071-583 9199 *fax* 071-583 5049.
£2.25. W. (£88.00 p.a.) News and features on all aspects of producing, manufacturing, marketing and retailing music. *Payment:* NUJ rates.

Musical Opinion (1877), Denby Richards, 2 Princes Road, St Leonards-on-Sea, East Sussex TN37 6EL *tel* (0424) 715167 *fax* (0424) 730052.
£1.50. M. Suggestions for contributions of musical interest, scholastic, educational, anniversaries, ethnic, and relating to the organ world. Record, opera, festival, book, music reviews. All editorial matter must be commissioned. *Payment:* on publication. *Illustrations:* b&w photos.

Musical Times (1844), Basil Ramsey, Orpheus Publications, 4th Floor, Centro House, Mandela Street, London NW1 0DU *tel* 071-387 3848 *fax* 071-388 8532.

£1.50. M. Musical articles, reviews, 150-2500 words. Intending contributors are advised to *study recent numbers of the journal. Payment:* by arrangement. *Illustrations:* photos and music.

My Weekly (1910), D.C. Thomson & Co. Ltd, 80 Kingsway East, Dundee DD4 8SL; and 185 Fleet Street, London EC4A 2HS.
33p. W. Serials, from 30,000-80,000 words, suitable for family reading. Short complete stories of 1500-5000 words with humorous, romantic or strong emotional theme. Articles on prominent people and on all subjects of feminine interest. All contributions should make their appeal to the modern woman. *No preliminary letter* required. *Payment:* on acceptance. *Illustrations:* colour and b&w.

My Weekly Story Library, D.C. Thomson & Co. Ltd, Courier Place, Dundee DD1 9QJ *tel* (0382) 23131 *fax* (0382) 22214; and 185 Fleet Street, London EC4A 2HS *tel* 071-242 5086 *fax* 071-404 5694.
35p. 4 p.m. 35,000-37,500-word romantic stories aimed at the post-teenage market. *Payment:* by arrangement; competitive for the market. No *illustrations.*

National Builder (1921), Michael Harnett, 82 New Cavendish Street, London W1M 8AD *tel* 071-580 5588 *telegraphic address* Natbuild, Westcent, London *fax* 071-631 3872. Ceased publication.
£2.00. M. Official journal of the Building Employers Confederation. Articles on building and constructional methods, management techniques, materials and machinery used in building. *Preliminary letter* advisable. *Length:* 750-1000 words, preferably with *illustrations. Payment:* by arrangement.

Natural World (1981), Linda Bennett, Sea Containers House, 20 Upper Ground, London SE1 9PF *tel* 071-928 2111 *fax* 071-620 1594.
Free to members. 3 p.a. Magazine of the Royal Society for Nature Conservation. Short articles on nature conservation; contributors normally have special knowledge of subjects on which they write. *Length:* up to 1500 words. *Payment:* by arrangement. *Illustrations:* line, half-tone, colour.

Naturalist (1875), Professor M.R.D. Seaward, MSc, PhD, DSc, The University, Bradford BD7 1DP *tel* (0274) 733466, ext. 8540 *telex* 51309 Unibfd G *fax* (0274) 305340.
£12.00 p.a. Q. Original papers on all kinds of British natural history subjects, including various aspects of geology, archaeology and environmental science. *Length:* immaterial. *Illustrations:* photos and line drawings. *Payment:* none.

Nature (1869), John Maddox, Macmillan Magazines Ltd, Little Essex Street, London WC2R 3LF *tel* 071-836 6633 *telex* 262024.
£2.50. W. Devoted to scientific matters and to their bearing upon public affairs. All contributors of articles have specialised knowledge of the subjects with which they deal. *Illustrations:* line, half-tone.

Nautical Magazine (1832), L. Ingram-Brown, FInstSMM, MBIM, MRIN, Brown, Son & Ferguson Ltd, 4-10 Darnley Street, Glasgow G41 2SD *tel* 041-429 1234 *telegraphic address* Skipper, Glasgow *fax* 041-420 1694.
£24.00 p.a. inc. postage; 3 years £72.00. M. Articles relating to nautical and shipping profession, from 1500-2000 words; also translations. *Payment:* by arrangement. No *illustrations.*

Navy International, Anthony J. Watts, Hunters Moon, Hogspudding Lane, Newdigate, Nr Dorking, Surrey RH5 5DS *tel* (0306) 77442.
£35.00 p.a. M. Geo-political, strategic and technical articles on current world naval affairs. *Length:* 1500-2000 words. *Payment:* £70 per 1000 words. *Illustrations* used.

New Beacon (1930) (as **Beacon,** 1917), Ann Lee, RNIB, 224 Great Portland Street, London W1N 6AA   *tel* 071-388 1266   *fax* 071-388 2034.
95p. M. Articles on all aspects of visual handicap. *Length:* from 500 words. *Payment:* £15 per 1000 words: *Illustrations:* half-tone. Also Braille edition (£3.00 p.a.).

New Blackfriars (1920), The English Dominicans (Rev. Allan White, OP), Blackfriars, Oxford OX1 3LY   *tel/fax* (0865) 278414.
£1.30. M. (£14.00 p.a.) Critical review, surveying the field of theology, philosophy, sociology and the arts, from the standpoint of Christian principles and their application to the problems of the modern world. Incorporates *Life of the Spirit. Length:* 2500-6000 words. *Payment:* by arrangement.

New Internationalist (1973), Vanessa Baird, Chris Brazier, David Ransom, Sue Shaw, 55 Rectory Road, Oxford OX4 1BW   *tel* (0865) 728181   *telegraphic address* Newint Oxford   *telex* 83147 Newint Viaorg   *fax* (0865) 793152.
£1.50. M. (£18.40 p.a.) World issues, ranging from food to feminism to peace – examines one subject each month. *Length:* up to 2000 words. *Illustrations:* line, half-tone, cartoons; colour – front cover only. *Payment:* £75 per 1000 words; b&w photos, £100 full page, £45 ¼ page.

New Library World (1898), MCB University Press, 62 Toller Lane, Bradford, West Yorkshire BD8 9BY   *tel* (0274) 499821.
£149.95 p.a. M. Professional and bibliographical articles. *Illustrated. Payment:* by arrangement.

New Musical Express, Danny Kelly, IPC Magazines Ltd, 25th Floor, King's Reach Tower, Stamford Street, London SE1 9LS   *tel* 071-261 5000.
55p. W. Authoritative articles and news stories on the world's rock and movie personalities. *Length:* by arrangement. *Preliminary letter or phone call* desirable. *Payment:* by arrangement. *Illustrations:* action photos with strong news-angle of recording personalities.

New Scientist, David Dickson, Holborn Publishing Group, King's Reach Tower, Stamford Street, London SE1 9LS   *tel* 071-261 5000   *fax* 071-261 6464   *electronic mailbox* Telecom Gold/Dialcom: 83:NSM007.
£1.40. W. Authoritative articles of topical importance on all aspects of science and technology are considered; *length:* 1000-3000 words. Preliminary letter or telephone call desirable. Short items from specialists also considered for *Science, This Week, Forum* and *Technology.* Intending contributors should study recent copies of the magazine. *Payment:* varies but average £150 per 1000 words. *Illustrations:* line, half-tone, colour.

New Statesman & Society (1988), Steve Platt, Foundation House, Perseverance Works, 38 Kingsland Road, London E2 8DQ   *tel* 071-739 3211.
£1.40. W. Interested in news and analysis of current political and social issues at home and overseas, plus book reviews and coverage of the arts, seen from the perspective of the British Left. *Length:* strictly according to the value of the piece. *Payment:* basic £77.50 per 1000 words.

New Theatre Quarterly (1985; as **Theatre Quarterly** 1971), Clive Barker, Simon Trussler, Great Robhurst, Woodchurch, Ashford, Kent TN26 3TB.
£9.00. Q. (individual subs. £19.00 p.a.) Articles, interviews, documentation, reference material covering all aspects of live theatre. An informed, factual and serious approach essential. Preliminary discussion and synopsis desirable. *Payment:* by arrangement. *Illustrations:* line, half-tone.

The New Welsh Review (1988), Belinda Humfrey, Department of English, St David's University College, Lampeter, Dyfed SA48 7ED   *tel* (0570) 423523.

£2.95. Q. (£12.00 p.a.) Articles, short stories, poetry; plus reviews, interviews and profiles. Especially, but not exclusively, concerned with Welsh literature in English. *Length:* (articles) up to 4000 words; short poems preferred. *Illustrations:* line, half-tone; colour cover. *Payment:* £7-£12 per page prose; £12-£20 per poem; £10-£20.

New Woman (1988), Gill Hudson, Fanum House, 48 Leicester Square, London WC2H 7FB   *tel* 071-930 9300   *fax* 071-976 1964.
£1.20. M. Features up to 3000 words. Considers unsolicited articles; enclose sae for return. *Payment:* at or above NUJ rates. *Illustrated.*

New World, United Nations Association, 3 Whitehall Court, London SW1A 2EL   *tel* 071-930 2931   *fax* 071-930 5893.
50p. 6 p.a. Review of UN activities, of UNA campaigns and of different viewpoints on major international issues confronting the United Nations.

News of the World (1843), Patricia Chapman, 1 Virginia Street, London E1 9XR   *tel* 071-782 4000   *fax* 071-583 9504.
45p. W.

19 (1968), Maureen Rice, IPC Magazines Ltd, King's Reach Tower, Stamford Street, London SE1 9LS   *tel* 071-261 6360.
£1.00. M. Glossy fashion and general interest magazine for young women aged 17 to 22 including beauty, music and social features of strong contemporary interest.

90 Minutes (1990), Dan Goldstein, 14 Rathbone Place, London W1P 1DE   *tel* 071-436 2545   *fax* 071-323 9343.
90p. W. Football features, news stories, match previews. *Length:* 500-1500 words. *Illustrations:* colour and b&w photos. *Payment:* £25-£50.

The Northern Echo (1870), Peter Sands, PO Box 14, Priestgate, Darlington, Co. Durham DL1 1NF   *tel* (0325) 381313   *fax* (0325) 380539.
25p. D. Articles of interest to North-East and North Yorkshire; *all material commissioned.* Literary tabloid pull-out published Q.; Echoes magazine W. *Preliminary study* of newspaper advisable. *Length:* 800-1000 words. *Illustrations:* in colour, half-tone and line; process and spot colour; mostly commissioned. *Payment:* by negotiation.

Nottingham Evening Post (1878), Forman Street, Nottingham NG1 4AB   *tel* (0602) 482000   *telex* 377884   *fax* (0602) 484116.
25p. D. Will consider material on local issues.

Number One (1983), Nicky Smith, BBC Magazines, 1st Floor, 35 Marylebone High Street, London W1M 4AA   *tel* 071-224 1554   *fax* 071-224 3097.
55p. W. Interviews and articles on pop stars, for the teenage market. *Illustrations:* colour, occasional cartoons. *Payment:* by negotiation.

Numismatic Chronicle (1839), c/o R.F. Bland, Department of Coins and Medals, British Museum, London WC1B 3DG.
£24.00 per annual volume. Journal of the Royal Numismatic Society. Articles on coins and medals. Memoirs relating to coins and medals are unpaid, and contributions should reach a high standard of quality.

Nursery World, Sue Hubberstey, The School House Workshop, 51 Calthorpe Street, London WC1X 0HH   *tel* 071-837 7224.
75p. W. For all grades of nursery and child care staff, nannies, foster parents and all concerned with the care of expectant mothers, babies and young children. Authoritative and informative articles, 750-1500 words, and photos, on all aspects of child welfare, from 0-7 years, in the UK. Practical ideas and

leisure crafts. *No* short stories. *Payment:* by arrangement. *Illustrations:* line, half-tone.

Nursing Times and Nursing Mirror (1905), Macmillan Magazines Ltd, 4 Little Essex Street, London WC2R 3LF *tel* 071-379 0970 *fax* 071-497 2664.
65p. W. Articles of clinical interest, nursing education and nursing policy. *Illustrated* articles not longer than 1500 words. Contributions from other than health professionals sometimes accepted. Press day, Friday. *Payment:* NUJ rates.

The Observer (1791), Donald Trelford, Chelsea Bridge House, Queenstown Road, London SW8 4NN *tel* 071-627 0700 *telegraphic address* Observer, London, SW8 *telex* 888963 Obs Ldn *fax* 071-627 5570/1/2.
60p. W. Ind. Some articles and illustrations commissioned.

The Observer Colour Magazine (1964), Angela Palmer, Chelsea Bridge House, Queenstown Road, London SW8 4NN *tel* 071-627 0700 *telegraphic address* Observer, London, SW8 *telex* 888963 Obs Ldn *fax* 071-627 5570/1/2.
Free with newspaper. W. Articles on all subjects. *Illustrations:* also accepted. *Payment:* by arrangement.

Office Secretary (1986), Onay Faiz, Trade Media Ltd, Brookmead House, Two Rivers, Station Road, Witney, Oxon OX8 3BH *tel* (0993) 775545 *fax* (0993) 778884.
£8.50 p.a. Q. Serious features on anything of interest to senior secretaries/working women. *Illustrations:* colour transparencies. *Payment:* £100 per 1000 words, or by negotiation.

Opera, Rodney Milnes, 1A Mountgrove Road, London N5 2LU *tel* 071-359 1037 *fax* 071-354 2700. Seymour Press Ltd, Windsor House, 1270 London Road, London SW16 4DH.
£1.95. 13 p.a. Articles on general subjects appertaining to opera; reviews; criticisms. *Length:* up to 2000 words. *Payment:* by arrangement. *Illustrations:* photos.

Opera Now (1989), Margaret Rand, 5th Floor, Castle House, 75 Wells Street, London W1P 3RE *tel* 071-323 5007 *fax* 071-636 7205.
£2.50. M. Articles, news, reviews on opera. *Length:* 150-2000 words. *Illustrations:* colour and b&w photos, line. *Payment:* £150 per 1000 words.

Options (1982), Jo Foley, IPC Magazines Ltd, King's Reach Tower, Stamford Street, London SE1 9LS *tel* 071-261 5000.
£1.30. M. Articles only, 1000-3000 words. Mostly commissioned. *Payment:* by arrangement.

Orbis (1968), Mike Shields, 199 The Long Shoot, Nuneaton, Warks. CV11 6JQ *tel* (0203) 327440.
£14.00 p.a. Q. Poetry, prose pieces (up to 1000 words), reviews, letters. Annual competition for rhymed poetry. *Payment:* by arrangement. *Illustrations:* line.

The Organ (1921), D.R. Carrington, 84 Park View Road, Lytham St Annes, Lancs. FY8 4JF *tel* (0253) 737859.
£3.00. Q. Articles, 1000-5000 words, relating to the organ: historical, technical and artistic. Reviews of music, records. *Payment:* small. *Illustrations:* line, half-tone, colour.

Our Dogs (1895), William Moores, Oxford Road Station Approach, Manchester M60 1SX *tel* 061-236 2660 *fax* 061-236 5534/0892.
90p. W. Articles and news on the breeding and showing of pedigree dogs. *Illustrations:* b&w photos. *Payment:* NUJ rates; £7.50 per photo.

Outdoor Action, Laura McCaffrey, Hawker Consumer Publications, 13 Park House, 140 Battersea Park Road, London SW11 4NB *tel* 071-720 2108.
£1.40. M. Anything outdoors with the emphasis on walking and lightweight backpacking; gear testing; conservation issues. *Preliminary letter* essential. *Illustrations:* colour transparencies and b&w prints. *Payment:* by arrangement.

Outposts Poetry Quarterly (1943), Roland John, 22 Whitewell Road, Frome, Somerset BA11 4EL *tel* (0373) 66653. *Founder:* Howard Sergeant, MBE.
£3.50. Q. (£10.00 p.a.) Poems, essays and critical articles on poets and their work. Poetry competitions. *Payment:* by arrangement.

Oxford Poetry (1983), Mark Wormald, Magdalen College, Oxford OX1 4AU.
£1.95. 3 p.a. Previously unpublished poems, both unsolicited and commissioned. *Payment:* none.

Parents (1976), Isobel McKenzie-Price, Emap Élan, Victory House, Leicester Place, London WC2H 7BP *tel* 071-437 9011 *fax* 071-434 0656.
£1.20. M. Articles on pregnancy, childbirth, general family health, food, fashion, child upbringing up to aged eight and marital relations. MSS with sae only. *Illustrations:* b&w or colour. *Payment:* in accordance with national magazine standards; by arrangement.

Parks & Sports Grounds (1935), Alan Guthrie, 61 London Road, Staines, Middlesex TW18 4BN *tel* (0784) 461326 *fax* (0784) 462073.
£25.00 p.a. M. Articles on the design, construction, maintenance and management of parks, sports grounds, golf courses, open spaces and amenity areas. *Length:* 750-2000 words. *Payment:* £65 per 1000 words. *Illustrations:* line, half-tone.

Peace News for nonviolence in action (1936), 55 Dawes Street, London SE17 1EL *tel* 071-252 7937 *fax* 071-708 2545.
50p. M. Political articles based on nonviolence in every aspect of human life. *Illustrations:* line, half-tone. *Payment:* none.

Penthouse Magazine, The International Magazine for Men (1965), Northern & Shell plc, The Northern & Shell Building, PO Box 381, Mill Harbour, London E14 9TW *tel* 071-987 5090 *fax* 071-987 2160.
£2.60. M. Serious and light articles on sex, motoring, star interviews, general interest. *Length:* 3000 words. *Payment:* by arrangement. *Illustrations:* colour and b&w photos, but by commission only.

The People, Bill Hagerty, Holborn Circus, London EC1P 1DQ *tel* 071-353 0246 *telex* 27286 *fax* 071-822 3405/3684.
45p. W. Sun. Features, single articles and series considered. Pictures should be supplied with contributions if possible. Features should be of deep human interest, whether the subject is serious or light-hearted. The first investigative newspaper, The People is particularly noted for its exposures of social evils, criminal activities, financial and other rackets and bureaucratic malpractices, in the public interest. Very strong sports following. Exclusive news and news-feature stories also considered. *Payment:* rates high, even for tips that lead to published news stories.

People's Friend (1869), D.C. Thomson & Co. Ltd, 80 Kingsway East, Dundee DD4 8SL; and 185 Fleet Street, London EC4A 2HS.
33p. W. Illustrated weekly appealing to women of all ages and devoted to their personal and home interests, especially knitting, fashions and cookery. Serials (60,000-70,000 words) and complete stories (1500-3000 words) of strong romantic and emotional appeal. Stories for children considered. *No preliminary letter* required. *Illustrations:* colour and b&w. *Payment:* on acceptance.

People's Friend Library, D.C. Thomson & Co. Ltd, 80 Kingsway East, Dundee DD4 8SL.
65p. 2 p.m. 50,000-55,000-word family and romantic stories aimed at 30 plus age groups. *Payment:* by arrangement. No *illustrations*.

Performance Car (1983), Dave Calderwood, EMAP National Publications Ltd, Bushfield House, Orton Centre, Peterborough PE2 0UW *tel* (0733) 237111.
£2.20. M. Articles, 2000-3000 words, on all aspects of cars. *Payment:* by arrangement. *Illustrations:* half-tone, colour.

Personal Computer World (1977), Guy Swarbrick, 32-34 Broadwick Street, London W1A 2HG *tel* 071-439 4242 *telex* 23918 VNU G.
£1.70. M. Articles about computers. *Length:* 2000-5000 words. Reviews. *Payment:* from £94 per 1000 words. *Illustrations:* line, half-tone.

Personnel Management, Susanne Lawrence, Personnel Publications Ltd, 57 Mortimer Street, London W1N 7TD *tel* 071-323 5717 *fax* 071-323 5770.
£3.50. M. (£48.00 p.a.) Journal of the Institute of Personnel Management. Features and news items on recruitment and selection, training and development; wage and salary administration; industrial psychology; employee relations; labour law; welfare schemes, working practices and new practical ideas in personnel management in industry and commerce. *Length:* up to 2500 words. *Payment:* by arrangement. *Illustrations:* photographers and illustrators should contact art editor.

The Pharmaceutical Journal (1841), D. Simpson, MRPharmS, 1 Lambeth High Street, London SE1 7JN *tel* 071-735 9141 *telegraphic address/cables* Pharmakon, London SE1 *fax* 071-735 7629.
£1.10. W. Official journal of the Royal Pharmaceutical Society of Great Britain. Articles on any aspect of pharmacy may be submitted. *Payment:* by arrangement. *Illustrations:* half-tone, colour.

Photo Answers, Steve Bavister, EMAP, Apex House, Oundle Road, Peterborough PE2 9NP *tel* (0733) 898100/898418 *fax* (0733) 231137.
£1.65. M. Magazine appealing to everyone interested in photography. Little opportunity for freelance writers, but always interested in seeing quality photos. *Payment:* upwards of £25 per published page, colour or mono. *Illustrations:* print, slide, line, half-tone.

Photography (1945), Mark Warford, Argus Specialist Publications, Argus House, Boundary Way, Hemel Hempstead, Herts. HP2 7ST *tel* (0442) 66551 *fax* (0442) 66998.
£1.95. M. Aimed at anyone with an interest in photography. Articles on photographers, the uses of photography and topical subjects such as the media, advertising and contemporary issues such as the environment. Important showcase for documentary photojournalism and historical photos. *Length:* according to subject. *Payment:* by arrangement. *Illustrations:* world-class photography or with very strong story only.

Physiotherapy, Jill Whitehouse, 14 Bedford Row, London WC1R 4ED *tel* 071-242 1941.
£3.50. M. Journal of the Chartered Society of Physiotherapists. Articles on physiotherapy and related subjects, technical items and news regarding activities of members of the Society. Contributions welcomed from physiotherapists and doctors. *Length:* 2000 words (average). *Payment:* £15 per published page for technical and medical articles. *Illustrations:* photos, line.

PIC (People in Camera) (1989), Colin Carron, PIC International Promotions Ltd, Lingley House, Commissioners Road, Strood, Rochester, Kent ME2 4EU *tel* (0634) 291115 *fax* (0634) 724761.

£1.95. M. Photographic or image-making articles, concentrating on people – models as well as photographers – generally illustrated with photos. *Length:* up to 2000 words. *Illustrations:* colour transparencies/prints. *Payment:* by negotiation.

Pig Farming, Bryan Kelly, Morgan-Grampian Farming Press, Wharfedale Road, Ipswich IP1 4LG   *tel* (0473) 241122   *fax* (0473) 240501.
£20.00 p.a. M. Practical, well-illustrated articles on all aspects of pigmeat production required, particularly those dealing with new ideas in pig management, feeding, housing and processing. *Length:* 1000-1400 words. *Payment:* by arrangement. *Illustrations:* line, half-tone, colour.

Pilot (1968), James Gilbert, The Clock House, 28 Old Town, Clapham, London SW4 0LB   *tel* 071-498 2506   *fax* 071-498 6920.
£1.80. M. Feature articles on general aviation, private and business flying. *Illustrations:* line, half-tone, colour. *Payment:* £100-£800 per article on acceptance; £25 for each photo used.

Planet (1970-9; relaunched 1985), John Barnie, Gwen Daves, PO Box 44, Aberystwyth, Dyfed SY24 5BS   *tel* (0970) 611255   *fax* (0970) 623311.
£2.00. 6 p.a. (£11.00 p.a.) Short stories, poems, topical articles on Welsh current affairs, politics and society; articles on minority cultures throughout the world. New literature in English. *Length* of articles: 1000-3500 words. *Payment:* £40 per 1000 words for prose; £20 minimum per poem. *Illustrations:* line, half-tone, cartoons.

Plays and Players, Vera Lustig, Media House, 55 Lower Addiscombe Road, Croydon CR0 6PQ   *tel* 081-681 7817   *fax* 081-688 9573.
£1.95. M. Articles, reviews and photos on world theatre. *Payment:* by arrangement. *Illustrations:* line, photos.

PN Review, formerly **Poetry Nation** (1973), Michael Schmidt, 208 Corn Exchange Buildings, Manchester M4 3BQ   *tel* 061-834 8730   *fax* 061-832 0084.
£2.75. Q. (£16.50 p.a.) Poems, essays, reviews, fiction, translations. *Payment:* by arrangement.

Poetry Durham (1982), David Hartnett, Michael O'Neill, Gareth Reeves, School of English, University of Durham, Elvet Riverside, New Elvet, Durham DH1 3JT   *tel* (091) 374 2730.
£4.50 p.a. 3 p.a. Poems and review essays on contemporary poetry. *Payment:* on publication.

Poetry London Newsletter (1988), Leon Cych, 26 Clacton Road, London E17 8AR   *tel* 081-520 6693.
£8.00 p.a. Q. Poems of the highest standard, articles/reviews on any aspect of modern poetry; listings. Contributors must be very knowledgeable about poetry. *Illustrations:* line or digitised photos, cartoons. *Payment:* £5 per item.

Poetry Nottingham (1941), Claire Piggott, Summer Cottage, West Street, Shelford, Notts. NG12 1EJ   *tel* (0602) 334540.
£1.75. Q. Poems. *Length:* not more than 40 lines. *Illustrations:* line. *Payment:* none, but complimentary copy.

Poetry Review, Peter Forbes, 21 Earls Court Square, London SW5 9DE   *tel* 071-373 7861/2   *fax* 071-244 7388.
£16.00 p.a. (£21.00 p.a. institutions, schools and libraries) Q. Poems, features and reviews. Send no more than six poems with sae. *Preliminary study* of magazine essential. *Payment:* £10-£15 per poem.

Poetry Wales (1965), Mike Jenkins, 26 Andrew's Close, Heolgerrig, Merthyr Tudful CF48 1SS, Cymru/Wales *tel* (0685) 76726.
£1.95. Q. (£8.00 p.a. inc. postage) Poems mainly in English and mainly by Welsh people or resident; other contributors (and Welsh language poetry) also published. Articles on Welsh literature in English and in Welsh, as well as on poetry from other countries. Special features; reviews on poetry and wider matters. *Payment:* by arrangement.

Police Journal (1928), R.W. Stone, QPM, Little London, Chichester, West Sussex PO19 1PG *tel* (0243) 787841 *fax* (0243) 779278.
£37.50 p.a. Q. Articles of technical or professional interest to the Police Service throughout the world. *Payment:* by negotiation. *Illustrations:* half-tone.

The Political Quarterly (1930), Basil Blackwell Ltd, 108 Cowley Road, Oxford OX4 1JF *tel* (0865) 791100. Editors: Colin Crouch (Trinity College, Oxford OX1 3BH *tel* (0865) 279879/279900 *fax* (0865) 279911) and David Marquand (University of Salford, Salford M5 4WT *tel* 061-736 5843). Literary Editor: James Cornford. Books for review to be sent to: James Cornford, Institute for Public Policy Research, 30/32 Southampton Street, London WC2E 7RA.
£10.20. Q. (£46.00 p.a.) Journal devoted to topical aspects of national and international politics and public administration; takes a progressive, but not a party, point of view. *Length:* average 5000 words. *Payment:* c. £50 per article.

Pony (1949), Managing Editor: Kate Austin, 296 Ewell Road, Surbiton, Surrey KT6 7AQ *tel* 081-390 8547 *fax* 081-390 8696.
90p. M. Lively articles and short stories with a horsy theme aimed at young readers, 8 to 16 years old. Technical accuracy and young, fresh writing essential. *Length:* up to 1000 words. *Payment:* by arrangement. *Illustrations:* drawings (commissioned) and interesting photos.

Popular Crafts, Brenda Ross, Argus Specialist Publications, Argus House, Boundary Way, Hemel Hempstead, Herts. HP2 7ST *tel* (0442) 66551.
£1.60. M. Covers all kinds of crafts. Projects with full instructions, profiles and successes of craftspeople, news on craft group activities, collecting crafts, personal anecdotes, general craft-related articles. Welcomes written outlines of ideas. *Payment:* by arrangement. *Illustrated.*

Port of London, Port of London Authority, Europe House, World Trade Centre, London E1 9AA *tel* 071-481 4306 *fax* 071-481 2458.
£2.50. Q. The magazine of the Port of London Authority. Articles up to 2500 words considered, semi-technical, historical or having bearing on trade and commerce of London essential. *Preliminary letter* essential. *Payment:* £75 per 1000 words. *Illustrations:* line, half-tone, colour.

The Post (1920), J. Jacques, UCW House, Crescent Lane, Clapham, London SW4 9RN *tel* 071-622 9977 *telex* 913585 *fax* 071-720 6853.
Free to members. M. Journal of the Union of Communication Workers. Articles on postal, telephone and telegraph workers in the UK and abroad and on other questions of interest to a trade union readership. *Length:* 1000 words or less. *Payment:* by arrangement. *Illustrations:* line and half-tone occasionally.

Poultry World, John Farrant, Reed Farmers Publishing Group, Greenfield House, 69-73 Manor Road, Wallington, Surrey SM6 0DE *tel* 081-661 3500.

£1.35. M. Articles on commercial poultry breeding, production, marketing and packaging. News of international poultry interest. *Payment:* by arrangement. *Illustrations:* photos, line.

The Powys Review (1977), Belinda Humfrey, Dept. of English, Saint David's University College, Lampeter, Dyfed SA48 7ED   *tel* (0570) 422351/422018. £3.75. Bi-annual. Articles and reviews on the writings of John Cowper Powys, T.F. Powys and Llewelyn Powys, and on related subjects and literature, especially of the period since 1890. *Payment:* by arrangement. *Illustrations:* line, photos.

PR Week (1984), Howard Smith, Haymarket Marketing Publications, 22 Lancaster Gate, London W2 3LP   *tel* 071-413 4520.
Controlled circulation. £40.00 p.a. W. News and features on public relations. *Length:* approx. 800 words. *Payment:* £125 per 1000 words. *Illustrations:* half-tone.

Practical Boat Owner (1967), George Taylor, Westover House, West Quay Road, Poole, Dorset BH15 1JG   *tel* (0202) 680593.
£2.00. M. Articles of up to 2000 words in *length*, about practical matters concerning the boating enthusiast. *Payment:* by negotiation. *Illustrations:* photos or drawings.

Practical Electronics (1964), Kenn Gurroch, 193 Uxbridge Road, London W12 9RA   *tel* 081-743 8888.
£1.50. M. Constructional and theoretical articles. *Length:* 1000-5500 words. *Payment:* £55-£90 per 1000 words depending upon type of article. *Illustrations:* line, half-tone and Mackintosh illustrations.

Practical Fishkeeping (1966), Steve Windsor, EMAP Pursuit Publishing Ltd, Bretton Court, Bretton, Peterborough PE3 8DZ   *tel* (0733) 264666.
£1.50. M. Instructional articles on fishkeeping with heavy emphasis on easily-absorbed information. *Payment:* by arrangement. *Illustrations:* line, half-tone, high quality colour transparencies of tropical fish.

Practical Gardening (1960), Adrienne Wild, EMAP Garden Publications, Apex House, Oundle Road, Peterborough PE2 9NP   *tel* (0733) 898100   *fax* (0733) 898433.
£1.45. M. 500-1000 words on inspirational gardening subjects, particularly if oriented towards ideas for garden improvement, and well illustrated. *Payment:* from £70 per 1000 words. *Illustrations:* line, half-tone, colour.

Practical Health (1987), Michele Simmons, IPC Magazines Ltd, King's Reach Tower, Stamford Street, London SE1 9LS   *tel* 071-261 5102   *fax* 071-261 6895.
£1.20. Bi-M. Covers all aspects of popular health. *Preliminary letter*; no unsolicited manuscripts. *Illustrated. Payment:* by arrangement.

Practical Householder (1955), Martyn Hocking, Greater London House, Hampstead Road, London NW1 7QQ   *tel* 071-388 3171.
£1.40. M. Articles about 1500 words in *length*, about practical matters concerning home improvement. *Payment:* according to subject. *Illustrations:* line, half-tone.

Practical Motorist (1934), Denis Rea, Unit 8, Forest Close, Ebblake Industrial Estate, Verwood, Wimborne, Dorset BH21 6DQ   *tel* (0202) 823581.
£1.30. M. Practical articles on upkeep, servicing and repair and customising and performance improvements of all makes of cars; also practical hints and tips. *Payment:* according to merit. *Illustrations:* b&w, colour prints or transparencies and line drawings.

Practical Parenting (1987), Davina Lloyd, IPC Magazines Ltd, King's Reach Tower, Stamford Street, London SE1 9LS *tel* 071-261 5058 *fax* 071-261 5366.
£1.00. M. Articles on parenting, baby and childcare, health, psychology, education, children's activities, personal birth/parenting experiences. *Send synopsis*, with sae. *Illustrations: commissioned only*; colour: photos, line, cartoons. *Payment:* £100-£150 per 1000 words; by agreement.

Practical Photography (1959), Richard Hopkins, EMAP, Bushfield House, Orton Centre, Peterborough PE2 0UW *tel* (0733) 237111.
£1.60. M. Features on any aspect of photography with practical bias. *Illustrations:* line, half-tone, colour. *Payment:* from £50 per 1000 words; from £10 b&w or colour.

Practical Wireless (1932), Rob Mannion, G3XFD, PW Publishing Ltd, Enefco House, The Quay, Poole, Dorset BH15 1PP *tel* (0202) 678558 *fax* (0202) 666244.
72p. M. Articles on the practical and theoretical aspects of amateur radio and communications. Constructional projects. *Illustrations:* b&w and colour photos, line drawings and wash half-tone for offset litho. *Payment:* by arrangement.

Practical Woodworking, Alan Mitchell, IPC Magazines Ltd, King's Reach Tower, Stamford Street, London SE1 9LS *tel* 071-261 6602.
£1.65. M. Articles of a practical nature covering any aspect of woodworking, including woodworking projects, tools, joints or timber technology. *Payment:* £50 per published page. *Illustrated.*

The Practitioner (1868), Howard Griffiths, Morgan-Grampian (Professional Press) Ltd, 30 Calderwood Street, London SE18 6QH *tel* 081-855 7777.
£6.50. M. (£42.00 p.a., overseas $98.00 p.a.) Articles of interest to GPs and vocational trainees, and others in the medical profession.

Prediction (1936), Jo Logan, Link House, Dingwall Avenue, Croydon CR9 2TA *tel* 081-686 2599 *telex* 947709 Linkho G.
£1.30. M. Articles on all occult subjects. *Length:* up to 2000 words. *Payment:* by arrangement. *Illustrations:* litho; full-colour cover.

Prep School, Anne Kiggell, Straight Ash, Ashampstead Common, Pangbourne, Berks. RG8 8QT *tel* (0635) 201385.
£7.00 p.a. (on subscription) 3 p.a. Journal of the Preparatory School world: the magazine of IAPS and SATIPS. Articles of educational interest covering ages 4-13. *Length:* about 1000 words. *Illustrations:* line, half-tone. *Payment:* by arrangement.

The Press and Journal (1748), Harry Roulston, Lang Stracht, Aberdeen AB9 8AF *tel* (0224) 690222; London Office: Marylebone House, 52 St John Street, EC1M 4DT *tel* 071-490 5581.
23p. D. Contributions of Scottish interest. *Payment:* by arrangement. *Illustrations:* half-tone.

Priests & People, Revd. D.C. Sanders, OP, Blackfriars, Buckingham Road, Cambridge CB3 0DD *tel* (0223) 359376.
£2.00. M. Journal of pastoral theology especially for parish ministry and for Christians of English-speaking countries. *Length* and *payment* by arrangement.

Prima (1986), Portland House, Stag Place, London SW1E 5AU *tel* 071-245 8700.
£1.10. M. Articles on fashion, crafts, health and beauty, cookery; features. *Illustrations:* half-tone, colour.

Printing World (1878), Gareth Ward, Benn Publications Ltd, Benn House, Sovereign Way, Tonbridge, Kent TN9 1RW   *tel* (0732) 364422   *fax* (0732) 361534.
£1.75. W. (£60.00 p.a., overseas £88.00 p.a.) Commercial, technical, financial and labour news covering all aspects of the printing industry in the UK and abroad. Outside contributions. *Payment:* by arrangement. *Illustrations:* line, half-tone, colour.

Private Eye (1962), Ian Hislop, 6 Carlisle Street, London W1V 5RG   *tel* 071-437 4017   *fax* 071-437 0705.
70p. F. Satire. *Payment:* by arrangement. *Illustrations:* b&w, line.

Professional Nurse (1985), Ann Shuttleworth, Austen Cornish Publishers Ltd, Brook House, 2-16 Torrington Place, London WC1E 7LT   *tel* 071-636 4622   *telex* 8814230   *fax* 071-637 3021.
£22.50 p.a. M. Articles of interest to the professional nurse. *Length:* articles: 2500-3000 words; factsheets: 1400 words; letters: 250-500 words. *Payment:* by arrangement. *Illustrations:* line, colour, half-tone.

Publishing News (1979), Fred Newman, 43 Museum Street, London WC1A 1LY   *tel* 071-404 0304.
80p. W. Articles and news items on books and publishers. *Payment:* £60-£80 per 1000 words. *Illustrations:* half-tone.

Pulse, Howard Griffiths, Morgan-Grampian (Professional Press) Ltd, Morgan-Grampian House, 30 Calderwood Street, Woolwich, London SE18 6QH   *tel* 081-855 7777   *fax* 081-855 2406.
£72.00 p.a. W. Articles and photos of direct interest to GPs. Purely clinical material can only be accepted from medically-qualified authors. *Length:* up to 750 words. *Payment:* £100 average. *Illustrations:* b&w and colour photos.

Punch (1841), David Thomas, 245 Blackfriars Road, London SE1 9UY   *tel* 071-921 5900   *fax* 071-928 2874.
£1.20. W. All features commissioned; *no* unsolicited manuscripts. Will consider brief synopses (max. 150 words) of proposed non-fiction features. Cartoons welcome, *payment:* by arrangement. *All* submissions must be accompanied by an sae. Illustration portfolios viewed by appointment.

Quaker Monthly (1921), Elizabeth Cave, Quaker Home Service, Friends House, Euston Road, London NW1 2BJ   *tel* 071-387 3601.
55p. M. (£8.65 p.a.) Articles, poems, reviews, expanding the Quaker approach to the spiritual life. Writers should be members or attenders of a Quaker meeting. *Illustrations:* line, half-tone. *Payment:* none.

Quarterly Journal of Medicine (1907), *Publisher:* Oxford University Press, Pinkhill House, Southfield Road, Eynsham, Oxford OX8 1JJ; *Executive editor:* Dr J.M. Holt, John Radcliffe Hospital, Oxford OX3 9DU.
£105.00 p.a. M. Devoted to the publication of original papers and critical reviews dealing with clinical medicine. *Payment:* none.

Radio Control Models and Electronics (1960), Geoff Clarke, Argus Specialist Publications, Argus House, Boundary Way, Hemel Hempstead, Herts. HP2 7ST   *tel* (0442) 66551   *fax* (0442) 66998.
£1.50. M. Well-illustrated articles on topics related to radio control. *Payment:* £30 per published page. *Illustrations:* line, half-tone, cartoons.

Radio Times, Nicholas Brett, BBC Enterprises, 35 Marylebone High Street, London W1M 4AA   *tel* 071-580 5577.
50p. W. Articles support and enlarge BBC Television and Radio programmes, and ITV, Channel 4 and satellite programmes, and are, therefore, on every

subject broadcast. *Length:* 600-2500 words. *Payment:* by arrangement. *Illustrations:* in colour and b&w; photos, graphic designs or drawings.

Railway Gazette International, Murray Hughes, Reed Business Publishing Group, Quadrant House, The Quadrant, Sutton, Surrey SM2 5AS   *tel* 081-661 3739   *telex* 892084 Reedbp G   *fax* 081-661 3738.
£5.00. M. Deals with management, engineering, operation and finance of railways world-wide. Articles of practical interest on these subjects are considered and paid for if accepted. Illustrated articles, of 1000-3000 words, are preferred. A *preliminary letter* is desirable.

Railway Magazine (1897), Prospect House, 9-13 Ewell Road, Cheam, Surrey SM1 4QQ   *tel* 081-661 6780.
£1.70. M. Illustrated magazine dealing with all railway subjects; no fiction or verse. Articles from 1500-2000 words accompanied by photos. *Preliminary letter* desirable. *Payment:* by arrangement. *Illustrations:* colour transparencies, half-tone and line.

Railway World (founded as **Railways** 1939), Handel Kardas, Terminal House, Station Approach, Shepperton TW17 8AS   *tel* (0932) 228950   *fax* (0932) 232366.
£1.70. M. Articles on railway and allied matters. *Length:* 500-3000 words. *Payment:* by arrangement. *Illustrations:* line, half-tone, colour.

Rattler's Tale (1989), Anthony North, BCM Keyhole, London WC1N 3XX   *tel* (0543) 373260.
£5.00 p.a. Bi-M. Mystery/SF/horror/crime/ghost stories, ideally with a twist. Articles on fringe of knowledge/paranormal/New Age philosophy. *Length:* approx. 500 words. *Payment:* approx. £5 per piece.

Reader's Digest, Russell Twisk, The Reader's Digest Association Ltd, Berkeley Square House, Berkeley Square, London W1X 6AB   *tel* 071-629 8144.
£1.50. M. Original anecdotes – £150 for up to 300 words – are required for humorous features.

Red Tape (1911), Barry A. Reamsbottom, Civil and Public Services Association, 160 Falcon Road, Clapham Junction, London SW11 2LN   *tel* 071-924 2727   *fax* 071-924 1847.
Free to members. 11 p.a. (non-members £4.00 p.a. + £2.00 inland, £5.00 overseas postage) Well-written articles on Civil Service, trade union and general subjects considered. *Length:* 750-1400 words. Also photos and humorous drawings of interest to Civil Servants. *Illustrations:* line, half-tone.

Reform (1972), Norman Hart, 86 Tavistock Place, London WC1H 9RT   *tel* 071-837 7661   *fax* 071-833 9262 (mark: for 'Reform').
50p. M. Published by United Reformed Church. Articles of religious or social comment. *Length:* 600-1000 words. *Illustrations:* line, half-tone, colour. *Payment:* by arrangement.

Report, 7 Northumberland Street, London WC2N 5DA   *tel* 071-930 6441   *fax* 071-930 1359.
£8.00 p.a. 8 p.a. (£12.00 p.a. overseas) Journal of the Assistant Masters and Mistresses Association. Features, articles, comment, news about primary, secondary and further education; no poems. *Payment:* minimum £60 per 1000 words.

Retail Attraction, Jan Myers, MBC Retail Publications, Warwick House, Swanley, Kent BR8 8JF   *tel* (0322) 69411   *telex* 892629   *fax* (0322) 614474.
£4.00. Bi-M. (£24.00 p.a. post free) Reviews, retail business orientated articles, features and news, preferably illustrated, of shop and store premises design, display, planning, construction and fitting, services and lighting.

Length: 750-1250 words (or longer by arrangement), or short paragraphs; features by arrangement. *Payment:* by arrangement. *Illustrations:* photos, plans and sketches.

Retail Week (1988), Consultant Editor: Patience Wheatcroft, Warwick House, Azalea Drive, Swanley, Kent BR8 8JF *tel* (0322) 669411 *fax* (0322) 614474. Controlled circulation. W. (£60.00 p.a.) Features and news stories on all aspects of retail. *Length:* up to 1000 words. *Illustrations:* colour and b&w photos. *Payment:* £120 per 1000 words; market rates.

The Rialto (1984), Michael Mackmin, John Wakeman, 32 Grosvenor Road, Norwich, Norfolk NR2 2PZ *tel* (0603) 666455.
£2.90. 3 p.a. (£8.00 p.a.) Poetry and criticism. Sae essential. *Illustrations:* line. *Payment:* by arrangement.

The Round Table (1910), Peter Lyon, Institute of Commonwealth Studies, 28 Russell Square, London WC1B 5DS *tel* 071-580 5876 *fax* 071-255 2160.
£74.00 p.a. Q. The Commonwealth Journal of International Affairs. Appropriate articles. *Payment:* £10 per 1000 words. *Illustrations* by agreement with editor.

Roy of the Rovers (1975), David Hunt, 3rd Floor, Greater London House, Hampstead Road, London NW1 7QQ *tel* 071-383 7156 X 6922 *fax* 071-383 7485.
50p. W. Football-based stories, articles and features. *Length:* by negotiation. *Illustrated. Payment:* by negotiation.

Running Magazine (1979), Nick Troop, 67-71 Goswell Road, London EC1V 7EN *tel* 071-250 1881.
£1.60. M. Articles on jogging, running and fitness. *Payment:* by arrangement. *Illustrations:* line, half-tone, colour.

RUSI Journal, Jane Allford, Whitehall, London SW1A 2ET *tel* 071-930 5854 *fax* 071-321 0943.
£6.00. Q. Journal of the Royal United Services Institute for Defence Studies. Articles on international security, the military sciences, defence technology and procurement, and military history; also book reviews and correspondence. *Length:* 3500-4500 words. *Illustrations:* b&w photos, maps and diagrams. *Payment:* £12.50 per printed page upon publication.

Safety Education (1966; founded 1937 as **Child Safety**; 1940 became **Safety Training**), Ian Edginton, Royal Society for the Prevention of Accidents, Cannon House, The Priory Queensway, Birmingham B4 6BS *tel* 021-200 2461.
£10.00 p.a. 3 p.a. Articles on every aspect of safety for children and in particular articles on the teaching of road, home, water and leisure safety by means of established subjects on the school curriculum. All ages. *Illustrations:* line, half-tone, colour. *Payment:* by negotiation.

Saga Magazine (1984), Paul Bach, The Saga Building, Middelburg Square, Folkestone, Kent CT20 1AZ *tel* (0303) 857523 *telex* 966331 *fax* (0303) 220391.
£1.20 (on subscription). 10 p.a. Articles relevant to interests of 55+ age group, and profiles of celebrities in same age group. *Length:* up to 1800 words. *Illustrations:* colour transparencies, commissioned colour artwork. *Payment:* negotiable, approx. £200 per 1200 words; £120 per page and pro rata.

Satellite Times (1988), John D. Bryant, Satellite House, 85-89 Church Road, Crystal Palace, London SE19 2TA *tel* 081-653 9933 *fax* 081-653 3291.
£1.75. M. Television personality articles and interviews, sports articles, music,

competitions. *Illustrations:* in colour, b&w and line. Cartoons and TV-related illustrations, e.g. stars' caricatures, considered. *Payment:* by negotiation.

Scale Models International, Chris Ellis, Argus House, Boundary Way, Hemel Hempstead, Herts. HP2 7ST *tel* (0442) 66551 *fax* (0442) 66998.
£1.60. M. Articles on scale models. *Length:* up to 2500 words. *Payment:* £30 per page. *Illustrations:* line, half-tone, colour.

School Librarian (1937), Editor: Sheila Ray; Review Editor: Keith Barker, The School Library Association, Liden Library, Barrington Close, Liden, Swindon, Wilts. SN3 6HF *tel* (0793) 617838.
£40.00 p.a. post free. Q. Official journal of the School Library Assoc. (free to members). Reviews of books from pre-school to young adult age range with articles on authors and illustrators; also articles on school library organisation, use and skills. *Length:* up to 3000 words. *Payment:* by arrangement.

Science Progress, Professor J.M. Ziman, FRS, Professor Patricia H. Clarke, FRS, Blackwell Scientific Publications Ltd, Osney Mead, Oxford OX2 0EL *tel* (0865) 240201 *fax* (0865) 721205.
£62.50 p.a. Q. Articles of 6000 words suitably illustrated on scientific subjects, written so as to be intelligible to workers in other branches of science. *Payment:* £1.50 per printed page. *Illustrations:* line, half-tone.

Scootering (1985), Stuart Lanning, PO Box 46, Weston-super-Mare, Avon BS23 1AF *tel* (0934) 414785.
£1.60. M. Custom, racing and vintage scooter features, plus technical information. Music features and related life style pieces. *Payment:* by arrangement. *Illustrations:* half-tone, colour.

Scotland on Sunday (1988), Andrew Jaspan, North Bridge, Edinburgh EH1 1YT *tel* 031-225 2468 *telex* 72255 *fax* 031-220 2443.
50p. W.

Scotland on Sunday Magazine (1989), Alexandra Henderson, Scotsman Publications Ltd, 20 North Bridge, Edinburgh EH1 1YT *tel* 031-225 2468 *telex* 72255/727600 *fax* 031-220 2443.
Free with Scotland on Sunday. M. Features of Scottish or major international significance. *Length:* 1500-3000 words. *Illustrations:* colour and b&w photos and line. *Payment:* £150 per 1000 words; varies.

The Scots Magazine (1739), D.C. Thomson & Co. Ltd, Bank Street, Dundee DD1 9HU *tel* (0382) 23131 *fax* (0382) 27159.
80p. M. Articles on all subjects of Scottish interest. Short stories, poetry, but must be Scottish. *Payment:* varies according to quality. *Illustrations:* colour and b&w photos, and drawings.

The Scotsman (1817), Magnus Linklater, 20 North Bridge, Edinburgh EH1 1YT *tel* 031-225 2468 *fax* 031-226 7420.
35p. D. Ind. Considers articles, 800-1000 words, on political, economic and general themes, which add substantially to current information. Prepared to commission topical and controversial series from proved authorities. *Illustrations:* outstanding news pictures.

Scottish Educational Journal, 46 Moray Place, Edinburgh EH3 6BH *tel* 031-225 6244 *fax* 031-220 3151.
50p. 8 p.a., plus Specials. Published by the Educational Institute of Scotland.

The Scottish Farmer (1893), Angus MacDonald, The Plaza Tower, The Plaza, East Kilbride, Glasgow G74 1LW *tel* (03552) 46444.
75p. W. Articles on agricultural subjects. *Length:* 1000-1500 words. *Payment:* by arrangement. *Illustrations:* line, half-tone.

Scottish Field (1903), Joe Stirling, George Outram & Co. Ltd (Magazine Division), The Plaza Tower, The Plaza, East Kilbride, Glasgow G74 1LW   *tel* (03552) 46444   *fax* (03552) 63013.
£1.60. M. (£16.75 p.a.) Will consider all material with a Scottish link and good photos. *Payment:* above average rates.

Scottish Historical Review (Company of Scottish History, Ltd), Dr A. Grant and Dr I.G.C. Hutchison. Distributed by Aberdeen University Press, Farmers Hall, Aberdeen AB9 2XT   *tel* (0224) 630724   *fax* (0224) 643286.
£15.00 p.a. 2 p.a. (£18.00 through booksellers) Contributions to the advancement of knowledge in any aspect of Scottish history. *Length:* up to 8000 words. *Payment:* none; contributors are given offprints. *Illustrations:* line, half-tone.

Scottish Home and Country (1924), Stella Roberts, 42A Heriot Row, Edinburgh EH3 6ES   *tel* 031-225 1934.
40p. M. Articles on crafts, cookery, travel, personal experience, village histories, country customs, DIY, antiques, farming; humorous rural stories; fashion, health, books. *Illustrations:* half-tone. *Length:* up to 1000 words, preference being given to those accompanied by photos, etc.

Scouting, David Easton, The Scout Association, Baden-Powell House, Queens Gate, London SW7 5JS   *tel* 071-584 7030   *fax* 071-581 9953.
£1.10. M. National Magazine of The Scout Association. Ideas, news, views, features and programme resources for Leaders and Supporters. Training material, accounts of Scouting events and articles of general interest with Scouting connections. *Illustrations:* photos – action shots preferred rather than static posed shots for use with articles or as fillers or cover potential. *Payment:* on publication by arrangement.

Screen International, Editor-in-Chief: Peter Noble; Editor: Oscar Moore, 7 Swallow Place, 249-259 Regent Street, London W1R 7AA   *tel* 071-491 9484   *telex* 27261 Screen G   *fax* 071-355 3337.
£1.25. W. International news and features on every aspect of films, television and associated media. *Length:* variable. *Payment:* by arrangement.

Sea Angler (1973), Melvyn Russ, EMAP Pursuit Publishing Ltd, Bretton Court, Bretton, Peterborough PE3 8DZ   *tel* (0733) 264666   *fax* (0733) 265515.
£1.50. M. Topical articles on all aspects of sea-fishing around the British Isles. *Payment:* by arrangement. *Illustrations:* line, half-tone, colour.

Sea Breezes (1919), C.H. Milsom, 202 Cotton Exchange Building, Old Hall Street, Liverpool L3 9LA   *tel* 051-236 3935.
£1.60. M. Factual articles on ships and the sea past and present, preferably illustrated. *Length:* up to 4000 words. *Payment:* by arrangement. *Illustrations:* colour, half-tone, line.

Secrets Story Library, D.C. Thomson & Co. Ltd, Courier Place, Dundee DD1 9QJ   *tel* (0382) 23131   *fax* (0382) 22214; and 185 Fleet Street, London EC4A 2HS   *tel* 071-242 5086   *fax* 071-404 5694.
35p. M. 66 pages. Exciting and romantic stories in text, 35,000-37,000 words.

She (1955), Linda Kelsey, National Magazine House, 72 Broadwick Street, London W1V 2BP   *tel* 071-439 5000   *fax* 071-437 6886.
£1.20. M. No unsolicited manuscripts. Ideas with synopses welcome on subjects ranging from health and relationships to child-care and careers. *Payment:* NUJ freelance rates. *Illustrations:* photos.

Ship & Boat International (incorporating **Small Craft**), Richard White, Royal Institution of Naval Architects, 10 Upper Belgrave Street, London SW1X 8BQ   *tel* 071-235 4622   *telex* 265844 Sinai G   *fax* 071-245 6959.

£46.00 p.a. M. Technical articles on the design, construction and operation of all types of specialised small ships and workboats. *Length:* 500-1500 words. *Payment:* by arrangement. *Illustrations:* line and half-tone, photos and diagrams.

Ships Monthly (1966), Robert Shopland, Waterway Productions Ltd, Kottingham House, Dale Street, Burton-on-Trent DE14 3TD   *tel* (0283) 64290. £1.60. M. Illustrated articles of shipping interest – both mercantile and naval, preferably of 20th century ships. Well-researched, factual material only. No short stories or poetry. 'Notes for Contributors' available. Mainly commissioned material; preliminary letter essential. *Payment:* by arrangement. *Illustrations:* half-tone and line, colour transparencies.

Shooting Times and Country Magazine (1882), Tim O'Nions, Burlington Publishing Co. Ltd, 10 Sheet Street, Windsor, Berks. SL4 1BG   *tel* (0753) 856061. £1.00. W. Articles on fieldsports especially shooting, and on related natural history and countryside topics. *Length:* up to 1000 words. *Payment:* by arrangement. *Illustrations:* photos, drawings, colour transparencies.

The Short Wave Magazine (1937), Dick Ganderton, G8VFH, Enefco House, The Quay, Poole, Dorset BH15 1PP   *tel* (0202) 678558   *fax* (0202) 666244. £1.75. M. (£19.00 p.a.) Technical and semi-technical articles, 500-20,000 words, dealing with design, construction and operation of radio receiving equipment. *Payment:* £52 per page. *Illustrations:* line, half-tone.

Sight and Sound (1932), Philip Dodd, 21 Stephen Street, London W1P 1PL   *tel* 071-255 1444   *telex* 27624 Bfildn G   *fax* 071-436 7950. Published by the British Film Institute.
£2.00. M. Topical and critical articles on the cinema of any country; book reviews; reviews of every film theatrically released in London; reviews of every video released; regular columns from the USA and Europe. *Length:* 1000-5000 words. *Payment:* by arrangement. *Illustrations:* relevant photos.

The Sign (1905), Chansitor Publications Ltd, St Mary's Works, St Mary's Plain, Norwich, Norfolk NR3 3BH   *tel* (0603) 615995.
5p. M. Leading national insert for C of E parish magazines. Unusual b&w photos, drawings considered. Items should bear the author's name and address; return postage essential. *Payment:* by arrangement.

Signal, Approaches to Children's Books (1970), Nancy Chambers, Lockwood, Station Road, South Woodchester, Stroud, Glos. GL5 5EQ   *tel* Amberley (0453 87) 3716/2208.
£2.90. 3 p.a. (£8.70 p.a.) Articles on any aspect of children's books or the children's book world. *Length:* no limit but average 2500-3000 words. *Payment:* £3 per printed page. *Illustrations:* line occasionally.

Signature (1953), Malcolm Tait, 3rd Floor, Greater London House, Hampstead Road, London NW1 7QQ   *tel* 071-377 4633   *fax* 071-383 7570.
£1.50. Bi-M. Articles on travel, leisure, food, wine, sport. *Payment:* by arrangement. No unsolicited manuscripts accepted.

Single Market News (1988), Bridget Mellor, Room 821, DTI, Bridge Place, London SW1V 1PT   *tel* 071-215 0859   *fax* 071-215 0823.
Free. Q. Published by the Department of Trade and Industry to promote and report on British trade and industry in the context of the European single market. Most material provided by the Department of Trade, but case studies welcomed from freelances. *Study* magazine first. *Length:* 750-1000 words. *Payment:* £175 per article. *Illustrations:* colour photos; occasional cartoons.

The Skier (inc. **Ski Magazine**) (1984), Frank Baldwin, Alpha House, Laser Quay, Medway City Estate, Rochester, Kent ME2 4HU *tel* (0634) 720202 *fax* (0634) 720188.
£1.50. 6 p.a. (Sept-Apr) Ski features, based around a good story. *Length:* 800-1000 words. *Illustrations:* colour action ski photos. *Payment:* £100 per 1000 words; £100 per page.

Slimmer Magazine (1972), Claire Crowther, Magazines International Ltd, Ward House, 5-7 Kingston Hill, Kingston-upon-Thames, Surrey KT2 7PW *tel* 081-547 2662 *fax* 081-547 1201.
£1.10. Bi-M. Features on health, nutrition, slimming. Personal weight loss stories. Sae essential. *Length:* 500 or 1500 words. *Payment:* £10 per 100 words.

Slow Dancer (1977), John Harvey, 58 Rutland Road, West Bridgford, Nottingham NG2 5DG.
£1.75. Bi-annual (Apr/Oct). Poetry, some short stories. *Payment:* none, but 3 complimentary copies of magazine. *Illustrations:* in b&w photos. *Preliminary study* of magazine essential. Reading period for submissions 1 Nov-30 Apr; send US poetry submissions to: Alan Brooks, Box 3010, RFD 1, Lubec, Maine 04652, USA.

Smallholder (1985), Liz Wright, Hook House, Hook Road, Wimblington, March, Cambs. PE15 0QL *tel* (0354) 740719/(0366) 501035 *fax* (0354) 741182.
£1.60. M. Articles of relevance to small farmers about livestock and crops; items relating to the countryside considered. *Payment:* £10 per 1000 words or by arrangement. *Illustrations:* line, half-tone.

Smash Hits, Mike Soutar, 52-55 Carnaby Street, London W1V 1PF *tel* 071-437 8050 *fax* 071-494 0851.
55p. F. News items on pop stars, puzzles. *Illustrations:* colour photos, cartoons. *Payment:* £100 per page; £100.

Snooker Scene (1971), Clive Everton, Cavalier House, 202 Hagley Road, Edgbaston, Birmingham B16 9PQ *tel* 021-454 2931 *fax* 021-452 1822.
£1.10. M. News and articles about snooker. *Payment:* by arrangement. *Illustrations:* photos.

The Sociological Review, Managing Editors: John Eggleston, Ronald Frankenberg, Gordon Fyfe, University of Keele, Keele, Staffs. ST5 5BG *tel* Newcastle under Lyme (0782) 621111 ext. 3620.
£34.00 p.a. (Institutions £50.00 p.a.) including Monograph. Q. Publishes a wide variety of subjects and discussions related to sociology. *Length:* 8000-10,000 words. *Illustrations:* line. *Payment:* none.

The Solicitors Journal (1856), 21-27 Lamb's Conduit Street, London WC1N 3NJ *tel* 071-242 2548 *fax* 071-831 8119.
£1.15. W. Articles, by practising solicitors or specialist journalists, on subjects of practical interest. *Length:* up to 2000 words, but preferably 750-1200.

Somerset & Avon Life (incorporating **Bristol Illustrated**) (1975), Group Editor: Bill Charlton, County Life Magazines, The Old Bank House, 7a Gosditch Street, Cirencester, Glos. GL7 2AG *tel* (0285) 652122 *fax* (0285) 641548.
£1.00. M. Feature articles of regional interest. *Length:* 1200 words. *Payment:* by arrangement. *Illustrations:* half-tone, colour.

Songwriting and Composing (1986), General Secretary: Carole Jones, Sovereign House, 12 Trewartha Road, Praa Sands, Penzance, Cornwall TR20 9ST *tel* (0736) 762826 *fax* (0736) 763328.
Free to members. Q. Magazine of the Guild of International Songwriters and Composers. Short stories, articles, letters relating to songwriting, publishing,

recording and the music industry. *Payment:* negotiable upon content £25-£60. *Illustrations:* line, half-tone.

Spaceflight (1956), Prof. G.V. Groves, 27-29 South Lambeth Road, London SW8 1SZ   *tel* 071-735 3160   *fax* 071-820 1504. Published by The British Interplanetary Society.
Free to members. M. (£1.70) Articles up to 2500 words dealing with topics of astronomy, space and astronautics. *Illustrations:* line, half-tone, colour. *Payment:* none.

Spare Rib, 27 Clerkenwell Close, London EC1R 0AT   *tel* 071-253 9792   *fax* 071-251 1773.
£1.40. M. (£12.00 p.a.) Progressive women's magazine; features, news and reviews by women about women. No unsolicited fiction. *Payment:* small.

The Spectator (1828), Dominic Lawson, 56 Doughty Street, London WC1N 2LL   *tel* 071-405 1706   *telex* 27124   *fax* 071-242-0603.
£1.40. W. Articles of a suitable character will always be considered. *Payment:* rate depends upon the nature and length of the article.

Speech and Drama (1951), Dr Paul Ranger, 4 Fane Road, Old Marston, Oxford OX3 0SA   *tel* (0865) 728304.
£6.50 p.a. 2 p.a. Specialist articles only. Photos welcome. Covers theatre, drama and all levels of education relating to speech and drama. Preliminary abstract of 300 words. *Length:* 1500-2000 words. *Payment:* none, complimentary copy.

Spoken English (1968), Mrs Margaret Edwards, English Speaking Board (International), 26A Princes Street, Southport, Merseyside PR8 1EQ   *tel* (0704) 501730.
£12.50 p.a. (includes full annual membership of ESB). 3 p.a. Articles on *all aspects* of oral English and drama at all levels of education and of a serious nature. Overseas as well as UK. *Length:* from 1000 words.

The Sport (1988), Peter Grimsditch, 19 Great Ancoats Street, Manchester M60 4BT   *tel* 061-236 4466   *fax* 061-236 4535   *Mercury Link* 19045750.
25p. 3 p.w. Factual stories and series. *Length:* up to 1000 words per episode. *Illustrations:* b&w and colour photos, cartoons. *Payment:* £30-£5000.

Sport and Leisure (1949), Louise Fyfe, The Sports Council, 16 Upper Woburn Place, London WC1H 0QP   *tel* 071-388 1277   *fax* 071-383 5740.
£2.00. 6 p.a. Articles on various sport development, physical education, sports politics, the leisure boom, sponsorship, facilities, equipment and outdoor activities. *Length:* 500-1000 words. *Payment:* £100 per 1000 words. *Illustrated.* Sports photographers encouraged; b&w photos.

The Sporting Life, Mike Gallemore, Mirror Group Newspapers Ltd, Orbit House, 1 New Fetter Lane, London EC4A 1AR   *tel* 071-822 3291   *telex* 263403   *fax* 071-583 3885.
50p. D.

Squash World (1986), Larry Halpin, Presswatch Ltd, The Spendlove Centre, Enstone Road, Charlbury, Oxford, Oxon OX7 3PQ   *tel* (0608) 811446   *fax* (0608) 811380.
£1.50. 9 p.a. Articles on players, events, equipment, clothing, sponsorship. *Payment:* by arrangement. *Illustrations:* half-tone, colour.

The Stage and Television Today (1880), Peter Hepple, Stage House, 47 Bermondsey Street, London SE1 3XT   *tel* 071-403 1818.

40p. W. Original and interesting articles on professional stage and television topics may be sent for the editor's consideration. *Length:* 500-800 words. *Payment:* £100 per 1000 words.

Stamp Lover (1908), Publisher: National Philatelic Society, British Philatelic Centre, 107 Charterhouse Street, London EC1M 6PT *tel* 071-251 5040. Editor: Michael Furnell.
£1.50. 6 p.a. Original articles on stamps and postal history. *Illustrations:* photos, half-tone and line. *Payment:* by arrangement; none.

Stamp Magazine (1934), Richard West, Link House, Dingwall Avenue, Croydon CR9 2TA *tel* 081-686 2599 *telex* 947709 Linkho G.
£1.35. M. Informative articles and exclusive news items on stamp collecting and postal history. *No preliminary letter. Payment:* by arrangement. *Illustrations:* line, half-tone.

Stamp Monthly, Hugh Jefferies, Stanley Gibbons Publications Ltd, 5 Parkside, Ringwood, Hants BH24 3SH *tel* (04254) 2363.
£1.35. M. (£16.20 p.a.) Articles on philatelic topics. Previous reference to the editor advisable. *Length:* 500-2500 words. *Payment:* by arrangement, £17 or more per 1000 words. *Illustrations:* photos.

Stamps (1979), Christina Harrison, CGB Publishing, Newspaper House, Tannery Lane, Penketh, Cheshire WA5 2UD *tel* (092572) 4234 *fax* (092572) 2617.
£1.30. M. Stamps. *Payment:* £40 per 1000 words. *Illustrations:* line, half-tone.

Stand Magazine (1952), Jon Silkin, Lorna Tracy, 179 Wingrove Road, Newcastle on Tyne NE4 9DA *tel* 091-273 3280/281 2614.
£2.50 (inc. p&p). Q. (£9.95 p.a.) Poetry, short stories, translations, literary criticism, art. Send sae for return. Biennial Short Story Competition for unpublished original short story in English (see **Literary Prizes and Awards**). *Payment:* £30 per 1000 words of prose; £30 per poem.

Staple (1982), Donald Measham, Bob Windsor, School of Humanities, Derbyshire CHE, Mickleover, Derby DE3 5GX *tel* (0332) 47181 *fax* (0332) 514323.
£6.00 p.a. 3 p.a. Mainstream poems and short stories. *Payment:* modest.

The Star (1887), M. Corner, York Street, Sheffield S1 1PU *tel* (0742) 767676 *fax* (0742) 725978.
22p. D. Well-written articles of local character. *Length:* about 800 words. *Payment:* by negotiation. *Illustrations:* topical photos, line drawings, graphics.

Steam Classic (1990), Peter Herring, Argus Specialist Publications, Argus House, Boundary Way, Hemel Hempstead, Herts. HP2 7ST *tel* (0442) 66551/(0932) 225330 *fax* (0442) 66998/(0932) 254639.
£1.50. M. Features on the history, design and performance of British-built steam locomotives; news stories and features on present-day steam locomotive preservation. *Length:* 2000-3000 words. *Illustrations:* archive and contemporary colour transparencies and b&w photos; apply for list of specific required material (topical material always welcome). *Payment:* approx. £50 per 1000 words; £20 colour, £10 b&w.

Street Machine (1979), Russ Smith, EMAP National Publications Ltd, Bushfield House, Orton Centre, Peterborough PE2 0UW *tel* (0733) 237111 *fax* (0733) 231137.
£1.50. M. Articles on all cars and bodywork. *Length:* 2000-3000 words. *Payment:* by arrangement. *Illustrations:* line, half-tone, colour.

Studies in Comparative Religion, Perennial Books Ltd, Pates Manor, Bedfont, Middlesex TW14 8JP   *tel* 081-890 2790.
£3.95. Q. Comparative religion, metaphysics, traditional studies, eastern religions, mysticism, holy places, etc. *Length:* 2000-4000 words.

Studio Sound (1959), Keith Spencer-Allen, Link House, Dingwall Avenue, Croydon CR9 2TA   *tel* 081-686 2599   *fax* 081-760 5154.
£2.00. M. Articles on all aspects of professional sound recording. Technical and operational features on the functional aspects of studio equipment: general features on studio affairs. *Length:* widely variable. *Payment:* by arrangement. *Illustrations:* line, half-tone, colour.

The Sun (1969), Kelvin MacKenzie, News Group Newspapers Ltd, Virginia Street, London E1 9XP   *tel* 071-782 4000   *telegraphic address* Sunnews, London   *telex* 262135 Sunews   *fax* 071-488 3253.
22p. D.

Sunday Express (1918), Eve Pollard, Ludgate House, 245 Blackfriars Road, London SE1 9UX   *tel* 071-928 8000   *cables* Lon Express   *telex* 21841/21842   *fax* 071-620 1656.
55p. W. Exclusive news stories, photos, personality profiles and features of controversial or lively interest. *Length:* 800-1000 words. *Payment:* top rates.

Sunday Express Magazine, Sue Peart, Ludgate House, 245 Blackfriars Road, London SE1 9UX   *tel* 071-928 8000   *cables* Lon Express   *telex* 21841/21842   *fax* 071-928 7262.
Free with newspaper. W. General interest features. *Length:* 1500 words. *Payment:* from £150 per 1000 words. *Illustrations:* colour, half-tone, artwork.

Sunday Magazine (1981), Sue Carroll, Phase 2, 5th Floor, 1 Virginia Street, Wapping, London E1 9BD   *tel* 071-782 7900   *fax* 071-782 7474.
Free with News of the World. W. Freelance writers' ideas and material always welcome. *Payment:* by arrangement.

Sunday Mail, Jim Cassidy, Anderston Quay, Glasgow G3 8DA   *tel* 041-242 3403   *fax* 041-242 3145; London Office: 33 Holborn Circus, EC1P 1DQ.
35p. W. Exclusive stories and pictures (in colour if possible) of national and Scottish interest. *Payment:* above average.

Sunday Mercury, Peter Whitehouse, Colmore Circus, Birmingham B4 6AZ   *tel* 021-236 3366   *telex* 337552   *fax* 021-233 0271.
30p. W. News specials or features of Midland interest. *Illustrations:* colour, b&w. Special rates for special matter.

Sunday Mirror (1915), Bridget Rowe, 33 Holborn, London EC1P 1DQ   *tel* 071-353 0246.
45p. W. Concentrates on human interest news features, social documentaries, dramatic news and feature photos. Ideas, as well as articles, bought. *Payment:* high, especially for exclusives.

Sunday Mirror Magazine (1988), Katharine Hadley, Third Floor, Orbit House, 1 New Fetter Lane, Holborn Circus, London EC1P 1DQ   *tel* 071-822 2298   *fax* 071-583 4151.
Free with Sunday Mirror. W. Human interest and celebrity articles. *Length:* 1000 words. *Illustrations:* colour photos. *Payment:* articles £250+; photos £50+.

Sunday Post, D.C. Thomson & Co. Ltd, 144 Port Dundas Road, Glasgow G4 0HZ; Courier Place, Dundee DD1 9QJ; and 185 Fleet Street, London EC4A 2HS   *tel* (Glasgow) 041-332 9933; (Dundee) (0382) 23131; (London) 071-404 0199   *fax* (Dundee) (0382) 22214; (London) 071-404 5694.

35p. W. Human interest, topical, domestic and humorous articles, and exclusive news; and short stories up to 2000 words. *Illustrations:* humorous drawings. *Payment:* on acceptance.

Sunday Sport (1986), Ian Pollock, 3rd Floor, Marten House, 39-47 East Road, London N1 6AH   *tel* 071-251 2544   *telex* 269277 Ssport   *fax* 071-608 1979. 45p. W.

The Sunday Sun (1919), Chris Rushton, Thomson House, Groat Market, Newcastle upon Tyne NE1 1ED   *tel* 091-232 7500   *fax* 091-230 0238.
30p. W. Immediate topicality and human sidelights on current problems are the keynote of the Sun's requirements. Particularly welcomed are special features of family appeal and news stories of special interest to the North of England. Photos used to illustrate articles. *Length:* 500-1200 words. *Payment:* normal lineage rates, or by arrangement. *Illustrations:* photos and line.

Sunday Telegraph, Trevor Grove, Peterborough Court at South Quay, 181 Marsh Wall, London E14 9SR   *tel* 071-538 5000.
60p. W.

The Sunday Times (1822), Andrew Neil, 1 Pennington Street, London E1 9XW   *tel* 071-782 5000.
70p. W. Special articles by authoritative writers on politics, literature, art, drama, music, finance and science, and topical matters. *Payment:* top rate for exclusive features. *Illustrations:* first-class photos of topical interest and pictorial merit very welcome; also topical drawings.

Sunday Times Magazine, Philip Clarke, 1 Pennington Street, London E1 9XW   *tel* 071-782 7000.
Free with paper. W. Articles and pictures. *Illustrations:* colour photos. *Payment:* £150 per 1000 words; £150 per page.

SuperBike, John Cutts, Link House Magazines Ltd, Link House, Dingwall Avenue, Croydon CR9 2TA   *tel* 081-686 2599   *fax* 081-760 0973.
£1.60. M. Anything to do with high-powered motorcycles and the associated life style, including touring stories and fiction. *Payment:* by arrangement. *Illustrations:* half-tone, colour.

The Tablet (1840), John Wilkins, 48 Great Peter Street, London SW1P 2HB   *tel* 071-222 7462   *fax* 071-222 4967.
£1.10. W. The senior Catholic weekly. Religion, philosophy, politics, society, the arts. Freelance work welcomed. Articles should not exceed 1500 words. *Payment:* by arrangement.

Take a Break (1990), Lori Miles, Shirley House, 25-27 Camden Road, London NW1 9LL   *tel* 071-284 0909   *fax* 071-482 2777.
38p. W. Lively, tabloid women's weekly. True life features, celebrities, health and beauty, family, travel; short stories (up to 1500 words); lots of puzzles. *Payment:* by arrangement. *Illustrated.*

The Tatler (1709), Jane Procter, Vogue House, Hanover Square, London W1R 0AD   *tel* 071-499 9080   *fax* 071-409 0451.
£2.00. 10 p.a. Smart society magazine favouring sharp articles, profiles, fashion and the arts. *Illustrations:* colour, b&w, but all arranged by the journal.

Telegraph Magazine (1964), Nigel Horne, Peterborough Court at South Quay, 181 Marsh Wall, London E14 9SR   *tel* 071-538 5000   *telegraphic address* Teleweek London.
Free with Sat. paper. W. Short profiles (about 1600 words), articles of topical interest. *Illustrations:* all types. *Preliminary study* of the magazine essential. *Payment:* by arrangement.

Television (1950), IPC Magazines Ltd, King's Reach Tower, Stamford Street, London SE1 9LS   *tel* 071-261 5752   *fax* 071-261 5546.
£1.80. M. Articles on the technical aspects of domestic TV and video equipment, especially servicing; long-distance television; constructional projects; satellite TV; video recording; teletext and viewdata; test equipment. *Payment:* by arrangement. *Illustrations:* photos and line drawings for litho.

Tempo, Calum MacDonald, Boosey & Hawkes, Music Publishers, Ltd, 295 Regent Street, London W1R 8JH   *tel* 071-580 2060   *fax* 071-436 5675.
£1.85. Q. (£10.00 p.a.) Authoritative articles about 2000-4000 words on contemporary music. *Payment:* by arrangement. *Illustrations:* music type, occasional photographic or musical supplements.

Tennis (1979), Charles Elder, Castle Lane Business Centre, 85 Castle Lane West, Bournemouth, Dorset BH9 3LH   *tel* (0202) 517555   *fax* (0202) 536439.
£1.40. M. Articles on any aspect of tennis, preferably player- or coach-oriented. Technical articles also considered. *Payment:* by arrangement. *Illustrations:* half-tone and colour of a superior quality.

Tennis World, Alastair McIver, Presswatch Ltd, The Spendlove Centre, Enstone Road, Charlbury, Oxford OX7 3PQ   *tel* (0608) 811446.
£1.80. 10 p.a. Tournament reports, topical features, personality profiles, instructional articles. *Length:* 600-1500 words. *Payment:* by arrangement. *Illustrations:* colour, b&w, line.

Theology (1920), Peter Coleman, Diocesan House, Palace Gate, Exeter EX1 1HX   *tel* (0392) 73509.
£2.00. Bi-M. Articles and reviews on theology, ethics, Church and Society. *Length:* up to 3500 words. *Payment:* none.

Therapy Weekly (1974 as **Therapy**), Simon Crompton, Macmillan Magazines Ltd, 4 Little Essex Street, London WC2R 3LF   *tel* 071-379 6144   *fax* 071-836 0798.
£36.00 p.a. Free to NHS and local authority therapists. W. Articles of interest to physiotherapists, occupational therapists and speech therapists. Guidelines to contributors available. *Send proposals only* initially. *Length:* up to 1000 words. *Illustrations:* colour and b&w photos, line. *Payment:* by arrangement.

Third Way (1977), 3 Mount Radford Crescent, Exeter, Devon EX2 4JW   *tel* (0392) 425992   *fax* (0392) 413317.
£2.50. 10 p.a. Aims to present a biblical perspective on a wide range of current issues, e.g. sociology, politics, education, economics, industry and the arts. *Payment:* for articles: on publication.

This Caring Business (1985), Michael J. Monk, 1 St Thomas's Road, Hastings, East Sussex TN34 3LG   *tel* (0424) 718406   *fax* (0424) 718460.
£25.00 p.a. M. Specialist contributions relating to the commercial aspects of nursing and residential care, including hospitals. *Payment:* £75 per 1000 words. *Illustrations:* line, half-tone.

This England (1968), Roy Faiers, PO Box 52, Cheltenham, Glos. GL50 1HT   *tel* (0242) 577775.
£2.50. Q. Articles on towns, villages, traditions, customs, legends, crafts of England; stories of people. *Length:* 250-2000 words. *Payment:* £20 per page and pro rata. *Illustrations:* line, half-tone, colour.

The Times (1785), Simon Jenkins, 1 Pennington Street, London E1 9XN   *tel* 071-782 5000   *telex* 262141   *fax* 071-782 5112.
35p. D. Ind. Outside contributions considered from (1) experts in subjects of current interest; (2) writers who can make first-hand experience or reflection

come readably alive. *No preliminary letter* is required, but telephone call to
appropriate section editor is recommended. *Length:* best up to 1200 words.

The Times Educational Supplement, Priory House, St John's Lane, London
EC1M 4BX   *tel* 071-253 3000   *telex* 24460 TTSupp   *fax* 071-251 4698.
75p. W. Articles on education written with special knowledge or experience.
News items. Books, arts and equipment reviews. *Illustrations:* suitable photos
and drawings of educational interest.

Times Higher Education Supplement (1971), Peter Scott, Priory House, St John's
Lane, London EC1M 4BX   *tel* 071-253 3000   *telex* 24460   *fax* 071-608 2349.
85p. W. Articles on higher education written with special knowledge or
experience, or articles dealing with academic topics. News items. *Illustrations:*
suitable photos and drawings of educational interest.

The Times Literary Supplement, Ferdinand Mount, Priory House, St John's
Lane, London EC1M 4BX   *tel* 071-253 3000   *telex* 24460 TTSupp   *fax* 071-
251 3424.
£1.40. W. Will consider poems for publication, literary discoveries and articles,
particularly of an opinionated kind, on literary and cultural affairs.

Times Scottish Education Supplement (1965), Willis Pickard, 37 George Street,
Edinburgh EH2 2HN   *tel* 031-220 1100   *fax* 031-220 1616.
75p. W. Articles on education, preferably 1100 words, written with special
knowledge or experience. News items about Scottish educational affairs.
Illustrations: line, half-tone.

Titbits (1881), Leonard Holdsworth, Caversham Communications, 2 Caversham
Street, London SW3 4AH   *tel* 071-351 4995.
99p. M. Human interest articles; also show business, pop stars and medical.
No fiction. *Illustrations:* colour transparencies and photos, cartoons. *No* b&w.
Payment: details on application; (colour only) cartoons £15, all others at
magazine rates.

Today (1986), Martin Dunn, 1 Virginia Street, London E1 9BS   *tel* 071-782
4600.
22p. D. Feature and news-type articles. *Length:* 300-3000 words. *Payment:*
by arrangement. *Illustrations:* line, half-tone, colour.

Today's Golfer (1988), Bob Warters, EMAP Pursuit Publishing Ltd, Bretton
Court, Bretton, Peterborough PE3 8DZ   *tel* (0733) 264666   *fax* (0733)
265515.
£1.90. M. Features and articles on golf. *Payment:* £100 per 1000 words.
Illustrations: line, half-tone, colour.

Today's Guide, Marina Brown, 17-19 Buckingham Palace Road, London SW1W
0PT   *tel* 071-834 6242   *fax* 071-828 8317.
85p. M. Official Monthly of the Girl Guides Association. Articles of interest
to Guides (aged 10-15) and general interest topics. Serials and short stories
with Guiding background (1000 words per instalment). Cartoons. *Payment:*
£40 per 1000 words. *Illustrations:* line, half-tone.

Today's Runner (1985), Paul Richardson, EMAP Pursuit Publishing, Bretton
Court, Bretton, Peterborough PE3 8DZ   *tel* (0733) 264666   *fax* (0733)
265515.
£1.40. M. Practical articles on all aspects of running, especially road running
training and events, and advice on health, fitness and injury. *Illustrations:*
mainly colour and b&w photos. *Payment:* by negotiation.

Together (1956), Church House Publishing, Church House, Great Smith Street, London SW1P 3NZ *tel* 071-222 9011. Editor: Mrs Pamela Egan, The National Society, Church House, Great Smith Street, London SW1P 3NZ. 70p. 9 p.a. Short, practical or topical articles dealing with all forms of children's Christian education or concerned with the development and psychology of children. *Length:* up to 1200 words. *Illustrations:* line, half-tone. *Payment:* by arrangement.

Town and Country Planning, 17 Carlton House Terrace, London SW1Y 5AS *tel* 071-930 8903/4/5. £40.50 p.a. M. Journal of the Town and Country Planning Association. Informative articles on town and country planning, regional planning, land use, new towns, green belts, countryside preservation, industrial, business and social life in great and small towns, environment in general and community development. *Length:* 1000 words. *Illustrations:* photos and drawings. *Payment:* none.

Toy Trader (1908), Neil Nixon, Turret-Group plc, 177 Hagden Lane, Watford, Herts. WD1 8LN *tel* (0923) 228577 *telex* 9419706 *fax* (0923) 221346. £36.80 p.a. M. Trade journal specialising in anything to do with games and toys, circulated to manufacturers and retailers. *Length:* by negotiation. *Payment:* by negotiation.

Transport (1980), David Robinson, Chartered Institute of Transport, 80 Portland Place, London W1N 4DP *tel* 071-636 9952 *fax* 071-637 0511. Free to Institute members; subscription rate on application. 10 p.a. Articles on all types/aspects of transport. *Length:* 1000-2000 words. *Payment:* £120 per 1000 words. *Illustrations:* b&w photos, line drawings, cartoons.

Travel Trade Gazette UK & Ireland (1953), Nigel Coombs, Morgan-Grampian House, 30 Calderwood Street, Woolwich, London SE18 6QH *tel* 081-855 7777 *telex* 896284 Ttgln G *fax* 081-316 7783. £57.00 p.a. W. Articles, features and news; cartoons. *Illustrations:* colour transparencies and b&w prints; colour prints if taken by a professional photographer. *Payment:* approx. 21/22p per line, £96.07 per page news articles, features varies; varies.

Traveller (1970), Wexas Ltd, 45 Brompton Road, London SW3 1DE *tel* 071-581 4130 *telegraphic address* Wexas London SW3 *telex* 297155 Wexas G *fax* 071-589 8418. £36.83 p.a. Q. Features on independent travel of all kinds but specialising in long-haul and offbeat destinations with first class photos. Articles giving useful tips on particular aspects of travel, country and city reports providing an insight and factual information of use to other travellers. Articles not strictly on travel but of related interest also welcomed. *Length:* 1000-2000 words. *Payment:* rates and leaflet giving full details of requirements available; sae required. *Illustrations:* colour transparencies.

Treasure Hunting (1977), Linda Wieland, Sovereign House, Brentwood, Essex CM14 4SE *tel* (0277) 219876. £2.25. M. Stories of interesting finds. Articles on all aspects of treasure hunting with or without a detector. *Payment:* £15 per 1000 words. *Illustrations:* half-tone, colour.

The Trefoil, Myra Street, C.H.Q., The Girl Guides Association, 17-19 Buckingham Palace Road, London SW1W 0PT *tel* 071-834 6242 *fax* 071-828 8317. Q. Official Journal of the Trefoil Guild. Articles on the activities of the Guild and of Guiding in the UK and overseas and on the work of voluntary organisations. *Length:* not more than 1000 words. No fiction. *Illustrations:* photos. *Payment:* by arrangement.

Tribune, Editor: Phil Kelly; Reviews Editor: Paul Anderson, 308 Gray's Inn Road, London WC1X 8DY   *tel* 071-278 0911.
80p. W. Political, literary, with Socialist outlook. Informative articles (about 800 words), news stories (250-300 words), some poetry. No unsolicited reviews or fiction. *Payment:* by arrangement. *Illustrations:* cartoons and photos.

Trout and Salmon (1955), Sandy Leventon, EMAP Pursuit Publishing Ltd, Bretton Court, Bretton Centre, Peterborough PE3 8DZ *tel* (0733) 264666   *fax* (0733) 265515.
£1.70. M. Articles of good quality with strong trout or salmon angling interest. *Length:* 400-2000 words, accompanied if possible by photos. *Payment:* by arrangement. *Illustrations:* line, half-tone, colour transparencies.

True Romances, Group Editor: Ann Jaloba, Argus Consumer Publications, 2-4 Leigham Court Road, Streatham, London SW16 2PD   *tel* 081-677 7538.
85p. M. First-person stories with strong love interest, aimed at the 16-19 reader, 2500-4000 words. But currently all material is anglicised from American magazines so *no freelance fiction can be considered.*

True Story, Group Editor: Ann Jaloba, 2-4 Leigham Court Road, Streatham, London SW16 2PD   *tel* 081-677 7538.
85p. M. First person short stories with a strong woman-interest plot, 2500-4000 words. But currently all material is anglicised from American magazines so *no freelance fiction can be considered.*

TV Guide (1989), Bernadette Clerkin, 214 Gray's Inn Road, London WC1X 8EZ *tel* 071-782 7000   *fax* 071-782 7887.
45p. M. News, views and previews on TV programmes, films and personalities. No unsolicited articles or illustrations accepted. *Payment:* fee, by arrangement, for commissioned work.

TV Times, Terry Pavey, 247 Tottenham Court Road, London W1P 0AU   *tel* 071-323 3222   *fax* 071-580 3986.
50p. W. Features with an affinity to ITV and Channel Four programmes and personalities and television generally. *Length:* from 500 words or by arrangement. *Photographs:* only those of outstanding quality. *Payment:* by arrangement.

Twinkle, D.C. Thomson & Co. Ltd, Albert Square, Dundee DD1 9QJ   *tel* (0382) 23131   *fax* (0382) 22214; and 185 Fleet Street, London EC4A 2HS   *tel* 071-242 5086   *fax* 071-404 5694.
33p. W. Picture stories, features and comic strips, specially for little girls. Drawings in line or colour for gravure. Special encouragement to promising writers and artists. *Payment:* on acceptance.

The Unesco Courier (1948), Bahgat Elnadi, Adel Rifaat, Unesco, PO Box 3.07, 7 place de Fontenoy, Paris 75700, France   *tel* (1) 45 68 47 15   *telegraphic address* Unesco, Paris   *fax* (1) 45 66 92 70.
£13.80 p.a. Monthly in 35 language editions. Illustrated feature articles in the fields of science, culture, education and communication; promotion of international understanding; human rights. *Length:* 2000 words. *Illustrations:* colour and b&w photos, drawings, graphs, maps.

The Universe (1860), Mrs Ann Knowles, 1st Floor, St James's Buildings, Oxford Street, Manchester M1 6FP   *tel* 061-236 8856   *fax* 061-236 8530.
40p. W. Newspaper and review for Catholics. News stories, features and photos on all aspects of Catholic life required. MSS should not be submitted without sae. *Payment:* by arrangement.

The Use of English, Roger Knight, School of Education, 21 University Road, Leicester LE1 7RF. *Publishers:* Scottish Academic Press Ltd, 139 Leith Walk, Edinburgh EH6 8NS *tel* 031-553 3649 *fax* 031-553 3705.
£8.50 p.a. 3 p.a. (£12.50 p.a. institutions) For teachers in all fields of English in Great Britain and overseas. *Length:* usually up to 3500 words. *Payment:* none.

The Vegan (1944), Richard Farhall, The Vegan Society, 7 Battle Road, St Leonards-on-Sea, East Sussex TN37 7AA *tel* (0424) 427393.
£1.25. Q. Articles on animal rights, nutrition, cookery, agriculture, Third World, health. *Length:* approx. 1500 words. *Payment:* by arrangement. *Illustrations:* photos, cartoons, line drawings – foods, animals, livestock systems, crops, people, events; colour for cover.

The Vegetarian, Nicola Graimes, ESG Publishing Ltd, Third Floor, 58 High Street, Sutton, Surrey SM1 1EZ *tel* 081-770 7337 *fax* 081-770 7283.
£1.20. Bi-M. Articles on animal welfare, nutrition, world food problems, vegetarian and alternative life styles. Interviews with vegetarian celebrities. *Payment:* by arrangement. *Illustrations:* photos and line drawings of foods, crops, relevant events, nature studies; colour.

Verse (1984), Robert Crawford, David Kinloch, Henry Hart, Nicholas Roe, Department of English, University of St Andrews, St Andrews, Fife KY16 9AL *tel* (0334) 76161 ext. 471.
£3.00. 3 p.a. Poems in English, Scots, or translation; critical pieces on contemporary poetry.

Victor, D.C. Thomson & Co. Ltd, Courier Place, Dundee DD1 9QJ *tel* (0382) 23131 *fax* (0382) 22214; and 185 Fleet Street, London EC4A 2HS *tel* 071-242 5086 *fax* 071-404 5694.
30p. W. Vigorous, well-drawn stories in pictures (line drawings) for boys and young men. War, adventure, sport. Instalments 2, 3, or 4 pages; 8 to 9 frames per page. *Payment:* on acceptance.

Video Week (1983), Steve Hurst, 23-27 Tudor Street, London EC4Y 0HR *tel* 071-583 9199 *fax* 071-583 2071.
£2.25. (Controlled circulation.) W. News and features on all aspects of producing, manufacturing, marketing and retailing video software programs; also cable and satellite TV, video games and computer software. *Payment:* NUJ rates.

Viz (1979), Chris Donald, John Brown Publishing Ltd, The Boat House, Crabtree Lane, Fulham Palace Road, London SW6 8NJ.
£1.00. 6 p.a. Cartoons, cartoon scripts, articles. *Illustrations:* half-tone, line, cartoons. *Payment:* £200 per page (cartoons).

Vogue, Elizabeth Tilberis, Vogue House, Hanover Square, London W1R 0AD *tel* 071-499 9080 *telex* 27338 Volon G.
£2.50. M. Fashion, beauty, health, decorating, art, theatre, films, literature, music, travel, food and wine. *Length:* articles from 1000 words. *Illustrated.*

The Voice (1982), Winsome Cornish, 370 Coldharbour Lane, London SW9 8PL *tel* 071-737 7377 *fax* 071-274 8994.
48p. W. News stories, general and arts features of interest to black readers. *Illustrations:* colour and b&w photos, cartoons. *Payment:* £100 per 1000 words; £20-£35.

Voice Intelligence Report (1972), Claud Morris, 15A Lowndes Street, London SW1X 9EY *tel* 071-235 5966 *fax* 071-259 6694.

£12.00. Q. (£40.00 p.a.) Background intelligence reports on the Press, media, Parliament with specific reference to Middle East. *Write* for specimen copy. *Length:* 500-1500 words. *Payment:* £150 per 1000 words. *Illustrations:* none.

Wales on Sunday (1989), Thomson House, Cardiff CF1 1WR *tel* (0222) 223333 *fax* (0222) 342462.
50p. W. Ind. General interest articles suitable for use in a national Sunday newspaper which offers comprehensive news, features, arts and entertainments coverage at a weekend, plus a particular focus on events from Wales.

War Cry (1879), Major Robert Street, 101 Queen Victoria Street, London EC4P 4EP *tel* 071-236 5222 *fax* 071-236 3491. Published by The Salvation Army.
15p. W. (£18.25 p.a. UK) Voluntary contributions, mostly by Salvationists. Puzzles. *Illustrations:* line and photos.

Warwickshire and Worcestershire Life (including **West Midlands**), William Amos, 27 Waterloo Place, Leamington Spa, Warks. CV32 5LF *tel* (0926) 422003/422372 *fax* (0926) 334050. Member of the Town & County Magazines Group.
£1.00. M. Articles of interest in the counties concerned based on first-hand experience dealing with work, customs and matters affecting urban and rural life. *Length:* 500-1500 words. *Illustrations:* preference given to articles accompanied by good photos relating to subject. *Payment:* by arrangement.

Wasafiri (1984), Susheila Nasta, PO Box 195, Canterbury, Kent CT2 7XB.
£10.00 p.a. Bi-annual. (£14.00 p.a. institutions) Published by the Association for the Teaching of Caribbean, African, Asian and Associated Literature. Short stories, poetry, biography. Submit MSS in duplicate, with an sae. *Illustrations:* b&w photos. *Payment:* none.

Waterways World (1972), Hugh Potter, Waterway Productions Ltd, Kottingham House, Dale Street, Burton-on-Trent, Staffs. DE14 3TD *tel* (0283) 64290.
£1.60. M. Feature articles on all aspects of inland waterways in Britain and abroad, including historical material. Factual and technical articles preferred. No short stories or poetry. *Payment:* by arrangement. *Illustrations:* b&w photos, colour transparencies, line.

Weekend Guardian, supplement of Saturday edition of The Guardian, Roger Alton, 119 Farringdon Road, London EC1R 3ER *tel* 071-278 2332 *telex* 8811746/7/8 Guardn G; 164 Deansgate, Manchester M60 2RR *tel* 061-832 7200.
Free with paper. W. Features on environment, world affairs, food and drink, home life, 'Fifth Dimension' (religions, New Age, alternative health, etc.), travel, leisure, etc. Also good reportage on social and political subjects. *Illustrations:* half-tone, line. *Payment:* apply for rates.

The Weekly News, D.C. Thomson & Co. Ltd, Courier Place, Dundee DD1 9QJ *tel* (0382) 23131; 139 Chapel Street, Manchester M3 6AA *tel* 061-834 2831-7; 144 Port Dundas Road, Glasgow G4 0HZ *tel* 041-332 9933; and 185 Fleet Street, London EC4A 2HS *tel* 071-242 5086.
30p. W. Real-life dramas of around 2000 words told in the first person. Non-fiction series with lively themes or about interesting people. Keynote throughout is strong human interest. Joke sketches. *Payment:* on acceptance.

West Africa, Editor-in-Chief: Kaye Whiteman, 43-45 Coldharbour Lane, London SE5 9AR *tel* 071-737 2946 *telex* 892420 West Af G *fax* 071-978 8334.
£1.00. W. Weekly summary of West African news, with articles on political, economic and commercial matters, and on all matters of general interest

affecting West Africa. Also book reviews. Covers Ghana, Nigeria, Sierra Leone, The Gambia, French-speaking African States, former Portuguese West Africa, Liberia, South Africa, Namibia and Zaire. *Length:* articles about 1200 words. *Payment:* as arranged. *Illustrations:* half-tone.

Western Daily Press (1858), Ian Beales, Temple Way, Bristol BS99 7HD *tel* (0272) 260080 *fax* (0272) 279568.
22p. D. National, international or West Country topics for features or news items, from established journalists, with or without *illustrations*. *Payment:* by negotiation.

Western Mail (1869), John Humphries, Thomson House, Cardiff CF1 1WR *tel* (0222) 223333 *fax* (0222) 220238.
30p. D. Ind. Articles of political, industrial, literary or general and Welsh interest are considered. *Illustrations:* topical general news and feature pictures. *Payment:* according to value; special fees for exclusive news.

The Western Morning News (1860), Colin Davison, 65 New George Street, Plymouth PL1 1RE *tel* (0752) 266626 *fax* (0752) 267580.
25p. D. Articles of 600-900 words, plus illustrations, considered on West Country subjects.

Which Computer (1977), Tim Wright, 34 Farringdon Lane, London EC1R 3AU *tel* 071-251 6222.
£2.25. M. Will consider proposals for equipment reviews and general features about business computing. *Preliminary letter* essential. *Payment:* by negotiation. *Illustrations:* line, half-tone, colour.

Wisden Cricket Monthly (1979), David Frith, 6 Beech Lane, Guildford, Surrey GU2 5ES *tel* (0483) 32573 *fax* (0483) 33153.
£1.40. M. Cricket articles of general interest. *Length:* up to 1000 words. *Payment:* by arrangement. *Illustrations:* half-tone, colour.

Woman (1937), David Durman, IPC Magazines Ltd, King's Reach Tower, Stamford Street, London SE1 9LS *tel* 071-261 5000.
43p. W. Practical articles of varying length on all subjects of interest to women. No unsolicited fiction. *Payment:* by arrangement. *Illustrations:* colour transparencies, photos, sketches.

Woman and Home (1926), Sue Dobson, IPC Magazines Ltd, King's Reach Tower, Stamford Street, London SE1 9LS *tel* 071-261 5423.
£1.00. M. Centres on the personal and home interests of the lively-minded woman with or without career and family. Articles dealing with leisure pursuits, crafts, gardening, dressmaking and fashion, needlework and knitting. Things to make and buy for the home. Features on people and places. Fiction: serial stories 3-5 instalments, and complete stories from 1000-5000 words in *length*, often with some romantic interest. *Illustrations:* commissioned photos and sketches for full-colour reproduction.

The Woman Journalist (1894), Jocelyn Glegg, 300 Hills Road, Cambridge CB2 2QG.
Free to members. 3 p.a. Organ of the Society of Women Writers and Journalists. Short articles of interest to professional writers. *Payment:* none.

Woman's Journal (1927), Deirdre Vine, IPC Magazines Ltd, King's Reach Tower, Stamford Street, London SE1 9LS *tel* 071-261 6622 *fax* 071-261 7061.
£1.50. M. Magazine devoted to the looks and lives of intelligent women. Contents include short stories of literary merit (3000 words maximum); interviews and articles (1000-2500 words) dealing in depth with topical subjects

and personalities; fashion, beauty and health, food and design. *Illustrations:* full colour, line and wash, first-rate photos.

Woman's Own, Keith McNeill, IPC Magazines Ltd, King's Reach Tower, Stamford Street, London SE1 9LS   *tel* 071-261 5474.
43p. W. Appealing to modern women of all ages, all classes, predominantly in the 20-35 age group. No unsolicited fiction accepted except for annual short story competition. Good, original feature ideas welcome from show business to human interest and sociological issues. *Illustrations:* in full colour and mono. Original knitting, crochet, craft designs, interior decorating and furnishing ideas, fashion. Please address work to relevant department editor.

Woman's Realm (1958), Ann Wallace, IPC Magazines Ltd, King's Reach Tower, Stamford Street, London SE1 9LS   *tel* 071-261 5000.
39p. W. Lively general interest weekly magazine aimed at women with growing families. Articles on personalities, topical subjects, cookery, fashion, beauty, home. Humorous pieces up to 600 words. Modern short stories of 1000-2500 words, preferably intriguing or with a twist. *Payment:* by arrangement. *Illustrations:* 4- and 2-colour drawings, photos in colour and b&w.

Woman's Story Magazine (1956), Group Editor: Ann Jaloba, 2-4 Leigham Court Road, Streatham, London SW16 2PD   *tel* 081-677 7538.
95p. M. Short stories with realistic characterisation and strong themes, 2500-4000 words. But currently all material is anglicised from American magazines so *no freelance fiction can be considered.*

Woman's Weekly (1911), Judith Hall, IPC Magazines Ltd, King's Reach Tower, Stamford Street, London SE1 9LS   *tel* 071-261 6131   *fax* 071-261 6322.
39p. W. Lively, family-interest magazine. Two serials, averaging 4500 words each instalment of strong romantic interest, and one short story of 1000-4000 words of general interest. Personality features with photos. Important biographies, and memoirs of celebrities. *Payment:* by arrangement. *Illustrations:* full colour fiction illustrations, small sketches and photos.

Woodworker, Nick Gibbs, Argus Specialist Publications, Argus House, Boundary Way, Hemel Hempstead, Herts. HP2 7ST   *tel* (0442) 66551   *telex* 827797   *fax* (0442) 66998.
£1.60. M. For the craft and professional woodworker. Practical illustrated articles on cabinet work, carpentry, wood polishing, wood turning, wood carving, rural crafts, craft history, antique and period furniture; also wooden toys and models; timber procurement, conditioning, seasoning; tool, machinery and equipment reviews. *Payment:* by arrangement. *Illustrations:* line drawings and photos.

Work Study, John Heap, Leeds Polytechnic Computing Services Unit, Calverley Street, Leeds LS1 3HE   *tel* (0532) 832600   *fax* (0532) 833145.
£44.95 p.a. Bi-M. Authoritative articles on all aspects of work study including work measurement, method study, O&M, industrial engineering, payment systems. *Length:* 2000-4000 words. *Payment:* by arrangement. *Illustrations:* line, half-tone.

Workbox (1984), Audrey Babington, 40 Silver Street, Wiveliscombe, Nr Taunton, Somerset TA4 2NY   *tel* (0984) 24033.
£1.25. Q. Features, of any length, on all aspects of needlecrafts. *No* 'how-to' articles. Send sae with enquiries and submissions. *Illustrations:* good b&w photos and colour transparencies; also line drawings. *Payment:* by agreement.

World Bowls (1954), Publisher: G.K. Browne, PO Box 17, East Horsley, Surrey KT24 5JU   *tel* (0372) 59319.

£1.20. M. Unusual features, fiction and news about all codes of bowling. *Payment:* by arrangement. *Illustrations:* half-tone, colour.

World Development, Pergamon Press plc, Headington Hill Hall, Oxford OX3 0BW   *tel* (0865) 794141.
DM1025 p.a. M. Multi-disciplinary international journal devoted to the study and promotion of world development.

World Fishing (1952), Nortide Ltd, Nortide House, Stone Street, Faversham, Kent ME13 8PG   *tel* (0795) 536536   *telex* 965770 Wfmag   *fax* (0795) 530244.
£30.00 p.a. M. International journal of commercial fishing. Technical and management emphasis on catching, processing, farming and marketing of fish and related products. Fishery operations and vessels covered world-wide. *Length:* 1000-2000 words. *Payment:* by arrangement. *Illustrations:* Photos and diagrams for litho reproduction.

World Magazine (1987), Mark Ausenda, World Publications Ltd (BBC Magazines), Hyde Park House, 5 Manfred Road, London SW15 2RS   *tel* 081-877 1080   *fax* 081-874 1845.
£1.80. M. People, places, wildlife and the environment. *Length:* 1500-2000 words. *Payment:* £100 per published page including pictures. *Illustrations:* colour slides – advise use of either Kodachrome 25 or 64, or Fuji 50; prefer 35 mm.

World Outlook, The Baptist Men's Movement. Editor: M.E. Putnam, 61 Hempstead Lane, Potten End, Berkhamsted, Herts. HP4 2RZ   *tel* (0442) 865245.
£2.50 p.a. Q. Articles on Christian ethics and world questions. *Length:* 1000-1200 words. *Illustrated.*

The World Today (1945), Christopher Cviic, The Royal Institute of International Affairs, Chatham House, 10 St James's Square, London SW1Y 4LE   *tel* 071-930 2233   *fax* 071-839 3593.
£1.80. M. Objective and factual articles on current questions of international affairs. *Length:* about 3500 words. *Payment:* £40 each article.

The World's Children (1920), Rosemary J. Brown, 17 Grove Lane, London SE5 8RD   *tel* 071-703 5400   *fax* 071-703 2278.
£5.00 p.a. Q. The magazine of The Save the Children Fund. Articles on child welfare related to Save the Children's work overseas and in the UK. *Length:* 700 words. *Payment:* by arrangement. *Illustrations:* photos for cover and article illustration.

Writers' Monthly (1984), Shirley Kelly, 29 Turnpike Lane, London N8 0EP   *tel* 081-342 8879   *fax* 081-347 8847.
£33.50 p.a. M. Articles and features of interest to the freelance writer. *Payment:* £35 per 1000 words. *Illustrations:* b&w.

Writers News (1989), Richard Bell, PO Box 4, Nairn IV12 4HU   *tel* (0667) 54441   *fax* (0667) 54401.
£34.90 p.a. M. News and articles on all aspects of writing. *Length:* 800-1500 words. *Illustrations:* line, half-tone. *Payment:* by arrangement.

Writing Women (1981), Linda Anderson, Cynthia Fuller, Rosemary O'Sullivan, Penny Smith, Margaret Wilkinson, 7 Cavendish Place, Newcastle upon Tyne NE2 2NE.
£2.00. 3 p.a. Poems, short stories, critical articles. *Payment:* £10 per poem or per 1000 words.

Y Faner (Banner and Times of Wales) (1843), Hafina Clwyd, County Press, Bala, Gwynedd LL23 7PG *tel* (0678) 521251 *fax* (0678) 521262.
85p. W. National weekly news review in Welsh; articles of economic, literary and political interest. Non-party. *Length:* 1000 words. *Payment:* minimum £7 per article. *Illustrations:* line and photos.

Yachting Monthly (1906), Andrew Bray, IPC Magazines Ltd, Room 2209, King's Reach Tower, Stamford Street, London SE1 9LS *tel* 071-261 6040 *fax* 071-261 6704.
£2.00. M. Technical articles, up to 2250 words, on all aspects of seamanship, navigation, the handling of sailing craft, and their design, construction and equipment. Well-written narrative accounts, up to 3000 words, of cruises in yachts. *Payment:* quoted on acceptance. *Illustrations:* b&w, colour transparencies, line or wash drawings.

Yachting World (1894), Dick Johnson, IPC Magazines Ltd, Quadrant House, The Quadrant, Sutton, Surrey SM2 5AS *tel* 081-661 3297 *fax* 081-643 2144.
£2.20. M. Practical articles of an original nature, dealing with sailing and boats. *Length:* 1500-2000 words. *Payment:* varies. *Illustrations:* b&w prints and colour transparencies, or drawings.

Yachts and Yachting (1947), Peter Cook, 196 Eastern Esplanade, Southend-on-Sea, Essex SS1 3AB *tel* (0702) 582245.
£1.55. F. Short articles which should be technically correct. *Payment:* by arrangement. *Illustrations:* line, half-tone, colour.

Yorkshire Evening Press (1882), Richard Wooldridge, York and County Press, PO Box 29, 76-86 Walmgate, York YO1 1YN *tel* (0904) 653051 *fax* (0904) 612853; London Office: Newspaper House, 8-16 Great New Street, EC4 *tel* 071-353 1030.
25p. D. Articles of Yorkshire or general interest, humour, personal experience of current affairs. *Length:* 500-1500 words. *Payment:* by arrangement. *Illustrations:* line, half-tone.

Yorkshire Gazette & Herald Series, P.A. Austin-Clarke, PO Box 29, 76-86 Walmgate, York YO1 1YN *tel* (0904) 653051 *fax* (0904) 611488.
25p. W. Stories, features and pictures of local interest. *Payment:* varies. *Illustrations:* line, half-tone, colour.

Yorkshire Life (1947), Brian Crowther, Town & County Magazines, Oyston Publications plc, Batley Business Centre, Ings Road, Batley, W. Yorks. WF17 8LT *tel* (0924) 440131 *fax* (0924) 474302.
£1.00. M. Topics of Yorkshire interest, with or without photos. *Length:* 200-500 words and 800-1500 words. *Payment:* varies. *Illustrations:* colour, tone or line.

Yorkshire Post (1754), Tony Watson, Wellington Street, Leeds LS1 1RF *tel* 432701 *telex* 55245 *fax* (0532) 443430; London Office: Ludgate House, 245 Blackfriars Road, SE1 9UY *tel* 071-921 5000.
32p. D. Authoritative and well-written articles elucidating new topics or on topical subjects of general, literary or industrial interests are preferred. *Length:* 1200-1500 words. *Payment:* by arrangement. Contributions to *People*, a column about personalities in the news, are welcomed. *Illustrations:* photos and frequent pocket cartoons (single column width), topical wherever possible.

Yorkshire Riding Magazine (1964), Winston Halstead, Barclays Bank Chambers, Sowerby Bridge, Yorkshire HX6 2DX *tel* (0422) 885678.
80p. Bi-M. Articles exclusively about people, life and character of the three Ridings of Yorkshire. *Length:* up to 1500 words. *Payment:* approx. £25-£35 per published page. *Illustrations:* line, half-tone, colour.

You (1982), Nicholas Gordon, Northcliffe House, 2 Derry Street, Kensington, London W8 5TS *tel* 071-938 6000 *telex* 28301 Ldm *fax* 071-938 1488.
Free with Mail on Sunday. W. Features on all subjects. *Length:* 1000-2500 words. *Payment:* by arrangement. *Illustrations:* line, half-tone, colour photos, generally commissioned.

Young People Now (1989), Jackie Scott, National Youth Bureau, 17-23 Albion Street, Leicester LE1 6GD *tel* (0533) 471200 *fax* (0533) 471043.
£1.75. M. (£18.60 p.a. on subscription) Informative, general interest articles, highlighting issues of concern to all those who work with young people – including youth, probation and social services, teachers and volunteers. Guidelines for contributors available on request. *Length:* 1000-1500 words. *Illustrations:* line, half-tone. *Payment:* £45 per 1000 words; by negotiation.

The Young Soldier (1881), Jean Bryant, 101 Queen Victoria Street, London EC4P 4EP *tel* 071-236 5222, ext. 2284 *fax* 071-236 3491.
15p. W. The Salvation Army's children's weekly. Stories, pictures, cartoon strips, puzzles etc., often on Christian themes. *Payment:* usual. *Illustrations:* half-tone, line and three-colour line.

Africa

KENYA

Daily Nation, Group Managing Editor: George Mbugguss; Managing Editor: Wangethi Mwangi, PO Box 49010, Nairobi *tel* 337691 *telex* 22239 *fax* 723992.
K.Sh. 6.00. D. News, features, etc. Pictures.

East African Medical Journal (1923), E.G. Kasili, MB, ChB, MD, PO Box 41632, Nairobi *tel* 724711/726073.
£95.00 p.a. M. Medical articles, preferably on tropical medicine, case reports, etc. *Illustrations:* photos.

The Standard, Ali S. Hafidh, PO Box 30080, Nairobi *tel* 540280 *telex* 24032 Newstad KE.
K.Sh. 6.00 daily; K.Sh. 7.00 Sun. News and topical articles of East African interest and the world in general.

Swara (1978), Justina E. Muchura, PO Box 20110, Nairobi *tel* 748170/1/2/3 *fax* 254-2-746868.
£18.00 p.a. 6 p.a. The Magazine of the East African Wild Life Society. Articles on wildlife, conservation and natural beauty of East Africa. *Payment:* by arrangement. *Illustrations:* photos, colour and b&w; line drawings occasionally.

NIGERIA

Monthly Life (1984), West African Book Publishers Ltd, Ilupeju Industrial Estate, PO Box 3445, Lagos, Nigeria *tel* 900760-4 *telex* 26144 Presac NG; UK: Magazine Production Ltd, 13 Southgate Street, Winchester, Hants SO23 9DZ *tel* (0962) 840088 *telegraphic address* Hambleside, Winchester *telex* 477357.
N.3.00. M. Features, human interest stories, short stories with a West African setting. *Illustrations:* line drawings, cartoons, colour and b&w photos – West African subjects. *Payment:* by arrangement.

SUDAN

Sudanow, Fath el Rahman Mahgoub, Ministry of Culture and Information, PO Box 2651, Khartoum   *tel* 77913   *telex* 22418/22419.
£S1.50. M. News stories, business stories, book reviews, travelogues – all about the Sudan. *Payment:* £S30 per column. *Illustrations:* line, half-tone.

TANZANIA

The Daily News, J.M. Mapunda, PO Box 9033, Dar es Salaam   *tel* 25318   *telex* 41071.
2½p. D.

Sunday News, Box 9033, Dar es Salaam   *tel* 29881   *telex* 41071.
4p. W.

UGANDA

The New Vision, PO Box 9815, Kampala   *tel* 235209   *fax* 235221.
200 shillings. D. News, topical features, news pictures.

Weekly Topic (1979), Wafula Oguttu, PO Box 1725, Kampala   *tel* 233834/ 231798/231854.
400 shillings. W. Non-sectarian, non-provocative, general interest articles. *Length:* up to 1000 words. *Illustrations:* b&w photos, line drawings, cartoons. *Payment:* 5000 shillings per article; 3000 shillings per illustration.

ZIMBABWE

The Chronicle (1894), Geoff Nyarota, PO Box 585, Bulawayo   *tel* 65471.
15c. D. (not Sun). Topical articles.

The Farmer, Modern Farming Publications (1928), Alistair Syme, Agriculture House, Leopold Takawira Street, PO Box 1622, Harare   *tel* 708245/6.
$45 p.a. W. Official journal of the Commercial Farmers Union. Articles on all aspects of agriculture. *Payment:* by arrangement. *Illustrated.*

The Herald (1891), T.A.G. Sithole, PO Box 396, Harare   *tel* 795771   *telegraphic address* Manherald, Harare   *telex* 26196   *fax* 791311.
20c. D. Topical articles of news value. *Payment:* varies, depends on length, content and news value. *Illustrations:* bromides, colour.

Mahogany, Gill Beach, PO Box UA589, Harare   *tel* 705412   *telex* 4748 ZW.
60c. F. Articles concerning events and personalities; standard women's magazine formula. Average *length:* 1500 words. *Payment:* by arrangement. *Illustrations:* line, half-tone, colour.

The Manica Post, A. Hamiwe, PO Box 960, Mutare   *tel* 61212.
25c. W. Non-fiction articles only. *Length:* up to 500 words. *Payment:* by arrangement. *Illustrations:* half-tone.

The Sunday Mail (1935), S. Mpofu, PO Box 396, Harare   *tel* 795771   *telegraphic address* Manherald, Harare.
20c. W. Topical articles of news value. *Payment:* varies, depends on length, content and news value. *Illustrations:* bromides, colour.

The Sunday News (1930), Lawrence Chikuwira, PO Box 585, Bulawayo   *tel* 65471.
27c. W. Topical articles.

AUSTRALIA

Newspapers are listed under the towns in which they are published.

(Adelaide) Advertiser (1858), Peter Blunden, 121 King William Street, Adelaide, South Australia 5000 *tel* (08) 218 9218 *telex* 82101 *fax* (08) 231 1147; London: 3rd Floor, Allen House, 70 Vauxhall Bridge Road, SW1V 2RP *tel* 071-834 9405 *telex* 267297 *fax* 071-828 6090 (news), 071-828 5833 (syndications).
50c., Sat. 80c. D. The only morning daily in S. Australia. Descriptive and news background material, 400-800 words, preferably with pictures.

(Adelaide) News (1923), Tony Baker, The News (South Australia) Pty Ltd, 112 North Terrace, Adelaide *tel* (08) 231-0351 *fax* (08) 212-2217.
25c. D. One feature page open for topical articles, but freelance articles rarely accepted. *Length:* preferably 600-750 words. *Payment:* by arrangement. *Illustrated* articles preferred.

(Adelaide) Sunday Mail (1912), K. Sullivan, 121 King William Street, Adelaide, South Australia 5000 *tel* (08) 218 9218 *fax* (08) 212 6264.

Australasian Sporting Shooter, Ray Galea, Yaffa Publishing Group, 17-21 Bellevue Street, Surry Hills, NSW 2010 *tel* (02) 281 2333 *fax* (02) 281 2750.
$3.50. M. All aspects of game shooting, collecting, antiques, archery (associated with hunting), pistol shooting, clay target shooting, reloading, ballistics and articles of a technical nature. *Payment:* by arrangement.

The Australian, David Armstrong, GPO Box 4245, Sydney, NSW 2000 *tel* (02) 288 3000.
50c. D. (except Sun) Will consider topical articles from freelance writers. *Length:* up to 1500 words. *Payment:* by arrangement.

Australian Angler's Fishing World, Gil Schott, Yaffa Publishing Group, 17-21 Bellevue Street, Surry Hills, NSW 2010 *tel* (02) 281 2333 *telex* AA 121887 *fax* (02) 281 2750.
$3.85. M. All aspects of rock, surf, stream, deep sea and game fishing, with comprehensive sections on gear, equipment and boats. *Payment:* by arrangement.

Australian Bookseller & Publisher (1921), John Nieuwenhuizen, D.W. Thorpe, 18 Salmon Street, Port Melbourne 3207 *tel* (03) 645 1511 *fax* (03) 645 3981.
UK agent: Bowker-Saur Ltd, 59 Grosvenor Street, London W1X 9DA.

The Australian Financial Review, Gerard Noonan, 235-243 Jones Street, Broadway, Sydney, NSW 2007; London: 12 Norwich Street, EC4A 1BH *tel* 071-353 9321; New York: Suite 2401, 1500 Broadway, NY 10036 *tel* 212-398-9494.
$1.00. M.-F. Investment business and economic news and reviews; government and politics, production, banking, commercial, and Stock Exchange statistics; company analysis. General features in Friday *Weekend Review* supplement.

Australian Flying, Lawry Cohen, Yaffa Publishing Group, 17-21 Bellevue Street, Surry Hills, NSW 2010 *tel* (02) 281 2333 *fax* (02) 281 2750; London: Robert Logan, 64 The Mall, Ealing, W5 *tel* 081-579 4836.
$4.15. 6 p.a. Appeals to light and medium aircraft owners, as well as those directly and indirectly associated with the aircraft industry. *Payment:* by arrangement.

Australian Historical Studies, John Rickard, Monash University, Clayton, Victoria 3168.

$30.00 p.a. 2 p.a. *Length:* 8000 words maximum. *Illustrations:* tables and maps. *Payment:* none.

Australian Home Beautiful (1913), A. Fawcett, 32 Walsh Street, West Melbourne, Victoria 3003   *tel* (03) 320 7000.
$3.00. M. Deals with home building, interior decoration, furnishing, gardening, cookery, etc. Short articles with accompanying photos with Australian slant accepted. *Preliminary letter* advisable. *Payment:* higher than Australian average.

Australian House and Garden (1948), Publisher: Richard Walsh, 54 Park Street, Sydney, NSW 2000   *tel* (02) 282 8000.
$3.50. M. Factual articles dealing with interior decorating, home design, gardening, wine, food. *Preliminary letter* essential. *Payment:* by arrangement. *Illustrations:* line, half-tone, colour.

Australian Journal of International Affairs, Dr James Cotton, Dept. of International Relations, Australian National University, GPO Box 4, Canberra, ACT 2601   *tel* (06) 249 4610   *telex* 61364 Ajrc   *fax* (06) 257 1893.
$28.00 p.a. in Australia and New Zealand; $39.00 p.a. elsewhere. 2 p.a. Scholarly articles on international affairs. *Length:* 4000-7000 words. *Payment:* none.

The Australian Journal of Politics and History, J.A. Moses, Department of History, University of Queensland Press, St Lucia, Queensland 4067   *tel* (07) 365 56477   *fax* (07) 365 6266.
$54.00. 3 p.a. (US $58.00, UK £33.00, inc. postage) Australian, Commonwealth, Asian, SW Pacific and international articles. Special feature: regular surveys of Australian Foreign Policy and State and Commonwealth politics. *Length:* 8000 words max. *Illustrations:* line, only when necessary. *Payment:* none.

Australian Mining, Lou Caruana, Thomson Publications Australia, 47 Chippen Street, Chippendale, NSW 2008   *tel* 699-2411   *postal address* PO Box 65, Chippendale, NSW 2008.
$56.00 p.a. in Australia.

The Australian Quarterly (1929), Dr Hugh Pritchard, Geraldine Walsh, Australian Institute of Political Science, Level 4, WEA House, 72 Bathurst Street, Sydney, NSW 2000   *tel* (02) 264 8923   *fax* (02) 267 7900.
$43.00 p.a. Q. ($55.00 p.a. overseas) Articles of high standard on politics, law, economics, social issues, etc. *Length:* 3500 words preferred. *Payment:* none.

The Australian Women's Weekly, Australian Consolidated Press Ltd, 54 Park Street, Sydney, NSW 2000   *tel* (02) 282 8000   *fax* (02) 282 8116.
$2.95. M. Fiction and features. *Length:* fiction 1000-10,000 words; features 750-2500 words plus colour or b&w photos. *Payment:* according to length and merit. *Fiction illustrations:* sketches by own artists and freelances.

(Brisbane) Courier-Mail, G. Chamberlin, Queensland Newspapers Pty Ltd, Campbell Street, Bowen Hills, Brisbane, Queensland 4006   *tel* (07) 252 6011   *fax* (07) 252 6696.
30c. D. Occasional topical special articles required. *Length:* 1000 words.

(Brisbane) Sunday Mail, Bob Gordon, GPO Box 130, Brisbane, Queensland 4001.
60c. W. Anything of general interest. *Length:* up to 1500 words. *Illustrations:* line, photos, b&w and colour. *Payment:* by arrangement. Rejected MSS returned if postage enclosed.

Cleo (1972), Lisa Wilkinson, 54 Park Street, Sydney, NSW 2000 *tel* (02) 282 8617 *fax* (02) 267 2150.
$3.50. M. Articles (relationship, emotional, self-help) up to 3000 words, short quizzes. *Payment:* articles $200 per 1000 words. *Illustrations:* colour, half-tone.

The Countryman, Russell C. Raymond, 219 St Georges Terrace, Perth, Western Australia 6000 *tel* (09) 482 3301 *telegraphic address* Westralian Perth *fax* (09) 322 7353.
50c. W. Agriculture, farming or country interest features and service columns. *Payment:* standard rates. *Illustrations:* line, half-tone.

Current Affairs Bulletin (1942), Dr Bob Howard, CAB, 72 Bathurst Street, Sydney, NSW 2000 *tel* (02) 264 5726 *fax* (02) 267 7900.
$3.00. M. ($40.00 p.a., $57.00 p.a. overseas) Authoritative well-documented articles on all national and international affairs: politics, economics, science, the arts, business and social questions. *Length:* 3000-5000 words. *Payment:* by arrangement. *Illustrations:* line, half-tone.

Dolly (1970), Assistant Editor: Suellen Topfer, 54 Park Street, Sydney, NSW 2000 *tel* (02) 282 8000 *fax* (02) 267 2150.
$2.40. M. Features on fashion, health and beauty, personalities, music, social issues and how to cope with growing up, etc. *Length:* not less than 1750 words. *Payment:* by arrangement.

Electronics Australia (incorporating **Radio, Television and Hobbies**) (1939), J. Rowe, Box 227, Waterloo, NSW 2017 *tel* (02) 693 6620 *fax* (02) 693 6613.
$4.50. M. Articles on technical television and radio, hi-fi, popular electronics, microcomputers and avionics. *Length:* up to 2000 words. *Payment:* by arrangement. *Illustrations:* line, half-tone.

Geo, Australasia's Geographical Magazine (1978), Publisher: Grant Young, 372 Eastern Valley Way, Willoughby, NSW 2068 *tel* (02) 415 9222 *fax* (02) 417 8478.
$5.95. Q. ($23.80 p.a.) Non-fiction articles on wild life and natural history. *Length:* 1500-3000 words. *Payment:* $400-$1200 by arrangement. *Illustrations:* photos, colour transparencies.

Herald of the South (1925), Editorial Board: Jennifer Lemon, Keith McDonald (Sec.), Lilian Alai, Janet Heteraka, Abbas Momtazi, GPO Box 283, Canberra, ACT 2601 *tel/fax* (09) 337 9525 (Sec.).
$20 p.a. (on subscription). Q. Baha'i magazine with particular emphasis on religious approach to unity. Features, fiction and non-fiction. *Length:* up to 3500 words. *Illustrations:* colour and b&w photos. *Payment:* by negotiation.

Labor News, Steve Harrison, Peter Kelly, F.I.A., 51-65 Bathurst Street, Sydney, NSW 2000 *tel* (02) 264-2877 *telex* 176770 *fax* (02) 261-1701.
Bi-M. Official Journal of Federated Ironworkers' Association of Australia.

(Launceston) Examiner, Michael Courtney, Box 99A, PO Launceston, Tasmania 7250 *tel* (003) 315111 *telegraphic address* Examiner, Launceston *fax* (003) 320 300.
45c. D.

(Melbourne) Age, M. Smith, David Syme & Co., Ltd, 250 Spencer Street, Melbourne, Victoria 3000 *tel* (03) 600 4211 *telex* 30331/30376/30449 *fax* (03) 670 7514; London: The London International Press Centre, 76 Shoe Lane, EC4A 3JB *tel* 071-353 5193.
50c. D. 70c. Sat. Independent liberal morning daily. Room occasionally for outside matter. An illustrated weekend magazine and literary review is published on Saturday. Accepts occasional freelance material.

(Melbourne) Australasian Post, Southdown Press, 32 Walsh Street, West Melbourne, Victoria 3003   *tel* (03) 320 7000.
$1.70. W. Opening for casual contributions of topical factual illustrated articles. All contributions must have Australian interest. General appeal. *Payment:* average $300 per 500 words plus $50 (minimum) per picture.

(Melbourne) Herald, Bruce Baskett, 44-74 Flinders Street, Melbourne, Victoria *tel* (03) 652 1111.
40c. D. Evening broadsheet; articles with or without illustrations. *Length:* up to 750 words. *Payment:* on merit. *Illustrations:* line, half-tone.

(Melbourne) Sun News Pictorial (1922), Colin Duck, 44-74 Flinders Street, Melbourne, Victoria 3000.
40c. D. Freelance articles with or without illustrations. *Payment:* on merit.

(Melbourne) The Sunday Age (1989), Steve Harris, 250 Spencer Street, Melbourne, Victoria 3000   *tel* (03) 600 4211   *fax* (03) 602 1856; London: The London International Press Centre, 76 Shoe Lane, EC4A 3JB   *tel* 071-353 5193.
70c. W. Features. *Length:* 500-2000 words. *Payment:* by arrangement; $250 for illustrations.

Modern Boating (1965), 180 Bourke Road, Alexandria, NSW 2015   *tel* (02) 693 6666   *fax* (02) 693 6613.
$4.50. M. Articles on all types of boats and boating. *Payment:* $130-$200 per 1000 words. *Illustrations:* half-tone, colour.

New Idea (1902), Mrs D. Boling, 32 Walsh Street, Melbourne, Victoria 3003   *tel* (03) 320 7000.
$1.50. W. General interest women's magazine; news stories, features, fashion, services, short stories of general interest to women of all ages. *Length:* stories, 500-4000 words: articles, 500-2000 words. *Payment:* on acceptance; minimum $150 per 1000 words.

Overland, Barrett Reid, PO Box 14146, Melbourne, Victoria 3000   *tel* (03) 850 4347   *fax* (03) 852 0527.
$6.00. Q. Literary and general. Australian material preferred. *Payment:* by arrangement. *Illustrations:* line, half-tone.

People Magazine (national weekly news-pictorial), P. Olszewski, 54 Park Street, Sydney, NSW 2000   *tel* (02) 282 8000   *fax* (02) 282 8722.
$2.10. W. Mainly people stories, but good documentary subjects needed. Photos depicting exciting happenings, candid camera pictures of events affecting Australians, glamour and show business, modern-living features, and complete series of any subject such as unusual occupations, rites, customs. *Payment:* highest Australian scale.

(Perth) Daily News (1840), Jack Harrison, 120 Roe Street, Northbridge, Perth, Western Australia 6000   *tel* (09) 427 1400   *fax* (09) 227 7351.
40c. D. (eve) Accepts special articles on subjects of outstanding interest. *Payment:* according to merit. *Illustrations:* line, half-tone.

(Perth) Sunday Times (1897), 34 Stirling Street, Perth, Western Australia 6000   *tel* (09) 326 8326.
80c. W. Topical articles to 800 words. *Payment:* on acceptance.

(Perth) The West Australian (1833), R.E. Cronin, 219 St Georges Terrace, Perth, Western Australia 6000   *tel* (09) 482 3111   *telegraphic address* Westralian, Perth   *fax* (09) 481 4615.

50c. M.-F. 60c. Sat. Articles and sketches about people and events in Australia and abroad. *Length:* 300-700 words. *Payment:* Award rates or better. *Illustrations:* line, half-tone.

Poetry Australia (1964), John Millett, South Head Press, Market Place, Berrima, NSW 2577   *tel* 048-771421.
$40 p.a. Q. Previously unpublished new poetry, and criticism. *Payment:* copy of magazine.

Quadrant, Robert Manne, 46 George Street, Fitzroy, Victoria 3065   *postal address* PO Box 1495, Collingwood, Victoria 3066   *tel* (03) 417 6855   *fax* (03) 416 2980.
$4.00. M. Articles, short stories, verse, etc. *Prose length:* 2000-5000 words. *Payment:* minimum $80 articles, $60 stories, $40 reviews, $30 poems.

Reader's Digest (Australian and New Zealand editions), Hugh Vaughan-Williams, 26-32 Waterloo Street, Surry Hills, NSW 2010   *tel* (02) 690 6111   *telegraphic address* Readigest, Sydney   *fax* (02) 699 8165.
$3.25. M. Articles on Australia and New Zealand subjects by commission only. No unsolicited manuscripts accepted. *Length:* 2500-3000 words. *Payment:* up to $4000 per article; brief filler paragraphs, $50-$200. *Illustrations:* half-tone, colour.

The Sun, T. Sweetman, 367 Brunswick Street, Fortitude Valley, Brisbane, Queensland 4006   *tel* (07) 253 3333.
50c. D.

Sunday Sun, Bill Murray, 367 Brunswick Street, Fortitude Valley, Brisbane, Queensland 4006   *tel* (07) 253 3333.
90c. W.

The Sun-Herald, David Hickie, GPO Box 506, Sydney, NSW 2001; London: John Fairfax (UK) Ltd, 12 Norwich Street, EC4A 1BH   *tel* 071-353 9321.
70c. W. Topical articles to 1000 words; sections on politics, social issues, show business, finance and fashion. *Payment:* by arrangement.

(Sydney) Bulletin (1880), James Hall, 54 Park Street, Sydney, NSW 2000   *tel* (02) 282 8200; London: Australian Consolidated Press, 112 Westbourne Park Road, W2   *tel* 071-221 3913; New York: Australian Consolidated Press, Lesa Tinker, 169 First Avenue, NY 10003   *tel* 212-979-0390.
$2.75. W. Concerned mainly with reporting Australia to Australians, or the world from an Australian aspect. Includes Australian edition of *Newsweek*. *Payment:* by arrangement.

(Sydney) Daily Mirror (1941), 2 Holt Street, Sydney, NSW 2010   *tel* (02) 288 3000.
40c. D. Accept modernly written feature articles and series of Australian or world interest. *Length:* 1000-2000 words. *Payment:* according to merit/length.

(Sydney) Daily Telegraph, D. Banks, News Limited, 2 Holt Street, Surry Hills, NSW 2010   *tel* (02) 288 3000   *fax* (02) 288 2300.
50c. D.

The Sydney Morning Herald (1831), Editor-in-Chief: J.H. Alexander, PO Box 506, Sydney, NSW 2001; London: 12 Norwich Street, EC4A 1BH   *tel* 071-353 9321.
50c. D. Saturday edition has pages of literary criticism and also magazine articles, plus glossy colour magazine. Topical articles 600-4000 words. *Payment:* varies, but minimum $100 per 1000 words. *Illustrations:* all types.

TraveLeisure (1987), PO Box 6495, Gold Coast Mail Centre, Queensland 4217   *tel* (075) 931 616   *fax* (075) 932 177.

$3.95. Q. Strongly travel oriented articles, *not* travelogues, plus entertainment, leisure and life style topics. *Study magazine* before submitting one-page query. All queries and submissions must be accompanied by an sae or envelope/ IRC. *Illustrations:* colour transparencies preferred. *Payment:* $300 per 1000 words; from $50 ($300 for a cover shot relating to an article).

Woman's Day, Nene King, 54-58 Park Street, Sydney, NSW 2000 *tel* (02) 282 8000 *fax* (02) 267 2150.
$1.50. W. National women's magazine; news, show business, fiction, fashion, general articles, cookery, home economy.

CANADA

Newspapers are listed under the towns in which they are published.

The Atlantic Advocate, Marilee Little, PO Box 3370, Fredericton, New Brunswick E3B 5A2 *tel* 506-452-6671.
$2.00. M. Non-fiction and short stories; focus must be on Atlantic Provinces. *Length:* up to 1500 words. *Payment:* up to 10 cents per word. *Illustrations:* line, half-tone.

Aviation & Aerospace (1928), Maclean-Hunter Ltd, 777 Bay Street, Toronto, Ontario M5W 1A7 *tel* 416-596-5789 *fax* 416-596-5810; London: EDP Press Associates, Hemingford Grey, Huntingdon, Cambs. PE18 9DF *tel* (0480) 63073.
$35.00 p.a. (UK). M. Stories with a Canadian angle, on civil or military aviation. *Payment:* $250-$700. *Illustrations:* photos; from $25.

The Beaver: Exploring Canada's History, Christopher Dafoe, Hudson's Bay Co., 450 Portage Avenue, Winnipeg, Manitoba R3C 0E7.
$19.00 p.a., Bi-M. ($25.00 elsewhere) Articles, historical and modern in the sphere of Hudson's Bay Company's activities and Canadian history. *Length:* 1500-5000 words, with illustrations. *Payment:* on acceptance, about 10 cents a word. *Illustrations:* b&w and colour photos or drawings.

Books in Canada (1971), Paul Stuewe, 366 Adelaide Street East, Suite 432, Toronto, Ontario M5A 3X9 *tel* 416-363-5426.
$2.95. 9 p.a. Commissioned reviews, informed criticism and articles on Canadian and international literary scene. *Query first* – do not send unsolicited material. *Payment:* by arrangement.

Broadcaster (1942), Lynda Ashley, 7 Labatt Avenue, Toronto, Ontario M5A 3P2 *tel* 416-363-6111 *fax* 416-861-9564.
$3.00. M. ($25.00 p.a.) Articles pertaining to broadcasting. *Length:* 500-1500 words. *Payment:* minimum $150.

Canadian Author and Bookman, 121 Avenue Road, Suite 104, Toronto, Ontario M5R 2G3.
$15.00 p.a. Q. ($20.00 p.a. overseas) Published by Canadian Authors Association. Interested in an international view on writing techniques, profiles, interviews, freelance opportunities for Canadian writers. *Query only.* *Payment:* $30 per printed page.

The Canadian Forum, Duncan Cameron, 251 Laurier Avenue W, Ottawa, Ontario *tel* 613-230-3078 *fax* 613-233-1458.
$2.00. 10 p.a. ($18.00 p.a.) Articles on public affairs and the arts. *Length:* up to 2500 words. *Payment:* $100 per article. *Illustrations:* line and photos.

Canadian Interiors, Lorraine Tierney, The Maclean Hunter Building, 777 Bay Street, Toronto, Ontario M5W 1A7 *tel* 416-596-5976 *telegraphic address* Macpub *fax* 416-593-3189.

$40.00 p.a. 8 issues p.a. ($89.00 elsewhere). Articles on all aspects of interior design; also technical and business articles. *Payment:* $100-$400 per article. *Illustrations:* half-tone, colour.

Canadian Literature (1959), W.H. New, 2029 West Mall, University of British Columbia, Vancouver, BC V6T 1Z2 *tel* 604-882-2780.
$10.00. Q. Articles on Canadian writers and writing in English and French. *Length:* up to 5000 words. *Payment:* $5 per printed page.

Chatelaine, 777 Bay Street, Toronto, Ontario M5W 1A7 *tel* 416-596-5425.
$2.00. M. Articles with woman's slant used; Canadian angle preferred. *Payment:* on acceptance; from $1000.

The Dalhousie Review, Dr Alan Andrews, Dalhousie University Press Ltd, Sir James Dunn Building, Suite 314, Halifax, NS B3H 3J5 *tel* 902-494-2541.
$5.50 (plus postage). Q. ($17.00 p.a., $25.00 p.a. outside Canada; or $40.00 for 3 years; $62.00 for 3 years outside Canada) Articles on literary, political, historical, educational and social topics; fiction; verse; book reviews. *Length:* prose, normally not more than 5000 words; verse, preferably less than 40 words. *Payment:* $1 per printed page for fiction; $3 for 1st poem, $2 for each subsequent poem (per issue). Contributors receive two copies of issue and 15 offprints of their work. Usually not more than two stories and about 10 or 12 poems in any one issue.

Equinox (1982), Bart Robinson, 7 Queen Victoria Road, Camden East, Ontario K0K 3N0 *tel* 613-378-6661.
$3.95. Bi-M. ($19.98 p.a. Canada; $24.98 p.a. USA; $28.98 elsewhere). Magazine of discovery in science and geography, especially ecology and earth sciences. Accepts articles on hard science topics (*length:* 100-500 words); welcomes queries (2-3-page outline) for specific environmental assignments. *Illustrations:* colour transparencies (preferably Kodachrome 35mm). *Payment:* by arrangement.

The Fiddlehead (1945), Don Mackay, Campus House, University of New Brunswick, PO Box 4400, Fredericton, NB E3B 5A3 *tel* 506-453-3501.
$6.00. Q. Reviews, poetry, short stories. *Payment:* approx. $10 per printed page. *Illustrations:* line, photos.

The Hamilton Spectator (1846), Publisher, Gordon Bullock, 44 Frid Street, Hamilton, Ontario L8N 3G3 *tel* 416-526-3333.
35 cents. M.-F. $1.00 Sat. Articles of general interest, political analysis and background; interviews, stories of Canadians abroad. *Length:* 800 words maximum. *Payment:* rate varies.

Journal of Canadian Studies, Michael Peterman, Michèle Lacombe, Trent University, Peterborough, Ontario K9J 7B8.
$25.00 p.a. Q. ($45.00 p.a. institutions) Major academic review of Canadian studies. Articles of general as well as scholarly interest on history, politics, literature, society, arts. *Length:* 2000-10,000 words.

Maclean's Magazine, Kevin Doyle, Maclean Hunter Building, 777 Bay Street, 7th Floor, Toronto, Ontario M5W 1A7 *tel* 416-596-5386 *telex* 065-24196 *fax* 416-596-7730. London: Suite 701, 25 St James's Street, SW1.
$2.00. W. News magazine articles of interest to Canadian readers, 500-3000 words. *Payment:* by arrangement. *Illustrations:* on assignment.

The Malahat Review (1967), Constance Rooke, University of Victoria, PO Box 3045, Victoria, BC V8W 3P4 *tel* 604-721-8524.
$15.00 p.a. Q. ($20.00 p.a. overseas) Short stories, poetry, short plays, reviews, some graphics and critical essays. *Payment:* prose: $40 per 1000 words; poetry: $20 per page. *Illustrations:* half-tone.

Performing Arts in Canada Magazine (1961), Patricia Michael, 263 Adelaide Street West, 5th Floor, Toronto, Ontario M5H IY2   *tel* 416-971-9516.
$8.00 p.a. Q. ($14.00 p.a. elsewhere) Feature articles on Canadian theatre, music, dance and film artists and organisations; technical articles on scenery, lighting, make-up, costumes, etc. *Length:* 1000-2000 words. *Payment:* $150-$250, one month after publication. *Illustrations:* b&w photos, colour slides.

Quebec Chronicle Telegraph (1764), Karen Macdonald, Quebec Chronicle-Telegraph Inc., 22 rue Ste-Anne, Quebec City, Quebec G1R 3X3   *tel* 418-692-0056.
40 cents. W. Covers local events within English community in Quebec City. Some feature articles.

Quill & Quire (1935), Ted Mumford, 70 The Esplanade, 4th Floor, Toronto, Ontario M5E 1R2   *tel* 416-360-0044.
$50.00 p.a. (in the UK). 12 p.a. Articles of interest about the Canadian book trade. *Payment:* from $100. *Illustrations:* line, half-tone. Subscription includes *Canadian Publishers Directory*, 2 p.a.

Reader's Digest, Alexander Farrell, 215 Redfern Avenue, Montreal, Quebec H3Z 2V9   *tel* 514-934-0751.
$2.49. M. Original articles on all subjects of broad general appeal, thoroughly researched and professionally written. Outline or query *only*. *Length:* 3000 words approx. *Payment:* from $2500. Also previously published material. *Illustrations:* line, half-tone, colour.

(Toronto) The Globe and Mail (1844), Publisher: A. Roy Megarry, Editor-in-Chief: William Thorsell, 444 Front Street West, Toronto, Ontario M5V 2S9. London: 164-167 Temple Chambers (2nd Floor), Temple Avenue, EC4Y 0EA   *tel* 071-353 5795.
50c. D.

Toronto Life (1967), Marq de Villiers, 59 Front Street East, Toronto, Ontario M5E 1B3   *tel* 416-364-3333.
$2.50. M. Articles, profiles on Toronto and Torontonians. *Illustrations:* line, half-tone, colour.

Toronto Star (1892), One Yonge Street, Toronto, Ontario M5E 1E6   *tel* 416-367-2000; London: Level 4A, PO Box 495, Virginia Street, E1 9XY   *tel* 071-833 0791.
30 cents. D. ($1.00 Sat, 75 cents Sun).

(Vancouver) Province (1898), Ian Haysom, Editor-in-Chief, 2250 Granville Street, Vancouver, BC V6H 3G2   *tel* 604-732-2484   *fax* 604-732-2720.
50 cents. M.-F. 75 cents Sunday.

Vancouver Sun, Editor-in-Chief: Nicholas Hills, 2250 Granville Street, Vancouver, BC V6H 3G2   *tel* 604-732-2111   *fax* 604-732-2323. London: Southam News, 8 Bouverie Street, 4th Floor, EC4Y 8AX   *tel* 071-583 7322.
50 cents. D. Fri, Sat. 75 cents (not Sun). Rates depending on arrangements. Very little outside contribution.

Wascana Review (1966), Joan Givner, c/o English Department, University of Regina, Regina, Sask. S4S 0A2   *tel* 306-585-4316.
$7.00 p.a. Bi-annual. ($8.00 p.a. outside Canada) Criticism, short stories, poetry, reviews. Manuscripts from freelance writers welcome. *Length:* prose, not more than 6000 words; verse, up to 100 lines. *Payment:* $3 per page for prose; $10 per printed page for verse; $3 per page for reviews. Contributors also receive two free copies of the issue.

Winnipeg Free Press (1872), John Dafoe, 300 Carlton Street, Winnipeg, Manitoba R3C 3C1   *tel* 204-943-9331.
   25 cents D., $1.25 Sat, 35 cents Sun. Some freelance articles. *Payment:* $100.

THE REPUBLIC OF IRELAND AND NORTHERN IRELAND

Africa: St Patrick's Missions, Rev. Brendan Cooney, St Patrick's, Kiltegan, Co. Wicklow   *tel* (0508) 73233.
   25p. 9 p.a. (£4.00 p.a.) Articles of missionary or topical religious interest. *Length:* up to 800 words. *Illustrations:* line, half-tone, colour

Belfast Telegraph (1870), 124-144 Royal Avenue, Belfast BT1 1EB   *tel* (0232) 321242   *telex* 74269   *fax* (0232) 242287 (editorial only).
   26p. D. Any material relating to Northern Ireland. *Payment:* by negotiation.

Books Ireland (1976), Jeremy Addis, 11 Newgrove Avenue, Dublin 4   *tel/fax* (01) 2692185.
   90p. £10.00 p.a. (M. except Jan, Jul, Aug) Reviews of Irish interest and Irish-author books, articles of interest to librarians, booksellers and readers. *Length:* 800-1400 words. *Payment:* £30 per 1000 words.

Church of Ireland Gazette (1885, New Series 1963), Rev. Canon C.W.M. Cooper, 36 Bachelor's Walk, Lisburn, Co. Antrim BT28 1XN   *tel* (0846) 675743.
   20p. W. Church news, articles of religious and general interest. *Length:* 600-1000 words. *Payment:* according to length and interest.

Commercial Transport (1970), Bridget Gavin, Rathcoole, Co. Dublin   *tel* (01) 589211.
   £1.00. M. Articles relating to transport on land, sea and air. *Payment:* £50-£60 per 1000 words. *Illustrations:* line, half-tone, colour.

Cyphers (1975), Leland Bardwell, Pearse Hutchinson, Eiléan Ní Chuilleanáin, Macdara Woods, 3 Selskar Terrace, Dublin 6   *tel* (01) 978866.
   £1.50. 2 or 3 p.a. Poems, fiction, articles on literary subjects, translations. *Payment:* £7 per page (verse), £5 per page (prose).

East Cork News, Peter Doyle, 25 Michael Street, Waterford   *tel* (051) 74951.
   40p. W. News articles. *Payment:* by arrangement. *Illustrations:* line, half-tone (web offset).

Evening Herald, 90 Middle Abbey Street, Dublin 1   *tel* (01) 731666.
   35p. D. Articles. *Payment:* by arrangement. *Illustrations:* line, half-tone.

Evening Press (1954), Sean Ward, Burgh Quay, Dublin 2   *tel* (01) 713333   *telex* 93752   *fax* (01) 713097.
   40p. D. News items, articles. *Payment:* NUJ rates.

Fortnight. An Independent Review of Politics and the Arts (1970), Robin Wilson, 7 Lower Crescent, Belfast BT7 1NR   *tel* (0232) 232353   *fax* (0232) 232650.
   £1.40. M. Current affairs analysis, reportage, opinion pieces, cultural criticism, book reviews, poems. *Illustrations:* line, half-tone, cartoons.

The Furrow (1950), Rev. Ronan Drury, St Patrick's College, Maynooth, Co. Kildare   *tel* (01) 6286215.
   £1.25. M. Religious, pastoral, theological, social articles. *Length:* 3500 words. *Payment:* average £10 per page (450 words). *Illustrations:* line or half-tone.

The Honest Ulsterman (1968), Robert Johnstone, Ruth Hooley, 102 Elm Park Mansions, Park Walk, London SW10 0AP.

£2.00. 3 p.a. Poetry, short stories, reviews, critical articles, poetry pamphlets. *Payment:* by arrangement.

Hotel and Catering Review, Frank Corr, Jemma Publications Ltd, 22 Brookfield Avenue, Blackrock, Co. Dublin   *tel* (01) 886946   *fax* (01) 881098.
£20.00 p.a. M. Short news and trade news pieces. *Length:* approx. 200 words. Features. *Payment:* £80 per 1000 words. *Illustrations:* half-tone and cartoons.

Image (1974), Jane McDonnell, 22 Crofton Road, Dun Laoghaire, Co. Dublin *tel* (01) 808415   *fax* (01) 808309.
£1.20. M. Short stories of a high literary standard and of interest to women. *Length:* up to 3000 words. Interviews with actors, writers, etc. Human interest stories. *Payment:* by arrangement.

In Dublin (1976), Tony Clayton-Lea, 129 Lower Baggot Street, Dublin 2   *tel* (01) 785411   *fax* (01) 785536.
95p. F. Articles, reviews: current affairs, arts, entertainment. *Length:* 200-5000 words. *Payment:* £80 per 1000 words. *Illustrations:* line, half-tone, cartoons.

Ireland of the Welcomes, Irish Tourist Board, Baggot Street Bridge, Dublin 2   *tel* (01) 765871   *fax* (01) 764765.
£1.50. Bi-M. Irish items with cultural, sporting or topographical background designed to arouse interest in Irish holidays. *Length:* 1200-1800 words. *Payment:* by arrangement. *Illustrations:* scenic and topical. Preliminary letter preferred; mostly commissioned.

Ireland's Eye (1979), Lynn Industrial Estate, Mullingar, Co. Westmeath   *tel* (044) 48868.
50p. M. Articles, features, short stories with an Irish flavour; cartoons. *Length:* 1200-2000 words. *Payment:* £10-£15; £4 for cartoons.

Ireland's Own (1902), Austin Channing, North Main Street, Wexford   *tel* (053) 22155   *fax* (053) 23801.
35p. W. Short stories (1500-2000 words); romances in particular, but with an Irish background; articles of interest to Irish readers at home and abroad (1000-3000 words); general and literary articles (1000-2500 words). Special issues for Christmas and St Patrick's Day. Jokes, funny stories, riddles, always welcome. Suggestions for new features considered. *Payment:* varies according to quality, originality and length. Serials of novel length, preliminary letter advisable, enclosing synopsis and sae, payment by arrangement. *Illustrations:* no restriction (web offset).

Irish Business (1975), Andrew Whittaker, 128 Lower Baggot Street, Dublin 2   *tel* (01) 619222/619236/619238   *fax* (01) 612417.
£1.20. M. (£13.00 p.a.) Topical articles on finance, banking, economics. *Length:* 900-1500 words. *Payment:* by arrangement. *Illustrations:* line, half-tone.

Irish Independent, Vincent Doyle, Independent House, 90 Middle Abbey Street, Dublin 1   *tel* (01) 731666   *fax* (01) 720304/731787.
65p. D. Special articles on topical or general subjects. *Length:* 700-1000 words. *Payment:* editor's estimate of value.

Irish Journal of Medical Science (1st series 1832, 6th series January 1926, Volume 160, 1991), Royal Academy of Medicine, 6 Kildare Street, Dublin 2   *tel* (01) 767650   *fax* (01) 611684.
£5.00. M. (GB and Ireland £40.00 post free; overseas £60.00 post free) Official Organ of the Royal Academy of Medicine in Ireland. Original contributions in medicine, surgery, midwifery, public health, etc.; reviews of professional books, reports of medical societies, etc. *Illustrations:* line, half-tone, colour.

Irish Medical Times, Dr John O'Connell, 15 Harcourt Street, Dublin 2 *tel* (01) 757461.
£1.00. W. Medical articles, also humorous articles with medical slant. *Length:* 850-1000 words. *Payment:* £60 per 1000 words. *Illustrations:* line, half-tone.

The Irish News and Belfast Morning News (1855), Nick Garbutt, 113-117 Donegall Street, Belfast BT1 2GE *tel* (0232) 322226 *fax* (0232) 231282.
25p. D. Articles of historical and topical interest. *Payment:* by arrangement.

Irish Press, Hugh Lambert, Burgh Quay, Dublin 2 *tel* (01) 713333.
50p. D. Topical articles about 1000 words. *Payment:* by arrangement. *Illustrations:* topical photos.

Irish Times, Conor Brady, 11-15 D'Olier Street, Dublin 2 *tel* (01) 6792022 *telex* 93639 *fax* (01) 6793910.
70p. D. Mainly staff-written. Specialist contributions (800 to max. 2000 words) by commission on basis of ideas submitted. *Payment:* at editor's valuation. *Illustrations:* photos and line drawings.

IT Magazine, Noelle Campbell-Sharp, The Village Centre, Ballybrack Village, Co. Dublin *tel* 826411.
£1.00. M. (£14.50 p.a.) Fashion and social magazine: beauty, interiors, health, books, wine and cookery, art, theatre, cinema, television, music, motoring, knitting and special monthly interviews. *Length:* 700-1500 words. *Payment:* by arrangement. *Illustrations:* half-tone.

Krino (1986), Gerald Dawe, Avril Forrest, Aodan MacPoilin, Glenrevagh, Corrandulla, Co. Galway.
£5.00. 2 p.a. Poetry; fiction; critical prose mostly on commissioned basis. *Payment:* none, but complimentary copies of the magazine. *Illustrations:* line, half-tone.

The Nationalist and Munster Advertiser (1890), Brendan Long, Queen Street, Clonmel, Co. Tipperary *tel* (052) 22211.
50p. W. Requirements by arrangement. *Payment:* £22 per 1000 words. *Illustrations:* artwork.

Poetry Ireland (1981), Máire Mhac an tSaoi, 44 Upper Mount Street, Dublin 2.
£3.50. Q. Poetry, short lyric and sections from long poems, articles and reviews. *Payment:* by arrangement.

Portadown Times & Craigavon News (1859), David Armstrong, 14 Church Street, Portadown BT62 1HY *tel* (0762) 336111.
44p. W. Articles. *Payment:* NUJ rates.

Reality (1936), Rev. K.H. Donlon, Redemptorist Publications, Orwell Road, Rathgar, Dublin 6 *tel* (01) 961488/961688.
70p. M. Illustrated magazine for Christian living. Articles on all aspects of modern life, including family, youth, religion, leisure. Illustrated articles, b&w photos only. Short stories. *Length:* 1000-1500 words. *Payment:* by arrangement; average £20 per 1000 words.

The Songwriter (1967), James D. Liddane, International Songwriters Association Ltd, Limerick City *tel* (061) 28837.
Available to members only as part of membership fee. 4 p.a. Articles on song writing and interviews with music publishers and recording company executives. *Length:* 400-5000 words. *Payment:* from £50 per page and by arrangement. *Illustrations:* photos.

Studies, An Irish quarterly review (1912), Rev. Noel Barber, SJ, 35 Lower Leeson Street, Dublin 2 *tel* (01) 766785 *fax* (01) 762984.

£3.00. Q. General review of social comment, literature, history, the arts. Articles written by specialists for the general reader. Critical book reviews. *Preliminary letter*. *Length:* 3500 words.

The Sunday Business Post (1989), Damien Kiberd, Merchants House, 27-30 Merchants Quay, Dublin 8   *tel* (01) 6799777   *fax* (01) 6796496/6796498.
85p. W. Features on financial, economic and political topics. Also life style, media and science articles. *Illustrations:* colour and b&w photos, graphics, cartoons. *Payment:* by negotiation.

Sunday Independent, Aengus Fanning, Independent House, 90 Middle Abbey Street, Dublin 1   *tel* (01) 731333   *fax* (01) 720304/731787.
70p. W. Special articles. *Length:* according to subject. *Payment:* at editor's valuation; good. *Illustrations:* topical or general interest.

Sunday Life (1988), Edmund Curran, 124 Royal Avenue, Belfast BT9 1EB   *tel* (0232) 331133   *telex* Belfast 74269   *fax* (0232) 248968.
35p. W. Items of interest to Northern Ireland Sunday tabloid readers. *Payment:* by arrangement. *Illustrations:* colour and b&w.

Sunday News (1965), Chris Harbinson, 51-67 Donegall Street, Belfast BT1 2GB   *tel* (0232) 244441.
30p. W. General topical articles of 500 words. *Payment:* by arrangement. *Illustrations:* line, half-tone.

The Sunday Press, Michael Keane, Burgh Quay, Dublin 2   *tel* (01) 713333   *telegraphic address* Sceala, Dublin   *telex* 93752   *fax* (01) 713097.
60p. W. Articles of general interest. *Length:* 1000 words. *Illustrations:* line, half-tone.

Technology Ireland (1969), Mary Mulvihill and Tom Kennedy, Eolas (Irish Science and Technology Agency), Glasnevin, Dublin 9   *tel* (01) 370101   *fax* (01) 379620.
£17.50 p.a. M. Articles, features and news on current science and technology. *Length:* 1500-2000 words. *Illustrations:* line, half-tone, colour. *Payment:* varies; none.

Theatre Ireland Magazine (1982), Lynda Henderson, 29 Main Street, Castlerock, Co. Derry BT51 4RA   *tel* (0265) 848130 (24 hours).
£2.00. Q. Irish and international: contemporary theatre practices, documentary and critical forum, book reviews. *Length:* 1000-3000 words. *Payment:* by arrangement. *Illustrations:* colour and b&w.

Ulster News Letter (1737), Geoff Martin, 51-67 Donegall Street, Belfast BT1 2GB   *tel* (0232) 244441.
28p. D. Unionist.

Waterford News & Star, Peter Doyle, 25 Michael Street, Waterford   *tel* (051) 74951.
60p. W. News articles. *Payment:* by arrangement. *Illustrations:* line and half-tone (web-offset).

Woman's Way (1963), Celine Naughton, Smurfit Publications Ltd, 126 Lower Baggot Street, Dublin 2   *tel* (01) 608264   *fax* (01) 619486.
60p. W. Short stories, personality interviews, general features. *Length:* 1500-2000 words. *Payment:* £50. *Illustrations:* half-tone, line and colour.

The Word (1936), Rev. Brother Paul Hurley, svd, (The Word Press, Hadzor, Droitwich), Divine Word Missionaries, Maynooth, Co. Kildare   *tel* (01) 6286391.

45p. M. Catholic illustrated magazine for the family. Illustrated articles of general interest up to 1000 words and good picture features. *Payment:* by arrangement. *Illustrations:* photos and large colour transparencies.

NEW ZEALAND

Newspapers are listed under the towns in which they are published.

(Auckland) New Zealand Herald (1863), P.J. Scherer, PO Box 32, Auckland *tel* (09) 795-050 *fax* (09) 366-1568.
50c. D. Topical and informative articles 800-1100 words. *Payment:* minimum $50-$150. *Illustrations:* half-tone blocks (65 screen).

Auckland Star (1870), Sue McPherson, Auckland Star Ltd, PO Box 1409, Auckland *tel* (09) 797-626.
50c. Monday to Friday.

(Christchurch) The Press, D.W.C. Wilson, Private Bag, Christchurch *tel* (03) 790-940 *fax* (03) 648-492.
40c. D. Articles of general interest not more than 1000 words. *Payment:* by arrangement. Extra for photos and line drawings.

Christchurch Star (1868), M.A. Fletcher, Tuam Street, Christchurch *tel* (03) 797-100 *fax* (03) 660-180.
45c. D. Topical articles.

(Dunedin) Otago Daily Times (1861), G.T. Adams, PO Box 181, Dunedin *tel* (03) 477-4760 *fax* (03) 477-8616.
45c. D. Any articles of general interest up to 1000 words, but preference is given to New Zealand writers. Topical illustrations and personalities. *Payment:* current New Zealand rates.

The Gisborne Herald (1874), Iain Gillies, PO Box 1143, 64 Gladstone Road, Gisborne *tel* (06) 867-2099 *telegraphic address* Herald, Gisborne.
12c. D. Topical features of local interest. *Length:* 1000-1500 words. *Payment:* by arrangement. *Illustrations:* bromides.

Hawke's Bay Herald Tribune (result of merger between Hawke's Bay Herald (1857), Hastings Standard (1896) and Hawke's Bay Tribune (1910)), J.E. Morgan, PO Box 180, Karamu Road, Hastings *tel* (06) 878-5155 *fax* (06) 878-5668.
45c. D. Limited requirements. *Payment:* $30+ for articles, $10+ for photos. *Illustrations:* web offset.

(Invercargill) The Southland Times (1862), C.A. Lind, PO Box 805, Invercargill *tel* (03) 218-1909 *telegraphic address* Times, Invercargill *fax* (03) 214-9905.
40c. D. Articles of up to 1000 words on topics of Southland interest. *Payment:* by arrangement. *Illustrations:* line, half-tone, colour.

Islands, Robin Dudding, 4 Sealy Road, Torbay, Auckland 10 *tel* (09) 403-9007.
$11. Q. ($33 p.a.; overseas: $16.50 single issue, $39.60 p.a.) Short stories, verse, criticism, reviews. No limits to *length.* Most critical work commissioned or prior letter preferred. *Payment:* about $1200 divided among contributors to a single issue. *Illustrations:* usually commissioned.

Kiwi Rider Magazine, Box 299, Kumeu, Auckland *tel* (09) 412-7658 *fax* (09) 412-7657.
$2.50. F. Reports, interviews, road tests about motor cycles. *Payment:* from $25. *Illustrations:* photos, technical drawings.

Landfall (1947), Editorial Board: Mark Williams, Michele Leggatt, Anna Smith, Iain Sharp, Judith Baker, The Caxton Press, PO Box 25-088, Christchurch *tel* (03) 668-516 *fax* (03) 657-840.
$41.50 p.a. Q. ($44.00 p.a. overseas) Literary and general material by NZ writers considered of any length. Illustrates the work of NZ painters, sculptors, architects, photographers. *Payment:* by arrangement.

Management, Profile Publishing, Box 5544, Auckland *tel* (09) 784-475 *fax* (09) 780-244.
$5.95. M. Articles on the practice of management skills and techniques, individual and company profiles, coverage of trends and topics of interest to the manager. A New Zealand/Australian angle or application preferred. *Length:* 2000 words. *Payment:* by arrangement; minimum 23c. per word. *Illustrations:* photos, line drawings.

(Napier) The Daily Telegraph (1871), K.R. Hawker, PO Box 343, Napier *tel* (06) 835-4488 *fax* (06) 835-1129.
50c. D. Limited market for features. *Payment:* $20 upwards per 1000 words; $10 a picture. *Illustrations:* line, half-tone, colour.

The Nelson Evening Mail, D.J. Mitchell, PO Box 244, 15 Bridge Street, Nelson *tel* (03) 548-7079 *fax* (03) 546-2802.
40c. D. Features, articles on New Zealand subjects. *Length:* 500-1000 words. *Payment:* up to $60 per 1000 words. *Illustrations:* half-tone, colour.

(New Plymouth) The Daily News (1857), D. Garcia, PO Box 444, New Plymouth *tel* (067) 80-559 *fax* (067) 84-653.
50c. D. Articles preferably with a Taranaki connection. *Payment:* by negotiation. *Illustrations:* half-tone.

New Truth and TV Extra, News Media Auckland Ltd, Hedley Mortlock, Glenside Crescent, Auckland, PO Box 1074 *tel* 794-780 *fax* 392-279.
$1.00. W. Bold investigative reporting, exposés. *Length:* 500-1000 words, preferably accompanied by photos. *Payment:* about $150 per 500 words, extra for photos.

New Zealand Farmer, Hugh Stringleman, NZ Rural Press Ltd, PO Box 4233, 540 Great South Road, Greenlane, Auckland 5 *tel* (09) 591-124 *fax* (09) 599-589.
F. Authoritative, simply written articles on new developments in livestock husbandry, grassland farming, cropping, farm machinery, marketing. *Length:* 500 words. *Payment:* $150 per 1000 words.

The New Zealand Listener, TV & Radio Times (1939), Terry Snow, PO Box 7, Auckland *tel* (09) 793-944 *fax* (09) 793-950.
$1.80. W. Topical features of New Zealand and international interest: also features related to television and radio programmes. *Length:* up to 2000 words. *Illustrations:* colour and b&w. *Payment:* by arrangement.

New Zealand Woman's Weekly (1932), Jenny Lynch, NZ Magazines Ltd (Wilson & Horton), Private Bag, Dominion Road, Auckland 3 *tel* (09) 688-177 *fax* (09) 609-128.
$2.00. W. Pictorial features. Illustrated articles of general, family, celebrity interest, particularly with a New Zealand slant. *Length:* articles 750-1750 words. *Payment:* by arrangement. *Illustrations:* b&w, colour.

NZ Engineering (1946), L.W. McEldowney, ʙᴀ, Engineering Publications Co. Ltd, PO Box 12241, Wellington *tel* (04) 739-444 *fax* (04) 732-324.
$4.50. M. Articles of interest to New Zealand engineers, not necessarily technical. *Preliminary letter* essential. *Payment:* by arrangement.

Sea Spray (1945), Shane Kelly, Private Bag 9, Parnell, Auckland   *tel* (09) 398-292   *fax* (09) 396-361.
$4.20. M. Features and photos, of New Zealand interest, on power or sail pleasure boating; also technical and how-to articles. *Payment:* $100 per 1000 words. *Illustrations:* line, half-tone, colour.

Sunday Star (1986), Jenny Wheeler, Auckland Star Ltd, PO Box 1409, Auckland   *tel* (09) 797-626.
$1.20. Sun.

The Timaru Herald, B.R. Appleby, PO Box 46, Bank Street, Timaru   *tel* (03) 68-44129   *fax* (03) 68-81042.
50c. D. Topical articles. *Payment:* by arrangement. *Illustrations:* screened bromides.

(Wellington) The Evening Post (1865), P.R. Cavanagh, PO Box 3740, 40 Boulcott Street, Wellington   *tel* (04) 740-444   *fax* (04) 740-237.
10c. D. General topical articles, 600 words. *Payment:* NZ current rates or by arrangement. News illustrations.

SOUTH AFRICA

Newspapers are listed under the towns in which they are published.

Argus South African Newspapers
The Argus, Cape Town, 60c. D.; **Weekend Argus** (Sat), R1.20; **The Star,** Johannesburg, 60c. D.; **The Sunday Star,** Johannesburg, R1.80; **The Daily News,** Durban, 60c. D.; **Sunday Tribune,** Durban, R1.80; **Pretoria News,** 60c, D; **The Diamond Fields Advertiser,** Kimberley, 50c. D. Accepts articles of general and South African interest. *Payment:* in accordance with an editor's assessment. Contributions should be addressed to the Foreign Editor, Argus South African Newspapers Ltd, 32-33 Hatton Garden, London EC1N 8DL   *tel* 071-831 0882   *fax* 071-831 2339, and not direct.

Bona, Republican Press (Pty) Ltd, PO Box 32083, Mobeni 4060, Natal   *tel* (031) 422041   *telegraphic address* Keur Durban; UK: Craven House, 121 Kingsway, London WC2B 6PA   *tel* 071-831 2965.
R1.50. M. Articles on fashion, cookery, sport, music of interest to black people. *Length:* up to 3000 words. *Payment:* by arrangement. *Illustrations:* line, half-tone, colour.

(Cape Town) Cape Times (1876), J.C. Viviers, Newspaper House, St George's Street, Cape Town   *tel* (021) 488-4911   *postal address* PO Box 11, Cape Town 8000; London Office: 1st Floor, 32-33 Hatton Garden, EC1N 8DL   *tel* 071-405 3742.
50c. D. Contributions must be suitable for daily newspaper and must not exceed 800 words. *Illustrations:* photos of outstanding South African interest.

Car (1957), David Trebett, PO Box 180, Howard Place 7450   *tel* 531-1391   *telegraphic address* Confrere   *telex* 526 933   *fax* 531-3333.
R3.20 + GST. M. New car announcements with pictures and full colour features of motoring interest. *Payment:* by arrangement. *Illustrations:* half-tone, colour.

(Durban) Natal Mercury (1852), J.M. Patten, Natal Newspapers (Pty) Ltd, 18 Osborne Street, Greyville 4001   *tel* 3082300   *fax* 3082333.
70c. D. (except Sun) Serious background news and inside details of world events. *Length:* 700-900 words. *Illustrations:* photos of general interest.

Fair Lady, Liz Butler, National Magazines, PO Box 1802, Cape Town 8000   *tel* (021) 254-878   *telegraphic address* Ladyfair; London: *tel* 071-823 5308.

R2.80. F. Fashion, beauty, articles and stories for women including showbiz, travel, humour. *Length:* articles up to 2000 words, short stories approx. 3000 words; short novels and serialisation of book material. *Payment:* on quality rather than length – by arrangement.

Farmer's Weekly (1911), M. Fisher, PO Box 32083, Mobeni 4060, Natal *tel* (031) 422041; UK: Craven House, 121 Kingsway, London WC2B 6PA *tel* 071-831 2965.
R1.85. W. Articles, generally illustrated, up to 1000 words in length dealing with all aspects of practical farming and research with particular reference to conditions in Southern Africa. *Payment:* according to merit. *Illustrations:* continuous-tone, full colour and line. Includes women's section which accepts articles suitably illustrated, on subjects of interest to women. *Payment:* according to merit.

Femina Magazine, Jane Raphaely, Associated Magazines, Box 3647, Cape Town 8000; UK: Craven House, 121 Kingsway, London WC2B 6PA *tel* 071-831 2965.
R2.50. M. For young married women and those who would like to be. Humour, good fiction, personalities, real-life drama, medical breakthroughs, popular science. *Payment:* by arrangement. *Illustrations:* line, half-tone, colour.

Garden and Home, Margaret Wasserfall, Republican Press (Pty.) Ltd, PO Box 32083, Mobeni 4060, Natal *tel* (031) 422041 *telegraphic address* Keur, Durban; UK: Craven House, 121 Kingsway, London WC2B 6PA *tel* 071-831 2965.
R3.30. M. Well-illustrated articles on gardening, suitable for Southern Hemisphere. Articles for home section on furnishings, flower arrangement, food. *Payment:* by arrangement. *Illustrations:* half-tone, colour.

(Johannesburg) Sunday Times, K.F. Owen, PO Box 1090, Johannesburg 2000 *tel* (011) 497-2300; London: South African Morning Newspapers Ltd, 32-33 Hatton Garden, EC1N 8DL *tel* 071-405 3742.
R2.20. Sun. Illustrated articles of political or human interest, from a South African angle if possible. Maximum 1000 words long and two or three photos. Shorter essays, stories and articles of a light nature from 500-750 words. *Payment:* average rate £100 a column. *Illustrations:* photos (colour or b&w) and line.

Living and Loving (1970), Angela Still, Republican Press (Pty.) Ltd, PO Box 32083, Mobeni 4060, Natal *tel* (031) 422041 *telegraphic address* Keur Durban; UK: Craven House, 121 Kingsway, London WC2B 6PA *tel* 071-831 2965.
R2.50. M. Romantic fiction, 1500-4000 words. Articles dealing with first-person experiences; baby, family and marriage, medical articles up to 3000 words. *Payment:* by merit.

Natal Witness (1846), D.J. Willers, 244 Longmarket Street, Pietermaritzburg, Natal 3201 *tel* (0331) 942 011 *telex* 6-43385 SA *fax* (0331) 940 468.
50c. D. Accepts topical articles. *Length:* 500-1000 words. *Payment:* average of R70 per 1000 words. All material should be submitted direct to the editor in Pietermaritzburg.

Personality, D. Mullany, Republican Press (Pty.) Ltd, PO Box 32083, Mobeni 4060, Natal *tel* (031) 422041 *telegraphic address* Keur, Durban; UK: Craven House, 121 Kingsway, London WC2B 6PA *tel* 071-831 2965.
R1.70. W. Illustrated. Primarily an entertainment-oriented magazine but also a market for articles about people and places, preferably with South African

angle. Strong news features and/or photojournalism, 1000-4000 words, with b&w and colour photos. Short stories 1500-5000 words. *Payment:* by arrangement. *Illustrations:* usually commissioned.

(Port Elizabeth) Eastern Province Herald, PO Box 1117, Port Elizabeth 6000 *tel* (041) 523470; London: 1st Floor, 32-33 Hatton Garden, EC1N 8DL *tel* 071-405 3742.
  25c. D. Contributions from 700-1500 words considered. *Payment:* £6 per 700 words minimum. *Illustrations:* topical photos.

Scope, D. Mullany, Republican Press (Pty.) Ltd, PO Box 32083, Mobeni 4060, Natal *tel* (031) 422041 *telegraphic address* Keur, Durban; UK: Craven House, 121 Kingsway, London WC2B 6PA *tel* 071-831 2965.
  R2.50. F. Strong news features, well illustrated, about people and places in all parts of the world. *Length:* up to 4000 words. Short stories 1500-5000 words, serials from 20,000 words. *Illustrations:* half-tone, colour.

South African Yachting (1957), Neil Rusch, PO Box 3473, Cape Town 8000 *tel* (021) 461-7472 *fax* (021) 461-3758.
  R4.00. M. Articles on yachting, boating or allied subjects. *Payment:* R8 per 100 words. *Illustrations:* line, half-tone; colour covers.

Southern Cross, PO Box 2372, 8000 Cape Town *tel* (021) 45-5007 *telegraphic address* Catholic.
  R1.00. W. National English language Catholic weekly. Catholic news reports, world and South African. 1000-word articles, cartoons of Catholic interest acceptable from freelance contributors. *Payment:* 45c. per column cm for all copy used. *Illustrations:* photos, R4 per column width.

World Airnews, Tom Chalmers, PO Box 35082, Northway, Durban 4065 *tel* (031) 84-1319.
  £12.50. M. Aviation news and features with an African angle. *Payment:* £75 per 1000 words. *Illustrations:* photos, £25 each (conditional).

Your Family, Angela Waller-Paton, Republican Press (Pty.) Ltd, PO Box 32083, Mobeni 4060, Natal *tel* (031) 422041 *telegraphic address* Keur, Durban; UK: Craven House, 121 Kingsway, London WC2B 6PA *tel* 071-831 2965.
  R2.50. M. Cookery, knitting, crochet and homecrafts. Short fiction, family drama, happy ending. *Payment:* by arrangement. *Illustrations:* continuous tone, colour and line.

UNITED STATES OF AMERICA

Because of the difficulties in providing an up-to-date list of US journals, the *Yearbook* does not contain a detailed list; instead we refer readers who are particularly interested in the US market to: *Writer's Market*, an annual guidebook giving editorial requirements and other details of over 4000 US markets for freelance writing, published by **Writer's Digest Books**, 1507 Dana Avenue, Cincinnati, Ohio 45207 ($25.95, plus $4.00 postage and handling); *The Writer's Handbook*, a substantial volume published by **The Writer Inc.,** 120 Boylston Street, Boston, Mass. 02116 ($28.95 plus $9.00 postage and handling). It contains 100 chapters, each written by an authority, giving practical instruction on a wide variety of aspects of freelance writing and including details of 2500 markets, payment rates and addresses. Also publishes books on writing fiction, non-fiction, poetry, articles, plays, etc.

The Writer Inc. also publish a monthly magazine *The Writer* ($35.00 p.a., must be in US funds) which contains articles of instruction on all writing fields, lists of markets for manuscripts and special features of interest to freelance writers everywhere.

Writer's Digest Books also publish the monthly magazine *Writer's Digest* ($25 per year) and the annual directories, *Novel and Short Story Writer's Market*, *Children's Writer's and Illustrator's Market*, *Poet's Market*, and many other books on creating and selling writing.

For availability in the UK details may be obtained from:

Freelance Press Services, Cumberland House, Lissadel Street, Salford M6 6GG   *tel* 061-745 8850   *fax* 061-745 8827.

SUBMISSION OF MSS

When submitting MSS to US journals send your covering letter with the MS together with any illustrations, stamped return envelope or International Reply Coupons. Make clear what rights are being offered for sale for some editors like to purchase MSS outright, thus securing world copyright, i.e. the traditional British market as well as the US market. MSS should be sent direct to the US office of the journal and not to any London office.

In many cases it is far better to send a preliminary letter giving a rough outline of your article or story. Enclose International Reply Coupons for reply. Most magazines will send a leaflet giving guidance to authors.

Writing for the European Community

BARBARA WOOD-KACZMAR

In 1992 all internal trading barriers will finally be removed and the EC will become a single market. For writers this means their home market will no longer be the UK, but Europe, the world's largest trader with 323 million people.

New opportunities for writers have already arisen in anticipation of 1992, as European publishers have launched new titles in the UK. The newcomers such as *Prima* and *Best* made such an impact that British publishers retaliated with their own new publications and writers now benefit from a larger market. And there is also the challenge of writing for magazines in the EC.

All speciality writers will find that, somewhere in the EC, there is a magazine which publishes their topic. The only difference in writing for an EC as opposed to a UK publication is that the language situation must be checked out first and various pitfalls need to be avoided (see below). Otherwise the usual rules of good writing apply: an article must be tailored to the magazine's style and written with respect for the sensitivities of its readers.

As part of the removal of trade barriers by 31 December 1992, standards and legislation concerning goods and services are being harmonised across the EC. Fortunately for journalists, none of these changes affects their work practices, but they do provide subject material to write about!

British writers should remember that 1992 also presents a challenge to other EC writers, and they are multi-lingual. Which group will seize these new opportunities?

HOW TO SUBMIT MSS TO EC MAGAZINES

Syndication (see page 121)

This is the easiest method for original MSS and also for articles previously published in the UK, if the UK rights only have been sold. Some syndicates (e.g. Features International) charge translation fees, while others (e.g. BIPS) don't. Illustrated material is preferred and popular topics include Royalty and specialised subjects such as fishing or science. Interesting events in Britain have a shelf life of six weeks on the Continent, but news items, women's interests and features on cars are not required.

Pan-European magazines

Pan-European magazines are publications sold throughout the EC and some aim for an all-European readership, e.g. *Eurobusiness*, *Euromoney* and *European Plastic News*. These English-language magazines pay well for freelance material tailored to their style. Subjects in demand are business, information technology, science and medicine, consumer marketing, pollution and law.

Other pan-Europeans change their language according to the country (e.g. *Prima*) and also their title (*Essentials* is called *Avantage* in France and *Pratica* in Italy). These publications are less easy to penetrate: each national title is geared to that market alone and there may be no connection between their different editions. *Vogue* (France) never buys from British writers – British writers must write for *Vogue* (UK) instead.

However, some magazine publishers e.g. Gruner and Jahr (International Marketing & Media Services Ltd, 7 Cavendish Square, London W1M 9HA   *tel* 071-580 8672) and Axel Springer (Springer Foreign News Service, Axel Springer Verlag AG, Suite 1/3, Ludgate House, 107-111 Fleet Street, London EC4A 2AB   *tel* 071-583 9986) will forward MSS from their London offices to their German counterparts. Ring the London offices of EC magazine publishers to find out.

Do it yourself

The go it alone approach is not difficult providing language and legal pitfalls are avoided. Choose a country you have some knowledge of and feel some affinity for. Then select a magazine from *Willings Press Guide*, the one essential tool. This lists major magazines and newspapers for each country, along with their publishers and UK advertising agents. Some London offices of pan-European publishers are also given.

Speciality writers will find the listings for magazines under the subjects published most helpful. English-language magazines are described as such so the few examples are easily located. However, English is the language of science and many English-language publications are academic journals, not commercial concerns.

Send a preliminary letter to the editor along with a synopsis, photocopies of previous work and an International Reply Coupon. Never send MSS or photos unless commissioned, and always stipulate that the material is being submitted for one use only in the country of publication. Otherwise the publisher can claim copyright and peddle the rights world-wide. Similarly, rates of pay should be agreed in advance. The magazine's UK agent may provide back copies for commissioned writers: s/he may also know if the editor speaks English.

The magazine may charge you for translation and/or require forms for double taxation exemption to be certified by your tax inspector before releasing the fees, but double taxation will disappear in 1992. Subjects in demand are environmental matters and interviews with famous people – it may be cheaper for an EC magazine editor to commission interviews from British writers who are on the spot. Hobbies, e.g. sailing, photography, camping and computers, are also popular. And high quality photos need no translation – articles with photos are usually easy to sell.

SOLVING THE LANGUAGE PROBLEM

English is the language of business in many EC countries. In descending order of English usage they are Ireland, Holland, Germany, Belgium, Denmark and Luxembourg, Portugal, Spain, France, Italy and Greece. Generally speaking, countries in the second half expect correspondence as well as articles to be in their own language. But, as areas popular with British tourists and expatriates, they have small English-language publishing sectors worth investigating.

Don't be tempted to translate your MSS yourself. The Institute of Translation and Interpreting (318a Finchley Road, London NW3 5HT   *tel* 071-794 9931 – see **Societies and Prizes**) maintains a national register of professional translators. Fees for French, German, Italian and Spanish start from £35 per 1000 words but Greek and Scandinavian languages cost more. Highly technical texts can cost from £60 per 1000 words. Local colleges may offer private translation facilities but few provide a 24-hour service.

SOURCES OF INFORMATION

1. **Willings Press Guide,** 1991. British Media Publications, 117th edn (see **Books, Research and Reference Sources**).
2. **Department of Trade and Industry Export Market Information Centre,** 1-19 Victoria Street, London SW1H 0ET (see **Government Offices and Public Services**). Each EC country has its own desk of experts at the Dti. Before you begin writing, obtain the Dti's profile on the country chosen (*tel* 071-215 5549). Also, the information pack 'Europe open for business' is essential reading (*tel* 081-200 1992). Visitors can use the Export Market Information Centre (for disabled access, *tel* 071-215 5444). These booklets are all free, but you may be charged for specific detailed enquiries.
3. **Embassies** (see **Government Offices and Public Services**). Most will supply lists of magazines and newspapers in their countries, publishers' and agents' addresses (useful as changes are frequent) as well as circulation figures and names of editors. Some lists are more comprehensive than others! Embassies usually know the UK addresses of their countries' major publishers.
4. **Chambers of Commerce** are comprehensive information centres. Visitors may study reference books on publishing or photocopies may be supplied on request. Some Cultural Institutes are located outside London.
5. **The European Commission** discusses its proposals with professionals before legislation. Phone the London office (071-222 8122) for information or to air your views.
6. The **European Parliament** is the only directly elected body in the EC. Your MEP or the London office (*tel* 071-222 0411) should know of changes in the legislative pipeline affecting writers or their specialities.

HELPFUL ASSOCIATIONS

1. The **National Union of Journalists** can raise grievances, such as non-payment or breach of copyright, with European publishers, either on its own or through its affiliated European unions. The NUJ maintains lists of EC unions of journalists (see **Societies and Prizes**).
2. **The Society of Authors** (see **Societies and Prizes**) normally advises on problems arising in the UK. However, it will refer a member having problems with a European publisher to the foreign authors' society, as all these belong to the Congress of European Writers' Organisations. However, if disputes arise over payments the cost of going to law may be prohibitive. Writers who regularly or solely write for an EC country should join the relevant authors' society. All EC countries are signatories to the Universal Copyright Convention and in many of them the author's moral right not to have his/her work distorted has been part of law for years.

3. **The Writers' Guild** (see **Societies and Prizes**) works out common European policies on Public Lending Rights and minimum terms publishing agreements through the biannual European Writers' Congress.

OPPORTUNITIES FOR BOOK AUTHORS

After 1992, competition will be fierce for the estimated total EC book sales of £9 billion. However, Western Europe is the UK's largest export market and the greatest growth is in English-language teaching materials.

A legal quirk will allow competing editions from the USA into the EC after 1992 and authors may be tempted to desert. UK publishers are therefore offering them a home royalty for the whole of Europe based on the UK price – this could double existing royalty payments.

NB. A British agent is essential for book and play authors to get the best deal on translation rights (see **Literary Agents**).

Recent UK Magazine Changes

The following changes have taken place since the last edition of the *Yearbook*.

CHANGES OF NAME AND MERGERS

Antique Clocks now Clocks
The Building Societies Gazette now Mortgage Finance Gazette
The Good Ski Guide now The Good Ski Guide A-Z
Financial Weekly now incorporated in Corporate Finance
The Fine Art Trade Guild Journal now Art Business Today
Information & Library Manager now merged with Logistics Information Management
Judy now merged with Mandy
Magazine Week now incorporated in UK Press Gazette
Power Farming now incorporated in Farmers Weekly
Secrets now merged with My Weekly
The Topper now merged with The Beezer
Voice of the Arab World Intelligence Report now Voice Intelligence Report

NEWSPAPERS AND MAGAZINES CEASED PUBLICATION

Argo
Blue Jeans
Business
Cheshire Times
Education and Training
Education Impact
Encounter
Engineering Materials and Design
Environment Now
Health Education Journal
Journalist's Week
Jump
The Listener
Margin
Mother
Music and Musicians
National Builder
New Socialist
Numbers
Performance Tuning & Sports Car
Popular Computing Weekly
Practical Computing
Road Racer Magazine
Spiritualist Gazette
Starblazer Library
The Sunday Correspondent
Tick-Tock
Today Magazine
20/20
Video Maker

Classified Index of Magazines

Commonwealth, Irish and South African Journals

This index can be only a broad classification. It should be regarded as a pointer to possible markets, and should be used with discrimination.

SHORT STORIES

This list does not include the women's journals requiring short stories, *see* WOMEN'S MAGAZINES; *see also* LITERARY

Ambit	Granta	*Personality (SA)
*Atlantic Advocate (Can.)	*Honest Ulsterman	*Quadrant (Aus.)
Catch	Interzone	Rattler's Tale
Chat	*Ireland's Eye	*Reality (Ire.)
Christian Herald	*Ireland's Own	*Scope (SA)
Company	Iron	Scots Magazine
Esquire	*Islands (NZ)	Slow Dancer
Essentials	*(Johannesburg) Sunday Times	Songwriting and Composing
Everywoman	(SA)	Stand
Family Circle	*Landfall (NZ)	Staple
Fantasy Tales	Literary Review	Sunday Post
Fear	London Magazine	SuperBike
*Fiddlehead (Can.)	Loving	Take a Break
Fly-Fishing & Fly-Tying	*Malahat Review (Can.)	*Wascana Review (Can.)
Good Housekeeping	*Monthly Life (Nigeria)	*Your Family (SA)

LONG COMPLETE STORIES

From 8000 words upwards (*See also under* WOMEN'S MAGAZINES)

*Landfall (NZ)	People's Friend Library	Secrets Story Library
My Weekly Story Library		

SERIALS

(*See also entries under* WOMEN'S MAGAZINES)

*Ireland's Own	People's Friend	Weekly News

CARTOONS

(*See also* CHILDREN'S AND YOUNG ADULT MAGAZINES)

Accountancy	Daily Star	Hi-Fi News
Annabel	Disability Now	*Hotel and Catering Review
Back Street Heroes	DR The Fashion Business	(Ire.)
Bella	Early Times	The Independent Magazine
Best	Eastern Evening News	*In Dublin (Ire.)
Catholic Gazette	Euromoney	Indian Bookworm's Journal
Catholic Pictorial	Everywoman	*Ireland's Eye
Celebrity	Family Tree Magazine	*Ireland's Own
Computer Weekly	*Fortnight (Ire.)	Just Seventeen
Countryman	Gay Times	Leisure Management
Coventry Evening Telegraph	Health & Efficiency	Local Government Chronicle
Crisis	Health & Fitness	MoneyMarketing

*Monthly Life (Nigeria)
Morning Star
New Internationalist
New Statesman & Society
Planet
Practical Parenting
Private Eye
Punch
Radio Control Models
Red Tape

Satellite Times
Scouting
Single Market News
Smash Hits
*Southern Cross (SA)
The Sport
*The Sunday Business Post (Ire.)
Sunday Post
Titbits
Today's Guide

Transport
Traveller
Tribune
Vegan
Viz
The Voice
Woman and Home
Yorkshire Post
Young Soldier

LETTERS TO THE EDITOR

Annabel
Art & Craft
*Australian Home Beautiful
*Australian Woman's Weekly
Autocar and Motor
Banking World
Best
British Deaf News
Choice
*Commercial Transport (Ire.)
Countryman
Daily Express
Devon Life
Do It Yourself
Empire
Family Circle
Film Monthly
Freelance Writing &
    Photography

*The Furrow (Ire.)
Garden News
Good Housekeeping
Good Ski Guide A-Z
Ideal Home
Jewish Telegraph
Journal of Alternative and
    Complementary Medicine
Living
*Living and Loving (SA)
Me
Mother & Baby
Motor Caravan Magazine
New Woman
19
Outdoor Action
Practical Gardening
Practical Householder
Practical Parenting

Practical Photography
Professional Nurse
Roy of the Rovers
Saga
Satellite Times
She
*Songwriter (Ire.)
Stamps
Street Machine
Sunday Mail
Take a Break
True Story
Viz
Weekly News
Woman
Woman's Own
Woman's Realm
*Woman's Way (Ire.)
Woman's Weekly

GOSSIP PARAGRAPHS

(Aberdeen) Press and
    Journal
Angler's Mail
Angling Times
Architectural Review
Art & Design
*Auckland Star (NZ)
Baptist Times
Birmingham Evening Mail
Bowls International
Bristol Evening Post
British Deaf News
Campaign
*(Cape Town) Cape Times (SA)
Catholic Herald
Catholic Pictorial
Cheshire Life
Christian Week
Church of England Newspaper
Coin Monthly
*Commercial Transport (Ire.)
Computing
Cosmetic World News
Country Homes & Interiors
Countryman
Coventry Evening Telegraph

Cricketer International
CTN
Daily Mail
Devon Life
Diver
Do It Yourself
DR The Fashion Business
Early Music
Eastern Evening News
Edinburgh Evening News
Engineering
EuroBusiness
The European
Evening Chronicle
Evening Standard
The Face
Family Tree Magazine
Fashion Weekly
The Field
Financial Weekly
*Fortnight (Ire.)
Freelance Writing &
    Photography
Garden News
Gas World
Gemmological Newsletter

Golf Monthly
Guiding
Health & Fitness
Hi-Fi News & Record Review
Horse & Pony
Hortus
*In Dublin (Ire.)
The Independent
The Independent on Sunday
Insurance Brokers' Monthly
*Irish Business
Jewish Telegraph
Just Seventeen
Justice of the Peace
Lancashire Evening Telegraph
Literary Review
Making Music
Marie Claire
*(Melbourne) Australasian Post
Melody Maker
The Mirror
Model Boats
90 Minutes
Parents
Penthouse
Popular Crafts

Poultry World
PR Week
Printing World
Private Eye
Radio Times
Satellite Times
Scotland on Sunday
Scottish Field
Somerset & Avon Life
*Songwriter (Ire.)
*Southern Cross (SA)
Sport and Leisure
Stage and Television Today
*The Sunday Age (Aus.)

*The Sunday Business Post (Ire.)
Sunday Express
*Sunday Life (Ire.)
Sunday Times
*(Sydney) Bulletin
Therapy Weekly
*Timaru Herald (NZ)
Times
Times Educational Supplement
Times Higher Education
  Supplement
Times Scottish Education
  Supplement
Treasure Hunting

Universe
*Weekly Topic (Uganda)
West Africa
Western Daily Press
Western Mail
Western Morning News
Woman's Realm
*Woman's Way (Ire.)
World Bowls
Writers' Monthly
Writers News
Yachts and Yachting
Yorkshire Life
Yorkshire Post

BRIEF FILLER PARAGRAPHS

(Aberdeen) Press and Journal
Aeroplane Monthly
African Business
Air Pictorial
Angler's Mail
Angling Times
Annabel
Architectural Design
Architectural Review
Art & Design
*Auckland Star (NZ)
*Australian Home Beautiful
Auto Express
Autocar & Motor
Balance
Baptist Times
Best
Birmingham Evening Mail
Bowls International
British Deaf News
Budgerigar World
Building
*(Cape Town) Cape Times (SA)
Caterer & Hotelkeeper
Catholic Herald
Catholic Pictorial
Cheshire Life
Christian Herald
Christian Week
Church of England
  Newspaper
Classical Music
Coin Monthly
*Commercial Transport (Ire.)
Cosmetic World News
Countryman
Cricketer International
CTN
Daily Star
Daily Telegraph
Dairy Industries International
Devon Life
Do It Yourself

DR The Fashion Business
Early Music
East Lothian Life
Eastern Evening News
Edinburgh Evening News
Electrical Review
*Electronics Australia
Engineering
Esquire
The European
Evening Standard
The Face
Family Tree Magazine
*Farmer's Weekly (SA)
Fashion Forecast International
Fashion Weekly
Fear
Freelance Writing &
  Photography
*The Furrow (Ire.)
Garden News
Gas World
Gay Times
Gemmological Newsletter
Golf Illustrated Weekly
Golf Monthly
Guiding
Health & Fitness
Hi-Fi News & Record Review
Homes and Gardens
Horticulture Week
Hortus
*Hotel and Catering Review
  (Ire.)
*Image (Ire.)
*In Dublin (Ire.)
*Irish Business
Jane's Defence Weekly
Jewish Telegraph
Just Seventeen
Lancashire Evening Telegraph
Literary Review
Liverpool Echo

Local Government Chronicle
Manx Life
Masonic Square
Melody Maker
Model Boats
Model Engineer
Motor Boat and Yachting
Nautical Magazine
New Musical Express
90 Minutes
Opera Now
Our Dogs
Penthouse
Pilot
Pony
Popular Crafts
Poultry World
Practical Fishkeeping
Printing World
Private Eye
Radio Times
Reader's Digest
Safety Education
Satellite Times
Scotland on Sunday
She
Ship and Boat International
Snooker Scene
Somerset & Avon Life
*Songwriter (Ire.)
*Southern Cross (SA)
Spare Rib
The Sport
Sport and Leisure
Steam Classic
*The Sunday Business Post (Ire.)
Sunday Express
*Sunday Life (Ire.)
Sunday Sun
Sunday Times
*(Sydney) Bulletin
Tennis World
*Theatre Ireland Magazine

*Timaru Herald (NZ)
Times Educational Supplement
Times Higher Education
  Supplement
Times Scottish Education
  Supplement
Today's Runner
Town and Country Planning

Treasure Hunting
Universe
Vegan
Viz
Waterways World
Western Daily Press
Woman's Realm

World Bowls
World Fishing
Writers' Monthly
Writers News
Yachting Monthly
Yachts and Yachting
Yorkshire Post

UK Regional Newspapers

Aberdeen Evening Express
Asian Times
Birmingham Evening Mail
The Birmingham Post
Bolton Evening News
Bristol Evening Post
Caribbean Times
The Courier and Advertiser
  (Dundee)
Coventry Evening Telegraph
Daily Post (Liverpool)
Daily Record (Glasgow)
Dundee Evening Telegraph &
  Post
Eastern Daily Press (Norwich)
Eastern Evening News
  (Norwich
Edinburgh Evening News

Evening Chronicle
  (Newcastle)
Evening Post (Chatham)
Evening Post (Reading)
Evening Standard (London)
Express and Star
  (Wolverhampton)
Glasgow Evening Times
Glasgow Herald
Inverness Courier
The Journal (Newcastle)
Kent Messenger
Lancashire Evening Post
Lancashire Evening Telegraph
Liverpool Echo
Manchester Evening News
The Northern Echo (Durham)
Nottingham Evening Post

The Press and Journal
  (Aberdeen)
The Star (Sheffield)
Sunday Mail (Glasgow)
Sunday Mercury (Birmingham)
Sunday Post (Dundee/
  Glasgow)
The Voice
The Weekly News (Scotland)
Western Daily Press (Bristol)
Western Mail (Cardiff)
The Western Morning News
  (Plymouth)
Yorkshire Evening Press
Yorkshire Gazette & Herald
  Series
Yorkshire Post

Women's Magazines

Home, Fashions, Children, Beauty, Fiction

Annabel
*Australian Women's Weekly
Bella
Best
*Bona (SA)
Catch
Chat
*Chatelaine (Can.)
Company
Cosmopolitan
Country Living
Elle (UK)
Essentials
Everywoman
*Fair Lady (SA)
Family Circle
*Femina (SA)
Girl About Town
Good Housekeeping
Harpers & Queen
Home and Country

Home Words
Homes and Gardens
*Image (Ire.)
*IT Magazine (Ire.)
Just Seventeen
Lady
Living
*Living and Loving (SA)
*Mahogany (Zimbabwe)
Marie Claire
Me
Mother & Baby
My Weekly
*New Idea (Aus.)
New Woman
*New Zealand Woman's
  Weekly
19
Nursery World
Office Secretary
Options

Parents
People's Friend
Practical Parenting
Prima
Scottish Home and Country
She
Spare Rib
Sunday Post
Take a Break
The Tatler
Vogue
Woman
Woman and Home
*Woman's Day (Aus.)
Woman's Journal
Woman's Own
Woman's Realm
*Woman's Way (Ire.)
Woman's Weekly
World's Children
*Your Family (SA)

Men's Magazines

Arena
Country
Esquire
For Him

Gay Times
GQ
Masonic Square
Mayfair

Men Only
Penthouse
Signature

Children's and Young Adult Magazines

The Beano
Beano Library
Beano Puzzle Library
Beezer-Topper
Blue Jeans Photo Novels
Brownie
Bunty
Bunty Library
Buster
Commando
Crisis
The Dandy

Dandy Cartoon Library
Dandy Library
Debbie Library
*Dolly (Aus.)
Early Times
Football Picture Story Library
Hi!
Horse & Pony
i-D Magazine
Jackie
Judy Library

Junior Bookshelf
Just Seventeen
Mandy/Judy
Mandy Library
Number One
Pony
Scouting
Smash Hits
Today's Guide
Twinkle
Victor

Subject Articles

ADVERTISING, DESIGN, PRINTING & PUBLISHING

(See also under LITERARY)

Arena
*Australian Bookseller &
 Publisher
Bookseller
British Journalism Review
British Printer
Campaign
*Canadian Interiors

Design
Designers' Journal
Exchange & Mart
The Face
Indexer
Interior Design
InterMedia
Journalist

Learned Publishing
Market Newsletter
Media Week
PR Week
Printing World
Publishing News
World of Interiors

AGRICULTURE AND GARDENING

Amateur Gardening
Country
Country Life
Countryman
*Countryman (Aus.)
Country-Side
Dairy Farmer
*The Farmer (Zimbabwe)
Farmer's Weekly

*Farmer's Weekly (SA)
Farming News
The Field
Fresh Produce Journal
*Garden and Home (SA)
Garden News
Grower
Horticulture Week

Hortus
*New Zealand Farmer
Pig Farming
Poultry World
Practical Gardening
Scottish Farmer
Smallholder
Town and Country Planning

ARCHITECTURE AND BUILDING

Architects' Journal
Architectural Design
Architectural Review
Building
Built Environment

Burlington Magazine
Construction Weekly
Contemporary Review
Country Homes & Interiors
Country Life

Design
Designers' Journal
Education
Homes and Gardens
House & Garden

House Builder	Local Historian	Museums Journal
Ideal Home	Metropolitan Home	Retail Attraction
International Construction	Mortgage Finance Gazette	Town and Country Planning

ART AND COLLECTING

(*See also under* PHILATELY)

Antique Collector	Artist's & Illustrator's	Country Life
Antique Dealer & Collectors	Magazine	Creative Camera
Guide	Arts Review	Design
Antiques Folio	Burlington Magazine	Gemmological Newsletter
Apollo	Clocks	Illustrated London News
Art & Design	Coin News	Leisure Painter
Art Business Today	Coin Monthly	Medal News
Artist	Contemporary Review	Museums Journal
		Numismatic Chronicle

AVIATION

Aeromodeller	*Aviation & Aerospace (Can.)	Spaceflight
Aeroplane Monthly	Flight International	Transport
Air Pictorial	Pilot	*World Airnews (SA)
*Australian Flying		

BLIND AND DEAF-BLIND

Published by the Royal National Institute for the Blind (see **United Kingdom Book Publishers**)

Braille Chess Magazine	Fleur de Lys	Nuggets
Braille Journal of	Gleanings	Physiotherapists' Quarterly
Physiotherapy	High Browse (in Braille and	Piano Tuners' Quarterly
Braille Music Magazine	print)	Rhetoric
Braille Radio Times	'Law Notes' Extracts	Roundabout
Braille Rainbow	Light of the Moon	Scientific Enquiry
Braille TV Times	Moon Magazine	Showcase (in Braille and print)
Channels of Blessing	Moon Messenger	Soundings
Contention	Moon Newspaper	Theological Times
Crusade Messenger	Moon Rainbow	Trefoil Trail
Daily Bread	New Beacon (in Braille and	The Weekender
Diane	print)	

BUSINESS, INDUSTRY AND MANAGEMENT

Achievement	European Plastic News	Millennium
Administrator	Fashion Forecast International	Office Secretary
Brewing & Distilling	Fashion Weekly	Personnel Management
International	Financial Director	Political Quarterly
Business Scotland	Information and Software	Post
Contemporary Review	Technology	Single Market News
Cosmetic World News	Involvement & Participation	Sociological Review
Dairy Industries International	IS	*The Sunday Business Post (Ire.)
Director	Land & Liberty	Woodworker
EuroBusiness	*Management (NZ)	Work Study
Euromoney	Management Today	

CINEMA AND FILMS

Campaign
Empire
Film Monthly
International Broadcast
    Engineer

New Statesman & Society
Screen International
Sight and Sound

Speech and Drama
Stand
Studio Sound

COMPUTERS

Computer Weekly
Computing

Personal Computer World

Which Computer?

ECONOMICS, ACCOUNTANCY AND FINANCE

Accountancy
Accountancy Age
Accounting World
African Business
*Australian Financial Review
Banker
Banking World
Business
Business Scotland
Certified Accountant
Choice
Contemporary Review

Dairy Industries
    International
Economic Journal
Economica
Economist
Euromoney
Financial Adviser
Financial Director
Financial Times
Financial Weekly
Grower
Insurance Brokers' Monthly

Investors Chronicle
*Irish Business
Land & Liberty
Local Government Chronicle
Money Week
MoneyMarketing
Mortgage Finance Gazette
New Statesman & Society
*Studies (Ire.)
Tribune
West Africa

EDUCATION

Amateur Stage
Art & Craft
La Brita Esperantisto
British Journal of Special
    Education
Child Education
Education
Guiding
Higher Education Quarterly
IS
Junior Bookshelf
Junior Education
Linguist
Local Historian
Modern Languages

Modus
Month
Museums Journal
Music Teacher
New Blackfriars
New Statesman & Society
Nursery World
Parents
Practical Parenting
Prep School
*Reality (Ire.)
Report
Safety Education
School Librarian
Scottish Educational Journal

Speech and Drama
Spoken English
Theology
Times Educational
    Supplement
Times Higher Education
    Supplement
Times Scottish Education
    Supplement
Together
Tribune
Unesco Courier
Use of English
World's Children
Young People Now

ENGINEERING AND MECHANICS

(*See also under* AGRICULTURE, ARCHITECTURE, AVIATION, BUSINESS, MOTORING, NAUTI-
CAL, RADIO, SCIENCES)

*Australian Mining
Buses
Car Mechanics
Construction Weekly
Control and Instrumentation
Design
Electrical Review
Electrical Times

*Electronics Australia
Engineer
Engineering
Everyday Electronics
Filtration & Separation
Gas World
International Construction
Model Engineer

*NZ Engineering
Practical Electronics
Practical Woodworking
Railway Gazette
Railway Magazine
Railway World
Spaceflight
Transport

HEALTH, MEDICINE AND NURSING

Balance
British Deaf News
British Journal of General
   Practice
British Medical Journal
Caring
Choice
Community Care
Dental Update
Disability Now
Doctor
*East African Medical Journal
   (Kenya)
Health & Efficiency
Health & Fitness

Here's Health
Hospitality
*Irish Journal of Medical Science
*Irish Medical Times
Journal of Alternative and
   Complementary Medicine
Lancet
New Statesman & Society
Nursery World
Nursing Times
Parents
Pharmaceutical Journal
Physiotherapy
Practical Health
Practical Parenting

The Practitioner
Professional Nurse
Pulse
Quarterly Journal of Medicine
Running Magazine
Saga
Slimmer Magazine
Therapy Weekly
This Caring Business
Today's Runner
Vegan
Vegetarian
Young People Now

HISTORY AND ARCHAEOLOGY

Albion
Bedfordshire Magazine
Coin & Medal News
Contemporary Review
Country Quest
English Historical Review

Geographical Magazine
Heythrop Journal
History
History Today
Illustrated London News
In Britain

Lancashire Life
Local Historian
Museums Journal
New Blackfriars
Scottish Historical Review
*Studies (Ire.)

HOME

(*See also* WOMEN'S MAGAZINES)

*Australian Home Beautiful
*Australian House and Garden
*Canadian Interiors
Choice
Country Homes & Interiors
Do It Yourself
Embroidery

*Garden and Home (SA)
Home and Family
House & Garden
House Beautiful
Ideal Home
Jewish Telegraph
Metropolitan Home

Modus
Parents
Practical Householder
Safety Education
Saga
*Your Family (SA)

HOTEL, CATERING AND LEISURE

Caterer and Hotelkeeper
Club Secretary
Hospitality

*Hotel and Catering Review
   (Ire.)
Leisure Management

Leisure Manager
Parks & Sports Grounds
Sport and Leisure

HUMOUR

Private Eye

Punch

Viz

LEGAL AND POLICE

The Criminologist
Family Law

Forensic Photography
Justice of the Peace

Police Journal
Solicitors' Journal

LITERARY

(See also under Poetry section)

Artrage
*Australian Bookseller &
  Publisher
Author
Book Collector
*Books in Canada
*Books Ireland
Books Magazine
Bookseller
British Book News
British Journalism Review
*Canadian Author
*Canadian Forum
*Canadian Literature
Cencrastus
Chapman
Contemporary Review
Critical Quarterly
*Dalhousie Review (Can.)
Dickensian
Edinburgh Review
*Fiddlehead (Can.)
Freelance Writing &
  Photography

Granta
Illustrated London News
Index on Censorship
Indexer
Indian Bookworm's Journal
*Islands (NZ)
*Journal of Canadian Studies
Journalist
Junior Bookshelf
*Landfall (NZ)
Learned Publishing
Library
Lines Review
Literary Review
Llais Llyfrau
London Magazine
London Review of Books
*Malahat Review (Can.)
Modern Languages
New Library World
New Statesman & Society
The New Welsh Review
Orbis

Outposts Poetry Quarterly
*Overland (Aus.)
Planet
Powys Review
Publishing News
*Quadrant (Aus.)
*Quill & Quire (Can.)
*Reality (Ire.)
Signal
Spectator
Stand
*Studies (Ire.)
Times Literary Supplement
Tribune
Use of English
Wasafiri
*Wascana Review (Can.)
Woman Journalist
Writers' Monthly
Writers News
Writing Women
Y Faner

LOCAL GOVERNMENT AND CIVIL SERVICE

Local Council Review
Local Government Chronicle

Local Government Review

Red Tape

MARKETING AND RETAILING

CTN
DR The Fashion Business
Fashion Weekly

Gifts International
Grocer
Incentive Today

Retail Attraction
Retail Week
Toy Trader

MOTORING AND CYCLING

Auto Express
Autocar & Motor
Back Street Heroes
Bicycle Action
Buses
Car
*Car (SA)
Car Mechanics
Caravan Magazine
Classic Cars

Commercial Motor
*Commercial Transport
  (Ire.)
Custom Car
Cycling
Dirt Bike Rider
*Kiwi Rider Magazine (NZ)
Mobile & Holiday Homes
Motor Caravan Magazine

Motor Cycle News
Motorcaravan and Motorhome
  Monthly
Performance Car
Practical Motorist
Scootering
Street Machine
Superbike
Transport

MUSIC AND RECORDING

Arena
Classical Music
Early Music
The Face
Gramophone

Hi-Fi News
High Fidelity
i-D Magazine
Jazz Journal International
Making Music

Melody Maker
Music and Letters
Music Review
Music Teacher
Music Week

Musical Opinion
Musical Times
New Musical Express
Number One

Opera
Opera Now
Organ
Smash Hits

*Songwriter (Ire.)
Songwriting and Composing
Studio Sound
Tempo

NATURAL HISTORY

(See also under AGRICULTURE, RURAL LIFE, COUNTRY)

Animal World
Aquarist and
  Pondkeeper
BBC Wildlife Magazine
British Birds
Budgerigar World
Cage and Aviary Birds
Cat World
Dalesman
Ecologist

Entomologist's Monthly
  Magazine
*Equinox (Can.)
European Racehorse
*Geo (Aus.)
Geographical Magazine
Green Magazine
Guiding
Heredity
Horse & Pony

Museums Journal
Natural World
Naturalist
Nature
Our Dogs
Pony
Practical Fishkeeping
*Swara (Kenya)
World Magazine

NAUTICAL AND MARINE

Diver
*Modern Boating (Aus.)
Motor Boat and Yachting
Nautical Magazine
Navy International

Port of London
Practical Boat Owner
Sea Breezes
*Sea Spray (NZ)
Ship & Boat International

Ships Monthly
Transport
Yachting Monthly
Yachting World
Yachts and Yachting

PHILATELY

Stamp Lover
Stamp Magazine

Stamp Monthly

Stamps

PHOTOGRAPHY

Amateur Photographer
British Journal of Photography
Creative Camera
Forensic Photography

Freelance Writing &
  Photography
Photo Answers

Photography
PIC (People in Camera)
Practical Photography

POETRY

(See Poetry section)

POLITICS

*Australian Journal of
  International Affairs
*Australian Journal of Politics
  and History
*Australian Quarterly
China Quarterly
Contemporary Review
*Current Affairs Bulletin (Aus.)
*Fortnight (Ire.)
Illustrated London News

International Affairs
Justice of the Peace
Liberal Democrats News
Local Government Chronicle
New Blackfriars
New Internationalist
New Statesman & Society
Peace News
Political Quarterly
Round Table

*Studies (Ire.)
*Times on Sunday (Aus.)
Town and Country Planning
Tribune
Unesco Courier
Voice Intelligence Report
West Africa
*Winnipeg Free Press (Can.)
World Development
World Today

RADIO, TELEVISION AND VIDEO

Broadcast
*Broadcast (Can.)
Campaign
*Electronics Australia
Empire
Gramophone
Hi-Fi News
InterMedia

International Broadcast
  Engineer
New Statesman & Society
*New Zealand Listener
Opera Now
Practical Wireless
Radio Times
Satellite Times

Short-Wave Magazine
Stage and Television Today
Studio Sound
Television
Tribune
TV Guide
TV Times
Video Week

RELIGION AND PHILOSOPHY

Baptist Times
Catholic Gazette
Catholic Herald
Catholic Pictorial
Christian Herald
Christian Week
Church of England Newspaper
*Church of Ireland Gazette
Church Times
Contemporary Review
Day by Day
Downside Review
Evangelical Quarterly
Faith and Freedom
Friend
*The Furrow (Ire.)
*Herald of the South (Aus.)

Heythrop Journal
Home and Family
Home Words
Inquirer
Jewish Chronicle
Jewish Quarterly
Jewish Telegraph
Life and Work
Methodist Recorder
Mind
Modern Churchman
Month
New Blackfriars
Priests & People
Quaker Monthly
*Reality (Ire.)

Reform
Sign
*Southern Cross (SA)
*Studies (Ire.)
Studies in Comparative
  Religion
Tablet
Theology
Third Way
Together
Universe
War Cry
West Africa
*Word (Ire.)
World Outlook
Young Soldier

RURAL LIFE AND COUNTRY

(*See also under* NATURAL HISTORY)

Bedfordshire Magazine
Cheshire Life
Country
Country Life
Country Quest
Countryman
Country-Side
Coventry Evening Telegraph
Cumbria
Dalesman
Derbyshire Life and
  Countryside
Devon Life
Dorset
East Lothian Life

Eastern Daily Press
Essex Countryside
The Field
Gloucestershire Life
Green Magazine
Hampshire
Hertfordshire Countryside
In Britain
Inverness Courier
*Ireland's Eye
Kent
Lady
Lancashire Evening Post
Lancashire Life
Lancashire Magazine

Local Historian
Manx Life
Scots Magazine
Scottish Field
Scottish Home and Country
Shooting Times and Country
  Magazine
Somerset & Avon Life
This England
Town and Country Planning
Warwickshire and Worcester-
  shire Life
Waterways World
Yorkshire Life
Yorkshire Riding

SCIENCES

(*See also under* AGRICULTURE, AVIATION, CINEMA, ENGINEERING, HEALTH, HISTORY, MOTORING, NATURAL HISTORY, NAUTICAL, PHOTOGRAPHY, RADIO, SPORTS, TRAVEL)

Criminologist
*Equinox (Can.)
Geological Magazine
Heredity

Impact of Science on Society
*Irish Press
Mind
Nature

New Scientist
Science Progress
*Technology Ireland

SERVICES: NAVAL, MILITARY, AIR, AND CIVIL

Air Pictorial
Army Quarterly & Defence
Journal

Jane's Defence Weekly
Red Tape

Round Table
RUSI Journal

SPORTS, GAMES, HOBBIES AND PASTIMES

(*See also under* AGRICULTURE, ART, AVIATION, CINEMA, HOME, MEN'S MAGAZINES, MOTORING, MUSIC, NATURAL HISTORY, NAUTICAL, PHILATELY, PHOTOGRAPHY, RADIO, TEHATRE, TRAVEL, WOMEN'S MAGAZINES)

Aeromodeller
Anglers' Mail
Angling Times
*Australasian Sporting Shooter
*Australian Angler's Fishing
  World
Boards
Bowls International
Bridge International
British Birds
British Chess Magazine
Camping & Walking
Climber and Hill Walker
Cricketer International
Darts World
Family Tree Magazine
The Field
Fly-Fishing & Fly-Tying
Gemmological Newsletter
Golf Illustrated Weekly
Golf Monthly
Golf World

Good Ski Guide A-Z
Great Outdoors
Guiding
Horse and Hound
Horse and Rider
In Britain
Military Modelling
Model Boats
Model Engineer
Model Railways
90 Minutes
Our Dogs
Outdoor Action
Popular Crafts
Radio Control Models
Railway World
Roy of the Rovers
Running Magazine
Scale Models International
Scottish Field
Scouting
Sea Angler

Shooting Times
The Skier
Snooker Scene
*South African Yachting
Sport and Leisure
Sporting Life
Squash World
Steam Classic
Tennis
Tennis World
Today's Golfer
Today's Runner
Trout and Salmon
Wisden Cricket Monthly
Woodworker
*Word (Ire.)
Workbox
World Bowls
World Fishing
Yachting Monthly
Yachting World
Yachts and Yachting

THEATRE, DRAMA AND DANCING

(*See also under* CINEMA, MUSIC)

Amateur Stage
Ballroom Dancing Times
*Canadian Forum
Celebrity
Contemporary Review
Dance & Dancers
Dancing Times
Illustrated London News

In Britain
*In Dublin
*Landfall (NZ)
New Statesman & Society
New Theatre Quarterly
*Performing Arts in Canada
Plays & Players

Radio Times
*Reality (Ire.)
Speech and Drama
Stage and Television Today
*Theatre Ireland Magazine
Tribune
TV Times

TRAVEL AND GEOGRAPHY

La Brita Esperantisto
British-Soviet Friendship
Bulletin of Hispanic Studies
Caravan Magazine
Contemporary Review
*Equinox (Can.)
*Geo (Aus.)

Geographical Journal
Geographical Magazine
Illustrated London News
In Britain
*Ireland of the Welcomes
Local Historian
*Natal Witness (SA)

Railway World
Town and Country Planning
Travel Trade Gazette
*TraveLeisure (Aus.)
Traveller
World Magazine

United Kingdom Magazine and Newspaper Publishers

The publishers included here are those who issue periodicals listed in the earlier pages of this *Yearbook*. For a fuller list of newspaper and magazine publishers, with the titles they publish, see *Willings Press Guide*.

Ian Allan Ltd, Terminal House, Station Approach, Shepperton, Surrey TW17 8AS   *tel* (0932) 228950   *telex* 929806 Iallan G   *fax* (0932) 232366.

Argus Consumer Publications, 2-4 Leigham Court Road, Streatham, London SW16 2PD   *tel* 081-677 7538.

Argus Specialist Publications, Argus House, Boundary Way, Hemel Hempstead, Herts. HP2 7ST   *tel* (0442) 66551   *fax* (0442) 66998.

Benn Industrial Publications Ltd, Sovereign Way, Tonbridge, Kent TN9 1RW   *tel* (0732) 364422   *telex* 95132 Benton G   *fax* (0732) 361534. *Directors:* John de Carle (chairman), John Brazier (managing), David Barrett, Roy Coxhead, Brian Downing, John Mann, Michael Staton.

Benn Retail Publications Ltd, Sovereign Way, Tonbridge, Kent TN9 1RW   *tel* (0732) 364422   *telex* 95132 Benton G   *fax* (0732) 361534. *Directors:* John de Carle (chairman), Christopher Leonard-Morgan (managing), Roy Coxhead, Brian Downing, John Mann, Felim O'Brien, Michael Staton, Patrick Wade.

Blackwell Scientific Publications Ltd (1939), Osney Mead, Oxford OX2 0EL   *tel* (0865) 240201   *fax* (0865) 721205; 25 John Street, London WC1N 2BL   *tel* 071-404 4101   *fax* 071-831 6745; 23 Ainslie Place, Edinburgh EH3 6AJ   *tel* 031-226 7232   *telex* 83355 Medbok G   *fax* 031-226 3803.

Cambridge University Press (1534), The Edinburgh Building, Shaftesbury Road, Cambridge CB2 2RU   *tel* (0223) 312393   *telegraphic address* Unipress, Cambridge   *telex* 817256 Cupcam   *fax* (0223) 315052. *Group director (journals)*: Richard L. Ziemacki, MA, PhD.

The Condé Nast Publications Ltd (1916), Vogue House, Hanover Square, London W1R 0AD   *tel* 071-499 9080   *telegraphic address* Volon, London   *telex* 27338 Volon G   *fax* 071-493 1345. *Directors:* Daniel Salem (chairman), R.S. Hill (managing), B. Tims, M.J.M. Garvin, D.J. Montgomery, Richard A. Shortway, S. Boler, P. Stuart, S. Quinn, J. Newhouse, B. Robertson, N. Coleridge.

EMAP Élan, Victory House, Leicester Place, London WC2H 7BP   *tel* 071-437 9011   *telex* 266400   *fax* 071-434 0656. *Managing director:* G.C. Butler.

EMAP Pursuit Publishing Ltd, Bretton Court, Bretton, Peterborough PE3 8DZ   *tel* (0733) 264666   *fax* (0733) 265515.

Express Newspapers plc, Ludgate House, 245 Blackfriars Road, London SE1 9UX   *tel* 071-928 8000   *cables* Lon Express   *telex* 21841/21842   *fax* 071-633 0244.

Harmsworth Magazines Ltd, 141/143 Drury Lane, London WC2B 5TB   *tel* 071-497 1199. *Group publishing director:* Andrew Warren.

Haymarket Publishing Group Ltd, 22-32 Lancaster Gate, London W2 3LP   *tel* 081-943 5000.

IPC Magazines Ltd, King's Reach Tower, Stamford Street, London SE1 9LS   *tel* 071-261 5000   *telex* 915748 Magdiv G.

Jane's Information Group, 163 Brighton Road, Coulsdon, Surrey CR5 2NH   *tel* 081-763 1030   *telex* 916907   *fax* 081-763 1005.

Justice of the Peace Ltd, Little London, Chichester, West Sussex PO19 1PG   *tel* (0243) 775552   *fax* (0243) 779174.

Link House Magazines Ltd, Dingwall Avenue, Croydon CR9 2TA   *tel* 081-686 2599   *fax* 081-760 0973. *Directors:* B.G.K. Downing (chairman), P.J. Cosgrove (managing), D.J.W. Browning, C.K. Gamm, C.D. Jakes, D.G. Shuard, R.J. Pyper.

Macmillan Magazines Ltd, 4 Little Essex Street, London WC2R 3LF   *tel* 071-836 6633   *telex* 262024 Macmil G. *Chairman:* N.G. Byam Shaw; *directors:* R. Barker (managing), Miss M. Waltham, J. Barnes, T. Tamsett, R. Hartgill.

Maxwell Business Communications Ltd, 33-35 Bowling Green Lane, London EC1R 0DA   *tel* 071-837 1212   *telex* 299049 Mbcbgl G   *fax* 071-278 4003.

Mirror Group Newspapers Ltd, Holborn Circus, London EC1P 1DQ   *tel* 071-353 0246   *telex* 27286/7 Mirror G   *fax* 071-822 3405/3864.

Morgan-Grampian plc, 30 Calderwood Street, London SE18 6QH   *tel* 081-855 7777   *fax* 081-854 7476.

The National Magazine Co. Ltd, National Magazine House, 72 Broadwick Street, London W1V 2BP   *tel* 071-439 5000   *telex* 263879 Natmag G   *fax* 071-437 6886.

Numismatic Publishing Company, Sovereign House, Brentwood, Essex CM14 4SE   *tel* (0277) 219876.

Pergamon Press (1948), Headington Hill Hall, Oxford OX3 0BW   *tel* (0865) 794141   *telegraphic address* Pergapress, Oxford   *telex* 83177   *fax* (0865) 60285.

Reed Business Publishing Group, Quadrant House, The Quadrant, Sutton, Surrey SM2 5AS   *tel* 081-661 3500   *telex* 892084 Reedbp G   *fax* 081-661 2071   *ad doc* DX 45550 Sutton 3.

Scholastic Publications Ltd, Villiers House, Clarendon Avenue, Leamington Spa, Warks. CV32 5PR   *tel* (0926) 887799   *fax* (0926) 883331.

Scripture Union (1867), Scripture Union House, 130 City Road, London EC1V 2NJ   *tel* 071-782 0013   *fax* 071-782 0014. Christian Publishers and Booksellers.

Thomson-Leng Publications, Dundee DD1 9QJ   *tel* (0382) 23131   *telegraphic address* Courier, Dundee   *telex* 76380   *fax* (0382) 22214; London: 185 Fleet Street, EC4A 2HS   *tel* 071-242 5086   *telegraphic address* Courier, London EC4   *fax* 071-404 5694.

Times Newspapers Ltd, PO Box 495, Virginia Street, London E1 9XY   *tel* 071-782 5000   *telex* 262141.

Town & County Magazines, Oyston Publications plc, Oyston Mill, Strand Road, Preston PR1 8UR   *tel* (0772) 722022   *fax* (0772) 736496. County magazines.

J. Whitaker & Sons Ltd, 12 Dyott Street, London WC1A 1DF   *tel* 071-836 8911   *fax* 071-836 2909. *Directors:* Peter Allsop, Louis Baum, R.F. Baum, Alan Mollison, T.E. Sweetman, David Whitaker, Sally Whitaker.

Syndicates, News and Press Agencies

In their own interests writers and others are strongly advised to make preliminary enquiries before submitting MSS, and to ascertain terms of work. Commission varies. The syndication details given in the following entries should be noted carefully; many news and press agencies do not syndicate articles.

Academic File (1985), Centre for Near East, Asia and Africa Research (NEAR), PO Box 571, Ground Floor, 172 Castelnau, London SW13 9DH   *tel* 081-741 5878   *telex* 940 12777 Near G   *fax* 081-741 5671. *Editor:* Sajid Rizvi. Feature and photo syndication with special reference to Middle East, North Africa and Asia.

Advance Features, Clarendon House, Judges Terrace, East Grinstead, West Sussex RH19 3AD   *tel* (0342) 328562. *Managing editor:* Peter Norman. Supplies text and visual services to the regional press in Britain and newspapers overseas. Editorial for advertising supplements on consumer and commercial themes. Instructional graphic panels on a variety of subjects. Text services (weekly); 'agony' columns (teenagers and general), property, careers, women's page editorial, general interest series, family finance, business editorial, daily and weekly crosswords. Legal and business articles for the specialist press. Daily and weekly cartoons for the regional press (not single cartoons).

Ameuropress (Main Office): *postal address* Clasificador 5, Tajamar, Providencia, Santiago, Chile; *located at* Daríos Urzúa 1523, Santiago   *tel* 40044   *cables* Europress   *telex* 340260   *fax* (56-2) 2351731. (Branch Office): *postal address* PO Box 3535, Buenos Aires 1000, Argentina; *located at* Av. Libertador 5560-8°B, Buenos Aires 1426   *tel* 785-3128   *cables* Ameuropres   *fax* (54-1) 4851. *Director:* José Gregorio Ríos. Illustrated features to newspapers and magazines world-wide. Specialising in Latin American subjects including travel, human interest stories, hobbies, science, animal features. Regularly supplies women's material including cookery, beauty, fashion, interior decorating, glamour. Also stock colour library for advertising, calendars and illustrations. Undertakes special requirements and local assignments.

ANPS (Australasian News & Press Services) (D.J. Varney & Associates 1964), Box T 1834, GPO, Perth, W Australia 6001   *tel* (09) 293-1455   *fax* (09) 293-4919. Australian correspondents and representatives for the international media. Services provided: features and news for colour photo magazines. Articles for consumer, trade, technical and professional journals. Trade news summaries and newsletters. Full range of professional public relations and market research services available including film, television and stage writing, production and talent services.

The Associated Press Ltd (News Department), The Associated Press House, 12 Norwich Street, London EC4A 1BP   *tel* 071-353 1515   *telegraphic address* Associated Londonpsy   *fax* 071-353 8118.

Australian Associated Press (1935), 85 Fleet Street, London EC4Y 1EH   *tel* 071-353 0153/4   *fax* 071-583 3563. News service to the Australian, New Zealand and Pacific Island press, radio and television.

BIPS—Bernsen's International Press Service Ltd, 9 Paradise Close, Eastbourne, East Sussex BN20 8BT   *tel* (0323) 28760. *Editor:* Harry Gresty. Specialise in photo-features, both b&w and colour. Want human interest, oddity, glamour, pin ups, scientific, medical, etc., material suitable for marketing through own branches (London, San Francisco, Paris, Hamburg, Milan, Stockholm, Amsterdam (for Benelux), Helsinki) in many countries. Give full information, well researched. Willing to syndicate abroad material already old in the UK, whether articles or photos. May buy outright or handle on commission. Query with ideas/suggestions.

Bulls Presstjänst AB, Tulegatan 39, Box 6519, S-11383 Stockholm, Sweden *tel* 23 40 20 *cables* Pressbull *telex* 19 482 *fax* 15 80 10; **Bulls Pressedienst GmbH,** Eysseneckstrasse 50, 0-6000 Frankfurt am Main 1, Germany *tel* 59 04 18 *cables* Pressbull *telex* 412117 *fax* 596 22 67; **Bulls Pressetjeneste A/S,** Ebbells Gate 3, N-0183, Oslo 01, Norway *tel* 20 56 01 *cables* Bullpress *fax* 20 49 78; **Bulls Pressetjeneste,** Vesterbrogade 14B, DK-1620 Copenhagen V, Denmark *tel* 21 37 27 *cables* Pressbull *fax* 21 14 05; **Bulls Finska Försäljnings AB,** Hämeentie 55 A, Pl 28, SF-00581, Helsinki, Finland *tel* 717 766 *fax* 701 273. *Market:* newspapers, magazines and weeklies in Sweden, Denmark, Norway, Finland, Iceland, Germany, Austria and German-speaking Switzerland. *Syndicates:* dramatic and human interest picture stories; topical and well-illustrated background articles and series; photographic features dealing with science, people, personalities, glamour; condensations and serialisations of best-selling fiction and non-fiction, cartoons, comic strips, merchandising, newspaper graphics.

The Canadian Press (1919), Stephen Ward (Chief Correspondent), The Associated Press House, 12 Norwich Street, London EC4A 1EJ *tel* 071-353 6355 *fax* 071-583 4238. London Bureau of the national news agency of Canada.

Capital Press Service, 2 Long Cottage, Church Street, Leatherhead, Surrey KT22 8EJ *tel* (0372) 377451. *Directors:* M. Stone, E.W. Stone; *news editor:* Nicholas Miller. Stories of trade, commerce and industry for trade papers in this country and abroad. Interested in tobacco, confectionery, air-cargo affairs and business travel (including hotels, luggage, guides, new routes via air, sea, road and train) for UK and US journals.

Caters News Agency Ltd, 42 Bartholomew Street, Digbeth, Birmingham B5 5QW *tel* 021-616 1100 *telegraphic address* Copy, Birmingham. *Managing director:* R.P. Blyth. Collection of news and pictures throughout Midlands. Representatives of Overseas, National and Provincial Press.

Central Press Features, 20 Spectrum House, 32/34 Gordon House Road, London NW5 1LP *tel* 071-284 1433 *fax* 071-284 4494. Supplies every type of feature to newspapers and other publications in 50 countries. Included in over 100 daily and weekly services are columns on international affairs, politics, sports, medicine, law, finance, computers, video, motoring, science, women's and children's features, strips, crosswords, cartoons and regular 6-12 article illustrated series of international human interest; also editorial material for advertising features.

Compass News Features (1984), 13/17 New Burlington Place, Regent Street, London W1X 2JP *tel* 071-287 3660 *telex* 911110 Concep G *fax* 071-734 0627. *Managing editor:* Gerard Loughran. News features and graphics agency specialising in subjects relating to the developing world.

J.W. Crabtree and Son (1919), 36 Sunbridge Road, Bradford BD1 2AA *tel* (0274) 732937 (office)/637312 (home). News, general, trade and sport; information and research for features undertaken.

Crocodile Press, GPO Box 4164, Darwin, NT 0801, Australia *tel* (089) 412287. *Directors:* Linda Donaldson, Murray Thompson. Supplies varied human interest features to magazines and newspapers in many parts of the world.

Specialises in 'Australiana', but has Australian markets for foreign items, the more wacky or unusual the better; risqué acceptable. Pictures must be good quality, colour or b&w. Suggest query first. Commission 50%. Also some assignments accepted.

The Daily Telegraph Syndication, Ewan MacNaughton Associates, Alexandra Chambers, 6 Alexandra Road, Tonbridge, Kent TN9 2AA *tel* (0732) 771116 *fax* (0732) 771160. News, features, photography. World-wide distribution and representation.

Europa-Press, Sveavägen 47, 4th Floor, Box 6410, S-113 82, Stockholm, Sweden *tel* 8-34 94 35 *cables* Europress *fax* 8-34 80 79. *Managing director:* Sven Berlin. *Market:* newspapers, magazines and weeklies in Sweden, Denmark, Norway and Finland. *Syndicates:* high quality features of international appeal such as topical articles, photo-features, b&w and colour, women's features, short stories, serial novels, non-fiction stories and serials with strong human interest, crime articles, popular science, cartoons, comic strips.

Europress Features (UK), 18 St Chads Road, Didsbury, near Manchester M20 9WH *tel* 061-445 2945. Representation of newspapers and magazines in Europe, Australia, United States. Syndication of top-flight features with exclusive illustrations – human interest stories – showbusiness personalities. 30-35% commission on sales of material successfully accepted; 40% on exclusive illustrations.

Express Enterprises, division of **Express Newspapers plc,** Ludgate House, 245 Blackfriars Road, London SE1 9UX *tel* 071-928 8000 *cable* Lon Express *telex* 21841/21842 *fax* 071-922 7966. Photo library, strips, cartoons, features, book serialisations and rights, merchandising.

Features International, Tolland, Lydeard St Lawrence, Taunton TA4 3PS *tel* (0984) 23014 *cables* Deadline, Taunton *fax* (0984) 23901. *Editorial director:* Anthony Sharrock. Syndicates features to magazines and newspapers throughout the world. The agency produces a wide range of material – mainly from freelance sources – including topical articles, women's features and weekly columns. Distributes directly to all English-language countries. Agents throughout the Common Market countries, Scandinavia, Japan, the Americas and Eastern Europe. Buys copy outright and welcomes story ideas. Sae essential.

Gemini News Service, 9 White Lion Street, London N1 9PD *tel* 071-833 4141 *telex* 262433 Monref G (ref. M 3172) *fax* 071-837 5118. *Editor:* Derek Ingram; *general manager:* Bethel Njoku. Network of correspondents and specialist writers all over the world. Some opening for freelance. Specialists in news-features of international, topical and development interest. Preferred *length* 1000-1200 words.

Global Syndication & Literary Agency, Limited, 323 N. Euclid, Fullerton, California 92632, USA. *President:* A.D. Fowler. Interested in previously published books for possible syndication and placement of subsidiary rights. Our book reviewers always looking for non-fiction titles. US postage required for return of material.

Graphic Syndication (1981), 2 Angel Meadows, Odiham, Hants RG25 1AR *tel* (0256) 703004. *Manager:* M. Flanagan. Cartoon strips and single frames supplied to newspapers and magazines in Britain and overseas. *Terms:* 50%.

India-International News Service, *Head office:* Jute House, 12 India Exchange Place, Calcutta, 700001, India *tel* 209563, 206572, 711009 *telegraphic address* Zeitgeist. *Proprietor:* Ing H. Kothari, BSc, DWP(Lond), FIMechE, FIE, FVI, FInstD. 'Calcutta Letters' and Air Mail news service from Calcutta. Specialists in industrial and technical news. Public relations and publicity consultants. Publishes trade and professional journals.

INS (International News Service)/Irish International News Service, *Editor & managing director:* Barry J. Hardy, PC; *photo dept:* Jan Vanek, 7 King's Avenue, Minnis Bay, Birchington-on-Sea, East Kent CT7 9QL   *tel* (0843) 45022. News, sport, book reviews, TV, radio, photographic department; also equipment for TV films, etc.

International Fashion Press Agency, Mumford House, Mottram Road, Alderley Edge, Cheshire SK9 7JF   *tel* (0625) 583537   *fax* (0625) 584344. *Directors:* P. Bentham (managing), P. Dyson, L.C. Bentham, S. Fagette, J. Fox. Monitors and photographs international fashion collections and developments in textile and fashion industry. Specialist writers on health, fitness, beauty and personalities. Undertakes individual commissioned features. Supplies syndicated columns and pages to press, radio and TV (NUJ staff writers and photographers). Associate Companies specialise in Management Consultancy and PR.

International Feature Service, 104 rue de Laeken, 1000 Brussels, Belgium   *tel* 217-03-42   *fax* 217-03-42. *Managing director:* Max S. Kleiter. Feature articles, serial rights, tests, cartoons, comic strips and illustrations. Handles English TV-features and books; also production of articles for merchandising.

The International Press Agency (Pty) Ltd (1934), PO Box 67, Howard Place 7450, South Africa   *tel* (021) 531 1926   *fax* (021) 531 8789. *Manager:* Mrs T. Temple; *UK Office:* Mrs U.A. Barnett, PhD (*Managing Editor*), 19 Avenue South, Surbiton, Surrey KT5 8PJ   *tel* 081-390 4414   *fax* 081-398 8723. South African agents for many leading British, American and Continental Press firms for the syndication of comic strips, cartoons, jokes, feature articles, short stories, serials, press photos for the South African market.

Knight Features (1985), 20 Crescent Grove, London SW4 7AH   *tel* 071-622 1467   *fax* 071-622 1522. *Director:* Peter Knight; *associates:* Ann King-Hall, Robin Mackay Miller, Caroline Figini. World-wide selling of strip cartoons and major features and serialisations. Exclusive agent in UK and Republic of Ireland for United Feature Syndicate and Newspaper Enterprise Association.

London News Service, 68 Exmouth Market, London EC1R 4RA   *tel* 071-278 5661   *fax* 071-278 8480   *telex* 21120 quote M 1317. *Editor:* John Rodgers. World-wide syndication of features and photos.

Maharaja Features Private Ltd, 5/226 Sion Road East, Bombay 400022, India   *tel* 484776   *telex* 011-74406 Pcod In ref. DR-016   *fax* 22-4135638 ref. DR-05. *Editor:* K.R.N. Swamy; *managing editor:* K.R. Padmanabhan. Syndicates feature and pictorial material, of interest to Asian readers, to newspapers and magazines in India, UK and abroad. Specialists in well-researched articles on India by eminent authorities for publication in prestige journals throughout the world. Also topical features 1000-1500 words. Represents PA NewsFeatures and Central Press Features of London in India. *Illustrations:* b&w prints and colour transparencies.

New Blitz TV, Via Cimabue 5, 00196 Rome, Italy   *tel* 32 01 489, 32 00 620   *fax* 32 19 014. *President:* Vinicio Congiu; *sales manager:* Gianni Piccione; *graphic dept:* Giovanni A. Congiu; *literary* and *television depts:* Giovanni A. Congiu. Syndicates cartoons, comic strips, humorous books with drawings, general books, feature and pictorial material, environment, travels, throughout the world and Italy. Television: importation and dubbing TV series, documentaries, educational films and video for schools. Material from freelance sources required. Average rates of commission 60-40%, monthly report of sales, payments on receipt of invoice.

New Zealand Press Association, 85 Fleet Street, London EC4P 4AJ *tel* 071-353 7040.

North West News & Sports Agency Ltd (1956), 148 Meols Parade, Meols, Wirral L47 6AN *tel* 051-632 5261. News and sports coverage, Birkenhead, Bebington, Wallasey and Wirral.

Orion Press, 55 1-Chome, Kanda-Jimbocho, Chiyoda-ku, Tokyo 101, Japan *tel* (03) 3295-1402 *telegraphic address* Orionserv, Tokyo *fax* (03) 3295-1430. International press service.

PA NewsFeatures (the Feature Service of the Press Association Ltd), 85 Fleet Street, London EC4P 4BE *tel* 071-353 7440. *NewsFeatures editor:* Neil Williams. World-wide syndication to newspapers, magazines and trade journals of text and strip services.

Chandra S. Perera, Cinetra, 437 Pethiyagoda, Kelaniya, Sri Lanka *tel* 521885 *cables* 521885 Colombo *telex* 22973 Vithy–CE Attn Chandra Perera *fax* 548427 Vithy Com. Attn Chandra Perera. Press and TV news, news films on Sri Lanka and Maldives, colour and b&w photo news and features, photographic and film coverages, screenplays and scripts for TV and films, Press clippings. Broadcasting, television and newspapers; journalistic features, news, broadcasting and TV interviews.

Pixfeatures, P.G. Wickman, 5 Latimer Road, Barnet, Herts. EN5 5NU *tel* 081-449 9946 *fax* 081-441 6246. Specialises in sale of picture features and news to British, European and South African press.

The Press Association Ltd (1868), 85 Fleet Street, London EC4P 4BE *tel* 071-353 7440 *telegraphic address* Press Association, London. *Chief executive:* R.B. Simpson; *editor-in-chief:* C.T. Webb; *finance director:* R.C. Henry. National News Agency: screen teleprinter and viewdata news and sports, photos, features. Distributes world agencies' news in British Isles outside London.

Christopher Rann & Associates Pty Ltd (1977), 185 Melbourne Street, North Adelaide, South Australia 5006 *tel* (08) 267 2299 *fax* (08) 267 5524. *Proprietors:* C.F. Rann, J.M. Jose. Former BBC and CBS News foreign correspondents offering full range of professional PR, press releases, special newsletters, commercial intelligence, media monitoring. Major clients in Australia, Britain and Scandinavia. Welcomes approaches from organisations requiring PR representation or press release distribution.

Reportage Bureau RBL, Kalevankatu 14 C, 00100 Helsinki-10, Finland *tel* (9)0-640 522 *cables* Reportage Helsinki *telex* 123949 rbl sf. Philip Laszlo.

Republican Press (London), Craven House, 121 Kingsway, London WC2B 6PA *tel* 071-831 2965 *fax* 071-831 2549.

Reuters Limited, 85 Fleet Street, London EC4P 4AJ *tel* 071-250 1122 *telex* 23222.

Anton Rippon Press Services, 20 Chain Lane, Mickleover, Derby DE3 5AJ *tel* (0332) 512379 *fax* (0332) 292755. News, sport and feature coverage of East Midlands.

St Albans Crown Court News Agency, 134 Marsh Road, Luton LU3 2NL *tel* (0582) 572222 *telex* 826634.

Sandesa News Agency, 23 Canal Row, Colombo 1, Sri Lanka   *tel* 21507.
Director: Gamini Navaratne, BSc(Econ)Lond. Supplies – news, features, photos
and press cuttings to local and overseas newspapers and agencies.

Singer Media Corporation Inc. (division of Media Transasia), 3164 Tyler
Avenue, Anaheim, California 92801, USA   *tel* 714-527-5650. *President:* Kurt
Singer; *chairman:* J.S. Uberoi. Use 25 features every week which are distributed to publications in 35 countries. Current needs for reprint rights (no
originals): profiles of famous people – 1-3 parts; men's fiction; women's fiction
(high standard only); adventure features (which are not blood-dripping or
over-sexed); travel articles with transparencies; Westerns – short stories and
books; modern romance books; books published by reputable publishers. 'We
accept only previously published material.' Interested in books for serial and
book rights. World-wide syndication of cartoons, strips and interviews with
celebrities.

Solo Syndication & Literary Agency Ltd (1978), 49-53 Kensington High Street,
London W8 5ED   *tel* 071-376 2165   *fax* 071-938 3165. *Chairman:* Don Short.
World-wide syndication of newspaper features, photos, cartoons, strips and
book serialisations. Professional journalists only. *Commission:* 50/50. Agency
represents the international syndication of the London Daily Mail group, IPC
Magazines (*Woman*, *Woman and Home*, *Woman's Own*, *Woman's Realm*,
Woman's Weekly), News Ltd of Australia, *New Idea* and *TV Week*, Australia
and the Guinness Book of Records strip cartoon.

Southern Media Services (division of Maximedia Pty Ltd), PO Box 268, Springwood, NSW 2777, Australia   *tel* (047) 514 967   *fax* (047) 515 545. *Directors:*
Nic van Oudtshoorn, Daphne van Oudtshoorn. Illustrated features (colour
and b&w) to newspapers and magazines in Australasia and many parts of the
world. Also stock colour library. Assignments (news and feature stories,
photos) accepted at moderate rates. Syndicates freelance features and photo
features in Australia and abroad, but query before submitting. Commission
50% or by arrangement.

Swedish Features, Wennerbergsgatan 10, S–105 16 Stockholm, Sweden   *tel* 8-
738 30 00   *telex* 17480   *fax* 8-618 28 72. *Managing director:* Herborg Ericson.
Market: newspapers, magazines and weeklies in Sweden, Norway, Denmark
and Finland. *Syndicates:* high quality features of international appeal such as
topical articles, photo-features, b&w and colour, women's features, short
stories, serial novels, non-fiction stories and serials with strong human interest,
popular science, cartoons, comic strips and TV features and TV personalities.

Syndication International Ltd, 4-12 Dorrington Street, London EC1N 7TB   *tel*
071-404 0004   *fax* 071-430 2437. Agents for Mirror Group Newspapers, BBC
News and Current Affairs photos; *The Financial Times* photos and computer-
generated graphics. Extensive world travel pictures from Berlitz, the British
Tourist Authority and the English Tourist Board. Major photo library
specialising in pop, Royalty and personalities.

Tass Agency, Swan House, 37-39 High Holborn, London WC1V 6AA. General
news service to USSR   *tel* 071-404 8701; economic and commercial news
service to USSR   *tel* 071-430 9828   *telex* 24201   *fax* 071-430 9839.

Peter Tauber Press Agency (1950), 94 East End Road, London N3 2SX   *tel*
081-346 4165   *telegraphic address* Tauberpres N3. UK and world-wide syndication of exclusive big name celebrity interviews, especially interviews
with their associates or ex-associates. Also unique human interest features.
Commission 25%.

THC Newsfeatures Agency (1984), PO Box 9175, Ikeja, Nigeria *tel* 01-961509 *telex* 27207 Magna NG. *Directors:* Babatunde Harrison, Mrs Jemima Harrison. West African correspondents for broadcast and print media in English-speaking parts of the world. Services include special newsletters, market research, commercial and intelligence clippings. Welcomes approaches from organisations abroad requiring PR representation or press release distribution.

TransAtlantic News Service, 7100 Hillside Avenue, Suite 304, Hollywood, California 90046, USA *tel* 213-874-1284. News and photo agency serving the British and Foreign press. Staffed by former Fleet Street reporters, TANS supplies entertainment news, features and columns from Hollywood, and topical news in general from California. Covers all Hollywood events and undertakes commissions and assignments in all fields. Candid photos of stars at major Hollywood events a speciality.

United Press International, 2 Greenwich View Place, Millharbour, London E14 9NN *tel* 071-538 5310 (news), 071-538 5460 (audio), 071-538 0933 (admin), 071-538 0939 (sports) *telex* 28829 *fax* 071-538 1051.

Visual Humour (1984), 5 Greymouth Close, Stockton-on-Tees, Cleveland TS18 5LF *tel* (0642) 581847/021-429 5861 *fax* (0642) 581847. *Contact:* Peter Dodsworth. Daily and weekly humorous cartoon strips; also single panel cartoon features (not single cartoons) for possible syndication in the UK and abroad. Picture puzzles also considered. Submit photocopy samples only initially, with sae.

Eric Whitehead, Picture Agency and Library (1984), PO Box 33, Kendal, Cumbria LA9 4SU *tel* (05396) 21002, and 24 hour (0860) 534767. News coverage of Lancaster to Carlisle, Lake District.

Yaffa Newspaper Service of New Zealand, PO Box 509, 10 Spencer Street, Wellington 4, New Zealand *tel* (04) 793 531 *fax* (04) 797 221.

See also the **Agents** section for literary agents.

Books

SUBMITTING MANUSCRIPTS

Care should be taken when submitting manuscripts to book publishers. A suitable publisher should be chosen either by examining publishers' lists of publications or by looking out for the names of suitable publishers in the relevant sections in libraries and bookshops. It is a waste of time and money to send the MS of a novel to a publisher who publishes no fiction, or poetry to one who publishes no verse, though all too often this is done. A preliminary letter is appreciated by most publishers, and this should outline the nature and extent of the MS and enquire whether the publisher would be prepared to read it (writers have been known to send out such letters of enquiry in duplicated form, an approach not calculated to stimulate a publisher's interest). It is desirable to enclose the cost of return postage (International Reply Coupons if writing from outside the UK) when submitting the MS and finally it must be understood that although every reasonable care is taken of material in the publishers' possession, responsibility cannot be accepted for any loss or damage thereto.

Publishers are busy people, who collectively receive thousands of unsolicited MSS each year. Be patient, therefore, in awaiting a decision on your work. Most publishers acknowledge receipt of a MS: if you do not hear within a few days, it is permissible to check that your work has arrived safely. Some publishers – especially if your material is topical – will then decide fairly quickly, but a two months' wait is more usual. If you have not then heard, write politely asking for a decision.

For more on the submission of manuscripts, see *Typescripts* in the **Preparation of Material, Resources** section. See also the article *Writing for the European Community*, especially page 105.

Authors are strongly advised not to pay for the publication of their work. If a MS is worth publishing, a reputable publisher will undertake its publication at their own expense, except possibly for works of an academic nature. In this connection attention is called to the paragraphs on *Self-publishing* and *Vanity Publishing*, at the end of this section, and to the article on *Publishers' Agreements* in the **Publishing Practice** section.

SMALL PRESSES

It is beyond the scope of the *Yearbook* to list all the many smaller publishers which have either a limited output, or who specialise in poetry, avant-garde or other fringe publishing. Details are given of some of the better-known small poetry houses, but for a comprehensive listing of some 300 UK small presses, the reader is referred to the *Small Press Yearbook 1992* (£7.99 inc. p&p), published by Small Press Group, BM BOZO, London WC12 3XX   *tel* (0234) 211606.

List of Book Publishers

UNITED KINGDOM

(For Northern Ireland publishers, see under Irish listings on page 196.)

* Members of the Publishers Association

*AA Publishing (1979), Automobile Association, Fanum House, Basingstoke, Hants RG21 2EA *tel* (0256) 20123 *telex* 858538 Aabas G *fax* (0256) 22575. *Managing director:* John Howard, *marketing director:* John Barrett; *editorial manager:* Michael Buttler.
Travel, atlases, maps, leisure interests, including Baedeker titles, leisure interests.

Abacus—see **Sphere Books Ltd.**

*Abelard-Schuman Ltd—subsidiary company of **Blackie Children's Books.**

*Abson Books (1970), Abson, Wick, Bristol BS15 5TT *tel* (0275) 822446. *Partners:* Anthea Bickerton, Pat McCormack.
English speaking glossaries, guides, West Region. Literary puzzle books. No fiction.

*Academic Press, 24-28 Oval Road, London NW1 7DX *tel* 071-267 4466 *telex* 25775 Acpres G. *Managing director:* Joan M. Fujimoto; *editorial director:* Conrad Guettler.

*Academy Editions (1967), member of the Academy Group Ltd, 7-8 Holland Street, Kensington, London W8 4NA. *Editorial:* 42 Leinster Gardens, London W2 3AN *tel* 071-402 2141 *telex* 896928 Academ G *fax* 071-723 9540. *Director:* Dr A.C. Papadakis; *business manager:* Sheila De Vallee; *sales manager:* Penny Padovani.
Art, architecture, crafts, design, photography, fashion, urbanism, philosophy. *Series include Architectural Design* Profiles, Architectural Monographs, *Art and Design* Profiles, Art Monographs, and *UIA Journal, Journal of Philosophy and the Visual Arts, What Is . . .?.*

*Acorn Editions—imprint of **James Clarke & Co. Ltd.** Local books on East Anglia.

Actinic Press Ltd, 311 Worcester Road, Malvern, Worcs. WR14 1AN *tel* (0684) 565045 *Directors:* Leslie Smith, Audrey Smith.
Chiropody.

*Addison-Wesley Publishers Ltd (1970), Finchampstead Road, Wokingham, Berks. RG11 2NZ *tel* (0734) 794000 *telex* 846136 *fax* (0734) 794035. *Directors:* R. Bristow, Ann Dilworth (USA), W.R. Stone (USA), N.W. White, Frans Gianotten.
Educational, pure and applied sciences, engineering, computing, software, business studies, economics.

*Adlard Coles Nautical—imprint of **A. & C. Black (Publishers) Ltd.** Sailing.

*Adlib, 7-9 Pratt Street, London NW1 0AE *tel* 071-284 4474 *fax* 071-284 4234. Imprint of **Scholastic Publications Ltd.**
Children's fiction and non-fiction. No unsolicited MSS.

Airlife Publishing Ltd (1976), 101 Longden Road, Shrewsbury, Shropshire SY3 9EB *tel* (0743) 235651 *fax* (0743) 232944. *Directors:* Alastair Simpson (chairman and managing), Robert Pooley.

Aviation, technical and general, military, travel, local interest, country pursuits.

Ian Allan Ltd, Terminal House, Station Approach, Shepperton, Surrey TW17 8AS　*tel* (0932) 228950　*telex* 929806 Iallan G　*fax* (0932) 232366. *Editorial director:* Simon Forty.
Transport: railways, aircraft, shipping, road; naval and military history; reference books and magazines; no fiction.

*Philip Allan Publishers Ltd—booklist acquired by **Simon & Schuster International.**

*George Allen & Unwin Publishers Ltd—acquired by **HarperCollins Publishers.**

*J.A. Allen & Co. Ltd (1926), 1 Lower Grosvenor Place, Buckingham Palace Road, London SW1W 0EL　*tel* 071-834 0090/5606　*telegraphic address* Allenbooks, London　*telex* 28905 ref 3810　*fax* 071-976 5836. *Managing director:* Joseph A. Allen; *publishing director:* Caroline Burt.
Specialist publishers of books on the horse and equestrianism including bloodstock breeding, racing, polo, dressage, horse care, carriage driving, breeds, veterinary and farriery. Technical books usually commissioned but willing to consider any serious, specialist MSS on the horse and related subjects. Also willing to consider exceptionally well-written horse/pony related fiction suitable for young and teenage readers.

W.H. Allen—imprint of **Virgin Publishing Ltd.** *Managing and publishing director:* Robert Shreeve. True crime, politics, current affairs, popular science.

Allison & Busby—imprint of **Virgin Publishing Ltd.** Art, biography and memoirs, current affairs, general, history, international fiction, literary criticism, poetry, politics, translations, writers' guides.

*Anaya Publishers Ltd (1988), 3rd Floor, Strode House, 44-50 Osnaburgh Street, London NW1 3ND　*tel* 071-383 2997　*fax* 071-383 3076. *Chairman:* Germán Sánchez Ruipérez; *deputy chairman:* Sue Thomson; *managing director:* Colin Ancliffe; *publisher:* Yvonne McFarlane.
Reference: health, cookery, gardening, arts and crafts, sports and leisure, biography.

Andersen Press Ltd (1976), 20 Vauxhall Bridge Road, London SW1V 2SA　*tel* 071-973 9720　*telegraphic address* Literarius, London　*telex* 261212 Lit Ldn G　*fax* 071-233 6263. *Managing director/publisher:* Klaus Flugge; *directors:* Philip Durrance, Denise Johnstone-Burt (editorial), Joëlle Flugge (company secretary).
Children's picture books and fiction; international coproductions.

Angus & Robertson (UK) Ltd, 77-85 Fulham Palace Road, Hammersmith, London W6 8JB　*tel* 081-741 7070　*telex* 25611 Colins G　*fax* 081-307 6408. *Managing director:* Barry Winkleman; *editorial director:* Valerie Hudson.
Biography, cinema and TV, humour, leisure, health and self-help, Australia, language, true crime, popular science, designer's guides.

Antique Collectors' Club (1965), 5 Church Street, Woodbridge, Suffolk IP12 1DS　*tel* (0394) 385501　*telex* 987271 Antbok G　*fax* (0394) 384 434. *Directors:* John Steel, Diana Steel.
Fine art, antiques, garden history, architecture.

Anvil Press Poetry (1968), 69 King George Street, London SE10 8PX　*tel* 081-858 2946. *Directors:* Peter Jay, Julia Sterland.
Poetry. Submissions only with sae.

Apple Press (1984), The Old Brewery, 6 Blundell Street, London N7 9BH   *tel* 071-700 6700   *fax* 071-700 4191. Imprint of **Quarto Publishing plc**, book packagers.
Leisure, domestic and craft pursuits; cookery, gardening, sport, transport, militaria, fine and decorative art.

***Aquarian Press Ltd** (1952), 77-85 Fulham Palace Road, Hammersmith, London W6 8JB   *tel* 081-741 7070   *telex* 25611 Colins G   *fax* 081-307 4440. *Publishing director:* Eileen Campbell. Imprint of **HarperCollins Publishers.**
Popular and serious books on all New Age subjects including astrology, magic and occultism, the Western mystery tradition, the paranormal, psychic awareness, tarot and divination, and mythology. **Mandala Books**—quality New Consciousness list covering the Eastern tradition, psychology and therapy, religion and spirituality, philosophy and new science.

Argus Books, Argus House, Boundary Way, Hemel Hempstead, Herts. HP2 7ST   *tel* (0442) 66551   *fax* (0442) 66998. *Publisher:* Rab MacWilliam.
Modelling, model engineering, woodworking, hobbies, sport, aviation, railways, military, crafts, electronics, amateur winemaking, home brewing.

***Arkana**—'mind, body and spirit' list (formerly owned by Routledge) of **The Penguin Group**.

***Armada** paperbacks—imprint of **HarperCollins Publishers.** Children's books.

***Arms & Armour Press**—imprint of **Cassell plc.** *Editorial director:* Rod Dymott.
Military subjects (tanks, ships, aircraft, small arms, etc.).

***E.J. Arnold Publishing Division**—see **Thomas Nelson & Sons Ltd.**

***Edward Arnold** (1890), Mill Road, Dunton Green, Sevenoaks, Kent TN13 2YA   *tel* (0732) 450111   *telegraphic address* Expositor, Sevenoaks   *telex* 957703   *fax* (0732) 461321. *Directors:* Richard Stileman (managing), Philip Walters, Nick Dunton, Dave Mackin. Division of **Hodder & Stoughton Ltd,** *q.v.*
Textbooks and advanced works in humanities, social sciences, pure and applied science, and medicine; journals.

***Arrow Books Ltd,** Random Century House, 20 Vauxhall Bridge Road, London SW1V 2SA   *tel* 071-973 9700   *telex* 299080 Random G   *fax* 071-233 6127. *Directors:* Anthony Cheetham (chairman), Simon Master (managing), Mike Broderick (deputy managing), Alison Berry (editorial, Red Fox), Frances Coady (editorial, Vintage), Alison Wood (finance). Division of **The Random Century Group Ltd.**
Fiction, non-fiction, children's, reference, science fiction, fantasy, crime, detective fiction.
Imprints: Arrow, Red Fox, Rowan, Vintage, Legend, Hutchinson Reference.

Art Trade Press Ltd, 9 Brockhampton Road, Havant, Hants PO9 1NU   *tel* (0705) 484943. *Editorial director:* J.M. Curley.
Publishers of *Who's Who in Art.*

Ashford, Buchan and Enright (1985), 31 Bridge Street, Leatherhead, Surrey KT22 8BN   *tel* (0372) 373355   *fax* (0372) 363550. *Managing director:* John Mole.
Travel, field sports, nautical, general and military history.

Ashgrove Press Ltd (1980), 4 Brassmill Centre, Brassmill Lane, Bath BA1 3JN   *tel* (0225) 425539   *telex* 449212 Lantel G, quote Ashgrove   *fax* (0225) 319137. *Directors:* Robin Campbell (managing), William Allberry, Keith Nelson.
Health, healing and diet, complementary medicine, esoteric, self-help.

Aslib (The Association for Information Management) (1924), 20-24 Old Street, London EC1V 9AP *tel* 071-253 4488 *telex* 23667 *fax* 071-430 0514. (For further details see entry under **Societies, Associations and Clubs**.)

Associated University Presses—see **Golden Cockerel Press**.

*The Athlone Press Ltd (1949), 1 Park Drive, London NW11 7SG *tel* 081-458 0888 *telex* 262433 ref 1334. *Directors:* Brian Southam, Doris Southam, Clive Bingley.
Anthropology, archaeology, architecture, art, economics, history, language, law, literature, medical, music, Japan, oriental, philosophy, politics, psychology, religion, science, sociology.

Aurum Press Ltd (1977), 10 Museum Street, London WC1A 1JS *tel* 071-379 1256 *fax* 071-580 2469. *Directors:* Bill McCreadie, Piers Burnett, Sheila Murphy.
General, illustrated and non-illustrated adult non-fiction: biography and memoirs, visual arts, film, life style, travel.

*Avebury—imprint of **Gower Publishing Group Ltd**. Social science research.

Bernard Babani (Publishing) Ltd, The Grampians, Shepherds Bush Road, London W6 7NF *tel* 071-603 2581/7296 *fax* 071-603 8203. *Directors:* S. Babani, M.H. Babani, BSc(Eng).
Practical handbooks on radio, electronics and computing.

Bailey Bros. & Swinfen Ltd—list acquired by Shelwing Ltd, 127 Sandgate Road, Folkestone, Kent CT20 2BL.

*Baillière Tindall (1826), 24-28 Oval Road, London NW1 7DX *tel* 071-267 4466 *telex* 25775 Acpres G. *Managing director:* Joan M. Fujimoto; *editor-in-chief:* Sean Duggan.
Medical, veterinary, nursing, pharmaceutical books and journals. Agents for Iowa State University Press.

*Bantam paperbacks—imprint of **Transworld Publishers Ltd**. General fiction and non-fiction; young adult titles.

*Bantam Little Rooster paperbacks—imprint of **Transworld Publishers Ltd**. Children's picture books.

*Bantam Press (1985), 61-63 Uxbridge Road, London W5 5SA *tel* 081-579 2652 *telegraphic address* Transcable *telex* 267974 Trnspb G *fax* 081-579 5479. *Directors:* Mark Barty-King, Ursula Mackenzie. Imprint of **Transworld Publishers Ltd**.
Fiction, general, cookery, craft, business, crime, child care, health and diet, history, humour, military, music, paranormal, photography, politics, self-help, science, travel and adventure.

Arthur Barker Ltd, 91 Clapham High Street, London SW4 7TA *tel* 071-622 9933 *telex* 918066 Wpwnab G *fax* 071-627 3361. *Chairman:* Lord Weidenfeld; *directors:* Richard Hussey, Bud Pauling, Christopher Falkus, Alan Miles. Imprint of **George Weidenfeld & Nicolson Ltd**.
Sport, humour, showbusiness biographies.

*Barrie & Jenkins, Random Century House, 20 Vauxhall Bridge Road, London SW1V 2SA *tel* 071-973 9670 *telex* 299080 Random G *fax* 071-233 6125. *Directors:* Anthony Cheetham (chairman), Peter Roche (group financial), Julian Shuckburgh (managing), Euan Cameron (editorial, non-fiction), Julian Agnew (non-executive). Division of **The Random Century Group Ltd**.
Fiction, non-fiction, biographies and memoirs.

*Bartholomew (1826), 12 Duncan Street, Edinburgh EH9 1TA   *tel* 031-667 9341   *telex* 728134 Barts G   *fax* 031-662 4282. *Managing director:* Robert W. Fisher.
Maps, atlases, guides.

*B.T. Batsford Ltd (1843), 4 Fitzhardinge Street, London W1H 0AH   *tel* 071-486 8484   *telex* 943763 Crocom G ref. Bat   *fax* 071-487 4296. *Chairman:* Stephen Quinn; *managing director:* Peter Kemmis Betty; *directors:* Timothy Auger (editorial), Robert Beard (marketing and sales), John Faulder (non-executive), A.N. Finlay (finance; company secretary), R.E. Huggins (production; US Sales).
Archaeology, architecture, building (Mitchell imprint), art, catering, cinema, chess, costume, countryside, country sports, travel, craft, needlecraft, lace, history, horticulture, literary criticism, music, school library reference, social work, agriculture, technical/professional.

*BBC Books, Woodlands, 80 Wood Lane, London W12 0TT   *tel* 081-576 2000   *telex* 934678 BBCENT G   *fax* 081-749 8766. Division of **BBC Enterprises Ltd.** *Joint head of editorial:* Sheila Ableman, Suzanne Webber.
Books related to television and radio programmes of all subjects.

*Bedford Square Press, National Council for Voluntary Organisations, 26 Bedford Square, London WC1B 3HU   *tel* 071-636 4066   *fax* 071-436 3188. *Managing editor:* Jacqueline Sallon.
Practical guides, directories and titles on social issues covering child welfare, women's and ethnic minority concerns, the environment, self help and community development, voluntary sector concerns. Reference books, social planning and policy studies.

*Belhaven Press—see **Pinter Publishers Ltd.**

Belitha Press Ltd (1980), 31 Newington Green, London N16 9PU   *tel* 071-241 5566   *telex* 8950511 Oneone G ref 32159001   *fax* 071-254 5325. *Directors:* Martin Pick, Neil Champion, Richard Hayes, Peter Osborn, Rachel Pick (non-executive), Peter West, ACA.
Children's books, mostly published in series on an international co-edition basis; books about children; books for children in association with non-publishing organisations and video companies. No unsolicited TSS please. Associated film production company Inner Eye Ltd.

*Bell & Hyman Ltd—acquired by **HarperCollins Publishers.**

*Ernest Benn Ltd—see **A. & C. Black plc.**

David Bennett Books Ltd (1989), 94 Victoria Street, St Albans, Herts. AL1 3TG   *tel* (0727) 55878   *fax* (0727) 864085. *Managing director:* David Bennett.
Children's fiction, highly illustrated general non-fiction, poetry.

Bible Society, Publishing Division, Stonehill Green, Westlea, Swindon, Wilts. SN5 7DG   *tel* (0793) 513713   *telex* 44283 Bibles G   *fax* (0793) 512539. *Publishing director:* Dave Halls.
Bibles, testaments, portions and selections in English and over 200 other languages; also books on use of Bible for personal, education, church situations.

*Clive Bingley Ltd (1965), 7 Ridgmount Street, London WC1E 7AE   *tel* 071-636 7543   *fax* 071-636 3627. Imprint of **Library Association Publishing Ltd.**
Library and information science, reference works.

A. & C. Black plc (1807), 35 Bedford Row, London WC1R 4JH   *tel* 071-242 0946   *telex* 32524 Acblac G   *fax* 071-831 8478. *Directors:* Charles Black (chairman and joint managing), David Gadsby (joint managing), Leonard

Brown, William Still (secretary), Jill Coleman. Proprietors of A. & C. Black (Publishers) Ltd, Ernest Benn Ltd, Nautical Publishing Co. Ltd, Stanford Maritime, Christopher Helm (Publishers) Ltd, Adlard Coles Ltd.

*A. & C. Black (Publishers) Ltd (1978), 35 Bedford Row, London WC1R 4JH *tel* 071-242 0946 *telex* 32524 Acblac G *fax* 071-831 8478. *Chairman:* Charles Black; *managing directors:* Charles Black, David Gadsby; *directors:* Leonard Brown (production), Jill Coleman (children's books), Paul Langridge (rights), William Still (company secretary). Subsidiary of **A. & C. Black plc.** Children's and educational books (including music) for 3-15 years; arts and crafts, calligraphy, drama (*New Mermaid* series), fishing, nautical, reference (*Who's Who*), sport, theatre, travel (*Blue Guides*).

*Black Swan paperbacks—imprint of **Transworld Publishers Ltd.** Quality fiction.

*Blackie & Son Ltd (1809), Bishopbriggs, Glasgow G64 2NZ *tel* 041-772 2311 *telegraphic address* Blackie, Glasgow *telex* 777283 Blacki G *fax* 041-762 0897. *London office* 7 Leicester Place, WC2H 7BP *tel* 071-734 7521 *fax* 071-734 7525. *Chairman and managing director:* R.M. Miller; *directors:* J.W.G. Blackie, Alexander D. Mitchell, Dr A. Graeme Mackintosh, A. Rosemary Wands, Tim J. Rix, Martin C. West.
Educational (infant, primary, secondary); children's books (fiction and non-fiction for all ages); professional, reference and text books (biological sciences, earth sciences, chemistry, food technology, engineering, physics, mathematics, business administration).

*Blackie Children's Books, 7 Leicester Place, London WC2H 7BP *tel* 071-734 7521 *telex* 777283 Blacki G *fax* 071-437 0498. *Directors:* R.M. Miller, A.D. Mitchell, Martin West (children's publisher); Catherine White (rights), John Smith (sales, UK/Europe).
Children's books, novelty, picture, young fiction, poetry.

Blackstaff Press Ltd—see Irish Book Publishers.

*Blackwell Publishers (Basil Blackwell Ltd) (1922), 108 Cowley Road, Oxford OX4 1JF *tel* (0865) 791100 *telex* 837022 *fax* (0865) 791347. *Directors:* Nigel Blackwell (chairman), David Martin, Julian Blackwell, Mark Houlton, John Davey, James Nash, René Olivieri (managing), Janet Joyce, Philip Carpenter, Charles Ashford, George Bain, Sue Corbett.
Economics, education (academic), geography, history, industrial relations, linguistics, literature and criticism, politics, psychology, social anthropology, social policy and administration, sociology, theology, business studies, professional, law, reference, feminism, information technology, philosophy. **NCC-Blackwell**—joint venture company.

*Blackwell Scientific Publications Ltd (1939), Osney Mead, Oxford OX2 0EL *tel* (0865) 240201 *cables* Research, Oxford *telex* 83355 Medbok G *fax* (0865) 721205 *telecom gold dialcom* 79:BSP001. *Chairman:* Nigel Blackwell; *managing director:* Robert Campbell; *directors:* Keith Bowker, Clark Brundin, Jonathan Conibear, Oluf Møller, John Robson, Peter Saugman, Martin Wilkinson.
Medicine, nursing, dentistry, veterinary medicine, life sciences, earth sciences, computer science, chemistry, professional.

*Blandford Press—imprint of **Cassell plc.** *Editorial director:* Clare Howell. Art, crafts, gardening, history, hobbies, militaria, music, natural history, practical handbooks, aviculture.

Bloodaxe Books Ltd (1978), PO Box 1SN, Newcastle upon Tyne NE99 1SN *tel* 091-232 5988. *Directors:* Neil Astley, Simon Thirsk.
Poetry, literary criticism, literary biography, photography.

*Bloomsbury Publishing Ltd (1986), 2 Soho Square, London W1V 5DE *tel* 071-494 2111 *telex* 21323 Blooms *fax* 071-434 0151. *Chairman:* Nigel Newton; *directors:* Nigel Newton (managing), David Reynolds (publishing), Liz Calder (publishing), Alan Wherry (marketing), Kathy Rooney (editorial), Sarah Beal (publicity), Nigel Batt (finance), Lucy Juckes (sales), Ruth Logan (rights).
Fiction, biography, illustrated, reference, travel in hardcover, trade paperback and mass market paperback.

Blue Murder—see **Xanadu Publications Ltd.**

*Blueprint—imprint of **Chapman & Hall Ltd.** *Publisher:* Charlotte Berrill. Books for the publishing and printing industries.

*Bodley Head—see **Jonathan Cape Ltd.**

*Bodley Head Children's—see **Random Century Children's Books.**

Boethius Press (UK) Ltd (1973), 3 The Science Park, Aberystwyth, Dyfed SY23 3AH *tel* (0970) 615393 *fax* (0970) 615840. *Directors:* L.J. Hewitt (chairman), J.M. Hewitt (managing), J.M. Hewitt (secretary), J. Bradley, E.C. Nelson.
Music, natural history, Irish studies in archaeology and history, topography and plate books.

*Bowker-Saur Ltd, 60 Grosvenor Street, London W1X 9DA *tel* 071-493 5841 *fax* 071-499 1590. *Directors:* G.R.N. Cusworth (chairman), K.G. Saur (chief executive), S. O'Neill (managing), N. McPherson, D. Day. *Affiliates overseas:* K.G. Saur Verlag GmbH & Co KG, West Germany; D.W. Thorpe, Australia, R.R. Bowker, USA, D.W. Thorpe, New Zealand.
Bibliographies, trade and reference directories, library and information science, electronic publishing, abstracts and indexes.

Boxtree Ltd (1986), 36 Tavistock Street, London WC2E 7PB *tel* 071-379 4666 *fax* 071-836 6741. *Directors:* S. Mahaffy (managing), P Roche, D. Inman, A. Sington, C. Brown.
TV tie-ins (adult non-fiction, children's fiction and non-fiction), film and TV reference, mass market paperbacks linked to TV, film, rock and sporting events.

*Marion Boyars Publishers Ltd, 24 Lacy Road, London SW15 1NL *tel* 081-788 9522 *fax* 081-789 8122. *Directors:* Marion Boyars, Arthur Boyars.
Belles-lettres and criticism, fiction, sociology, open forum series, history of ideas, ideas in progress series, critical appraisals series, signature series, Iris series, music, travel, drama, cinema, dance, biography.

Boydell & Brewer Ltd (1969), PO Box 9, Woodbridge, Suffolk IP12 3DF.
Medieval history, literature, art history, country and sporting books. *No unsolicited MSS.*

Brassey's (UK) Ltd (1886), 50 Fetter Lane, London EC4A 1AA *tel* 071-377 4881 *fax* 071-377 4888. *Directors:* Maj. Gen. Anthony J. Trythall, cb, ma (executive deputy chairman), Jenny Shaw, BSc(Econ). MA (publishing). Member of the **Maxwell Macmillan Pergamon Publishing Corporation.**
Defence and national security, international relations, weapons technology, military affairs, military biography, military history, Soviet studies, reference.

*Brimax Books Ltd (1948), 4/5 Studlands Park Industrial Estate, Exning Road, Newmarket, Suffolk CB8 7AU *tel* (0638) 664611 *telex* 817625 Brimax G *fax* (0638) 665220. *Managing director:* Patricia Gillette. Subsidiary of **Reed International Ltd.**

Children's full colour gift books, early readers, pre-school, fiction and non-fiction.

*The British Library (Publications) (1973), Marketing & Publishing Office, Humanities & Social Sciences, 41 Russell Square, London WC1B 3DG   *tel* 071-323 7704   *telex* 21462   *fax* 071-323 7736. *Head of marketing & publishing:* Jane Carr; *managers:* David Way (publishing), Colin Wight (sales and retail), Anne Young (product development).
Bibliography, book arts, music, maps, oriental, manuscript studies, history, literature, facsimiles.

*British Museum Press (1973), 46 Bloomsbury Street, London WC1B 3QQ   *tel* 071-323 1234   *telex* 28592 Bmpubs G   *fax* 071-436 7315. *Directors:* H.J.F. Campbell, W.V. Davies, Sir Claus Moser, Graham C. Greene, HRH the Duke of Gloucester, Sir David Attenborough, Peter Bagnall, Sir Peter Harrop, KCB, Professor Peter Lasko, H.A. Stevenson, The Rt. Hon. Lord Windlesham, CVO, PC.
Art history, archaeology, numismatics, history, oriental art and archaeology, horology.

James Brodie Ltd (1926), 15 Springfield Place, Lansdown, Bath BA1 5RA   *tel* (0225) 317706. *Directors:* Corinne Wimpress (secretary), Jeremy Wimpress.
Educational (primary and secondary) books; literal classical translations.

Brown, Son & Ferguson, Ltd (1860), 4-10 Darnley Street, Glasgow G41 2SD   *tel* 041-429 1234 (24 hours)   *telegraphic address* Skipper, Glasgow   *fax* 041-420 1694. *Editorial director:* L. Ingram-Brown.
Nautical books; Scottish books and Scottish plays. Scout, Cub Scout, Brownie and Guide story books.

Burke Publishing Co. Ltd—stock acquired by **Harrap Publishing Group Ltd.**

Burns & Oates Ltd (1847), Publishers to the Holy See, Wellwood, North Farm Road, Tunbridge Wells, Kent TN2 3DR   *tel* (0892) 510850   *telex* 957258 Search G   *fax* (0892) 515903. *Directors:* Charlotte de la Bedoyere, Alfred Zimmermann.
Theology, philosophy, spirituality, church history, books of Catholic interest and children's books with religious themes.

Ed. J. Burrow & Co. Ltd (1900), Publicity House, Streatham Hill, London SW2 4TR   *tel* 081-674 1222   *fax* 081-674 8489. *Managing director:* Graham Horley.
Guide books, street plans and maps, industrial and economic development handbooks.

Business Books, Random Century House, 20 Vauxhall Bridge Road, London SW1V 2SA   *tel* 071-973 9670   *telex* 299080 Random G   *fax* 071-233 6125. *Directors:* Anthony Cheetham (chairman), Peter Roche (group financial), Lucy Shankleman (publishing), Ivan Fallon (non-executive). Division of **The Random Century Group Ltd.**
Business, management, advertising, communication, marketing, selling, investment, financial.
Imprint: Hutchinson Business Books.

*Butterworth & Co. (Publishers), Ltd—see **Butterworths.**

*Butterworth Architecture, Linacre House, Jordan Hill, Oxford OX2 8DP   *tel* (0865) 310366   *fax* (0865) 310898. *Editorial director:* Peter Dixon.
Architecture, the environment, planning, townscape, building technology; general.

*Butterworth-Heinemann, Linacre House, Jordan Hill, Oxford OX2 8DP *tel* (0865) 310366 *telex* 83111 Bhpoxf G *fax* (0865) 310898. *Directors:* Eric Newman (chief executive), Douglas Fox (managing), Peter Dixon, Charles Fry, Kathryn Grant, Chris Hunt (finance), Tony Llewelyn, Tom McGorry. Subsidiary of **Reed International Books Professional Division.**
Books and journals in business and management, engineering and technology, medicine and nursing, applied science and Made Simple Books.

*Butterworths (1818), 88 Kingsway, London WC2B 6AB *tel* 071-405 6900; and Borough Green, Sevenoaks, Kent TN15 8PH *tel* (0732) 884567 *telegraphic address* Butterworth, London *telex* 95678 Butwth G. *Directors:* G.R.N. Cusworth (chairman and chief executive), D.A. Day, I.A.N. Irvine, D.J. Jackson, P. Kirk, G. Marshall, A. Martin, P.J. Robinson, D.L. Summers, E.J. Newman, K.G. Saur.
Law, taxation, accountancy, banking.

*J. Calder Publications Ltd, 9-15 Neal Street, London WC2H 9TU *tel* 071-497 1741. *Director:* John Calder.
European, international and British fiction and plays, art, literary, music and social criticism, biography and autobiography, essays, humanities and social sciences, European classics. *No unsolicited typescripts.* Series include: Scottish Library, New Writing and Writers, Platform Books, Opera Library, Historical Perspectives. Publishers of *Gambit*, the drama magazine, and the *Journal of Beckett Studies*.

*Cambridge University Press (1534), The Edinburgh Building, Shaftesbury Road, Cambridge CB2 2RU *tel* (0223) 312393 *telex* 817256 Cupcam *telegraphic address* Unipress, Cambridge *fax* (0223) 315052; *USA* 40 West 20th Street, New York; NY 10011. *Australia* 10 Stamford Road, Oakleigh, Melbourne, Victoria 3166. *University printer and chief executive of the Press:* Geoffrey A. Cass, MA; *deputy chief executive and managing director (publishing division):* Anthony K. Wilson, MA; *deputy managing director and Press editorial director:* Jeremy Mynott, PhD; *director, American branch:* Alan Winter, MA; *director, Australian branch:* Kim W. Harris.
Archaeology, art and architecture, computer science, educational (primary, secondary, tertiary), educational software, English language teaching, history, language and literature, law, mathematics, medicine, music, oriental, philosophy, reference, science (physical and biological), social sciences, theology and religion. The Bible and Prayer Book. In 1990 CUP took over **Eyre & Spottiswoode Publishers,** a leading publisher of bibles and prayer books.

Canongate Press plc (1973), 16 Frederick Street, Edinburgh EH2 2HB *tel* 031-220 3800 *telex* 72165 Canpub *fax* 031-220 3888. *Chairman:* The Rt Hon. Lord Balfour of Burleigh; *directors:* Stephanie Wolfe Murray (managing), Neville Moir, R. Shanks.
Adult general non-fiction and fiction. **Canongate Classics**. Children's books. **Kelpie** paperbacks.

*Jonathan Cape Ltd, Random Century House, 20 Vauxhall Bridge Road, London SW1V 2SA *tel* 071-973 9730 *telex* 299080 Random G *fax* 071-233 6117. *Directors:* Tom Maschler, David Godwin (managing), Tim Chester (production), Tony Colwell (editorial, Cape), Chuck Elliot (editorial, Bodley Head), Jill Black (editorial, Bodley Head), Racheal Kerr (publicity), Georgina Capel (deputy managing and rights), Pete Dyer (art), Gaye Poulton (contracts). Division of **The Random Century Group Ltd.**
Archaeology, biography and memoirs, children's books, current affairs, drama, economics, fiction, history, philosophy, poetry, sociology, travel. *Imprints:* Jonathan Cape, Bodley Head.

Carcanet Press Ltd (1969), 208 Corn Exchange Buildings, Manchester M4 3BQ *tel* 061-834 8730. *Director:* Michael Schmidt (Mexico).
Poetry, memoirs (literary), Fyfield Books, translations, biography, fiction.

Cardinal—see **Sphere Books Ltd.**

Frank Cass & Co. Ltd (1958), Gainsborough House, 11 Gainsborough Road, London E11 1RS *tel* 081-530 4226 *telegraphic address* Simfay, London E11 *fax* 081-530 7795. *Directors:* Frank Cass (managing), A.E. Cass, M.P. Zaidner.
History, African studies, Middle East studies, economic and social history, military and strategic studies, international affairs, development studies, academic and law journals.

*****Cassell plc** (1848), Villiers House, 41-47 Strand, London WC2N 5JE *tel* 071-839 4900 *fax* 071-839 1804. *Chairman and managing director:* Philip Sturrock; *editorial directors:* Stephen Butcher (academic and educational), Clare Howell (general non-fiction/Ward Lock); *sales and marketing directors:* David Holmes (general non-fiction), Stephen Lustig (academic and educational); *sales managers:* Jonathan King (UK general non-fiction), Judith Entwisle-Baker (UK academic and educational), John Mills (export/general non-fiction), Liz White (export/academic and education), David Williams (special sales); *rights and permissions:* Chris White.
General, reference, religion, gardening, cookery, sport and pastimes, art and craft, natural history, education (primary, secondary, tertiary), business and professional, military, ELT.
Imprints Arms & Armour Press, Blandford Press, Cassell, Geoffrey Chapman, Mansell Publishing, Mowbray, New Orchard Editions, Studio Vista, Tycooly, Ward Lock, Wisley Handbooks.

*****Castle House Publications Ltd** (1978), 28-30 Church Road, Tunbridge Wells, Kent TN1 1JP *tel* (0892) 39606 *fax* (0892) 39609. *Director:* D. Reinders; *editor:* W. Reinders.
Medical.

Kyle Cathie Ltd (1990), 3 Vincent Square, London SW1P 2LX *tel* 071-834 8027/233 6674 *fax* 071-821 9258. *Publisher and managing director:* Kyle Cathie; *sales and marketing director:* Laura Beckwith.
History, natural history, health, biography, food and drink; poetry; translations of Classic texts.

Catholic Truth Society (1868), 38-40 Eccleston Square, London SW1V 1PD *tel* 071-834 4392 *telex* 295542 Pavis G. *Chairman:* Rt Revd Bishop Patrick Kelly, STL. PhL; *general secretary:* David Murphy, MA.
General books of Roman Catholic and Christian interest, Bibles, prayer books and pamphlets of doctrinal, historical, devotional, or social interest. MSS of 4000 to 5000 words or 2500 to 3000 words with up to six illustrations considered for publication as pamphlets.

Caxton & English Educational Programmes International Ltd, 52 Fetter Lane, London EC4 1AA *tel* 071-377 4899 *fax* 071-822 3319.
Encyclopedias, language courses, general interest.

CBD Research Ltd (1961), 15 Wickham Road, Beckenham, Kent BR3 2JS *tel* 081-650 7745 *fax* 081-650 0768. *Directors:* G.P. Henderson, S.P.A. Henderson, C.A.P. Henderson.

Directories, reference books, bibliographies, guides to business and statistical information.

Centaur Press Ltd (1954), Fontwell, Arundel, West Sussex BN18 0TA   *tel* Eastergate (0243) 543302. *Directors:* Jon Wynne-Tyson, Jennifer M. Wynne-Tyson, M.S. Cover, S.J. Cover, C.A. Vacher, C.G. Vacher.
Philosophy, environment, humane education, biography, the arts, reference. A preliminary letter should be sent before submitting MS.
Imprint: Linden Press.

*Century Publishing Ltd, Random Century House, 20 Vauxhall Bridge Road, London SW1V 2SA   *tel* 071-973 9670   *telex* 299080 Random G   *fax* 071-233 6125. *Directors:* Anthony Cheetham (chairman), Peter Roche (group financial), Rosemary Cheetham (publishing, fiction), Hilary Arnold (publishing, non-fiction), Caroline Upcher (editorial, fiction), Mark Booth (editorial, non-fiction), Fran Johnson (production), Louise Weir (publicity), Dallas Manderson (sales), Denise Lie (rights), Richard Trinder (financial), Chris Custance (home sales). Division of **The Random Century Group Ltd.**
Fiction, non-fiction, oriental religion and philosophy, mysticism and meditation, biographies and memoirs, romance, thrillers.
Imprints: Century, Rider, Barrie & Jenkins.

*W. & R. Chambers Ltd (1820), 43-45 Annandale Street, Edinburgh EH7 4AZ   *tel* 031-557 4571   *telegraphic address* Chambers, Edinburgh   *telex* 727967 Words G   *fax* 031-557 2936. *Chairman:* W.G. Henderson; *managing director:* J.C. Clement; *directors:* J. Osborne, C. McLaren, D. Crystal, R.A.C. Drew.
Dictionaries and reference books; educational (secondary, including mathematics, business studies, history, modern studies, social studies); Scottish books for tourists and home market.
Imprint Blackie-Chambers.

Chansitor Publications Ltd, St Mary's Works, St Mary's Plain, Norwich, Norfolk NR3 3BH   *tel* (0603) 615995   *fax* (0603) 624483. *Publisher:* G.A. Knights.
Religious, moral, personal and social education; Church Pulpit Year Book; *The Sign*, monthly religious news inset.

*Chapman & Hall Ltd, 2-6 Boundary Row, London SE1 8HN   *tel* 071-865 0066   *telex* 290164 Chapma G   *fax* 071-522 9623. *Directors:* P. Gardner (managing), A. Watkinson (publishing), J. Lavender (marketing), G. McDonald (book production), A. J. Davies (finance).
Scientific, technical, medical and professional publishers.

*Geoffrey Chapman—imprint of **Cassell plc.** *Publisher:* Ruth McCurry. Religion and theology.

Paul Chapman Publishing Ltd (1987), 144 Liverpool Road, London N1 1LA   *tel* 071-609 5315/6   *fax* 071-700 1057. *Directors:* P.R. Chapman (managing), Marianne Lagrange (editorial).
Business, management, accounting, finance, economics, geography, education, information technology.

*Chapmans Publishers (1989), 141-143 Drury Lane, Covent Garden, London WC2B 5TB   *tel* 071-379 9799   *fax* 071-497 2728. *Directors:* F.I. Chapman (chairman and managing), Marjory S. Chapman (editor-in-chief), Greg Hill (marketing and production), David North (sales).
Wide range of fiction and general non-fiction.

*Chatto & Windus, Random Century House, 20 Vauxhall Bridge Road, London SW1V 2SA   *tel* 071-973 9740   *telex* 299080 Random G   *fax* 071-233 6123.

Directors: John Charlton (chairman), Carmen Callil (managing), Catherine Eccles (deputy managing), Jenny Uglow (editorial, Hogarth), Jonathan Burnham (editorial, Chatto), Rupert Lancaster (editorial, Fodor), Gail Lynch (publicity), Barry Featherstone (production), Stuart Biles (sales). Division of **The Random Century Group Ltd.**

Archaeology, art, belles-lettres, biography and memoirs, cookery, crime/thrillers, current affairs, drama, essays, fiction, history, illustrated books, poetry, politics, psychoanalysis, translations, travel, hardbacks and paperbacks.

Imprints: Chatto & Windus, Hogarth Press, Fodor Guides.

Church of Scotland Department of Communication—see **The Saint Andrew Press.**

***Churchill Livingstone** (medical division of **Longman Group UK Ltd**), Robert Stevenson House, 1-3 Baxter's Place, Leith Walk, Edinburgh EH1 3AF *tel* 031-556 2424 *telex* 727511 Longman G *fax* 031-558 1278. *Managing director:* Andrew Stevenson; *directors:* Peter Shepherd (sales and marketing); Peter Richardson (publishing), John Richardson (publishing services), Sally Morris (Churchill Livingstone journals); *publishing managers:* Tim Horne, Mary Law, Simon Fathers.

Medical books and journals for students, trainees and practitioners; books and journals in nursing, midwifery, physiotherapy, complementary medicine, and other allied health disciplines.

Churchill Livingstone are the agent in Britain, Europe and Africa for the medical publications of Little, Brown.

Cicerone Press (1969), 2 Police Square, Milnthorpe, Cumbria LA7 7PY *tel* (05395) 62069 *fax* (05395) 63417. *Managing and sales director:* Dorothy Unsworth; *editorial director:* Walt Unsworth; *production director:* R.B. Evans. Guidebooks to the great outdoors – walking, climbing, etc. – Britain, Europe and world-wide; general books about the North of England. *No* fiction or poetry.

***Clarendon Press**—see **Oxford University Press.**

Robin Clark Ltd (1976), 27-29 Goodge Street, London W1P 1FD *tel* 071-636 3992 *fax* 071-637 1866. *Director:* N.I. Attallah (chairman). Member of the **Namara Group.**

Fiction, biography, social history.

T. & T. Clark (1821), 59 George Street, Edinburgh EH2 2LQ *tel* 031-225 4703 *telex* 728134 *fax* 031-220 4260. *Managing director:* Geoffrey F. Green, MA, PhD.

Law, philosophy, theology.

***James Clarke & Co. Ltd** (1859), PO Box 60, Cambridge CB1 2NT *tel* (0223) 350865 *fax* (0223) 66951. *Managing director:* Adrian Brink.

Theology, academic, reference books.

***Collets (Publishers) Ltd,** Denington Estate, Wellingborough, Northants. NN8 2QT *tel* (0933) 224351 *telex* 317320 Collet G *fax* (0933) 76402. *Directors:* Dr Eva Skelley, Steve Lytton.

Politics, art, music studies, travel guides, Russian and East European language study materials.

***W.H. & L. Collingridge Ltd**—imprint of **The Octopus Publishing Group.** Gardening and horticulture.

Rex Collings Ltd (1969), Chaceside, Coronation Road, South Ascot, Berks. SL5 9LB *tel* (0344) 872453 *fax* (0344) 872858; and 38 King Street, Covent

Garden, London WC2E 8JS *tel* 071-836 8634 *telex* 337340 Bookps G *fax* 071-497 9320. *Publisher:* Eric Agume Opia.
Children's books (12 years upwards), Africana, poetry, reference books.

Collins & Brown (1989), Mercury House, 195 Knightsbridge, London SW7 1RE *tel* 071-584 2002 *fax* 071-584 0138. *Publisher:* Mark Collins; *chairman:* Cameron Brown; *directors:* Gillian Hawkins (sales and marketing), Roger Bristow (art), Gabrielle Townsend (editorial).
Literature, history, practical photography, natural history, crafts, music, biography.

*****Collins Harvill**—imprint of **HarperCollins Publishers.** Africana; quality illustrated books; literature; literature in translation (especially Russian, Italian, French); quality thrillers.

Columbus Books Ltd—incorporated with **Harrap Publishing Group Ltd.**

The Condé Nast Publications—imprint of **The Random Century Group Ltd.** Highly illustrated home interest books.

*****Conran Octopus Ltd** (1984), 37 Shelton Street, London WC2H 9HN *tel* 071-240 6961 *telex* 296249 Conoct G *fax* 071-836 9951. *Directors:* Alison Cathie (managing), Anne Furniss (editorial), Mary Evans (art), Serena Harrison (production), Anne Dixon (marketing), Marlis Ironmonger (financial controller).
Interior design, DIY, crafts and hobbies, cookery, gardening, travel, antiques, photography, cinema, health and beauty, children's books.

Conservative Political Centre (1945), 32 Smith Square, London SW1P 3HH *tel* 071-222 9000 *telex* 8814563. *Director:* Alistair B. Cooke, OBE.
Politics, current affairs.

*****Constable & Co. Ltd** (1890), 3 The Lanchesters, 162 Fulham Palace Road, London W6 9ER *tel* 081-741 3663 fax 081-748 7562. *Chairman and managing director:* Benjamin Glazebrook; *directors:* Anthony Cheetham, Richard Dodman, Miles Huddleston, Richard Tomkins, Robin Baird-Smith, Jeremy Potter.
Fiction: general, thrillers, historical. General non-fiction: literature, biography, memoirs, history, politics, current affairs, food, travel and guide books, social sciences, psychology and psychiatry, counselling, social work, sociology, mass media.

Consumers' Association (1957), 2 Marylebone Road, London NW1 4DX *tel* 071-486 5544 *telex* 918197 *fax* 071-935 1606. *Chief executive:* John Beishon; *assistant director (book publishing):* Kim Lavely; *publishing manager:* Gillian Rowley.
Travel, restaurant, hotel and wine guides, medical, law and personal finance for the layman, gardening, education – including *Which?* titles.

Conway Maritime Press Ltd (1972), 101 Fleet Street, London EC4Y 1DE *tel* 071-583 2412 *fax* 071-936 2153. *Directors:* W.R. Blackmore (Managing), D.C. Greening, Catherine V. Blackmore.
Maritime and naval history, ship modelling.

Leo Cooper Ltd, 190 Shaftesbury Avenue, London WC2H 8JL *tel* 071-836 3141 *telex* 8954961 *fax* 071-240 9247. Imprint of **Pen & Sword Books Ltd.**
Specialist military publisher.

*****Corgi** paperbacks—imprint of **Transworld Publishers Ltd.** General fiction and non-fiction.

Cornwall Books—see **Golden Cockerel Press.**

*Coronet—imprint of **Hodder & Stoughton Ltd.** Fiction and non-fiction paperbacks.

Council for British Archaeology (1944), 112 Kennington Road, London SE11 6RE *tel* 071-582 0494. *Director:* Henry Cleere; Northern Office: The King's Manor, York YO1 2EP *tel* (0904) 433925. *Managing editor:* Julie Gardiner. British archaeology – academic; practical pocket handbooks; no general books.

*Country Life—imprint of **The Octopus Publishing Group.** Non-fiction.

Countryside Books (1976), 6 Pound Street, Newbury, Berks. RG14 7AB *tel* (0635) 43816. *Partners:* Nicholas Battle, Suzanne Battle.
County guides – walking, outdoor activity, local history; genealogy.

Cressrelles Publishing Co. Ltd, 311 Worcester Road, Malvern, Worcs. WR14 1AN *tel* (0684) 565045. *Directors:* Leslie Smith, Audrey Smith.
Children's and general publishing.

*Croom Helm Ltd—incorporated in **Routledge.**

The Crowood Press (1982), The Stable Block, Ramsbury, Marlborough, Wilts. SN8 2HR *tel* (0672) 20320 *telex* 449703 Telser G *fax* (0672) 20280. *Directors:* John Dennis (chairman and managing), Ken Hathaway, Rob Henderson, Neville Burrell.
Sport, equestrian, fishing, shooting and country sports, climbing and mountaineering, animal and land husbandry, gardening, dogs, health and social issues, crafts, transport, travel.

James Currey Ltd (1985), 54b Thornhill Square, London N1 1BE *tel* 071-609 9026 *telex* 262433 W6327 *fax* 071-609 9605. *Directors:* James Currey, Clare Currey, Keith Sambrook.
Academic studies of Africa, Caribbean, Third World: history, archaeology, economics, agriculture, politics, literary criticism, sociology.

Terrence Dalton Ltd (1966), Water Street, Lavenham, Sudbury, Suffolk CO10 9RN *tel* (0787) 247572 *fax* (0787) 248267. *Directors:* T.R. Dalton (chairman), T.A.J. Dalton, E.H. Whitehair (managing).
Maritime and aeronautical history, East Anglian interest and history.

The C.W. Daniel Company Ltd (1902), 1 Church Path, Saffron Walden, Essex CB10 1JP *tel* (0799) 21909 *fax* (0799) 513462. *Directors:* Ian Miller, Jane Miller.
Natural healing, homoeopathy, aromatherapy, mysticism.

Dartmouth Publishing Co. Ltd—associate company of **Gower Publishing Group Ltd.** International relations and international law.

*Darton, Longman & Todd Ltd (1959), 89 Lillie Road, London SW6 1UD *tel* 071-385 2341 *telegraphic address* Librabook, London SW6 *fax* 071-381 4556. *Directors:* C.J. Ward (managing), L.L. Kay, M.J. Pritchard.
Bibles, ethics, theology and religion, spirituality.

Darwen Finlayson Ltd—see **Phillimore & Co. Ltd.**

David & Charles plc (1960), Brunel House, Newton Abbot, Devon TQ12 4PU *tel* (0626) 61121 *telex* 42904 Books G *fax* (0626) 64463. *Chairman:* S.N. McRae; *managing director:* T.K. Stubbs; *directors:* N. Loasby, A. Paetke, C. Sage; *company secretary:* N. Page; *associate directors:* M. Clarke (sales and marketing), P. Spence (editorial).
Practical non-fiction: art, country, DIY and building, equestrian, fishing, gardening, general, hard craft, health, maritime, natural history and pets, photography, railways and transport, soft craft, Victorian Ordnance Survey maps,

walking and climbing. Preliminary letter with outline welcomed. *Authors' Guide* available on receipt of first class stamp.

Christopher Davies Publishers Ltd (1949), PO Box 403, Sketty, Swansea SA2 9BE *tel* (0792) 648825. *Directors:* Christopher Talfan Davies, K.E.T. Colayera, D.M. Davies.
History, leisure books, sport, general, Welsh interest, Welsh dictionaries, *Triskele Books*.

*Dean's—imprint of **The Octopus Publishing Group**. Children's books.

J.M. Dent & Sons Ltd (1888), 91 Clapham High Street, London SW4 7TA *tel* 071-622 9933 *telex* 918066 Wpwnab G *fax* 071-627 3361 *telegraphic address* Nicobar, London, SW4. *Directors:* Lord Weidenfeld (chairman), Richard Hussey, Alan Miles, Christopher Falkus. Subsidiary of **George Weidenfeld & Nicolson Ltd.**
Everyman's Encyclopaedia, Everyman's Reference Library, Everyman Paperbacks, Everyman Fiction, Classic Thrillers, Mastercrime, Healthright, Master Musicians.
Archaeology, biography, children's books (fiction, non-fiction), cookery, gardening, health and nutrition, humour, military history, music, natural history, photography, reference, science fact, literary fiction (no poetry). Preliminary letter/synopsis and sae requested before submitting MSS.

*André Deutsch Ltd (1950), 105-106 Great Russell Street, London WC1B 3LJ *tel* 071-580 2746 *cables* Adlib London WC1 *fax* 071-631-3253. *Chairman and managing director:* T.G. Rosenthal; *president and founder:* André Deutsch; *directors:* Christobel Kent, Laura Morris, Pamela Royds, Jeffrey Sains, Anthony Thwaite, Julian Tobin, Esther Whitby; *literary adviser:* Diana Athill.
Art, belles-lettres, biography and memoirs, fiction, general, history, humour, politics, travel, photography.

*André Deutsch Children's Books, 7-9 Pratt Street, London NW1 0AE *tel* 071-284 4474 *fax* 071-284 4234. Imprint of **Scholastic Publications Ltd**.
Children's fiction and non-fiction. No unsolicited MSS.

Dial Industry—see **Reed Information Services Ltd.**

*Dinosaur Publications—imprint of **HarperCollins Publishers**. Children's books.

John Donald Publishers Ltd (1973), 138 St Stephen Street, Edinburgh EH3 5AA *tel* 031-225 1146 *fax* 031-220 0567. *Directors:* Gordon Angus, D.L. Morrison (managing), Don Morrison (sales).
British history, archaeology, ethnology, local history, vernacular architecture, general non-fiction. **Sportsprint**—sports imprint.

Dorling Kindersley Ltd (1974), 9 Henrietta Street, Covent Garden, London WC2E 8PS *tel* 071-836 5411 *telex* 8954527 Deekay G *fax* 071-836 7570. *Chairman:* Peter Kindersley; *deputy chairman and publishing director:* Christopher Davis; *managing director:* Richard Harman; *directors:* Ruth Sandys (international sales), Clyde Hunter (UK sales), Alan Buckingham (adult), Mike Strong (children's), Rod Hare (continuity), Stuart Jackman (art), John Adams (special sales), Martyn Longly (production), Lyn Blackman (finance).
High quality illustrated books on non-fiction subjects, including health, cookery, gardening, crafts and reference; also children's non-fiction. Specialists in international co-editions.

*Doubleday (UK) (1989), 61-63 Uxbridge Road, London W5 5SA *tel* 081-579 2652 *telegraphic address* Transcable *telex* 267974 Trnspb G *fax* 081-579

5479. *Directors:* Mark Barty-King, Marianne Velmans, Sally Gaminara. Imprint of **Transworld Publishers Ltd.**
General fiction and non-fiction.

Downlander Publishing (1978), 88 Oxendean Gardens, Lower Willingdon, Eastbourne, East Sussex BN22 0RS *tel* (0323) 505814. *Patron:* Jane Gow, DBE; *directors:* Derek Bourne-Jones, MA(Oxon). FRSA, Hilary Bourne-Jones.
Poetry of a high literary standard. Preliminary letter and sae essential; no unsolicited MSS.

Dr Who—imprint of **Virgin Publishing Ltd.** Paperbacks.

Dragon's World Ltd, Paper Tiger Books (1975), High Street, Limpsfield, Surrey RH8 0DY *tel* (0883) 715044   *fax* (0883) 716032; and 26 Warwick Way, London SW1V 1RX *tel* 071-976 5477   *fax* 071-976 5429. *Directors:* H.A. Schaafsma, C.M.A. Schaafsma, Pippa Rubinstein (editorial), Leslie Cramphorn (sales and marketing).
High quality illustrated books on fantasy illustration and mythology, natural history, DIY and general interest subjects. Children's illustrated classics, natural history and general non-fiction.

Richard Drew Publishing Ltd—acquired by **W. & R. Chambers Ltd,** *q.v.*

Dryad, PO Box 38, Leicester LE1 9BU *tel* (0533) 510405   *telex* 341766 Dryad G *fax* (0533) 515015. *General manager:* J.A. Green.
Dryad *500 series* full colour craft booklets, workcards, patterns.

Gerald Duckworth & Co. Ltd (1898), 48 Hoxton Square, London N1 6PB *tel* 071-729 5986   *fax* 071-729 0015. *Directors:* D.C. Blake, R.J. Davies, M.J. Estorick, C.B. Haycraft (chairman and managing), H.G.L. Russell, D. Shutt, T. Smith, M. Village.
General, fiction, and academic.

Eagle Books Ltd (1988), 5 Castle Road, London NW1 8PR *tel* 071-284 4441   *fax* 071-284 3031. *Directors:* David Howgrave-Graham (managing), Elizabeth Hamilton (rights).
Children's information books: science, nature, astronomy, history, geography, social sciences.

Earthscan Publications Ltd (1987), 3 Endsleigh Street, London WC1H 0DD *tel* 071-388 2117   *telex* 261681 Eascan G   *fax* 071-388 2826. *Directors:* Neil Middleton (managing), Kate Griffin (marketing), Jonathan Sinclair-Wilson (publicity).
Third World issues including politics, sociology, feminism, cultural questions, environment, economics, current events.

***East-West Publications (UK) Ltd** (1977), 8 Caledonia Street, London N1 9DZ *tel* 071-837 5061   *fax* 071-278 4429. *Chairman:* L.W. Carp. *Editor:* B. Thompson.
General non-fiction, travel, Eastern studies, sufism. Children's imprint: **Gallery Children's Books.**

***Ebury,** Random Century House, 20 Vauxhall Bridge Road, London SW1V 2SA *tel* 071-973 9680   *telex* 299080 Random G   *fax* 071-233 6129. *Directors:* Gail Rebuck (chairman), Amelia Thorpe (managing), Derek Morrison (production), Barry Milton (special sales), Robert Gwyn-Palmer (rights), Nicky Cowan (publicity), Fiona McIntyre (editorial, Ebury), Romy Sinfield (editorial, Century Benham). Division of **The Random Century Group Ltd.**
Cookery, health, beauty, photography, travel, transport, humour, crafts, antiques, hobbies, gardening, natural history, DIY, diaries, stationery. Publishes books from *Good Housekeeping, Cosmopolitan, Harpers & Queen, She.*
Imprints: Ebury Press, Cresset, Century Benham.

Edinburgh House Press. All enquiries to: **Lutterworth Press,** *q.v.*

*Edinburgh University Press, 22 George Square, Edinburgh EH8 9LF *tel* 031-650 4218 *telegraphic address* Edinpress *telex* 727442 Unived G *fax* 031-662 0053.
Academic and general publishers. Archaeology, Islamic studies, information technology, sociology and anthropology, politics, history, social and economic history, visual arts, biological sciences, linguistics, literature (criticism), philosophy, medico-legal issues, law, Scottish studies. Imprint: **Polygon.**

Educational Explorers (1962), 11 Crown Street, Reading, Berks. RG1 2TQ *tel* (0734) 873103. *Directors:* M.J. Hollyfield, D.M. Gattegno.
Educational, mathematics: *Numbers in colour with Cuisenaire Rods*, languages: *The Silent Way*, literacy, reading: *Words in Colour*, educational films.

Element Books (1978), The Old School House, The Courtyard, Bell Street, Shaftesbury, Dorset SP7 8BP *tel* (0747) 51448 *fax* (0747) 51394. *Directors:* Michael Mann, Annie Walton, Jean Allen, David Alexander, David Porteous. Philosophy, mysticism, religion, psychology, travel, complementary medicine and therapies, astrology and esoteric traditions. Also practical art, antiques and general original non-fiction under **Broadcast** imprint.

Edward Elgar Publishing Ltd—associate company of **Gower Publishing Group Ltd.** Economics.

Elliot Right Way Books (1946), Kingswood Buildings, Brighton Road, Lower Kingswood, Tadworth, Surrey KT20 6TD *tel* Mogador (0737) 832202. Clive Elliot, Malcolm Elliot.
Independent specialist publishers of practical 'how to' paperbacks. The low-price *Paperfronts* series includes games, pastimes, horses, pets, motoring, sport, health, business, financial and legal, cookery, home and garden, family subjects and etiquette. Welcomes new ideas; editorial help provided.

ELM Publications (1977), Seaton House, Kings Ripton, Huntingdon, Cambs. PE17 2NJ *tel* (048 73) 238 *fax* (048 73) 359. Sheila Ritchie.
Educational books and resources (especially history); books and training aids (tutor's packs and software) for business and management; languages; library and information studies.

*Elsevier Science Publishers Ltd (1963), Crown House, Linton Road, Barking, Essex IG11 8JU *tel* 071-594 7272 *telegraphic address* Elsbark, Barking *telex* 896950 Appsci G *fax* 071-594 5942. *Publishers:* D.J. Haank (chief executive), R. Lomax, N. Paskin.
Agriculture, architectural science, building and civil engineering, chemistry, food technology, materials science, petroleum technology, pollution, polymers, plastics technology.

*Encyclopaedia Britannica International Ltd, Carew House, Station Approach, Wallington, Surrey SM6 0DA *tel* 081-669 4355 *telex* 23866 Enbri G *fax* 081-773 3631. *Managing director:* Joe D. Adams.

Enitharmon Press (1969), BCM Enitharmon, London WC1N 3XX. *Director:* Stephen Stuart-Smith.
Poetry, literary criticism, translations, art and photography. No unsolicited MSS.

Epworth Press, Wesley Methodist Church, Christ's Pieces, Cambridge CB1 1LB *tel* (0223) 355982/311085. *Editorial committee:* Dr Valerie Edden,

Professor Harold Guite (hon. sec.), Revd Dr Ivor H. Jones, Revd Graham Slater (chairman), Revd Michael Townsend.
Religion, theology, church history.

Ethnographica (1976), 19 Westbourne Road, London N7 8AN *tel* 071-607 4074. *Directors:* Stuart Hamilton, Jane Hansom.
Ethnography, history, anthropology, social studies, arts and crafts; catalogues and books produced for museums, galleries and universities in UK and overseas.

Eurobook Ltd—see **Peter Lowe (Eurobook Ltd).**

Euromonitor Publications (1972), 87-88 Turnmill Street, London EC1M 5QU *tel* 071-251 8024 *telex* 21120 Monref G 2281 *fax* 071-608 3149. *Directors:* T.J. Fenwick (managing), R.N. Senior (chairman).
Business and commercial reference, marketing information, European and International Surveys, directories.

Europa Publications Ltd, 18 Bedford Square, London WC1B 3JN *tel* 071-580 8236 *telex* 21540 Europa G *fax* 071-636 1664. *Directors:* C.H. Martin (chairman), P.A. McGinley (managing), J.P. Desmond, R.M. Hughes, P.G.C. Jackson, M.R. Milton, A.G. Oliver, J. Quinney.
Directories, international relations, reference, year books.

Evangelical Press of Wales (1955), Bryntirion, Bridgend, Mid Glamorgan CF31 4DX *tel* (0656) 655886 *fax* (0656) 656095. *Director:* E.W. James.
Theology and religion (in English and Welsh).

*Evans Brothers Ltd (1905), 2A Portman Mansions, Chiltern Street, London W1M 1LE *tel* 071-935 7160 *telegraphic address* Byronitic, London, W1 *telex* 8811713 Evbook G *fax* 071-487 5034. *Directors:* S.T. Pawley (managing), D.J. Ellis (sales and marketing), B.O. Bolodeoku (Nigeria).
Educational books, particularly primary and secondary for Africa, the Caribbean and Hong Kong, general books for Europe and Africa; pre-school and school library books for the UK.

Exley Publications Ltd (1976), 16 Chalk Hill, Watford, Herts. WD1 4BN *tel* Watford (0923) 50505 *telex* 927500 *fax* (0923) 818733. *Directors:* Richard Exley, Helen Exley, Lincoln Exley, Dalton Exley.
Humour, cartoon series, gift books, children's biographies, children's activity books, anthologies for special occasions. No unsolicited MSS; sae essential.

*Eyre & Spottiswoode Publishers—see **Cambridge University Press.**

*Faber & Faber Ltd (1929), 3 Queen Square, London WC1N 3AU *tel* 071-465 0045 *telex* 299633 Faber G *fax* 071-465 0034 *telegraphic address* Fabbaf London WC1. *Chairman and managing director:* Matthew Evans; *vice-chairman:* Tom Pasteur; *directors:* John Bodley, Dennis Crutcher, Patrick Curran, Giles de la Mare, T.E. Faber, Joanna Mackle, Robert McCrum, Peter Simpson (company secretary), Brigid Macleod, Susanne McDadd.
High quality general fiction and non-fiction; all forms of creative writing. For current lists, write to the above address.
Address all submissions (with sae or return postage) to the Editorial Department. In the case of MSS, preliminary letter required.

Faber & Faber (Publishers) Ltd (1969), 3 Queen Square, London WC1N 3AU *tel* 071-465 0045 *telegraphic address* Fabbaf, London, WC1 *telex* 299633 Faber G *fax* 071-465 0034. *Directors:* T.E. Faber (chairman), P. Crawley, G. de la Mare, T. Faber, N. Smith, Peter Simpson. Holding company of **Faber & Faber Ltd,** *q.v.*

Fabian Society (1884), 11 Dartmouth Street, London SW1H 9BN   *tel* 071-222 8877   *fax* 071-976 7153 (also controls **NCLC Publishing Society Ltd**).
Current affairs, economics, educational, political economy, social policy.

Facts on File (1941 USA; 1984 UK), Collins Street, Oxford OX4 1XJ   *tel* (0865) 728399   *telex* 83147 Viaor G   *fax* (0865) 244839. *Directors:* Alan Goodworth (managing), Sheila Dallas (editorial).
Arts, business, current affairs, dictionaries, general interest, history, literature and language, natural history, sciences, medical, sport, professional reference, politics, music, young adult.

*Fantail (1988), mass market children's imprint of **The Penguin Group,** 27 Wrights Lane, London W8 5TZ   *tel* 071-416 3000   *telex* 917181/2   *fax* 071-416 3099. *Editor:* Richard Scrivener.
Teenage media books, licensed character publishing, novelties, graphic novels, film and TV tie-ins.

Farming Press Books (1951), 4 Friars Courtyard, 30-32 Princes Street, Ipswich, Suffolk IP1 1RJ   *tel* (0473) 241122   *fax* (0473) 240501. *Manager:* Roger Smith.
Agriculture, humour, veterinary.

Fernhurst Books (1979), 33 Grand Parade, Brighton, East Sussex BN2 2QA   *tel* (0273) 623174   *fax* (0273) 623175. *Publisher:* Tim Davison.
Sailing, watersports, skiing, motoring.

Filmscan Lingual House, Longman House, Burnt Mill, Harlow, Essex CM20 2JE   *tel* (0279) 426721   *telex* 81259 Longmn G   *fax* (0279) 31059. *Managing director:* T.M. Hunt.
Educational video/book publishers. English Language Teaching (school and self-study material).

*Firefly Books—see **Wayland (Publishers) Ltd.**

Fishing News Books Ltd (1953), Osney Mead, Oxford OX2 0EL   *tel* (0865) 240201   *telex* 83355 Medbok G   *fax* (0865) 721205. *Manager:* Philip Saugman.
Commercial fisheries, aquaculture and allied subjects.

*Flamingo—imprint of **HarperCollins Publishers.** Paperback literary fiction; non-fiction.

*Focal Press, Linacre House, Jordan Hill, Oxford OX2 8DP   *tel* (0865) 310366   *telex* 83111 Bhpoxf G   *fax* (0865) 310898. *Publishing director:* Peter Dixon. Photography and media imprint of **Butterworth-Heinemann.**
Professional, technical and academic books on photography, broadcasting, film, television, radio, audio visual and communication media.

*Fodor Guides—imprint of **Chatto & Windus.** World-wide annual travel guides.

*Fontana—imprint of **HarperCollins Publishers.** Mass market, paperback fiction and non-fiction.

*Fontana Lions—imprint of **HarperCollins Publishers.** Paperback children's books.

G.T. Foulis & Co. Ltd, Sparkford, Yeovil, Somerset BA22 7JJ   *tel* North Cadbury (0963) 40635   *telex* 46212 Haynes G   *fax* (0963) 40825. *Directors:* J.H. Haynes (executive chairman), J. Scott (managing), R.T. Grainger, R.J. Stagg, A.C. Haynes, R.J. Henwood. Imprint of **Haynes Publishing Group.**
Motoring/motorcycling, marque and model history, practical maintenance and renovation, related biographies, motor/motorcycle sport, aircraft, nautical, aviation.

W. Foulsham & Co. Ltd (1819), Yeovil Road, Slough, Berks. SL1 4JH *tel* (0753) 26769 *telex* 849041 Sharet G *fax* (0753) 811409. *Editorial director:* B.A.R. Belasco.
General manuals, children's activity, educational, school library, popular occult, do-it-yourself, hobbies and games, sport, travel, art directories, collectibles.

The Foundational Book Co. Ltd, Trade: PO Box 659, London SW3 6SJ *tel* 071-584 1053. *Editorial director:* Mrs Peggy M. Brook.
Spiritual science.

Foundery Press—ecumenical imprint of **Methodist Publishing House.**

*****Fount Paperbacks**—imprint of **HarperCollins Publishers.** Religious.

Fourth Estate Ltd (1984), 289 Westbourne Grove, London W11 2QA *tel* 071-727 8993/243 1382 *fax* 071-792 3176. *Directors:* Victoria Barnsley, Michael Mason, John Newall, Giles O'Bryen, Patric Duffy, Andrew Gifford, Jim Markwick.
Current affairs, literature, guide books, popular culture, fiction, humour, architecture, design. Imprints: Guardian Books, Blueprint Monographs.

L.N. Fowler & Co. Ltd (1880), 1201-3 High Road, Chadwell Heath, Romford, Essex RM6 4DH *tel* 081-597 2491/2 *fax* 081-598 2428. *Editorial director:* C.J. Nagle.
Astrology, healing, creative thinking.

Free Association Books (1984), 26 Freegrove Road, London N7 9RQ *tel* 071-609 5646 *fax* 071-700 0330. *Directors:* R.M. Young, M. Arnold, L. Levidow.
Psychoanalysis and psychotherapy; political and cultural aspects of science, technology and medicine; history; biography, autobiography and memoirs, cultural studies.

W.H. Freeman & Co. Ltd (1959), 20 Beaumont Street, Oxford OX1 2NQ *tel* (0865) 726975 *fax* (0865) 790391. *Directors:* L. Chaput, G. Voaden, F. Fochetta, H. Morgan.
Science, technical, medicine, economics, psychology, archaeology.

*****Freeway**—paperback imprint of **Transworld Publishers Ltd.** Young adult books.

*****Samuel French Ltd** (1830), 52 Fitzroy Street, London W1P 6JR *tel* 071-387 9373 *fax* 071-387 2161. *Branches:* New York, Hollywood, Toronto. *Agents:* Cape Town, Dublin, Harare, Johannesburg, Nairobi, Sydney, Valletta, Wellington. *Directors:* Abbott Van Nostrand (chairman), John Bedding (managing), Neil Peters, Amanda Smith, Jerry Stalworth, Paul Taylor.
Publishers of plays and agents for the collection of royalties.

David Fulton Publishers Ltd (1987), 2 Barbon Close, Great Ormond Street, London WC1N 3JX *tel* 071-405 5606 *fax* 071-831 4840. *Editorial director:* David Fulton.
Education, educational psychology, special education, geography, office skills and personal computing, psychiatry.

Futura, 165 Great Dover Street, London SE1 4YA *tel* 071-334 4800 *fax* 071-334 4905/6. Division of **Macdonald & Co. (Publishers) Ltd.**
General paperback fiction and non-fiction. Imprints: Orbit, Troubadour.

Gaia Books Ltd, 66 Charlotte Street, London W1P 1LR *tel* 071-323 4010 *telex* 914074 Gaia G *fax* 071-323 0435; and 20 High Street, Stroud, Glos. GL5 1AS *tel* (0453) 752985 *fax* (0453) 752987. *Managing director:* Joss Pearson; *directors:* Imogen Bright, Robin Hayfield, FCA, Patrick Nugent, David Pearson, Susan Walby; *environmental consultant:* Norman Myers.
Illustrated reference books on ecology, natural living, health, mind.

Gairm Publications, incorporating Alex MacLaren & Sons, (1875), 29 Waterloo Street, Glasgow G2 6BZ   *tel* 041-221 1971. *Editorial director:* Derick Thomson.
(Gaelic and Gaelic-related only) dictionaries, language books, novels, poetry, music, children's books, quarterly magazine.

*Gallery Children's Books—imprint of **East-West Publications (UK) Ltd.**

Gateway Books (1982), The Hollies, Wellow, Nr Bath, Avon BA2 8QJ   *tel* (0225) 835127   *telex* 449212 Lantel G ref 197   *fax* (0225) 840012. *Publisher:* Alick Bartholomew.
Popular psychology, spirituality, health and healing, ecology, self help and metaphysics.

The Gay Men's Press—see **GMP Publishers Ltd.**

Gee & Son (Denbigh) Ltd (1808), Chapel Street, Denbigh, Clwyd LL16 3SW *tel* Denbigh (0745) 812020. *Director:* E. Evans.
Oldest Welsh publishers. Books of interest to Wales, in Welsh and English.

*Geographia—now **Bartholomew,** *q.v.*

Geographical Publications Ltd (1933), The Keep, Berkhamsted Place, Berkhamsted, Herts. HP4 1HQ   *tel* (0442) 862981. *Directors:* A.N. Clark, G.N. Clark, G.N. Blake, D.R. Denman; *secretary:* G.N. Clark.
Books on geography and land affairs, both on own account and jointly with other publishers. Publishers and general agents to World Land Use Survey and International Geographical Union.

*Stanley Gibbons Publications Ltd (1856), Parkside, Christchurch Road, Ringwood, Hants. BH24 3SH   *tel* (0425) 472363   *fax* (0425) 470247. *Managing director:* S. Northcote.

Robert Gibson & Sons Glasgow, Ltd (1885), 17 Fitzroy Place, Glasgow G3 7SF   *tel* 041-248 5674. *Directors:* R.D.C. Gibson, R.G.C. Gibson, Dr J.S. McEwan, M. Pinkerton, H.C. Crawford, N.J. Crawford.
Educational.

*Ginn & Company Ltd (1867), Prebendal House, Parson's Fee, Aylesbury, Bucks. HP20 2QZ   *tel* (0296) 88411   *telex* 83535 Ginn G   *fax* (0296) 25487. *Chairman:* N. Thompson; *managing director:* W.P. Shepherd; *directors:* C. Bushnell-Wye, D.J. Miller, N.G. Hall, Ann Foster.
Educational (pre-school to age 12).

*Mary Glasgow Publications Ltd (1956), Avenue House, 131-133 Holland Park Avenue, London W11 4UT   *tel* 071-603 4688   *telex* 311890 Mgpubs   *fax* 071-602 5197. *Directors:* J.-P. Dubois (chairman), P. St C. Proctor (managing), W.D. Antrobus, A.K. Scott.
Secondary Level modern language books and magazines; file publications (design and technology, French, German, geography, media studies and music).

GMP Publishers Ltd (1979), PO Box 247, London N17 9QR   *tel* 081-365 1545   *fax* 081-365 1252. *Directors:* Aubrey Walter, David Fernbach, James Sprague.
The Gay Men's Press imprint: modern, popular, historical/literary fiction, including translations from European languages, biography and memoir, history, drama, health, social and political questions, poetry, literary criticism, male photography, art; *Gay Verse:* collections of modern and past gay poets; *Gay Modern Classics:* reprints of gay fiction/non-fiction from past 100 years;

Édition Aubrey Walter: male photography both art and glamour, fine-art editions of gay artists. Also **Heretic Books,** *q.v.*

Godfrey Cave Associates Ltd (1975), 42 Bloomsbury Street, London WC1B 3QJ *tel* 071-636 9177 *telegraphic address* Godave London WC1 *telex* 266945 Macrol G *fax* 071-636 9091. *Directors:* John Maxwell, Jack Cooper. General non-fiction, reprints, remainders.

Golden Cockerel Press, 25 Sicilian Avenue, London WC1A 2QH *tel* 071-405 7979 *fax* 071-404 5504. *Directors:* Tamar Yoseloff, Thomas Yoseloff (USA). Academic. Imprints: **Associated University Presses**—literary criticism, art, music, history, film, theology, philosophy, Jewish studies, politics, sociology; **Cornwall Books**—antiques, history, film, general.

*Victor Gollancz Ltd (1927), 14 Henrietta Street, London WC2E 8QJ *tel* 071-836 2006 *telex* 265033 Vgbook G *fax* 071-379 0934. *Directors:* Stephen Bray, David Burnett, Jane Blackstock, Chris Kloet, Elizabeth Dobson, Joanna Goldsworthy, Liz Knights, Adrienne Maguire, Jo Henry, Lionel Foot, Richard Evans, Ian Craig, Ian Smith; *consultant:* Livia Gollancz.
Biography and memoirs, children's books, current affairs, fiction, crime fiction, science fiction, fantasy and macabre, history, music, mountaineering, natural history, sociology, travel. In association with Peter Crawley: Master Bridge Series, historical architecture, cookery, general.

Gomer Press (1892), Llandysul, Dyfed SA44 4BQ *tel* (055 932) 2371 *fax* (055 932) 3758. *Directors:* J. Huw Lewis, John H. Lewis.
Books in Welsh; biography, local history.

*Gower Publishing Group Ltd (1967), Gower House, Croft Road, Aldershot, Hampshire GU11 3HR *tel* (0252) 331551 *fax* (0252) 344405. *Chairman:* N.A.E. Farrow.
Practical management and business reference, library science, engineering, industrial technology. Academic monographs on the social sciences. Reference and scholarly works in art, architecture, music, humanities. Imprints: Avebury, Dartmouth Publishing Co. Ltd, Edward Elgar Publishing Ltd, Gower, Scolar Press, Variorum, Wildwood House Ltd.

*Grafton Books—imprint of **HarperCollins Publishers.** Paperback fiction and non-fiction.

Graham & Trotman Ltd (1972), Sterling House, 66 Wilton Road, London SW1V 1DE *tel* 071-821 1123 *telegraphic address* Infobooks London *telex* 298878 Gramco G *fax* 071-630 5229. *Directors:* A.M.W. Graham, S. Willcox, F.W.B. Van Eysinga, A. Visser, H.A. Pabbruwe, G. Monkhorst, P. le Bosquet.
International business, international law, finance and banking.

Granta Publications Ltd (1982), 2/3 Hanover Yard, Noel Road, Islington, London N1 8BE *tel* 071-704 9776 *fax* 071-704 0474. *Editor:* W.H. Buford; *managing director:* Derek Johns.
Fiction, autobiography, political non-fiction.

Green Books (1987), Ford House, Hartland, Bideford, Devon EX39 6EE *tel* (0237) 441621 *fax* (0237) 441203. *Chairman:* Satish Kumar; *managing director:* John Elford.
Ecology, philosophy, the arts.

Green Print—see **Merlin Press Ltd.**

Gresham Books, The Gresham Press, PO Box 61, Henley-on-Thames, Oxon RG9 3LQ *tel* (0734) 403789. *Chief executive:* Mrs M.V. Green.
Hymn books, prayer books, wood engraving.

Grisewood & Dempsey Ltd (1973), Elsley House, 24-30 Great Titchfield Street, London W1P 7AD *tel* 071-631 0878 *telex* 27725 *fax* 071-323 4694. *Managing director:* Daniel Grisewood; *directors:* Duncan Baird (managing), J.M. Bourgois, Librairie Nathan S.A., Margaret Barrett (accounts, company secretary), Jane Olliver, John Richards (production), John Grisewood, Henryk Wesolowski (sales and marketing). Publishing imprint: *Kingfisher Books.*
Children's reference, picture information books, activity books, history and geography, science, encyclopedias, story collections, anthologies, picture books; adult guides and reference.

Grub Street (1981), The Basement, 10 Chivalry Road, London SW11 1HT *tel* 071-924 3966/738 1008 *fax* 071-738 1009. *Director:* John B. Davies.
Adult non-fiction: aviation history, cookery, gifts and humour.

*****Guinness Publishing Ltd** (1954), 33 London Road, Enfield, Middlesex EN2 6DJ *tel* 081-367 4567 *cables* Mostest Enfield *telex* 23573 Gbrldn G *fax* 081-367 5912.
General reference books.

Gwasg Gee—see **Gee & Son (Denbigh) Ltd.**

Peter Halban Publishers Ltd (1986), 42 South Molton Street, London W1Y 1HB *tel* 071-491 1582 *fax* 071-629 5381. *Directors:* Martine Halban, Peter Halban.
General fiction and non-fiction; history and biography; Jewish subjects and Middle East.

Robert Hale Ltd (1936), Clerkenwell House, 45-47 Clerkenwell Green, London EC1R 0HT *tel* 071-251 2661 *telegraphic address* Barabbas, London EC1 *fax* 071-490 4958. *Managing director:* John Hale; *directors:* Eric Restall (production), Robert Kynaston (financial), Martin Kendall (marketing), Betty Weston (rights).
Adult general non-fiction and fiction.

*****Hamish Hamilton Ltd** (1931), 27 Wrights Lane, London W8 5TZ *tel* 071-416 3200 *telex* 917181/2 *fax* 071-416 3295. *Publishing director:* Andrew Franklin; *directors:* Jane Nissen, Trevor Glover, John Rolfe, John Webster, Karen Geary, Ruth Salazar, Nigel Sisson, Joy Harrison, Alexandra Pringle. A **Penguin Group** company.
Belles-lettres, biography and memoirs, children's books (fiction, non-fiction), current affairs, fiction, general, history, literature, music, politics, travel, psychology.

*****Hamish Hamilton Children's Books**—imprint of **The Penguin Group**. *Editorial director:* Jane Nissen. Children's fiction and picture books.

*****Hamlyn Publishing** (1947), Michelin House, 81 Fulham Road, London SW3 6RB *tel* 071-581 9393 *telex* 920191 *fax* 071-589 8419. *Executive director:* Tony Bovill; *publishing director:* Emma Blackley. Parent Company: **The Octopus Publishing Group.**
General non-fiction.

*****Patrick Hardy Books**—imprint of **Lutterworth Press**. Children's fiction.

*****Harper & Row**—acquired by **HarperCollins Publishers**. Medical, nursing.

*****HarperCollins Publishers** (1819), General, Children's, Educational and Religious Book Publishing Offices, 77-85 Fulham Palace Road, Hammersmith, London W6 8JB *tel* 081-741 7070 *telex* 25611 Colins G *fax* 081-307 4440. *Printing and distribution offices and editorial offices* for Bibles and reference books, Westerhill Road, Bishopbriggs, Glasgow G64 2QT *tel* 041-772 3200.

Chairman: T. Kitson; *chief executive:* E. Bell; directors: (trade) J. Lloyd (managing), J. Boothe (publishing); (children's) W. Mitchell (managing), G. Penston (publishing).

Archaeology, architecture, art, belles-lettres, Bibles, biography and memoirs, children's books (fiction, non-fiction, picture books, audio), current affairs, dictionaries, directories or guide books, educational (infants, primary, secondary), essays, fiction, general history, humour, liturgical books, maps and atlases, natural history, philosophy, practical handbooks, reference, science (history of), sports, games and hobbies, travel, theology and religion. Crime Club, Flamingo paperbacks, Fontana, Fontana Press, Fount Religious Paperbacks, Armada Children's paperbacks, Collins Harvill, Grafton Paperbacks, Paladin Books.

Harrap Publishing Group Ltd, Chelsea House, 26 Market Square, Bromley, Kent BR1 1NA   *tel* 081-313 3484   *telex* 28673 Consol G   *fax* 081-313 0702. *Directors:* E.R. Dobby (managing), J.L. Barbanneau (deputy managing), M.L. Hughes (deputy managing), I. Leggett (financial), J.-M. Bourgois, N. Solomon.

Dictionaries, reference, self-study language courses, travel and maps.

*Harvester Wheatsheaf (1969), Wolsey House, Wolsey Road, Hemel Hempstead, Herts. HP2 4SS   *tel* (0442) 231900   *telex* 82445   *fax* (0442) 252544. *Editorial director:* Robert Bolick. Division of **Simon & Schuster International Group.** History, English literature, philosophy, psychology, women's studies, cognitive science, economics, politics.

J.H. Haynes & Co. Ltd (trading as **Haynes Publishing Group**), Sparkford, Yeovil, Somerset BA22 7JJ   *tel* North Cadbury (0963) 40635   *telex* 46212 Haynes G   *fax* (0963) 40825. *Directors:* J.H. Haynes (chairman), Max Pearce (chief executive), J. Scott (managing), A.C. Haynes, Barry Squance, R.J. Stagg, P.B. Ward, R.T. Grainger, A. Bish.

Car and motorcycle owners workshop manuals, car handbooks/servicing guides, do-it-yourself books, aircraft, trains, nautical.

Haynes Publishing Group—see **J.H. Haynes & Co. Ltd.**

Headline Book Publishing plc (1986), Headline House, 79 Great Titchfield Street, London W1P 7FN   *tel* 071-631 1687   *telex* 268326 Headln G   *fax* 071-631 1958. *Chairman:* The Earl of Donoughmore (non-executive); *managing director:* Tim Hely Hutchinson; *directors:* Sue Beavan (production), Alan Brooke (non-fiction publishing), Jeremy Dawson, Sue Fletcher (joint deputy managing, editorial), Paul Coley (financial), Sian Thomas (joint deputy managing, sales and publicity), Christopher Weston, Jane Morpeth.

Fiction, biography, humour, food and wine, design, British heritage and countryside, military history, art history, sport, music, cinema, TV and film tie-ins, hardbacks and both trade and mass-market paperbacks.

Health Science Press—imprint of **The C.W. Daniel Company Ltd.** Homeopathy.

*William Heinemann Ltd, Michelin House, 81 Fulham Road, London SW3 6RB   *tel* 071-581 9393   *telex* 920191   *fax* 071-589 8437. Subsidiary of **The Octopus Publishing Group.** *Directors:* Helen Fraser (publisher), John Potter (publishing), Amanda Conquy, Peter Kilborn, Annie Garwood, Martin Cowell, Tom Weldon.

Art, biography and memoirs, belles-lettres, fiction, history, humour, travel. No unsolicited manuscripts considered.

*Heinemann Children's Reference—division of **Heinemann Educational Books Ltd.**

*Heinemann Educational—division of **Heinemann Educational Books Ltd.**

*Heinemann Educational Books Ltd, Halley Court, Jordan Hill, Oxford OX2 8EJ *tel* (0865) 311366 *telex* 837292 Hebox G *fax* (0865) 310043. *Directors:* N. Thompson (chairman), David Fothergill (managing), Bob Osborne (managing, Heinemann Educational), Mike Esplen (managing, Heinemann International), Richard Balkwill (managing, Heinemann Children's Reference), Vicky Unwin (managing, international literature and textbooks), Stephen Ashton, Guy Gerlach, Mark Stanton, Richard Gale, Yvonne De Henseler, Simon Watts, Kay Symons. Subsidiary of **Reed International Books.**
African studies, African writers, biology, chemistry, physics, mathematics, English, drama, history, geography, economics, business studies, home economics, modern languages, education, primary, English as a foreign language, library books.

*Heinemann International—division of **Heinemann Educational Books Ltd.**

*Heinemann Newnes—imprint of **Butterworth-Heinemann.**

*Heinemann Young Books, 38 Hans Crescent, London SW1 0LZ *tel* 071-581 9393 *telex* 920191 *fax* 071-584 0530. *Publisher:* Ingrid Selberg. Member of **The Octopus Publishing Group.**
Quality fiction, picture books and poetry for pre-school to mid-teens age range; some non-fiction for under-elevens.

*Christopher Helm—imprint of **A. & C. Black (Publishers) Ltd.** Ornithology, natural history, travel.

*Her Majesty's Stationery Office: *Head Office:* St Crispins, Duke Street, Norwich NR3 1PD *tel* (0603) 622211 *telex* 97301. *Distribution and order point:* PO Box 276, London SW8 5DT *tel* 071-873 0011 *telex* 297138. *Government Bookshops* (retail): 49 High Holborn, London WC1V 6HB *tel* 071-873 0011; 9-21 Princess Street, Manchester M60 8AS *tel* 061-834 7201; 71 Lothian Road, Edinburgh EH3 9AZ (wholesale and retail) *tel* 031-228 4181; 258 Broad Street, Birmingham B1 2HE *tel* 021-643 3740; Southey House, Wine Street, Bristol BS1 2BQ *tel* (0272) 264306; 80 Chichester Street, Belfast BT1 4JY *tel* (0232) 238451.
Archaeology, architecture, art, current affairs, directories or guide books, educational (primary, secondary, technical, university), general, history, naval and military, practical handbooks, reference, science, sociology, year books. As the Government Publisher, **HMSO** publishes only material sponsored by Parliament, Government Departments and other official bodies. Consequently it cannot consider unsolicited work submitted by private citizens.

*Herbert Press Ltd (1972), 46 Northchurch Road, London N1 4EJ *tel* 071-254 4379 *telex* 8952022 Ctytel G *fax* 071-254 4332. *Directors:* David Herbert, Brenda Herbert.
Art, architecture, design, crafts, art nostalgia, fashion and costume, natural history, archaeology, biography, illustrated non-fiction.

Heretic Books (1982), PO Box 247, London N17 9QR *tel* 081-365 1545 *fax* 081-365 1252. *Directors:* David Fernbach, Aubrey Walter.
Ecology, animal liberation, green politics, third world.

Nick Hern Books (1988), 20 Vauxhall Bridge Road, London SW1V 2SA *tel* 071-973 9000 *telex* 299080 Random G *fax* 071-233 6125. *Publisher:* Nick Hern. *Managers:* Jackie Bodley (editorial), Diane Petherick (sales). Division of **The Random Century Group Ltd.**
Theatre, plays.

*Adam Hilger, Techno House, Redcliffe Way, Bristol BS1 6NX *tel* (0272) 297481 *telex* 449149 Instp G *fax* (0272) 294318. Book imprint of the **Institute of Physics.**

Monographs, graduate texts, conference proceedings, in physics and physics-related science and technology, and popular science titles.

Hilmarton Manor Press (1964), Calne, Wilts. SN11 8SB   *tel* Hilmarton (0249 76) 208   *fax* (0249 76) 379. *Editorial director:* Charles Baile de Laperriere. Fine art, photography, antiques, visual arts.

*Hippo Books (1980), 7-9 Pratt Street, London NW1 0AE   *tel* 071-284 4474   *fax* 071-284 4234. Imprint of **Scholastic Publications Ltd.** Children's paperbacks – fiction and non-fiction. *No* unsolicited MSS.

Hippopotamus Press (1974), 22 Whitewell Road, Frome, Somerset BA11 4EL   *tel* Frome (0373) 66653. *Editors:* Roland John, Anna Martin. Poetry, essays, criticism. Publishes *Outposts Poetry Quarterly.* Poetry submissions from new writers welcome.

Hobsons Publishing plc (1974), Bateman Street, Cambridge CB2 1LZ   *tel* (0223) 354551   *fax* (0223) 323154. *Directors:* Adrian Bridgewater (chairman), T.G.P. Rogers, Vivian Coghill, Robert Baker, Roger Dalzell, Martin Morgan (managing), David Hepburn, Roger Gilbert, Andrew Round.
Careers guidance, PSIE, science, business studies, leisure, *Johansens Guides, Business of Horse Racing.* Publishers under licence to CRAC – Careers Research & Advisory Centre.

*Hodder & Stoughton Ltd (1868), Mill Road, Dunton Green, Sevenoaks, Kent TN13 2YA   *tel* (0732) 450111   *cables* Expositor Sevenoaks   *telex* 95122 Hodder G   *fax* (0732) 460134. *Editorial offices* Hodder & Stoughton, 47 Bedford Square, London WC1B 3DP   *tel* 071-636 9851   *telegraphic address* Expositor   *fax* 071-631 5248. *Executive chairman:* Philip Attenborough; *directors: fiction and paperback publishing:* Michael Attenborough; *non-fiction publishing:* Tom Biggs-Davison, Eric Major; *educational publishing:* Brian Steven; *academic publishing:* Richard Stileman; *divisional directors:* David Grant (children's books), J.A.G. Wilson (production).
Fiction (hardback and paperback), non-fiction, religious, children's (hardback and paperback), schoolbooks, further education, academic (medical, humanities, science, engineering and technology). See also: **Edward Arnold.**

*Hogarth Press—see **Chatto & Windus.**

*Holmes McDougall—list acquired by **HarperCollins Publishers.**

*Holt, Rinehart & Winston, 24-28 Oval Road, London NW1 7DX   *tel* 071-267 4466   *telex* 25775 Acpres G. *Managing director:* Joan M. Fujimoto. Educational books (school, college, university) in all subjects.

Horizon Books (1988), Plymbridge House, Estover Road, Plymouth, Devon PL6 7PZ   *tel* (0752) 705251   *telex* 45635 Hardis G   *fax* (0752) 695699. *Directors:* B.R.W. Hulme, M.W. Beevers, FCA (secretary). Travel.

Ellis Horwood Ltd (1973), Market Cross House, Cooper Street, Chichester, West Sussex PO19 1EB   *tel* (0243) 789942   *cables* Horwood Chichester   *telex* 86516 Elwood G   *fax* (0243) 778855. *Consultant:* Ellis Horwood, MBE; *directors:* Clive Horwood (managing), J. Gillison (production), Sue Horwood (consultant). Acquired by **Simon & Schuster International Group.**
Chemical science and engineering, computer science, artificial intelligence, cognitive science, cybernetics, engineering, environmental science, mathematics, medical science, physics, water science, food science, space science and space technology, aquaculture and fisheries support, biomedicine, applied science and industrial technology, information technology, biochemistry,

robotics, metallurgy, geology, entomology, corrosion science, energy and fuel science, polymer science, inorganic, organic, photo and physical chemistry.

How To Books Ltd (1991), Plymbridge House, Estover Road, Plymouth, Devon PL6 7PZ *tel* (0752) 705251 *telex* 45635 Hardis G *fax* (0752) 695699. *Managing director:* R.E. Ferneyhough; *secretary:* M.W. Beevers, FCA. *How To* series of achievement paperbacks covering student life, careers, employment and expatriate topics, business skills, education, parenting, community and life style development.

Hugo's Language Books (1864), Old Station Yard, Marlesford, Woodbridge, Suffolk IP13 0AG *tel* (0728) 746546 *fax* (0728) 746236. Hugo's language books and courses; distributors for Beekay & Pisces.

*Hulton Educational Publications Ltd—merged with **Stanley Thornes (Publishers) Ltd.**

Hunt & Thorpe (1989), 66 High Street, Alton, Hants GU34 1ET *tel* (0420) 83301 *fax* (0420) 83432. *Partners:* John Hunt, Debbie Thorpe. Children's and religious.

*C. Hurst & Co. (Publishers) Ltd (1967), 38 King Street, London WC2E 8JT *tel* 071-240 2666, (night) 081-852 9021 *fax* 071-240 2667. *Directors:* Christopher Hurst, Michael Dwyer. 'Area studies' covering contemporary history, politics, political economy, social studies, comparative religion of the developing world.

*Hutchinson Books Ltd, Random Century House, 20 Vauxhall Bridge Road, London SW1V 2SA *tel* 071-973 9680 *telex* 299080 Random G *fax* 071-233 6129. *Directors:* Gail Rebuck (chairman), Robyn Sisman (managing), Anthony Whittorme (editorial, Hutchinson), Paul Sidey (editorial, Muller), Neil Belton (editorial, Radius), Heather Schiller (rights), Bridget Sleddon (publicity), Dallas Manderson (sales), Stephen Esson (production). Division of **The Random Century Group Ltd.** Fiction, non-fiction, biographies and memoirs. *Imprints:* Hutchinson, Muller, Radius.

Hutchinson Business Books—see **Business Books.**

*Hutchinson Children's—see **Random Century Children's Books.**

*Hutchinson Education—list acquired by **Stanley Thornes (Publishers) Ltd.**

*Hutchinson Reference—imprint of **Arrow Books Ltd.** Encyclopedias, reference.

*International Textbook Co. Ltd, Bishopbriggs, Glasgow G64 2NZ *tel* 041-772 2311 *telex* 777283 Blacki G *fax* 041-762 0897. *Directors:* Dr Graeme Mackintosh, Michael Miller. Member of **The Blackie Group.** Professional, reference and text books in engineering, hotel and tourism management, business administration, food technology, chemistry, physics, biological sciences. Imprints: International Textbook Company, Leonard Hill, Surrey University Press.

*Inter-Varsity Press, 38 De Montfort Street, Leicester LE1 7GP *tel* (0533) 551700 *fax* (0533) 555672. Theology and religion.

Arthur James Ltd (1935), 1 Cranbourne Road, London N10 2BT *tel* 081-883 1831/2201/8307 and (0386) 446566 *fax* (0386) 446566/081-883 8307. *Directors:* D.M. Duncan, Jillian Tallon. Religion, sociology, psychology.

Jane's Information Group, 163 Brighton Road, Coulsdon, Surrey CR5 2NH *tel* 081-763 1030 *telex* 916907 *fax* 081-763 1005. *Managing director:* Michael Goldsmith.
Military, aviation, naval, non-fiction, reference.

Jarrold Publishing (1770), Barrack Street, Norwich NR3 1TR *tel* (0603) 763300 *telex* 97497 *fax* (0603) 662748. *Managing director:* Antony Jarrold; *publications manager:* Caroline Jarrold. Division of **Jarrold & Sons Ltd.**
Travel, sport, natural history.

Jewish Chronicle Publications, 25 Furnival Street, London EC4A 1JT *tel* 071-405 9252 *telex* 01 940 11415. *Executive director:* M. Weinberg.
Theology and religion, reference; *Jewish Year Book*, *Jewish Travel Guide*.

*****Johnson Publications Ltd** (1946), 130 Wigmore Street, London W1H 0AT *tel* 071-486 6757 *fax* 071-487 5436. *Directors:* M.A. Murray-Pearce, Z.M. Pauncefort.
Perfume, cosmetics, beauty culture and aromatherapy, including presentation/ *objets d'art*, advertising, marketing, biography and memoirs. Return postage should be sent with unsolicited manuscripts.

Jordan & Sons Ltd (1836), 21 St Thomas Street, Bristol BS1 6JS *tel* (0272) 230600 *telex* 449119 *fax* (0272) 230063 *DX* 78161 Bristol. *Publishing director:* Richard Hudson.
Law, particularly company and family (including the *Family Law Journal*), company administration, business, finance, looseleaf services.

*****Michael Joseph Ltd** (1935), 27 Wrights Lane, London W8 5TZ *tel* 071-416 3100 *telex* 917181/2 *fax* 071-416 3293. A **Penguin Group** company. *Publishing director:* Susan Watt; *directors:* Jenny Dereham, Nellie Flexner, Trevor Glover, John Rolfe, Ruth Salazar, Nigel Sisson, John Webster.
Belles-lettres, biography and memoirs, current affairs, fiction, general, history, humour, illustrated books (including **Mermaid** trade paperbacks).

The Journeyman Press—imprint of **Pluto Publishing Ltd.** Socialist, feminist, graphics, biography, social history, politics, philosophy, media handbooks.

Karnak House (1979), 300 Westbourne Park Road, London W11 1EH *tel* 071-221 6490 *fax* 071-229 3086. *Directors:* Dada A. Imarogbe (chairman), Amon Saba Saakana (editorial), Susan Harding (administration).
Anthropology, children's stories, education, Egyptology, fiction, history, language, linguistics, literary criticism, music, parapsychology, philosophy, poetry, prehistory.

Kelly's—see **Reed Information Services Ltd.**

Kelpie Books—see **Canongate Press plc.**

The Kenilworth Press Ltd (1990; incorporates **Threshold Books**, 1970), Addington, Buckingham MK18 2JR *tel* (029 672) 5101 *fax* (029 672) 5148. *Directors:* David Blunt, Deirdre Blunt.
Equestrian, including official publications for the British Horse Society and the Pony Club.

Kenyon-Deane Ltd, 311 Worcester Road, Malvern, Worcs. WR14 1AN *tel* (0684) 565045. *Directors:* Leslie Smith, Audrey Smith.
Plays and drama textbooks. Specialists in plays for women.

Kingfisher Books—publishing imprint of **Grisewood & Dempsey Ltd.** Children's books and general non-fiction.

Jessica Kingsley Publishers (1986), 118 Pentonville Road, London N1 9JN *tel* 071-833 2307 *fax* 071-837 2917. *Director:* Jessica Kingsley.

Psychology, therapy, social work, higher education policy, regional studies, education, engineering history.

*Kingsway Publications Ltd, 1 St Anne's Road, Eastbourne, East Sussex BN21 3UN *tel* (0323) 410930 *fax* (0323) 411970. *Directors:* Ray Bodkin, Bob Clark, Tony Collins, Nigel Coltman, Richard Herkes, Gordon Scutt (chairman), David Nickalls, Jon Paculabo, Peter Fenwick (executive chairman). Evangelical Christian books: testimony, teaching, children's books. Submit synopsis/2 sample chapters *only.*

Kluwer Publishing (1972), Croner House, London Road, Kingston-upon-Thames, Surrey KT2 6SY *tel* 081-549 1455. *Directors:* Hans Staal (managing), Chris Hilton-Childs (finance), Mike Brace (marketing). Subsidiary of Croner Publications Ltd.
Law, taxation, finance, insurance, business management, medicine, farming, looseleaf information services, books, databases, conferences.

*Knight—imprint of **Hodder & Stoughton Ltd.** Children's paperbacks.

Charles Knight Publishing, Tolley House, 2 Addiscombe Road, Croydon, Surrey CR9 5AF *tel* 081-686 9141 *fax* 081-686 3155. *Business publisher:* M.G. Pomel; *managing editor:* S.C. Cotter. Member of the **Benn Group.**
Looseleaf legal works on local government, offshore oil industry, construction industry, and technical subjects.

*Kogan Page Ltd (1967), 120 Pentonville Road, London N1 9JN *tel* 071-278 0433 *telex* 263088 Kogan G *fax* 071-837 6348. *Managing director:* Philip Kogan; *directors:* Pauline Goodwin (editorial), Peter Chadwick (production), Praba Kan (financial), Ben Kogan, Mark McNeish (sales), Dolors Black (associate, editorial).
Education, training, educational and training technology, journals, business and management, human resource management, transport and distribution, marketing, sales, advertising and PR, finance and accounting, directories, small business, careers and vocational, personal finance.

Kompass—see **Reed Information Services Ltd.**

*Ladybird Books Ltd (1924), Beeches Road, Loughborough, Leicestershire LE11 2NQ *tel* (0509) 268021 *telegraphic address* Ladybird, Loughborough *telex* 341347 Ldbird G *fax* (0509) 234672. *Chairman:* Paula Kahn; *managing director:* Anthony Forbes Watson; *directors:* M.G. Banks, D.P. Collington, B.D.L. Cotton, M.H. Gabb, R. Smith, A.T. Warren, J.D. Williamson.
Children's books, general and educational (infants, primary, junior and secondary).

*Allen Lane The Penguin Press, academic hardcover imprint of **The Penguin Group,** 27 Wrights Lane, London W8 5TZ *tel* 071-416 3000 *telex* 917181/2 *fax* 071-416 3099. *Chief editor:* Paul Keegan.
Non-fiction titles of academic and intellectual interest, principally but not exclusively the humanities.

Lawrence & Wishart Ltd, 144A Old South Lambeth Road, London SW8 1XX *tel* 071-820 9281 *telegraphic address* Interbook, London, SW8 *fax* 071-587 0469. *Directors:* R. Simon, J. Skelley, S. Davison, S. Sedley, S. Hayward, E. Munro, W. Norris, J. Taylor, J. Rodrigues, B. Kirsch.
Current affairs, economics, history, socialism and Marxism, literary criticism, philosophy, political economy, sociology, biography.

*Legend—imprint of **Arrow Books Ltd.** Science fiction and fantasy.

*Leicester University Press (1951), Fielding Johnson Building, University of Leicester, University Road, Leicester LE1 7RH *tel* (0533) 523333 *telex*

347250　*fax* (0533) 522200. *Publisher:* Alec McAulay. Division of **Pinter Publishers.**
Academic books, especially in history (including English local history and urban history), archaeology, politics and international relations, defence studies, English and foreign literature, museum studies and law.

Lennard Publishing, Windmill Cottage, Mackerye End, Harpenden, Herts. AL5 5DR　*tel* (0582) 715866　*fax* (0582) 715121. *Directors:* K.A.A. Stephenson, R.H. Stephenson. Division of **Lennard Associates Ltd.**
General adult non-fiction.

*****Charles Letts & Company Ltd** (1761), Diary House, Borough Road, London SE1 1DW　*tel* 071-407 8891　*fax* 071-403 6729. *Directors:* A.A. Letts (chairman), J.M. Letts, T.R. Letts, R.W. Aitken, J.W.B. Gibbs, C.J. Nott (managing), P.J. Casben (finance and company secretary), C. Saunders, R.D. Hall, N.E.M. Cuthertson.
Adult general non-fiction; diaries.

Lewis Masonic (1870), Terminal House, Shepperton TW17 8AS　*tel* Walton-on-Thames (0932) 222211　*telex* 929806 Iallan G　*fax* (0932) 232366. *Managing director:* C. Beach.
Masonic books; *Masonic Square Magazine.*

*****H.K. Lewis & Co. Ltd** (1844)—imprint of **Chapman & Hall Ltd.** Science, medical.

John Libbey & Co. Ltd (1979), 13 Smiths Yard, Summerley Street, London SW18 4HR　*tel* 081-947 2777　*telex* 94013503 John G　*fax* 081-947 2664. *Directors:* John Libbey, G. Cahn.
Medical: nutrition, obesity, epilepsy, neurology, diabetes, biological psychiatry; media communications.

*****Library Association Publishing Ltd** (1981), 7 Ridgmount Street, London WC1E 7AE　*tel* 071-636 7543　*telex* 21897 Laldn G　*fax* 071-636 3627. *Chairman:* E.M. Broome, OBE, FLA; *deputy chairman:* G. Cunningham, BA, BSc(Econ); *directors:* Jamie Cameron, MA (managing), R. Attwood, S.A. Brewer, MA, ALA, FBIM, B. Jover, BA, DipLIB, G. Page, J.M. Potter, MA, ALA, A.G.D. White, FBIM, ALA.
Library and information science, reference works, directories, bibliographies.

*****Lime Tree**—imprint of **Methuen London.** *Publisher:* Elsbeth Lindner; *publishing director:* John Potter. Fiction, cultural studies, current affairs, feminism, sexual politics, psychology, biography and autobiography, opera and classical music.

Frances Lincoln Ltd (1977), Apollo Works, 5 Charlton Kings Road, London NW5 2SB　*tel* 071-482 3302　*telex* 21376 Fralin G　*fax* 071-485 0490. *Directors:* Frances Lincoln (managing), Erica Hunningher (editorial, adult books), Janetta Otter-Barry (editorial, children's books).
Illustrated, international co-editions: gardening, interiors, design, health, crafts, children's books.

*****Lion Publishing plc** (1972), Peter's Way, Sandy Lane West, Oxford OX4 5HG　*tel* (0865) 747550　*telex* 837161 Lion G　*fax* (0865) 747568. *Directors:* David Alexander, Pat Alexander, Tony Wales, Mark Beedell, Robin Keeley, Denis Cole.
Reference, paperbacks, illustrated children's books, educational, gift books, religion and theology; all reflecting a Christian position.

Little, Brown and Company (UK) Ltd (1988), Beacon House, 30 North End Road, London W14 0SH　*tel* 071-603 1456　*fax* 071-603 0503. *Directors:*

Terry Melia (managing), Ian Sinclair, Robert Hyde. Subsidiary of **Little, Brown and Company**, Boston, USA.
Art, photography, gardens, travel, crafts, cookery, fiction, children's, calendars, stationery.

***Liverpool University Press** (1901), Robin Bloxsidge (Publisher), PO Box 147, Liverpool L69 3BX   *tel* 051-794 2231/7 (7 lines) *telex* 627095 Unilpl G   *fax* 051-708 6502.
Academic and scholarly books in a range of disciplines. Special interests: education, literature, social, political, economic and ancient history, archaeology, medicine, veterinary science and urban and regional planning.

London & International Publishers Ltd (1984), 49 St James's Street, London SW1A 1JT   *tel* 071-493 4561   *fax* 071-629 4435. *Directors:* S.J. Slater, J.A. Miller.
Publishing under The Stock Exchange Press in finance, investment, the securities industry.

***Longman Group Ltd** (1724), 5 Bentinck Street, London W1M 5RN   *tel* 071-935 0121   *telegraphic address* Longman, London, W1; Longman House, Burnt Mill, Harlow, Essex CM20 2JE   *tel* (0279) 426721   *telex* 81259 Longmn G   *telegraphic address/cables* Longman, Harlow   *fax* (0279) 431059/451946   *Chairman:* P. Kahn; *Directors:* R.G.B. Duncan, C.J. Rea, P. Warwick, J.D. Williamson (finance), M.G.P. Wymer (operations and planning), L.W. Herbert, A. Stevenson, M. Todd. *Associated companies:* Spain, Italy, France, West Germany, Netherlands, Greece, USA, Canada, Australia, New Zealand, Japan, Hong Kong, Singapore, Malaysia, Egypt, Nigeria, Zimbabwe, Kenya, Botswana, South Africa.
Atlases, audio-visual aids, children's, school, further education, university, scholarly, undergraduate, post-graduate, academic, scientific and technical, legal, financial, business education, dictionaries, reference, English language teaching, directories, learned journals; micro computer software, videos. Africana (including African studies and African and Caribbean literature). Medical—see **Churchill Livingstone**. Preliminary letter recommended before submitting MSS.

***Longman Law Tax and Finance,** 21-27 Lamb's Conduit Street, London WC1N 3NJ   *tel* 071-242 2548   *fax* 071-831 8119. *Directors:* L.W. Herbert (managing), R.E.M. Baynes, A.R. Wells, M.G. Smith, E.A.O. Bramwell, J.D. Williamson, J.E. Robinson, P. Warwick.
Books and professional journals on law, business, taxation, pensions, insurance, government contracting, finance and accountancy.

Peter Lowe (Eurobook Ltd) (1968), PO Box 52, Wallingford, Oxon OX10 0XU   *tel* (086732) 8333   *fax* (086732) 8263. *Directors:* P.S. Lowe, R. Lowe.
Illustrated general information books, natural history, gardening, books for children, young people and adults. *No* young children's picture books, children's or general fiction.

Lund Humphries Publishers Ltd, 16 Pembridge Road, London W11 3HL   *tel* 071-229 1825. *Directors:* Clive Bingley, Charlotte Burri, Lionel Leventhal, John Taylor.
Art, architecture, graphic art and design, Arabic language.

***Lutterworth Press** (1799), PO Box 60, Cambridge CB1 2NT   *tel* (0223) 350865   *fax* (0223) 66951. Subsidiary of **James Clarke & Co. Ltd.**
The arts, biography, children's books (fiction, non-fiction, picture, rewards), educational, environmental, general, history, leisure, philosophy, science, sociology, theology and religion.

Macdonald & Co. (Publishers) Ltd, 165 Great Dover Street, London SE1 4YA *tel* 071-334 4800 *fax* 071-334 4905/6. *Directors:* N. Webb (managing), B. Boote (Sphere), A. Samson (general), T. Bulgarelli (finance), P. Crosby (distribution).
Hardback and paperback fiction, general non-fiction and illustrated books. *Divisions/imprints* Abacus, Cardinal, Futura, Macdonald, Macdonald Illustrated, Noddy, Optima, Orbit, Queen Anne Press, Scribners, Scribners Crime, Sphere.

Macdonald Illustrated—imprint of **Macdonald & Co. (Publishers) Ltd.** *Director:* Hilary Foakes. Large illustrated and pocket books covering art, sciences, DIY, design and decoration, food and wine, popular encyclopedias.

*****McGraw-Hill Book Company (UK) Ltd,** McGraw-Hill House, Shoppenhangers Road, Maidenhead, Berks. SL6 2QL *tel* (0628) 23432 *telegraphic address* McGraw-Hill, Maidenhead *telex* 848484 Mchill G *fax* (0628) 770224. *Managing director:* Stephen White; *directors:* Roger Horton (editorial), Dan Jennings (financial).
Technical, scientific, professional reference, medical.

*****Macmillan Academic and Professional Ltd** (formerly **The Macmillan Press Ltd**), 4 Little Essex Street, London WC2R 3LF *tel* 071-836 6633. *Chairman:* A. Soar; *directors:* C. Paterson (managing), T.M. Farmiloe, J.F.K. Ashby, A. Gordon, R. Hartgill, H. Holt, D. Knight, J.W. Peacock.
Academic, scientific and technical works, learned journals, economics and world affairs, publishers of The Statesman's Year-Book, and other reference works.

*****Macmillan Education Ltd,** Brunel Road, Houndmills, Basingstoke, Hants RG21 2XS *tel* (0256) 29242. *Chairman:* A. Soar; *directors:* J.E. Jackman (managing), D. Knight, P. Murby, Prof. J.J. Thompson, C.R. Harrison, R. Jones-Parry, S. Kennedy, J. Winckler, G.W. Lennox, D.I. Robertson.
Primary, secondary, college and university textbooks.

*****Macmillan London Ltd,** 18-21 Cavaye Place, London SW10 9PG *tel* 071-373 6070 *fax* 071-370 0746. *Chairman:* A. Gordon Walker; *directors:* Felicity Rubinstein (managing), B.J. Davies, R. Philipps, J. Wood, S. Lutyens, N. McDowell, A. Kay, T. Florance, D. Macmillan, M. Fenton.
General fiction, biography and memoirs, history, military history, politics, cookery, gardening, crime/thrillers.

Julia MacRae Books (1979), 20 Vauxhall Bridge Road, London SW1V 2SA *tel* 071-473 9000 *telex* 299080 *fax* 071-233 6058. *Managing director:* Julia MacRae. Division of **The Random Century Group Ltd.**
Children's books, music and general non-fiction.

Magi Publications (1987), 55 Crowland Avenue, Hayes, Middlesex UB3 4JP *tel* 071-387 0610/388 9832 *fax* 071-383 5003. *Director:* M.S. Bhatia.
Children's picture books.

Mainstream Publishing Co. (Edinburgh) Ltd (1978), 7 Albany Street, Edinburgh EH1 3UG *tel* 031-557 2959 *fax* 031-556 8720; *London office:* 19 Minford Gardens, W1H 0AP *tel* 071-602 4558 *fax* 071-602 7263. *Directors:* Bill Campbell, Peter MacKenzie.
Literature, fiction, biography, history, politics, sport, alternative medicine, current affairs, popular paperbacks, art, photography, architecture.

*****Mammoth**—see **Mandarin Paperbacks.**

*****Manchester University Press** (1912), Oxford Road, Manchester M13 9PL *tel* 061-273 5530/5539 *telex* 666517 Uniman G *fax* 061-274 3346.

Works of academic scholarship: literary criticism, art, architecture, urban studies, cultural studies, history, politics, economics, life sciences. General books on North of England, specialises in international law, non-linear science, Spanish, Italian, German and French texts; social anthropology, sociology, special education. Sixth form/student texts.

*Mandala Books—see **Aquarian Press.**

*Mandarin Paperbacks (1989), Michelin House, 81 Fulham Road, London SW3 6RB *tel* 071-581 9393 *telex* 920191 *fax* 071-589 8450. *Publisher:* John Potter; *directors:* Max Eilenberg (editorial), Sue Freestone (editorial), Jane Carr (editorial), Robert Snuggs (sales). Member of **The Octopus Publishing Group.**
Paperback fiction, crime/thriller, humour, romance, TV tie-in, military, biography, business; imprints: **Mandarin, Minerva.** Children's fiction and non-fiction paperbacks; imprint: **Mammoth.**

The Mandeville Press (1974), 2 Taylor's Hill, Hitchin, Herts. SG4 9AD *tel* (0462) 450796. *Editor/proprietor:* Peter Scupham; *editor:* John Mole. Contemporary poetry.

*Mansell Publishing—imprint of **Cassell plc.** *Editorial director:* Stephen Butcher. Bibliographies in all academic subject areas and monographs in urban and regional planning, Islamic studies, librarianship, history.

Marshall Cavendish Books Ltd (1969), 58 Old Compton Street, London W1V 5PA *tel* 071-734 6710 *telex* 23880 Marcav G. *Directors:* Lim Chin Geok (chief executive), Reg Wright (publishing), Sarah Dixon (production). Cookery, crafts, gardening, do-it-yourself, general non-fiction.

Marshall Pickering (1928), 77-85 Fulham Palace Road, London W6 8JB *tel* 081-741 7070 *fax* 081-307 4064. *Managing director:* Ron Chopping. Imprint of **HarperCollins Publishers.**
Theology, music, popular religions, illustrated, children's, wide range of Christian books.

Martin Books, Fitzwilliam House, 32 Trumpington Street, Cambridge CB2 1QY *tel* (0223) 66733 *fax* (0223) 461428. Imprint of **Simon & Schuster International Group.**
Cookery, gardening and other popular subjects.

Martin Brian & O'Keeffe Ltd (1971), 78 Coleraine Road, Blackheath, London SE3 7PE *tel* 081-858 5164. *Director:* Timothy O'Keeffe.
General literature including biography, fiction, history, travel, science, economics and poetry.

Martin Robertson & Co. Ltd—now merged with **Blackwell Publishers.**

*Kenneth Mason Publications Ltd (1958), 12A North Street, Emsworth, Hants PO10 7DQ *tel* (0243) 377977 *fax* (0243) 379136. *Directors:* Kenneth Mason, M.A. Mason, P.A. Mason.
Nautical history, football, slimming and patent licensing. No poetry. Technical journals, high court law reports.

Meadowfield Press Ltd (1976), I.S.A. Building, Hackworth Industrial Park, Shildon, Co. Durham DL4 1LH *tel* Bishop Auckland (0388) 773065. *Directors:* Dr J.G. Cook, M. Cook, J.A. Verdon, A.M. Creasey.
Microbiology, zoology, archaeology, botany, biology.

Medici Society Ltd, 34-42 Pentonville Road, London N1 9HG *tel* 071-837 7099.
Publishers of the Medici Prints, greeting cards and other colour reproductions of Old Masters and Modern Artists.

Art, nature and children's books. Preliminary letter with brief details of the work requested.

Melrose Press Ltd (1969), 3 Regal Lane, Soham, Ely, Cambs. CB7 5BA *tel* Ely (0353) 721091 *fax* (0353) 721839. *Directors:* Ernest Kay, R.A. Kay, J.M. Kay, B.J. Wilson, N.S. Law, C. Emmett, FCA, V.A. Kay.
International biographical reference works, including *International Authors & Writers Who's Who.*

Mercury Books, Gold Arrow Publications Ltd, 862 Garratt Lane, London SW17 0NB *tel* 081-682 3858 *fax* 081-682 3859. *Directors:* N. Dale-Harris, A. Finn, B. Tomes, R. Postema.
Business books.

Merehurst Ltd (1982), Ferry House, 51/57 Lacy Road, Putney, London SW15 1PR *tel* 081-780 1177 *fax* 081-780 1714. *Group chief executive:* Edward Cox; *publisher:* Liz Allen; *sales and marketing director:* Clair Lister; *editorial director:* Shirley Patton.
Crafts and hobbies, cake decorating, cookery, floristry.

Merlin Press Ltd, 10 Malden Road, London NW5 3HR *tel* 071-267 3399 *fax* 071-284 3092. *Directors:* M.W. Eve, Jon Carpenter.
Green Print: green politics and the environment; **Seafarer Books:** traditional sailing. *No* unsolicited MSS please.

*****Mermaid**—see **Michael Joseph Ltd.**

Merrow Publishing Co. Ltd (1951), I.S.A. Building, Hackworth Industrial Park, Shildon, Co. Durham DL4 1LH *tel* Bishop Auckland (0388) 773065. *Directors:* J.G. Cook, M. Cook, J.A. Verdon, A.M. Creasey.
Textiles, plastics, popular science, scientific.

Methodist Church, Division of Education and Youth, 2 Chester House, Pages Lane, Muswell Hill, London N10 1PR *tel* 081-444 9845 *fax* 081-365 2471. Theology and religion.

Methodist Publishing House (1773), 20 Ivatt Way, Peterborough PE3 7PG *tel* (0733) 332202 *fax* (0733) 331201.
Hymn and service books, general religious titles, church supplies. **Foundery Press:** ecumenical titles.

*****Methuen Academic**—incorporated in **Routledge.**

*****Methuen Children's Books,** 38 Hans Crescent, London SW1X 0LZ *tel* 071-581 9393 *telex* 920191 *fax* 071-823 9406. *Publisher:* Rona Selby; *rights manager:* Kate Wilson. Member of **The Octopus Publishing Group.**
Children's books (picture, fiction, non-fiction, for young children to early teens).

*****Methuen London,** Michelin House, 81 Fulham Road, London SW3 6RB *tel* 071-581 9393 *telex* 920191 *fax* 071-589 8419. *Directors:* John Potter (publishing), Geoffrey Strachan (publishing), Ann Mansbridge (non-fiction), Pam Edwardes (drama), Anne Nicholson (rights). Member of **The Octopus Publishing Group.**
General fiction, biography and memoirs, history, current affairs, topography, humour. Performing arts under **Methuen Drama** imprint. Please write with synopsis before submitting MSS.

Michelin Tyre plc (1989), Davy House, Lyon Road, Harrow, Middlesex HA1 2DQ *tel* 081-861 2121 *telex* 919071 *fax* 081-863 0680. *Head of tourism department:* D.C. Brown.
Tourist guides, maps and atlases, hotel and restaurant guides.

Milestone Publications (1967), 62 Murray Road, Horndean, Hants PO8 9JL *tel* (0705) 592255 *fax* (0705) 591975. *Directors:* Nicholas J. Pine (managing), Lynda J. Pine.
Heraldic china, antique porcelain, business, economics.

*Harvey Miller Publishers (1968), 20 Marryat Road, London SW19 5BD *tel* 081-946 4426 *fax* 081-944 6082 *BTG:* 84:DDS 2017. *Directors:* H.I. Miller, E. Miller.
Art history, medical atlases.

J. Garnet Miller Ltd (1951), 311 Worcester Road, Malvern, Worcs. WR14 1AN *tel* (0684) 565045. *Directors:* Leslie Smith, Audrey Smith.
Drama, theatre, plays.

*Mills & Boon (Publishers) Ltd (1908), Eton House, 18-24 Paradise Road, Richmond, Surrey TW9 1SR *tel* 081-948 0444 *telex* 24420 Milbon G *fax* 081-940 5899. *Chairman:* J.T. Boon, CBE; *managing director:* R.J. Williams; *directors:* A.W. Boon, M.J. Westwell (financial), M.N. Saraceno (production), R. Hedley (export sales), F. Whitehead (editorial), N. Peters (direct marketing), H. Walton (retail marketing), G. Howe (paperback sales); *managers:* S. Lomax (export), C. Stevens (sales operations).
Romantic fiction in paperback and hardback. Imprints: **Silhouette, Worldwide.**

*Minerva—see **Mandarin Paperbacks.**

*Mitchell Beazley, Michelin House, 81 Fulham Road, London SW3 6RB *tel* 071-581 9393 *telex* 920191 *fax* 071-584 8268. *Directors:* Richard Charkin (executive), Simon McMurtrie (publishing), Tony Cobb (creative), Donald Porter (sales). Incorporating: Mitchell Beazley International Ltd, Mitchell Beazley London Ltd, Mitchell Beazley Encyclopaedias Ltd. Division of **The Octopus Publishing Group.**
Wine and food, antiques, architecture, interior style, art, gardening, photography, travel, health, reference.

*Monarch Publications Ltd, 1 St Anne's Road, Eastbourne, East Sussex BN21 3UN *tel* (0323) 410930 *fax* (0323) 411970. *Directors:* Ray Bodkin, Bob Clark, Tony Collins, Nigel Coltman, Richard Herkes, Gordon Scutt (chairman), David Nickalls, Jon Paculabo, Peter Fenwick (executive chairman).
Christian books: the arts, poetry, adult fiction and mission books (evangelism). Submit synopsis/2 sample chapters *only*.

Moorland Publishing Co. Ltd (1972), Moor Farm Road, Ashbourne, Derbyshire DE6 1HD *tel* (0335) 44486 *telex* 377106 Chacom G MPC *fax* (0335) 46397. *Directors:* Dr J.A. Robey (chairman and editorial director), C.L.M. Porter (managing), Mrs J.A. Cundy (administration), J. Angell.
Travel, collecting, countryside, gardening.

Morgan-Grampian Business Information Services (1977), Royal Sovereign House, 40 Beresford Street, Woolwich, London SE18 6BQ *tel* 081-855 7777 *telex* 896238 *fax* 081-316 0512. *General manager:* Glen Wilders.
Directories for the travel trade and engineering industries.

The Mothers' Union (1876), 24 Tufton Street, London SW1P 3RB *tel* 071-222 5533.
Religious, educational and social subjects connected with marriage and the family; religious books for adults and children; quarterly magazine *Home & Family*.

*Mowbray—imprint of **Cassell plc.** *Publisher:* Ruth McCurry. Religion and theology.

*Frederick Muller Ltd—imprint of **Hutchinson Books Ltd.** Biography and autobiography, cinema, fiction, history, humour.

*John Murray (Publishers) Ltd (1768) 50 Albemarle Street, London W1X 4BD *tel* 071-493 4361 *telegraphic address* Guidebook, London, W1 *telex* 21312 Murray G *fax* 071-499 1792. *Chairman:* John R. Murray (general books marketing); *managing director:* Nicholas Perren; *directors:* Grant McIntyre (general editorial), John G. Murray, CBE; Judith Reinhold (educational marketing); *company secretary:* John Roberts; *managers:* Beverley Waldron (production), Carlotta Lowe (rights).

General: art and architecture, biography, autobiography, fiction, letters and diaries, travel, exploration and guidebooks, Middle East, Asia, India and sub-continent, general history, health education, aviation, craft and practical. *No* unsolicited MSS please.

Educational: biology, chemistry, physics, business studies, economics, management and law, English, geography and environmental studies, history and social studies, mathematics, modern languages, technical subjects. Also self teaching in all subjects in *Success Studybook* series.

*National Christian Education Council (incorporating **Hillside Publishing** and **International Bible Reading Association**), Robert Denholm House, Nutfield, Redhill RH1 4HW *tel* Nutfield Ridge (0737) 82411 *fax* (0737) 822116.

Books on all aspects of Christian education. Material for children's work in the Church, also RE material for day schools. Activity, visual and resource material, religious drama and religious music.

The Natural History Museum (1881), Cromwell Road, London SW7 5BD *tel* 071-938 8963/9365 *fax* 071-938 9267.

Natural sciences; entomology, botany, geology, palaeontology, zoology.

*Nautical Books—now **Adlard Coles Nautical,** *q.v.*

*Thomas Nelson & Sons, Ltd (1798), Nelson House, Mayfield Road, Walton-on-Thames, Surrey KT12 5PL *tel* (0932) 246133 *telegraphic address* Thonelson, Walton-on-Thames *telex* 929365 Nelson G *fax* (0932) 246109. Subsidiary in Hong Kong. *Directors:* M.E. Thompson (managing), M.J. Givans, Brian Snaith, John Tuttle, Barry Hinchmore, Pamela Hutchinson.

Educational (infant, primary, secondary), school atlases and dictionaries, English language teaching world-wide, educational books for Africa, Caribbean and SE Asia.

New Beacon Books (1966), 76 Stroud Green Road, London N4 3EN *tel* 071-272 4889. *Directors:* John La Rose, Sarah White, Michael La Rose, Janice Durham.

Small specialist publishers: general non-fiction, fiction, poetry, critical writings, mainly concerning the Caribbean, Africa, Afro-America, Black Europe.

New Cavendish Books (1973), 3 Denbigh Road, London W11 2SJ *tel* 071-229 6765 *telex* 8951182 Gecoms G *fax* 071-792 0027. **White Mouse Editions Ltd** (1979).

Specialist books for the collector.

*New English Library Ltd (1957), Mill Road, Dunton Green, Sevenoaks, Kent TN13 2YA *tel* (0732) 450111 *cables* Expositor, Sevenoaks *telex* 95122 *fax* (0732) 460134. *Editorial offices:* 47 Bedford Square, London WC1B 3DP *tel* 071-636 9851 *telex* 885887 *fax* 071-631 5248. *Directors:* P.J. Attenborough, M.F. Attenborough, E.P. Major; *divisional director:*

Clare Bristow (publisher, NEL hardcover books). Division of **Hodder & Stoughton Ltd**, *q.v.*
Fiction and non-fiction.

***New Holland Publishers,** 37 Connaught Street, London W2 2AZ   *tel* 071-258 0204   *telex* 995448 Tythan G   *fax* 071-262 6184. *Managing director:* John Beaufoy; *editorial director:* Charlotte Parry-Crooke.
Illustrated books on natural history and travel, cookery, cake decoration, needlecrafts and handicrafts, gardening.

***New Orchard Editions**—imprint of **Cassell plc.** *Publishing director:* David Holmes. Antiques and collecting, children's, cookery, wines and spirits, gardening, history and antiquarian, illustrated and fine editions, military and war, natural history, reference and dictionaries, transport, travel and topography.

***Newnes**—imprint of **The Octopus Publishing Group.** Maps and non-fiction.

Nexus—imprint of **Virgin Publishing Ltd.**

***NFER-NELSON Publishing Co. Ltd** (1981), Darville House, 2 Oxford Road East, Windsor, Berks. SL4 1DF   *tel* (0753) 858961   *telex* 937400 Onecom G ref. 24966001   *fax* (0753) 856830. *Editorial director:* Keith Nettle.
Educational, occupational and psychological tests and assessments, educational research.

***Nicholson** (1967), HarperCollins Publishers, 77-85 Fulham Palace Road, Hammersmith, London W6 8JB   *tel* 081-741 7070   *telex* 25611 Colins G   *fax* 081-307 4440. *Publishing manager:* Louise Cavanagh.
London maps and guides. Waterways map and guides.

James Nisbet & Co. Ltd (1810), 78 Tilehouse Street, Hitchin, Herts. SG5 2DY   *tel* (0462) 438331   *fax* (0462) 431528. *Directors:* Miss E.M. Mackenzie-Wood, Mrs R.M. Mackenzie-Wood, Mrs A.A.C. Bierrum.
Dictionaries, educational (infants, primary, secondary).

The Nonesuch Press Ltd—see **Reinhardt Books Ltd.**

Northcote House Publishers Ltd (1985), Plymbridge House, Estover Road, Plymouth, Devon PL6 7PZ   *tel* (0752) 705251   *telex* 45635 Hardis G   *fax* (0752) 1695699. *Directors:* B.R.W. Hulme, M.W. Beevers, FCA.
Business and professional text and reference books, careers and training, accountancy, banking, economics, education, management, educational dance and drama, English literature.

W.W. Norton & Company (1980), 10 Coptic Street, London WC1A 1PU   *tel* 071-323 1579   *telegraphic address* Gavia, London WC1   *fax* 071-436 4553. *Directors:* Alan Cameron (managing), Donald Lamm (USA), Victor Schmalzer (USA), Eric Swenson (USA), Lord Bullock, FBA, Robin Denniston
History, biography, current affairs, sailing, English and American literature, economics, music, psychology, science.

***The Octopus Publishing Group** (1971), Michelin House, 81 Fulham Road, London SW3 6RB   *tel* 071-581 9393   *telex* 920191   *fax* 071-589 8419. *Directors:* Ian Irvine (chairman), Richard Charkin (chief executive), Tony Bovill, Sandy Grant, Arthur Philo, Mark Radcliffe, Nicolas Thompson, Gwyn Williams.
Subsidiaries: Hamlyn Publishing Group, William Heinemann Ltd, Secker & Warburg, Octopus Group, Brimax Books Ltd, Ginn & Co., Mitchell Beazley Ltd, George Philip Ltd, Heinemann Educational Books Ltd,

Heinemann Professional Publications Ltd, The Parent and Child Programme.

The Oleander Press (1960), 17 Stansgate Avenue, Cambridge CB2 2QZ *tel* (0223) 244688 *telegraphic address* Oleander. *Managing director:* P. Ward. Language, literature, Libya, Arabia and Middle East, Indonesia and Far East, Cambridgeshire, travel, medical history, reference. Preliminary letter required before submitting MSS; please send sae for reply.

Oliver & Boyd, Longman House, Burnt Mill, Harlow, Essex CM20 2JE *tel* (0279) 426721 *fax* (0279) 431059 *telex* 81259 Longman G. *Directors:* Chris Kington (divisional managing), Brian Willan (editorial). Division of **Longman Group Ltd.**
Educational material for primary and secondary schools; Scottish school books.

Michael O'Mara Books Ltd (1985), 9 Lion Yard, Tremadoc Road, London SW4 7NQ *tel* 071-720 8643 *fax* 071-627 8953. Michael O'Mara (chairman), Lesley O'Mara (managing director), David Roberts (editorial director).
General fiction and non-fiction: Royal books, murder and mystery anthologies, illustrated classics; children's books.

Omnibus Press/Music Sales Ltd (1976), 8/9 Frith Street, London W1V 5TZ *tel* 071-434 0066 *telex* 21892 Msldn G *fax* 071-439 2848. *Directors:* Robert Wise (managing – Music Sales Group), Frank Warren (Omnibus Press).
Rock music biographies, books about music.

Open Books Publishing Ltd (1974), Beaumont House, New Street, Wells, Somerset BA5 2LD *tel* (0749) 77276. *Directors:* P. Taylor (managing), C. Taylor.
Academic and general non-fiction; education, child development, medicine, human behaviour, local history.

Open University Press (1977), Celtic Court, 22 Ballmoor, Buckingham MK18 1XW *tel* (0280) 823388 *fax* (0280) 823233. *Directors:* John Skelton (managing), Richard Baggaley (editorial), Sue Hadden (production), Barry Clarke (financial).
Cultural studies, education, health studies, literature, politics, psychology, sociology.

Optima (1987), 165 Great Dover Street, London SE1 4YA *tel* 071-334 4800 *fax* 071-334 4905/6. *Director:* Harriet Griffey. Division of **Macdonald & Co. (Publishers) Ltd.**
Health, alternative medicine, women's studies, the environment, popular psychology, self-help.

Orbit—imprint of **Futura.** *Director:* John Jarrold. Science fiction and fantasy paperbacks.

Orchard Books (1985), 96 Leonard Street, London EC2A 4RH *tel* 071-739 2929 *telex* 262655 Groluk G *fax* 071-739 2318. *Directors:* Judith Elliott (managing/publisher), Marlene Johnson (finance/operations), Rita Ireland (production). Division of **The Watts Group.**
Children's picture books, fiction, poetry, novelty books.

Osprey (1968), 59 Grosvenor Street, London W1X 9DA *tel* 071-493 5841 *telex* 27278 *fax* 071-491 3803.
Aviation, automotive, military. See also **George Philip Ltd.**

Outposts Publications (1956), 72 Burwood Road, Walton-on-Thames, Surrey KT12 4AL *tel* (0932) 240712. *Founder:* Howard Sergeant, MBE; *director:* Jean Sergeant.
Poetry.

*Peter Owen Ltd, 73 Kenway Road, London SW5 0RE *tel* 071-373 5628/370 6093 *fax* 071-373 6760. *Managing director:* Peter L. Owen.
Art, belles-lettres, biography and memoirs, fiction, general, theatre.

Oxford Illustrated Press Ltd, Sparkford, Yeovil, Somerset BA22 7JJ *tel* (0963) 40635 *telex* 46212 Haynes G *fax* (0963) 40825. *Editorial:* The Gables, Newington, Oxford OX9 8AH *tel* Oxford (0865) 890026. *Directors:* J.H. Haynes (executive chairman), J. Scott (managing), Jane Marshall (editorial), R.J. Stagg, A.C. Haynes, R.J. Henwood. Imprint of **Haynes Publishing Group.**
Well-illustrated non-fiction books, sport, leisure and travel guides, car books, art books, general.

Oxford Publishing Company (1976), Sparkford, Yeovil, Somerset BA22 7JJ *tel* (0963) 40635 *telex* 46212 Haynes G *fax* (0963) 40825. *Chairman:* J.H. Haynes; *editor:* P. Nicholson. Imprint of **Haynes Publishing Group.**
Railway transport.

*Oxford University Press (1478), Walton Street, Oxford OX2 6DP *tel* (0865) 56767 *telex* 837330 Clarpress *fax* (0865) 56646 *cables* Clarendon Press, Oxford. *Chief executive and secretary to the delegates:* Sir Roger Elliott; *deputy secretary and finance director:* W.R. Andrewes; Art and Reference Division: *managing director:* Ivon Asquith; *directors:* Simon Wratten (sales and marketing, and dictionary publishing), B. Townsend (production), George Taylor (UK sales); head of rights: David Wynn. Science, Medical and Journals Division: *managing director:* John Manger, *marketing director:* Kate Jury. Education Division: *managing director:* Fiona Clarke; *sales director:* Martin Cuss. ELT Division: *managing director:* Peter Mothersole; *sales director:* David Stewart.
Branches or offices in New York, Toronto, Melbourne, Auckland, Delhi, Bombay, Calcutta, Madras, Karachi, Lahore, Cape Town, Johannesburg, Durban, Nairobi, Dar es Salaam, Kuala Lumpur, Singapore, Hong Kong, Taipei, Tokyo, Beijing; *ELT Offices* in Buenos Aires, St Philip, Rio de Janiero, São Paulo, Kyoto, Montesson (France), Athens, Florence, Mexico DF, Ibadan, Lima, Madrid, Barcelona, Bilbao, Port of Spain, Montevideo; *Associated companies:* University Press Ltd, Ibadan; Libris (Thailand) Co. Ltd, Bangkok.
Anthropology, archaeology, architecture, art, belles-lettres, bibles, bibliography, biography and memoirs, children's books (fiction, non-fiction, picture), commerce, current affairs, dictionaries, drama, economics, educational (infants, primary, secondary, technical, university), English language teaching, essays, general history, hymn and service books, journals, law, maps and atlases, medical, music, oriental, philosophy, poetry, political economy, prayer books, reference, science, sociology, theology and religion, educational software. Academic books published under the imprint **Clarendon Press.** Trade paperbacks published under the imprint of **Oxford Paperbacks.**

*Paladin Books—imprint of **HarperCollins Publishers.** Paperback literary fiction and non-fiction.

*Pan Books Ltd (1944), Cavaye Place, London SW10 9PG *tel* 071-373 6070 *telex* 917466 *fax* 071-370 0746. *Chairman:* Nicholas Byam Shaw; *managing director:* Alan Gordon Walker; *directors:* David Bleasdale, Ian Chapman, Brian Davies, Ian Metcalfe. Member of **The Macmillan Trade Publishing Group.**

Paperback originals/reprints of notable fiction/non-fiction, including novels, detective fiction, travel, adventure, war books, biography, memoirs, current affairs, humour, reference, crafts, practical handbooks, sci-fi, fantasy and horror. **Piccolo**—children's non-fiction; **Piper**—children's fiction/picture books; **Picador**—outstanding international fiction/non-fiction.

Education: study aids for school and college students including *Brodie's Notes on English Literature*; books for adult education, particularly in languages, business, management and professional education.

*Pandora Press—imprint of **HarperCollins Publishers.** Feminist press publishing. General fiction, crime fiction, biography, arts, media, health, current affairs, travel, humour, reference.

*Papermac—imprint of **Macmillan London Ltd.**

*The Parent and Child Programme—imprint of **The Octopus Publishing Group.** Home education: children's books, 0-9 years, and parents' guides.

*Partridge Press (1987), 61-63 Uxbridge Road, London W5 5SA   *tel* 081-579 2652   *telegraphic address* Transcable   *telex* 267974 Trnspb G   *fax* 081-579 5479. *Director:* Mark Barty-King; *manager:* Debbie Beckerman. Division of **Transworld Publishers Ltd.**
Sport and leisure.

*The Paternoster Press Ltd, Paternoster House, 3 Mount Radford Crescent, Exeter, Devon EX2 4JW   *tel* (0392) 50631   *fax* (0392) 413317.
Biblical studies, Christian theology, philosophy, ethics, history, mission.

*Stanley Paul, Random Century House, 20 Vauxhall Bridge Road, London SW1V 2SA   *tel* 071-973 9680   *telex* 299080 Random G   *fax* 071-233 6129. *Directors:* Gail Rebuck (chairman), Roddy Bloomfield (publishing), Susan Lamb (non-executive). Division of **The Random Century Group Ltd.**
Sport, games, hobbies and handicrafts, sporting biographies, practical books on breeding, care, training and general management of dogs. *Imprint:* Popular Dogs.

Pavilion Books (1980), 196 Shaftesbury Avenue, London WC2H 8JL   *tel* 071-836 1306   *telex* 268639 Eperon G   *fax* 071-240 7684. *Joint chairmen:* Tim Rice, Michael Parkinson; *directors:* Colin Webb, Pamela Webb, Jonathan Hayden, Paul Warren, Robert Christie.
Cookery, travel, humour, cinema, theatre, music, sport, children's.

*Pelham Books (1959), 27 Wrights Lane, London W8 5TZ   *tel* 071-416 3100   *telex* 917181/2   *fax* 071-416 3293. Imprint of **Michael Joseph Ltd.** *Publishing director:* Roger Houghton.
Pears Cyclopaedia, Junior Pears Encyclopaedia. Autobiographies of men and women in sport, sports handbooks, hobbies, crafts and pastimes, practical handbooks on dogs and others pets, country pursuits.

Pen & Sword Books Ltd, 47 Church Street, Barnsley, S. Yorks. S70 2AS   *tel* (0226) 734222   *fax* (0226) 734437. *Chairman:* Sir Nicholas Hewitt, Bt; *managing director:* Leo Cooper; *director/company secretary:* T.G. Hewitt. Military history.

*Penguin Books Ltd, Bath Road, Harmondsworth, West Drayton, Middlesex UB7 0DA   *tel* 081-899 4000   *telex* 933349   *fax* 081-899 4099. *London office* 27 Wrights Lane, W8 5TZ   *tel* 071-416 3000   *telex* 917181/2   *fax* 071-416 3099. *Founder:* Sir Allen Lane; *chief executive:* Peter Mayer; *managing director:* Trevor Glover; *directors:* Elizabeth Attenborough, Peter Carson, Stephen Hall, Brenda Johnson, Tony Lacey, John Peck,

John Rolfe, John Webster, Nigel Williams, Patrick Wright, Jonathan Yglesias, Sally Floyer, Andrew Franklin, Susan Watt, Clare Alexander.
For more than fifty years the publishers of one of the largest paperback lists in the English language. The Penguin list embraces, both as originals and as reprints, fiction and non-fiction, poetry and drama, classics, works of reference, and many areas of more specialised interest.
See also Arkana, Fantail, Hamish Hamilton, Michael Joseph, Allen Lane The Penguin Press, Puffin, Viking, Viking Children's Books, Frederick Warne.

Pergamon Press plc (1948), Headington Hill Hall, Oxford OX3 0BW   *tel* (0865) 794141   *telegraphic address* Pergapress, Oxford   *telex* 83177   *fax* (0865) 60285. *Directors:* James Kels (chairman), Michael Boswood (managing), Tim Davies, Ian Liddiard, A.F. Moon, B. Cox, D. Sar (international marketing).
Economics, educational (secondary, technical, university), medical research, science, technology, engineering, sociology, energy, environment, chess, general, electronic databases.

Peterloo Poets (1976), 2 Kelly Gardens, Calstock, Cornwall PL18 9SA   *tel* (0822) 833473. *Managing director:* Harry Chambers; *trustees:* Richard H. Francis, John Ashbrook, David Selzer.
Poetry.

*Phaidon Press Ltd, 140 Kensington Church Street, London W8 4BN   *tel* 071-221 5656   *fax* 071-221 8474. *Joint chairmen and managing directors:* Mark Futter, Richard Schlagman; *directors:* Andrew Price (financial), Roger Sears (editorial), Alan Peebles (production); *managers:* Mark Eastment (rights), Claire Sawford (publicity), Issy Thomas (designer).
Fine arts, the history of art and civilisation, architecture, decorative and performing arts, design, archaeology, history, music, photography, art instruction, reference, theatre.

*George Philip Ltd (1834), 59 Grosvenor Street, London W1X 9DA   *tel* 071-493 5841   *telex* 27278   *fax* 071-491 3803. *Chairman:* Tony Bovill; *publishing director:* John Gaisford; *directors:* Roger Bonnett, Moira McCann, W.J. Croser, A. Poynter, D. Rivers, B.M. Willett. Member of **The Octopus Publishing Group.**
Educational, reference and road maps and atlases. Globes. Travel, countryside and astronomy.
Imprint: Osprey.

Phillimore & Co. Ltd (incorporating **Darwen Finlayson Ltd**), Shopwyke Hall, Chichester, West Sussex PO20 6BQ   *tel* (0243) 787636. *Directors:* Philip Harris, JP (chairman and managing), Noel Osborne, MA(Cantab) (editorial), Ian Macfarlane, FCA, Hilary Clifford Brown.
Local and family history; architectural history, archaeology, genealogy and heraldry; also Darwen County History Series. *The Local Historian* (Q.) Journal of the British Association for Local History.

Piatkus Books (1979), 5 Windmill Street, London W1P 1HF   *tel* 071-631 0710   *fax* 071-436 7137. *Managing director:* Judy Piatkus; *directors:* Philip Cotterell (marketing), Gill Cormode (editorial); *managers:* Jana Sommerlad (publicity), Diane Hill (sales), Simon Colverson (production), David Harris (financial).
Business, fiction, leisure, women's interest, parenting, health, mind, body and spirit, arts, business, biography, how to and practical, gift books, fashion, beauty.

*Picador—see **Pan Books Ltd.**

Piccadilly Press (1983), 5 Castle Road, London NW1 8PR *tel* 071-267 4492, *fax* 071-267 4493. *Directors:* Brenda Gardner (chairman and managing), Philip Durrance (secretary).
Children's hardback books.

*Piccolo—see **Pan Books Ltd.**

*Picture Corgi paperbacks—imprint of **Transworld Publishers Ltd.** Children's picture books.

*Pinter Publishers Ltd (1973) 25 Floral Street, London WC2E 9DS *tel* 071-240 9233 *telex* 912881 Cwuktx G Attn PIN *fax* 071-379 5553. *Chairman:* Ann Weyman; *managing director:* Frances Pinter; *directors:* Pamela Fulton (marketing), Iain Stevenson (editorial), Robert Macleod, Christopher Conolly-Smith, Mark Hawksworth.
Academic and professional publishers specialising in social sciences including international relations, politics, economics, new technology, linguistics and humanities. **Belhaven Press** focuses on environmental topics such as geography, earth sciences and life sciences. Division: **Leicester University Press,** *q.v.*

*Piper—see **Pan Books Ltd.**

*Pitkin Pictorials Ltd (1941), Healey House, Dene Road, Andover, Hants SP10 2AA *tel* (0264) 334303 *telex* 47214 *fax* (0264) 334110. *Director:* Ian Corsie. Imprint of **The Octopus Publishing Group.**
Colour guidebooks to cathedrals, palaces and major tourist attractions.

*Pitman Publishing (1845), 128 Long Acre, London WC2E 9AN *tel* 071-379 7383 *telegraphic address* Ipandsons, London, WC2 *telex* 261367 Pitman *fax* 071-240 5771 Pitman Ldn.
Secretarial studies, business education, management, professional studies, information technology, computer science, M & E Handbooks.

Plexus Publishing Ltd (1973), 26 Dafforne Road, London SW17 8TZ *tel* 081-672 6067 *fax* 081-672 1631. *Directors:* Terence Porter (managing), Sandra Wake (editorial). Also **Eel Pie Publishing.**
Film, music, biography, popular culture, fashion.

Pluto Publishing Ltd (1968), 345 Archway Road, London N6 5AA *tel* 081-348 2724 *telex* 262433 *fax* 081-348 9133. *Directors:* Roger van Zwanenberg (managing), Anne Beech (editorial).
Social and political science including economics, history; cultural, international, women's studies.

Poetry Wales Press (1981), Andmar House, Trewsfield Industrial Estate, Tondu Road, Bridgend, Mid Glamorgan CF31 4LJ *tel* (0656) 767834. *Director:* Mick Felton.
Poetry, fiction, drama, history, film, literary criticism, biography – mostly with relevance to Wales.

Polity Press (1983), 65 Bridge Street, Cambridge CB2 1UR *tel* (0223) 324315 *fax* (0223) 461385. *Directors:* Anthony Giddens, David Held, John Thompson.
Social and political theory, politics, sociology, history, economics, psychology, media and cultural studies, philosophy, theology, literary theory, feminism, human geography, anthropology.

*Polygon, 22 George Square, Edinburgh EH8 9LF *tel* 031-650 4689 *fax* 031-662 0053.

New international fiction, including translations, oral history, general, Scottish, social and political (Determination series).

*Popular Dogs—imprint of **Stanley Paul**. Practical books on breeding, care, training and general management of dogs.

PRION–Multimedia Books Ltd (1986), Unit L, 32-34 Gordon House Road, London NW5 1LP   *tel* 071-482 4248   *telex* 295941 Atid G   *fax* 071-482 4203. *Managing director:* Arnon Orbach.
Psychology and health, food, environment, photography, animals, space and aviation.

Prism Press Book Publishers Ltd (1974), 2 South Street, Bridport, Dorset DT6 3NQ   *tel* (0308) 27022   *fax* (0308) 421015. *Directors:* Julian King, Colin Spooner.
Non-fiction, including health, food, building, new age, feminism, politics, ecology.

P.S.I. Policy Studies Institute, 100 Park Village East, London NW1 3SR   *tel* 071-387 2171   *fax* 071-388 0914. *Director:* W.W. Daniel; *head of external relations:* Nicholas Evans; *secretary:* Eileen M. Reid.
Economic, industrial and social policy, political institutions, social sciences.

*Puffin, children's paperback imprint of **The Penguin Group,** 27 Wrights Lane, London W8 5TZ   *tel* 071-416 3000   *telex* 917181/2   *fax* 071-416 3099. *Publishing director:* Elizabeth Attenborough.
Children's paperback books – mainly reprints. Fiction, poetry, picture books, limited non-fiction.

*Purnell Books—see **Simon & Schuster Young Books.**

Putnam & Co. Ltd (1916), 101 Fleet Street, London EC4Y 1DE   *tel* 071-583 2412   *telex* 8814206 Popper G   *fax* 071-936 2153. *Directors:* W.R. Blackmore (managing), D.C. Greening.
Putnam Aeronautical Books: technical and reference.

*Pyramid Books—imprint of **The Octopus Publishing Group.** Lifestyle, reference, sport and leisure.

Quantum—imprint of **W. Foulsham & Co. Ltd.** *Editor:* Bill Anderton. Popular philosophy, practical psychology.

Quartet Books Ltd (1972), 27-29 Goodge Street, London W1P 1FD   *tel* 071-636 3992   *telex* 919034 Namara G   *fax* 071-637 1866. *Chairman:* N.I. Attallah; *editorial director:* S. Pickles. Member of the **Namara Group.**
General fiction and non-fiction, foreign literature in translation, history, sociology, politics, topical issues, classical music, jazz, biography, original paperbacks.

Queen Anne Press, 165 Great Dover Street, London SE1 4YA   *tel* 071-334 4800   *fax* 071-334 4905/6. *Director:* Caroline North. Division of **Macdonald & Co. (Publishers) Ltd.**
Sports reference and celebrity books; heritage, travel, biography.

Quiller Press Ltd, 46 Lillie Road, London SW6 1TN   *tel* 071-499 6529   *telex* 21120 Monref G   *fax* 071-381 8941. *Directors:* J.J. Greenwood, A.E. Carlile. Publishers of sponsored books.
Guide books, history, industry, humour, architecture, cookery, aviation, nature.

*Radius—imprint of **Hutchinson Books Ltd.** Politics and economics.

*Random Century Children's Books, Random Century House, 20 Vauxhall Bridge Road, London SW1V 2SA   *tel* 071-973 9750   *telex* 299080 Random

G   *fax* 071-233 6057. *Directors:* Piet Snyman (chairman), Clare Conville (publishing), Caroline Roberts (publishing), Alan Lee (production), Jill Taylor (rights). Division of **The Random Century Group Ltd.**
Children's books: fiction and non-fiction, picture books.
Imprints: Bodley Head Children's, Hutchinson Children's, Random House Children's.

*The Random Century Group Ltd, Random Century House, 20 Vauxhall Bridge Road, London SW1V 2SA   *tel* 071-973 9000   *telex* 299080 Random G   *fax* 071-233 6058. *Chairman:* A.J.V. Cheetham; *deputy chairman:* S.H. Master; *directors:* D.J. Attwooll, C.T. Callil, R.M.F. Cheetham, D.J. Godwin, J.M. Mottram, G.R. Rebuck, P.C.K. Roche, P.G.W. Snyman. Antiques and collecting, art, biography and memoirs, children's books (fiction and non-fiction, toy and picture books), animals (care and breeding), current affairs, essays, fiction, general, history, humour, music, mysticism and meditation, oriental religion and philosophy, poetry, reference, classics, romance, sport, thrillers, travel, films, graphics, fashion, illustrated editions, cookery.
Divisions: Century, Ebury, Business Books, Arrow, Jonathan Cape, Chatto & Windus, Hutchinson, Stanley Paul, Barrie & Jenkins, Random Century Children's Books.

Rapp & Whiting Ltd. All books published by Rapp & Whiting have been taken over by **André Deutsch Ltd.**

*The Reader's Digest Association, Ltd, Berkeley Square House, Berkeley Square, London W1X 6AB   *tel* 071-629 8144   *telegraphic address* Readigest, London, W1   *telex* 264631   *fax* 071-499 9751. *Directors:* S.N. McRae (managing), B.C. Gray, A.T. Lynam-Smith, R.G. Twisk, H. van Wyk, R.S. Hosie, M.L. Stockton, F.K. Ross, K.A. Gordon.
Monthly magazine, condensed and series books; also DIY, car maintenance, gardening, medical, handicrafts, law, touring guides, encyclopaedias, dictionaries, nature, folklore, atlases, cookery.

*Red Fox—imprint of **Arrow Books Ltd.** Children's books.

Reed Information Services Ltd (1983), Windsor Court, East Grinstead House, East Grinstead, West Sussex RH19 1XA   *tel* (0342) 326972   *telegraphic address* Infoservices, East Grinstead   *telex* 95127 Infser G   *fax* (0342) 315130. *Directors:* R.J.E. Dangerfield (chief executive), J.R. Clayton, P.A. Oram, K. Burton, W.J. Irlam, G. McVey, J. Siebert, D. Barr.
Publishers of commercial and industrial directories under the **Reed Information Services, Kompass, Dial Industry** and **Kelly's** imprints.

Reinhardt Books Ltd, including **The Nonesuch Press Ltd,** 27 Wrights Lane, London W8 5TZ   *tel* 071-938 2200. *Directors:* Max Reinhardt (chairman), Joan Reinhardt, John R. Hews, FCA; *assistant publisher:* Amanda Hargreaves; *consultants:* John Ryder, Judy Taylor.
Biography, fiction, essays, belles-lettres, children's books. *No* unsolicited MSS.

Religious and Moral Education Press—acquired by **Chansitor Publications Ltd,** *q.v.*

*Rider—imprint of **Century Publishing Ltd.** Oriental religion and philosophy, mysticism and meditation.

Rivelin Grapheme Press (1984), The Annexe, Kennet House, 19 High Street, Hungerford, Berks. RG17 0NL   *tel* (0488) 684645   *fax* (0488) 683018.
Director: Snowdon Barnett.
Poetry.

Robinson Publishing (1983), 11 Shepherd House, Shepherd Street, London W1Y 7LD *tel* 071-493 1064 *telex* 2622433 Monref G ref 778 *fax* 071-409 7226. *Publisher:* Nicholas Robinson.
General fiction and non-fiction, including paperback fiction omnibuses, fantasy and science fiction, crime, film, health, country. Letters/synopses only please.

*Robson Books (1973), Bolsover House, 5-6 Clipstone Street, London W1P 7EB *tel* 071-323 1223/637 5937 *telegraphic address* Robsobook, London, W1 *fax* 071-636 0798. *Managing director:* Jeremy Robson.
General, biography, music, humour.

*George Ronald (1939), 46 High Street, Kidlington, Oxford OX5 2DN *tel* (0865) 841515 *telegraphic address* Talisman, Oxford *telex* 837646 Talism *fax* (0865) 841230. *Managers:* W. Momen, E. Leith.
Religion, specialising in the Baha'i Faith.

*Routledge, 11 New Fetter Lane, London EC4P 4EE *tel* 071-583 9855 *telex* 263398 Rout G *cables* Elegiacs, London EC4. *Managing director:* David Croom; *publishers:* Peter Sowden (business), Gill Davies (social and behavioural science), Janice Price (humanities), Wendy Morris (reference); *marketing director:* Malcolm Campbell; *production director:* Tony Short. Division of **Routledge, Chapman & Hall Ltd.**
Access, addiction, archaeology, anthropology, art, business and management, counselling, criminology, development and environment, dictionaries, economics, education, geography, history, Japanese studies, literary criticism, Middle East studies, philosophy, political economy, psychiatry, psychology, reference, social administration, sociology, women's studies.

*Routledge & Kegan Paul—incorporated in **Routledge.**

*Rowan—imprint of **Arrow Books Ltd.** Women's fiction.

Royal National Institute for the Blind (1868), PO Box 173, Peterborough, Cambs. PE2 0WS *tel* (0733) 370777 *fax* (0733) 371555.
Magazines and books for blind people, in Braille and Moon embossed types. Also tape-recorded books (*Talking Books* and cassette library). For complete list of magazines see **Classified Index.**

*Sage Publications Ltd (1971), 6 Bonhill Street, London EC2A 4PU *tel* 071-374 0645 *fax* 071-374 8741. *Directors:* David Hill (managing), Lynn Adams, Ian Eastment, Stephen Barr, Mike Birch, S. Jones, David F. McCune (USA), Sara Miller McCune (USA).
Sociology, psychology, political and social sciences.

The Saint Andrew Press, 121 George Street, Edinburgh EH2 4YN *tel* 031-225 5722 *telegraphic address* Free, Edinburgh, EH2 4YN *telex* 727935 Chscot G *fax* 031-220 3113. Section of **Church of Scotland Department of Communication.**
Theology and religion, church history.

St George's Press (1969), 37 Manchester Street, London W1M 5PE *tel* 071-486 5481. *Directors:* C.M. Ardito (chairman), R.A. Duparc, The Hon. Julian Fane, J.M. Hatwell.
General (fiction and non-fiction), belles-lettres, educational (English as a foreign language).

St James Press (1968), 2-6 Boundary Row, London SE1 8HP *tel* 071-865 0190 *fax* 071-865 0192. *Company president:* George Walsh; *managing director:* Daniel Kirkpatrick; *publicity manager:* Kate Berney; *marketing manager:* Andrew Parker.

Reference books for libraries – literature, arts, performing arts, film and television, biography, history and social sciences.

David St John Thomas Publisher (1982), PO Box 4, Nairn IV12 4HU   *tel* (0667) 54441   *fax* (0667) 54401.
Railways and transport, writing, Scotland, general.

St Paul Publications (1954), St Paul's House, Middlegreen, Slough, Berks. SL3 6BT   *tel* (0753) 20621   *fax* (0753) 74240.
Theology, philosophy, ethics, spirituality, biography, education, ecology, children's books with religious themes, general books of Roman Catholic and Christian interest.

St Paul's Bibliographies (1974), West End House, 1 Step Terrace, Winchester, Hants SO22 5BW   *tel* (0962) 860524   *fax* (0962) 842409. *Managing director:* Robert S. Cross.
Bibliography and scholarly books on books and the book trade.

Salamander Books Ltd (1973), 129-137 York Way, London N7 9LG   *tel* 071-267 4447   *cables* Salamander London N7   *telex* 261113 Salama G   *fax* 071-267 5112. *Directors:* Jef Proost (chairman), Ray Bonds (managing), Keith Allen Jones, David Spence, Philip Hughes.
Military, natural history, music, gardening, hobbies, cookery, crafts, pets.

Salvationist Publishing and Supplies Ltd, 117-121 Judd Street, London WC1H 9NN   *tel* 071-387 1656.
Devotional books, theology, biography, world-wide Christian and social service, children's books, music.

***W.B. Saunders Co. Ltd,** 24-28 Oval Road, London NW1 7DX   *tel* 071-267 4466   *telex* 25775 Acpres G. *Managing director:* Joan M. Fujimoto.
Medical and scientific.

***K.G. Saur Ltd**—see **Bowker-Saur Ltd.**

***Sceptre**—imprint of **Hodder & Stoughton Ltd.** Fiction and non-fiction paperbacks.

Schofield & Sims Ltd (1901), Dogley Mill, Fenay Bridge, Huddersfield HD8 0NQ   *tel* (0484) 607080   *telegraphic address* Schosims, Huddersfield   *telex* 51458 Comhud G for Schosims   *fax* (0484) 606815. *Directors:* John S. Nesbitt (chairman), J. Stephen Platts (managing), J. Brierley (sales).
Educational (infants, primary, secondary, technical, music for schools, children's books).

***Scholastic Hardcover** (1990), 7-9 Pratt Street, London NW1 0AE   *tel* 071-284 4474   *fax* 071-284 4234. Imprint of **Scholastic Publications Ltd.**
Children's hardbacks – fiction and non-fiction. *No* unsolicited MSS.

***Scholastic Publications Ltd** (1964), Villiers House, Clarendon Avenue, Leamington Spa, Warks. CV32 5PR   *tel* (0926) 887799   *fax* (0926) 883331. *London office:* 7-9 Pratt Street, London NW1 0AE   *tel* 071-284 4474   *fax* 071-284 4234. *Directors:* D.M.R. Kewley (managing), M.R. Robinson Jr (USA), R.M. Spaulding (USA), D.J. Walsh (USA).
Children's division (London) Publishers of fiction and non-fiction hardbacks and paperbacks under the imprints **André Deutsch Children's Books, Scholastic Hardcover, Adlib, Hippo.** *Educational division* (Leamington) Publishers of books for teachers (Bright Ideas and other series), primary classroom resources and magazines for teachers (*Child Education, Junior Education* and others). *Direct Marketing* (Leamington) children's book clubs and school book fairs.

Scientific Publishing Co. Ltd, 40 Dalton Street, Manchester M4 4JP   *tel* 061-205 1514.
Engineering textbooks.

*SCM Press Ltd (1929), 26-30 Tottenham Road, London N1 4BZ   *tel* 071-249 7262   *fax* 071-249 3776. *Managing director and editor:* John Bowden; *directors:* Margaret Lydamore (associate editor and company secretary), Linda Foster (bookroom), Roger Pygram (finance).
Theological books with special emphasis on biblical, philosophical and modern theology; books on sociology of religion and religious aspects of current issues.

*Scolar Press—imprint of **Gower Publishing Group Ltd.** Arts and humanities.

Scottish Academic Press Ltd (1969), 139 Leith Walk, Edinburgh EH6 8NS   *tel* 031-553 3649   *fax* 031-553 3705. *Directors:* Douglas Grant, A.A. Rodwell, H. Whittaker.
All types of academic books and books of Scottish interest.

The Scout Association, Baden-Powell House, Queen's Gate, London SW7 5JS   *tel* 071-584 7030   *telegraphic address* Scouting   *fax* 071-581 9953. *General editor:* David Easton.
Technical books dealing with all subjects relevant to Scouting and monthly journal *Scouting.*

Scribners—imprint of **Macdonald & Co. (Publishers) Ltd.** *Director:* Alan Samson. Hardback upmarket fiction and non-fiction.

Scribners Crime—imprint of **Macdonald & Co. (Publishers) Ltd.** *Director:* Hilary Hale. Hardback crime fiction.

*Scripture Union Publishing (1867), Scripture Union House, 130 City Road, London EC1V 2NJ   *tel* 071-782 0013   *fax* 071-782 0014. Christian Publishers and Booksellers.
Music, bible reading aids, Sunday school materials and Christian books especially for children and young people.

B.A. Seaby Ltd (1926), 7 Davies Street, London W1Y 1LL   *tel* 071-495 2590   *fax* 071-491 1595. *Directors:* E.R. Cox, D. Kidd, G. Manton, B. Reeds.
Numismatics, archaeology, history, antiquities.

Seafarer Books—see **Merlin Press Ltd.**

Search Press Ltd (1962), Wellwood, North Farm Road, Tunbridge Wells, Kent TN2 3DR   *tel* (0892) 510850   *telex* 957258 Search G   *fax* (0892) 515903. *Directors:* Charlotte de la Bedoyère, John M. Todd, The Hon. G.E. Noel, Ruth B. Saunders.
Philosophy, arts, crafts, leisure, cookery, gardening.

*Martin Secker & Warburg Ltd (founded 1910; reconstructed and enlarged 1936), Michelin House, 81 Fulham Road, London SW3 6RB   *tel* 071-581 9393   *telex* 920191   *fax* 071-589 8421. *Directors:* John Potter (publishing), Dan Franklin (publishing), Peter Kilborn (production), Martin Cowell (sales), Serena Davies (publicity), Robin Robertson (editorial), Margaret Halton (rights). Member of **The Octopus Publishing Group.**
Art, belles-lettres, biography and memoirs, cinema, fiction, history, poetry, jazz, crime, politics, theatre, travel.

Serpent's Tail (1986), 4 Blackstock Mews, London N4 2BT   *tel* 071-354 1949   *fax* 071-704 6467. *Director:* Peter Ayrton.
Modern fiction in paperback: literary and experimental work, first novels and work in translation.

Settle Press (1983), Wigmore House Publishing Ltd, 10 Boyne Terrace Mews, London W11 3LR *tel* 071-243 0695. *Directors:* D. Settle (managing), M. Carter (editorial).
Travel and guidebooks, general, fiction.

Severn House Publishers (1974), 35 Manor Road, Wallington, Surrey SM6 0BW *tel* 081-773 4161 *fax* 081-773 4143. *Chairman:* Edwin Buckhalter.
Adult fiction: romances, thrillers, detective, adventure, war, western, science fiction; film and TV tie-ins.

Shakespeare Head Press (1904), Basil Blackwell Ltd, 108 Cowley Road, Oxford OX4 1JF *tel* (0865) 791100. *Editorial director:* John Davey.
Finely printed books; scholarly works.

Sheed & Ward Ltd (1926), 2 Creechurch Lane, London EC3A 5AQ *tel* 071-283 6330. *Directors:* M.T. Redfern, K.G. Darke. Publishers of books, mostly by Catholics.
History, philosophy, theology, catechetics, scripture and religion.

Sheldon Press, Holy Trinity Church, Marylebone Road, London NW1 4DU *tel* 071-387 5282 *telegraphic address* Futurity, London *fax* 071-388 2352. *Editorial director:* Judith Longman; *senior editor:* Joanna Moriarty.
Popular medicine, health, self-help, psychology, practical management.

Shepheard-Walwyn (Publishers) Ltd (1971), Suite 34, 26 Charing Cross Road, London WC2H 0DH *tel* 071-240 5992 *fax* 071-379 5770. *Directors:* A.R.A. Werner, M.M. Werner.
History, political economy, philosophy, religion; books in calligraphy; Scottish interest.

John Sherratt & Son Ltd, Hotspur House, 2 Gloucester Street, Manchester M1 5QR *tel* 061-236 9963 *fax* 061-236 2026.
Educational (primary, secondary, technical, university), medical, practical handbooks, collectors' books.

Shire Publications Ltd (1966), Cromwell House, Church Street, Princes Risborough, Aylesbury, Bucks. HP17 9AJ *tel* (08444) 4301 *fax* (08444) 7080. *Directors:* J.P. Rotheroe, J.W. Rotheroe.
Discovering paperbacks, Shire Albums, Shire Archaeology, Shire Natural History, Shire Ethnography, Shire Egyptology, Shire Garden History.

*Sidgwick & Jackson Ltd (1908), 18-21 Cavaye Place, London SW10 9PG *tel* 071-373 6070 *fax* 071-370 0746. *Directors:* Alan Gordon Walker (chairman), William Armstrong (managing), Morven Knowles, Hilary Engel, Brian Davies, David Macmillan, Margaret Heriot, Mike Fenton. Member of **The Macmillan Trade Publishing Group.**
Archaeology, biography, cinema, current affairs, fiction, future history, gardening, history, military history, music (pop and classical), political economy, show business, sociology, sport, travel, wine, cookery, crafts.

*Silhouette—imprint of **Mills & Boon (Publishers) Ltd.** Popular romantic fiction.

*Simon & Schuster Ltd (1986), West Garden Place, Kendal Street, London W2 2AQ *tel* 071-724 7577 *telex* 21702 *fax* 071-402 0639. *Directors:* Nick Webb (managing), Maureen Waller (editorial, fiction), Carol O'Brien (editorial, non-fiction), Jonathan Atkins, Lesley Toll, Fenella Smart, Penelope McNeile.
Fiction, non-fiction.

*Simon & Schuster Young Books/Simon & Schuster Education (incorporating **Macdonald Educational, Blackwell Education, Macdonald Children's**

Books, Purnell Books), Wolsey House, Wolsey Road, Hemel Hempstead, Herts. HP2 4SS   *tel* (0442) 231900   *fax* (0442) 214467. *Publisher:* Philippa Stewart. Division of **Simon & Schuster International Group.**
Educational and information books; picture books and fiction for children from pre-school to teenage.

*__Sinclair-Stevenson Ltd__ (1989), 7/8 Kendrick Mews, London SW7 3HG   *tel* 071-581 1645   *fax* 071-581 1699. *Directors:* Christopher Sinclair-Stevenson (managing), Stephen Langton and Peter Tummons (financial), Penelope Hoare (editorial), John Lyon (sales), Angela Martin (publicity), Lorraine Abraham (production).
Fiction, biography, history, travel, politics and current affairs.

*__Colin Smythe Ltd__ (1966), PO Box 6, Gerrards Cross, Bucks. SL9 8XA   *tel* (0753) 886000   *telegraphic address* Smythebooks, Gerrardscross   *fax* (0753) 886469. *Directors:* Colin Smythe (managing), Peter Bander van Duren, A. Norman Jeffares, Ann Saddlemyer, Leslie Hayward.
Biography, histories, parapsychology, literary criticism, folklore, fantasy fiction (sword & sorcery only), Irish interest and Anglo-Irish literature. Also **Dolmen Press** books.

*__Society for Promoting Christian Knowledge__ (1698), Holy Trinity Church, Marylebone Road, London NW1 4DU   *tel* 071-387 5282   *telegraphic address* Futurity, London   *fax* 071-388 2352. *General secretary:* Patrick Gilbert; *editorial director:* Judith Longman; *editors:* Philip Law (senior editor), Rachel Boulding (editor, Triangle imprint).
Theology and religion. See also **Sheldon Press.**

Southside (Publishers) Ltd (1968)—subsidiary of **Canongate Press plc.**

*__Souvenir Press Ltd__, 43 Great Russell Street, London WC1B 3PA   *tel* 071-580 9307-8 and 637 5711/2/3   *telegraphic address* Publisher, London   *telex* 24710 Souvnr G   *fax* 071-580 5064. *Managing director:* Ernest Hecht, BSc(Econ). BCom; *executive directors:* Rodney King, Jeanne Manchee.
Archaeology, biography and memoirs, children's books (non-fiction, rewards), educational (secondary, technical), fiction, general, humour, practical handbooks, psychiatry, psychology, sociology, sports, games and hobbies, travel, supernatural, parapsychology, illustrated books.

*__SPCK__—see **Society for Promoting Christian Knowledge.**

Neville Spearman Ltd—imprint of **The C.W. Daniel Company Ltd.** Mysticism.

Spellmount Ltd, Publishers (1983), 12 Dene Way, Speldhurst, Tunbridge Wells, Kent TN3 0NX   *tel* (0892) 862860   *fax* (0892) 863861. *Directors:* Ian Morley-Clarke, Kathleen Morley-Clarke.
Militaria, cricket, London historical guides.

Sphere Books Ltd (1966), 165 Great Dover Street, London SE1 4YA   *tel* 071-334 4800   *fax* 071-334 4905/6. *Directors:* Barbara Boote (publishing), Mary Loring (Abacus), Peter Cotton (art), Richard Beswick (Cardinal). Part of the **Macdonald Group.**
Paperbacks: original fiction and non-fiction, reprints; **Abacus** and **Cardinal** trade paperbacks and reference.

*__Spindlewood__ (1980), 70 Lynhurst Avenue, Barnstaple, Devon EX31 2HY   *tel* (0271) 71612. *Directors:* Michael Holloway, Anne Holloway.
Children's picture books; adult and children's fiction. History, travel and education titles.

*__E. & F.N. Spon Ltd__ (1834), 2-6 Boundary Row, London SE1 8HN   *tel* 071-865 0066   *telex* 290164 Chapma G   *fax* 071-522 9623. *Directors:* P.

Gardner (managing), P. Read (publishing), G. McDonald (book production), A.J. Davis (finance), J. Lavender (marketing). Division of **Chapman & Hall Ltd.**
Architecture, building, surveying, engineering, applied science, energy studies, leisure studies, construction, planning.

Sportsprint—imprint of **John Donald Publishers Ltd.** Sports.

*****Spring Books**—imprint of **The Octopus Publishing Group.** Non-fiction.

Stacey International (1974), 128 Kensington Church Street, London W8 4BH *tel* 071-221 7166 *telex* 298768 Stacey G *fax* 071-792 9288. *Directors:* Tom Stacey, C.S. Stacey, Geoffrey Milne (managing).
Illustrated non-fiction, encyclopaedic books on regions and countries, Islamic and Arab subjects, world affairs, art.

Stainer & Bell Ltd (1906), PO Box 110, 82 High Road, London N2 9PW *tel* 081-444 9135 *fax* 081-365 2770. *Directors:* Bernard Braley, ACIS (chairman), Allen Percival, CBE (deputy chairman), Keith Wakefield (joint managing), Carol Wakefield (joint managing/secretary), Joan Braley, John Hosier, CBE, Scott Stroman, Antony Kearns.
Books on music, religious communication.

*****Stanford Maritime**—see **A. & C. Black plc.**

*****Harold Starke Publishers Ltd,** Pixey Green, Stradbroke, Eye, Suffolk IP21 5NG *tel* (0379) 388334 *fax* (0379) 388335; and 203 Bunyan Court, Barbican, London EC2Y 8DH *tel* 071-588 5195. *Directors:* Harold K. Starke, Naomi Galinski.
Specialist, scientific, medical, reference, biography and memoirs.

Patrick Stephens Ltd (1967), Sparkford, Yeovil, Somerset BA22 7JJ *tel* North Cadbury (0963) 40635 *fax* (0963) 40825. *Chairman:* J.H. Haynes; *editorial director:* Darryl Reach. Imprint of **Haynes Publishing Group.**
Aviation, biography, collecting, the countryside, walking and mountaineering, maritime, military and wargaming, model making, motor cycling, motoring and motor racing, railways and railway modelling.

The Sterling Publishing Group plc (1978), PO Box 839, 86-88 Edgware Road, London W2 2YW *tel* 071-258 0066 *telex* 8953130 Espepe G *fax* 071-723 5766. *Chairman:* R.M. Cohen; *managing director:* R.M. Summers; *directors:* D.M. Coughlan, R.G.B. Heller, V.L. Lewis, M.D. Preston, A.D.L. Robinson, B.L. Manfrey.
Reference, management and technology directories, leisure, commemorative publishing.

Stevens and Sons Ltd (founded 1799; incorporated 1889), South Quay Plaza, 184 Marsh Wall, London E14 9FT *tel* 071-538 8686 *telex* 929089 Itpinf G *fax* 071-538 8625. *Directors:* C.D.O. Evans (chairman and managing), J. Jenkins, A. Kinahan, B. Grandage, C. Tullo, D. Tebbutt, R. Greener, G. Francis, S. Harris. Subsidiary of International Thomson Professional Information/Thomson Information Services.
Law.

Stillit Books Ltd, 72 New Bond Street, London W1Y 0QY *tel* 071-493 1177 *telex* 23475. *Director:* Gerald B. Stillit.
Stillitron audio-visual, direct method, programmed, instantaneously electronically corrected, language systems. French, German, Spanish, Italian, Arabic and English as a foreign language.

Stride Publications (including **Taxus Press** and **Apparitions Press**) (1980), 37 Portland Street, Newtown, Exeter, Devon EX1 2EG. *Proprietor:* Rupert M. Loydell.
Poetry, short stories, novels, visual arts, theology.

Studio Publications (Ipswich) Ltd—see **Sunbird Publishing Ltd.**

*****Studio Vista**—imprint of **Cassell plc.** *Senior commissioning editor:* Christopher Fagg. Art, antiques and collecting, architecture and design, fine art and art history, illustrated and fine editions, photography.

The Sumach Press (1990), 29 Mount Pleasant, St Albans, Herts. AL3 4QY *tel* (0727) 47032 *fax* (0727) 50479. *Managing/publishing director:* Heather Godwin; *financial directors:* Anthony Cheetham, Peter Roche. Imprint of **The Random Century Group Ltd.**
The land, the landscape, country matters, county histories; some fiction.

*****Sunbird Publishing Ltd** (formerly **Studio Publications (Ipswich) Ltd**), Windmill Road, Loughborough, Leics. LE11 1XD *tel* (0509) 233339 *fax* (0509) 236846. Subsidiary of **Ladybird Books Ltd.**
Children's novelty and early learning titles including fairy stories. Imprints include: **Playskool, Stick-A-Tale** and **Balloon Books.**

Sunflower Books, 12 Kendrick Mews, London SW7 3HG *tel* 071-589 1862 *telex* 269388 Lonhan G *fax* 071-225 1033. *Directors:* P.A. Underwood (USA), J.G. Underwood, S.J. Seccombe.
Travel guide books.

Sussex University Press (1971)—publications distributed by **Scottish Academic Press Ltd,** *q.v.* Academic books.

Alan Sutton Publishing Ltd (1978), Phoenix Mill, Far Thrupp, Stroud, Glos. GL5 2BU *tel* (0453) 731114 *fax* (0453) 731117. *Directors:* Alan Sutton, Peter Clifford, Richard Bryant, Kaye Montgomery, Christopher Sackett, Nicholas Mills, Dave Prigent.
General and academic publishers of high quality fully illustrated books. Subjects include: history, travel, military, countryside, topography, railways, literature, biography and archaeology.

Swedenborg Society, 20-21 Bloomsbury Way, London WC1A 2TH *tel* 071-405 7986.
The writings of Swedenborg.

*****Sweet & Maxwell Ltd** (founded 1799; incorporated 1889), South Quay Plaza, 183 Marsh Wall, London E14 9FT *tel* 071-538 8686 *telex* 929089 Itpinf G *fax* 071-538 8625. *Directors:* C.D.O. Evans (chairman and managing), J. Jenkins, A. Kinahan, B. Grandage, C. Tullo, D. Tebbutt. Subsidiary of International Thomson Professional Information/Thomson Information Services.
Law.

I.B. Tauris & Co. Ltd (1983), 110 Gloucester Avenue, London NW1 8JA *tel* 071-483 2681 *telex* 262433/3166 Tauris *fax* 071-483 4541. *Directors:* I. Bagherzade, G.W. Green.
Modern history, politics, international relations, economics and current affairs.

*****Tavistock Publications Ltd**—incorporated in **Routledge.**

Taylor & Francis Ltd, 4 John Street, London WC1N 2ET *tel* 071-405 2237-9. *President:* Professor Sir Nevill Mott, MS, DSC, FIinstP, FRS; *directors:* Professor B.R. Coles, BSc, DPhil, FInstp, FRS (chairman), Professor K.W. Keohane, CBE, BSc, PhD, FInstP (vice-chairman), A.R. Selvey, FCCA, FBIM (managing), E. Ferguson, MA, S.M.A. Banister, MA, Professor H. Baum, K.R. Courtney, S.B. Neal, BSc.

Educational (university), science: physics, and mathematics, chemistry, electronics, natural history, pharmacology and drug metabolism, medical science, astronomy, technology, history of science, ergonomics, production engineering, Falmer Press Ltd.

Telegraph Books (1920), Daily Telegraph, Peterborough Court at South Quay, 181 Marsh Wall, London E14 9SR   *tel* 071-538 6829   *fax* 071-538 6950. *Publishing director:* Marilyn Warnick.
Business, personal finance, crosswords, sport, travel and guides, cookery and wine, general, history – all co-published with major publishing houses.

Thomas Telford Ltd (1972), Thomas Telford House, 1 Heron Quay, London E14 4JD   *tel* 071-987 6999   *telex* 298105 Civils G   *fax* 071-538 5746. *Directors:* A.G. Dawson (managing), A. Levett, H. Ferguson.
Professional and technical books, journals and magazines on civil engineering and associated areas.

*Thames and Hudson Ltd, 30-34 Bloomsbury Street, London WC1B 3QP   *tel* 071- 636 5488   *telegraphic address* Thameshuds, London WC1   *telex* 25992 Thbook G   *fax* 071-636 4799. *Chairman:* E.U. Neurath; *managing director:* T.M. Neurath; *directors:* E. Bates (company secretary), J.R. Camplin (editorial), T.L. Evans (sales), C.A. Ferguson (production), W. Guttmann, S. Huntley (sales), C.M. Kaine (design), I.H.B. Middleton (rights), N. Stangos (editorial).
Art, archaeology and anthropology, architecture, photography, travel, social, classical history, fashion, literature and criticism, practical guides, design, cultural history, craft, mythology and religion, philosophy, music.

Thames Publishing (1970), 14 Barlby Road, London W10 6AR   *tel* 081-969 3579. *Publishing manager:* John Bishop.
Books about music, particularly by British composers. Preliminary letter essential.

Thomson-Leng Publications, Dundee DD1 9QJ   *tel* (0382) 23131 *telegraphic address* Courier, Dundee   *telex* 76380   *fax* (0382) 22214. *London Office:* 185 Fleet Street, EC4A 2HS   *tel* 071-242 5086   *telegraphic address* Courier, London, EC4   *fax* 071-404 5694. Publishers of newspapers and periodicals. Children's books (annuals), fiction.

*Stanley Thornes (Publishers) Ltd (and **Hulton**), Old Station Drive, Leckhampton, Cheltenham, Glos. GL53 0DN   *tel* (0242) 228888   telex 43593 Sthorn G   *fax* (0242) 221914. *Managing director:* R.M. Kendall; *directors:* M.M. Van de Weijer, J.C. Richardson, B. Carvell, J. de Courcy, J.P. Dubois.
Educational – primary, secondary, further education.

*Thorsons (1930), 77-85 Fulham Palace Road, Hammersmith, London W6 8JB   *tel* 081-741 7070   *telex* 25611 Colins G   *fax* 081-307 4440. *Managing director:* Eileen Campbell. Imprint of **HarperCollins Publishers.**
Complementary medicine, health and nutrition, business and management, self-help and positive thinking, popular psychology, parenting and childcare, and environmental issues.

Threshold Books—acquired by **The Kenilworth Press Ltd,** *q.v.*

*Times Books—imprint of **HarperCollins Publishers.** *Managing director:* Barry Winkleman. Atlases, reference.

*Alec Tiranti Ltd—taken over by **Academy Editions,** *q.v.*

Titan Books Ltd (1981), Panther House, 38 Mount Pleasant, London WC1X 0AP *tel* 071-833 3777 *fax* 071-278 1089. *Publisher and managing director:* Nick Landau; *managing editor:* Katy Wild.
Graphic novels, paperbacks and albums, including Judge Dredd and Batman, featuring comic strip material for both children and adults; film and TV tie-ins, including Dr Who and Star Trek; science fiction and fantasy. *No* unsolicited material without preliminary letter please.

Tolley Publishing Co. Ltd (1918), Tolley House, 2 Addiscombe Road, Croydon, Surrey CR9 5AF *tel* 081-686 9141. *Directors:* B.G.K. Downing (chairman), H.L. King (managing), A.J. Fisher, N.H. Parmee, R.E. Webb, K.D. Ladbrook, K.R. Tingley, R. McKay, A.P. Diggles.
Taxation, accountancy, company law and secretarial practice, employment law, social security and other law.

*****Transworld Publishers Ltd,** 61-63 Uxbridge Road, London W5 5SA *tel* 081-579 2652 *telex* 267974 Trnspb G *fax* 081-579 5479. Subsidiary of **Bertelsmann AG.** *Managing director and chief executive:* Paul Scherer.
Imprints Corgi, Bantam, Bantam Press, Young Corgi, Picture Corgi, Black Swan, Partridge Press, Doubleday, Freeway, Bantam Little Rooster, Yearling.

*****Trentham Books Ltd** (1968), Unit 13/14 Trent Trading Park, Botteslow Street, Hanley, Stoke-on-Trent, Staffs. ST1 3LY *tel* (0782) 274227 *fax* (0782) 281755. *Directors:* Professor S.J. Eggleston (managing), Gillian Klein, Barbara Wiggins. *Editorial office:* 28 Hillside Gardens, London N6 5ST *tel* 081-348 2174.
Education (including specialist fields – multicultural issues, design and technology, early years), social policy, sociology of Europe.

*****Triangle**—imprint of **Society for Promoting Christian Knowledge.** Popular religion paperbacks.

Triton Publishing Company Ltd (1964), 1A Montagu Mews North, London W1H 1AJ *tel* 071-706 0486. *Directors:* G. Golledge, Carolyn Whitaker.
Fiction and general non-fiction.

Trotman & Company Ltd (1970), 12-14 Hill Rise, Richmond, Surrey TW10 6UA *tel* 081-940 5668. *Director:* A.F. Trotman; *publications manager:* Kathryn Woodvine.
Higher education guidance, careers, lifeskills.

Troubadour—imprint of **Futura.** Historical romance paperbacks.

Two-Can Publishing (1987), 27 Cowper Street, London EC2A 4AP *tel* 071-251 4232 *telex* 261234 Tlsyst G *fax* 071-251 1610. *Directors:* Andrew Jarvis (chairman), Ian Grant (managing), Sara Lynn (creative), Brian Privett (production).
Children's magazines and non-fiction and activity books.

*****Tycooly Publishing**—imprint of **Cassell plc.** *Editorial director:* Stephen Butcher. Natural resources, agriculture and environment, scientific policy for economy of tropical and developing world.

Unicorn Books, 16 Laxton Gardens, Paddock Wood, Kent TN12 6BB *tel* (0892) 833648 *fax* (0892) 833577. *Directors:* R. Green, M.D. Green.
Militaria, music, transport and collecting books.

University of Exeter Press (1958), Reed Hall, Streatham Drive, Exeter, Devon EX4 4QR *tel* (0392) 263066 *telex* 42894 Exuniv G *fax* (0392) 263108. *Secretary to the University Press:* Elizabeth Saxby.

American and Commonwealth arts, archaeology, Classical studies, English literature, Exeter and the South West, general, history, linguistics, maritime studies, mining, modern languages and literature.

University of Wales Press (1922), 6 Gwennyth Street, Cathays, Cardiff CF2 4YD *tel* (0222) 231919 *fax* (0222) 230908.
Academic and educational (Welsh and English). Publishers of *Bulletin of the Board of Celtic Studies, Welsh History Review, Studia Celtica, Llen Cymru, Y Gwyddonydd, Efrydiau Athronyddol, Contemporary Wales, Welsh Journal of Education, Journal of Celtic Linguistics.*

*Unwin Hyman Ltd—acquired by **Routledge, Chapman & Hall.**

Usborne Publishing (1973) Usborne House, 83-85 Saffron Hill, London EC1N 8RT *tel* 071-430 2800 *telex* 8953598 *fax* 071-430 1562. *Directors:* T.P. Usborne, Jenny Tyler, Robert Jones, David Lowe, Keith Ball, C. Rawson, D. Harte, L. Hunt.
Children's books: reference, practical, craft, natural history, computers.

Vallentine, Mitchell & Co. Ltd (1950), Gainsborough House, 11 Gainsborough Road, London E11 1RS *tel* 081-530 4226 *telegraphic address* Valmico, London *fax* 081-530 7795. *Directors:* F. Cass (managing), M.P. Zaidner.
Jewish studies.

*Van Nostrand Reinhold (INT.) Co. Ltd, 2-6 Boundary Row, London SE1 8HN *tel* 071-865 0066 *telex* 290164 Chapma G *fax* 071-522 9623. *Directors:* P.A. Gardner (managing), A.J. Davis (finance), D. Recaldin (publishing), J. Lavender (marketing), G. McDonald (book production). Division of **Chapman & Hall.**
Academic, aeronautics, architecture, electrical and electronics, engineering, mathematics, professional, reference, pure and applied science, technology, computers, management, accountancy, finance, food technology.

*Variorum—imprint of **Gower Publishing Group Ltd.** Historical studies.

The Vegetarian Society (UK) Ltd, Parkdale, Dunham Road, Altrincham, Cheshire WA14 4QG *tel* 061-928 0793 *fax* 061-926 9182.
Vegetarianism, recipes, wholefood nutrition and cookery courses; travel guide and handbook; bi-monthly magazine.

Verso Ltd (1970), 6 Meard Street, London W1V 3HR *tel* 071-437 3546/434 1704 *fax* 071-734 0059. *Directors:* Colin Robinson (managing), Robin Blackburn (chairman), Ellen Wood.
Politics, biography, sociology, economics, history, philosophy, cultural studies.

*Viking, hardcover imprint of **The Penguin Group,** 27 Wrights Lane, London W8 5TZ *tel* 071-416 3000 *telex* 917181/2 *fax* 071-416 3099. *Publishing director:* Clare Alexander.
Fiction, general non-fiction; history, literature, art, architecture, biography, current affairs and science.

*Viking Children's Books, children's hardcover imprint of **The Penguin Group,** 27 Wrights Lane, London W8 5TZ *tel* 071-416 3000 *telex* 917181/2 *fax* 071-416 3099. *Publishing director:* Elizabeth Attenborough.
Fiction, poetry, picture books, limited non-fiction.

*Vintage—imprint of **Arrow Books Ltd.** Quality fiction and non-fiction.

Virago Press (1974), 20-23 Mandela Street, Camden Town, London NW1 0HQ *tel* 071-383 5150 *telegraphic address* Caterwaul London NW1

fax 071-383 4892. *Chairwoman:* Carmen Callil; *managing director:* Harriet Spicer; *directors:* Lennie Goodings, Ruth Petrie, Gil McNeil, Lynn Knight, Susan Sandon, Karen Cooper, Ursula Owen.
Books for the general and educational market which highlight all aspects of women's lives. Fiction and non-fiction, educational.

Virgin Books—imprint of **Virgin Publishing Ltd.** Youth-oriented popular non-fiction.

Virgin Publishing Ltd, 26 Grand Union Centre, 338 Ladbroke Grove, London W10 5AH *tel* 081-968 7554 *fax* 081-968 0929. *Chairman:* Robert Devereux; *directors:* Robert Shreeve (managing), Sally Holloway (editorial).
Biography and memoirs, current affairs, literary, fiction, films, general, history, humour, illustrated, practical handbooks, rock music, television, theatre, true crime.
Imprints: W.H. Allen, Allison & Busby, Dr Who, Nexus, Virgin Books.

Virtue & Co. Ltd (1819), 25 Breakfield, Coulsdon, Surrey CR5 2UE *tel* 081-668 4632 *telex* 262433 Monref G *fax* 081-668 4102. *Directors:* Michael Virtue, Joan Tolman.
Books for the catering trade and the home.

Vision Press Ltd (1946), 28 Phillimore Walk, Kensington, London W8 7SA *tel/fax* 071-938 2929. *Directors:* Alan Moore, BA (managing), Amber G. Moore.
Art, film, history, literary criticism, music, theatre. **Artemis Press** imprint: education.

Walker Books Ltd (1979), 87 Vauxhall Walk, London SE11 5HJ *tel* 071-793 0909 *telex* 8955572 *fax* 071-587 1123. *Directors:* David Ford, David Heatherwick, Wendy Boase, David Lloyd, Amelia Edwards, Judy Burdsall, Harold G. Gould, OBE.
Children's – mainly picture books; junior and teenage fiction.

Warburg Institute, University of London, Woburn Square, London WC1H 0AB *tel* 071-580 9663 *fax* 071-436 2852.
Cultural and intellectual history, with special reference to the history of the classical tradition.

*Ward Lock—imprint of **Cassell plc.** *Publishing director:* David Holmes.
Cookery, gardening, sports and adventure pursuits, popular reference books and fishing.

Ward Lock Educational Co. Ltd (1952), 1 Christopher Road, East Grinstead, West Sussex RH19 3BT *tel* (0342) 318980 *fax* (0342) 410980. *Directors:* Au Bak Ling (chairman Hong Kong), Vincent Winter, Au King Kwok (Hong Kong), Au Wai Kwok (Hong Kong), Albert Kw Au (Hong Kong), Au Chun Kwok (Hong Kong); Quentin Hockliffe (sales).
Primary and secondary pupil materials, Kent Mathematics Project, Reading Workshops, teachers' books, music books, history, religious education, environmental studies.

*Frederick Warne & Co. Ltd, 27 Wrights Lane, London W8 5TZ *tel* 071-416 3000 *telex* 917181/2 *fax* 071-416 3099. *Directors:* Sally Floyer (publisher), Trevor Glover, John Rolfe, Stephen Hall, John Webster. A **Penguin Group** company.
Beatrix Potter, Flower Fairies, Orlando, Huxley Pig, Bunnykins, Observer's Pocket Series.

*Franklin Watts (1969, London; 1942, New York), 96 Leonard Street, London EC2A 4RH *tel* 071-739 2929 *telex* 262655 Groluk G *fax* 071-739 2318.

Directors: Chester Fisher (publishing), Marlene Johnson (finance/operations), Rita Ireland (production). Division of **The Watts Group.**
Children's illustrated non-fiction, reference, education.

*The Watts Group, 96 Leonard Street, London EC2A 4RH *tel* 071-739 2929 *telex* 262655 Groluk G *fax* 071-739 2318. Division of **The House of Grolier Ltd.** *Directors:* Judith Elliot (publisher: Orchard), Chester Fisher (publisher: Franklin Watts), Marlene Johnson (managing), Rita Ireland (production).
Children's picture books, fiction, poetry, novelty books, non-fiction, reference, education. Imprints: Orchard Books, Franklin Watts.

*Wayland (Publishers) Ltd (1969), 61-61A Western Road, Hove, East Sussex BN3 1JD *tel* (0273) 722561 *telex* 878170 Wayland G *fax* (0273) 29314. *Chairman:* J.-P. Dubois; *managing director:* J.W. Lewis; *directors:* S. White-Thomson (editorial), F.M. Jane (finance), K. Lilley (international sales), B. Nevin (UK sales).
Children's information books for ages 5-18. **Firefly Books** (1989). *Publishing manager:* F. Underwood. Elementary fiction/non-fiction imprint for ages 3-8.

Webb & Bower (Publishers) Ltd (1978), 5 Cathedral Close, Exeter, Devon EX1 1EZ *tel* (0392) 435362 *cables* Webbower Exeter *telex* 42544 Webbow *fax* (0392) 211652. *Directors:* Richard Webb, Delian Bower.
Specialises in publishing illustrated non-fiction books for the UK, USA and international co-edition markets. Arts, crafts, biography, topography, travel, nostalgia, gardening, food, wine, reference, general.

George Weidenfeld & Nicolson Ltd (1948), 91 Clapham High Street, London SW4 7TA *tel* 071-622 9933 *telex* 918066 Wpwnab G *fax* 071-627 3361 *telegraphic address* Nicobar London SW4. *Chairman:* Lord Weidenfeld; *managing directors:* Alan Miles, Richard Hussey; *directors:* Michael Dover, Christopher Falkus, Allegra Huston, Fiona Kennedy, Nick Williams (editorial), Bud Maclennan (rights), Diane Rowley (publicity), Mark Streatfeild (group sales), Graham Long (accounts).
Architecture, art, biography and memoirs, business, current affairs, economics, fiction, general, history, politics, sport, humour, cookery, crime, crafts and hobbies, gardening, science, sociology, travel.

*Wheatsheaf Books Ltd—see **Harvester Wheatsheaf.**

Wheldon & Wesley Ltd, Lytton Lodge, Codicote, Hitchin, Herts. SG4 8TE *tel* Stevenage (0438) 820370 *telex* 825562 Chacom G Wheld *fax* (0438) 821478 *Email* 78: ITE 001.
Natural history booksellers and publishers. Agency of the British Museum (Natural History) and Hunt Botanical Library.

*J. Whitaker & Sons Ltd, 12 Dyott Street, London WC1A 1DF *tel* 071-836 8911 *fax* 071-836 2909. *Directors:* Peter Allsop, Louis Baum, Robin Baum, Alan Mollison, T.E. Sweetman, David Whitaker (chairman), Sally Whitaker (managing).
Reference including *Whitaker's Almanack* (1869), *The Bookseller* (1858), *Whitaker's Books in Print* (1874), *Whitaker's Book List* (1924), and other book trade directories.

Whittet Books Ltd (1976), 18 Anley Road, London W14 0BY *tel* 071-603 1139 *telex* 826542 Teltex G (Whit) *fax* 043871 5247. *Directors:* Annabel Whittet, John Whittet, Marion Kovach.
Natural history, countryside, transport.

*Wildwood House Ltd—associate company of **Gower Publishing Group Ltd.** Business and general.

*John Wiley & Sons Ltd (incorporating **Interscience Publishers**), Baffins Lane, Chichester, West Sussex PO19 1UD   *tel* (0243) 779777   *telegraphic address and cables* Wilebook, Chichester   *telex* 86290 Wibook G   *fax* (0243) 775878   *BTG* 83 JWP001. *Chairman:* W.B. Wiley (USA); *managing director:* M.B. Foyle; *directors:* P.W. Ferris, M. Bide, J. Jarvis, C.J. Dicks, The Duke of Richmond, C.R. Ellis, D.E. Wiley. Subsidiary of **John Wiley & Sons Inc.,** New York.
Behavioural sciences and management, chemistry and earth sciences, biomedical sciences, engineering.

Wiley-Heyden Ltd—associate company of **John Wiley & Sons Ltd.**

*Philip Wilson Publishers Ltd (1975), 26 Litchfield Street, London WC2H 9NJ   *tel* 071-379 7886   *telex* 22158   *fax* 071-836 7049. *Directors:* Philip Wilson, Juliana Powney, Anne Jackson, Adrian Burton, Mary Osborne. Art.

*Wisley Handbooks—imprint of **Cassell plc.** *Trade publisher:* Barry Holmes. Gardening.

*H.F. & G. Witherby Ltd, 14 Henrietta Street, London WC2E 8QJ   *tel* 071-836 2006. *Directors:* David Burnett (managing), Stephen Bray, Michael Goff; *consultant:* Antony Witherby. Subsidiary of **Victor Gollancz Ltd.**
Natural history, fishing, ornithology, dogs, travel, cookery, wine, adventure.

The Woburn Press (1968), Gainsborough House, 11 Gainsborough Road, London E11 1RS   *tel* 081-530 4226   *fax* 081-530 7795. *Directors:* Frank Cass (managing), A.E. Cass, M.P. Zaidner.
Non-fiction, Woburn Educational Series.

*Wolfe Publishing Ltd, Brook House, 2-16 Torrington Place, London WC1E 7LT   *tel* 071-636 4622   *telegraphic address* Wolfebooks London   *telex* 8814230   *fax* 071-637 3021. *Chairman:* John F. Dill (USA); *managing director:* Michael Manson; *directors:* Pat Daly, Daniel J. Doody (USA), Peter Heilbrunn, Colin MacPherson, Derrick Holman, Geoffrey Greenwood, Elizabeth Horne.
Text and reference books in medicine, surgery, dentistry, nursing, veterinary medicine, pure and applied sciences.

Oswald Wolff Books, 8 Circus Lodge, Circus Road, London NW8 9JL   *tel* 071-286 5654. *Director:* Mrs Ilse Wolff.
German and European studies: literature and the arts, history, biography, current affairs.

The Women's Press (1978), 34 Great Sutton Street, London EC1V 0DX   *tel* 071-251 3007   *fax* 071-608 1938. *Directors:* Kathy Gale (publishing), Mary Hemming (sales).
Books by women in the areas of fiction, autobiography, history, art, health, politics. Imprint: Livewire Books for Teenagers.

Woodhead Publishing Ltd (1989), Abington Hall, Abington, Cambridge CB1 6AH   *tel* (0223) 891358   *telex* 81883 Weldex G   *fax* (0223) 893694. *Managing director:* Martin Woodhead; *finance director:* Duncan Leeper.
Engineering, electronics, finance, investment.

Woodhead-Faulkner (Publishers) Ltd (1972), Fitzwilliam House, 32 Trumpington Street, Cambridge CB2 1QY   *tel* (0223) 66733   *telex* 818454 Wfpubl G   *fax* (0223) 461428. *Directors:* H. Hirschberg (Chairman), P. Williams, J. Owens, O. Davies. Subsidiary of **Simon & Schuster International Group.**
Finance and investment, management, technical, social and welfare topics.

World International Publishing Ltd, Egmont House, PO Box 111, Great Ducie Street, Manchester M60 3BL   *tel* 061-834 3110   *telex* 668609 World G   *fax* 061-834 0059   *telegraphic address* World, Manchester. *Directors:* Tony Palmer (managing), Tony Paulaskas, Michael Herridge, David Sheldrake, Don Smith, Jeffrey Nobbs.
Children's humour, early learning, activity, gift and information books and annuals.

*****Worldwide Books**—imprint of **Mills & Boon.** Contemporary fiction, thriller, mystery, romance.

Xanadu Publications Ltd (1984), 19 Cornwall Road, London N4 4PH   *tel* 071-272 4895   *fax* 071-263 7708. *Director:* Richard Glyn Jones.
Blue Murder imprint, crime/thrillers, food and travel guides, general fiction, non-fiction, biography. *No* unsolicited MSS please.

*****Yale University Press London** (1961), 23 Pond Street, London NW3 2PN   *tel* 071-431 4422   *telegraphic address* Yalepress, London   *telex* 896075 Yupldn G   *fax* 071-431 3755.
Art, architecture, history, economics, political science, literary criticism, Asian and African studies, religion, philosophy, psychology, history of science.

*****Yearling** paperbacks—imprint of **Transworld Publishers Ltd.** Fiction for ages 8-11.

*****Young Corgi** paperbacks—imprint of **Transworld Publishers Ltd.** Fiction for ages 5-9.

Young Library Ltd (1982), 3 The Old Brushworks, 56 Pickwick Road, Corsham, Wiltshire SN13 9BX   *tel* (0249) 712025   *fax* (0249) 715558. *Director:* Roger Cleeve.
Highly illustrated non-fiction for children's libraries, including geography, history, natural history, social and urban studies, science and technology, and reference.

*****Zed Books Ltd** (1976), 57 Caledonian Road, London N1 9BU   *tel* 071-837 4014 (general)   071-837 0384 (editorial)   *fax* 071-833 3960. *Managing editor:* Robert Molteno.
Social sciences on international and Third World issues; women's studies, development and environmental studies; area studies (Africa, Asia, Caribbean, Latin America, Middle East and the Pacific).

*****Hans Zell Publishers,** PO Box 56, Oxford OX1 3EL   *tel* (0865) 511428   *fax* (0865) 311534/793298. Imprint of **Bowker-Saur Ltd.**
Bibliographies, directories and other reference works. African studies, African literature (criticism only).

Zwan Publishing Ltd—incorporated into **Pluto Publishing Ltd.**

A. Zwemmer Ltd (1951), 26 Litchfield Street, London WC2H 9NJ   *tel* 071-379 7886   *telex* 22158   *fax* 071-836 7049.
Architecture, photography, music history.

AUSTRALIA

*Members of Australian Book Publishers Association

Access Press (1979), 35 Stuart Street, Northbridge, WA 6000   *postal address* PO Box 132, Northbridge, WA   *tel* (09) 328 9188   *fax* (09) 328 4605.

Directors: John Harper-Nelson (chairman), Helen Weller (managing). Australiana, fiction, poetry, children's, history, general. Privately financed books published and distributed.

*Allen & Unwin Pty Ltd, PO Box 764, 8 Napier Street, North Sydney, NSW 2059   *tel* (02) 922 6399   *fax* (02) 955 3155. General trade, including fiction and children's books, academic, especially social science and history.

Edward Arnold (Australia) Pty Ltd (1975), 80 Waverley Road, Caulfield East, Victoria 3145   *postal address* PO Box 234, Caulfield East, Victoria 3145   *tel* (03) 572 2211   *cables* Edarnold   *fax* (03) 572 2095. *Directors:* Michael Duffett (managing), Graham Foxcroft, Richard Morris (UK). Educational, secondary, academic, professional, technical, medical.

*Australasian Publishing Co. Pty Ltd—now known as **Random Century Australia Pty Ltd.**

*The Australian Council for Educational Research Ltd, PO Box 210, Hawthorn, Victoria 3122   *tel* (03) 819 1400   *fax* (03) 819 5502. Range of books and kits: for teachers, trainee teachers, parents, psychologists, counsellors, students of education, researchers.

Blackwell Scientific Publications (Australia) Pty Ltd, 54 University Street, Carlton, Victoria 3053   *tel* (03) 347 0300   *telegraphic address* Blackwell, Melbourne   *telex* 107 16421 via Keylink   *fax* (03) 347 5001.

Brooks Waterloo Publishers—imprint of **Jacaranda Wiley Ltd.**

*Butterworths Pty Limited, 271-273 Lane Cove Road, North Ryde, NSW 2113   *tel* (02) 887 3444   *fax* (02) 887 4555.

*Cambridge University Press Australian Branch, 10 Stamford Road, Oakleigh, Melbourne, Victoria 3166   *tel* (03) 568 0322   *fax* (03) 563 1517; and 35 Sophia Street, Surry Hills, Sydney, NSW 2010   *tel* (02) 211 0604. *Director:* Kim W. Harris.

*Collins/Angus & Robertson Publishers, 4 Eden Park, 31 Waterloo Road, North Ryde, NSW 2113   *tel* (02) 888 4111   *fax* (02) 888 9972   *postal address* PO Box 290, North Ryde, NSW 2113. *Directors:* T.J. Kitson, S. MacDonald, P. Montgomery, D.M. Boyd. General fiction and non-fiction, Australiana, poetry, popular medicine, self-discovery, humour.

Craftsman House (1981), 20 Barcoo Street, Roseville East, NSW 2069   *postal address* PO Box 480, Roseville, NSW 2069   *tel* (02) 417 1670   *fax* (02) 417 1501. *Directors:* Nevill Drury (managing), Martin Gordon. Australian and European fine arts.

Elephas Books (1989), 361 Orrong Road, Kewdale, WA 6105   *tel* (09) 470 1080   *fax* (09) 470 3922. *Chairman:* Gail White; *managing director:* Michael Woodhouse. How-to and informational subjects.

Samuel French Ltd, represented by Dominie Pty Ltd, Drama Department, 8 Cross Street, Brookvale, NSW 2100   *tel* (02) 905 0201   *fax* (02) 905 5209. Publishers of plays and agents for the collection of royalties for Samuel French Ltd, incorporating Evans Plays and Samuel French Inc., The Society of Authors, ACTAC, and Bakers Plays of Boston.

*William Heinemann Australia—see **Octopus Publishing Group Australia.**

*Hill of Content Publishing Co. Pty Ltd (1965), 86 Bourke Street, Melbourne, Victoria 3000   *tel* (03) 654 3144   *fax* (03) 662 2527. *Directors:* M. Slamen, M.G. Zifcak, Michelle Anderson. Australiana, health, history, educational, general.

*****Hodder & Stoughton (Australia) Pty Ltd,** 10-16 South Street, (PO Box 386), Rydalmere, NSW 2116 *tel* (02) 638 5299 *telex* 24858 *fax* (02) 684 4942. *Directors:* Michael Duffett (managing), Philip Attenborough, John Clarke, Graham Foxcroft, Bert Hingley, Richard Morris, David Wilson. Fiction, general, educational, children's, religious, hardback and paperback.

Horwitz Grahame Pty Ltd, including **Horwitz Publications, Martin Educational** and **Carroll's,** 506 Miller Street, Cammeray 2062 *tel* (02) 929-6144 *telex* 127833 *fax* (02) 957 1814. *Directors:* S.D.L. Horwitz (chairman), P.D.L. Horwitz (chief executive), L.J. Moore, R.B. Fuller. Magazine and book publishers: non fiction, educational (primary, secondary and tertiary), reference books, technical, cookery, humour.

*****Jacaranda Wiley Ltd,** 33 Park Road, Milton, Queensland 4064 *tel* (07) 369 9755 *telex* AA 41845 *fax* (07) 369 9155; 90 Ormond Road, Elwood, Victoria 3184 *tel* (03) 531 8677; Suite 4, Level 4, Building 1, 1 Thomas Holt Drive, North Ryde, NSW 2113 *tel* (02) 805 1100 *fax* (02) 805 1597. Also New Zealand, Hong Kong, *q.v. Managing director:* K.J. Collins; *general managers:* Q. Smith, P. Donoughue, B. Brennan, F. Shea. Educational, technical, atlases, software.

*****Kangaroo Press Pty Ltd** (1980), 3 Whitehall Road, Kenthurst, NSW 2156 *tel* (02) 654 1502 *telex* AA 176432 Duroff *fax* (02) 654 1338. *Directors:* David Rosenberg, Priscilla Rosenberg. Gardening, craft, Australian history and natural history, collecting, fitness.

*****The Law Book Company Ltd,** 44-50 Waterloo Road, North Ryde, NSW 2113 *tel* (02) 887 0177 *telex* 27995 *fax* (02) 888 9706.

*****Longman Cheshire Pty Ltd,** Longman Cheshire House, Kings Gardens, 95 Coventry Street, South Melbourne, Victoria 3205 *tel* (03) 697 0666 *telex* AA33501 *fax* (03) 699 2041. *Managing director:* N.J. Ryan. Educational publishers.

*****Lothian Publishing Co. Pty Ltd,** 11 Munro Street, Port Melbourne, Victoria 3207 *tel* (03) 645 1544 *fax* (03) 646 4882. *Directors:* P. Lothian (chairman & managing), K.A. Lothian, E. McDonald, G. Matthews. Juveniles, health, gardening, general literature.

*****The Macmillan Company of Australia Pty Ltd,** 107 Moray Street, South Melbourne, Victoria 3205 *tel* (03) 699 8922 *telegraphic address* Scriniaire, Melbourne *telex* AA34454 *fax* (03) 690 6938; 6-8 Clarke Street, Crows Nest, NSW 2065 *tel* (02) 438 2988 *fax* (02) 438 1984. *Directors:* Brian Stonier (executive chairman), John Rolfe (managing), N. Byam Shaw (UK), Brian McCurdy, Marek Palka, Julia Stanton; *company secretary/financial controller:* Terry White. All types of books.

*****The Macquarie Library**—division of **Weldon International Pty Ltd.** The *Macquarie Dictionary*; dictionaries with lexicons appropriate to Australia and South-East Asia; reference.

*****Melbourne University Press,** 268 Drummond Street, Carlton, Victoria 3053 *tel* (03) 347 3455 *fax* (03) 344 6214 *postal address* PO Box 278, Carlton South, Victoria 3053. *Chairman:* Professor J.R.V. Prescott; *director:* J. Iremonger. Prepared to consider works of academic, scholastic or cultural interest, educational textbooks and books of reference. Representatives: North America, International Specialized Book Services Inc *tel* 503-287-3093; Tokyo, Hong Kong and Singapore, United Publishers Services Ltd.

*****Thomas Nelson Australia,** 102 Dodds Street, South Melbourne, Victoria 3205 *tel* (03) 685 4111 *fax* (03) 685 4199. Educational books.

*Octopus Publishing Group Australia Pty Ltd, 22 Salmon Street, Port Melbourne, Victoria 3207 *tel* (03) 646 6688 *fax* (03) 646 6925. *Managing Director:* Sandy Grant. General fiction and non-fiction, children's books, reference.

*Oxford University Press, Australia, 253 Normanby Road, South Melbourne, Victoria 3205 *postal address* GPO Box 2784Y, Melbourne, Victoria 3001 *tel* (03) 646 4200 *cables* Oxonian, Melbourne *telex* AA 35330 ref. Oxonian *fax* (03) 646 3251. *Managing director:* Sandra McComb. Australian history, biography, literary criticism, general, including children's books, but excluding fiction. School books in all subjects.

Pacific Publications (Aust.) Pty Ltd, division of News Ltd, 4th Floor, 46 Kippax Street, Surry Hills, NSW 2010 *tel* (02) 288 3000 *telex* AA20124 *fax* (02) 288 3322 *postal address* GPO Box 4245, Sydney, NSW 2001. General and reference for Pacific Islands market and agricultural/technical.

*Penguin Books Australia Ltd (1946), (PO Box 257), 487 Maroondah Highway, Ringwood, Victoria 3134 *tel* (03) 871 2400 *telegraphic address* Penguinook, Melbourne *fax* (03) 870 9618. *Directors:* P.W. Dart (information services), P.J. Field (managing), R.E. Ford (trade services), T.D. Glover (chairman), P.M. Mayer, T.V. Moloney (sales), N.J. Ryan, R.P. Sessions (publishing), J.C. Strike (finance and administration), J.W. Webster. Fiction, general non-fiction, current affairs, sociology, economics, environmental, travel guides, anthropology, politics, children's.

*Pitman Publishing Pty Ltd—imprint of Longman Cheshire Pty Ltd.

*Random Century Australia Pty Ltd, 1st Floor, 20 Alfred Street, Milsons Point, NSW 2061 *tel* (02) 954 9966 *fax* (02) 954 4562. *Directors:* J.E. Bullivant, A.J.V. Cheetham (chairman), J.D. Cody, A. Davidson, S. Delmont, R.J. Ford, S. Guthrie, M.J. Kelly (editorial/rights and permissions), E.F. Mason (managing), J.M. Mottram. General, non-fiction, fiction, children's.

Reed Books Pty Ltd, Suite 3, 470 Sydney Road, Balgowlah, NSW 2093 *tel* (02) 907 9966 *fax* (02) 907 9664. *Directors:* D.A. MacLellan, W.A. Templeman (publishing), J.B. Broadley. General.

Rigby International—subsidiary of Weldon International Pty Ltd. Educational resources.

Sun Books Pty Ltd (1965), 107 Moray Street, South Melbourne, Victoria 3205 *tel* (03) 699 8922 *telegraphic address* Sunbooks. *Directors:* K.B. Stonier, J. Rolfe, N.G. Byam Shaw. Paperbacks – fiction, non-fiction, educational, especially Australian titles. Subsidiary of The Macmillan Company of Australia Pty Ltd.

*University of Queensland Press (1948), PO Box 42, St Lucia, Queensland 4067 *tel* (07) 365 2127 *telex* Univqld AA40315 Press *fax* (07) 365 1988. *General manager:* L.C. Muller. Scholarly works, tertiary texts, Australian fiction, young adult fiction, poetry, history, and general interest.

*Viking O'Neil (1987), 56 Claremont Street, South Yarra, Victoria 3141 *tel* (03) 241 9901 *fax* (03) 241 0913. *Associate director:* Lloyd J. O'Neil; *publisher:* Peter Hyde; *managing editor:* Helen Duffy. Imprint of Penguin Books Australia Ltd. Pictorial and general works relating to Australia, cartographic publications, craft, health, cookery, gardening, sport.

Weldon International Pty Ltd, 372 Eastern Valley Way, Willoughby, NSW 2068 *tel* (02) 415 9222 *telex* AA 121546 *fax* (02) 417 6919. *Chairman:* Kevin Weldon. Incorporates publishing divisions of Weldon Publishing, Weldon Russell, Weldon Owen, Weldon New Zealand, Weldon Young, The Macquarie Library and Rigby International.

Weldon Owen—division of **Weldon International Pty Ltd.** Cookery, natural science, aerial photography books, travel.

Weldon Publishing—division of **Weldon International Pty Ltd.** Non-fiction including gardening, cookery, Australiana, sport, natural history, health and life style, Aboriginal subjects.

Weldon Russell—division of **Weldon International Pty Ltd.** Non-fiction including Australiana, natural history, cookery, gardening, general reference books and gift books.

Weldon Young Productions—division of **Weldon International Pty Ltd.** Magazines. Incorporates Lansdowne Editions: reference works in limited editions.

*__Wild & Woolley P__ (1974), PO Box 41, Glebe, NSW 2037   *tel* (02) 692 0166   *fax* (02) 552 4320. *Director:* Pat Woolley. Australian authors only.

CANADA

The following is a selected list; it includes only a few of the very many smaller firms, and of the specialist publishers.

*Members of the Canadian Book Publishers' Council
†Members of the Association of Canadian Publishers

The Book Society of Canada, Limited—see **Irwin Publishing.**

*__Butterworths,__ 75 Clegg Road, Markham, Ontario L6G 1A1   *tel* 416-479-2665   *fax* 416-479-2826.

*__Canada Publishing Corporation__ (1844), 164 Commander Boulevard, Agincourt, Ontario M1S 3C7   *tel* 416-293-8141   *fax* 416-293-9009. Publishers of elementary, secondary, post-secondary, university textbooks, medical and general reading publications. Professional and reference material, technical video production, electronic courseware.
Agents for: Fraser Institute, Harrap's Ltd (Trade), Andrews & McMeel, Wm. Morrow, Scott Foresman Inc., Wilshire Book, Bordas (Paris), C.B.I., Hearst Books, Ivory Tower, Quill, Green Willow, Chivers Large Print Books, Orchard Books, Microsoft, IDG Books, Taylor & Francis, Aspen Publishing, Productivity Press, Source Books (trade).

Canadian Stage and Arts Publications Ltd, George Hencz, 263 Adelaide Street West, 5th Floor, Toronto, Ontario M5H 1Y2   *tel* 416-971-9516   *fax* 416-971-9517. Primarily interested in children's books of an educational nature, art books. Also publishes *Performing Arts in Canada*, a quarterly covering all aspects of the performing arts (*editor:* Sarah B. Hood).

The Carswell Company Ltd, 2330 Midland Avenue, Agincourt, Ontario M1S 1P7   *tel* 416-291-8421   *telex* 065-25289   *fax* 416-291-3426. *President:* Alan Turnbull. Law, professional and reference.

Wm. Collins Sons & Co. (Canada) Ltd—see **HarperCollins Canada.**

*__Copp Clark Pitman,__ 2775 Matheson Boulevard East, Mississauga, Ontario L4W 4P7   *tel* 416-238-6074   *telex* 06-960413   *fax* 416-238-6075. *President:* Stephen J. Mills; *publication director:* Marion Elliott. Educational textbooks for elementary, secondary and college, technical and business education. Preliminary letter required before submitting manuscript.

*__Doubleday Canada Ltd__ (1937), 105 Bond Street, Toronto, Ontario M5B 1Y3   *tel* 416-977-7891/416-340-0777   *fax* 416-977-8087/416-977-8488. General trade fiction and non-fiction; book clubs.

†**Douglas & McIntyre Ltd** (1964), 1615 Venables Street, Vancouver, BC V5L 2H1 *tel* 604-254-7191/416-537-2501 *fax* 604-254-9099/416-537-4647. General list including Canadian biography, art and architecture, natural history, history, North American anthropology/ethnology, Canadian fiction. Children's division (Groundwood Books) specialises in fiction and illustrated flats. Educational division in elementary social studies, health and reading. Agents for Thames and Hudson and Walker Books.

†**ECW Press** (1979), 307 Coxwell Avenue, Toronto, Ontario M4L 3B5 *tel* 416-694-3348. *President:* Jack David; *secretary-treasurer:* Robert Lecker. Literary criticism, indexes, bibliographies.

†**Fitzhenry & Whiteside Limited** (1966), 195 Allstate Parkway, Markham, Ontario L3R 4T8 *tel* 416-477-0030 *fax* 416-477-9179 *toll free* 1-800-387-9776. *Directors:* R.I. Fitzhenry, Sharon Fitzhenry, Robert W. Read, Thomas Richardson. Trade, educational, college books.

***Gage Educational Publishing Company**—see **Canada Publishing Corporation.**

***Harlequin Enterprises Ltd** (1949), 225 Duncan Mill Road, Don Mills, Ontario M3B 3K9 *tel* 416-445-5860 *telex* 06-966697 *fax* 416-445-8655. *Chairman:* David A. Galloway; *president and ceo:* Brian E. Hickey. Romance, action adventure.

HarperCollins Canada, 1995 Markham Road, Scarborough, Ontario M1B 5M8 *tel* 416-321-2241 *fax* 416-321-3033; **HarperCollins Publishers Ltd,** Suite 2900, Hazelton Lanes, 55 Avenue Road, Toronto, Ontario M5R 3L2 *tel* 416-975-9334 *fax* 416-975-9884. Publishers of general literature, trade and reference, bibles, religious, mass market paperbacks, audio cassettes, children's books. Publishers in Canada for HarperCollins Publishers, Harvill Press Ltd, Fontana, Farrar, Straus & Giroux, Armada Books, Carnival, Collins Willow, Dinosaur, Flamingo, Fount, Grafton, Hill & Wang, Lions, Noonday Press, Paladin, Picador Books, Piccolo Books, Picture Lions, Piper, Young Lions, Ballinger Pub., Barnes & Noble, Basic Books, T.Y. Crowell, Caedmon, Carousel, Colophon, Icon Editions, J.B. Lippincott Jr, Perennial Library, Torch, Trophy, Unwin Hyman, Bartholomew.

***Holt, Rinehart & Winston of Canada, Ltd,** 55 Horner Avenue, Toronto, Ontario M8Z 4X6 *tel* 416-255-4491 *fax* 416-255-4046.

†**Hurtig Publishers** (1967), 1302 Oxford Tower, 10235 101 Street, Edmonton, Alberta T5J 3G1 *tel* 403-426-2359 *fax* 403-429-5996. *President:* M.G. Hurtig. Reference, humour, biography, political science, Canadiana, energy, environment, The Canadian Encyclopedia, The Junior Encyclopedia of Canada.

***Irwin Publishing,** division of **General Publishing Co. Ltd,** 30 Lesmill Road, Don Mills, Ontario M3B 2T6 *tel* 416-445-3333 *fax* 416-445-5967. *President:* Brian O'Donnell; *chairman:* Jack Stoddart. Educational books at the elementary, high school and college levels.
Represent in Canada: B.T. Batsford, Unwin Hyman (Educational), Heinemann Educational, Heinemann Medical, John Murray, McDougal Littell & Co., Cambridge University Press, Paul Chapman Publishing, EMC Publishing, Multilingual Matters, Paradigm Publishing.

†**Kids Can Press Ltd,** 585 1/2 Bloor Street West, Toronto, Ontario M6G 1K5 *tel* 416-534-6389 *fax* 416-534-6152. *Publisher:* Valerie Hussey. Juvenile and young adult books.

McClelland & Stewart Inc. (1906), 481 University Avenue, Suite 900, Toronto, Ontario M5G 2E9 *tel* 416-598-1114 *fax* 416-598-7764. *Chairman/president and ceo:* Avie Bennett. General and educational.

†**McGill-Queen's University Press** (1969), 3430 McTavish Street, Montreal, Quebec H3A 1X9 *tel* 514-398-3750 *telex* 05-268510 *fax* 514-398-4333; and Watson Hall, Queen's University, Kingston, Ontario K7L 3N6 *tel* 613-545-2155 *fax* 613-545-6822. Academic.

*McGraw-Hill Ryerson Ltd, 300 Water Street, Whitby, Ontario L1N 9B6 *tel* 416-430-5000 *fax* 416-430-5020. Educational and trade books.

*Macmillan of Canada (1905), division of **Canada Publishing Corporation,** 29 Birch Avenue, Toronto, Ontario M4V 1E2 *tel* 416-963-8830 *telex* 062 18018 *fax* 416-923-4821. Trade book publishers.

*Maxwell Macmillan Canada (1958), 1200 Eglinton Avenue East, Suite 200, Don Mills, Ontario M3C 3N1 *tel* 416-449-6030 *fax* 416-449-0068. *President:* Ray Lee. Academic, technical, medical, educational, children's and adult, trade, computer books and software.

Nelson Canada (1914), 1120 Birchmount Road, Scarborough, Ontario M1K 5G4 *tel* 416-752-9100 *telex* 06-963813 *fax* 416-752-9646. *Directors:* Alan G. Cobham (president), Ronald Fior, Martin Keast, Peter McBride, Ben Wentzell, Ron Munro. Elementary, high school, college textbooks; measurement and guidance; children's library.

†**Oberon Press,** 400-350 Sparks Street, Ottawa, Ontario K1R 7S8 *tel* 613-238-3275. General.

*Oxford University Press, Canada, 70 Wynford Drive, Don Mills, Ontario M3C 1J9 *tel* 416-441-2941 *fax* 416-441-0345. *Manager:* M. Morrow. General, educational, juvenile and academic.

*Pippin Publishing Ltd, 150 Telson Road, Markham, Ontario L3R 1E5 *tel* 416-513-6966 *fax* 416-513-6977.

*Prentice-Hall Canada, Inc. (1960), 1870 Birchmount Road, Scarborough, Ontario M1P 2J7 *tel* 416-293-3621 *telex* 065-25184 *fax* 416-293-0571. *Directors:* John P. Schram, E.E. Campbell, R.E. Snyder. Educational (elementary, secondary, post-secondary), general history, natural history, politics, sports.

*Stoddart Publishing Co. Ltd, 34 Lesmill Road, Don Mills, Ontario M3B 2T6 *tel* 416-445-3333 *fax* 416-445-5967. Fiction and non-fiction.

Tundra Books Inc., 1434 St Catherine Street West, Suite 303, Montreal, Quebec H3G 1R4 *tel* 514-932-5434 *cables* Tunbooks *fax* 514-861-6426. *President:* May Cutler. General trade and juvenile books; art books.

†**University of Toronto Press,** 10 St Mary Street, Suite 700, Toronto M4Y 2W8 *tel* 416-978-5171 (editorial); 416-978-2239 (administration).

INDIA

*Members of the Federation of Indian Publishers

*Ajanta Books International (1975), 1-UB Jawahar Nagar, Bungalow Road, Delhi 110007 *tel* 2926182. *Proprietor:* S. Balwant. Social sciences and humanities, specialising in: politics, sociology, management, history, literature (Indian and Western), education, linguistics, philosophy, archaeology, library science, fiction.

Allied Publishers Limited, 15 J.N. Heredia Marg, Ballard Estate, Bombay 400038 *tel* 2617926 *telex* 011-86506. *Managing director:* S.M. Sachdev. Publishers of school and college textbooks; economics, education, psychology, sociology, and general books on current affairs and Oriental art. Exclusive agents in India for: A. & C. Black (Publishers) Ltd, W. and R. Chambers Ltd, Gerald Duckworth & Co. Ltd, Elsevier Applied Science Publishers Ltd, Graham & Trotman Ltd, MTP Press Ltd.

Atma Ram & Sons (1909), Post Box 1429, Kashmere Gate, Delhi 110006 *tel* 2518159, 2523082 *cables* Books Delhi. *Managing proprietor:* Ish Kumar Puri; *senior director:* Sushil Puri. *Branch:* 17 Ashok Marg, Lucknow. Art, literature, reference, biography, fiction, economics, politics, education, history, philosophy, psychology, science, technology. Books published in English and Hindi languages. Translations and reprints of foreign books undertaken. Booksellers and importers of foreign books on a large scale.

B.I. Publications Pvt. Ltd, 54 Janpath, New Delhi 110001 *tel* 3325313 *telex* 031 63352 BI IN *fax* 91-11-3323138. *Chairman:* R.D. Bhagat. Scientific, technical, medical, business and industrial management, educational, children's, reference and general.

*S. Chand & Co. Ltd (1917), Ram Nagar, New Delhi 110055 *tel* 772080 *telegraphic address* Eschand, New Delhi *telex* 316-1310. *Directors:* Rajendra Kumar Gupta, Ravindra Kumar Gupta. Science, technology, medicine, educational books, children's books.

*Children's Book Trust (1957), Nehru House, 4 Bahadur Shah Zafar Marg, New Delhi 110002 *tel* 3316970 *telegraphic address* Childtrust, New Delhi. *Founder:* K. Shankar Pillai. Children's books.

English Book Depot (1923), 15 Rajpur Road, Dehra Dun (UP) 248001 *tel* 23792/23187 *telex* 583 345 Ebd IN *fax* 91-135-28392. *Directors:* Snehlata and Sandeep Dutt. Military science, agriculture, forestry, geology and petroleum.

*Heritage Publishers (1973), 4348 Madan Mohan Street, 4c Ansari Road, Daryaganj, New Delhi 110002. *Proprietor:* B.R. Chawla. Social science, Indology, humanities.

*Hind Pocket Books Pvt Ltd, G.T. Road, Dilshad Garden, Delhi 110095 *tel* 3320014, 2282046 *telegraphic address* Pocketbook Delhi. *Managing director:* D.N. Malhotra. Paperbacks in Indian languages and English.

Indian Press (Publications) Private, Limited, 36 Pannalal Road, Allahabad (UP) *tel* 600858/9 *telegraphic address* Publikason. *Managing director:* D.P. Ghosh. Branches and agencies in all principal towns of India. Publishers of *Saraswati Hindi Monthly Magazine*, and school, college, university and general books in Hindi, Bengali, English; Gurumukhi, Urdu, Marathi, Nepali languages.

*Jaico Publishing House (1946/7), 121-125 Mahatma Gandhi Road, Bombay 400023 *tel* 276702, 276802 *telegraphic address* Jaicobooks Bombay *telex* 11-3369 Jai In *fax* 91-22-2041673. *Managing director:* Ashwin J. Shah. History, politics, sociology, management, economics, psychology, philosophy, religion, law, crime.

Kothari Publications, Jute House, 12 India Exchange Place, Calcutta 700001 *tel* 20-9563, 20-6572, 711-009 *cables* Zeitgeist. *Proprietor:* Ing. H. Kothari of Sujangarh, Rajasthan. Technical, general and reference books. *Who's Who* series in India. Agents for many foreign publishers.

The Little Flower Co. (1929), Bhurangam Buildings, P.B. 1028, 43 Ranganathan Street, Thyagarayanagar, Madras 600017 *tel* 441538 *telegraphic address* Lifco, Madras. Lifco books. General, fiction, technical, dictionaries, astrology, medicine, legal, commercial, educational and religious.

Macmillan India Ltd, 50/4 Palace Road, Bangalore 560052. *Branches:* Mercantile House, Magazine Street, Reay Road (East), Bombay 400010; 21 Patullos Road, Royapettah, Madras 600002. Associate Company of Macmillan Publishers Ltd, London. Publishers of educational, scientific, humanities, literature, technical, medical, and general books. Agents in India, Burma, Ceylon, Nepal and Bangladesh for: Gill & Macmillan Ltd, Dublin, The Hamlyn Publishing Group Ltd.

National Book Trust, India (1957), A-5 Green Park, New Delhi 110016 *tel* 664667, 664020, 664540 *telex* 031-73034 Nbt In.

*Orient Longman Ltd, 3-6-272 Himayat Nagar, Hyderabad 500029 *tel* 240 305/306, 240 294/297/391 *telex* 425 6803 Olex IN; and regional offices at Kamani Marg, Ballard Estate, Bombay 400 038; 17 Chittaranjan Avenue, Calcutta 700 072; 160 Anna Salai, Madras 600 002; 1/24 Asaf Ali Road, New Delhi 110 002; 80/1 Mahatma Gandhi Road, Bangalore 560 001; Birla Mandir Road, Patna 800 004; S C Goswami Road, Pan Bazar, Guwahati 781 001; Patiala House 16-A, Ashok Marg, Lucknow 226 001. Fiction and non-fiction, biography, history, philosophy, reference, children's literature, paperbacks, medicine, psychology, engineering, general and social science, technology, university, secondary and primary textbooks, educational materials. Associated with Longman Group Ltd, Sangam Books Ltd, The Universities Press (India) Pvt. Ltd, The Sangam Books (India) Pvt. Ltd. Agents and distributors in India for Longman Group Ltd, Penguin Books Ltd, Ladybird Books Ltd, Cambridge University Press, UNESCO, Paris.

Oxford & IBH Publishing Co. Pvt. Ltd (1964), 66 Janpath (2nd Floor), New Delhi 110001 *tel* 3324578, 3320518, 3315896 *telegraphic address* Indamer *telex* 3161990 Am In *fax* 91-11-3322639. Agricultural sciences, biology, zoology, civil engineering, mechanical engineering, botany, economics and management.

*Oxford University Press (Indian Branch). *General manager:* S.K. Mookerjee. *Head office:* Post Box 43, YMCA Library Building, Jai Singh Road, New Delhi 110001 *tel* 350490/351312/352769 *cables* Oxorient, Delhi *telex* 61108 Oxon IN; *branch offices:* Post Box 7035, 2/11 Ansari Road, Daryaganj, New Delhi 110002 *tel* 3273841/3273842/3277812 *cables* Oxonian, Delhi *telex* 62269 Oxon IN; Post Box 31, Oxford House, Apollo Bunder, Bombay 400039 *tel* 202-1029/202-1198/202-1396 *cables* Oxonian, Bombay *telex* 6737 Oxon IN; GPO Box 530, 5 Lala Lajpat Rai Sarani (Third Floor), Calcutta 700020 *tel* 475735 *cables* Oxonian, Calcutta *telex* 4090 Oxon IN; Post Box 1079, Oxford House, Anna Salai, Madras 600006 *tel* 47-2267/47-2268/47-2299 *cables* Oxonian, Madras *telex* 6504 Oxon IN. Publishers in all subjects. Agents in India, Burma, Sri Lanka and Nepal for Blackwell Scientific Publications Ltd, Faber & Faber Ltd and Ginn & Co. Ltd. Distributors for the following university presses: Harvard, Princeton and Stanford.

Penguin Books India (P) Ltd (1985), B4/246 Safdarjung Enclave, New Delhi 110029 *tel* 608246, 607157 *telex* 62062 Peng IN *fax* 91-11-6875611. *Directors:* Patrick Wright (chairman), Peter Mayer, Aveek Sarkar (managing), Peter Carson, Arup Sarkar, John Webster, Ganes Nag, Shobha Subramaniam, V.S.T. Shankardass, Rani Shankardass; *publisher:* David Davidar. Fiction, non-fiction, history, biography, autobiography, belles-lettres, social sciences, management, humour, sports, classics, poetry, children's books.

Prentice-Hall of India Pvt Ltd, M-97 Connaught Circus, New Delhi 110011 *tel* 332 1779 *cables* Prenhall New Delhi *telex* 3161808 Ph In. *Chairman/managing director:* Asoke K. Ghosh. Textbooks. *Associate companies:* Prentice-Hall, UK, Prentice-Hall, Inc., USA.

*Rajpal & Sons, PO Box 1064, Delhi 110006 *tel* 2523904, 2519104 *telegraphic address* Rajpalsons, Delhi. *Managing partner:* Vishwanath. Literary criticism, social and general, humanities, textbooks, juvenile literature, Hindi and English.

Rupa & Co., PO Box 12333, 15 Bankim Chatterjee Street, Calcutta 700073 *tel* 321291, 316597, 326335 *telegraphic address* Rupanco, Calcutta-73. Art, education, history, literature, fiction, philosophy, religion, sport pastimes. Representatives for HarperCollins, Eyre & Spottiswoode, Foulsham, Wm. Heinemann, Merlin Press, Pan, Search Press, Sidgwick & Jackson, Souvenir Press, Spokesman, Frederick Warne.

Sage Publications India Pvt Ltd, 2nd Floor, 32 M-Block Market, Greater Kailash-I, New Delhi 110048 *tel* 6419884, 6444958 *cables* Sagepub New Delhi 110048. *Managing director:* Tejeshwar Singh. Social sciences. *Associate companies:* Sage Publications Ltd, UK, Sage Publications, Inc., USA.

Shiksha Bharati (1955), Madarsa Road, Kashmere Gate, Delhi 110006 *tel* 2519104. *Managing partner:* Veena Malhotra. Textbooks, popular science and children's books in Hindi and English; also juvenile literature.

*Sterling Publishers Pvt. Ltd (1964), L-10 Green Park Extension, New Delhi 110016 *tel* 669560/660904 *fax* 11-6839157. *Directors:* O.P. Ghai (chairman), S.K. Ghai (managing), Mrs Vimla Ghai. Biography, computer science, cookery, economics and commerce, education, history and Indology, language and literature, law, library science, management, military, philosophy and religion, politics, psychology and sociology.

*D.B. Taraporevala Sons & Co., Private, Ltd (Original firm established 1864), 210 Dr Dadabhai Naoroji Road, Bombay 400001 *tel* 204-1433. *Directors:* Mrs Manekbai J. Taraporevala and Miss Sooni J. Taraporevala; *chief executive:* Prof. Russi J. Taraporevala; Books on India and on Indian interest, fine arts, handicrafts, pictorial albums, business, economics, education, electronics, psychology, cookery, domestic economy, pets, hobbies, reference, languages, religion, philosophy, mysticism, occult sciences, law, history, culture, mythology, sociology, health, medical, sex, science, technology, self-improvement, self-instruction, sports, Indian classics.

*Tata McGraw-Hill Publishing Co. Ltd (1970), 4/16 Asaf Ali Road, New Delhi 110002 *tel* 278251-2-3 *telegraphic address* Corinthian, New Delhi *telex* 31-61979 Tmhd IN. *Directors:* J.J. Bhabha (chairman), S.A. Sabavala, Dr Francis A. Menezes, Dr Malcolm S. Adiseshiah, J.C. Dastur, N.R. Subramanian, R. Radhakrishnan, Joseph L. Dionne, J.G. Wrede, Frederick G. Perkins. Engineering, sciences, management, humanities, social sciences, computer science, electronics.

Thacker & Co., Ltd, 18-20 Kaikushroo Dubash Marg (Rampart Row), Bombay 400023 *tel* 242667, 242683, 242745 *telegraphic address* Booknotes, Bombay. *Chairman:* K.M. Diwanji; *chief executive:* Dhanraj K. Bhagat; *managing director:* J.M. Chudasama. Banking, gardening, cooking. Distributors for Ladybird Books, RotoVision, Walter Foster, Pan, Fontana, Hamlyn.

The Theosophical Publishing House, Adyar, Madras 600020 *tel* 410238 *telegraphic address* Theotheca, Madras 600020. Theosophical, mystical and occult literature. Publishers of *The Theosophist*, official organ of the

President, Theosophical Society. *Editor:* Mrs Radha Burnier, International President of The Theosophical Society. *Manager:* R. Gopalaratnam.

***Vikas Publishing House Pvt Ltd** (1969), 576 Masjid Road, Jangpura, New Delhi 110014 *tel* 615313, 4624605, 4624902 *telegraphic address* Vikasbooks, New Delhi *fax* 011-3313503 Vikas. *Managing director:* Narendra Kumar. Science and technology, humanities and social sciences, college level textbooks, school level textbooks, children's books, paperbacks.

***Vision Books Pvt. Ltd** (1975). Head Office: Madarsa Road, Kashmere Gate, Delhi 110006 *tel* 2517001, 2514274, 2512267; Editorial Office: 36-c Connaught Place, New Delhi 110 001 *tel* 332-8898, 332-9357 *telegraphic address* Visionbook New Delhi. *Directors:* Sudhir Malhotra (managing), Kapil Malhotra, Vishwanath. Fiction (including Indo-Anglian and translation from Indian languages and other languages), Indian culture, politics, biography, travel, poetry, drama management, military, religion, anthropology, mountaineering, education, international relations. *Imprints:* Vision Books, Orient Paperbacks, Anand Paperbacks, Naya Sahitya.

***Wiley Eastern Ltd** (1966), 4835/24 Ansari Road, Daryaganj, New Delhi 110002 *tel* 3276802, 3261487, 3267996 *telegraphic address* Wileyeast *telex* 031-66507 Welin. *Branches:* Bangalore, Bombay, Calcutta, Guwahati, Hyderabad, Lucknow, Madras, Pune, Rewa. *Directors:* W. Bradford Wiley, John Collins, Charles Ellis, E.B. Desai, A. Machwe, F.N. Mulla, A.R. Kundaji. Biology, physics, chemistry, mathematics, engineering sciences, humanities and social sciences.

THE REPUBLIC OF IRELAND AND NORTHERN IRELAND

*Members of the Irish Publishers' Association

***Appletree Press Ltd** (1974), 7 James Street South, Belfast BT2 8DL *tel* (0232) 243074 *telex* 9312100435 *fax* (0232) 246756; and Suite 521, Irish Life Centre, Talbot Street, Dublin *tel* (01) 746611. *Director:* John Murphy. Academic, biography, cookery, educational, guide books, history, literary criticism, music, photographic, social studies, sport, travel.

***Attic Press** (1984), 4 Upper Mount Street, Dublin 2 *tel* (01) 616128 *fax* (01) 616176. *Directors:* Aileen Cashman, Róisín Conroy, Paulyn Marrinan BL, Ailbhe Smyth. Books for and about women in the areas of social and political comment, fiction, women's studies, humour, reference guides and handbooks.

***Blackstaff Press Ltd** (1971), 3 Galway Park, Dundonald BT16 0AN *tel* (0232) 487161 *fax* (0232) 489552. *Chairman:* Michael Burns; *managing director:* Anne Tannahill. Fiction, poetry, biography, history, art, academic, natural history, sport, politics, music, education, fine limited editions.

The Blackwater Press—imprint of **Folens & Co. Ltd,** *q.v.* General non-fiction, Irish interest.

Brandon Book Publishers Ltd (1982), Cooleen, Dingle, Co. Kerry *tel* (066) 51463 *fax* (066) 51234. *Directors:* Steve MacDonogh, Bernard Goggin. Biography, literature, politics, fiction, travel (Ireland), history, folklore.

Brophy Educational Books Ltd (1977), 108 Sundrive Road, Dublin 12 *tel* (01) 973061/971617. *Directors:* Kevin T. Brophy (Managing), Mary Brophy. School texts.

Brophy International Publishing Ltd, 108 Sundrive Road, Dublin 12 *tel* (01) 973061/971617. *Directors:* K.T. Brophy, M. Brophy. General non-fiction, religion, sport, entertainment, drama. Imprints: **Brophy Books, Canavaun Books.**

Catholic Communications Institute of Ireland, Inc.—see **Veritas Publications.**

Dolmen Press Ltd. Stock acquired by **Colin Smythe Ltd**—see UK list.

The Educational Company of Ireland, PO Box 43a, Ballymount Road, Walkinstown, Dublin 12 *tel* (01) 500611 *fax* (01) 500993. *Executive directors:* F.J. Maguire (chief executive), S. O'Neill, Ursula Ní Dhálaigh, R. McLoughlin. A trading unit of Smurfit Services Ltd. Educational MSS on all subjects in English or Gaelic.

C.J. Fallon (1927), Lucan Road, Palmerstown, Dublin 20 *tel* (01) 265777 *fax* (01) 268225. *Directors:* H.J. McNicholas (managing), P. Tolan (secretary), N. White (editorial). Educational text books.

Folens & Co. Ltd, Airton Road, Tallaght, Co. Dublin *tel* (01) 515311 *fax* (01) 515306.
Educational (primary, secondary, comprehensive, technical, in English and Irish), educational children's magazines.

*****Four Courts Press** (1969), Kill Lane, Blackrock, Co. Dublin *tel* (01) 892922 *fax* (01) 893072. *Directors:* Michael Adams, Gerard O'Flaherty. Theology.

The Gallery Press (1970), Loughcrew, Oldcastle, Co. Meath *tel* (049) 41779. *Editor and publisher:* Peter Fallon. *Allied company:* Deerfield Publications Inc., Massachusetts. Poetry, drama, occasionally fiction by Irish authors. Also, hand-printed limited editions poetry.

*****Gill & Macmillan Ltd** (1968), Goldenbridge, Inchicore, Dublin 8 *tel* (01) 531005 *telex* 92197 Gilm EI *fax* (01) 541688. Biography or memoirs, educational (primary, secondary, university), history, philosophy, sociology, theology and religion, literature.

The Goldsmith Press (1972), Newbridge, Co. Kildare *tel* (045) 33613. *Directors:* D. Egan, V. Abbott, Peter Kavanagh; *secretary:* Peter Mulreid. Literature, art, Irish interest, poetry. *ERA Review* (occasional).

*****Institute of Public Administration** (1957), 57-61 Lansdowne Road, Dublin 4 *tel* (01) 686233; Publications: (01) 697011 *telegraphic address* Admin, Dublin. *Deputy assistant director and head of publishing:* James D. O'Donnell; *assistant manager:* Iain MacAulay. Government, economic, law, social policy and administrative history.

*****Irish Academic Press** (1974), Kill Lane, Blackrock, Co. Dublin *tel* (01) 892922 *fax* (01) 893072. Publishes under the imprints **Irish University Press, Irish Academic Press** and **Ecclesia Press.** *Directors:* Michael Adams, Frank Cass, Gilbert Raff, Michael Philip Zaidner. Scholarly books especially in history and law.

The Kavanagh Press Ltd (1989), Newbridge, Co. Kildare *tel* (045) 33613 *fax* (045) 33885. *Directors:* Desmond Egan, Vivienne Abbott. Poetry, Irish interest, literary criticism, Irish history, art; cassettes.

Longman, Browne & Nolan—now incorporated in **The Educational Company of Ireland,** *q.v.*

*****The Mercier Press** (1945), PO Box 5, 4 Bridge Street, Cork *tel* (021) 504022 *telex* 75463 *fax* (021) 504216. *Directors:* Capt. J.M. Feehan, D.J. Keily, C.U.O. Marcaigh, M. Feehan, L. McNamara, J.F. Spillane. Irish literature, folklore, history, politics, humour, ballads, education, theology, law.

O'Brien Educational (1976), 20 Victoria Road, Rathgar, Dublin 6 *tel* (01) 979598 and 740354 *fax* (01) 979274. *Directors:* Michael O'Brien, Bride Rosney. Humanities, science, environmental studies, history, geography, English, Irish, art, commerce, music, careers, media studies.

The O'Brien Press Ltd (1974), 20 Victoria Road, Rathgar, Dublin 6 *tel* (01) 979598 *fax* (01) 979274. *Directors:* Michael O'Brien, Valerie O'Brien. Folklore, nature, fiction, architecture, topography, history, general, illustrated books, sport, anthropology, children, biography, tapes for children series include *Lucky Tree Books*, *Junior Biography Library*, *Urban Heritage*.

*Poolbeg Press Ltd (1976), Knocksedan House, Forrest Great, Swords, Co. Dublin *tel* (01) 407433 *fax* (01) 403753. *Directors:* Philip MacDermott (managing), Breda Purdue (marketing), Jo O Donoghue (editorial), Kieran Devlin (finance). Fiction, public interest, women's interest, history, politics, current affairs, Children's Poolbeg and Young Poolbeg (teens).

*Raven Arts Press (1979), PO Box 1430, Finglas, Dublin 11. *Publisher:* Dermot Bolger. Modern Irish poetry and literature.

School and College Publishing Ltd (1968), Taney Road, Dundrum, Dublin 14 *tel* (01) 983544 *fax* (01) 988554. *Directors:* Patrick M. O'Brien, Gilbert Brosnan, Mark Kavanagh, Michael Kelly. Educational books for primary and secondary schools.

*Stationery Office (1922), Bishop Street, Dublin 8 *tel* (01) 781666 *telegraphic address* Enactments Dublin. Parliamentary publications.

*Town House and Country House (1981), 41 Marlborough Road, Donnybrook, Dublin 4 *tel* (01) 686700 *fax* (01) 687808. *Directors:* Treasa Coady, Jim Coady. Environmental and natural history, general non-fiction and popular fiction.

*Veritas Publications, a division of the **Catholic Communications Institute of Ireland, Inc.,** Veritas House, 7/8 Lower Abbey Street, Dublin 1 *tel* (01) 788177 *fax* (01) 786507. *UK:* Veritas Book & Video Distribution Ltd, Lower Avenue, Leamington Spa, Warks. CV31 3NP *tel* (0926) 451 730 *fax* (0926) 451 733. Religion, including social and educational works, and material relating to the media of communication.

Wolfhound Press (1974), 68 Mountjoy Square, Dublin 1 *tel* (01) 740354. *Publisher:* Seamus Cashman; *publishing manager:* Siobhan Campbell. Literary studies and criticism, fiction, art, biography, history, children's, law.

NEW ZEALAND

*Membership of the New Zealand Book Publishers' Association

*Ashton Scholastic Ltd (1962), 165 Marua Road, Panmure, Auckland *postal address* Private Bag 1, Penrose, Auckland *tel* (09) 579-6089 *fax* (09) 579-3860. *Managing director/publisher:* Graham Beattie; *company secretary:* David Peagram. Children's books.

*Auckland University Press (1966), University of Auckland, Private Bag, Auckland *tel* (09) 737-654 *fax* (09) 366-0702. *Chairman of University Press Committee:* N. Alcorn; *managing editor:* Elizabeth Caffin. Represented by Oxford University Press. New Zealand studies – especially history and literature. Works of scholarship in general.

*David Bateman Ltd (1979), PO Box 100-242, North Shore Mail Centre, Auckland 10 *tel* (09) 444-4680 *fax* (09) 444-0389. *Directors:* David L. Bateman (managing), Janet Bateman, Paul Bateman, Paul Parkinson. Natural history, gardening, encyclopedias, sport, art books, cookbooks, historical, juvenile, travel, motoring, maritime history, business.

*Bush Press Communications Ltd (1979), 4 Bayview Road, Haurak Corner, Takapuna, Auckland 1309 *postal address* PO Box 33-029, Takapuna, Auckland 1309 *tel/fax* (09) 486-2667. *Governing director and publisher:* Gordon Ell. All New Zealand books: outdoor, wildlife, architecture, crafts, Maori, popular history; children's books.

*Butterworths of New Zealand Ltd, 205-207 Victoria Street, Wellington *tel* (04) 851-479 *fax* (04) 851-598.

*The Caxton Press, 113 Victoria Street, Christchurch, PO Box 25-088 *tel* (03) 668-516 *fax* (03) 657840. *Directors:* B.C. Bascand, E.B. Bascand. Fine printers and publishers since 1935 of New Zealand books of many kinds, including verse, fiction, biography, history, natural history, travel, gardening, children's books. Publish literary quarterly *Landfall* (*q.v.*).

*William Collins Publishers Ltd, PO Box 1, Auckland *tel* (09) 444-3740 *fax* (09) 444-1086. Publishers of general literature, teen fiction, non-fiction, reference books, trade paperbacks.

*Heinemann Education—see Octopus Publishing Group (NZ) Ltd.

*Heinemann Publishers (NZ) Ltd—see Octopus Publishing Group (NZ) Ltd.

*Hodder & Stoughton Ltd, PO Box 3858, Auckland 1. *Showroom:* 46 View Road, Glenfield, Auckland 10 *tel* (09) 444-3640 *telegraphic address* Expositor, Auckland *fax* (09) 444-3646.

Jacaranda Wiley Ltd, 236 Dominion Road, 1st Floor, Mt Eden, Auckland 3 *tel* (09) 687-070 *fax* (09) 606-843 *postal address* CPO Box 2259, Auckland 1. *Head office:* Milton, Queensland 4064, Australia, *q.v.*

*Longman Paul Limited, Private Bag, Takapuna, Auckland 9 *tel* (09) 444-4968 *fax* (09) 444-4957. Publishers of New Zealand educational books.

*John McIndoe Ltd (1968), 51 Crawford Street, PO Box 694, Dunedin *tel* (024) 4770-355 *fax* (024) 4771-982. *Directors:* I. Frame, B. Munro. All categories.

*Mallinson Rendel Publishers Ltd (1980), 7 Grass Street, PO Box 9409, Wellington *tel* (04) 857-340 *fax* (04) 854-235. *Directors:* Ann Mallinson, David Rendel. Children's, general New Zealand books, aviation.

*Nelson Price Milburn Ltd, 1 Te Puni Street, Petone *tel* (04) 687179 *fax* (04) 682-115 *postal address* PO Box 33005, Petone. Children's fiction, primary school texts, especially school readers and social studies, secondary and tertiary educational, general adult non-fiction.

*New Zealand Council for Educational Research (1933), Box 3237, Education House, 178-182 Willis Street, Wellington 1 *tel* (04) 847-939 *fax* (04) 847-933. Education, including educational administration and planning, vocational education and adult learning, special education, families, women and parents, rural education, early childhood education, higher education, Maori schooling, educational achievement tests, etc.

*Octopus Publishing Group (NZ) Ltd, incorporating **Reed Books, Paul Hamlyn, Mandarin** and **Heinemann Education,** Private Bag, Birkenhead, Auckland 10 *tel* (09) 480-6039 *fax* (09) 419-1212. *Agencies:* George Philip, John Murray, Conran Octopus, Mitchell Beazley, Sterling Publishing, Octopus Publishing Group Australia Pty Ltd, Ventura Publishing Ltd, BBC Enterprises

Ltd, Pan Britannica, Heinemann Young Books, Secker & Warburg, Kings-
wood, Cedar, Methuen Drama, Brimax, Daily Express, Budget Books Pty
Ltd, Octopus Publishing Group, Ginn & Company, Grandreams, Heinemann
Education Books, Rigby Heinemann (Australia), Ragged Bears, Heinemann
Education Books Inc. (USA). *Chairman:* Nicolas Thompson; *managing direc-
tor:* Alan Smith; *director:* Kath Downie (trade); *financial controller:* A.
Stratton. New Zealand literature, specialist and technical titles, secondary
and tertiary textbooks.

*****Oxford University Press,** 1A Matai Road, Greenlane, Auckland 5   *postal address*
PO Box 11-149 Ellerslie, Auckland 5   *tel* (09) 523-3134/523-3702   *cables*
Oxonian, Auckland   *fax* (09) 524-6723. *NZ manager:* Jeff Olson; *managing
editor:* Anne French.

Pitman New Zealand—imprint of **Longman Paul Ltd.** Technical, educational,
general, commercial, legal, art and crafts.

*****Random Century New Zealand Ltd** (1977), Private Bag, North Shore Mail
Centre, Glenfield, Auckland 10   *tel* (09) 444-7197   *fax* (09) 444-7524. *Directors:* J. Mottram (chairman), J. Rogers (managing), D. Ling, M.L. Burnett,
S. Lai, A.J.V. Cheetham. Fiction, junior books, educational and university,
sports and pastimes, religion, non-fiction.

*****Reed Methuen Publishers Ltd**—see **Octopus Publishing Group (NZ) Ltd.**

*****Ray Richards Publisher** (1977), 3-49 Aberdeen Road, Castor Bay, Auckland
postal address PO Box 31240 Milford, Auckland   *tel* (09) 410-5681   *fax*
(09) 410-6389. *Partners:* Ray Richards, Barbara Richards. Publishers for
organisations; especially history, science, bibliography, military, equestrian,
agriculture.

Sweet & Maxwell—imprint of The Law Book Co., CPO Box 3139, Auckland.
Attention: Peter Stuart.

*****Victoria University Press** (1974), Victoria University of Wellington, PO Box 600,
Wellington   *tel* (04) 721-000   *fax* (04) 711-700. *Chairman of the publications
committee:* Professor G.R. Hawke; *editor:* Fergus Barrowman. Academic,
scholarly books on New Zealand history, sociology, political history, architecture, economics, law, zoology, biology; also fiction, plays.

Viking Sevenseas Ltd, 23b Ihakara Street, Paraparaumu   *tel* 058-
71990   *telegraphic address* Vikseven   *fax* 058-72040. *Managing director:*
M.B. Riley. Factual books on New Zealand only.

Weldon New Zealand—division of **Weldon International Pty Ltd,** Australia
(*q.v.*). Cookery, photographic books on New Zealand landscape, gardening,
road atlases and guides.

Other Commonwealth Publishers

GHANA

Emmanuel Publishing Services, PO Box 5282, Accra. *Director:* E. K. Nsiah.
Representing Oxford University Press, Faber & Faber Ltd, George Philip
Ltd, University Press Ltd, Ibadan, Nigeria.

Moxon Paperbacks (1967), PO Box M 160, Accra   *tel* 665397   *telegraphic
address* Moxon, Accra. *Partners:* James Moxon, Oliver Carruthers, Mark
Gilbey. Crime, current affairs, biography, travel, fiction.

Sedco Publishing Ltd, Sedco House, Tabon Street, North Ridge, Accra *tel* 221332 *cables* Sedco, Accra *telex* 2456 Sedco GH *fax* 220107 *postal address* PO Box 2051, Accra.

HONG KONG

Jacaranda Wiley Ltd, 42-48 Paterson Street, 10A Causeway Bay, Hong Kong *tel* 8905738 *fax* 5761813. *Head office:* Milton, Queensland 4064, Australia, *q.v.*

Longman Group (Far East) Ltd, GPO Box 223, Hong Kong *tel* 8118168 *telex* 73051 Lghk HX *fax* 5657440.

Macmillan Publishers (China) Limited, Warwick House, East Wing, 19th Floor, Taikoo Trading Estate, 28 Tong Chong Street, Quarry Bay, Hong Kong *tel* 811 8781 *telex* 85969 Penhk Hx *fax* 8110743. *Directors:* Nicholas Byam Shaw (chairman), Ken Derrick, Yiu Hei Kan, Rupert Li, Michael Hamilton, Brian Stonier. Educational and general books.

Oxford University Press, 18/F Warwick House, Taikoo Trading Estate, 28 Tong Chong Street, Quarry Bay, Hong Kong *tel* (852) 565 1351-8, (852) 561 0221-4 *cables* Oxonian, Hong Kong *telex* HX65522 *fax* (852) 565 8491.

KENYA

Heinemann Kenya Ltd (1967), PO Box 45314, Nairobi *tel* 750711/222144 *telegraphic address* Hebooks Nairobi *fax* 750715. *Managing director:* Henry Chavaka. Academic and educational books.

Longman Kenya Ltd, PO Box 18033, Nairobi *tel* 541345-7 *telex* 24101 *fax* 540037. *Chairman:* F.T. Nyammo; *managing director:* Dr E.M. Mugiri. Primary and secondary school course books; tertiary: languages, humanities, business education and technical; novels.

Oxford University Press (East & Central Africa), POB 72532, 2nd Floor, ABC Place, Waiyaki Way, Nairobi *tel* 748 090/1/2/3. *Regional manager:* Abdulla Ismaily.

MALAYSIA

Longman Malaysia Sdn. Berhad, 2nd Floor, 3 Jalan Kilang A, off Jalan Penchala, 46050 Petaling Jaya, Selangor *tel* 03-7920466 *telegraphic address* Free-grove, Kuala Lumpur *telex* LMSB MA37600 *fax* 03-7918005.

Oxford University Press (South-East Asian Publishing Unit), 7 Jalan Semangat, PO Box 523, Jalan Sultan, 46760 Petaling Jaya, Selangor Darul Ehsan *tel* 7551744, 7551841, 7551958 *telex* MA37283 *fax* 03-7568119. *Manager:* Azlina Yunus.

NIGERIA

African Universities Press, Pilgrim Books Ltd, PMB 5617 Ibadan. *Head office:* Plot 1, Block P., New Oluyole Industrial Estate, Phase 2, Ibadan-Lagos Ex-pressway, Ibadan *tel* 022-317218 *cables* Pilgrim Ibadan *telex* 20311-Box 078. *Directors:* Emmanuel A. Jaja, J.E. Leigh, Nicholas Perren. Educational, Africana.

Evans Brothers (Nigeria Publishers), Ltd, Jericho Road, PMB 5164, Ibadan *tel* 417570, 417601, 417626 *telex* 31104 Edbook NG.

Longman Nigeria, Ltd, Private Mail Bag, 21036, Ikeja *tel* Lagos 964370, 901150-9 *telex* 26639.

Macmillan Nigeria Publishers Ltd, Oluyole Industrial Estate, Scheme 2, Lagos-Ibadan Expressway, Near Methodist High School, PO Box 1463, Ibadan, Oyo State *tel* 316894, 316896-7. *Warehouse and accounts:* Ilupeju Industrial Estate, Mushin, PO Box 264, Yaba, Lagos *tel* 961188. *Directors:* Sir J.O. Immanuel (chairman), Dr A.I. Adelekan (managing), Nze E.C. Ohuka, J. Ademokun, C.R. Harrison, Dr Tai Solarin, Dr S.O. Omotoso.

University Press Limited (in association with **Oxford University Press**), Three Crowns Building, Jericho, Ibadan *postal address* Private Mail Bag 5095, Ibadan *tel* Ibadan 0-22 411356, 412386, 412313, 413117 *telegraphic address/cable* Oxonian Ibadan. *Managing director:* M.O. Akinleye.

SINGAPORE

Butterworth Asia, 3 Shenton Way, Unit 14-03, Shenton House, Singapore 0106 *tel* 2241622/2203684 *telex* RS 42890 Bgasia *fax* 2252939/2255026.

Federal Publications (S) Pte Ltd (1957), Times Centre, 1 New Industrial Road, Singapore 1953 *tel* 2848844 *cables* Fedpubs, Singapore *telex* RS 25713 Times S *fax* 2889254. *Vice president & general manager:* Y.H. Mew. Educational, children's, general reference and academic books.

Heinemann Publishers Asia (Pte) Ltd (1963), 37 Jalan Pemimpin, Apartment 07-04, Block B, Union Industrial Building, Singapore 2057 *tel* 2583255 *telex* RS 24299 Hebooks *fax* 2588279.

Oxford University Press Pte Ltd, Unit 221, Ubi Avenue 4, Singapore 1440 *tel* 7431066 *telex* RS 37960 Oxpres *cables* Oxonian, Singapore *fax* 7425915.

TANZANIA

Oxford University Press (East & Central Africa), POB 5299, Maktaba Road, Dar es Salaam *tel* Dar es Salaam 29209 *cables* Oxonian, Dar es Salaam.

ZIMBABWE

The College Press (Pvt) Ltd, PO Box 3041, Harare *tel* 66335/66641 *telex* 22558 *fax* 66645. *Contact:* Engelbert Luphahla.

William Collins International Ltd, PO Box 2800, Harare *tel* 721413.

Longman Zimbabwe (Pvt.) Ltd, PO Box ST 125, Southerton, Harare *tel* Harare 62711, 65945 *telegraphic address* Longman, Harare *telex* 22566 Lonzim ZW *fax* 263-4-62716.

Oxford University Press, represented by The College Press (Pvt) Ltd (*q.v.*).

SOUTH AFRICA

*Members of South African Publishers' Association

Books of Africa (Pty) Ltd, 39 Atlantic Road, Muizenberg 7951 *tel* (021) 888-316. *Directors:* T.V. Bulpin, M. Bulpin. Books on any subject about Africa.

***Butterworth Publishers (Pty) Ltd,** 8 Walter Place, Waterval Park, Mayville, Durban 4091 *tel* (031) 294247 *telegraphic address/cables* Butterlaw,

Durban *telex* 620730SA *fax* (031) 283255 *postal address* PO Box 792, Durban 4000.

Collins Publishers (SA) (Pty) Ltd, 10-14 Watkins Street, Denver Ext. 4, Johannesburg. (PO Box 33977, Jeppestown 2043) *tel* (011) 622-2900 *cables* Fontana, Johannesburg *fax* (011) 622-3553. General publications, fiction, reference books, bibles, juveniles, school textbooks and paperbacks.

Delta Books (Pty) Ltd (1980), PO Box 2105, Parklands 2121. Gallo House, 6 Hood Avenue, Rosebank, Johannesburg 2196 *tel* (011) 880-3116 *fax* (011) 880-1008. *Director:* Adriaan Donker. Natural history, gardening, cookery, sport, health, practical and pictorial books.

Ad Donker (Pty) Ltd (1973), PO Box 2105, Parklands 2121. Gallo House, 6 Hood Avenue, Rosebank, Johannesburg 2196 *tel* (011) 880-3116 *fax* (011) 880-1008. *Directors:* Adriaan Donker, J.A.B. Ball, G. Schahat, B.P.I. Trisk. Africana, literature, history, academic, biography, socio-political.

*****Juta & Company Ltd** (1853), PO Box 14373, Kenwyn 7790 *tel* (021) 797-5101 *fax* (021) 761-5010. Educational, academic, professional and legal publishers. General and educational booksellers and importers.

Longman Penguin Southern Africa (Pty) Ltd—see **Maskew Miller Longman (Pty) Ltd.**

*****Lovedale Press,** PO Lovedale 5702. Educational, religious and general book publications for African market.

*****Maskew Miller Longman (Pty) Ltd,** Howard Drive, Pinelands 7405 *tel* (021) 531-7750 *telex* 526053 *fax* (021) 531-4049 *postal address* PO Box 396, Cape Town 8000. Educational and general publishers and booksellers; school stationery requirements.

*****Oxford University Press (Southern African Branch),** Smuts Beyers (managing director), 5th Floor, Harrington House, 37 Barrack Street, Cape Town 8001 *postal address* PO Box 1141, Cape Town 8000 *tel* (021) 45-7266 *fax* (021) 45-7265; *Transvaal* Poovan Moodley (regional manager), Suite 206 Willowbrook, Willowbrook Close, off Atholl Oaklands Road, Melrose North 2196 *postal address* PO Box 41390, Craighall 2024 *tel* (011) 788-3617; *Natal* Bheki Sithomo (education), 12th Floor, Maritime House, Cnr Salmon Grove and Esplanade Road, Durban 4001 *postal address* PO Box 37166, Overport 4067 *tel* (031) 304-7202.

David Philip Publishers (Pty) Ltd (1971), PO Box 23408, Claremont 7735, Cape Province *tel* (021) 64-4136 *telegraphic address* Philipub, Capetown *fax* (021) 64-3358. *Directors:* David Philip, Marie Philip. Academic, history, social sciences, politics, theology, biography, belles-lettres, reference books, fiction, learners' texts, children's books.

Pitman Publishing Co. SA (Pty) Ltd (1974), PO Box 396, Cape Town 8000 *tel* (021) 5317750 *fax* (021) 5314049. Division of **Maskew Miller Longman (Pty) Ltd.**

Ravan Press (Pty) Ltd (1972), 3rd Floor, Standard House, 40 De Korte Street, Braamfontein, Johannesburg *postal address* PO Box 31134, Braamfontein 2017 *tel* (011) 403-3925-9 *fax* (011) 339-2439. *Manager:* Glenn Moss. African studies: history, politics, theology, social studies. Fiction, literature, children's, educational.

*****Shuter and Shooter (Pty) Ltd** (1925), 230 Church Street, and 199 Pietermaritz Street, Pietermaritzburg 3201, Natal *postal address* PO Box 109, Pietermaritzburg 3200 *tel* (0331) 946830/948881 *telegraphic address* Shushoo *fax* (0331) 943096. *Directors:* M.N. Prozesky (managing), J.S.

Craib, C.L.S. Nyembezi, E.O. Oellermann, C.A. Roy, D.F. Ryder, W.N. Vorster, R.J. Watkinson.

*Southern Book Publishers (Pty) Ltd, PO Box 3103, Halfway House, Transvaal 1685 *tel* (011) 315-3633/7 *fax* (011) 315-3810. Publishers of academic, educational and general books as well as those of South African interest.

Struik Winchester Publishers, PO Box 1144, Cape Town 8000. A division of Struik Publishers (Pty) Ltd *tel* (021) 216740 *fax* (021) 216744 *telex* 5-26713SA. *Managing director:* Peter Borchert. Natural history, cultural history, Africana.

Struik Publishers, PO Box 1144, Cape Town 8000. An operating division of The Struik Group (Pty) Ltd *tel* (021) 216740 *telex* 5-26713 SA *fax* (021) 216744. *Managing director:* Peter Borchert. General non-fiction.

*J.L. Van Schaik (1914), 1064 Arcadia Street, Hatfield, Pretoria 0083 *tel* (012) 342-2765 *fax* (012) 43-3563. Publishers of books in English, Afrikaans and African languages. Specialists in Afrikaans non-fiction, dictionaries and text-books.

Witwatersrand University Press, Private Bag 3, Wits 2050 *tel* (011) 716-2023 *telex* 4-27125 SA *fax* (011) 339-3559.

UNITED STATES OF AMERICA

The following is a selected list; it includes only a few of the very many smaller firms, and of the specialist publishers.

*Members of the Association of American Publishers Inc.

Abingdon Press, Editorial and Business Offices: 201 Eighth Avenue S, Nashville, TN 37202 *tel* 615-749-6403 *fax* 615-749-6512. Editorial offices for academic books: 2495 Lawrenceville Highway, Decatur, GA 30033 *tel* 404-636-6001 *fax* 404-636-5894. *Editor-in-chief:* Neil M. Alexander. General interest, professional, academic and reference – primarily directed to the religious market.

Academy Chicago Publishers (1975), 213 West Institute Place, Chicago, IL 60610 *tel* 312-751-7302 *fax* 312-751-7306. *Directors:* Anita Miller, Jordan Miller. Fiction, mystery, biography, travel, books of interest to women; quality reprints.

And/Or Press Inc. (1974), PO Box 2246, Berkeley, CA 94702 *tel* 415-548-2124. Health and nutrition, life styles. No unsolicited work.

Andrews & McMeel, 4900 Main Street, Kansas City, MO 64112 *tel* 816-932-6700 *fax* 816-932-6706. *Vice-president and editorial director:* Donna Martin. General trade publishing, with emphasis on humour and consumer reference.

Arcade Publishing, 141 Fifth Avenue, New York, NY 10010 *tel* 212-475-2633 *fax* 212-353-8148. *President and editor-in-chief:* Richard Seaver. General, including adult hard cover and paperbacks, children's and young adult books.

Ashley Books Inc. (1971), 4600 W. Commercial Blvd, Tamarac, FL 33319 *tel* 305-739-2221 *fax* 305-485-2287. *Directors:* Simeon Paget (managing), Billie Young (president); *associate editor:* Gwen Costa. Fiction, especially emotional page turners, but no erotica; medicine, health, vitamins, diet and natural foods; controversy, how-to, humour, reference, self-help and technical.

*Atheneum Publishers (1960), division of Macmillan Publishing Company, 866 Third Avenue, New York, NY 10022   tel 212-614-1300   telex 23-9532 UR   fax 212-319-4220. General, fiction, poetry, juveniles.

*Atlantic Monthly Press, 19 Union Square West, New York, NY 10003   tel 212-645-4462   fax 212-727-0180. MSS of permanent interest, fiction, biography, autobiography, history, current affairs, social science, belles-lettres, natural history, travel adventure, gardening, cookbooks.

Avon Books (1941), The Hearst Corporation, 1350 Avenue of the Americas, New York, NY 10019   tel 212-261-6800   fax 212-261-6895. President and publisher: Carolyn Reidy. All subjects, fiction and non-fiction.

Walter H. Baker Company (1845), 100 Chauncy Street, Boston, MA 02111   tel 617-482-1280   fax 617-482-7613. President: M. Abbott Van Nostrand; Editor: John B. Welch. Plays and books on the theatre. Also agents for plays. London agents: Samuel French Ltd, 52 Fitzroy Street, London W1P 6JR.

*Bantam Doubleday Dell Publishing Group Inc., 666 Fifth Avenue, New York, NY 10103   tel 212-765-6500   cables Bantambook New York   telex 7608009   fax 212-765-3869. Chairman and chief executive officer: Paul D. Neuthaler; president and chief operating officer: Jack Hoeft; svp and chief financial officer: John Choi; svp, president and publisher, international: Alun Davies. Fiction, classics, biography, health, business, general non-fiction, social sciences, religion, sports, science, audio tapes, computer books.

A.S. Barnes & Co., PO Box 119, Stamford, CT 06904   tel 203-322-8977   fax 203-322-2417. Imprint of Oak Tree Publications Inc. General publishers.

Beacon Press, 25 Beacon Street, Boston, MA 02108   tel 617-742-2110   fax 617-723-3097. Director: Wendy Strothman. General non-fiction in fields of religion, ethics, philosophy, current affairs, gender studies, environmental concerns, African-American studies, anthropology and women's studies, nature, children's books.

*Bergh Publishing, Inc. (1983), 276 Fifth Avenue, New York, NY 10001   tel 212-686-8551   fax 212-779-2290. Chairman and ceo: Sven-Erik Bergh. Quality popular non-fiction and occasional fiction with unusual theme and setting, crime, thrillers; juveniles and picture books of outstanding merit.

*R.R. Bowker Co., 245 West 17th Street, New York, NY 10011   tel 212-645-9700. Outside North America: R.R. Bowker (a subsidiary of Butterworths), Borough Green, Sevenoaks, Kent TN15 8PH, England. Bibliographies and reference tools for the book trade and literary and library worlds, available in hardcopy, on microfiche, on-line and CD-ROM. Reference and 'how-to' books for graphic arts, music, art, corporate communications, computer industry, cable industry and information industry.

*Bradbury Press—hardcover imprint of Macmillan Publishing Company. Children's books.

Brassey's (US), Inc. (1984), member of the Maxwell Macmillan Pergamon Publishing Company, 8000 Westpark Drive, 1st Floor, McLean, VA 22102   tel 703-442-0900. President and director of publishing: Franklin D. Margiotta, PhD. Foreign policy defence, international affairs.

George Braziller Inc. (1954), 60 Madison Avenue, Suite 1001, New York, NY 10010   tel 212-889-0909   fax 212-689-5405. President: George Braziller. Science, art, architecture, history, biography, fiction, poetry.

*Cambridge University Press (American branch), 40 West 20th Street, New York, NY 10011   tel 212-924-3900   fax 212-691-3239. Director: Alan Winter, MA.

Carroll & Graf Publishers, Inc. (1983), 260 Fifth Avenue, New York, NY 10001 *tel* 212-889-8772. *President:* Herman Graf; *publisher:* Kent Carroll; *subrights:* James Mason. Mystery and science fiction, history, biography, literature, business, psychology.

*Columbia University Press, 562 West 113th Street, New York, NY 10025 *tel* 212-316-7100 *fax* 212-316-7169; *UK:* 10 Watlington Road, Cowley, Oxford OX4 5NF *fax* (0865) 7458401. Scholarly work in all fields, translations and serious non-fiction of more general interest.

Concordia Publishing House (1869), 3558 S. Jefferson Avenue, St Louis, MO 63118 *tel* 314-664-7000. Religious books, Lutheran perspective. Few freelance manuscripts accepted. Query first.

Contemporary Books Inc., 180 North Michigan Avenue, Chicago, IL 60601 *tel* 312-782-9181 *fax* 312-782-2157. *President:* Harvey Plotnick; *vice president and editorial director:* Nancy Crossman; *subsidiary rights:* Christine Albritton. Non-fiction.

The Continuum Publishing Corp. (1980), 370 Lexington Avenue, New York, NY 10017 *tel* 212-532-3650 *telex* 4974569 Conti *fax* 212-532-4922. *Chairman and chief executive officer:* Werner Mark Linz. General non-fiction, education, literature, psychology, politics, sociology, literary criticism.

*Cornell University Press (including **Comstock Publishing Associates**) (1869), 124 Roberts Place, Ithaca, NY 14851 *tel* 607-257-7000 *fax* 607-257-3552. Scholarly books. *Agents overseas:* Trevor Brown Associates, Suite 7B, 26 Charing Cross Road, London WC2H 0LN *tel* 071-240 8774 *fax* 071-497 2486.

Crown Publishers, Inc., 201 East 50th Street, New York, NY 10022 *tel* 212-572-2568. *Executive:* Betty A. Prashker. General fiction, non-fiction, illustrated books.

Devin-Adair Publishers, Inc. (1911), 6 North Water Street, Greenwich, CT 06830 *tel* 203-531-7755. Conservative politics, health and ecology, Irish topics, gardening and travel topics, homeopathy and holistic health books.

*Doubleday, a division of **Bantam Doubleday Dell Publishing Group Inc.,** 666 Fifth Avenue, New York, NY 10103 *tel* 212-765-6500. *London:* 61-63 Uxbridge Road, W5 5SA *tel* 081-579 2652. Trade, general fiction and non-fiction. Anchor Press. Books For Young Readers. Foundation. Religious.

Dryden Press—see **Harcourt Brace Jovanovich Inc.**

E.P. Dutton, division of Penguin USA, 375 Hudson Street, New York, NY 10014 *tel* 212-366-2000 *fax* 212-366-2933. General publishers. General non-fiction, including biographies, adventure, history, travel; fiction, mysteries, juveniles, quality paperbacks.

Facts On File Inc. (1940), 460 Park Avenue South, New York, NY 10016 *tel* 212-683-2244 *cables* Factsfile New York *telex* 238552 *fax* 212-213-4578. *UK:* Collins Street, Oxford OX4 1XJ *tel* (0865) 728399. *President:* Howard Epstein; *executive vice president and publisher:* Edward W. Knappman; *UK and European manager:* Alan Goodworth. Information books and services for colleges, libraries, schools and general public.

Farrar, Straus & Giroux Inc., 19 Union Square West, New York, NY 10003 *tel* 212-741-6900 *telegraphic address* Farrarcomp, New York *telex* 667428 *fax* 212-633-9385. General publishers.

Fearon/Janus/Quercus, 500 Harbor Boulevard, Belmont, CA 94002 *tel* 415-592-7810. **Fearon Education** – young adult basic education, ESL and special education materials in all academic areas; fiction; **Janus Books** – special education supplementary textbooks for middle, junior and senior high school and adult education; **Quercus** – special needs materials for junior high and high school.

*****Four Winds Press**—hardcover imprint of **Macmillan Publishing Company.** Children's books.

Samuel French Inc., 45 West 25th Street, New York, NY 10010 *tel* 212-206-8990 *fax* 212-206-1429. Play publishers and authors' representatives (dramatic).

David R. Godine, Publisher Inc. (1970), Horticultural Hall, 300 Massachusetts Avenue, Boston, MA 02115 *tel* 617-536-0761 *fax* 617-421-0934. *President:* David R. Godine. Fiction, photography, history, natural history, art, biography, children's.

Greenwillow Books, a division of **William Morrow & Co., Inc.,** 1350 Avenue of the Americas, New York, NY 10019 *tel* 212-261-6500 *fax* 212-261-6595. *Senior vice-president/editor-in-chief:* Susan Hirschman. Children's books.

*****Grosset & Dunlap, Inc.,** 200 Madison Avenue, New York, NY 10016 *tel* 212-951-8400. Children's mass market and picture books, series books, activity books.

Grove Weidenfeld (1986), 841 Broadway, New York, NY 10003 *tel* 212-614-7860 *telex* 6711993 *fax* 212-614-7915. *Chairman:* Lord Weidenfeld. Non-fiction: history, biography, current events; fiction: popular and literary.

Harcourt Brace Jovanovich Inc., 1250 Sixth Avenue, San Diego, CA 92101 *tel* 619-231-6616. General publishers. Fiction, history, biography, etc.; college and school textbooks of all kinds; children's; technical; reference; religious; dictionaries. Imprints: **Holt Rinehart and Winston, Dryden Press, Saunders College.**

*****HarperCollins Publishers** (1817), 10 East 53rd Street, New York, NY 10022 *tel* 212-207-7000 *cables* Harpsam, NY *telex* 12-5741(dom.), 62-501(intl). *President and chief executive officer:* George Craig. Religious books division: Icehouse One, Suite 401, 151 Union Street, San Francisco, CA 94111 *tel* 415-477-4400 *fax* 415-421-5865. *London:* HarperCollins Publishers, 77-85 Fulham Palace Road, Hammersmith, London W6 8JB. Fiction, history, biography, poetry, science, travel, juvenile, educational, business, technical, medical and religious.

Hastings House, 141 Halstead Avenue, Mamaroneck, NY 10543 *tel* 914-835-4005 *fax* 914-835-1037. *President:* Hy Steirman; *director of operations:* Richard Cadier. Non-fiction, general, consumer, travel, cooking, juveniles and how-to.

*****D.C. Heath and Co.,** international division of **Raytheon Co.,** 125 Spring Street, Lexington, MA 02173 *tel* 617-860-1340 *fax* 617-860-1508. Elementary, secondary, college textbooks.

Hill & Wang (1956), division of **Farrar, Straus & Giroux Inc.,** 19 Union Square West, New York, NY 10003 *tel* 212-741-6900 *telex* 667428 *fax* 212-741-6973. *Editor-in-chief:* Arthur W. Wang; *publisher:* Arthur J. Rosenthal. General non-fiction, drama, history.

*****Holiday House** (1935), 40 East 49th Street, New York, NY 10017 *tel* 212-688-0085 *fax* 212-241-6134. *Directors:* John Briggs (president), Margery Cuyler, Kate Briggs, David R. Rogers. General children's books.

Henry Holt and Company, Inc. (1866), 115 West 18th Street, New York, NY 10011   *tel* 212-886-9200   *telex* 424632 Hhc   *fax* 212-633-0748. *President and ceo:* Bruno A. Quinson; *associate publisher adult books:* William Strachan; *editor-in-chief books for young readers:* Brenda Bowen; *publisher reference books:* Richard Staron. History, biography, nature, science, self-help, novels, mysteries; books for young readers.

Holt, Rinehart and Winston—see Harcourt Brace Jovanovich Inc.

*****Houghton Mifflin Company** (1832), One Beacon Street, Boston, MA 02108   *tel* 617-725-5000   *telex* 4430255 Hmhq UI   *fax* 617-573-4916 (trade), 617-227-5409 (school and college). Fiction, biography, history, works of general interest of all kinds, both adult and juvenile; also school and college textbooks in all departments, and standardised tests. Best length: 75,000-180,000 words; juveniles, any reasonable length.

Keats Publishing Inc. (1971), 27 Pine Street, PO Box 876, New Canaan, CT 06840   *tel* 203-966-8721. *Directors:* Nathan Keats (president); Norman Goldfind (vice president, marketing). Natural health, nutrition and medical books.

Alfred A. Knopf Inc. (1915), division of **Random House, Inc.,** 201 East 50th Street, New York, NY 10022   *tel* 212-751-2600   *telegraphic address* Knopf, New York   *fax* 212-572-2593. General literature, fiction, belles-lettres, sociology, politics, history, nature, science, etc.

David S. Lake Publishers—now Fearon/Janus/Quercus, *q.v.*

J.B. Lippincott Co. (1792), a Wolters Kluwer company, East Washington Square, Philadelphia, PA 19106   *tel* 215-238-4200   *cables* Lippcot, Phila. Medical and nursing books and journals.

Little, Brown & Company, 34 Beacon Street, Boston, MA 02108   *tel* 617-227-0730   *cables* Brownlit, Boston. General literature, especially fiction, non-fiction, biography, history, trade paperbacks, books for boys and girls, law, medical books. Art and photography books under the **Bulfinch Press/New York Graphic Society Books** imprint.

Lothrop, Lee & Shepard Books (1859), division of **William Morrow & Co., Inc.,** 1350 Avenue of the Americas, New York, NY 10019   *tel* 212-261-6500   *fax* 212-261-6595. *Vice-president/editor-in-chief:* Susan Pearson. Children's books only.

Lyons & Burford, 31 West 21st Street, New York, NY 10010   *tel* 212-620-9580   *fax* 212-929-1836. Outdoor sport, natural history, general sports, art.

*****McGraw-Hill Book Co.,** 1221 Avenue of the Americas, New York, NY 10020   *tel* 212-512-2000. Professional and reference: engineering, scientific, business, architecture, encyclopaedias. College textbooks. High school and vocational textbooks: business, secretarial, career. Trade books. Micro-computer software; training courses for industry. See also McGraw-Hill Book Company (UK) Ltd, McGraw-Hill House, Maidenhead, England, and McGraw-Hill Ryerson Ltd of Canada.

David McKay Co., Inc., division of **Times Books/Random House,** 201 East 50th Street, New York, NY 10022   *tel* 212-872-8104   *telegraphic address* Davmacay   *fax* 212-872-8244. *Editor:* Ruth Fecych. Non-fiction.

*****Macmillan Publishing Company** (1896), division of **Macmillan Inc,** 866 Third Avenue, New York, NY 10022   *tel* 212-702-2000   *telegraphic address* Pachamac, NY. *President and publisher:* Barry Lippman. General books.

Julian Messner, division of **Simon & Schuster,** Prentice Hall Building, Englewood Cliffs, NJ 07632 *tel* 201-592-2966 *fax* 201-461-8178. General nonfiction for ages 7 through high school.

*****The MIT Press** (1961), 55 Hayward Street, Cambridge, MA 02142 *tel* 617-253-5646 *telex* 92.1473 Mit Cam *fax* 617-258-6779. *Director:* Frank Urbanowski; *managing editor:* Helen Osborne. *UK:* The MIT Press, 126 Buckingham Palace Road, London SW1W 9SA. Architecture and design, cognitive sciences and linguistics, computer science and artificial intelligence, economics and management sciences, aesthetic criticism, philosophy, environment and ecology, natural history.

Morehouse Publishing Co., PO Box 1321, Harrisburg, PA 17105 *tel* 717-541-8130 *fax* 717-541-8128. *Chairman:* Stanley Kleiman; *president & publisher:* E. Allen Kelley. Religious books, religious education, texts, seminary texts, children's books.

Morrow Jr. Books, division of **William Morrow & Co., Inc.,** 1350 Avenue of the Americas, New York, NY 10019 *tel* 212-261-6500 *fax* 212-261-6595. *Vice-president/editor-in-chief:* David Reuther. Children's books only.

William Morrow & Co., Inc., 1350 Avenue of the Americas, New York, NY 10019 *tel* 212-261-6500 *fax* 212-261-6595. Allen Marchioni (chairman and ceo), James D. Landis (senior vp, publisher, adult trade), Susan Hirschman (senior vp editor-in-chief Greenwillow Books), Susan Pearson (vp editor-in-chief Lothrop, Lee & Shepard), David Reuther (vp, editor-in-chief Morrow Jr. Books), Paulette Kaufman (editor-in-chief Tambourine Books). General literature, fiction and juveniles. Interested in works dealing with American and non-fiction foreign life and history. Royalty.

Thomas Nelson, Inc. (1978), Nelson Place at Elm Hill Pike, PO Box 141000, Nashville, TN 37214-1000 *tel* 615-889-9000. Publishers of bibles, religious, non-fiction and fiction general trade.

W.W. Norton & Company, Inc., 500 Fifth Avenue, New York, NY 10110 *tel* 212-354-5500 *fax* 212-869-0856. General fiction and non-fiction, music, boating, psychiatry, economics, family therapy, social work, reprints, college texts, science.

Ottenheimer Publishers Inc. (1890), 300 Reisterstown Road, Baltimore, MD 21208 *tel* 301-484-2100 *fax* 301-486-8301. *Directors:* Allan T. Hirsh, Jr., Allan T. Hirsh, III. Juvenile and adult non-fiction, reference.

*****The Overlook Press,** 149 Wooster Street, 4th Floor, New York, NY 10012 *tel* 212-477-7162 *fax* 212-477-7525. Non-fiction, fiction, how-to manuals.

*****Oxford University Press, Inc.,** 200 Madison Avenue, New York, NY 10016 *tel* 212-679-7300 *fax* 212-725-2972. Scholarly, professional, reference, all nonfiction, bibles, college textbooks, religion, medicals, music.

*****Pantheon Books,** division of **Random House, Inc.,** 201 East 50th Street, New York, NY 10022 *tel* 212-751-2600. Fiction, mysteries, belles-lettres, translations, philosophy, history and art, sociology, psychology, juvenile.

*****Penguin USA,** 375 Hudson Street, New York, NY 10014 *tel* 212-366-2000 *fax* 212-366-2666. General books, fiction, non-fiction, biography, sociology, poetry, art, travel, children's books.

Clarkson N. Potter, Inc. (1962), 201 East 50th Street, New York, NY 10022 *tel* 212-572-6160 *fax* 212-572-6192. *Editor-in-chief:* Carol Southern; *executive editor:* Lauren Shakely; *art director:* Howard Klien. Life style, food, biography, travel, self-help, photography; quality fiction; juveniles.

Praeger Publishers, imprint of **Greenwood Publishing Group Inc.**, One Madison Avenue, New York, NY 10010 *tel* 212-685-5300 *fax* 212-685-0285. Non-fiction on international relations, social sciences, economics, reference, contemporary issues, urban affairs, psychology, education.

*Prentice-Hall, Inc. (1913), subsidiary of **Simon & Schuster**, Englewood Cliffs, NJ 07632 *tel* 201-767-4990. Text, technical and general non-fiction, business selling and management books, juveniles; biographies and autobiographies. Free-lance artists' and designers' work used.

*The Putnam Berkley Group Inc., 200 Madison Avenue, New York, NY 10016 *tel* 212-576-8900. Publications of books in all divisions of literature. History, economics, political science, natural science, and standard literature. Also an important group of fiction. Children's books.

Quill Trade Paperbacks, division of **William Morrow & Co., Inc.,** 1350 Avenue of the Americas, New York, NY 10019 *tel* 212-889-3050. *Editor:* Andrew Dutter. General non-fiction.

*Rand McNally, PO Box 7600, Chicago, IL 60680 *tel* 708-673-9100. *Chairman:* Andrew McNally III; *president:* Andrew McNally IV. Maps, guides, atlases, educational publications and globes.

*Random House, Inc., 201 East 50th Street, New York, NY 10022 *tel* 212-751-2600. General publishers.

*Rawson Associates, division of **Macmillan Publishing Company,** 866 Third Avenue, New York, NY 10022 *tel* 212-702-3436 *fax* 212-319-1216. Adult non-fiction and fiction.

Fleming H. Revell Co., 184 Central Avenue, Old Tappan, NJ 07675 *tel* 201-768-8060 *fax* 201-768-2749. Religious books.

Rizzoli International Publications, Inc. (1976), 300 Park Avenue South, New York, NY 10010 *tel* 212-387-3400 *fax* 212-387-3535/212-982-3866. *President/ceo:* Gianfranco Monacelli. Art, architecture, photography, fashion, gardening, design; children's books.

*Rodale Press, Inc. (1930), 33 East Minor Street, Emmaus, PA 18098 *tel* 215-967-5171 *fax* 215-967-3044. *President, book division:* Pat Corpora; *editorial director, book division:* Bill Gottlieb. Health, gardening, environment, woodworking.

Ronin Publishing Inc., Box 1035, Berkeley, CA 94701 *tel* 415-540 6278. Management, health, comics. Preliminary letter essential; no unsolicited manuscripts or art work.

Routledge, Chapman & Hall, Inc., 29 West 35th Street, New York, NY 10001 *tel* 212-244-3336 *telegraphic address* Algernon New York *telex* 6801368 *fax* 212-563-2269. *Directors:* John von Knorring (president), Edward R. Sands (secretary/treasurer), William P. Germano (editorial). Literary criticism, history, philosophy, psychology and psychiatry, politics, women's studies, life sciences, ecology, mathematics and statistics.

*St Martin's Press, Inc., 175 Fifth Avenue, New York, NY 10010 *tel* 212-674-5151 *fax* 212-420-9314 *telegraphic address* Saintmart, New York. Trade, reference, college.

Saunders College—see **Harcourt Brace Jovanovich Inc.**

*Schocken Books Inc. (1945), imprint of **Random House,** 201 East 50th Street, New York, NY 10022 *tel* 212-572-2517. Education, Judaica and holocaust studies, women's studies, social sciences, literature, literary criticism.

Charles Scribner's Sons (1846), division of **Macmillan Inc.**, 866 Third Avenue, New York, NY 10022 *tel* 212-702-2000 *fax* 212-319-1216. General publishers of standard books in education, biography, history, science, fiction, belles-lettres, juveniles.

*Simon & Schuster, 1230 Avenue of the Americas, New York, NY 10020 *tel* 212-698-7000. *Chairman:* Richard Snyder; *president and chief operating officer:* Jonathan Newcomb; *president, trade division:* Charles Hayward; *editor-in-chief, trade division:* Michael V. Korda. General non-fiction, fiction, biography, detective, humour, occasional novelty books. Manuscripts not addressed to an editor by name will be returned unread.

*Stanford University Press, Stanford, CA 94305 *tel* 415-723-9434 *cables* Stanpress *fax* 415-725-3457. Scholarly non-fiction.

Strawberry Hill Press (1973), 2594 15th Avenue, San Francisco, CA 94127 *tel* 415-664-8112. *President:* Jean-Louis Brindamour, PhD; *executive vice-president and art director:* Ku Fu-Sheng; *treasurer:* Edward E. Serres. Health, self-help, cookbooks, philosophy, religion, history, drama, science and technology, biography, mystery, Third World. No unsolicited MSS; preliminary letter and return postage essential.

*Taplinger Publishing Co., Inc. (1955), PO Box 1324, New York, NY 10185 *tel* 201-432-3257 *telegraphic address* Taplinpub. Calligraphy, literature (including translated works into English), music, art and art criticism, non-fiction.

*Taylor & Francis, New York, member of the Taylor & Francis Group, 79 Madison Avenue, New York, NY 10016 *tel* 212-725-1999 *fax* 212-867-1076. Strategy and foreign affairs, oceanography and marine sciences, biological and biomedical sciences, scientific journals.

Theatre Arts Books, division of **Routledge, Chapman & Hall Inc.,** 29 West 35th Street, New York, NY 10001 *tel* 212-244-3336. *President:* John von Knorring; *editorial director:* William Germano. Successor to the book publishing department of Theatre Arts (1921-1948). Theatre, dance and allied books – costume, materials, tailoring, etc., a few plays.

*Charles E. Tuttle Co., Inc. (1949), 28 South Main Street (PO Box 410), Rutland, VT   05701-0410   *tel*   802-773-8930/802-773-8229   *cables*   Tuttbooks *fax* 802-773-6993. *President:* Donald E. Berg; and Suido I-chome, 2-6 Bunkyo-ku, Tokyo 112, Japan *tel* 811-7106-9 *cables* Tuttbooks, Tokyo *telex* 0272-3170 Tutbks J *fax* 811-6953. *President:* Nicholas J. Ingleton. Oriental art, culture, history, manners and customs, Americana.

*University of California Press, 2120 Berkeley Way, Berkeley, CA 94720. Publishes scholarly books, books of general interest, series of scholarly monographs and scholarly journals. *UK:* University Presses of California, Columbia, and Princeton, Avonlea, 10 Watlington Road, Cowley, Oxford OX4 5NF *tel* (0865) 748405 *fax* (0865) 748401.

*University of Chicago Press, 5801 South Ellis Avenue, Chicago, IL 60637 *tel* 312-702-7700 *fax* 312-702-9756. Scholarly books and monographs, religious and scientific books, general trade books, and 51 scholarly journals.

*University of Illinois Press (1918), 54 East Gregory Drive, Champaign, IL 61820 *tel* 217-333-0950 *fax* 217-244-8082. *Director:* Richard L. Wentworth. American studies (history, music, literature), poetry, working-class and ethnic studies, communications, regional studies, art and photography, architecture, short fiction and women's studies.

Van Nostrand Reinhold (1848), 115 Fifth Avenue, New York, NY 10003   *tel* 212-254-3232   *cables* Readbooks Newyork   *telex* 272562 Vnrc UR   *fax* 212-254-9499, 212-475-2548. *President & ceo:* Chester C. Lucido, Jr. Reference, encyclopedias, handbooks: architecture, design, occupational health and safety, science and engineering, hospitality and tourism.

*Viking—see **Penguin USA.**

Walker & Co. (1960), 720 Fifth Avenue, New York, NY 10019   *tel* 212-265-3632   *fax* 212-307-1764. *President:* Samuel S. Walker Jr. General publishers, biography, history, religion, natural history, and adventure, popular science, health, business, mystery/suspense, thrillers, romances, westerns, juveniles, early childhood education, parenting.

Warner Books Inc. (1973), 666 Fifth Avenue, New York, NY 10103   *tel* 212-484-2900   *telegraphic address* Warcom   *fax* 212-484-2713. *President:* Laurence J. Kirshbaum. Fiction and non-fiction, hardcovers, trade paperbacks, mass market paperbacks.

Franklin Watts Inc., subsidiary of **Grolier Inc.**, 387 Park Avenue South, New York, NY 10016   *tel* 212-686-7070   *telex* 236537   *fax* 212-213-6435.

*Westminster/John Knox Press,** 100 Witherspoon Street, Louisville, KY 40202-1396   *tel* 502-569-5043   *fax* 502-569-5018. Religious, academic, reference, general.

Writer's Digest Books, 1507 Dana Avenue, Cincinnati, OH 45207   *tel* 513-531-2222   *fax* 513-531-4744. Market Directories, books for writers, photographers, songwriters, plus selected how-to trade titles. **North Light** imprint: fine art and graphic arts instruction books.

*Yale University Press,** 302 Temple Street, New Haven, CT 06520   *tel* 203-432-0960   *telex* 963531   *fax* 203-432-0948. *postal address* 92A Yale Station, New Haven, CT 06520. *Director:* John G. Ryden; *London:* 23 Pond Street, Hampstead, NW3 2PN   *tel* 071-431 4422   *fax* 071-431 3755. Scholarly books.

Top Hundred Chart of
1990 Paperback Fastsellers

ALEX HAMILTON

In the pages that follow this preamble readers will find a table of the 100 highest sales figures for paperbacks uttered during 1990 by British publishers. It is an annual survey, which I have compiled for *The Guardian* newspaper since 1979, but for readers encountering it for the first time it would perhaps be useful to describe its terms of reference and indicate certain limitations.

An important distinction has first to be made between 'bestsellers' and the term used here – 'fastsellers'. The former have the real commercial pedigree. Sometimes, but not always, they have made a very visible showing in the fastseller lane, but among bestselling authors there are hundreds whose books have made a slow start and only through the cumulative sales over many years demonstrate the faith of the original publisher. Among many examples of those whose sales in their lifetimes was modest but the posthumous interest spectacular, two obvious cases are D.H. Lawrence and George Orwell.

Again, while serious poets never repeat Lord Byron's success in becoming a bestseller and 'famous overnight', and the only two works with short lines in a decade of fastsellers were collections of comic verse, a poet like T.S. Eliot, not to mention Shakespeare and Chaucer, will over the long haul rack up sales in millions. In fact the bread and butter of the publishing trade, year in and year out, continues to be Bibles, classic authors, cookbooks, dictionaries and other reference books. Although the larger bulk of counter sales, and of library borrowings, consists of fiction, the topselling individual titles for this century, with figures over 20 million copies, include most of these categories.

However, it must also be said that the gross figures world-wide, hardcover and paperback, with translations, of prolific authors like Agatha Christie, Alistair MacLean, Mickey Spillane, Ed McBain and Catherine Cookson prompt claims between 50 million and 300 million copies. The individual titles of such popular authors would generally show up in topical bestseller lists, but not always. Dennis Wheatley, for instance, had a very big following in Britain, but the 'British' quality he prided himself on did not travel, and overseas he was hardly read. As another instance, none of the romances of Barbara Cartland has ever sold enough in one year to qualify for my fastseller list, despite a figure of over 100 million copies for the totality of her oeuvre. The presumption must be that it is divided between over 400 titles in many translations.

The fastselling tank which follows consists of the outpourings of the parish pump. That is to say that it is limited to paperbacks which have appeared for the first time in that year from British publishers (regardless of their hardcover provenance) and which have sold over 100,000 copies by the end of the calendar year. (Since 1979 there have always been between 102 and 125 of these.) Though one has a natural inclination to suspect a distortion for the titles published at the end of the period, one finds (checking some months later) that it has rarely made much difference. The significant sale of new paperpacks, particularly by authors with a regular following, takes place within a very few weeks of their appearance on the racks. This can be said even though very few of them advance into the magic circle of bestsellers: during the eighties the highest cumulative sales were for books by Sue Townsend and Jeffrey Archer, each passing five million, which had sold 400,000 and a million respectively in their first year of publication.

It was never the intention behind this list to make it into a competition, and it would be a total misinterpretation to use it as a comparative index of the sales efficiency or business health of the publishers involved. It is possible to go broke with a runaway fastseller on your list – it may even be the cause of a failure if its success entails an unrealistic expansion – and on the other hand there are a number of attractive and profitable imprints which have never come within hailing distance of having a title in this list in the whole time of its collection. The best way to look at it is as a reflection of current popular taste.

As such it indicates a rather conservative attitude on the part of the public. It is very unusual for a book to appear in the top 20 (which earn between them much the same as the rest of the list put together) which has not appeared somewhere else on the list before. Once properly established on the list, an author has only to turn in a similar performance to stay on it year after year. The stalwarts and dominant figures of the eighties were Wilbur Smith (who has now 20 novels with a sale over a million), Barbara Taylor Bradford, Dick Francis, Len Deighton, Stephen King, Catherine Cookson, Jeffrey Archer, Danielle Steel and Victoria Holt, with Jilly Cooper in the later stages strengthening her hand, particularly in the UK market. It is a fair bet that these will be among the dominant figures of the nineties, for as long as they produce new books. It is the author's name that has the most influence, for which good evidence lies in the fact that of a thousand titles only three have been volumes of short stories, two with sales over 750,000 copies, because they were by Frederick Forsyth and Jeffrey Archer, joined this year by Rosamund Pilcher.

Some 80 per cent of the bulk is usually fiction, and the regular features of the non-fiction remainder are diet books, the horoscope division of astrology, movie exploitations, joke books, and showbiz lives. Of the fiction, genres take up most of the slots, particularly adventure yarns, thrillers, horror stories, family sagas and a mixed bag of romances, from historical to Gothic to the now faded bodice-ripper, and a variety of 'shopping romances' and career conflict stories under the vague umbrella of 'women's fiction'. (There seems to be no overt category of 'men's fiction' that might perhaps once have included authors like Mickey Spillane and Harold Robbins.) It is curious, in view of the fact that more than half the buyers of paperbacks are said to be women, that hardly more than a quarter of the authors are women – at least, for the first eight years it remained a steady 25%, and only in the last years has it risen a few points. One should be asking if this figure corresponds to the percentages in publishing as a whole.

Science fantasy is more likely to appear in the list than science fiction of a harder, more experimental kind. Westerns never figure at all, despite the fame on the range of authors like Louis L'Amour and J.T. Edson. There are rarely more than ten or a dozen in any list that could count on reviews from serious book pages, and most of these appear some way down the list, though in recent years, broadly since the leverage given it by television focus, the Booker Prize has taken the winners into the fastseller list. At present the Booker seems to establish the book rather than the author, and the only winner who has kept a place with subsequent books is Anita Brookner. No other literary award has yet resulted in a 100,000 paperback sale for the author.

The highest selling title for the eighties happens to have been a juvenile, *The Secret Diary of Adrian Mole Aged 13¾*, whose author Sue Townsend is said to have been embarrassed when she heard that the publishers had a print of 70,000 in hand, and begged them to reduce it because she could not bear to think of their losing a lot of money on her behalf. With this and a sequel she very nearly equals the total sale for 11 titles of the best-known author in children's fiction, Roald Dahl, and in the long run probably the only one capable of an international sale rivalling that of Dr Seus.

The most successful child author, and the youngest of the list so far registered, wrote a book about solving Rubik's Cube. In the juvenile field it should also be mentioned that a genre of Dungeons and Dragons books had a fairly extended vogue, though it has now lapsed.

Nevertheless books for children, important though they are as an element of general education, and whose rude health in the market place has been one of the few cheering factors in a generally depressed commercial sector, do not as a rule command many places in the fastseller list. So it is a very peculiar phenomenon indeed which is revealed in the current list beginning over the page.

The unexpected change was created by the success of toy manufacturers with the humanoid turtle image of the film, from which books were only part of the merchandising. There was a distinct danger in this one year that the ship would turn turtle with the number of of subteens climbing aboard. Children on their own can't make a fastseller, but when they're combined with pretty infantile adults you get some very impressive results. Previous examples have included exploitations of humanoid fantasies such as ET and Star Wars, and the odd episode of Rubik's Cube, but these were one-offs, on nothing like the scale of the mutanteens deployed in book form to correspond with the film and TV projections of the toy industry.

Perhaps it was just as well for publishing economics that they came on the scene when they did, because they gave a lift to the bookselling business which was generally sagging. Even their presence did not save the graph of the total unit sale of the 100 top fastsellers from its first ever downturn (though their gross retail value continued to rise).

In the department of sums, to save readers long toil with an abacus, it can be stated that the total of books sold by the hundred titles was 24,401,888, a drop of 2,128,895 on the previous year. The total product was £103,345,530 – an increase of £1,070,834, almost all of it from the top 10, even though these grossed 600,000 fewer copies. For the first time a single title, Frederick Forsyth's, achieved £5 million within 12 months. The average cost per unit rose from £3.88 to £4.25, though the presence of so many lower-priced children's books depressing the average should be taken into account by anybody looking for a figure for the paperback trade as a whole.

Six of the authors have died, all but one fairly recently. That one is Virginia Andrews, a well-established fastseller over the years with her own brand of creepy fiction, who departed this life in 1986, having apparently left in her safe a bundle of unpublished MSS of her uncanny works, and her legacy has been very cannily and imaginatively deployed ever since.

No	Title	Genre	Author	Imprint
1	The Negotiator	Thriller	Frederick Forsyth (Br)	Corgi
2	A Time to Die	Thriller	Wilbur Smith (Br)	Pan
3	Star	Fiction	Danielle Steel (US)	Sphere
4	Sands of Time	Saga	Sidney Sheldon (US)	Fontana
5	The Black Candle	Saga	Catherine Cookson (Br)	Corgi
6	The Harrogate Secret	Saga	Catherine Cookson (Br)	Corgi
7	Straight	Thriller	Dick Francis (Br)	Pan
8	The Dark Half	Horror	Stephen King (US)	NEL
9	The Russia House	Novel	John le Carré (Br)	Coronet
10	Gates of Paradise	Saga	Virginia Andrews (US)	Fontana
11	Inch Loss Plan	Health	Rosemary Conley (Br)	Arrow
12	Spy Line	Thriller	Len Deighton (Br)	Grafton
13	Clear and Present Danger	Novel	Tom Clancy (US)	Fontana
14	A Season in Hell	Thriller	Jack Higgins (Br)	Pan
15	True Conf. Adrian Mole	Humour	Sue Townsend (Br)	Mandarin
16	The Pillars of the Earth	Saga	Ken Follet (Br)	Pan
17	Trevayne	Thriller	Robert Ludlum (US)	Grafton
18	Ambition	Novel	Julie Burchill (Br)	Corgi
19	TMHT: Red Herrings	TV tie-in	Dave Morris (Br)	Yearling
20	The Greek Key	Thriller	Colin Forbes (Br)	Pan
21	Home Run	Novel	Gerald Seymour (Br)	Fontana
22	TMHT: Buried Treasure	TV tie-in	Dave Morris (Br)	Yearling
23	The Business	Novel	Charlotte Bingham (Br)	Bantam
24	Daughters of the Prince	Novel	Noel Barber (Br)	Coronet
25	TMHT: Six...Shurikens	TV tie-in	Dave Morris (Br)	Yearling
26	Midnight	Fiction	Dean R. Koontz (US)	Headline
27	TMHT: Sky High	TV tie-in	Dave Morris (Br)	Yearling
28	1991 Horoscopes	Astrology	Russell Grant (Br)	Virgin
29	Old Sins	Romance	Penny Vincenzi (Br)	Arrow
30	Horoscopes 1991	Astrology	Various (US)	Grafton
31	Silence of the Lambs	Thriller	Thomas Harris (US)	Mandarin
32	Superhoroscopes	Astrology	Various	Arrow
33	French Kiss	Thriller	Eric Van Lustbader (US)	Grafton
34	Devices & Desires	Crime	P.D. James (Br)	Faber
35	Foucault's Pendulum	Novel	Umberto Eco (Ita)	Picador
36	A History...Chapters	Novel	Julian Barnes (Br)	Picador
37	Teenage...Turtles	TV tie-in	B.B. Hiller (US)	Yearling
38	Enter the Turtles	TH Mutant	Greg Steddy (Br)	Hippo
39	The Blue Bedroom	Stories	Rosamund Pilcher (Br)	Coronet
40	The Bridesmaid	Crime	Ruth Rendell (Br)	Arrow
41	Return of the Shredder	TH Mutant	Greg Steddy (Br)	Hippo
42	The Remains of the Day	Novel	Kazuo Ishiguro (Br)	Faber
43	Rhyme	Fiction	Roald Dahl (Br)	Puffin
44	Great & Secret Show	Novel	Clive Barker (Br)	Fontana
45	A Prayer for Owen Meany	Novel	John Irving (US)	B Swan
46	London Fields	Fiction	Martin Amis (Br)	Penguin
47	The Diamond Throne	Fantasy	David Eddings (US)	Grafton
48	The Power of One	Novel	Bryce Courtenay (Aus)	Mandarin
49	The Fortune	Novel	Michael Korda (US)	Pan
50	Doctors	Novel	Erich Segal (US)	Bantam

Price £	Month	Home	Export	Total	Gross £	No
4.99	Feb	553,380	496,158	1,049,538	5,237,194	1
4.99	Jun	396,050	553,521	949,571	4,738,359	2
3.99	Jul	392,270	195,151	587,421	2,343,809	3
3.99	Jan	273,601	312,445	586,046	2,338,323	4
4.99	Oct	429,807	149,094	578,901	2,888,715	5
3.99	Mar	431,691	123,839	555,530	2,216,564	6
3.99	Dec	310,122	217,444	527,566	2,104,988	7
4.99	Oct	326,320	188,061	514,381	2,566,761	8
4.50	May	281,564	228,479	510,043	2,295,193	9
3.99	Sep	295,888	212,145	508,033	2,027,051	10
6.99	Jan	443,444	59,561	503,005	3,516,004	11
3.99	Sep	271,230	228,795	500,025	1,995,099	12
4.99	Jun	236,403	246,297	482,700	2,408,673	13
3.99	Mar	261,244	169,014	430,258	1,716,729	14
2.99	Oct	253,991	130,452	384,443	1,149,484	15
4.99	Aug	182,892	198,104	380,996	1,901,170	16
4.50	Jun	184,064	166,213	350,277	1,576,246	17
3.99	May	261,915	87,899	349,814	1,395,757	18
1.99	Feb	222,095	90,798	312,893	622,657	19
4.50	Jan	184,895	124,627	309,522	1,392,849	20
3.99	May	172,125	124,531	296,656	1,183,657	21
1.99	Mar	200,460	89,311	289,771	576,644	22
4.99	Jun	187,217	100,969	288,186	1,438,048	23
4.99	Dec	156,276	120,697	276,973	1,382,095	24
1.99	Feb	181,323	91,149	272,472	542,219	25
4.50	Mar	171,749	98,089	269,838	1,214,271	26
1.99	Mar	176,323	90,110	266,433	530,201	27
2.50	Jun	168,500	86,900	255,400	638,500	28
4.50	Jul	145,014	108,928	253,942	1,142,739	29
2.50	Jul	121,248	131,616	252,864	632,160	30
3.99	Apr	129,965	121,273	251,238	1,002,439	31
3.50	Jun	146,317	100,482	246,799	863,796	32
4.50	May	110,122	136,562	246,684	1,110,078	33
6.99	Apr	210,108	35,729	245,837	1,718,400	34
6.99	Nov	140,979	101,311	242,290	1,693,607	35
4.99	Jul	195,316	36,394	231,710	1,156,232	36
2.50	Oct	139,917	89,849	229,766	574,415	37
2.99	Apr	226,720	0	226,720	677,892	38
3.50	Nov	187,883	32,834	220,717	772,509	39
3.99	Apr	174,414	35,035	209,449	835,701	40
2.99	Jun	209,122	0	209,112	625,244	41
4.99	May	145,023	60,781	205,804	1,026,961	42
3.50	Oct	151,892	52,131	204,023	714,080	43
4.99	Oct	134,581	62,503	197,084	983,449	44
5.99	May	93,314	103,606	196,920	1,179,550	45
4.99	Sep	160,435	34,425	194,860	972,351	46
4.50	Jul	111,352	83,505	194,857	876,856	47
3.99	Feb	75,966	114,873	190,839	761,447	48
4.50	Apr	92,770	93,959	186,729	840,280	49
3.99	Jan	93,609	91,693	185,302	739,354	50

No	Title	Genre	Author	Imprint
51	Curse of the Evil Eye	TH Mutant	Greg Steddy (Br)	Hippo
52	Turtle Power	TH Mutant	Greg Steddy (Br)	Hippo
53	Eve's Apples	Fiction	Lena Kennedy (US)	Futura
54	A Year in Provence	Travel	Peter Mayle (Br)	Pan
55	Beverly Hills	Romance	Pat Booth (Br)	Arrow
56	The House of Bonneau	Saga	Elvi Rhodes (Br)	Corgi
57	Mitla Pass	Novel	Leon Uris (US)	Corgi
58	Pyramids	Fantasy	Terrry Pratchett (Br)	Corgi
59	Ultimate Prizes	Novel	Susan Howatch (Br)	Fontana
60	Night Watch	Novel	Alastair MacNeil (Br)	Fontana
61	House of Cards	Novel	Michael Dobbs (Br)	Fontana
62	Ironmonger's Daughter	Saga	Harry Bowling (Br)	Headline
63	Secret... Laura Palmer	TV tie-in	Lynch & Frost (US)	Penguin
64	Heretic's Apprentice	Crime	Ellis Peters (Br)	Futura
65	Caribbean	Novel	James Michener (US)	Mandarin
66	The Captive	Romance	Virginia Holt (Br)	Fontana
67	The Naked Heart	Saga	Jacqueline Briskin (Br)	Corgi
68	Magic Sword of Nowhere	TH Mutant	Greg Steddy (Br)	Hippo
69	Passing Glory	Romance	Reay Tannel ? (?)	Penguin
70	Guards! Guards!	Fantasy	Terry Pratchett (Br)	Corgi
71	A Rare Benedictine	Crime	Ellis Peters (Br)	Headline
72	Paragon Place	Saga	Harry Bowling (Br)	Headline
73	Dickie	Romance	Sheelagh Kelly (Br)	Arrow
74	The Wench is Dead	Crime	Colin Dexter (Br)	Pan
75	By Sun and Candlelight	Saga	Susan Sallis (Br)	Corgi
76	Seasons of My Life	Autobiog	Hannah Hauxwell (Br)	Arrow
77	Orders For New York	Thriller	Leslie Thomas (Br)	Penguin
78	Spy Shadow	Thriller	Tim Sebastian (Br)	Bantam
79	Rivals	Fiction	Janet Dailey (US)	Sphere
80	Sorceress of Darshiva	Fantasy	David Eddings (US)	Corgi
81	Hungry Women	Glitz	Laramie Dunaway (US)	NEL
82	Silent Partner	Fiction	Jonathan Kellerman (US)	Futura
83	Super Rockesteady	TH Mutant	Greg Steddy (Br)	Hippo
84	The Crosskiller	Thriller	Marcel Montecino (US)	Grafton
85	The White Guns	Adventure	Douglas Reeman (Br)	Pan
86	God's Highlander	Saga	E.V. Thompson (Br)	Pan
87	TNMT – The Movie	TN Mutant	Greg Steddy (Br)	Hippo
88	Prince of Blood	Fantasy	Reymond E. Feist (US)	Grafton
89	Duncton Found	Fiction	William Horwood (Br)	Arrow
90	What Am I Doing Here?	Memoir	Bruce Chatwin (Br)	Picador
91	While...Sleeps	Thriller	Mary Higgins Clark (US)	Arrow
92	Brotherhood of the Tomb	Thriller	Daniel Easterman (Br)	Grafton
93	The Blackbird's Tale	Fiction	Emma Blair (Br)	Sphere
94	A Natural Curiosity	Fiction	Margaret Drabble (Br)	Penguin
95	Truckers	Fantasy	Terry Pratchett (Br)	Corgi
96	Presumed Innocent	Thriller	Scott Turow (US)	Penguin
97	Billy Bathgate	Novel	E.L. Doctorow (US)	Picador
98	Nemesis	SF	Isaac Asimov (US)	Bantam
99	Teenage...Turtles	TV tie-in	Dave Morris (Br)	Bantam
100	Cloning of Joanna May	Novel	Fay Weldon (Br)	Fontana

Price £	Month	Home	Export	Total	Gross £	No
2.99	Jun	183,284	0	183,284	548,019	51
2.99	Apr	180,029	0	180,029	538,286	52
3.99	Aug	161,728	6,761	168,489	672,271	53
4.99	Apr	147,404	17,525	164,929	822,995	54
3.99	Mar	102,846	61,436	164,282	655,485	55
3.99	Jul	159,290	3,502	162,792	649,540	56
4.99	Apr	54,670	107,745	162,415	810,450	57
3.50	Jun	131,729	30,385	162,114	567,399	58
4.50	Jun	78,501	82,026	160,527	722,371	59
3.50	Dec	91,866	67,889	159,755	559,142	60
3.99	Mar	130,436	28,973	159,409	636,041	61
3.99	Jan	158,104	1,043	159,147	634,996	62
3.99	Nov	145,328	6,949	152,277	607,585	63
3.50	Mar	128,627	19,656	148,283	518,990	64
4.99	Nov	65,852	80,684	146,536	731,214	65
3.99	Oct	83,639	60,645	144,284	575,693	66
4.50	Mar	92,571	49,666	142,237	640,066	67
1.95	Oct	142,005	0	142,005	276,909	68
4.99	Jun	82,110	58,004	140,114	699,168	69
3.99	Nov	125,513	14,283	139,796	557,786	70
2.99	Oct	105,085	31,962	137,047	409,770	71
4.99	Dec	135,196	1,028	136,224	679,757	72
4.99	Aug	113,668	21,079	134,747	672,387	73
3.99	Jul	114,051	19,657	133,708	533,494	74
3.99	Apr	129,881	3,784	133,665	533,323	75
3.99	Jul	130,228	417	130,645	521,273	76
3.99	Jun	99,126	29,709	128,925	514,410	77
3.99	Apr	89,142	37,483	126,625	505,233	78
3.99	Jan	76,448	49,985	126,433	504,467	79
4.99	Dec	78,061	48,204	126,265	630,062	80
3.99	Aug	112,142	13,316	125,458	500,577	81
4.50	Oct	47,197	76,888	124,085	558,382	82
1.95	Oct	123,783	0	123,783	241,376	83
4.50	Feb	69,746	53,469	123,215	554,467	84
3.99	Jul	84,252	38,082	122,334	488,112	85
4.50	Feb	92,040	29,120	121,160	545,220	86
3.25	Nov	119,703	0	119,703	389,034	87
3.99	Jan	57,725	61,701	119,426	476,509	88
4.99	Jun	74,829	42,358	117,187	584,763	89
4.99	May	72,476	44,120	116,596	581,814	90
3.99	Oct	41,149	75,140	116,289	463,993	91
4.50	Oct	41,870	73,752	115,622	520,299	92
3.99	Jun	108,386	6,880	115,266	459,911	93
4.50	Nov	60,597	52,184	112,781	507,514	94
2.99	Sep	98,432	13,732	112,164	335,370	95
4.99	Sep	97,863	13,943	111,806	557,911	96
3.50	Sep	40,929	68,337	109,266	382,431	97
3.99	Sep	67,010	41,328	108,338	432,268	98
2.99	Oct	104,784	2,137	106,921	319,693	99
3.99	May	50,719	55,231	105,950	422,740	100

Book Packagers

Many modern illustrated books are created by book packagers, whose special skills are in the areas of book design and graphic content. Children's interests and informational how-to are the usual subject areas; such books match up the expertise of specialist writers, artists and photographers, usually freelances, with the craftsmanship of in-house desk editors and art editors.

Packaged books are often expensive to produce, beyond the cost parameters set by traditional publishers for their own markets; the packager recoups the expense by pre-selling titles to publishers in various countries. Thus packaged books are usually international in content and approach, avoiding local interests such as cricket or Cornish cream teas.

The working style in most packagers' offices is more akin to magazine publishing than to traditional book publishing, with creative groups concentrating on the complexities of integrating words and pictures for individual titles rather than merely manuscript editing for a broad publishing list.

The many opportunities for freelance writers, specialist contributors and consultants, photographers and illustrators will usually be short-term and high pressure; packagers rarely spend more than a year on any title. As packaged books are frequently the work of more than one 'author' and because of the complications of the overseas rights deals that will be made and the formulae for packager's earnings, which are obviously only a proportion of a book's retail price, flat fees are often suggested rather than royalty agreements. Where royalties are appropriate, they will be based on the packager's receipts, but the expectation is that there will be more foreign language editions than a traditional publisher can achieve.

The Book Packagers Association (*Secretary:* Rosemary Pettit, 93a Blenheim Crescent, London W11 2EQ) is the forum for the exchange of creative and commercial experience in this branch of the publishing industry. The BPA has devised standard contracts to cover members' relationships with contributors and customers.

* Members of the Book Packagers Association

Aladdin Books Ltd (1980), 28 Percy Street, London W1P 9FF   *tel* 071-323 3319   *telex* 21115 Aladin G   *fax* 071-323 4829. *Directors:* Charles Nicholas, Lynn Lockett. Full design and book packaging facility.

Albion Press Ltd (1984), PO Box 52, Princes Risborough, Aylesbury, Bucks. HP17 9PR   *tel* (084 44) 4018   *fax* (084 44) 3358. *Directors:* Emma Bradford, Neil Philip. Quality integrated illustrated titles specialising in literature, social history, fine and graphic arts, cookery, children's books. Supply finished books. Publishers' commissions undertaken.

*Alphabet & Image Ltd (1972), Alpha House, South Street, Sherborne, Dorset DT9 3LU *tel* (0935) 814944   *fax* (0935) 816717. *Directors:* Anthony Birks-Hay, Leslie Birks-Hay. Complete editorial, picture research, photographic, design and production service for illustrated books on ceramics, beekeeping, horticulture, architecture, history, etc.

*Amanuensis Books Ltd (1986), 12 Station Road, Didcot, Oxon OX11 7LL   *tel* (0235) 811066   *telex* 94016837 Aman G   *fax* (0235) 510134. *Directors:* Loraine Fergusson, Kit Maunsell. High quality, illustrated non-fiction for the international co-edition market; all general subjects, specialising in medical handbooks for the layman. Opportunities for freelances.

Andromeda Oxford Ltd (1986), 11-15 The Vineyard, Abingdon, Oxon OX14 3PX *tel* (0235) 550296 *telex* 838075 *fax* (0235) 550330. *Directors:* M. Ritchie (managing), M. Desebrock (group publishing), J. Taylor (finance), Erik Skipper Larsen, Michael Cordsen, Jette Juliusson, J.G. Bateman, D.M. Halford, L. Clarke, J. Ridgeway, C. Sparling. Illustrated reference titles for the international market.

Antler Books Ltd (1980), PO Box 420, Warminster, Wilts. BA12 9XB *tel* (0985) 40189. *Directors:* John Stidolph, Dr Susan Abbott. Packaging – production and printing of books and magazines. Picture research, editorial, design services. Supplies film to publishers. Part of **Berkswell Publishing Co. Ltd.**

Beanstalk Books Ltd (1983), The Gardens House, Hever Castle Gardens, Nr Chiddingstone, Kent TN8 7NE *tel* (0892) 870912 *telex* 957320 Telexus G *fax* (0732) 863550. *Directors:* Shona McKellar, Penny Kitchenham. Specialists in highly illustrated books for adults and children and novelties; editorial, design and production service.

*Belitha Press Ltd (1980), 31 Newington Green, London N16 9PU *tel* 071-241 5566 *telex* 8950511 Oneone G ref. 32159001. *Directors:* Martin Pick, Richard Hayes, Rachel Pick (non-executive), Neil Champion, Peter Osborn, Peter West, ACA; *Associate:* Marilyn Malin. Conception, editing, design and production of finished books, offering authors and illustrators close involvement at each stage. Specialises in high quality international co-editions for children, preferably with potential for television or video tie-ins. Associated film production company, Inner Eye Ltd.

Bison Books Ltd (1974), Kimbolton House, 117a Fulham Road, London SW3 6RL *tel* 071-823 9222 *telex* 888014 Bison G *fax* 071-244 7139. *President and ceo:* S.L. Mayer. Non-fiction illustrated titles principally history, military history, weaponry, natural history, transport, travel, sport, art, entertainment.

BLA Publishing Ltd (1981), Christopher Road, East Grinstead, West Sussex RH19 3BT *tel* (0342) 318980 *fax* (0342) 410980. *Directors:* Au Bak Ling (chairman Hong Kong), Vincent Winter, Au King Kwok (Hong Kong), Au Chun Kwok (Hong Kong), Albert Kw Au (Hong Kong), Au Wai Kwok (Hong Kong); Quentin Hockliffe (sales). High quality illustrated reference books, particularly science dictionaries and encylopaedia, for the international market.

Book Packaging and Marketing (1990), 3 Murswell Lane, Silverstone, Towcester, Northants. NN12 8UT *tel/fax* (0327) 858380. *Proprietor:* Martin F. Marix Evans. Illustrated general and informational non-fiction for adults and children. Product development and project management; editorial and marketing consultancy. Opportunities for freelances.

*Breslich & Foss (1978), Golden House, 28-31 Great Pulteney Street, London W1R 3DD *tel* 071-734 0706 *fax* 071-494 0854. *Directors:* Paula G. Breslich, K.B. Dunning. Books produced from MS to bound copy stage from in-house ideas. Specialising in the arts, sport, health, crafts, gardening, children's.

Brown Wells and Jacobs Ltd (1981), 2 Vermont Road, London SE19 3SR *tel* 081-653 7670 *fax* 081-771 1765. *Director:* Graham Brown. Design, editorial, illustration and production of high quality non-fiction illustrated children's books. Specialities include pop-ups and novelties. Opportunities for freelances.

Bycornute Books (1986), 76a Ashford Road, Eastbourne, East Sussex BN21 3TE *tel* (0323) 26819 *fax* (0323) 649053 Bycorn/Cresc. *Director:* Ayeshah Abdel-Haleem. Development of projects for production by publishers, including editing, picture research and commissioning illustrations. Specialising in art history, mythology, comparative religion, New Age, cosmology, astronomy, iconography. Opportunities for freelances.

John Calmann and King Ltd (1976), 71 Great Russell Street, London WC1B 3BN *tel* 071-831 6351 *telex* 298246 Owls G *fax* 071-831 8356. *Directors:* Robin Hyman, Laurence King, Stanley Kekwick, Judy Rasmussen, Rosemary Bradley, David Lewis. Illustrated books on design, art, history, nature, architecture for international co-editions.

Cameron Books (1976), PO Box 1, Moffat, Dumfriesshire DG10 9SU *tel* (0683) 20808 *fax* (0683) 20012. *Directors:* Ian A. Cameron, Jill Hollis. Illustrated non-fiction including architecture, design, fine arts, the decorative arts and crafts, antiques, collecting, natural history, social history, films, food. **Edition** (1975). Design, editing, typesetting, production work from concept to finished book for other publishers.

*****Philip Clark Ltd** (1981), 53 Calton Avenue, Dulwich Village, London SE21 7DF *tel* 081-693 5605 *fax* 081-299 4647. *Director:* Philip Clark. Illustrated non-fiction for the international co-edition market, including books on wine, travel, natural history, windsurfing and other sports, children's reference and sponsored titles.

Diagram Visual Information Ltd (1967), 195 Kentish Town Road, London NW5 8SY *tel* 071-482 3633 *fax* 071-482 4932. *Director:* Bruce Robertson. Research, writing, design and illustration of reference books, supplied as film or manufactured copies. Opportunities for freelances.

Earthscape Editions (1987), 86 Peppard Road, Sonning Common, Reading, Berks. RG4 9RP *tel* (0734) 723751 *fax* (0734) 724488. *Partners:* B.J. Knapp, D.L.R. McCrae. High quality, full colour, illustrated children's books, including co-editions, for education, library and trade market. Opportunities for freelances.

*****Eddison Sadd Editions Ltd** (1982), St Chad's Court, 146B Kings Cross Road, London WC1X 9DH *tel* 071-837 1968 *telex* 929879 ESE G *fax* 071-837 2025. *Directors:* Nick Eddison, Ian Jackson, Marjorie Nelson. Illustrated non-fiction books for the international co-edition market.

Elvendon Press (1978), The Old Surgery, High Street, Goring-on-Thames, Reading, Berks. RG8 9AW *tel* (0491) 873003 *fax* (0491) 874233. *Directors:* Ray Hurst, Bernice Hurst. Complete packaging service. Business, professional and popular consumer titles; magazines, directories and all types of publications for publishers, commercial companies and institutions.

Equinox (Oxford) Ltd—acquired by **Andromeda Oxford Ltd,** *q.v.*

Sadie Fields Productions Ltd (1983), 3D Westpoint, 36/37 Warple Way, London W3 0RQ *tel* 081-746 1171 *fax* 081-746 1170. *Directors:* Sheri Safran, David Fielder. Creates and produces international co-productions of pop-up, novelty and picture and board books for children.

Graham-Cameron Publishing (1984), 10 Church Street, Willingham, Cambridge CB4 5HT *tel* (0954) 60444 *fax* (0954) 61453. *Directors:* Mike Graham-Cameron, Helen Graham-Cameron. Children's books; biographies; sponsored publications. Editorial, illustration and production services. *No* unsolicited MSS please.

Hamilton House Publishing (1975), 17 Staveley Way, Brixworth Industrial Park, Northampton NN6 9EU *tel* (0604) 881889 *fax* (0604) 880735. *Directors:* Tony Attwood, Philippa Attwood. Mostly secondary school text books; TV and radio tie-ins and business books.

*Johnson Editions (1980), 15 Grafton Square, London SW4 0DQ *tel* 071-622 1720 *fax* 071-720 9114. *Managing director:* Lorraine Johnson. Practical and art-related books on gardening, cookery, interior design, fashion, architecture.

Lennard Books, Windmill Cottage, Mackerye End, Harpenden, Herts. AL5 5DR *tel* (0582) 715866 *fax* (0582) 715121. *Directors:* K.A.A. Stephenson, R.H. Stephenson. Division of Lennard Associates Ltd. Sport, personalities, TV tie-ins, humour.

Lexus Ltd (1980), 205 Bath Street, Glasgow G2 4HZ *tel* 041-221 5266 *fax* 041-226 3139. *Director:* P.M. Terrell. Reference book publishing (especially bilingual dictionaries) as contractor, packager, consultant. Translation.

Lionheart Books (1985), 10 Chelmsford Square, London NW10 3AR *tel* 081-459 0453. *Partners:* Lionel Bender, Madeleine Bender, Ben White. Handle all aspects of editorial and design packaging of, mostly, children's illustrated science, natural history and history projects. Opportunities for freelances.

*Market House Books Ltd (1981), 2 Market House, Market Square, Aylesbury, Bucks. HP20 1TN *tel* (0296) 84911 *fax* (0296) 437073. *Directors:* Dr Alan Isaacs, Dr John Daintith, P.C. Sapsed. Compilation of dictionaries and reference books.

*Marshall Editions Ltd (1977), 170 Piccadilly, London W1V 9DD *tel* 071-629 0079 *telegraphic address* Marsheds, London W1 *fax* 071-834 0785. *Directors:* Bruce Marshall, John Bigg, Barbara Anderson, Barry Baker. Highly illustrated non-fiction, for the co-edition market, including aviation, business and industry, photography and video, cookery, wines and spirits, crafts and hobbies, DIY, fashion and costume, beauty, gardening, health, military and war, natural history, nautical, science and technical.

Oyster Books (1985), Sparrow Hill Way, Upper Weare, Nr Axbridge, Somerset BS26 2LA *tel* (0934) 732251 *fax* (0934) 732514. *Directors:* Jenny Wood, Tim Wood, Ali Brooks. Development of projects from conception through to CRC, film or finished books, including editorial, design and production service. Specialising in children's books (fiction, non-fiction and educational).

Parke Sutton Ltd (1982), High-Tec House, 10 Blackfriars Street, Norwich NR3 1SF *tel* (0603) 667021 *fax* (0603) 760284. *Directors:* Ian S. McIntyre (managing), Cris de Boos (financial), Geoff Staff (studio), Alan Boardman. Packagers of non-fiction books. Also publish newspapers, magazines and reference books for specific organisations. Opportunities for freelances.

Playne Books (1987), New Inn Lane, Avening, Tetbury, Glos. GL8 8NB *tel* (0453) 835155 *fax* (0453) 835590. *Director:* David Playne. Book packaging and production service. All stages of production undertaken from initial concept (editorial, design and manufacture) to delivery of completed books.

*Mathew Price Ltd (1983), Old Rectory House, Marston Magna, Yeovil, Somerset BA22 8DT *tel* (0935) 851158 *telex* 46720 Mprice G *fax* (0935) 851285. *Chairman:* Mathew Price. Illustrated fiction and non-fiction children's books for all ages for the international market.

*Quarto Publishing plc (1976), Quintet Publishing Ltd (1984), Atlas Photography Ltd (1948), The Old Brewery, 6 Blundell Street, London N7 9BH *tel* 071-700 6700 *telegraphic address* Quartopub *fax* 071-700 4191. *Directors:* L.F. Orbach, R.J. Morley, M.J. Mousley, J.M.A. Manstead. International co-editions.

Roxby Press Ltd (1974), 126 Victoria Rise, London SW4 0NW *tel* 071-720 8872 *fax* 071-622 9528. Hugh Elwes (managing director), Lady Francis Seymour (editor), Anne Hunt (foreign rights editor). International book packagers.

*****Savitri Books Ltd** (1983), 115 J Cleveland Street, London W1P 5PN *tel* 071-436 9932 *fax* 071-580 6330. *Director:* Mrinalini S. Srivastava. Packaging, design, production.

Sceptre Books (1982), Time and Life Building, New Bond Street, London W1Y 0AA *tel* 071-499 4080 *telex* 22557. *Managing director:* David Owen. Conceive, design, edit and produce finished books; work with publishers on joint ventures.

*****Sheldrake Press Ltd** (1979), 188 Cavendish Road, London SW12 0DA *tel* 081-675 1767 *fax* 081-675 7736. *Director:* Simon Rigge. Original illustrated non-fiction; travel, home improvement, cookery, history of technology, music; children's stationery.

Sports Editions Ltd (1987), 3 Greenlea Park, Prince George's Road, London SW19 2JD *tel* 081-640 1116 *telex* 8955022 Asport G *fax* 081-648 5240. *Directors:* Richard Dewing, Steve Powell. Packagers of sports and leisure books, offering full service of design, production and print.

Swallow Books (1982), 260 Pentonville Road, London N1 9JY *tel* 071-278 1483 *fax* 071-278 7277. *Directors:* Michael Edwards, Richard Hayes, Erik Pordes. Illustrated non-fiction: reference, cookery, gardening, art and design, natural history, travel, popular science.

Tango Books—imprint of **Sadie Fields Productions Ltd.**

*****Templar Publishing Co.,** Pippbrook Mill, London Road, Dorking, Surrey RH4 1JE *tel* (0306) 76361. *Directors:* Richard Carlisle (chairman and managing), Del Tucker (deputy managing), Amanda Wood (editorial), Co Van Woerkom (production). Children's picture and illustrated information books; also adult illustrated non-fiction. Most titles aimed at international co-edition market. Established links with major co-publishers in UK, USA, Australia and throughout Europe.

Thames Head, division of **BLA Publishing Ltd,** Christopher Road, East Grinstead, West Sussex RH19 3BT *tel* (0342) 318980 *fax* (0342) 410980. *Sales:* Quentin Hockliffe. Illustrated international co-editions: general non-fiction, militaria, history, travel guides and practical crafts.

*****Toucan Books Ltd** (1985), Albion Courtyard, Greenhills Rents, London EC1M 6BN *tel* 071-251 3921 *fax* 071-251 1692. *Directors:* Robert Sackville West, Adam Nicolson, John Meek. International co-editions; editorial, design and production services.

Touchstone Publishing Ltd (1989), 68 Florence Road, Brighton, East Sussex BN1 6DJ *tel* (0273) 561689 *fax* (0273) 550415. *Directors:* Roger Coote (managing), Edwina Conner (publishing). High quality, illustrated children's fiction and non-fiction for trade and institutional markets world-wide. Supply CRC, film or finished books. Publishers' commissions undertaken.

Ventura Publishing Ltd, 11-13 Young Street, London W8 5EH *tel* 071-221 6395 *telex* 8953658 Venpub G *fax* 071-938 3575. *Directors:* R.D. Ellis (managing), D. Hall. Specialise in production of high quality children's novelty books including the *Spot* books by Eric Hill. Illustrated adult leisure and general interest non-fiction for the international co-edition market.

*Victoria House Publishing Ltd (1980), Victoria House, 4 North Parade, Bath BA1 1LF   *tel* (0225) 463401   *telex* 449218 Josmor G   *fax* (0225) 460942. *Directors:* Derek Hall, Martyn Lewis, Joanna Verney, Michael J. Morris, William Gaspero. International children's co-editions.

*Wordwright (1987), 2-6 Ellington Place, Ellington Road, London N10 3DG   *tel* 081-444 0505   *fax* 081-444 0695. *Directors:* Charles Perkins, Veronica Davis. Full packaging service – research, editorial, design and production. Also assesses and prepares MSS for the US market. Opportunities for freelances.

Doing It On Your Own
Self-publishing for Writers

PETER FINCH

Why bother?
You've tried all the usual channels and been turned down; your work is uncommercial, specialised, technical; you are concerned with art while everyone else is obsessed with cash; you need a book out quickly; you want to take up small publishing as a hobby; you've heard that publishers make a lot of money out of their authors and you'd like a slice – all reason enough. But be sure you understand what you are doing before you begin.

But isn't this cheating? It can't be real publishing – where is the critical judgement? Publishing is a respectable activity carried out by firms of specialists. Writers of any ability never get involved
But they do. Start self-publishing and you'll be in good historical company: Horace Walpole, Balzac, Walt Whitman, Virginia Woolf, Gertrude Stein, John Galsworthy, Rudyard Kipling, Beatrix Potter, Lord Byron, Thomas Paine, Mark Twain, Upton Sinclair, W.H. Davies, Zane Grey, Ezra Pound, D.H. Lawrence, William Carlos Williams, Alexander Pope, Robbie Burns, James Joyce, Anais Nin and Lawrence Stern. All these at some time in their careers dabbled in doing it themselves. William Blake did nothing else. He even made his own ink, handprinted his pages and got Mrs Blake to sew on the covers.

But today it's different
Not necessarily. This is not vanity publishing we're talking about although if all you want to do is produce a pamphlet of poems to give away to friends then self-publishing will be the cheapest way. Doing it yourself today can be a valid form of business enterprise. Look at the huge success in recent times of the late Aeron Clement with his story of badgers, *The Cold Moons*: 8000 self-produced hardbacks sold in three months and it was then brought out as a best-selling paperback by Penguin. Clement self-published with the help of his local publican from Llandeilo in West Wales – hardly a base from which to take the book world by storm but this is just what he did. And now best-selling author of *A Month in the Country*, J.L. Carr, taking the bull by the horns, has formed The Quince Tree Press to republish his novels as their licences with Penguin lapse. Why? He enjoys the control and gets a better financial return.

Can anyone do it?
Certainly. If you are a writer then a fair number of the required qualities will already be in hand. If, in addition, you can put up a shelf then the manufacture of the book to go on it will not be beyond you. The more able and practical you are then the cheaper the process will be. The utterly inept will need to pay others to help them, but it will still be self-publishing in the end.

Where do I start?
With research. Read up on the subject. Make sure you know what the parts of a book are. Terms like *verso*, *recto*, *prelims*, *dummy*, *typeface* and *point size* all have to lose their mystery. You will not need to become an expert but you will need a certain familiarity. Don't rush. Learn.

What about ISBN numbers?

International Standard Book Numbers – a standard bibliographic code, individual to each book published, are used by booksellers and librarians alike. They are issued free of charge by the Standard Book Numbering Agency, 12 Dyott Street, London WC1A 1DF. Write giving the basic details of your proposed book and, if appropriate, you will receive an ISBN by return.

Next?

Put your book together – be it the typed pages of your novel, your selected poems or your nature notes and drawings – and see how large a volume it will make. Follow the details on preparation of typescript given elsewhere in this yearbook. No real idea of what your book should look like? Anything will not do. Go to your local bookshop and hunt out a few contemporary examples of volumes produced in a style you would like to emulate. Ask the manager for advice. Take your typescript and your examples round to a number of local printers (find these through *Yellow Pages*) and ask for a quote. This costs nothing and will give you an idea of what the enterprise is likely to involve. Anthony Rowe Ltd (Bumper's Way, Bristol Road, Chippenham SN14 6LM) are specialists in low runs from camera ready copy, and will quote you a price.

How much?

It depends. How long is a piece of string? You will not get a pamphlet of poems out for less than a few hundred pounds while a hardbacked work of prose will come in well above £3000. Unit cost is important. The larger the number of copies you have printed the less each will cost. Print too many and the total bill will be enormous. Books are no longer cheap; perhaps they never were.

Can I make it cost less?

Yes. Do some of the work yourself. If it's poems and you are prepared to manage with text set on a typewriter then that can make a considerable saving. Could you accept home production and run the pages off on a borrowed duplicator? Or staple together sheets produced on an office photocopier? Text prepared on a word processor with a daisy-wheel printer can be very presentable. Access to one running a desktop publishing program with a laser printer will give even better results. Home binding, if your abilities lie in that direction, can save a fair bit. What it all comes down to is the standard of production you want and indeed at whom your book is aimed. Books for the commercial market place need to look like their fellows, specialist publications can afford to be more eccentric.

Who decides how it looks?

You do. No one should ever ask a printer simply to produce a book. You should plan the design of your publication with as much care as you would a house extension. Books which sell are those which stand out in the bookshop. Spend as much time and money as you can on the cover. It is the part of the book your buyer will see first. Look at the volumes in bookshop displays especially those in the window. Imitate British paperback design, it's the best in the world.

How many copies should I produce?

Small press poetry pamphlets sell about 300 copies, new novels sometimes manage 1500, literary paperbacks 10,000, mass-market blockbusters over a million. But that is generally where there is a sales team and whole distribution organisation behind the book. You are an individual. You must do all yourself. Do not on the one hand end up with a prohibitively high unit cost by ordering too few copies. One hundred of anything is usually a waste of time. On the other hand can you really sell 3000? Will shops buy in dozens? They will probably only want twos and threes. Take care. Research your market first.

How do I sell it?

With all your might. This is perhaps the hardest part of publishing. It is certainly as time consuming as both the writing of the work and the printing of it put together. To succeed here you need a certain flair and you should definitely not be of a retiring nature. If you intend selling through the trade (and even if you don't you are bound to come into contact with bookshop orders at some stage) your costing must be correct and *worked out in advance*. Shops will want at least 33% of the selling price as discount. You'll need about the same again to cover your distribution, promotion and other overheads leaving the final third to cover production costs and any profit you may wish to make. Take your unit production cost and multiply by at least 4. Commerical publishers often multiply by as much as 9.

Do not expect the trade to pay your carriage costs. Your terms should be 33% post free on everything bar single copy orders. Penalise these by reducing your discount to 25%. Some shops will suggest that you sell copies to them on *sale or return*. This means that they only pay you for what they sell and then only after they've sold it. This is a common practice with certain categories of publications and often the only way to get independent books into certain shops; but from the self-publisher's point of view it should be avoided if at all possible. Cash in hand is best but expect to have your invoices paid by cheque at a later date. Buy a duplicate pad in order to keep track of what's going on. Phone the shops you have decided should take your book or turn up in person and ask to see the buyer. Letters and sample copies sent by post will get ignored. Get a freelance distributor to handle all of this for you if you can. Check the trade section of Cassell's *Directory of Publishing* or advertise for one in *The Bookseller*. They will want another 12% or so commission on top of the shops' discount – but expect to have to go it alone.

What about promotion?

A vital aspect often overlooked by beginners. Send out as many review copies as you can, all accompanied by slips quoting selling price and name and address of the publisher. Never admit to being that person yourself. Invent a name, it will give your operation a professional feel. Ring up newspapers and local radio stations ostensibly to check that your copy has arrived but really to see if they are prepared to give your book space. Try to think of an angle for them, anything around which they can write a story. Buying advertising space rarely pays for itself but good local promotion with 100% effort will generate dividends.

What if I can't manage all this myself?

You can employ others to do it for you. If you are a novelist and you opt for a package covering everything, it could set you back more than £10,000. A number of publishers and associations advertise such services in writers' journals and in the Sunday classifieds. *Authors. Publish with us.* is a typical ploy. They will do a competent job for you, certainly, but you will still end up having to do the bulk of the selling yourself. It is a costly route, fraught with difficulty. Do the job on your own if you possibly can.

And what if it goes wrong?

Put all the unsolds under the bed or give them away. It has happened to lots of us. Even the big companies who are experienced at these things have their regular flops. It was an adventure and you did get your book published. On the other hand you may be so successful that you'll be at the London Book Fair selling the film rights and wondering if you've reprinted enough. Whichever way it goes – good luck.

Where to learn more
Peter Finch, *How To Publish Yourself*, Allison & Busby, 1991.
Harry Mulholland, *Guide to Self Publishing*, Mulholland Wirral, 1984.
Ian Templeton, *Publish it Yourself and Make it Pay*, Pikers Pad, 1985.

Organisations which can help
Association of Little Presses, 89a Petherton Road, London N5 2QT *tel* 071-226 2657. Membership £10. Offers advice, publishes a catalogue of small independent publications, produces a newsletter, organises book fairs.

Small Press Group, BM Bozo, London WC1N 3XX *tel* (0234) 211606. Membership £15. Campaigns on behalf of small presses in Britain, publishes a yearbook (see page 128), a monthly magazine, organises book fairs.

Password (Books) Ltd, 23 New Mount Street, Manchester M4 4DE *tel* 061-953 4009. Runs publishing training courses for small and self-publishers.

See also the articles on word processing and desktop publishing in the **Preparation of materials, resources** section.

Vanity Publishing

A reputable publisher very rarely asks an author to pay for the production of his work, or to contribute to its cost, or to undertake to purchase copies. The only exception is in the case of a book of an extremely specialised nature, with a very limited market or perhaps the first book of poems by a new writer of some talent. In such instances, especially if the book is a good one making a contribution to its subject, an established and reliable publisher will be prepared to accept a subvention from the author to make publication possible, and such financial grants often come from scientific or other academic foundations or funds. This is a very different procedure from that of the *vanity publisher* who claims to perform, for a fee to be paid by the author, all the many functions involved in publishing a book.

In his efforts to secure business the vanity publisher will usually give exaggerated praise to an author's work and arouse equally unrealistic hopes of its commercial success. The distressing reports we have received from embittered victims of vanity publishers underline the importance of reading extremely carefully the contracts offered by such publishers. Often these will provide for the printing of, say, 2000 copies of the book, usually at a quite exorbitant cost to the author, but will leave the 'publisher' under no obligation to bind more than a very limited number. Frequently, too, the author will be expected to pay the cost of any effective advertising, while the 'publisher' makes little or no effort to promote the distribution and sale of the book. Again, the names and imprints of vanity publishers are well known to literary editors, and their productions therefore are rarely, if ever, reviewed or even noticed in any important periodical. Similarly, such books are hardly ever stocked by the booksellers.

We repeat, therefore: except in rare instances, never pay for publication, whether for a book, an article, a lyric, or a piece of music. If a work is worth publishing, sooner or later a publisher will be prepared to publish it at his own expense. But if a writer cannot resist the temptation of seeing his work in print, in book form, he should consider the possibility of self-publishing. If, after all, he decides to approach a vanity publisher, even though he has to pay a substantial sum, he should first discover just how much or how little the publisher will provide and will do in return for the payment demanded.

See also the **Agents** section for literary agents.

Poetry

Poetry Publishing Today

PETER FORBES
Editor, Poetry Review

and

JONATHAN BARKER
Literature Officer, The British Council

As the 1980s *Zeitgeist* recedes and the 1990s start to take shape the messages for poetry are mixed. The good news is that a new generation of gifted poets, born mostly around 1960–63, has started to make its mark: Glyn Maxwell, Jackie Kay, Robert Crawford, Simon Armitage and Gerard Woodward have made an unusual impact with their first books (in Jackie Kay's case, even before her first book), and the excitement of arrival is good for poetry.

The bad news is the recession and the decline of literary magazines. Two magazines that were once influential outlets for poetry, the *Listener* and *Encounter*, folded in 1991; the *Times Literary Supplement* was revamped under new Editor Ferdinand Mount to arrest falling sales, and the position of the *New Statesman & Society* is precarious. If this tendency goes on, outlets for poetry will soon be restricted to the book publishers and the little magazines, clearly an unhealthy state of affairs.

The recession has also led to restructuring and lay-offs among the major publishers, but so far the poetry lists seem to have escaped without serious damage. A development worth recording is that Craig Raine has left Faber after nearly ten years as Poetry Editor to become a Fellow of New College, Oxford. His successor is Christopher Reid, who had been Children's Poetry Editor. Faber will be eagerly watched for signs of Reid's emerging editorial policy.

No doubt there will be further upheavals in both magazines and book publishers, but for a while it looks as if competition for space in magazines and on publishers' lists is going to be even more intense. It is thus more important than ever for poets to understand the system if they seriously want to be published.

So, what is this system? The first thing to bear in mind is that there are literally hundreds of 'established' poets in this country. This means that they publish poems in the recognised poetry magazines, followed by volume publication with a major poetry publisher. But, unless you are already involved in the poetry world, you're unlikely to be able to name more than a handful of them. And for every poet achieving that coveted first volume there are dozens with plausible track records knocking on the door. In other words, the fame and fortune accruing to poets, in an increasingly publicity-conscious age, is strictly limited. Many begin sending out their work with totally unreal expectations. Only the likes of Tony Harrison, Seamus Heaney and Ted Hughes achieve anything like the glamour associated with writers of fiction and biography. On the other hand, only those who are not in the end cut out to be poets will fail to understand the true rewards of writing and publishing poetry – most poetic reputations are extremely hard won and deserved.

So where do you start? Most budding poets are afflicted by excessive self-consciousness and anxiety concerning questions of protocol, copyright and the like. This article will answer those questions; but the first rule is to realise that submitting poetry is a very down-to-earth business – there is no magic formula, and personal revelations will not help the cause of your work. The first question to ask, before the envelope is sealed, is should I really be sending my work out at all? If, in answer to the question, how many books of contemporary poetry have you read in recent years? the answer is, none, almost certainly the postage would be better saved and spent on those unread volumes. Anybody writing poetry needs to have read some representative poetry of the time, and very many really gifted poets begin by imitating some master. The place to start is in the anthologies. Some worth looking at are: Blake Morrison and Andrew Motion's *Penguin Book of Contemporary British Poetry* (Penguin, 1982), Dannie Abse's *Hutchinson Book of Post-War British Poets* (Hutchinson, 1989), Carol Rumens' *Making for the Open* (Chatto, 1985), Fraser Steel's *Poetry Book Society Anthology: New Series No. 1* (Hutchinson, 1990) and Anne Stevenson's *Poetry Book Society Anthology: New Series No. 2* (Hutchinson, 1991). The poetry magazines listed below will give a good flavour of contemporary verse, together with reviews of the new collections. Like any other subject, the more you know, the easier it is to learn more.

So, you have read a good deal of contemporary verse – what next? Ideally you should do two things. You should subscribe and submit to a few magazines that publish the kind of poetry you feel sympathetic to, and you should join a poetry group or workshop.

MAGAZINES

There are two main kinds of magazine outlet for poetry: general literary magazines which print some poems, and specialist poetry magazines: the little magazines. The first category is of little interest to the beginner, normally printing work by experienced poets, even if not yet published in book form. The little magazines are the place to start. But which one? There are literally hundreds of little poetry magazines – almost all are run as part-time activities by one or two dedicated people. A few have Arts Council or Regional Arts Board Grants, a track record, and a reasonable expectation of survival long enough to print your poem when accepted. As you might expect, these are rather freer with rejection slips than with acceptances. Emerging poets usually get to know the little magazine scene well. There are always newish magazines coming along which have a livelier profile and a greater openness to new contributors; established magazines sometimes gain a new editor with a vigorous policy. It helps to know all this, but only experience will teach it. A common error among beginner poets is to assume that it must be easy to publish in the less-well-known magazines. It is always difficult to gain acceptance anywhere, and that first acceptance is a significant step. To impress just one person, who's read your work cold amongst the work of dozens of other people's, is a real feat.

Most poetry magazines have circulations of less than a thousand, but the big little magazines – *London Magazine, PN Review, Poetry Review, Stand* – have considerably more – up to 5000 (*London Magazine, PN Review* and *Stand* also feature other kinds of writing but their reputation as poetry magazines is high). Newish poetry magazines of considerable liveliness include *Acumen, Bête Noire, The North, The Rialto* and *Verse*. Certain magazines have a particular character: *Ambit* has always featured a blend of sci-fi, street-cred and quality illustrations; *Agenda* is – among other things – one of the few outlets for translations from pre-twentieth-century poetry; *Poetry World* is devoted to contemporary translation; and so on. A few magazines have traditionally been popular with new poets: *Outposts*, run for over 40 years until his death by Howard Sergeant, and now edited by Roland John; *Orbis*; *Poetry Wales* (for which you don't have to be Welsh but it helps). Although *Poetry Review*, as the Poetry Society's magazine, is the highest circulation strictly poetry magazine and one of the most prestigious, it is extremely hospitable to new writers.

Payment in the little magazines is unlikely to be more than £15 and could be no more than a free copy of the magazine. The other magazines which publish some poetry can be more financially rewarding, but this sector is currently a disaster area. As we said at the start of this article, two major magazines, the *Listener* and *Encounter*, have gone and a question mark hangs over the viability of the literary magazine as a species. So far, there is no sign of any other outlet, newspapers for example, filling the gap. Exceptions to the gloom are the *Spectator*, the most successful weekly, whose Poetry Editor, P.J. Kavanagh, smuggles an increasing number of poems into the books pages, the *London Review of Books*, which is now the principal serious literary magazine in the country, and which sometimes gives space to extremely long poems, and the *Observer*, which prints a poem most weeks these days, and not just by the most obvious names. The *Literary Review* has become a vehicle for Editor Auberon Waugh's crusade for what he calls 'real poetry'. Poems (which must rhyme and scan) have to be on a set theme advertised in each issue. The prizes are good.

It must be stressed that anyone seriously hoping to appear in the little poetry magazines should, in principle, subscribe to at least two or three. The magazines are the lifeblood of poetry and all have great difficulty in making ends meet. Their habitual postbags contain dozens of submissions for every single new subscription, and editors learn to love the small envelope and fear the large one: the smallest envelopes almost always contain subscriptions or at least enquiries, and 'the larger the envelope the worse the submission' is a kind of Murphy's Law of poetry editing – which brings us to the mechanics of submission.

How to submit poems to magazines

1. Your poems must be typed, preferably on A4 and only one poem to the page. Your name and address should appear on each poem.
2. Send no more than six poems at a time. Never send a book-length collection unless a large batch is requested by the editor.
3. Always send an adequate stamped addressed envelope. Adequate means two things: it should be neither too small nor too large an envelope and the postage should be correct. If only six poems are sent the postage will be the standard rate. Too large or small envelopes make life miserable for the editor. Handling the sheer bulk of mail is always a problem. *Poetry Review* receives about 5000 submissions, or more than 30,000 poems a year. Trying to stuff too many poems into tiny envelopes is not conducive to a judicial editorial frame of mind. On the other hand, it is wrong to put A4 typescript into a large envelope with card stiffening and DO NOT BEND written on it, or to insert poems into bulky ring binders or plastic wallets. Typescript is not precious artwork – it

can and will be bent. So, *fold* your poems once and put them in an envelope about 10″ × 7″, with a similar self-addressed and stamped envelope folded inside. Submissions from outside the UK or submissions to foreign magazines must include return postage – either adequate postage stamps of the relevant country or International Reply Coupons, obtainable from post offices. It is helpful when sending poems abroad to specify that the poems needn't be returned – postage can then be kept to the minimum necessary for a letter in reply. Editors are not obliged to return work without return postage and most simply cannot afford to. So sending a submission without an sae is a complete waste of time.

4. Do not write to editors asking for free sample copies. Buy one. Send a cheque. If you don't know the price, send the magazine a note, including sae, asking for details.

5. Given the size of the postbag and the fact that most poetry magazines are quarterly or less frequent, don't expect (though you may sometimes get) a quick response. And don't pester the editor – who has a magazine to produce – by phoning. If after two months you haven't heard, it's a good idea to send a reminder. Unfortunately, decisions sometimes take even longer than this. If you feel you must try your poems elsewhere, simply write to the editor withdrawing the poems. They are then free and he has no rights over them, whether he replies or not.

6. Always keep copies of your poems. Editors generally accept no responsibility for unsolicited material. It is your responsibility to make sure your work is not lost.

7. Don't use special pleading in your covering letter. If you have published before, in any reputable outlet, it is worth telling the editor, otherwise the covering letter is a mere formality, offering the poems for publication. If and when an editor accepts work he will usually then want to know a bit about you – not before.

8. Don't ask the editor for advice, however politely. If he or she is seriously interested advice may well be tendered freely, but the editor is not there as a counsellor but to produce the best magazine possible. The Poetry Society (21 Earls Court Square, London SW5 9DE) runs a Critical Service specifically to provide what the editor cannot. It costs money of course, as it should, since providing a critique is a time-consuming business.

Markets – poetry magazines

Full details of those magazines marked with an asterisk can be found in earlier sections of the *Yearbook*. The Poetry Library publishes a regularly updated list of poetry magazines – write, sending a large sae, to: The Poetry Library, South Bank Centre, Royal Festival Hall, London SE1 8XX. A fuller list of poetry magazines appears in *Small Presses and Little Magazines of the UK and Ireland*, 9th edition, £5.50 inc. p&p from Oriel Bookshop, The Friary, Cardiff CF1 4AA.

*Acumen	*Krino (Ire)
*Agenda	Lines Review
*Ambit	New Spokes
Bête Noire	The North
*Chapman	*Orbis
*Cyphers (Ire)	Ore
The Echo Room	*Outposts
*Envoi	*Oxford Poetry
The Gairfish	Pennine Platform
*Honest Ulsterman (N Ire)	*PN Review
*Iron	*Poetry Durham
Joe Soap's Canoe	*Poetry Ireland Review (Ire)

*Poetry London Newsletter
*Poetry Nottingham
*Poetry Review
*Poetry Wales
*The Rialto
 Rhinoceros
*The Salmon (Ire)
*Slow Dancer

 Smoke
*Stand Magazine
*Staple
*Verse
 Westwords
 Weyfarers
 The Wide Skirt
 Writing Women

Markets – literary magazines, weeklies and others which publish poetry

Artrage
Cencrastus
The Countryman
Critical Quarterly
The Green Book
Kunapipi
The Literary Review
London Review of Books

New Statesman & Society
The New Welsh Review
The Observer
Planet
The Spectator
The Times Literary Supplement
Wasafiri: Caribbean, African,
    Asian and associated literatures
Writing Ulster

BOOK PUBLICATION

Submitting a collection of poems to a book publisher should not be considered lightly. If at least half of the poems have been published in magazines listed in this *Yearbook* and/or you've won a few prizes, you should definitely consider it. A collection is usually 40-50 poems (the standard length of a poetry collection is 64 pages). In submitting a collection, you must keep a copy of the MS, send return postage, and be prepared to wait – six months is not unusual.

Major trade publishers

These are the household names everyone dreams of being published by. In recent years, though, many have removed themselves from the poetry market completely, leaving a few who maintain active lists and who do occasionally take on new poets. These are Faber & Faber, Chatto & Windus, Oxford University Press, Hutchinson, Secker & Warburg, Collins Harvill, Paladin and Penguin/ Viking. A few other publishers have the occasional star poet: Deutsch with Geoffrey Hill, Macmillan with Charles Causley, Cape with Roger McGough and Methuen with Michèle Roberts. Some of these publishers are very unlikely to take on a new poet, although Methuen have recently signed Katie Campbell. Penguin specialise in selected poems by poets like U.A. Fanthorpe, James Fenton, Tony Harrison, Geoffrey Hill and Jeremy Reed, who have already made considerable reputations with other publishers, and Paladin have a modernist list, often publishing in paperback books previously published by Carcanet Press. So, only Faber, Secker, OUP, Chatto, Hutchinson and Collins Harvill are seriously in the market for new poets.

As previously mentioned, all eyes will be on Faber for signs of their new direction. Most of the publishers have taken on new poets recently, thanks to the boom in talent mentioned at the beginning of this article, although some of the best new poets – Glyn Maxwell and Simon Armitage for example – have been snapped up by the leading independent poetry press Bloodaxe rather than by the traditional majors. But Chatto have signed Robert Crawford and Gerard Woodward, Secker Sarah Maguire and John Burnside, OUP Jamie McKendrick and Collins Harvill Michael O'Neill and Michael Hulse. Whether the recession will put an end to this list building is still uncertain.

It is worth remembering that many of the poets signed to major publishers have already published books by other publishers. Poets are poached and some are dropped. The newcomer is thus in competition with established names. In recent years, there has been an increasing tendency for the major publishers to favour poets who have won one of the major competitions, the Poetry Society's National Poetry Competition or the biennial Arvon Competition. Faber have long had a series called *Poetry Introduction* in which about six poets are given anthology space and the Faber imprint as a way of floating them in the big pool. This practice has now been taken up by other publishers, including Chatto, and by Peterloo, Anvil, Bloodaxe and Seren amongst the specialist poetry presses, and is a welcome innovation.

Another important source of early recognition for poets are the annual Eric Gregory Awards run by the Society of Authors (see page 570). These are cash awards, made to promising poets under 30 years of age on the basis of merit and circumstances. An anthology of the winners is usually produced, about every two years, but the Award is prestigious enough to carry weight irrespective of such publication. *Poetry Review* publishes an issue devoted to new poets (no age limit) about every three years, with the aim of alerting publishers to promising new poets. Eight poets were featured in 1987 and eleven in 1990.

Specialist poetry presses

There have always been small poetry presses, but as the trade publishers were drawing in their poetic horns in the 1970s, some of the subsidised small presses began to take on a new dimension. A few of these now constitute the main outlet for poetry book publication, and match the majors in attractive production, prestige, and often in marketing flair. Bloodaxe Books, in particular, based in Newcastle, has become legendary for a very full and imaginative publishing programme, including Tony Harrison, Miroslav Holub, Ken Smith, R.S. Thomas, Sylvia Kantaris and Irina Ratushinskaya, and many new poets. *The New Women Poets* anthology (1990) launched 25 new poets, three of whom, Jackie Kay, Eva Salzman and Elizabeth Garrett, are already contracted for first volumes with Bloodaxe.

The big league comprises Bloodaxe, Carcanet, Peterloo, Anvil, Seren (formerly Poetry Wales Press), Enitharmon and Littlewood·Arc. All of these are more prolific than the majors. In 1989 Peterloo published its 100th volume, and has a reputation for publishing late-starters, although it is equally hospitable to the young poet. In 1989 it won the £12,000 Ralph Lewis Award for its commitment to publishing new poets. Anvil and Carcanet are both committed to poetry in translation but have published a substantial number of British and Irish poets, such as Carol Ann Duffy, Dick Davis, Tim Dooley, Dennis O'Driscoll, John Birtwhistle, David Hartnett, Philip Holmes, E.A. Markham, Thomas McCarthy and Anthony Howell (Anvil) and Alison Brackenbury, Gillian Clarke, Charles Boyle, Robert Wells, Clive Wilmer, Alistair Elliot, Roger Garfitt, Ian McMillan, Peter Sansom, Sujata Bhatt and Vikram Seth (Carcanet).

Enitharmon, based in Hampshire, has an increasingly impressive catalogue of established names like Jeremy Reed, David Gascoyne, Edwin Brock, and new poets like Martyn Crucefix and Michael Henry. Hippopotamus Press has published poets such as A.L. Hendriks, Debjani Chatterjee and Peter Dale, and Stride have become prolific publishers recently, with poets like Chris Bendon, Jay Ramsay and Evangeline Paterson.

There has been a surge of poetry activity in the North in recent years, much of it expressed in pamphlet form. Littlewood·Arc is the leading publisher of quality paperbacks in this area, with poets like Mick North, Wes Magee, David Craig and Tariq Latif. Smith-Doorstop in Huddersfield have now begun to move from pamphlets to books. Headland Publications are based in Liverpool and publish poets such as Elizabeth Bartlett, Ian Caws and John Cotton.

Some of these publishers are represented by the Password Distribution Service, whose catalogue (free on receipt of an A4 sae, with 46p stamp, from Password Books, 23 New Mount Street, Manchester M4 4DE) is a good introduction to the range of work currently being produced. In autumn 1991 Password launched a distribution service to back up their repping of small-press titles. This should lead to wider availability of these books. Many of the poetry presses and magazines in Yorkshire are members of the Yorkshire Federation of Small Presses – for details send an sae to Richard Mason, Flat 7, 4 Chestnut Avenue, Leeds LS6 1BA.

In Scotland, Polygon and Mainstream maintain small poetry lists, southern Ireland has Beaver Row, Dedalus, Gallery, Raven Arts and Salmon, and Northern Ireland Blackstaff.

All of the presses mentioned so far are mainstream publishers. There are presses dedicated to more specialised genres. Pig Press in Durham are devoted to modernist and avant-garde poetry. Allardyce, Barnett have produced collected poems by poets such as Douglas Oliver and Veronica Forrest-Thompson. In addition, there are numerous small presses working in this area which belong to the Association of Little Presses: they organise book-fairs, and produce a newsletter and a catalogue, including names and addresses of publishers (available at £2.40 plus 60p p&p from the Association of Little Presses, 89a Petherton Road, London N5 2QT). More information on small presses is available in Oriel Bookshop's *Small Presses and Little Magazines of the UK and Ireland* (address given earlier). The Small Press Group of Britain (BM BOZO, London WC1N 3XX *tel* (0234) 211606) organise exhibitions and an annual book fair, and issue newsletters, a monthly small press magazine, and the *Small Press Yearbook 1992*, price £7.99 inc. p&p.

A new generation of Black British poets has been a vital force injecting new rhythms and styles into British poetry over the last ten years. Influential anthologies such as James Berry's *News for Babylon* (Chatto) and E.A. Markham's *Hinterland* (Bloodaxe) have ensured that Black British poets such as James Berry, Fred D'Aguiar, Grace Nichols, John Agard and E.A. Markham have appeared in mainstream publishers' lists. Several publishers, though, specialise in Black poetry, including New Beacon Books, Dangaroo Press, Bogle L'Ouverture and Peepal Tree Press. Sangam Books is an interesting new press specialising in South Asian poetry. South Asian poets living in Britain or on the continent have appeared with various publishers: Sujata Bhatt (Carcanet), Debjani Chatterjee (Hippopotamus), Tariq Latif (Littlewood · Arc). Magazines specialising in Afro-Caribbean and Asian writing include *Artrage*, *Kunapipi* and *Wasafiri*. *Poetry Review* has produced an Afro-Asian-Caribbean Focus issue (Winter 1990–91) with a wide range of work from Britain, the Caribbean, Africa and South Asia.

The Poetry Library produces a useful current awareness list of Asian and Afro-Caribbean poetry, including a list of bookshops and distributors specialising in Black writing, competitions, libraries, publishers and magazines (send a large sae). Lambeth Libraries produce a useful booklist entitled *Black Poetry*, available from Lambeth Amenity Services, 8th Floor, International House, Canterbury Crescent, London SW9 7QE. New Beacon Books, 76 Stroud Green Road, London N4, has a good stock of Black poetry from all over the world.

Of the feminist presses, Virago has the largest poetry list, with poets such as Gillian Allnutt, Amryl Johnson and Alison Fell. Onlywomen Press publish some poetry, as do the Gay Men's Press.

Poetry book publishers

Allardyce, Barnett	Beaver Row Press
Anvil Press Poetry	Blackstaff Press (N Ire)

Bloodaxe Books
Bogle L'Ouverture
Marion Boyars
John Calder
Jonathan Cape
Carcanet Press
Chatto & Windus
Collins Harvill
Dangaroo
Dedalus (Ire)
André Deutsch
Enitharmon Press
Faber & Faber
Forest Books
Gallery Press (Ire)
GMP Publishers
Headland Publications
Hippopotamus Press
Hutchinson
Littlewood · Arc
Macmillan
Mainstream
Mandeville Press
Methuen

New Beacon Books
Onlywomen Press
Peter Owen Ltd
Oxford University Press
Paladin
Peepal Tree Press
Penguin
Peterloo Poets
Pig Press
Polygon
Priapus Press
Race Today
Raven Arts (Ire)
Redcliffe Press
Salmon Press (Ire)
Sangam Books
Secker & Warburg
Seren Books
Serpent's Tail
Slow Dancer
Smith/Doorstop
Stride Publications
Viking
Virago

VANITY PUBLISHING

Attention is drawn to the separate article on vanity publishing. There are many publishers who will offer to publish your poetry for a fee. This is not a last resort but no resort at all. If a reputable publisher will not accept your work, or if you are not content with magazine publication, there are two real options: one is to abandon ambitions of volume publication; the other is self-publication. The latter is expensive and usually fruitless (magazines almost never review such books), but at least does not carry the stigma that attaches to vanity publication.

COPYRIGHT

The copyright act defines a poem, be it four or 400 lines long, as a complete work. It is therefore not permitted to photocopy poems published in books and periodicals without permission until 50 years after the death of the author when the work comes out of copyright.

In Britain all works are protected by copyright as soon as written. The person who creates a work is the prime owner of 'intellectual property'. There is no actual need to put the copyright symbol © on each poem you send out to a magazine, although, for practical reasons, it is advisable to put your name and address on each poem you send to a magazine editor for consideration. Each and every poem you write is automatically protected by copyright and you as the author have the right to be identified as the author, and to choose where it should be published *if* an editor wants to publish it. You can retain the serial rights of a poem published in a magazine and submit it elsewhere if you choose so long as you include a note of where it has appeared previously. But, that said, you will find that magazine editors will not generally be interested in publishing work which has already appeared in other magazines, and you must never submit work to more than one outlet at a time. The Society of Authors produce a Quick Guide entitled *Copyright* (£1.00 inc. p&p), available from The Society of Authors, 84 Drayton Gardens, London SW10 9SB.

Organisations

ARVON FOUNDATION AND OTHER WRITING COURSES

1. **Arvon Foundation**

Everyone who has been involved in writing for any length of time should eventually seriously consider attending one of the Arvon Foundation's creative writing courses. These are residential, last for five days, and the course fee includes all accommodation, food and tuition. The tutors are themselves professional writers, and students benefit both from their guidance, and – just as important – from discussion with other students. There are courses on a wide range of types of writing, including poetry, playwriting, fiction, television and radio. There are two separate centres running five day residential courses, from whom annual details of courses are available.

The Arvon Foundation at Totleigh Barton, Sheepwash, Beaworthy, Devon EX21 5NS

The Arvon Foundation at Lumb Bank, Hebden Bridge, West Yorkshire HX7 6DF

The Arvon Foundation also organise a major international poetry competition every two years (see Competitions).

2. **Writing courses at Tŷ Newydd**

A more recent development in the area of writing courses is Tŷ Newydd, a residential writers' centre based in Wales which was set up by the Taliesin Trust, to encourage and promote writing in both English and Welsh. Courses last $4\frac{1}{2}$ days and, as with Arvon, there are a wide range of courses tutored by professional writers. More details and the annual programme of courses are available from: Taliesin Trust, Tŷ Newydd, Llanystumdwy, Criccieth, Gwynedd LL52 0LW, Wales.

3. **Other writing courses**

Some Regional Arts Boards, such as Eastern Arts and East Midlands Arts, organise short residential writing courses. Look out for details in your local library or ask the Literature Officer of your Regional Arts Board (see **Societies** for addresses). Details of other writing courses are kept in the Poetry Library (see Poetry Library).

AWARDS AND PRIZES

See **Literary prizes and awards** section, or there is a complete list in the *Guide to literary prizes, grants and awards in Britain and Ireland* compiled by Book Trust and the Society of Authors, 6th edition 1990, £3.75 inc. p&p, available from Book Trust, 45 East Hill, Wandsworth, London SW18 2QZ.

BOOK SHOPS

As has already been explained, it is impossible to learn to write poetry without reading a good deal of the poetry of our own day and of the past. It is also important to support publishers of contemporary poetry and buy books and magazines, as without a reading public (in addition to a writing public) poetry can hardly survive. There are quite a number of bookshops up and down the country with a stock of contemporary poetry. Most sell new books, others will provide books by post, or specialise in areas such as Black British poetry, or second-hand literary firsts, etc. The branch of Waterstones within the Royal Festival Hall in London's South Bank Centre has a poetry section and is open from 11am–10pm, seven days a week. An annotated national list is available from the Poetry Library on receipt of an A4 sae (see Poetry Library).

COMPETITIONS

As already mentioned, publishers are increasingly impressed by competition success. Entering competitions and submitting to magazines are complementary activities. Both have strengths and weaknesses. To win a major competition clearly makes a bigger splash than publication in the most prestigious magazine, but one of the smaller prizes is probably worth less than a good magazine appearance. Reputable competitions always charge an entry fee and offer prizes to the winners. There are dozens of competitions, but two dominate the field: The Poetry Society's annual National Poetry Competition and the biennial Arvon Foundation International Poetry Competition.

1. **National Poetry Competition**
This annual competition, founded by the Poetry Society in 1978, is for previously unpublished poems written in the English language. Entries are now accepted from anywhere in the world. First prize is £2000 and there are other cash prizes ranging from £1000 to £50. An annual booklet is produced of each year's winners, who have included Tony Harrison, Carol Ann Duffy, James Berry, Philip Gross, Jo Shapcott and Carole Satyamurti. Full details on entry fee, etc., from The National Poetry Competition, The Poetry Society, 21 Earls Court Square, London SW5 9DE.

2. **Arvon Foundation International Poetry Competition**
This competition, founded in 1980, is awarded biennially for previously unpublished poems written in the English language. Entries are accepted from Great Britain and elsewhere. The next competition should be scheduled for 1993 with a first prize of £5000 and a range of other cash prizes. An anthology is produced of the winners, who have included Andrew Motion, John Hartley Williams, Oliver Reynolds and Selima Hill. Full details on entry fee, etc., from Arvon Foundation Poetry Competition, Kilnhurst, Kilnhurst Road, Todmorden, Lancashire OL14 6AX.

These main two apart, there is a clutch of substantial other competitions and each year brings a new crop. A few are as follows. Details and an entry form will be sent on receipt of an sae:

Bridport Arts Centre Creative Writing Competition, 9 Pier Terrace, West Bay, Bridport, Dorset DT6 4ER
City of Cardiff International Poetry Competition, PO Box 438, Cardiff CF1 6YA, Wales
Leek Arts Festival International Poetry Competition, 44 Rudyard Road, Biddulph Moor, Stoke-on-Trent, Staffs. ST8 7JN
Peterloo National Poetry Competition, 2 Kelly Gardens, Calstock, Cornwall PL18 9SA

For a regularly updated list of poetry competitions, send an A4 sae to the Poetry Library (see Poetry Library).

EDUCATION

Children's poetry competitions

In addition to the competitions listed above there are others specifically intended for children/young people, two of the best established are as follows:

1. WH Smith Young Writers Competition

The longest established of children's competitions. Anyone in Britain who is not yet 17 by the time of the closing date for entries is eligible to enter with poems, stories, articles or plays. An anthology is produced of the winning entries. Teachers should write for more information to: WH Smith Young Writers Competition, Strand House, 7 Holbein Place, Sloane Square, London SW1W 8NR.

2. Shell Young Poet of the Year Award

Now organised by the Poetry Society and the Schools' Poetry Association, this competition brings the winner a cash prize and publication of an individual collection of poetry. Entry is open to young people aged under 19. For more information contact the Education Officer at the Poetry Society (see Poetry Society).

Poetry in the classroom

1. Some courses organised by the **Arvon Foundation** are intended for younger writers (see Arvon Foundation).
2. The **Poetry Society Education Department** offers a range of activities and services for children and teachers. They administer a national writing scheme for young people, the WH Smith Poets-in-Schools Scheme, and organise children's poetry events at the Society. Education Department staff offer up-to-date advice and information to teachers on all aspects of poetry in the classroom, run the Shell Young Poet of the Year Competition, produce a poetry newsletter for under 18s, and co-ordinate an INSET programme for teachers. For full information, write enclosing an sae to Education Department, The Poetry Society, 21 Earls Court Square, London SW5 9DE.
3. **Poems on the Underground** produce poems by known poets for display on the London Underground. These make excellent and relatively inexpensive display material in classrooms. Distribution is now handled by the Education Department of the Poetry Society (see entry above).
4. The **South Bank Centre Poetry Library** houses the Signal Poetry Collection within a newly developed children's section including over 3000 modern poetry books written for and by children, and a separate teachers' section. The library produces a free Information Pack for teachers, with over 20 items, including free bibliographical lists of poetry books for children, poetry competitions and magazines for children and other information. Class visits and Teachers' Days are arranged. Children's poetry events are timetabled in at the Voice Box. All services are free. More information is available on receipt of an A4 sae sent to: Children's Librarian, South Bank Centre Poetry Library, Royal Festival Hall, London SE1 8XX.
5. The **Schools' Poetry Association** initiated the Young Poet of the Year Award and has published important magazines and posters for teachers. It is involved in running workshops and in-service sessions for schools. For further details of services and publications contact: The Schools' Poetry Association, 27 Pennington Close, Colden Common, near Winchester, Hants SO21 1UR.
6. The **Northern Association of Writers in Education** publish *NAWE News* (36 Sterndale Road, Sheffield S7 2LD), which reports on the involvement of poets in education within the region.

7. The **Children's Book Foundation** aims to promote reading and offers advice and information on all aspects of children's reading and books. Its library holds children's books published over the last two years, after which they are transferred to the Poetry Library. The CBF organises a Children's Book Week, publishes CBF News and Authorbank, which offers information on authors of books for children. Each year a volume titled *Children's Books of the Year* is published by the Anderson Press and CBF. For information on membership fees, etc. contact: The Children's Book Foundation, 45 East Hill, London SW18 2QZ.

8. **Books for Keeps** is a children's book magazine. It produces an annotated bibliography *Poetry 0–16* edited by Morag Styles and Pat Triggs (1988, £5.50) which is a major bibliographical information resource for teachers, librarians and parents. For more information contact: Books for Keeps, 6 Brightfield Road, Lee, London SE12 8QF.

GROUPS AND WORKSHOPS

Poetry workshops are inevitably less formal than printed outlets: they are as varied as the people who run them. Some have quasi-official status, being run by writers in residence attached to Regional Arts Boards, colleges, libraries, or local authority evening classes or arts departments. Others are loose groupings of individuals who meet in their own homes. Some have impressive records of success in terms of members getting into print.

A good workshop will provide what the hard-pressed editor cannot: detailed comment on work-in-progress with the aim of better realising the writer's intentions. Of course, in such a situation personalities intrude and not all advice may be well meant, but a real workshop, and there are many, will sharpen up a developing poet's style quicker than anything else. A workshop also comprises an invaluable swap shop of knowledge about the magazines. It is common for a rash of poems from one workshop to appear in a magazine after an initial success by a member. And if members sometimes attend the best workshops of all, those of the Arvon Foundation (see above), a link is made to the big 'real' world of poetry.

Local poetry workshops vary in standard, but you should certainly try to make contact if there is one near to you. Unfortunately there is no complete register, and provision varies widely. The places to look are: your local Regional Arts Board (see **Societies** for addresses) (but they may well not know of all in your area), local arts centre and library; sometimes the local press will carry an article about a new workshop starting up. A list for London is produced by the Poetry Library – write, sending a large sae (see under Poetry Library). Also the quarterly magazine *Poetry London Newsletter* includes substantial listings of poetry activities in all the London boroughs (26 Clacton Road, London E17). In the north, The Poetry Business, publishers of *The North*, provide workshops and a poetry advisory service (51 Byram Arcade, Westgate, Huddersfield, West Yorkshire HD1 1ND). If there is a magazine based in your region, you could, as a last resort, write to the editor, but as with all such requests, you must send an sae. If you're keen and there is one, you'll find it.

LITERARY FESTIVALS

There are now literature festivals in parts of Britain as diverse as: Bath, Birmingham, Brighton, Cardiff, Cheltenham, Edinburgh, Hay-on-Wye, Kent and Lancaster. Your local Regional Arts Board (see **Societies** for addresses) will be able to let you know if there is an annual literature festival in your area. If there is one it will probably include events connected with poetry. These festivals are a good way of getting to hear other writers read from and talk about their work. They often have bookshops with a selection of current literary publications too. The Poetry Society administers the Literature Festivals Council, which has all the main literature festivals in membership (see Poetry Society). The Poetry Library produces a regularly updated list of literary and poetry festivals. Send an sae for a copy (see Poetry Library).

PERFORMANCE VENUES

In London, poetry readings and poetry in performance events are regularly held at the Poetry Society and the South Bank Centre (see entries). There are numerous other, generally smaller scale and youth-based, poetry in performance organisations of which the best established is Apples & Snakes, 'London's unique Poetry Cabaret Company', which regularly holds events at a number of London venues. Apples & Snakes have recently expanded and appointed a UK poetry touring co-ordinator and an education worker, proof of their success. Information on events is listed in *Time Out* or in the Poetry Library. For venues outside London contact your local Regional Arts Board (see also Literary Festivals).

POETRY BOOK SOCIETY

The Poetry Book Society is a book club, founded in 1953, devoted to contemporary poetry. Like all book clubs it offers books to members at discount prices, and other inducements to membership. Each year members receive four quarterly books of new poetry chosen by independent selectors appointed by the Board of Management. With the book comes the free quarterly *Bulletin* containing information on the books recommended each quarter and, at Christmas, a free annual anthology of new poems. A membership form with further information is available from the Membership Department, Poetry Book Society Ltd, 21 Earls Court Square, London SW5 9DE.

POETRY LIBRARY AND OTHER LIBRARIES

1. The **Poetry Library** was set up by the Arts Council in 1954 and is the central national bibliographical information resource in the subject area of modern English language poetry. Membership is free. Books are available for reference and loan, and may be borrowed via your local library through the LASER national interlibrary loan network. The collection includes all the current poetry magazines and over 35,000 items dating from 1912 to the present, including books, pamphlets, poster poems, poemcards, pictures of poets, press cuttings, and audio and video cassettes, which may be played in the library. The library has a current awareness information service on poetry events and publications, and disseminates information in the form of regularly updated lists of poetry magazines, competitions, groups and workshops in and around London, bookshops selling poetry, etc. available free on receipt of an A4 sae. The library, now renamed The Saison Poetry Library, is part of the South Bank Literature Centre in London and is open seven days a week, 11 am–8 pm. Write for information to The Librarian, Poetry Library, South Bank Centre, Royal Festival Hall, London SE1 8XX (see also South Bank Centre).

2. The **Scottish Poetry Library** organises poetry readings and houses a collection of twentieth-century poetry written in Scotland in English, Scots and Gaelic, as well as older Scottish poetry and a selection of poetry from other countries. Books are available by post in Scotland and a newsletter, *Splash*, is issued to members. Details are available from The Librarian, Scottish Poetry Library, Tweedale Court, 14 High Street, Edinburgh EH1 1TE.

3. The **Northern Arts Poetry Library** is a collection of over 6000 books published in Britain since 1968 and loans books free by post to members resident in the North-East and Cumbria. Write for information on membership to The Librarian, Northern Arts Poetry Library, County Library, The Willows, Morpeth, Northumberland NE61 1TA.

4. **Poetry Ireland** run the Austin Clarke Library, a collection of 6000 volumes of modern poetry. Poetry Ireland also organise readings, produce a magazine, *Poetry Ireland Review*, and provide both a newsletter and a book club offering four of the best new poetry books published in Ireland each year. For more information on membership contact: Poetry Ireland, The Austin Clarke Library, 44 Upper Mount Street, Dublin 2, Republic of Ireland.

5. All these specialist libraries are centres for information. Your local branch library can also be an invaluable information resource. It will normally have details of poetry groups and workshops in your area, may have details of national poetry competitions and, through its shelves, you will be able to discover some of the poetry publishers of today. If your local library does not have work by an author you want, ask to borrow something from the Poetry Library at the South Bank Centre through the national interlibrary loan network, for a small fee, by filling in a book requisition form with bibliographical details of the title you want to read.

THE POETRY SOCIETY AT THE NATIONAL POETRY CENTRE

The Poetry Society is situated at the National Poetry Centre in London, and organises a wide range of services for the entire poetry community, including an effective Education Service, administering the National Poetry Competition and awards such as the European Poetry Translation Prize, helping organise poetry readings and tours nationally and running a Critical Service which provides professional advice for a fee for poets. Membership brings all this, plus a subscription to *Poetry Review* and reduced price admittance to all events at the Society's headquarters. In season, readings are organised at the Society on Tuesday or Thursday evenings. For more information contact the Membership Department, The Poetry Society, 21 Earls Court Square, London SW5 9DE.

REGIONAL ARTS BOARDS

A list of the Literature Officers of each of the Regional Arts Boards is available from the Research and Information Unit of the Arts Council, 14 Great Peter Street, London SW1P 3NQ on receipt of an A4 sae. You can contact the Regional Arts Board in your area (see **Societies** for addresses) and discover if there are writers' groups and workshops or a literary festival nearby, or perhaps a local writer in residence who may be able to offer advice on your work. Some Regional Arts Boards produce Newsletters with information on literature events. Others, such as Eastern Arts, South East and South West Arts, run schemes whereby your work will be commented on by a professional writer for a fee.

SOUTH BANK CENTRE

In recent years an important location for literary events in London has been created within the South Bank Centre with the Poetry Library as its base. The South Bank Centre literature programme aims to reflect the diversity of writing within the British Isles and beyond. Most literature events take place in the Voice Box situated next to the Poetry Library, others in the Purcell Room and Queen Elizabeth Hall. The continuing New Voices series presents the work of emerging poets, novelists and short story writers, and the literature programme includes one-off readings, thematic series, international poetry festivals and writers' workshops. For more information and to be placed on the mailing list contact the Literature Officer, South Bank Centre, Royal Festival Hall, London SE1 8XX (see also Poetry Library).

FURTHER READING TO BUY OR CONSULT

Michael Baldwin, *The way to write poetry*, Hamish Hamilton
Sandy Brownjohn, *Does it have to rhyme: teaching children to write poetry*, Hodder
Tracey Chevalier (ed), *Contemporary poets*, 5th edition, 1991, St James Press. (The standard reference book listing living English-language poets.)
Tony Curtis, *How to study modern poetry*, Macmillan
Rosalind Fergusson (ed.), *The Penguin rhyming dictionary*, Penguin
Peter Finch, *How to publish your poetry*, Allison & Busby
G.S. Fraser, *Metre, rhyme and free verse*, Methuen
John Mole, *Passing judgements: poetry in the eighties*, Bristol Classical Papers
Jack Myers and Michael Sims, *The Longman dictionary of poetic terms*, Longman
Philip Davies Roberts, *How poetry works: the elements of English poetry*, Penguin

---

See also the **Agents** section for literary agents; the **Illustration and design** section for verses in greetings cards; the **Societies and prizes** section.

Scripts for theatre, radio, tv and film

Marketing a play

JULIA JONES
Society of Authors

As soon as a play is written, it is protected under the copyright laws of this country. No formalities are necessary here to secure copyright protection but it is a good plan to deposit a copy with the bank and take a dated receipt for it, so as to be able to prove the date of its completion, if this should be necessary at some time either, for example, to enforce a claim for infringement of copyright or to rebut such a claim. The copyright belongs to the author unless and until he parts with it and this he should never do, since the copyright is in effect the sum total of all his rights in his work. He should, so far as possible, deal separately with the component rights which go to make up the copyright and grant limited licences for the principal rights with, where customary or necessary, limited interests in the ancillary rights. A West End production agreement (see below) illustrates this principle.

The author can try to market the play himself, but once a play is accepted, it is wise to have professional assistance. All aspects of a contract are open for negotiation and the contractual complications are best handled by a reputable literary agent.

Although most ambitious young playwrights visualise a West End opening for their plays, the first step, except for the established dramatist, is usually to try to place the play with a repertory company known to be interested in presenting new plays. It is wise to write to the company first, giving salient details, such as type of play, size of cast, number of sets, etc., and ask if the management would be willing to read it. This saves the frustration and expense of copies of the play being kept for long periods by managements who have no interest in it. (Do not send your only copy of the play away – this seems obvious, but many authors have suffered the torment of having to rewrite from memory when the only copy has been lost.) It is also possible to get a first production by entering the play for the various competitions which appear from time to time, but in this case great care should be taken to study the rules and ensure that the organisers of the competition do not acquire unreasonably wide rights and interests in the entries.

Many repertory companies will give a new play a try-out production in the hope that it will be seen by London managements and transfer to the West End. For the run at the repertory company's own theatre the company will receive a licence for a given period from a fixed date and pay the author a royalty of between 6 per cent and 10 per cent calculated on the gross box office receipts. In return for the risk involved in presenting a new play, the repertory company will expect a share in the author's earnings from subsequent professional stage productions of the play during a limited period (usually two years). Sometimes on transfer the West End management will agree to take over responsibility for part or all of this payment.

The contract, for repertory or West End production, or for the use of any other rights in the play, should specify precisely the rights to which it refers, the territory covered, the period of time covered, the payments involved and make it clear that all other rights remain the property of the author.

For a first-class production in the West End of London, usually preceded by a short provincial tour, the author's contract will include clauses dealing with the following main heads of agreement. The substance, as well as the phrasing of these clauses will vary considerably, but those given below probably represent the average, as do the figures in brackets, which must not be assumed to be standard:

1. UK option

In consideration of a specified minimum sum (between £500 and £1000) as a non-returnable advance against royalties, the Manager shall have the exclusive option for a specified period (usually six months) to produce the play in a first-class theatre in the West End of London (preceded possibly by a tour of a specified number of weeks) with an extension for a further period upon payment of a further similar sum.

2. UK licence

When the Manager exercises his option he shall have the UK licence for a specified period (three or five years) from the date of the first performance under the licence such licence to terminate before the expiry of the specified period if
(a) the play is not produced before a specified date;
(b) (i) less than a specified number (between 50 and 75) of consecutive professional performances are given and paid for in any year; or
(ii) the Manager has not paid at the beginning of any year a non-returnable advance against royalties. This variant on clause (b) (i) prevents the rights being tied up for a year while waiting to check if the qualifying performances have been given and is thus desirable from the author's point of view.

3. US option

If the Manager gives a specified number (usually 24) of consecutive performances in the West End he shall have an option exercisable within a specified period of the first West End performance (six weeks) to produce the play on Broadway on payment of a specified non-returnable advance on royalties (between £500 and £1000).

4. US licence

When the Manager exercises his option the Broadway licence shall be for a specified period (three years) on terms not less favourable than those specified in the Minimum Basic Agreement of the Dramatists' Guild of America.

5. Other rights

Provided the play has run for the qualifying period (usually 24 performances) the Manager acquires interests in some of the other rights as follows:
(i) *Repertory*. The author should reserve these rights paying the Manager a share (one-third) of his royalties for a specified period (two years after the end of the West End run or the expiry of the West End licence whichever is the shorter). The author agrees not to release these rights until after the end of the West End run without the Manager's consent, this consent not to be unreasonably withheld. It is recommended that a play should be released to theatres on

the A list immediately after the end of the West End run, and to theatres on the B list within three months from the end of the West End run, if an option for a tour has not been taken up by then, otherwise at the end of the tour. The Theatres on these lists are those recommended by the Theatres' National Committee for immediate and early release of plays to repertory.

(ii) *Amateur.* The author should reserve these rights and pay the Manager no share in his royalties, but should undertake not to release these rights for an agreed period, to allow the repertory theatres to have maximum clear run.

(iii) *Radio, Television and Video.* The author should reserve these rights but it may well be in his interest not to release them until some time after the end of the West End run. During the run of the play in the West End, however, the Manager may arrange for an extract from the play to be broadcast or televised for publicity purposes, the author's fee for such broadcast or television performances being paid to him in full without any part of it going to the Manager.

(iv) *Film.* If the Manager has produced the play for the qualifying period it is expected that the author will pay him a percentage (often 20 per cent) of the author's net receipts from the disposal of the film rights, if these rights are disposed of within a specified period (one year) from the last West End performance. If the Manager has also produced the play on Broadway for the qualifying period the author is expected to allow him a further percentage (20 per cent) of the author's net receipts from the disposal of the film rights if the rights are disposed of within a specified time (one year) of the last Broadway performance. This is a field where the established dramatist can, not unnaturally, strike a much better bargain than the beginner. In no case, however, should the total percentage payable to the Manager exceed 40 per cent.

(v) *Foreign Language.* These rights should be reserved to the author, the Manager receiving no share of the proceeds.

(vi) *Cassette.* These rights should be specifically reserved to the author.

Other clauses which should appear include:

(a) A royalty clause setting out the royalties which the author shall receive from West End and touring performances of the play – usually a scale rising from 5 per cent through $7\frac{1}{2}$ per cent to 10 per cent. If the author is registered for VAT, provision for VAT should be included here.

(b) Cast approval, etc. The author should be consulted about the casting and the director of the play, and in some cases may be able to insist on approval of the casting of a particular part.

(c) Rehearsals, scripts, etc. The author should be entitled to attend all rehearsals of the play and no alteration in the title or script should be made without the author's consent. All approved alterations in or suggestions for the script should become the author's property. In this clause also should appear details about supply of tickets for the author for opening performances and any arrangements for tickets throughout the West End run.

(d) Credits. Details of billing of the author's name on posters, programmes and advertising matter should be included.

(e) Lord Chamberlain's Licence. The Theatres Act 1968 abolishes the power of the Lord Chamberlain to censor stage plays and play licences are no longer required. However, it is obligatory for managers to deposit a copy of the script on which the public performance of any new play is based with the Keeper of Manuscripts, British Library, London WC1, within one month of the performance.

(f) The author will normally warrant that the play contains nothing that is obscene or defamatory or that infringes copyright.

There must also be:

(g) An accounting clause giving details of payment and requiring a certified statement of box office receipts.

(h) A clause giving the conditions under which the agreement may be assigned or sub-leased.

(i) A termination clause, stating the conditions under which the agreement shall terminate.

ARRANGEMENTS FOR OTHER RIGHTS AFTER THE FIRST-CLASS RUN OF THE PLAY

Repertory

The author or his representative will license repertory performances for a fixed royalty on the gross box office receipts – usually 10 per cent for a new play immediately after its West End run, dropping perhaps to 7½ per cent in later years.

Amateur

The author or his representative will license amateur performances of the play for a flat fee (normally between £20 and £30).

Publication

A firm specialising in acting editions of plays may offer to publish the play in which case it will expect to license amateur performances and collect the fees on a commission basis (20 per cent to 50 per cent). The publication contract will also usually provide for the author to receive a royalty of 10 per cent of the published price of every copy sold.

Radio and television

Careful negotiation is required and care should be taken that repeat fees for repeat performances are included in the contract in addition to the initial fee for the first broadcast.

Film rights

Professional advice is absolutely necessary when dealing with a film contract as there are many complications. The rights may be sold outright or licensed for a number of years – usually not less than 7 or 10 or more than 15. The film company normally acquires the right of distribution throughout the world in all languages and expects a completely free hand in making the adaptation of the play into a film.

Foreign rights

It is usual to grant exclusive foreign language rights for the professional stage to an agent or translator who will arrange for a translation to be prepared and produced – it is wise to ask for evidence of the quality of the translator's work unless the translator is very well known. The financial arrangement is usually an advance against royalties for a given period to enable a translation to be prepared and then a licence to exploit the translation for a further period after production (usually five years).

Markets for Stage Plays

It is not easy for a new or comparatively unknown writer to find a management willing to present his play. The English Stage Company at the Royal Court Theatre and some other similarly enterprising organisations present a number of plays by new authors. The new and inexperienced writer may find it easier to persuade amateur drama groups or provincial repertory theatres to present his work. A further possible market may be found in the smaller fringe theatre companies.

The Stage reports productions of most new plays first produced by repertory theatres and a study of this journal may reveal other potential new markets for plays.

The Arts Council of Great Britain publishes a brochure, *Theatre Writing Schemes*, which gives details of various forms of assistance available to playwrights and to theatres wishing to commission new plays. The help given by the Arts Council includes Bursaries (including the John Whiting Award) and help to writers who are being commissioned or encouraged by a theatre company. There is a number of Resident Dramatists' Attachment Awards available and some support is available towards the costs of writers' workshops. Some assistance to playwrights' organisations is also available. Copies of the brochure and further information may be obtained from The Drama Director, The Arts Council of Great Britain, 14 Great Peter Street, London SW1P 3NQ.

It is probable that competitions for full-length and one-act plays and other special opportunities for new plays will be announced after the *Yearbook* has gone to press, and writers with plays on the stocks would do well to watch carefully for announcements in the Press. *The Observer*, *The Author*, *Amateur Stage*, and *The Stage*, are the journals in which announcements are most likely to appear.

Sketches for revues and broadcasting and plays for youth organisations are in demand. Sketches are usually bought outright, but in any case authors should make quite certain of what rights they will be disposing before accepting any offer.

In every case it is advisable to send a preliminary letter before submitting a manuscript. Suggestions for the preparation of manuscripts will be found in the article **Typescripts**.

Writers of plays are also referred to **Marketing a Play** and to the sections on **Radio** and **Television**, media which provide a very big market for the writers of plays.

LONDON

Bush Theatre, Shepherd's Bush Green, London W12 8QD *tel* 071-602 3703 *fax* 071-602 7614.

Michael Codron Ltd, Aldwych Theatre Offices, Aldwych, London WC2B 4DF *tel* 071-240 8291 *fax* 071-240 8467.

Ray Cooney Presentations Ltd, Duchess Theatre, Catherine Street, London WC2B 5LA *tel* 071-497 7701 *fax* 071-497 8130.

English Stage Company Ltd, Royal Court Theatre, Sloane Square, London SW1W 8AS *tel* 071-730 5174.

Clare Fox Associates Ltd, 9 Plympton Road, London NW6 7EH *tel* 071-372 2301.

John Gale, Lisden Productions Ltd, 185 Walm Lane, London NW2 3AY *tel* 081-452 8086. Please write first with details. No unsolicited scripts accepted.

Greenwich Theatre Ltd, Greenwich Theatre, Crooms Hill, London SE10 8ES *tel* 081-858 4447.

Half Moon Theatre, 213 Mile End Road, London E1 4AA *tel* 071-791 1141.

Hampstead Theatre, Swiss Cottage Centre, London NW3 3EX *tel* 071-722 9224 *fax* 071-722 3860.

Bill Kenwright Ltd, 59 Shaftesbury Avenue, London W1V 7AA *tel* 071-439 4466 *fax* 071-437 8370.

King's Head Theatre, 115 Upper Street, London N1 1QN *tel* 071-226 1916/ 8561 *fax* 071-226 8507. *Contact:* Helen Webb.

Brian Kirk Associates, 5 Dryden Street, Covent Garden, London WC2E 9NW *tel* 071-829 8448 *fax* 071-734 0254.

Knightsbridge Theatrical Productions Ltd, 2nd Floor, Winchmore House, 15 Fetter Lane, London EC4A 1JJ *tel* 071-583 8687 *fax* 071-583 0046.

Lyric Theatre Hammersmith, King Street, London W6 0QL *tel* 081-741 0824 *fax* 081-741 7694.

Orange Tree Theatre, 1 Clarence Street, Richmond, Surrey TW9 2SA *tel* 081-940 0141.

Polka Children's Theatre, 240 The Broadway, London SW19 1SB *tel* 081-542 4258 *fax* 081-542 7723.

Questors Theatre, Mattock Lane, Ealing, London W5 5BQ *tel* 081-567 0011.

Royal National Theatre, South Bank, London SE1 9PX *tel* 071-928 2033 *telex* 297306 Nattre G *fax* 071-620 1197.

Royal Shakespeare Company, Barbican Theatre, Barbican, London EC2Y 8BQ *tel* 071-628 3351 *fax* 071-374 0818.

Peter Saunders Ltd, Vaudeville Theatre Offices, 10 Maiden Lane, London WC2E 7NA *tel* 071-240 3177 *fax* 071-497 9505.

Soho Theatre Company, 24 Goodge Street, London W1P 1FG *tel* 071-436 3594.

Tabard Theatre, 2 Bath Road, Turnham Green, Chiswick, London W4 1LW *tel* 081-995 6035/747 8256.

Theatre Royal, Stratford East, Gerry Raffles Square, Newham, London E15 1BN *tel* 081-534 7374 *fax* 081-534 8381.

The Tricycle Theatre Company, Tricycle Theatre, 269 Kilburn High Road, London NW6 7JR *tel* 071-372 6611 *fax* 071-328 0795.

Triumph Proscenium Productions Ltd, Suite 4, Waldorf Chambers, 11 Aldwych, London WC2B 4DA *tel* 071-836 0186 *fax* 071-240 7511.

Turnstyle, Monro House, 40-42 King Street, Covent Garden, London WC2E 8JS *tel* 071-240 9891 *fax* 071-379 5748.

Unicorn Theatre for Children, Arts Theatre, 6-7 Great Newport Street, London WC2H 7JB *tel* 071-379 3280. Plays for children up to age of 12 only.

Warehouse Theatre, Dingwall Road, Croydon CR0 2NF *tel* 081-681 1257. Sponsors South London Playwrights' Festival (see **Literary prizes and awards**).

Michael White, 13 Duke Street, St James's, London SW1Y 6DB   *tel* 071-839 3971   *fax* 071-839 3836.

The Young Vic, 66 The Cut, London SE1 8LZ   *tel* 071-633 0133.

PROVINCIAL

Abbey Theatre, Lower Abbey Street, Dublin 1, Republic of Ireland   *tel* (01) 748741   *fax* (01) 729177. The Abbey Theatre mainly produces plays written by Irish authors or on Irish subjects. Foreign plays are however regularly produced.

Yvonne Arnaud Theatre Management Ltd, Yvonne Arnaud Theatre, Millbrook, Guildford, Surrey GU1 3UX   *tel* (0483) 64571   *fax* (0483) 64071.

Belgrade Theatre, Belgrade Square, Coventry CV1 1GS   *tel* (0203) 256431   *fax* (0203) 550680.

Birmingham Repertory Theatre Ltd, Broad Street, Birmingham B1 2EP   *tel* 021-236 6771   *fax* 021-236 7883.

Bristol Old Vic Company, Theatre Royal, King Street, Bristol BS1 4ED   *tel* (0272) 277466.

The Byre Theatre of St Andrews Ltd, Abbey Street, St Andrews KY16 9LA   *tel* (0334) 76288.

Chester Gateway Theatre Trust Ltd, Gateway Theatre, Hamilton Place, Chester CH1 2BH   *tel* (0244) 344238.

Chichester Festival Theatre Productions Company Ltd, Chichester Festival Theatre, Oaklands Park, Chichester, West Sussex PO19 4AP   *tel* (0243) 784437.

Churchill Theatre Trust Ltd, High Street, Bromley, Kent BR1 1HA   *tel* 081-464 7131   *fax* 081-290 6968.

Theatr Clwyd, Mold, Clwyd CH7 1YA   *tel* (0352) 56331   *fax* (0352) 58323.

Colchester Mercury Theatre Ltd, Balkerne Gate, Colchester, Essex CO1 1PT   *tel* (0206) 577006.

The Coliseum Theatre, Fairbottom Street, Oldham OL1 3SW   *tel* 061-624 1731   *fax* 061-624 5318.

Contact Theatre Company, Oxford Road, Manchester M15 6JA   *tel* 061-274 3434   *fax* 061-273 6286.

Crucible Theatre Trust Ltd, The Crucible Theatre, Norfolk Street, Sheffield S1 1DA   *tel* (0742) 760621   *fax* (0742) 701532.

Derby Playhouse Ltd, Theatre Walk, Eagle Centre, Derby DE1 2NF   *tel* (0332) 363271   *fax* (0332) 294412.

Druid Theatre Company, Druid Lane Theatre, Chapel Lane, Galway, Republic of Ireland   *tel* (091) 68617/68660.

The Duke's Playhouse, Moor Lane, Lancaster LA1 1QE   *tel* (0524) 67461.

Dundee Repertory Theatre, Tay Square, Dundee DD1 1PB   *tel* (0382) 27684.

Everyman Theatre, Regent Street, Cheltenham, Glos. GL50 1HQ   *tel* (0242) 512515   *fax* (0242) 224305.

Farnham Repertory Company Ltd, The Redgrave Theatre, Brightwells, Farnham, Surrey GU9 7SB   *tel* (0252) 727000   *fax* (0252) 712350.

Grand Theatre, Singleton Street, Swansea SA1 3QJ   *tel* (0792) 475242   *fax* (0792) 475379.

Harrogate Theatre, Oxford Street, Harrogate, North Yorkshire HG1 1QF *tel* (0423) 502710.

The Hornchurch Theatre Trust Ltd, The Queen's Theatre, Billet Lane, Hornchurch, Essex RM11 1QT *tel* (040 24) 56118 *fax* (040 24) 52348.

Horseshoe Theatre Co., The Shrubbery, Cliddesden Road, Basingstoke, Hants RG21 3ER *tel* (0256) 55844.

Leicester Haymarket Theatre, Belgrave Gate, Leicester LE1 3YQ *tel* (0533) 530021.

Liverpool Repertory Theatre Ltd, Liverpool Playhouse, Williamson Square, Liverpool L1 1EL *tel* 051-709 8478 *fax* 051-709 7113.

Lyceum Theatre, Sheffield Theatres Ltd, 55 Norfolk Street, Sheffield S1 1DA *tel* (0742) 760621 *fax* (0742) 701532.

Merseyside Everyman Theatre Company Ltd, 5-9 Hope Street, Liverpool L1 9BH *tel* 051-708 0338 *fax* 051-709 0398.

New Victoria Theatre, Etruria Road, Newcastle under Lyme ST5 0JG *tel* (0782) 717954. New purpose built theatre in the round, presenting new plays, major classics, adaptations, documentaries.

Northampton Repertory Players Ltd, The Royal Theatre, Guildhall Road, Northampton NN1 1EA *tel* (0604) 38343 *fax* (0604) 602408.

Northcott Theatre, Stocker Road, Exeter, Devon EX4 4QB *tel* (0392) 56182.

Northern Stage Company, 67A Westgate Road, Newcastle upon Tyne NE1 1SG *tel* (091) 232 3366 *fax* (091) 261 9699.

Nottingham Playhouse, Nottingham Theatre Trust Ltd, Wellington Circus, Nottingham NG1 5AF *tel* (0602) 474361 *fax* (0602) 475759.

Nuffield Theatre, University Road, Southampton SO9 5NH *tel* (0703) 671871 *fax* (0703) 676862.

Octagon Theatre, Howell Croft South, Bolton BL1 1SB *tel* (0204) 29407.

The Oxford Stage Company, 15-19 George Street, Oxford OX1 2AU *tel* (0865) 723238 *fax* (0865) 790625.

Palace Theatre, Clarendon Road, Watford, Herts. WD1 1JZ *tel* (0923) 35455 *fax* (0923) 819664.

Palace Theatre Trust Ltd, London Road, Westcliff-on-Sea, Essex SS0 9LA *tel* (0702) 347816.

Peacock Theatre, The Abbey Theatre, Lower Abbey Street, Dublin 1, Republic of Ireland *tel* (01) 748741 *fax* (01) 729177. The experimental theatre associated with the Abbey Theatre; presents mostly new writing as well as exploring the entire canon of world drama.

Perth Theatre Ltd, 185 High Street, Perth PH1 5UW *tel* (0738) 38123 *fax* (0738) 24576.

Plymouth Theatre Royal, Theatre Royal, Royal Parade, Plymouth, Devon PL1 2TR *tel* (0752) 668282 *telex* 45115 Troyal G *fax* (0752) 671179.

Royal Exchange Theatre Company Ltd, The Royal Exchange, St Ann's Square, Manchester M2 7DH *tel* 061-833 9333 *fax* 061-832 0881.

Royal Lyceum Theatre Company Ltd, Royal Lyceum Theatre, Grindlay Street, Edinburgh EH3 9AX *tel* 031-229 7404 *fax* 031-228 3955.

Salisbury Playhouse, Malthouse Lane, Salisbury, Wilts. SP2 7RA *tel* (0722) 20117.

Scarborough Theatre Trust Ltd, Stephen Joseph Theatre in the Round, Valley Bridge, Scarborough, North Yorkshire YO11 2PL   *tel* (0723) 370540.

Sherman Theatre (1974), Senghennydd Road, Cardiff CF2 4YE   *tel* (0222) 396844. Plays mainly for 15-25 age range.

Swan Theatre, The Moors, Worcester WR1 3EF   *tel* (0905) 726969   *fax* (0905) 723738.

Thorndike Theatre, Church Street, Leatherhead, Surrey KT22 8DF   *tel* (0372) 376211   *fax* (0372) 362595.

Towngate Theatre, Pagel Mead, Basildon, Essex SS14 1DW   *tel* (0268) 531343   *fax* (0268) 525415.

Traverse Theatre, 112 West Bow, Grassmarket, Edinburgh EH1 2HH   *tel* 031-225 1974   *fax* 031-225 3308.

Watermill Theatre Ltd, Bagnor, Newbury, Berks. RG16 8AE   *tel* (0635) 45834.

The West Yorkshire Playhouse, Quarry Hill Mount, Leeds LS9 8AW   *tel* (0532) 442141   *fax* (0532) 448252. Twin auditoria complex – with a policy of encouraging new writing; community theatre; Young People's Theatre programme.

Windsor Theatre Company (Capoco Ltd), Theatre Royal, Windsor, Berks. SL4 1PS   *tel* (0753) 863444   *fax* (0753) 831673.

The Wolsey Theatre, Civic Drive, Ipswich, Suffolk IP1 2AS   *tel* (0473) 218911.

York Citizens' Theatre Trust Ltd, Theatre Royal, St Leonard's Place, York YO1 2HD   *tel* (0904) 658162   *fax* (0904) 611534.

TOURING COMPANIES

Black Theatre Co-Operative Ltd, 8 Bradbury Street, London N16 8JN   *tel* 071-249 9150.

Compass Theatre Company, The Leadmill, 6-7 Leadmill Road, Sheffield S1 4SF   *tel* (0742) 755328   *fax* (0742) 786931.

Compass Theatre Ltd, The Dean Clough Complex, Halifax, West Yorks. HX3 5AX   *tel* (0422) 345631.

Gay Sweatshop, Interchange Studios, Dalby Street, London NW5 3NQ   *tel* 071-485 5799   *fax* 071-482 5292 marked attn Gay Sweatshop.

Hull Truck Theatre Co. Ltd, Spring Street Theatre, Spring Street, Hull HU2 8RW   *tel* (0482) 224800   *fax* (0482) 228546.

Live Theatre, 8 Trinity Chare, Quayside, Newcastle upon Tyne NE1 3DF   *tel* (091) 261 2694.

The London Bubble (Bubble Theatre Company), 3/5 Elephant Lane, London SE16 4JD   *tel* 071-237 4434   *fax* 071-231 2366.

M6 Theatre Company, Hamer C.P. School, Albert Royds Street, Rochdale, Lancs. OL6 2SU   *tel* (0706) 355898.

Major Road Theatre Company, 29 Queens Road, Bradford, West Yorks. BD8 7BS   *tel* (0274) 480251   *fax* (0274) 548528.

Manx National Theatre Company, 4 Athol Terrace, Castletown, Isle of Man   *tel* (0624) 823182   *fax* (0624) 824339. Primarily interested in comedy. Send MSS to Vanessa Stead, Literary Manager, enclosing International Reply Coupons.

Monstrous Regiment, 190 Upper Street, Islington, London N1 1RQ *tel* 071-359 9842 *fax* 071-359 5773.

Northumberland Theatre Company, The Playhouse, Bondgate Without, Alnwick, Northumberland NE66 1PQ *tel* (0665) 602586.

Orchard Theatre Company, 108 Newport Road, Barnstaple, North Devon EX32 9BA *tel* (0271) 71475 *fax* (0271) 71825.

Paines Plough, The Writers Company, Interchange Studios, 15 Wilkin Street, London NW5 3NG *tel* 071-284 4483 *fax* 071-284 4506. Contact: Robin Hooper (literary manager).

Perspectives Theatre Co-operative Ltd, c/o Mansfield Community Arts Centre, Leeming Street, Mansfield, Notts. NG18 1NG *tel* (0623) 635225. Has a policy of employing writers for new work. Regret unsolicited scripts returned.

Prometheus Touring Th. Co., Box Prom, c/o Housman's Bookshop, 5 Caledonian Road, London N1 9DX *tel* (0865) 245448.

Quicksilver Theatre for Children (formerly Theatre of Thelema), 4 Enfield Road, London N1 5AZ *tel* 071-241 2942.

Red Ladder Theatre Co., Cobden Avenue, Lower Wortley, Leeds LS12 5PB *tel* (0532) 792228.

Red Shift Theatre Company, Battersea Arts Centre, Lavender Hill, London SW11 5TF *tel* 071-223 3256 *fax* 071-978 5207.

Solent People's Theatre, The Heathfield Centre, Valentine Avenue, Sholing, Southampton SO2 8EQ *tel* (0703) 443943.

Temba Theatre Company, Dominion House, 101 Southwark Street, London SE1 0JH *tel* 071-261 0991 *fax* 071-261 9715.

Theatre Centre, Hanover School, Noel Road, Islington, London N1 8BD *tel* 071-354 0110 *fax* 071-359 7562.

Women's Theatre Group, 5 Leonard Street, London EC2A 4AQ *tel* 071-251 0202. Women writers only.

PUBLISHERS SPECIALISING IN THE PUBLICATION OF PLAYS

Walter H. Baker Company, 100 Chauncy Street, Boston, MA 02111, USA *tel* 617-482-1280.

Faber & Faber Ltd, 3 Queen Square, London WC1N 3AU *tel* 071-465 0045.

Samuel French Ltd, 52 Fitzroy Street, London W1P 6JR *tel* 071-387 9373 *fax* 071-387 2161.

Samuel French Inc., 45 West 25th Street, New York, NY 10010, USA *tel* 212-206-8990 *fax* 212-206-1429.

Nick Hern Books, 20 Vauxhall Bridge Road, London SW1V 2SA *tel* 071-973 9000 *telex* 299080 Random G *fax* 071-233 6125.

Kenyon-Deane Ltd, 311 Worcester Road, Malvern, Worcs. WR14 1AN *tel* (0864) 565045.

Methuen Drama, Michelin House, 81 Fulham Road, London SW3 6RB *tel* 071-581 9393 *fax* 071-225 0933.

J. Garnet Miller Ltd, 311 Worcester Road, Malvern, Worcs. WR14 1AN *tel* (0684) 565045.

New Playwrights' Network, 35 Sandringham Road, Macclesfield, Cheshire SK10 1QB   *tel/fax* (0625) 425312.

(For a list of periodicals dealing with the Theatre see the **Classified Index.**)

Writing for Broadcasting

JOCELYN HAY
Chairman, Voice of the Listener

Since the 1990 Broadcasting Act was passed there has been a fundamental change in the nature of commercial radio and television: the underlying philosophy now is based on 'market' theories rather than public service. Among the changes is the abolition of the Independent Broadcasting Authority (IBA) and its replacement by two new bodies with much narrower remits, the Independent Television Commission (ITC) and the Radio Authority (see page 264).

The Act renamed the ITV network as Channel 3 and it requires the licences for the Channel 3 network, now due for renewal, to be auctioned to the highest bidder in all but the most exceptional circumstances. At the same time the Act creates three new independent national radio networks (INR), the licences for which will be sold in a straight auction.

The names of the winning licence applicants were to be announced in October 1991, until when the industry faced months of uncertainty during which no one made firm programme plans. It is particularly unfortunate that this occurred when ITV suffered a 25 per cent fall in its income due to the recession, with knock-on effects on Channel 4. The fledgling cable and satellite industries have been hit even harder.

Meantime the BBC's income has been squeezed by the Government's decision to reduce the level of the licence fee for this year. This has forced the BBC to embark on a series of economies, including the dismantling of the radio and television script units. There is no recognised route now for unsolicited scripts in television. Writers with an agent should use one. Writers without an agent should study the programme output, note the names of directors whose work they enjoy, and write to them with a copy of their completed script and an sae, hoping for a sympathetic reading. Writers should also remember that the biggest demand is in series and serials where script editors are always looking for new talent. The Script Editor of BBC 2's 'Screen Play' is receptive to innovative work and requires plays of over an hour's length. Writers wishing to submit other original material should now send it to the Script Administrator, BBC Television Centre, London W12 7RJ.

Otherwise, the biggest area of change, so far as writers are concerned, arises from the Act's requirement that both the BBC and Channel 3 must now commission 25 per cent of their programmes from independent producers. Most will belong to the Independent Programme Producers Association (50-51 Berwick Street, London W1A 4RD   *tel* 071-439 7034), from whom a list of members may be obtained (see entry in **Societies**).

While this is probably the most difficult year for anyone wanting to break into television, things should improve once the recession and the uncertainty are over. In the meantime, radio provides the best market in broadcasting. Radios 3 and 4 between them broadcast about 500 plays a year, at least 50 of which will be from new writers. Follow the same procedure as for television: send a copy of your script with an sae to a producer whose work you enjoy, or, if you are really stuck, send it to: The Literary Manager, BBC Radio, Broadcasting House, London W1A 1AA. Remember too that Radio 5, the BBC network for educational and youth programmes, wants material suitable for children and young people. Ask for details from the Head of Drama, Radio 5, Broadcasting House, London W1A 1AA   *tel* 071-580 4468.

British Broadcasting Corporation

For fuller information see *Writing for the BBC* – a guide for writers on possible markets for their work within the BBC. The 8th edition is available from major booksellers at £3.99.

TELEVISION

Drama

Original 60-minute plays and 90-minute film screenplays dealing with contemporary situations are sought. Plays and screenplays needing few locations and small casts are advantageous. No standardised layout or technical instructions are expected in scripts or screenplays. Dialogue should be laid out in ways which clearly distinguish it from 'stage directions' of any kind. Series and serials represent the bulk of the Drama output, but new writers should always present sample scripts with any submission of ideas for either form.

Since the BBC has opened its doors to national and international drama markets, competition is fierce. Unsolicited scripts will therefore be rigorously sifted and a large proportion will be returned unread.

Clearly typed and well-presented scripts should be submitted to: Script Administration, Drama Group, Room 5103, BBC Television Centre, Wood Lane, London W12 7RJ.

Light Entertainment Television

The Comedy Department is looking for new narrative thirty-minute series, preferably mainly studio based. Original formats are always in demand rather than variations on existing programmes.

The requirements for sketch material vary depending on which series are currently in production.

All scripts and enquiries should be addressed to the Comedy Script Unit, Room 4010, Television Centre, Wood Lane, London W12 7RJ   *tel* 081-576 1900.

RADIO

Short stories

Short stories specially written for broadcasting will be considered. A short story written for a 15-minute broadcasting space should be between 2300 and 2500 words in length.

Drama Department

The Department broadcasts several hundred new plays and adaptations every year, in addition to series and serials, and readings. There is therefore a very large market regularly available to the freelance writer. A free leaflet, *Notes on Radio Drama*, giving basic guidance on the technique of radio writing and also on the market is available from the Literary Manager (Radio Drama), BBC, Broadcasting House, Portland Place, London W1A 1AA to whom all submissions should be addressed.

Music

The music policy of the BBC, dedicated to the encouragement of the best music old and new, continues to enlarge its range. Audition sessions for professional soloists and ensembles are held every other week, except in July and August, with an outside professional assessor on the listening panel.

A Music Panel of distinguished musicians meets regularly to advise on the suitability for performance of the large number of MSS constantly submitted. The BBC also commissions from British composers works of various kinds. These have included opera and works for special occasions. Incidental music is also commissioned for features and drama. In the case of music commissioned by the BBC the original score is now returned to the composer at his request and not as in the past automatically retained by the BBC.

Light Entertainment

Light Entertainment Radio is interested in receiving scripts or ideas for series of half hour sitcoms or panel games, principally for Radios 2 and 4. Before submitting material, please read the leaflet – explaining such matters as length, layout, structure and so on – available from the Script Editor (Light Entertainment Radio), Room 107, 16 Langham Place, London W1A 1AA, where all material should ultimately be sent.

Two programmes, *Week Ending* and *The News Huddlines*, are interested in using unsolicited topical sketches during the course of their run. *Week Ending* holds a weekly writers' meeting at which anyone is welcome, at the above address. Details (and times of deadlines) can be obtained by ringing 071-580 4468 and asking for the production office of the programme concerned. All fees are a matter for negotiation with the Corporation's Copyright Department.

BROADCASTING RIGHTS AND TERMS

Contributors are advised to check latest details of fees with the BBC.

Specially written material for television

For the period to 31st July 1991 the rates for one performance of a 60-minute original television play were a minimum of £4000 for a play written by a beginner and a 'going rate' of £6300 for an established writer, or *pro rata* for shorter or longer timings. Fees for submitted material are paid on acceptance, and for commissioned material half on commissioning and half on acceptance as being suitable for television. Fees for a 50-minute episode in a series during the same period were a minimum of £3295 for a beginner and a 'going rate' of £4760 for an established writer. Fees for a 50-minute dramatisation were a minimum of £2305 for a beginner and a £3390 'going rate' for an established writer. All fees were subject to negotiation above the minima.

Specially written material for radio

Fees are assessed on the basis of the type of material, its length, the author's status and experience in writing for radio. For the period to 31st December 1992 fees for two performances of specially written radio dramas in English (other than educational programmes) are £34.61 a minute for beginners and a 'going rate' of £52.70 a minute for established writers. Fees for submitted material are paid on acceptance, and for commissioned material half on commissioning and half on acceptance as being suitable for broadcasting.

Short stories specially written for radio

Fees range from £102.00 for 15 minutes.

Stage plays for television

Fees for stage plays are negotiable.

Published material for radio (for the period to 30th June 1991)

Domestic service: Dramatic works: £9.36 per minute; Prose works: £9.76 per minute; Prose works required for dramatisation: £7.61 per minute; Poems: £9.76 per *half* minute.

External Services: English language services: Dramatic works: £4.88 per minute for up to five broadcasts; Prose works: £4.88 per minute for up to five broadcasts; Prose works required for dramatisation: £3.80 per minute for up to five broadcasts; Poems: £4.88 per *half* minute for up to five broadcasts. For Foreign language services one fifth of the rate for English language services.

Published prose and poems for television

Prose works, £15.23 per minute; poems £17.68 per minute.

Repeats in BBC programmes

Further proportionate fees are payable for repeats.

Use abroad of recordings of BBC programmes

If the BBC sends abroad recordings of its programmes for use by overseas broadcasting organisations on their own networks or stations, further payments accrue to the author, usually in the form of additional percentages of the basic fee paid for the initial performance or a royalty based on a percentage of the distributors' receipts. This can apply to both sound and television programmes.

Value Added Tax

A self-billing system for VAT was introduced in January 1978 for programmes made in London. This now covers radio, external services and television.

TALKS FOR TELEVISION

Contributors to talks will be offered the standard Television talks contract which provides the BBC certain rights to broadcast the material in a complete, abridged and/or translated manner, and which provides for the payment of further fees for additional usage of the material whether by television, domestic radio or external broadcasting. The contract also covers the assignment of material and limited publication rights. Alternatively a contract taking all standard rights may be negotiated. Fees are arranged by the contract authorities in London and the Regions.

TALKS FOR RADIO

Contributors to talks for domestic Radio and World Service broadcasting may be offered either: the standard talks contract which takes rights and provides for residual payments, as does the Television standard contract above; or be offered an STC (Short Talks Contract) which takes all rights except print publication rights where the airtime of the contribution does not exceed five minutes and which has set fees or disturbance money payable; or an NFC (No Fee Contract) where no payment is made which provides an acknowledgement that a contribution may be used by the BBC.

ADDRESSES

Letters addressed to speakers c/o the BBC will be forwarded, but may be opened before being forwarded. Letters marked 'Personal' are forwarded unopened.

LONDON

Head Office: Broadcasting House, London W1A 1AA *tel* 071-580 4468 *telegraphic address/cables* Broadcasts, London *telex* 265781.

Television: Television Centre, Wood Lane, London W12 7RJ *tel* 081-743 8000 *telegraphic address/cables* Telecasts, London *telex* 265781.

Publications: 35 Marylebone High Street, London W1M 4AA *tel* 071-580 5577 *telegraphic address/cables* Broadcasts, London *telex* 265781.

External Broadcasting: PO Box 76, Bush House, Strand, London WC2B 4PH *tel* 071-240 3456 *telegraphic address/cables* Broadbrit, London *telex* 265781.

ENGLAND

Birmingham: Broadcasting Centre, Pebble Mill Road, Birmingham B5 7SA *tel* 021-414 8888.

Bristol: Broadcasting House, Whiteladies Road, Bristol BS8 2LR *tel* (0272) 732211.

Caversham: Caversham Park, Reading, Berks. RG4 8TZ *tel* (0734) 472742.

Elstree: BBC Elstree Centre, Clarendon Road, Borehamwood, Herts. WD6 1JF *tel* 081-953 6100.

Norwich: St Catherine's Close, All Saints Green, Norwich, Norfolk NR1 3ND *tel* (0603) 619331.

Nottingham: Willson House, Derby Road, Nottingham N91 5HX *tel* (0602) 472395.

Manchester: New Broadcasting House, PO Box 27, Oxford Road, Manchester M60 1SJ *tel* 061-200 2020.

Milton Keynes: OUPC, Walton Hall, Milton Keynes MK7 6BH *tel* (0908) 74033.

Newcastle: BBC Broadcasting Centre, PO Box, Barrack Road, Newcastle upon Tyne NE99 2NE *tel* 091-232 1313.

Leeds: Broadcasting Centre, Woodhouse Lane, Leeds LS2 9PX *tel* (0532) 441188.

Plymouth: Broadcasting House, Seymour Road, Mannamead, Plymouth PL3 5BD *tel* (0752) 229201.

Southampton: South Western House, Canute Road, Southampton SO9 1PF *tel* (0703) 226201.

NORTHERN IRELAND

Belfast: Broadcasting House, Ormeau Avenue, Belfast BT2 8HQ *tel* (0232) 244400.

SCOTLAND

Glasgow: Broadcasting House, Queen Margaret Drive, Glasgow G12 8DG *tel* 041-339 8844/330 2345.

Edinburgh: Broadcasting House, Queen Street, Edinburgh EH2 1JF   *tel* 031-225 3131.

Aberdeen: Broadcasting House, Beechgrove Terrace, Aberdeen AB9 2ZT   *tel* (0224) 635233.

Dundee: 12-13 Dock Street, Dundee   *tel* (0382) 25025.

BBC Radio Highland: 7 Culduthel Road, Inverness IV2 4AD   *tel* (0463) 221711.

BBC Radio Nan Eilean: Rosebank, Church Street, Stornoway, Isle of Lewis   *tel* (0851) 5000.

BBC Radio Orkney: Castle Street, Kirkwall   *tel* (0856) 3939.

BBC Radio Shetland: Brentham House, Lerwick, Shetland   *tel* (0595) 4747.

BBC Radio Solway: Lavers Walk, Dumfries   *tel* (0387) 68008/9.

BBC Radio Tweed: Municipal Buildings, High Street, Selkirk   *tel* (0750) 21884.

WALES

Cardiff: Head Office, Broadcasting House, Llandaff, Cardiff CF5 2YQ   *tel* (0222) 564888.

Bangor: Broadcasting House, Meirion Road, Bangor, Gwynedd LL57 2BY   *tel* (0248) 362214.

Gabalfa: Broadcasting House, Llandaff, Cardiff CF5 2YQ   *tel* (0222) 610061.

Swansea: 32 Alexandra Road, Swansea SA1 5DZ   *tel* (0792) 54986.

BBC Radio Clwyd: The Old School House, Glanrafon Road, Mold, Clwyd   *tel* (0352) 59111.

OVERSEAS OFFICES

USA: 630 Fifth Avenue, New York, NY 10111   *tel* 212-581-7100   *cables* Broadcasts, New York City   *telex* 620150.
2030 M Street NW, Suite 607, Washington, DC 20036   *tel* 202-223-2050.

Cairo Bureau: PO Box 2642, Cairo, Egypt   *tel* Cairo 770040/741931   *telex* 94169 Nytim Un.

South East Asia Bureau: 26 Olive Road, Singapore 1129   *tel* 250 3100.

South American Office: Casilla de Correo, 1566 Buenos Aires, Argentina   *tel* 3926439   *telex* Florida 734.

Australia and New Zealand: Suite 101, 80 William Street, Sydney, NSW 2011, Australia   *tel* (02) 3317744.

India: 1 Nizamuddin East, New Delhi 110013   *tel* 616108/616102   *cables* Loncalling, Newdelhi   *telex* 31 2927 Bbc IN.

France: 155 rue du Faubourg Saint-Honoré, BP 487 08, 75366 Paris, Cedex 08   *tel* 561-9700   *cables* Broadbrit, Paris   *telex* 650341.

Germany: BBC Buro, Savignyplatz 6, D-1 Berlin   *tel* Berlin 316773/3133063. Prestehaus 1/429, Heussallee 2 - 10, D-5300 Bonn   *tel* 228 215625.

Belgium: BBC Office, PO Box 50, International Press Centre, 1 Boulevard Charlemagne, Brussels 1040   *tel* 322 2302120   *telex* 25912 Bbcbre B.

BBC LOCAL RADIO STATIONS

Local Radio also affords opportunities for writers to submit short stories and plays. A number of stations hold play-writing or short story competitions where the winners have their work broadcast. Others consider original work from local writers. Material should be submitted to the Programme Organiser.

Bedfordshire: BBC Radio Bedfordshire, PO Box 476, Hastings Street, Luton, Beds. LU1 5BA *tel* (0582) 459111 *telex* 825979 *fax* (0582) 23318.

Birmingham: BBC Radio WM, Pebble Mill Road, Birmingham B5 7SD *tel* 021-414 8484 *telex* 339210 *fax* 021-472 3174.

Bristol: BBC Radio Bristol, 3 Tyndalls Park Road, Bristol BS8 1PP *tel* (0272) 741111 *telex* 449170 *fax* (0272) 732549.

Cambridgeshire: BBC Radio Cambridgeshire, Broadcasting House, 104 Hills Road, Cambridge CB2 1LD *tel* (0223) 315970 *telex* 817776 *fax* (0223) 460832.

Cleveland: BBC Radio Cleveland, Broadcasting House, Newport Road, Middlesbrough, Cleveland TS1 5DG *tel* (0642) 225211 *telex* 58203 *fax* (0642) 211356.

Cornwall: BBC Radio Cornwall, Phoenix Wharf, Truro, Cornwall TR1 1UA *tel* (0872) 75421 *telex* 45728 *fax* (0872) 75045.

Cumbria: BBC Radio Cumbria, Hilltop Heights, London Road, Carlisle CA1 2NA *tel* (0228) 31661 *telex* 64165 *fax* (0228) 511195.

Derby: BBC Radio Derby, 56 St Helen's Street, Derby DE1 3HY *tel* (0332) 361111 *telex* 37257 *fax* (0332) 290794.

Devon: BBC Radio Devon, PO Box 100, Exeter, Devon EX4 4DB *tel* (0392) 215651 *telex* 42440 *fax* (0392) 215628; PO Box 5, Catryn Street, Plymouth PL1 2AD *tel* (0752) 260323 *fax* (0752) 222679.

Gloucestershire: BBC Radio Gloucestershire, London Road, Gloucester GL1 1SW *tel* (0452) 308585 *telex* 437434 *fax* (0452) 306541.

Guernsey: BBC Radio Guernsey, Commerce House, Les Banques, St Peter Port, Guernsey, CI *tel* (0481) 28977 *telex* 4191456 *fax* (0481) 713557.

Humberside: BBC Radio Humberside, 63 Jameson Street, Hull HU1 3NU *tel* (0482) 23232 *telex* 597031 *fax* (0482) 226409.

Jersey: BBC Radio Jersey, Broadcasting House, Rouge Bouillon, St Helier, Jersey, CI *tel* (0534) 70000 *telex* 4192381 *fax* (0534) 32569.

Kent: BBC Radio Kent, 30 High Street, Chatham, Kent ME4 4EZ *tel* (0634) 46284 *telex* 965011.

Lancashire: BBC Radio Lancashire, King Street, Blackburn, Lancs. BB2 2EA *tel* (0254) 62411 *telex* 63491 *fax* (0254) 680821.

Leeds: BBC Radio Leeds, Broadcasting House, Woodhouse Lane, Leeds LS2 9PN *tel* (0532) 442131 *telex* 557230 *fax* (0532) 420652.

Leicester: BBC Radio Leicester, Epic House, Charles Street, Leicester LE1 3SH *tel* (0533) 27113 *telex* 34401 *fax* (0533) 511463.

Lincolnshire: BBC Radio Lincolnshire, Radio Buildings, Newport, Lincoln LN1 3EU *tel* (0522) 40011 *telex* 56186 *fax* (0522) 510124.

London: BBC Radio London, 35a Marylebone High Street, London W1A 4LG *tel* 071-486 7611 *telex* 267223 *fax* 071-487 2908.

Manchester: Greater Manchester Radio, New Broadcasting House, Oxford Road, Manchester M60 1SJ *tel* 061-200 2000 *telex* 668708 *fax* 061-228 6110.

Merseyside: BBC Radio Merseyside, 55 Paradise Street, Liverpool L1 3BP *tel* 051-708 5500 *telex* 62364 *fax* 051-708 5356.

Newcastle: BBC Radio Newcastle, Barrack Road, Newcastle upon Tyne NE99 1RN *tel* 091-232 4141 *telex* 537007 *fax* 091-232 5082.

Norfolk: BBC Radio Norfolk, Norfolk Tower, Surrey Street, Norwich, Norfolk NR1 3PA *tel* (0603) 617411 *telex* 975515 *fax* (0603) 633692.

Northampton: BBC Radio Northampton, PO Box 1107, Northampton NN1 2BE *tel* (0604) 20621 *telex* 311812 *fax* (0604) 230709.

Nottingham: BBC Radio Nottingham, York House, Mansfield Road, Nottingham NG1 3JB *tel* (0602) 415161 *telex* 37464 *fax* (0602) 481482.

Oxford: BBC Radio Oxford, 242-254 Banbury Road, Oxford OX2 7DW *tel* (0865) 53411 *telex* 837658 *fax* (0865) 512506.

Sheffield: BBC Radio Sheffield, Ashdell Grove, 60 Westbourne Road, Sheffield S10 2QU *tel* (0742) 686185 *telex* 54400 *fax* (0742) 664375.

Shropshire: BBC Radio Shropshire, PO Box 397, Shrewsbury, Shropshire SY1 3TT *tel* (0743) 248484 *telex* 35187 *fax* (0743) 271702.

Solent: BBC Radio Solent, South Western House, Canute Road, Southampton SO9 4PJ *tel* (0703) 631311 *telex* 47420 *fax* (0703) 339648.

Stoke-on-Trent: BBC Radio Stoke, Conway House, Cheapside, Hanley, Stoke-on-Trent, Staffs. ST1 1JJ *tel* (0782) 208080 *telex* 36104 *fax* (0782) 289115.

Sussex: BBC Radio Sussex, Marlborough Place, Brighton, East Sussex BN1 1TU *tel* (0273) 680231 *telex* 87313 *fax* (0273) 571754.

Swindon: BBC Wiltshire Sound, Broadcasting House, 56-58 Prospect Place, Swindon, Wilts. SN1 3RW *tel* (0793) 513626 *fax* (0793) 512617.

York: BBC Radio York, 20 Bootham Row, York YO3 7BR *tel* (0904) 641351 *telex* 57444 *fax* (0904) 610937.

Independent Broadcasting

Independent Television Commission (ITC), 70 Brompton Road, London SW3 1EY *tel* 071-584 7011 *telex* 24345 *fax* 071-589 5533. Licenses and regulates all commercially funded UK television services, including cable and satellite services as well as the terrestrial UHF services.

The Radio Authority, 70 Brompton Road, London SW3 1EY *tel* 071-581 2888 *fax* 071-823 9113. Licenses and regulates Independent Radio. The Authority plans frequencies, awards licences, regulates (as necessary) programming and radio advertising, and plays an active role in the discussion and formulation of policies which affect the radio industry and its listeners.

REGIONAL TELEVISION

The programme contractors listed below were correct at the time of going to press. New franchises were to be awarded late 1991, and will start broadcasting

on 1 January 1993. Details of the new franchise holders may be obtained from
the Independent Television Commission (address above).

It is advisable to check before submitting any ideas/material – in all cases,
scripts are preferred to synopses. Programmes should be planned with natural
breaks for the insertion of advertisements. These companies also provide some
programmes for Channel 4.

Anglia Television Ltd, Anglia House, Norwich NR1 3JG   *tel* (0603) 615151   *fax*
(0603) 631032; 48 Leicester Square, London WC2H 7FB   *tel* 071-321
0101   *fax* 071-930 8499. Provides programmes for the East of England
during the whole week and drama and natural history programmes. Drama
submissions only through an accredited agency or similar source.

Border Television plc, The Television Centre, Carlisle CA1 3NT   *tel* (0228)
25101. Provides programmes for The Borders and the Isle of Man, during the
whole week. Occasionally scripts are commissioned from outside sources.
Suggestions should be sent to the Controller of Programmes in Carlisle.

Central Independent Television plc, Central House, Broad Street, Birmingham
B1 2JP   *tel* 021-643 9898; East Midlands Television Centre, Nottingham NG7
2NA   *tel* (0602) 863322. Provides programmes to the ITV Network and the
East and West Midlands seven days a week. Central's requirements are
constantly changing, and interested professional writers are asked to contact
the Script Unit in Nottingham for information. Writers are advised to send
photo-copies rather than original unsolicited manuscripts.

Channel Television, The Television Centre, St Helier, Jersey, CI   *tel* (0534)
68999   *fax* (0534) 59446. Provides programmes for the Channel Islands during
the whole week relating mainly to Channel Islands news and current affairs.

Grampian Television plc, Queens Cross, Aberdeen AB9 2XJ   *tel* (0224)
646464   *telex* 73151   *fax* (0224) 635127; Albany House, 68 Albany Road,
West Ferry, Dundee DD5 1NW   *tel* (0382) 739363; 23-25 Huntly Street,
Inverness IV3 5PR   *tel* (0463) 242624. Provides programmes for North Scotland during the whole week.

Granada Television Ltd, Granada Television Centre, Manchester M60 9EA   *tel*
061-832 7211; and 36 Golden Square, London W1R 4AH   *tel* 071-734 8080.
The ITV franchise holder for the North West of England. Produces programmes across a broad range for both its region and the ITV network. It is
advisable for writers to make their approach through agents who would have
some knowledge of Granada's current requirements.

HTV Ltd, HTV Wales, The Television Centre, Culverhouse Cross, Cardiff CF5
6XJ   *tel* (0222) 590590; HTV West, The Television Centre, Bristol BS4
3HG   *tel* (0272) 778366; 126 Baker Street, London W1M 1FH   *tel* 071-224
4048; The Civic Centre, Mold, Clwyd CH7 1YA   *tel* (0352) 55331. Provides
programmes for Wales and West of England during the whole week. Produces
programmes for home and international sales.

LWT, South Bank Television Centre, London SE1 9LT   *tel* 071-620 1620.
Provides programmes for Greater London and much of the Home Counties
area from Friday 5.15 p.m. to Monday 6.00 a.m.

Scottish Television plc, Cowcaddens, Glasgow G2 3PR   *tel* 041-332 9999   *telex*
77388   *fax* 041-332 6982. Provides programmes for Central Scotland during
the whole week, *Material:* scripts for contemporary series and ideas and
formats for programmes with a Scottish or international flavour. Approach
in the first instance to the Controller of Drama, Robert Love.

Thames Television plc, 306 Euston Road, London NW1 3BB   *tel* 071-387 9494; 149 Tottenham Court Road, London W1P 9LL   *tel* 071-387 9494. Provides programmes for London and the South East from Monday 6.00 a.m. to Friday 5.15 p.m.
Currently not accepting unsolicited programme material. Enquiries only, in writing to: Central Registry, Thames Television plc, Teddington Studios, Broom Road, Teddington, Middlesex TW11 9NT   *tel* 081-977 3252.

TSW-Television South West Ltd, Derry's Cross, Plymouth PL1 2SP   *tel* (0752) 663322   *telex* 45566   *fax* (0752) 671970. Provides programmes for South-West England during the whole week.

TVS Television Ltd, Television Centre, Southampton SO9 5HZ   *tel* (0703) 634211   *telex* 477217   *fax* (0703) 211428; Television Centre, Vinters Park, Maidstone ME14 5NZ   *tel* (0622) 691111; 84 Buckingham Gate, London SW1E 6PD   *tel* 071-976 7199; and 60-61 Buckingham Gate, London SW1E 6AJ   *tel* 071-828 9898. Provides programmes for the South and South East of England during the whole week.

Tyne Tees Television Ltd, The Television Centre, City Road, Newcastle upon Tyne NE1 2AL   *tel* 091-261 0181   *telex* 53279   *fax* 091-222 0013; 15 Bloomsbury Square, London WC1A 2LJ   *tel* 071-405 8474   *telex* 266316   *fax* 071-242 2441; Ground Floor, United House, Piccadilly, York YO1 1PQ   *tel* (0904) 610666   *fax* (0904) 610236; Corporation House, Corporation Road, Middlesbrough TS1 2RX   *tel* (0642) 219181   *fax* (0642) 249961. Serving the North of England seven days a week, 24 hours a day.

Ulster Television plc, Havelock House, Ormeau Road, Belfast, Northern Ireland BT7 1EB   *tel* (0232) 328122   *fax* (0232) 246695; 6 York Street, London W1H 1FA   *tel* 071-486 5211. Provides programmes for Northern Ireland during the whole week. Company staff provide majority of scripts, but occasionally they are commissioned from other sources.

Yorkshire Television Ltd, The Television Centre, Leeds LS3 1JS   *tel* (0532) 438283   *telex* 557232; Television House, 32 Bedford Row, London WC1R 4HE   *tel* 071-242 1666   *telex* 295386. Yorkshire Television is a Network Company which produces many programmes for the ITV Network and the Yorkshire area throughout the week.

NATIONAL AND SATELLITE TELEVISION

British Sky Broadcasting, 6 Centaurs Business Park, Grant Way, off Syon Lane, Isleworth, Middlesex TW7 5QD   *tel* 071-782 3000   *fax* 071-782 3030.

Channel Four Television Company Ltd, 60 Charlotte Street, London W1P 2AX   *tel* 071-631 4444   *fax* 071-637 4872. Commissions and purchases programmes (does not make them) for broadcast during the whole week throughout the United Kingdom (except Wales).

Independent Television Association, Knighton House, 56 Mortimer Street, London W1N 8AN   *tel* 071-636 6866.

Independent Television News Ltd, 200 Gray's Inn Road, London WC1X 8XZ   *tel* 071-833 3000   *cables* Telindep, London PS4. Provides the national and international news programmes for all ITV areas.

Oracle Teletext, Craven House, 25-32 Marshall Street, London W1V 1LL   *tel* 071-434 3121.

TV-am plc, Breakfast Television Centre, Hawley Crescent, London NW1 8EF   *tel* 071-267 4300. A national service of Independent breakfast television seven days a week.

INDEPENDENT LOCAL RADIO

Aberdeen: NorthSound Radio, 45 King's Gate, Aberdeen AB2 6BL   *tel* (0224) 632234.

Ayr: West Sound, Radio House, 54 Holmston Road, Ayr KA7 3BE   *tel* (0292) 283662.

Belfast: Classic Trax BCR, Russell Court, Claremont Street, Lisburn Road, Belfast, Northern Ireland BT9 6JX   *tel* (0232) 438500   *fax* (0232) 23050.

Belfast: Cool FM, PO Box 974, Belfast, Northern Ireland BT1 1RT   *tel* (0247) 817181.

Belfast: Downtown Radio, Kiltonga Industrial Estate, Newtownards, Co. Down, Northern Ireland BT23 4ES   *tel* (0247) 815555.

Birmingham: BRMB-FM/XTRA-AM, PO Box 555, Radio House, Aston Road North, Aston, Birmingham B6 4BX   *tel* 021-359 4481   *fax* 021-359 1117.

Birmingham: Buzz FM, The Spencers, Augusta Street, Birmingham B18 6JA   *tel* 021-236 6777/4888   *fax* 021-236 0956.

Borders: Radio Borders, Tweedside Park, Galashiels TD1 3TD   *tel* (0896) 59444.

Bournemouth: Two Counties Radio, 5 Southcote Road, Bournemouth BH1 3LR   *tel* (0202) 239170.

Bradford: Sunrise FM, 30 Chapel Street, Little Germany, Bradford BD1 5DN   *tel* (0274) 735043.

Bradford/Huddersfield & Halifax: Pennine FM Radio, Forster Square, Bradford BD1 5NP   *tel* (0274) 731521.

Brighton: South Coast Radio 'Light & Easy', Radio House, PO Box 2000, Brighton, East Sussex BN41 2SS   *tel* (0273) 430111   *fax* (0273) 430098.

Brighton: Southern Sound Classic Hits, Radio House, PO Box 2000, Brighton, East Sussex BN41 2SS   *tel* (0273) 430111   *fax* (0273) 430098.

Bristol: Galaxy Radio, 25 Portland Square, Bristol BS2 8NN   *tel* (0272) 240111.

Bristol: GWR Radio, PO Box 2000, Bristol BS99 7SN   *tel* (0272) 279900.

Bury St Edmunds: Saxon Radio, Long Brackland, Bury St Edmunds, Suffolk IP33 1JY   *tel* (0284) 701511.

Cambridge & Newmarket: CN.FM 103, PO Box 1000, The Vision Park, Chivers Way, Histon, Cambridge CB4 4WW   *tel* (0223) 235255   *fax* (0223) 235161.

Cardiff: Red Dragon FM, West Canal Wharf, Cardiff CF1 5XJ   *tel* (0222) 384041.

Coventry: Mercia FM, Hertford Place, Coventry CV1 3TT   *tel* (0203) 633933.

Coventry: Radio Harmony, Ringway House, Hill Street, Coventry CV1 4AN   *tel* (0203) 525656   *fax* (0203) 551744.

Doncaster: Hallam, PO Box 194, Sheffield S1 1GP   *tel* (0742) 766766.

Dumfries: South West Sound, Campbell House, Bankend Road, Dumfries DG1 4TH   *tel* (0387) 50999   *fax* (0387) 65629.

Dundee/Perth: Radio Tay, PO Box 123, 6 North Islast, Dundee DD1 9UF *tel* (0382) 200800.

East Kent: Invicta FM, 15 Station Road East, Canterbury, Kent CT1 2RB *tel* (0227) 767661.

Eastbourne/Hastings: Southern Sound, PO Box 2000, Brighton, East Sussex BN41 2SS *tel* (0273) 430111.

Easterhouse (East Glasgow): East End Radio, The Greater Easterhouse Business Centre, 19 Blairtummock Road, Glasgow G33 4AN *tel* 041-774 5335.

Edinburgh: Radio Forth REM, Forth House, Forth Street, Edinburgh EH1 3LF *tel* 031-556 9255.

Exeter/Torbay: Devonair Radio, 35-37 St David's Hill, Exeter, Devon EX4 4DA *tel* (0392) 430703.

Glasgow: Clyde One and Clyde Two, Clydebank Business Park, Clydebank, Glasgow G81 2RX *tel* 041-306 2200.

Gloucester & Cheltenham: Severn Sound, Old Talbot House, 67 Southgate Street, Gloucester GL1 2DQ *tel* (0452) 423791.

Guildford: First Gold Radio, Chertsey Road, Woking, Surrey GU21 5XY *tel* (0483) 740066.

Hereford/Worcester: Radio Wyvern, Barbourne Terrace, Worcester WR1 3JZ *tel* (0905) 612212.

Hounslow & Ealing: Sunrise Radio, PO Box 212, Hounslow, Middlesex TW3 2AD *tel* 081-569 6666.

Humberside: Viking, Commercial Road, Hull HU1 2SG *tel* (0482) 25141.

Inverness, Moray Firth Radio, PO Box 271, Inverness IV3 6SF *tel* (0463) 224433 *fax* (0463) 713318.

Ipswich: Radio Orwell, Electric House, Lloyds Avenue, Ipswich IP1 3HZ *tel* (0473) 216971.

Isle of Wight: Isle of Wight Radio, Dodnor Park, Newport, Isle of Wight PO30 5XE *tel* (0983) 822557   (0933) 821777 (newsroom) *fax* (0983) 821690.

Kettering: KCBC, PO Box 1530, Kettering, Northants. NN16 8PU *tel* (0536) 412413 *fax* (0536) 517390.

Leeds: Aire FM/Magic 828, PO Box 2000, Leeds LS3 1LR *tel* (0532) 452299 *fax* (0532) 421830   (0532) 343985 (newsroom).

Leicester: Leicester Sound, Granville House, Granville Road, Leicester LE1 7RW *tel* (0533) 551616.

Liverpool: Radio City, PO Box 967, Liverpool L69 1TQ *tel* 051-227 5100.

London (General and Entertainment Service): Capital Radio, Euston Tower, London NW1 3DR *tel* 071-388 1288.

London (News & Information Service): LBC (London Broadcasting Company), Crown House, 72 Hammersmith Road, London W14 8YE *tel* 071-371 1515.

London (Brixton): Choice FM, 16-18 Trinity Gardens, London SW9 8DP *tel* 071-738 7969.

London (Haringey): London Greek Radio, Florentia Village, Vale Road, London N4 1TD *tel* 081-800 8001.

London (Haringey): WNK Radio, 185b High Road, Wood Green, London N22 6BA *tel* 081-889 1547 *fax* 081-889 1571.

London, Greater: Jazz FM, 26/27 Castlereagh Street, London W1H 5YR *tel* 071-706 4100 *fax* 071-723 9742.

London, Greater: Spectrum Radio, Endeavour House, Brent Cross, London NW2 1JT *tel* 081-905 5151 *fax* 081-209 1029.

Luton/Bedford: Chiltern Radio, Chiltern Road, Dunstable, Beds. LU6 1HQ *tel* (0582) 666001.

Maidstone & Medway: Invicta Radio, 15 Station Road East, Canterbury, Kent CT1 2RB *tel* (0227) 767661.

Manchester: Piccadilly Radio, 127-131 The Piazza, Piccadilly Plaza, Manchester M1 4AW *tel* 061-236 9913.

Manchester: Sunset Radio, 23 New Mount Street, Manchester M4 4DE *tel* 061-953 5353.

Milton Keynes: Horizon Radio, Broadcast Centre, Crownhill, Milton Keynes MK8 0AB *tel* (0908) 269111.

Newport (Gwent): Red Dragon FM, West Canal Wharf, Cardiff CF1 5XJ *tel* (0222) 384041.

Northampton: Northants Radio, PO Box 96.6, Northampton NN1 2NR *tel* (0604) 29811.

Norwich & Great Yarmouth: Radio Broadland, St George's Plain, Colegate, Norwich NR3 1DB *tel* (0603) 630621 *fax* (0603) 666353.

Nottingham/Derby: Trent FM, 29-31 Castle Gate, Nottingham NG1 7AP *tel* (0602) 581731.

Oxford/Banbury: Fox FM, Brush House, Pony Road, Hotspath Estate, Cowley, Oxford OX4 2XR *tel* (0865) 748787.

Peterborough: Hereward Radio, PO Box 225, Queensgate Centre, Peterborough, Cambs. PE1 1XJ *tel* (0733) 346225 *fax* (0733) 342714.

Plymouth: Plymouth Sound, Earl's Acre, Plymouth PL3 4HX *tel* (0752) 227272.

Portsmouth: Ocean Sound Classic Hits, Whittle Avenue, Segensworth West, Fareham, Hants PO15 5PA *tel* (0489) 589911.

Preston & Blackpool: Red Rose Radio, PO Box 301, St Paul's Square, Preston, Lancs. PR1 1YE *tel* (0772) 556301.

Reading/Basingstoke & Andover: 210 FM, PO Box 210, Reading, Berks. RG3 5RZ *tel* (0734) 413131 *fax* (0734) 431215.

Reigate & Crawley: Radio Mercury, Broadfield House, Brighton Road, Crawley, West Sussex RH11 9TT *tel* (0293) 519161.

Sheffield & Rotherham/Barnsley/Doncaster: Hallam FM, PO Box 194, Sheffield S1 1GP *tel* (0742) 766766.

Southend/Chelmsford: Essex Radio, Radio House, Clifftown Road, Southend-on-Sea, Essex SS1 1SX *tel* (0702) 333711.

Stirling: Central FM Radio, PO Box 967, Stirling FK7 7RP *tel* (0786) 51188 *fax* (0786) 61883.

Stockport: KFM Radio, Regent House, Heaton Lane, Stockport, Cheshire SK4 1BX *tel* 061-480 5445.

Stoke-on-Trent: Signal Radio, Studio 257, Stoke Road, Stoke-on-Trent, Staffs. ST4 2SR *tel* (0782) 747047.

Sunderland: Wear FM, The Forster Building, Sunderland Polytechnic, Chester Road, Sunderland, Tyne and Wear   *tel* 091-515 2103   *fax* 091-515 2270.

Swansea: Swansea Sound, Victoria Road, Gowerton, Swansea, West Glamorgan SA4 3AB   *tel* (0792) 893751   *fax* (0792) 898841.

Swindon/West Wiltshire: GWR Radio, PO Box 2000, Swindon, Wilts. SN4 7EX   *tel* (0793) 853222.

Teesside: TFM Radio, 74 Dovecot Street, Stockton-on-Tees, Cleveland TS18 1HI   *tel* (0642) 615111.

Tendring: Mellow 1557, PO Box 1557, Colchester, Essex CO15 2DF   *tel* (0255) 675303.

Thamesmead: RTM (Independent Radio Thamesmead), 19 Tavy Bridge, Thamesmead, London SE2 9UG   *tel* 081-311 3112.

Tyne and Wear: Metro Radio, Long Rigg, Swalwell, Newcastle upon Tyne NE99 1BB   *tel* 091-488 3131.

Wolverhampton & Black Country/Shrewsbury & Telford: Beacon Radio, 267 Tettenhall Road, Wolverhampton WV6 0DQ   *tel* (0902) 757211.

Wrexham & Deeside: Marcher Sound/Sain-Y-Gororau, The Studios, Mold Road, Wrexham, Clwyd LL11 4AF   *tel* (0978) 752202.

Yeovil/Taunton: Orchard FM, Haygrove House, Shoreditch, Taunton, Somerset TA3 7BT   *tel* (0823) 338448.

Association of Independent Radio Contractors (AIRC) and **Radio Marketing Bureau (RMB),** Radio House, 46 Westbourne Grove, London W2 5SH   *tel* 071-727 2646   *telex* 24543   *fax* 071-229 0352. AIRC is the trade association for Independent Radio companies.

IRN (Independent Radio News), Crown House, 72 Hammersmith Road, London W14 8YE   *tel* 071-333 0011   *telex* 261281   *fax* 071-371 2199. National news provider to all UK commercial radio stations, including live news bulletins, sport and financial news, and coverage of the House of Commons. **IRN International (IRNI),** a wholly owned subsidiary, provides news to other radio stations around the world.

Overseas Radio and Television Companies

AUSTRALIA

Australian Broadcasting Corporation, Box 9994, GPO, Sydney, NSW 2001. Manager for Europe: Australian Broadcasting Corporation, 54 Portland Place, London W1N 4DY. The Australian Broadcasting Corporation is a statutory authority established by Act of Parliament and responsible to Parliament. It provides television and radio programmes in the national broadcasting service and operates Radio Australia. It operates six symphony orchestras and stages concerts throughout Australia.

ABC television restricts its production resources to work closely related to the Australian environment. For this reason scripts submitted from outside Australia in the field of television drama and short stories have little chance of success. ABC radio also looks principally to Australian writers for the basis of its drama output. However, ABC radio is interested in reading or auditioning new creative material of a high quality from overseas sources and this may be submitted in script or taped form. No journalistic material is required. Talks on international affairs are commissioned.

Federation of Australian Commercial Television Stations, 44 Avenue Road, Mosman, NSW 2088 *tel* (02) 960 2622 *fax* (02) 969 3520. FACTS is the industry association representing the commercial television stations in Australia.

The following six stations accept freelance material:

ATN Channel 7, Australian Television Network, Amalgamated Television Services Pty Ltd, Television Centre, Epping, NSW 2121 *tel* (02) 877 7777 *telegraphic address* Telecentre, Sydney *telex* AA 20250 *fax* (02) 877 7886. Willing to consider original television material of all types, especially 60-minute drama series/serials, 30-minute situation-comedy series and children's drama series/serials that have received a 'C' classification. Material should have an *Australian* background and deal with *Australian* characters. For series submit sample script with some future story-lines.

BTQ Channel 7, Brisbane TV Limited, Sir Samuel Griffith Drive, Mt Coot-Tha, GPO Box 604, Brisbane 4001 *tel* (07) 369 7777 *fax* (07) 368 2970. Writers should be Australian-based. Children's Educational-type series, children's entertainment programmes and local drama (Queensland writers only).

HSV Channel 7, HSV Channel 7 Pty Ltd, 119 Wells Street, South Melbourne, Victoria 3205 *tel* (03) 697 7777. For requirements see ATN Channel 7.

National Nine Network (TCN 9 Sydney; GTV 9 Melbourne; QTQ 9 Brisbane; NWS 9 Adelaide; STW 9 Perth), c/o TCN Channel 9 Sydney, 24 Artarmon Road, Willoughby, NSW 2068 *tel* (02) 906 9999 *fax* (02) 958 2279. *Director of programs Nine Network:* Ross Plapp; *assistant director of programs:* Jim Blomfield; *director/producer entertainment:* Kris Noble. Interested in receiving material from freelance writers strictly on the basis of payment for material or ideas used. No necessity for writers to be Australian-based, but membership of the Australian Writers' Guild is helpful.

NSW Channel 9, Southern Television Corporation Pty Ltd, 202 Tynte Street, PO Box 9, North Adelaide, South Australia 5006 *tel* (08) 267 0111 *fax* (08) 267 3996.

STW Channel 9, Swan Television & Radio Broadcasters Ltd, PO Box 99, Tuart Hill, Western Australia 6060 *tel* (09) 349 9999 *telegraphic address* Swantel, Perth *telex* AA92142 *fax* (09) 349 2110. Writers should be Australian-based.

CANADA

Canadian Broadcasting Corporation, PO Box 8478, Ottawa, Ontario K1G 3J5 *tel* 613-724-1200 *fax* 613-738-6887.

Canadian Radio-television and Telecommunications Commission, Ottawa, Ontario K1A 0N2. *General information tel* 819-997-0313 *fax* 819-994-0218; *Visual Ear* 819-994-0423. The federal authority which regulates telecommunications and the broadcasting system in Canada.

INDIA

All India Radio, Akashvani Bhavan, Parliament Street, New Delhi 110001 (*telex* AVDG 031-6585) is a part of the Ministry of Information and Broadcasting of the Government of India which operates the broadcasting network in the country. There are 100 stations covering almost the entire area of the country and catering to the various social, cultural and linguistic needs of the people. Programmes consist of news, music, talks, plays, discussions, documentary features and special audience programmes for women, children, industrial workers and rural audiences.

External Services Division of All India Radio broadcasts programmes in 23 languages. The object of these programmes is to entertain Indians abroad and keep them in touch with the events and developments in India.

The Commercial Service is broadcast over 29 AIR stations.

The National Channel commenced in May 1988.

Television: Director General, Doordarshan India (Television), Mandi House, Copernicus Marg, New Delhi 110001 *tel* 382094 *telex* 3166143. Covers most of India, providing a wide variety of programmes, both educational and for entertainment. Some commercial advertising.

IRELAND

Radio Telefis Eireann, Donnybrook, Dublin 4, Republic of Ireland *tel* (01) 643111 *telex* 643080 *fax* (01) 643080. The Irish national broadcasting service operating radio and television.

Television: script requirements: original television plays, length 52 minutes, preferably set in Ireland or of strong Irish interest. Plays should be sent to the Head of Drama. Guidelines on writing plays for television are available from the Head of Television Drama. Before submitting material to Current Affairs, Drama, Features or Young People's programmes, authors are advised to write to the department in question.

Radio: talks and short stories (length 14 minutes) in Irish or English suitable for broadcasting: features, dramatic or narrative and plays are welcomed and paid for according to merit. Plays should run 30, 60 or 90 minutes. Guidelines on writing for radio are available from the RTE Radio Drama Department, Radio Centre, Donnybrook, Dublin 4, Republic of Ireland.

Recent broadcasting lesiglation allowed for the setting up of the **Irish Radio and Television Commission:** Marine House, Clanwilliam Court, Dublin 2, Republic of Ireland *tel* (01) 760966.

Independent, commercial, national and community radio services were in operation in 1990, and an independent national television service should be set up by the end of 1991.

NEW ZEALAND

Radio New Zealand Ltd, Chief Executive, Beverley Wakem, PO Box 2092, Wellington, C1 *tel* (04) 4741-555 *telex* NZ31031 *fax* (04) 4741-440. A 24 hour state-owned radio enterprise, with editorial and programming independence, controlling a NZ-wide group of commercial community stations and three public service non-commercial networks, and a shortwave service directed primarily to the Pacific area.

Television New Zealand Ltd, PO Box 3819, Auckland *tel* (09) 770-630 *telex* NZ 63047 Tvnzho *fax* (09) 750-916. *Chairman:* Brian Corban; *chief executive:* Julian Mountner.

Auckland Television Centre *tel* (09) 770-630. TVNZ is a state-owned enterprise with stations in all four main centres. It owns and operates Television One,

Channel 2 and three subsidiary companies, South Pacific Pictures Ltd, Avalon Ltd and Broadcast Communications Ltd.

TVNZ Avalon Ltd, PO Box 30945, Lower Hutt, Wellington *tel* (04) 666-969 *fax* (04) 678-959. *Managing director:* Reg Russ.

TVNZ Christchurch, PO Box 1945, Christchurch *tel* (03) 792-680 *fax* (03) 657-882.

TVNZ Dunedin & TVNZ Natural History Unit, PO Box 474, Dunedin *tel* (024) 799-799 *fax* (024) 799-917.

South Pacific Pictures Ltd, PO Box 35 656, Browns Bay, Auckland 10 *tel* (09) 479-3000 *fax* (09) 479-3007. *Managing director:* John McRae.

Broadcast Communications Ltd, PO Box 2396, Wellington *tel* (04) 826-000 *fax* (04) 859-652. *Managing director:* Dr Gerry Moriarty.

SOUTH AFRICA

South African Broadcasting Corporation, Private Bag XI, Auckland Park 2006 *tel* (011) 714-9111 *fax* (011) 714-3106. Operates five national networks: Radio South Africa, Radio Suid-Afrika, Radio 5, Radio Orion, Radio Allegro, and seven regional services, Radio Highveld, Radio Port Natal, Radio Good Hope, Radio Lotus, Radio Jacaranda, Radio Algoa, Radio Oranje. The nine radio services in Nguni and Sotho languages broadcast in Zulu, Xhosa, Southern Sotho, Northern Sotho, Tswana, Venda, Tsonga, Swazi and Ndebele. The External Service known as Radio RSA, *The Voice of South Africa*, transmits programmes to Africa and the India Ocean islands. The service which makes the greatest use of written material in English is Radio South Africa.

Drama. One-hour plays of all kinds are welcomed, both original works and adaptations/dramatisations – comedies, domestic dramas, thrillers, 'social' plays, etc. Half-hour plays are occasionally broadcast in a 'double bill' format, and about five 90-minute plays are broadcast annually. A series of weekly half-hour self-contained episodes (about 13 per series) is also broadcast. Serials (up to 65 15-minute episodes) are broadcast daily. These may be dramatisations or originals.

Radio Suid-Afrika also accepts quality material for translation into Afrikaans.

Short Stories. Short stories of all kinds, of between 1500 and 1800 words, are welcomed.

Children's Programmes. Short stories, plays and serials (maximum 15 minutes) may be submitted.

Talks. Most are locally commissioned, but outstanding material of particular interest may be submitted (3-10 minutes).

Television. There are four television services in seven languages.

Markets for Screenplays

JEAN McCONNELL

There have been setbacks for the British film industry recently. Nevertheless, a market still exists – particularly material being made for television or for videograms, with which many film companies are now very actively engaged.

The recommended approach is through a recognised literary agent, but most film companies have a story department to whom material can be sent for consideration. But it is a good idea to check with the company first to make sure it is worth your while.

It is a fact that many of the feature films these days are based on already best-selling books, but there are some companies, particularly those with a television outlet, which will sometimes accept unsolicited material if it seems to be exceptionally original. It is obviously sensible to try to sell your work to a company which is currently in active production, such as those listed below. *But again remember the best way to achieve success is through the knowledge and efforts of a literary agent.*

When a writer submits material direct to a company, some of the larger ones, usually those American based, may request that a Release Form be signed before they are prepared to read it. This document is ostensibly designed to absolve the company from any charge of plagiarism if they should be working on a similar idea; also to limit their liability in the event of any legal action. The writer must make up his own mind whether he wishes to sign this but, in principle, it is not highly recommended.

Markets for Screenplays and Television Programmes

Chapman Clarke TV (CCTV) (1983), Osborne House, 24 Pembroke Road, Clifton, Bristol BS8 3BB   *tel* (0272) 239270   *fax* (0272) 732170. *Contact:* Dr Jane Chapman. Films for cinema and TV; drama-documentaries; factual and educational programmes.

Children's Film and Television Foundation Ltd, Elstree Studios, Borehamwood, Herts. WD6 1JG   *tel* 081-953 0844   *fax* 081-207 0860.

The Walt Disney Company Ltd, 31-32 Soho Square, London W1V 6AP   *tel* 071-734 8111/734 5619. Screenplays not accepted by London office. *Must be submitted by an agent* to The Walt Disney Studios in Burbank, California

Mark Forstater Productions Ltd, 8a Trebeck Street, London W1Y 7RL   *tel* 071-408 0733   *telex* 8954665 Vbstlx G ref MFP   *fax* 071-499 8772. Films.

Hammer Film Production Ltd, Elstree Studios, Borehamwood, Herts. WD6 1JG   *tel* 081-953 1600   *fax* 081-905 1127.

HandMade Films (1978), 26 Cadogan Square, London SW1X 0JP   *tel* 071-581 1265 (will only consider material submitted through an agent known to the company).

Tony Klinger: Avton Communications and Entertainment Inc., 19 Watford Road, Radlett, Herts. WD7 8LF   *tel* (0923) 853255   *fax* (0923) 855757. Films.

London Film Productions Ltd, 44A Floral Street, London WC2E 9DA   *tel* 071-379 3366   *telex* 896805   *fax* 071-240 7065. *Managing director:* Steven North. No unsolicited material considered.

Merchant Ivory Productions Ltd (1962), Hanover House, 14 Hanover Square, London W1R 0BE   *tel* 071-437 1200/439 4335   *fax* 071-734 1579.

Paramount Pictures (UK) Ltd, Paramount House, 162-170 Wardour Street, London W1V 4AB   *tel* 071-287 6767   *fax* 071-734 0387. Material only accepted through agents.

Paravision (UK) Ltd (1989), 114 The Chambers, Chelsea Harbour, London SW10 0XF   *tel* 071-351 7070   *fax* 071-352 3645. *Contacts:* Linda Agran, Nick Barton. Films; drama and factual TV programmes.

Portman Entertainment Ltd (1970), Pinewood Studios, Iver Heath, Bucks. SL0 0NH   *tel* (0753) 630366   *telex* 849516   *fax* (0753) 630332. *Script editor:* Steve Matthews. Films for cinema and TV.

Twentieth Century Fox Productions Ltd, Twentieth Century House, 31-32 Soho Square, London W1V 6AP   *tel* 071-437 7766   *fax* 071-434 1435 (will not consider unsolicited material).

Tyburn Productions Ltd, Pinewood Studios, Iver Heath, Bucks. SL0 0NH   *tel* (0753) 651700   *telex* 847505   *fax* (0753) 656844. Submissions to Gillian Garrow, Director of Research and Development.

Warner Bros. Productions Ltd, 135 Wardour Street, London W1V 4AP   *tel* 071-437 5600 (will only consider material submitted through an agent).

Zenith Productions Ltd, 43-45 Dorset Street, London W1H 4AB   *tel* 071-224 2440   *cables* Zenithfilms London W1   *telex* 23348 Zenith   *fax* 071-224 3194. *Development manager:* Sarah Golding. No unsolicited scripts.

Literary Agents Specialising in Plays, Films, Television and Radio

Full particulars about these and other agents will be found in the section beginning on page 330.

*US Literary Agents

A & B Personal Management Ltd
Aquarius Literary Agency
Terence Baker Ltd
Yvonne Baker Associates
*Georges Borchardt, Inc.
*Brandt & Brandt Literary Agents, Inc.
Rosemary Bromley Literary Agency
*James Brown Associates, Inc.
Casarotto
Jonathan Clowes
Elspeth Cochrane Agency
Rosica Colin Ltd
Jane Conway-Gordon
Cruickshank Cazenove Ltd
Curtis Brown
*Liz Darhansoff Literary Agency
Reg Davis-Poynter
Felix De Wolfe
Susan Dunnett Management
*Ann Elmo Agency
Fact & Fiction Agency Ltd
Film Rights Ltd
Laurence Fitch Ltd
Jill Foster Ltd
John French Artists Agency Ltd
Kerry Gardner Management
Eric Glass
David Grossman Literary Agency
David Higham Associates Ltd
Valerie Hoskins
ICM/Duncan Heath Associates
Michael Imison Playwrights Ltd
International Scripts
Juvenilia
*Ben F. Kamsler
Frances Kelly Agency
Dieter Klein Associates
Peter Knight Agency
Lemon Unna & Durbridge Ltd
*Ellen Levine Literary Agency, Inc.
Barbara Levy Literary Agency

Christopher Little Literary Agent
London Independent Books Ltd
L.R. Associates
Andrew Mann Ltd
Blanche Marvin
MBA Literary Agents
*Peter Miller Agency, Inc.
Richard Milne
William Morris Agency (UK) Ltd
*Harold Ober Associates, Inc.
*Fifi Oscard Associates, Inc.
Mark Paterson & Associates
Penman Literary Agency
The Peters Fraser & Dunlop Group Ltd
PVA Management Ltd
Radala & Associates
Douglas Rae
Margaret Ramsay Ltd
*Marie Rodell-Frances Collin Literary Agency
Rostrum Literary Agency Ltd
Tessa Sayle Agency
*Susan Schulman
*Scott Meredith Literary Agency, Inc.
James Sharkey Associates Ltd
The Sharland Organisation Ltd
Anthony Sheil Associates Ltd
*Shukat Co. Ltd
*Singer Media Corporation
Micheline Steinberg Playwrights' Agent
*Sterling Lord Literistic, Inc.
*Roslyn Targ Literary Agency, Inc.
Jon Thurley
Lorna Vestey
*Austin Wahl Agency, Inc.
*Wallace Literary Agency, Inc.
Warner Chappell Plays Ltd
A.P. Watt Ltd
*Rhoda Weyr Agency
*Williams Wesley Winant

Illustration and design

Opportunities for Freelance Artists

CAMILLA BRYDEN-BROWN

FINE ART

Opportunities for freelance artists are more numerous than is generally supposed. For fine art such as painting, it is best to contact galleries, of which there are many in this country, particularly in London. It is worth remembering, though, that they have the choice of a large market and specialise in a fairly limited field. If you want to exhibit at these galleries, perhaps to have a one-man show, it is advisable to find out about the type of exhibitions they hold. This you can do by visiting each gallery yourself and assessing the current work. It is best to visit likely galleries frequently in order to get to know their work and how they function. *The Arts Review Yearbook* (£13.95, plus £2.00 postage and packing), published by Arts Review, 69 Faroe Road, London W14 0EL   *tel* 071-603 7530/8533, contains a guide to London and Regional Galleries – including a description of the type of work in which they specialise – and also a list of Art Organisations. If you decide to approach a gallery, it is usual to write to the director with a short description, and photographs of some of your work, with an sae for their return. The photographs should be clear, but not necessarily up to reproduction quality. It is possible to take the photographs yourself, but most towns have commercial photographers who work freelance for industry. Ask for an estimate first. Some of the greetings-card manufacturers listed in this book are interested in paintings for reproduction. It would be wiser to write to them, if possible enclosing good colour transparencies of your work, before becoming involved in the expense of packing and sending paintings by post or carrier. Other useful reference books for the artist are the *London Art and Artists Guide*, 5th edition (£6.95) and *The Artists Directory*, 3rd edition (£8.95); both published by Art Guide Publications, 35 Bedford Row, London WC1R 4JH   *tel* 071-242 0946.

One of the best methods of displaying and selling paintings is at the annual Summer Exhibition at the Royal Academy in London. Anyone can submit work, which is put to the Selection Committee and the Hanging Committee. Sending in days are in April and these dates must be strictly adhered to. A handling fee allows artists to enter up to three pieces of work at currently £9.00 per entry. Should any subsequently be hung and sold the Royal Academy charges commission at 25% plus VAT. Full details will be found in the leaflet of regulations entitled *Notice to Artists* which is obtainable from early February each year by sending an sae to The Registry, 'Summer Exhibition', The Royal Academy of Arts, Piccadilly, London W1V 0DS   *tel* 071-439 7438. This leaflet refers to the exhibition of the coming summer of that year. If requests for it are sent at other times of the year the Royal Academy can only send the leaflet from the previous February. Other exhibitions are listed in *Arts Review* (£2.20 fortnightly), which has a comprehensive exhibition guide for the whole of Great Britain, and *The Artist's & Illustrator's Magazine* (£1.85 monthly).

ILLUSTRATION AND DESIGN

For a career in the field of illustration and design it is advisable to have a training in illustration, and also in typography if possible. Although the latter is not absolutely essential, it is helpful to the artist and to the publisher. Now that desktop publishing and illustration software programs are available on personal computers the possibility of producing work with integrated type and drawing is fact. These programs and the printers and scanners are being improved at such speed that in the near future it will be practicable for an illustrator to present some work ready for press. Artists who launch into freelance work often do so gradually from the security of full-time employment, probably in the same field. It is useful to have the experience of working with a publisher or in an advertising agency or a studio first, as this gives the artist valuable background knowledge of suppliers and sources of work. Training in illustration can be obtained through a recognised course at art school, or through employment in a studio. Either method is an advantage, for even the most brilliantly gifted illustrator should know how to think in terms of printed work and to realise how work will reduce and reproduce.

Once an artist feels competent to accept commissions it is important to be available and reliable. Both these attributes are essential, and busy clients will not be bothered with artists who say vaguely that they had to go away or that the children were ill. Freelance work is a business, and will stand or fall by the competence or otherwise of the staff – you.

THE FOLIO

Artists who have already been in full-time employment in an advertising agency or publishing house will know of clients who are prepared to give them commissions, and if one commission is a success it will very often lead to another. For all artists, but particularly those with no connections, it is essential to make up a professional folio of work, spending some time and money on it, and showing as versatile a range of work as possible. For instance, it should include work in line, pencil, ink, line and tone, two or more colour line and full colour, and be on a variety of subjects. There are excellent folders, plastic envelopes or elaborate specimen books or cases containing plastic folders, for sale at most shops which stock equipment for designers. An overall colour scheme for your presentation helps to make your work look well-organised and professional. Designs or samples should be neatly trimmed and mounted on coloured cover paper (try black if in doubt) of a size to fit the folder or envelope. Paste the specimens of work on the cover paper, but do not use petroleum-based rubber solution if the sample of work is to be enclosed in a plastic envelope.

Gradually you will collect together printed specimens as the commissions increase, and your folio of work should be brought up to date all the time. Always get as many samples as you can beg, although if it is a book you may receive only one copy. In this case, see if you can get some extra dust-jackets so that should the first one become worn you can replace it; if necessary buy more copies of the book if that should also become worn. The publisher may well give you a discount on books on which you have worked. Any book specimens should be kept separately in plastic bags, but it would be expedient to ask for spare block pulls of your illustrations early on in the proceedings, and they should be mounted up in your specimen book. Try to keep your specimens immaculate.

PUBLISHERS

When the specimen folder is complete it is time to type letters to the production manager or art director of as many publishing houses as practicable, asking for an interview in order to show your work, whether for illustrations or for book-jackets, or both. It would be wise to design an attractive personal stationery range which can be an excellent advertisement of your work. There are print shops that will produce your design very well and advise you if you are not skilled in typography or finished artwork. Usually they print by lithography quickly and at a reasonable price. A letterheading, preferably A4 because this is the most popular size and therefore is easily filed, can also be used as a compliment slip, invoice and estimate if necessary. A business card can be very useful. Space these letters out, or you may find yourself with too many appointments in one week. The production managers will usually grant you interviews (be on time), since they are interested in seeing new work, and they will probably be helpful about prices too, if you have no experience in this field. Book-publishing houses as a rule are not able to pay as highly as advertising agencies or popular magazines but they are usually fair. Do not overlook educational departments of publishing houses for there is considerable scope for illustrating modern school books. You may have to accept low fees to begin with until you know your market and your worth, but you will be gaining valuable knowledge and experience. Newspapers are another source of work, also magazines.

At each interview it would be a good idea to ask if there is anyone else in the firm who would be interested in seeing your work, such as editors, who occasionally commission artists. Do not expect to be seen by other people in the firm at the same time as your first interview, but be prepared to come back another time. It would be better not to leave your samples to be seen by other people, particularly if you have only one folio. You will be needing your folio for other interviews, and there is a very real danger that it will go astray, or that specimens will be damaged beyond use, with no redress. If your work is liked and your first commission is satisfactory, you will often find that you will be recommended to other people in similar fields.

You would be very wise to make a contract with the publisher when commissioned. Some of the well-known illustrators have fought hard and long for fair conditions. The Society of Illustrators have produced a Standard Form of Contract. It is important for illustrators to realise that the artwork remains the property of the artist, and so does the copyright, and this includes commissioned work. You should make clear from the outset that the work belongs to you and that definitely you want it returned. Publishers have a sad history of losing artwork.

ARTISTS' AGENTS

Advertising agencies frequently use the services of artists' agents, who can be good or bad, but if you are accepted on the books of a good one life will be much easier for you. Agents generally work very hard on behalf of both clients and artists: they take the brief, negotiate the price and commission you to do the work, usually taking 25 to 30 per cent of the fee. Although this percentage may seem high, you should remember that they do a lot of work on your behalf and invariably manage to get a more professional fee for you than you can obtain for yourself, even after the percentage has been deducted.

FEES

There is no definite rule in assessing fees. A simple method of calculation is to decide upon a weekly salary and the number of hours of work for a normal week. This salary is then divided by the number of hours, which gives a basic hourly rate. Rent, rates, heating, telephone and other general studio costs should be considered, materials bought especially for a commission have to be added to the invoice concerned. As a rough guide one third of a fee will be payable to the Inland Revenue. Time spent at meetings with clients and the travelling time and cost involved should be added to the time sheet.

This solution may appear to be simple but it will be seen that the hourly rate is high. Many clients offer low fees and it is sometimes necessary to choose between accepting work at little or no return when the result is a good specimen of work, or to do without work. One of the greatest problems to the freelance artist is the artist in full-time employment who is prepared to accept commissions out of hours for a lower fee. With no studio overheads and a regular salary the market is spoilt for the serious professional.

ADVERTISING AGENCIES

Advertising agencies employ art buyers who are very skilled and capable people and should be approached by a letter similar to that previously described, giving details of the type of work at which you are best. Here again, once you have obtained the interview and shown your work, you might ask if there is anyone else who would be interested, not necessarily at that moment.

STUDIOS

Studios exist in most cities, and the type of their work varies; some specialise in purely commercial work in finished lettering and finished artwork, and they employ highly skilled and extremely able artists. Often their work involves the use of airbrushes and photographic skills, but they do sometimes employ freelance artists for specific commissions, and may well like to have photocopies of your work on file in case they need drawings or diagrams for catalogues or similar uses. Technical drawing is called technical drawing with good reason and requires specific training. If you feel your work would be of interest to a studio, write to the studio manager and ask for an interview. Should they ask for photographs of your work, a commercial photographic studio will prepare these for you. If you wish to have photographs made, the photographic studio will help you with the details and give you prices before they take on the work. Photocopies may be acceptable, especially now that colour copying is available. The studio might offer to photocopy work which they might like to keep for future reference.

GRAPHIC DESIGNERS

A graphic designer, who may be running a one-man studio of his own and doing freelance design and typography (designing for printing), may also use illustrators from time to time. They will not be able to use your work all the time, even if they like it, as not all their commissions require drawings. The more versatile you are the more opportunities are available to you, and artists skilled only in very specialised fields, such as lettering and illumination, usually know where to offer their work.

IMPORTANCE OF RELIABILITY

Remember also that once you have started to get commissions, you must be accurate and reliable, as well as available. If you are given a date for the work, it must be presented on time, even if this means sitting up half the night before. Do not, for example, fall back on the excuse of mild illness or you will lose sympathy and understanding should you have the misfortune to be more seriously ill. Once you have received the commission you are part of a team, even though you may not know the other members of it. There are often unforeseen events which hold up production anyway, and it is as well to see that you do not come to be considered one. It is wise to take trouble over the presentation, and you have only yourself to blame if you have not protected your finished work adequately. It is distressing to have one's precious work destroyed or damaged, the more so if it means doing it all again.

You will discover that once you have started freelance work your commissions will build up gradually, although most artists have some periods when there is little work available. Use these 'rests' advantageously to prepare more specimen drawings and to experiment with new techniques and equipment, and to make sure your folio is ready to show again. At such times you should be looking for new outlets, visiting more agencies and publishers, or checking with the ones you have visited in the past.

Above all decide whether or not you really want to do this work: are you sure it is not just a pleasant day-dream with the appeal of being called an artist. It is hard work, but if you have ability and are consistent, reliable, enthusiastic and optimistic, even at those times when there is a lull, then you will be happy and successful.

Markets for Artists

ART AGENTS AND COMMERCIAL ART STUDIOS

In their own interests, artists are advised to make preliminary enquiries before submitting work, and to ascertain terms of work. Commission varies but averages 25-30 per cent. **The Association of Illustrators** (full details under **Societies**) provides a valuable service for illustrators, agents and clients.

A.L.I. Press Agency, Ltd, Boulevard Anspach 111-115, B9–1000 Brussels, Belgium   *tel* 02 512 73 94   *fax* 02 514 17 19. *Director:* G. Lans. Cartoons, comics, strips, puzzles, entertainment features, illustrations for covers. All feature material for newspapers and magazines. Large choice of picture stories for children and adults. Market for transparencies. Paintings, portraits, nudes, landscapes, handicrafts.

Allied Artists Ltd, 24 York Street, London W1H 1FE   *tel* 071-487 2750   *fax* 071-487 2753. *Director:* Gary Mills. Represents over 30 artists specialising in highly finished realistic figure illustration for magazines, books, video and advertising, ranging from watercolour to airbrush. Also offers extensive library of second rights illustrations for syndication.

Associated Freelance Artists Ltd, 124 Elm Park Mansions, Park Walk, Chelsea, London SW10 0AR   *tel* 071-352 6890. *Directors:* Eva Morris, Doug Fitz-Maurice. Freelance illustrators mainly in children's and educational fields; strip illustration; and lots of greeting cards.

Beint & Beint (1976), 3 Leigh Street, London WC1H 9EW   *tel* 071-383 4363   *fax* 071-387 7206. *Proprietor:* Michele Beint. Illustrations in a variety of styles for advertising, design groups and some publishing.

Ian Fleming Associates Ltd (1970), 1 Wedgwood Mews, 12-13 Greek Street, London W1V 5LW   *tel* 071-734 8701   *fax* 071-439 3400. *Managing director:* Ian Fleming. Illustration and lettering for advertising and publishing. *Rate of commission:* 33⅓%.

Garden Studio (1929), 23 Ganton Street, Soho, London W1V 1LA   *tel* 071-297 9191   *fax* 071-287 9131. *Agents:* John Havergal, Harry Lyon-Smith. World-wide all-round coverage. *Commission:* 33⅓% (publishing 25%).

Simon Girling & Associates (1985), 61B High Street, Hadleigh, Suffolk IP7 5DY   *tel* (0473) 824083   *fax* (0473) 827846. Illustrations for book publishing (children's and adult), encyclopaedias, magazines, dust jackets, greeting cards. *Commission:* 28%.

Graham-Cameron Illustration (1988), 10 Church Street, Willingham, Cambridge CB4 5HT *tel* (0954) 60444   *fax* (0954) 61453. *Partners:* Mike Graham-Cameron, Helen Graham-Cameron. All forms of illustration for book publishers, advertising agencies, magazines and journals. Specialises in children's and educational markets.

The Guild of Aviation Artists (1971), Bondway Business Centre, 71 Bondway, London SW8 1SQ   *tel/fax* 071-735 0634. *President:* Michael Turner, PGAvA; *secretary:* Hugo Trotter, DFC. Professional body of 300 artists specialising in aviation art in all mediums. The Guild sells, commissions and exhibits members' work. *Rate of commission:* 25%.

Hambleside Design and Marketing Ltd (1990), 13 Southgate Street, Winchester, Hants SO23 9DZ   *tel* (0962) 840088   *telex* 477357 Hamble G   *fax* (0962) 840144. *Directors:* D.R. Yellop, R.A. Jeffery, R.B. Gamble (USA). Graphic art and design studio specialising in advertising and marketing materials. Enquiries from freelance illustrators, photographers welcome.

John Hodgson Agency (1965), 38 Westminster Palace Gardens, Artillery Row, London SW1P 1RR   *tel* 071-580 3773   *fax* 071-222 4468. Illustrations for advertising, publishing, design, editorial. Sae with samples please. *Commission:* 25%.

Image by Design (1987), 46 Castle Street, Frome, Somerset BA11 3BW   *tel/ fax* (0373) 61323. *Partners:* John R. Brown, Burniece M. Brown. Artwork for prints, greeting cards, calendars, posters, stationery, book publishing, jigsaw puzzles, tableware, ceramics. *Commission:* negotiable.

Image Directory (1987), 2 Eiffel Street, Hebden Bridge, West Yorks. HX7 8DE   *tel* (0422) 844647   *fax* (0422) 844647. *Proprietor:* Linda Brill. Illustrations in all styles and media suitable, in particular, for advertising and design groups, based in the North. *Commission:* 30%.

David Lewis Illustration Agency (1974), Worlds End Studios, 134 Lots Road, London SW10 0RJ   *tel* 071-351 4333   *telex* 893851 Wrenst G   *fax* 071-351 5044. *Contacts:* David Lewis and Matthew Doyle. All types of illustration for a variety of applications. Sae with samples essential. *Average commission:* 30%.

Libba Jones Associates (1983), Hopton Manor, Hopton, Nr Wirksworth, Derbyshire DE4 4DF   *tel* (062 985) 353   *fax* (062 985) 577. High quality artwork and design for china, greetings cards and gift wrap, jigsaw puzzles, calendars, prints, posters, stationery, book illustration, fabric design. Submission of samples required for consideration.

Juvenilia, Avington, Winchester, Hants SO21 1DB   *tel* (096278) 656   *fax* (0962) 64649. *Proprietor:* Mrs Rosemary Bromley. Professional artwork for the children's market considered. Picture books – particularly author illustrated. No games or play books. Preliminary letter with sae. *Commission:* 20%. Return postage for artwork and acknowledgement imperative.

London Art Services Ltd, 140 Southwark Street, London SE1 0SW   *tel* 071-928 1884. Artists, designers, illustrators and photographers. Art studio offering service in illustration, lettering, general art work, photography.

John Martin Artists, Ltd, 26 Danbury Street, Islington, London N1 8JU   *tel* 071-734 9000   *fax* 071-226 6069. *Directors:* W. Bowen-Davies, C.M. Bowen-Davies, B.L. Bowen-Davies; *production manager:* W. Bowen-Davies. Illustrations for children (educational and fictional), dust jackets, paperbacks, magazines, encyclopaedias, advertising. Return postage for any artwork sent please.

Meiklejohn (1971), 28 Shelton Street, Covent Garden, London WC2H 9JN   *tel* 071-240 2077   *fax* 071-836 0199. All types of illustration.

N.E. Middleton Ltd, 44 Great Russell Street, London WC1B 3PA   *tel* 071-580 1999   *fax* 071-436 8760. General.

Montague Ward (1989), Lime Trees, Cousley Wood, Wadhurst, East Sussex TN5 6EY   *tel* (0892 88) 3673/(0892) 890383. *Owner:* Mrs Kate Wilson. Country gallery, showing original paintings, which places artwork for publication for cards, prints, books, giftwrap, calendars. Please send samples and sae. *Commission:* by arrangement.

Maggie Mundy Illustrators' Agency, The Studio, 206 Hammersmith Road, London W6 *tel* 081-741 5862 *fax* 081-748 5532. Represents 40 artists in varying styles of illustration in publishing, editorial and advertising.

Oxford Illustrators Ltd (1968), Aristotle Lane, Oxford OX2 6TR *tel* (0865) 512331 *fax* (0865) 512408. Studio of 30 full-time illustrators working for publishers, business and industry – science, technical, airbrush, graphic, medical, biological, botanical, figure, cartoon, maps, diagrams, graphs. Macintosh generated artwork with Linotronic 300 output.

Rogers & Co., Artists' Agents—now **Temple Rogers Artists' Agency.**

Russell & Russell Associates (1987), 128 Wellington Road North, Stockport, Cheshire SK4 2LL *tel* 061-474 7131 *fax* 061-480 3358. *Partners:* George Russell, Janice Russell. All artwork considered for greeting cards, calendars, posters, book publishing, advertising and design. *Commission:* 30%.

Specs Art Agency (1982), 1 Clarence Road, Cheltenham, Glos. GL52 2AY *tel* (0242) 515951 *fax* (0242) 518862. *Director:* Roland Berry. High quality illustration work for advertisers, publishers and all other forms of visual communication.

Temple Rogers Artists' Agency, 120 Crofton Road, Orpington, Kent BR6 8HZ *tel/fax* (0689) 826249. Illustrations for children's educational books, picture strips and magazine illustrations. *Commission:* by arrangement.

Vicki Thomas Associates (1985), 22 Hickman Close, Fulmer Road, London E16 3TA *tel* 071-476 3086 *telex* 334003 Ref 42268 *fax* 071-407 3068. *Consultant:* Vicki Thomas. Considers the work of illustrators and designers working in greetings and gift industries, and promotes such work to gift, toy, publishing and related industries. Written application and samples required. *Commission:* from 25%.

Michael Woodward Licensing (1980), Parlington Hall, Parlington, Aberford, West Yorks. LS25 3EG *tel* (0532) 813913 *fax* (0532) 813911. *Proprietor:* Michael R. Woodward. International art agency and art library with offices in New York and Antwerp. Specialists in greeting cards, posters, prints, calendars. Character merchandising division. Terms on application. Freelance artists please send samples.

Young Artists (1970), 144 Royal College Street, London NW1 0TA *tel* 071-267 9661 *fax* 071-284 0486. Book covers, editorial, advertising. *Average commission:* 30%.

DRAWINGS, DESIGNS AND VERSES FOR CARDS, ETC.

In their own interest, artists are advised to write giving details of the work which they have to offer, and asking for requirements before submitting the work.

*Member of the Greeting Card and Calendar Association

Arnold Barton Cards Ltd—see **Hambledon Studios.**

Athena International, PO Box 918, Harlow, Essex CM20 2DU *tel* (0279) 641125. *Art directors:* P. Rodriguez, T. Jones, T. Taffs. Designs for greetings cards. Paintings and illustrations of a professional standard for reproduction as prints and posters. Sae essential for return of work.

Carlton Cards Ltd, Mill Street East, Dewsbury, West Yorkshire WF12 9AW *tel* (0924) 465200.

C.C.A. Stationery Ltd, Eastway, Fulwood, Preston PR2 4WS *tel* (0772) 794508. Publishers of personalised wedding stationery and Christmas cards. Pleased to consider original artwork, preferably of relevant subject matter, but verses not required.

Fine Art Graphics Ltd (incorporating **Raphael Tuck & Sons Ltd**), Dawson Lane, Dudley Hill, Bradford BD4 6HW *tel* (0274) 689514 *telex* 517669 *fax* (0274) 651218. *Managing director:* D.B. Roxburgh; *creative director:* D. Nicholls. Greeting card and calendar publishers.

*****Giesen & Wolff** (1908), Kaygee House, Dallington, Northampton NN5 7QW *tel* (0604) 755411 *telex* 311009 Kaygee G *fax* (0604) 759157. *Director:* Gordon Wood. Illustrations: floral studies, child and baby figures. Will consider verses.

Greetings Cards By Noel Tatt Limited (1954/1988), Unit 17, Roper Close, Canterbury, Kent CT2 7EP *tel* (0227) 455540 *fax* (0227) 458976. *Directors:* Noel Tatt, Vencke Tatt, Jarle Tatt, Diane Tatt, Paul Tatt. Greetings cards and gift wrap.

Hambledon Studios Ltd, Hambledon House, Marlborough Road, Accrington, Lancs. BB5 6BX *tel* (0254) 872266 *telex* 635169 Cardac G *fax* (0254) 872079. *Brands:* Arnold Barton, Donny Mac, Reflections, New Image. *Art managers:* D. Jaundrell, J. Ashton, D. Fuller; *creative directors:* D. Meloy, M. Smith. Designs suitable for reproduction as greetings cards.

*****Hayes Greeting Card Publishers Ltd** (1984), Thames View, Newtown Road, Henley-on-Thames, Oxon RG9 1HQ *tel* (0491) 410454. *Directors:* M.S. Belsten, R.H. Parker. Artwork: floral, cute, traditional.

*****Jarrold & Sons Ltd** (1770), Jarrold Publishing, Barrack Street, Norwich NR3 1TR *tel* (0603) 763300 *telegraphic address* Jarrold, Norwich *telex* 97497 *fax* (0603) 662748. *Managing director:* Antony Jarrold; *publication manager:* Caroline Jarrold. Drawings, transparencies (35mm or larger). Postcards, calendars, pictorial books on natural history, topography, hobbies, architecture. No verses.

Kardonia Ltd, Farrier Street, Worcester WR1 3BH *tel* (0905) 611294.

Thomas Leach Ltd, 54 Ock Street, Abingdon-on-Thames, Oxon OX14 5DE *tel* (0235) 520444 *fax* (0235) 554270. *Contact:* David J. Leach. Line drawings of religious subjects suitable for reproduction as Christmas or Easter Cards.

Leeds Postcards (1979), PO Box 84, Leeds LS1 1HU *tel* (0532) 468649 *fax* (0532) 436730. Workers co-operative. Publishers and producers of campaign postcards for the labour, environmental, women's and international justice movements.

*****Henry Ling & Son (London) Ltd,** Chiddingstone Causeway, Nr Tonbridge, Kent TN11 8JP *tel* (0892) 870333 *telex* 8813271 Gecoms G ref H087 *fax* (0892) 870466. Artwork for greeting cards; no verses. Address to: Product Manager – Greeting Cards.

The Medici Society Ltd, 34-42 Pentonville Road, London N1 9HG *tel* 071-837 7099. Requirements: paintings suitable for reproduction as large prints or greeting cards. Preliminary letter with brief details of work requested.

*Panache Studio Ltd (1985), Station Road, Henley-on-Thames, Oxon RG9 1LQ	*tel* (0491) 578383	*telex* 847279 HMK HO G	*fax* (0491) 578817. Drawings; humorous greetings card editorial.

*Photo Production Ltd, Featherby Road, Gillingham, Kent ME8 6PJ	*tel* (0634) 33241. Artwork for greeting card design. Will consider verses.

*Rainbow Cards Ltd (1977), Albrighton Business Park, Albrighton By-pass, Albrighton, Wolverhampton, West Midlands WV7 3QH	*tel* (090237) 4347. *Directors:* M. Whitehouse, R. Fellows, J. Whitehouse, I. Mackintosh. Artwork for greeting cards. No verses.

Reeves Dryad, PO Box 38, Leicester LE1 9BU	*tel* (0533) 510405	*telex* 341766 Dryad G	*fax* (0533) 515015. Dryad *500 Series,* full colour craft booklets, workcards and patterns.

Felix Rosenstiel's Widow & Son Ltd, Fine Art Publishers, 33-35 Markham Street, London SW3 3NR	*tel* 071-352 3551. Invite offers of originals of a professional standard for reproduction as picture prints for the picture framing trade. Oil paintings and strong watercolours. Any type of subject considered. Also subjects for decorative stationery trade.

*Royle Publications Ltd, Royle House, Wenlock Road, London N1 7ST	*tel* 071-253 7654. *Publishing director:* Barry M. Everitt. Greeting cards, calendars, fine art reproductions and social stationery. Only accept work in colour.

*Scandecor Ltd (1967), 3 The Ermine Centre, Hurricane Close, Huntingdon, Cambs. PE18 6XX	*tel* (0480) 456395	*telex* 32365	*fax* (0480) 456269. *Directors:* G. Huldtgren, A. Inghammar. Drawings all sizes.

*W.N. Sharpe Ltd, Bingley Road, Bradford BD9 6SD	*tel* (0274) 542244	*telex* 51408	*fax* (0274) 496099. Greetings cards, gift wrap. Artwork in colour; verses considered.

Solomon & Whitehead (Guild Prints) Ltd, Lynn Lane, Shenstone, Staffs. WS14 0DX	*tel* (0543) 480696	*fax* (0543) 481619. Fine Art prints and limited editions, framed and unframed.

Noel Tatt Ltd (1954), Coombe Valley Road, Dover, Kent CT17 0EU	*tel* (0304) 211644	*fax* (0304) 240470. *Directors:* Noel Tatt, Vencke Tatt, Derek Bates, Anthony Sharpe, Paul Tatt, Robert Dixon. Greetings cards, prints, postcards.

*United Greeting Card Co. (UK) Ltd (1969), River Park, Billet Lane, Berkhamsted, Herts. HP4 1EL	*tel* (0442) 871381. *Directors:* R.H. Seddon, M. Howard. Ideas and artwork for humorous greeting cards.

*Valentines of Dundee, Ltd, PO Box 74, Kinnoull Road, Dundee DD1 9NQ	*tel* (0382) 833338. Everyday greetings cards, Christmas cards, gift wraps, social stationery, St Valentine's Day, Easter, Mother's Day, Father's Day, calendars. Address to *The Director of Product Management.*

Webb Ivory Ltd, Queen Street, Burton-on-Trent, Staffs. DE14 3LP   *tel* (0283) 66311. Greeting card designs, particularly Christmas, suitable for charities and up-market ranges.

> See also the **Articles, reports and short stories** and the **Books** sections for lists of magazines, book publishers and packagers; the **Agents** section for literary agents (particularly for children's book illustration).
> It is recommended that artists read the article on copyright in the **Law and regulations** section; the **Publishing practice** section for information about formal agreements.

Photography

The Freelance Photographer and the Agent

BRUCE COLEMAN

Photographic agencies and libraries have a dual role in the service they provide. They meet the needs and demands of picture editors, picture researchers and art buyers and, at the same time, provide a service to the freelance photographer. The enterprising photographer, wishing to penetrate the publishing market, would do well to consider employing the services of an agent whose knowledge of current trends and client contact will gear the photographer's output to the requirements of the markets. The complexities of reproduction rights are best left to an agent – that's if the photographer wishes to protect the copyright of his work!

Selecting the right agent very much depends on the type of work the photographer is producing and he should, therefore, take a look at several agencies before choosing the one he thinks will be of advantage to him. Some agents, for example, work in the syndication area, selling news and topical pictures to the world's press; others are in the stock business maintaining a library of photographers' work orientated to the editorial market. Agents normally do not sell pictures outright but lease them for a specific use and fee from which they deduct a commission. A good photograph in the hands of a good agent can be published several times over and bring in royalties for many years.

Before submitting your work to an agent, a preliminary letter is recommended enquiring whether he is accepting new photographers and asking for details of his specific needs.

The agent will wish to see an initial presentation of at least two hundred photographs and the photographer should indicate the number of photographs he plans to submit in the course of a year. Agents are keen to encourage the active photographer who can supply a regular stream of good quality work. Serious attention should be given to the caption of every picture as this can often mean the difference between a sale or a rejection. A caption should be brief and legible and an example of a good nature caption would be:

> Spotted Hyena (*C. crocuta*)
> Serengeti
> Aggressive behaviour

or, a geographical caption:

> Canada: Northwest Territories
> Eskimo fur trappers and dogsled

Some time spent on the presentation of your work, editing for composition, content, sharpness and, in the case of transparencies, colour saturation, will create a favourable impression. When submitting original colour transparencies, to ensure they are protected from damage and also to facilitate easy examination, place them in clear plastic sleeves, never between glass. Do not submit transparencies which you may require for personal use as it is quite impossible for an agent to recall pictures at short notice from his client.

One final point, never supply similar photographs to more than one agent as the problems created by almost identical pictures appearing, say, on a calendar or a greeting card can be embarrassing and costly to rectify. Indeed, for this reason, many agents insist on an exclusive arrangement between themselves and their photographers.

How to run your own Picture Library

JOHN FELTWELL

Photographers seeking to have someone else place their work should consider the possibilities of engaging a photographic agency (*see* Bruce Coleman's piece above). Photographers wishing to market their work themselves, either as specialist libraries listed below, or those wishing to establish a library, might find useful the following guidelines and tips.

It is important to draw up strict terms of business to cover items such as search fee, holding fee, and particularly loss or damage to original transparencies (£100 to £500 per transparency. See also *Picture Research* article.) A month is reasonable time for transparencies to be reviewed, thereafter a weekly holding fee per transparency is recommended, unless stated otherwise. Search fees (up to £30) may or may not be waived if transparencies are accepted. Reproduction rights should be calculated according to territorial limitations, whether non-exclusive UK only, English speaking countries, world rights, etc., as well as size (small 'editorial' size to front cover). Sliding scales are required. Agree fees, including future fees, before publication.

Beware of and budget for use of transparencies by editors for preparation of 'dummies'; pictures used may not be accounted for in-house by the resident picture researcher if acquired by editors, sub-editors, etc. Forbid any slide projection of transparencies. Be wary of the use of transparencies from which artists can derive ideas, unless arranged, and of publicity/advertising companies who generate computer models and logos and bill accordingly. Beware of supplying private individuals (or freelances) who are naive to procedures. Some libraries ask for an official letter of request from the publisher.

The photographer's transparencies are treasured possessions. Unfortunately *some* publishers and magazines do not see it like that and treat them as dispensable and with some irreverence. You can be sure that picture researchers who are members of SPREd (full details at end of *Picture Research* article) know all about looking after transparencies and they are safe in their hands.

Make sure that dispatched transparencies (all sleeved) are well packed by whatever means (messenger, recorded, registered post) and are properly insured – and that the recipient knows when his or her liability starts and finishes. This includes transit to printers away from publishers' premises. Once accepted, transparencies may lie up for several months waiting to be used, this can run on to a year, unless strictly controlled. Arrange for payment six months after acceptance or on publication, whichever happens first, otherwise it might be on publication, some time off. Specify that transparencies are returned from printers in a clean condition without any printers' solvents, but with original mounts.

The *British Association of Picture Libraries and Agencies* (BAPLA) (13 Woodberry Crescent, London N10 1PJ *tel* 081-883 2531) mostly represents commercial and institutional libraries. Smaller libraries, who are perhaps more vulnerable to disputes, can only be assisted (the right is reserved) by BAPLA after first year membership (full £240 + VAT).

Pictures into Print

DAVID ASKHAM

Imagine completing a book-length manuscript, accompanied by a fine selection of your own photographs, only to discover that the publisher requires colour *transparencies*, whereas your illustrations are in the form of colour *prints*!

To an author such a set-back can be highly demoralising. Apart from the frustrations of lost time and opportunities, there is the daunting prospect of a major re-shoot of the photography, a costly conversion of negatives into transparencies, or facing up to hiring photographs from a picture library at a cost probably not included in the original budget.

Of course the street-wise photographer would probably not make such a fundamental mistake. Increasingly, however, more and more writers are undertaking the provision of their own photographs to illustrate their written work. And why not? Modern cameras are well-endowed with automatic features to simplify the task and are quite capable of yielding results perfectly acceptable for reproduction.

So this article is intended primarily for writers who wish to make a success of supplying their own photography. It will not transform them into multi-talented professional photographers. That would be wildly optimistic. Rather it will help them avoid basic mistakes, such as that mentioned earlier, and give some useful pointers to success.

It should be stressed, however, that an author should know and respect the upper limits of his or her photographic capabilities. A publisher will not thank you for second-rate results. If in doubt, consider engaging a talented colleague, though your agreement needs to take account of the ultimate division of labour. At all times be honest with your editor about the degree of confidence you have in providing acceptable photography.

On the positive side, many authors have acquired and developed photographic skills to the point where their work is highly accomplished in its own right. But first – back to basics.

BASIC REQUIREMENTS

Before embarking on any photography it is essential first to elicit a publisher's or editor's requirements. In the case of a book-length project the contract should set out, precisely, what the author accepts and is obliged to produce in terms of numbers of pictures and their breakdown, where appropriate, into colour or monochrome images. With illustrated features, it is less usual to have a written contract prior to production. Nevertheless, a letter should spell out the salient facts concerning the provision of pictures.

The question of fees and reproduction rights should also be addressed, not only for text but also for the illustrations. Publishers have budgets for their editorial needs and prior agreement on fees is essential if the contributing author is not to finish the commitment unwittingly well out of pocket. While photographic film may appear a relatively inexpensive item, travel to distant locations can inflate overall costs. Thought, therefore, must be given to the question of expenses.

Where colour is concerned, transparencies (derived from colour reversal or slide film) provide the better source for high quality reproduction than do colour prints. Of course there are exceptions and reproduction techniques are always improving. To be safe, however, always check with your publisher before deviating from industry standards. If in any doubt when, for example, you are producing pilot material to form the basis of a book proposal, do use colour slide film. Then, if the proposal is accepted, you have already made a valuable start with your photography.

Editors rarely influence the choice of pictorial content of images produced by authors, provided the pictures offered meet certain criteria and accepted standards. So, while the author would appear to enjoy unbridled freedom in deciding what pictures to take and supply to the publisher, the editor will only be satisfied if your pictures are truly relevant to the manuscript and the aim of your work, and are also of a satisfactory quality. Let us now look at these aspects in more detail.

PICTURE RELEVANCE

Images should complement and help to clarify the text. Additionally they can beautify and add interest. Picture subjects often suggest themselves. However there is a potential trap in sacrificing relevance when the most appropriate pictures are unavailable or difficult to acquire.

Take an example of a non-fiction book about London Midland and Scottish Railway locomotives which would clearly require illustrations of some, if not all, of the models described. It would be quite misleading to intermix pictures of the London and North Western Railway locomotives unless a specific point of comparison or contrast was being made. Without such justification, readers could become confused, misled and eventually lose interest in the book. The author's credibility would suffer. Fortunately such lack of relevance should be spotted at the editorial stage and the author would be required to rectify the error.

A biographer seeking to illustrate the boyhood home environment of an historical figure would be lucky indeed to find the actual dwelling, let alone the atmosphere of the period, unless immortalised in a museum. In the absence of contemporary artwork, it becomes acceptable to show the current locale provided captions clearly account for the time-shift.

Occasionally a publisher will have preferences or fixed ideas on the need for certain illustrations. Provided these ideas are feasible and reasonable they should be respected and added to the author's list of picture requirements.

PICTURE QUALITY

Next to relevance comes picture quality which is vitally important. Photographs should be *sharp* and *clear*. Modern cameras are capable of yielding high definition results provided the lens is correctly focused on the principal subject and the camera is held steady at the time of exposure. The latter calls for practice and suggestions for success appear in instruction manuals and books.

Paradoxically, a photograph may appear to be sharp but at the same time suffer from lack of clarity. Why should this be?

Usually the cause of such obfuscation is conflict and confusion in the picture area, caused by lack of thought at the time of exposure. Remedies lie in isolating the main subject by using certain simple techniques such as careful framing, differential focus or employing contrasting tones or colour.

It should be realised that no amount of camera automation will substitute for skill on the part of the photographer. Only the photographer can compose the picture in such a way as to communicate his or her ideas clearly and unambiguously to the reader.

Quality results also depend on reliable equipment, films, processing and presentation. Avoid skimping in any of these areas. It is not necessary to invest a small fortune in photographic equipment. A modern 35mm camera of a reputable make will serve an author well. Choose wisely taking counsel from a learned colleague or trusted dealer. Use fresh films and have them processed by a professional laboratory rather than a cut-price corner shop.

While the emphasis has been on colour photography, most of the principles apply equally to monochrome pictures. Black and white photography will continue to be an important source of illustration in publishing.

It is becoming more difficult to find good processors of black and white films which is why many photographers set up a small darkroom to print their own $10'' \times 8''$ or whole plate enlargements. In extremis, however, publishers can derive impressive black and white illustrations from colour transparency originals, albeit at a cost.

ADMINISTRATION

Once you start producing your own pictures for publication, it is important to consider their administration.

Each picture should be presented in such a way that your name, address, telephone number, reference and caption is clearly related to the subject. Records should be kept of pictures stored in your library and of those held by publishers. Despite all reasonable care losses will occasionally occur. Depending on circumstances, compensation should be claimed.

Colour transparencies need to be mounted, handled, stored and transmitted with extreme care if damage is to be avoided. Never mount colour transparencies intended for publication in glass.

Depending on urgency, pictures can be dispatched by post or courier services. In all cases they should be carefully packed and insured, if so inclined, according to their value.

Questions of copyright are addressed in detail in a separate chapter of this book (see page 391). Normally an author retains copyright both of his or her literary and artistic works unless these are assigned to a publisher. It is customary to assign only limited rights (eg First British Serial Rights for an article, or Single Reproduction Rights (qualified by territory and time if appropriate)) for pictures unless special circumstances prevail.

Occasionally problems arise in the reproduction of historic photographs, such as those produced, for example, by Henry Fox Talbot and other pioneering practitioners. By any definition these old pictures would be out of copyright by virtue of the time elapsed since the photographer's death. However trustees or independent commercial libraries often levy hire charges if material in their possession is subsequently reproduced.

In summary, authors are well placed to produce their own photography to illustrate their literary works. With sensible understanding of publishers' requirements and thoughtful application with the camera, writers will derive extra pleasure and profit from seeing their pictures, as well as words, in print.

List of Agencies and Picture Libraries

*Member of the British Association of Picture Libraries and Agencies

*A-Z Botanical Collection Ltd, Bedwell Lodge, Cucumber Lane, Essendon, Hatfield, Herts. AL9 6JB *tel* (0707) 49091 *fax* (0707) 46613. Colour transparencies of plant life world-wide, 5 × 4, 6 × 6, 35 mm.

Academic File News Photos (1985), Centre for Near East, Asia and Africa Research (NEAR), PO Box 571, 172 Castelnau, London SW13 9DH *tel* 081-741 5878 *telex* 940 12777 Near G *fax* 081-741 5671. *Director:* Sajid Rizvi. Daily news coverage in UK and general library of people and places, with special reference to the Middle East, North Africa and Asia. New photographers welcomed to cover UK and abroad.

*Ace Photo Agency (1980), 22 Maddox Street, London W1R 9PG *tel* 071-629 0303 *fax* 071-495 6100. General library: people, industry, travel, commerce, skies, sport, music and natural history. World-wide syndication. *Terms:* 50%. Sae for enquiries.

*Action Plus (1986), 54-58 Tanner Street, London SE1 3LL *tel* 071-403 1558 *fax* 071-403 1526. Comprehensive and creative coverage of action, venues and personalities in over 120 sports and leisure activities, worldwide. Extensive colour and b&w library of high quality work from staff and contributing photographers. *Terms:* 50%.

Lesley and Roy Adkins Picture Library (1989), Longstone Lodge, Aller, Langport, Somerset TA10 0QT *tel* (0458) 250075. Colour library covering archaeology and heritage; prehistoric, Roman and medieval sites and monuments; landscape, countryside, architecture, towns and villages.

Aerofilms Ltd (1919), Gate Studios, Station Road, Borehamwood, Herts. WD6 1EJ *tel* 081-207 0666 *fax* 081-207 5433. Comprehensive library of vertical and oblique aerial photographs of UK, large areas with complete cover.

Air Photo Supply (1963), 42 Sunningvale Avenue, Biggin Hill, Kent TN16 3BX *tel* (0959) 74872. Aircraft and associated subjects, South-East England, colour and monochrome. No other photographers' material required.

Al Ahram (1983), Barry Davies, Dyffryn, Bolahaul Road, Cwmffrwd, Carmarthen, Dyfed SA31 2LP *tel* (0267) 233625. Natural history, landscape (especially waterfalls), Egypt, children, outdoor activities. Formats 35 mm, 6 × 6 cm, 5 × 4 in. Other photographers' work not accepted.

Bryan and Cherry Alexander Photography (1973), Higher Cottage, Manston, Sturminster Newton, Dorset DT10 1EZ *tel* (0258) 73006 *fax* (0747) 51474. Arctic regions with emphasis on Eskimos, Lapps and the modern Arctic.

*All-Sport Photographic Ltd (1972), All-Sport House, 3 Greenlea Park, Prince George's Road, Colliers Wood, London SW19 2JD *tel* 081-685 1010 *telex* 8955022 *fax* 081-648 5240. International sport and leisure.

Rev. J. Catling Allen, St Giles House, Little Torrington, Devon EX38 8PS *tel* (0805) 22497. Library of colour transparencies (35 mm) and b&w photos of Bible Lands, including archaeological sites and the religions of Christianity, Islam and Judaism. Medieval abbeys and priories, cathedrals and churches in Britain. Also historic, rural and scenic Britain. (Not an agent or buyer.)

American History Picture Library, 3 Barton Buildings, Bath BA1 2JR *tel* (0225) 334213. Photographs, engravings, colour transparencies covering the exploration, social, political and military history of North America from 15th to 20th century. Conquistadores, Civil War, gangsters, Moon landings, etc. Prints and photos purchased.

*Ancient Art & Architecture Photo Library, 6 Kenton Road, Harrow-on-the-Hill, Middlesex HA1 2BL   *tel* 081-422 1214   *fax* 081-426 9479. Specialising in the history of civilisations of the Middle East, Mediterranean countries, Europe, Asia, Americas, from ancient times to recent past, their arts, architecture, beliefs and peoples.

Andes Press Agency (1983), 26 Padbury Court, London E2 7EH   *tel/fax* 071-739 3159. *Director:* Carlos Reyes. Social, political and economic aspects of Latin America, Africa, Asia, Europe and Britain. Specialising in contemporary world religions.

*Heather Angel, Highways, 6 Vicarage Hill, Farnham, Surrey GU9 8HJ   *tel* (0252) 716700   *fax* (0252) 727464. Colour transparencies (35 mm and $2\frac{1}{4}$ in square) and monochrome prints with world-wide coverage of natural history and biological subjects including animals, plants, landscapes, gardens, close-ups and underwater images; also China. Detailed catalogues on request.

*Animal Photography (1955), 4 Marylebone Mews, New Cavendish Street, London W1M 7LF   *tel* 071-935 0503   *fax* 071-487 3038. Horses, dogs, cats, East Africa, Galapagos.

Aqua Pics, 73 Rosehill Drive, Bransgore, Christchurch, Dorset BH23 8NR   *tel* (0425) 73430. Fishing: trout, coarse, sea, big game, tropical reef; whaling, travel, flora, fauna, scrimshaw, yachting, windsurfing.

*Aquarius Picture Library (1977 in UK), PO Box 5, Hastings, East Sussex TN34 1HR   *tel* (0424) 721 196. *Contact:* David Corkill. Colour and b&w library specialising in showbusiness: film stills, candids, portraiture, archive material to present. Also television, pop, opera, ballet and stage. World-wide representation and direct sales. Collections considered, either outright purchase or 50%-50% marketing.

*Aquila Photographics, Haydon House, Alcester Road, Studley, Warks. B80 7AN   *tel* (052 785) 2357   *fax* (052 785) 7507. Specialists in ornithological subjects, but covering all aspects of natural history, also pets and landscapes, in both colour and b&w.

Arctic Camera, Derek Fordham (1978), 66 Ashburnham Grove, Greenwich, London SE10 8UJ   *tel* 081-692 7651. Colour transparencies of all aspects of Arctic life and environment.

*Ardea London Ltd, 35 Brodrick Road, London SW17 7DX   *tel* 081-672 2067   *fax* 081-672 8787. Su Gooders. Specialist world-wide natural history photographic library of animals, birds, plants, fish, insects, reptiles.

*Aspect Picture Library Ltd (1971), 40 Rostrevor Road, London SW6 5AD   *tel* 071-736 1998/731 7362   *fax* 071-731 7362. General library including wildlife, tribes, cities, industry, science, Space.

The Associated Press Ltd, News Photo Department, The Associated Press House, 12 Norwich Street, London EC4A 1BP   *tel* 071-353 1390 (b&w library direct no.), 071-353 0354 (colour library direct no.)   *fax* 071-583 0218. News, feature pictures, sports.

*Aviation Photographs International (1970), 15 Downs View Road, Swindon, Wilts. SN3 1NS   *tel* (0793) 497179   *fax* (0793) 49179. All types of aviation and military subjects. Assignments undertaken.

*Aviation Picture Library (Austin J. Brown) (1970), 35 Kingsley Avenue, West Ealing, London W13 0EQ   *tel* 081-566 7712   *fax* 081-566 7714   *cellphone*

(0860) 292661. World-wide aviation photographic library, dynamic views of aircraft. Travel library including Europe, Caribbean, USA, and East and West Africa. Material taken since 1960. Specialising in air to air and air to ground commissions.

B. & B. Photographs (1974), Prospect House, Clifford Chambers, Stratford upon Avon, Warks. CV37 8HX *tel* (0789) 298106 *fax* (0789) 292450. 35 mm colour library of horticulture (especially pests and diseases) and biogeography (world-wide), natural history (especially Britain) and biological education. Other photographers' work not represented.

Alan Band Associates (Bandphotos), 25 Longdown Road, Farnham, Surrey GU10 3JL *tel* (0252) 713022 *fax* (0252) 737719. International news and feature picture service for British and overseas publishers.

*Barnaby's Picture Library, 19 Rathbone Street, London W1P 1AF *tel* 071-636 6128/9 *fax* 071-637 4317. Requires photographs for advertising and editorial publication. Photographs not purchased, sender retains copyright.

*BBC Hulton Picture Library—see Hulton Picture Company.

Dr Alan Beaumont, 52 Squires Walk, Lowestoft, Suffolk NR32 4LA *tel* (0502) 560126. World-wide collection of monochrome prints and colour transparencies (35 mm and 6 × 7 cm) of natural history, countryside, windmills and aircraft. Subject lists available. No other photographers required.

Bee Photographs—see Heritage & Natural History Photography.

Stephen Benson Slide Bureau, 45 Sugden Road, London SW11 5EB *tel* 071-223 8635. World: agriculture, archaeology, architecture, commerce, everyday life, culture, environment, geography, science, tourism. Speciality: South America, the Caribbean, Australasia and Nepal. Assignments undertaken.

BIPS-Bernsen's International Press Service Ltd, 9 Paradise Close, Eastbourne, East Sussex BN20 8BT *tel* (0323) 28760. (For full details see page 121.)

*John Birdsall Photography (1980), 75 Raleigh Street, Nottingham NG7 4DL *tel* (0602) 782645 *fax* (0602) 785546. *Contact:* Clare Marsh. Multicultural, contemporary social documentary library covering children/youth, education, old age, housing, work/services; also Nottingham and surrounding area.

*The Anthony Blake Photo Library, 54 Hill Rise, Richmond, Surrey TW10 6UB *tel* 081-940 7583 *fax* 081-948 1224. Food and wine around the world, including shops, restaurants, markets, agriculture and viticulture. Commissions undertaken. Contributors welcome.

*John Blake Picture Library (1975), 7 High Street, Thornbury, Bristol, Avon BS12 2AE *tel* (0454) 418321/413240 *fax* (0454) 416636. England, Scotland and Wales: landscapes, architecture, churches, gardens, countryside, towns and villages. General topography of Europe, the Americas and Middle and Far East. Horse Trials covered including Badminton and Gatcombe Park. *Terms:* 50%.

Blitz International News & Photo Agency (1988), Blitz Photographic Studios, 41a London Road, Bognor Regis, West Sussex PO21 1PQ *tel* (0243) 830407. *Contact:* Simon Green. Comprehensive library of colour transparencies and monochrome prints (35 mm, medium and large formats). Action and sports photography (especially yachting and motorsport, including Le Mans 24hr race), travel, natural history, landscapes and aerial, reportage, personalities, news, advertising shots, general. Commissions undertaken and photographers accepted. *Terms:* 50%. Catalogue on request.

Bodleian Library, Oxford OX1 3BG   *tel* (0865) 277000/277214   *fax* (0865) 277182. Photographic library of 30,000 35 mm (5 × 4 in to order) colour transparencies, of subjects mostly from medieval manuscripts with iconographical index to illuminations.

***Janet and Colin Bord,** Melysfan, Llangwm, Corwen, Clwyd LL21 0RD   *tel* (049 082) 472   *fax* (049 082) 321. Library of b&w photos and colour transparencies, specialising in the prehistoric and Roman sites of Britain, but also covering rural and scenic Britain in general, e.g. landscapes, wild flowers, villages, churches. Also strange phenomena. Do not act as agents for other photographers.

Boxing Picture Library, 3 Barton Buildings, Bath BA1 2JR   *tel* (0225) 334213. Prints, engravings and photos of famous boxers, boxing personalities and famous fights from 18th century to recent years.

***Bridgeman Art Library,** 19 Chepstow Road, London W2 5BP   *tel* 071-727 4065/ 229 7420   *fax* 071-792 8509. Documentary and fine art collection; specialists in top quality colour transparencies relating to the arts: European and Oriental paintings and prints, Christmas material, antiques, arms and armour, history, natural history, maps, manuscripts, sculpture, topography, transport and many other subjects. Represents many major UK museums and art galleries. Catalogue available.

***Britain on View Photographic Library,** official photographic library for British Tourist Authority and English Tourist Board. Colour library operated on their behalf by **Syndication International** *q.v.* For details of b&w, contact Manager, Design, BTA, Thames Tower, Black's Road, London W6 9EL   *tel* 081-846 9000   *fax* 081-563 0302. General UK travel including many special subjects.

Hamish Brown, 21 Carlin Craig, Kinghorn, Fife KY3 9RX   *tel* (0592) 890422. Photographs and 35 mm transparencies of Scottish sites and topographical, Morocco, mountain ranges of Europe, Africa, India and South America. Commissions undertaken. No pictures purchased.

***Camera Press Ltd** (1947), Russell Court, Coram Street, London WC1H 0NB   *tel* 071-837 4488/9393/1300/0606   *telex* 21654 Camrap G   *fax* 071-278 5126. B&w prints and colour transparencies covering British Royalty, portraits of world statesmen, politicians, entertainers, sportspersons, etc., documentary, animals, fashion, human interest. *Terms:* 50%.

***Camerapix**—see **C.P.L. (Camerapix Picture Library).**

***J. Allan Cash Photolibrary (J. Allan Cash Ltd),** 74 South Ealing Road, London W5 4QB   *tel* 081-840 4141   *fax* 081-566 2568. World-wide photographic library: travel, landscape, natural history, sport, industry, agriculture. Details available for photographers interested in contributing.

***Celtic Picture Library** (1985), Trefnant, St Asaph, Clwyd   *tel/fax* (0745) 730395. All subjects relating to Wales: ancient monuments, crafts and customs, conservation, farming, industry, landscapes, tourism, environment, wildlife.

***The Central Press Photos Ltd**—see **Hulton Picture Company.**

***Cephas Picture Library,** 20 Trafalgar Drive, Walton-on-Thames, Surrey KT12 1NZ   *tel/fax* (0932) 241903. People, places, agriculture, industry, religion, architecture, travel, food and wine, crafts; wine industry and vineyards. *Terms:* 50%.

***City Syndication Ltd**—see **Monitor Syndication.**

Bruce Coleman Inc., 381 Fifth Avenue, New York, NY 10016-3314, USA *tel* 212-683-5227 *telex* 429093 Bcinc *fax* 212-689-6140. *President:* Norman Owen Tomalin. Specialising exclusively in colour transparencies. All formats from 35 mm acceptable. All subjects required.

*Bruce Coleman Ltd, Unit 16, Chiltern Business Village, Arundel Road, Uxbridge, Middlesex UB8 2SN *tel* (0895) 57094 *fax* (0895) 72357. Colour transparencies on natural history, ecology, environment, geography, archaeology, anthropology, agriculture, science, scenics and travel.

*Collections (1990), 13 Woodberry Crescent, London N10 1PJ *tel* 081-883 0083 *fax* 081-883 9215. Traditional British customs, bridges, castles, horticulture, babies, children, pregnancy, steam trains, and lots of other British things.

Colorific Photo Library, Unit C1, Enterprise Business Estate, Mastmaker Road, London E14 9TE *tel* 071-723 5031 *fax* 071-262 6870. Handling photos of top international photographers, most subjects currently on file, upwards of 150,000 images. Represent *Sports Illustrated*. New York agencies: Black Star, Contact Press Images Inc., Wheeler Pictures, Picture Group, Visages, Los Angeles; Cosmos, Paris; Focus, Germany; Camara Tres, Brazil.

*C.P.L. (Camerapix Picture Library), 8 Ruston Mews, London W11 1RB *tel* 071-221-0077 *telex* 263996 *fax* 071-792 8105; and PO Box 45048 Nairobi, Kenya *tel* 223511/334398 *telex* 22576 *fax* 217244. Africa, Middle East, Pakistan, Nepal, Maldives, India; portraits, agriculture, industry, tribal cultures, landscapes. Wildlife including rare species. Islamic portfolio; Mecca, Medina, Muslim pilgrimage. News material available and special assignments arranged. Further material available from collection held in Nairobi.

Crafts Council Picture Library (1973), 44a Pentonville Road, Islington, London N1 9BY *tel* 071-278 7700 *fax* 071-837 6891. Large, medium and small format transparencies available for reproduction and an extensive collection of slides available for loan only. Subjects covered include ceramics, jewellery, textiles, metal and silver, furniture, wood, glass, knitting, weaving, bookbinding, fashion accessories, toys and musical instruments. Information Service available.

*Lupe Cunha (1987), 843-845 Green Lanes, London N21 2RX *tel* 081-360 0144 *fax* 081-886 6812. Specialist library on all aspects of childhood from pregnancy to school age, including large section devoted to health and child development. Commissioned photography undertaken. Also represents collection on Brazil for Brazil Photo Agency. *Terms:* 50%.

The Dance Library (1983), PO Box 6, Moreton-in-Marsh, Glos. GL56 0RQ *tel* (0608) 74414 *fax* (0608) 74555. Contemporary and historical dance: classical ballet, jazz, tap, disco, popping, ice dancing, musicals, variety, folk, tribal rites and rituals.

Das Photo (1975), Cherry Trees, 1 Chatton Row, Bisley, Surrey GU24 9AP *tel* Brookwood (04867) 3395; and Chalet le Pin, Domaine de Bellevue 181, 6940 Septon, Belgium *tel* (086) 32 24 26. Arab countries, Americas, Europe, Amazon, folklore, world festivals, archaeology, people, biblical, markets, sailing, motor bikes.

Dennis Davis Photography (1984), The Flat, Himbleton Manor, Droitwich, Worcs. WR9 7LE *tel* (090) 569 506. Rare breeds of domestic livestock, agricultural landscapes, country life, architecture – interiors and exteriors, landscape and coastal.

*James Davis Travel Photography, 30 Hengistbury Road, New Milton, Hants BH25 7LU *tel* (0425) 610328 *fax* (0425) 638402. *Proprietor:* James Davis. Stock transparency library specialising in world-wide travel photos. Supply tour operators, publishers, advertising agents, etc. Submissions of larger format transparencies, 6 × 6 cm or larger, considered. 35 mm only of specialised subjects, e.g. underwater, etc. *Terms:* 50%.

*Peter Dazeley; Extensive Golf Library from 1970. The Studios, 5 Heathmans Road, Parsons Green, London SW6 4TJ *tel* 071-736 3171 *fax* 071-736 3356. Players, tournaments, courses world-wide and various related material. Colour, b&w.

Derbyshire Scene (1989), 66 Norfolk Street, Glossop, Derbyshire SK13 9RA *tel* (0457) 862997. The Derbyshire County and all its aspects: people, places, life and natural history. Commissions undertaken. *Terms:* 50%.

George A. Dey (1986), 'Drumcairn', Aberdeen Road, Laurencekirk, Kincardineshire, Scotland AB30 1AJ *tel* (05617) 8845. Scottish Highland landscapes, Highland Games, forestry, castles of NE Scotland, gardens, spring, autumn, winter scenes, veteran cars, North Holland.

*Douglas Dickins Photo Library (1946), 2 Wessex Gardens, Golders Green, London NW11 9RT *tel* 081-455 6221. World-wide collection of colour transparencies (mostly 6 × 6 cm, some 35 mm) and b&w prints (10 × 8 in originals), specialising in Asia, particularly India and Indonesia; also, USA, Canada, France, Austria and Switzerland.

Gordon Dickson (1975) Flagstones, 72 Catisfield Lane, Fareham, Hants PO15 5NS *tel* (0329) 42131. Colour transparencies of fungi, in natural habitat; also butterflies, moths, beetles. No other photographers required.

*C.M. Dixon, The Orchard, Marley Lane, Kingston, Canterbury, Kent CT4 6JH *tel* (0227) 830075. Europe and Ethiopia, Iceland, Sri Lanka, Tunisia, Turkey, USSR. Main subjects include agriculture, archaeology, architecture, clouds, geography, geology, horses, industry, meteorology, mosaics, mountains, occupations, people.

Ecoscene (1987), Sally Morgan, 4 Heatherview Cottages, Shortfield, Frensham, Surrey GU10 3BH *tel* (025125) 4395 *fax* (025125) 5695. Natural history, specialising in the environment and ecology. Subjects include animal and plant species, habitats, conservation, energy, industry, all forms of pollution; world-wide coverage. *Terms:* 55% to photographer.

Edifice (1987), 14 Doughty Street, London WC1N 2PL *tel* 071-405 9395 *fax* 071-267 3632. Architecture (especially detail), landscape, gardening. No other photographers' material required.

T. Malcolm English, BA, LRPS, MRAeS, 3 The Bakery, Silver Street, Stevington, Beds. MK43 7QN *tel* (02302) 4150. Aviation photographic library specialising in military, historic and air weapons.

*English Heritage Photo Library (1984), Room 517, Fortress House, 23 Savile Row, London W1X 1AB *tel* 071-973 3338/3339 *fax* 071-973 3001. Wide range of large format colour transparencies ranging from ancient monuments to artefacts, legendary castles to stone circles, elegant interiors to industrial architecture.

*Greg Evans Photo Library (1979), 91 Charlotte Street, London W1P 1LB *tel* 071-636 8238 *fax* 071-637 1439. World-wide travel and winter skiing; UK travel, people, industrial, commercial, social, animals, food and sports. Commissions undertaken. *Terms:* 50%. No search/service fee.

*__Mary Evans Picture Library,__ 59 Tranquil Vale, Blackheath, London SE3 0BS *tel* 081-318 0034 *fax* 081-852 7211. Over two million historical illustrations from antiquity to the recent past. Also runs of British and foreign illustrated periodicals. Special collections: Sigmund Freud Copyrights, Society for Psychical Research, Fawcett Library (women's rights), Bruce Castle Museum, Ernst Dryden Collection, London University Harry Price Collection and many individual photographers 1930s–1960s.

*__Eyeline Photos__ (1979), 259 London Road, Cheltenham, Glos. GL52 6YG *tel* (0242) 513567 *telex* 43432 DSA G ref Eyeline *fax* (0242) 573498. Watersports, particularly sailing and powerboating, world-wide; equestrian events. *Terms:* 50%.

*__Feature-Pix Colour Library (World Pictures),__ 85a Great Portland Street, London W1N 5RA *tel* 071-437 2121 *fax* 071-439 1307. *Directors:* Gerry Brenes, Joan Brenes, David Brenes. Colour transparencies (2¼ in sq or larger), on travel and allied subjects. Undertake photography on assignment for tour operators, National Tourist Offices. *Terms:* 50%.

__Vivien Fifield__ (1981), 10 Claremont Road, Teddington, Middlesex TW11 8DG *tel* 081-943 3516. Engravings, drawings and b&w photos covering the history of science, medicine and technology up to the late 1930s.

__Focus Picture Library,__ 75A Selby Road, Garforth, Leeds LS25 1LR *tel* (0532) 863016. Transparencies, 35 mm/6 × 9 cm. Landscapes, rivers, buildings, British Isles, especially Yorkshire and Northern Counties. Also popular European regions, especially Greece. Assignments undertaken. No new photographers required.

__Ron and Christine Foord,__ 155b City Way, Rochester, Kent ME1 2BE *tel* (0634) 847348. Colour picture library of 1000 species of wild flowers, British insects, garden flowers, pests and diseases, indoor plants, cacti, countryside views.

*__Werner Forman Archive__ (1975), 36 Camden Square, London NW1 9XA *tel* 071-267 1034 *telex* 295931 Unicom G *fax* 071-267 6026. Art, architecture, archaeology, history and peoples of ancient, oriental and primitive cultures.

__Fortean Picture Library,__ Melysfan, Llangwm, Corwen, Clwyd LL21 0RD *tel* (049 082) 472 *fax* (049 082) 321. Library of colour and b&w pictures covering all strange phenomena: UFOs, Loch Ness Monster, ghosts, Bigfoot, witchcraft, etc.

__Fotoccompli–The Picture Library__ (1989), 11 Ampton Road, Edgbaston, Birmingham B15 2UH *tel* 021-454 3305 *fax* 021-454 9257. Comprehensive library, ranging from aircraft to wildlife, serving the Birmingham and West Midlands areas. *Terms:* 50%; minimum retention period – two years.

__Fotomas Index,__ 5 Highland Croft, Beckenham, Kent BR3 1TB *tel* 081-663 6628 *fax* 081-650 7429. Specialises in supplying pre-20th century (mostly pre-Victorian) illustrative material to publishing and academic worlds, and for television and advertising. Complete production back-up for interior décor, exhibitions and locations.

__Fotosports International__ (1969), The Barn, Swanbourne, Bucks. MK17 0SL *tel* (0296) 720773 *fax* (0296) 728181; 227 27th Manhattan Beach, CA 90266, USA *tel* 213-546-7078 *fax* 213-545-6175. Sports events and players, domestic, European, international. American football, athletics, baseball, cricket, golf, motor sport, tennis, soccer.

*__Fox Photos—see Hulton Picture Company.__

Freelance Focus (1988), 7 King Edward Terrace, Brough, North Humberside HU15 1EE *tel* (0482) 666036 *fax* (0482) 665680. *Contact:* Gary Hicks. UK/international network of stock-shooting photographers. Over two million stock pictures available, covering all subjects, world-wide, at competitive rates. Assignments undertaken for all types of clients. Further details/subject list available on request.

Frost Historical Newspaper Collection, 8 Monks Avenue, New Barnet, Herts. EN5 1DB *tel* 081-440 3159. (For full details see **Historical Newspaper Loan Service** under **Editorial, Literary and Production Services.**)

Brian Gadsby Picture Library, Route de Maubourguet, Labatut-Riviere 65700, Hautes Pyrenees, France *tel* 62 96 38 44. Colour (2¼ in sq, 6 × 4.5 cm, 35 mm) and b&w prints. Wide range of subjects but emphasis on travel, natural history, children.

Colin Garratt—see **Railways and Locomotives of the World Photo Library.**

*****Genesis Space Photo Library** (1990), Peppercombe Lodge, Horns Cross, Bideford, Devon EX39 5DH *tel* (0237) 451 756 *fax* (0237) 451 600. *Contact:* Tim Furniss. Specialises in rockets, spacecraft, spacemen, Earth, Moon, planets.

*****GeoScience Features,** 6 Orchard Drive, Wye, Kent TN25 5AU *tel* Wye (0233) 812707 *fax* (0233) 812707. *Director:* Dr Basil Booth. Colour library (35 mm to 5 × 4 in). Natural history, ecology, geology, geography, macro/micro, natural phenomena. Americas, Africa, Australasia, Europe, Indian subcontinent, SE Asia. Incorporates K.S.F. colour library.

Geoslides, 4 Christian Fields, London SW16 3JZ *tel* 081-764 6292. *Library director:* John Douglas. Geographical and general interest subjects from Africa, Asia, Antarctic, Arctic and sub-Arctic areas. Australian cover through Associate Picture Library: Blackwoods S.A. Interested only in large recent collections of relevant colour transparencies, regionally based. *Terms:* 50% on UK sales. Photographs for all types of publications, television, advertising.

Mark Gerson Photography, 3 Regal Lane, Regents Park Road, London NW1 7TH *tel* 071-286 5894/267 9246. Portrait photographs of personalities, mainly literary, in colour and b&w from 1950 to the present. No other photographers' material required.

Global Syndications (1990), Chartwood Towers, Punchbowl Lane, Dorking, Surrey RH5 4ED *tel* (0306) 741213 *fax* (0306) 875347. *Managing editor:* Sam Hall. Colour transparencies of all aspects of Arctic life and environment, particularly Eskimo (Inuit) and Lapps (Sami); Scandinavia and UK (landscapes, people, etc.). Assignments undertaken. No other photographers required.

John Glover (1979), 2 Struan Cottages, Church Fields, Witley, Godalming, Surrey GU8 5PP *tel/fax* (0428) 683322. Gardening, UK landscapes, native flora. Commissions undertaken.

*****Martin and Dorothy Grace** (1984), 40 Clipstone Avenue, Mapperley, Nottingham NG3 5JZ *tel* (0602) 208248 *fax* (0602) 626802. General British natural history, specialising in native trees, shrubs, flowers, habitats and ecology.

Tim Graham (1970), 31 Ferncroft Avenue, London NW3 7PG *tel* 071-435 7693 *fax* 071-431 4312. British Royal Family in this country and on tours; background pictures on royal homes, staff, hobbies, sports, cars, etc. English and foreign country scenes.

Greater London Photograph Library, 40 Northampton Road, London EC1R 0HB *tel* 071-606 3030 ext. 3823 *fax* 071-833 9136. Over 350,000 photographs of London and the London area from *c.*1860 to 1986. Especially strong on local authority projects – schools, housing, open spaces, etc.

Greek Island Photos (1985), Willowbridge Publishers, Bridge House, Southwick Village, Nr Fareham, Hants PO17 6DZ *tel* (0705) 375570. Country and urban facets of most Greek islands. Commissions undertaken.

Robert Haas Photo Library (1978), 11 Cormont Road, Camberwell, London SE5 9RA *tel* 071-326 1510. Holland, Greek Islands, Morocco, Scottish oil industry, Notting Hill Carnival, skies. *Specialities:* people; New York City, Lloyd's of London, Docklands.

*Robert Harding Picture Library, 58-59 Great Marlborough Street, London W1V 1DD *tel* 071-287 5414 *fax* 071-631 1070. Photographic library. Require photographs of outstanding quality for editorial publications. Telephone or write for details.

Harper Horticultural Slide Library, 219 Robanna Shores, Seaford, VA 23696, USA *tel* 804-898-6453. 150,000 35 mm slides of plants and gardens.

Heritage & Natural History Photography, Dr John B. Free, 37 Plainwood Close, Summersdale, Chichester, West Sussex PO19 4YB *tel* (0243) 533822. Archaeology, history, agriculture: Mexico, Mediterranean countries, Oman, Iran, USSR, India, Nepal, Thailand, Japan, UK. Bees and bee keeping, insects and small invertebrates, tropical crops and flowers.

Christian Him, Jazz Picture Library (1979), 12 Greystoke Lodge, Hanger Lane, Ealing, London W5 1EW *tel* 081-998 1232. Comprehensive library of b&w photos and colour transparencies of blues and jazz musicians. Buy/sell other photographers' work. *Terms:* 50%.

Historical Picture Service, 3 Barton Buildings, Bath BA1 2JR *tel* (0225) 334213. Engravings, prints and photos on all aspects of history from ancient times to 1920. Special collection Old London: buildings, inns, theatres, many of which no longer exist.

Pat Hodgson Library, Jasmine Cottage, Spring Grove Road, Richmond, Surrey TW10 6EH *tel* 081-940 5986. Small social history collection of 19th century engravings. Special picture research in 19th century periodicals, prints, etc. also undertaken. Modern b&w photos: topographical and archaeological.

*Holt Studios Photographic Library (Agricultural) (1981), The Courtyard, 24 High Street, Hungerford, Berks. RG17 0NF *tel* (0488) 683523 *fax* (0488) 683511. World-wide agriculture: crop production and protection, including healthy crops and relevant weeds, pests, diseases and deficiencies; farming, people, machines, landscapes and environmental factors; livestock. Assignments undertaken.

Horizon International Creative Images (1978), 7 Bury Place, London WC1A 2LA *tel* 071-831 1109 *fax* 071-831 9005. Transparencies: models, Space, travel, people, sport, special effects, abstracts and illustrations. Specialist collections on Australia, New Zealand, China and the Far East.

David Hosking, ARPS, Pages Green House, Stowmarket, Suffolk IP14 5QA *tel* (0728) 861113 *fax* (0728) 860222. Natural history subjects, especially birds covering whole world. Also Dr D.P. Wilson's unique collection of marine photos.

Houses & Interiors Photographic Features Agency (1987), 2D The Colonnade, Rye Road, Hawkhurst, Kent TN18 4ES *tel* (0580) 754078 *fax* (0580) 754197. *Contact:* Richard Wiles. Stylish house interiors and exteriors, home dossiers, renovations, architectural details, interior design. Also step-by-step photographic sequences of practical subjects. Colour and b&w. Commissions undertaken. *Commission:* Library 50%, Agency negotiable.

*Hulton Picture Company, Unique House, 21-31 Woodfield Road, London W9 2BA   *tel* 071-266 2662   *fax* 071-289 6392. One of the largest picture resources in Europe, with many millions of b&w and colour images. Specialises in social history, Royalty, transport, war, fashion, sport, entertainment, people, places and early photography. Collections include *Picture Post*, *Express*, *Evening Standard*, Keystone, Fox and Topical Press. Exclusive UK agents for Bettmann Archive, New York.

*The Hutchison Library (1976), 118b Holland Park Avenue, London W11 4UA   *tel* 071-229 2743   *fax* 071-792 0259. General colour library; world-wide subjects: agriculture, environments, festivals, human relationships, industry, landscape, peoples, religion, towns, travel.

*The Illustrated London News Picture Library, 20 Upper Ground, London SE1 9PF   *tel* 071-928 2111   *fax* 071-928 1469. Engravings, photos, illustrations in b&w and colour from 1842 to present day, especially 19th and 20th century social history, wars, portraits, Royalty. Travel archive including The Thomas Cook collection.

*The Image Bank (1979), 7 Langley Street, London WC2H 9JA   *tel* 071-240 9621   *fax* 071-831 1489. Hi-tech, special effects, food, still life, sports, scenic, people, industry, medical, business and concepts. Free catalogue featuring 1200 images from 450 photographers available on request.

*Images of Africa Photo Bank (1983), 11 The Windings, Lichfield, Staffs. WS13 7EX   *tel* (0543) 262898   *fax* (0543) 417154. *Contact:* David Keith Jones. Colour and b&w covering wildlife, traditional and modern people, land, resources, beauty, tourist attractions, hotels and lodges, National Parks and Reserves. *Terms:* 50%.

*Imperial War Museum (1917), Department of Photographs, Lambeth Road, London SE1 6HZ   *tel* 071-416 5000   *fax* 071-416 5374. National archive of over five million photos, dealing with war in the twentieth century involving the armed forces of Britain and the Commonwealth countries. Visitors' Room open by appointment Mon-Fri; restricted service on Sat. Enquiries should be as specific as possible; prints made to order.

International Press Agency (Pty) Ltd (1934), PO Box 67, Howard Place 7450, South Africa   *tel* (021) 531 1926   *fax* (021) 531 8789. Press photos for South African market.

JS Library International (1979) 101A Brondesbury Park, London NW2 5JL   *tel* 081-451 2668   *fax* 081-459 0223. The Royal Family, world-wide travel pictures, particularly the African continent, stage and screen celebrities, authors, world-wide general material. New material on any subject, in any quantity, always urgently required. Assignments undertaken.

*Keystone Collection—see **Hulton Picture Company.**

Lakeland Life Picture Library (1979), Langsett, Lyndene Drive, Grange-over-Sands, Cumbria LA11 6QP   *tel* (05395) 33565. English Lake District: industries, crafts, sports, shows, customs, architecture, people. Not an agency. Catalogue available on request.

*Landscape Only (1986), Dufours Place Studio, 14a Dufours Place, Broadwick Street, London W1V 1FE   *tel* 071-437 2655/734 7344   *fax* 071-287 0126. Outdoor subjects: villages, countryside, places, landscape, countries, travel, towns, cities. *Terms:* 50%.

*Frank Lane Picture Agency Ltd, Pages Green House, Wetheringsett, Stowmarket, Suffolk IP14 5QA   *tel* (0728) 860789   *fax* (0728) 860222. Natural history and meteorology.

Michael Leach, Brookside, Kinnerley, Oswestry, Shropshire SY10 8DB   *tel* (069 185) 639. General wildlife and natural history subjects, particularly mammals and owls. Special emphasis on urban wildlife.

Lears Magical Lanterns Museum, Spa Road, Llandrindod Wells, Powys D1 5EJ   *tel* (0597) 824737. 10,000 lantern slides, mainly Victorian, some Edwardian; all subjects.

*The MacQuitty International Collection, 7 Elm Lodge, River Gardens, Stevenage Road, London SW6 6NZ   *tel* 071-385 6031. 300,000 photos covering aspects of life in 70 countries: archaeology, art, buildings, flora and fauna, gardens, museums, people and occupations, scenery, religions, methods of transport, surgery, acupuncture, funeral customs, fishing, farming, dancing, music, crafts, sports, weddings, carnivals, food, drink, jewellery and oriental subjects. Period: 1920 to present day.

Mander & Mitchenson Theatre Collection (a Registered Charity), The Mansion, Beckenham Place Park, Beckenham, Kent BR3 2BP   *tel* 081-658 7725. Prints, drawings, photos, programmes, etc., theatre, opera, ballet, music hall, and other allied subjects including composers, playwrights, etc. All periods. Available for books, magazines, TV.

Mansell Collection Ltd, 42 Linden Gardens, London W2 4ER   *tel* 071-229 5475.

John Massey Stewart, 20 Hillway, Highgate, London N6 6QA   *tel* 081-341 3544. Large collection Russia/USSR: topography, people, culture, etc., plus Russian and Soviet history, 2000 pre-revolutionary PCs, etc. Also Britain, Europe, Asia (including Mongolia and South Korea), Alaska, USA, Israel, Sinai, etc.

*S. & O. Mathews, Stitches Farm House, Eridge, East Sussex TN3 9JB   *tel* Rotherfield (089 285) 2848. Country life, landscapes, gardens and flowers.

Chris Mattison, 138 Dalewood Road, Beauchief, Sheffield S8 0EF   *tel* (0742) 364433. Colour library specialising in reptiles and amphibians; other natural history subjects; habitats and landscapes in SE Asia, South America, USA, Mexico, Mediterranean. Captions or detailed copy supplied if required. No other photographers' material required.

Robin May Collection, 23 Malcolm Road, London SW19 4AS   *tel* 081-946 8965. Library specialising in Western Americana and the theatrical arts.

Merseyside Photo Library (1989), 65 Woodside Business Park, Woodside, Birkenhead, Wirral L41 1EH   *tel* 051-647 6898   *fax* 051-647 6803 (operated by Ron Jones Associates). Library specialising in images of Liverpool and Merseyside; now being expanded to include NW England, other destinations and general stock photos.

*Microscopix (1986), Middle Travelly, Beguildy, Nr Knighton, Powys LD7 1UW   *tel* (054 77) 242. Scientific photo library specialising in high quality colour photomicrographs for technical and aesthetic purposes. Commissioned work, both biological and non-biological, undertaken offering a wide variety of applicable micropical techniques.

Military History Picture Library, 3 Barton Buildings, Bath BA1 2JR   *tel* (0225) 334213. Prints, engravings, photos, colour transparencies covering all aspects of warfare and uniforms from ancient times to present.

*Monitor Syndication (1960), 17 Old Street, London EC1V 9HL   *tel* 071-253 7071   *telex* 24718   *fax* 071-251 4405. *General manager:* David Willis. Specialists in portrait photos of leading national and international personalities from politics, trade unions, entertainment, sport, Royalty and well-known buildings in London. Incorporates the **City Syndication** library.

Mountain Visions (1984), Graham and Roslyn Elson, 25 The Mallards, Langstone, Havant, Hants PO9 1SS   *tel* (0705) 478441. Colour transparencies of mountaineering, skiing, and associated travel, in Europe, Africa, Himalayas, Arctic, Far East and Australia. Do not act as agents for other photographers.

*David Muscroft Snooker Photography and **David Muscroft Picture Library** (1977), 16 Broadfield Road, Heeley, Sheffield S8 0XJ   *tel* (0742) 589299   *fax* (0742) 550113. Snooker; most other sports, Northern England news, personalities, features, events. Falkland Islands from 1880.

The Mustograph Agency, 19 Rathbone Street, London W1P 1AF   *tel* 071-636 6128/9   *fax* 071-637 4317. Britain only. General subjects of countryside life, work, history and scenery.

National Motor Museum, Beaulieu, Photographic Library, Beaulieu, Hants SO42 7ZN   *tel* (0590) 612345   *fax* (0590) 612655. All aspects of motoring, cars, commercial vehicles, motor cycles, traction engines, etc. Illustrations of period scenes and motor sport. Also large library of 5×4 in and smaller colour transparencies of veteran, vintage and modern cars, commercial vehicles and motor cycles.

*Natural History Photographic Agency—see **NHPA**.

Natural Image, Dr Bob Gibbons (1982), 49 Bickerley Road, Ringwood, Hants BH24 1EG   *tel/fax* (0425) 478742. Colour library covering natural history, gardening, countryside and travel. Special emphasis on conservation. Commissions undertaken. *Terms:* 60% to photographer.

New Blitz TV, Via Cimabue 5, 00196 Rome, Italy   *tel* 32 01 489/32 00 620   *fax* 32 19 014 (see page 124).

Newsfocus Press Photograph Agency Ltd (1989), 18 Rosebery Avenue, London EC1R 4TD   *tel* 071-833 8691   *fax* 071-278 9180. *Contact:* David Fowler. Specialises in colour and b&w portrait photos of leading British and international personalities, especially politics, entertainment, Royalty, trade unions, media. No search/service fees to clients. *Terms:* 50%; occasional outright purchase.

*NHPA, Little Tye, 57 High Street, Ardingly, West Sussex RH17 6TB   *tel* (0444) 892514   *fax* (0444) 892168. Represents 50 of the world's leading natural history photographers covering a wide range of fauna and flora, landscapes and environmental subjects. Specialisations include high-speed photography, a large Kalahari Bushmen collection, and the wildlife of North America and southern Africa. UK agents for Australasian Nature Transparencies.

Frank Nowikowski (1985), 3 Bush Drive, Rugeley, Staffs. WS15 2AO   *tel* (0889) 584885. 4×5in Scottish scenics; Africa: animals, landscape, social; South America: Argentina, Peru, Uruguay, people, animals, scenics; Italy: Rome, Florence; Paris, Barcelona, Brussels; children, education, environmental themes.

Operation Raleigh Picture Library (1978), The Powerhouse, Alpha Place, Flood Street, London SW3 5SZ   *tel* 071-351 7541   *fax* 071-351 9372. *Manager:* Mark Bainbridge. Colour and b&w library, including original artwork by expedition artists, covering expeditions and locations in over 50 countries.

Material ranges from adventure to architecture, trekking to tribal customs. Will advise on photographers to accompany expeditions. *Terms:* 50%.

Orion Press, 55 1-Chome, Kanda Jimbocho, Chiyoda-ku, Tokyo 101, Japan   *tel* (03) 3295-1400   *telex* J2 4447 Orionprs   *fax* (03) 3295-0227.

Christine Osborne Pictures/Inc. Middle East Pictures (1975), 53a Crimsworth Road, London SW8 4RJ   *tel/fax* 071-720 6951. Muslim countries of the Middle East and North Africa; South-East Asia and Pacific basin; Indo-Pak. sub-continent – travel, environment, socio-economic. Colour and b&w. Over 60 countries.

*Oxford Scientific Films Ltd, Photo Library, Long Hanborough, Oxford OX7 2LD   *tel* (0993) 881881   *telex* 83147 Viaor OSF   *fax* (0993) 882808. Comprehensive collection of colour transparencies of wildlife and scenics worldwide. Illustrated articles on natural history topics. UK agents for *Animals Animals*, New York and *Okapia*, Frankfurt. Representatives in New York, Tokyo, Milan, Barcelona, Frankfurt, Copenhagen, Paris, Amsterdam.

*Panos Pictures (1986), 9 White Lion Street, London N1 9PB   *tel* 071-278 1111   *telex* 9419293 Panos G   *fax* 071-278 0345. All aspects of Third World rural and urban life; deforestation, desertification, pollution, agriculture, health, etc. *Terms:* 50%.

Rosemary Pardoe, Flat One, 36 Hamilton Street, Hoole, Chester CH2 3JQ. Heraldic subjects, especially royal arms in churches, hatchments; also inn signs (heraldic and general). Not an agency.

Ann & Bury Peerless, 22 King's Avenue, Minnis Bay, Birchington-on-Sea, Kent CT7 9QL   *tel* Thanet (0843) 41428. Art, architecture, geography, history, social and cultural aspects in India, Pakistan, Bangladesh, Sri Lanka, Thailand, Malaysia and parts of the Middle East, Egypt and Africa. Specialist material on world religions: Hinduism, Buddhism, Jainism, Christianity, Islam, Sikhism.

*Photo Flora (1982), 46 Jacoby Place, Priory Road, Birmingham B5 7UN   *tel* 021-471 3300. Comprehensive collection of British wild plants; Mediterranean botany and travel; Egypt, North India, Tibet, China, Nepal.

*Photo Library International, PO Box 75, Leeds LS7 3NZ   *tel* (0532) 623005   *telex* 55293 Chacom G/PLI   *fax* (0532) 625366. Colour transparencies 35 mm to 10 × 8 in. Most subjects. New material always welcome.

Photo Link (1990), Unit 101B, The Argent Centre, 60 Frederick Street, Birmingham B1 3HS   *tel* 021-236 2152   *fax* 021-236 7842. *Contact:* Mike Vines. Colour and b&w aviation library, covering subjects from 1909 to the present day. Specialises in air-to-air photography. Assignments undertaken.

*Photofusion (previously **The Photo Co-op**) (1979), 17A Electric Lane, Brixton, London SW9 8LA   *tel* 071-228 8949   *fax* 071-738 1462. Collection of colour and b&w photos on contemporary social issues, including health, housing, homelessness, education, family and work.

*The Photographers' Library (1978), 81A Endell Street, Covent Garden, London WC2H 9AG   *tel* 071-836 5591. Requires material on world-wide travel, industry, agriculture, commerce, sport, people, leisure, girls, scenic. Colour only. *Terms:* 50%.

*Photo Resources, The Orchard, Marley Lane, Kingston, Canterbury, Kent CT4 6JH   *tel* (0227) 830075. Ancient civilisations, art, archaeology, world religions, myth, and museum objects covering the period from 30,000 BC to AD 1900. European birds, butterflies, trees.

Pictor International Ltd, Twyman House, 31-39 Camden Road, London NW1
9LR *tel* 071-482 0478 *fax* 071-267 1396. International photographic library –
all subjects, especially industry technology, people. *Rates:* 50%. Offices also
in Paris, Milan, Munich, New York and Washington.

****Picturepoint Ltd,** Hurst House, 157-169 Walton Road, East Molesey, Surrey
KT8 0DX *tel* 081-941 4520 *fax* 081-979 6671. Have ready world-wide
markets for high quality colour transparencies. Any subject other than *news*.
Minimum of 250 pictures in first submission. Send by Registered Mail enclosing
stamps or IRC for returns. *Terms:* 5-year contract, 50% commission.

Sylvia Pitcher (1968), 75 Bristol Road, Forest Gate, London E7 8HG *tel* 081-
552 8308. Specialist in rural south-east USA, including musicians, blues, jazz,
old time country.

Pixfeatures (Mr P.G. Wickman), 5 Latimer Road, Barnet, Herts. EN5 5NU *tel*
081-449 9946 *fax* 081-441 6246. Picture-features, preferably topical.
Especially for sale to British, German, South African, Spanish and American
magazines. *Terms:* 35% of all sales, unless otherwise arranged.

****Planet Earth Pictures: Seaphot Ltd** (1969), 4 Harcourt Street, London W1H
1DS *tel* 071-262 4427 *fax* 071-706 4042. Marine, surface and underwater;
natural history and environments on land and underwater; people, places;
Space.

****Popperfoto (Paul Popper Ltd),** 24 Bride Lane, London EC4Y 8DR *tel* 071-353
9665/6 *telex* 8814206 *fax* 071-583 1019. Offer documentary and feature
photos (b&w and colour) from all countries of the world. Collection includes
Exclusive News Agency, Odhams Periodicals Photo Library, Conway Picture
Library, Reuters, United Press International (UPI) Library, Planet, Agence-
France Presse and European Pressphoto Agency.

Power Pix International Picture Library—see **S. & I. Williams Power Pix
International Picture Library.**

****Premaphotos Wildlife,** 2 Willoughby Close, King's Coughton, Alcester, Warks.
B49 5QJ *tel/fax* (0789) 762938. Library of 35 mm transparencies of own
work only by K.G. Preston-Mafham and Dr R.A. Preston-Mafham. Wide
range of natural history subjects from around the world. All work done in
the field.

Press Association Photos (news picture service of The Press Association), 85
Fleet Street, London EC4P 4BE *tel* 071-353 7440 *telex* 922330 *fax* 071-
936 2363.

Pro-file Photo Library (1982), 4th Floor, Min Yip Building, 67 Jervois Street,
Hong Kong *tel* 5442255 *fax* 5459263. *Director:* Neil Farrin. General photographic library; also pictures of old Hong Kong. *Terms:* 50%.

Punch Cartoon Library (1841), *Punch*, 245 Blackfriars Road, London SE1
9UZ *tel* 071-921 5900 *fax* 071-928 2874. Comprehensive collection of
cartoons and illustrations, indexed under subject categories: humour, historical events, politics, fashion, sport, etc.

****Railways and Locomotives of the World Photo Library** (1969), The Square,
Newton Harcourt, Leics. LE8 0FQ *tel* (053759) 2068. Thousands of professional railway photos from Colin Garratt's world-wide collection. Steam
trains of all shapes and sizes, in every climate and mood. British preserved
stock and tourist lines, plus modern traction. Colour transparencies, b&w.
Captions, editorial, articles and book production. New colour brochure available on request.

*Retna Pictures Ltd (1984), 1 Fitzroy Mews, Cleveland Street, London W1P 5DQ *tel* 071-388 3444 *fax* 071-383 7151. Library of colour transparencies and b&w prints of rock and pop performers, show business personalities, celebrities, actors and actresses, travel and general stock library.

*Retrograph Archive (1984), 164 Kensington Park Road, London W11 2ER *tel* 071-727 9378/9426 *fax* 071-229 3395. Specialised picture library offering international graphic design, 1860-1960, drawn from rare sources. In most cases originals held, copied to specification on request.

Rich Research (1978), 1 Bradby House, Carlton Hill, St John's Wood, London NW8 9XE *tel* 071-624 7755. *Director:* Diane Rich. Speedy and innnovative picture research service. Visuals found for all sectors of publishing and the media. Stock images, commissioned photography and artwork. Negotiations of rights and fees.

*Ann Ronan Picture Library, Wheel Cottage, Bishops Hull, Taunton, Somerset TA1 5EP *tel* (0823) 252737 *fax* (0823) 336785. Woodcuts, engravings, etc., of history of science and technology from *c.*1500-*c.*1900.

The Royal Photographic Society (1853), The Octagon, Milsom Street, Bath BA1 1DN *tel* (0225) 462841 *fax* (0225) 448688. Exhibitions; library of books, photos and photographic equipment.

Royal Society for Asian Affairs, 2 Belgrave Square, London SW1X 8PJ *tel* 071-235 5122. Archive library of original 19th and 20th century b&w photos, glass slides, etc., of Asia. Publishes *Asian Affairs* 3 times p.a.

*Science Photo Library (1979), 112 Westbourne Grove, London W2 5RU *tel* 071-727 4712 *fax* 071-727 6041. Scientific photography of all kinds – medicine, technology, Space, nature.

Scotland in Focus Picture Library (1988), 22 Fleming Place, Fountainhall, Galashiels, Selkirkshire TD1 2TA *tel* (05786) 256. Library specialising in all aspects of Scotland, plus Europe, wildlife and natural history. All Scottish subjects required on 35 mm and upwards and b&w print. Photographers must enclose return postage. *Commission:* 50%.

SCR Photo Library (1943), Society for Cultural Relations with the USSR, 320 Brixton Road, London SW9 6AB *tel* 071-274 2282 *telex* 888941 Lcci G attn SCR. Russian and Soviet life and history. Comprehensive coverage of cultural subjects: art, theatre, folk art, costume, music. Also posters and theatre props, artistic reference and advice. Research by appointment only.

*Sealand Aerial Photography (1976), Goodwood Airfield, Goodwood, Chichester, West Sussex PO18 0PH *tel* (0243) 781025 *fax* (0243) 531422. Aerial photo coverage of any subject that can be photographed from the air in the UK. Most stock on 2¼ in format colour negative/transparency. Subjects constantly updated from new flying.

*Sefton Photo Library, 30-30A Mason Street, Manchester M4 5EY *tel* 061-832 7670 *fax* 061-834 9423. *Director:* S. Samuels. General library covering Britain, the world, sport, leisure, etc. Submissions considered from other photographers. Assignments undertaken.

S & G Press Agency Ltd, 68 Exmouth Market, London EC1R 4RA *tel* 071-278 1223. Press photos and vast photo library. Send photos, but negatives preferred.

Mick Sharp (1981), Eithinog, Waun, Penisarwaun, Caernarfon, Gwynedd LL55 3PW *tel* Llanberis (0286) 872425. Archaeology, ancient monuments, architecture, churches, countryside, environment, history, landscape, travel and tourism. Emphasis on British Isles, but material from many other countries including France, Iraq, Morocco and USA. Access to other similar photo collections. B&w prints from 5 × 4 in negatives, and 35 mm colour transparencies.

Brian and Sal Shuel—see **Collections.**

*****Skyscan Balloon Photography** (1984), Oak House, Toddington, Cheltenham, Glos. GL54 5BY *tel* (0242) 621357 *fax* (0242) 621343. Aerial views of British landscapes, cities, heritage sites, etc., taken from remotely controlled cameras suspended beneath a tethered balloon.

The Slide File (1978), 79 Merrion Square South, Dublin 2, Republic of Ireland *tel* (01) 766850 *fax* (01) 608332. Specialise in Eire and Northern Ireland: landscapes, Irish natural history, agriculture and industry, Irish people and their traditions, Celtic archaeological heritage.

Patrick Smith Associates (1964), Gloucester House, High Street, Borth, Dyfed SY24 5NZ *tel* (0970) 871296. South London 1950-1977, mid-Wales, aviation. The Patrick Smith Collection, comprised of London photos, now in The Museum of London.

Society for Anglo-Chinese Understanding (1965), Sally & Richard Greenhill Photo Library, 357a Liverpool Road, London N1 1NL *tel* 071-607 8549. Colour and b&w prints of China, late 1960s-1989.

Society for Cultural Relations with the USSR—see **SCR Photo Library.**

Source Photographic Archives (1974), 66 Claremont Road, Sandymount, Dublin 4, Republic of Ireland *tel* (01) 607090. *Director:* Thomas Kennedy. Mostly recent photos by living photographers on many different subjects.

Southern Media Services, division of **Maximedia Pty Ltd**, PO Box 268, Springwood, NSW 2777, Australia *tel* (047) 514967 *fax* (047) 515545. *Directors:* Nic van Oudtshoorn, Daphne van Oudtshoorn. Stock colour library, also illustrated features.

*****Spectrum Colour Library,** 146 Oxford Street, London W1N 9DL *tel* 071-637 2108. Require high quality colour transparencies for all markets. Need all subjects except topical or 'hot news' pictures – list of requirements available on receipt of sae.

*****Sporting Pictures (UK) Ltd,** 7A Lambs Conduit Passage, Holborn, London WC1R 4RG *tel* 071-405 4500 *fax* 071-831 7991. *Director:* Crispin J. Thruston; *librarians:* Mark Whitmore, Ellis Badillo. Specialising in sports, sporting events, sportsmen.

Peter Stiles Picture Library, 50 Chippers Road, Worthing, West Sussex BN13 1DG *tel* (0903) 61978. Specialising in horticulture, plus natural history, pictorial views. Sequences and illustrated features. Own pictures only. Commissions undertaken.

*****Stockphotos,** 7 Langley Street, London WC2H 9JA *tel* 071-240 7361 *fax* 071-831 1489. Stock colour library covering travel, people, business, industry, scenics, sport and leisure. Free catalogue available on request.

*****Tony Stone Worldwide,** Worldwide House, 116 Bayham Street, London NW1 0BA *tel* 071-267 7166 *fax* 071-722 9305. International photo library. Subjects required: travel, people, natural history, commerce, industry, technology, sport, etc. Check first with Creative Department. *Terms:* 50%.

*****Survival Anglia Photo Library** (1960), 48 Leicester Square, London WC2H 7FB *tel* 071-321 0101 *fax* 071-493 2598. Outstanding natural history collection, by some of world's top wildlife photographers, the result of over 30 years of the award-winning ITV programme 'Survival'. *Terms:* 50%.

Sutcliffe Gallery, 1 Flowergate, Whitby, North Yorkshire YO21 3BA   *tel* (0947) 602239. Collection of 19th century photography, all by Frank M. Sutcliffe, Hon. FRPS (1853-1941). Especially inshore fishing boats and fishing community, also farming interests. Period covered 1872 to 1910.

*Syndication International Ltd, 4-12 Dorrington Street, London EC1N 7TB   *tel* 071-404 0004   *telex* 267503   *fax* 071-430 2437. Photo library specialising in pop, Royalty and personalities. Agents for Mirror Group Newspapers, BBC News and Current Affairs photos; the *Financial Times* photos and computer generated graphics. Extensive world travel pictures from Berlitz, the British Tourist Authority and the English Tourist Board.

Charles Tait Photo Library (1978), Kelton, St Ola, Orkney KW15 1TR   *tel* (0856) 3738   *fax* (0856) 5313. Orkney, Shetland, Western Isles, North Scotland, France, especially Paris, Provence, including wildlife, archaeology, transport, events, farming, fishing, people. Panoramic landscape transparencies a speciality. Publisher of postcards, calendars and guidebooks.

*The Telegraph Colour Library, Unit C1, Enterprise Business Estate, Mastmaker Road, London E14 9TE   *tel* 071-987 1212   *fax* 071-538 3309. Collection covers a wide range of subjects, including photography commissioned by *The Telegraph Magazine* since 1964. Representations include Space Frontiers, a comprehensive collection of space photography and images. Sameday service for all UK clients. Free catalogues available upon request.

Theatre Museum, 1E Tavistock Street, Covent Garden, London WC2E 7PA   *tel* 071-836 7891 ext. 129   *fax* 071-836 5148. The Theatre Museum is not a picture library, but has extensive collections of prints, drawings, playbills, programmes, press cuttings, photos, theatre documents including the Enthoven Collection, the Guy Little Photographic Collection, the London Archives of the Dance, the Dame Marie Rambert-Ashley Dukes Ballet Collection, the M.W. Stone Toy Theatre Collection, the Gerald Morice Puppetry Collection, the British Puppet Theatre Guild's Collection of Puppets, the Harry R. Beard Theatre Collection, the Antony Hippisley Coxe Circus Collection, the British Council's and the Arts Council of Great Britain's collections of theatre designs and the collections of the British Theatre Museum Association and the Friends of the Museum of Performing Arts. Much of the material in the collections is being reorganised into a new archive housed in Olympia and is temporarily unavailable, but full details may be obtained from the above address.

*Three Lions—see **Hulton Picture Company.**

*Topham Picture Source (1928), PO Box 33, Edenbridge, Kent TN8 5PB   *tel* Cowden (0342) 850313   *telex* 95351   *fax* (0342) 850244. Historic library: personalities, warfare, Royalty, topography, France, natural history. World news file from original sources: UPI, INP, Press Association, Central News, Planet News, Alfieri, Pictorial Press, Syndicated Features Ltd, etc.

*B.M. Totterdell Photography (1989), Constable Cottage, Burlings Lane, Knockholt, Kent TN14 7PE   *tel* (0959) 32001. Specialist volleyball library, covering all aspects of the sport.

Transworld Feature Syndicate (UK) Ltd, Scope Features, 26 St Cross Street, London EC1N 8UH   *tel* 071-405 2997.

Travel Photo International, 8 Delph Common Road, Aughton, Ormskirk, Lancs. L39 5DW   *tel/fax* (0695) 423720. Touristic interest including scenery, towns, monuments, historic buildings, archaeological sites, local people. Specialising in travel brochures and books. *Terms:* 50%.

Travel Trade Photography, Colour Library, 22 Princedale Road, London W11 4NJ *tel* 071-727 5471. *Principal:* Teddy Schwarz. Landscapes, townscapes, ancient monuments and buildings of historical interest in England and foreign countries, peoples, and their customs. Return postage essential. *Terms:* 50%.

*****Tropix Photographic Library** (1973), 156 Meols Parade, Meols, Wirral, Merseyside L47 6AN *tel/fax* 051-632 1698. All human and environmental aspects of tropics, sub-tropics and non-tropical developing countries. Environmental issues are accepted from locations world-wide. New collections welcome but preliminary enquiry in writing essential. *Terms:* 50%.

Ulster Photographic Agency (1985), 22 Casaeldona Park, Belfast, Northern Ireland BT6 9RB *tel* (0232) 795738. Motoring and motorsport. *Terms:* 50%.

*****Universal Pictorial Press & Agency, Ltd** (1929), New Bridge Street House, 30-34 New Bridge Street, London EC4V 6BN *tel* 071-248 6730 *telex* 8952718 Unipix G *fax* 071-489 8982. Suppliers of a daily press and library service to the national and provincial press, periodicals and television companies throughout the British Isles and overseas. Notable Royal, political, company, academic, legal, diplomatic, church, military, pop, arts, entertaining and sports personalities and well-known views and buildings.

*****USSR Photo Library** (1988), Conifers House, Cheapside Lane, Denham, Uxbridge, Middlesex UB9 5AE *tel* (0895) 834814. *Library manager:* Mark Wadlow. Colour photo library specialising in cities, towns, famous landmarks and the people of the USSR. Do not accept other photographers' work.

Van Hallan, Bill Bates, 16 Blenheim Road, Basing, Basingstoke, Hants RG24 0HP *tel* (0256) 465217.

John Vickers Theatre Collection, 27 Shorrolds Road, London SW6 7TR *tel* 071-385 5774. Archives of British theatre and portraits of actors, writers and musicians by John Vickers from 1938-1974.

Vidocq Photo Library (1983), 162 Burwell Meadow, Witney, Oxon OX8 7GD *tel* (0993) 778518. Extensive coverage of wide range of subjects. Register of Photographers includes many specialists who market their work exclusively through the library. New photographers welcome. *Terms:* 60% to the photographer.

*****Viewfinder Colour Photo Library** (1984), The Production House, 147A St Michaels Hill, Bristol BS2 8DB *tel* (0272) 237268/239449 *fax* (0272) 239198. Colour library covering industry, agriculture, transport, people, world-wide travel; detailed sections on South West England and Wales. *Terms:* 50% to photographer.

Wales Scene, Melysfan, Llangwm, Corwen, Clwyd LL21 0RD *tel* (049 082) 472 *fax* (049 082) 321. Library of b&w photos and colour transparencies on the landscape of Wales: scenery, towns and villages, churches, antiquities, rural life. Do not act as agents for other photographers.

Simon Warner, Whitestone Farm, Stanbury, Keighley, West Yorkshire BD22 0JW *tel* Haworth (0535) 644644. Landscape photographer with own stock pictures of northern England, North Wales and NW Scotland.

*****Waterways Photo Library** (1976), 39 Manor Court Road, London W7 3EJ *tel* 081-840 1659. *Contact:* Derek Pratt. British inland waterways; canals, and rivers; bridges, aqueducts, locks and all waterside architectural features; waterway holidays, boats, fishing; town and countryside scenes.

Weimar Archive (1983), 8-9 The Incline, Coalport, Telford, Shropshire TF8 7HR *tel* (0952) 680050 *fax* (0952) 587184. Modern Germany, specialising in Weimar Republic; also all aspects of social, political and cultural life in central Europe from Middle Ages until 1945; plus a comprehensive collection of German painting and sculpture.

Welfare History Picture Library (1975), Heatherbank Museum of Social Work, 163 Mugdock Road, Milngavie, Glasgow G62 8ND *tel* 041-956 2687. Social history and social work, especially child welfare, workhouses, prisons, hospitals, slum clearance, women's movement, social reformers and their work. Catalogue on request.

Western Americana Picture Library, 3 Barton Buildings, Bath BA1 2JR *tel* (0225) 334213. Prints, engravings, photos and colour transparencies on the American West, cowboys, gunfighters, Indians, including pictures by Frederic Remington and Charles Russell, etc. Interested in buying pictures on American West.

Roy J. Westlake, ARPS, Photo Library, 31 Redwood Drive, Plympton, Plymouth PL7 3FS *tel* (0752) 336444. Britain, especially the West Country. Landscape subjects suitable for book illustrations, calendars, greeting cards, travel brochures, etc. Also camping, caravanning and inland waterways subjects in Britain, including rivers and canals. Other photographers' work not accepted.

*Eric Whitehead Picture Agency and Library (1984), PO Box 33, Kendal, Cumbria LA9 4SU *tel* (05396) 21002 and (0860) 534767 (24 hours). Covers assignments for news contacts and publishers and operates a picture library specialising in news, sport (mainly snooker), landscapes, mountaineering, northern subjects and general interest. Assignments undertaken for public relations clients and the media.

Derek G. Widdicombe, Worldwide Photographic Library, 'Oldfield', High Street, Clayton West, Huddersfield HD8 9NS *tel/fax* (0484) 862638. Landscapes, seascapes, architecture, human interest of Britain and abroad. Moods and seasons, buildings and natural features. Holds copyright of Noel Habgood, FRPS, Collection.

Wilderness Images (1977), 70 Foster Road, Kempston, Bedford MK42 8BU *tel* (0234) 854848. The Canadian Rockies, British Columbia, Alberta.

*Wilderness Photographic Library, Mill Barn, Broad Raine, Sedbergh, Cumbria LA10 5ED *tel* (05396) 20196 *fax* (05396) 21293. *Director:* John Noble, FRGS. Mountain and wilderness regions, travel and adventure world-wide, and associated aspects.

Wildlife Matters Photographic Library (1980), Dr John Feltwell, Marlham, Henley Down, Battle, East Sussex TN33 9BN *tel* (042 483) 566 *fax* (042 483) 224. 2¼ in sq and 35 mm colour transparencies: ecology, conservation and environment; habitats and pollution; agriculture and horticulture; general natural history, especially entomology; Mediterranean wildlife; rainforests; oblique aerial pics of countryside UK, Europe. **Plants 3000**—special collection of over 3000 garden plants world-wide including trees, grasses, herbs; 300 garden portfolios in Europe and USA; garden design and architecture, plantation gardens.

*S. & I. Williams, Power Pix International Picture Library (1968), Castle Lodge, Wenvoe, Cardiff CF5 6AD *tel* (0222) 595163 *telex* 995411 *fax* (0222) 593905. World-wide travel, people and views, girl and 'mood-pix', sub-aqua, aircraft, flora, fauna, agriculture, children. Agents world-wide.

Timothy Woodcock (1983), 45 Lyewater, Crewkerne, Somerset TA18 8BB *tel* (0460) 74488 *mobile* (0860) 826072 *fax* (0460) 74988. British and Eire landscape, seascape, architecture and heritage; children, parenthood and education; gardens, containers and gardening. Location commissions undertaken. *Terms:* 50%.

*****Woodmansterne Publications Ltd,** Watford Business Park, Watford, Herts. WD1 8RD   *tel* (0923) 228236   *fax* (0923) 245788. Britain, Europe, Holy Land; architecture, cathedral and stately home interiors; general art subjects; museum collections; natural history, butterflies, geography, volcanoes, transport, Space; opera and ballet; major state occasions; British heritage.

Murray Wren Picture Library, 3 Hallgate, London SE3 9SG   *tel* 081-852 7556. Outdoor nudes; nudist holiday resorts and activities in Europe and elsewhere; historic and erotic art of the nude through the ages.

Markets for Photographers

Photographers are advised to study carefully the detailed requirements of journals at the beginning of the *Yearbook*. Book publishers, especially those issuing technical books and school books, will be glad to know the range of subjects covered by a photographer.

GREETINGS, VIEWCARD, CALENDAR AND COLOUR SLIDES

A preliminary letter to ascertain requirements is advisable.

So far as colour is concerned, and most of the firms mentioned below are concerned with colour, usually colour transparencies are required. Very few firms will consider 35 mm frames; 5 × 4 in is preferred, and 3¼ × 2¼ is acceptable. 2¼ in sq is the minimum size acceptable to libraries and agencies. Only top quality transparencies should be submitted; inferior work is never accepted. *Postage for return of photographs should be enclosed.*

*Member of the Greeting Card and Calendar Association

Arnold Barton Cards Ltd—see **Hambledon Studios.**

Athena International, PO Box 918, Harlow, Essex CM20 2DU *tel* (0279) 641125. *Art directors:* P. Rodriguez, T. Jones, T. Taffs. Professional quality transparencies for posters, prints and postcards, preferably not 35 mm. Sae essential for return of work.

C.C.A. Stationery Ltd, Eastway, Fulwood, Preston PR2 4WS *tel* (0772) 794508. Personalised wedding stationery, Christmas cards.

E.T.W. Dennis & Sons Ltd, Printing House Square, Melrose Street, Scarborough, North Yorkshire YO12 7SJ *tel* (0723) 500555 *fax* (0723) 500545. Interested in first-class transparencies for reproduction as local view postcards and calendars. 3¼ × 2¼ in or 35 mm transparencies ideal for postcard reproduction.

*Giesen & Wolff (1908), Kaygee House, Dallington, Northampton NN5 7QW *tel* (0604) 755411 *telex* 311009 Kaygee G *fax* (0604) 759157. *Director:* Gordon Wood. Transparencies, 2¼ in sq minimum: views, floral, cute characters, wedding, sympathy, juvenile age subjects, traditional landscapes, humour – anything suitable for everyday and all seasonal occasions.

Hambledon Studios Ltd, Hambledon House, Marlborough Road, Accrington, Lancs. BB5 6BX *tel* (0254) 872266 *telex* 635169 Cardac G *fax* (0254) 872079. *Brands:* Arnold Barton, Donny Mac, Reflections, New Image. *Art managers:* D. Jaundrell, J. Ashton, D. Fuller; *creative directors:* D. Meloy, M. Smith. Photographs for reproduction as greeting cards.

*Hayes Greeting Card Publishers Ltd (1984), Thames View, Newtown Road, Henley-on-Thames, Oxon RG9 1HQ *tel* (0491) 410454. *Directors:* M.S. Belsten, R.H. Parker. Transparencies 35 mm upwards.

Jane's Information Group, Sentinel House, 163 Brighton Road, Coulsdon, Surrey CR5 2NH *tel* 081-763 1030 *telex* 916907 Janes G *fax* 081-763 1005. Considers defence, aerospace and transportation transparencies.

Kardonia Ltd, Farrier Street, Worcester WR1 3BH *tel* (0905) 611294.

Leeds Postcards (1979), PO Box 84, Leeds LS1 1HU   *tel* (0532) 468649   *fax* (0532) 436730. Workers co-operative. Publishers and producers of campaign postcards for the labour, environmental, women's and international justice movements.

Lowe Aston Calendars Ltd, Saltash, Cornwall PL12 4HL   *tel* (0752) 842233. Calendar printers.

The Medici Society Ltd, 34-42 Pentonville Road, London N1 9HG   *tel* 071-837 7099. Photos suitable for reproduction as greeting cards. Preliminary letter with brief details of work requested.

*****Panache Studio Ltd** (1985), Station Road, Henley-on-Thames, Oxon RG9 1LQ   *tel* (0491) 578383   *telex* 847279 HMK HO G   *fax* (0491) 578817. Photos of finished artwork and transparencies.

*****Photo Production Ltd,** Featherby Road, Gillingham, Kent ME8 6PJ   *tel* (0634) 33241. Colour transparencies for greetings cards.

*****Royle Publications Ltd,** Royle House, Wenlock Road, London N1 7ST   *tel* 071-253 7654. Colour transparencies required for two calendars, *Moods of Nature* and *Gardens of Britain*. Natural landscape photography taken in Britain and abroad or pictures of ornate flower gardens in Britain.

*****J. Salmon Ltd,** 100 London Road, Sevenoaks, Kent TN13 1BB   *tel* (0732) 452381   *fax* (0732) 450951. Picture postcards, calendars and greeting cards.

*****Scandecor Ltd** (1967), 3 The Ermine Centre, Hurricane Close, Huntingdon, Cambs. PE18 6XX   *tel* (0480) 456395   *telex* 32365   *fax* (0480) 456269. *Directors:* G. Huldtgren, A. Inghammar. Transparencies all sizes.

Noel Tatt Ltd (1954), Coombe Valley Road, Dover, Kent CT17 0EU   *tel* (0304) 211644   *fax* (0304) 240470. *Directors:* Noel Tatt, Vencke Tatt, Derek Bates, Anthony Sharpe, Paul Tatt, Robert Dixon. Greeting cards, prints and postcards.

See also the **Articles, reports and short stories** and the **Books** sections for lists of magazines and publishers.

Picture research

Picture Research

JENNIE KARRACH

Picture research is the art of obtaining pictures – photos and illustrations – suitable for reproduction, which suit the project's brief, budget and deadline. It also includes the clearance of permissions, copyright, the negotiation of rights and fees, and the eventual return of pictures to their owners at the end of the project. Given the incidence of pictures in daily life it can be appreciated that picture researchers are responsible for supplying a vast range of clients, in the book and magazine industry, both publishers and packagers, advertising agencies, film, television and video companies, newspapers and exhibition organisers. Although the skills involved in picture research are relevant in all these contexts, the type of pictures required varies enormously. As a result researchers tend to specialise in the type of work they undertake, and they may well have a specialist knowledge of one particular area, such as science and technology.

Picture researchers are employed either as staff members or freelance by the hour, day, for the duration of the project, as appropriate. An employee working full time on a long-running project may have time to carry out extensive research, but freelance work is often constrained by the client's budget and schedule. It is here that experience counts. Knowing where to find material quickly to suit the brief saves time and therefore money. The researcher's fees are often included in the total budget, so that although the final deadline for delivery of pictures to the client may be a month away, the total allowed for picture research amounts to three days' work. It may be that this is unrealistic, and that the job will require five days. These details all need to be clarified at the outset and some sort of agreement listing the picture brief, deadlines, budget and invoicing particulars needs to be drawn up. It is important to put everything in writing so that in the event of dispute both parties can refer back to the agreement. Pictures themselves are often worth large amounts of money, and in the event of loss it will become difficult to agree who will pay compensation unless this has been pre-arranged. It can also prove difficult to collect payment for work completed, so it may be advisable to agree upon regular payments and an advance to cover expenses such as travel, postage and telephone, etc.

THE BRIEF

It is important to clarify the brief so that both parties, the picture researcher and the editor/design team, are agreed upon the image required. It may be that the picture requested needs no further description – a work of art, by a well-known artist, e.g. *The Mona Lisa* by Leonardo da Vinci, to be used in colour. Or it may be that the picture is to depict an historical event which occurred long before the advent of photography. What is required? A photo of a contemporary manuscript which describes the incident, or perhaps a contemporary illumination exists. Or does the client have in mind an illustration executed by a more recent artist, perhaps a nineteenth-century engraving? Or perhaps a photograph of the remains of an historic site? It may be that the client has no one image in mind, but rather needs to evoke a specific mood, or provoke a reaction. This is often the case in advertising campaigns. Pictures are highly subjective, and what is evocative to some will appear bleak to others. A good picture researcher is able to capture the image conjured up in a picture meeting, responding to the ideas of an art director or editor.

It may be that the picture required must be a specific shape – portrait (upright) or landscape (horizontal), or it may need to have an area lacking in detail, such as sky, into which text can fit. Or a dark area suitable for text reversal. If there are too many design constraints it may be cost effective to commission a photographer, rather than to search for a non-existent 'existing' photo.

THE BUDGET, RIGHTS AND DEADLINE

Once the brief has been agreed, the budget, rights and deadline must be confirmed. These are interdependent. Picture fees increase according to the size and use made of the image; for instance, a picture used at quarter-page size in a school text book will cost less than one used quarter-page size in a glossy, adult non-fiction book. Fees are calculated also according to the rights requested. The larger the territory, the larger the fee, although the percentage increase between the various categories will vary from agency to agency. The territories sold are usually: UK only; UK and first foreign edition; English language, world rights, excluding US; English language, world rights, including US; world rights, all languages. It may well be that, as the European Community attempt to remove trade barriers, the rights available will change. The print run will also have an effect on the fees charged.

Other fees will need to be budgeted for. Many commercial picture agencies charge 'research' or 'service' fees. These may be linked to the amount of material they are loaning or there may be a fixed charge levied. In both cases the source should advise of this at the initial enquiry stage. Some will only charge if a personal visit is not possible and pictures are despatched by a member of their staff. The levying of these fees can erode the total picture budget quickly. It is not unusual to receive a service fee of £30, which may be acceptable if this is the only source used, and the pictures obtained are accepted by the client. However, on projects where a selection of pictures to cover a wider range of topics is required, many sources will have to be approached. It is worth discussing service fees at the outset. It is not unknown for agencies to waive or reduce them if it increases the likelihood of a sale. Some only charge the service fee if all pictures are returned and none selected for use. Other sources do not loan out material but instead sell copy transparencies or prints. This is usually the case with museums who can supply a transparency of a particular object or manuscript, but are unable to respond to a vague request for a selection of pictures for possible use. A transparency of reproduction quality may cost £20, or more, if a 'rush job' surcharge is added on.

Most commercial picture libraries or agencies operate on a loan system. Pictures are selected and loaned for an agreed period, usually a month. After this time material not required should be returned and some indication given as to the fate of the pictures still held. Is a subsequent picture selection to be made, or are those retained going to be used? If material is kept longer than the agreed loan period, then holding fees may be charged. These should only be levied if a reminder sent fails to elicit news of the pictures or return. (Freelance picture researchers need to make sure that such reminders are forwarded to them either by the source or sent on by the client.) Holding fees are charged per picture, per week over the deadline, and are usually waived if a reasonable extension to the free loan period is requested.

PICTURE SOURCES

Sources are many and various. They included government departments, institutions, companies, libraries, commercial picture libraries and agencies, individual collectors, and individual photographers. Some of these sources supply pictures without charge, but that is not to say that they are necessarily easy to obtain, or that no copyright pertains. Many sources are not primarily concerned with the supply of pictures and give it low priority. Access to the collection may be limited to research students and those who hold readers' cards. Enquiries may have to be made in writing, and the idea of urgency is an alien one. Or lack of resources may prevent an efficient service.

There is no one source book which lists all picture sources and if one existed it would run to many volumes and be in need of constant updating. Commercial libraries and agencies maintain a high profile, advertising by mail shots to prospective clients. The larger ones produce glossy catalogues, usually free, which include a selection of their images, enough to give a flavour of the type of stock held. 'General stock libraries' hold pictures which fall into the following broad categories: travel, architecture, food, business, science/medicine, people, sport, nature, animals, transport, etc. They would almost certainly hold pictures of famous foreign landmarks, e.g. the Eiffel Tower, photographed from the ground, the air, by night, by day, with lovers . . . It is much more difficult to find pictures of less glamorous sites. Street furniture, cars and pedestrians date quickly, and some agencies, keen to keep pictures saleable for as long as possible, will attempt to keep such features to a minimum. The result is strange; London, peopled only by bobbies and red buses, Venice reduced to St Mark's Square and gondoliers on the Grand Canal, Los Angeles depicted by traffic on freeways. This problem extends to the 'people' pictures, which tend to be stereotypes posed by models. It is not impossible to find pictures of 'real' people going about everyday activities, but it can be time-consuming. Directories cannot hope to express the nuances of photographic collections, and it is only over time, after visits to many sources, that an overview of the range available will emerge. Specialist picture libraries are usually one-subject libraries, and cover the whole range of picture needs. The level of captioning is usually higher in specialist sources as the photographer has expert knowledge. It can be the case that a good quality photograph badly captioned is rendered useless. A photo filed in the 'elderly people' category of a general stock agency showed a woman standing in a slight depression in the desert somewhere. The woman was actually a famous anthropologist, but her name meant nothing to the library so she had been miscaptioned and then wrongly filed. It may be that for certain purposes any train, boat, car, etc. will be acceptable, but if the picture required is of a specific model then it is frustrating to find insubstantial captions and undated pictures.

USE OF PHOTOS

Once pictures have been found which fit the brief, the next stage is clearance for use. Permission must be sought from the copyright holder for use of particular photos in set contexts. The supply of photos does not automatically guarantee permission to reproduce. It may be that the agency or picture source is not the copyright holder, and permission has to be sought elsewhere. This is often the case with photos of works of art still in copyright. The artist, or the artist's estate, may be represented by a copyright protection society such as DACS (Design and Artists Copyright Society – see page 528), which will approach the estate or artist on behalf of a picture researcher and, if permission is granted, often subject to conditions, issue a licence. Conditions could include the right to approve colour proofs. The production department or designer of the project would therefore need to be informed to allow time in the schedule. DACS have reciprocal representation agreements with similar copyright protection societies in some 26 countries. This simplifies a copyright enquiry considerably but sufficient time should be allowed for clearance. It may take a day or several weeks. If the copyright holder and the supplier of the photograph are not one and the same, then a fee may be due to both parties.

It may be that the context in which the photo is to appear is a sensitive one, perhaps an article about child abuse, divorce, AIDS, or that the caption is to make some derogatory statement about the subject. If this is the case it is important to be honest about the context with the supplier of the photo. If the article is educational and positive in its approach, then the photo will play a different role from one appearing in an exposé of shameful goings on. It is prudent to enquire whether the photographer has obtained 'model release' from the subject in the photo. In return for a sum of money the model grants the photographer the right to sell the photos taken. This is standard procedure at photo sessions, where a particular shot has been commissioned by a client, or a personality has granted a shoot. The release may have certain riders attached as to use, precisely to avoid certain contexts.

It may be that the agency grants permission to use the photo in a sensitive area, but insists on a declaration appearing with it or with the photo credits 'all photos posed by models'. Or it may be that the agency or photographer do not have model release for the photo. At present in the UK, if a person is photographed in public they cannot prevent that photo being published. Hence the breed of paparazzi photographers. There is as yet no law protecting against the invasion of privacy. (The situation is different in the USA.) As a result many British photo libraries hold photos of members of the public, taken 'in the public domain' for which they hold no model release. Most agencies reproduce the following or similar statement in their Terms & Conditions: 'although the agency takes all reasonable care, the agency shall not be liable for any loss or damage suffered by the client or by any third party arising from any defect in the picture or its caption, or in any way from its reproduction.' The onus is put onto the picture user. It is fair to say that if the context of the photo is an innocent one, most members of the public are pleased to be in the spotlight, and require no more than a complimentary copy of the book, magazine, or whatever.

CAPTIONS

It is important for picture researchers to make caption writers aware that litigation may result from derogatory or inappropriate captions. Staff researchers should attempt to prevent pictures which were obtained for one project, e.g. a book on health care, being transferred to another, such as a booklet on safe sex. Freelance researchers would be well advised to include a paragraph in the agreement mentioned above which would disclaim responsibility for use by the client of pictures supplied in any use other than that stated in the brief, and any subsequent copyright infringement by the client. It is not unknown for clients to withhold information or mislead picture researchers as to the length of the print run, or the production of foreign language editions.

Picture researchers do not generally write captions themselves but may be asked to provide information for captions. This can be very time-consuming if the pictures do not already have a reasonable amount of caption information attached, supplied by the source or photographer.

CREDITS AND COPYRIGHT

Once pictures have been selected, captioned, and sized for the project in hand, the credit or acknowledgement list will need to be drawn up. This usually includes a courtesy line thanking the various picture sources for permission to reproduce photographs. Sources are either listed alphabetically, with page numbers as to where their pictures appear, or the name of the source appears next to the picture.

Under the provisions of the Copyright, Designs and Patents Act 1988, photographers have 'moral rights' which include the right to be identified as the author of a photograph (see page 398). Newspapers, magazines, encyclopedias, and other works of reference, are exempt from crediting contributors, but most will include credits as a matter of course. Under the terms of the 1988 Act photography is now copyright for the same duration and in the same way as other works of art. At present this is for 50 years after the death of the photographer. However harmonisation of EC legislation may bring about an extension of this period in line with other EC countries such as Germany, where the duration is 70 years. Commissioned work, where previously the copyright belonged to the commissioner, is now the property of the photographer. This means that photos can only be kept for a limited period after a photo session, and rights must be agreed in the same way as for stock library images. All photos, used and unused, must be returned to the photographer. Staff photographers as employees do not own copyright on their photos.

A short booklet, *The Photographer's Guide to the 1988 Copyright Act*, has been produced by the British Photographers Liaison Committee (BPLC) which summarises the changes in copyright relevant to photographers brought about by the 1988 Act. This is available from the Association of Photographers (address below), £3.50 (inc. p&p), cheque made payable to BPLC.

LAST STAGES

The pictures are now ready to go off to the printers. A final check should be made to see that they have not been damaged by any of the people who have handled them – editors, designers, etc. If the printer returns photos damaged it will be easier to refute claims that pictures were already scratched if everything is checked as a matter of course. If prints or transparencies are damaged, a fee to compensate the agency or photographer is due. This will vary in amount according to whether the picture was an original or a duplicate. Some photographs are irreplaceable. The amount due for loss is stated in the Terms & Conditions listed on the reverse of most delivery notes. This may be in the region of £400 for an original. Sometimes pictures are not damaged irreparably but are returned by the printer with torn mounts, or still sticky from origination. It is best to return such pictures to the printer for cleaning, in case any damage occurs during a DIY cleaning session. Pictures should then be returned to their owners and one or two copies of the book or proofs supplied as evidence of use, as stated in the Terms & Conditions of the source.

GETTING INTO PICTURE RESEARCH

This can be difficult as employers are loath to employ people without experience, and some picture sources are nervous about loaning pictures. A job with a picture library would give an insight into that particular source and might lead into a job as a picture researcher. Jobs in picture libraries, and picture research work, are advertised in the Arts/Media section of *The Guardian* on Saturdays and Mondays. Sometimes such ads appear in *The Bookseller*, the weekly publishing journal, and *Campaign*, the weekly advertising magazine. These may all be available at the local library. Salaries tend to be low initially as one learns the skills involved. The idea of working freelance may appeal but it is difficult to obtain enough freelance work without the contacts amassed over a period of time. Many picture researchers build up experience working for an employer full time, and then go freelance. This is not without risks. Getting enough work; getting paid for work completed; sorting out tax; National Insurance; motivation; and loneliness are some of the problems which may arise.

USEFUL DIRECTORIES

Picture Sources UK, Rosemary Eakins, Macdonald, 1985. Now out of print but may be available through a library.

Picture Researcher's Handbook, Hilary & Mary Evans, 4th edition, Van Nostrand Reinhold (UK), £24.95. Also available from The Mary Evans Picture Library, 59 Tranquil Vale, London SE3 0BS   *tel* 081-318 0034   *fax* 081-852 7211.

BAPLA Directory, £10. This lists all the current members of the British Association of Picture Libraries and Agencies (BAPLA), at present totalling around 300. Copies available from Sal Shuel, BAPLA Administrator, 13 Woodberry Crescent, London N10 1PJ   *tel* 081-883 2531   *fax* 081-883 9215.

USEFUL ORGANISATIONS

BAPLA – see above.

DACS (Design and Artists Copyright Society), St Mary's Clergy House, 2 Whitechurch Lane, London E1 7QR   *tel* 071-247 1650   *fax* 071-377 5855.

Association of Photographers, 9-10 Domingo Street, London EC1Y 0TA   *tel* 071-608 1441. Includes fashion and advertising photographers amongst its members.

SPREd (The Society of Picture Researchers and Editors) – see opposite.

Picture Research Course

The Book House Training Centre offers training in picture research in the form of a two-day course, which is also offered as an evening class, designed for those working in book publishing. The objective of the course is to give a professional approach to the search for and use of suitable sources; to make picture researchers aware of all the implications of their task: suitability for reproduction, legal and financial aspects, efficient administration.

Details of the course, with the outline of the programme, may be obtained from Book House Training Centre, 45 East Hill, Wandsworth, London SW18 2QZ   *tel* 081-874 2718/4608.

The London School of Publishing now offers a course in picture research twice a year – spring and autumn. Each course lasts eight weeks and there is one lecture a week. Further details may be obtained from Mark Featherstone-Witty, 47 Red Lion Street, London WC1R 4PF   *tel* 071-405 9801.

The Art of Picture Research by Hilary Evans (David & Charles) is a useful introduction to picture research as a profession. It covers everything from qualifications needed to do picture research to everyday aspects of the job and also covers career opportunities. Now out of print, but a new edition should be available late 1992.

SPREd (Society of Picture Researchers and Editors)

SPREd was formed in 1977 as a professional body for picture researchers and picture editors. It is not a trade union but a society for people who work in similar fields, and who wish to share problems and exchange information on all aspects of dealing with illustrations.

Its main aims are:

1. To promote the recognition of picture research as a profession, requiring particular skills and knowledge.
2. To promote and maintain professional standards and ethics within the profession.
3. To bring together those involved in the research and publication of visual material and to provide a forum for the exchange of information.
4. To encourage the use of trained researchers throughout publishing and other media, and to ensure common professional standards in all areas of picture use.
5. To provide guidance and advice to its members.

All picture researchers need a wide circle of contacts and a good knowledge of sources. Picture researchers tend to encounter the same problems and have the same need for up-to-date information, but they tend to work in isolation from each other. SPREd sets out to be a clearing house for information. More importantly, it provides an opportunity for researchers to meet each other informally and to exchange ideas and discuss problems. It can be a great relief to discover that others have already met and overcome the very difficulties that are worrying you.

To this end SPREd runs monthly meetings for members, and publishes a quarterly magazine to which non-members may subscribe. Advertising space may be purchased in this magazine.

SPREd members sign a Code of Practice which sets out the professional standards expected from a SPREd member and states the responsibilities of a picture researcher.

For further details about SPREd contact The Secretary, BM Box 259, London WC1N 3XX   *tel* 071-404 5011.

See also the **Books** section for lists of publishers; the **Photography** section.

Music

Music Publishers

UNITED KINGDOM

Copyright in musical compositions comprises (a) the right of publication in print and sale of printed copies; (b) the right of public performance; and (c) the right to use the work for the purpose of making gramophone records, sound films or other similar contrivances. The musical composer should bear all three in mind when entering into an agreement for the publication of his work.

Rutland Boughton's warning to amateurs given many years ago, still stands. He said that amateurs, 'like the more hardened professional composers, find pleasure in seeing their musical thoughts in print. Because of that human weakness they become the prey of tenth-rate publishers, who offer to issue their music for them (however poor and ineffective it may be) *if they will pay for the privilege. If a piece of music is worth publishing a publisher will be willing to pay for it in cash or royalty.*' Music publishers requiring work for issue on cash or royalty terms no more advertise in the public press for music and lyrics than a first-class publisher of books advertises for MSS on that basis.

The publishers in the following list are all members of the Performing Right Society except those marked . The list does not include all publisher-members of the Performing Right Society.

Lyrics without a musical setting are not accepted unless stated by individual firms

ATV Music Ltd—see **EMI Music Publishing Ltd.**

Banks Music Publications (Ramsay Silver), The Old Forge, Sand Hutton, York YO4 1LB *tel* (0904) 86472 *fax* (0904) 86679. Publishers of choral and instrumental music.

Bardic Edition (1987), 6 Fairfax Crescent, Aylesbury, Bucks. HP20 2ES *tel/ fax* (0296) 28609. Piano, vocal, chamber, choral, educational, orchestral, Grainger Society Edition.

Belwin-Mills Music Ltd—now distributed by **International Music Publications.**

A. & C. Black (Publishers) Ltd (1978), 35 Bedford Row, London WC1R 4JH *tel* 071-242 0946 *telex* 32524 Acblac *fax* 071-831 8478. Song books and instrumental books for children.

†**Boethius Press (UK) Ltd** (1973/1988), 3 The Science Park, Aberystwyth, Dyfed SY23 3AH *tel* (0970) 615393 *fax* (0970) 615840. *Directors:* L.J. Hewitt, J.M. Hewitt, Mrs J.M. Hewitt, E.C. Nelson, J. Bradley. Early music in facsimile and edition, opera, history of musical education.

Boosey & Hawkes Music Publishers, Ltd, 295 Regent Street, London W1R 8JH *tel* 071-580 2060 *telex* 8954613 Boosey G *fax* 071-436 5675. General and educational.

Bosworth & Co. Ltd (1889), 14-18 Heddon Street, London W1R 8DP *tel* 071-734 4961 *fax* 071-734 0475. Orchestral, chamber, instrumental, operetta, church, educational, piano, string, recorder and recorder ensemble, and part-songs.

Bourne Music Ltd, 34-36 Maddox Street, London W1R 9PD *tel* 071-493 6412/6583. Popular and educational music.

Cambridge University Press (1534). The Edinburgh Building, Shaftesbury Road, Cambridge CB2 2RU *tel* (0223) 312393 *telegraphic address* Unipress, Cambridge *telex* 817256 Cupcam *fax* (0223) 315052. *University Printer and chief executive of the Press:* Geoffrey A. Cass, MA; *deputy chief executive and managing director* (publishing division): Anthony K. Wilson, MA; *deputy managing director and Press editorial director:* Jeremy Mynott, PhD. Books on music and history of music; music books for schools.

Campbell Connelly Group of Companies, 8-9 Frith Street, London W1V 5TZ *tel* 071-434 0066 *telex* 21892 *fax* 071-439 2848. General and popular.

Chester Music London (1860), 8-9 Frith Street, London W1V 5TZ *tel* 071-434 0066 *telex* 21892 *fax* 071-439 2848. Concert and educational works.

Cramer Music (1824), 23 Garrick Street, London WC2E 9AX *tel* 071-240 1612. General and educational.

De Wolfe Ltd, 80-88 Wardour Street, London W1V 3LF *tel* 071-439 8481-6 *fax* 071-437 2744. Symphonic recorded orchestral (English and foreign). Comprehensive library of recorded music on CD and tape. Extensive effects library. Original film scores. Recording studio.

Dix Ltd (1922)—see **EMI Music Publishing Ltd.**

†**East-West Publications (UK) Ltd** (1977), 8 Caledonia Street, London N1 9DZ *tel* 071-837 5061 *fax* 071-278 4429. *Chairman:* L.W. Carp; *editor:* B. Thompson. Piano, guitar, recorder and vocal music.

Emerson Edition Ltd (1972), Windmill Farm, Ampleforth, North Yorkshire YO6 4HF *tel* (043 93) 324. *Managing director:* June Emerson. Specialist publisher of music for wind instruments only.

EMI Music Publishing Ltd, 127 Charing Cross Road, London WC2H 0EA *tel* 071-434 2131 *telemessages/cables* Emimus *telex* 269189 *fax* 071-434 3531. Comprising ATV Music Ltd, Dix Ltd, EMI Songs Ltd, EMI United Partnership Ltd, B. Feldman & Co. Ltd, Francis, Day & Hunter Ltd, KPM Music Group, The Peter Maurice Music Co. Ltd, Northern Songs, Keith Prowse Music Publishing Co. Ltd, Reynolds Music, Robbins Music Corp. Ltd, Screen Gems-EMI Music Ltd, Lawrence Wright Music Ltd.

Faber Music Ltd (1966), 3 Queen Square, London WC1N 3AU *tel* 071-278 7436 *telegraphic address* Fabbaf, London, WC1 *telex* 299633 Faber G *fax* 071-278 3817. *Directors:* Donald Mitchell (president), Robin Boyle (chairman & chief executive), Martin Kingsbury (vice-chairman & director of publishing), Sally Cavender, Piers Hembry, Thomas H. Pasteur, Wendy Thompson. A general list of the highest quality, comprising both old and new music, and music books.

B. Feldman & Co. Ltd—see **EMI Music Publishing Ltd.**

Fentone Music Ltd, Fleming Road, Earlstrees, Corby, Northants. NN17 2SN *tel* (0536) 60981 *cables* Fentone, Corby *telex* 312305 Hondel G *fax*

(0536) 401075. Agents for Fenette Music, Earlham Press, Mimram Music, all of Corby, F.E.C. Leuckart of Munich, Edizioni Bèrben, Ancona, Italy, F & R. Walsh Publications, London, Notaset, Wiesbaden.

First Time Music (Publishing) UK Ltd (1986), Sovereign House, 12 Trewartha Road, Praa Sands, Penzance, Cornwall TR20 9ST   *tel* (0736) 762826   *fax* (0736) 763328. *Managing director:* Roderick G. Jones. Popular, country, folk, gospel music. Music for choirs – in all styles.

Forsyth Bros. Ltd (1857), 126 Deansgate, Manchester M3 2GR   *tel* 061-834 3281   *fax* 061-834 0630. Educational piano and instrumental music. Modern Teaching material. UK Distributors of *Music Minus One* and *Pocket Songs*.

Francis, Day & Hunter Ltd—see **EMI Music Publishing Ltd.**

Glocken Verlag Ltd (1946), 12-14 Mortimer Street, London W1N 7RD   *tel* 071-580 2827   *cables* Operetta, London W1   *fax* 071-436 9616. *Directors:* R.M. Toeman, R.G. Holt. Musical works by Franz Lehar.

†**Gresham Books,** The Gresham Press, PO Box 61, Henley-on-Thames, Oxon RG9 3LQ   *tel* (0734) 403789. *Chief executive:* Mrs M.V. Green. Hymn books and prayer books for churches and schools.

Gwynn, Cwmni Cyhoeddi (Cyf.), Y Gerlan, Heol Y Dŵr, Penygroes, Gwynedd LL54 6LR   *tel* Penygroes (0286) 881797. Publishers of Welsh Educational and International Choral Music. Official music publishers to the Welsh Folk Song Society, The Welsh Folk Dance Society, The Court of the National Eisteddfod.

Hughes & Son, Publishers (1820), Parc Tŷ Glas, Llanishen, Cardiff CF4 5DU   *tel* (0222) 343421   *telex* 94017032 Sian G   *fax* (0222) 341643. Welsh music, Welsh language, television related material, educational publications, novels.

Hymns Ancient & Modern Ltd, trading under the imprint of **The Canterbury Press Norwich,** St Mary's Works, St Mary's Plain, Norwich, Norfolk NR3 3BH   *tel* (0603) 612914/616563   *fax* (0603) 624483. *Directors:* The Very Revd Professor Henry Chadwick, KBE (chairman), The Revd Canon Cyril V. Taylor, Dr Allan Wicks, Dr Lionel Dakers, Sir Richard O'Brien; *publisher:* Gordon Knights. The leading hymn book publisher in the UK for churches, schools and other institutions.

International Music Publications, Woodford Trading Estate, Southend Road, Woodford Green, Essex IG8 8HN   *tel* 081-551 6131   *fax* 081-551 3919. Standard and popular, educational, instrumental tutors, band and choral music. Sole representatives of **Columbia Pictures Publications.**

Janus Music (1978), 22 Ivybridge Close, Twickenham TW1 1EA   *tel* 081-892 1833. *Proprietor:* C.J. Gordon. Recorder music, contemporary wind music, contemporary piano music. Woodwind ensembles for schools/amateurs. Duets for equal/mixed wind instruments.

Alfred A. Kalmus Ltd, 2-3 Fareham Street, Dean Street, London W1V 4DU   *tel* 071-437 5203/4   *fax* 071-437 6115. *Trade:* 38 Eldon Way, Paddock Wood, Tonbridge, Kent TN12 6BE   *tel* (0892) 833422   *telex* 95374   *fax* (0892) 836038. Sole representatives of Universal Edition AG, Vienna, Universal Edition (London) Ltd, Universal Edition AG, Zurich, Universal Edition SpA, Milan; Theodore Presser Co, Lea Pocket Scores, International Music Co, Boelke-Bomart Inc., European American Music Corp., Bourne Music, Belmont Music, Kelton Publications, Trio Associates, all USA; Doblinger Edition, Vienna, Polish Editions, Cracow (complete Chopin-Paderewski), Supraphon, Prague, Harmonia Uitgave, Hilversum, Artia, Prague, Panton,

Prague, Berandol, Canada, Boccaccini and Spada, Italy, Aldo Bruzzichelli, Italy, Breitkopf & Härtel, Wiesbaden, Germany, Musikwissenschaftlicher Verlag, Austria, Musica Rara, France, Fraser-Enoch, Kent; Olivan Press, London; Broekmans & Van Poppel, Amsterdam, Loux Music Publishing, USA, Zen-On, Japan; Power Music, West Yorkshire, Virgo Music, West Midlands. Serious music of all types.

KPM Music Group—see **EMI Music Publishing Ltd.**

Alfred Lengnick & Co. Ltd (1892), 7-8 Greenland Place, London NW1 0AP   *tel* 071-267 9736   *fax* 071-485 5133. Music publishers and importers. Publishers of works by Malcolm Arnold, Alun Hoddinott, Robert Simpson. Specialise in educational music, leading publishers of English contemporary music. Always ready to consider MSS of any type. Agents for CeBeDeM (Brussels); Iceland Music Information Centre (Iceland).

The Peter Maurice Music Co. Ltd—see **EMI Music Publishing Ltd.**

M.S.M. Music Publishers (incorporating **Leonard, Gould & Bolttler**), 406 Roding Lane South (off Woodford Avenue), Woodford Green, Essex IG8 8EY   *tel* 081-551 1282. General and educational.

Music Sales Ltd, 8-9 Frith Street, London W1V 5TZ   *tel* 071-434 0066   *telex* 21892   *fax* 071-439 2848. General and popular.

Northern Songs—see **EMI Music Publishing Ltd.**

Novello & Co. Ltd (1811), 8-10 Lower James Street, London W1R 3PL   *tel* 071-287 5060   *fax* 071-287 0816. Classical and modern orchestral, instrumental, vocal and choral music, church music, school and educational music books.

Novello Hire Library, incorporating **Goodwin & Tabb,** Unit 17, The Orchard Business Centre, Vale Road, Tonbridge, Kent TN9 1QF   *tel* (0732) 771588   *fax* (0732) 361425. Vocal, choral and orchestral hire library.

Octava Music Co. Ltd (1938), 12-14 Mortimer Street, London W1N 7RD   *tel* 071-580 2827   *cables* Operetta, London W1   *fax* 071-436 9616.

Oxford University Press (Oxford University Press established 1478. Music Dept. constituted 1923), Music Department, Walton Street, Oxford OX2 6DP   *tel* (0865) 56767   *telex* 837330   *fax* (0865) 56646. Orchestral, instrumental, operatic, choral, vocal works, church and organ music by early and modern composers, educational music, courses, and books on music.

Paterson's Publications Ltd—acquired by **Novello & Co. Ltd,** *q.v.*

Peters Edition Ltd (1938), 10-12 Baches Street, London N1 6DN   *tel* 071-253 1638. Copyright/Hire: *tel* 071-251 5094; Promotion/Editorial: *tel* 071-251 6732   *fax* 071-490 4921. Peters Edition, Hinrichsen Edition, Collection Litolff. Classical and modern (piano, organ, other instrumental, vocal, choir and brass band) music.

Keith Prowse Music Publishing Co. Ltd—see **EMI Music Publishing Ltd.**

Reynolds Music—see **EMI Music Publishing Ltd.**

G. Ricordi & Co. (London), Ltd (1808), The Bury, Church Street, Chesham, Bucks. HP5 1JG   *tel* (0494) 783311   *telegraphic address* Ricordi, Chesham   *fax* (0494) 784427. Publishers of Italian opera, music for piano, classical and contemporary, operatic arias, songs, choral large scale works and part songs for all voices, orchestral works, classical and contemporary, instrumental, string, woodwind, brass tutors, exercises, etc., guitar music of all types.

Roberton Publications, The Windmill, Wendover, Aylesbury, Bucks. HP22 6JJ *tel* (0296) 623107. *Partners:* Kenneth Roberton, Margaret Roberton. Choral and educational; also piano, chamber, orchestral, and music for all instruments. Represent Albert House Press, London; Hardie Press, Edinburgh; Leslie Music Supply, Oakville, Ontario.

Schott & Co. Ltd (1835), 48 Great Marlborough Street, London W1V 2BN *tel* 071-437 1246 *fax* 071-437 0263. Music of a serious and educational nature.

Sea Dream Music (1976), 236 Sebert Road, Forest Gate, London E7 0NP *tel* 081-534 8500. *Senior partner:* S.A. Law. Christian-based rock, blues and folk.

Shapiro Bernstein & Co. Ltd, 8-9 Frith Street, London W1V 5TZ *tel* 071-434 0066 *telex* 21892 *fax* 071-439 2848. General and popular.

R. Smith & Co., Ltd (1857), PO Box 367, Aylesbury, Bucks. HP22 4LJ; *Delivery:* Unit 10, Upper Wingbury Farm, Wingrave, Bucks. *tel* (0296) 682220 *fax* (0296) 681989.

†Sphemusations, Gramercy House, 12 Northfield Road, Onehouse, Stowmarket, Suffolk IP14 3HF *tel* (0449-61) 3388. Serious music, brass band, choral, instrumental and educational. Records of modern works. Tapes.

Stainer & Bell Ltd, PO Box 110, 82 High Road, East Finchley, London N2 9PW *tel* 081-444 9135 *fax* 081-365 2770. Book and music publishers including the imprints of **Augener, Belton Books, Galliard, Stainer & Bell, A. Weekes, Joseph Williams.**

Sylvester Music Co. Ltd, 80-82 Wardour Street, London W1V 3LF *tel* 071-437 4933/4 *fax* 071-437 2744. Popular and orchestral music. Comprehensive library of recorder music on CD and tape. Extensive effects library. Specially composed scores. Transfers to tape and film.

Thames Publishing (1970), 14 Barlby Road, London W10 6AR *tel* 081-969 3579. Serious music of all types, particularly vocal, choral and instrumental. Manuscripts welcome *but should always be preceded by a letter*.

United Music Publishers Ltd (1932), 42 Rivington Street, London EC2A 3BN *tel* 071-729 4700 *fax* 071-739 6549. Agents for the principal French music publishing houses and specialists in the distribution of French, Spanish and other foreign music. Also contemporary English works.

Universal Edition (London) Ltd, 2-3 Fareham Street, Dean Street, London W1V 4DU *tel* 071-437 5203/6880. Serious music of all types.

Warner Chappell Music Ltd, 129 Park Street, London W1Y 3FA *tel* 071-629 7600. Brussels, Munich, Johannesburg, Los Angeles, Madrid, Milan, Bussum, Nashville, New York, Paris, Stockholm, Sydney, Tokyo, Toronto, Zurich.

†Warren & Phillips (1906), 126 Deansgate, Manchester M3 2GR *tel* 061-834 3281 *fax* 061-834 0630. Educational piano and instrumental music. Modern teaching material.

Josef Weinberger Ltd (1885), 12-14 Mortimer Street, London W1N 7RD *tel* 071-580 2827 (4 lines) *cables* Operetta, London, W1 *fax* 071-436 9616. *Directors:* R.G. Holt, R.M. Toeman; *executive directors:* G. Barker, K. Dixon, G. Kingsley, J. Schofield. Theatrical and music publishers.

Workers' Music Association (1936), 240 Perry Rise, Forest Hill, London SE23 2QT *tel* 081-699 2250. General music organisation with emphasis on the social aspects of music. Publications, music courses.

Lawrence Wright Music Ltd—see **EMI Music Publishing Ltd.**

UNITED STATES OF AMERICA

Associated Music Publishers, Inc., 225 Park Avenue South, New York, NY 10003 *tel* 212-254-2100 *telex* 428351 *fax* 212-254-2013.

Boosey & Hawkes, Inc., 24 East 21st Street, New York, NY 10010-7200 *tel* 212-228-3300 *fax* 212-473-5730. Symphonic, opera, ballet, concert and educational music.

Bourne Co., 5 West 37th Street, New York, NY 10018 *tel* 212-391-4300 *fax* 212-391-4306; *London office:* 34-36 Maddox Street, W1R 9PD *tel* 071-493 6412. Publishers of popular, standard, choral, educational wind band, instrumental, production and film music.

John Church Company (1854)—see **Theodore Presser Co.**

Roger Dean Publishing, 501 East Third Street, Dayton, OH 45401-0802 *tel* 513-228-6118. Division of **The Lorenz Corporation**. Manuscripts for schools and colleges.

Oliver Ditson Company (1793)—see **Theodore Presser Co.**

Elkan-Vogel, Inc.—see **Theodore Presser Co.**

Heritage Music Press, 501 East Third Street, Dayton, OH 45401-0802 *tel* 513-228-6118. Division of **The Lorenz Corporation.** Manuscripts for elementary, junior-high and high schools (secondary schools).

Hinrichsen Edition, C.F. Peters Corporation, 373 Park Avenue South, New York, NY 10016 *tel* 212-686-4147. Classical and contemporary music.

International Music Company, 5 West 37th Street, New York, NY 10018 *tel* 212-391-4200 *fax* 212-391-4306. Subsidiary of **Bourne Co.** Publishers of performing editions of classical, romantic and modern chamber music for piano, instrumental solo, duet, trio, quartet, quintet, large ensembles, voice; study scores, opera scores; concerto and aria orchestral parts on hire.

Laurel Press, 40 Music Square East, Nashville, TN 37203 *tel* 615-244-5588. Division of **Lorenz Creative Services.** Gospel music.

Lorenz Publishing Co., 501 East Third Street, Dayton, OH 45401-0802 *tel* 513-228-6118. Considers for purchase anthems and church organ voluntaries. Division of **The Lorenz Corporation.**

Mercury Music Corporation—see **Theodore Presser Co.**

Merion Music, Inc. (1953)—see **Theodore Presser Co.**

C.F. Peters Corporation, 373 Park Avenue South, New York, NY 10016 *tel* 212-686-4147. (Edition Peters, Hinrichsen Edition, and other European music publications, in USA.)

Theodore Presser Co. (1783), Bryn Mawr, PA 19010 *tel* 215-525-3636 *fax* 215-527-7841. Considers suitable MSS from composers. Does not use or buy songs or lyrics unless with a musical setting. Publication at the firm's expense only.

The Sacred Music Press, 501 East Third Street, Dayton, OH 45401-0802 *tel* 513-228-6118. *Editor:* Dale Wood. Division of **The Lorenz Corporation.**

G. Schirmer Inc., 225 Park Avenue South, New York, NY 10003 *tel* 212-254-2100 *telex* 428351 *fax* 212-254-2013.

The Sengstack Tree Group, Ltd (1876), 180 Alexander Street, Princeton, NJ 08540 *tel* 609-497-3900. *President:* David K. Sengstack.

Sonshine Productions, 40 Music Square East, Nashville, TN 37203   *tel* 615-244-5588. Division of **Lorenz Creative Services.** Contemporary sacred music.

Triune Music Inc., 40 Music Square East, Nashville, TN 37203   *tel* 615-244-5588. Division of **Lorenz Creative Services.** Sacred music.

Warner/Chappell Music Inc., 9000 Sunset Boulevard, Penthouse, Los Angeles, CA 90069   *tel* 213-273-3323   *cables* Wang, Los Angeles. Includes, among others, the following companies: WB Music Corp., Warner-Tamerlane Publishing Corp., Harms Inc., M. Witmark, Remick, Advanced, New World Music Corp., Pepamar Music Corp., Schubert Music Publishing Corp., Weill-Brecht-Harms Company Inc., Viva Music Inc., Zapata Music Inc., Curtom Publishing Co. Inc., Rodart Music Corp., Jalynne Corp., Twentieth Century Fox Music Corp., House of Gold Music, Foster Frees Music Inc., Pendulum Music, Chappell Music, Unichappell, Rightsongs, Ricks Music, Delightful Music, Summy Birchard, Mighty Three Music, Bellboy Music.

Agents

Literary Agents

The Association of Authors' Agents (see **Societies**) is the trade association of British agents. Members meet regularly and commit themselves to observe a code of practice in the conduct of their business. They are designated with an asterisk in the following list. All agents listed below were circulated with a questionnaire with a view to providing pertinent information and are asked to keep this information up to date.

It should be noted that most agents do not charge a fee for marketing or placing manuscripts. Some firms charge a reading fee which is refunded on acceptance of the material. Most agents in this list will suggest revision of worthwhile manuscripts where necessary, suggesting in the first instance that revision should be done by the author. In certain cases, an agency is prepared to recommend a qualified person not connected with their agency to undertake revision. In a few cases where agencies themselves are prepared to undertake revision, this fact is clearly stated. In their own interests writers are strongly recommended to think twice before agreeing to pay for revision. Some agents are prepared to give an author a report and advice on a MS and they make an appropriate charge for this. Any reference to 'Short MSS' is almost invariably to short stories and not to journalistic articles.

Literary agents exist to sell saleable material. It must be remembered that, while they are looking for new writers and are often prepared to take immense pains with a writer whose work, in their opinion, shows potential quality or distinctive promise, agents do not exist to teach people how to write. Short manuscripts, unless they are of an exceptional nature, are unlikely to be profitable or even to pay an agent for the work involved. Writers must not expect agents, publishers or editors to comment at length on unsuitable work submitted to them, although often they are asked to do so. Every writer must expect disappointments, especially at the outset of his career, but if he has something to say and knows how to say it, then eventually (if he is patient) he will learn how to satisfy an editor's requirements, or alternatively he will learn that he should give up attempting to write and turn to some other form of activity. He must not expect other people to tell him his mistakes, although not infrequently a new writer is helped in this way by an agent, editor or publisher who has detected a spark of promise in a manuscript submitted to him.

If a writer of some proven ability is contemplating using an agent, he is advised in his own interests *to write a preliminary letter* to ascertain whether the agent will consider him as a potential client. He should also enquire the agent's terms if they are not given in the entry in the following pages. Reputable agents do not accept work unless they consider it to be of a marketable standard and an author submitting work to an agent for the first time *should therefore enclose return postage.* Most agents prefer a synopsis and specimen chapters to be sent in the first instance. This enables the agent to react faster. It is not advisable for a writer to send work to more than one agent at the same time. This is not only a waste of time, but could cause complications.

This list of literary agents does not purport to be exhaustive. If any who are not included would like to receive a copy of the questionnaire and to be considered for inclusion, application should be made to the publishers.

UNITED KINGDOM

*Membership of The Association of Authors' Agents

A & B Personal Management Ltd (1982), 5th Floor, Plaza Suite, 114 Jermyn Street, London SW1Y 6HJ   *tel* 071-839 4433   *telegraphic address* Abpersman London SW1   *fax* 071-930 5738. *Directors:* R.W. Ellis, R. Ellis.
Full-length MSS (home 12½%, overseas 15%), performance rights (12½%). Synopsis required initially from writers submitting work for first time. No reading fee for synopsis, plays or screenplays, but fee charged for full-length MSS. Return postage required.

***Aitken & Stone Ltd,** incorporating **Hughes Massie Ltd,** 29 Fernshaw Road, London SW10 0TG   *tel* 071-351 7561   *telex* 298391   *fax* 071-376 3594. *Directors:* Gillon Aitken, Brian Stone, Sally Riley, Andrew Wylie (USA).
Full-length MSS (home 10%, USA 15%, translations 20%). USA associates: Wylie, Aitken & Stone Inc., Suite 2106, 250 West 57th Street, New York, NY 10107   *tel* 212-246-0069. Preliminary letter and return postage essential.

***Jacintha Alexander Associates** (1981), 47 Emperor's Gate, London SW7 4HJ   *tel* 071-373 9258   *fax* 071-373 4374. *Proprietor:* Jacintha Alexander; *associate:* Julian Alexander.
Full length MSS. General fiction and non-fiction (home 15%, abroad 20%). No poetry or plays. Will sometimes suggest revision. Works in conjunction with agents in New York and Europe. No reading fee, but preliminary letter with sae essential.

Darley Anderson, MA, Estelle House, 11 Eustace Road, London SW6 1JB   *tel* 071-385 6652   *fax* 071-386 5571.
Specialises in all types of commercial women's fiction, especially family saga, historical, romance and glitz; also crime, thrillers, horror; non-fiction: showbusiness, diet, health, self-help, practical books for women, devotional, popular religion, supernatural. No poetry, plays, academic or children's books. Will consider short stories. Full-length MSS (home 15%, USA and translation 20%). Offers world-wide representation; can arrange PR and author publicity through associated PR company, and also specialist financial advice; editorial guidance on selected MSS. Preliminary letter, synopsis and return postage essential.

Aquarius Literary Agency & Picture Library (1973 in UK), PO Box 5, Hastings, East Sussex TN34 1HR   *tel* (0424) 721 196. *Directors:* David P. Corkill, Gilbert Gibson (SA).
Showbusiness only, including biography and autobiography. No fiction. Full-length and short MSS (home 10-15%, overseas 20-30%); performance rights (home 10%, overseas 20%). Works in conjunction with overseas agents. Will suggest revision. Preliminary letter; no unsolicited material. No reading fee.

Yvonne Baker Associates (1987), 8 Temple Fortune Lane, London NW11 7UD   *tel* 081-455 8687   *fax* 081-458 3143.

Theatre, television and film scripts primarily. No books, short stories, poetry. Theatre, radio (10%), television, films (12½%). No reading fee but preliminary enquiry appreciated and sae essential.

*Blake Friedmann Literary, TV & Film Agency Ltd (1977), 37-41 Gower Street, London WC1E 6HH   *tel* 071-631 4331   *telex* 262433 ref W6867   *fax* 071-323 1274. *Directors:* Carole Blake, Julian Friedmann, Barbara Jones, Conrad Williams.
Full-length MSS. Fiction: thrillers, contemporary and historical women's novels and literary fiction; non-fiction: investigative books, biography, travel; no poetry or plays (home 15%, overseas 20%). Specialise in film, television and video rights; place journalism and short stories. Represented in France, Germany, Greece, Holland, Israel, Italy, Scandinavia, Spain, Turkey, Canada, South America, Latin America, Japan; and in USA by Writers House Inc. Preliminary letter, synopsis and first two chapters preferred. No reading fee.

David Bolt Associates, 12 Heath Drive, Send, Surrey GU23 7EP   *tel* Woking (0483) 721118   *fax* (0483) 222878.
Specialises in biography, fiction, theology. Full-length MSS (home 10%, overseas 19%; all other rights including film, video and television 10%). No unsolicited short stories or play scripts. Will sometimes suggest revision. Works in association with overseas agencies world-wide. Preliminary letter essential.

Rosemary Bromley Literary Agency, Avington, Winchester, Hants SO21 1DB   *tel* (096278) 656   *fax* (0962) 64649.
Specialises in biography, travel, leisure. Full-length fiction and non-fiction (home 10%, overseas from 15%.) No poetry. No reading fee. Preliminary letter with return postage essential. For children's books see **Juvenilia.**

*Felicity Bryan, 2A North Parade, Banbury Road, Oxford OX2 6PE   *tel* (0865) 513816   *fax* (0865) 310055.
Fiction and general non-fiction – no light romance, science fiction, short stories, plays, children's (home 10%, overseas 20%). Performance rights handled by Curtis Brown; translation rights handled by Andrew Nurnberg Associates; works in conjunction with US agents. Return postage essential.

Diane Burston (1984), 46 Cromwell Avenue, Highgate, London N6 5HL   *tel* 081-340 6130.
General fiction and non-fiction, full-length MSS (home 10%, overseas 20%, USA 15%). Sae necessary. Preliminary enquiry essential; no unsolicited MSS. Reading service available on request.

Bycornute Books, 76a Ashford Road, Eastbourne, East Sussex BN21 3TE   *tel* (0323) 26819   *fax* (0323) 649053 Bycorn/Cresc. *Director:* Ayeshah Abdel-Haleem.
Specialises in illustrated books on sacred art, comparative religion, mythology, cosmology, astrology, iconography, spiritual development (*not* psychic studies or psychology); associated cardboard novelties. Full-length and short MSS (10%). Will suggest revision; fee by arrangement. Marketing fee: 10%.

*Campbell Thomson & McLaughlin Ltd, 31 Newington Green, London N16 9PU   *tel* 071-249 2971   *fax* 071-923 1375. *Directors:* John McLaughlin, John Parker, Charlotte Bruton, Hal Cheetham.
Full-length book MSS (home 10%, overseas up to 20% including commission to foreign agent). No poetry, plays or television scripts or short stories. USA agents represented: Raines & Raines, 71 Park Avenue, New York, NY 10016; The Fox Chase Agency, Inc., The Public Ledger Building, Independence

Square, Philadelphia, PA 19106. Representatives in most European countries. No reading fee, but return postage required. Subsidiary company: **Peter Janson-Smith Ltd.**

*Carnell Literary Agency (1951), Danes Croft, Goose Lane, Little Hallingbury, Herts. CM22 7RG   *tel* (0279) 723626. *Proprietor:* Pamela Buckmaster.
All MSS except poetry. Specialises in science/fantasy fiction. Works in conjunction with many foreign agents (home 10%, overseas 10% or 19% through sub-agent). No reading fee, but sae for acknowledgement. Outline plus first two chapters initially – return postage essential.

Casarotto Company Ltd (1989), National House, 60-66 Wardour Street, London W1V 3HP   *tel* 071-287 4450   *fax* 071-287 9128. *Directors:* Jenne Casarotto, Giorgio Casarotto.
Specialises in cinema, television and theatre (10%). Will suggest revision. No reading fee.

Judith Chilcote (1990), 8 Wentworth Mansions, Keats Grove, London NW3 2RL   *tel* 071-794 3717   *fax* 071-794 7431.
Fiction, non-fiction – celebrity and Royal books, TV tie-ins; journalists (home 15%, overseas 20-25%). Works in conjunction with overseas agents and New York affiliate. UK representative for Jonathon Lazear Agency, Miller Press, Cader Books and John Boswell Associates. No reading fee but preliminary letter essential.

Christy & Moore Ltd—see **Sheil Land Associates Ltd.**

*Serafina Clarke (1980), 98 Tunis Road, London W12 7EY   *tel* 081-749 6979   *fax* 081-740 6862.
Full-length MSS (home 10%, overseas 15-20%). Works in conjunction with agents overseas. No reading fee, but preliminary letter and return postage essential.

Robert Clarson-Leach (1985), 29 Ravensbourne Park Crescent, London SE6 4YJ   *tel* 081-690 4616.
Biography, autobiography, other non-fiction; full-length fiction occasionally handled (home 10%, overseas 20%), film, TV rights negotiated. Will suggest revision where appropriate. No reading fee; preliminary letter with sae essential.

*Jonathan Clowes Ltd (1960), Iron Bridge House, Bridge Approach, London NW1 8BD   *tel* 071-722 7674   *fax* 071-722 7677. *Directors:* Jonathan Clowes, Ann Evans, Brie Burkeman.
Full-length MSS (home and Europe 10%, USA 15%). Theatre, films, television and sound broadcasting. Works in association with agents in most foreign countries. Not actively seeking new clients.

Elspeth Cochrane Agency (1967), 11-13 Orlando Road, London SW4 0LE   *tel* 071-622 0314   *fax* 071-622 9456. *Director:* Miss Elspeth Cochrane.
Full-length MSS (home and overseas 12½%), performance rights (12½%). No reading fee.

Dianne Coles Literary Agency (1980), The Old Forge House, Sulgrave, Banbury, Oxon OX17 2RP   *tel* (0295) 76692/266631   *fax* (0295) 271454. *Contact:* Dianne Coles, Philip Gosling.
Full-length MSS. Non-fiction: investigative journalism, craft and leisure, human interest, biography, travel; fiction: thrillers and literary fiction (home/radio/TV/film 15%, overseas/translation 20%, journalism/short stories 25%). Own US office. Preliminary letter and return postage essential.

Rosica Colin Ltd (1949), 1 Clareville Grove Mews, London SW7 5AH   *tel* 071-370 1080   *telegraphic address* Colrep, London, SW7   *fax* 071-244 6441. *Directors:* Sylvie Marston, Joanna Marston.
All full-length MSS (home 10%, overseas 20%), performance rights (10%). Works in USA, European countries and overseas. No reading fee.

*****Jane Conway-Gordon** (1982), 1 Old Compton Street, London W1V 5PH   *tel* 071-494 0148   *fax* 071-287 9264.
Full length MSS, performance rights (home 10%, overseas 20%). Represented in all foreign countries. No reading fee but preliminary letter and return postage essential.

*****Rupert Crew Ltd** (founded by F. Rupert Crew, 1927), King's Mews, London WC1N 2JA   *tel* 071-242 8586   *telegraphic address* Authorship, Holb., London   *fax* 071-831 7914. *Directors:* Kathleen A. Crew, Doreen Montgomery, Shirley Russell.
International business management, available to a limited clientele, for authors seeking world representation: the agency specialises in promoting major book projects – non-fiction, general and women's fiction – especially those having serialisation potential. Preliminary letter and sae. Commission 10-20% by arrangement. No reading fees. Also acts independently as publishers' consultants.

Cruickshank Cazenove Ltd (1983), 97 Old South Lambeth Road, London SW8 1XU   *tel* 071-735 2933   *fax* 071-820 1081. *Director:* Harriet Cruickshank.
Fiction and non-fiction, film, television, theatre and radio scripts (home 10%, overseas varies). Works with agents abroad. No reading fee but preliminary letter essential with sae. Also agent for directors and designers.

Curtis Brown & John Farquharson, 162-168 Regent Street, London W1R 5TB   *tel* 071-872 0331   *cables* Browncurt, London W1   *telex* 920379   *fax* 071-872 0332. *Chairman:* Robert Loder; *managing director:* Daniel Edelman (USA); *directors:* Diana Baring, Sebastian Born, Tim Curnow (Australia), Sue Freathy, Jane Gelfman (John Farquharson, NY), Antony Harwood, Perry Knowlton (USA), Diana Mackay, Anne McDermid, Anthea Morton-Saner, Peter Murphy, Leah Schmidt, Vivienne Schuster, Michael Shaw, Elizabeth Stevens. Part owner of Curtis Brown Ltd, New York, 10 Astor Place, New York, NY 10003, USA   *tel* 212-473-5400, and of Curtis Brown Canada Ltd   *tel* 516-537-7924   *fax* 516-537-7365. Sole owner of Curtis Brown (Australia) Pty Ltd, 27 Union Street or PO Box 19, Paddington, Sydney, NSW 2021, Australia   *tel* (02) 331 5301 and of John Farquharson (NY), 250 West 57th Street, Suite 1007, New York, NY 10107, USA   *tel* 212-245-1993.
Agents for the negotiation in all markets of novels, general non-fiction, children's books and associated rights (home 10%, USA 15-20%, Canada and foreign 20%). Preliminary letter required; no reading fee. MSS for films, theatre, television and radio. Also agents for directors and designers.

The Caroline Davidson and Robert Ducas Literary Agency (1988), 5 Queen Anne's Gardens, London W4 1TU   *tel* 081-995 5768   *fax* 081-994 2770.
Specialises in highly illustrated general interest MSS and literary fiction (12½%). Will suggest revision. Works in conjunction with Robert Ducas (350 Hudson Street, New York, NY 10014, USA   *tel* 212-924-8120   *fax* 212-924-8079) and overseas agents. No reading fee.

Merric Davidson Literary Agency (1990), Oakwood, Ashley Park, Tunbridge Wells, Kent TN4 8UA   *tel/fax* (0892) 514282.
Fiction and general non-fiction; popular music (home 10%, overseas 20%). Will suggest revision. No reading fee, but preliminary letter essential.

Reg Davis-Poynter, 118 St Pancras, Chichester, West Sussex PO19 4LH *tel* (0243) 779047; and 11 Bolt Court, Fleet Street, London EC4A 3DQ *tel* 071-353 9365.
Specialising in contemporary history, politics, sociology, popular science, modern music, jazz. Full-length MSS (home 15%, overseas 20%), performance rights (10%). Works with agents in Germany, Scandinavia, Japan, Italy, France, USA. No reading fee but preliminary letter and return postage essential. Also acts as publishing consultant.

Felix De Wolfe (1946), Manfield House, 376 Strand, London WC2R 0LR *tel* 071-379 5767 *fax* 071-836 0337.
Theatre, films, television, sound broadcasting, fiction. Works in conjunction with many foreign agencies.

Denniston and Lownie (1991), 16a Inverleith Row, Edinburgh EH3 5LS *tel* 031-556 8949 *fax* 031-558 3853.
Fiction and general non-fiction, specialising in history, biography, current affairs and espionage (home 10%, overseas 20%). Own representation in USA. No reading fee but preliminary letter, synopsis and return postage essential.

Dorian Literary Agency (1986), 35 Longcroft Avenue, Brixham, Devon TQ5 0DS *tel* (0803) 859390. *Proprietor:* Dorothy Lumley.
Full-length MSS. Specialises in women's writing, SF, fantasy and horror, crime and thrillers (home 10%, USA 15%, translations 20-25%), performance rights (10%). No poetry or children's. Works in conjunction with agencies in most countries; negotiates direct with USA. No reading fee; preliminary letter with sample material preferred, with return postage. *Note* – initial enquiry by telephone, change of address expected.

Anne Drexl (1988), PO Box 541, 8 Roland Gardens, London SW7 3PH *tel* 071-244 9645.
Full-length MSS, fiction and non-fiction, especially romantic, suspense, crime novels/short stories, children's books (home 12½%, overseas 20-23%). No science fiction, scripts, plays or poetry. Works in conjunction with foreign agencies and negotiates direct with foreign publishers. No reading fee, but no unsolicited MSS; return postage and preliminary letter essential.

Susan Dunnett Management (1987), 27 Bryantwood Road, London N7 7BG *tel* 071-609 5294.
Drama, drama comedy, light entertainment (10%). Works in conjunction with foreign agencies. No unsolicited material.

Faith Evans Associates (1987), 5 Dryden Street, Covent Garden, London WC2E 9NW *tel* 071-829 8425 *fax* 071-240 5600.
Specialises in editorial support (fee by arrangement) as well as representation of fiction and non-fiction (home 15%, overseas 20%). Also offers independent advice service for authors and publishers. No scripts or unsolicited MSS; preliminary letter essential. No reading fee.

Fact & Fiction Agency Ltd, 16 Greenway Close, London NW9 5AZ *tel* 081-205 5716. *Directors:* Roy Lomax, Vera Lomax.
Television, radio (home 10%, overseas 15%). By introduction only.

***John Farquharson Ltd**—see **Curtis Brown & John Farquharson.**

Film Link Literary Agency (1979), 31 Oakdene Drive, Tolworth, Surrey KT5 9NH *tel* 081-330 3182. *Director:* Yvonne Heather.
Specialising in fiction for women's market and children's fiction; will consider general fiction and non-fiction. Full-length MSS (home 10%, overseas 15-20%). No short stories or poetry. Will suggest revision where appropriate.

Works in conjunction with overseas agents. Preliminary letter, synopsis and sae essential.

Film Rights Ltd (1932), 483 Southbank House, Black Prince Road, Albert Embankment, London SE1 7SJ *tel* 071-735 8171. *Directors:* D.M. Sims, Maurice Lambert, Laurence Fitch.
Theatre, films, television and sound broadcasting (10%). Represented in USA and abroad.

Laurence Fitch Ltd (1952) (incorporating The London Play Company) (1922), 483 Southbank House, Black Prince Road, Albert Embankment, London SE1 7SJ *tel* 071-735 8171. *Directors:* F.H.L. Fitch, Joan Potts, Brendan Davis.
Theatre, films, television and sound broadcasting. Also works with several agencies in New York and in Europe.

Jill Foster Ltd (1978), 3 Lonsdale Road, London SW13 9ED *tel* 081-741 9410 *fax* 081-741 2916.
Theatre, films, television, sound broadcasting (10%). Particularly interested in film and television comedy and drama. No novels or short stories. No reading fee. Preliminary letter essential.

*Fraser & Dunlop Ltd—see **The Peters Fraser & Dunlop Group Ltd.**

*Fraser & Dunlop Scripts Ltd—see **The Peters Fraser & Dunlop Group Ltd.**

John French Artists Agency Ltd, 24 St Anselm's Place, London W1Y 1FG *tel* 071-495 1598 *fax* 071-499 4336. *Director:* John French.
All MSS, home and overseas (10%). Novels, theatre, films, television, radio (10%). Reading service available, details on application. Sae must be enclosed with all MSS.

Vernon Futerman Associates (1984), Garden Flat A, 159 Goldhurst Terrace, London NW6 3EU *tel* 071-625 9601 *fax* 071-372 1282. *Directors:* Vernon Futerman (managing), Jenny Goodstone, Wendy Futerman.
Specialises in academic (science, humanities), art, education, politics, current affairs, literary criticism, showbusiness, travel and business books. Full-length MSS (home $12\frac{1}{2}$-$17\frac{1}{2}$%, overseas $17\frac{1}{2}$-$22\frac{1}{2}$%), performance rights ($12\frac{1}{2}$-$17\frac{1}{2}$%). Works in conjunction with overseas agents. Will suggest revision. No reading fee; preliminary letter with synopsis and sae essential. No unsolicited MSS.

Jüri Gabriel, 35 Camberwell Grove, London SE5 8JA *tel* 071-703 6186.
Literary fiction; quality non-fiction (current specialisations: medical, military, academic). Full-length MSS (home 10%, overseas 20%), performance rights (10%); will suggest revision where appropriate. No short stories, articles, verse or books for small children. No reading fee; return postage essential.

Kerry Gardner Management (1975), 15 Kensington High Street, London W8 5NP *tel* 071-937 4478 *fax* 071-376 2587.
Specialises in performance rights – represents playwrights, and film, TV and radio scriptwriters (10%). Will suggest revision. Works in conjunction with overseas agents. No reading fee.

Eric Glass Ltd (1932), 28 Berkeley Square, London W1X 6HD *tel* 071-629 7162 *telegraphic address* Blancheric, London, W1 *telex* 296759 Kallin G ref 101 *fax* 071-499 6780. *Directors:* Eric Glass, Janet Crowley.
Full-length MSS only. Theatre, films, television, and sound broadcasting. Will occasionally recommend someone for revision of promising material if the author is unable to undertake it. No reading fee. Sole representatives of the French Society of Authors (Societé des Auteurs et Compositeurs Dramatiques).

*Christine Green (Author's Agent) Ltd (1984), 2 Barbon Close, London WC1N 3JX   *tel* 071-831 4956   *fax* 071-831 4840.
Fiction and general non-fiction. Full-length MSS (home 10%, overseas 20%). Works in conjunction with agencies in Europe and Scandinavia. No reading fee, but preliminary letter and return postage essential.

*Elaine Greene Ltd (1962), 37 Goldhawk Road, London W12 8QQ   *tel* 081-749 0315   *fax* 081-749 0318. *Directors:* Elaine Greene (USA), Carol Heaton, Timothy Webb.
Full-length MSS, fiction and non-fiction (home 10%, overseas 15-20%, translation 20%). Works in conjunction with agencies in most countries. No reading fee. No unsolicited MSS accepted without an introductory letter describing the work and enclosing return postage.

*The Jane Gregory Agency (1982)—see **Gregory & Radice Authors' Agents.**

Gregory & Radice Authors' Agents (1982), Riverside Studios, Crisp Road, Hammersmith, London W6 9RL   *tel* 081-741 3646   *fax* 081-846 9039. *Partners:* Jane Gregory, Dr Lisanne Radice; *US serial translation:* Karin Joseph.
Full-length MSS; fiction and non-fiction. Specialise in crime fiction, thrillers and politics (home 15%, articles, USA and translation 20%). No short stories, plays, film scripts, science fiction, poetry, academic or children's books. UK representative for Simon & Schuster Inc., New York. No reading fee, editorial advice given. No unsolicited MSS: preliminary letter and synopsis essential plus return postage.

David Grossman Literary Agency Ltd (1976), 110-114 Clerkenwell Road, London EC1M 5SA   *tel* 071-251 5046/7   *telex* 263404 Bk Biz G   *fax* 071-490 2702.
Full-length MSS (home 10-15%, overseas 15-20% including foreign agent's commission), performance rights (15%). Works in conjunction with agents in New York, Europe, Japan. No reading fee, but preliminary letter required.

The June Hall Literary Agency Ltd (member of The Peters Fraser & Dunlop Group Ltd), 504 The Chambers, Chelsea Harbour, Lots Road, London SW10 0XF   *tel* 071-352 4233   *fax* 071-352 7356. *Directors:* Kenneth Ewing (joint chairman), Michael Sissons (joint chairman & managing director), Shân Morley Jones (deputy managing director), Lucinda Culpin, Rosemary Canter, Tim Corrie, Mark Lucas, Caroline Dawnay; *consultant:* June Hall.
Specialists in the negotiation of all rights in general fiction and non-fiction (home/overseas 10-20%). No unsolicited manuscripts accepted without an introductory letter from the author describing the work and return postage. No reading fee.

*A.M. Heath & Co. Ltd (1919), 79 St Martin's Lane, London WC2N 4AA   *tel* 071-836 4271   *telegraphic address* Script, London, WC2   *cables* Script, London   *telex* 27370   *fax* 071-497 2561. *Directors:* Mark Hamilton, Michael Thomas, William Hamilton, Sara Fisher.
Full-length MSS (home 10%, USA 20%, translation 20%), performance rights (15%). Agents in USA and all European countries and Japan. No reading fee.

Duncan Heath Associates Ltd—see **ICM/Duncan Heath Associates.**

*David Higham Associates Ltd (1935), 5-8 Lower John Street, Golden Square, London W1R 4HA   *tel* 071-437 7888   *telex* 8955509   *fax* 071-437 1072. *Directors:* Bruce Hunter, Jacqueline Korn, Anthony Crouch, John Rush, Elizabeth Cree, Anthony Goff, Ania Corless.
Agents for the negotiation of all rights in fiction, general non-fiction, plays, film and television scripts (home 10%, USA 15%, translation 20%). USA

Associate Agency: Harold Ober Associates Inc. Represented in all foreign markets. Preliminary letter and return postage essential. No reading fee.

Pamela Hodgson Agency (1990), 38 Westminster Palace Gardens, Artillery Row, London SW1P 1RR *tel/fax* 071-222 4468.
Books for children from babies to teens (home 15%). Will suggest revision where appropriate. No reading fee.

Vanessa Holt Associates Ltd (1989), 59 Crescent Road, Leigh-on-Sea, Essex SS9 2PF *tel* (0702) 73787 *fax* (0702) 471890. Also based in London.
General adult fiction and non-fiction (home 10%, overseas 20%). Works in conjunction with many foreign agencies. No reading fee, but preliminary letter essential.

Valerie Hoskins (1983) at Noel Gay Artists, 19 Denmark Street, London WC2H 8NA *tel* 071-836 3941 *fax* 071-379 7027. *Proprietor:* Valerie Hoskins at Noel Gay Artists.
Film, television, theatre and radio only (10% home and maximum 20% overseas). No reading fee, but sae appreciated. Works in conjunction with overseas agents. *No* unsolicited MSS; preliminary letter essential.

*Tanja Howarth (1970), 19 New Row, London WC2N 4LA *tel* 071-240 5553 *fax* 071-379 0969. *Partners:* Tanja Howarth, Charlotte Oldfield.
Full-length MSS, fiction and non-fiction (home 10%, USA 15%, translation 20%). No reading fee.

Hughes Massie Ltd—see **Aitken & Stone Ltd.**

ICM/Duncan Heath Associates, Paramount House 162-170 Wardour Street, London W1V 3AT *tel* 071-439 1471 *telex* 263361 ParaUK *fax* 071-439 7274. *Directors:* Duncan Heath, Susan Rodgers, Michael Foster, Ian Amos, Steve Bailie.
Specialising in scripts for film, theatre, TV, radio (home 10%, overseas 10%). Part of International Creative Management Inc., Los Angeles and New York. No reading fee.

Michael Imison Playwrights Ltd (formerly Dr Jan Van Loewen Ltd), 28 Almeida Street, London N1 1TD *tel* 071-354 3174 *fax* 071-359 6273. *Directors:* Michael Imison, MA, Tamsyn Imison, BSc.
Specialise in stage plays, also cover radio, TV, film (home 10%, overseas 15%), no fiction or general MSS. Represented in all major countries. No reading fee, but preliminary letter and sae essential.

Intercontinental Literary Agency (1965), The Chambers, Chelsea Harbour, Lots Road, London SW10 0XF *tel* 071-351 4763 *telegraphic address* Interlitag, London *fax* 071-351 4809. Anthony Guest Gornall and Nicki Kennedy.
Concerned only with translation rights exclusively for The Peters Fraser & Dunlop Group Ltd, including The June Hall Literary Agency, London, Harold Matson Company, Inc., New York, Sterling Lord Literistic, Inc., New York.

International Copyright Bureau Ltd (1905), 22A Aubrey House, Maida Avenue, London W2 1TQ *tel* 071-724 8034 *telegraphic address* Volscius London *fax* 071-724 7662. *Directors:* Joy Westendarp, J.C.H. Hadfield (secretary).
Theatre, films, television, radio (home 10%, overseas 19%). Works in conjunction with agents in New York and most foreign countries. Preliminary letter essential.

International Scripts (1979), 1 Norland Square, Holland Park, London W11 4PX *tel* 071-229 0736 *fax* 071-792 3287. *Directors:* H.P. Tanner, J. Lawson; *agent:* Yvonne Weaver.

Specialising in full-length contemporary and women's fiction, general non-fiction (home 10%, overseas 20%). First works 15%. Films, television, radio, theatre (10-20%). No poetry. Works with overseas agents world-wide. Return postage required for MSS plus a £20.00 reading fee (for which a report will be provided).

Mary Irvine (1974), 11 Upland Park Road, Oxford OX2 7RU *tel* (0865) 513570.
Specialising in women's fiction and family sagas. No plays, scripts, children's books or poetry (home 10%, USA 15%, translations 20%). Works with agents in USA, Europe, Japan. No reading fee. No unsolicited MSS. Preliminary letter and return postage required.

*John Johnson (Authors Agent) Ltd (1956), Clerkenwell House, 45-47 Clerkenwell Green, London EC1R 0HT *tel* 071-251 0125 *fax* 071-251 2172.
Full-length and short MSS (home 10%, overseas 10%, if foreign agent is concerned maximum of 20%). Works in conjunction with agents in USA and many European countries. Strictly no MSS without preliminary letter and sae first.

*Jane Judd Literary Agency (1986), 18 Belitha Villas, London N1 1PD *tel* 071-607 0273 *telex* 444 322 *fax* 071-607 0623.
Full-length MSS only (home 10%, overseas 20%). Works with agents in USA and most foreign countries. No reading fee, but preliminary letter and sae essential.

Juvenilia (1973), Avington, Winchester, Hants SO21 1DB *tel* (096278) 656 *fax* (0962) 64649. *Proprietor:* Mrs Rosemary Bromley.
Full-length MSS for the children's market, fiction and non-fiction (home 10%, overseas from 15%). No verse. Short stories only if specifically for picture books, radio or TV. Theatre, films, television, radio (10%). No unsolicited MSS.; preliminary letter with sae and full details essential. No reading fee. Postage for acknowledgement and return of material imperative.

J.W. Productions Literary Associates (1986), Suite 3, 123/125 Gloucester Place, London W1H 3PJ. *Director:* Marjorie Windsor; *consultant:* Jennifer Watts.
Mainly interested in full-length MSS suitable for dramatisation after publication (15-20%); will suggest revision where appropriate. Reading fee from £20; report given. Send return postage with script.

*Frances Kelly Agency (1978), 111 Clifton Road, Kingston-upon-Thames, Surrey KT2 6PL *tel* 081-549 7830 *fax* 081-547 0051.
Full-length and short MSS (home 10%, overseas 20%), television, radio (10%). Non-fiction: general and academic, reference and professional books; all subjects. *US Associate:* The Balkin Agency, 850 West 176 Street, New York, NY 10033. No reading fee, but no unsolicited MSS; return postage and preliminary letter requested.

Dieter Klein Associates—see **Patricia Robertson.**

Peter Knight Agency (1985), 20 Crescent Grove, London SW4 7AH *tel* 071-622 1467 *fax* 071-622 1522. *Director:* Peter Knight; *associates:* Ann King-Hall, Robin Mackay Miller, Caroline Figini.
Full-length MSS but no short stories, or poetry (home 10%, overseas 20%), performance rights (15%). Works in conjunction with agents world-wide. Reading fee.

Lemon Unna & Durbridge Ltd, 24 Pottery Lane, Holland Park, London W11 4LZ *tel* 071-727 1346 *telex* 27618 Author G *fax* 071-727 9037. *Directors:* Stephen Durbridge, Sheila Lemon, Girsha Reid, Wendy Gresser, Nigel Britten, Bethan Evans.

Specialises in theatre, film, television and radio. Novels represented only for existing clients. Commission 10% unless sub-agents employed overseas; works in conjunction with agents in USA and all foreign countries. No reading fee, but return postage and preliminary letter essential.

*Barbara Levy Literary Agency (1986), 21 Kelly Street, London NW1 8PG   *tel* 071-485 6037   *fax* 071-284 0292. *Director:* Barbara Levy; *associate:* John Selby.
Full-length MSS only; also films, television and radio (home 10%, overseas by arrangement). No reading fee, but preliminary letter and return postage essential.

Christopher Little Literary Agent (1976), 49 Queen Victoria Street, London EC4N 4SA   *tel* 071-236 5881   *fax* 071-236 7625.
Specialising in non-fiction, full-length fiction; thrillers, crime, historical, romance. Full-length MSS (home 20%, overseas 20%). Films, television (20%). Reading fee £35 + VAT.

London Independent Books Ltd (1971), 1A Montagu Mews North, London W1H 1AJ   *tel* 071-706 0486. *Directors:* Carolyn Whitaker, Patrick Whitaker.
Specialises in travel, fantasy fiction, cinema, jazz, show business. Full-length MSS (home 15%, overseas 20%). Films, television and sound broadcasting (15%). Will suggest revision of promising MSS. No reading fee.

Andrew Lownie Associates (1988), 15/17 Heddon Street, London W1R 7LF   *tel* 071-734 1510   *fax* 071-287 5118. *Associate office:* Denniston and Lownie, *q.v.*
Fiction and general non-fiction, specialising in history, biography, current affairs (home 10%, overseas 20%). No reading fee, but preliminary letter, synopsis and return postage essential.

MacLean Dubois (Writers & Agents)—see **Alexandra Nye, Writers & Agents.**

*Andrew Mann Ltd (1974), 1 Old Compton Street, London W1V 5PH   *tel* 071-734 4751   *fax* 071-287 9264. *Directors:* Anne Dewe, Tina Betts.
Full-length MSS (home 10%, USA 19%, Europe 19%), performance rights (10%). Associated with agents in Europe and USA. No reading fee, but no unsolicited MSS without preliminary enquiry and sae.

Manuscript ReSearch (1988), PO Box 33, Bicester, Oxon OX6 8BU   *tel* (0869) 252992. *Proprietors:* T.G. Jenkins, V. Miller.
Specialising in crime/thrillers, historical romance, biographies. Full-length MSS (home 10%, overseas 20%), performance rights (15%); short MSS only from established clients. Will suggest and undertake revision where appropriate (from £50 per script; retyping service extra). No reading fee, but sae for script return essential.

Marsh & Sheil Ltd (1985), 19 John Street, London WC1N 2EA   *tel* 071-405 9351   *fax* 071-405 5239. Paul Marsh, Susanna Nicklin, Anthony Sheil, Sonia Land.
Translation rights only.

Judy Martin (1990), 20 Powis Mews, London W11 1JN   *tel* 071-229 8764   *fax* 071-792 3635.
Fiction, non-fiction, film and TV tie-ins, film and TV scripts, journalism; *no* plays or poetry (home 10%, overseas 20%), performance rights (10-15%). Foreign rights handled by Marsh & Sheil. No reading fee, but sae required for all unsolicited MSS, together with details of publishing history.

M.C. Martinez Literary Agency (1988), 60 Oakwood Avenue, Southgate, London N14 6QL   *tel* 081-886 5829. *Proprietor:* Mary Caroline Martinez.

Fiction, children's books, arts and crafts, DIY, cookery, travel, business books, educational books (home 15%, overseas 20%), performance rights (15%); will suggest revision where appropriate. Works in conjunction with foreign agencies. Preliminary letter and sae required; no reading fee. Full desktop publishing service using Ventura is offered to both publishers and authors.

Blanche Marvin, 21A St John's Wood High Street, London NW8 7NG   *tel/fax* 071-722 2313.
Full-length MSS (home $12\frac{1}{2}$% + $12\frac{1}{2}$% overseas), performance rights. No reading fee but return postage essential.

*MBA Literary Agents Ltd (1971), 45 Fitzroy Street, London W1P 5HR   *tel* 071-387 2076/4785   *fax* 071-387 2042. *Directors:* Diana Tyler, John Richard Parker, Meg Davis, Ruth Needham.
Full-length MSS (home 10%, overseas 20%), theatre, television, radio (10%), films – negotiable. No reading fee. Works in conjunction with agents in most countries.

Richard Milne Ltd (1956), 28 Makepeace Avenue, Highgate, London N6 6EJ   *tel* 081-340 7007. *Directors:* R.M. Sharples, K.N. Sharples.
Specialising in scripts for films, television, sound broadcasting (10%). Unable to represent any additional authors at present.

*William Morris Agency (UK) Ltd (1965), 31/32 Soho Square, London W1V 5DG   *tel* 071-434 2191   *fax* 071-437 0238. *Contacts:* Stephen M. Kenis (Films), Jane Annakin (Television and Theatre), Lavina Trevor (Books).
World-wide theatrical and literary agency with offices in New York, Beverly Hills and Nashville, and associates in Rome, Munich and Sydney. Represents theatre, television, film and radio scripts; fiction and general non-fiction (television, theatre, film and UK book 10%, US book and translation 20%). Writers should approach by letter with synopsis/sample chapters and an sae. No unsolicited material or MSS. No reading fee.

Negotiate Ltd (1986), 22 Braid Avenue, Edinburgh EH10 6EE   *tel* 031-452 8404   *fax* 031-452 8388. *Directors:* Gavin Kennedy, John Benson, Trevor Webster.
Specialise in the negotiation of the author's contract and all rights.

*Maggie Noach Literary Agency (1982), 21 Redan Street, London W14 0AB   *tel* 071-602 2451   *fax* 071-603 4712.
General fiction and non-fiction; non-illustrated children's books. Full-length MSS (home 10-15%, overseas 20%). Works with agents in USA and all foreign markets. No reading fee but preliminary letter with sae essential.

*Andrew Nurnberg Associates Ltd, Clerkenwell House, 45-47 Clerkenwell Green, London EC1R 0HT   *tel* 071-251 0321   *cables* Nurnbooks, London   *telex* 23353   *fax* 071-251 0584.
Specialise in the sale of translation rights of English and American authors into European languages.

Alexandra Nye, Writers & Agents (successor to **Maclean Dubois (Writers & Agents)**; 1991), 115 Buccleuch Street, Edinburgh EH8 9NG   *tel* 031-668 4103. *Director:* Alexandra Nye.
Literary fiction, thrillers, biographies. No poetry or plays (home 10%, overseas 20%, translation 15%). Will suggest revision where appropriate. Unsolicited MSS welcome if accompanied by return postage.

David O'Leary Literary Agency (1988), 10 Lansdowne Court, Lansdowne Rise, London W11 2NR   *tel* 071-229 1623   *telex* 27636 Aezra G   *fax* 071-221 7185.

General fiction and non-fiction: special interests Russia, Ireland, history,
archaeology (home 10%, overseas 20%), performance rights (15%). Will
suggest revision; no reading fee. Write or call before submitting MSS.

*Deborah Owen Ltd (1971), 78 Narrow Street, Limehouse, London E14 8BP   *tel*
071-987 5119/5441   *fax* 071-538 4004. Deborah Owen, Rosemary Scoular.
Full-length MSS (home 10%, overseas 15%). All types of literary material
except plays, scripts, children's books or poetry. No unsolicited MSS without
preliminary letter and sae.

*Mark Paterson & Associates (1955), 10 Brook Street, Wivenhoe, Colchester,
Essex CO7 9DS   *tel* (0206) 825433/4   *telex* 987562MP Cochac G   *fax* (0206)
822990.
Full-length MSS, specialising in psychoanalysis, psychotherapy, clinical psychology and psychiatry (20% including sub-agent's commission). No short
stories or articles. Preliminary letter required.

John Pawsey (1981), 60 High Street, Tarring, Worthing, West Sussex BN14
7NR   *tel* (0903) 205167   *fax* on application.
Full-length popular fiction and non-fiction MSS, television and radio (home
10-15%, overseas 19%). No unsolicited material, poetry, short stories or
original film and stage scripts. Preliminary letter and return postage with all
correspondence essential. Works in association with agencies in the USA,
Europe and the Far East. Will suggest revision if MS sufficiently promising.
No reading fee.

Maggie Pearlstine Authors' Agent (1989), 31 Ashley Gardens, Ambrosden
Avenue, Westminster, London SW1P 1QE   *tel* 071-828 4212   *fax* 071-834
5546.
Full-length MSS, fiction and general non-fiction – commercial fiction and
illustrated life style books a speciality (home 10% basic, overseas 20%),
performance rights (20%). Will suggest revision where appropriate. Works
in conjunction with foreign agents. No unsolicited MSS considered without
preliminary letter describing work and giving publishing history; return postage with MSS essential. No reading fee.

Penman Literary Agency (1950), 175 Pall Mall, Leigh-on-Sea, Essex SS9
1RE   *tel* Southend (0702) 74438. *Director:* Leonard G. Stubbs, FRSA.
Full-length novel MSS (home 10%, overseas 15%), performance rights (10%).
Revision undertaken by agency at author's request; fees depending upon
amount of revision required. No reading fee.

*A.D. Peters & Co. Ltd—see **The Peters Fraser & Dunlop Group Ltd.**

†The Peters Fraser & Dunlop Group Ltd, 503/4 The Chambers, Chelsea Harbour,
Lots Road, London SW10 0XF   *tel* 071-376 7676   *fax* 071-352 7356/351
1756. *Directors:* Kenneth Ewing (joint chairman), Michael Sissons (joint
chairman & managing director), Anthony Jones, Pat Kavanagh, Tim Corrie,
Maureen Vincent, Norman North, Anthony Baring. *Incorporating* A.D.
Peters & Co. Ltd, Watergate Film Services Ltd, Fraser & Dunlop Scripts
Ltd, Fraser & Dunlop Ltd, The June Hall Literary Agency Ltd. *Associated
agencies:* Intercontinental Literary Agency, Sterling Lord Literistic (New
York), Icone (Paris).
Specialists in the negotiation of all rights in general fiction and non-fiction,
film and television scripts, plays, and certain specialist and academic works
(home/overseas 10-20%). No unsolicited manuscripts accepted. We ask for
an introductory letter from the author describing the work offered, with sae.
No reading fee.

Laurence Pollinger Ltd, 18 Maddox Street, London W1R 0EU   *tel* 071-629 9761   *telegraphic address* Laupoll, London, W1   *fax* 071-629 9765. *Directors:* Gerald J. Pollinger, Margaret Pepper; *secretary:* Denzil De Silva.
Authors' agents for all material with the exception of original film stories, poetry and freelance journalistic articles. Dramatic associate, Micheline Steinberg. Terms are a commission of 15% of the amounts obtained, except on translation sales, where the total commission of 20% may include the commission to the associate in the territory concerned. No reading fee. An editorial contribution may be requested.

*Murray Pollinger (1969), 222 Old Brompton Road, London SW5 0BZ   *tel* 071-373 4711   *telegraphic address/cables* Chopper, London, SW5   *fax* 071-373 3775.
Agents for the negotiation in all markets of adult fiction and non-fiction, children's fiction and picture books (home 10%, overseas 20%). Preliminary letter and synopsis required; also names of agents and publishers previously contacted. No reading fee.

Shelley Power Literary Agency Ltd (1976), PO Box 149a Surbiton, Surrey KT6 5JH   *tel* 081-398 7723   *fax* 081-398 8723.
General fiction and non-fiction. Full-length MSS (home 10%, USA and translations 19%). No children's books, poetry or plays. Works in conjunction with agents abroad. No reading fee, but preliminary letter with sae essential.

PVA Management Ltd, Alpha Tower, Paradise Circus, Birmingham B1 1TT   *tel* 021-643 4011   *fax* 021-633 3947. *Managing director:* Paul Vaughan.
Full-length and short MSS (home 15%, overseas 20%), performance rights (15%).

Radala & Associates (1970), 17 Avenue Mansions, Finchley Road, London NW3 7AX   *tel* 071-794 4495   *telex* 295441   *fax* 071-209 1231. *Directors:* Richard Gollner, István Siklós; *Associates:* Neil Hornick, Anna Swan.
Full-length MSS (10% UK, 15% overseas). Fiction and non-fiction. Books, films, television, sound broadcasting. Electronic publishing division, including video, audio tape, computer program packages for multi-media publishing production companies.

Douglas Rae (Management) Ltd (1975), 28 Charing Cross Road, London WC2H 0DB   *tel* 071-836 3903/4.
Full-length MSS (home 10%, overseas 15%), theatre, films, television (10%).

Margaret Ramsay Ltd (1953), 14A Goodwin's Court, St Martin's Lane, London WC2N 4LL   *tel* 071-836 7403/240 0691   *fax* 071-836 6807. *Directors:* M. Ramsay, Tom Erhardt.
MSS – theatre, films, television, sound broadcasting only (commission 10%). Works in conjunction with agents in USA and in all foreign countries. Preliminary letter essential. No reading fee.

Jim Reynolds Associates (1988), Westbury Mill, Westbury, Nr Brackley, Northants. NN13 5JS   *tel* (0280) 701582   *fax* (0280) 701945 ref Jim Reynolds. *Director:* Ann Reynolds.
Full-length MSS – biography, social, political and military history, current affairs, investigative journalism, cricket (home 10%, overseas 19%); will suggest revision where appropriate. Works in conjunction with foreign agencies. No reading fee.

Patricia Robertson (1985), Flat 1, 87 Caledonian Road, London N1 9BT   *tel* 071-278 9982   *fax* 071-837 3486.
General fiction and non-fiction. Full-length MSS only (home 10%, USA 15%, translation 20%). No playscripts or poetry. Works in conjunction with agents

overseas; for dramatic rights works in conjunction with The Sharland Organisation Ltd; manages the interests of Dieter Klein Associates. No reading fee. Preliminary letter and sae please.

*Rogers, Coleridge & White Ltd (1967), 20 Powis Mews, London W11 1JN   *tel* 071-221 3717   *telegraphic address* Debrogers, London, W11   *telex* 25930 Debrog G   *fax* 071-229 9084. *Directors:* Deborah Rogers, Gill Coleridge, Patricia White (USA); *consultant:* Ann Warnford-Davis.
Full-length book MSS, including children's books (home 10%, USA 15%, translations 20%). *USA Associate:* International Creative Management, 40 West 57th Street, New York, NY 10019. No unsolicited MSS considered without a preliminary letter describing work and giving publishing history. No reading fee but return postage with MSS essential.

Rostrum Literary Agency Ltd (1986), 2nd Floor, Basil House, 105-107 Portland Street, Manchester M1 6DF   *tel* 061-456 8035   *fax* 061-483 4747. *Directors:* Eric Falk, Marj Falk; *drama associate:* Andrew Burton.
Fiction and non-fiction; biography, autobiography (home 10%, overseas 19%), theatre, films, TV (15%). Preliminary letter and return postage essential. No reading fee.

Herta Ryder (1984), c/o Toby Eady Associates Ltd, 18 Park Walk, London SW10 0AQ   *tel* 081-948 1010.
Specialises in novels for older children, adult fiction and non-fiction. Full-length MSS (home 10%, USA 15%, overseas 20%). Represented by agents in all major foreign countries. No reading fee. Preliminary letter welcomed.

*Tessa Sayle Agency, 11 Jubilee Place, London SW3 3TE   *tel* 071-823 3883 (5 lines)   *fax* 071-823 3363. *Associates – publishing:* Tessa Sayle; *film, TV and theatre:* Penny Tackaberry.
Full-length MSS (home 10%, overseas 20%), performance rights (10%). USA Associates: Liz Darhansoff Literary Agency, 1220 Park Avenue, New York, NY 10028. Represented in all foreign countries. No reading fee, but preliminary letter and return postage essential.

The Sharland Organisation Ltd (1988), 9 Marlborough Crescent, Bedford Park, London W4 1HE   *tel* 081-742 1919   *fax* 081-995 7688. *Directors:* Mike Sharland, Alice Sharland.
Mainly performance rights; also full-length book MSS (home 15%, overseas 20%); will suggest revision where appropriate. Also assist TV and film directors to find suitable material. Work in conjunction with overseas agents. Sae required.

*Sheil Land Associates Ltd (1962), incorporating Christy & Moore Ltd (1912) and Richard Scott Simon Ltd (1971), 43 Doughty Street, London WC1N 2LF   *tel* 071-405 9351   *telegraphic address* Novelist, London   *telex* 94013094 Asap G   *fax* 071-831 2127. *Agents:* Sonia Land, Anthony Sheil, Giles Gordon, Paul Marsh, Janet Fillingham, Mic Cheetham, Vivien Green, Eunice McMullen (children's).
Full-length MSS, children's (home 10%, USA 20%, translations 20%). Film, television scripts, plays (home/overseas 10-20%). Preliminary letter and return postage essential. Translations: see **Marsh & Sheil Ltd.**

*Caroline Sheldon Literary Agency (1985), 71 Hillgate Place, London W8 7SS   *tel* 071-727 9102.
Full-length MSS (home 10%, overseas 20%). General fiction, women's fiction, and children's books longer than 10,000 words. No reading fee. Synopsis and first three chapters with return postage required initially.

*Dasha Shenkman Associates (1987). Ceased trading.
   Full-length MSS, non-fiction and fiction, but no short stories, poetry, plays or film/TV scripts (home 15%, USA 15%, overseas 20%), performance rights (15%). Represented in all foreign markets. No reading fee, but preliminary letter required.

Sheri Safran Literary Agency Ltd (1979), 3D Westpoint, 36/37 Warple Way, London W3 0RQ *tel* 081-746 1171 *telex* 262433 ref 1255 *fax* 081-746 1170.
   Non-fiction titles for, by and about women; and children's books (home 15%, overseas 20%). Preliminary letter with outline or partial MSS together with return postage and sae essential. No reading fee. See also: **Sadie Fields Productions Ltd (Book Packagers).**

Jeffrey Simmons, 10 Lowndes Square, London SW1X 9HA *tel* 071-235 8852 *fax* 071-235 9733.
   Specialises in adult fiction, biography, autobiography, show business, law, crime, politics, world affairs. Full-length MSS (home from 10%, overseas from 15%). Will suggest revision. No reading fee, but preliminary letter essential.

*Richard Scott Simon Ltd—see **Sheil Land Associates Ltd.**

*Carol Smith (1976), 25 Hornton Court, Kensington High Street, London W8 7RT *tel* 071-937 4874 *fax* 071-938 5323.
   Full-length and short MSS (home 10%, USA and translation 20%). Will suggest revision of promising MSS. Works in conjunction with many foreign agencies. No reading fee, but preliminary letter essential. Please enclose return postage.

Solo Literary Agency Ltd (1978), 49-53 Kensington High Street, London W8 5ED *tel* 071-376 2166 *fax* 071-938 3165. *Directors:* Don Short (managing), Wendy Short (secretary).
   Specialising in celebrity and autobiographical books. Fiction from established authors only (home 15%, overseas 20%).

Spokesmen—see **Curtis Brown & John Farquharson.**

*Abner Stein, 10 Roland Gardens, London SW7 3PH *tel* 071-373 0456/370 7859 *fax* 071-370 6316.
   Full-length and short MSS (home 10%, overseas 19%). No reading fee, but no unsolicited MSS; return postage and preliminary letter required.

Micheline Steinberg Playwrights' Agent (1987), 110 Frognal, London NW3 6XU *tel* 071-433 3980 *fax* 071-794 8355.
   Full-length MSS – theatre, films, television, radio (home 10%, overseas 15%). Dramatic Associate for Laurence Pollinger Ltd; works in conjunction with agents in USA and other countries. No reading fee, but preliminary letter essential and return postage with MSS.

Peter Tauber Press Agency (1950), 94 East End Road, London N3 2SX *tel* 081-346 4165. *Directors:* Peter Tauber, Martha Tauber, Robert Tauber.
   Well-researched, epic women's saga fiction, glitzy novels and international thrillers; quality literature; also celebrity auto/biographies (20% world-wide). No poetry, short stories, plays, children's or foreign books. Preliminary letter with synopsis, author's CV, copies of all previous rejections and sae essential.

Jon Thurley, MA (1976), 213 Linen Hall, 156-170 Regent Street, London W1R 5TA *tel* 071-437 9545/6 *fax* 071-287 9208.

Literary and dramatic work for all media (home 10%, overseas 20%). American and European representation arranged geared to specific projects. No reading fee.

Jane Turnbull (1986), 13 Wendell Road, London W12 9RS　*tel* 081-743 9580　*fax* 081-749 6079.
Fiction and non-fiction (home 10%, North America 15%, translations 20%), performance rights (15%); will suggest revision where appropriate. No children's books. Works in conjunction with Aitken & Stone for sale/translation rights; negotiates direct with USA and Canada. Preliminary letter essential; no reading fee.

*Harvey Unna & Stephen Durbridge (1975) Ltd—see **Lemon Unna & Durbridge Ltd.**

Dr Jan Van Loewen Ltd—see **Michael Imison Playwrights Ltd.**

*Vardey & Brunton Associates (1985), Studio 8, 125 Moore Park Road, London SW6 4PS　*tel* 071-384 1248　*fax* 071-384 1246. *Directors:* Lucinda Vardey, Carolyn Brunton.
Full-length MSS – all general fiction and non-fiction (home 10%, overseas 20%); will suggest revision where appropriate. No children's books, science fiction or academic. Works in conjunction with overseas agents. No reading fee.

Lorna Vestey (1971), 33 Dryburgh Road, London SW15 1BN.
Full-length MSS (home 10%, USA 15%, other overseas 20%). Films, television, sound broadcasting (10%). No unsolicited MSS.

*Ed Victor Ltd (1976), 162 Wardour Street, London W1V 3AT　*tel* 071-734 4795　*telegraphic address* Victorious, London W1　*fax* 071-494 3400. *Directors:* Ed Victor, Graham C. Greene, CBE, Carol Ryan, Leon Morgan, Margaret Phillips.
Full-length MSS but no short stories, film/TV scripts, poetry or plays (home 15%, USA 15%, translation 20%), performance rights (15%). Represented in all foreign markets. No unsolicited MSS.

S. Walker Literary Agency (1939), 96 Church Lane, Goldington, Bedford MK41 0AS　*tel* (0234) 216229. *Partners:* Alan Oldfield, Cora-Louise Oldfield; *consultant:* E.K. Walker.
Full-length novels only (home 10%, overseas 20% including 10% to overseas agent). Do not handle short topical articles or poetry. Works in conjunction with agencies in most European countries, and also negotiates directly with foreign publishers. No reading fee but preliminary letter and return postage essential.

Warner Chappell Plays Ltd (formerly **English Theatre Guild, Ltd**) (1938), part of **Warner Chappell Music Ltd**, 129 Park Street, London W1Y 3FA　*tel* 071-629 7600　*telex* 268403　*fax* 071-499 9718.
Specialises in stage plays. Works in conjunction with overseas agents. Preliminary letter essential.

Watergate Film Services Ltd—see **The Peters Fraser & Dunlop Group Ltd.**

*Watson, Little Ltd, 12 Egbert Street, London NW1 8LJ　*tel* 071-722 9514　*fax* 071-586 7649. *Directors:* Sheila Watson, Amanda Little.
Full-length MSS (home 10%, overseas 19%; all other rights including film, video and television 10%). No short stories or play scripts. Will sometimes suggest revision. Works in association with US agency and many foreign agencies. Preliminary letter please.

*A.P. Watt Ltd (1875), 20 John Street, London WC1N 2DR *tel* 071-405 6774 *fax* 071-831 2154. *Directors:* Hilary Rubinstein, Caradoc King, Linda Shaughnessy, Rod Hall, Imogen Parker, Lisa Eveleigh.
Full-length MSS; dramatic works for all media (home 10%, US and foreign 20% including commission to US or foreign agent). No poetry. Works in conjunction with agents in USA and most European countries and Japan. No reading fee. Preliminary letter please.

*Dinah Wiener Ltd, 27 Arlington Road, London NW1 7ER *tel* 071-388 2577 *fax* 071-388 7559.
Full-length MSS only, fiction and general non-fiction; no plays, scripts, poetry, short stories or children's books (home 15%, overseas 20%), film and television in association (20%). US office: Suite 21a, 7-13 Washington Square North, New York, NY 10003. No reading fee, but preliminary letter and return postage essential.

Elisabeth Wilson (1979), 24 Thornhill Square, London N1 1BQ *tel* 071-609 1965 *telex* 946797 Pronto G *fax* 071-863 6460.
Rights agent and consultant on illustrated books, also Australian rights in UK and vice versa (home/overseas 10%). No reading fee.

UNITED STATES OF AMERICA

*Membership of the Society of Authors' Representatives

The Society of Authors' Representatives, Inc. is a voluntary association of agents, whose individual members subscribe to a strict code of ethical practices. The SAR regrets that it cannot recommend individual member agents.
In all cases, and in their own interests, writers are advised to send a preliminary letter with a self-addressed, stamped envelope (or an International Reply Coupon if writing from outside the USA) and to ascertain terms before submitting MSS.

American Play Company Inc., 19 West 44th Street, Suite 1206, New York, NY 10036 *tel* 212-921-0545. *President:* Sheldon Abend.

*Julian Bach Literary Agency Inc., 747 Third Avenue, New York, NY 10017 *tel* 212-753-2605 *cables* Turtles, New York *telex* 668359 *fax* 212-688-8297.

The Balkin Agency Inc., 317 South Pleasant Street, Amherst, MA 01004 *tel* 413-253-5073. *Director:* Richard Balkin.
Full-length MSS – adult non-fiction only (home 15%, overseas 20%). Query first. May suggest revision. Agents in all major countries. *British representative:* Barbara Levy. No reading fee.

Virginia Barber Literary Agency, Inc. (1974), 353 West 21st Street, New York, NY 10011 *tel* 212-255-6515 *telex* 212-493-3790 *fax* 212-691-9418. *Directors:* Virginia Barber, Mary Evans.
General fiction and non-fiction (home 10-15%, overseas 20% for new authors), performance rights (10-15% for new authors); will suggest revision. Has co-agents in all major countries; Abner Stein handles UK rights. No reading fee.

*Lois Berman, The Little Theatre Building, 240 West 44th Street, New York, NY 10036 *tel* 212-575-5114.
Dramatic writing only (and only by recommendation).

*Georges Borchardt Inc. (1967), 136 East 57th Street, New York, NY 10022 *tel* 212-753-5785 *telegraphic address* Literary, New York *fax* 212-838-6518. *Directors:* Georges Borchardt, Anne Borchardt.

Full-length and short MSS (home 10%, British 15%, translations 20%), performance rights (10%). Agents in most foreign countries. No unsolicited MSS. No reading fee.

*Brandt & Brandt Literary Agents Inc., 1501 Broadway, New York, NY 10036 *tel* 212-840-5760 *telegraphic address* Bromasite, New York.
Full-length and short MSS (home 10%, overseas 15-20%), performance rights (10%). *British representative:* A.M. Heath & Co. Ltd. No reading fee.

*The Helen Brann Agency Inc., 94 Curtis Road, Bridgewater, CT 06752 *tel* 203-354-9580 *fax* 203-355-2572.

*James Brown Associates Inc.—see **Curtis Brown Ltd.**

Maria Carvainis Agency, Inc., 235 West End Avenue, New York, NY 10023 *tel* 212-580-1559 *fax* 212-877-3486. *President:* Maria Carvainis.
General fiction; mystery, thrillers and suspense; women's fiction; children's and young adult; non-fiction, including popular sciences, biography, investigative journalism, true crime. Full-length and short MSS (home 15%, overseas 20%), films (10-15%). Works in conjunction with foreign agents. No reading fee; will suggest revision.

*Curtis Brown Ltd, 10 Astor Place, New York, NY 10003 *tel* 212-473-5400. *Chairman:* Perry Knowlton; *president:* Peter Ginsberg.

*John Cushman Associates Inc.—see **Curtis Brown Ltd.**

Liz Darhansoff Literary Agency, 1220 Park Avenue, New York, NY 10128 *tel* 212-534-2479 *fax* 212-996-1601.
Full-length and short MSS (home 10%, overseas 20%), performance rights (15%). Works with agents throughout Europe; Tessa Sayle Agency in UK. No reading fee.

*Joan Daves Literary Agency (1952), 21 West 26th Street, New York, NY 10010 *tel* 212-685-2663 *fax* 212-685-1781/914-234-0730.
Full-length MSS or a detailed outline of n-f projects (home 15%, overseas 20%). No reading fee. No unpublished writers.

*Anita Diamant, 310 Madison Avenue, New York, NY 10017 *tel* 212-687-1122.

*Candida Donadio & Associates, Inc., 231 West 22nd Street, New York, NY 10011 *tel* 212-691-8077.
Literary book agents, fiction and non-fiction.

Dorese Agency, 1400 Ambassador Street, Los Angeles, CA 90035 *tel* 213-556-0710. Alyss Barlow Dorese.

Ethan Ellenberg (1983), 548 Broadway, 5-C, New York, NY 10012 *tel* 212-431-4554 *fax* 212-941-4652.
First novels, thrillers, mysteries, science fiction and fantasy, quality fiction, horror; non-fiction: biography, history, military, current events. Full-length and short MSS (home 15%, overseas 10%), performance rights (15%). Submit one-page outline and first three sample chapters, plus return postage (US stamps or US$ international money order). Works in conjunction with overseas agents. Will suggest revision. No reading fee.

*Ann Elmo Agency, Inc., 60 East 42nd Street, New York, NY 10165 *tel* 212-661-2880. *Directors:* Ann Elmo, Lettie Lee.
Full-length fiction and non-fiction MSS (home 15%, overseas 20%), theatre, films, television (15%). Will suggest revision when MSS is promising. Works with foreign agencies. No reading fee.

Frieda Fishbein Ltd, 2556 Hubbard Street, Brooklyn, NY 11235 *tel* 212-247-4398.

Forthwrite Literary Agency (1988), PO Box 922101, Sylmar, CA 91392 *tel* 818-365-3400. *Owner:* Wendy L. Zhörne.
Non-fiction, general fiction including juvenile, historical and non-denominational Christian, and scripts. No explicit sex or violence, horror or religious zealot (home/Canada 10%, overseas 15%), performance rights 10%. Send sase with query. $35 reading/short critique fee.

*The Fox Chase Agency Inc., The Public Ledger Building, Room 930, Independence Square, Philadelphia, PA 19106 *tel* 215-625-2450.

*Robert A. Freedman Dramatic Agency, Inc. (formerly **Harold Freedman Brandt & Brandt Dramatic Dept., Inc.**), 1501 Broadway, Suite 2310, New York, NY 10036 *tel* 212-840-5760.

*Samuel French Inc., 45 West 25th Street, New York, NY 10010 *tel* 212-206-8990 *fax* 212-206-1429. *President:* M. Abbott Van Nostrand.

Jay Garon-Brooke Associates Inc., 415 Central Park West, New York, NY 10025 *tel* 212-866-3654 *fax* 212-666-6016. Writer must be referred by an editor or a client. Will not read unsolicited MSS. *London:* Abner Stein *tel* 071-373 0456.

Goodman Associates, Literary Agents (1976), 500 West End Avenue, New York, NY 10024 *tel* 212-873-4806 *fax* 212-580-3278. *Partners:* Arnold P. Goodman, Elise Simon Goodman.
Adult book length fiction and non-fiction (home 15%, overseas 20%). No reading fee.

Sanford J. Greenburger Associates, Inc., 55 Fifth Avenue, New York, NY 10003 *tel* 212-206-5600 *fax* 212-463-8718.

*John Hawkins & Associates, Inc. (formerly **Paul R. Reynolds, Inc.**) (1893), 71 West 23rd Street, Suite 1600, New York, NY 10010 *tel* 212-807-7040 *cables* Carbonato, New York *fax* 212-807-9555. *President:* John Hawkins; *vice-president:* William Reiss; *foreign rights:* Elsie Stern; *permissions:* Sharon Friedman.

Frederick Hill Associates (1979), 1842 Union Street, San Francisco, CA 94123 *tel* 415-921-2910 *fax* 415-921-2802; *branch office:* 1325B North Olive Drive, West Hollywood, CA 90069 *tel* 213-650-4092 *fax* 213-650-4093.
Full-length fiction and non-fiction (home 15%, overseas 20%). Will suggest revision. Works in conjunction with agents in Scandinavia, France, Germany, Holland, Japan, Spain. No reading fee.

*International Creative Management, Inc., 40 West 57th Street, New York, NY 10019 *tel* 212-556-5600 *telex* 125422 or 661562 Icmnyk *fax* 212-556-5665.

*JCA Literary Agency Inc., Suite 1103, 27 West 20th Street, New York, NY 10011 *tel* 212-807-0888.

Ben F. Kamsler Ltd (1990), 5501 Noble Avenue, Van Nuys, CA 91411 *tel* 818-785-4167 *fax* 818-988-8304. *Directors:* Ben Kamsler, Irene Kamsler.
Full-length MSS, plays, TV specials (home 10%, overseas 20%), performance rights (10%). Will suggest revision on promising MSS. No reading fee, but preliminary letter with sase essential.

Daniel P. King (1974), 5125 North Cumberland Boulevard, Whitefish Bay, WI 53217 *tel* 414-964-2903 *telex* 724389 *fax* 414-964-6860.
Specialist in mystery and crime fiction, mainstream fiction, romance, science fiction and general non-fiction.

*Lucy Kroll Agency, 390 West End Avenue, New York, NY 10024 *tel* 212-877-0627 *fax* 212-769-2832.

*The Robert Lantz-Joy Harris Literary Agency, 888 Seventh Avenue, New York, NY 10106 *tel* 212-262-8177 *fax* 212-262-8707.

Michael Larsen-Elizabeth Pomada Literary Agents (1972), 1029 Jones Street, San Francisco, CA 94109 *tel* 415-673-0939. *Partners:* Michael Larsen and Elizabeth Pomada.
Full-length MSS (home 15%, overseas 20%). Works in conjunction with agents in Hollywood, Europe, Israel, Japan, South America. Preliminary letter, with sae, essential.

*Lescher & Lescher Ltd (1966), 67 Irving Place, New York, NY 10009 *tel* 212-529-1790 *telegraphic address* Micawber. *Directors:* Robert Lescher, Susan Lescher.
Full-length and short MSS (home 10-15%, overseas 20%). No reading fee.

*Ellen Levine Literary Agency (1980), Suite 1801, 15 East 26th Street, New York, NY 10010 *tel* 212-899-0620.
Full-length MSS (home 10-15%, overseas 20%). In conjunction with co-agents, theatre, films, television (10%). Will suggest revision. Works in conjunction with agents in Europe, Japan, Israel, Brazil, Argentina. *UK representative:* A.P. Watt. No reading fee; preliminary letter essential.

*Literistic Ltd—see **Sterling Lord Literistic, Inc.**

*Gerald McCauley Agency, Inc., PO Box AE, Katonah, NY 10536 *tel* 914-232-5700.

Kirby McCauley/The Pimlico Agency Inc., 155 East 77th Street, Suite 1A, New York, NY 10021 *tel* 212-628-9729 *fax* 212-535-7861. *Contact:* Ann Ducharme, Christopher Shepard; *directors:* Kirby McCauley, Kay McCauley.

Anita D. McClellan Associates, 50 Stearns Street, Cambridge, MA 02138 *tel* 617-864-3448. *Director:* Anita D. McClellan.
General fiction and non-fiction. Full-length MSS (home 15%, overseas 20%). Will suggest revision for agency clients. No unsolicited manuscripts. Send preliminary letter and sase.

McIntosh, McKee & Dodds, Inc., 276 Fifth Avenue, New York, NY 10001 *tel* 212-679-4490 *cables* Halmatson *fax* 212-545-1224.

*McIntosh & Otis Inc. (1928), 310 Madison Avenue, New York, NY 10017 *tel* 212-687-7400 *fax* 212-687-6894.

Mildred Marmur Associates Ltd (1987), 310 Madison Avenue, Suite 607, New York, NY 10017 *tel* 212-949-6055 *fax* 212-687-6894. *President:* Mildred Marmur.
Serious non-fiction, literary fiction, juveniles. Full-length and short MSS (home 15%, overseas 20%), performance rights (15%). Works with co-agents in all major countries. No reading fee.

*Elisabeth Marton, 96 Fifth Avenue, New York, NY 10011 *tel* 212-225-1908 *fax* 212-691-9160. *Partners:* Elisabeth Marton, Tonda Marton.

*Harold Matson Company, Inc. (1937), 276 Fifth Avenue, New York, NY 10001 *tel* 212-679-4490 *cables* Halmatson *fax* 212-545-1224.
Full-length MSS (home 10%, UK 19%, translation 19%). No unsolicited MSS. No reading fee.

*Helen Merrill Ltd, 435 West 23rd Street, Suite 1A, New York, NY 10011 *tel* 212-691-5326 *fax* 212-727-0545.

Peter Miller Agency Inc. (1976), PO Box 760, Old Chelsea Station, New York, NY 10011 *tel* 212-929-1222 *fax* 212-206-0238. *President:* Peter Miller.

Full-length MSS, specialising in biography, true crime, Hollywood history and all books with film and television production potential (home 15%, overseas 25%), films, television (10-20%). Works in conjunction with agents in Germany, Japan, Spain. Preliminary enquiry with synopsis and resumé essential.

Robert P. Mills Ltd, c/o Richard Curtis Associates, 164 East 64th Street, New York, NY 10021   *tel* 212-371-9481   *fax* 212-750-9142.

*William Morris Agency Inc., 1350 Avenue of the Americas, New York, NY 10019   *tel* 212-586-5100.

New Wave—see **Pegasus International Inc.**

*Harold Ober Associates Inc., 425 Madison Avenue, New York, NY 10017   *tel* 212-759-8600   *telegraphic address* Litober   *fax* 212-759-9428. *Directors:* Claire M. Smith, Phyllis Westberg.
Full-length MSS (home 10%, British 15%, overseas 20%), performance rights (10%). Will suggest revision. *London representative:* David Higham Associates. No reading fee.

*Fifi Oscard Associates Inc., 19 West 44th Street, New York, NY 10036   *tel* 212-764-1100   *fax* 212-870 5019. *President:* Fifi Oscard; *directors:* Ivy Fischer Stone, Kevin McShane, Nancy Murray.
Full-length MSS (home 15%, overseas 20%), performance rights (10%). Will suggest revision. Works in conjunction with many foreign agencies. No reading fee, but no unsolicited submissions.

Pegasus International Inc., literary and film agents. PO Box 5470, Winter Park, FL 32793-5470   *tel* 407-831-1008. *Director:* Gene Lovitz; *client contact and assistant director:* Carole Morling.
All non-fiction/fiction genres. Specialises in: regency and historical romances, gothic, horror, mystery, mainstream, science fiction, juveniles, medicine and health; TV/film scripts (home 10%, overseas 15%). Literary assistance to unpublished authors. Evaluation fee charged (returned when published). MSS with high film potential need not be submitted in screenplay form. Personal telephone calls returned anywhere in the world (call at any hour).

Perkins' Literary Agency, PO Box 48, Childs, MD 21916   *tel* 301-398-2647.
Full-length MSS (home 15%, overseas 20%), film/television (20%); will suggest revision. Reading fee. Query first.

Porter, Dierks & Lovitz—see **Pegasus International Inc.**

*Raines & Raines (1961), 71 Park Avenue, New York, NY 10016   *tel* 212-684-5160. *Directors:* Theron Raines, Joan Raines, Keith Korman.
Full-length MSS (home 15%, overseas 20%). Works in conjunction with overseas agents. No unsolicited MSS.

*Flora Roberts Inc., 157 West 57th Street, New York, NY 10019   *tel* 212-355-4165.

*Marie Rodell-Frances Collin Literary Agency (1948), 110 West 40th Street, New York, NY 10018   *tel* 212-840-8664   *cables* Rodellitag, New York. *Director:* Frances Collin.
Full-length MSS (home 15%, overseas 25%), performance rights (20%). Works in conjunction with agents throughout the world. No reading fee. No unsolicited MSS accepted.

*Rosenstone/Wender, 3 East 48th Street, 4th Floor, New York, NY 10017   *tel* 212-832-8330   *fax* 212-759-4524.

*Russell & Volkening Inc., 50 West 29th Street, New York, NY 10001   *tel* 212-684-6050   *fax* 212-889-3206.

Schaffner Agency (1948), 6625 N. Casas Adobes Road, Tucson, AZ 85704   *tel* 602-797-8000   *fax* 602-797-8271. *Director:* Timothy Schaffner.
Full-length MSS (home 15%, foreign 15-20%). British/translation representatives: A.M. Heath & Co. Ltd. No reading fee.

Susan F. Schulman Literary & Dramatic Agents Inc., 454 West 44th Street, New York, NY 10036   *tel* 212-713-1633   *fax* 212-581-8830.
Agents for negotiation in all markets (with co-agents) of fiction, general nonfiction, children's books, academic and professional works, and associated subsidiary rights including plays, film and television (home 15%, UK 7½%, overseas 20%). Return postage required.

Scott Meredith Literary Agency Inc. (1941), 845 Third Avenue, New York, NY 10022   *tel* 212-245-5500   *cables* Scottmere   *telegraphic address* Esemela 224705   *fax* 212-755-2972. *President:* Scott Meredith; *vice-presidents:* Jack Scovil, Theodore Chichak; *subsidiary rights:* William T. Haas.
Full-length and short MSS (home 10%, overseas 20%), performance rights (10%). Will read unsolicited MSS, queries, outlines. Single fee charged for readings, criticism and assistance in revision. *London:* Mark Hamilton, A.M. Heath & Co. Ltd.

Charlotte Sheedy Literary Agency, Inc., 41 King Street, New York, NY 10014   *tel* 212-633-2288   *fax* 212-633-6261.

*The Shukat Company Ltd, 340 West 55th Street, Suite 1A, New York, NY 10019   *tel* 212-582-7614   *telex* 6502224600 MC1 UW   *fax* 212-315-3752. Scott Shukat.
Theatre, films, novels, television, radio (15%). No reading fee. No unsolicited material accepted.

Singer Media Corporation, 3164 West Tyler Avenue, Anaheim, CA 92801   *tel* 714-527-5650   *fax* 714-527-0268. *Directors:* Katherine Haw (executive vice-president), Kurt Singer (president).
Full-length MSS, including romance, mysteries, westerns, biography; also teenage romance (age 12-16) (home 15%, overseas 20%); short MSS (home 10%, overseas 15%). Films, television, radio (15%, overseas 20%). Represented in most countries abroad.

*Philip G. Spitzer Literary Agency, 788 Ninth Avenue, New York, NY 10019   *tel* 212-265-6003   *fax* 212-765-0953.

*Sterling Lord Literistic, Inc., One Madison Avenue, New York, NY 10010   *tel* 212-696-2800   *fax* 212-686-6976   *cables* Literistic New York. *Directors:* Peter Matson, Sterling Lord, Michael Sissons, Anthony Jones.
Full-length and short MSS (home 10%, overseas 19%). Theatre, films, television, radio (10%). Will suggest revision. Represented in Europe by Intercontinental Literary Agency. UK representative: The Peters Fraser & Dunlop Group Ltd. No reading fee.

H.N. Swanson, Inc. (1934), 8523 Sunset Boulevard, Los Angeles, CA 90069   *tel* 213-652-5385   *fax* 213-652-3690. *Founder and president:* H.N. Swanson; *vice-president:* N.V. Swanson; *head of operations:* Thomas J. Shanks.
Full-length MSS (home 10%, overseas 20%), performance rights. No reading fee.

*Roslyn Targ Literary Agency, Inc., 105 West 13th Street, New York, NY 10011   *tel* 212-206-9390   *cables* Rosbooks, New York   *telex* 62193   *fax* 212-989-6233.
Full-length MSS (home 10%, unpublished authors 15%, overseas 20%). Films, television, radio (10%). Affiliates in most foreign countries. No reading fee; preliminary letter with sase essential.

Ralph Vicinanza Ltd, 111 8th Avenue, Suite 1501, New York, NY 10011   *tel* 212-924-7090   *telex* 4945337   *fax* 212-691-9644.
No unsolicited MSS (home 10%, overseas 20%).

Austin Wahl Agency, Ltd (1935), Suite 342, Monadnock Building, 53 West Jackson Boulevard, Chicago, IL 60604   *tel* 312-922-3331. *President:* Thomas Wahl.
Full-length and short MSS (home 15%, overseas 20%). Theatre, films, television (10%). No reading fee; professional writers only.

*****Wallace Literary Agency, Inc.** (1988), 177 East 70th Street, New York, NY 10021   *tel* 212-570-9090   *fax* 212-772-8979. *Directors:* Lois Wallace, Thomas C. Wallace.
Full-length MSS (home 10%, UK 20%, overseas 20%). Film, television, theatre for agency clients (10%). Will suggest revision. No unsolicited manuscripts.

Watkins/Loomis Agency, Inc., 150 East 35th Street, New York, NY 10016   *tel* 212-532-0080   *cables* Anwat, Newyork   *fax* 212-889-0506. *London:* Abner Stein (UK), Marsh & Sheil Ltd (foreign).

*****Rhoda Weyr Agency** (1983), 151 Bergen Street, Brooklyn, NY 11217   *tel* 718-522-0480.
General non-fiction and fiction with particular interest in science, history, biography. Full-length MSS for fiction; proposal for n-f (home 15%, overseas 20%), performance rights (15%). Co-agents in all foreign markets. Sase required.

Writers House Inc. (1974), 21 West 26th Street, New York, NY 10010   *tel* 212-685-2400   *telex* 620103 Writers   *fax* 212-685-1781. *President:* Albert Zuckerman; *executive vice-president:* Amy Berkower.
Full-length MSS (home 15%, overseas 20%). No reading fee.

*****Mary Yost Associates, Inc.** (1958), 59 East 54th Street, New York, NY 10022   *tel* 212-980-4988   *telegraphic address* Mybooks.
Full-length and short MSS (home and overseas 10%). Works with individual agents in all foreign countries. Will suggest revision. No reading fee.

Others

Most of the agents whose names and addresses are given below work in association with an agent in London.
In all cases, and in their own interests, writers are advised to send a preliminary letter and to ascertain terms before submitting MSS or books.

ARGENTINA

International Editors Co., Avenida Cabildo 1156, 1426 Buenos Aires   *tel* 786-0888   *telex* 24518 Blibro AR   *fax* 541-786-0888.

Lawrence Smith, BA (1938), Avenida de los Incas 3110, 1426 Buenos Aires   *tel* 552-5012   *cables* Litagent, Baires   *fax* 54-1-8045508.

AUSTRALIA

Curtis Brown (Australia) Pty Ltd, 27 Union Street, Paddington, NSW 2021   *tel* (02) 331 5301/361 6161   *cables* Browncurt   *fax* (02) 360 3935.

BRAZIL

Agencia Literária Balcells Mello e Souza Riff, Rua Visconde de Pirajá, 414 s1 1108 Ipanema, 22410 Rio de Janeiro, RJ *tel* 287-6299 *fax* 267-6393. Cristina de Mello e Souza, Lucia Riff.

Karin Schindler, Rights Representative (formerly **Dr J.E. Bloch Literary Agency**), Caixa Postal 19051, 04599 São Paulo, SP *tel* 241-9177 *cables* Copyright Sãopaulo *fax* 241-9077.

CANADA

Curtis Brown Canada Ltd, Janet Turnball Irving, PO Box 757, Dorset, VT 05251, USA *tel* 802-326-5165 *fax* 802-362-5166.

CZECHOSLOVAKIA

Dilia Theatrical and Literary Agency, Vyšehradská 28, 128 24 Prague 2 *tel* 29 66 51-5 *telex* 121 367 dili c *fax* 297695.

Lita Slovak Literary Agency, Zámočnicka 9, 815-30 Bratislava *tel* 334801, 334806, 334346 *telegraphic address* Lita, Bratislava *fax* 42 7 334288.

FRANCE

Bureau Littéraire International Marguerite Scialtiel, 14 rue Chanoinesse, 75004 Paris *tel* (1) 43 54 71 16. Geneviéve Ulmann.

Robert Fouques Duparc (1986), 37 boulevard Saint-Michel, 75005 Paris *tel* (1) 43 54 69 08 *fax* (1) 40 51 07 25.

Agence Hoffman, 77 boulevard Saint-Michel, 75005 Paris *tel* (1) 43 26 56 94 *cables* Aghoff *telex* 203605.

Mme Michelle Lapautre, 6 rue Jean Carriès, 75007 Paris *tel* (1) 47 34 82 41 *fax* (1) 47 34 00 90.

Donine Mouche, Agent Littéraire (formerly **McKee & Mouche**), 12 rue du Regard, 75006 Paris *tel* (1) 45 48 45 03/42 22 42 33.

La Nouvelle Agence, 7 rue Corneille, 75006 Paris *tel* (1) 43 25 85 60 *fax* (1) 43 25 47 98. Mary Kling.

Mme Greta Strassova, 4 rue Git-Le-Coeur, 75006 Paris *tel* (1) 46 33 34 57.

GERMANY

Brigitte Axster, Dreieichstr. 43, D-6000 Frankfurt/Main 70 *tel* 069-629856 *fax* 069-623526.

Geisenheyner & Crone, Gymnasiumstrasse 31B, 7000 Stuttgart-1 *tel* 0711-293738 *telex* 722664 Wdpat *fax* 0711-2261748.

Agence Hoffman, Bechsteinstrasse 2, D-8000 Munich 40 *tel* (089) 308 48 07 *telex* 5215661 *fax* (089) 308 21 08.

Andrew Hunter Lee (1988), Neidenburger Str. 1, D-7500 Karlsruhe *tel* 0721-688403. *Directors:* A. Lee, Eva Herz, Angélica Bohne. Full-length MSS, medicine, pharmacy, plants and general (home/overseas 10%): will suggest revision (10%). Works in conjunction with UK and German agencies. Reading fee for non-European languages only.

Thomas Schlück, Literary Agency, Hinter der Worth 12, 3008 Garbsen 9 *tel* 05131-93053 *fax* 05131-93045.

HONG KONG

Holmes Literary Agency (1989), 1/F, 90 Stanley Main Street, Stanley, Hong Kong *tel* 852 8132068 *fax* 852 8132094. *Directors;* Stephanie Holmes, Christopher Holmes. General fiction and non-fiction. Full-length and short MSS (overseas 15%); performance rights (15%). Will suggest revision; no reading fee.

HUNGARY

Artisjus. Agency for Literature, Theatre and Music of the Hungarian Bureau for the Protection of authors' rights, Vörösmarty tér 1, Budapest V *postal address* H-1364 Budapest PB 67 *tel* 11-84-704 *cables* Artisjus *telex* 226527 Arjus H *fax* 11-85-597.

ISRAEL

Rogan Pikarski Literary Agency (1977), 200 Hayarkon Street, PO Box 4006, Tel Aviv 61040 *tel* 03-231880/5440159 *fax* 03-5440160. *Director:* Ilana Pikarski. General trade publishing.

ITALY

Agenzia Letteraria Internazionale SRL, Via Fratelli Gabba 3, 20121 Milan *tel* (02) 86 54 45/87 93 06/86 15 72 *telex* 323574 Linali I *fax* (02) 87 62 22.

ILA—International Literary Agency—USA (1969), I-18010 Terzorio-IM *tel/fax* (0184) 48 72 92. Publishers' agent, interested in bestsellers and mass market books. *Speciality:* Books on collecting and antiques.

Living Literary Agency (1976), Via Fra Cristoforo 2, 20142 Milan *tel* (02) 84 39 413 *fax* (02) 84 36 522. *Director:* Elfriede Pexa.
Full-length MSS, English-language fiction and general non-fiction (home 10%, overseas 20%); films/television (5%), radio (10%); will suggest revision. Reading fee. Only handle Italian translation rights in English language books.

New Blitz TV, Via Cimabue 5, 00196 Rome *tel* (06) 32 01 489/32 00 620 *fax* (06) 32 19 014.

Irina Reylander Literary Agency (1989), Viale Monza 167/A, 20125 Milan *tel* (02) 28 42 603 *fax* (02) 28 47 828. *Director:* Dr Irina Reylander. Full-length MSS (15%). Marketing fee.

JAPAN

Orion Literary Agency, 1-58 Kanda-Jimbocho, Chiyoda-ku, Tokyo 101 *tel* 03-295-1405 *telegraphic address* Orionagy, Tokyo *telex* J24408 Orionagy *fax* 03-295-4366.

NETHERLANDS

International Drama Agency, Ilperveldstraat 82, 1024 PJ Amsterdam *tel* (020) 636 77 54/634 08 04 *fax* (020) 636 73 55. Francis Lonnee.

Internationaal Literatuur Bureau B.V., Postbus 10014, 1201 DA, Hilversum   *tel* (035) 21 35 00   *telex* 73201 ILB   *fax* (035) 21 57 71. Menno Kohn.

United Dutch Dramatists, de Perponcherstraat 116, 2518 TA The Hague   *tel* (070) 34 69 738   *fax* (070) 36 09 827. Hemmo B. Drexhage.

NEW ZEALAND

Glenys Bean Literary Agency (1989), 15 Elizabeth Street, Freeman's Bay, Auckland 2   *tel/fax* (09) 786-287. Adult and children's fiction, educational, non-fiction, film, TV, radio (home 10%, overseas 15%). Represented in New York by Diane Cleaver; translations Marsh & Sheil (UK). Preliminary letter, synopsis and sae required.

Richards Literary Agency (1976), 3-49 Aberdeen Road, Castor Bay, Auckland 9   *postal address* PO Box 31240, Milford, Auckland 9   *tel* (09) 410-5681   *fax* (09) 410-6389. *Partners:* Ray Richards, Barbara Richards. Full-length MSS, fiction, non-fiction, juvenile, educational, academic books; films, television, radio (home 10%, overseas 10-20%). Preliminary letter, synopsis with sae required. No reading fee.

NIGERIA

Joe-Tolalu & Associates (Nigeria) Limited (1983), 5A Oremeji Street, Off Medical Road, PO Box 7031, Ikeja-Lagos   *tel* 01-932929, 01-931505. *Directors:* Joseph Omosade Awolalu, Tosin Awolalu, Foluke Awolalu, Dimeji Popoola. Full-length MSS, fiction and non-fiction, short MSS, picture books only (home 10-15%, overseas 15-20%), performance rights (10%), translations (15%); will suggest revision. Works in conjunction with overseas agents. Preliminary letter essential; no reading fee.

PORTUGAL

Ilidio da Fonseca Matos, Rua de S. Bernardo, 68-3, 1200 Lisbon   *tel* 66 97 80   *cables* Ilphoto   *fax* 715 44 45.

SCANDINAVIA, including FINLAND

Arlecchino Teaterförlag, Gränsvägen 14, S-131 41 Nacka, Sweden   *tel* 08-718 17 18.

A/S Bookman, Fiolstraede 12, DK-1171, Copenhagen K, Denmark   *tel* 33 14 57 20   *fax* 33 12 00 07.

Gösta Dahl & Son, AB, Aladdinsvägan 14, S-161 38 Bromma, Sweden   *tel* 08 25 62 35   *fax* 08 25 11 18.

Leonhardt Literary Agency aps, Studiestraede 35, DK-1455 Copenhagen K, Denmark   *tel* 33 13 25 23   *cables* Leolitag   *fax* 33 13 49 92.

Licht & Licht, Maglemosevej 46, DK-2920 Charlottenlund, Denmark   *tel* 31 61 09 08   *cables* Literagent   *telex* 21131 licht dk   *fax* 31 61 11 05.

Suzanne Palme Literary Agency, Oscarsgt. 60, Oslo 2, Norway   *postal address* PO Box 7112, Homansbyen, 0307 Oslo 3, Norway   *tel* 44 81 74   *fax* 02-55 80 46.

Gustaf von Sydow (1988), Lorensbergsvägen 76, S 136 69 Haninge, Sweden   *tel* 46-8-776 10 54. *Directors:* Gustaf von Sydow, Elizabeth von Sydow. Handles television, film, celebrity and news features in Sweden, Norway, Denmark and Finland.

SOUTH AFRICA

Frances Bond Literary Agency (1985), 32B Stanley Teale Road, Westville North 3630, Natal   *tel* (031) 824532   *fax* (031) 822620   *postal address* PO Box 223, Westville 3630.

Elizabeth Crompton-Lomax Agency (1985), 6 Eagle Hill, Yellowwood Park, Durban, Natal 4001   *tel* (031) 421732   *fax* (031) 421732.

International Press Agency (Pty) Ltd, PO Box 67, Howard Place 7450   *tel* (021) 5311926   *fax* (021) 5318789. *Manager:* Terry Temple. *UK office:* Ursula A. Barnett, 19 Avenue South, Surbiton, Surrey KT5 8PJ   *tel* 081-390 4414   *fax* 081-398 8723.

Sandton Literary Agency (1982), PO Box 785799, Sandton 2146   *tel* (011) 4428624. *Directors:* J. Victoria Canning, M. Sutherland. Full-length MSS and screenplays; lecture agents. Letter or telephone call first, please. Works in conjunction with: (*UK*) Joan Beakbane, Jacob's Ladder, Low Habberley, Kidderminster, Worcs. DY11 5RF, (*USA*) H.N. Swanson, Inc., Los Angeles.

SPAIN

Miss Carmen Balcells, Agencia Literaria Carmen Balcells, Diagonal 580, Barcelona 08021   *tel* 200-89-33, 200-85-65   *cables* Copyright, Barcelona   *telex* 50459 Copy E and 50936 Kopi E   *fax* 200-70-41.

International Editors Co., S.A., Rambla Cataluña 63, 3º-1ª, 08007 Barcelona   *tel* 215-88-12   *fax* 487-35-83.

Julio F. Yañez, Agencia Literaria, Via Augusta 139, 6º-2ª, 08021 Barcelona   *tel* 200-71-07   *telex* 97348 GNLT-E   *fax* 209-48-65.

SWITZERLAND

Paul & Peter Fritz AG Literary Agency, Jupiterstrasse 1, 8032 Zürich   *postal address* Postfach, 8032 Zürich   *tel* (01) 53 41 40   *fax* (01) 53 20 35.

Liepman AG., Maienburgweg 23, 8044 Zürich   *tel* (01) 261 76 60   *cables* Litagent   *fax* (01) 261 01 24. Dr Ruth Liepman, Eva Koralnik, Ruth Weibel.

Mohrbooks Literary Agency, Klosbachstrasse 110, CH-8032 Zürich   *tel* (01) 251 16 10   *fax* (01) 262 52 13. Rainer Heumann.

Niedieck Linder AG, Wehrenbachhalde 34, CH-8053 Zürich, Postbox 153   *tel* (01) 53 65 92   *telex* 817 585 120 Com ch.   *E-Mail (Geomail)* Net 1: Nck.

See also **Scripts for theatre, radio, tv and film** section for agents specialising in these fields.

Character Merchandisers

A number of agents specialise in the handling of rights connected with the promotion of characters from books, television programmes, etc., or with the books and programmes themselves. This is a selective listing, both of agents and of properties handled.

BBC Licensing, BBC Enterprises Ltd, Room A2106, Woodlands, 80 Wood Lane, London W12 0TT *tel* 081-576 2550 *telex* 934678 *fax* 081-743 0393. Representing BBC TV and Radio and a selection of copyright owners.
Properties include *The Archers, Antiques Roadshow, Doctor Who, EastEnders, Every Second Counts, Going Live, Grange Hill, Howards' Way, Jimbo and the Jet Set, Magic Roundabout, P.C. Pinkerton, A Question of Sport, Radio 1, 2, 3 and 4, Top of the Pops, Victorian Kitchen Garden, Telly Addicts, Watch with Mother, The Brollies, Edd the Duck, Animals of Farthingwood, Blue Peter, Narnia Chronicles, Only Fools and Horses, Neighbours, Fireman Sam, Gordon T. Gopher, Noddy.*

Copyright Promotions Ltd, 12th Floor, Metropolis House, 22 Percy Street, London W1P 9FF *tel* 071-580 7431 *telex* 28992 Cpl Ldn *fax* 071-631 1147.
Properties include *Alfred J. Kwak, Aspects of Love, The Bash Street Kids, Cats, Cluedo, Dan Dare, Dennis the Menace, Desperate Dan, Fiddley Foodle Bird, Ivy Cottage, Judge Dredd, Korky the Cat, Little Miss, Mask, Monopoly, Mr Men, My Little Pony, The Pink Panther, The Phantom of the Opera, Pictures in the Post, Playskool, Spitting Image, Starlight Express, Teenage Mutant Hero Turtles, Tom & Jerry, Tonka, The Wizard of Oz, World Championship Wrestling.*

The Copyrights Company Ltd, 22 Crawford Place, London W1H 1JE *tel* 071-723 6034 *fax* 071-723 0463; *Head office:* Manor Barn, Milton, Nr Banbury, Oxon OX15 4HH *tel* (0295) 721188 *fax* (0295) 720145.
Properties include *Beatrix Potter, Paddington Bear, Brambly Hedge, Flower Fairies*, and other book-related properties for merchandise licensing.

JWE Special Projects Ltd, 16 Owen Mansions, Queens Club Gardens, London W14 9RS *tel* 071-385 5072 *fax* 071-385 6274.

Link Licensing Ltd (1986), United Newspapers Building, 23-27 Tudor Street, London EC4Y 0HR *tel* 071-353 7305/6 *fax* 071-583 3479. *Directors:* Claire L. Derry, David A. Hamilton.
Properties: *Barney, Count Duckula, Trap Door, What-a-Mess, Hippo & Duck, Dogtanian, Victor & Hugo, Joshua Jones, Barbie.*

Marvel Licensing, Arundel House, 13-15 Arundel Street, London WC2R 3DX *tel* 071-497 2121.
Properties include *The Marvel Super-Heroes, The Real Ghostbusters, Sesame Street, The Sylvanian Families, James Bond Junior.*

Noddy Enterprises Ltd, The Macdonald Group, 165 Great Dover Street, London SE1 4YA *tel* 071-334 4800 *telex* 885233 Macdon G *fax* 071-334 4905/6. *Contact:* Sylvia Rosen.
Property: *Noddy.*

Patrick, Sinfield (PSL) (1980), 95 White Lion Street, London N1 9PF *tel* 071-837 5440 *telex* 295209 Psluk G *fax* 071-837 5334. *Directors:* Christopher Patrick, John Sinfield.

Represent properties of: Twentieth Century Fox (inc. *The Simpsons*, *Attack of the Killer Tomatoes*, *Fern Gully*), United Feature Syndicate (inc. *Garfield*, *Peanuts*, *Fido Dido*), Leisure Concepts (inc. *Nintendo*, *Captain Planet*), MGM, Carolco, Viacom International and all London Weekend Television productions.

Michael Woodward Creations (1990), Parlington Hall, Parlington, Aberford, West Yorks. LS25 3EG   *tel* (0532) 813913   *fax* (0532) 813911. *Directors:* Michael R. Woodward, Ian C. Bond.
Teddy Tum Tum, *Mello*, *Mr Frimble*, *Ginger Spike*, *Professor Plonker*, *Baby Su*, *Dolly Mice*, *Davy Croc*, *Edwardian Hedgerow*, *Charles Dickens Heritage Ltd*. New concepts and characters needed. Please forward samples of work for consideration.

PART TWO

General Information

Finance

Income Tax for Writers and Artists

PETER VAINES, FCA, ATII
Chartered Accountant
Barrister at Law

This article is intended to explain the impact of taxation on writers and others engaged in similar activities. Despite attempts by many Governments to simplify our taxation system, the subject has become increasingly complicated and the following is an attempt to give a broad outline of the position. At the time of writing the proposals in the Budget have been set out in detail in the Finance Bill which will emerge in due course as the Finance Act 1991. The changes proposed in the Finance Bill are reflected in this article.

HOW INCOME IS TAXED

(a) Generally

Authors are usually treated for tax purposes as carrying on a profession and are taxed in a similar fashion to other professional persons, i.e. as self-employed persons assessable under Schedule D. This article is directed to self-employed persons only, because if a writer is employed by another in whatever capacity he will be subject to the rules of Schedule E where different considerations apply – substantially to his disadvantage. Attempts are often made by employed persons to shake off the status of 'employee' and to attain 'freelance' status so as to qualify for the advantages of Schedule D, such attempts meeting with varying degrees of success. The problems involved in making this transition are considerable and space does not permit a detailed explanation to be made here – proper advice is necessary if the difficulties are to be avoided.

Particular attention has been paid by the Inland Revenue to Fleet Street journalists and to those engaged in the TV and film industry with a view to reclassifying them as employees so that PAYE is deducted from their earnings. This blanket treatment has been extended to other areas and, although it is obviously open to challenge by individual taxpayers, it is always difficult to persuade the Inland Revenue to change their views.

There is no reason why an employed person cannot carry on a freelance business in his spare time. Indeed, aspiring authors, painters, musicians, etc., often derive so little income from their craft that the financial security of an employment, perhaps in a different sphere of activity, is necessary. The existence of the employment is irrelevant to the taxation of the freelance earnings although it is most important not to confuse the income or expenditure of the employment with the income or expenditure of the self-employed activity. The Inland Revenue are aware of the advantages which can be derived by an individual having 'freelance' income from an organisation of which he is also an employee, and where such circumstances are contrived, it is of course extremely difficult to convince an Inspector of Taxes that a genuine freelance activity is being carried on.

For those starting in business or commencing work on a freelance basis the Inland Revenue produce a very useful booklet entitled 'Starting in Business (IR28)', which is available from any tax office.

(b) Income

For income to be taxable it need not be substantial, nor even the author's only source of income; earnings from casual writing are also taxable but this can be an advantage, because occasional writers do not often make a profit from their writing. The expenses incurred in connection with writing may well exceed any income receivable and the resultant loss may then be used to reclaim tax paid on other income. There may be deducted from the income certain allowable expenses and capital allowances which are set out in more detail below. The possibility of a loss being used as a basis for a tax repayment is fully appreciated by the Inland Revenue who sometimes attempt to treat casual writing as a hobby so that any losses incurred cannot be used to reclaim tax; of course by the same token any income receivable would not be chargeable to tax. This treatment may sound attractive but it should be resisted vigorously because the Inland Revenue do not hesitate to change their mind when profits begin to arise. However, in the case of exceptional or non-recurring writing, such as the autobiography of a sports personality or the memoirs of a politician, it could be better to be treated as pursuing a hobby and not as a professional author. Sales of copyright are chargeable to capital gains tax only (and not income tax), unless the recipient is a professional author.

(c) Royalties

However, where the recipient is a professional author, a series of cases has laid down a clear principle that sales of copyright are taxable as income and not as capital receipts. Similarly, lump sums on account of, or in advance of royalties are also taxable as income in the year of receipt, subject to a claim for spreading relief (see below).

Copyright royalties are generally paid without deduction of Income Tax. However, if royalties are paid to a person who normally lives abroad, tax will be deducted by the payer or his agent at the time the payment is made unless arrangements are made with the Inland Revenue for payments to be made gross.

(d) Arts Council Grants

Persons in receipt of grants from the Arts Council or similar bodies have been concerned for some time whether or not such grants were liable to Income Tax. In 1979, the Arts Council and other interested bodies engaged in detailed discussions with the Inland Revenue which culminated in the issue of a Statement of Practice regarding the tax treatment of those awards. Grants and other receipts of a similar nature have now been divided into two categories – those which are to be treated by the Inland Revenue as chargeable to tax and those which are not. Category A awards are considered to be taxable and arise from the following:

(1) Direct or indirect musical, design or choreographic commissions and direct or indirect commission of sculpture and paintings for public sites.
(2) The Royalty Supplement Guarantee Scheme.
(3) The contract writers' scheme.
(4) Jazz bursaries.
(5) Translators' grants.
(6) Photographic awards and bursaries.
(7) Film and video awards and bursaries.
(8) Performance Art Awards.
(9) Art Publishing Grants.
(10) Grants to assist with a specific project or projects (such as the writing of a book) or to meet specific professional expenses such as a contribution towards copying expenses made to a composer or to an artist's studio expenses.

Awards made under category B are not chargeable to tax and are as follows:
(1) Bursaries to trainee directors.
(2) In-service bursaries for theatre directors.
(3) Bursaries for associate directors.
(4) Bursaries to people attending full time courses in arts administration (the practical training course).
(5) In-service bursaries to theatre designers and bursaries to trainees on the theatre designers' scheme.
(6) In-service bursaries for administrators.
(7) Bursaries for actors and actresses.
(8) Bursaries for technicians and stage managers.
(9) Bursaries made to students attending the City University Arts Administration courses.
(10) Awards, known as the Buying Time Awards, made not to assist with a specific project or professional expenses but to maintain the recipient to enable him to take time off to develop his personal talents. These at present include the awards and bursaries known as the Theatre Writing Bursaries, awards and bursaries to composers, awards and bursaries to painters, sculptures and print makers, literature awards and bursaries.

This Statement of Practice has no legal force and is used merely to ease the administration of the tax system. It is open to anyone in receipt of a grant or award to disregard the agreed statement and challenge the Inland Revenue view on the merits of their particular case. However, it must be recognised that the Inland Revenue do not issue such statements lightly and any challenge to their view would almost certainly involve a lengthy and expensive action through the Courts.

The tax position of persons in receipt of literary prizes will generally follow a decision by the Special Commissioners in connection with the Whitbread Literary Award. In that case it was held that the prize was not part of the author's professional income and accordingly not chargeable to tax. The precise details are not available because decisions of the Special Commissioners are not reported unless an appeal is made to the High Court and the Inland Revenue chose not to appeal against this decision. Elsewhere in this *Yearbook* will be found details of the many literary awards which are given each year and this decision is of considerable significance to the winners of each of these prizes. It would be unwise to assume that all such awards will be free of tax as the precise facts which were present in the case of the Whitbread award may not be repeated in another case; however it is clear that an author winning a prize has some very powerful arguments in his favour, should the Inland Revenue seek to charge tax on the award.

ALLOWABLE EXPENSES

To qualify as an allowable business expense, expenditure has to be laid out wholly and exclusively for business purposes. Strictly there must be no 'duality of purpose', which means that expenditure cannot be apportioned to reflect the private and business usage, e.g. food, clothing, telephone, travelling expenses, etc. However, the Inland Revenue do not usually interpret this principle strictly and are prepared to allow all reasonable expenses (including apportioned sums) where the amounts can be commercially justified. It should be noted carefully that the expenditure does not have to be 'necessary', it merely has to be incurred 'wholly and exclusively' for business purposes; naturally, however, expenditure of an outrageous and wholly unnecessary character might well give rise to a presumption that it was not really for business purposes. As with all things, some expenses are unquestionably allowable and some expenses are equally unquestionably not allowable – it is the grey area in between which gives rise to all the difficulties and the outcome invariably depends on negotiation with the Inland Revenue.

Great care should be taken when claiming a deduction for items where there is a 'duality of purpose' and negotiations should be conducted with more than usual care and courtesy – if provoked the Inspector of Taxes may well choose to allow nothing. An appeal is always possible although unlikely to succeed as a string of cases in the Courts has clearly demonstrated. An example is the case of *Caillebotte* v. *Quinn* where the taxpayer (who normally had lunch at home) sought to claim the excess cost of meals incurred because he was working a long way from his home. The taxpayer's arguments failed because he did not eat only in order to work, one of the reasons for his eating was in order to sustain his life; a duality of purpose therefore existed and no tax relief was due. Other cases have shown that expenditure on clothing can also be disallowed if it is the kind of clothing which is in everyday use, because clothing is worn not only to assist the pursuit of one's profession but also to accord with public decency. This duality of purpose may be sufficient to deny relief – even where the particular type of clothing is of a kind not otherwise worn by the taxpayer. In the recent case of *Mallalieu* v. *Drummond* a lady barrister failed to obtain a tax deduction for items of sombre clothing purchased specifically for wearing in Court. The House of Lords decided that a duality of purpose existed because clothing represented part of her needs as a human being.

Despite the above Inspectors of Taxes are not usually inflexible and the following expenses are among those generally allowed:

(a) Cost of all materials used up in the course of preparation of the work.

(b) Cost of typewriting and secretarial assistance, etc.; if this or other help is obtained from one's spouse then it is entirely proper for a deduction to be claimed for the amounts paid for the work. The amounts claimed must actually be paid to the spouse and should be at the market rate although some uplift can be made for unsocial hours, etc. Payments to a wife (or husband) are of course taxable in her (or his) hands and should therefore be most carefully considered. The wife's earnings may also be liable for National Insurance contributions and if care is not taken these contributions can more than outweigh the tax savings.

(c) All expenditure on normal business items such as postage, stationery, telephone, fax and answering machines, agent's fees, accountancy charges, photography, subscriptions, periodicals, magazines, etc., may be claimed. The cost of daily papers should not be overlooked if these form part of research material. Visits to theatres, cinemas, etc., for research purposes may also be permissible (but not of course the cost relating to guests). Unfortunately expenditure on all types of business entertaining is specifically denied tax relief.

(d) If work is conducted at home, a deduction for 'use of home' is usually allowed providing the amount claimed is reasonable. If the claim is based on an appropriate proportion of the total costs of rent, light and heat, cleaning and maintenance, insurance, etc. (but not the personal community charge), then care should be taken to ensure that no single room is used *exclusively* for business purposes, because this may result in the Capital Gains Tax exemption on the house as the only or main residence being partially forfeited. However, it would be a strange household where one room was in fact used exclusively for business purposes and for no other purpose whatsoever (e.g. storing personal bank statements and other private papers); the usual formula is to claim a deduction on the basis that most or all of the rooms in the house are used at one time or another for business purposes, thereby avoiding any suggestion that any part was used exclusively for business purposes.

(e) The appropriate business proportion of motor running expenses may also be claimed although what is the appropriate proportion will naturally depend on the particular circumstances of each case; it should be mentioned that the well-known scale benefits, whereby one is taxed according to the size and cost of the car, do not apply to self-employed persons.

(f) It has been long established that the cost of travelling from home to work (whether employed or self-employed) is not an allowable expense. However, if home is one's place of work then no expenditure under this heading is likely to be incurred and difficulties are unlikely to arise.

(g) Travelling and hotel expenses incurred for business purposes will normally be allowed but if any part could be construed as disguised holiday or pleasure expenditure, considerable thought would need to be given to the commercial reasons for the journey in order to justify the claim. The principle of 'duality of purpose' will always be a difficult hurdle in this connection – although not insurmountable.

(h) If a separate business bank account is maintained, any overdraft interest thereon will be an allowable expense. This is the *only* circumstance in which overdraft interest is allowed for tax purposes and care should be taken to avoid overdrafts in all other circumstances.

(i) Where capital allowances (see below) are claimed for a television, video, record or tape player, etc., used for business purposes an appropriate proportion of the costs of maintenance and repair of the equipment may also be claimed.

Clearly many other allowable items may be claimed in addition to those mentioned above. Wherever there is any reasonable business motive for some expenditure it should be claimed as a deduction although one should avoid an excess of imagination as this would naturally cause the Inspector of Taxes to doubt the genuineness of other expenses claimed.

The question is often raised whether the whole amount of an expense may be deducted or whether the VAT content must be excluded. Where VAT is reclaimed from the Customs and Excise (on the quarterly returns made by a registered person), the VAT element of the expense cannot be treated as an allowable deduction. Where the VAT is not reclaimed, the whole expense (inclusive of VAT) is allowable for Income Tax purposes.

CAPITAL ALLOWANCES

(a) Allowances

Where expenditure of a capital nature is incurred, it cannot be deducted from income as an expense – a separate and sometimes more valuable capital allowance being available instead. Capital allowances are given for many different types of expenditure, but authors and similar professional people are likely to claim only for 'plant and machinery'; this is a very wide expression which may include motor cars, typewriters, computers and other business machines, televisions, record and cassette players used for business purposes, books – and even a horse! Plant and machinery qualify for a 25% allowance in the year of purchase and 25% of the reducing balance in subsequent years.

The reason these allowances can be more valuable than allowable expenses is that they may be wholly or partly disclaimed in any year that full benefit cannot be obtained – ordinary business expenses cannot be similarly disclaimed. Where, for example, the income of an author does not exceed his personal allowances, he would not be liable to tax and a claim for capital allowances would be wasted. If the capital allowances were to be disclaimed their benefit would be carried forward for use in subsequent years.

Careful planning with claims for capital allowances is therefore essential if maximum benefit is to be obtained, especially where the spouse also has income chargeable to tax.

As an alternative to capital allowances claims can be made on the 'renewals' basis whereby all renewals are treated as allowable deductions in the year; no allowance is obtained for the initial purchase, but the cost of replacement (excluding any improvement element) is allowed in full. This basis is no longer widely used, as it is considerably less advantageous than claiming capital allowances as described above.

Leasing is a popular method of acquiring fixed assets, and where cash is not available to enable an outright purchase to be made, assets may be leased over a period of time. Whilst leasing may have financial benefits in certain circumstances, in normal cases there is likely to be no *tax* advantage in leasing an asset where the alternative of outright purchase is available. Indeed, leasing can be a positive disadvantage in the case of motor cars with a new retail price of more than £8000. If such a car is leased, only a proportion of the leasing charges will be tax deductible.

(b) Books

The question of whether the cost of books is eligible for tax relief has long been a source of difficulty. The annual cost of replacing books used for the purposes of one's professional activities (e.g. the annual cost of a new *Writers' & Artists' Yearbook*) has always been an allowable expense; the difficulty arose because the initial cost of reference books etc. (for example when commencing one's profession) was treated as capital expenditure and no allowances were due as the books were not considered to be 'plant'. However, the matter has now been clarified by the case of *Munby* v. *Furlong* in which the Court of Appeal decided that the initial cost of law books purchased by a barrister was expenditure on 'plant' and eligible for capital allowances. This is clearly a most important decision, particularly relevant to any person who uses expensive books in the course of exercising his profession.

PENSION CONTRIBUTIONS

(a) Personal pensions

Where a self-employed person pays annual premiums under an approved personal pension policy, tax relief may now be obtained each year for the following amounts:

Age at 6/4/91	Maximum %
35 and under	17.5% (max) £12,495
36 – 45	20% (max) £14,280
46 – 50	25% (max) £17,850
51 – 55	30% (max) £21,420
56 and over	35% (max) £24,990

These figures do not apply to existing retirement annuity policies; these remain subject to the old limits which are unchanged.

These arrangements can be extremely advantageous in providing for a pension as premiums are usually paid when the income is high (and the tax relief is also high) and the pension (taxed as earned income when received) usually arises when the income is low and little tax is payable. The reduction in the rates of income tax to a maximum of 40% makes this decision a little more difficult because the tax advantages could go into reverse. When the pension is paid it could, if rates rise again, be taxed at a higher rate than the rate of tax relief at the moment. One would be deferring income in order to pay more tax on it later. However, this involves a large element of guesswork, and many people will be content simply with the long-term pension benefits.

(b) Class 4 National Insurance Contributions

Allied to pensions is the payment of Class 4 National Insurance contributions, although no pension or other benefit is obtained by the contributions; the Class 4 contributions are designed solely to extract additional amounts from self-employed persons and are payable in addition to the normal Class 2 (self-employed) contributions. The rates are changed each year and for 1991/92 self-employed persons will be obliged to contribute 6.3% of their profits between the range £5900-£20,200 per annum, a maximum liability of £900.90 for 1991/92. This amount is collected in conjunction with the Schedule D Income Tax liability and appears on the same assessment; the comments below regarding assessments, appeals and postponement apply equally to Class 4 contributions although interest does not ordinarily accrue on their late payment. Tax relief is available for one half of the Class 4 contributions.

SPREADING RELIEF

(a) Relief for copyright payments

Special provisions enable authors and similar persons who have been engaged on a literary, dramatic, musical or artistic work for a period of more than twelve months, to spread certain amounts received over two or three years depending on the time spent in preparing the work. If the author was engaged on the work for a period exceeding twelve months, the receipt may be spread backwards over two years; if the author was engaged on the work for more than 24 months, the receipt may be spread backwards over three years. (Analogous provisions apply to sums received for the sale of a painting, sculpture or other work of art.)

The relief applies to:

a. lump sums received on the assignment of copyright, in whole or in part;

b. sums received on the grant of any interest in the copyright by licence;

c. non-returnable advances on account of royalties;

d. any receipts of or on account of royalties or any periodical sums received within two years of first publication.

A claim for spreading relief has to be made within eight years from 5th April following the date of first publication.

(b) Relief where copyright sold after ten years

Where copyright is assigned (or a licence in it is granted) more than ten years after the first publication of the work, then the amounts received can qualify for a different spreading relief. The assignment (or licence) must be for a period of more than two years and the receipt will be spread forward over the number of years for which the assignment (or licence) is granted – but with a maximum of six years. The relief is terminated by death, but there are provisions enabling the deceased author's personal representatives to re-spread the amounts if it is to the beneficiaries' advantage.

The above rules are arbitrary and cumbersome, only providing a limited measure of relief in special circumstances. The provisions can sometimes be helpful to repair matters when consideration of the tax position has been neglected, but invariably a better solution is found if the likely tax implications are considered fully in advance.

COLLECTION OF TAX

Assessments

In order to collect the tax which is due on the profits of authorship the Inland Revenue issue an assessment based on the income for the relevant period. Normally the income to be assessed will be that for the previous year (e.g. the 1991/92 assessment will be based on the accounts made up to some date in 1990/91 – perhaps 31st December 1990 or 5th April 1991). However, there are complicated rules for determining the income to be assessed in the years immediately after commencement, and in the years immediately prior to the discontinuance of the profession, and if for any reason there is a change in the date to which accounts are made up. When an assessment is received it should be examined carefully.

(a) If it is correct, the tax should be paid on the dates specified. Usually the tax is payable in two equal instalments, on 1st January in the year of assessment and on the following 1st July. If payment is delayed then interest may arise – see below.

(b) If the assessment is incorrect (for example, if it is estimated), then prompt action is required. An appeal must be lodged within 30 days of the date of issue of the assessment specifying the grounds of the appeal. An appeal form usually accompanies the notice of assessment. (If for some reason an appeal cannot be lodged within the 30 days the Inland Revenue are often prepared to accept a late appeal, but this is at their discretion and acceptance cannot be guaranteed.) If there is any tax charged on an incorrect assessment it cannot simply be forgotten, because it will become payable despite any appeal, unless an application for 'postponement' is also made. (This may be done by completing the bottom half of the appeal form.) Tax can be postponed only where there are grounds for believing that too much tax has been charged, and the Inspector of Taxes will agree to postpone tax only if these grounds are reasonable. The tax which is not postponed will usually be payable on the normal due dates. It is necessary to consider claims for postponement most carefully to ensure that approximately the correct amount of tax remains payable; otherwise an unfortunate (and expensive) charge to interest could arise. It is important to recognise that 'postponement' does not mean elimination; it simply means that payment of tax may be deferred, and after six months interest will start to run on any tax which has been postponed but which is ultimately found to be payable. As agreement of the final liability may take a long time, a large amount of interest can arise unless a reasonably accurate amount has been paid on time.

Interest

Interest is chargeable on overdue tax at a variable rate, currently approximately 11% per annum and does not rank for any tax relief, which makes the Inland Revenue a very expensive source of credit. Where the amount of interest is less than £30 in any year it is not usually collected but should the interest exceed £30 the full amount will be payable and it is sometimes difficult to persuade the Inland Revenue to withdraw a charge to interest – even where the delay is their fault.

However, the Inland Revenue can also be obliged to pay interest at the same rate (known as repayment supplement) tax-free where repayments are delayed. The rules relating to repayment supplement are less beneficial and even more complicated than the rules for interest payable but they do exist and can be very welcome if a large repayment has been delayed for a long time.

Example

Author's accounts made up to 30th April 1990 showing profits of £10,000 giving rise to tax of (say) £1500.

Assessment issued in September 1991 for 1991/92 in an estimated figure of £15,000 – tax charged £2500.

Appeal must be made within 30 days of issue.

Application for postponement must also be made within 30 days to postpone £1000 of the tax charged.

Tax therefore becomes payable thus:

	1st Jan. 1992	£750
	1st July 1992	£750

(If no application for postponement were to be made £1250 would become payable on each of these dates. When the final liability is agreed the excess of £1000 would be refunded but that could take some time, and repayment supplement might not apply.)

Unfortunately life is never as simple as the above illustration would suggest, but it serves to demonstrate the principle.

VALUE ADDED TAX

The activities of writers, painters, composers, etc., are all 'taxable supplies' within the scope of VAT and chargeable at the standard rate. (Zero rating which applies to publishers, booksellers, etc., on the supply of books does not extend to the work performed by writers; the position is less clear with regard to authors writing for foreign persons. Changes were made in the VAT rules from 1st January 1978 with the effect that zero rating does not always apply. Proper advice should be sought if there is any doubt regarding the correct treatment.) Accordingly, authors are obliged to register for VAT if their income for the past twelve months exceeds £35,000.

Delay in registering can be a most serious matter because if registration is not effected at the proper time, the Customs and Excise can (and invariably do) claim VAT from all the income received since the date on which registration should have been made. As no VAT would have been included in the amounts received during this period the amount claimed by the Customs and Excise must inevitably come straight from the pocket of the author.

He may be entitled to seek reimbursement of the VAT from those whom he ought to have charged VAT but this is obviously a matter of some difficulty and may indeed damage his commercial relationships. Apart from the commercial disadvantages there is now a penalty for late registration. The rules are extremely harsh and are imposed automatically even in cases of innocent error. It is therefore extremely important to monitor the income very carefully because if in any period of twelve months the income exceeds the £35,000 limit, the Customs and Excise must be notified within 30 days of the end of the period. Failure to do so will give rise to an automatic penalty of up to 30% of the VAT which should have been paid; this will always be a substantial amount. It should be emphasized that this is a penalty for failing to submit a form and has nothing to do with any real or potential loss of tax. Furthermore, whether the failure was innocent or deliberate will not matter. Only the existence of a 'reasonable excuse' will be a defence to the penalty. However, a reasonable excuse does not include ignorance, error, a lack of funds or reliance on any third party. It should be particularly noted that neither the Customs and Excise nor the VAT Appeal Tribunal have any power to reduce the amount of any penalty for failing to register for VAT. It has also been announced that further and equally harsh penalties are to be introduced concerning the late submission of returns and underdeclarations of VAT in addition to those which already exist.

However it is possible to regard VAT registration as a privilege and not a penalty, because only VAT registered persons can reclaim VAT paid on such expenditure as stationery, telephone, professional fees, etc., even typewriters and other plant and machinery (excluding cars). However, many find that the administrative inconvenience – the cost of maintaining the necessary records and completing the necessary forms – more than outweighs the benefits to be gained from registration and prefer to stay outside the scope of VAT for as long as possible.

OVERSEAS MATTERS

The general observation may be made that self-employed persons resident and domiciled in the United Kingdom are not well treated with regard to their overseas work, being taxable on their world-wide income. It is important to emphasise that if fees are earned abroad, no tax saving can be achieved merely by keeping the money outside the country. Although exchange control regulations no longer exist to require repatriation of foreign earnings, such income remains taxable in the UK and must be disclosed to the Inland Revenue; the same applies to interest or other income arising on any investment of these earnings overseas. Accordingly whenever foreign earnings are likely to become substantial, prompt and effective action is required to limit the impact of UK and foreign taxation. In the case of non resident authors it is important that arrangements concerning writing for publication in the UK, e.g. in newspapers, are undertaken with great care. A recent case concerning the wife of one of the great train robbers who provided detailed information for a series of articles in a Sunday newspaper is most instructive. Although she was acknowledged to be resident in Canada for all the relevant years, the income from the articles was treated as arising in this country and fully chargeable to UK tax.

The United Kingdom has double taxation agreements with many other countries and these agreements are designed to ensure that income arising in a foreign country is taxed either in that country or in the United Kingdom. Where a withholding tax is deducted from payments received from another country (or where tax is paid in full in the absence of a double taxation agreement), the amount of foreign tax paid can usually be set off against the related UK tax liability. Many successful authors can be found living in Eire because of the complete exemption from tax which attaches to works of cultural or artistic merit by persons who are resident there. However, such a step should only be contemplated having careful regard to all the other domestic and commercial considerations and specialist advice is essential if the exemption is to be obtained and kept; a careless breach of the conditions could cause the exemption to be withdrawn with catastrophic consequences.

COMPANIES

When an author becomes successful the prospect of paying tax at the higher rate may drive him to take hasty action such as the formation of companies, etc., which may not always be to his advantage. Indeed some authors seeing the exodus into tax exile of their more successful colleagues even form companies in low tax areas in the naive expectation of saving large amounts of tax. The Inland Revenue are fully aware of the opportunities and have extensive powers to charge tax and combat avoidance. Accordingly such action is just as likely to *increase* tax liabilities and generate other costs and should never be contemplated without expert advice; some very expensive mistakes are often made in this area which are not always able to be remedied.

To conduct one's business through the medium of a company can be a most effective method of mitigating tax liabilities, and providing it is done at the right time and under the right circumstances very substantial advantages can be derived. However, if done without due care and attention the intended advantages will simply evaporate. At the very least it is essential to ensure that the company's business is genuine and conducted properly with regard to the realities of the situation. If the author continues his activities unchanged, simply paying all the receipts from his work into a company's bank account, he cannot expect to persuade the Inland Revenue that it is the company and not himself who is entitled to, and should be assessed to tax on, that income. It must be strongly emphasised that many pitfalls exist which can easily eliminate all the tax benefits expected to arise by the formation of the company. For example, company directors are employees of the company and will be liable to pay much higher National Insurance contributions; the company must also pay the employer's proportion of the contribution and a total liability of nearly 20% of gross salary may arise. This compares most unfavourably with the position of a self-employed person. Moreover on the commencement of the company's business the individual's profession will cease and the Inland Revenue have the power to re-open earlier years assessments and may be able to increase the liabilities for previous years; this is always a crucial factor in determining the best moment when the changeover to a company should take place.

No mention has been made above of personal reliefs and allowances (for example the single and married persons allowances, etc.); this is because these allowances and the rates of tax are subject to constant change and are always set out in detail in the explanatory notes which accompany the Tax Return. The annual Tax Return is an important document and should not be ignored because it is crucial to one's tax position. Indeed, it should be completed promptly with extreme care because the Inland Revenue treat failures to disclose income very harshly, invariably exacting interest and penalties – sometimes of substantial amounts. If filling in the Return is a source of difficulty or anxiety, comfort may be found in the Consumer Association's publication *Money Which? – Tax Saving Guide*; this is published in March of each year and includes much which is likely to be of interest and assistance.

Social Security Contributions

J. PHILIP HARDMAN, FCA. FTII
Chartered Accountant

INTRODUCTION

In general, every individual who works in Great Britain either as an employee or as a self-employed person is liable to pay social security contributions. The law governing this subject is complicated and the following should only be regarded as a summary of the position.

All contributions are payable in respect of years ending on 5 April, the classes of contributions being as follows:

Class 1 These are payable by employees (primary contributions) and their employers (secondary contributions) and are based on earnings.

Class 1A Use of company car, and fuel, for private purposes.

Class 2 These are flat rate contributions, payable weekly by the self-employed.

Class 3 These are weekly flat rate contributions, payable on a voluntary basis in order to provide, or make up entitlement to, certain social security benefits.

Class 4 These are payable by the self-employed in respect of their trading or professional income and are based on earnings.

EMPLOYED OR SELF-EMPLOYED?

The question as to whether a person is employed under a contract *of* service and is thereby an employee liable to Class 1 contributions, or performs services (either solely or in partnership) under a contract *for* service and is thereby self-employed liable to Class 2 and Class 4 contributions, often has to be decided in practice. One of the best guides can be found in the case of *Market Investigations Limited* v. *Minister of Social Security* (1969 2 WLR 1) when Cooke J. remarked as follows:

'. . . the fundamental test to be applied is this: "Is the person who has engaged himself to perform these services performing them as a person in business on his own account?" If the answer to that question is "yes", then the contract is a contract for services. If the answer is "no", then the contract is a contract of service. No exhaustive list has been compiled and perhaps no exhaustive list can be compiled of the considerations which are relevant in determining that question, nor can strict rules be laid down as to the relative weight which the various considerations should carry in particular cases. The most that can be said is that control will no doubt always have to be considered, although it can no longer be regarded as the sole determining factor; and that factors which may be of importance are such matters as

—whether the man performing the services provides his own equipment,
—whether he hires his own helpers,
—what degree of financial risk he takes,

—what degree of responsibility for investment and management he has, and
—whether and how far he has an opportunity of profiting from sound
management in the performance of his task.'

There have been three cases in recent years, all dealing with musicians, which
provide further guidance on the question as to whether an individual is employed
or self-employed.

Midland Sinfonia Concert Society Ltd v. *Secretary of State for Social Services*
(1981 ICR 454)

A musician, employed to play in an orchestra by separate invitation at irregular
intervals and remunerated solely in respect of each occasion upon which he does
play, is employed under a contract for services. He is therefore self-employed,
not an employed earner, for the purposes of the Social Security Act 1975,
and the orchestra which engages him is not liable to pay National Insurance
contributions in respect of his earnings.

Addison v. *London Philharmonic Orchestra Limited* (1981 ICR 261)

This was an appeal to determine whether certain individuals were employees
for the purposes of section 11(1) of the Employment Protection (Consolidation)
Act 1978.

The Employment Appeal Tribunal upheld the decision of an industrial tribunal
that an associate player and three additional or extra players of the London
Philharmonic Orchestra were not employees under a contract of service, but
were essentially freelance musicians carrying on their own business.

The facts found by the industrial tribunal showed that, when playing for the
orchestra, each appellant remained essentially a freelance musician, pursuing
his or her own profession as an instrumentalist, with an individual reputation,
and carrying on his or her own business, and they contributed their own
skills and interpretative powers to the orchestra's performances as independent
contractors.

Winfield v. *London Philharmonic Orchestra Limited* (ICR 1979, page 726)

This case dealt with the question as to whether an individual was an employee
within the meaning of section 30 of the Trade Union and Labour Relations Act
1974.

The following remarks by the appeal tribunal are of interest in relation to the
status of musicians:

'. . . making music is an art, and the co-operation required for a performance
of Berlioz's *Requiem* is dissimilar to that required between the manufacturer
of concrete and the truck driver who takes the concrete where it is needed. . .
It took the view, as we think it was entitled on the material before it to do,
that the company was simply machinery through which the members of the
orchestra managed and controlled the orchestra's operation . . . In deciding
whether you are in the presence of a contract of service or not, you look at
the whole of the picture. This picture looks to us, as it looked to the industrial
tribunal, like a co-operative of distinguished musicians running themselves
with self and mutual discipline, and in no sense like a boss and his musician
employees.'

Other recent cases have concerned a professional dancer and holiday camp
entertainers, and there are special arrangements for workers in the film industry.
In two recent cases income from part-time lecturing was held to be from an
employment.

Accordingly, if a person is regarded as an employee under the above rules,
he will be liable to pay contributions even if his employment is casual, part time
or temporary.

Furthermore, if a person is an employee and also carries on a trade or
profession either solely or in partnership, there will be a liability to more than
one class of contributions (subject to certain maxima – see below).

Exceptions

There are certain exceptions to the above rules, those most relevant to artists and writers being:

(a) The employment of a wife by her husband, or vice versa, is disregarded for social security purposes unless it is for the purposes of a trade or profession (for example, the employment of his wife by an author would not be disregarded and would result in a liability for contributions if her salary reached the minimum levels).

(b) The employment of certain relatives in a private dwelling house in which both employee and employer reside is disregarded for social security purposes provided the employment is not for the purposes of a trade or business carried on at those premises by the employer. This would cover the employment of a relative (as defined) as a housekeeper in a private residence.

(c) In general, lecturers, teachers and instructors engaged by an educational establishment to teach on at least four days in three consecutive months are regarded as employees, although this rule does not apply to fees received by persons giving public lectures.

Freelance film workers

As regards the status of workers in the film and allied industries, the Inland Revenue made the following announcement on 30 March 1983:

'The Inland Revenue has recently carried out a review of the employment status of workers engaged on "freelance" terms within the industry. Following this review there has been an extensive series of discussions with representative bodies in the industry, including Independent Programme Producers Association, British Film and Television Producers Association, Advertising Film and Video Tape Producers Association, National Association of Theatrical and Kine Employees, and Association of Cinematograph, Television and Allied Technicians.

As a result of that review and the subsequent discussions, the Inland Revenue consider that a number of workers engaged on "freelance" terms within the industry are engaged as employees under contracts of service, either written or oral, and should be assessed under Schedule E. Many workers in the industry already pay employee's National Insurance contributions.

The Inland Revenue, however, accept that a number of "freelance" workers in certain types of work within the industry are likely to be engaged under contracts for services, as people in self-employment, and should therefore be assessed under Schedule D. Any individual who does not agree with the Revenue's determination of his position has the normal right of appeal to the independent Income Tax Commissioners.'

There is a list of grades in the film industry in respect of which PAYE need not be deducted and who are regarded as self-employed for tax purposes.

Further information can be obtained from the March 1991 edition of the Inland Revenue guidance notes on the application of PAYE to casual and freelance staff in the film industry. In view of the Inland Revenue announcement that the same status will apply for PAYE and DSS purposes, no liability for employee's and employer's contributions should arise in the case of any of the grades mentioned above. However, in the film industry this general rule is not always followed in practice, and various special arrangements exist. There are also special rules for personnel appearing before the camera, short engagements, payments to limited companies and payments to overseas personalities.

Artistes, performers and non-performers

From 6 April 1990 artistes and performers (excluding established performers with 'reserved Schedule D status' and guest artistes engaged by opera companies) working under standard Equity contracts are treated as employees for income tax purposes so far as earnings from such employments are concerned. This will bring the income tax treatment into line with that for social security, as it has been the view of the DSS for many years that the vast majority of performers are employees for social security contribution purposes because of the general conditions under which they usually work. The DSS has always acknowledged, however, that there is some scope for self-employment for performers (especially 'act as known' engagements), and specific claims to self-employment are looked into in detail.

The DSS does, however, permit subsistence allowances to be paid without liability to contributions.

The industry also uses standard agreements for the engagement of non-performers. The Inland Revenue has looked at some of these and concluded that some are normally contracts *for* services (self-employed) and others contracts *of* service (employed).

CLASS 1 CONTRIBUTIONS BY EMPLOYEES AND EMPLOYERS

As mentioned above, these are related to earnings, the amount payable depending upon whether the employer has applied for his employees to be 'contracted-out' of the State earnings-related pension scheme; such application can be made where the employer's own pension scheme provides a requisite level of benefits for his employees and their dependents.

Up to 6 October 1985, when earnings reached the lower earnings limit primary and secondary Class 1 contributions were payable on earnings up to the upper earnings limit, although for contracted-out employments there were reduced rates of contributions on earnings between the lower and upper limits.

From 6 October 1985 the upper earnings limit for secondary contributions, but not for primary contributions, was removed, and contribution rates on lower earnings reduced.

Contributions are normally collected via the PAYE tax deduction machinery, and there are penalties for late submission of returns and for errors therein.

Employees liable to pay contributions

These are payable by any employee who is aged 16 years and over (even though he may still be at school) and who is paid an amount equal to, or exceeding, the lower earnings limit (see below).

Nationality is irrelevant for contribution purposes and, subject to special rules covering employees not normally resident in Great Britain, Northern Ireland or the Isle of Man, or resident in countries with which there are reciprocal social security agreements, contributions must be paid whether the employee concerned is a British subject or not provided he is gainfully employed in Great Britain.

Employees exempt from liability to pay contributions

Persons over pensionable age (65 for men and 60 for women) are exempt from liability to pay primary contributions, even if they have not retired.

However, the fact that an employee may be exempt from liability does not relieve an employer from liability to pay secondary contributions in respect of that employee.

Rate of employees' contributions

For earnings paid after 5 October 1989, the rate of employees' contributions, where the earnings are not less than the lower earnings limit, is 2% of earnings to the lower earnings limit and 9% of earnings between the lower and upper earnings limits (7% for contracted-out employments).

Certain married women who made appropriate elections before 12 May 1977 may be entitled to pay a reduced rate of 3.85%. However, these ladies will have no entitlement to benefits in respect of these contributions.

Employers' contributions

All employers are liable to pay contributions on the gross earnings of employees. As mentioned above, an employer's liability is not reduced as a result of employees being exempted from, or being liable to pay only the (3.85%) reduced rate of, contributions.

For earnings paid on or after 6 April 1991 employers are liable at rates of 4.6%, 6.6%, 8.6% or 10.4% on earnings paid (without any upper earnings limit) depending upon the particular band into which the earnings fall (see below). The rate of contributions attributable to the band into which the earnings fall is applied to *all* those earnings and not merely to the earnings falling into that band. The above four rates of secondary contributions are reduced to 0.8%, 2.8%, 4.8% and 6.6% in respect of earnings above the lower earnings limit and up to and including the upper earnings limit for contracted-out employments from 6 April 1991.

The employer is responsible for the payment of both employees' and employer's contributions, but is entitled to deduct the employees' contributions from the earnings on which they are calculated. Effectively, therefore, the employee suffers a deduction in respect of his social security contributions in arriving at his weekly or monthly wage or salary.

Special rules apply to company directors and persons employed through agencies.

Rates of Class 1 contributions and earnings limits from 6 April 1991

Earnings per week £	Rates payable on all Earnings			
	Contracted In		Contracted Out	
	Employee	Employer %	Employee	Employer %
Below 52.00	—	—	—	—
52.00 – 84.99	2% to lower	4.6	2% to lower	*4.6/0.8
85.00 – 129.99	earnings limit,	6.6	earnings limit,	*6.6/2.8
130.00 – 184.99	9% between	8.6	7% between	*8.6/4.8
185.00 – 390.00	lower and	10.4	lower and	*10.4/6.6
Over £390.00	upper earnings limits	10.4	upper earnings limits	†10.4/6.6

* The first figure is the rate to the lower earnings limit and the second is to the top of the earnings.

† 10.4% to lower earnings limit and above upper earnings limit; 6.6% between these limits.

Items included in, or excluded from, earnings

Contributions are calculated on the basis of a person's gross earnings from his employment. This will normally be the figure shown on the tax deduction card, except where the employee pays superannuation contributions and, from 6 April 1987, charitable gifts – these must be added back for the purposes of calculating

Class 1 liability. Profit-related pay exempt from income tax is not exempt from social security contributions.

Earnings include salary, wages, overtime pay, commissions, bonuses, holiday pay, payments made while the employee is sick or absent from work, payments to cover travel between home and office, and payments under the statutory sick pay and maternity pay schemes.

However, certain payments, some of which may be regarded as taxable income for income tax purposes, are ignored for social security purposes. These include certain gratuities paid other than by the employer, redundancy payments and most payments in lieu of notice, certain payments in kind, reimbursement of specific expenses incurred in the carrying out of the employment, benefits given on an individual basis for personal reasons (e.g. wedding and birthday presents), compensation for loss of office, and meal vouchers which can only be redeemed for food or drink.

DSS booklet NI 269 (April 1991) gives a list of items to include in or exclude from earnings for Class 1 contribution purposes.

Maximum contributions

There is a limit to the total liability for social security contributions payable by a person who is employed in more than one employment, or is also self-employed or a partner.

Where only non contracted-out Class 1 contributions, or non contracted-out Class 1 and Class 2 contributions, are payable, the maximum contribution is limited to 53 primary Class 1 contributions at the maximum weekly non-contracted-out standard rate. For 1991/92 the maximum will thus be £1667.38.

However, where contracted-out Class 1 contributions are payable, the maximum primary Class 1 contributions payable for 1991/92 where all employments are contracted-out are £1309.10.

Where Class 4 contributions are payable in addition to Class 1 and/or Class 2 contributions, *the Class 4 contributions are restricted* so that they shall not exceed the excess of £1178.89 (i.e. 53 Class 2 contributions plus maximum Class 4 contributions) over the aggregate of the Class 1 and Class 2 contributions.

Miscellaneous rules

There are detailed rules covering a person with two or more employments; where a person receives a bonus or commission in addition to a regular wage or salary; and where a person is in receipt of holiday pay. From 6 April 1991 employers' social security contributions can arise in respect of the private use of a company car, and of fuel provided for private use therein.

CLASS 2 CONTRIBUTIONS BY THE SELF-EMPLOYED

Rate

Class 2 contributions are payable at the rate of £5.15 per week as from 6 April 1991.

Exemptions from Class 2 liability

These are as follows:
(1) A man over 65 or a woman over 60.
(2) A person who has not attained the age of 16.
(3) A married woman or, in certain cases, a widow could elect prior to 12 May 1977 not to pay Class 2 contributions.
(4) Persons with small earnings (see below).
(5) Persons not ordinarily self-employed (see below).
(6) Persons in receipt of invalid care allowance.

(7) Persons in receipt of sickness or invalidity benefits or unemployability supplements, or maternity allowances, or incapable of work or in prison or legal custody.

Small earnings

Any person who can show that his net self-employed earnings per his profit and loss account (as opposed to taxable profits):
(1) for the year of application are expected to be less than a specified limit (£2900 in the 1991/92 tax year); or
(2) for the year preceding the application were less than the limit specified for that year (£2600 for 1990/91) and there has been no material change of circumstances;
may apply for a certificate of exception from Class 2 contributions. Certificates of exception must be renewed in accordance with the instructions stated thereon. At the Secretary of State's discretion the certificate may commence up to 13 weeks before the date on which the application is made. Despite a certificate of exception being in force, a person who is self-employed is still entitled to pay Class 2 contributions if he wishes, in order to maintain entitlement to social security benefits.

Persons not ordinarily self-employed

Part-time self-employed activities as a writer or artist are disregarded for contribution purposes if the person concerned is not ordinarily employed in such activities and has a full-time job as an employee. There is no definition of 'ordinarily employed' for this purpose but the DSS regard a person who has a regular job and whose earnings from spare-time occupation are not expected to be more than £800 per annum as falling within this category. Persons qualifying for this relief do not require certificates of exception. It should be noted that many activities covered by this relief would probably also be eligible for relief under the small earnings rule (see above).

Method of payment

Class 2 contributions may be paid by purchasing stamps to be fixed to contribution cards, or alternatively application may be made to pay contributions by direct debit through a bank account or the Post Office giro system.

Overpaid contributions

If, following the payment of Class 2 contributions, it is found that the earnings are below the exception limit (e.g. the relevant accounts are prepared late), the Class 2 contributions that have been overpaid can be reclaimed for tax years 1988/89 onwards, provided a claim is made between 6 April and 31 December immediately following the end of the tax year.

CLASS 3 CONTRIBUTIONS

These are payable voluntarily, at the rate of £5.05 per week from 6 April 1991 by persons aged 16 or over with a view to enabling them to qualify for a limited range of benefits if their contribution record is not otherwise sufficient. In general, Class 3 contributions can be paid by employees, the self-employed and the non employed.

Broadly speaking, no more than 52 Class 3 contributions are payable for any one tax year, and contributions are not payable after the end of the tax year in which the individual concerned reaches the age of 64 (59 for women).

Class 3 contributions may be paid by purchasing stamps to be fixed to contribution cards, or by direct debit through a bank account or the Post Office giro system.

CLASS 4 CONTRIBUTIONS BY THE SELF-EMPLOYED

Rate

In addition to Class 2 contributions, self-employed persons are liable to pay Class 4 contributions. These are calculated at the rate of 6.30% on the amount of profits or gains chargeable to income tax under Schedule D Case I or II which exceed £5900 per annum but which do not exceed £20,280 per annum for 1991/92. Thus the maximum Class 4 contribution is 6.30% of £14,380 – i.e. £905.94 for 1991/92.

For the tax year 1991/92, Class 4 contributions are based on the income tax assessment for 1991/92 (for example, the profits of the year ending 31 December 1990) and so on for subsequent years.

The income tax assessment on which Class 4 contributions are calculated is after deducting capital allowances and losses, but before deducting personal tax allowances or retirement annuity or personal pension plan premiums.

Class 4 contributions produce no additional benefits, but were introduced to ensure that self-employed persons as a whole pay a fair share of the cost of pensions and other social security benefits without the self-employed who make only small profits having to pay excessively high flat rate contributions.

For 1985/86 and subsequent years, one half of the Class 4 contributions (as finally settled) is deductible in computing total income. It should be noted that this deduction is given in arriving at total income for income tax purposes and not in arriving at the profits assessable under Schedule D. Although the legislation states that a claim is necessary, in practice the deduction will be given automatically. This deduction is broadly equivalent to that available to employers for tax purposes in respect of their secondary contributions, and was introduced to rectify the previous anomaly in that employers, but not the self-employed, were eligible for tax relief for the contributions they bore. Where deferment of Class 2 and 4 contributions has been obtained, it should be ensured that the eventually assessed Class 4 contributions, if any, are allowed for income tax purposes.

Payment of contributions

In general, contributions are calculated and collected by the Inland Revenue together with the income tax under Schedule D Case I or II, and accordingly the contributions are due and payable at the same time as the income tax liability on the relevant profits.

Persons exempt from Class 4 contributions

The following persons are exempt from Class 4 contributions:
(1) Men over 65 and women over 60 at the commencement of the year of assessment (i.e. on 6 April).
(2) An individual not resident in the United Kingdom for income tax purposes in the year of assessment.
(3) Persons whose earnings are not 'immediately derived' from carrying on a trade, profession or vocation (for example, sleeping partners and, possibly, limited partners).
(4) A child under 16 on 6 April of the year of assessment.
(5) Persons not ordinarily self-employed (see above as for Class 2 contributions).

Calculation of liability for married persons and partnerships

Under independent taxation of husband and wife from 1990/91 onwards, each spouse is responsible for his or her Class 4 liability.

In partnerships, each partner's liability is calculated separately, and the Inland Revenue will normally collect each partner's Class 4 liability in the partnership name as is the case with the income tax liability of the partnership under

Schedule D. If a partner also carries on another trade or profession, the profits of all such businesses are aggregated for the purposes of calculating his Class 4 liability; in these circumstances the Class 4 liability in respect of his share of partnership profits may be assessed separately and not in the partnership name.

When an assessment has become final and conclusive for the purposes of income tax, it is also final and conclusive for the purposes of calculating Class 4 liability.

SOURCES OF FURTHER INFORMATION

Further information can be obtained from the many booklets published by the Department of Social Security, and from Accountants Digests Nos 247 and 267 published by The Institute of Chartered Accountants in England and Wales. Individuals resident abroad should address their enquiries to the DSS Overseas Branch, Newcastle upon Tyne NE98 1YX.

Social Security Benefits

K.D. BARTLETT, FCA
Chartered Accountant

Social security benefits are quite difficult to understand. There are many leaflets produced by the Department of Social Security and this article is written to try to simplify some of the more usual benefits that are available under the Social Security Acts. It deliberately does not cover every aspect of the legislation but the references given should enable the relevant information to be easily traced. These references are to the leaflets issued by the Department of Social Security.

It is usual for only one periodical benefit to be payable at any one time. If the contribution conditions are satisfied for more than one benefit it is the larger benefit that is payable. Benefit rates shown below are those payable from week commencing 8 April 1991.

Employed persons (Category A contributors) are covered for all benefits. Certain married women and widows (Category B contributors) who elected to pay at the reduced rate receive only attendance allowance, guardian's allowance and industrial injuries benefits. Other benefits may be available dependent on their husbands' contributions.

Self-employed persons (Class 2 and Class 4 contributors) are covered for all benefits except earnings-related supplements, unemployment benefit, widow's and invalidity pensions and widowed mother's allowance.

The major changes, which take place from the week beginning 8 April 1991, are:

- Child benefit increases by £1.00 a week for all families by an additional payment for the oldest or only child.
- Statutory Maternity Pay rises from £39.25 to £44.50 a week and Maternity Allowance from £35.70 to £40.60 a week.
- Retirement Benefit will rise by £5.10 a week for a single person and £8.15 for a couple.
- There will be a £45 a week increase in the Income Support limits for the main category of nursing homes catering for the elderly (£55 a week for nursing homes in Greater London).
- Unemployment Benefit will rise from £37.35 to £41.40 for a single person and from £60.40 to £66.95 for a couple; and sickness benefit from £35.70 to £39.60 for a single person and from £57.80 to £64.10 for a couple.
- Widows' pensions will be uprated and the new payment for pre-1973 war widows will go up from £40 to £44.36 per week.
- Income support increases for a single person under 25 from £28.80 to £31.15 and for a family of two by £7.75 a week to £103.30 plus mortgage interest or rent.

FAMILY BENEFITS

Child Benefits (CH 1)

Child Benefit is payable for all children who are either under 16 or under 19 and receiving full-time education at a recognised educational establishment. The rate is £8.25 for the first or eldest child and £7.25 a week for each subsequent child. It is payable to the person who is responsible for the child but excludes foster parents or people exempt from United Kingdom tax. A higher benefit (£5.60 a week more) is payable for the first or only child in a one parent family.

Maternity Benefits

Help with maternity expenses is given to selected people from the Social Fund. To be eligible the claimant must be receiving Income Support or Family Credit. £100 is paid for each new or adopted baby reduced by the amount of any savings over £500 held by the claimant or his or her family. A payment can be obtained from the Social Fund for an adopted baby provided the child is not more than 12 months old when application is made. The claimant has three months to make the claim from when adoption has taken place.

Maternity Pay (NI 17A)

Statutory Maternity Pay (SMP) was introduced for female employees who leave employment because of pregnancy.

SMP is applicable to those who have worked for 26 weeks by the 15th week before the expected date of confinement. This 15th week is known as the qualifying week (QW). The other qualifying conditions are that the woman must:
(1) be pregnant at the 11th week before the expected week of confinement, or already have been confined;
(2) have stopped working for her employer wholly or partly because of pregnancy or confinement;
(3) have average earnings of not less than the lower earnings limit for the payment of National Insurance Contributions which is in force during her QW;
(4) provide her employer with evidence of her expected week of confinement;
(5) provide her employer with notice of her maternity absence.

Rates of SMP

There is a higher and a lower rate. The higher rate of SMP is 90% of an employee's weekly earnings and is paid for the first 6 weeks for which there is entitlement to SMP. To be eligible for the higher rate, a woman must meet all the qualifying conditions and have been employed by the employer for a continuous period of at least two years if she worked for more than 16 hours a week. Her service must continue into the QW.

The lower rate of SMP is a set rate reviewed each year. The rate for the tax year beginning 6 April 1991 is £44.50 per week. It is paid for 18 weeks to those not entitled to the higher amount and for up to 12 weeks to those who receive the higher rate for the first six weeks.

SMP is taxable and also subject to National Insurance contributions. The gross amount of SMP and the employer's portion of National Insurance payable on the SMP can be recovered from the State by deducting the amounts from the amount normally due for PAYE and National Insurance deductions payable to the Collector of Taxes.

Guardian's Allowance (NI 14)

This is paid at the rate of £9.70 a week for the first or eldest child and £10.70 for each subsequent child to people who have taken orphans into their own family. Usually both of the child's parents must be dead and at least one of them must have satisfied a residence condition.

The allowance can only be paid to the person who is entitled to child benefit for the child (or to that person's spouse). It is not necessary to be the legal guardian. The claim should be made within three months of the date of entitlement.

BENEFITS FOR HANDICAPPED OR DISABLED PEOPLE

Mobility Allowance (NI 211)

This is a non-contributory benefit payable to persons aged between 5 and 65 who are unable to walk because of physical disablement. The allowance is £29.10 per week. It is not taxable.

Attendance Allowance (NI 205)

This is payable to help those who are so severely disabled physically or mentally that they require frequent attention during the day or night or frequent attention for both day and night. A higher rate (£41.65 a week) is payable if attention is required day and night and a lower rate of £27.80 is payable if attention is required only in the day or in the night. The attendance allowance board decide whether, and for how long, a person is eligible for this allowance. Attendance allowance is not taxable.

BENEFITS FOR THE ILL OR UNEMPLOYED

Statutory Sick Pay (NI 27, NI 16 and NI 244)

In the majority of cases the employer now has the responsibility of paying Sick Pay to its employees. The payment is dependent on satisfying various conditions in respect of periods of incapacity, periods of entitlement, qualifying days and rules on notification of absence. The rules are quite complicated and reference should be made to the relevant booklets for further clarification but the key points are:
(1) Payment is made by the employer.
(2) There is a possibility of two rates of payment dependent on the employee's gross average earnings.
(3) The employee must not be capable of work and must do no work on the day concerned.
(4) SSP is not usually payable for the first three working days.
(5) The maximum entitlement is 28 weeks in any period of incapacity.
(6) Notification must be made by the employer but this procedure must be within statutory guidelines.
(7) Payment can be withheld if notification of sickness is not given in due time.
   The employer can only recover 80% of all SSP payments made in respect of 1991/92, as compensation for their share of National Insurance Contributions paid on SSP.

Invalidity Benefit (NI 16A)

An invalidity pension is substituted for sickness benefit or SSP after this has been paid for 168 days of incapacity. To qualify one must be unable to work and have been entitled to sickness benefit for 168 days in a period of interruption of employment. This pension is currently £52.00 a week.

   An invalidity allowance is payable with invalidity pension to those who are more than five years away from retirement age. The rates are as follows:

Standard rate of invalidity pension:

	£
Single person	52.00
Spouse or adult dependant	31.25

Invalidity allowance:	
(i) Higher rate	11.10
(ii) Middle rate	6.90
(iii) Lower rate	3.45

For each dependent child £9.70 is payable for the first or eldest child and £10.70 for each subsequent child.

Severe Disablement Allowance (NI 252)

This is a benefit for people under pensionable age who cannot work because of physical or mental ill health and do not have sufficient NI contributions to qualify for sickness or invalidity benefit. The basic allowance is £31.25 a week. There are increases of £18.70 a week for adult dependants and £9.70 for the first or eldest child and £10.70 for each subsequent child.

Invalid Care Allowance (NI 212)

This is a taxable benefit paid to people of working age who cannot take a job because they have to stay at home to look after a severely disabled person. The basic allowance is £31.25 per week. An extra £18.70 is paid for each adult dependant and £9.70 is payable for the first or eldest child and £10.70 for each subsequent child.

Unemployment Benefit (NI 12)

Unemployment benefit is payable for a maximum period of one year in any period of interruption of employment. Once this year's unemployment pay is reached a claimant cannot qualify again until he has worked as an employee for at least 13 weeks in the period of 26 weeks immediately before the claim, each week being work of at least 16 hours.

To be eligible the claimant must be unemployed but available for work but can be disqualified from receiving benefit for a period of up to six weeks if he lost his employment without just cause or failed to accept suitable employment offered.

Unemployment benefit is not payable for the first three days of a period of interruption of employment, in the same way as for sickness benefit.

Persons over 18 should register for work at their local Employment Office or Job Centre and should go to their local unemployment benefit office to claim benefit. Either a P45 or a note of their national insurance number should be produced. Persons under 18 should register for work at their local Youth Employment Office. Unemployment benefit is reduced, pound for pound, for those claimants over 55 years of age, whose pensions exceed £35.00 per week.

The standard rate of unemployment benefit is £41.40 for a single person and £25.55 for a wife or other adult dependant.

PENSIONS AND WIDOW'S BENEFITS (NP 23, NP 35, NP 31)

The State Pension is divided into two parts – the basic pension, presently £52.00 per week for a single person or £83.25 per week for a married couple, and the State Earnings Related Pension Scheme, which will after it matures on the present basis pay a pension of 25% of revalued earnings between the lower and upper earnings limits.

The cost of the State Earnings Related Pension Scheme (SERPS) has been a major political consideration for some time. In order to reduce the long-term cost of the Scheme, benefits will be reduced for those retiring or widowed after the year 2000. The benefits will be reduced as follows:
(1) The pension will be based on lifetime average earnings rather than the best 20 years as at present.
(2) The pension will be calculated on the basis of 20% of earnings between the lower and upper earnings limit rather than 25%. This will be phased in over ten years from the tax year 2000/2001.

(3) Presently all of a member's State Earnings Related Benefit is inherited by a surviving spouse. For deaths occurring after April 2000 this will be reduced to 50%.

Women paying standard rate contributions into the Scheme are eligible for the same amount of pension as men but five years earlier, from age 60. If a woman stays at home to bring up her children or to look after a person receiving attendance allowance she can have her basic pension rights protected without paying contributions.

The widow's pension and widowed mother's allowance also consists of a basic pension and an additional earnings related pension. The full amount of the additional pension applies only if the husband has contributed to the new Scheme for at least 20 years.

Widow's Benefits

From 11 April 1988 there are three main widow's benefits:
(1) Widow's payment, which has replaced the widow's allowance which has been abolished;
(2) Widowed mother's allowance;
(3) Widow's pension.

Widow's payment
This is a new allowance, currently a lump sum payment of £1000 payable to widows who were bereaved on or after 11 April 1988. It is payable immediately on the death of the husband. Entitlement to this benefit is based on the late husband's contribution record but no payment will be made if the widow is living with another man as husband and wife at the date of death. The late husband must have actually paid contributions on earnings of at least 25 times the weekly or lower earnings limit for a given tax year in any tax year ending before his death (or ending before he reached pensionable age if he was over 65 when he died). The equivalent number of Class 2 or voluntary Class 3 contributions will be sufficient.

When claiming, the widow should complete the form on the back of the death certificate and send it to the local social security office. On receipt of this information the DSS will send the claimant a more detailed form (BD8) which, once completed, has to go back to the social security office. It is important to claim the benefit within twelve months of the husband's death.

Widowed mother's allowance (NP 45)
If a widow is left with children to look after she is entitled to a widowed mother's allowance provided that her late husband had paid sufficient national insurance contributions. These contributions are:
(a) 25 Class 1, 2 or 3 contributions before age 65 and before 6 April 1975; or
(b) contributions in any one tax year after 6 April 1975 on earnings of at least 25 times the weekly lower earnings limit for that year.

It is important that the widow is looking after either her own child or her husband's child and that the child is under 16 or, if between the age of 16 and 19, is continuing in full-time education.

The allowance stops immediately if the widow remarries and will be suspended if she lives with a man as his wife. From 8 April 1991 the amounts payable are as follows:

	£
Basic allowance	52.00
Increase for first or oldest child	9.70
Increase for each subsequent child	10.70

Where a husband's contributions only satisfied the first test above, the basic allowance may be payable at a reduced rate. This reduction does not alter the rate of an increase for a child.

Widow's pension (NP 45)

A widow who is over the age of 45 when her husband dies may be eligible for a widow's pension unless she is eligible for the widowed mother's allowance. In this situation the widow's pension becomes payable when the widowed mother's allowance ends, provided she is still under the age of 65. However, where a woman had been receiving widowed mother's allowance, she becomes entitled to a widow's pension if she is between the ages of 45 and 65 when the allowance ends, no matter what her age may have been when her husband died. Before 11 April 1988 a widow aged 40 or over could qualify for a widow's pension.

Qualification conditions
(a) The contributions conditions must be satisfied and these conditions are the same as those for the widowed mother's allowance above.
(b) The widow must not be receiving the widowed mother's allowance.
(c) When her husband died she was aged between 45 and 65 or she was entitled to widowed mother's allowance and is aged between 45 and 65 when her widowed mother's allowance finished.

Cessation of Widow's Pension
(a) Entitlement finishes if the widowed mother's allowance stops because she has remarried.
(b) Widow's pension must not be claimed when the payment of the widowed mother's allowance has been suspended because the widow is in pension or is living with a man as his wife.

From 11 April 1988 both the basic and additional pension are paid at a reduced rate if the widow was aged under 55:

(a) when her husband died, if she did not subsequently become entitled to widowed mother's allowance; or
(b) when her widowed mother's allowance ceased to be paid. The relevant rates from 8 April 1991 are as follows (the ages given in parentheses apply to women for whom widow's pension was payable before 11 April 1988):

Age related	£
Age 54 (49)	48.36
53 (48)	44.72
52 (47)	41.08
51 (46)	37.44
50 (45)	33.80
49 (44)	30.16
48 (43)	26.52
47 (42)	22.88
46 (41)	19.24
45 (40)	15.60

Funeral Expenses
The death grant was abolished from 6 April 1987. It has been replaced by a payment from the Social Fund where the claimant is in receipt of Supplementary Benefit, Family Income Supplement or Housing Benefit. The full cost of a reasonable funeral is paid, reduced by any savings over £500 held by the claimant or his family (£1000 for couples over 60).

FAMILY CREDIT

Family credit replaced family income supplement (FIS) with effect from 11 April 1988. Family credit is a tax-free benefit payable to families in Great Britain where:

(1) the claimant or partner is engaged in remunerative work for 24 hours or more per week; and

(2) there is at least one child under 16 in the family (or under 19 if in full-time education up to and including A level or OND standard) for whom the claimant and/or partner is responsible.

Entitlement to family credit is determined by comparing the family's normal income with a prescribed amount, known as the 'applicable amount'. The current applicable amount is £57.60. Eligible families fall into two income groups: (i) those whose total income does not exceed the applicable amount. Such families will be entitled to the appropriate maximum amount of family credit payable; and

(ii) those whose total income does exceed the applicable amount but by an amount which still allows some entitlement. To determine eligibility, a prescribed percentage (currently 70%) of the excess income (over and above the applicable amount) is deducted from the appropriate maximum family credit. If there is an amount left (i.e. the figure is a plus sum of at least 50p) the family will be able to receive family credit equal to this amount, rounded to the nearest penny.

Maximum family credit benefit rates (from 8 April 1991)

Adult	£38.30
Child	
aged less than 11 years	£ 9.70
aged 11 to 15 years	£16.10
Young Person	
aged 16 to 17 years	£20.05
aged 18 years	£27.95

An award is normally made for a period of 26 weeks. Changes of circumstances during this period will not usually affect the award.

Capital and income

Families where the claimant and partner together hold capital in excess of £8000 will not be entitled to family credit. The resources of a family taken into account as income for family credit are the aggregate of their normal net earnings and other income plus any tariff income. Certain payments are disregarded in the calculation of income. For those with capital of between £3000 and £8000, the rate of benefit will be affected. For every £250 (or part of £250) held in excess of £3000, a 'tariff' income of £1.00 will be added to the family's other income.

INCOME SUPPORT (SBI, SB20)

Income support has replaced supplementary benefit. It is usually only payable to eligible persons who are unemployed or people who work less than 24 hours a week. If a person or partner works for 24 hours or more on average per week in 'remunerative' work, then no income support is payable.

Income support gives financial assistance towards regular weekly needs only. Claimants with exceptional needs will now have to apply for payments (in the form of a loan or grant) from the social fund.

The person's income must be insufficient to bring him up to the designated minimum level of income, known as the 'applicable amount'. The applicable amount is made up of a 'basic' personal allowance plus 'additional' premiums for those with additional needs, e.g. pensioners. People who are entitled to income support and who have no income at all will be entitled to the appropriate applicable amount in full. Those who have an income will receive income support equal to the difference between their income and the appropriate applicable amount.

As with supplementary benefit, there is a limit to the amount of capital a person can hold before income support is affected. Those who have capital above £8000 are disqualified from receiving income support altogether. Capital up to £3000 is disregarded but savings between £3000 and £8000 affect Income Support in the same way as for Family Credit.

As in the case of supplementary benefit, eligibility for income support is, in most instances, dependent on the claimant being 'available for work'. Where a person is disqualified from receiving unemployment benefit (or would be if it were otherwise payable), for such reasons as being dismissed from his or her former job because of misconduct, entitlement to income support will also be affected.

GRANTS FROM LOCAL AUTHORITIES

Community Charge Benefit

Prior to 1 April 1990 those on Income Support will have received claims from the DSS. Those who wish to make a claim since 1 April 1990 must apply direct to their Local Authority. If they are claiming Income Support, then they must make a claim to the DSS who have to send on the application forms to the Local Authority.

The amount of benefit is calculated by comparing a claimant's relevant income with their applicable amount. The applicable amount is the total of specific scale allowances to which their circumstances or needs entitle them.

The above does not set out to cover every aspect of the Social Security Acts legislation.

Further information can be obtained from the local office of the Department of Social Security or from Accountants Digest No. 263 published by the Institute of Chartered Accountants in England and Wales. Readers resident abroad who have queries should write to the Department's Overseas Branch, Newcastle upon Tyne NE98 1YX.

Law and regulations

British Copyright Law

AMANDA L. MICHAELS, MA
Barrister

INTRODUCTION

Copyright is a creature of statute. There have been a series of Copyright Acts over the years, gradually extending the scope of this area of the law so as to offer protection to the widening range of media used by writers, artists and communicators of all types.

On 1 August 1989, the Copyright Act 1956, previously the major Act in this field, was replaced by the Copyright, Designs and Patents Act 1988 ('the Act'). The Act sets out to restate the law of copyright. Much of the law in it is a true restatement of the pre-existing law, especially in so far as it relates to the essentials of what may be a copyright work and how they may be protected. To this end, section 172 of the Act in particular provides that mere changes of expression from the old law do not denote a substantive change in the law, whilst prior decisions may be referred to as an aid to the construction of the new Act.

However, there is a good deal in the new Act which is innovatory (see, for instance, the comments below on the new design right, and the repercussions upon infringement actions of section 51), as well as a number of provisions where one might well ask whether all that is intended is a change of expression from the old law, or whether a change of words implies a change of substance.

The general reader should therefore be aware that the old law, and old texts on the subject, may not apply to new copyright works. There are also complicated transitional provisions (in Schedule 1 to the Act) relating to pre-existing works and infringements, and reference may need to be made to these and to the old law for some years to come, as well as to the numerous Orders in Council made under the Act. Users of this handbook may particularly need to note that forms of publishing and licensing agreements suitable for use under the old law may need revision in the light of the new Act.

In an article of this length, it is not possible to deal fully with all the changes in the law effected by the new Act, nor indeed with all the complexities of this technical area of the law. The purpose of the article is rather to set out the basic principles of copyright protection, and to identify topics which may be of particular interest to readers of this general handbook.

WORKS CAPABLE OF COPYRIGHT PROTECTION

Copyright protection has always protected the *form* in which the artist/author has set out his inspiration, not the underlying idea. So, plots, artistic ideas, systems and themes cannot be protected by copyright. Whilst an idea remains no more than that, it can be protected only by the law relating to confidential information (contrast the cases of *Green* v. *Broadcasting Corp. of New Zealand* [1989] RPC 700: no copyright in 'format' of *Opportunity Knocks* and *Fraser* v. *Thames TV Ltd* [1984] QB 44: plot of a projected TV series protected by law of confidence). The law of copyright prevents the copying of the material form in which the idea has been presented, or of a substantial part of it, measured in terms of quality, not quantity.

The Act therefore starts out, in section 1, by setting out a number of different categories of works which can be the subject of copyright protection. These are:

(a) original literary, dramatic, musical or artistic works,
(b) sound recordings, films, broadcasts, or cable programmes, and
(c) typographical arrangements of published editions.

These works are further defined in sections 3 to 8. The definitions are not identical to those in the 1956 Act. A literary work, for instance, is defined as: 'any work, other than a dramatic or musical work, which is written, spoken or sung, and accordingly includes: (a) a table or compilation, and (b) a computer program.' A musical work means: 'a work consisting of music, exclusive of any words or action intended to be sung, spoken or performed with the music.' An artistic work means: '(a) a graphic work, photograph, sculpture or collage, irrespective of artistic quality, (b) a work of architecture being a building or model for a building, or (c) a work of artistic craftsmanship.'

The definitions of literary and musical works do not, however, contradict the basic rule that copyright protects the form and not the idea, such that works can be protected *before* being reduced into tangible form. Section 3 (2) specifically provides that no copyright shall subsist in a literary, musical or artistic work until it has been recorded in writing or otherwise.

On the other hand, all that is required to achieve copyright protection is to record the original work in any appropriate medium. Once that has been done copyright will subsist in the work (assuming that the qualifying features set out below are present) without any formality of registration or otherwise. As long as the work is produced in some tangible form there is, for instance, no need for it to be published in any way for the protection to attach to it. (Please note, however, that although this lack of formality applies here and in most European countries, the law of the USA does differ – see article: **US Copyright**). The common idea that one must register a work at Stationers Hall, or send it to oneself or to, say, a bank, in a sealed envelope so as to obtain copyright protection is incorrect. All that this precaution may do is provide some proof in an infringement action (whether as plaintiff or defendant) of the date of creation of one's work.

ORIGINALITY

Section 1 provides that, in order to gain copyright protection, literary, dramatic, artistic and musical works must be original. Similarly, there are provisions which exclude from copyright protection sound recordings or films which are mere copies of pre-existing sound recordings and films, broadcasts which infringe rights in another broadcast or cable programmes which consist of immediate retransmissions of broadcasts.

The test of originality may not be quite that expected by the layman. Over a number of years, the courts have held that a work need not be original in the sense of showing innovative or cultural merit, but that it needs only to have been the product of skill and labour on the part of the author. Nonetheless, merely making a 'slavish copy' of a drawing does not suffice: see *Interlego AG v. Tyco Industries* [1988] 1 WLR 678. This can be seen from various sections in the Act, for instance in the definition of certain artistic works, and in the fact that it offers copyright protection to works such as compilations (like football pools coupons or directories) and tables (including mathematical tables).

On the other hand, 'works' comprising the titles of books or periodicals, or advertising slogans, which may have required a good deal of original thought, generally are not accorded copyright protection, because they are too short to be deemed literary works.

See, too, the limited protection given to drawings of a functional or engineering type in the sections on infringement and design right below.

QUALIFICATION

The Act is limited in its effects to the UK (and to colonies to which it may be extended by Order in Council). It is aimed primarily at protecting the works of British citizens, or works which were first published here. However, in line with the requirements of various international conventions to which the UK is a party, copyright protection in the UK is also accorded to the works of nationals of many foreign states which are also party to these conventions, as well as to works first published in those states.

The importance of these rules (which largely repeat similar provisions of the 1956 Act) mainly arises when one is trying to find out whether a pre-existing foreign work is protected by copyright here, for instance, if one wishes to make a film based upon a foreign novel. Within the confines of this article, all that can be said is that there have been numerous different Orders in Council regulating the position for most of the major countries of the world, including the other member states of the EEC and the USA, and further Orders continue to be made, but that in every case it will be wise to check the position.

OWNERSHIP

The general rule is that a work will initially be owned by its author, the author being the creator of the work, or in the case of a film or sound recording, the person who makes the arrangements necessary for it to be made.

One essential exception to the general rule is that the copyright in a work of an employee produced in the course of his employment will belong to his employer, subject to any agreement to the contrary.

There can be joint authorship of a work where the work is produced by several people in such collaboration that the contribution of one is not distinct from the contribution of the other. Where two people collaborate to write a song, one producing the lyrics and the other the music, there will be two separate copyright works, the copyright in which will be owned by each of the authors separately. But where two people write a play, each rewriting what the other produces, there will be a joint work. The importance of knowing whether the work is joint or not arises firstly in working out the duration of the copyright (see below) and secondly from the fact that joint works can only be exploited with the agreement of all the joint authors so that all of them have to join in any licence, although each of them can sue for infringement.

DURATION OF COPYRIGHT

Copyright in a literary, dramatic, artistic or musical work expires fifty years after the end of the calendar year in which the author dies. If there were joint authors, the fifty-year period will run from the end of the year in which the last of them dies. However, there is an important exception to this general rule in the case of artistic works which have been industrially exploited, limiting the length of copyright protection to twenty-five years from the date of first marketing of articles made according to the design (see section 52).

If the author is unknown, the copyright will expire fifty years after the work is first made available to the public, by being performed, broadcast, exhibited, etc, depending upon the nature of the work (see section 12(2) of the Act).

If the work is 'computer-generated', copyright will expire fifty years from the date when the work was made. Copyright in a typeface runs for only twenty-five years from when it was first published.

Sound recordings will lose their copyright fifty years from the end of the year in which they are made, unless they have been released during that period, when they will enjoy copyright protection for fifty years after release. Similarly, copyright in broadcasts will expire fifty years after the end of the year in which they are made and that in cable programmes, fifty years after they are included in a cable programme.

These provisions are not identical with those under earlier Acts. Where one is dealing with a work made before the Act came into force, one needs to look at the law in force when it was made, as well as at the transitional provisions of the 1956 Act (for pre-1957 works) and/or of the Act (for pre-1989 works).

DEALING WITH COPYRIGHT WORKS: ASSIGNMENT AND LICENSING

As will be seen below, ownership of the copyright in a work confers upon the owner the exclusive right to deal with the work in a number of ways, and essentially stops all unauthorised exploitation of the work. Copyright works can be exploited by their owners in two ways: the whole right in the work may be sold, with the owner retaining no interest in it (except, possibly, for payment by way of royalties); this is what is known as assignment. Alternatively, the owner may grant a licence to another to exploit the right, whilst retaining overall ownership. Agreements dealing with copyright should make it clear whether an assignment or a licence is being granted, and should clearly define the scope of any assignment or licence. The question of the new moral rights (see below) will also have to be considered by parties negotiating an assignment or licence.

An assignment must be in writing, signed by or on behalf of the assignor, but no other formality is required. One can make an assignment of future copyright (under section 91). Where the author of a projected work agrees in writing that he will assign the rights in a future work to another, the copyright vests in the assignee immediately upon the creation of the work, without further formalities. This facility may be used where works are commissioned from the author, as the specific provisions as to ownership of commissioned works which existed in the 1956 Act are not reproduced as such in the new Act, save in respect of works protected by the new design right (see below).

These rules do not, apparently, affect the pre-existing common law as to beneficial interests in copyright. Essentially, where someone had been commissioned to create a work for another, in circumstances in which copyright did not vest automatically in the latter, and the court found that it was the parties' mutual intention that the copyright should belong to the 'commissioner', it would hold that the 'commissioner' was the equitable or beneficial owner of the copyright, and the author would be obliged to assign the copyright to him.

Licences do not need to take any form in particular, and may indeed be granted orally. However, an exclusive licence (i.e. one which excludes even the copyright owner himself from exploiting the work in the manner foreseen by the licence) must be in writing, if the licensee is to enjoy rights in respect of infringements concurrent with those of the copyright owner.

Both assignments and licences can, and most frequently do, split up the various rights contained within the copyright. So, for instance, a licence might be granted to one person to publish a novel in hardback and to another to publish in softback, a third person might be granted the film, television and video rights, and yet a fourth the right to translate the novel into other languages.

In practice, assignments may, and licences usually do, confer rights according to territory, dividing the USA from the EEC or different EEC countries one from the other. Two comments must be made about this. Firstly, it must be appreciated that any such agreement would be dealing with a bundle of different national copyrights, as each country's law generally extends only to its own borders; it must be noted that each country's law on copyright protection, on licensing and on infringement may differ. Secondly, when purporting to divide rights between different territories of the EEC there is a danger that one will infringe the competition rules of the EEC (in the main Articles 30-36 and 85-86 of the Treaty of Rome), and professional advice should be taken to ensure that one is not in breach of these rules, which would render the parties liable to large fines, as well as making the agreement void in whole or in part.

Licences can also, of course, be of varying lengths. There is no need for a licence to be granted for the whole term of copyright; indeed this would be unusual, if not foolish. Well-drafted licences will provide for termination on breach, including the failure of the licensee to exploit the work properly, and on the bankruptcy or winding up of the licensee.

Copyright may be assigned by will, and where a bequest is given of an original document, etc., embodying an unpublished copyright work, the bequest will carry the copyright.

INFRINGEMENT

Copyright is infringed by doing any of a number of specified acts in relation to the copyright work, without the authority of the owner. In all forms of infringement, it suffices if a substantial part of the original is used, and the question is one to be judged according to quality not quantity (see, e.g., *Ravenscroft* v. *Herbert* [1980] RPC 193).

The form of infringement common to all forms of copyright works is that of copying. This means reproducing the work in any material form.

In the case of a two-dimensional artistic work, reproduction can mean making a copy in three dimensions, and vice versa, although there is an important limitation on this general rule in section 51 of the Act, which provides that in the case of a 'design document or model' (defined as a record of a design of any aspect of the shape or configuration, internal or external, of the whole or part of an article, other than surface decoration) for something which is not itself an artistic work, it is no infringement to make an article to that design. This would appear to mean that whilst it would be an infringement to make an article from a design drawing for, say, a sculpture, it will not be an infringement of copyright to make a handbag from a copy of the design drawing therefor, or from a handbag which one has purchased. In order to protect such designs one will have to rely upon the new design right or upon a registered design (for both see below). However, under the transitional provisions, the right to rely upon copyright protection for any such designs made before the commencement of the new Act will continue until 1st August 1999 (see Schedule 1, para. 19).

Copying of a film, broadcast or cable programme can include making a copy of the whole or a substantial part of any one image forming part thereof (see section 17(4)). Presumably this means that copying one frame of the film would be an infringement, as it was under the previous law (see *Spelling Goldberg Productions* v. *BPC* [1981] RPC 283).

Copying is generally proved by showing substantial similarities between the original and the alleged copy, plus an opportunity to copy. Surprisingly often, minor errors in the original are reproduced by an infringer.

Copying need not be direct, so that, for instance, where the copyright is in a fabric design, copying of the material, without ever having seen the original drawing, will still be an infringement.

Issuing copies of a work to the public when it has not previously been put into circulation in the UK is also an infringement of all types of work.

Other acts which may amount to an infringement depend upon the nature of the work. It will be an infringement of the copyright in a literary, dramatic or musical work to perform it in public, whether by live performance or by playing recordings. Similarly, it is an infringement of the copyright in a sound recording, film, broadcast or cable programme to play or show it in public.

One rather different form of infringement is to make an adaptation of a literary, dramatic or musical work. An adaptation includes, in the case of a literary work, a translation, in the case of a non-dramatic work, making a dramatic work of it, and in the case of a dramatic work, making a non-dramatic work of it. An adaptation of a musical work is a transcription or arrangement of it.

There are also a number of 'secondary' infringements. These consist not of making the infringing copies, but of dealing with them in some way. So, it is an infringement to import an infringing copy into the UK, and to possess in the course of business, or to sell, hire, offer for sale or hire, or distribute in the course of trade an infringing copy. However, none of these acts will be an infringement unless the alleged infringer knew or had reason to believe that the articles were infringing copies.

Other secondary infringements consist of permitting a place to be used for a public performance in which copyright is infringed and supplying apparatus to be used for infringing public performance, again, in each case, with safeguards for innocent acts.

EXCEPTIONS TO INFRINGEMENT

The Act provides a large number of exceptions to the rules on infringement, many of which are innovatory. They are far too numerous to be dealt with here in full, but they include:

- fair dealing with literary, dramatic, musical or artistic works for the purpose of research or private study;
- fair dealing for the purpose of criticism or review or reporting current events;
- incidental inclusion of a work in an artistic work, sound recording, film, broadcast, or cable programme;
- various educational exceptions (see sections 32-36);
- various exceptions for libraries (see sections 37-44);
- various exceptions for public administration (see sections 45-50);
- dealing with a work where the author cannot be identified and the work seems likely to be out of copyright;
- public recitation, if accompanied by a sufficient acknowledgement;

– recording broadcasts or cable programmes at home for use at a more convenient time.

REMEDIES FOR INFRINGEMENT

The copyright owner has all the remedies offered to other owners of property. Usually the owner will want one or both of two things: firstly, to prevent the repetition or continuation of the infringement, and, secondly, compensation.

In almost all cases an injunction will be sought at trial, stopping the continuation of the infringement. A very useful remedy offered by the courts is the 'interlocutory injunction'. This is a form of interim relief, applied for at short notice, with a view to stopping damaging infringement at an early stage, without having to await the outcome of a full trial. Interlocutory injunctions are not always granted in copyright cases, but it is generally worth considering the matter when first an infringement comes to notice, for delay in bringing the interlocutory application may be fatal to its success. Where an infringement is threatened, the courts will in appropriate cases make a 'quia timet' injunction to prevent the infringement ever taking place.

Otherwise, financial compensation may be sought in one of two forms. Firstly, damages may be granted for infringement. These will usually be calculated upon evidence of the loss caused to the plaintiff, frequently upon the basis of what would have been a proper licence fee had the defendant sought a licence for the acts complained of. Additional damages may be awarded in rare cases for flagrant infringements.

Under the old law, a plaintiff could also claim conversion damages, which were often assessed at a much higher level than infringement damages. However, these cannot be claimed under the Act.

Damages will not be awarded for infringements where the infringer did not know, and had no reason to believe, that copyright subsisted in the work. This exception may of course be hard to rely upon where, although the infringer had no actual knowledge of the copyright, the work was of such a nature that he should have known that copyright would subsist in it.

An alternative to a claim for damages will be a claim for an account of profits; this is an equitable remedy, however, and is therefore discretionary.

A copyright owner may also apply for delivery up of infringing copies of his work (sections 99 and 113-15).

Finally, there are various criminal offences relating to the making, importation, possession, sale, hire, distribution, etc., of infringing copies (see sections 107-10).

DESIGN RIGHT

Many industrial designs which would previously have been protected by copyright will now be excluded from copyright protection, by reason of the provisions of section 51 of the Act, described above. However, they may instead be protected by the new 'design right' created by sections 213-64 of the Act.

The protection of the new right will be given to original designs consisting of the shape or configuration (internal or external) of the whole or part of an article. A design is not to be considered original if it was commonplace in the design field in question at the time of its creation. Nor will designs be protected if they consist of a method or principle of construction, or are dictated by the shape, etc., of an article to which the new article is to be connected or of which it is to form part.

The new right will be granted only to designs made by qualifying persons (in this part of the Act meaning UK and EEC citizens or residents or others to whom the right may be extended) or commissioned by a qualifying person, or first marketed in the UK, another EEC state or any other country to which the provision may be extended by Order in Council.

The design right lasts only fifteen years from the end of the year in which it was first recorded or an article made to the design, or (if shorter) ten years from the end of the year in which articles made according to the design were first sold or hired out.

The designer will be the owner of the right, unless he made it in pursuance of a commission, in which case the commissioner will be the first owner of the right. The same rule applies as in copyright, that an employee's designs made in the course of his employment will belong to the employer.

The right given to the owner of a design right is the exclusive right to reproduce the design for commercial purposes. The rules as to assignments and licensing and as to infringement, both primary and secondary, are substantially similar to those described above in relation to copyright, as are the remedies available.

This new design right will co-exist with the scheme of registered designs of the *Registered Designs Act* 1949 (as amended by the Act), which provides a monopoly right renewable for up to twenty-five years in respect of designs which have been accepted on to a register. Registered designs must contain features which appeal to and are judged by the eye, unlike designs protected by the design right.

MORAL RIGHTS

Another new departure in the Act is the provision of 'moral rights', commonly known as the rights of 'paternity' and 'integrity'.

The right of 'paternity' is for the author of a copyright literary, dramatic, musical or artistic work, and the director of a copyright film, to be identified as the author/director in a number of different situations, largely whenever the work is published, performed or otherwise commercially exploited (section 77).

However, the right does not arise unless it has been 'asserted' by the author or director, by appropriate words in an assignment, or otherwise by an instrument in writing (section 78), or in the case of an artistic work by ensuring that the artist's name appears on the frame, etc. Writers should therefore aim to ensure that all copies of their works carry a clear assertion of their rights under this provision, so that all who read their works are bound thereby (see end).

There are exceptions to the right, in particular, where the first ownership of the copyright vested in the author's or director's employer.

The right of 'integrity' is not to have one's work subjected to 'derogatory treatment'. This is defined as meaning an addition to, deletion from, alteration to or adaptation of a work (save for a translation of a literary or dramatic work or an arrangement of a musical work involving no more than a change of key or register) which amounts to distortion or mutilation of the work or is otherwise prejudicial to the honour or reputation of the author/director.

Again, infringement of the right takes place when the maltreated work is published commercially or performed or exhibited in public. There are various exceptions set out in section 81 of the Act, in particular where the publication is in a newspaper, etc., and the work was made for inclusion therein or made available therefor with the author's consent.

Where the copyright in the work vested first in the author's or director's employer, he has no right to 'integrity' unless he was identified at the time of the relevant act or was previously identified on published copies of the work.

These rights subsist for as long as the copyright in the work subsists.

A third moral right conferred by the Act is not to have a literary, dramatic, musical or artistic work falsely attributed to one as author, or to have a film falsely attributed to one as director, again where the work in question is published, publicly performed, etc.

This right subsists until twenty years after a person's death.

None of these rights can be assigned during the person's lifetime, but all of them either pass on the person's death as directed by his will or fall into his residuary estate.

A fourth but rather different moral right is conferred by section 85. It gives a person who has commissioned the taking of photographs for private purposes a right to prevent copies of the work being issued to the public, etc.

The remedies for breach of these moral rights are those for breach of a statutory duty. Both damages and an injunction can be sought in appropriate cases, although section 103(2) specifically foresees the granting of an injunction qualified by a right to the defendant to do the acts complained of, albeit subject to a suitable disclaimer.

NOTICE

I, AMANDA LOUISE MICHAELS, hereby assert and give notice of my right under section 77 of the Copyright, Designs and Patents Act 1988 to be identified as the author of the foregoing article.

AMANDA MICHAELS

FURTHER READING

The Copyright Acts

Copyright, Designs and Patents Act 1988, HMSO, £16.65 net
Numerous Orders in Council made under the Act
Design Copyright Act 1968, HMSO
Copyright Act 1956, HMSO
 Amendments: 1971; 1982; 1983
Cable and Broadcasting Act 1984, HMSO
Copyright (Computer and Software) Amendment Act 1985, HMSO
Copyright Act 1911, HMSO

Other books

Black, T. *Intellectual Property in Industry*, Butterworths, 1989.
Dworkin, G. and Taylor, R. *Blackstone's Guide to the Copyright, Designs and Patents Act 1988*, Blackstone Press, 1989.
Laddie, Prescott and Vitoria. *The Modern Law of Copyright*, Butterworths, 1980. o.p. 2nd ed. in preparation; expected 1992.
Skone James, E. P., J. F. Mummery and J. Rayner James. *Copinger and Skone James on Copyright*, Sweet and Maxwell, 13th ed. 1991, £150.00.

US Copyright

GAVIN McFARLANE, LLM, PhD
Barrister

THE SYSTEM OF INTERNATIONAL COPYRIGHT

The international copyright conventions

There is no general principle of international copyright which provides a uniform code for the protection of right owners throughout the world. There are however two major international copyright conventions which lay down certain minimum standards for member states, in particular requiring members to accord to right owners of other members the same protection which is granted to their own nationals. One is the higher standard Berne Convention of 1886, the most recent revision of which was signed in Paris in 1971. The other is the Universal Copyright Convention signed in 1952 with lower minimum standards, and sponsored by Unesco. This also was most recently revised in Paris in 1971, jointly with the Berne Convention. To this latter Convention the United States has belonged since 1955. On 16 November 1988, the Government of the United States deposited its instrument of accession to the Paris Revision of the Berne Convention. The Convention entered into force as regards the United States on 1 March 1989.

Summary of the Universal Copyright Convention

(1) The fundamental intent is to accord reciprocally in each member state to nationals of all other member states the same protection as that member grants to its own nationals.
(2) The minimum term of protection is the life of the author and twenty-five years after his death (by contrast with the Berne Convention which demands a term of the life of the author and a post-mortem period of fifty years).
(3) Any national requirement as a condition of copyright of such formalities as deposit, registration, notice, payment, or manufacture or publication within that state shall be satisfied for all works first published outside its territory and of which the author is not one of its nationals if all copies bear the symbol © accompanied by the name of the copyright owner and the year of first publication.
(4) Publication for the purposes of the Universal Copyright Convention means the reproduction in tangible form and the general distribution to the public of copies of a work from which it can be read or otherwise visually perceived.
(5) The effect of American ratification of the Universal Copyright Convention on 16 September 1955 was to alter completely the nature of the protection granted by the United States to copyright works originating abroad. The previous policy of American domestic law had been extremely restrictive for foreign authors, particularly those writing in the English language. But in consequence of ratification American law was amended to exempt from many of these restrictions works published in other member states, or by nationals of other member states. Recent amendments have relaxed the position even further.

Effect on British copyright owners

The copyright statute of the United States having been brought into line with the requirements of the Universal Copyright Convention, compliance with the formalities required by American law is all that is needed to acquire protection for the work of a British author first published outside the United States. Even these formality requirements have been largely removed now that the United States has joined the Berne Convention, although caution is still required.

SUMMARY OF UNITED STATES COPYRIGHT LAW

Introduction of new law

After many years of debate, the new Copyright Statute of the United States was passed on 19 October 1976. The greater part of its relevant provisions came into force on 1 January 1978. It has extended the range of copyright protection, and further eased the requirements whereby British authors can obtain copyright protection in America. New Public Law 100-568 of 31 October 1988 has made further amendments to the Copyright Statute which were necessary to enable ratification of the Berne Convention to take place.

Works protected in American law

Works of authorship include the following categories:

(1) literary works;

Note: Computer programs are classified as literary works for the purposes of United States copyright. In *Whelan Associates Inc.* v. *Jaslow Dental Laboratory Inc.* (1987) F.S.R.1, it was held that the copyright of a computer program could be infringed even in the absence of copying of the literal code if the structure was part of the expression of the idea behind a program rather than the idea itself.

(2) musical works, including any accompanying words;

(3) dramatic works, including any accompanying music;

(4) pantomimes and choreographic works;

(5) pictorial, graphic and sculptural works;

(6) motion pictures and other audiovisual works;

(7) sound recordings, but copyright in sound recordings is not to include a right of public performance.

The rights of a copyright owner

(1) To reproduce the copyrighted work in copies or phonorecords;

(2) to prepare derivative works based upon the copyrighted work;

(3) to distribute copies or phonorecords of the copyrighted work to the public by sale or other transfer of ownership, or by rental, lease or lending;

(4) in the case of literary, musical, dramatic and choreographic works, pantomimes, and motion pictures and other audiovisual works, but NOT sound recordings, to perform the copyrighted work publicly;

(5) in the case of literary, musical, dramatic, and choreographic works, pantomimes, and pictorial, graphic, or sculptural works, including the individual images of a motion picture or other audiovisual work, to display the copyrighted work publicly.

(6) By the Record Rental Amendment Act 1984, s.109 of the Copyright Statute is amended. Now, unless authorised by the owners of copyright in the sound recording and the musical works thereon, the owner of a phonorecord may not, for direct or indirect commercial advantage, rent, lease or lend the phonorecord. A compulsory licence under s.115(c) includes the right of a maker of a phonorecord of non-dramatic musical work to distribute or authorise the distribution of the phonorecord by rental, lease, or lending, and an additional royalty is payable in respect of that.

(7) The Semiconductor Chip Protection Act 1984 adds to the Copyright Statute a new chapter on the protection of semiconductor chip products.

Manufacturing requirements

With effect from 1 July 1982, these ceased to have effect. Prior to 1 July 1982, the importation into or public distribution in the United States of a work consisting preponderantly of non-dramatic literary material that was in the English language and protected under American law was prohibited unless the portions consisting of such material had been manufactured in the United States or Canada. This provision did not apply where, on the date when importation was sought or public distribution in the United States was made, the author of any substantial part of such material was not a national of the United States or, if a national, had been domiciled outside the United States for a continuous period of at least one year immediately preceding that date.

Thus since 1 July 1982, there is no manufacturing requirement in respect of works of British authors. Certain interested groups in the United States still lobby for the restoration of the manufacturing clause in American law. Countries such as Britain will no doubt oppose this vigorously through diplomatic channels. With American ratification of the Berne Convention, the formalities previously required in relation to copyright notice, deposit and registration have been greatly modified.

Formalities: notice, deposit and registration

(1) Notice of copyright

Whenever a work protected by the American Copyright Statute is published in the United States or elsewhere by authority of the copyright owner, a notice of copyright shall be placed on all publicly distributed copies. This shall consist of (i) either the symbol © or the word 'Copyright' or the abbreviation 'Copr.' plus (ii) the year of first publication of the work, plus (iii) the name of the copyright owner.

(2) Deposit

Unless exempted by the Register of Copyrights, the owner of copyright or the exclusive right of publication in a work published with notice of copyright in the United States shall within three months of such publication deposit in the Copyright Office for the use or disposition of the Library of Congress two complete copies of the best edition of the work (or two records, if the work is a sound recording). Penalties are provided for failure to comply with the requirement of deposit.

(3) Registration

While deposit is mandatory, registration for copyright in the United States is optional. However, any owner of copyright in a work first published outside the United States may register a work by making application to the Copyright Office with the appropriate fee, and by depositing one complete copy of the work. This requirement of deposit may be satisfied by using copies deposited for the Library of Congress. But it is vital to note that no action may be brought for infringement of copyright in the United States until registration of the claim to copyright has been made according to the statutory provisions.

(*Note:* These requirements have been made discretionary now that the United States has joined the Berne Convention.)

Duration of copyright

An important change in the new American law is that in general, copyright in a work created on or after 1 January 1978 endures for a term of the life of the author, and a period of fifty years after the author's death. This brings the United States into line with most other advanced countries, and with the further amendments made by Public Law 100-568 of 31 October 1988 has enabled her government to ratify the higher standard Berne Convention. Copyright in a work created before 1 January 1978, but not published or copyrighted before then, subsists from 1 January 1978, and lasts for the life of the author and a post-mortem period of fifty years.

Any copyright, the first term of which under the previous law was still subsisting on 1 January 1978, shall endure for twenty-eight years from the date when it was originally secured, and the copyright proprietor or his representative may apply for a further term of forty-seven years within one year prior to the expiry of the original term. In default of such application for renewal and extension, the copyright shall end at the expiration of twenty-eight years from the date copyright was originally secured.

The duration of any copyright, the renewal term of which was subsisting at any time between 31 December 1976 and 31 December 1977, or for which renewal registration was made between those dates, is extended to endure for a term of seventy-five years from the date copyright was originally secured.

These alterations are of great importance for owners of existing American copyrights.

All terms of copyright provided for by the sections referred to above run to the end of the calendar year in which they would otherwise expire.

Public performance

Under the previous American law the provisions relating to performance in public were less generous to right owners than those existing in the copyright law of the United Kingdom. In particular, performance of a musical work was formerly only an infringement if it was 'for profit'. Moreover, the considerable American coin-operated record-playing machine industry (juke boxes) had obtained an exemption from being regarded as instruments of profit, and accordingly their owners did not have to pay royalties for the use of copyright musical works.

Now by the new law one of the exclusive rights of the copyright owner is, in the case of literary, musical, dramatic and choreographic works, pantomimes, and motion pictures and other audiovisual works, to perform the work publicly, without any requirement of such performance being 'for profit'. By Section 114 however, the exclusive rights of the owner of copyright in a sound recording are specifically stated not to include any right of public performance.

The position of coin-operated record players (juke boxes) is governed by the new Section 116A, inserted by Public Law 100-568 of 31 October 1988. It covers the position of negotiated licences. Limitations are placed on the exclusive right if licences are not negotiated.

These extensions of the scope of the right of public performance should augment the royalty income of authors, composers and publishers of musical works widely performed in the United States. All such right owners should ensure that their American interests are properly taken care of.

Mechanical right – alteration of the rate of royalty

Where sound recordings of a non-dramatic musical work have been distributed to the public in the United States with the authority of the copyright owner, any other person may, by following the provisions of the law, obtain a compulsory licence to make and distribute sound recordings of the work. This right is known in the United Kingdom as 'the mechanical right'. Notice must be served on the copyright owner, who is entitled to a royalty in respect of each of his works recorded of either two and three fourths cents or one half of one cent per minute of playing time or fraction thereof, whichever amount is the larger. Failure to serve or file the required notice forecloses the possibility of a compulsory licence and, in the absence of a negotiated licence, renders the making and distribution of such records actionable as acts of infringement.

Transfer of copyright

Under the previous American law copyright was regarded as indivisible, which meant that on the transfer of copyright, where it was intended that only film rights or some other such limited right be transferred, the entire copyright nevertheless had to be passed. This led to a cumbersome procedure whereby the author would assign the whole copyright to his publisher, who would return to the author by means of an exclusive licence those rights which it was not meant to transfer.

Now it is provided by Section 201(d) of the Copyright Statute that (1) the ownership of a copyright may be transferred in whole or in part by any means of conveyance or by operation of law, and may be bequeathed by will or pass as personal property by the applicable laws of intestate succession and (2) any of the exclusive rights comprised in a copyright (including any subdivision of any of the rights set out in *The rights of a copyright owner* above) may be transferred as provided in (1) above and owned separately. The owner of any particular exclusive right is entitled, to the extent of that right, to all the protection and remedies accorded to the copyright owner by that Statute. This removes the difficulties which existed under the previous law, and brings the position much closer to that existing in the copyright law of the United Kingdom.

Copyright Royalty Tribunal

A feature of the new United States law is the establishment of a Copyright Royalty Tribunal, with the purpose of making adjustments of reasonable copyright royalty rates in respect of the exercise of certain rights, mainly affecting the musical interests. The Tribunal is to consist of five commissioners appointed by the President with the advice and consent of the Senate for a term of seven years each. This body will perform in the United States a function similar to the new Copyright Tribunal in the United Kingdom.

The new American law spells out the economic objectives which its Copyright Tribunal is to apply in calculating the relevant rates. These are:

(1) to maximise the availability of creative works to the public;
(2) to afford the copyright owner a fair return for his creative work and the copyright user a fair income under existing economic conditions;
(3) to reflect the relative roles of the copyright owner and the copyright user in the product made available to the public with respect to relative creative contribution, technological contribution, capital investment, cost, risk, and contribution to the opening of new markets for creative expression and media for their communication.
(4) to minimise any disruptive impact on the structure of the industries involved and on generally prevailing industry practices.

Every final determination of the Tribunal shall be published in the Federal Register. It shall state in detail the criteria that the Tribunal determined to be applicable to the particular proceeding, the various facts that it found relevant to its determination in that proceeding, and the specific reasons for its determination. Any final decision of the Tribunal in a proceeding may be appealed to the United States Court of Appeals by an aggrieved party, within thirty days after its publication in the Federal Register.

Fair use

One of the most controversial factors which held up the introduction of the new American copyright law for at least a decade was the extent to which a balance should be struck between the desire of copyright owners to benefit from their works by extending copyright protection as far as possible, and the pressure from users of copyright to obtain access to copyright material as cheaply as possible – if not completely freely.

The new law provides by Section 107 that the fair use of a copyright work, including such use by reproduction in copies or on records, for purposes such as criticism, comment, news reporting, teaching (including multiple copies for classroom use), scholarship or research is not an infringement of copyright. In determining whether the use made of a work in any particular case is a fair use, the factors to be considered shall include:

(1) the purpose and character of the use, including whether such use is of a commercial nature or is for non-profit educational purposes;
(2) the nature of the copyrighted work;
(3) the amount and substantiality of the portion used in relation to the copyrighted work as a whole; and
(4) the effect of the use upon the potential market for or value of the copyrighted work.

It is not an infringement of copyright for a library or archive, or any of its employees acting within the scope of their employment, to reproduce or distribute no more than one copy of a work, if:

(1) the reproduction or distribution is made without any purpose of direct or indirect commercial advantage;
(2) the collections of the library or archive are either open to the public or available not only to researchers affiliated with the library or archive or with the institution of which it is a part, but also to other persons doing research in a specialised field; and
(3) the reproduction or distribution of the work includes a notice of copyright.

It is not generally an infringement of copyright if a performance or display of a work is given by instructors or pupils in the course of face to face teaching activities of a non-profit educational institution, in a classroom or similar place devoted to instruction.

Nor is it an infringement of copyright to give a performance of a non-dramatic literary or musical work or a dramatico-musical work of a religious nature in the course of services at a place of worship or other religious assembly.

It is also not an infringement of copyright to give a performance of a non-dramatic literary or musical work other than in a transmission to the public, without any purpose of direct or indirect commercial advantage and without payment of any fee for the performance to any of the performing artists, promoters or organisers if either (i) there is no direct or indirect admission charge or (ii) the proceeds, after deducting the reasonable costs of producing the performance, are used exclusively for educational, religious or charitable purposes and not for private financial gain. In this case the copyright owner has the right to serve notice of objection to the performance in a prescribed form.

Note the important decision of the Supreme Court in *Sony Corporation of America* v. *Universal City Studios*. (No. 81-1687, 52 USLW 4090.) This decided that the sale of video-recorders to the public does not amount to contributory infringement of the rights in films which are copied as a result of television broadcasts of them. (The practice known as time-switching.) Among other reasons for their decision advanced by the majority of the judges was their opinion that even unauthorised time-switching is legitimate fair use.

REMEDIES FOR COPYRIGHT OWNERS

Infringement of copyright

Copyright is infringed by anyone who violates any of the exclusive rights referred to in *The rights of a copyright owner* above, or who imports copies or records into the United States in violation of the law. The owner of copyright is entitled to institute an action for infringement so long as that infringement is committed while he or she is the owner of the right infringed. Previously, no action for infringement of copyright could be instituted until registration of the copyright claim had been made, but this requirement has been modified now that the United States has ratified the Berne Convention.

Injunctions

Any court having civil jurisdiction under the copyright law may grant interim and final injunctions on such terms as it may deem reasonable to prevent or restrain infringement of copyright. Such injunction may be served anywhere in the United States on the person named. An injunction is operative throughout the whole of the United States, and can be enforced by proceedings in contempt or otherwise by any American court which has jurisdiction over the infringer.

Impounding and disposition of infringing articles

At any time while a copyright action under American law is pending, the court may order the impounding on such terms as it considers reasonable of all copies or records claimed to have been made or used in violation of the copyright owner's exclusive rights; it may also order the impounding of all plates, moulds, matrices, masters, tapes, film negatives or other articles by means of which infringing copies or records may be reproduced. A court may order as part of a final judgement or decree the destruction or other disposition of all copies or records found to have been made or used in violation of the copyright owner's exclusive rights. It also has the power to order the destruction of all articles by means of which infringing copies or records were reproduced.

Damages and profits

An infringer of copyright is generally liable either for the copyright owner's actual damage and any additional profits made by the infringer, or for statutory damages.

(1) The copyright owner is entitled to recover the actual damages suffered by him as a result of the infringement, and in addition any profits of the infringer which are attributed to the infringement and are not taken into account in computing the actual damages. In establishing the infringer's profits, the copyright owner is only required to present proof of the infringer's gross revenue, and it is for the infringer to prove his or her deductible expenses and the elements of profit attributable to factors other than the copyright work.

(2) Except where the copyright owner has persuaded the court that the infringement was committed wilfully, the copyright owner may elect, at any time before final judgement is given, to recover, instead of actual damages and profits, an award of statutory damages for all infringements involved in the action in respect of any one work, which may be between $250 and $10,000 according to what the court considers justified.

(3) However, where the copyright owner satisfies the court that the infringement was committed wilfully, the court has the discretion to increase the award of statutory damages to not more than $50,000. Where the infringer succeeds in proving that he was not aware that and had no reason to believe that his acts constituted an infringement of copyright, the court has the discretion to reduce the award of statutory damages to not less than $100.

Costs: time limits

In any civil proceedings under American copyright law, the court has the discretion to allow the recovery of full costs by or against any party except the Government of the United States. It may also award a reasonable sum in respect of an attorney's fee.

No civil or criminal proceedings in respect of copyright law shall be permitted unless begun within three years after the claim or cause of action arose.

Criminal proceedings in respect of copyright

(1) Anyone who infringes a copyright wilfully and for purposes of commercial advantage and private financial gain shall be fined not more than $10,000 or imprisoned for not more than one year, or both. However, if the infringement relates to copyright in a sound recording or a film, the infringer is liable to a fine of not more than $25,000 or imprisonment for not more than one year or both on a first offence, which can be increased to a fine of up to $50,000 or imprisonment for not more than two years or both for a subsequent offence.

(2) Following a conviction for criminal infringement a court may in addition to these penalties order the forfeiture and destruction of all infringing copies and records, together with implements and equipment used in their manufacture.

(3) It is also an offence knowingly and with fraudulent intent to place on any article a notice of copyright or words of the same purport, or to import or distribute such copies. A fine is provided for this offence of not more than $2500. The fraudulent removal of a copyright notice also attracts the same maximum fine, as does the false representation of a material particular on an application for copyright representation.

Counterfeiting

By the Piracy and Counterfeiting Amendment Act 1982, pirates and counterfeiters of sound recordings and of motion pictures now face maximum penalties of up to five years imprisonment or fines of up to $250,000.

Colouring films

The United States Copyright Office has decided that adding colour to a black and white film may qualify for copyright protection whenever it amounts to more than a trivial change.

Satellite home viewers

The position of satellite home viewers is now controlled by the Satellite Home Viewer Act of 1988. (Title II of Public Law 100-667 of 16 November 1988.)

GENERAL OBSERVATIONS

The copyright law of the United States has been very greatly improved as a result of the new statute passed by Congress on 19 October 1976. (Title 17, United States Code.) Apart from lifting the general standards of protection for copyright owners to a much higher level than that which previously existed, it has on the whole shifted the balance of copyright protection in favour of the copyright owner and away from the copyright user in many of the areas where controversy existed. But most important for British and other non-American authors and publishers, it has gone a long way towards bringing American copyright law up to the same standards of international protection for non-national copyright proprietors which have long been offered by the United Kingdom and the other major countries, both in Europe and elsewhere in the English-speaking world. The ratification by the United States of the Berne

Convention with effect from 1 March 1989 is an action which finally puts American copyright law on par with the protection offered by other major countries.

Libel

JAMES EVANS and ANTONY WHITAKER

What follows is an outline of the main principles of the law of Libel, with special reference to points which appear most frequently to be misunderstood. But it is no more than that, and specific legal advice should be taken when practical problems arise. The law discussed is the law of England and Wales. Scotland has its own, albeit somewhat similar, rules.

LIBEL: LIABILITY TO PAY DAMAGES

English law draws a distinction between defamation published in permanent form and that which is not. The former is libel, the latter slander. 'Permanent form' includes writing, printing, drawings and photographs and radio and television broadcasts. It follows that it is the law of libel rather than slander which most concerns writers and artists professionally, and the slightly differing rules applicable to slander will not be mentioned in this article.

Publication of a libel can result in a civil action for damages, an injunction to prevent repetition and/or in certain cases a criminal prosecution against those responsible, who include the writer (or artist or photographer), the printers, the publishers, and the editor, if any, of the publication in which the libel appeared. Prosecutions are rare. Certain special rules apply to them and these will be explained below after a discussion of the question of civil liability, which in practice arises much more frequently.

Civil libel cases, for which legal aid is not available, are usually heard by a judge and jury, and it is the jury who decide the amount of any award, which is tax-free. It is not necessary for the plaintiff to prove that he has actually suffered any loss, because the law presumes damage. While the main purpose of a libel claim is to compensate the plaintiff for the injury to his reputation, a jury may give additional sums either as 'aggravated' damages, if it appears a defendant has behaved malevolently or spitefully, or as 'exemplary', or 'punitive', damages where a defendant hopes the economic advantages of publication will outweigh any sum awarded against him. Damages can also be 'nominal' if the libel complained of is trivial. It is generally very difficult to forecast the amounts juries are likely to award, though recent awards against newspapers have disclosed a tendency towards considerable generosity.

In an action for damages for libel, it is for the plaintiff to establish that the matter he complains of (1) has been published by the defendant, (2) refers to himself, (3) is defamatory. If he does so, the plaintiff establishes a *prima facie* case. However, the defendant will escape liability if he can show he has a good defence. There are five defences to a libel action. They are Justification, Fair Comment, Privilege, S.4 of the Defamation Act, 1952, Apology, etc., under the Libel Acts, 1843 and 1845. A libel claim can also become barred under the Limitation Acts, as explained below. These matters must now be examined in detail.

THE PLAINTIFF'S CASE

(1) 'Published' in the legal sense means communicated to a person other than the plaintiff. Thus the legal sense is wider than the lay sense but includes it. It

follows that the content of a book is published in the legal sense when the manuscript is first sent to the publishing firm just as much as it is when the book is later placed on sale to the public. Both types of publication are sufficient for the purpose of establishing liability for libel, but the law differentiates between them, since the scope of publication can properly be taken into account by the jury in considering the actual amount of damages to award.

(2) The plaintiff must also establish that the matter complained of refers to himself. It is of course by no means necessary to mention a person's name before it is clear that he is referred to. Nicknames by which he is known or corruptions of his name are just two ways in which his identity can be indicated. There are more subtle methods. The sole question is whether the plaintiff is indicated to those who read the matter complained of. In some cases he will not be unless it is read in the light of facts known to the reader from other sources, but this is sufficient for the plaintiff's purpose. The test is purely objective and does not depend at all on whether the writer intended to refer to the plaintiff.

It is because it is impossible to establish reference to any individual that generalisations, broadly speaking, are not successfully actionable. To say boldly 'All lawyers are crooks' does not give any single lawyer a cause of action, because the statement does not point a finger at any individual. However, if anyone is named in conjunction with a generalisation, then it may lose its general character and become particular from the context. Again if one says 'One of the X Committee has been convicted of murder' and the X Committee consists of, say, four persons, it cannot be said that the statement is not actionable because no individual is indicated and it could be referring to any of the committee. This is precisely why it is actionable at the suit of each of them as suspicion has been cast on all.

(3) It is for the plaintiff to show that the matter complained of is defamatory. What is defamatory is decided by the jury except in the extreme cases where the judge rules that the words cannot bear a defamatory meaning. Various tests have been laid down for determining this. It is sufficient that any one test is satisfied. The basic tests are: (i) Does the matter complained of tend to lower the plaintiff in the estimation of society? (ii) Does it tend to bring him into hatred, ridicule, contempt, dislike or disesteem with society? (iii) Does it tend to make him shunned or avoided or cut off from society? The mere fact that what is published is inaccurate is not enough to involve liability; it is the adverse impact on the plaintiff's reputation that matters.

'Society' means right-thinking members of society generally. It is by reference to such people that the above tests must be applied. A libel action against a newspaper which had stated that the police had taken a statement from the plaintiff failed, notwithstanding that the plaintiff gave evidence that his apparent assistance to the police (which he denied) had brought him into grave disrepute with the underworld. It was not by their wrongheaded standards that the matter fell to be judged.

Further, it is not necessary to imply that the plaintiff is at fault in some way in order to defame him. To say of a woman that she has been raped or of someone that he is insane imputes to them no degree of blame, but nonetheless both statements are defamatory.

Sometimes a defamatory meaning is conveyed by words which on the face of them have no such meaning. 'But Brutus is an honourable man' is an example. If a jury finds that words are meant ironically they will consider this ironical sense when determining whether the words are defamatory. In deciding therefore whether or not the words are defamatory, the jury seek to discover what, without straining the words or putting a perverse construction on them, they will be understood to mean. In some cases this may differ substantially from their literal meaning.

Matter may also be defamatory by innuendo. Strictly so called, an innuendo is a meaning that words acquire by virtue of facts known to the reader but not stated in the passage complained of. Words, quite innocent on the face of them, may acquire a defamatory meaning when read in the light of these facts. For example, where a newspaper published a photograph of a man and a woman, with the caption that they had just announced their engagement, it was held to be defamatory of the man's wife since those who knew that she had cohabited with him were led to the belief that she had done so only as his mistress. The newspaper was unaware that the man was already married, but some of its readers were not.

DEFENCES TO A LIBEL ACTION

Justification

English law does not protect the reputation that a person either does not or should not possess. Stating the truth therefore does not incur liability, and the plea of justification – namely, that what is complained of is true in substance and in fact – is a complete answer to an action for damages. However, this defence is by no means to be undertaken lightly. For instance, to prove one instance of using bad language will be insufficient to justify the allegation that a person is 'foulmouthed'. It would be necessary to prove several instances, and the defendant is obliged in most cases to particularise in his pleadings giving details, dates and places. However, if there are two or more distinct charges against the plaintiff the defence will not fail by reason only that the truth of every charge is not proved, if the words not proved to be true do not materially injure the plaintiff's reputation having regard to the truth of the remaining charges. It is for the defendant to prove that what he has published is true, not for the plaintiff to disprove it, though if he can do so, so much the better for him.

One point requires special mention. It is insufficient for the defendant to prove that he has accurately repeated what a third person has written or said or that such statements have gone uncontradicted when made on occasions in the past. If X writes 'Y told me that Z is a liar', it is no defence to an action against X merely to prove that Y did say that. X has given currency to a defamatory statement concerning Z and has so made it his own. His only defence is to prove that Z is a liar by establishing a number of instances of Z's untruthfulness. Nor is it a defence to prove that the defendant genuinely believed what he published to be true. This might well be a complete answer in an action, other than a libel action, based on a false but non-defamatory statement. For such statements do not incur liability in the absence of fraud or malice, which, in this context, means a dishonest or otherwise improper motive. Bona fide belief, however, may be relevant to the assessment of damages, even in a libel action.

Special care should be taken in relation to references to a person's convictions, however accurately described. Since the Rehabilitation of Offenders Act, 1974, a person's convictions may become 'spent' and thereafter it may involve liability to refer to them. Reference to the Act and orders thereunder must be made in order to determine the position in any particular case.

Fair comment

It is a defence to prove that what is complained of is fair comment made in good faith and without malice on a matter of public interest.

'Fair' in this context means 'honest'. 'Fair comment' means therefore the expression of the writer's genuinely held opinion. It does not necessarily mean opinion with which the jury agree. Comment may therefore be quite extreme and still be 'fair' in the legal sense. However, if it is utterly perverse the jury may be led to think that no one could have genuinely held such views. In such a case the defence would fail, for the comment could not be honest. 'Malice' here includes the popular sense of personal spite, but covers any dishonest or improper motive.

The defence only applies when what is complained of is comment as distinct from a statement of fact. The line between comment and fact is notoriously difficult to draw in some cases. Comment means a statement of opinion. The facts on which comment is made must be stated together with the comment or be sufficiently indicated with it. This is merely another way of saying that it must be clear that the defamatory statement is one of opinion and not of fact, for which the only defence would be the onerous one of justification. The exact extent to which the facts commented on must be stated or referred to is a difficult question, but some help may be derived in answering it by considering the purpose of the rule, which is to enable the reader to exercise his own judgement and to agree or disagree with the comment. It is quite plain that it is not necessary to state every single detail of the facts. In one case it was sufficient merely to mention the name of one of the Press lords in an article about a newspaper though not one owned by him. He was so well known that to mention his name indicated the substratum of fact commented upon, namely his control of his group of newspapers. No general rule can be laid down, save that, in general, the fuller the facts set out or referred to with the comment the better. These facts must always be true, except that in an action for libel partly in respect of allegations of fact and partly of expressions of opinion, a defence of fair comment will not fail by reason only that the truth of every allegation of fact is not proved, if the expression of opinion is fair comment, having regard to such of the facts alleged or referred to in the matter complained of as are proved.

The defence only applies where the matters commented on are of public interest, i.e. of legitimate concern to the public or a substantial section of it. Thus the conduct of national and local government, international affairs, the administration of justice, etc., are all matters of public interest, whereas other people's private affairs may very well not be, although they undoubtedly interest the public, or provoke curiosity.

In addition, matters of which criticism has been expressly or impliedly invited, such as publicly performed plays and published books, are a legitimate subject of comment. Criticism need not be confined merely to their artistic merit but equally may deal with the attitudes to life and the opinions therein expressed.

It is sometimes said that a man's moral character is never a proper subject of comment for the purpose of this defence. This is certainly true where it is a private individual who is concerned, and some authorities say it is the same in the case of a public figure even though his character may be relevant to his public life. Again, it may in some cases be exceeding the bounds of fair comment to impute a dishonourable motive to a person, as is frequently done by way of inference from facts. In general, the imputation is a dangerous and potentially expensive practice.

Privilege

In the public interest, certain occasions are privileged so that to make defamatory statements upon them does not incur liability. The following are privileged in any event: (i) fair, accurate, and contemporaneous reports of public judicial proceedings in England published in a newspaper, (ii) Parliamentary papers published by the direction of either House, or full republications thereof. The following are privileged provided publication is made only for the reason that the privilege is given and not for some wrongful or indirect motive: (i) fair and accurate but non-contemporaneous reports of public judicial proceedings in

England, whether in a newspaper or not, (ii) extracts of Parliamentary papers, (iii) fair and accurate reports of Parliamentary proceedings, (iv) a fair and accurate report in a newspaper of the proceedings at any public meeting held in the United Kingdom. The meeting must be bona fide and lawfully held for a lawful purpose and for the furtherance or discussion of·any matter of public concern. Admission to the meeting may be general or restricted. In the case of public meetings, the defence is not available, if it is proved that the defendant has been requested by the plaintiff to publish in the newspaper in which the original publication was made a reasonable letter or statement by way of explanation or contradiction, and has refused or neglected to do so, or has done so in a manner not adequate or not reasonable having regard to all the circumstances. This list of privileged occasions is by no means exhaustive, but they are those most commonly utilised.

S.4 of the Defamation Act, 1952

The defence provided by the above section is only available where the defamation is 'innocent'. As has been seen, liability for libel is in no way dependent on the existence of an intention to defame on the part of the defendant and the absence of such an intention does not mean that the defamation is 'innocent'.

Defamation is innocent if the publisher did not intend to publish the matter complained of about the plaintiff and did not know of circumstances by virtue of which it might be understood to refer to him, or, if the matter published was not defamatory on the face of it, if the publisher did not know of circumstances by virtue of which it might be understood to be defamatory. Further the publisher must have exercised all reasonable care in relation to the publication. If the publisher has published matter innocently, he should make an 'offer of amends' to the party aggrieved. This consists of an offer to publish a correction and apology and as far as practicable to inform others to whom the alleged libel has been distributed that the matter is said to be defamatory. If the offer of amends is accepted, it is a bar to further proceedings against the person making the offer. If rejected, the making of the offer affords a defence provided the defendant can prove that he did publish innocently and made the offer as soon as practicable after learning that the matter published was or might be defamatory. The offer must not have been withdrawn and must have been expressed to be for the purposes of the defence under S.4 and have been accompanied by an affidavit. It is vital that the offer should be made swiftly, but it is inadvisable to make it without professional advice owing to its technicality.

An example of the first type of innocent publication is where a reference to a person by name has been understood to refer to another person of the same name and this could not reasonably have been foreseen.

An example of the other type of innocent publication is the case referred to earlier in this article of the man pictured with 'his fiancée'. The publishers did not know that he was already married and that accordingly the picture and caption could be understood to be defamatory of his wife.

In practice all the conditions for a successful defence under this section are infrequently fulfilled.

Apology under the Libel Acts, 1843 and 1845

This defence is rarely utilised, since if any condition of it is not fulfilled, the plaintiff must succeed and the only question is the actual amount of damages. It only applies to actions in respect of libels in newspapers and periodicals. The defendant pleads that the libel was inserted without actual malice and without gross negligence and that before the action commenced or as soon afterwards as possible he inserted a full apology in the same newspaper, etc., or had offered to publish it in a newspaper, etc., of the plaintiff's choice, where the original newspaper is published at intervals greater than a week. Further a sum must be paid into court with this defence to compensate the plaintiff.

Limitation

In general, unless an action is started within three years of publication, a libel claim becomes 'statute-barred' through lapse of time. But successive and subsequent publications, such as the issue of later editions of the same book, or the sale of surplus copies of an old newspaper, can give rise to fresh claims.

Insurance

For an author, the importance of at least an awareness of this branch of law lies first, in the fact that most book contracts contain a clause enabling the publisher to look to him should any libel claims result; and second, in the increasingly large awards of damages. It is therefore advisable to check what libel insurance a publisher carries, and whether it also covers the author who, if he is to have the benefit of it, should always alert the publisher to any potential risk. One company which offers libel insurance for authors is the Sun Alliance of 1 Leadenhall Street, London EC3V 1PP. Premiums start at £1000, and can be substantially higher if the book is tendentious or likely to be controversial. The company generally insists on the author obtaining, and paying for, a legal opinion first. Indemnity limits vary between £50,000 and £1 million, and the author is required to bear at least the first £5000, and 10 per cent of the remainder, of any loss. It is worth remembering that 'losses' include legal costs as well as damages, which they can often exceed. Libel insurance can also be obtained through a Lloyds broker.

CRIMINAL LIABILITY IN LIBEL AND RELATED AREAS

Whereas the object of a civil action is to obtain compensation for the wrong done or to prevent repetition, the object of criminal proceedings is to punish the wrongdoer by fine or imprisonment or both. There are four main types of writing which may provoke a prosecution:

(1) defamatory libel
(2) obscene publications
(3) sedition and incitement to racial hatred
(4) blasphemous libel

(1) The publication of defamatory matter is in certain circumstances a crime as well as a civil wrong. But whereas the principal object of civil proceedings will normally be to obtain compensation, the principal object of a criminal prosecution will be to secure punishment of the accused, for example by way of a fine. Prosecutions are not frequent, but there have been signs of late of a revival of interest. There are important differences between the rules applicable to criminal libel and its civil counterpart. For example, a criminal libel may be 'published' even though only communicated to the person defamed and may be found to have occurred even where the person defamed is dead, or where only a group of persons but no particular individual has been maligned. During election campaigns, it is an 'illegal practice' to publish false statements about the personal character or conduct of a candidate irrespective of whether they are also defamatory.

(2) It is an offence to publish obscene matter. By the Obscene Publications Act, 1959, matter is obscene if its effect is such as to tend to deprave and corrupt persons who are likely, having regard to all relevant circumstances, to read, see or hear it. 'To deprave and corrupt' is to be distinguished from 'to shock and

disgust'. It is a defence to a prosecution to prove that publication of the matter in question is justified as being for the public good, on the ground that it is in the interests of science, literature, art or learning, or of other objects of general concern. Expert evidence may be given as to its literary, artistic, scientific or other merits. Playwrights, directors and producers should note that the Theatres Act, 1968, though designed to afford similar protection to stage productions, does not necessarily prevent prosecutions for indecency under other statutes.

(3) Writings which tend to destroy the peace of the Realm may be prosecuted as being seditious or as amounting to incitement to racial hatred. Seditious writings include those which advocate reform by unconstitutional or violent means or incite contempt or hatred for the Monarch or Parliament. These institutions may be criticised stringently, but not in a manner which is likely to lead to insurrection or civil commotion or indeed any physical force. Prosecutions are a rarity, but it should be remembered that writers of matter contemptuous of the House of Commons, though not prosecuted for seditious libel are, from time to time, punished by that House for breach of its Privileges, although, if a full apology is made, it is often an end of the matter. The Public Order Act 1986 makes it an offence, irrespective of the author's or publisher's intention, to publish, or put on plays containing, threatening, abusive or insulting matter if hatred is likely to be stirred up against any racial group in Great Britain.

(4) Blasphemous libel consists in the vilification of the Christian religion or its ceremonies. Other religions are not protected. The offence lies essentially in the impact of what is said concerning, for instance, God, Christ, the Bible, the Book of Common Prayer, etc.; it is irrelevant that the publisher does not intend to shock or arouse resentment. While temperate and sober writings on religious topics however anti-Christian in sentiment will not involve liability, if the discussion is 'so scurrilous and offensive as to pass the limit of decent controversy and to outrage any Christian feeling', it will.

The Florence Agreement and its Nairobi Protocol

This Agreement, on the Importation of Educational, Scientific and Cultural Materials, generally known as the Florence Agreement, was adopted by the Unesco General Conference in Florence in 1950 and came into force on 21 May 1952. It is concerned with the free flow of a wide variety of articles including books and the removal of tariff and trade obstacles. The principal undertaking of the contracting states is the exemption of books and other educational, scientific and cultural imports from customs duties, and the granting of licences and foreign exchange as far as possible for their importation. Books of every sort are included in the Agreement, not exempting those printed abroad from the work of an author in the importing country. Unbound sheets do not come under the Agreement.

The following is an up-to-date list of the States parties to the Agreement: Afghanistan, Austria, Barbados, Belgium, Bolivia, Burkina-Faso, Cameroon, Congo, Cuba, Cyprus, Democratic Kampuchea, Denmark, Egypt, El Salvador, Fiji, Finland, France, Gabon, Germany, Ghana, Greece, Guatemala, Haiti, Holy See, Hungary, Iran, Iraq, Ireland, Israel, Italy, Ivory Coast, Japan, Jordan, Kenya, Lao People's Democratic Republic, Liechtenstein, Luxembourg, Madagascar, Malawi, Malaysia, Malta, Mauritius, Monaco, Morocco, Netherlands, New Zealand, Nicaragua, Niger, Nigeria, Norway, Oman, Pakistan, Philippines, Poland, Portugal, Romania, Rwanda, San Marino, Sierra Leone, Singapore, Socialist People's Libyan Arab Jamahiriya, Solomon Islands, Spain, Sri Lanka, Sweden, Switzerland, Syrian Arab Republic, Tanzania (United Republic of), Thailand, Tonga, Trinidad and Tobago, Tunisia, Uganda, United Kingdom, United States of America, Viet-Nam (Socialist Republic of), Yugoslavia, Zaire, Zambia.

A Protocol to the Florence Agreement or Nairobi Protocol adopted by the Unesco General Conference in Nairobi in 1976 came into force on 2 January 1982. It is open only to states which are parties to the Agreement. The Protocol broadens the scope of the Agreement by extending the benefits it offers to additional objects and by granting further benefits to a number of materials. The following States adhere to the Protocol: Barbados, Belgium, Denmark, Egypt, Finland, France, Germany, Greece, Holy See, Iraq, Ireland, Italy, Luxembourg, Netherlands, Portugal, San Marino, United Kingdom, Yugoslavia.

Mechanical-Copyright Protection Society Ltd

The Society was formed in 1910 by a group of music publishers in anticipation of the introduction of new legislation which for the first time would provide for the protection of copyright material by mechanical reproduction.

This became effective on the introduction of the Copyright Act 1911 when only the music box, piano roll, cylinder and disc recordings were known.

Since those days the Society has grown with the technical advances into sound, film, radio and television recordings, magnetic tape and videocassettes, and now grants licences in all matters affecting recording rights, both in the UK and throughout the world by virtue of its affiliation with other similar organisations and agencies.

Membership of the Society is open to all music copyright owners, composers, lyric writers and publishers. There is no entrance fee or subscription.

Enquiries for membership should be addressed to the Membership Department, Elgar House, 41 Streatham High Road, London SW16 1ER *tel* 081-769 4400 *fax* 081-769 8792.

The Performing Right Society Ltd

The Performing Right Society is an Association of Composers, Authors and Publishers of copyright musical works, established in 1914 to collect royalties for the public performance, broadcasting and diffusion by cable of such works and their use by diffusion services; also to restrain unauthorised use thereof.

Licences are granted which convey the necessary permission for the public performance of any of the works of its members and those of the affiliated national societies of more than 30 other countries. The combined membership thus represented by the Society is about 500,000. Over 200,000 places of entertainment are covered by the Society's licence in the British Isles alone.

The Society does not control the performance of non-musical works (plays, sketches, etc.), but its licence is required for the use of its international repertoire in variety, as overture, entr'acte or exit music, or for any other form of live or mechanical performances (excluding operas, operettas, musical plays, specially written music for plays, revues or pantomimes (apart from interpolations therein of independent items) and ballets).

The constitution of the Society is that of a Company limited by guarantee having no share capital. The General Council consists of twelve composers and authors and twelve music publishers elected by the members from among their own number. The Society is not a profit-making organisation, the whole of the royalties it collects being distributed amongst its members and the affiliated societies after deduction of administration expenses and contributions to the PRS Members' Fund, established for the benefit of necessitous members and their dependants.

There are two distributions of general performing fees each year, and two distributions of broadcasting fees. The Annual General Meeting is usually held in July.

Applicants for membership are required to pay an initial admission fee, but no further subscriptions or fees are charged. All composers of musical works and authors of lyrics or poems which have been set to music are eligible for membership, provided that they satisfy the current membership criteria.

The Society has available for free loan a new film entitled *PRS – The Movie*. For details of this and for further information contact the Public Relations Department at PRS, 29-33 Berners Street, London W1P 4AA   *tel* 071-580 5544.

Public Lending Right

FOR WRITERS AND ILLUSTRATORS OF BOOKS

Outline

Under the PLR system, payment is made from public funds to authors (writers, translators, illustrators and some editors/compilers) whose books are lent out from public libraries. Payment is made once a year, in February, and the amount each author receives is proportionate to the number of times (established from a sample) that his books were borrowed during the previous year (July to June).

The legislation

PLR was created, and its principles established, by the Public Lending Right Act 1979 (HMSO, 30p). The Act required the rules for the administration of PLR to be laid down by a scheme. That was done in the Public Lending Right Scheme 1982 (HMSO, £2.95), which includes details of transfer (assignment), transmission after death, renunciation, trusteeship, bankruptcy, etc. Amending orders made in 1983, 1984, 1988, 1989 and 1990 were consolidated in December 1990 (S.I. 2360, £3.90).

How the system works

From the applications he receives, the Registrar of PLR compiles, to hold on his computer, a register of authors and books. A representative sample is recorded, consisting of all loans from thirty public libraries. This is then multiplied in proportion to total library lending to produce, for each book, an estimate of its total annual loans throughout the country. Each year the computer compares the register with the estimated loans to discover how many loans are credited to each registered book for the calculation of PLR payments. The computer does this using code numbers – in most cases the ISBN printed in the book.

Parliament allocates a sum each year (£4,750,000 in 1991/92) for PLR. This Fund pays the administrative costs of PLR and reimburses local authorities for recording loans in the sample libraries. The remaining money is then divided in order to work out how much can be paid for each estimated loan of a registered book.

Limits on payments

(1) *Bottom limit*. If all the registered interests in an author's books score so few loans that they would earn less than £1 in a year, no payment is due.
(2) *Top limit*. If the books of one registered author score so high that the author's PLR earnings for the year would exceed £6000, then only £6000 is paid. No author can earn more than £6000 in PLR in any one year.

Money that is not paid out because of these limits belongs to the Fund and increases the amounts paid that year to other authors.

The sample

The basic sample represents only public libraries (no academic, private or commercial ones) and only loans made over the counter (not consultations of books on library premises). The reference sections of public libraries are not included in PLR. It follows that only those books which are loaned from public libraries can earn PLR and make an application worthwhile.

The sample consists of the entire loans records for a year in thirty public libraries representatively spread through England, Scotland, Wales and Northern Ireland. Sample loans are about 1.7% of the national total. It is intended to change to a situation where all computerised sampling points in an authority contribute loans data – not just single sampling points. This change will be introduced gradually, starting in July 1991. The aim is to increase the sample to 7-8 per cent by 1995, without any significant increase in costs. In order to counteract sampling error, libraries in the sample change every two to three years. Loans are totalled every twelve months for the period 1 July to 30 June.

An author's entitlement to PLR depends, under the 1979 Act, on the loans scored by his books in the sample. This score is multiplied to produce regional and national estimated loans.

ISBNs

PLR depends on the use of code numbers to identify books lent and to correlate loans with entries on the register so that payment can be made. Chiefly the system uses the International Standard Book Number – the ISBN – which consists of ten digits and is usually printed with the publishing information on the back of the title page; it may also be on the back or back flap of the jacket or cover. Examples are: 0 10 541079 9 and 185036110x.

Some books – particularly those published before 1970 – lack an ISBN; where such books have no ISBN, the Registrar has allocated to it another code number so that it can still score loans and earn PLR. However, where there is an ISBN, an author who applies for registration is asked to give it on his application form. From July 1991 an ISBN is required for all new registrations. Different editions (for example, 1st, 2nd, hardcover, paperback, large print) of the same book have different ISBNs.

Authorship

In the PLR system the author of a book is the writer, illustrator, translator, compiler, editor or reviser. His name must be on the book's title page. He is eligible for PLR as an author even if he does not own the copyright. PLR and copyright are different. Note also that:

(1) Illustrators include photographers, provided that the photographer is (in the words of section 48 of the Copyright Act 1956) 'the person who, at the time when the photograph is taken, is the owner of the material on which it is taken'.
(2) For the registration of an author who is less than 18 years old the application must be made by his parent or guardian. Upon reaching the age of 18, the author should apply for the PLR to be registered in his own name: until this is done the PLR belongs to the parent or guardian.
(3) A compiler or editor must also have written at least 10% of the book's contents or more than ten pages of text.
(4) A reviser may be regarded as an editor.
(5) A translator receives a fixed 30% share.

The sole writer of a book may not be its sole author because, for PLR, all the eligible contributors named on the title page are its co-authors.

Co-authorship/illustrators

In the PLR system the authors of a book are those writers, translators, editors, compilers and illustrators whose names appear on the title page. Authors must apply for registration before their books can earn PLR. Books with *no more* than three named writers (excluding translators, editors and compilers) or illustrators can be registered for PLR. (Some changes to the title page rules are currently under consideration.)

Applications from writers and/or illustrators

At least one must be eligible and they must jointly agree what share of PLR each will take. This agreement is necessary even if one or two are ineligible or do not wish to register for PLR. If they are not all eligible, those who are will receive a share(s) specified in the application. PLR can be any whole percentage. Illustrators and joint writers may only register more than 50% if justified by their actual contribution to the book. Detailed advice is available from the PLR office. The change to allow single applications for joint-author books was introduced in 1990.

Applications from translators

Translators may apply, without reference to other authors, for a 30% fixed share (to be divided equally between joint translators). Translators do not have to be named on the title page but must be credited in the book.

Applications from editors and compilers

An editor or compiler who has also made a significant written contribution to the book, and who is named on the title page, may apply, either with others or without reference to them, to register a 20% share provided he has written 10% of the book or more than ten pages of text: this should be substantiated by photocopies of the title and contents pages. The share of joint editors/compilers is 20% in total to be divided equally.

An application from an editor or compiler to register a greater percentage share must be accompanied by supporting documentary evidence of actual contribution. A special form is available from the PLR Office.

Dead or missing co-authors

Where it is impossible to agree shares with a co-author because that person is dead or untraceable, then the surviving co-author or co-authors may submit an application without the dead or missing co-author, but must name the co-author and provide supporting evidence as to why that co-author has not agreed shares. The living co-author(s) will then be able to register a share in the book which will be 20% for the illustrator (or illustrators) and the residual percentage for writer (or writers).

If this percentage is to be divided between more than one writer or illustrator, then this will be in equal shares unless some other apportionment is requested and agreed by the Registrar.

Writers or illustrators may apply for a different percentage apportionment, and the Registrar will register different percentage shares if it is reasonable in relation to the authors' contribution to the particular book. Detailed advice and forms are available from the PLR Office.

The PLR Office keeps a file of missing authors (mostly illustrators) to help applicants locate co-authors. Help is also available from publishers, the writers' organisations, and The Association of Illustrators, 1 Colville Place, London W1P 1HN.

Life and death

Authors can only be registered for PLR during their lifetime. However, for authors so registered, books can later be registered if first published within one year before their death or ten years afterwards. New versions of titles registered by the author can be registered posthumously.

Eligible authors

If he is (in the senses described above) the author or a co-author of a book that is eligible (as described below), then he is eligible for PLR registration provided that he is resident in the United Kingdom or Germany. A resident in these countries (for PLR purposes) has his only home there or his principal home there. The United Kingdom does not include the Channel Islands or the Isle of Man.

Eligible books

In the PLR system each separate edition of a book is registered and treated as a separate book.

A book is eligible for PLR registration provided that:
(1) it has an eligible author (or co-author) named on its title page (or is translated by an eligible author);
(2) it is printed and bound (paperbacks counting as bound);
(3) copies of it have been put on sale (i.e. it is not a free handout and it has already been published);
(4) it is not a newspaper, magazine, journal or periodical;
(5) it does not have more than three writers or illustrators named on the title page;
(6) the authorship is personal (i.e. not a company or association) and the book is not crown copyright;
(7) it is not wholly or mainly a musical score;
(8) it has an ISBN.

Notification and payment

Every registered author earning a payment receives from the Registrar an annual statement of estimated loans for each book and the PLR due.

SAMPLING ARRANGEMENTS

Libraries

The scheme specifies the eight regions within which authorities and sampling points have to be designated. With such a small sample, random selection would not necessarily produce a statistically more accurate result than consciously aiming for a reasonable spread – considering as many factors as possible likely to influence the result.

From July 1991 the sampling points, designated in close collaboration with the public libraries and local authorities involved, are at: *Wales*: Llanelli (3 service points), Cardiff Central, Denbigh, Ruthin Mobile; *Scotland*: Dumfries & Galloway (3 service points), Cardonald (Glasgow), Dundee Central; *Northern Ireland*: Newry, Chichester Road (Belfast); *London*: Barbican, Ilford Central, Cheam, Swiss Cottage; *Metropolitan Boroughs*: Sefton (all service points), Shirley (Solihull), South Shields, Sheffield Central, Pontefract; *Counties S&E*: Rayleigh (Essex), Tonbridge, Redhill, Hadleigh (Suffolk), Portslade (East Sussex); *Counties S&W*: Devon (11 service points), Yate (Avon), Lillington (Warwickshire), Penzance; *Counties N*: Bransholme (Humberside), Lancs. (Lancaster & Fleetwood), Durham City, Runcorn Shopping City.

Participating local authorities are reimbursed on an actual cost basis for additional expenditure incurred in providing loans data to the PLR Office. The extra PLR work mostly consists of modifications to computer programs to accumulate data already held in the local authority computer and to produce a monthly magnetic tape to be sent to the PLR Office at Stockton-on-Tees.

SUMMARY OF THE EIGHTH YEAR'S RESULTS

Registration: authors

When registration closed for the eighth year (30 June 1990) the number of books registered was 168,587 for 18,976 authors. This included 610 German authors.

Library loans

The ISBN was used for 95% of the loans; the remaining 5% were identified by author and title referring to the PLR database.

The sample loans were 1.75% of total issues from UK public libraries – 583 million per annum.

Because the sampling strength is different in each region, the calculation is done in two stages. For example the loans recorded in Wales are multiplied by 32 because issues in the three Welsh sampling points represent 3% of borrowings from all public libraries in Wales; but in London the multiplication factor is 52 since 2% of issues from all London libraries have been sampled.

Eligible loans

Of these 583 million estimated loans, 239 million belong to books on the PLR register. The loans credited to registered books – 41% of all library borrowings – qualify for payment. The remaining 59% of loans relate to books that are ineligible for various reasons, to books written by dead or foreign authors, and to books that have simply not been applied for.

Money and payments

Most of the setting up and computer system was paid for in previous financial years: £372,000 in 1981/82, £350,000 in 1982/83 and £107,000 in 1983/84.

Operating the Scheme this year cost £513,000 plus payments to local authorities of £35,000. The Rate per Loan for 1990/91 was set at 1.37 pence and calculated to distribute all the £2,969,000 available. The total of PLR distribution and costs is therefore the full £3.5 million which the Government provided in 1990/91.

Within this £2,969,000, some £300,600 would have gone to the most popular authors – but the maximum limit of £6000 per author has in effect transferred this money to increase payments to other authors.

The numbers of authors in various payment categories are as follows:

		£
55	payments at	6,000 maximum
25	payments at	5,000-5,999
148	payments between	2,500-4,999
405	payments between	1,000-2,499
575	payments between	500-999
3,062	payments between	100-499
11,211	payments between	1-99
15,481	TOTAL	

There were also 3495 registered authors whose books earned them *nil* payment.

MOST BORROWED AUTHORS IN UK PUBLIC LIBRARIES

Based on PLR sample loans July 1989-June 1990. Includes all writers, both registered and unregistered, but not illustrators where the book has a separate writer. Writing names are used; pseudonyms have not been combined. (C) indicates a children's book author.

Top 100 Authors (82,752,000 loans = 14.2%)

Jean & Gareth Adamson (C)	Jeffrey Archer	Maeve Binchy	Barbara Taylor Bradford
Allan & Janet Ahlberg (C)	Isaac Asimov	Val Biro (C)	Simon Brett
Ted Allbeury	Revd W. Awdry (C)	Ursula Bloom	Iris Bromige
Virginia Andrews	Desmond Bagley	Judy Blume (C)	Dick Bruna (C)
Evelyn Anthony	Tessa Barclay	Enid Blyton (C)	Philippa Carr

Barbara Cartland	Catherine Gaskin	Alexander Kent	Dudley Pope
James Hadley Chase	René Goscinny (C)	Stephen King	Claire Rayner
Agatha Christie	Iris Gower	Dick King-Smith (C)	Miss Read
Jon Cleary	Winston Graham	Louis L'Amour	Douglas Reeman
Virginia Coffman	John Harris	Charlotte Lamb	Ruth Rendell
Jackie Collins	James Herbert	Norah Lofts	Harlold Robbins
Catherine Cookson	Georgette Heyer	Robert Ludlum	Gerald Seymour
Jilly Cooper	Jack Higgins	Helen MacInnes	Tom Sharpe
John Cunliffe (C)	Eric Hill (C)	Alistair MacLean	Sarah Shears
Roald Dahl (C)	Jane Aiken Hodge	Ngaio Marsh	Sidney Sheldon
Janet Daily	Victoria Holt	Graham Masterton	Wilbur Smith
Len Deighton	Susan Howatch	Ed McBain	Danielle Steel
R.F. Delderfield	Shirley Hughes (C)	Philip McCutchan	Jessica Stirling
Daphne Du Maurier	Pat Hutchins (C)	Maisie Mosco	Leslie Thomas
Elizabeth Ferrars	Hammond Innes	Betty Neels	E.V. Thompson
Colin Forbes	P.D. James	Christopher Nicole	John Wainwright
Helen Forrester	Penny Jordan	Pamela Oldfield	Phyllis A. Whitney
Dick Francis	Marie Joseph	Helen Oxenbury (C)	Kate Williams (C)
Christine M. Fraser	Carolyn Keene (C)	Ellis Peters	Sara Woods
John Gardner	Lena Kennedy	Jean Plaidy	Margaret Yorke

RECIPROCAL ARRANGEMENTS

In 1981-1982 reciprocal arrangements with West Germany were demanded by the writers – fearful that they might lose the West German PLR they had enjoyed since 1974. The West German Scheme, although loan based, is very different in most other respects. There is no question of harmonisation, but simple reciprocity was brought into effect in January 1985. Authors can apply for German PLR through the Authors' Licensing and Collecting Society. (Comparison of PLR schemes internationally and consideration of prospects for reciprocity are covered in the Registrar's Report to the Advisory Committee, *PLR in Practice*, John Sumsion, 2nd edn, 1991, £14.50 inc. UK postage, from the PLR office.)

ADVISORY COMMITTEE

The PLR Advisory Committee was reconstituted in 1988 under the chairmanship of Mr David Whitaker to advise both the Minister for the Arts and the Registrar on matters concerning PLR.

CRITICAL FEATURES REVIEWED

On the question of practical feasibility, the central question has been how a writer can collect when the value of each transaction is so small that, with conventional methods, the cost of collecting the money would be far greater than its value. (There is an obvious parallel here with photocopying.)

There is now a basically satisfactory way of calculating PLR remuneration. The objections to PLR as being infeasible or impractical have been completely overcome through the use of the latest available library computing technology and an approach familiar to businessmen dealing with stock control problems.

An important result has been the provision of information on book loans and author payments so that future developments and improvements in PLR can be based on a factual review of public library lending. This is described in *PLR in Practice* (op. cit.) and also in *PLR Loans – A Statistical Exploration*, Part 2, A. Hasted *et al.*, £16.50 from the PLR office.

PLR application forms, information and publications can be obtained from The Registrar, PLR Office, Bayheath House, Prince Regent Street, Stockton-on-Tees, Cleveland TS18 1DF *tel* (0642) 604699 *fax* (0642) 615641. The Minister's Annual Report to Parliament and the statutory accounts may be obtained from this address or from HMSO.

This report was written by the first Registrar of Public Lending Right, John Sumsion, and his staff. In August 1991 he retired and moved to direct the Library and Information Statistics Unit at the University of Loughborough. From August 1991 the Registrar is Dr James Parker.

The Authors' Licensing and Collecting Society Ltd

ALCS was set up in 1977 to collect and distribute money to writers for payments which authors and other copyright holders are unable to collect individually.

ALCS is a company limited by guarantee (i.e. not having a share capital). It is run by members through a Council of Management on which the Society of Authors and Writers' Guild of Great Britain are represented.

ALCS is a member of CISAC (International Confederation of Authors and Composers Societies) and IFRRO (International Federation of Reprographic Rights Organisation) and through them maintains constant links with continental European and other overseas collecting societies.

ADMINISTRATION

The Council of Management has twelve members, all of whom are active writers. Four are elected by and from the Ordinary Members of ALCS, four are nominated by the Society of Authors and four by the Writers' Guild. The ALCS is served by the Secretary General and a small staff who manage the office and arrange the regular distributions.

POWER

On joining, members transfer to the Society the power to administer on their behalf specific rights which they are unable to exercise as individuals. Under the Society's constitution ALCS may administer (a) in the United Kingdom and the Republic of Ireland and (b) in other Countries:

    lending right (not British PLR);
    reprographic (photocopying) right;
    cable transmission right;
    private recording right;
    off-air recording right;
    right of public reception of broadcasters.
Where such a right can be exercised by an individual, the Society does not normally intervene.

From time to time ALCS may add other rights by special Resolution of a General Meeting to reflect the development of technology.

DISTRIBUTIONS

Foreign PLR

ALCS distributes annually some £80,000 from the collecting society, VG WORT, in the German Federal Republic. Further money is held in Germany on behalf of British writers who have not yet joined ALCS. Those eligible to receive German PLR through ALCS are:

     living British authors resident anywhere;
     heirs of British authors through successor membership;
     foreign writers resident in Britain, writing in English;
     British illustrators.

Reprography

Set up in 1983 by ALCS together with the Publishers Licensing Society, the Copyright Licensing Agency (CLA) is now well-established and offers licences for reprography. ALCS is responsible for paying writers their share in any fees collected from such licences. (See the following article.)

Cable retransmission

ALCS collects fees for the retransmission of BBC 1 and 2 to Belgium and Holland and of BBC World Service Television to other European countries. ALCS also collect fees in Switzerland for British writers whose work is cabled into Switzerland from neighbouring countries.

Educational off-air recording

ALCS is part of the Educational Recording Agency Ltd (ERA) set up to license educational establishments to record off-air under the provisions of the 1988 Copyright Act.

GENERAL

ALCS is represented on the British Copyright Council and the Secretary General is a member of the PLR Advisory Committee. ALCS maintains a watching brief on all matters affecting copyright both in Great Britain and abroad and is recognised internationally as expert on writers' collective rights. ALCS increasingly operates as a central international information exchange.

TO JOIN

The current subscription is £5.00 (excl. VAT). Application forms from: The Membership Secretary, 33/34 Alfred Place, London WC1E 7DP   *tel* 071-255 2034.

     Members of The Society of Authors and the Writers' Guild have free membership of ALCS.

The Copyright Licensing Agency Ltd
CLA

Eighteen years have passed since 1973, when interest groups in the UK started to prepare submissions to the government-appointed committee under the Hon. Mr Justice Whitford about ways of regulating copying from books, journals and periodicals. These interest groups, representing owners of copyright, were seeking both a mechanism of control and just recompense for authors and publishers while at the same time continuing to satisfy the reasonable demands of a modern information-driven society.

When it was eventually published in 1977, the Whitford Report on Copyright and Designs Law suggested, as the best likely solution to the problem, a collective administration system for copying rights organised by the rights owners themselves.

This recommendation spawned first the Wolfenden Committee that brought together representatives of authors' societies and publishers' associations, and then the de Freitas committee that hammered out and fashioned, with these two sometimes antagonistic groups, a mutually acceptable constitution for such a licensing body. The outcome was the formation of the Copyright Licensing Agency, CLA, in April 1982 and its incorporation in January 1983 as a non-profit making company limited by guarantee. The Agency, which is primarily concerned with licensing 'heavy user' groups, issued its first licence in May 1984.

CLA is 'owned' by the Authors' Licensing & Collecting Society (ALCS) and the Publishers Licensing Society (PLS) in that they are its members. ALCS's members are the Society of Authors (SoA), the Writers' Guild of Great Britain (WGoGB) and the Association of Authors' Agents (AAA); and PLS's members are the Publishers Association (PA), the Periodical Publishers Association (PPA) and the Association of Learned and Professional Society Publishers (ALPSP). All are represented on CLA's board of twelve directors, six being ALCS nominations and six PLS nominations.

CLA has six main functions and these are:

> to obtain mandates from publishers and authors in association with ALCS and PLS;
>
> to license users for copying extracts from books, journals and periodicals;
>
> to collect fees from licensed users for such copying;
>
> to maintain a system of record-keeping sufficient to provide statistically acceptable information on which to calculate a fair apportionment of the distributable income;
>
> to pay ALCS and PLS their correct shares of the distributable income and provide sufficient data to enable these societies to pay individual authors and publishers;
>
> to institute such legal proceedings as may be necessary for the enforcement of the rights entrusted to the Agency.

CLA sees its principal licensing areas in the UK as being *education*, *government* and *industry*. Each of these broad categories has three or four sub-groups. In company with nearly all other Reprographic Rights Organisations (RROs) around the world, CLA started licensing in the general education sector. The first major development occurred in April 1986, when three-year voluntary licensing agreements with the country's local education authorities (LEAs) came into effect; in April 1989 these licences were extended for a further three years; copying in all thirty thousand or so state colleges and schools is now covered by such licences. The Agency also licenses the independent education sector through its licensing scheme for independent schools.

With the general education sector (5 to 16 years) covered, CLA next turned its attention to higher and further education (HE & FE) and during 1989, after several years of negotiating, finalised arrangements whereby universities, polytechnics, independent colleges and language schools, etc. all became licensed from 1 January 1990. Three-year licences once again were the norm.

Having successfully negotiated the local education authority licences with a joint committee of representatives appointed by the Association of County Councils (ACC), the Association of Metropolitan Authorities (AMA) and the Convention of Scottish Local Authorities (CoSLA), CLA will try to license the non-LEA parts of local government in one fell swoop with a similar committee but expanded to include representatives of the Association of District Councils (ADC) and the Association of London Authorities (ALA).

It is the Agency's intention to deal with central government on a ministry by ministry basis, starting with the Department of Trade & Industry (DTI) as the sponsors of the Copyright, Designs and Patents Act 1988; the Department of Education and Science (DES), as educational institutions are already licensed; and the National Health Service (NHS) which, with 1.25 million employees, is the largest employer in western Europe.

Public bodies, i.e. those organisations for which government ministers have some accountability (e.g. The British Council), may have to be dealt with in some non-collective manner.

Trade, industry, commerce and the professions present CLA with its greatest challenge because of their size and diversity. A first step has already been taken, however, with the setting up of a joint task force with the Confederation of British Industry (CBI). This CBI/CLA working party, chaired by an industrialist, will examine the best way or ways forward, concentrating initially on manufacturing industry, with particular emphasis on R&D-driven sectors such as pharmaceuticals, chemicals, engineering, electronics, aerospace and oil fuel.

Basically, CLA is a banking operation with legal overtones: it collects fees from licensed users in respect of acts of photocopying from books and serials and other copying such as microfiche printing and, after deducting its administration costs and any reserves or provisions the Board may decide, distributes the balance to ALCS and PLS for them to pay to authors and publishers.

CLA currently offers two basic services, that is, licences to copy, authorised by many individual owners of copyright, both of which offer the collective repertoire of copyright works mandated to CLA by those owners:

> a *collective user* arrangement such as that made with the associations representing local education authorities for state colleges and schools;

> a *transactional user* service for those institutions where a suitable representative organisation, such as an LEA, is unable or unwilling to provide the level of administrative support which a collective user scheme requires, e.g. implementation and supervision of a sampling system, single cheque payment, etc.

Both types of licence are valid for a specific period, usually two or three years.

Under a collective user arrangement the level of copying for a group of institutions is mutually agreed and a global fee set; this fee total is then apportioned by the organising body amongst its constituents and paid by them to CLA on presentation of an invoice from CLA. With the transactional user scheme, fees are paid on a straight cost per copy-page basis; returns to CLA are made at regular, agreed intervals, and a self-billing system is used.

Importantly, from the user community's standpoint, CLA indemnifies all licensees against any inadvertent infringement of copyright.

Right from the outset, the authors' representatives insisted first that writers should benefit individually and directly from the copying of their works and that the money should not go to authors' societies for 'social benefit' purposes, as is the case in some parts of the world. Secondly, they insisted that the individual authors' shares should be paid to them directly, and not through the accounting systems of their publishers.

In order to fulfil these requirements CLA had to devise a title-based distribution system and a form of record-keeping suitable for a stratified and statistically sound sample of the licensees. Some form of itemised record-keeping, therefore, is necessary on the part of both categories of licence holders. With *collective user* licensing, a rotating sample of about 5% of institutions in each broad category is required to maintain records of their copying, which are returned to CLA at agreed intervals, where they are checked and analysed. *Transactional user* licensees are required to keep records of all their copying.

Controlled record-keeping is crucial to CLA because the statistical information extracted from these records of copying is used as the basis for making payments to copyright owners whose works have been copied.

Once a licence has been issued, it has been relatively simple, so far, to collect fees. It is quite another matter, however, to edit, process and analyse the returns of copying, and to calculate the correct amounts due to copyright owners.

In the distribution CLA made in the autumn of 1987 which covered the period since the issue of the first licence in May 1984 to September 1986, the works of some 10,000 authors on 1600 publishing imprints were copied.

On return to the Agency, the record-keeping forms, which are regarded and treated as strictly confidential documents, some of which are deemed to be personal data under the Data Protection Act 1984, are:

> checked by the licensing officer responsible to ensure that the conditions of the licence are being adhered to;

> scrutinised by the data preparation department to validate the information being submitted, e.g. missing ISBN/ISSNs etc. are searched for;

> keyed for computer analysis;

> subjected to a final edit for data quality.

The results are analysed and summaries produced showing pages copied, by ISBN/ISSN, by title, by author, and by publisher. Apportionments are then calculated, statements produced and cheques drawn.

The existence of the International Standard Book Number (ISBN) and the International Standard Serial Number (ISSN) systems is a great benefit to CLA and makes the Agency's task that much easier than it would otherwise be.

The CLA Board decided that the first distribution to members would be £1.4 million (US$2.3 million) and would be paid in two parts: the first tranche of just over £500,000 in October 1987, and the balance of around £900,000 in March/April 1988. Thereafter, payments to rights owners would be made every six months. At the time of writing CLA has distributed nearly £4.7 million to members.

The returns submitted by state colleges and schools on CLA's structured sample enabled statisticians to confirm that copying in this sector is now in the order of 110 million pages per annum from copyright books and serials, which supports the estimates produced by earlier surveys on which the initial LEA global fee was based.

It must be emphasised that a CLA licence is not a carte blanche to copy without restrictions. The conditions are clearly set down and are required to be displayed alongside every copying machine within the control of the licensee. The wording of the notices may vary slightly depending on the category of the licensee, but the core message is always the same! CLA also produces various user guides for issue to employees, and there is a warning sticker that goes on top of machines to act as a reminder to copier users.

For CLA there is comfort in knowing that it is not alone in pioneering the collective administration of copying rights. Counterpart organisations to CLA now exist in sixteen other countries – Australia, Austria, Canada, Denmark, Finland, France, Germany, Iceland, the Netherlands, New Zealand, Norway, South Africa, Spain, Sweden, Switzerland and the United States – nearly all of them in membership of IFRRO, the International Federation of Reproduction Rights Organisations. RROs are also presently being formed in Italy and Japan.

Finally, the broader the repertoire an RRO can offer its licensees the better, and it is a priority of CLA to secure reciprocal agreements with counterpart organisations overseas, particularly those in English-speaking countries where UK books, journals and periodicals are being widely and extensively copied, and, equally, where much publishing in the English language takes place.

Critics of collecting societies say that they spend pounds to distribute pennies. From the start, this is a potential criticism of which the CLA directors were acutely conscious. As far back as November 1982 the board designate set down in its minutes that on no account were CLA's administration costs to exceed 20% of the fee income. The Agency has done much better than that: CLA's overhead is working out at about 15% of the fee income, and it continually strives to reduce that level where possible. It is, however, in the business of handling large numbers of documents and processing a great deal of information, and to do so efficiently in this day and age a high degree of office automation is required and technological wizardry does not come cheap.

CLA's aim is to distribute as much as it can, as fast as it can, and as efficiently as it can. It believes that £4.7 million, distributed between October 1987 and April 1990, speaks louder than any words, and demonstrates better than anything else the Agency's resolve to achieve its objectives.

Further information from The Secretary, The Copyright Licensing Agency Ltd, 90 Tottenham Court Road, London W1P 9HE   *tel* 071-436 5931.

Publishing practice

Agreements

PUBLISHERS' AGREEMENTS

ROYALTY AGREEMENTS

The royalty agreement is now the most usual arrangement between author and publisher, and almost invariably the most satisfactory for the author. It provides for the payment to the author of a royalty of an agreed percentage on all copies of the book which are sold. The rate of royalty varies with circumstances: for hardback general books it is often ten per cent of the published price (or the equivalent percentage of the sum received by the publisher). Lower rates will be payable on copies sold at a high discount, for example in some export areas, to major wholesalers and to book clubs. There may be a provision for the rate to rise after the sale of a specified number of copies. Similarly, most authors can secure in their contracts provision for an advance from the publisher in anticipation and on account of the specified royalties, and the amount of this advance will depend largely upon the publisher's estimate of the book's prospect of sales.

Because many publishers' invoicing and stock control are now computerised there is a trend towards paying royalties on the price received – which can easily be read from a computer printout – rather than on the published price. Appropriate adjustments are of course made to the royalty figure, and the arrangement is of no intrinsic disadvantage to the author. Royalties are usually paid on either a six-monthly or yearly basis, and the author should check the frequency at the time of signature of the agreement.

Most publishing houses nowadays have printed or word-processed agreement forms in which blanks are left for the insertion of the proposed royalty rates, the sum payable in advance, and so on. The terms are usually agreed between author and publisher before the form is completed, but the fact that a printed form or word-processed agreement has been signed by the publisher does not mean that an author, before signing it, cannot discuss any of its clauses with the publisher. The majority of publishers value the establishment of confidence and understanding between themselves and their authors and are willing to make reasonable amendments.

It is impossible to set out in detail here the numerous provisions of publishing agreements or to comment on the differing effects of these upon different sorts of book. Every sensible author will scrutinise any agreement carefully before signing it, will not hesitate to ask the publisher to explain any point in it which is not clear, and if in any doubt will seek professional advice from a reliable literary agent, or the Society of Authors, or one of the few firms of solicitors who specialise in authors' business.

The careful author will look for a comprehensive clause setting out the contingencies in which the contract is to terminate, what happens if the publisher goes out of business or is taken over, and whether the publisher can sell his rights in the book to a third party without consulting the author.

The agreement should specify the respective responsibilities of author and publisher in the provision of illustrations, indexes, etc. Unexpected fees for reproducing illustrations can swiftly eat up an advance.

The author will examine the clauses covering the handling of overseas sales, American rights and subsidiary rights (film, serial, broadcasting, etc.) which for some books may well bring in more than the book publication rights. A clause covering merchandising rights may also be included. This has more relevance to children's books, but there is a growing potential for adult books.

Consider carefully clauses giving the publisher an option to publish future works and clauses which may restrict a specialist author's future output by preventing him or her from writing other books on the same subject. The author should also be sure that he or she understands what the contract proposes in relation to cheap editions, 'remainders', sheet sales, reprints and new editions.

There should be a clause covering moral rights in the agreement unless the author has consciously waived them. (See the section on moral rights in the article **British Copyright Law**.)

OUTRIGHT SALE

Outright sale of copyright for an agreed sum is rarely suggested by a publisher, and hardly ever to be recommended, though it may be justified in special cases, as when an author is commissioned to supply a small amount of text as a commentary for a book which consists primarily of illustrations, particularly if the author did not originate the idea for the book. It is a survival from the days when copyright meant, for all practical purposes, merely the exclusive right of publication in book form. So long as it was possible to gauge approximately a book's potential sales and the profit to be anticipated, the value of a copyright could be fairly accurately estimated. But to-day, anything from a thousand to a million copies of a book may be sold, and when the various subsidiary rights – the film rights in particular – may prove either valueless or worth thousands of pounds, any arrangement for an outright sale of copyright must be a gamble in which the author is likely to be the loser.

PROFIT-SHARING AND COMMISSION AGREEMENTS

Under a profit-sharing agreement the publisher bears the cost of production, but the author makes no money until the book shows a profit, at which point the profit is divided in agreed proportions between author and publisher. In theory this sounds fair, but it is rarely satisfactory in practice. Such agreements can lend themselves readily to abuse, largely because of the difficulty of defining the term 'profit'.

Under a commission agreement the author bears the cost of production and pays the publisher a commission for marketing the book. If no publisher is prepared to publish a work on the normal royalty basis, the chances are that the author who decides to finance his or her own publication will lose most, if not all, of the money outlaid. In consequence commission agreements, save in exceptional circumstances, are to be discouraged. Many good publishers refuse to handle books on commission in any circumstances whatsoever; others confine their commission publishing to authoritative books of a highly specialised or scholarly nature. The specialist author who decides that commission publishing is justified by special circumstances should make sure that the firm which offers such an arrangement is reputable and able to market the book efficiently.

No firm of standing will publish fiction or poetry on commission, and publishers offering to do so should be given a wide berth. There are a few firms ready to exploit the vanity of a would-be author. Such firms ask the author for a large sum as 'a contribution towards the cost' of producing the book. Too often it more than covers the cost of bringing out a small and shoddy edition, which the 'publisher' makes no effort to distribute.

Further reading

Sir Stanley Unwin, *The Truth About Publishing*, 8th edn 1976, Unwin Hyman O.P.

ed. Charles Clark, *Publishing Agreements: A Book of Precedents*, 3rd edn 1988, Unwin Hyman.

Society of Authors, *Quick Guide: Publishing Contracts*, free to members or £1.50, including postage.

NET BOOK AGREEMENT

The Net Book Agreement is an arrangement, approved by the Restrictive Practices Court as operating in the public interest, designed to improve the availability of a wide range of books to the public through a wide range of outlets. The Agreement, operated by the Publishers Association, enables (but does not require) any publishers who are signatories (whether or not in membership of the PA) to enforce a minimum retail price (the net price) for individual titles, then known as 'net books'. In this way, booksellers are encouraged to hold wide-ranging stocks, secure in the knowledge that the prices of their books, and the value of their stocks, will not be undermined by other retailers who do not provide similar levels of stock or customer-service, such as handling special orders. The Restrictive Practices Court held that, without such a system, the availability of books and the number of booksellers would be reduced, book prices would overall be higher, and fewer titles would be published, with particular loss to those of literary and scholastic value.

Under the arrangement, libraries open to the public, schools and school and church book agencies may be supplied by booksellers at permitted discounts on the net price. School books are normally sold non-net (not subject to the Agreement).

Book Clubs

Book clubs provide their members with selected books (offered either as a main choice or alternative choice) at book club prices, usually through the mail on a regular basis. In order to acquire selected books at special prices book club members are required to commit to the purchase of a number of selections over a given period.

Book clubs can enjoy relatively secure sales and offer savings to their members by buying or printing considerable numbers of copies and offering them to members who have indicated their interest in the type of books offered. These sales can provide valuable revenues to the authors and the publishers of the selected books.

In the case of books otherwise sold as 'net books' through booksellers (see **Net Book Agreement**), the conduct of book clubs is regulated by Book Club Regulations administered by the Publishers Association. These regulations are designed to ensure fairness between book clubs and booksellers offering the same titles.

Sales to book clubs are usually made by the original publisher under the terms of the contract between publisher and author – usually providing a royalty on the number of copies sold.

Artists' Choice (Quarterly) Artists' Choice Ltd, PO Box 3, Huntingdon, Cambs. PE18 0QX   *tel* Bythorn (080 14) 201   *fax* (080 14) 488.

BCA, 87 Newman Street, London W1P 4EN   *tel* 071-637 0341   *fax* 071-631 3262.

Monthly Book Clubs	*Quarterly Book Clubs*
Ancient & Medieval History Book Club	Arts Guild
Childrens Book of the Month Club	Cricket Book Club
History Guild	Encounters
The Literary Guild	Executive World
Military and Aviation Book Society	Home Computer Club
Mystery & Thriller Guild	On the Road
World Books	Quality Paperbacks Direct
	Railway Book Club
	Readers Choice

Bookmarx Club (Quarterly), IS Books Ltd, 265 Seven Sisters Road, London N4 2DE   *tel* 081-802 6145.

Books for Children (Monthly), BFC Limited, Whiteway Court, The Whiteway, Cirencester, Glos. GL7 7BA   *tel* (0285) 657081   *fax* (0285) 657086.

The Bookworm Club, Children's Club in Schools (6 p.a.), Heffers Booksellers, 20 Trinity Street, Cambridge CB2 3NG   *tel* (0223) 358351.

Computer Users Book Club (Cub Club) (Quarterly), Merit Computer Solutions, Merit Business Centre, Crown Avenue, Tredegar, Gwent NP2 4EF   *tel* (0495) 711927   *fax* (0495) 256728.

The Folio Society, 202 Great Suffolk Street, London SE1 1PR   *tel* 071-407 7411   *fax* 071-378 6684. *Showroom:* The Folio Gallery, 5 Royal Arcade, 28 Old Bond Street, London W1X 3HB   *tel* 071-629 6517.

Letterbox Library (Quarterly), Childrens Books Co-operative, 2nd Floor, Leroy House, 436 Essex Road, London N1 3QP   *tel* 071-226 1633   *fax* 071-226 1768.

New Left Review Editions, 6 Meard Street, London W1V 3HR   *tel* 071-734 8839   *fax* 071-734 0059.

Odhams Leisure Group Ltd (Subsidiary of K.L.P. Group plc), Denington Road, Wellingborough, Northants. NN8 2PY   *tel* (0933) 228848. Women's interest series: cookery, needlecraft, children's products.

Poetry Book Society, 21 Earls Court Square, London SW5 9DE   *tel* 071-244 9792.

Pooh Corner Book Club, For all things Pooh, High Street, Hartfield, East Sussex TN7 4AE   *tel* (0892) 770453.

Readers Union Ltd, PO Box 6, Brunel House, Newton Abbot, Devon TQ12 2DW   *tel* (0626) 61121   *telex* 42904 Books G   *fax* (0626) 664463/331374.

Anglers Book Society
Belief: The Religious Book
  Society
Birds and Natural History Book
  Society
Country Book Society
Country Sports Book Society
Craft Book Society
Craftsman Book Society
Design Book Club
Equestrian Book Society

Gardeners Book Society
Maritime Book Society
Music Book Society
Needlecraft Book Society
Photographic Book Society
Popular Science Book Society
Ramblers and Climbers Book
  Society
World of Nature incorporating
  Travel Book Society

Red House Children's Book Club (12 p.a.), Cotswold Business Park, Witney, Oxon OX8 5YF   *tel* (0993) 771144   *fax* (0993) 776813.

Scholastic Publications Ltd, Villiers House, Clarendon Avenue, Leamington Spa, Warks. CV32 5PR   *tel* (0926) 887799   *fax* (0926) 883331.

Travel Book Club (Quarterly), 248-250 Lavender Hill, London SW11 1LJ   *tel* 071-228 6730   *fax* 071-924 1139.

The Women's Press Bookclub (Quarterly), The Women's Press Ltd, 34 Great Sutton Street, London EC1V 0DX   *tel* 071-253 0009   *fax* 071-608 1938.

International Standard Book Numbering (ISBN)

The Standard Book Numbering (SBN) system was introduced in this country in 1967. It became the International Standard Book Numbering (ISBN) system three years later.

The overall administration of the international system is done from Berlin, by the International ISBN-Agentur, Staatsbibliothek Preussicher Kulturbesitz, D-1000 Berlin 30, Postfach 1407, Germany.

In this country the system is administered by the Standard Book Numbering Agency Ltd, 12 Dyott Street, London WC1A 1DF. The Agency was set up before the scheme became international, which is why that word does not appear in its title.

Over the years a number of misconceptions have grown up about ISBNs, and this article endeavours to put right some of these.

The Standard Book Numbering Agency gets a large number of telephone calls, many of which follow a common pattern. For instance:

Are they legal? Do we have to have them?

There is no legal requirement for a book to carry an ISBN. But it is useful to educational authorities, certain library suppliers, public libraries and some computer using distributors, and is now essential to booksellers using the teleordering system. The introduction of Public Lending Right has also made ISBNs of importance to authors.

I am about to publish a book. Must I deposit a copy with the ISBN Agency to obtain copyright?

No. Copyright is obtained by the simple act of publication. However, by law, a copy of every new book must be deposited at the Legal Deposit Office of the British Library, Boston Spa, Wetherby, West Yorkshire LS23 7BY. The copyright office issues a receipt, and this has, in the past, proved useful when a dispute has arisen over the date of publication.

Titles deposited are catalogued by the British National Bibliography, which records ISBNs where available. Perhaps a confusion about copyright and ISBNs arises from this, but the ISBN, of itself, has nothing to do with copyright.

What are the fees for ISBNs?

No charge is made for the allocation of an ISBN. Various publishers who allocate their own usually ask the Agency to supply a computer print out of all the ISBNs available to the publisher, with check digits calculated. A small charge is made for this print out.

If the publisher does not allocate his own ISBNs, not only is there no charge, he may not even know about them. For a few years after the system was introduced, books catalogued by the BNB or Whitaker's may have been assigned ISBNs by the Agency for listing purposes, without reference to the publisher. However, with the widespread use of numbers it is now customary to consult all publishers before any are assigned.

Are you a Government Department?

No. Our parent company pays taxes; we get no subsidy from anyone. In most other countries the costs *are* borne by the state, through the national library system which frequently administers the scheme overseas.

Do I need an ISBN for a Church Magazine?

No. But you may need an ISSN (International Standard Serial Number). These are obtainable from the UK National Serials Data Centre, the British Library, 2 Sheraton Street, London W1V 4BH.

Incidentally, a yearbook can have both an ISBN and an ISSN.

We would prefer to have our own identifier as we do not consider ourselves within the English speaking group.

This comes from publishers with devolution in mind. Usually Welsh, less often Irish. The group system within the ISBN scheme is not quite so categoric as to be dictated by language considerations only. A group is defined as a 'language, geographic or other convenient area'. There is no strict logic applied, just pragmatism as to what is most *convenient* for trading purposes.

I would prefer not to be involved with ISBNs, but there is this Public Lending Right, and the author says . . .

Well, yes. ISBNs have now taken on a new significance; they help authors towards a little more money. The recording system for PLR dues is machine based, and uses ISBNs where available. It is more convenient for the libraries who provide the sample loan statistics if ISBNs are printed in books, but this is not a legal requirement and the system *can* work without ISBNs. However, it works better, and with lower overheads (and so more money available to be allocated to authors) if ISBNs *are* in books.

I want my book to reach as wide a market as possible, so I must have an ISBN.

The ISBN will not automatically sell a book. If the book, like that famous mousetrap, is a better one, the world will beat a path to its door. However, the ISBN will oil the wheels of distribution and it is therefore advisable to have one.

Will you supply an ISBN for a carton of assorted painting books?

No. In the words of the ISBN manual (available from the SBN agency at £3.50, cash with order), 'an ISBN identifies one title, or edition of a title, from one specific publisher, and is unique to that title or edition'. It is now additionally used to identify computer software and maps. It is not designed for a carton of assorted painting books.

How does a publisher who knows nothing about the system and does not want regularly to allocate his own numbers get an ISBN?

The Agency is willing to supply ISBNs for future books, to all the small publishers who have neither the continuity of staff nor the facilities for assigning their own. This offer extends not only to new books, but also to new editions and reprints. If they have not had ISBNs before, publishers should ask the SBN Agency for a standard application form. Written answers are required to six basic questions. Publishers already in the Agency records can obtain ISBNs on request, provided that they can quote firm details of title, edition and the kind of binding.

If, at any stage, a publisher who has not previously assigned his own ISBNs wishes to take over the allocation of his own numbers from the Agency he will be welcome to do so. But it is essential that due warning is given. Otherwise the publisher may assign one number to a given title, and the Agency may well assign a completely different number.

Reproduced by kind permission of the Standard Book Numbering Agency Ltd.

Preparation of materials, resources

Books, Research and Reference Sources for Writers

MARGARET PAYNE, ALA

Almost every writing project will involve the use of books or research at some stage. Some references are quickly found; others require accumulating numerous books or information files on a specific topic and visits to specialist libraries or other relevant places or people. Although research can be an interest or pleasure in itself, it can also be time-consuming, cutting into writing or earning time. Even checking a single fact can take hours or days if you ask the wrong question or check the wrong source first. No article or book can hope to solve all problems – sometimes there are no answers, or the lack of information is itself the answer – but a few guidelines as to routines and sources may save much time and money. The following is an introduction to printed sources. For a more detailed approach, including guides to original and unpublished material, it is recommended you consult Ann Hoffmann's *Research for Writers*, Black, 1986, £7.99, a most useful book which covers methods, sources, specific organisations and specialist libraries.

Suggestions for a core collection of reference books to own are given below under the WRITER'S REFERENCE BOOKSHELF. The final choice of title often depends on personal preference and interests, space, the frequency with which it needs to be consulted, its cost and the proximity of your nearest public reference library. Anyone living in or near a large city has an advantage over the country dweller. Those living within easy reach of London have the best advantage of all: a choice of major reference libraries; a variety of specialist sources such as headquarters of various societies, companies and organisations; academic and other specialist libraries and the government. Often a question can be answered much nearer home, but you may find the further back in time you go, or the more detailed your research, the further afield you need to travel.

CHECKING A FACT

What do you really want to know?

Clarifying your question in advance can save much work for you or your researcher. If you want to check someone's date of birth and know the person is alive or very recently dead and in *Who's Who*, then ask for that book, or phrase your telephone request so that the librarian goes straight to that source. Do not start with general questions such as 'Where are the biographies?' In a branch library you may be shown sections of individual lives; on the telephone you are adding to British Telecom's profits and your telephone bill, as well as wasting time. If the person is dead, did he or she die recently enough to have a newspaper obituary – it often mentions the date of birth – or long enough ago to be in a volume of *Who Was Who* or the *Dictionary of National Biography*? Never assume that information that you know is necessarily common knowledge; it needs to be specified.

Go straight to the index.

Most reference books are arranged in alphabetical order but, if not, they should have an index. Some indexes may seem inadequate, but have you used the right key word? A good index should refer you from the one not used. For example, some will use carpentry and ignore woodwork as an entry. Others will ignore both and go straight to the object to be made or repaired. If there is no index, turn first to the contents page, as in some books the index is at the front rather than the back.

Is it important to be up to date?

Most books have the date of publication on the back of the title page. Is the answer given one which may be surpassed or superseded? Despite some instant publishing, when dealing with statistics most books have a built in obsolescence. There is a cut off date when the text goes to the printer and the updating must wait for the next edition. Some current events are too recent to be found in books at all, although well documented at the time in newspapers and magazines (see below).

If in doubt, re-check your answer.

If the answer is of importance, try not to depend on one source. Mistakes can occur in print or in transcribing. Sometimes it is necessary to check another source for verification or to obtain another point of view. In all cases you should . . .

Note your source.

Even if you think you will remember, always note where you find your information, preferably next to the answer, or in a card file or book where it can be easily found. Note the title, author, publisher and date of publication as well as the page number. Nothing is more annoying than having to undertake the same search twice.

RESEARCHING A SUBJECT

Reference has already been made to Ann Hoffmann's book for detail, but Kipling's six honest serving men can still be the basis for any subject: What? Why? When? How? Where? Who? cover aspects of most enquiries. The starting point depends on the writer's personal knowledge of the subject. Where it is unfamiliar always start from the general and go on to the particular. An article in an encyclopedia can fill in the background and often recommend bibliographies or other references. If an article in the *Encyclopaedia Britannica* is too detailed or too complex, try *The World Book*. The latter may be in the children's library, but because it has to appeal to a wider readership, the text and illustrations are clearer. Avoid a detailed book on the subject until you need it; it may tell you more than you want to know.

The following sources are suggestions as sources of information, but not all will be relevant to your subject.

Reference Libraries. Use the largest one in your vicinity for encylopedias, specialised reference books, annuals and for back numbers of newspapers and periodicals. Ask for *Walford's Guide to Reference Material*. The three volumes list the standard reference works of subjects, most of which should be available for consultation.

Lending Libraries. Find the class number of the books you want, and see what is available.

Special Libraries. *The Aslib Directory of Information Sources in the United Kingdom* should be available in your reference library. It gives details of special libraries of industries, organisations and societies.

Catalogues, bibliographies and subject guides. Some libraries publish their catalogues, but this is becoming less frequent. There is a series of subject catalogues to the British Library (formerly the British Museum Library) up to 1975 and the *British National Bibliography* updates this (*see* COMPILING A BIBLIOGRAPHY below).

Newspapers and bibliographies. There is a monthly index to *The Times*, cumulated annually, which often provides the date of an event. The index also includes the *The Times Supplements*. For periodical articles, begin with the *British Humanities Index*, and, if necessary, check also the specialist indexes and abstracting journals such as *Current Technology Index*. Your public library can often locate runs of periodicals and magazines, and the interloan service can obtain specific periodical articles if you have the details. *Profile*, an on line index to quality newspapers, is the most up to date available, but retrospective only to 1985 and few libraries have the facility as yet.

COMPILING A BIBLIOGRAPHY

Checking what books are already available may reveal both the range of titles already in print and the potential market for your work. If yours is to be the tenth book on the subject published in the last two years, saturation point may be near. On the other hand, if you know the books and believe you can do better, or have evolved a different approach, you can mention this in a covering letter to a potential publisher. A quick way to evaluate what is available is by checking the shelves of a public library or bookstore, but it should be remembered that in a library, many of the best books will be on loan. This practice also makes one aware of publishers' interests.

A more comprehensive and systematic list of recent books can be compiled by consulting the *British National Bibliography*, a cumulating list based on the copyright books in the British Library, with advance notice (up to three months) of new books through the Cataloguing in Publication scheme. The arrangement is by the Dewey Decimal Classification used in all public libraries. Other subject lists are less satisfactory to consult. The British Museum (now British Library) has a series of subject indexes up to 1975, and many British books are included in the American *Cumulative Book Index* (1928 on). *Whitaker's Books in Print* is predominantly an author-title list, but does index some books under the key word of a subtitle; as its name implies, out of print books are excluded.

Facilities now exist to obtain a bibliography on any subject by using one of the computer data banks based on the British Library, the Library of Congress or commercial firms. The difficulties are expense (£25.00 per hour) and, at the time of going to press, some initial teething problems.

OBTAINING BOOKS

Books in print. In 1990 63,980 different books were published in the United Kingdom alone, joining the many thousands of other titles still in print from previous years. The number of books available means that the chances of finding a copy of what you want on your bookseller's shelf, when you want it, may be slim. But if it is in print it can be ordered for you, although delivery times vary with each publisher. Most large bookshops and libraries now have the monthly microfiche editions of *Whitaker's Books in Print* giving details of author, publisher, price, number of pages and international standard book number (ISBN). The latter is often useful for speeding the order.

Out of print books present more difficulty. Generally the older the book, the more difficult it may be to obtain. Such books are no longer available from the publishers, who retain only a file copy, all other stocks having been sold. Therefore unless you are lucky enough to find an unsold copy on a bookseller's shelves, it must be sought in the second-hand market or through a library loan. There are many specialist second-hand and antiquarian booksellers, and a number of directories listing them and their interests. The most well known are *Sheppard's Book Dealers in the British Isles*, now published by Europa, and Peter Marcan's *Directory of Specialist Book Dealers in the United Kingdom*. Copies of these should be in your local reference library. Many advertise in *Book and Magazine Collector*, a monthly magazine, which has an extensive 'wants' column.

Public libraries should be able to obtain books for you, whether or not they are in print, either from their own stock, from other libraries in the system or through the interloan scheme. This operates through the British Lending Library, but all requests must go through your library as you cannot apply direct. Your local library tickets may sometimes be used in other libraries, but different issuing systems have discouraged this in recent years.

A WRITER'S REFERENCE BOOKSHELF

However good and accessible a public library may be, there are some books required for constant or instant consultation, which should be within easy reach of the desk or typewriter. The choice of title may vary, but the following list is offered as suggestions for a core collection.

1. **Dictionaries.** With the use of word processor packages, a dictionary is no longer quite so essential for spelling checks, although still needed to clarify definitions and meanings. A book is often easier to consult, and portable. The complete *Oxford English Dictionary* is not, and although the definitive work, neither the full nor the compact edition with its magnifying glass, nor the two volume *Shorter Oxford Dictionary* is easy to handle for quick reference, so a one volume dictionary is more practical. The number of new words and meanings coming into vogue suggests a replacement every five years or so, or supplementing your choice by a good paperback edition. If you use an old copy, you will be surprised by the improved format and readability of the new editions.

The most popular one volume dictionaries are the *Concise Oxford Dictionary* (8th ed. 1990, £10.95 – 80,000 definitions), *Chambers' English Dictionary* (5th ed. 1991, £18.95 – 150,000 entries, appealing to crossword addicts), *The Collins English Dictionary* (£19.99 – 110,000 entries). A recommended paperback dictionary is *Oxford Paperback Dictionary* (1988, £3.95 – 50,000 entries). If you write for the American market, it is advisable also to have an American dictionary to check variant spellings and meanings. The equivalent of the Oxford family of dictionaries is Webster's, the most popular one volume edition being *Webster's New World Dictionary* (Merriam U.S., 3rd ed. 1988, £14.50).

2. **Roget's Thesaurus.** When the exact word or meaning eludes you, the thesaurus may help clear a mental block. There are many versions of Roget available, both in hardback and paperback, including a revision by E.M. Kirkpatrick (Longman, 1987, £14.95) and a paperback edition from Penguin (1984, £4.95).

3. **Grammar and English usage.** A wide choice is available but Fowler's *Modern English Usage* remains a standard work (2nd ed. revised Sir Ernest Gowers, Oxford UP, £10.95 and £5.95 paperback). Many prefer Sir Ernest Gowers' *Complete Plain Words* (3rd ed. 1986 revised Sidney Greenbaum and Jane Whitcut, HMSO, £5.50; Penguin 1987, £4.99). More recent works are *The Oxford Guide to English Language* (Oxford UP, 1984, £17.50 and £5.99) and *Bloomsbury Good Word Guide* (Bloomsbury, 2nd ed. 1990, £16.99), and Michael Legat's *The Nuts and Bolts of Writing* (Hale, 1989, £9.95 and £4.95).

4. **Encyclopedias and annuals.** Multi-volume encyclopedias are both expensive and space consuming. They are best left for consultation at the nearest reference library, where the most up-to-date versions should be available, unless your need justifies ownership. Of the single volumes, *Pears Cyclopaedia* contains a surprising amount of general information and a new edition is issued annually (Pelham Books, 99th ed. 1990, £12.95). For those concerned with current affairs, the complete edition of *Whitaker's Almanack* has valuable statistics and information on government and countries, as well as many miscellaneous facts not found elsewhere. For annual replacement if constantly used.

5. **Atlases, gazetteers and road maps.** These also need replacing with updated editions from time to time. An old edition can be misleading with recent changes of placenames and metrication. The *The Times Atlas of the World* is the definitive work, but it is expensive and bulky for quick reference. The *The Times Concise Atlas of the World* (Times Books, 1986, £29.50) has the most comprehensive gazetteer-index. It is a little more manageable but still requires special shelving.

With the building of the M25 and other motorways, many existing road atlases of Britain may be out of date and need replacing. There are many paperback editions at 3 miles to 1 inch (1:190,080) for less than £5.00, but most detailed is *AZ Great Britain Road Atlas* (Geographers AZ, 1990, £5.99; 1:250,000) with 31,000 place names and 56 town maps. Hardbacks recommended by *Which?* magazine are *AZ Great Britain Road Atlas* (1990, £12.95; 1:200,000) and *Ordnance Survey Touring Atlas of Great Britain* (Hamlyn, 1990, £19.95). The *Reader's Digest Driver's Atlas of the British Isles* (1988, £19.95) includes Ireland. For London and environs *Greater London Street Atlas* (AA/Geographia, 6th ed., 1989, £8.99 paperback) is a detailed 3.12 miles to 1 inch street map for the whole M25 area.

6. **Literary companions and dictionaries.** There are many to choose from, and frequency of consultation will determine whether all or some of the following are desirable. *Brewer's Dictionary of Phrase and Fable* (14th ed., Cassell, 1991, £16.95 and £9.95) avoids many distractions and diversions by settling queries, as does *The Oxford Companion to English Literature* (5th ed. edited by Margaret Drabble, Oxford UP, 1985, £19.95). This new edition complements rather than replaces Sir Paul Harvey's earlier editions. Either can be used for checking an author's work, but the definitive and exhaustive lists are to be found in the *New Cambridge Bibliography of English Literature*. The four volumes and the index volume can be found in major reference libraries.

7. **Books of quotations.** Once divorced from their text and unattributed, quotations are not easy to trace. This should be a warning to any writer or researcher to note author, title and page number to any item copied. Tracing quotations

often needs resort to more than one collection, but the most popular anthologies are *The Oxford Dictionary of Quotations* (3rd ed., Oxford UP, 1985, £25.00) and the *Bloomsbury Dictionary of Quotations* (Bloomsbury, 2nd ed. 1991, £17.99). The *Oxford Dictionary of Modern Quotations* (Oxford UP, 1991, £14.95) and *The Twentieth Century Quotations* (Sphere, 1987, £4.99).

8. **Biographical dictionaries.** *Pears Cyclopaedia* contains a brief but useful section, but for a fuller working tool the standard works are *Chambers' Biographical Dictionary* (Chambers, 5th ed. 1990, £30.00, paperback £17.99 – 15,000 entries) or the American-biased *Webster's New Biographical Dictionary* (Merriam U.S., 1990, £21.00 – 150,000 entries). Frequency of consultation will determine whether you need a personal copy of *Who's Who* or the *Concise Dictionary of National Biography*, which are available in most libraries.

9. **Dates, anniversaries and names.** A brief guide to anniversaries is included in the Journalists' Calendar section of this book (see **Index**). *Chambers' Dates* (Chambers, 1989, £5.99 paperback), is the most used work. Leslie Dunkling's *Guinness Book of Names* (Guinness, 4th ed. 1991, £8.99) is an encyclopedic source on its subject from first names to places and pubs, with a comprehensive index.

10. **Working directories for writers.** A current copy of *Writers' & Artists' Yearbook* is essential, as recent moves and mergers have made so many publishers' details out of date. It is useful for very much more information besides that found in the first section. Browse through, or use the index, in spare moments to familiarise yourself with its contents for future reference.

Frequency of consultation will determine whether you also need *Willings Press Guide* (annual, British Media Publications). *Benn's Media Directory* (Benn, 2 vols. annual) is expensive; both are very comprehensive in their coverage of British and overseas newspapers, magazines and other media information. *Cassell's Directory of Publishing* complements all the above, but gives more information about publishing personnel not found elsewhere.

SOME BOOKS ABOUT WRITING AND THE BOOK TRADE

The book trade has changed considerably in the last decades. The paperback explosion of the seventies appears to have settled down, as has the bookshop chain development. In publishing, computerisation is beginning to affect many aspects and recent mergers and takeovers of publishing companies large and small are now leading to many staff changes, though not as yet reducing the number of titles published annually. Partly for that reason, much material in older books is inapplicable, although a few remain important for historical reasons. The following is a selection from recent publications. It does not include any of the many books on writing specific types of novels or articles which are best examined in a library or book shop before purchase.

Bolt, David. *The Author's Handbook*. Piatkus Books, 1986. £7.95 & £3.95. Written to fill some of the gaps in the author's search for information.
Bonham-Carter, Victor. *Authors by Profession, volume 2: From the Copyright Act 1911 until the End of 1981*. Bodley Head, 1984, o.p. Volume 1 published by the Society of Authors covered the history of authorship up to 1911; the present volume brings it closer to date.
Clark, Giles N. *Inside Book Publishing: a career builder's guide*. Blueprint, 1988. £6.95. Intended to give an overview to young publishers, it describes the processes and business of modern publishing.

Curwen, Peter. *The World Book Industry*. Euromonitor, 1986, £38.00. The only book attempting a world survey, but marred by a lack of index. To be dipped into rather than read.

Legat, Michael. *An Author's Guide to Publishing*. Robert Hale, 1987. £4.95. Assumes no experience of publishing; a useful, clear introduction with a glossary.

Legat, Michael. *Writing for Pleasure and Profit*. Robert Hale, 1987. £5.95. The best of the recent introductions to writing, covering novels, non-fiction and other topics briefly but clearly.

Mumby, F.A. *Publishing and Bookselling in the Twentieth Century*. Unwin Hyman, 6th ed. paperback 1984. £8.95. Revised by Ian Norrie to include events up to 1970, this is the best historical survey.

Owen, Peter (ed.) *Publishing – the Future*. Peter Owen, 1988. £6.95. A collection of articles by leading figures on various aspects of the book trade today.

Waterhouse, Keith. *Waterhouse on Newspaper Style*. Viking, 1989. £9.95. Based on the *Daily Mirror* house style, it contains much information on writing succinctly and clearly.

Journalists' Calendar
1992

SELECTED ANNIVERSARIES

JANUARY

1 1942 **United Nations Declaration;** 26 nations signed the pact in Washington, to (i) employ full war resources against axis powers, and (ii) co-operate with co-signatories, and make no separate peace or armistice.

2 1892 Death of **Sir George Airy,** English Astronomer Royal who modernised the Greenwich Observatory.

1892 Birth of J(ohn) R(onald) R(euel) **Tolkien.** *The Hobbit.* (Died 1973.)

4 1967 **Donald Campbell** killed on Coniston Water in *Bluebird K7* during an attempt to break his own **Water Speed Record.**

5 1942 Birth of **Maurizio Pollini,** Italian pianist.

6 1367 Birth of **King Richard II.**

8 1642 Death of **Galileo,** Italian mathematician, physicist and astronomer.

10 1917 Death of **William Frederick Cody,** known as **'Buffalo Bill',** American Indian fighter and showman.

13 1842 Birth of **Heinrich Hofmann,** German pianist and composer.

14 1742 Death of **Edmund Halley,** English Astronomer Royal.

17 1942 Birth of **Cassius Clay, (Muhammad Ali).** (See also 8 May 1967.)

18 1892 Birth of **Oliver Hardy,** American film actor, of the comedy partnership **Laurel & Hardy.**

20 1942 **The Wannsee Conference** held in secret in Berlin, at which the SS outlined plans for Germany's final solution to the 'Jewish problem'.

22 1942 Death of **Walter Sickert,** British painter.

23 1967 **Milton Keynes** designated as a **new town** for 250,000 Londoners.

24 1917 Birth of American film actor **Ernest Borgnine.** *Marty.*

29 1942 **BBC Radio:** First transmission of **Desert Island Discs.** Comedian and actor Victor Oliver was the first guest.

31 1892 Birth of American comedian **Eddy Cantor** (born Edward Israel Iskowitz). (Died 1964.)

FEBRUARY

6 1952 Death of **King George VI.**

1952 Accession of **Queen Elizabeth II.**

10 1567 Murder of **Henry, Lord Darnley,** second husband of **Mary Queen of Scots** and father of **James I.**

13 1542 Execution of **Catherine Howard,** fifth wife of **Henry VIII.**

1692 **Glencoe Massacre;** Scottish Highlands. The **Macdonald** clan was massacred by the **Campbells.**

15 1942 **WWII: British naval base at Singapore** surrendered to the Japanese. 60,000 British and Empire troops captured. 9000 British, Indian and Australian troops died during the battle.

18 1967 Death of **Robert Oppenheimer,** American physicist who led the team that developed the **atomic bomb.**

19 1717 Birth of **David Garrick,** English actor and theatre manager.

23 1792 Death of **Sir Joshua Reynolds,** English portrait painter. First President of the **Royal Academy.**

29 1792 Birth of **Gioacchino Rossini,** Italian composer. *The Barber of Seville* and *William Tell.*

MARCH

1 1867 **Nebraska** became the 37th state of the Union.

3 1792 Death of **Robert Adam,** Scottish architect and interior designer.

6 1967 Death of **Nelson Eddy,** American singer.

7 1792 Birth of **Sir John Herschel,** English astronomer.

8 1717 Death of **Abraham Darby,** English ironmaster and first person to use coke to smelt iron, a process that revolutionised the iron and steel industry.

1917 Death of **Count Ferdinand von Zeppelin,** German airship pioneer.

10 1892 Birth of **Arthur Honegger,** French composer. *King David* and *Pacific 231.*

11 1982 Trident: John Nott, Secretary for Defence, told the House of Commons that Britain was to purchase the American **Trident D5** nuclear missile system at a price of $7.5bn.

12 1917 Izvestia, the official newspaper of the USSR, was founded, following the February revolution. (See 5 May 1912: *Pravda.*)

15 1767 Birth of **Andrew Jackson, 'Old Hickory',** 7th American President.

1842 Death of **Luigi Cherubini,** Italian-born French composer. *The Water Carrier* (opera).

1892 Jesse W. Reno of New York patented the **first commercially successful escalator.**

1917 Russia: Tsar Nicholas II forced to abdicate, thus ending over 300 years of Romanov rule and nearly 1000 years of imperial rule. His son was ruled out of succession in favour of the Tsar's brother, **Grand Duke Michael.** He in turn refused, in favour of a provisional government.

18 1967 The oil tanker **Torrey Canyon** carrying 120,000 tons of crude oil was wrecked on the Pollard Rock between the Isles of Scilly and Land's End.

20 1917 Birth of **Dame Vera Lynn** (born Vera Welch), known as **'The Forces Favourite'.**

21 1967 First North Sea Gas was pumped ashore at Easington, County Durham.

23 1842 Death of French novelist **Stendhal.** (Real name **Marie Henri Beyle.**)

25 1867 Birth of **Arturo Toscanini,** Italian conductor and musical director.

26 1892 Death of **Walt Whitman,** American poet.

27-28 1942 WWII: Commandos made a night raid on French port of **St Nazaire. 'Operation Chariot',** in which an old destroyer, the *Campbeltown,* full of explosives, was rammed against the main dock gate in order to put the port out of action for the rest of the war.

28 Women's Army Auxiliary Corps founded.

1942 Birth of **Neil Kinnock,** leader of the Labour Party.

30 1842 Dr Crawford Long performed the **first operation under anaesthetic** using ether.

1867 Alaska acquired by the United States from Russia for $7.2m. (Less than two cents an acre.)

APRIL

1 1917 Death of **Scott Joplin,** American pianist and composer of **'ragtime'.**

1967 Sir Edmund Compton took office as Great Britain's first **Ombudsman** (Parliamentary Commissioner for Administration).

2 1982 Falklands War: Argentina invaded the Falkland Islands.

4 1617 Death of **John Napier,** Scottish mathematician and inventor of **logarithm tables.**

5 1982 Falklands War: Lord Carrington resigned as Foreign Secretary. His place was taken by **Francis Pym.** The British Task Force set sail for the Falklands.

6 1917 WWI: USA declared war on Germany. (The first US troops arrived in France on 26 June.)

7 1947 Death of **Henry Ford,** American automobile manufacturer.

8 1492 Death of **Lorenzo de Medici,** Italian statesman and patron of the arts. **'Lorenzo the Magnificent',** he is considered the most brilliant of the Medici.

9 1917 WWI: Battle of Vimy Ridge. Canadian forces captured Vimy Ridge and 6000 German prisoners. The Germans lost 20,000 men, the Canadians 3000.

1942 WWII: Japanese bombers sank aircraft carrier **HMS Hermes** off Ceylon. The **Bataan Peninsula** in the Philippines fell to the Japanese. Some 35,000 American and Filipino troops fell into Japanese hands making it the largest ever American surrender. Prisoners began the forced **'Bataan Death March'** from Balanga to San Fernando, in which thousands died.

13 1742 First ever performance of Handel's 'Messiah', at the Music Hall, Dublin.

1892 Birth of **Arthur Harris, 'Bomber Harris',** English air force Commander.

1917 Birth of **Howard Keel,** American actor and singer. *Annie Get Your Gun.*

14 1892 **Rudolf Diesel** patented his engine design.

1917 Death of **Dr Ludwig Zamenhof,** Russian linguist and creator of **Esperanto.**

16 1867 Birth of **Wilbur Wright,** American aviation pilot. (Brother of Orville Wright.)

1942 WWII: Island of **Malta** awarded the **George Cross Medal.** (The island had to withstand 2000 air raids in a period of just four months.)

19 1892 Birth of **Germaine Tailleferre** (born Taillefesse), French composer.

1967 Death of **Konrad Adenauer,** West German statesman and first post-war Chancellor.

21 1967 **Military coup in Greece.** Monarchy deposed. Constantine Kollias appointed Prime Minister. Military rule ended 23 July; democracy restored November 1974.

23 1967 Soviet spaceship **Union 1** launched. Crashed on 24th when parachute failed, killing Col. Komarov. First recorded space fatality.

24 1892 Birth of **Jack Hulbert,** English actor. (Died 1978.)

25 1792 **The guillotine** used for the first time in Paris. The victim was a young highwayman named Pelletier.

1792 The '**Marseillaise**' composed by **Claude Joseph Rouget de Lisle** during the French Revolution. Originally entitled *War Song of the Army of the Rhine* or *Chant de guerre de l'armée du Rhin,* the anthem came to be called '**La Marseillaise**' because of its popularity with volunteer army units from Marseille. Was not adopted as the National Anthem until July 1795.

26 1942 **The world's worst mine disaster** took place in Hinkeiko Colliery, in China. 1572 died.

28 1942 Birth of **Mike Brearley,** former Middlesex and England cricketer.

1442 Birth of **King Edward IV.**

MAY

2 1892 Birth of **Baron Manfred von Richthofen, 'The Red Baron',** German Air Ace of WWI. (Died 1918.)

1982 **Falklands War:** Argentine cruiser **General Belgrano,** the country's second largest warship, was hit by Tigerfish torpedoes fired from British submarine **HMS Conqueror.** Around 800 men were rescued from crew of 1042.

1982 **The Mail on Sunday** launched. Great Britain's first new national newspaper for 21 years.

4 1982 **Falklands War: HMS Sheffield,** type 42 destroyer, was hit by Argentine Exocet missile, fired from a Super Etendard fighter-bomber. Ship caught fire and 20 died in the blaze.

4-8 1942 **WWII: Battle of the Coral Sea:** First naval battle fought entirely by planes launched from aircraft carriers.

5 1912 First issue of **Pravda,** Russian newspaper. (See 12 March 1917: *Izvestia.*)

1967 Great Britain's **first satellite Ariel III** was launched from Vandenberg air base in California.

7 1892 Birth of **Josep Broz Tito,** Yugoslav statesman and post-war President of Yugoslavia. (Died 1980.)

8 1967 **Muhammad Ali (Cassius Clay)** was stripped of his title by the World Boxing authorities for refusing to serve in the US army. He was sentenced to five years' imprisonment on 20 June, but the decision was reversed in 1971. (See 17 January 1942.)

1962 **Trolleybuses ran for the last time in London.** No. 1521 on Route 604, Wimbledon to Fullwell Depot. (See 5 July 1952: Last Tram in London.)

11 1892 Birth of **Margaret Rutherford,** English actress. (Died 1972.)

12 1842 Birth of **Jules Massenet,** French composer. (Died 1912.)

13 1842 Birth of **Sir Arthur Sullivan,** English composer of light operas in collaboration with **W.S. Gilbert.**

1717 Birth of **Maria Theresa,** Empress of Austria.

14 1842 **The Illustrated London News** first published.

1967 **Liverpool's Roman Catholic cathedral** opened by Cardinal Heenan. (Nicknamed 'The Mersey Funnel'.)

15 1567 Birth of **Claudio Monteverdi,** Italian composer.

1967 Death of **Edward Hopper,** American painter.

21 1982 Falklands War: British troops
landed at Port San Carlos, East Falkland,
and established a bridgehead. Some three
hours later Argentine planes attacked
ships anchored in Falkland Sound.
Despite suffering heavy losses they
managed to destroy HMS *Ardent*.

1917 Birth of **Raymond Burr**, American
film actor. *Ironside*.

24 1792 Death of **Lord Rodney (George
Bridges),** British Admiral. Famous
victory at the **'Battle of the Saints'**.

25 1982 Falklands War: HMS Coventry
attacked and sunk by Argentine
bombers. A container ship *Atlantic
Conveyer,* used by the Navy to carry
munitions, also sunk.

1967 Celtic, the Scottish champions,
became the first British football club to
win the **European Cup,** beating
Internazionale, 2-1 in Lisbon.

27 1867 Birth of (Enoch) **Arnold Bennett,**
English novelist. *The Old Wives' Tale*.

1942 WWII: Assassination by Czech
resistance of **Reinhard Heydrich,** Deputy
Commander of the SS in Bohemia and
Moravia. Died of his wounds 4.6.42. (See
9 June: Lidice Massacre.)

28 1967 Francis Chichester arrived back at
Plymouth after sailing single handed
round the world in the yacht *Gipsy Moth
IV.* (See 7 July 1967.)

1982 Falklands War: British forces
launched attack on Port Darwin, the
islands' second largest settlement, and
Goose Green. Port Darwin captured on
the same day, Goose Green surrendered
on 28th; official surrender signed on 29th.

29 1917 Birth of **John Fitzgerald Kennedy,**
American statesman and 35th President.
(Assassinated 1963.)

1942 Death of **John Barrymore,**
American actor, called **'The Great
Profile'**.

**30 1942 WWII: First 1000-bomber raid on
Cologne** by the RAF. 39 aircraft lost and
1455 tons of bombs dropped.

1967 Death of **Claude Rains,** British-
born actor.

1967 Biafra declared itself an
independent republic, and no longer part
of the Nigerian federation.

JUNE

1 1977 Police Complaints Board was set
up. Name changed to Police Complaints
Authority in April 1986.

1792 Kentucky became the 15th state of
the Union.

3 1942 Birth of **Curtis Mayfield,** American
rhythm and blues singer, songwriter,
producer and guitarist.

4 1792 Death of **John Burgoyne,** British
general and playwright.

4-6 1942 WWII: Battle of Midway
commenced. The Japanese were forced
to retreat, marking a turning point in the
war in the Pacific.

5 1967 'Six Day' War began between
Egypt (with support from Jordan, Syria,
Iraq and Lebanon) and Israel, following
serious provocation by Arab and Israeli
attack against their airfields.
6th: UN Security Council met in
emergency session; oil supplies to UK
and USA cut off by several Arab
countries following Egypt's accusations
of Anglo-American aid to Israel; the Suez
Canal was closed; Israeli forces advanced
into Jordan and Egypt.
7th: Israel and then Jordan agreed to UN
ceasefire call.
8th: Egypt followed suit and Syria gave
in on the **9th.** War ended on the **10th,**
though minor skirmishes continued.
Israel had captured the old city of
Jerusalem, the West Bank, the Sinai,
Gaza Strip and the Golan Heights.

6 1982 Israel invaded Lebanon with the
objective of destroying the strongholds of
the PLO.
7th: UN Resolution 509 called for the
immediate Israeli withdrawal.
14th: Israelis completed the encirclement
of Beirut and laid siege to the capital,
where at least 6000 Palestinian guerrillas
were trapped.
19th: Israelis moved into the centre of
Beirut and took up positions along the
'green line' separating the Christian east
from the Muslim west.

8 1982 Falklands War: HMS **Plymouth,**
frigate, and landing ships, **Sir Galahad**
and **Sir Tristram,** were attacked and
damaged by Argentine jets. Over 40 men
were killed and nearly 60 injured.

1867 Birth of **Frank Lloyd Wright,**
American architect and writer. Pioneered
the design of modern American housing.
Designed the Guggenheim Museum,
New York City.

10 1692 Execution of **Bridget Bishop,** first
of the **'Salem Witches'** to be hanged.

1942 WWII: Lidice Massacre: On direct orders of Hitler, Nazi troops shot the entire male population of Lidice (199 men) in retaliation for the assassination of SS Commander Reinhard Heydrich (see 27 May). The 195 women residents of Lidice were imprisoned in concentration camps, and the 98 children of the village were sent to other penal institutions.

1967 Death of **Spencer Tracy,** American film actor.

11 1667 Second Anglo-Dutch War: Raiding of the Medway. The Dutch fleet under Admiral de Ruyter sailed up the Medway, bombarding Sheerness and landing 800 men on the Isle of Sheppey. **12th:** Destroyed the dockyard and six ships at Chatham, carrying off the flagship *Royal Charles*.

12 1842 Death of **Thomas Arnold,** English educationalist, who pioneered the reform of the English public school system.

13 1977 The Commission for Racial Equality established.

1892 Birth of **Basil Rathbone,** English stage and film actor, best known for his role in *Sherlock Holmes*. (Died 1967.)

15 1982 Falklands War: Surrender document signed. Announcing the surrender in the Commons, Mrs Thatcher said an unexpected total of 15,000 Argentine prisoners had been taken: the victory at Port Stanley was won by 6000 soldiers and marines who were opposed by an Argentine garrison of 11,000.

1962 Great Britain's first commercial nuclear power station, at Berkeley, Gloucestershire, came on line and began supplying power to the National Grid.

17 1917 Birth of **Dean Martin** (born Dino Paul Crocetti), American actor and entertainer.

1967 China exploded her first **H-bomb.**

18 1942 Birth of **Paul McCartney,** English musician.

1982 Roberto Calvi, chairman of Italy's largest banking group Banco Ambrosiano, was found hanging from scaffolding beneath Blackfriars Bridge, London. He had been due to appear in court in Italy on 21st to appeal against a gaol sentence for currency offences. (Death soon followed and was later to become linked with the P2 masonic lodge scandal, which involved many high-ranking Italian officials and public figures.)

21 1892 Birth of **Hilding Rosenberg,** Swedish composer.

1942 WWII: Fall of Tobruk. German Afrika Corps under Rommel took over 30,000 prisoners. Rommel was promoted to Field Marshal on the 26th for his victories against the 8th Army.

22 1917 Death of **Sir Joseph Lyons,** chairman and founder of the business **J. Lyons Ltd** – originator of the Lyons corner houses and teashops.

24 1717 The Grand Lodge of Freemasons inaugurated in London. Anthony Sayer elected first Grand Master.

25 1767 Death of **Georg Philipp Telemann,** German composer.

1967 First world-wide tv programme: Our World was seen via live satellite link in 26 countries by an estimated 400 million viewers.

26 1917 WWI: First contingent of the American Expeditionary Force landed in France, with General John Pershing as their commander-in-chief. (See 6 April 1917.)

1892 Birth of **Pearl Buck** (born Pearl Sydenstricker), American author. Winner of 1938 Nobel Prize for Literature. *The Good Earth*.

1967 Barclays became the **first high street bank** to introduce cash dispenser cards. (Enfield branch.)

29 1967 Death of **Jayne Mansfield,** American film actress, killed in a car crash in New Orleans.

JULY

1 1892 Birth of US novelist **James Cain.** *The Postman Always Rings Twice*. (Died 1977.)

1817 Sovereigns became legal tender for the first time in Great Britain, by Royal Proclamation. (Ceased to be legal tender on 28.2.1891.)

1967 BBC2 began the **first colour tv transmissions** in Europe.

4 1892 James Keir Hardie of Holytown, Lanarkshire, became **first Socialist to be elected as Member of Parliament** in the General Election of 1892. (At this time Hardie did not represent the Labour Party. Elected as an Independent in the seat of West Ham South.)

1862 Alice in Wonderland: On a picnic Charles Lutwidge Dodgson told the story of what happened to a girl named Alice after she fell down a rabbit hole. Ten-year-old Alice Liddell, the model for the heroine, insisted that he wrote it down. Dodgson did so under the pen-name Lewis Carroll and the book was called *Alice's Adventures in Wonderland.* (Published 1865.)

5 **1942 WWII:** Russian-bound **PQ-17 shipping convoy** came under severe German aircraft and U-boat attack. 22 US and 11 British merchant ships were lost. As a result of these severe losses, all shipping convoys to the Soviet Union were suspended until September, which in turn strained UK/US relations with Stalin. Only 11 ships reached USSR.

1952 London's last tram in passenger service, No. 1951 on Route 40, made its last journey from Perrot Street, Woolwich, to New Cross Depot. Journey ended in the early hours of 6th. (See also 8 May 1962: Last Trolleybus in London.)

6 **1917 WWI: Lawrence of Arabia (T.E. Lawrence),** leading Sheik Faisal's army, captured the strategic port of Aqaba from the Turks. Victory gave a much needed boost to the Arab forces following a series of British setbacks. The capture removed the danger of a Turkish raid through the Sinai against the Suez Canal or British army communication lines in Palestine.

1892 Dadabhai Naoroji, Liberal, was elected Great Britain's **first coloured Member of Parliament,** for Finsbury Central in London.

7 **1967 Francis Chichester,** publicly dubbed a Knight, at Greenwich. The Queen used Sir Francis Drake's sword. (See 28 May 1967.)

8 **1967** Death of **Vivien Leigh,** English film actress. *Gone with the Wind.*

9 **1942 Anne Frank,** aged 13, **went into hiding with her family** and several other Jews in a secret apartment in an Amsterdam office-block/warehouse. (Remained hidden until 1944; died in a concentration camp.)

10 **1962 Launch of Telstar,** the world's first active telecommunications satellite. Began transmitting live television pictures from the USA on the 11th.

1792 Birth of **Frederick Marryat,** English writer of novels on sea life. *The Little Savage* and *The Children of the New Forest.*

11 **1767** Birth of **John Quincy Adams,** 6th President of the USA 1825-29 and son of John Adams, 2nd President. Considered one of America's greatest diplomats. As Secretary of State he was chiefly responsible for drafting the **Monroe Doctrine** which established America's claim to be a hemispheric power and the right to intervene to protect its areas of influence.

12 **1967 USA: Race riots** broke out in Newark, New Jersey, following reports of police beating a black man. Over 20 people were killed and at least 1000 injured after the National Guard were called in.
24th: President Johnson ordered troops into Detroit; over the next six days between 35 and 45 people kiled, 5000 arrested and $16m of damage caused.

13 **1962 'The Night of the Long Knives':** Prime Minister Macmillan announced sweeping changes in his government; seven out of 21 ministers left the Cabinet, including Selwyn Lloyd, the Lord Chancellor. Further changes were announced on the 16th.

17 **1917 WWI: The Royal Family** adopted the name **House of Windsor** in place of House of Saxe-Coburg-Gotha.

18 **1817** Death of **Jane Austen,** English novelist. *Pride and Prejudice* and *Emma.*

1892 Death of **Thomas Cook,** English travel agent, pioneer and founder of the agency bearing his name.

23 **1892** Birth of **Haile Selassie,** Emperor of Ethiopia. One of the longest reigning monarchs in the world. (Died 1975.)

27 **1967 The Sexual Offences Act 1967** came into force, legalising homosexual acts between consenting men over 21, in private.

28 **1917** Formation of the **Royal Tank Regiment** of the British Army.

31 **1917 WWI: The Battle of Passchendaele.** Major offensive launched by Sir Douglas Haig from near Ypres to capture high ground in NW Belgium from which the Germans had dominated British positions since 1914. Ended on 6 November when the Allies captured the village of Passchendaele. The British suffered at least 240,000 casualties.

AUGUST

3 **1492 Christopher Columbus** set sail from Spain with three ships, the **Santa Maria, Pinta** and **Niña,** in an expedition to find a new route to the Indies but which

resulted in the discovery of America. (Sighted land on 12 October.)

1792 Death of **Sir Richard Arkwright,** English inventor who developed the mechanical cotton spinning process. A pioneer of power-driven machinery, and the Industrial Revolution.

4 1792 Birth of **Percy Bysshe Shelley,** English poet.

5 1792 Death of **Lord Frederick North,** Prime Minister 1770-82, during the American War of Independence.

6 1917 Birth of **Robert Mitchum,** American actor.

7 1942 **Mohandas K. Gandhi** called on nationalist followers in India to begin a mass campaign of non-violent civil disobedience.
9th: British authorities outlawed the Congress Party and arrested and imprisoned Gandhi, as well as 200 other nationalist Indian leaders.

1867 Birth of **Emile Nolde,** German Expressionist painter and graphic artist. Specialised in religious themes. *Dance round the Golden Calf.*

1942 WWII: Approximately 15,000 Americans landed at **Guadalcanal,** in the Solomon Islands group: **'Operation Watchtower'.** The first allied offensive undertaken against the Japanese in the SW Pacific.

9 1967 Death of **Joe Orton,** English playwright. Murdered by his lover, Kenneth Haliwell. *Entertaining Mr Sloane.*

11 1942 Barnes Wallis patented his **bouncing bomb** invention. (The patent was filed on this date but acceptance and publication was delayed until 1963 for security reasons.)

14 1867 Birth of **John Galsworthy,** English novelist and dramatist. Winner of the Nobel Prize for Literature in 1932. *The Forsyte Saga.*

15 1967 Death of **René François Ghislain Magritte,** Belgian painter. Founder of the Surrealist movement.

16 1977 Death of **Elvis Presley,** American singer and film actor.

17 1892 Birth of **Mae West,** American stage and film actress, producer and director. *She Done Him Wrong.* (Died 1980.)

19 1942 WWII: The Dieppe raid, a dummy run for the invasion of Europe, ended in disaster for the combined Anglo-Canadian force. In six hours of fighting over 3500 men were killed, wounded or captured. The British lost nearly 100 planes to the Germans in fighting over the area, more planes than on any other day of the war. It was the greatest Anglo-German air battle since September 1940. Codenamed 'Operation Jubilee'.

1977 Death of **Julius 'Groucho' Marx** of the Marx Brothers, American film comedians. *A Night at the Opera* and *Duck Soup.*

22 1917 Birth of **John Lee Hooker,** American blues guitarist and singer.

1642 Start of the English Civil War when Charles I raised his standard at Nottingham. (See 23 October 1642.)

1967 Death of **Gregory Pincus,** American biologist, co-developer of **the Pill.**

1892 Birth of **Percy Fender,** Surrey and England cricketer. (Died 1985.)

1942 Death of **Michel Fokine,** Russian dancer and choreographer.

24 1892 Goodison Park, home of Everton Football Club in Liverpool, opened.

25 1867 Death of **Michael Faraday,** English physicist and founder of the science of electro-magnetism. Invented the first **dynamo.**

27 1967 Death of **Brian Epstein,** manager of The Beatles.

29 1842 Hong Kong leased to Great Britain under the **Treaty of Nanking** which ended the Opium War 1839-42.

30 1917 Birth of **Denis Healey,** Labour Member of Parliament and former Defence Secretary and Chancellor of the Exchequer.

SEPTEMBER

1 1912 Death of **Samuel Coleridge-Taylor,** English composer.

1967 Death of **Siegfried Sassoon,** English poet and critic. Remembered for his poems about WWI and his autobiography, *Memoirs of a Fox-Hunting Man.*

2 1192 The Crusades: King Richard I and Sultan Saladin concluded a treaty for a 3-5 year truce, so ending the 3rd Crusade. (See 11 December 1192.)

1792 The French Revolution: The Reign of Terror began when over 1500 people being held in Paris prisons were murdered by the mob. Nearly a quarter of those killed were political prisoners. The massacre had been sparked off by rumours that the gaols were full of counter-revolutionaries plotting to restore the Monarchy. (The Terror lasted for almost two years.)

7 1917 Birth of **Group Captain Leonard Cheshire, VC,** founder of homes for the disabled.

13 1592 Death of **Michel de Montaigne,** French essayist and diarist.

17 1967 BBC tv: First transmission of **The World this Weekend.**

18 1967 Death of **Sir John Cockcroft,** British physicist. Creator of the Atomic Research Establishment at Harwell. Together with Ernest Walton, he split the atom. Awarded the Nobel Prize for Physics in 1951.

20 1842 Birth of **Sir James Dewar,** Scottish physicist, chemist and inventor of the **vacuum flask.**

1967 Cunard liner **QE2** launched at Clydebank, Scotland.

22 1942 WWII: German troops entered the cenre of **Stalingrad.** (See 19 November 1942.)

1792 French Revolution: First Republic came into existence and began using the French Revolutionary Calendar. (The Republic lasted until 1804, when the First Empire was declared under Napoleon Bonaparte.)

24 1717 Birth of **Horace Walpole,** the first British Prime Minister.

26 1942 Death at age 95 of **Wilson Carlile,** English clergyman and founder of the Church Army in 1882.

27 1792 Birth of **George Cruikshank,** English illustrator and engraver. *Sketches by 'Boz'* by Charles Dickens.

1917 Death of **Edgar Degas,** French Impressionist painter.

30 1917 Birth of **Buddy Rich,** American jazz drummer and bandleader.

1967 BBC Radio 1 went on the air and the Light Programme, Third Programme and the Home Service began broadcasting as Radios 2, 3 and 4, respectively.

OCTOBER

1 1967 Majority jury verdicts came into force as part of the Criminal Justice Act 1967. (The first verdict was given on the 5th when Saleh Kassem was found guilty of theft by a 10-2 majority verdict at Brighton Crown Court.)

2 1942 British cruiser *Curacao* sank off the coast of Donegal with the loss of 338 lives following a collision with the liner *Queen Mary.*

1967 London Bridge put up for sale; bought by McCullock Properties, for rebuilding in Lake Havasu, Arizona. Building of new London Bridge began on 6 November.

3 1867 Birth of **Pierre Bonnard,** French painter, designer and graphic artist. A member of the group of artists called Nabis, who specialised in painting domestic scenes, and a leader of the Intimists. Considered one of the leading recorders of France's 'Belle Epoque'.

1967 Death of **Sir Malcolm Sargent,** English conductor.

4 1892 Birth of **Engelbert Dolfuss,** Austrian Fascist dictator, responsible for the destruction of the Austrian Republic and the formation of the one-party state. In an effort to avoid a takeover by the Nazis, he almost made Austria an Italian satellite state. (Assassinated by the Nazis in 1934.)

5 1942 Oxfam – Oxford Committee for Famine Relief – held its first meeting in the Old Library, University Church of Oxford.

6 1892 Death of **Alfred, Lord Tennyson,** Poet Laureate 1850-92. *Locksley Hall.*

8 1967 Death of **Clement Attlee,** British Statesman and Labour Prime Minister 1945-51.

9 1967 Death of **Ernesto 'Che' Guevara,** Argentine revolutionary and guerrilla. One of Fidel Castro's principal lieutenants in the overthrow of the Battista regime in Cuba (1956-58) and later a member of his government. Killed while fighting with guerrillas in Bolivia.

1967 The Breathalyser introduced.
(Legislation came into force at midnight
of the 8th.) Under the 1966 Road Traffic
Act it became an offence, for the first
time, to drive with more than a specified
quantity of alcohol in the bloodstream,
regardless of the person's ability to drive.
The first person to be caught was Thomas
McCrory at 12.15 am.

12 **1492 The 'New World' was discovered
when Christopher Columbus reached the
West Indies.** He sighted the island of
Guanahini in the Bahamas group, later
renamed San Salvador. He was still
convinced he had reached the Orient.
Columbus Day in the USA. (See also 23
August 1492.)

17 **1967 Hair,** the musical, opened in New
York. (British première at the
Shaftesbury Theatre was on 27.9.1968.)

1892 Birth of Herbert Howells, English
composer. (Died 1983.)

1972 EEC: British membership. The
European Communities Act 1972
received the Royal Assent and became
law.

18 **1922 The British Broadcasting Company
formed.** (See also 14 November 1922:
2LO.)

**1967 The USSR achieved the first 'soft'
landing** of an instrument capsule on the
surface of **Venus.**

20 **1842 Death of Grace Darling,** English
heroine of the wreck of the *Forfarshire*
in 1838.

21 **1917** Birth of **'Dizzy' Gillespie,** American
jazz trumpeter and bandleader.

22 **1962 The Cuban missile crisis:** President
Kennedy revealed the building of a Soviet
missile base in Cuba and ordered a partial
blockade of the island.
24th: Blockade went into effect.
28th: Kennedy and Krushchev reached
agreement on a formula to end the crisis.
2 Nov: President Kennedy announced
the dismantling of the base.
20 Nov: Blockade lifted.

23 **1642 English Civil War: The Battle of
Edgehill,** in the Cotswolds. First major
conflict of the war. Although Prince
Rupert's cavalry charge
broke through the enemy line, he failed
to regroup fast enough believing the
Parliamentarians broken. But they
managed to reform and counter-
attacked, nearly overrunning the royal
army. Rupert returned in time to prevent
defeat, but both sides claimed it as a
victory. (See 22 August 1642.)

1942 WWII: The 2nd **Battle of El
Alamein** began. The British, heavily
reinforced and under Lt-Gen. Bernard
Montgomery, attacked Rommel,
inflicting heavy losses and driving the
Germans and Italians back over 1000
miles to Tunisia. Battle continued until
3/4 November.

24 **1917** Death of **Sir William James
Herschel,** English inventor of the finger-
print identity system.

1917 WWI: The Battle of Caporetto.
German/Austrian forces under Gen.
Otto von Bulow defeated the 2nd Italian
Army at Caporetto on the Isonzo river,
forcing them to retreat 70 miles. The
Italians lost 275,000 men as prisoners,
with 45,000 casualties. (Direct result of
the defeat was the Rapallo Conference,
which set up a Supreme War Command,
to co-ordinate a unified system of
command and so avoid such surprise
attacks and defeats.)

26 **1967 Mohammed Reza Pahlavi** crowned
himself and his wife, Farah Diba, as Shah
and Queen of Iran.

28 **1792** Death of **John Smeaton,** English
engineer. Built Eddystone Lighthouse;
founder of the civil engineering
profession in Great Britain.

30 **1967 Cosmos 186** and **Cosmos 188,** Soviet
satellites, achieve the first automatic
rendezvous and docking. Flew together
for three and a half hours before
separating into different orbits.

31 **1517 Martin Luther nailed his 95 Theses
to the church door** at Wittenberg. The
start of the Reformation.

1517 Death of **Fra Bartolommeo,** Italian
High Renaissance painter. Specialised in
religious subjects.

NOVEMBER

2 **1982 Channel 4 launched.** Great Britain's
first new tv channel for 18 years.

1917 The British Government issued the
Balfour Declaration recognising Palestine
in principle as 'a national home' for the
Jewish people.

3 **1917** Birth of **Connor Cruise O'Brien,**
Irish author, newspaper columnist and
politician.

**1892 World's first automatic telephone
exchange began operating** at La Porte,
Indiana. Designed and patented by
Almon B. Strowger.

5 1942 Death of **George M(ichael) Cohan,** American actor, playwright and songwriter. *Yankee Doodle Dandy.*

6 1892 Birth of **Sir John Alcock,** English aviator. Together with A.W. Brown he completed the first flight across the Atlantic.

7 1967 Declaration of the **Elimination of Discrimination against Women** adopted by the UN General Assembly.

1867 Birth of **Marie Curie** (born **Sklodowska**), Polish-French physicist and radiochemist. Pioneer in the handling and analysis of radioactive substances. Together with her husband she laid the foundation of the **science of radiochemistry.**

1917 The 'October' Russian Revolution: The Bolsheviks under Lenin seized power and overthrew the Kerensky government, transferring power to the 2nd All Russian Congress of Soviets. (It is called the 'October Revolution' because at the time Russia was still using the Julian calendar and not the Gregorian or Western calendar.)

8 1967 BBC Radio Leicester, the first local radio station, opened.

1942 WWII: The 'Second' Front: British and American troops landed in French N. Africa.
9th: Vichy France severed diplomatic relations with the USA, who immediately reciprocated.
11th: French forces under Admiral Jean Darlan surrendered.
13th: Darlan announced he had assumed full responsibility for French interests in N. Africa with US approval. (An announcement which caused controversy and which forced President Roosevelt to state that this would be only a temporary arrangement.)
15th: Darlan appointed General Giraud commander-in-chief of French forces in N. Africa.

12 1942 WWII: The naval **Battle of Guadalcanal** began; finished on the 15th. Sometimes known as the Battle of the Solomon Islands. The Japanese lost 28 ships to America's nine. With these losses the Japanese could no longer resupply units in Guadalcanal; the garrison was effectively cut off and isolated, turning stalemate into an American victory (See 7 August 1942.)

1817 Birth of **Baha Allah** (also spelt **Ullah**), Iranian founder of the Bahai faith. (Died 1892.)

1842 Birth of **Lord Rayleigh (John William Strutt),** English physicist. Winner of the 1904 Nobel Prize. Although he specialised in acoustics and optics, his most famous work is *The Theory of Sound.* Rayleigh is remembered for his discovery and the isolation of the gas **Argon.**

14 1922 BBC: First daily programmes from 2LO in London. (See also 18 October 1922.)

15 1942 Birth of **Daniel Barenboim,** Argentine-born Israeli pianist and conductor.

17 1917 Death of **Auguste Rodin,** French sculptor.

1942 Birth of **Martin Scorsese,** American film director.

18 1967 Sterling Crisis: Sterling devalued by 14.3%; the pound fell from $2.80 to $2.40; the bank rate rose from 6.5% to 8%; $100m cut in defence spending; $100m cut in public spending.
20th: Banks and the Stock Exchange closed.
21st: Heavy trading in sterling on currency markets. In the following days Spain, Denmark, Eire and Israel devalued.
23rd: Prime Minister Wilson described the decision to devalue as a 'setback and defeat'.
29th: James Callaghan resigned as Chancellor of the Exchequer and became Home Secretary in a swop with Roy Jenkins.
30th: Publication of Government letter to the IMF which promised curbs on pay and spending in return for standby credit of $1400m.

942 Death of **St Odo of Cluny,** Benedictine monk who named the notes of the **diatonic scale** from A·to G.

19 1917 Birth of **Indira Gandhi,** Indian stateswoman. Prime Minister of India 1966-77 and 1979-84. (Assassinated 1984.)

1692 Death of **Thomas Shadwell,** English playwright and poet. *Epsom Wells* and *The Sullen Lovers.*

1942 WWII: The Battle of Stalingrad. Soviet forces in the Stalingrad area went on the offensive, taking nearly 50 miles from the Germans.
23rd: The German 6th Army cut off from the rest of the German forces.
24th: Soviet forces, advancing from the north, reached the defenders of Stalingrad and relieved the city. (The

Battle was not won until 1943.) (See 22 September 1942.)

20 1942 The Beveridge Report: Publication of Sir William Beveridge's Report on 'Social Insurance and Allied Services'. Main recommendations: establishment of a Ministry of Social Security; rationalisation of insurance contributions in order to ensure a flat rate contribution from the whole working population; medical treatment to be separated from benefits; and the setting up of a comprehensive medical service for use by everyone, to be administered by a Department of Health.

1917 WWI: The Battle of Cambrai: First massed use of tanks in warfare – over 350 British tanks attacked the German 2nd Army and broke through the Hindenberg Line, south-west of Cambrai. Although initially forced to retreat, mechanical problems and inadequate support for the British forces allowed the Germans to counter-attack and by 4 December they had recaptured all their ground. The British lost nearly 45,000 men, the Germans 50,000.

21 1942 Death of **James Barry Munnik Hertzog,** Prime Minister of South Africa 1924-39. Pro-Nazi, he opposed South Africa's declaration of war against Germany in WWII. Resigned in September 1939. (Succeeded by General Smuts.)

22 1967 Birth of **Boris Becker,** German tennis player. Youngest winner of the Men's Singles Championship, Wimbledon, 1985 and 1986.

24 1642 Abel Janszoon Tasman discovered Van Diemen's Land. (Nearly two centuries later its notoriety as a convict prison caused the authorities to rename it Tasmania.) (See also 13 December 1642: New Zealand discovered.)

27 WWII: The French fleet scuttled in Toulon. Action taken by the French navy as the Germans marched into the city. On the same day the Germans announced the dissolution of the French army, which had been left to the Vichy government under the terms of the 1940 Armistice. In one day France was deprived of its army and navy.

29 1967 Aden: The last British troops left Aden. The colony declared its independence at midnight and changed its name from the Protectorate of South Arabia to the South Yemen People's Republic.

30 1667 Birth of **Jonathan Swift,** Anglo-Irish author and clergyman. *Gulliver's Travels.*

DECEMBER

2 1942 World's first nuclear chain reaction took place. The experiment, known as the **Argonne Project,** was conducted by physicists Enrico Fermi and Arthur Compton in a laboratory at Stagg Field, on the campus of the University of Chicago.

3 1967 The Tridentine Mass, used in England since 1510, was replaced by the English Mass in all Roman Catholic churches in Great Britain.

1967 World's first heart transplant carried out by Dr Christiaan Barnard at the Groote Schuur Hospital, Cape Town, South Africa. Louis Washansky, aged 56, received the heart of Denise Darvall, aged 24. Washansky died on the 21st.

4 1642 Death of **Cardinal Richelieu.** Known as the 'Red Eminence' or 'L'Eminence Rouge', the Cardinal and Duke of Richelieu was the chief minister to Louis XIII during 1624 to 1642 and the most powerful man in France.

1892 Birth of **General Francisco Franco,** Spanish dictator from 1939 until his death in 1975.

5-8 1952 Great London Smog, during which an estimated 4000 people died.

6 1917 Finland declared its independence from Russia after 118 years of rule as a Russian autonomous grand-duchy and centuries of Swedish rule.

7 1817 Death of **Admiral William Bligh,** English naval commander, captain of HMS *Bounty.*

8 1542 Birth of **Mary, Queen of Scots.** (See also 14th.)

11 1192 King Richard I captured near Vienna on his way home from the 3rd Crusade, by Leopold, Duke of Austria. Leopold was forced to hand Richard over to his suzerain, the Holy Roman Emperor, Henry VI, in February 1193. Richard was eventually ransomed and returned to England in early 1194. (There is a legend that the troubador Blondel found him in prison.) (See 2 September 1192.)

1792 The French Revolution: The trial began of King Louis XIV; charged with treason. Trial ended 14 January 1793. Executed on 21 January 1793.

1967 Prototype Anglo-French **Concorde** made its **first public appearance** at Toulouse, France.

12 **1917 World's worst train accident** happened at Modane, France. 543 were killed when an overloaded troop train, returning home from the Western Front for Christmas, ran off the tracks on a sharp bend. (Because the train had been forced to overload by senior officers, against the wishes of the train's engineer, the crash was not revealed for nearly 15 years. Some sources speculated that the true death toll exceeded 1000.)

13 **1642 New Zealand** was discovered by Dutch navigator, **Abel Tasman.** (See also 24 November 1642: Tasmania discovered.)

14 **1542** Death of **King James V** of Scotland.

1967 Scientists at Stanford University, USA, succeeded in producing for the first time **a synthetic version of DNA** (deoxyribonucleic acid).

15 **1917 WWI: The Treaty of Brest-Litovsk signed.** Russo-German armistice. (Negotiations connected with the treaty did not end until the early months of 1918.) Provisional suspension of hostilities from 17 December.

1892 Birth of **Jean Paul Getty,** American oil magnate. At his death in 1976 he was reputed to be the richest man in the world.

16 **1917** Birth of **Arthur C. Clarke,** British novelist. *2001: A Space Oddity.*

1742 Birth of **Gebhard von Blücher,** Prussian field marshal in the Napoleonic Wars. Played an important part in the Battle of Waterloo.

17 **1917** Death of **Elizabeth Garrett Anderson,** Great Britain's first woman doctor and England's first woman mayor, at Aldeburgh.

18 **1442** Death of **Pierre Cauchon,** French bishop of Beauvais, who conducted the trial of (St) **Joan of Arc,** and condemned her to death.

1912 The Piltdown Man 'discovery' on Piltdown Common, East Sussex, by Charles Dawson, announced to the world. Also known as Swanscombe Man. Until 1953, when the 'discovery' was proved to be a hoax, it was thought that Piltdown Man was the so-called 'missing link' in the history of the evolution of man. In actual fact, Dawson had attached an ape's jaw to a human skull. (Now celebrated as the most famous hoax in the history of archaeology.)

24 **1167** Birth of **King John I.**

25 **1892** Birth of **Dame Rebecca West** (pseudonym of **Cecily Isabel Andrews** *née* **Fairfield),** author, journalist and critic. *The Meaning of Treason.* (Died 1983.)

1642 Birth of **Sir Isaac Newton,** mathematician and astronomer. *Philosophiae Naturalis Principia Mathematica.*

26 **1792** Birth of **Charles Babbage,** English mathematician and inventor. Credited with constructing the **first automatic digital computer.**

Typescripts

PREPARATION

Many publishers refuse even to consider handwritten manuscripts. No publisher will accept them as final copy. If you cannot afford to have the whole script typed before acceptance, there are ways round the problem. See below under PRELIMINARY LETTER.

NEATNESS

The first impression made on a publisher and a publisher's reader may be vital. They will try to discount the physical appearance of your typescript, but a tatty typescript covered with handwritten corrections, on different sizes of paper and with inadequate margins and spacing, will perhaps not receive benign consideration first thing on a Monday morning.

Even if you have followed the advice below and have a signed contract in your pocket, and the publisher is awaiting the final manuscript with impatience, there are other reasons for neatness. The publisher's copy editor needs a 'clean' manuscript in order to avoid spending an unnecessary amount of time on marking it up for the printer. The manuscript then has to go to a printer for setting. The typesetting keyboard operator is basically a copy typist, working a complicated and expensive set of equipment. He must be able to read your typescript quickly and accurately, and at the same time he must interpret a code of marks which the copy editor or designer will have made all over it.

TYPING

Authors are increasingly using word processors for the advantages they have to offer over the traditional typewriter (see article **Word Processing**).

For ordinary typescripts, use the black ribbon. For plays, use red for names of characters, stage directions, etc., and black for dialogue. If a two-colour ribbon is not available use capitals for character names and underline stage directions in red by hand. Keep a fairly new ribbon in the typewriter so that it is black but not splodgy. Remember that typewriter maintenance is a tax-deductible expense!

The paper used should be uniform in size, preferably the standard size A4, which has replaced the old foolscap and quarto sizes. Neither flimsy paper nor very thick paper should be used. If in doubt, ask the stationer for a standard A4 typewriter paper. Use one side of the paper only. It is helpful but not essential if manuscripts are typed to a width of sixty characters per line. This makes it easier for printers and publishers to calculate the extent of a work and so – using copyfitting tables – to work out the space occupied when it is printed.

Margins

Good margins are essential, especially on the left hand side. This enables the copy editor to include instructions to the printer. On A4 paper a left hand margin of 1½-2 inches allows sufficient space.

Double spacing

This is necessary if you are to make any corrections to the typescript, and there are always some improvements which you will want to make; they can only be made clear to the printer if there is space available between the lines. The copy editor too needs this extra space. Double spacing means a *full* line of space between two lines of copy – not half a line of space.

Consistency

Be as consistent as possible in your choice of variant spellings, use of sub-headings, etc.

Authors who want to know more about the technicalities of preparing a manuscript for the printer should consult *Copy-editing* by Judith Butcher, Cambridge University Press, 3rd edn 1991, £19.95. Much of this is outside the author's scope, but dipping into this book will make him aware of points of style and consistency, particularly with reference to the use of inverted commas, roman and arabic numerals, italic and roman, rendering of foreign words, etc.

Numbering

Pages (or folios as publishers prefer to call them to distinguish them from the pages of the final book) should be numbered throughout. If you need to include an extra folio after, say, folio 27, call it 27a and write at the foot of folio 27: 'Folio 27a follows'. Then write at the foot of 27a: 'Folio 28 follows'. Don't do this too often or you will confuse and irritate your readers.

CORRECTIONS TO TYPESCRIPT

Corrections to the final typescript should be kept to a minimum. Often the publisher's editor will want to suggest a few additional changes – this happens even to the best authors – and once all or some of these are included, the typescript may have become very messy. If the publisher then feels it is not in a fit state for the printer he may well ask you to have it retyped.

BINDING

Printers prefer to handle each folio separately, so do not use a binder which will make this impossible. Ring binders are acceptable. Alternatively you can use a cardboard envelope folder. In this case it will help if you can clip the pages of each chapter together, but never staple them.

PROTECTION OF TYPESCRIPTS

This can be achieved by placing a stiffer piece of paper at front and back. On the first folio of the typescript itself, give the title, your name and, most important of all, your address. It is worth including your address on the last page also, just in case the first folio becomes detached.

SUBMISSION

The terms 'manuscript' and 'typescript' are interchangeable in present usage, though different editors may favour one or the other.

CHOOSING YOUR PUBLISHER

It will save you time and postage if you check first that you are sending your typescript to a firm that will consider it. Publishers specialise. It is no use sending a work of romantic fiction to a firm that specialises in high-brow novels translated from obscure languages just because they are described in this book as fiction publishers. It is still less use to send it to a firm which publishes no fiction at all. The way to avoid the more obvious mistakes is to look in your library or bookshop for books which are in some way similar to yours, and find out who publishes them. Remember, though, that paperbacks are often editions of books published first in cased editions.

PRELIMINARY LETTER

This again will save you time, money and probably frustration. The letter by itself will tell the publisher very little; what he or she would in most cases prefer to see is a brief preliminary letter together with a synopsis of the book and the first couple of chapters from it. From this material the publisher will be able to judge whether the book would perhaps fit the list, in which case you will be asked to send the complete manuscript. This is one way of avoiding paying a typing bill until it looks as though the investment in the manuscript may be worthwhile.

There is no point whatsoever in asking for a personal interview. The publisher will prefer to consider the manuscript on its own merits, and will not want to be influenced by a personal meeting.

POSTAGE OF MANUSCRIPTS

Always send postage to cover the return of your manuscript or, if you prefer, explain that you will arrange to pick it up from the publisher's office. (Again, if your manuscript has been rejected the publisher will not be willing to discuss the reasons in person.)

Manuscripts are best sent by recorded delivery. Registered post is not recommended. You are unlikely to agree with the Post Office on the value of your lost manuscript, and if anyone does rob the mail, they head for the registered packets first. Recorded delivery is useful because you can check that the publisher has received the manuscript. Whether you send it first or second class depends entirely on how fast you want it to arrive. A properly packed parcel almost always arrives by either rate.

Packing is important. It is not enough to put the manuscript in an envelope. Padded bags are a good idea and are available in several sizes from many stationers.

At all costs, *keep a duplicate*, with all the latest changes to the text included on it.

ESTIMATING

To estimate the length or *extent* of a manuscript, calculate the average number of words per page over, say, eight pages. Multiply the average by the number of pages in the manuscript, making allowances for half-pages at the end of chapters, etc.

WHAT IS THE PUBLISHER DOING WITH YOUR MANUSCRIPT?

Whether or not the publisher finally accepts or rejects the manuscript, there is usually a considerable interval between submission and the publisher's decision. Most publishers acknowledge receipt of manuscript, and if you do not receive an acknowledgement it is advisable to check that the manuscript has arrived. Apart from that, it is not worth chasing the publisher for a quick decision: if pressed, the publisher will probably reject, purely because this is the safer decision.

You should hear from the publisher within about two months. During this time he will either have had the manuscript read 'in-house' or will have sent it to one or more advisers whose opinions he respects. Favourable readers' reports may mean that the publisher will immediately accept the manuscript, particularly if it fits easily into his current publishing programme.

On the other hand, a reader's report may be glowing, but the publisher may still hesitate. He knows he has a good book, but he wants to be sure he will be able to sell it. He is, after all, considering an investment of at least £5000 and frequently more. He may need time to obtain further opinions, and also to obtain estimates from printers, to judge whether the book could be produced at a reasonable price. The worst delays occur when the publisher is attracted to a manuscript but cannot see how he can publish it successfully.

If you have not had a decision after two months, write either a tactful letter saying 'I don't want to rush you, but . . . . .' or alternatively request an immediate decision and be prepared to start again with another publisher.

If your book is topical you have a right to a speedy decision, but it is as well to establish this early on.

ILLUSTRATIONS

If illustrations form a large part of your proposed book and you expect to provide them yourself, then they should be included with the manuscript. If you are sending specimen pages you should include also some sample illustrations. This applies largely to children's picture books and to travel and technical books. It is prudent to send duplicate photographs, photocopies of line drawings and so on so that little harm is done if illustrations go astray.

In the case of a children's book, if you intend to illustrate it yourself, obviously one finished piece of artwork is essential, plus photocopies of roughs for the rest (one must bear in mind that the final artwork may have to be drawn to a particular size and the number of illustrations fixed according to the format chosen by the publisher). If you have written a children's story, or the text for a picture book, do *not* ask a friend to provide the illustrations. The publisher who likes your story may well not like your friend's artwork: you will have considerably lengthened the odds against the story being accepted. Of course this does not apply when an artist and author work closely together to develop an idea, but in that case it is best to start by finding a publisher who likes the artist's work before submitting the story.

Travel manuscripts should be accompanied by a sketch map to show the area you are writing about. The publisher will have an atlas in his reference shelves, but it may not have sufficient detail with which to follow your manuscript. Irreplaceable material should not be sent speculatively.

Many illustrated books these days have illustrations collected by the publishers. If your proposed book is to be illustrated, it is best to establish early on who is responsible for the illustration costs: an attractive royalty offer might be less attractive if you have to gather the pictures, obtain permission for use, and foot the bills.

QUOTATIONS

It is normally the author's responsibility to obtain (and pay for) permission to quote written material which is still in copyright. Permission should always be sought from the publisher of the quoted work, not from the author. Fees for quotation vary enormously: for fashionable modern writers permission may be costly, but in other cases only a nominal fee of a few pounds is charged. There is no standard scale of fees. It is permissible to quote up to about 200 words for the purpose of criticism or review, but this does not apply to use in anthologies, nor does it apply to poetry. And it is a concession, not a right. Even though this is your area of responsibility, your publisher will be able to give you some advice.

PROOF READING

There are many ways of producing books, especially with the advent of modern printing processes, but they all have certain points in common from the author's point of view, and it is as well to be forewarned.

As author you will see either one or two stages of proofs. Sometimes you will be shown the finalised copy of the typescript immediately before it goes to the printer. If so, this is really your last chance to make changes which will not tend to sour relations with your publisher! Take the opportunity to comb through the manuscript, and if there are changes which you suspect you will want to make in proof, make them now. (See also **Corrections to Proofs.**)

CORRECTIONS TO PROOFS

There was a time when authors could virtually rewrite their books in galley proof, and revise them again at page. Do not be seduced by biographies of Victorian writers into thinking this is the way the professional writer works!

Modern printing is highly mechanised, but corrections are time-consuming and may involve extensive handwork. This makes corrections far more costly than the original setting. You will probably have signed a contract undertaking to pay the cost of corrections (other than printer's errors) over say 10 per cent or 15 per cent of the cost of composition. This does not mean that you can change ten or fifteen lines in every hundred.

The cost of adding a comma at galley stage, in modern processes, is insignificant. But if you add a word in one line of a paragraph, it will probably mean resetting down to the end of the paragraph. If you add a word at page stage, and this results in the paragraph being longer, many pages may have to be adjusted by one line until the end of the chapter is reached. What to you seemed a simple improvement may take an hour's work on expensive equipment.

STAGES OF PROOFS

Increasingly often only one stage of proofs is used in book production, and there is rarely any need for the author to see more than one stage. The proofs may be in several forms. Ask your editor how many stages of proofs you will see. It could be that you will be asked to check computer print-outs which bear no resemblance to the finished book but which do contain everything that will appear in that book!

Galley proofs hold columns of continuous text. They were originally a rough print taken from metal type. Modern typesetting methods most often produce proofs from a master print or direct from computer data by the Laserprint process.

Page proofs have been made up into pages, including page numbers, headlines, and so on. It is prohibitively expensive to make corrections at this stage, except to the printer's own errors.

It is worth noting that during the production of some books which have illustrations in the text, such as children's or 'coffee table' books, the editor or designer has to do a scissors and paste job to put the whole thing together. This may require some minor modifications to the text to make the final result come together happily.

Screenplays for Films

JEAN McCONNELL

Despite the old saying that the plot of the best movie can be written on a postcard, film companies do not actually welcome a plot on a postcard. Nor is it enough simply to send a story in narrative form. You should be prepared to write your idea into a full screenplay. In consequence, it is advisable to check as far as possible in case a company is already working on a similar idea and your efforts are likely to be wasted.

LAYOUT

1. Use A4 size typing paper.
2. It is not necessary to put in elaborate camera directions. A shooting script will be made later. Your job is to write the master scenes, clearly broken down into each incident and location.
3. Your screenplay will tell your story in terms of visual action and dialogue spoken by your characters. If you intend it to be a full-length feature film, running about 1½ hours, your script will be about 100-130 pages long.
4. The general layout of a page of screenplay can be seen from the specimen page. The following points should be noted.
(a) Each scene should be numbered on the left and given a title which indicates whether the scene is an interior or an exterior, where it takes place, and the lighting conditions, i.e. Day or Night. The situation of each scene should be standardised; don't call your 'sitting room' a 'lounge' the next time you come to it, or people will think you mean a different place.
(b) Note that the dialogue is spaced out, with the qualifying directions such as '(frowning)' on a separate line, slightly inset from the dialogue. Double space each speech from the previous one.
(c) Always put the names of the characters in CAPITALS, except when they occur in the actual dialogue. Double space the stage directions from the dialogue, but single space the lines of the stage directions themselves.
(d) Leave at least a 1½ inch margin on the left hand and a reasonably wide right-hand margin. It is false economy to cram the page. You will, of course, type on one side of the sheet only.
(e) If you have to make a correction, cross it out neatly and type the whole section out again. But don't irritate your reader with too many corrections. Better to re-type the page.
(f) Only give the camera directions when you feel it to be essential. For instance, if you want to show something from a particular character's point of view, or if you think you need it to make a point, i.e. 'HARRY approaches the cliff edge and looks down. LONG SHOT – HARRY'S POINT OF VIEW. ALICE fully-clad is walking into the sea. CUT TO: CLOSE UP OF HARRY'S HORRIFIED FACE.' Note the camera directions are put in capital letters on a separate line, as in the specimen page.

PREPARATION OF MANUSCRIPT

1. Make at least two copies, and never send your very last copy out to anyone. It will invariably be lost.

13   (continued)

She moves across the barn to the door, where she turns.

ELIZABETH
I still think the police ought to know.

She goes out. ALAN stands immobile until her
footsteps retreat, and then he sighs with relief.
He darts quickly to the large wine vat, climbs
up and begins heaving at the lid.

CUT TO:

14   EXT. FARMYARD DAY

DONALD intercepts ELIZABETH as she crosses yard.

DONALD
What does he say?

ELIZABETH
Nothing.

DONALD
(frowning)

Right! Now it's my turn.

He starts for the barn. ELIZABETH watches him
anxiously.

CUT TO:

15   INT. BARN DAY

DONALD's shadow falls across the threshold.
He hesitates while his eyes get used to the gloom.

DONALD
Alan?

ALAN lets the lid of the vat fall and jumps down.
He stands quite still as DONALD crosses the barn
and stands staring at him. The two men are silent
a moment.

DONALD
(then, with realisation)
You knew it was there, didn't you?

CLOSE SHOT — DONALD'S POINT OF VIEW
ALAN'S face is haggard.

ALAN
I hoped to God it wouldn't be.
Nobody will ever understand.

2. The length of your manuscript will depend on whether you are submitting a feature film, a short film for children, say, or a documentary. But it is better to present a version which is too short rather than too long.

3. Prepare the title page in the same way as for a story or article to an editor, except that it is not necessary to state the number of words.

4. If you give a list of characters, do not suggest the actor or actress you would like to play it. This is a decision to be made elsewhere and relies on many factors about which you cannot know. Don't attach character sketches, as these should appear in the body of the screenplay.

5. Bind your screenplay, giving it a front and back cover, and securing the pages firmly.

SUBMISSION

Attach a stamped, addressed envelope to your manuscript whether sending it through an agent or direct. But do remember that if film companies state that they will only consider material sent through an agent, they definitely mean it.

Most companies have Story Departments to which you should address your material. As Story Editors are very busy people, you can make their life easier by complying with the following rules.

1. If you have based your screenplay on someone else's published work you should make the fact clear in a covering letter, stating *(a)* that the material is no longer in copyright, or *(b)* that you yourself own the copyright, or at least an option on it, or *(c)* that you have not obtained the copyright but have reason to believe that there would be no difficulty in doing so.

2. Apart from a note of any relevant credits you may already possess, do not regale the Editor with your personal details, unless they bear a direct relation to the material submitted. For instance, if your story concerns a brain surgeon, then it would be relevant for the Editor to know that you actually are one. Otherwise, trust your work to stand on its own merit.

3. There is no need to mention if your work has been turned down by other companies, however regretfully. The comments of others will not influence a Story Editor one way or the other.

4. Don't pester the company if you don't get a reply, or even an acknowledgement, for some weeks. Most companies will formally acknowledge receipt and then leave you in limbo for at least six weeks. However, after a passage of three months or more, a brief letter asking politely what has happened is in order. A telephone call is unlikely to be helpful. It is possible the company may have liked your work enough to have sent it to America, or to be getting further readers' opinions on it. This all takes time. If they don't like it, you will certainly get it back in due course.

5. Accept that this is really a tough market; for this there are at least three reasons. One, films cost so much to make these days that the decision to go ahead is only taken after a great many important factors have been satisfied and an even greater number of important people are happy about it. Two, the number of films made is small in relation to, say, books published or TV plays produced. Three, writing a screenplay calls for knowledge and appreciation of the technicalities of film-making, as well as the ability to combine dialogue, action and pictures, visualising the story throughout in the language of the cinema.

6. Try to get an agent. A good agent will give you a fair opinion of your work. If he thinks it worthwhile, then he is the one who will know the particular film company to whom he can sell it.

(A list of agents who handle film material will be found at the end of the section on **Scripts for theatre, radio, tv and film.**)

Writing for Television

BILL CRAIG
Past-President of The Writers' Guild of Great Britain

'Television drama' is a generic term which covers several varied and specialist areas of writing for the domestic screen. Since each differs from the others in terms of requirements and rewards and since each is definable in copyright terms, let's start by identifying them.

The television play is a one-off creation of a single mind and talent and absolutely the property of its author. As a form it is the vehicle for the talents of newest and least-experienced writers in the medium and also for those who are held in the highest regard. It is (for practical reasons) the traditional point of entry for the tyro. There has been some reduction in the number of plays produced annually but the BBC and certain ITV companies are still in the market for 30, 60 and 90 minute slot-length works. If the bad news is that they get several thousand unsolicited manuscripts every year, the good news is that they are all read. No script-unit will risk missing out on an undiscovered genius.

The same observations (with some modification) would apply to the original series or serial: that is, a multi-part work of sole authorship and of finite length. They tend to be written by established television writers who have a proven ability to go the necessary distance, but a new writer with an attractive idea can come in through this door.

What's the procedure? Invest some time and talent and write the play. A commission on a synopsis is unlikely without some evidence that you can write interesting action, dialogue and characters. With the finite series/serial – write the first episode and synopsise the rest.

The situation-comedy is the most highly paid area of television writing – and understandably so. It calls for a quirky and idiosyncratic mind, and its overriding imperative – to make the viewer laugh – subordinates all of the other dramatic tools to this end. If it's difficult to play Beethoven's *Ninth* on a one-stringed fiddle, then it's Hell to do it for a run of six episodes. The sit-com is unique in screen drama in so far as most of them are played before live studio audiences. Once upon a time, they were constructed around individual comedians. Some still are, but for several years now the practice has been to cast according to the script with actors who can play comedy. And that's not a bad thing, is it?

Again, this form is an original in copyright terms, though dual authorships are not uncommon. A synopsis is pretty useless (ever tried to explain a joke?), so write the pilot-script and briefly indicate where you can go with other episodes.

We now come to a significant point of departure and go into those areas where the copyright is split with another party.

First, the drama-series: *Lovejoy*, *The Bill*, *The Chief*, et al. These are definable as a series of original and self-contained scripts using the same characters and backgrounds throughout. The format – that is, the characters and general ambience – will be owned or leased by the production organisation. They represent a substantial part of television drama, but it is rare for a writer without previous screen experience to be commissioned to write for them. It is quite pointless to submit a speculative script or synopsis: the series you are seeing now was recorded months ago.

The daily or bi-weekly serial (*Coronation Street*, *Brookside*, *Take the High Road*, *Emmerdale Farm*) will occasionally try out new writers, but the production pressures on reliability and deadline delivery dates don't allow for too many risks to be taken outside what is usually an established and pretty permanent writing team.

Dramatisation and Adaptation are terms which are interchanged in an ignorantly casual manner; they are not the same thing. A dramatisation is the conversion of a prose-work to a screenplay. An adaptation is a similar conversion of a dramatic work. The difference is considerable, and the screen credit should reflect this fact.

There has been a great increase in the number of dramatisations made from novels. Again, these are usually written by writers with a track record in television, but occasionally the author of the book to be dramatised will be approached to write the screenplay. If you don't come under either of those headings, then you probably wouldn't get very far by simply suggesting that you'd like to dramatise this or that novel. Adaptations are usually 'in-house' works.

All of this leaves uncovered an odd and often lucrative area – the format. It is possible to sell an idea for a series without ever having written a script. But make sure that your submission is as detailed as it possibly can be in terms of background, main characters and development. Doing it the simple way in this instance can mean finding out that fifty other people have had the same simple idea. And selling an idea carries no guarantee that you'll be asked to write the scripts.

Script layout and presentation. Use A4. Type it or have it typed. Blank margin about four inches on the left hand side. Directions and character names in capitals, dialogue in capitals and lower case, double spaced. Don't go mad with directions; keep them functional and indicative. Don't be intimidated by camera directions; use them only when they make a dramatic point you want to get across.

Number and head the scenes thus: 1. INT. JOE'S ROOM. DAY

Avoid nonsense action directions such as 'Her inner resilience manifests itself in a way reminiscent of the wind howling across her native moors'. If you mean she's from Yorkshire, just say it.

There are several books on the subject of layout and technique. Two which come to mind are *Writing for Television* by Gerald Kelsey (Black) and *The Way to Write for Television* by Eric Paice (Elm Tree Books). *Writing for the BBC* (BBC Books) could be money well spent.

Given success to your efforts, you will be contracted under the terms of the relevant agreement between the British Broadcasting Corporation or the Independent Television Companies Association and the Writers' Guild of Great Britain, 430 Edgware Road, London W2 1EH. The Guild has sole bargaining rights in the television drama rates, its agreements are complex and comprehensive and several of the rights and benefits contained in them are available to Guild members only.

Payments are made in stages: BBC – half on commission, half on acceptance; ITCA – half on commission, a quarter on delivery, a quarter on acceptance.

The foregoing comments apply mainly to programmes produced by the British Broadcasting Corporation or the ITV companies. The increasingly-important independent production sector should not, however, be ignored, since many of their productions are primarily intended for television screening.

These programmes are made by either entirely independent production organisations or subsidiaries of the ITV companies (e.g. *Minder*, Euston Films/Thames Television).

Generally speaking, the scripts are laid out in film format (see **Screenplays for Films**) although some, since they produce on tape, might prefer the television format. The procedures described above for submitting unsolicited work should be observed.

Contracts should conform to the terms laid down by the agreement between the Writers' Guild of Great Britain and the British Film and Television Producers Association/Independent Programme Producers Association. Again, the Agreement is comprehensive and covers all forms and aspects of screen drama. Payment is made in four stages: treatment, first draft, second draft and principal photography. Further exploitation is also covered.

Further useful information and addresses may be found in a booklet called *Contacts*. The 1991-92 edition is available, price £6.00 including postage, from *The Spotlight*, 7 Leicester Place, London WC2H 7BP.

Word Processing
A Guide for Authors

RANDALL McMULLAN

Writers never used to read much about typewriters, let alone pens and pencils, so perhaps it is a pity that we need an article about word processors for writers. Approach this knowledge with a similar attitude to collecting information about a new car. You don't wish to be a mechanic but there are certain automotive ideas and terms that you accept in order to make an appropriate choice of car and to get use from it.

Acquiring a word processor and learning to 'drive' the device is an investment of effort comparable to using a car and word processing offers similar gains in productivity, and convenience. If you do happen to enjoy extra technical features like power steering or central locking then you will find the equivalent in extra features associated with word processors, but they are not essential.

WRITING WITH A WORD PROCESSOR

A word processor should have a benign effect on your writing habits because the system encourages a fundamental rule of writing – to keep going. You do not stop typing at the end of a line because the word processor does that sort of housekeeping for you. You do not stop for any typing mistakes during 'text input' (writing) because the errors on screen are only transient until you decide to make them permanent. It is more efficient to fix mistakes during a separate editing pass over the screen. Indeed, you should learn to let the computer dictionary pick up the typos and automatically correct them, with a watchful eye from yourself. If you can't spell a word then you just need to make a best guess.

Initially you may miss the act of ripping pages from the typewriter and hurling them at the wastepaper basket but you can learn new and equally satisfying ways of savaging your text. Once the text is fixed then it need never be keyed again. Most publishers will be happy to accept your disk fresh from the word processor without further work from you, and you will be saved proofreading for typesetting mistakes. For some authors the electronic file from the word processor is the starting point for desktop publishing or for self-publishing, as described in the companion articles on pages 475 and 226 respectively.

WHAT EQUIPMENT IS NEEDED?

A word processor is essentially a device which accepts the input of text from a keyboard and displays it on screen for you to change and move about as you please. This text is then electronically stored for reuse and transport, like a cassette in a tape recorder, and the text can be printed on to paper at any time.

Being loath to lose sight of their paper, even temporarily, authors are often drawn towards new generations of electronic typewriters which can store some text and show it on a small screen for correction. At the most, you can only view a few lines at one time and it becomes difficult and discouraging to process pages of text. Electronic typewriters have their uses, especially if cheap, but they also run the risk of giving word processors a bad name.

Modern word processors are actually desktop computers for which a 'program' of word processing instructions is just one of many 'software' packages. The computer 'hardware' is neutral about what it does and can run other programs such as databases, accounts or even games. This ability can be regarded as a bonus but should not distract a writer while choosing a word processor. It is usually more satisfactory for all parties if children, for example, are given separate games machines to use in another room!

Most computers for word processing are various models of the 'PC' or 'Personal Computer' range which are produced by a large number of manufacturers, small and large. Although IBM originally set the standards for this family of computers, IBM now produce machines which are not especially compatible with the *de facto* standards used by the rest of the industry. The importance of the PC standard is that you can read and write your disks on other machines, like a tape cassette, or you can plug-in parts from other people's machines, such as keyboards or display screens. Some ranges of computer, such as the Apple Macintosh or Amstrad PCW, are not compatible with PC computers but have a moderate-sized base of users.

Word processing packages

Hundreds of different brands of word processing software have been produced for PC computers. As with the hardware, there are great advantages in choosing from the half dozen word processing packages which are established as standards. You will then have access to the training and general community help associated with a widely used product.

Like different models of cars, word processors are perhaps 90 per cent identical in their word processing capabilities although manufacturers, and some users, will declare that the difference or the extra features are of great importance. Without becoming too partisan however, you may certainly wish to observe different styles of word processor and look ahead to any desktop publishing ambitions.

The 'text editor' style, used in a traditional word processor, allows you to input and edit your text while you view a screen which shows the correct arrangements of lines on the page. The characters seen on screen are neutral in matters of style, although special text such as bold, superscript or subscript will be highlighted. But in such editing mode you will not expect to see the exact size and style of the type fonts.

The 'graphical interface' of some later word processors takes the concept of WYSIWIG (What You See Is What You Get) further, in that your text is displayed on screen in the same size and style of type that will be used by your current printer. The characters are usually shown as black on a white screen. If your printer can produce the appropriate varieties of size and style then you will be able to achieve a simple form of desktop publishing.

The graphical display of text will not necessarily replace the use of a simpler text editor screen. For intensive processing of words, rather than arrangement of print style, the 'clean' screen can be more efficient. If the text is to be used later by a desktop publishing program, or by a typesetter, then it should *not* be formatted with print styles. This difference in screen styles is not necessarily crucial in the later versions of well-known word processors, such as WordPerfect and WordStar, because they offer the option of previewing your text in graphical form.

Word processors also differ in the style by which you give them 'commands'. Learners and casual users often appreciate visible menus of options on screen which are activiated by moving arrow keys on the keyboard, or even by moving a mouse. As a constant keyboardist you may soon find such selection methods tedious and probably need keyboard commands. Fortunately, the mainstream packages offer a choice of command methods and screen clutter which can be reset at any time.

Other features of modern word processors include large dictionaries used for checking spelling and supplying an instant Thesaurus. The dictionaries are usually in 'British English' and you can add your own lists of specialised words. Remember that the spellchecker can not check for context although it should be smart enough to recognise and suggest automatic corrections for well-known typos such as 'hte' or 'the the'.

Most word processors have the ability to generate 'mailshots' of apparently personalised letters, like those promoting unique and unrepeatable timeshare offers. 'Indexing' and 'Footnoting' features sound alluring to authors but all of them rely on systematic coding by the writer before they spring into action. Such features are often optimised for technical publications and can never replace the skills of a good indexer.

If you choose a word processing program from outside the well-known names then you will be on your own. A minority of writing tasks may be better handled by programs which specialise in the layout of mathematical and scientific symbols. Foreign languages are another special area and there are word processors which can be set to display non-Roman scripts. You must expect the use of such a specialised package to be more of a lonely challenge.

Computers

The word processing 'computer' is usually a metal or plastic box connected by cables to the keyboard and display screen. Some of the components in the box can be varied to suit the requirements of the software that you wish to run. Typical decisions involve the speed of the processor chip, the amount of memory (RAM), the type of disk drives, and the type of display screen to be used. Some minimum technicalities are given in the later section about purchasing your word processor.

The computer will come with an *operating system*, the software which co-ordinates the tasks of the computer such as interpreting keystrokes, displaying characters on screen and storing them on disk in magnetic 'files'. A reasonable minimum knowledge of the operating system is needed to name the files, which contain your precious work, and to make backups of them.

The *keyboard* of a standard modern desktop computer is attached to the computer box by cable and can therefore be used in any convenient position. Good keyboards are constructed with springs beneath each key and an escapement mechanism to give a 'positive' feel. The keyboard works in the same way as a QWERTY typewriter keyboard and has some special keys such as the Control and Alt keys which give special effects. Computer keyboards have also gained some extra keys such as arrows to move the cursor about on screen, duplicate numeral keys, and 'function' keys for shortcut commands within programs.

Disks

Your writing is electronically stored on to a disk covered with a magnetic coating, like an audio or video tape. Yes, it is usually spelt 'disk' rather than disc. A 'floppy' disk can be taken in and out of a slot in the computer and the contents can be copied on to a blank disk. Unlike a tape recorder, you don't need two floppy disk drives to duplicate a floppy disk. Several sagas of text can easily be stored on a single floppy disk and they cost around £1.00 each. Like most information, writing is best stored and organised as separate 'files' of data, usually no longer than a chapter per file.

One advantage of accepted technical standards for computers is that the floppy disk, containing your work, written by one computer can be read by another computer. There are some variations in 'standards' but in general you should aim to be able to use your disk in other computers. For example, you may wish to use a portable computer, or to produce a printout on another style of printer at another site.

A 'hard disk' or 'fixed disk' can not be removed from the computer but holds much more information than a floppy disk and works more quickly. A hard disk is not an essential requirement for the storage of text and you should always keep a recent copy of your text on a floppy disk, stored in a safe place away from the computer. But hard disks are now relatively cheap and are needed to store the complex files of modern programs. The latest versions of word processors have so many features, like large dictionaries, that they are difficult or impossible to run from floppy disks.

Display screens

The display screen or 'monitor' on which you view your text work has some electronics in common with a TV but produces a higher resolution of dots in order to display at least 80 characters across the screen. It is expensive to have a monitor which can display the full length of an A4 page on screen, and it is not usually necessary as you can easily pan the screen over your text.

A monochrome display system has a good resolution suitable for word processing or desktop publishing. Monochrome screens are available in green or in amber. A high resolution colour display can add significantly to the cost of a system and is not a necessity for word processing or desktop publishing. It is relatively easy to upgrade to a colour display should it become desirable or affordable.

There are continuing investigations into possible radiation hazards from display screens which are either as significant or as negligible as sitting close to a TV set. Regular rest periods are the recommended methods of avoiding visual strain or muscular strain from word processing or from any other desk activities, such as handwriting.

Printers

The product of your word processing is the 'hard copy' on paper. The same text stored on disk can be printed out many times in different styles and on different printers. You will be generating a lot of paper so printers need to be fast, more robust than the average typewriter, and be able to feed paper automatically. Fortunately modern printers can offer these features at reasonable prices.

PURCHASING

The simple guideline for choosing your word processor is to buy what everyone else is using. If you do have any difficulties help will be available quickly and cheaply. Friends or colleagues, for example, may be able to loan equipment in an emergency or to provide a printout. The common makes of word processing equipment are accompanied by abundant training, help and advice available from books, magazines and acquaintances.

The following technical considerations are centred around the 'PC' standard of desktop computers which occupies over 90 per cent of the business market. National and local newspapers carry regular computer advertisements from well-known chains of retailers and you will find that they also use this jargon to describe their offers.

Computers

Although IBM set the original standard for modern desktop personal computers, most people now buy IBM-compatible machines or 'clones' offered under a variety of brand names over a range of prices. The particular brand name on the computer box is not as important as you might think. The electronic components are all made in countries far away and, fortunately, are usually interchangeable.

A reasonable minimum choice for a modern professional word processing system is a machine based on the '286' processing chip running at a clockrate of 12 MHz (megahertz). The later and more powerful '386' and '486' chips are becoming cheaper and run programs faster. These speed considerations will not affect simple word processing but do have a noticeable effect on the speed of desktop publishing.

The computer should have at least 640 KB (kilobytes) or 1 MB (megabyte) of RAM (Random Access Memory). Most designs allow you to add more memory later if programs require it. The fixed or hard disk should have at least 20 MB (megabytes) of storage and there will be at least one floppy disk drive. The format of this floppy disk drive may be either 5.25 inch or 3.25 inch. There is a definite trend towards the smaller size of disk but the 5.25 inch disk was used throughout the 1980s and will be with us for some time. For about £60 extra you can have a second floppy disk drive of either format built into the computer box and many vendors offer this option.

Display systems

A display system consists of a video monitor (screen) accompanied by a matching video adaptor card which plugs into a slot inside the computer. You pay significantly more money for increased resolution (fineness) on screen, especially in colour. VGA is currently the leading colour standard and the EGA standard is adequate for word processing. Monochrome VGA or Monochrome Graphics (Hercules) are also adequate for simple word processing and a lot cheaper.

Word processing software

There are around half a dozen major brands of professional word processing programs for the PC. WordPerfect, WordStar and Word are found in general use, while DisplayWrite and MultiMate are generally confined to corporate offices. Word for Windows and Ami Professional are from a newer generation of graphical word processors which need the power of later models of PC.

Most of these word processors have evolved during the last ten years and later versions are often significantly different from earlier versions although the transitions between them are easy. Locoscript is a program which started life on the Amstrad PCW machines and is now also available on the PC. There are many other worthy word processors with enthusiastic users but they are not as widespread as the 'majors'. If you receive any word processor program 'bundled' free with your computer then it will be suitable for learning.

Printers

Dot-matrix printers are cheap, reasonably quiet, and can produce a variety of type styles ranging between fast dotty styles and slower NLQ (near-letter-quality) where the dot structure is hard to detect. Most dot-matrix printers use continuous paper with perforated 'tractor' margins but they will also print single sheets. Daisy-wheel printers, which work like a typewriter, are slow and noisy and have become obsolete.

Laser printers and inkjet printers have replaced daisy-wheel printers for the production of office-quality text and both types of printer quietly feed on plain A4 paper. These printers can also produce different styles and sizes of text (fonts) when driven by an appropriate desktop publishing program. The prices of inkjet printers are comparable to many dot-matrix printers and laser printers are also decreasing in price. An A4 page of dense text or graphics may use several pence worth of toner or ink and these costs should be considered when buying a laser printer or inkjet printer.

Portables

Writers have some good reasons for being tempted to buy a portable PC which will run any of the well-known word processing programs. The portables range in size from 'luggable' suitcases, through 'laptops' for people with strong knees, to 'notebooks' for large briefcases. All of the portables make various compromises in the size of memory and storage, the quality of keyboard and the display. None of them runs on batteries for extended periods, if at all, but they may fit a special need such as travel in places with unreliable electricity supplies.

Costs

It is possible to acquire a professional word processing setup, including printer, for between £700 and £1200, depending on its technical specification and your shopping acumen. You can buy the same equipment from well-known stores or from reputable discount warehouses. Computer equipment is as reliable as any consumer electronics and most likely to show a fault in the early hours when it is under warranty.

Unless you are spending corporate money it will not be sensible to take a maintenance contract. If continuous use of a word processor becomes really important to you then it is usually more economic to buy a standby machine, such as a portable or second-hand computer. Another common strategy is to have plenty of friends or neighbours who can oblige with a printout on their computers with the same ease as they can give you a lift in their cars.

Desktop Publishing

RICHARD WILLIAMS

WHAT IS DESKTOP PUBLISHING?

Most writers will have heard of word processing, even if they do not use a word processor themselves, but desktop publishing (dtp) is a less familiar concept. It is important not to confuse it with self-publishing, which is dealt with elsewhere in this book (see page 226). Desktop publishing is a misnomer since a desktop publishing computer program does the work, not so much of a publisher, but of the specialists who prepare books or magazines for printing. Perhaps the best way to explain what it does is to look at the stages in producing a book or magazine by conventional methods, and then to see how desktop publishing can take over some of these.

Using conventional methods, manuscripts for books or magazines are delivered by the author as typewritten pages. Before being sent to the typesetter these pages have first to be marked up to indicate the different sizes and styles of type to be used. The typeset text comes back in the form of galleys, long strips of paper with the type in its final width.

The galleys then have to be pasted up on boards by a graphics designer or layout artist to produce the page layout – a comparatively simple task for some books, but more complex for illustrated books and magazines. It is then known as camera ready copy, since the next stage is to photograph the boards, and use the resulting film to produce the plates from which the book or magazine is printed. At each stage the copy has to be proofread, and corrections made if necessary.

Desktop publishing programs can take over most of these stages. Instead of specialists setting type from the manuscript, a file from a word processor is transferred to a computer disk, and fed into the desktop publishing program. From this it emerges as the instructions from which camera ready copy can be produced. All the processes can be carried out by a desktop computer (hence the name) and indeed by a single operator.

So what does desktop publishing offer authors and illustrators? At the most, effectively the ability to control their own books, right from the original idea through to the final printed version. Even for those who do not want to go to these lengths, the ability of these programs to cut out the rekeying of text by accepting manuscripts on disk, and to integrate typesetting and layout, should cut publishing costs, and hopefully some of this saving will accrue to the author. Magazines are increasingly being produced by desktop publishing, and graphic designers, after initial suspicion of the new method, are adopting it for their work.

HOW DOES IT WORK?

Although desktop publishing programs differ in their features, most work in basically the same way. Instead of being marked up manually, and then typeset, the text is given invisible 'tags'. These specify the typeface, including its style and size, the letter, word and line spacing, and the alignment of the text. The program uses this information to format the text automatically in the equivalent of galleys. Some programs also have facilities for setting complicated tables, or mathematical equations.

Simultaneously the program lays out the text on the page (the equivalent of pasting up) in accordance with the instructions it has been given for page size, margins and number of columns. Illustrations can be positioned wherever required, and the text can be made to flow automatically around them. The other information needed on the page, such as headers, footers and page numbers, can be specified once and is then added automatically to each page. Some programs go further, and will automatically number sections as well as pages, and produce the index and table of contents for a book.

The end result is a complete page layout which can be viewed on-screen. The great advantage of this is that anything can be changed quickly and with immediate feedback. The change can be as simple as rewriting a few words so that the text fits a particular space, or as complex as changing the whole page layout with a different typeface, or a different number of columns. Various possibilities can be quickly tried out, and any obvious non-starters discarded as quickly, without needing to print out a page.

In practice it is necessary to print out a certain number of drafts, if only for proofreading, because the screen cannot show as much detail as the printed page – except for the most expensive systems the choice is between readable text on part of the page, or a full page view which only gives a general impression. These proofs can be produced relatively quickly, even on an inexpensive computer printer.

Once satisfied with the appearance of the document, the final printed version can be produced. If only a small number of copies are required, these can be produced on a laser printer. For larger print runs, such a printer can also be used to produce camera ready copy. This can then be reproduced by a photocopier, or photographed for platemaking and conventional printing. For the highest quality the camera ready copy can be produced on a special version of the normal typesetter which can take files direct from a desktop publishing program.

WHAT SORT OF EQUIPMENT IS NEEDED?

Anyone with a personal computer used for word processing can probably use it to make a start in desktop publishing, since there are now programs available for most machines. (If you do not already have a computer, and need some explanation of how they work, then turn to the article on word processing on page 469.) The three essentials are a screen which can display the page in sufficient detail for the text to be read easily, a printer to produce draft copies of the documents, and a mouse to operate the program.

Some screens such as the low resolution colour types found in cheaper computers are not suitable for desktop publishing, but higher resolution mono-chrome screens give quite acceptable results. The absence of colour is often no disadvantage since a great deal of printed matter is in black and white.

Although a laser printer is normally the minimum needed for high quality finished work, a surprising number of cheaper printers can produce draft versions which give a reasonable impression of the final result. You can then send a disk to a service bureau to have this run off on a laser printer or typesetter.

Most desktop publishing programs can be used with some dot matrix printers, and often with other types such as inkjets. As you might expect, inexpensive programs are more likely to cater for inexpensive printers, and vice versa.

Nowadays many computers are already equipped with a mouse (a small device which can be moved around the desktop to control an on-screen pointer). If not, models are now available to suit most types of computer and can be added relatively easily and cheaply.

Using your existing equipment with a relatively cheap program allows you to try your hand at dtp at little cost and if your requirements are simple this may well be all you need. If your requirements are more complex then it may well be worth spending more to allow work to be done more easily and quickly.

Updating a desktop publishing document on-screen is much more demanding than updating the text screen of an ordinary word processor. It will therefore be slower on a basic computer than on a more powerful machine. More expensive displays can also show more detail, and allow you to see more of the page on-screen while keeping the text readable.

Similarly non-laser printers usually take longer to print than lasers and their quality is not normally good enough for final prints. An inkjet printer like the HP Deskjet can give quality approaching a laser, at lower cost, but is still significantly slower. You may decide that the convenience of having your own laser justifies the cost.

Another piece of equipment which may be useful is a scanner. These convert photographs or drawings into electronic form for inclusion in desktop published documents. (This is not essential, since these can be pasted into camera ready copy in the conventional way, but it may be more convenient.) With special software, scanners can also convert typed or printed text into word processor files. Full page scanners are relatively expensive, but handheld versions covering a smaller area are much cheaper.

IS A SPECIAL PROGRAM NECESSARY?

When desktop publishing programs were first introduced word processing software was still producing much the same sort of output as an electric typewriter. Since then heavyweight word processors have added more and more desktop publishing-type features, such as multiple columns, headers and footers, the ability to include graphics, and to use a wide range of typefaces and sizes.

It is now claimed that it is possible to achieve much the same results with one of these programs as with true desktop publishing software. Is this true? The answer depends on what sort of work is to be done. The new generation of word processors is probably best suited to the business world, where there is a relatively narrow range of documents each with a standard format.

These programs tend not to have the flexibility in page layout needed for newsletters or magazines, or the more specialised features for longer documents which desktop publishing programs offer. Although the final results can be previewed on screen, these usually have to be achieved by giving instructions to the program, rather than changing the screen image directly.

A DETAILED LOOK AT PARTICULAR COMPUTERS

This section looks at the main types of computer, and the desktop publishing programs which are available for them. Printers can normally be used with any type of computer, and so are considered separately at the end. A certain amount of knowledge about the technicalities of computers is assumed – if you are unsure about some of the terms used these are explained in the article on word processing (see page 469).

IBM personal computers and compatibles

These are the predominant type of machine, in the business sector at least, and have the widest selection of hardware and software. At the basic level there are floppy disk machines, with just the basic 640k of memory, but these have been supplemented by machines with hard disks, more powerful processors, and more machine memory (RAM). The newer machines are faster but inevitably they are considerably more expensive. As a rough guideline you can buy a basic machine for well under £1000 but machines based on the 386 chip will cost at least twice as much as the basic model.

To a considerable extent the choice of machine will determine the choice of desktop publishing program since the heavyweight programs require a hard disk and at least one megabyte (sometimes two) of machine memory. The two leading contenders in this category are PC Pagemaker and Ventura Publisher. Their latest editions offer a wide range of facilities for producing complex page layouts and large books, with detailed and precise control over the size and positioning of print and illustrations, and also include index and table of contents compilation. A less well known but similarly heavyweight program is 3B2 by Advent. Inevitably such powerful programs are relatively costly (about the same as a basic machine).

Users of more modest machines may have to be content with programs at the other end of the spectrum, such as Timeworks Desktop Publisher. These cost only a fraction of the price of the heavyweights already mentioned but inevitably offer fewer facilities. Such programs would not be suitable for intensive book or magazine production but would be adequate for occasional use or as an introduction to desktop publishing.

Make sure however that these include the essentials of being able to tag text, incorporate illustrations, and adjust the resulting layout with the mouse until the on-screen result is satisfactory (some cheaper programs do not).

In between these two extremes are programs such as Deskpress or Gem Desktop Publisher which offer some of the facilities of the heavyweights at something like half their price. The disadvantage is that, if they prove inadequate for your needs, you will lose more than if you had bought a cheaper program.

A complicating factor is that, unlike the other programs mentioned, Pagemaker and the newer version of Ventura work only with the Windows program, which may have to be bought separately (though it is now often included with machines). However this can also be used with an increasing number of other programs such as word processors, spreadsheets and database programs.

There are a variety of display standards for IBM machines, of which Hercules monochrome is the minimum suitable for desktop publishing. In ascending order of resolution (and price) there are also EGA, VGA and Super VGA. VGA displays have fallen in price and are rapidly becoming the standard for all but the cheapest machines – the monochrome version is cheaper than colour, and perfectly adequate for desktop publishing. It can of course also be upgraded to colour later. Super VGA is a higher resolution, which allows more of a page to be shown on screen with readable characters.

Beyond this there are large screen displays which can show a whole page or a two page spread at actual size. These are intended for professional users for whom the time saved justifies the price of £2000 or more for a colour screen.

The Apple Macintosh (Mac)

Although selling in smaller numbers than IBM compatibles, these are the only other machine to make a significant impact on the business sector. Because the standard machine has all the necessary features they are particularly popular for graphic design and desktop publishing work.

Pagemaker originated on the Mac, but the other established heavyweight program is Quark Express – Ventura has only just appeared in a Mac version. A hard disk is essential for all of these, with minimum machine memory of one megabyte for Pagemaker, and two megabytes for Ventura and Quark Express. As with other programs which are available on both machines the Mac versions are cheaper than the IBM, but hitherto there have been no equivalents of the cheaper IBM programs. A new program, Personal Press, has now filled this gap. The machines themselves have tended in the past to be more expensive than IBM compatibles, but relatively cheap new basic models have changed that.

Macs offer a choice of monochrome or colour screens in different resolutions. Unlike IBM even the cheapest Mac provides a satisfactory display for desktop publishing, but large screen displays are available at a price for professional work.

Other machines

All the other machines suitable for this purpose have at least one desktop publishing program available. Programs for the Acorn and Amiga are offered by the makers of these machines, but the Atari has probably the widest choice, with heavyweight programs such as Calamus, Fleet Street Publisher, and Pagestream. There is also a version of Timeworks for this machine.

PRINTERS

Although it was the laser printer that helped to start desktop publishing, other types of printer such as the dot matrix or inkjet can be used. Dot matrix printers are usually 9 pin or 24 pin – the latter are more expensive, but give quicker and better quality output. Look for compatibility with the Epson range (FX for 9 pin, LQ for 24 pin) as these are most likely to be supported by desktop publishing programs. The wider range of built in fonts in more expensive machines is no advantage for desktop publishing (though it may be useful for other programs).

Inkjet printers are quieter than dot matrix but tend to cost more. The best known make is Hewlett Packard, whose Deskjet can produce quality almost as good as a laser and at a lower price (though rather more slowly). With all types of printer make sure that you can connect them to your computer. (There are different types of connection, and cables often have to be bought separately.)

Laser printers fall into two categories, Postscript or Postscript compatibles (such as the Apple Laserwriter) and the HP Laserjet and compatibles (also known as PCL printers). Originally the distinction between them was clear – PCL printers cost much less than Postscript, but lacked some of its features, such as the ability to generate a wide variety of type styles and sizes within the printer and to print reverse text (white on black) or very large size letters.

Now the situation is much more complex. On the one hand the difference between the price of Postscript and other laser printers is much less than it was. On the other hand many non-Postscript lasers can now be upgraded to full Postscript compatibility relatively cheaply, so that buying them does not foreclose the Postscript option.

Even without such an upgrade newer PCL printers such as the Laserjet III can generate a wider variety of typefaces and sizes internally in the same way as Postscript. For non-Postscript lasers, Hewlett Packard is the *de facto* standard, so if buying another make you should ensure that it is HP compatible.

FURTHER READING

Inevitably in a short article such as this it is only possible to give a brief introduction to the subject. There are too many books dealing with individual programs or topics to list individually, but the following books on general topics may be useful:

DTP The Complete Guide to Corporate Desktop Publishing by Robert Jones (Cambridge University Press)
Design for Desktop Publishing by John Miles (John Taylor Book Ventures)

Correcting Proofs

The following notes and table are extracted from BS 5261: Part 2: 1976 and are reproduced by permission of the British Standards Institution, 2 Park Street, London W1A 2BS, from whom copies of the complete Standard may be obtained.

NOTES ON COPY PREPARATION AND PROOF CORRECTION

The marks to be used for marking-up copy for composition and for the correction of printers' proofs shall be as shown in table 1.

The marks in table 1 are classified in three groups as follows.

(a) Group A: general.

(b) Group B: deletion, insertion and substitution.

(c) Group C: positioning and spacing.

Each item in table 1 is given a simple alpha-numeric serial number denoting the classification group to which it belongs and its position within the group.

The marks have been drawn keeping the shapes as simple as possible and using sizes which relate to normal practice. The shapes of the marks should be followed exactly by all who make use of them.

For each marking-up or proof correction instruction a distinct mark is to be made:

(a) in the text: to indicate the exact place to which the instruction refers;

(b) in the margin: to signify or amplify the meaning of the instruction.

It should be noted that some instructions have combined textual and marginal mark.

Where a number of instructions occur in one line, the marginal marks are to be divided between the left and right margins where possible, the order being from left to right in both margins.

Specification details, comments and instructions may be written on the copy or proof to complement the textual and marginal marks. Such written matter is to be clearly distinguishable from the copy and from any corrections made to the proof. Normally this is done by encircling the matter and/or by the appropriate use of colour (see below).

Proof corrections shall be made in coloured ink thus:

(a) printer's literal errors marked by the printer for correction: green;

(b) printer's literal errors marked by the customer and his agents for correction: red;

(c) alterations and instructions made by the customer and his agents: black or dark blue.

Table 1. Classified list of marks

NOTE. The letters M and P in the notes column indicate marks for marking-up copy and for correcting proofs respectively.

Group A   General

Number	Instruction	Textual mark	Marginal mark	Notes
A1	Correction is concluded	None	/	P Make after each correction
A2	Leave unchanged	- - - - - - under characters to remain	(√)	M P
A3	Remove extraneous marks	Encircle marks to be removed	X	P e.g. film or paper edges visible between lines on bromide or diazo proofs
A3.1	Push down risen spacing material	Encircle blemish	⊥	P
A4	Refer to appropriate authority anything of doubtful accuracy	Encircle word(s) affected	(?)	P

Group B   Deletion, insertion and substitution

Number	Instruction	Textual mark	Marginal mark	Notes
B1	Insert in text the matter indicated in the margin	ʎ	New matter followed by ʎ	M P Identical to B2
B2	Insert additional matter identified by a letter in a diamond	ʎ	ʎ Followed by for example ◇A	M P The relevant section of the copy should be supplied with the corresponding encircled letter marked on it e.g. ◇A
B3	Delete	/ through character(s) or ⊢—————⊣ through words to be deleted	♪	M P
B4	Delete and close up	⌢/⌣ through character or ⊨⊐⊏⊨ through characters e.g. charaͤcter charaͣcter	⌢♪	M P

Table 1 *(continued)*

Number	Instruction	Textual mark	Marginal mark	Notes
B5	Substitute character or substitute part of one or more word(s)	/ through character or ⊢————⊣ through word(s)	New character or new word(s)	M P
B6	Wrong fount. Replace by character(s) of correct fount	Encircle character(s) to be changed	⊗	P
B6.1	Change damaged character(s)	Encircle character(s) to be changed	✕	P This mark is identical to A3
B7	Set in or change to italic	——— under character(s) to be set or changed	⊔⊔	M P Where space does not permit textual marks encircle the affected area instead
B8	Set in or change to capital letters	≡≡≡ under character(s) to be set or changed	≡	
B9	Set in or change to small capital letters	══ under character(s) to be set or changed	══	
B9.1	Set in or change to capital letters for initial letters and small capital letters for the rest of the words	≡ under initial letters and ══ under rest of the word(s)	≡	
B10	Set in or change to bold type	∼∼∼∼∼ under character(s) to be set or changed	∼	
B11	Set in or change to bold italic type	∼∼∼∼∼ under character(s) to be set or changed	⊔⊔∼	
B12	Change capital letters to lower case letters	Encircle character(s) to be changed	≢	P For use when B5 is inappropriate

Table 1 *(continued)*

Number	Instruction	Textual mark	Marginal mark	Notes
B12.1	Change small capital letters to lower case letters	Encircle character(s) to be changed	≠	P For use when B5 is inappropriate
B13	Change italic to upright type	Encircle character(s) to be changed	ᰔ	P
B14	Invert type	Encircle character to be inverted	↻	P
B15	Substitute or insert character in 'superior' position	/ through character or ʌ where required	⌐ under character e.g. ⌐2	P
B16	Substitute or insert character in 'inferior' position	/ through character or ʌ where required	⌐ over character e.g. /2	P
B17	Substitute ligature e.g. fh for separate letters	⊢———⊣ through characters affected	⌒ e.g. f͡h	P
B17.1	Substitute separate letters for ligature	⊢———⊣	Write out separate letters	P
B18	Substitute or insert full stop or decimal point	/ through character or ʌ where required	⊙	M P
B18.1	Substitute or insert colon	/ through character or ʌ where required	⦂	M P
B18.2	Substitute or insert semi-colon	/ through character or ʌ where required	;	M P

Table 1 *(continued)*

Number	Instruction	Textual mark	Marginal mark	Notes
B18.3	Substitute or insert comma	/ through character *or* ⋋ where required	و	M P
B18.4	Substitute or insert apostrophe	/ through character *or* ⋋ where required	⸲	M P
B18.5	Substitute or insert single quotation marks	/ through character *or* ⋋ where required	⸲ and/or ⸲	M P
B18.6	Substitute or insert double quotation marks	/ through character *or* ⋋ where required	⸲ and/or ⸲	M P
B19	Substitute or insert ellipsis	/ through character *or* ⋋ where required	•••	M P
B20	Substitute or insert leader dots	/ through character *or* ⋋ where required	(•••)	M P Give the measure of the leader when necessary
B21	Substitute or insert hyphen	/ through character *or* ⋋ where required	⊨	M P
B22	Substitute or insert rule	/ through character ⋋ where required	⊢	M P Give the size of the rule in the marginal mark e.g. ⊢1 em⊣ ⊢4 mm⊣

Table 1 *(continued)*

Number	Instruction	Textual mark	Marginal mark	Notes
B23	Substitute or insert oblique	/ through character or ⅄ where required	⊘	M P

Group C Positioning and spacing

Number	Instruction	Textual mark	Marginal mark	Notes
C1	Start new paragraph			M P
C2	Run on (no new paragraph)			M P
C3	Transpose characters or words	between characters or words, numbered when necessary		M P
C4	Transpose a number of characters or words	3 2 1 | | |	123	M P To be used when the sequence cannot be clearly indicated by the use of C3. The vertical strokes are made through the characters or words to be transposed and numbered in the correct sequence
C5	Transpose lines			M P
C6	Transpose a number of lines		——— 3 ——— 2 ——— 1	P To be used when the sequence cannot be clearly indicated by C5. Rules extend from the margin into the text with each line to be transposed numbered in the correct sequence
C7	Centre	enclosing matter to be centred	[ ]	M P
C8	Indent			P Give the amount of the indent in the marginal mark

Table 1 *(continued)*

Number	Instruction	Textual mark	Marginal mark	Notes
C9	Cancel indent			P
C10	Set line justified to specified measure	and/or		P Give the exact dimensions when necessary
C11	Set column justified to specified measure			M P Give the exact dimensions when necessary
C12	Move matter specified distance to the right	enclosing matter to be moved to the right		P Give the exact dimensions when necessary
C13	Move matter specified distance to the left	enclosing matter to be moved to the left		P Give the exact dimensions when necessary
C14	Take over character(s), word(s) or line to next line, column or page			P The textual mark surrounds the matter to be taken over and extends into the margin
C15	Take back character(s), word(s), or line to previous line, column or page			P The textual mark surrounds the matter to be taken back and extends into the margin
C16	Raise matter	over matter to be raised under matter to be raised		P Give the exact dimensions when necessary. (Use C28 for insertion of space between lines or paragraphs in text)
C17	Lower matter	over matter to be lowered under matter to be lowered		P Give the exact dimensions when necessary. (Use C29 for reduction of space between lines or paragraphs in text)
C18	Move matter to position indicated	Enclose matter to be moved and indicate new position		P Give the exact dimensions when necessary

Table 1 *(continued)*

Number	Instruction	Textual mark	Marginal mark	Notes
C19	Correct vertical alignment	‖ ‖	‖ ‖	P
C20	Correct horizontal alignment	Single line above and below misaligned matter e.g. mi₅aligned	― ―	P The marginal mark is placed level with the head and foot of the relevant line
C21	Close up. Delete space between characters or words	linking ⌒⌣ characters	⌒⌣	M P
C22	Insert space between characters	| between characters affected	Y	M P Give the size of the space to be inserted when necessary
C23	Insert space between words	Y between words affected	Y	M P Give the size of the space to be inserted when necessary
C24	Reduce space between characters	| between characters affected	⟰	M P Give the amount by which the space is to be reduced when necessary
C25	Reduce space between words	⟰ between words affected	⟰	M P Give amount by which the space is to be reduced when necessary
C26	Make space appear equal between characters or words	| between characters or words affected	Ⴘ	M P
C27	Close up to normal interline spacing	(each side of column linking lines)		M P The textual marks extend into the margin

Marked galley proof of text

(B9.1) =/

(B13) ⊣/

(C7) []/

(C9) ⊐/

(B12) ≠/

(B18.5) ˘/

(B18.5) ˘/

(B6) Ⓚ/

(B17) ʈ̂/

(C8) ⊐/

(B14) Ω/

(A4) ⑦/
(B7) ɯ/

(A3.1) ⊥/
(B18.1) ⊙/

(B15) ˘/

(C26) ⅄/

(B8) ≡/
(B6) Ⓧ/

(C27)

(B18) ⊙/

(C27)

(B18.3) '/

(C21) ⊃/

(C19) |||/

(C22) Ƴ/

(B10) ᴡ/

(B9) =/

(B1) i⅃/

(A2) ✓/
(B19) .../

(C23) Ƴ/
(C1) ⌐/

(B5) t/

(B3) ∂/

(C3) ⌐/

(B7) ɯ/

(C20) ═/

(B2) ⟨Ⓐ/

(A3) ✗/

(B12.1) ≠/

(C2) ⌐/
(B4) ∂/

(B22) Hɪ/
(C14)

(B21) Hɪ/
(C6) 3/

(C25) Ƴ/

(C28) (+1pt

(C29))−1pt

At the sign of the red plate

The Life and Work of William Caxton, by H W Larken

[An Extract]

Few people, even in the field of printing, have any clear conception of what William Caxton did or, indeed, of what he was. Much of this lack of knowledge is due to the absence of information that can be counted as factual and the consequent tendency to vague generalisation.

Though it is well known that Caxton was born in the county of Kent, there is no information as to the precise place. In his prologue to the *History of Troy*, William Caxton wrote "for in France I was never and was born and learned my English in Kent in the Weald where I doubt not is spoken as broad and rude English as in any place of England." During the fifteenth century there were a great number of Flemish cloth weavers in Kent; most of them had come to England at the instigation of Edward III with the object of teaching their craft to the English. So successful was this venture that the English cloth trade flourished and the agents who sold the cloth (the mercers) became very wealthy people. There have been many speculations concerning the origin of the Caxton family and much research has been carried out. It is assumed often that Caxton's family must have been connected with the wool trade in order to have secured his apprenticeship to an influential merchant.

W. Blyth Crotch (*Prologues and Epilogues of William Caxton*) suggests that the origin of the name Caxton (of which there are several variations in spelling) may be traced to Cambridgeshire but notes that many writers have suggested that Caxton was connected with a family at Hadlow or alternatively a family in Canterbury.

Of the Canterbury connection a William Caxton became freeman of the City in 1431 and William Pratt, a mercer who was the printer's friend, was born there. H. R. Plomer suggests that Pratt and Caxton might possibly have been schoolboys together, perhaps at the school St. Alphege. In this parish there lived a John Caxton who used as his mark three cakes over a barrel (or tun) and who is mentioned in an inscription on a monument in the church of St. Alphege.

In 1941, Alan Keen (an authority on manuscripts) secured some documents concerning Caxton; these are now in the BRITISH MUSEUM. Discovered in the library of Earl Winterton at Shillinglee Park by Richard Holworthy, the documents cover the period 1420 to 1467. One of Winterton's ancestors purchased the manor of West Wratting from a family named Caxton, the property being situated in the Weald of Kent.

There is also record of a property mentioning Philip Caxton and his wife Dennis who had two sons, Philip (born in 1413) and William.

Particularly interesting in these documents is one recording that Philip Caxton junior sold the manor of Little Wratting to John Christemasse of London in 1436, the deed having been witnessed by two aldermen, one of whom was Robert Large, the printer's employer. Further, in 1439 the other son, William Caxton, con Wratting to John Christemasse, and an indenture of 1457 concerning this property mentions one William Caxton veyed his rights in the manor Bluntes Hall at Little alias Causton. It is an interesting coincidence to note that the lord of the manor of Little Wratting was the father of Margaret, Duchess of Burgundy.

In 1420, a Thomas Caxton of Tenterden witnessed the will of a fellow townsman; he owned property in Kent and appears to have been a person of some importance.

[1] See 'William Caxton'.

Ⓐ *attached to Christchurch Monastery in the parish of*

AT THE SIGN OF THE RED PALE

The Life and Work of William Caxton, *by H W Larken*

An Extract

FEW PEOPLE, even in the field of printing, have any clear conception of what William Caxton did or, indeed, of what he was. Much of this lack of knowledge is due to the absence of information that can be counted as factual and the consequent tendency to vague generalisation.

Though it is well known that Caxton was born in the county of Kent, there is no information as to the precise place. In his prologue to the *History of Troy*, William Caxton wrote '. . . for in France I was never and was born and learned my English in Kent in the Weald where I doubt not is spoken as broad and rude English as in any place of England.'

During the fifteenth century there were a great number of Flemish cloth weavers in Kent; most of them had come to England at the instigation of Edward III with the object of teaching their craft to the English. So successful was this venture that the English cloth trade flourished and the agents who sold the cloth (the mercers) became very wealthy people.

There have been many speculations concerning the origin of the Caxton family and much research has been carried out. It is often assumed that Caxton's family must have been connected with the wool trade in order to have secured his apprenticeship to an influential merchant.

W. Blyth Crotch (*Prologues and Epilogues of William Caxton*) suggests that the origin of the name Caxton (of which there are several variations in spelling) may be traced to Cambridgeshire but notes that many writers have suggested that Caxton was connected with a family at Hadlow or alternatively a family in Canterbury.

Of the Canterbury connection: a William Caxton became freeman of the City in 1431 and William Pratt, a mercer who was the printer's friend, was born there. H.R. Plomer[1] suggests that Pratt and Caxton might possibly have been schoolboys together, perhaps at the school attached to Christchurch Monastery in the parish of St. Alphege. In this parish there lived a John Caxton who used as his mark three cakes over a barrel (or tun) and who is mentioned in an inscription on a monument in the church of St. Alphege.

In 1941, Alan Keen (an authority on manuscripts) secured some documents concerning Caxton; these are now in the British Museum. Discovered in the library of Earl Winterton at Shillinglee Park by Richard Holworthy, the documents cover the period 1420 to 1467. One of Winterton's ancestors purchased the manor of West Wratting from a family named Caxton, the property being situated in the Weald of Kent. There is also record of a property mentioning Philip Caxton and his wife Dennis who had two sons, Philip (born in 1413) and William.

Particularly interesting in these documents is one recording that Philip Caxton junior sold the manor of Little Wratting to John Christemasse of London in 1436— the deed having been witnessed by two aldermen, one of whom was Robert Large, the printer's employer. Further, in 1439, the other son, William Caxton, conveyed his rights in the manor Bluntes Hall at Little Wratting to John Christemasse, and an indenture of 1457 concerning this property mentions one William Caxton alias Causton. It is an interesting coincidence to note that the lord of the manor of Little Wratting was the father of Margaret, Duchess of Burgundy.

In 1420, a Thomas Caxton of Tenterden witnessed the will of a fellow townsman; he owned property in Kent and appears to have been a person of some importance.

[1] See 'William Caxton'.

Table 1 *(continued)*

Number	Instruction	Textual mark	Marginal mark	Notes
C28	Insert space between lines or paragraphs		*(or)*	M P The marginal mark extends between the lines of text. Give the size of the space to be inserted when necessary
C29	Reduce space between lines or paragraphs		*(or)*	M P The marginal mark extends between the lines of text. Give the amount by which the space is to be reduced when necessary

Editorial, Literary and Production Services

The following list of specialists offer a wide variety of services to writers (both new and established), to publishers, journalists and others. Services include advice on MSS, editing and book production, indexing, translation, research, writing, marketing and publicity.

Abbey Writing Services (1989), 30 Palmerston Street, Romsey, Hants SO51 8GG *tel* (0794) 515939 *fax* 0794 3c. *Director:* John McIlwain. Offers a comprehensive editorial service: editing, copy-editing, proof-reading. Writing of all types. Advisory service on educational matters.

Academic File (Centre for Near East, Asia and Africa Research Limited) (1985), PO Box 571, Ground Floor, 172 Castelnau, London SW13 9DH *tel* 081-741 5878 *telex* 940 12777 Near G *fax* 081-741 5671. *Directors:* Sajid Rizvi, Shirley Rizvi. Research, advisory and consultancy services related to politics, economics (oil, etc.) and societies of the Middle East, Asia and North Africa and related issues in Europe: editing, editorial assessment, art and design and desktop publishing.

Academic Projects/Research Factors (Features & Editorial Services), 84 Rupert Street, Norwich NR2 2AT *tel* (0603) 615416/620301. *Editors:* Dr Dennis Chaplin, Caroline du Sautoy. Features, backgrounders, research briefs for press and broadcasting. Subjects include: defence, politics, technology, medicine, economics, finance, business, marketing, PR, advertising. Also: press releases, promotorials, special feature projects, ghosted books/features, book editing, typing, word processing, house journals, speeches, magazine/ newspaper editing/design/typesetting (desktop). Researchers always needed (CVs only).

Airplay (1988), PO Box 175, Bath BA1 2FX *tel* (0225) 743782/318335. Consists of a major radio-drama producer, mainstream actors and editors with access to full stereo recording studio facilities for the production of pilot tapes for new musicals, screen and teleplays and stage plays. This fusion means that Airplay can offer very favourable terms. Full details by return.

Alpha Word Power (1985), 84 Claypath, Durham DH1 1RG *tel* 091-384 7219 *fax* 091-384 3767 *modem* 091-384 3767. Publishing services: camera-ready copy, word processing, desk editing, proof-reading, liaison with printers/ binders/graphic design; full secretarial services; business services. Specialise in speed of turnaround.

Anvil Editorial Associates (1966), Lleifior, Malltraeth, Bodorgan, Anglesey, Gwynedd LL62 5AF *tel* Bodorgan (0407) 840688 *fax* (0407) 840180. *Director:* Dr H. Bernard-Smith. Comprehensive editorial service, including editing, indexing, copy-editing and proof-reading. Planning, preparation, writing and editing of books, house journals, company histories, reports, brochures, promotional literature, pamphlets and scripts. Full MS service.

Archaeological Consultants, Lesley and Roy Adkins, Longstone Lodge, Aller, Langport, Somerset TA10 0QT *tel* (0458) 250075. Work with an archaeological, historical and heritage theme undertaken, including all types of research, critical assessment of manuscripts, contract writing for publishers, indexing, some illustration, and picture research.

Arioma Editorial Services. Gloucester House, High Street, Borth, Dyfed SY24 5HZ *tel* (0970) 871 296. *Partners:* Moira Smith, Patrick Smith. Research, co-writing, ghost-writing, indexing; manuscripts prepared for monographs. *Speciality:* military aviation history.

Authors' Advisory Service (1972), 21 Campden Grove, Kensington, London W8 4JG   *tel* 071-937 5583. All typescripts professionally evaluated in depth and edited by long-established publishers' reader specialising in constructive advice to new writers and with wide experience of current literary requirements. Critic and reader for literary awards. Lecture service on the craft and technique of writing for publication.

Authors in Science Consultancy (1987), Sally Crawford, 112 Great Titchfield Street, London W1P 7AJ   *tel* 071-637 1759. Experienced medical editor, publishers' reader and health writer offers general/technical editing service to publishers. Good rapport with authors new and established.

Authors' Research Services (1966), Richard Wright, 32 Oak Village, London NW5 4QN   *tel/fax* 071-284 4316. Offers comprehensive research service to writers, academics and business people world-wide, including fact checking, bibliographical references and document supply. Specialises in English history, social sciences, business.

Laraine Bamrah, 61 rue de Parmain, 95430 Butry sur Oise, Auvers sur Oise, France   *tel* (1) 34 73 09 75. British freelance writer and researcher resident in France's 'Impressionist' valley. Editorial, commercial picture and script research. Covers most fields including fashion, tourism, World War II, human interest. Production assistant and liaison for radio, TV and film. Translations from French.

Benn's Media Information Service (BEMIS), established 1978 in association with *Benn's Media Directory*, Benn Business Information Services Ltd, PO Box 20, Sovereign Way, Tonbridge, Kent TN9 1RQ   *tel* (0732) 362666   *telex* 95454 Bbis G   *fax* (0732) 770483. Primarily an updating service for subscribers to *Benn's Media Directory*. Spot enquiries by telephone regarding the Press or Broadcasting media – either in the UK or elsewhere in the world – answered normally without charge. Enquiries needing in-depth research (current or historical) are individually costed before the work is undertaken.

Beswick Writing Services (1988), Francis Beswick, 19 Haig Road, Stretford M32 0DS   *tel* 061-865 1259. Manuscript criticism/advice, creative and copy-editing, ghost writing, information books, proof-reading. Special interests: religious, ecology, outdoor activities, philosophical and educational. Expertise in correspondence courses.

Book Doctor (1990), 65 Albion Road, London N16 9PP   *tel* 071-923 2480/ 081-560 2751   *fax* 071-923 2480. *Partners:* Susan Moore, Joy Chamberlain. Troubleshooting service for publishers, packagers and agents: co-authorship with specialists, ghost writing, re-writing, translation fine tuning, re-drafting.

Book Production Consultants (1973), 47 Norfolk Street, Cambridge CB1 2LE   *tel* (0223) 352790   *fax* (0223) 460718. *Directors:* A.P. Littlechild, C.S. Walsh. Complete book production service: editing, designing, illustrating, translating, indexing, artwork; production management of printing and binding. For books, journals, manuals, reports, diaries, promotional products.

Bookwatch Ltd (1982), 15-up, East Street, Lewin's Yard, Chesham, Bucks. HP5 1HQ   *tel* (0494) 792269   *fax* (0494) 784850. *Directors:* Peter Harland, Jennifer Harland, Simon Westcott. Market research, bestseller lists, syndicated reviews, features. Publishers of *Books in the Media*, weekly for booksellers and librarians.

Harriet Bridgeman and Elizabeth Drury, 19 Chepstow Road, London W2 5BP   *tel* 071-229 7420/727 4065   *fax* 071-792 8509. Editors; specialists in fine art book production and design.

Brooke Associates (Manchester) Ltd (1979, incorporated 1987), 21 Barnfield, Urmston, Manchester M31 1EW   *tel* 061-746 8140   *telex* 265871 Monref G, ref 72 Mag 20263   *fax* 061-746 8132. Research, editing and contract writing. Specialises in business, management, tourism, history, biography, social science.

Mrs D. Buckmaster (1966), 51 Chatsworth Road, Torquay TQ1 3BJ   *tel* (0803) 294663. General editing of MSS, specialising in traditional themes in religious, metaphysical and esoteric subjects. Also success and inspirational books or articles.

Bucks Literary Services (1983), 73 Vicarage Road, Marsworth, Nr Tring, Herts. HP23 4LU   *tel* Cheddington (0296) 668630. *Partners:* J.L.N. Stobbs, A.M.B. Stobbs. Authors' advisory, editorial and typing service.

Causeway Resources (1989), 8 The Causeway, Teddington, Middlesex TW11 0HE   *tel* 081-977 8797/943 3290. *Director:* Keith Skinner. Genealogical, biographical and historical research, specialising in family and police history.

Central Office of Information, Hercules Road, London SE1 7DU   *tel* 071-928 2345. Commissions feature articles on British affairs for publication in overseas newspapers, magazines and trade press. Commissions photography, illustrations, artwork and design.

Karyn Claridge Book Production (1989), 244 Bromham Road, Biddenham, Bedford MK40 4AA   *tel* (0234) 347909. Complete book production management service offered to publishers from manuscript to bound copies; graphic services also available.

Judy Corbett, Freelance Researches (1987), Dolbelidr, Trefnant, St Asaph, Clwyd LL17 0BB   *tel* (074 574) 659. Offers comprehensive research and typing service covering all topics including genealogy.

Ingrid Cranfield (1972), 16 Myddelton Gardens, Winchmore Hill, London N21 2PA   *tel* 081-360 2433. Advisory and editorial services for authors and media, including critical assessment, rewriting, proof-reading, copy-editing, writing of marketing copy, indexing, research, interviews and transcripts. Special interests: geography, travel, exploration, adventure (own archives), language, education, youth training. Translations from German and French.

Creative Comics, Denis Gifford, 80 Silverdale, Sydenham, London SE26   *tel* 081-699 7725. Specialises in strip cartoons and comics for both adults and children, custom-tailored to clients' requirements. Everything from jokes, puzzles, and single strips to serials and complete comics, books, supplements and giveaways.

David A. Cross, West Wing, Isel Hall, Cockermouth, Cumbria CA13 0QG   *tel* 0900-827555. Research and information service; editing texts, specialising in art history, English literature, biography and genealogy; creative writing tutorials.

Margaret Crush (1980), Moonfleet, Burney Road, West Humble, Dorking, Surrey RH5 6AU   *tel* (0306) 884347. Editing, copy-editing, writing, rewriting and proof-reading for publishers, especially illustrated books and children's books.

Meg and Stephen Davies, 31 Egerton Road, Ashton, Preston, Lancs. PR2 1AJ   *tel* (0772) 725120   *fax* (0772) 723853. Indexing to general and post-graduate level in the arts and humanities. Can offer indexes on PC disk. Also proof-reading and copy-editing. Registered Indexer with Society of Indexers since 1971, founder member of Society of Freelance Editors and Proofreaders.

DD Editorial Services (1983), Gosford House, Gosford Road, Beccles, Suffolk NR34 9QX   *tel* (0502) 717735. *Partners:* D. Derbyshire, J. Nicholls. Proof-reading, copy-editing, indexing, index repagination, compilation of diaries.

Andrew Duncan (1986), 19 Rainham Road, London NW10 5DL   *tel* 081-969 8332. A professional researcher working in historical and contemporary sources.

Editorial/Visual Research (1973), Angela Murphy, 21 Leamington Road Villas, London W11 1HS   *tel* 071-727 4920   *fax* on application. Comprehensive research service including historical, literary, film and picture research for writers, publishers, film and television companies. Services also include copy-writing, editing, and travel and feature writing.

Dr Martin Edwards (1985), 2 Highbury Hall, 22 Highbury Road, Weston-super-Mare, Avon BS23 2DN   *tel* (0934) 621261. Specialist editorial and research service in the medico-scientific field: including copy-editing, co-editorial/-authorship, proof-reading, abstracting and conference productions. Special interest in the improvement of foreign texts.

FIVE SEVEN NINE ONE: Caroline White Communications (1985), 78 Howard Road, Walthamstow, London E17 4SQ   *tel* 081-521 5791. Technical editing of illustrated books and journals, particularly medicine, ecology, history. Research and writing of features for newspapers, magazines and radio, specialising in medical and social issues. Corporate literature.

Brian J. Ford, Rothay House, 6 Mayfield Road, Eastrea, Cambs. PE7 2AY   *tel* (0733) 350888. Scientist and adviser on scientific matters; author, producer/director scientific films and programmes in addition to editor/contributor to many leading books and journals. Has hosted many leading BBC television and radio programmes, and overseas documentaries.

Sydney Francis (1987), 19 Rainham Road, London NW10 5DL   *tel* 081-969 8332. Editor, non-fiction (illustrated or unillustrated). Editorial planning of books or series, development of projects, project management, editorial services, rewriting. Specialist interests: history and travel.

Freelance Editorial Services (1975), Bill Houston, BSc, DipLib, MPhil. 45 Bridge Street, Musselburgh, Midlothian EH21 6AA   *tel* 031-665 7825. Editing, proof-reading, indexing, abstracting, translations, bibliographies; particularly scientific and medical.

Freelance Press Services (1967), Cumberland House, Lissadel Street, Salford M6 6GG   *tel* 061-745 8850   *fax* 061-745 8827. A Market Research Department for the freelance writer and photographer. Issues a monthly Market News service the *Freelance Market News*; £21.00 p.a. A good rate of pay made for news of editorial requirements. (Small amounts are credited until a worthwhile payment is reached.) Agents for the UK for the books of the American Writer Inc. and Writer's Digest Books, including *The Writer's Handbook*; also the American *Writer's Market*. Writers' market guides for Canada and Australia.

Jean Gay (1965), April Cottage, Hatch Lane, Tisbury, Salisbury, Wilts. SP3 6NT   *tel* (0747) 871201. *Director:* Mrs Jean Ayres-Gay. Copy-editing, proof-reading, indexing, index-refolioing.

Geo Group & Associates, 4 Christian Fields, London SW16 3JZ   *tel* 081-764 6292. Visual aid production services: slide packs; filmstrips; colour to monochrome processing; packaging. Photo library. Commission photography. Specialist work for educational publishing. Audio tape production.

C.N. Gilmore (1987), 19B St Michael's Road, Bedford MK40 2LY *tel* (0234) 261853. Sub-editing, copy-editing, slush-pile reading, reviewing. Will also collaborate. Undertakes work in all scholarly and academic fields as well as fiction and practical writing.

Graphic Design and Illustration (1988), R.J. Billington, Thorneydown Cottage, Policeman's Corner, Winterbourne Gunner, Salisbury, Wilts. SP4 6LN *tel* (0980) 610760 *fax* (0980) 610164. Offers all types of artwork support to authors and publishers, from graphs, diagrams and line drawings to professional cartography and full-colour illustration, including children's. Quotations sent by return on receipt of rough/brief or faxes same day. Over fifteen major publishers on client list.

Guildford Reading Services (1978), 31 Southway, Guildford, Surrey GU2 6DA *tel* (0483) 504325/(0252) 317950. *Director:* B.V. Varney. Proofreading, press revision, copy preparation, sub-editing.

John Hassell (1973), Mayfield House, Clench, Marlborough, Wilts. SN8 4NT *tel* (0672) 810 384. *Director:* John Hassell. Advisory and editorial work for authors.

Bernard Hawton, 137 Park Road, Chandler's Ford, Hants SO5 1HT *tel* (0703) 267400. Proof-reading, copy-editing.

Historica Consultancy (1986), 8-9 The Incline, Coalport, Telford, Shropshire TF8 7HR *tel* (0952) 680050 *fax* (0952) 587184. Consultants for drama, documentary and fiction, specialising in European history and culture.

Historical Newspaper Loan Service (1972), 8 Monks Avenue, New Barnet, Herts. EN5 1DB *tel* 081-440 3159. *Proprietor:* John Frost. Headline stories from 40,000 British and overseas newspapers reporting major events since 1850.

Holland-Ford Associates (Robert), 103 Lydyett Lane, Barnton, Northwich, Cheshire CW8 4JT *tel* (0606) 76960. *Director:* Robert Holland-Ford. Impresarios, Concert/Lecture Agents.

Rosemary Horstmann, 43 Westcombe Park Road, Blackheath, London SE3 7QZ *tel* 081-853 4706. Broadcasting scripts evaluated. General consultancy on editorial and marketing matters. Tuition in interviewing and taperecording, lectures, writing workshops. Send sae for brochure.

E.J. Hunter, 6 Dorset Road, London N22 4SL *tel* 081-889 0370. Editing, copyediting, proof-reading. Appraisal of typescripts. Special interests: novels, short stories, drama, children's stories; primary education, alternative medicine, New Age.

Hurst Village Publishing (1989), Henry and Elizabeth Farrar, High Chimneys, Davis Street, Hurst, Reading RG10 0TH *tel* (0734) 345211 *fax* (0734) 320348. Offers design, photography, typesetting, printing and binding services, using the latest desktop publishing programs, photographic equipment and high-quality laser printers.

Society of Indexers, 16 Green Road, Birchington, Kent CT7 9JZ (see **Societies** and **Article** for further details).

Indexing Specialists (1965), 202 Church Road, Hove, East Sussex BN3 2DJ *tel* (0273) 23309 *fax* (0273) 208278. *Director:* Richard Raper, BSc, DTA. Indexes for books, journals and reference publications on professional, scientific and general subjects. *Consultancy:* indexing projects, their design and cost.

The Information Bureau (formerly **Daily Telegraph Information Bureau**), 51 The Business Centre, 103 Lavender Hill, London SW11 5QL   *tel* 071-924 4414. *Manager:* Jane Hall. Offers an on-demand research service on a variety of subjects including current affairs, business, marketing, history, the arts, media and politics. Resources include range of cuttings amassed by the bureau since 1948.

Ken Jackson (1985), 30 The Boundary, Langton Green, Tunbridge Wells, Kent TN3 0YB   *tel* (0892) 545198. Commissioning, copy-editing, proof-reading, indexing, particularly of technical or religious manuscripts.

Sara Kerruish Literary Agency (1985), Fuaran, Coldwell End, Youlgreave, Derbyshire DE4 1UY   *tel* (0629) 636731. Editing, copy-editing, proof-reading, indexing.

Hugh Lamb (1983), 10 The Crescent, Westmead Road, Sutton, Surrey SM1 4HU   *tel* 081-661 1936. Experienced journalist, proof-reader and anthologist offers proof-reading for publishers and typesetters, sub-editing, rewrite work, etc.; experienced in book, magazine and institution work.

Laserbacks (1987), Ann Kritzinger Ltd, 20 Shepherds Hill, London N6 5AH   *tel* 081-341 7650. *Directors:* Ann Kritzinger (managing), Kim Spanoghe (technical), Michael Davis (secretary). Fast high-tech production of cost-effective short-run books for self-publishers, from typescript (or disk) to bound copies (hardbacks or paperbacks, sewn or unsewn).

Leeds Postcards (Northern Trading Co-operative Ltd) (1979), PO Box 84, Leeds, West Yorkshire LS1 4HT   *tel* (0532) 468649   *fax* (0532) 436730. *Directors:* Richard Honey, Christine Hankinson, Alison Sheldon, Stephen Edwards, Dinah Clark. Publishing, printing and distribution service for artists, campaigns and unions, specialising in postcards and greeting cards.

Library Research Agency (1974), Burberry, Devon Road, Salcombe, Devon TQ8 8HJ   *tel* (0548 84) 2769. *Directors:* D.J. Langford, MA, B. Langford. Research and information service for writers, journalists, artists, businessmen from libraries, archives, museums, record offices and newspapers in UK, USA and Europe. Sources may be in English, French, German, Russian, Serbo-Croat, Bulgarian.

London Media Workshops (1978), 101 King's Drive, Gravesend, Kent DA12 5BQ   *tel* (0474) 564676. *Booking secretary:* Linda Forbes. Short courses run by top working professionals in writing for radio, television, video and the press.

Kenneth Lysons (1986), MA, MEd, DPA, DMS, FCIS, FInstPS, FBIM, Lathom, Scotchbarn Lane, Whiston, nr Prescot, Merseyside L35 7JB   *tel* 051-426 5513. Company and institutional histories, support material for organisational management and supervisory training, house journals, research and reports service. Full secretarial support.

Duncan McAra (1988), 30 Craighall Crescent, Edinburgh EH6 4RZ   *tel* 031-552 1558. Consultancy on all aspects of general trade publishing; editing; proof correction; reading, assessing and placing typescripts with suitable publishers. Main subjects include art, architecture, archaeology, biography, film, military and travel.

Sally McCann (1987), MA, 18 Devonshire Drive, Alderley Edge, Cheshire SK9 7HT   *tel* (0625) 584260. Editing, author liaison and proofing of non-fiction works (especially academic and educational) in the arts, social sciences and humanities.

McText (1986), Denmill, Tough, By Alford, Aberdeenshire AB3 8EP *tel/fax* (09755) 62582. *Partners:* K. and Duncan McArdle. Editing, proof-reading, copywriting for: ads and promotion, brochures, catalogues, DTP (incl. production), house journals, manuals. French, German translation.

Manuscript Appraisals (1984), 95 Bramble Road, Eastwood, Leigh-on-Sea, Essex SS9 5HA *tel* (0437) 563822. *Proprietor:* Raymond J. Price; *consultants:* N.L. Price, MBIM, Mary Hunt. An independent appraisal of authors' MSS (fiction and non-fiction, but no poetry) with full editorial guidance and advice. Proof-reading if required. Interested in the work of new writers.

Marlinoak (1984), 22 Eve's Croft, Birmingham B32 3QL *tel* 021-475 6139. *Proprietors:* Alan L. Billing, MBIM, Hazel J. Billing, JP, BA, DipEd. Preparation of scripts, plays, books, MSS service, ghostwriting, proof reading, research. Audio-transcription, word processing and full secretarial facilities.

James Moore Associates (1975), 51 Firs Chase, West Mersea, Essex CO5 8NN *tel* (0206) 382073 *fax* (0206) 382326. *Partners:* James Moore, BCom, Inge Moore. Editorial from MSS to printing. Special subjects: educational (especially language courses), music, travel, sailing, ships and the sea. Picture research, organises artwork and photography, proof-reading, translation from/into German, from French.

Morley Adams Ltd (1917), 20 Spectrum House, 32/34 Gordon House Road, London NW5 1LP *tel* 071-284 1433 *fax* 071-284 4494. *Directors:* M.J. Gay, E. Rayner, R. Simpson. Specialists in the production of crosswords and other puzzles, quizzes, etc. Experts in handling advertisers' competitions.

Elizabeth Murray (1975), 3 Gower Mews Mansions, Gower Mews, London WC1E 6HR *tel/fax* 071-636 3761. Literary, biographical, historical research for authors, radio, theatre and television.

Andrew Nash (1981), 15 Cedar Road, Farnborough, Hants GU14 7AU *tel* (0252) 514466. Non-fiction. Writing, rewriting and editing including joint authorship with subject specialists. Reworking of books, leaflets, etc., to chosen reading level. Rewriting of specialist and technical material in plain English. For texts thus written or edited, preparation of artwork brief, glossary, and/or index. Also copy-editing and proof-reading.

Paul Nash (1979), Rhandir Isaf, Croesaubach, Oswestry, Shropshire SY10 9BG *tel* (0691) 652650. Indexing of technical publications; proof-reading. Registered indexer with Society of Indexers.

Paul H. Niekirk (1976), 40 Rectory Avenue, High Wycombe, Bucks. HP13 6HW *tel* (0494) 27200. Text editing for works of reference and professional and management publications, particularly texts on law. Freelance writing. Editorial consultancy and training. Marketing consultancy and research.

Northern Writers Advisory Services (1986), 77 Marford Crescent, Sale, Cheshire M33 4DN *tel* 061-969 1573. *Proprietor:* Jill Groves. Offers word processing, copy-editing, proof-reading and desktop publishing to small publishers, societies and authors.

Northgate Training (1978), Scarborough House, 29 James Street West, Bath, Avon BA1 2BT *tel* (0225) 339733. *Directors:* M.R. Lynch, J.M. Bayley. Editorial services for education and training, including writing and design of educational resources (audio-visual aids, games, booklets) and of management games and training packs. Specialising in distance and open learning training packages.

Sabine Oppenländer Associates (1990), 36 Cranfield Road, London SE4 1UG *tel* 081-692 4158. Picture research, photographic agent, information research and advisory services. Special areas: art, history, architecture and design, natural history, science, contemporary German history, gardens, English and German copyright.

Oriental Languages Bureau, Lakshmi Building, Sir P. Mehta Road, Fort, Bombay 400001, India   *tel* 2861258   *telegraphic address* Orientclip. *Partner:* Rajan K. Shah. Undertakes translations and printing in all Indian languages and a few foreign languages.

Ormrod Research Services (1982), Weeping Birch, Burwash, East Sussex TN19 7HG   *tel* (0435) 882541. Comprehensive research service; literary, historical, academic, biographical, commercial. Critical reading with report, editing, indexing, proof-reading, ghosting.

Oxprint (1974), Aristotle House, Aristotle Lane, Oxford OX2 6TR   *tel* (0865) 512331   *fax* (0865) 512408. *Directors:* Per Saugman, John Webb (managing), I.W. Goodgame, FCA. Design, typesetting, editorial, illustrating scientific, educational and general books. Specialists in taking complete projects from start to finish. Macintosh desktop and bureau facilities, computer aided design and illustration.

Pageant Publishing (1978), 5 Turners Wood, London NW11 6TD   *tel* 081-455 3703   *fax* 081-209 0726. *Director:* Gillian Page. Consultancy on all aspects of academic publishing: publication of academic journals.

Geoffrey D. Palmer (1987), 47 Burton Fields Road, Stamford Bridge, York YO4 1JJ   *tel/fax* (0759) 72874. Editorial and production services, including STM and general copy-editing, artwork editing, proof-reading and indexing. Specialising in mathematics, ecology, economics, engineering, geography and geology. Other interests include: architecture, gardening and horticulture, Green issues, road and rail transport history and policy.

Margaret Parker, 17 North Street, Norton St Philip, Bath, Avon BA3 6LE   *tel* (0373) 834 616. Experienced university press editor offers copy-editing and proof-reading services to publishers or academics in non-technical subjects (monographs or journal articles).

The Penman Literary Service (1950), 175 Pall Mall, Leigh-on-Sea, Essex SS9 1RE   *tel* (0702) 74438. Preparation of authors' MSS for submission, from typing, with any necessary attention to punctuation, spelling and general lay-out, to full revision and re-typing if requested. Charges depend upon work recommended and/or desired in the particular case.

Christopher Pick, 41 Chestnut Road, London SE27 9EZ   *tel* 081-761 2585. Writer, publishing consultant, editor. Author and editor of non-fiction books and articles for all popular markets. Special interests: modern social and political history, travel, heritage and current affairs. Non-fiction title and series planning and development projects undertaken; re-writing, but only for publishers on already contracted manuscripts. Consultancy advice and project management for commercial and voluntary organisations.

Picture Research Agency, Pat Hodgson, Jasmine Cottage, Spring Grove Road, Richmond, Surrey TW10 6EH   *tel* 081-940 5986. Illustrations found for books, films and television. Written research also undertaken particularly on historical subjects, including photographic and film history. Small picture library.

Reginald Piggott (1962), Decoy Lodge, Decoy Road, Potter Heigham, Norfolk NR29 5LX   *tel* (0692) 670384. Cartographer to the University Presses and academic publishers in Britain and overseas. Maps and diagrams for academic and educational books.

Keith Povey Editorial Services (1980), North Burrow, Bratton Clovelly, Oke-hampton, Devon EX20 4JJ   *tel* (083 787) 296   *fax* (083 787) 369. Copy-editing, indexing, proof-reading, publisher/author liaison. In 1989 partnership with T & A Typesetting Services, 6 Heald Drive, Rochdale, Lancs. OL12 7HH   *tel* (0706) 32789   *fax* (0706) 861673. Specialist book-typesetting to CRC and negs, graphic design.

Prefis Ltd (Book Machine) (1982), 64 Baldock Street, Ware, Herts. SG12 9DT   *tel/fax* (0920) 465890. *Director:* Paul Procter, BA. Originator of a word-processing and page-make-up system (the **Book Machine**) specifically designed for the author, publisher's editor and designer, and the typesetter, running on standard IBM compatible microcomputers.

Victoria Ramsay (1981), Abbots Rest, Chilbolton, Stockbridge, Hants SO20 6BE   *tel* (0264) 860251. Freelance editing, copy-editing and proof-reading; non-fiction research and writing of promotional literature and pamphlets. Any non-scientific subject undertaken. Special interests include education, cookery, travel, African and Caribbean works and works in translation from French.

Research Ireland (1985), Pamela Bradley, Fair View, Kindlestown Hill, Delgany, Co. Wicklow, Republic of Ireland   *tel* (01) 287 4034. Research service for writers, specialising in Irish history, biography, genealogy.

S. Ribeiro (1986), 42 West Heath Court, North End Road, Golders Green, London NW11 7RG *tel* 081-458 9082. Editor and writing tutor. Services include: review, revision and editing of completed MSS, guidance towards possible markets. New writers welcome, but please write or telephone with initial enquiry. Special interests: Americanisation, fiction, autobiography and academic articles.

Rich Research (1978), 1 Bradby House, Carlton Hill, St John's Wood, London NW8 9XE   *tel* 071-624 7755. *Director:* Diane Rich. Speedy and innovative picture research service. Visuals found for all sectors of publishing and the media. Stock images, commissioned photography and artwork. Negotiation of rights and fees.

Anton Rippon Press Services, 20 Chain Lane, Mickleover, Derby DE3 5AJ   *tel* (0332) 512379/384235   *fax* (0332) 292755. Writer and researcher on historical, sociological and sporting topics. Features, programmes, brochures produced; ghost writing.

Vernon Robinson Editorial Services (1973), 114 Blinco Grove, Cambridge CB1 4TT   *tel* (0223) 244414. Copy-editing and proof-reading of all educational books. Competitive rates. Specialise: science, maths, engineering, economics, computer science, biology, etc.

Roger Smithells Ltd, Editorial Services, Garth Cottage, 26 High Street, Buriton, Petersfield, Hants GU31 5RX   *tel* (0730) 62369   *fax* (0730) 60722. Journal-istic specialists in everything relating to travel and holidays; newspaper and magazine articles; TV and radio scripts; compilers of travel books.

Sarratt Information Services (1986), Willow View House, 52 Church Lane, Sar-ratt, Herts. WD3 6HL   *tel* 081-422 4384. *Directors:* D.M. Brandl, MIInfSci, G.H. Kay, BSc. CEng. MIChem. EMBCS. A.C. Rickard, BA. MIInfSci. Research, bib-liographies compiled, references checked, indexes compiled, translations, abstracting, data entry. Specialists in medical engineering.

Science Unit, Rothay House, 6 Mayfield Road, Eastrea, Cambs. PE7 2AY   *tel* (0733) 350888. Independent scientific consultancy specialising in microscopical matters. Advises on programmes and publications in general scientific field.

Activities are world-wide, with publications in many overseas and foreign-language editions.

Scriptmate (1985), 20 Shepherd's Hill, London N6 5AH   *tel* 081-341 7650. Ann Kritzinger (managing). Reports and revision suggestions given on unpublished work in the fields of fiction, non-fiction and drama by team of 80 specialist readers.

Mrs Ellen Seager, Baytrees, Burnham Road, Little Bookham, Surrey KT23 3AU   *tel* (0372) 58746. Critical assessment of fiction and non-fiction work with helpful direction, tuition and advice. Creative writing tutor. Ghost writing. Publishing and market information.

Seminar Cassettes Ltd (1973), Drake Educational Associates, St Fagans Road, Fairwater, Cardiff CF5 3AE   *tel* (0222) 560333   *fax* (0222) 554909. Spoken word cassettes on current affairs, psychology, metaphysics, ecology and inter-views with literary and artistic figures. Widely used in English language teaching and in universities, polytechnics, school libraries and bookshops as unique and authentic source material.

Christine Shuttleworth (1981), Flat 1, 25 St Stephen's Avenue, London W12 8JB   *tel* 081-749 8797. Indexing (with MACREX program), copy-editing, proof-reading, non-technical translation from German. Registered Indexer and Council member, Society of Indexers; Committee member, Society of Freelance Editors and Proofreaders; member, Translators' Association.

Robert and Jane Songhurst (1976), 3 Yew Tree Cottages, Grange Lane, Sandling, Nr Maidstone, Kent ME14 3BY   *tel* Maidstone (0622) 757635. Literary consultants, authors' works advised upon (fees by agreement), literary and historical research, feature writing, reviewing, editing.

Strand Editorial Services (1974) 16 Mitchley View, South Croydon, Surrey CR2 9HQ   *tel* 081-657 1247. *Joint principals:* Derek and Irene Bradley. Providing a comprehensive service to publishers, editorial departments, and public relations and advertising agencies at any stage in the production process.

Tamar Literary Services (1988), 18 Barton Close, Landrake, Saltash, Cornwall PL12 5BA   *tel* (0752) 851451. *Director:* Dr Brian Gee. General editing (non-fiction). Specialist editing in technical and scientific fields. Also editing on disc (MS WORD/SPELLCHECK).

Hans Tasiemka Archives (1950), 80 Temple Fortune Lane, London NW11 7TU   *tel* 081-455 2485   *fax* 081-455 0231. *Proprietor:* Mrs Edda Tasiemka. Comprehensive newspaper cuttings library from 1850s to the present day on all subjects for writers, publishers, picture researchers, film and TV companies.

Lyn M. Taylor, 1 Eglinton Crescent, Edinburgh EH12 5DH   *tel* 031-225 6152. Comprehensive editorial service. Copy-editing and proof-reading in all subjects. Specialising in scientific and medical.

Technidraught (Cartography) (1984), 3 Rayleigh Road, Basingstoke, Hants RG21 1TJ   *tel* (0256) 28186. *Partners:* P.J. Corcoran, Rosemary Corcoran. Cartographic design and draughting service for publishers and authors, research and editing facilities, specialising in academic, education, travel and related fields.

Tecmedia Ltd (1972), Unit 1, The Courtyard, Whitwick Business Park, Stenson Road, Coalville LE6 3JP   *tel* (0530) 815800   *fax* (0530) 813452. *Managing director:* J.D. Baxter. Specialists in the design, development and production of mixed media training packages, newsletters and brochures.

Hilary Thomas (1974), 27 Grasvenor Avenue, Barnet, Herts. EN5 2BY   *tel* 081-440 5662. Genealogical, literary and historical research.

3 & 5 Promotion (1985), 5 Church Street, Harston, Cambridge CB2 5NP *tel* (0223) 871028. *Proprietor:* Rosemary Dooley. Publicity services for publishers, specialising in music, academic humanities, health care, travel, including book exhibitions.

Elaine Towns Editorial Services (1978), 3 The Priory, Atlantic Way, Westward Ho, Bideford, Devon EX39 1JA *tel* Bideford (0237) 477722. Copy-editing, proof-reading, indexing, MSS assessment; complete editorial, design and production service for books. Fully computerised operation – can deal with authors' disks in MS DOS or Apple format.

Carolina Tucker, BA, ALA (1986), Ford Cottage, Lymore Valley, Milford-on-Sea, Nr Lymington, Hants SO41 0TW *tel* (0202) 472380, (0590) 642441 (evening). MSS reading and evaluation for publishers. Advisory and editorial service for authors. Full revision and re-typing of MSS if required. Research and writing of travel brochures (UK).

John Vickers, 27 Shorrolds Road, London SW6 7TR *tel* 071-385 5774. Archives of British Theatre photographs by John Vickers, from 1938-1974.

Gordon R. Wainwright, 22 Hawes Court, Sunderland SR6 8NU *tel* 091-548 9342. Criticism, advice, revision and all other editorial work for publishers, especially those concerned with educational and how-to books. Articles on education and training matters supplied to newspapers, journals and magazines. Training in report writing, rapid reading, effective meetings, etc. Lecture service. Consultancy service in all aspects of communication. Travel writing assignments undertaken.

Joan Wilkins Associates, 54 Church Street, Tisbury, Salisbury, Wilts. SP3 6NH *tel* Tisbury (0747) 870490 *fax* (0747) 871027. Comprehensive editorial (editing, sub editing, indexing, proof-reading) and preparation of reports. Word processing. Conference services include recording, verbatim reporting and tape transcribing. Rates on application.

Rita Winter, Translation and Editorial Services (1988), Kilrubie, Eddleston, Peeblesshire, Scotland EH45 8QS *tel* (07213) 353. Ex-academic librarian offers comprehensive editorial service including: proof-reading, copy-editing, research, word-processing, indexing and index repagination. Also reading service/critical assessment of Dutch texts and translations from/into Dutch. Special interests: arts/humanities, social sciences, reference, general.

Della Woodman (1973), Laurel Glen, 244 Chichester Road, Copnor, Portsmouth PO2 0AU *tel* (0705) 698830. *Proprietors:* Mrs D. Emmerson, N. Emmerson. Typesetting, paste-up, camera-ready artwork, design and preparation of books to print stage, illustration, proof-reading, indexing, general editing and research services.

Richard M. Wright (1977), 32 Oak Village, London NW5 4QN *tel/fax* 071-284 4316. Indexing, copy-editing, specialising in politics, history, business, social sciences.

Write Line Critical Service (1988), 130 Morton Way, Southgate, London N14 7AL *tel* 081-886 1329. Criticism and assessment of poetry, fiction (including short stories) and general articles. Suggestions for revision/development of work, advice about publication outlets. Special interest: poetry. Enquiries by phone or write with sae.

Write on. . . (1989), PO Box 360, 62 Kiln Lane, Headington, Oxford OX3 8DQ *tel* (0865) 61169 *fax* (0865) 69216. *Director:* Yvonne Newman. Seminars on writing and marketing articles and non-fiction books; advisory service for unpublished authors; travel, business, open-learning and general writing assignments undertaken.

Writerlink Ltd (1984), Bolsover House, 5 Clipstone Street, London W1P 7EB   *tel* 071-323 4323. *Directors:* Charles Dawes, John Hare, John Bennett, Sally Cartwright. Expert individual reports made and issued to authors by a team of readers widely experienced in publishing.

The Writers' Exchange (1977), 14 Yewdale, Clifton Green, Swinton, Manchester M27 2GN   *tel* 061-793 4606. *Directors:* Peter Collins, John Michael Wright. Reading and appraisal service for writers preparing to submit material to, or having had material rejected by, literary agents and/or publishers. We offer a constructive, objective evaluation service, particularly for those who cannot get past the standard rejection slip barrier or who have had MSS rejected by publishers and need an impartial view on why it did not sell. Novels, short stories, film and TV, radio and stage plays; sae for details.

Hans Zell, Publishing Consultant (1987), 11 Richmond Road, PO Box 56, Oxford OX1 3EL   *tel* (0865) 511428   *telex* 94012872 Zell G   *fax* (0865) 793298. Consultancies, project evaluations, market assessments, feasibility studies, research and surveys, funding proposals, freelance editorial work, commissioning, journals management, exhibition services. Specialises in services to publishers and the book community in Third World countries and provides specific expertise in these areas.

Indexing

The Society of Indexers maintains a Register of members whose practical competence in compiling indexes has been tested and approved by its Assessors. Introductions are freely available to authors, publishers and others responsible for commissioning indexes by contacting the Society's Registrar, Mrs E. Wallis, 25 Leyborne Park, Kew Gardens, Surrey TW9 3HB   *tel* 081-940 4771.

In addition, there are some 200 general and specialist indexers listed in the Society's annual booklet *Indexers Available*, which is obtainable by sending a SAE (at least $6\frac{1}{2} \times 8\frac{1}{2}$) to the Secretary, 16 Green Road, Birchington, Kent CT7 9JZ.

For other details of the Society of Indexers, see the entry under **Societies, Associations and Clubs.**

Translation

The role of the translator in enabling literature to pass beyond its national frontiers is receiving growing recognition. In view of the general increase of activity in this field, it is not surprising that many people with literary interests and a knowledge of languages should think of adopting freelance translating as a full- or part-time occupation. Some advice may be usefully given to such would-be translators.

The first difficulty the beginner will encounter is the unwillingness of publishers to entrust a translation to anyone who has not already established a reputation for sound work. The least the publisher will demand before commissioning a translation is a fairly lengthy specimen of the applicant's work, even if unpublished. The publisher cannot be expected to pay for a specimen sent in by a translator seeking work. If, on the other hand, a publisher specifically asks for a lengthy specimen of a commissioned book the firm will usually pay for this specimen at the current rate. Perhaps the best way the would-be translator can begin is to select some book of the type which he feels competent and anxious to translate, ascertain from the foreign author or publisher that the English-language rights are still free, translate a substantial section of the book and then submit the book and his specimen translation to an appropriate publisher. If he is extremely lucky, this may result in a commission to translate the book. More probably, however – since publishers are generally very well informed about foreign books likely to interest them and are rarely open to a chance introduction – the publisher will reject the book as such. But if he is favourably impressed by the translation, he may very possibly commission some other book of a similar nature which he already has in mind.

In this connection it is important to stress that the translator should confine himself to subjects of which he possesses an expert knowledge. In the case of non-fiction, he may have to cope with technical expressions not to be found in the dictionary and disaster may ensue if he is not fully conversant with the subject. The translation of fiction, on the other hand, demands different skills (e.g. in the writing of dialogue) and the translator would be wise to ask himself whether he possesses these skills before taking steps to secure work of this nature.

Having obtained a commission to translate a book, the translator will be faced with the question of fees. These vary considerably from publisher to publisher but for the commoner European languages they should range from £40.00 upwards per thousand words. Translators should be able to obtain, in addition to the initial fee, a royalty of 2½%. However, some publishers will consent to pay royalties of this nature, if at all, only on second editions and reprints. In the past it was common practice for a translator to assign his copyright to the publisher outright, but this is no longer the rule. Most reputable publishers will now sign agreements specifying the rights they require in the translation and leaving the copyright in the translator's hands.

Advice regarding fees, copyright, Public Lending Right and other matters may be obtained from the Translators Association of the Society of Authors (see **Societies, Associations and Clubs**).

Technical translators are catered for by the Institute of Translation and Interpreting (see **Societies, Associations and Clubs**). Annual prizes are awarded for translations from the German, the Italian and the French languages (see **Literary Prizes and Awards**). There are also prizes for translations from Swedish and Portuguese.

Press-cutting Agencies

UNITED KINGDOM

In the following section it should be noted that no agency can check every periodical, local paper, etc., and that some agencies cover more than others. Special attention should be given to the time limit specified by certain agencies.

Contemporary Music Press Bureau (1982), 46 Grange Road, Orpington, Kent BR6 8EA *tel* (0689) 851811. Music press articles from 1970; specialises in pop, rock, soul, jazz, reggae. *Subscription:* £15 search fee, cuttings free.

Durrant's Press Cuttings Ltd (1880), 103 Whitecross Street, London EC1Y 8QT *tel* 071-588 3671 *fax* 071-374 8171. *Directors:* A.M. Kennedy, T.W. Lorenzen. Press cutting service for publishers and art galleries from a guaranteed comprehensive reading list. *Subscription rates:* from £115.

International Press-Cutting Bureau (1920), 224-236 Walworth Road, London SE17 1JE *tel* 071-708 2113 *telegraphic address* Adverburo, London, SE1 *fax* 071-701 4489. *Subscription rates:* on application. *Representatives:* Brussels, Copenhagen, Geneva, Madrid, Milan, Paris, Lisbon, Stockholm, Berlin, Helsinki, The Hague.

Newsclip (incorporating **Apcut Ltd**), 26 Aylmer Road, London N2 0BX *tel* 081-341 0091 *fax* 081-348 3927. *Subscription rates:* on application.

Press Information (Scotland), Ltd, Virginia House, 62 Virginia Street, Glasgow G1 1TX *tel* 041-552 6767. Comprehensive Scottish cuttings service. *Subscription rates:* on application.

Romeike & Curtice Ltd (1852), Hale House, 290-296 Green Lanes, London N13 5TP *tel* 081-882 0155 *telex* 896462 Inform G *fax* 081-882 6716. *Directors:* Paul J. Morgan, Simon H. Lanyon, John F. Colleran, Ian A. Duncan, Stephen D. George. Provides a media monitoring service to over 5500 clients in different industries, covering more than 3000 newspapers and magazines as well as national radio and TV. *Subscription rates:* £34.00 per month and £0.60 per clipping. Minimum contract: 3 months.

We Find It Press Clippings, 103 South Parade, Belfast, Northern Ireland BT7 2GN *tel* (0232) 646008. Northern Ireland press coverage; fast, up-to-date, accurate feedback. *Subscription rates:* on application.

Overseas

AUSTRALIA

Australian Press Cuttings Agency, 11-15 Albert Street, Richmond, Victoria 3121 *tel* 4298388 *fax* 4299229. $75 per month and 65 cents per cutting.

CANADA

Canadian Press Clipping Services, 720 King Street West, Suite 515, Toronto, Ontario M5V 2T3 *tel* 416-362-0140 *fax* 416-362-5655.

INDIA

International Clipping Service, Lakshmi Building, Sir P. Mehta Road, Fort, Bombay 400001   *tel* 2861258   *telegraphic address* Orientclip. *Partner:* Rajan K. Shah. Supplies press cuttings of news, editorials, articles, advertisements, press releases, etc., from all India papers. Undertakes compilation of statistical reports on competitive press advertising pertaining to all products.

NEW ZEALAND

Chong Press Clippings Bureau, PO Box 13330, Onehunga, Auckland   *tel* (09) 640-463   *fax* (09) 667-607. All NZ newspapers and most magazines read and clipped for subscribers on any topic; metro papers only from $60 per month. Information consultants. Data searches.

SOUTH AFRICA

S.A. Press Cutting Agency, 52/57 Mitrie House, 110 Stanger Street, Durban 4001, Natal   *tel* 370403   *fax* DBN-374-307. English and Afrikaans newspapers and trade journals from Zambia to the Cape. *Minimum rates:* R.80.00 per 100 cuttings plus reading fee R.20.00 per month plus postage.

SPAIN

Express Mail (1961), Apartado 14762, 28080 Madrid   *tel* 881 58 23. Comprehensive Spanish and Portuguese cuttings service. Individual attention. Undertakes full investigations.

UNITED STATES OF AMERICA

Burrelle's Press Clipping Service (1888), 75 East Northfield Avenue, Livingston, NJ 07039   *tel* 201-992-6600.

Luce Press Clippings, Inc., 420 Lexington Avenue, New York, NY 10170   *tel* 212-889-6711.

New England Newsclip Agency, Inc., 5 Auburn Street, PO Box 9128, Framingham, MA 01701-9128   *tel* 508-879-4460   *fax* 508-620-1719.

Government Offices and Public Services

Enquiries, accompanied by a stamped addressed envelope, should be sent to the Public Relations Officer.

AEA Technology (United Kingdom Atomic Energy Authority), 11 Charles II Street, London SW1Y 4QP   *tel* 071-389 6515   *telex* 22565   *fax* 071-389 6906 ext 517/274.

Agriculture, Fisheries and Food, Ministry of, 3-8 Whitehall Place, London SW1A 2HH   *tel* 071-270 3000   *telex* 01-889351   *fax* 071-270 8125.

Arts Council of Great Britain, 14 Great Peter Street, London SW1P 3NQ   *tel* 071-333 0100.

Australia, High Commissioner for Commonwealth of, Australia House, Strand, London WC2B 4LA   *tel* 071-379 4334   *telex* 27565   *fax* 071-240 5333.

Austrian Embassy, 18 Belgrave Mews West, London SW1X 8HU   *tel* 071-235 3731   *telex* 28327   *fax* 071-235 8025.

Bahamas High Commission, Bahamas House, 10 Chesterfield Street, London W1X 8AH   *tel* 071-408 4488   *fax* 071-499 9937.

Bangladesh High Commission, 28 Queen's Gate, London SW7 5JA   *tel* 071-584 0081-4/589 4842-4.

The Bank of England, Threadneedle Street, London EC2R 8AH   *tel* 071-601 4444.

Barbados High Commission, 1 Great Russell Street, London WC1B 3NH   *tel* 071-631 4975   *telex* 262081 Barcom G   *fax* 071-323 6872.

Belgian Embassy, 103 Eaton Square, London SW1W 9AB   *tel* 071-235 5422   *telex* 22823   *fax* 071-259 6213.

Bodleian Library, Oxford OX1 3BG   *tel* (0865) 277000   *telex* 83565   *fax* (0865) 277182.

Botswana High Commission, 6 Stratford Place, London W1N 9AE   *tel* 071-499 0031.

British Broadcasting Corporation, Broadcasting House, London W1A 1AA   *tel* 071-580 4468.

British Coal, Hobart House, Grosvenor Place, London SW1X 7AE   *tel* 071-235 2020   *telex* 882161 Cbhob G   *fax* 071-235 3747.

The British Council, 10 Spring Gardens, London SW1A 2BN   *tel* 071-930 8466   *telex* 895220 Bricon G   *fax* 071-839 6347.

British Film Institute, 21 Stephen Street, London W1P 1PL   *tel* 071-255 1444   *telex* 27624 Bfildng   *fax* 071-436 7950.

The British Library, 2 Sheraton Street, London W1V 4BH   *tel* 071-636 1544   *telex* 21462 Blref G   *fax* 071-323 7039.

British Library, Document Supply Centre, Boston Spa, Wetherby, West Yorkshire LS23 7BQ   *tel* Boston Spa (0937) 546000   *telex* 557381   *fax* (0937) 546333.

British Library Newspaper Library, Colindale Avenue, London NW9 5HE   *tel* 071-323 7353   *fax* 071-323 7379.

British Museum, Great Russell Street, London WC1B 3DG   *tel* 071-636 1555   *fax* 071-323 8480.

British Railways Board, Euston House, 24 Eversholt Street, PO Box 100, London NW1 1DZ   *tel* 071-928 5151   *telex* 299431 Brhqln G   *fax* 071-922 6994.

BSI (British Standards Institution), Customer information: *Library:* Linford Wood, Milton Keynes, Bucks. MK14 6LE   *tel* (0908) 220022   *telex* 825777 Bsimk G   *fax* (0908) 320856. *Head office:* 2 Park Street, London W1A 2BS   *tel* 071-629 9000.

British Technology Group, 101 Newington Causeway, London SE1 6BU   *tel* 071-403 6666.

British Tourist Authority/English Tourist Board, Thames Tower, Black's Road, London W6 9EL   *tel* 081-846 9000   *telex* 21231   *fax* 081-563 0302.

Broadcasting Standards Council, 5-8 The Sanctuary, London SW1P 3JS   *tel* 071-233 0544   *fax* 071-233 0397.

Bulgaria, Embassy of the People's Republic of, 186-188 Queen's Gate, London SW7 5HL   *tel* 071-584 9400/9433, 071-581 3144 (5 lines)   *fax* 071-584 4948.

Cadw, Welsh Historic Monuments, Brunel House, 2 Fitzalan Road, Cardiff CF2 1UY   *tel* (0222) 465511.

Canadian High Commission, Cultural Affairs Section, Canada House, Trafalgar Square, London SW1Y 5BJ   *tel* 071-629 9492 ext 2246   *telex* 261592 Cdaldn   *fax* 071-491 3968.

Central Office of Information, Hercules Road, London SE1 7DU   *tel* 071-928 2345. In the UK conducts press, television, radio and poster advertising; produces booklets, leaflets, films, radio and television material, exhibitions and other visual material. For the Foreign and Commonwealth Office supplies British information posts overseas with press, radio and television material, publications and briefing material, films, exhibitions and display and reading-room material.

College of Arms or Heralds' College, Queen Victoria Street, London EC4V 4BT   *tel* 071-248 2762   *fax* 071-248 6448.

Commonwealth Institute, Kensington High Street, London W8 6NQ   *tel* 071-603 4535   *fax* 071-602 7374. Permanent exhibitions on over 50 Commonwealth countries. Temporary thematic and visual arts exhibitions. Full educational programme for all ages. Range of holiday events. Public Information Centre. Educational Resource Centre for use by teachers and youth workers. Theatre. Compix commercial picture library and mail order publications service. Room hire facilities.

Countryside Commission, John Dower House, Crescent Place, Cheltenham, Glos. GL50 3RA   *tel* (0242) 521381   *fax* (0242) 584270/224962.

Countryside Commission for Scotland, Battleby, Redgorton, Perth PH1 3EW   *tel* (0738) 27921 ext 218   *fax* (0738) 30583.

Court of the Lord Lyon, HM New Register House, Edinburgh EH1 3YT   *tel* 031-556 7255   *fax* 031-557 2148.

Cyprus High Commission, 93 Park Street, London W1Y 4ET   *tel* 071-499 8272   *telex* 263343   *fax* 071-491 0691

Czech and Slovak Federal Republic, Embassy of the, 25 Kensington Palace Gardens, London W8 4QY   *tel* 071-229 1255   *fax* 071-727 5824.

Royal Danish Embassy, 55 Sloane Street, London SW1X 9SR   *tel* 071-333 0200   *fax* 071-333 0270.

Data Protection Registrar, Office of the Data Protection Registrar, Springfield House, Water Lane, Wilmslow, Cheshire SK9 5AX   *tel Enquiries:* (0625) 535777; *Administration:* (0625) 535711   *fax* 0625 524510.

Defence, Ministry of, Main Building, Whitehall, London SW1A 2HB   *tel* 071-218 9000.

The Design Council, 28 Haymarket, London SW1Y 4SU   *tel* 071-839 8000   *telex* 8812963   *fax* 071-925 2130.

DTI: Department of Trade and Industry, Ashdown House, 123 Victoria Street, London SW1E 6RB   *tel* (*general enquiries*) 071-215 5000   *telex* 8813148 Dthq G   *fax* 071-583 4900   *other tel Enterprise Initiative* 0800 500 200   *Single European Market* 081-200 1992   *Environmental Enquiry Point* 0800 585 794.

Education and Science, Department of, Elizabeth House, York Road, London SE1 7PH   *tel* 071-934 9000   *fax* 071 934 0513/9082/9731.

Electricity Regulation, Office of,   Hagley House, Hagley Road, Birmingham B16 8QG   *tel* 021-456 2100   *fax* 021-456 4664.

Employment, Department of, Information Branch, Caxton House, Tothill Street, London SW1H 9NF   *tel* 071-273 3000 (main switchboard). *Public enquiries:* 071-273 6969.

Energy, Department of, 1 Palace Street, London SW1E 5HE   *tel* 071-238 3000, 071-238 3042 (library)   *telex* 918777.

English Heritage, Fortress House, 23 Savile Row, London W1X 1AB   *tel* 071-973 3000   *fax* 071-973 3001.

Environment, Department of the, 2 Marsham Street, London SW1P 3EB   *tel* 071-276 3000.

Equal Opportunities Commission, Overseas House, Quay Street, Manchester M3 3HN   *tel* 061-833 9244   *fax* 061-835 1657.

European Parliament, UK Information Office, 2 Queen Anne's Gate, London SW1H 9AA   *tel* 071-222 0411   *fax* 071-222 2713.

Fair Trading, Office of, Field House, 15-25 Bream's Buildings, London EC4A 1PR   *tel* 071-242 2858   *telex* 269009 Oftrin G   *fax* 071-269 8800.

Foreign and Commonwealth Office, King Charles Street, London SW1A 2AH   *tel* 071-270 3000   *telex* 287711 (a/b Prdrme G).

Forestry Commission, 231 Corstorphine Road, Edinburgh EH12 7AT   *tel* 031-334 0303   *fax* 031-334 3047.

French Embassy, 58 Knightsbridge, London SW1X 7JT   *tel* 071-235 8080; *Cultural department:* 23 Cromwell Road, London SW7 2EL   *tel* 071-581 5292.

Gambia High Commission, 57 Kensington Court, London W8 5DG   *tel* 071-937 6316   *fax* 071-376 0531.

General Register Office, now part of the **Population Censuses and Surveys, Office of,** *q.v.*

Germany, Embassy of the Federal Republic of, 23 Belgrave Square, London SW1X 8PZ   *tel* 071-235 5033   *fax* 071-235 0609.

Ghana, High Commission for, 13 Belgrave Square, London SW1X 8PR   *tel* 071-235 4142/5.

Greece, Embassy of, 1A Holland Park, London W11 3TP   *tel* 071-727 8040.

Guyana High Commission, 3 Palace Court, Bayswater Road, London W2 4LP *tel* 071-229 7684/8.

Hayward Gallery, South Bank Centre, Belvedere Road, London SE1 8XZ *tel* 071-928 3144.

Health, Department of, Richmond House, 79 Whitehall, London SW1A 2NS *tel* 071-210 3000.

Historic Scotland, 20 Brandon Street, Edinburgh EH3 5RA *tel* 031-244 3107 *fax* 031-244 3030.

HMSO Books, St Crispins, Duke Street, Norwich NR3 1PD *tel* (0603) 622211 *telex* 97301 *fax* (0603) 695317.

Home Office, Queen Anne's Gate, London SW1H 9AT *tel* 071-273 3000. *Public relations branch:* Director of information services: A.E. Moorey.

Hungary, Embassy of the Republic of, 35 Eaton Place, London SW1X 8BY *tel* 071-235 4048/7191 *fax* 071-823 1348.

Independent Television Commission, 70 Brompton Road, London SW3 *tel* 071-584 7011 *telex* 24345 *fax* 071-589 5533.

India, High Commission of, Press & Information Wing, India House, Aldwych, London WC2B 4NA *tel* 071-836 8484 ext 147, 286 *fax* 071-836 4331.

Inland Revenue, Board of, Somerset House, London WC2R 1LB *tel* 071-438 6622.

Ireland, Embassy of, 17 Grosvenor Place, London SW1X 7HR *tel* 071-235 2171 *telex* 916104 Iverna G *fax* 071-245 6961.

Israel, Embassy of, 2 Palace Green, Kensington, London W8 4QB *tel* 071-937 8050 *fax* 071-937 5184.

Italian Embassy, 14 Three Kings Yard, Davies Street, London W1Y 2EH *tel* 071-629 8200.

Jamaican High Commission, 1-2 Prince Consort Road, London SW7 2BZ *tel* 071-823 9911 *telex* 263304 Jamcom G *fax* 071-589 5154.

Japan, Embassy of, 101-104 Piccadilly, London W1V 9FN *tel* 071-465 6500.

Kenya High Commission, 45 Portland Place, London W1N 4AS *tel* 071-636 2371/5 *telex* 262551 *fax* 071-323 6717.

The Legal Deposit Office, The British Library, Boston Spa, Wetherby, W. Yorks. LS23 7BY *tel* (0937) 546267/546268 *telex* 557381 *fax* (0937) 546586.

Lesotho, High Commission of the Kingdom of, 10 Collingham Road, London SW5 0NR *tel* 071-373 8581/2.

London Museum—see Museum of London.

London Records Office, Corporation of City of, Guildhall, London EC2P 2EJ *tel* 071-260 1251.

London Transport, 55 Broadway, London SW1H 0BD *tel* 071-222 5600 (Administration).

Luxembourg, Embassy of, 27 Wilton Crescent, London SW1X 8SD *tel* 071-235 6961 *fax* 071-235 9734.

Malawi High Commission, 33 Grosvenor Street, London W1X 0DE *tel* 071-491 4172/7 *telex* 263308 *fax* 071-491 9916.

Malaysian High Commission, 45 Belgrave Square, London SW1X 8QT *tel* 071-235 8033 *telex* 262550 *fax* 071-235 5161.

Malta High Commission, 16 Kensington Square, London W8 5HH   *tel* 071-938 1712-6   *telex* 261102 Mlt Ldn G   *fax* 071-937 8664.

Mauritius High Commission, 32-3 Elvaston Place, London SW7 5NW   *tel* 071-581 0294/6.

Monopolies and Mergers Commission, New Court, 48 Carey Street, London WC2A 2JT   *tel* 071-324 1467/8.

Museum of London, London Wall, London EC2Y 5HN   *tel* 071-600 3699   *fax* 071-600 1058. Amalgamating the collections of the London Museum and the Guildhall Museum.

Museum of Mankind (Ethnography Department of the British Museum), 6 Burlington Gardens, London W1X 2EX   *tel* 071-323 8043 (information).

National Economic Development Office, Millbank Tower, Millbank, London SW1P 4QX   *tel* 071-217 4000   *fax* 071-821 1099.

National Gallery, Trafalgar Square, London WC2N 5DN   *tel* 071-839 3321   *fax* 071-930 1681   *press office fax* 071-930 4764.

National Maritime Museum, Greenwich, London SE10 9NF, including the Queen's House and the Old Royal Observatory   *tel* 081-858 4422.

National Savings, Department for, Marketing and Information Division, Charles House, 375 Kensington High Street, London W14 8SD   *tel* 071-605 9432/ 9438   *fax* 071-605 9446.

The National Trust for Scotland, 5 Charlotte Square, Edinburgh EH2 4DU   *tel* 031-226 5922   *fax* 031-220 6266.

Natural Environment Research Council, Polaris House, North Star Avenue, Swindon, Wilts. SN2 1EU   *tel* (0793) 411500   *fax* (0793) 411501.

The Natural History Museum, Cromwell Road, London SW7 5BD   *tel* 071-938 9123   *fax* 071-938 8754.

Royal Netherlands Embassy, 38 Hyde Park Gate, London SW7 5DP   *tel* 071-584 5040.

New Zealand, High Commissioner for, New Zealand House, Haymarket, London SW1Y 4TQ   *tel* 071-930 8422   *telex* 24368   *fax* 071-839 4580.

Nigeria High Commission, Nigeria House, 9 Northumberland Avenue, London WC2N 5BX   *tel* 071-839 1244   *fax* 071-839 8746.

Northern Ireland Office, Whitehall, London SW1A 2AZ   *tel* 071-210 3000. Also Stormont House, Belfast BT4 3ST   *tel* (0232) 63255.

Northern Ireland Tourist Board, River House, 48 High Street, Belfast BT1 2DS   *tel* (0232) 231221   *telex* 748087   *fax* (0232) 240960. *Press only: tel* (0232) 235906.

Royal Norwegian Embassy, 25 Belgrave Square, London SW1X 8QD   *tel* 071-235 7151   *telex* 22321   *fax* 071-245 6993.

Patent Office (An Executive Agency of the Department of Trade and Industry), Cardiff Road, Newport, Gwent NP9 1RH   *tel* (0633) 81400. *Copyright enquiries:* Industrial Property and Copyright Department, Hazlitt House, 45 Southampton Buildings, Chancery Lane, London WC2A 1AR   *tel* 071-438 4778.

PLR Office, Bayheath House, Prince Regent Street, Stockton-on-Tees, Cleveland TS18 1DF   *tel* (0642) 604699   *fax* (0642) 615641. Address enquiries to The Registrar of Public Lending Right.

Poland, Embassy of the Republic of, 47 Portland Place, London W1N 3AG   *tel* 071-580 4324   *telex* 265691   *fax* 071-323 4018.

Population Censuses and Surveys, Office of, St Catherine's House, 10 Kingsway, London WC2B 6JP   *tel* 071-242 0262   *fax* 071-430 1779.

Portuguese Embassy, 11 Belgrave Square, London SW1X 8PP   *tel* 071-235 5331   *fax* 071-245 1287.

Post Office Headquarters, 30 St James's Square, London SW1Y 4PY   *tel* 071-490 2888.

Public Record Office, *Modern Departmental Records:* Ruskin Avenue, Kew, Richmond, Surrey TW9 4DU   *tel* 081-876 3444; *Medieval, Early Modern and Legal Records* and the *Census Returns:* Chancery Lane, London WC2A 1LR   *tel* 081-876 3444   *fax* Kew 081-878 8905, Chancery Lane 081-878 7231.

Public Trust Office, Stewart House, 24 Kingsway, London WC2B 6JX   *tel* 071-269 7000   *fax* 071-831 0060.

Racial Equality, Commission for, Elliot House, 10-12 Allington Street, London SW1E 5EH   *tel* 071-828 7022   *fax* 071-630 7605.

The Radio Authority, 70 Brompton Road, London SW3 1EY   *tel* 071-581 2888   *fax* 071-823 9113.

Regional Arts Associations, Council of (CORAA), Litton Lodge, 13A Clifton Road, Winchester, Hants SO22 5BP   *tel* (0962) 51063   *fax* (0962) 842033.

Romania, Embassy of, 4 Palace Green, London W8 4QD   *tel* 071-937 9666   *telex* 22232 Romcom G   *fax* 071-937 8069.

Royal Commission on the Ancient and Historical Monuments of Scotland, 54 Melville Street, Edinburgh EH3 7HF   *tel* 031-225 5994   *fax* 031-220 6851.

Royal Commission on the Ancient and Historical Monuments in Wales, Crown Building, Plas Crug, Aberystwyth, Dyfed SY23 2HP   *tel* (0970) 624381-2.

Royal Commission on Historical Manuscripts, Quality House, Quality Court, Chancery Lane, London WC2A 1HP   *tel* 071-242 1198   *fax* 071-831 3550.

Royal Commission on the Historical Monuments of England, Fortress House, 23 Savile Row, London W1X 2JQ   *tel* 071-973 3500   *fax* 071-494 3998.

Royal Mint, Llantrisant, Pontyclun, Mid-Glamorgan CF7 8YT   *tel* Llantrisant 222111; 7 Grosvenor Gardens, London SW1W 0BH   *tel* 071-828 8724/8.

Science and Engineering Research Council, Polaris House, North Star Avenue, Swindon, Wilts. SN2 1ET   *tel* (0793) 411000.

Science Museum, Exhibition Road, South Kensington, London SW7 2DD   *tel* 071-938 8000   *fax* 071 938 8118. *Enquiries: Information Desk* 071-938 8080/8008. *Press Office tel* 071-938 8181   *fax* 071-938 8112.

Scotland, National Galleries of, The Mound, Edinburgh EH2 2EL   *tel* 031-556 8921.

Scotland, National Library of, George IV Bridge, Edinburgh EH1 1EW   *tel* 031-226 4531   *telex* 72638 Nlsedi G   *fax* 031-220 6662.

The Scottish Office, Dover House, Whitehall, London SW1A 2AU   *tel* 071-270 6755.

Scottish Office Information Directorate, New St Andrew's House, Edinburgh EH1 3TD   *tel* 031-244 1111; and Dover House, Whitehall, London SW1A 2AU   *tel* 071-270 6744.

Scottish Record Office, HM General Register House, Edinburgh EH1 3YY   *tel* 031-556 6585.

Scottish Tourist Board, 23 Ravelston Terrace, Edinburgh EH4 3EU *tel* 031-332 2433 *telex* 72272 *fax* 031-343 1513.

Serpentine Gallery, Kensington Gardens, London W2 3XA *tel* 071-402 6075 *fax* 071-402 4103. *Recorded information:* 071-723 9072. International exhibitions of modern and contemporary art.

Seychelles High Commission, 111 Baker Street, 2nd Floor, Eros House, London W1M 1FG *tel* 071-224 1660.

Sierra Leone, High Commissioner for, 33 Portland Place, London W1N 3AG *tel* 071-636 6483-5.

Singapore High Commission, 9 Wilton Crescent, London SW1X 8SA *tel* 071-235 8315 *telex* 262564 Shciuk G *fax* 071-245 6583.

Social Security, Department of, Richmond House, 79 Whitehall, London SW1A 2NS *tel* 071-210 3000. *Overseas branch:* Central Office, Long Benton, Newcastle upon Tyne NE98 1YX *tel* 091-213 5000.

South Africa, Republic of, South African Embassy, Trafalgar Square, London WC2N 5DP *tel* 071-930 4488.

Spanish Embassy, 24 Belgrave Square, London SW1X 8QA *tel* 071-235 5555.

Sri Lanka, High Commission for the Democratic Socialist Republic of, 13 Hyde Park Gardens, London W2 2LU *tel* 071-262 1841 *fax* 071-262 7970.

Swaziland High Commission, 58 Pont Street, London SW1X 0AE *tel* 071-581 4976 *telex* 28853 *fax* 071-589 5332.

Swedish Embassy, 11 Montagu Place, London W1H 2AL *tel* 071-724 2101 *fax* 071-724 4174.

Switzerland, Embassy of, 16-18 Montagu Place, London W1H 2BQ *tel* 071-723 0701 *telex* 28212 Amswis G *fax* 071-724 7001.

Tanzania High Commission, 43 Hertford Street, London W1Y 8DB *tel* 071-499 8951.

Tate Gallery, Millbank, London SW1P 4RG *tel* 071-821 1313 *fax* 071-931 7512.

Telecommunications, Office of, Export House, 50 Ludgate Hill, London EC4M 7JJ *tel* 071-822 1665/1688 *telex* 883584 *fax* 071-822 1643.

Transport, Department of, 2 Marsham Street, London SW1P 3EB *tel* 071-276 0888.

HM Treasury, Treasury Chambers, Parliament Street, London SW1P 3AG *tel* 071-270 3000.

Trinidad and Tobago High Commission, 42 Belgrave Square, London SW1X 8NT *tel* 071-245 9351 *fax* 071-823 1065.

Trinity House, London, Tower Hill, London EC3N 4DH *tel* 071-480 6601 *telex* 987526 Navaid G *fax* 071-480 7662. The General Lighthouse Authority for England, Wales and the Channel Islands, a Charitable Organisation for the relief of Mariners and a Deep Sea Pilotage Authority.

Turkish Embassy, 43 Belgrave Square, London SW1X 8PA *tel* 071-235 5252 *telex* 884236 Turkel G *fax* 071-235 8093.

Uganda High Commission, Uganda House, 58-59 Trafalgar Square, London WC2N 5DX *tel* 071-839 5783/5 *fax* 071-839 8925.

United States Embassy, 24 Grosvenor Square, London W1A 1AE *tel* 071-499 9000.

USSR, Embassy of the, 13 Kensington Palace Gardens, London W8 4QX *tel* 071-229 3628.

Victoria and Albert Museum, South Kensington, London SW7 2RL *tel* 071-938 8500 *telex* 268831 Vicart G *fax* 071-938 8341.

Wales, The National Library of, Aberystwyth, Dyfed SY23 3BU *tel* (0970) 623816 *telex* 35165 *fax* (0970) 615709.

Wales Tourist Board, Brunel House, 2 Fitzalan Road, Cardiff CF2 1UY *tel* (0222) 499909 *telex* 497269 *fax* (0222) 485031.

Water Services, Office of, 13th Floor, Centre City Tower, 7 Hill Street, Birmingham B5 4UA *tel* 021-625 1300 *fax* 021-625 1400.

Wellington Museum, Apsley House, 149 Piccadilly, Hyde Park Corner, London W1V 9FA *tel* 071-499 5676. Closed Mondays.

Welsh Office, Gwydyr House, Whitehall, London SW1A 2ER *tel* 071-270 0567 *fax* 071-270 0570; and Cathays Park, Cardiff, CF1 3NQ *tel* (0222) 825111 *fax* (0222) 823036.

West India Committee (The Caribbean), Commonwealth House, 18 Northumberland Avenue, London WC2N 5RA *tel* 071-976 1493 *fax* 071-976 1541.

Yugoslavia, Embassy of the Socialist Federal Republic of, 5-7 Lexham Gardens, London W8 5JJ *tel* 071-370 6105 *telex* 928542 *fax* 071-370 3838.

Zambia High Commission, 2 Palace Gate, Kensington, London W8 5NG *tel* 071-589 6655 *telex* 263544 *fax* 071-581 1353.

Zimbabwe High Commission, Zimbabwe House, 429 Strand, London WC2R 0SA *tel* 071-836 7755.

In *Whitaker's Almanack* will be found names and addresses of many other public bodies.

See also the **Picture research** section.

Societies and prizes

Societies, Associations and Clubs

Academi Gymreig Yr. *President:* Prof. J.E. Caerwyn Williams; *chairman:* Gwenlyn Parry; *treasurer:* Prof. Dafydd Jenkins; *administrator:* Dafydd Rogers, 3rd Floor, Mount Stuart House, Mount Stuart Square, The Docks, Cardiff CF1 6DQ *tel* (0222) 492064. The society was founded in 1959 to promote creative writing in the Welsh language. Existing members elect new members on the basis of their contribution to Welsh literature or criticism. The society publishes a literary magazine, *Taliesin*, books on Welsh literature, and translations of modern European classics into Welsh. It is currently engaged in the production of a new English/Welsh Dictionary. The society's activities are open to all.

Academi Gymreig, Yr: English Language Section. *President:* Roland Mathias; *chairman:* Gillian Clarke; *director:* Kevin Thomas, 3rd Floor, Mount Stuart House, Mount Stuart Square, The Docks, Cardiff CF1 6DQ *tel* (0222) 492025. This section was founded in 1968 to provide a meeting-point for writers in the English language who are of Welsh origin and/or take Wales as a main theme of their work. Membership open to all those who are deemed to have made a contribution to the literature of Wales, whether as writers, editors or critics. Associate Membership is open to all interested individuals or organisations. Although it is an autonomous body, members of the English Language Section co-operate with members of the parent body for joint conferences and similar activities.

Agricultural Journalists, Guild of. *President:* Charles Jarvis; *chairman:* Raymond Vale; *hon. general secretary:* Don Gomery, Charmwood, 47 Court Meadow, Rotherfield, East Sussex TN6 3LQ *tel* (089 285) 3187. Established to promote a high standard among journalists who specialise in agricultural matters and to assist them to increase their sources of information and technical knowledge. Membership is open to those earning their livelihood wholly or mainly from agricultural journalism.

American Correspondents in London, Association of. *President:* Maureen Johnson, c/o Associated Press, 12 Norwich Street, London EC4A 1BP *tel* 071-353 6322 *fax* 071-353 8118.

American Publishers, Association of, Inc. (1970). *President:* Nicholas A. Veliotes; *executive vice president:* Thomas D. McKee, 220 East 23rd Street, New York, NY 10010, USA *tel* 212-689-8920 *fax* 212-696-0131. Confederation of approximately 250 member houses which is the major voice of the publishing industry in the United States. Members drawn from all regions of the country publish the great majority of printed materials sold to American schools, colleges and libraries, bookstores, and by direct mail to homes. Their basic products comprise books in the categories of school and college textbooks, general trade, reference, religious, technical, professional, scientific, and medical – both hard cover and paperback. They also publish scholarly journals, and produce a range of educational materials including computer software, classroom periodicals, maps, globes, films and filmstrips, audio and video tapes, records, cassettes, slides, transparencies, and test materials.

Art and Design, National Society for Education in (1888), 7A High Street, Corsham, Wilts. SN13 0ES   *tel* (0249) 714825   *fax* (0249) 716138. *General secretary:* John Steers, NDD, ATC, DAE. Professional association of principals and lecturers in colleges and schools of art and of specialist art, craft and design teachers in other schools and colleges. Has representatives on National and Regional Committees which are the concern of those engaged in Art and Design Education. Publishes *Journal of Art and Design Education* (3 p.a.).

Artists Union (1972), 9 Poland Street, London W1V 3DG   *tel* 071-437 1984. Trade union for painters, sculptors and other visual artists.

Artists, Federation of British, 17 Carlton House Terrace, London SW1Y 5BD   *tel* 071-930 6844   *fax* 071-839 7830. Administers 9 major National Art Societies at The Mall Galleries, The Mall, London SW1.

Artists, International Guild of, Ralston House, 41 Lister Street, Riverside Gardens, Ilkley, West Yorkshire LS29 9ET   *tel* (0943) 609075. *Director:* Leslie Simpson, FRSA. The guild offers artists a service and insight into the opportunities in the art world as well as help with art problems and exhibition. *Membership:* by invitation.

Arts (1863), 40 Dover Street, London W1X 3RB   *tel* 071-499 8581. *Secretary:* Jackie Downing. For men and women connected with or interested in the arts. *Subs:* £345.

Arts Council of Great Britain, 14 Great Peter Street, London SW1P 3NQ   *tel* 071-333 0100. *Chairman:* Peter Palumbo; *secretary-general:* Anthony Everitt. To develop and improve the knowledge, understanding and practice of the arts, and to increase their accessibility to the public throughout Great Britain. The arts with which the Council is mainly concerned are dance and mime, drama, literature, music and opera, and the visual arts, including photography and arts films.

Aslib, The Association for Information Management (1924), Information House, 20-24 Old Street, London EC1V 9AP   *tel* 071-253 4488   *telex* 23667   *fax* 071-430 0514. Promotes the effective management and use of information in industry, central and local government, education and the professions. Provides publications, training, independent advice and recruitment services to the information sector. For particulars of membership apply: Chief Executive.

Assistant Librarians, Association of (1895), c/o The Library Association, 7 Ridgmount Street, London WC1E 7AE (Group of the Library Association, *qv.*). *President:* Jonathan Willson, BA, MA; *hon. secretary:* Christine Wise, BA, DipLib, ALA. Publishes library text books and bibliographical aids.

Australia, Children's Book Council of, *National Executive:* PO Box 420, Dickson, ACT 2602, Australia. The Council, a non-profit organisation, exists to encourage reading among children of all ages, to promote better writing, illustration and book production, and to encourage the sharing of literature. *Reading Time*, the official journal of the Council, is published 4 times a year. *Subscription:* $20.00. Entries for awards for 1991 and 1992 should be forwarded to Box 202, Sandy Bay, Tasmania 7005.

Australia Council, PO Box 74, Chippendale, NSW 2008, Australia   *located at* 181 Lawson Street, Redfern, NSW 2016, Australia   *tel* (02) 950 9000. *Chairperson:* Professor Rodney Hall, AO.

The Australia Council is a statutory authority which provides a broad range of support for the arts in Australia. Established in 1968 as the Australian Council for the Arts (supporting mainly the performing arts), it was restructured in 1973 to embrace music, theatre, film/radio/television, literature, visual arts, crafts, Aboriginal arts and community arts. (In June 1976 the activities of the film/radio/television Board were transferred to the Australian Film Commission.) In March 1975, by Act of Parliament, the Australia Council was established as an independent authority.

The Council is involved in the administration of grants, public information services, policy development, research, international activities, and advisory services to many other arts organisations including government bodies. A wide range of projects and activities, both individual and group, receive Australia Council funds. Support includes grants made to enable artists to study, and living allowances to permit others (notably writers) to 'buy time' to follow their creative pursuits. Some of the major initiatives of the Council in past years, include: negotiation with international bodies for the touring of exhibitions, a Public Lending Right scheme for Australian authors; copyright protection; moral rights for artists; art and working life; women in the arts; Arts Law Centre; a Provident Fund for performers; Artist-in-Residence schemes at tertiary institutions; and increased employment for Australian artists in all fields. Australia Council publications include information booklets, directories, research reports, newsletters, program reviews and an Annual Report.

The Literature Board, Australia Council, PO Box 74, Chippendale, NSW 2008, Australia   *tel* (02) 950 9000   *fax* (02) 950 9111. Because of its size and isolation and the competition its literature meets from other English-speaking countries, Australia has always needed to subsidise writing of creative and cultural significance. The Literature Board, one of the Boards of the Australia Council, was created in 1973, taking over the duties of the earlier Commonwealth Literary Fund, established in 1908.

The Board's chief objective is the support of the writing of all forms of creative literature – novels, short stories, poetry, plays, biographies, history and works on the humanities. The Board also assists with the publication of literary magazines and periodicals. It has a publishing subsidies scheme and it initiates and supports projects of many kinds designed to promote Australian literature both within Australia and abroad.

About two-thirds of the Board's expenditure in recent years has gone to writers in the form of direct grants including Fellowships and Writers' Project Grants (living allowances), and Emeritus Fellowships. Category A Fellowships (valued at $31,000 per year) are living allowances to assist published writers of substantial achievement to complete a major project or projects. Category B Fellowships (valued at $22,000 per year) are living allowances for developing writers of potential who may or may not have had a work published or performed. Writers' Project Grants (maximum value $10,000) are to assist writers to meet living expenses while writing a particular literary work. Emeritus Fellowships are paid at varying rates to senior writers of distinction.

Australian Book Publishers Association, 89 Jones Street, Ultimo, NSW 2007, Australia   *tel* (02) 281 9788   *fax* (02) 281 1073. Aims to foster original and licensed publishing in Australia, to help improve the Australian book industry as a whole. Has over 150 member firms.

Australian Library and Information Association, PO Box E441, Queen Victoria Terrace, ACT 2600, Australia   *tel* (06) 285 1877   *fax* (06) 282 2249. *Executive director:* Sue Kosse. Australia-wide organisation first incorporated by Royal

Charter in 1964 and supplemented in 1988, with about 7500 members, of whom about 5500 are professional members. The objects of the Association are to promote and improve the services of libraries and other information agencies; to improve the standard of library and information personnel and foster their professional interests; to represent the interests of members to governments, other organisations and the community; and to encourage people to contribute to the improvement of library and information services by supporting the Association. It publishes the *Australian Library Journal* four times per year and the newsletter *InCite* twenty times a year, as well as a range of specialist publications to cater for the interests of members in different types of library and information services. The governing body of the Association is the General Council.

The Australian Society of Authors, PO Box 315, Redfern, NSW 2016, Australia *located at* Suite 4, 245 Chalmers Street, Redfern, NSW 2016, Australia   *tel* (02) 318 0877   *fax* (02) 318 0530. *President:* Tom Keneally; *executive officer:* Gail Cork; *chairman:* Blanche d'Alpuget.

Australian Writers' Guild Ltd (1962), 60/60A Kellett Street, Kings Cross, NSW 2011, Australia   *tel* 357 7888   *fax* 357 7776. *Executive officer:* Janette Paramore. Trade union and professional association dedicated to promoting and protecting the professional interests of writers for stage, screen, television and radio. *Subscription:* full members: entrance fee $130, annual fee $130-$500 dependent on income from writing; associate members: entrance fee $65, annual fee $66.

Authors (1891) (at the Arts Club), 40 Dover Street, London W1X 3RB   *tel* 071-499 8581. *Secretary:* Huldine Ridgway. *Subscription:* £345.

Authors, The Society of, 84 Drayton Gardens, London SW10 9SB   *tel* 071-373 6642. *Chairman:* Penelope Lively, OBE; *general secretary:* Mark Le Fanu. Founded in 1884 by Sir Walter Besant with the object of representing, assisting and protecting authors. It is a limited company and an independent trade union. The Society's scope has been continuously extended; specialist associations have been created for translators, broadcasters, educational, medical, technical and children's writers (details will be found elsewhere in this issue). Members are entitled to legal as well as general advice in connection with the marketing of their work, their contracts, their choice of a publisher, problems with publishers, etc. *Subscription:* £65 (£60 by direct debit) p.a. Full particulars of membership from the Society's offices. (See article: **The Society of Authors.**)

Authors' Agents, The Association of (1974), 79 St Martin's Lane, London WC2N 4AA   *tel* 071-836 4271. *President:* Carole Blake; *secretary:* Sara Fisher; *treasurer:* Caroline Dawnay. Maintains a code of professional practice to which all members of the association commit themselves; holds regular meetings to discuss matters of common professional interest; and provides a vehicle for representing the view of authors' agents in discussion of matters of common interest with other professional bodies.

Authors' Guild of Ireland Ltd, 282 Swords Road, Dublin 9, Republic of Ireland   *tel* 375974. *Directors:* John K. Lyons, Mrs Iseult McGuinness. Society for the protection of copyright owned and managed, on a non-profit basis, by Full Members who must be owners of copyright in literary or dramatic works by reason of authorship, or who are the personal successors of such authors. Agents for the control of performing rights and collection of royalties in Ireland. *Secretary:* Tom Mooney.

The Authors League of America, Inc. (1912), 330 West 42nd Street, New York, NY 10036, USA   *tel* 212-564-8350   *fax* 212-564-8363. National membership organisation to promote the professional interest of authors and dramatists, procure satisfactory copyright legislation and treaties, guard freedom of expression, and support fair tax treatment for writers.

Authors' Licensing and Collecting Society Ltd (ALCS), 33/34 Alfred Place, London WC1E 7DP *tel* 071-255 2034. *President:* Lord Willis. Independent collecting society for the collective administration of literary and dramatic rights in the spheres of reprography, lending right, off-air recording and cable television. Membership, £5.88 annually, open to authors, successor membership to authors' heirs. See **ALCS** article.

Authors' Representatives, Inc., Society of (1928), Ten Astor Place, 3rd Floor, New York, NY 10003, USA *tel* 212-353 3709.

Aviation Artists, The Guild of (incorporating the Society of Aviation Artists), The Bondway Business Centre, 71 Bondway, Vauxhall Cross, London SW8 1SQ *tel* 01-735 0634. *President:* Michael Turner, PGAvA; *secretary:* Hugo Trotter, DFC. Guild of artists formed in 1971 to promote all forms of aviation art through the organisation of exhibitions and meetings. Annual open exhibition in June/July in London. £1000 prize for 'The Aviation Painting of the Year'. Quarterly members' journal. Entrance fee £25. Associates £30. Members £40 (by invitation). Non-exhibiting artists and friends £15.

BAPLA (British Association of Picture Libraries and Agencies) (1975). *Administrator:* Sal Shuel, BAPLA, 13 Woodberry Crescent, London N10 1PJ *tel* 081-444 7913 *fax* 081-883 9215. Trade association formed to promote fair and honest trading within the profession, and between members and their clients. Publishes a Code of Professional Standards and Fair Practice and a set of Recommended Terms and Conditions for the Submission and Reproduction of Photographs. BAPLA makes a constant effort to promote the fact that photographs, prints, drawings, have a copyright and that this copyright has a commercial value, that if any picture has the impact to promote a product, sell a book, it also has a market value for being so used. Publishes an annual Directory of Members and a quarterly Journal.

The E.F. Benson Society (1984), 88 Tollington Park, London N4 3RA *tel* 071-272 3375. *Secretary:* Allan Downend. To promote interest in E.F. Benson and the Benson family. The Society arranges two literary evenings a year and has an annual outing to Rye in July. Holder of an Archive, including the Austin Seckersen Collection, transcriptions of the Benson diaries and letters. Publishes post cards, and an annual journal, *The Dodo. Annual subscription:* £5.00 single, £6.00 two people at same address; £10.00 overseas. Affiliated to the Alliance of Literary Societies.

E.F. Benson: The Tilling Society (1982), Martello Bookshop, 26 High Street, Rye, East Sussex TN31 7JJ *tel* (0797) 222242. *Secretaries:* Cynthia and Tony Reavell. To bring together enthusiasts for E.F. Benson and his Mapp & Lucia novels. News and information is exchanged through two lengthy annual newsletters. Annual gathering in Rye. *Annual subscription:* £7, overseas £9; full starters membership (including all back newsletters) £13, overseas £18.

Bibliographical Society (1892), British Library, Collection and Preservation, Great Russell Street, London WC1B 3DG. *President:* B.C. Bloomfield; *hon. secretary:* Mrs M.M. Foot. Acquisition and dissemination of information upon subjects connected with historical bibliography.

The Blackpool Art Society (1884). *President:* Mrs Audrey Singleton; *hon. secretary:* Denise Fergyson, 29 Stafford Avenue, Poulton-le-Fylde, Blackpool FY6 8BJ *tel* (0253) 884645. *Studio:* Wilkinson Avenue, Blackpool FY3 9HB.

Summer and Autumn exhibition (members' work only). Studio meetings, practical, lectures, etc., out-of-door sketching.

Book Development Council—see **Publishers Association.**

Book House Ireland (1983), 65 Middle Abbey Street, Dublin 1, Republic of Ireland *tel* (01) 730108. *Administrator:* Cecily Golden. Represents Clé: The Irish Book Publishers' Association and The Booksellers' Association of Great Britain and Ireland (Irish Branch); provides a joint secretariat for both associations; book trade information and resource centre; produces regular newsletters, runs courses, has function rooms, a library and co-ordinates trade and social events for the Irish book industry.

Book Packagers Association (1985), 93a Blenheim Crescent, London W11 2EQ *tel* 071-221 9089. *Secretary:* Rosemary Pettit. Aims to represent the interests of book packagers; to exchange information; to provide services such as standard contracts and meeting facilities at book fairs.

Book Trust (formerly **National Book League**), Book House, 45 East Hill, Wandsworth, London SW18 2QZ *tel* 081-870 9055 *fax* 081-874-4790. Founded in 1925 as the National Book Council, and incorporated as an educational charity. The name and the constitution of the National Book League were changed in September 1986 and it is now known as **Book Trust**. *Patron:* HRH Prince Philip, Duke of Edinburgh; *chairman:* Michael Turner; *chief executive:* Keith McWilliams. Book Trust exists to open up the world of books and reading to people of all ages and cultures. Its services include the Book Information Service, a unique, specialist information and research service for all queries on books and reading. Details about subscription rates and research charges are available on request.

Book Trust's Prizes and Publicity Department administers 11 literary prizes including the £20,000 Booker Prize, and is responsible for the quarterly newsletter, *Book News* (annual subscription £25). The Publications and Exhibitions Department produces a wide range of books, pamphlets and leaflets designed to make books more easily accessible to the public. A number of touring book exhibitions are available for hire. For more details contact the Publicity Office.

The Children's Book Foundation is the children's division of Book Trust. It offers information and advice on all aspects of children's books and reading, and holds a collection of every title published for children in the UK during the last 24 months. The CBF runs its own membership scheme (subscription £40 + VAT) and Authorbank – a comprehensive information bank about authors and illustrators. It produces a termly newsletter for its members and organises Children's Book Week each year.

Book Trust (Scotland) (1960), 15A Lynedoch Street, Glasgow G3 6EF *tel* 041-332 0391 *fax* 041-331 2645. With a particular responsibility towards Scottish writing, being especially active in the field of children's writing, Book Trust Scotland exists to promote literature and reading, and aims to reach (and create) a wider reading public than has existed before. It also organises exhibitions, readings and storytellings, operates an extensive reference library available to everyone and administrates literary prizes such as the Kathleen Fidler Award. Book Trust Scotland also publishes short biographies, literary guides and directories and advises other relevant art organisations.

Books Across the Sea, The English-Speaking Union of the Commonwealth, Dartmouth House, 37 Charles Street, London W1X 8AB *tel* 071-493 3328 *fax* 071-495 6108; The English Speaking Union of the United States, 16 East 69th Street, New York, NY 10021, USA. World voluntary organisation devoted to the promotion of international understanding and friendship.

Exchanges books with its corresponding BAS Committees in New York, Australia, Canada and New Zealand. The books exchanged are selected to re..ect the life and culture of each country and the best of its recent publishing and writing. The books are circulated among members and accredited borrowers, bulk loans are made to affiliated schools and public libraries. New selections are announced by bulletin, *The Ambassador Booklist*.

Booksellers Association of Great Britain and Ireland (1895), 272 Vauxhall Bridge Road, London SW1V 1BA *tel* 071-834 5477 *fax* 071-834 8812. *Director:* T.E. Godfray. To protect and promote the interests of booksellers engaged in selling new books.

Botanical Artists, Society of (1985), Burwood House, 15 Union Street, Wells, Somerset BA5 2PU *tel* (0749) 674472 (during exhibitions 071-222 2723). *Founder president:* Suzanne Lucas; *hon. treasurer:* Pamela Davis; *hon. secretary:* Christine Hart-Davies; *executive secretary:* Mrs S.M. Burton. Aims to honour and strive to continue in the great tradition of talent, beauty and infinite care apparent in the art of botanical painting through the ages. An exhibition is held in March each year at the Westminster Gallery, Westminster Central Hall, Storey's Gate, London SW1H 9NU. Artists who use more recent techniques in style and interpretation are welcome, and non-members may submit work. Information from the executive secretary. *Membership fee:* £30; lay members £10.

British Academy, 20-21 Cornwall Terrace, London NW1 4QP *tel* 071-487 5966 *telex* 2631947 *fax* 071-224 3807. *President:* Dr A.J.P. Kenny; *foreign secretary:* Professor J.B. Trapp; *treasurer:* Dr E.A. Wrigley; *publications secretary:* Professor D.E. Luscombe; *secretary:* P.W.H. Brown.

British Amateur Press Association (1890), Michaelmas, Cimarron Close, South Woodham Ferrers, Essex CM3 5PB. To promote the fellowship of writers, artists, editors, printers, publishers and other craftsmen/women, and to encourage them to contribute to, edit, print or publish, *as a hobby*, magazines and literary works produced by letterpress and other processes.

British American Arts Association (UK), 116 Commercial Street, London E1 6NF *tel* 071-247 5385 *fax* 071-247 5256. *Director:* Jennifer Williams. Acts as an information service and clearing house for exchange between Britain and the United States in all the arts fields – literature, poetry, theatre, dance, music, visual arts. Counsels artists, administrators, organizations and sponsors on opportunities to promote, perform, show and tour their work; does not run programmes or give funds.

The British Association of Industrial Editors (1949), 3 Locks Yard, High Street, Sevenoaks, Kent TN13 1LT *tel* (0732) 459331 *fax* (0732) 461757. The objects include development of the qualifications of those engaged in the management, editing and production of internal corporate communication media. BAIE defines internal corporate communication to include such audiences as employees, customers, suppliers and shareholders. Membership is open to those engaged in, or have a valid interest in, corporate communication.

The British Copyright Council, Copyright House, 29-33 Berners Street, London W1P 4AA. *Chairman:* Maureen Duffy; *vice chairmen:* Anne Bolt, Jüri Gabriel, Graham Whettam; *secretary:* Geoffrey Adams; *treasurer:* Charles Clark. Its purposes are to defend and foster the true principles of creators' copyright and their acceptance throughout the world, to bring together bodies representing all who are interested in the protection of such copyright, and to keep watch on any legal or other changes which may require an amendment of the law.

The British Council, 10 Spring Gardens, London SW1A 2BN *tel* 071-930 8466 *telex* 8952201 Bricon G *fax* 071-839 6347. *Chairman:* Sir David Orr, MC, LLD; *Director General:* Sir Richard Francis, KCMG. The British Council promotes Britain abroad. It provides access to British ideas, talents and experience in education and training, books and the English language, information, the arts, the sciences and technology.

The Council is represented in 90 countries. Around the world the Council runs 155 offices, 116 libraries and 56 English language schools and employs 1800 staff in its London headquarters and in university towns around England, Scotland, Wales, Northern Ireland and the Republic of Ireland.

The Council's lending and reference libraries throughout the world stock material appropriate to the Council's priorities in individual countries. Where appropriate the libraries act as show-cases for the latest British publications. They vary in size from small reference collections and information centres to comprehensive libraries equipped with reference works, CD-ROM, on-line facilities and a selection of British periodicals. Bibliographies of British books on special subjects are prepared on request.

Working in close collaboration with book trade associations, the British Council organises book and electronic publishing exhibitions for showing overseas. These exhibitions range from small specialist displays of 100 or so titles to a big trade exhibit of 3000 titles representing 500 British publishers which is mounted annually at Frankfurt and elsewhere.

The Council publications include *British Book News*, a monthly guide to forthcoming books published in Britain. It also publishes a series of literary bibliographies, including *The Novel in Britain since 1970* and *Shakespeare*; *Contemporary Writers*, a series of over 30 pamphlets on modern British writers; and exhibitions on literary topics such as *Writers Abroad: British Travel Writing* (a catalogue of these and other literature publications is available on request).

A catalogue of other publications, covering the arts, books, libraries and publishing, education and training, English language teaching and information for and about overseas students, is also available on request.

The Council acts as the agent of the Overseas Development Administration for book aid projects for developing countries.

In 1990/91 the Council also supported over 1000 events in the visual arts, film and television, drama, dance and music, ranging from the classical to the contemporary.

The Council is an authority on teaching English as a second or foreign language and gives advice and information on curriculum, methodology, materials and testing through its English Language and Literature Division. It also promotes British literature overseas through writers' tours, academic visits, seminars and exhibitions.

Further information about the work of the British Council is available from the Press and Public Relations Department at the headquarters in London or from British Council offices and libraries overseas.

British Film Institute, 21 Stephen Street, London W1P 1PL *tel* 071-255 1444 *telex* 27624. *Director:* Wilf Stevenson.

The general object of the British Film Institute is 'to encourage the development of the art of the film, to promote its use as a record of contemporary life and manners, to foster study and appreciation of it from these points of view, to foster study and appreciation of film for television and television programmes generally, to encourage the best use of television'. Its divisions include the National Film Archive and the National Film Theatre on the South Bank. The Institute has also helped to set up 40 Film Theatres outside London. Through its Information Service, its monthly publication *Sight and Sound* (which gives credit and reviews of every feature film released in Britain, as well as feature articles by leading British and US writers on film and television) and its Education Department, it provides materials and services for film and television education. The BFI Library contains Britain's largest collection of printed material relating to film and television, open to BFI members only. The annual subscription for Members £13.90 including *BFI Film and Television Handbook* and NFT monthly programme. Annual Members are entitled to a BFI Library Pass £15.00 and/or *Sight and Sound* subscription £16.50. Students, senior citizens, registered disabled and unemployed £8.00.

British Institute of Professional Photography (founded 1901, incorporated 1921), Amwell End, Ware, Herts. SG12 9HN   *tel* Ware (0920) 464011. *Principal objects:* Professional Qualifying Association; to represent all who practise photography as a profession in any field; to improve the quality of photography; establish recognised examination qualifications and a high standard of conduct; to safeguard the interests of the public and the profession. *Membership:* approx. 5000. Admission can be obtained either via the Institute's examinations, or by submission of work and other information to the appropriate examining board. Fellows, Associates and Licentiates are entitled to the designation Incorporated Photographer or Incorporated Photographic Technician. *Meetings:* The Institute organises numerous meetings and conferences in various parts of the country throughout the year. *Publications:* a monthly journal, *The Photographer* and an annual Register of Members and *guide to buyers of photography*, plus various pamphlets and leaflets on professional photography.

British Kinematograph, Sound and Television Society (founded 1931, incorporated 1946), 547-549 Victoria House, Vernon Place, London WC1B 4DJ   *tel* 071-242 8400   *fax* 071-405 3560. *Secretary:* R.B. Mobsby. Aims to encourage technical and scientific progress in the industries of its title. Publishes technical information, arranges international conferences and exhibitions, lectures and demonstrations, and encourages the exchange of ideas. Monthly journal *Image Technology*.

The British Science Fiction Association Ltd (1958). *President:* Arthur C. Clarke; *membership secretary:* Jo Raine, 29 Thornville Road, Hartlepool, Cleveland TS26 8EW. For authors, publishers, booksellers and readers of science fiction, fantasy and allied genres. Publishes informal magazine, *Matrix*, of news and information, *Focus*, an amateur writers' magazine, *Vector*, a critical magazine, and *Paperback Inferno*, paperback and magazine reviews (all enquiries to membership secretary).

British Science Writers, Association of, c/o British Association for the Advancement of Science, Fortress House, 23 Savile Row, London W1X 1AB   *tel* 071-494 3326   *fax* 071-734 1658. *Chairman:* Pearce Wright; *secretary:* Dr Peter Briggs. Association of science writers, editors, and radio, film, and television producers concerned with the presentation and communication of science, technology and medicine. Its aims are to improve the standard of science writing and to assist its members in their work. Activities include visits to research establishments, luncheon meetings for those concerned with scientific policy, and receptions for scientific attachés and Parliamentarians.

Broadcasting Entertainment and Cinematograph Technicians' Union, Writers Section (1946), 111 Wardour Street, London W1V 4AY   *tel* 071-437

8506   *fax* 071-437 8268. *National organiser:* Bob Hamilton; *general secretary:* D.A. Hearn. To defend the interests of writers in film, television and radio. By virtue of its industrial strength, the union is able to help its writer members to secure favourable terms and conditions. In cases of disputes with employers, the union can intervene in order to ensure an equitable settlement. Its specialised production agreement with the BFTPA lays down minimum terms for writers working in the documentary area.

Broadcasting Group, The Society of Authors (1979), 84 Drayton Gardens, London SW10 9SB   *tel* 071-373 6642. Specialist unit within the framework of the Society of Authors exclusively concerned with the interests and special problems of radio and television writers.

The Brontë Society, Brontë Parsonage, Haworth, Keighley, West Yorkshire BD22 8DR   *tel* Haworth (0535) 642323   *fax* (0535) 647131. *President:* Lord Briggs of Lewes, MA, BSc, FBA; *chairman of the council:* Michael J.P. Steed; *hon. secretary:* Catherine M. Geldard; *hon. editor:* Mark Seaward, PhD, DSc. Examination, preservation, illustration of the memoirs and literary remains of the Brontë family; exhibitions of MSS. and other subjects. Publishes: *The Transactions of the Brontë Society* (bi-annual) and *The Brontë Gazette.* Affiliated to the Alliance of Literary Societies.

The Browning Society (1881, refounded 1969), 10 Pembridge Square, London W2 4ED   *tel* 071-221 5748   *fax* 071-792 0730. *Secretary:* Dr M.B.M. Calcraft. Aims to widen the appreciation and understanding of the lives and poetry of Robert Browning and Elizabeth Barrett Browning, and other Victorian writers and poets. *Membership fee:* £10.

The John Buchan Society (1979). *Hon. secretary:* Russell Paterson, Limpsfield, 16 Ranfurly Road, Bridge of Weir, Renfrewshire PA11 3EL   *tel* (0505) 613116. Promotes a wider understanding and appreciation of the life and works of John Buchan. Encourages publication of a complete annotated edition of Buchan's works, and supports the John Buchan Centre and Museum at Broughton, Borders. Holds regular meetings and social gatherings; produces a Newsletter and a Journal. *Subscription:* £8.00 p.a. full/overseas; other rates on application. Affiliated to the Alliance of Literary Societies.

Byron Society (International) (1971), Byron House, 6 Gertrude Street, London SW10 0JN   *tel* 071-352 5112. *Hon. director:* Mrs Elma Dangerfield, OBE. To promote research into the life and works of Lord Byron by seminars, discussions, lectures and readings. Publishes *The Byron Journal* (annual). *Subscription:* £15.00 p.a.

Cable Television Association (1934), The Fifth Floor, Artillery House, Artillery Row, London SW1P 1RT   *tel* 071-222 2900   *fax* 071-799 1471. Trade body representing the interests of companies involved in the provision of cable television and telecommunications in the United Kingdom. Associate membership open to individuals.

Randolph Caldecott Society (1983). *Secretary:* Kenn Oultram, Clatterwick Hall, Little Leigh, Northwich, Cheshire CW8 4RJ   *tel* (0606) 891303 (office hours). To encourage an interest in the life and works of Randolph Caldecott, the Victorian artist, illustrator and sculptor. Meetings: Chester. *Subscription:* £5.00-£8.00 p.a. Newsletter bi-annually. Affiliated to the Alliance of Literary Societies.

Canada, Periodical Writers Association of (1976), 24 Ryerson Avenue, Toronto, Ontario M5T 2P3, Canada   *tel* 416-868-6913   *fax* 416-860-0826. To protect and promote the interests of periodical writers in Canada.

Canada, The Writers' Union of, The Writers' Centre, 24 Ryerson Avenue, Toronto, Ontario M5T 2P3, Canada *tel* 416-868-6914 *fax* 416-860-0826. *Chair:* Trevor Ferguson.

Canadian Authors Association, 275 Slater Street, Suite 500, Ottawa, Ontario K1P 5H9, Canada *tel* 613-238-2296 *fax* 613-235-8237. *President:* Mary E. Dawe.

Canadian Book Publishers' Council. Consists of 41 educational and trade publishers; maintains offices at 250 Merton Street, Suite 203, Toronto, Ontario M4S 1B1, Canada *tel* 416-322-7011 *fax* 416-322-6999. *Executive director:* Jacqueline Hushion. Interested in advancing the cause of the publishing business by co-operative effort and encouragement of high standards of workmanship and service. Co-operates with other organisations interested in the promotion and distribution of books. Canadian Book Publishers' Council has three divisions: the School Group concerned with primary and secondary school instructional materials, the College Group concerned with post-secondary materials, and the Trade Group concerned with general interest adult and children's books.

Canadian Magazine Publishers Association (1989), 2 Stewart Street, Toronto, Ontario M5V 1H6, Canada *tel* 416-362-2546 *fax* 416-362-2547. *Executive director:* Catherine Keachie. Trade association representing members' interests to provincial and federal governments, and providing services to Canadian magazines, including retail distribution. Resource centre for information about Canadian magazines.

Canadian Poets, League of (1966), 24 Ryerson Avenue, Toronto, Ontario M5T 2P3, Canada *tel* 416-363-5047 *fax* 416-860-0826. *Executive director:* Angela Rebeiro; *executive assistant:* Dolores Ricketts. To promote the interests of poets and to advance Canadian poetry in Canada and abroad.

Canadian Publishers, Association of (1976; formerly Independent Publishers Association 1971), 260 King Street East, Toronto, Ontario M5A 1K3, Canada *tel* 416-361-1408 *fax* 416-361-0643. *Director:* Roy MacSkimming. Represents the interests of Canadian publishers in Canada and abroad; facilitates the exchange of information and professional expertise among its members.

(Daresbury) Lewis Carroll Society (1970). *Secretary:* Kenn Oultram, Clatterwick Hall, Little Leigh, Northwich, Cheshire CW8 4RJ *tel* (0606) 891303 (office hours). To encourage an interest in the life and works of Lewis Carroll, author of *Alice's Adventures*. Meetings at Carroll's birth village (Daresbury). *Subscription:* £5.00 p.a. Newsletter (*Stuff & Nonsense*) bi-annually.

The Lewis Carroll Society (1969), 16 Parkfields Avenue, London NW9 7PE. *Secretary:* Anne Clark Amor. To promote interest in the life and works of Lewis Carroll (Revd Charles Lutwidge Dodgson) and to encourage research. Activities include regular meetings and publication of *Jabberwocky* quarterly and newsletter *Bandersnatch*. *Annual subscription:* ordinary £8.00 ($20.00); institutions £10.00 ($23.00); students and retired £5.00 ($15.00). Affiliated to the Alliance of Literary Societies.

Cartoonists Club of Great Britain. *Secretary:* Charles Sinclair, 2 Camden Hill, Tunbridge Wells, Kent TN2 4TH *tel* (0892) 28938. Aims to encourage social contact between members and endeavour to promote the professional standing and prestige of cartoonists. Fee on joining: provisional, full or associate £30; thereafter annual fee £15.

The Chartered Society of Designers, 29 Bedford Square, London WC1B 3EG *tel* 071-631 1510 *fax* 071-580 2338. *Director:* Brian Lymbery. The leading professional body for designers, the Society represents 8000 designers in 17 categories under the main sections of product design, fashion and textiles, interiors, graphics, design management and design education. It provides a range of services to members including general information, guidance on copyright and other professional issues, access to professional indemnity insurance, a credit-checking/debt collection service; etc. Members may use the rooms available at the Society's headquarters. Activities in the regions are included in an extensive yearly programme of events and training courses. As the representative association for designers, the Society works to promote and regulate standards of competence, professional conduct and integrity. This includes representation on government and official bodies, design education and competitions. The Society's Code of Conduct has recently been revised and republished.

The Chesterton Society (1974), 11 Lawrence Leys, Bloxham, Nr Banbury, Oxon OX15 4NU　*tel* (0295) 720869. To promote interest in the life and work of Chesterton and those associated with him or influenced by his writings. *Subscription:* £15 p.a., includes journal *The Chesterton Review* (Q.) and newsletters. Affiliated to the Alliance of Literary Societies.

Children's Book Foundation, Book Trust, Book House, 45 East Hill, London SW18 2QZ　*tel* 081-870 9055　*fax* 081-874 4790. The Foundation provides practical help and advice on all aspects of children's books and reading. On joining, members receive Bookfax, a file of information regularly updated with information on authors, prizes, costume characters, exhibitions, etc. Membership is made up mainly of publishers, schools, colleges, libraries and book shops. *Annual membership:* £40 + VAT.

Children's Writers and Illustrators Group, 84 Drayton Gardens, London SW10 9SB　*tel* 071-373 6642. *Secretary:* Diana Shine. Subsidiary organisation for writers and illustrators of children's books, who are members of the Society of Authors.

Civil Service Authors, Society of. *Secretary:* Mrs J.M. Hykin, 8 Bawtree Close, Sutton, Surrey SM2 5LQ. The Society's aim is to encourage authorship by present and past members of the Civil Service (and some other public service bodies). There are annual competitions for poetry, short stories, etc., open to members only, and an annual 'Writer of the Year' award. The Society's magazine, *The Civil Service Author*, is free to members. *Annual subscription:* £8.50. Sae for enquiries.

The John Clare Society (1981), The Stables, 1a West Street, Helpston, Peterborough PE6 7DU　*tel* (0733) 252678. Promotes a wider appreciation of the life and works of the poet John Clare. *Annual subscription:* ordinary/libraries/ institutions £7.50, joint £10.00, retired £6.00, student (no voting rights) £3.00; overseas rates on application. Affiliated to the Alliance of Literary Societies.

Classical Association. *Secretary (Branches):* Mrs M.O. Baldock, 52 Alma Road, St Albans, Herts. AL1 3BL; *Secretary (Council):* Dr M. Schofield, St John's College, Cambridge CB2 1TP.

The William Cobbett Society (1976), *Secretary:* R.F. Hatt, Combe Wood, Burnt Hill Way, Boundstone, Farnham, Surrey GU10 4RN　*tel* (0252) 3543. To make the life and work of William Cobbett better known. *Subscription:* £5.00 p.a.

An Comann Leabhraichean (Gaelic Books Council) (1968), Department of Celtic, University of Glasgow, Glasgow G12 8QQ　*tel* 041-330 5190. *Chairman:* Professor Derick S. Thomson. Stimulates Scottish Gaelic publishing by awarding publication grants for new books, commissioning authors, setting literary competitions and providing editorial services and general assistance to writers and readers. Also publishes a catalogue of all Scottish Gaelic books in print and a magazine of book news. Runs a mobile bookselling service in the Highlands and Islands of Scotland and supports, and sometimes organises, literary evenings. Enquiries to the Chief Executive.

Comedy Writers Association of Great Britain (1981). Ken Rock, 61 Parry Road, Wolverhampton WV11 2PS *tel* (0902) 722729. Aims to develop and promote comedy writing in a professional and friendly way. *Membership:* £40 p.a.

Comics Enthusiasts, The Association of (1978). *Founder:* Denis Gifford, 80 Silverdale, Sydenham, London SE26 4SJ. Society for those interested in comics and strip cartoons from both the collecting and professional angles. *Comic Cuts*, the society's journal (8 p.a.). Annual membership £8; specimen issue £1.

The Composers' Guild of Great Britain, 34 Hanway Street, London W1P 9DE *tel* 071-436 0007 *fax* 071-436 1913. The Composers' Guild was created in June 1945 under the aegis of The Incorporated Society of Authors, Playwrights, and Composers. In 1948 it was formed into an independent body under the title of The Composers' Guild of Great Britain. Its function is to represent and protect the interests of composers of music in this country and to advise and assist its members on problems connected with their work. *Annual subscription:* £30.00, Associate membership £22.50. Further particulars obtained from the General Secretary of the Guild.

The Arthur Conan Doyle Society (1989). *Secretary:* Christopher Roden, Grasmere, 35 Penfold Way, Dodleston, Chester CH4 9ML *tel* (0244) 660988. Promotes the study of the life and works of Sir Arthur Conan Doyle. Publishes a bi-annual Journal and regular Newsletters. *Subscription:* £12.00 p.a., overseas £15.00 p.a. (airmail extra). Affiliated to the Alliance of Literary Societies.

Confédération Internationale des Sociétés d'Auteurs et Compositeurs, 11 rue Keppler, 75116 Paris, France *tel* 47-20-59-37 *telegraphic address* Interauteurs, Paris *telex* 649940 Cisac F.

The Joseph Conrad Society (UK) (1973). *Chairman:* Mrs Juliet McLauchlan; *president:* Philip Conrad; *secretary:* Hugh Epstein; *editor of the Conradian:* R.G. Hampson, The English Dept., Royal Holloway and Bedford New College, Egham Hill, Egham, Surrey TW20 0EX. Maintains close and friendly links with the Conrad family. Activities include an Annual Gathering, with lectures and discussions; publication of the *Conradian* and a series of pamphlets; and maintenance of a study centre in London.

Contemporary Arts, Institute of, The Mall, London SW1Y 5AH *tel* 071-930 3647. Centre which aims at encouraging collaboration between the various arts, the promotion of experimental work and the mutual interchange of ideas. Exhibitions, theatre, music, dance, poetry, lectures, cinema and discussions, all play a part in the programme. Open noon to 11 p.m. every day.

Copyright Clearance Center, Inc. (1978), 27 Congress Street, Salem, MA 01970, USA *tel* 508-744-3350 *fax* 508-741-2318. Operates a centralised photocopy authorisations and payment system in the US, serving photocopy users in their efforts to comply with the law, and foreign and domestic copyright owners in their efforts to protect their printed works. *Free registration* to rights holders.

The Copyright Licensing Agency Ltd (1983), 90 Tottenham Court Road, London W1P 9HE *tel* 071-436 5931 *fax* 071-436 3986. *Secretary:* Colin P. Hadley. Formed by the Authors' Licensing & Collecting Society (ALCS) and the Publishers Licensing Society (PLS) in 1982, CLA administers collectively photocopying and other copying rights that it is uneconomic for writers and publishers to administer for themselves. The Agency issues collective and transactional licences, and the fees it collects, after the deduction of its administration costs, are distributed every six months to authors and publishers via their respective societies. Since 1987 CLA has distributed £4.7m. See article on page 427.

Crime Writers' Association (1953), PO Box 172, Tring, Herts. HP23 5LP. For professional writers of crime novels, short stories, plays for stage, television and sound radio, or of serious works on crime. Associate membership open to publishers, journalists, booksellers specialising in crime literature. Publishes *Red Herrings* monthly.

The Critics' Circle (1913). *President:* William Hall; *vice-president:* David Dougill; *hon. general secretary:* Peter Hepple, 47 Bermondsey Street, London SE1 3XT *tel* 071-403 1818. *Objects:* To promote the art of criticism, to uphold its integrity in practice, to foster and safeguard the professional interests of its members, to provide opportunities for social intercourse among them, and to support the advancement of the arts. Membership is by invitation of the Council. Such invitations are issued only to persons engaged professionally, regularly and substantially in the writing or broadcasting of criticism of drama, music, films or ballet.

The Cromwell Association (1935), *Press liaison officer:* B. Denton, 10 Melrose Avenue, off Bants Lane, Northampton NN5 5PB *tel* (0604) 582516. Encourages the study of Oliver Cromwell and his times, holds academic lectures and meetings, publishes annual journal *Cromwelliana*, erects memorials at Cromwellian sites. *Subscription:* £10.00 p.a.

Cyngor Llyfrau Cymraeg—see Welsh Books Council.

The De Vere Society (1986), Canonteign, Nr Exeter, Devon EX6 7RH. *Secretary:* Earl of Burford. Aims to seek and, if possible, to establish the truth concerning the authorship of the Shakespeare plays and poems and, in addition, to promote research into the family of de Vere, Earls of Oxford. Please write for details.

Design and Artists Copyright Society (1983), St Mary's Clergy House, 2 Whitechurch Lane, London E1 7QR *tel* 071-247 1650 *telex* 885130 Fabrix G *fax* 071-377 5855. *Secretary:* Adrian Barr-Smith; *chief executive:* Rachel Duffield; *administrator:* Janet Tod. Aims to protect and administer visual artists' copyright, nationally and internationally. DACS licenses users of artwork and charges fees which are paid on to the artist less a small administration charge. The society advises on and pursues copyright infringement where appropriate. *Life membership:* £17.63 (inc. VAT).

Dickens Fellowship (1902), *Headquarters:* The Dickens House, 48 Doughty Street, London WC1N 2LF *tel* 071-405 2127. *Hon. Secretary:* Hylton Craig. House occupied by Dickens 1837-9. Membership rates and particulars on application. Publishes *The Dickensian*, 3 p.a. Affiliated to the Alliance of Literary Societies.

Directory Publishers Association (1970). *Secretary:* Rosemary Pettit, 93a Blenheim Crescent, London W11 2EQ *tel* 071-221 9089. Maintains a code of professional practice; aims to raise the standard and professional status of UK directory publishing and to protect (and promote) the legal, statutory and common interests of directory publishers; provides for the exchange of technical, commercial and management information. *Subscription:* £100-£600 p.a.

Sean Dorman Manuscript Society (1957), Cherry Trees, Crosemere Road, Cockshutt, Ellesmere, Shropshire SY12 0JP *tel* (0939 270) 293. *Director:* Mary Driver. The Society's aim is to provide mutual help among part-time writers in England, Scotland and Wales. Members regularly receive circulating manuscript parcels affording constructive criticism of their work and providing opportunities for technical and general discussion. *Subscription:* £5.00 p.a. Full details available on request.

Royal Dutch Publishers' Association (Koninklijke Nederlandse Uitgeversbond), Keizersgracht 391, 1016 EJ Amsterdam, The Netherlands *tel* (020) 626 77 36. *Secretary General:* R. M. Vrij.

Early English Text Society (1864). *Executive secretary:* Dr H.L. Spencer, Department of English, University of Bristol, 3/5 Woodland Road, Bristol BS8 1TB; *hon. director:* Professor John Burrow. To bring unprinted early English literature within the reach of students in sound texts. *Annual subscription:* £15.00.

Edinburgh Bibliographical Society (1890), c/o New College Library, Mound Place, Edinburgh EH1 2LU *tel* 031-225 8400, ext. 256. *Secretary:* M.C.T. Simpson; *treasurer:* E.D. Yeo.

Educational Publishers Council—see **Publishers Association.**

Educational Writers Group, 84 Drayton Gardens, London SW10 9SB *tel* 071-373 6642. Specialist unit within the membership of The Society of Authors.

The Eighteen Nineties Society, 17 Merton Hall Road, Wimbledon, London SW19 3PP. *President:* Countess of Longford, CBE; *chairman:* Martyn Goff, OBE; *secretary:* Dr G. Krishnamurti. Founded in 1963 as The Francis Thompson Society, it widened its scope in 1972 to embrace the entire artistic and literary scene of the eighteen-ninety decade. Its activities include exhibitions, lectures, poetry readings. Publishes biographies of neglected authors and artists of the period; also check lists, bibliographies, etc. Its Journal appears periodically, and includes biographical, bibliographical and critical articles and book reviews. The Journal is free to members, and is not for public sale. All correspondence to the *hon. secretary,* 97-D Brixton Road, London SW9 6EE.

The George Eliot Fellowship (1930). *President:* Jonathan G. Ouvry; *secretary:* Mrs K.M. Adams, 71 Stepping Stones Road, Coventry CV5 8JT *tel* (0203) 592231. Promotes an interest in the life and work of George Eliot and helps to extend her influence. Meetings are arranged; an annual magazine and a quarterly newsletter are produced. *Annual subscription:* £7.00. Affiliated to the Alliance of Literary Societies.

English Association, The Vicarage, Priory Gardens, Bedford Park, London W4 1TT *tel* 081-995 4236. *Chairman:* Professor Martin Dodsworth; *secretary:* Dr Ruth Fairbanks-Joseph.

English Speaking Board (International) Ltd, 26A Princes Street, Southport, Merseyside PR8 1EQ *tel* (0704) 501730. *President:* Christabel Burniston, MBE; *chairman:* Arthur Ridings. Aims to foster all activities concerned with English speech. The Board conducts examinations and training courses for teachers and students where stress is on individual oral expression. The examination auditions include talks, prepared and unprepared. Examinations are also held for those engaged in technical or industrial concerns, and for those using English as an acquired language. Three times a year, in January, May and September, members receive the English Speaking Board Journal, *Spoken English.* Articles are invited by the editor on any special aspect of spoken English. Members can also purchase other publications at reduced rates. Residential summer conference held annually, July-August. AGM in the spring. *Membership:* individuals, £12.00 p.a.

Fabian Society, 11 Dartmouth Street, London SW1H 9BN *tel* 071-222 8877 *fax* 071-976 7153.

Fantasy Society, The British (1971), 15 Stanley Road, Morden, Surrey SM4 5DE *tel* 081-540 9443. *President:* Ramsay Campbell. *Secretary:* Di Wathen. The Society was formed for devotees of fantasy, horror and related fields, in literature, art and the cinema. Publications include *British Fantasy Newsletter* (Quarterly) featuring news and reviews and approx. four annual booklets, including: *Dark Horizons*; *Winter Chills*, an all-fiction publication; *Masters of Fantasy* on individual authors; and *Mystique*, containing fiction. There is a small-press library and an annual convention and fantasy awards sponsored by the Society. *Membership:* £12.00 p.a.

The Fine Art Trade Guild (1910), 16-18 Empress Place, London SW6 1TT *tel* 071-381 6616 *fax* 071-381 2596. *Clerk to the Guild:* John D. Mountford. Principal aim is to improve and regulate working practices within the fine art and framing industry, and to promote the benefits of dealing with Guild members to the public. The Guild offers a unique 'Business in Art' service to trade, consumers and media providing information on technology, market trends, supply and education.

The Folklore Society (1878), c/o University College, Gower Street, London WC1E 6BT *tel* 071-387 5894. *Hon. secretary:* Marion Bowman. Collection, recording and study of folklore.

Foreign Press Association in London (1888). *President:* Patricia Layman; *secretary:* Davina Crole and Catherine Flurry. *Registered Office:* 11 Carlton House Terrace, London SW1Y 5AJ *tel* 071-930 0445/8883 *fax* 071-925 0469. Aims to promote the professional interests of its members. Membership open to overseas professional journalists, men or women, residing in the United Kingdom. Entrance fee, £110.45; annual subscription, £89.30.

Free Painters & Sculptors, Loggia Gallery and Sculpture Garden, 15 Buckingham Gate, London SW1E 6LB *tel* 071-828 5963. *Hon. secretary:* Philip Worth. Exhibits progressive work of all artistic allegiances and provides opportunities for FPS members to meet and discuss their work in either one-person or group shows. (Weekdays 6-8 p.m., Sat. and Sun. 2-6 p.m.)

Freelance Editors and Proofreaders, Society of (1988). *Secretary:* Jane Sugarman, 16 Brenthouse Road, London E9 6QG *tel* 081-986 4868. A professional Society whose aims are to promote high editorial standards and to achieve recognition of its members' professional status. These aims are furthered through the dissemination of information, advice and training; the provision of a network of contacts; the fostering of good relations between members and their clients; and advice on how to overcome the sense of isolation often experienced by freelances. The SFEP meets these aims through local and national meetings, a yearly conference, a monthly newsletter and a programme of workshops/training sessions provided at reasonable rates. These sessions help newcomers to acquire basic skills and experienced editors (whether in-house or freelance) to update, and/or improve their skills and develop or broaden their competence. They also cover aspects of professional practice or business matters for the self-employed. The SFEP also provides other services, including a yearly directory, which is made available to publishers, and the opportunity to buy reference books at publishers' discount prices. In addition, the Society supports moves towards recognised standards and accreditation for editors and proofreaders. Publishers and individuals interested in learning more about the Society should send an sae to the Secretary.

Freelance Photographers, Bureau of (1965), Focus House, 497 Green Lanes, London N13 4BP   *tel* 081-882 3315. *Head of administration:* John Tracy. To help the freelance photographer by providing information on markets, and free advisory service. Publishes monthly *Market Newsletter*. *Membership:* £32.50 p.a.

French Publishers' Association (Syndicat National de l'Edition), 35 Rue Grégoire de Tours, 75279 Paris 06, France   *tel* 43-29-75-75   *telex* 270838 Lifran F   *fax* 43-25-35-01.

Gaelic Books Council—see **An Comann Leabhraichean.**

The Gaskell Society (1985). *Hon. secretary:* Mrs Joan Leach, Far Yew Tree House, Over Tabley, Knutsford, Cheshire WA16 0HN   *tel* (0565) 634668. Promotes and encourages the study and appreciation of the work and life of Elizabeth Cleghorn Gaskell. Holds regular meetings and visits; produces an annual Journal and bi-annual Newsletters. *Subscription:* £5.00 p.a.

Gay Authors Workshop (1978), Kathryn Byrd, BM Box 5700, London WC1N 3XX. To encourage writers who are lesbian or gay. Quarterly newsletter. *Membership:* £4.00; unwaged £2.00.

General Practitioners Writers Association (1985). *Membership secretary:* Mrs G. Byrne, The Cottage, 102A High Street, Henley in Arden, West Midlands B95 5BY   *tel* (0564) 794894. The Society's aim is the improvement of writing by, for, from or about general medical practice. It publishes its own journal, *The GP Writer*, twice a year with a register of members' writing interests which is sent to medical editors and publishers.

German Publishers' and Booksellers' Association (Börsenverein des Deutschen Buchhandels e.V.), Postfach 10 04 42, 6000 Frankfurt am Main 1, Germany   *tel* (069) 13060   *telex* 413573 buchv d   *fax* (069) 13063201. *General manager:* Dr Hans-Karl von Kupsch.

The Ghost Story Society (1988), 2 Looe Road, Croxteth, Liverpool L11 6LJ   *tel* 051-546 2287. *Secretary:* Jeffrey A. Dempsey. Devoted mainly to supernatural fiction in the literary tradition of M.R. James, Walter de la Mare, Arthur Machen, Algernon Blackwood, etc. Thrice-yearly newsletter and annual journal, *All Hallows*. *Membership:* £7 (£8/$16 overseas).

Graphic Fine Art, Society of (1919), 9 Newburgh Street, London W1V 1LH. *President:* Mrs Lorna B. Kell, FSBA, FRSA. A fine art society holding an annual open exhibition. Membership by election, requires work of high quality with an emphasis on good drawing, whether by pen, pencil (with our without wash), water colour, pastel or any of the forms of print making.

The Greeting Card and Calendar Association, 6 Wimpole Street, London W1M 8AS   *tel* 071-637 7692   *telex* 21201   *fax* 071-436 3137. Publishes *Greetings* bi-monthly.

Guernsey Arts Council (1981), St James Concert and Assembly Hall, St Peter Port, Guernsey, CI   *tel* (0481) 721902. *Secretary:* Jennifer Seth-Smith. Co-ordinates the organisations under the council's umbrella, presents artistic events, sponsors reports, aims to bring about the creation of an arts centre in Guernsey and to encourage all the arts in Guernsey, Alderney and Sark. *Membership fee:* £5, under 18 £2.

Hakluyt Society (1846), c/o The Map Library, The British Library, Great Russell Street, London WC1B 3DG   *tel* (0986) 86359. *President:* Sir Harold Smedley, KCMG, MBE; *Hon. Secretaries:* Mrs Sarah Tyacke and Dr W.F. Ryan. Publication of original narratives of voyages, travels, naval expeditions, and other geographical records.

The Thomas Hardy Society Ltd (1967). *Secretary:* Mrs Kate N. Fowler, Park Farm, Tolpuddle, Dorchester, Dorset DT2 7HG *tel* Puddletown (0305) 848651. Publishes *The Thomas Hardy Journal* (3 p.a.). *Subscription:* £9.00 (£12.00 overseas) p.a. Affiliated to the Alliance of Literary Societies.

Harleian Society (1869), College of Arms, Queen Victoria Street, London EC4V 4BT. *Chairman:* J. Brooke-Little, cvo, ma, fsa, Norroy and Ulster King of Arms; *secretary:* P. Ll. Gwynn-Jones, ma. Lancaster Herald of Arms. Instituted for transcribing, printing and publishing the heraldic visitations of Counties, Parish Registers and any manuscripts relating to genealogy, family history and heraldry.

Heraldic Arts, Society of (1987), 46 Reigate Road, Reigate, Surrey RH2 0QN *tel* (0737) 242945. *Secretary:* John Ferguson, arca, sha, frsa. The objectives of the society are to serve the interests of heraldic artists, craftsmen, designers and writers, to provide a 'shop window' for their work, to obtain commissions on their behalf and to act as a forum for the exchange of information and ideas. The society also offers an information service to the public. Candidates for admission as members should be artists or craftsmen whose work comprises a substantial element of heraldry and is of a sufficiently high standard to satisfy the requirements of the society's advisory council. *Associate membership:* £10.00 p.a.; *full membership:* £15.00 p.a.

The Sherlock Holmes Society of London (1951). *President:* Frank A. Allen, fps; *chairman:* Mrs Shirley A. Purves, mcsp; *hon. secretary:* Cdr. G.S. Stavert, mbe, ma, rn (ret'd), 3 Outram Road, Southsea, Hants PO5 1QP *tel* (0705) 812104. *Objects:* to bring together those who have a common interest as readers and students of the literature of Sherlock Holmes; to encourage the pursuit of knowledge of the public and private lives of Sherlock Holmes and Dr Watson; to organise meetings and lectures for the discussion of these topics; to co-operate with other bodies at home and abroad that are in sympathy with the aims and activities of the Society. *Subscription*, including two issues of *The Sherlock Holmes Journal*: £10.00 p.a. UK, £11.00 Europe, £14.00 Far East, US$23.00 Americas.

Hesketh Hubbard Art Society, 17 Carlton House Terrace, London SW1Y 5BD *tel* 071-930 6844 *fax* 071-839 7830. *President:* Colin McMillan. Weekly drawing workshops open to all.

Illustrators, The Association of (1973), 1 Colville Place, London W1P 1HN *tel* 071-636 4100. Non-partisan, non-profitmaking trade association established in order to support illustrators, and to promote illustration and to encourage professional standards in the industry. Membership open to all involved with illustration. Bi-monthly magazine, and gallery space available for hire. All services give maximum support and assistance to members.

Illustrators, Society of Architectural and Industrial (1975), PO Box 22, Stroud, Glos. GL5 3DH *tel* Brimscombe (0453) 882563. *Administrator:* Eric Monk. Professional body to represent all who practise architectural, industrial and technical illustration, including the related fields of model making and photography.

Independent Literary Agents Association, Inc., 15 East 26th Street, Suite 1801, New York, NY 10010, USA.

Independent Programme Producers Association (IPPA), 50-51 Berwick Street, London W1A 4RD *tel* 071-439 7034 *fax* 071-494 2700. *Contacts:* Margaret Windham Heffernan (director)/Fred Hasson (deputy director). The trade association for British independent television producers. Services to members include an industrial relations unit; model contracts; publication of a regular journal, an annual members' directory and specialist guidebooks; a seminar programme, business affairs and sponsorship advice services; a European producers' network, plus links with Commonwealth countries and advice on all matters relating to independent production for television and satellite. IPPA led the successful campaign, now UK law, for 25% of new British television programmes to be made by independent producers and has established comprehensive trading guidelines with Channel 4, BBC and ITV. IPPA maintains an active lobby to ensure that the needs of the sector are heard both by broadcasters and Governments in Britain and Europe.

Independent Publishers Guild (1962), 25 Cambridge Road, Hampton, Middlesex TW12 2JL   *tel* 081-979 0250. Full membership is open to new and established publishers and book packagers; supplier membership is available to specialists in fields allied to publishing (but not printers and binders). The Guild offers a forum for the exchange of ideas and information and represents the interests of its members. *Membership:* £54.00 (+VAT) p.a.

Indexers, Society of. *Secretary:* Mrs H.C. Troughton, 16 Green Road, Birchington, Kent CT7 9JZ   *tel* (0843) 41115. Objects: (1) to improve the standard of indexing; (2) to maintain a Register of Indexers (for details see article on page 503); (3) to act as an advisory body on the qualifications and remuneration of indexers; (4) to publish or communicate books, papers and notes on the subject of indexing; (5) to raise the status of indexers and to safeguard their interests; (6) to publish and run an open-learning indexing course, 'Training in Indexing'. Membership is open to those who are interested in indexing and all aspects of information retrieval. There is no entrance fee. *Annual subscription:* £20.00, corporate £25.00. Copies of the Society's journal, *The Indexer*, are sent free to members.

Indian Publishers, The Federation of, Federation House, 18/1-C Institutional Area, J.N.U. Road, New Delhi 110067, India   *tel* 654847.

International Amateur Theatre Association. *Secretariat:* 19 Abbey Park Road, Grimsby DN32 0HJ   *tel* (0472) 343424. To encourage, foster and promote exchanges of theatre; student, educational, adult, puppet theatre activities at international level. To organise international seminars, workshops, courses and conferences, and to collect and collate information of all types for national and international dissemination.

International Publishers Association (1896), 3 avenue de Miremont, CH-1206 Geneva, Switzerland   *tel* (022) 46-30-18   *cable address* Inpublass   *telex* 421883   *fax* (022) 475717. *President:* Andrew H. Neilly; *secretary-general:* J. Alexis Koutchoumow.

International Songwriters & Composers, The Guild of, Sovereign House, 12 Trewartha Road, Praa Sands, Penzance, Cornwall TR20 9ST   *tel* (0736) 762826   *fax* (0736) 763328. *Secretary:* Carole Ann Jones. Gives advice to members on contractual and copyright matters; assists with protection of members rights; assists with analysis of members' works; international collaboration register free to members; outlines requirements to record companies, publishers, artists. *Subscription:* £18 p.a. UK, £20 p.a. EEC, £25 p.a. overseas. Publishers of quarterly magazine, *Songwriting & Composing*.

International Translations Centre (1961), Schuttersveld 2, 2611 WE Delft, Netherlands   *tel* (015) 14-22-42   *telex* 38104   *fax* (015) 15-85-35. *Director:* M. Risseeuw. A non-profit-making international clearing house facilitating access to existing translations of scientific and technical literature in Western and other languages.

Irish Book Publishers Association, Book House Ireland, 65 Middle Abbey Street, Dublin 1, Republic of Ireland *tel* (01) 730108. *President:* Alex Miller. *administrator:* Cecily Golden.

Irish Composers, Association of (1969), Liberty Hall, Room 804, Dublin 1, Republic of Ireland *tel* (01) 740070. *Secretary:* Fergus Johnston. To protect the rights of Irish composers and to foster and promote the writing of contemporary music in Ireland. *Annual subscription:* IR£20.

Irish Playwrights, Society of (1969), Liberty Hall, Room 804, Dublin 1, Republic of Ireland *tel* (01) 740070. *Secretary:* Patricia Martin. To safeguard the rights of Irish playwrights and to foster and promote Irish playwriting. *Annual subscription:* IR£25.

The Richard Jefferies Society (1950), 45 Kemerton Walk, Swindon, Wilts. SN3 2EA *tel* (0793) 521512. *President:* Prof. W.J. Keith (Toronto). *hon. secretary:* Cyril Wright. Promotes interest in the life, works and associations of Richard Jefferies; helps to preserve buildings and memorials, and co-operates in the development of a Museum in his birthplace; provides a service to students, lecturers, readers and writers. The Society arranges regular meetings in Swindon, and occasionally elsewhere. Outings and displays are organised. The membership is world-wide. *Annual subscription:* £3.00. Affiliated to the Alliance of Literary Societies.

The Johnson Society, Johnson Birthplace Museum, Breadmarket Street, Lichfield, Staffs. WS13 6LG *tel* (0543) 264972. *Hon. general secretary:* Patricia A. Wilmot. To encourage the study of the life and works of Dr Samuel Johnson; to preserve the memorials, associations, books, manuscripts, letters of Dr Johnson and his contemporaries; preservation of his birthplace.

Johnson Society of London (1928). *President:* The Revd Dr E.F. Carpenter, kcvo; *secretary:* Miss Stella Pigrome, Round Chimney, Playden, Rye, East Sussex TN31 7UR *tel* Iden (079 78) 252. To study the life and works of Doctor Johnson, and to perpetuate his memory in the city of his adoption.

Journalists, The Chartered Institute of. *Director:* Bill Tadd, fcij, 2 Dock Offices, Surrey Quays Road, London SE16 2XL *tel* 071-252 1187 *fax* 071-232 2302. The senior organisation of the profession, founded in 1884 and incorporated by Royal Charter in 1890. Men and women equally eligible for Fellowship (fcij) and Membership (mcij). The Chartered Institute maintains an employment register and has accumulated funds for the assistance of members. A Freelance Division links editors and publishers with freelances and a Directory is published of freelance writers, with their specialisations. There are special sections for broadcasters, motoring correspondents and public relations practitioners. Occasional contributors to the media may qualify for election as Affiliates.

The trade union interests of members are protected under the umbrella of the Federation of Professional Associations, an organisation of certificated independent unions not affiliated to the TUC. This provides full union representation and free legal advice to members in relation to their employment and professional activities. *Subscription:* related to earnings – maximum £160, minimum £50; Affiliate £75.

Keats-Shelley Memorial Association (1903). *Chairman:* K.V. Prichard-Jones; *patron:* HM Queen Elizabeth the Queen Mother; *hon. secretary:* Leonora Collins, Flat 1, 33 Aberdeen Road, London N5 2UG *tel* 071-354 3874. Occasional meetings; annual *Review* and progress reports. Supports house in

Rome where John Keats died, and celebrates the poets Keats, Shelley, Byron, and Leigh Hunt. Subscription to 'Friends of the Keats-Shelley Memorial', minimum £5.00 p.a.

Kent and Sussex Poetry Society, centre Tunbridge Wells, formed in 1946 to create a greater interest in Poetry. *President:* Laurence Lerner; *chairman:* Mary Colloff; *hon. secretary:* Madeline Munro, Pendips, Furzefield Avenue, Speldhurst, Tunbridge Wells, Kent TN3 0LD *tel* (0892) 863275. Well-known poets address the society, a Folio of members' work is produced and a full programme of recitals, discussions and readings is provided. *Annual subscription:* adults, £5.00; country members £3.00; students, £1.00.

The Kipling Society. The Secretary, 2nd Floor, Schomberg House, Pall Mall, London SW1Y 5HF. *Secretary:* Norman Entract *tel* (0428) 652709. *Aims:* To honour and extend the influence of Kipling, to assist in the study of Kipling's writings, to hold discussion-meetings, to publish a quarterly journal and to maintain a Kipling Reference Library. Membership details on application.

The Lancashire Authors' Association (1909). *President:* G. A. Wormleighton, MBE, FCA; *general secretary:* Eric Holt, 5 Quakerfields, Westhoughton, Bolton BL5 2BJ *tel* (0942) 816785. 'For writers and lovers of Lancashire literature and history.' Publishes *The Record* (Q.). *Subscription:* £7.00 p.a.

The Lancashire Dialect Society (1951). *Secretary:* Peter Wright, 30 Broadoak Road, Stockport, Cheshire SK7 3BL. Fosters the study of Northern dialects and their preservation in speech and writing. Journal and Newsletter published annually. *Annual subscription:* £3.00.

The T.E. Lawrence Society (1985). *Secretary:* Gordon Button, 75 Teevan Road, Addiscombe, Croydon, Surrey CR0 6RQ *tel* 081-654 4507. Promotes the memory of T.E. Lawrence and furthers knowledge by research into his life. Publishes bi-annual *Journal* and *Newsletter*. *Subscription:* £8.00 p.a., overseas £12.00 p.a. Affiliated to the Alliance of Literary Societies.

Learned and Professional Society Publishers, The Association of (1972). Aims to promote and develop the publishing activities of learned and professional organisations which produce journals and other publications. Membership is open to professional and learned societies and to individuals with publishing interests: details are available from the Secretary, Professor B.T. Donovan, 48 Kelsey Lane, Beckenham, Kent BR3 3NE *tel* 081-658 0459.

The Library Association (1877), 7 Ridgmount Street, London WC1E 7AE *tel* 071-636 7543 *telex* 21897 Laldn G *fax* 071-436 7218. *Chief executive:* G. Cunningham, BA. BSc(Econ). For over a century, The Library Association has promoted and defended the interests of the Library and Information Service profession, those working within it and the people who use the services. The monthly journal, *The Library Association Record*, is distributed free to all members. *Subscription* varies according to income.

Limners, The Society of (1986), 2 Glentrammon Close, Green Street Green, Orpington, Kent BR6 6DL *tel* (0689) 851158. *Founder/president:* Elizabeth Davys Wood, PSLM. SWA. Aims to promote an interest in miniature painting (in any medium), calligraphy and heraldry and encourage their development to a high standard. New members are elected after the submission of four works of acceptable standard and guidelines are provided for new artists. Members receive four newsletters a year and an annual exhibition is arranged. *Membership:* £15.

Linguists, Institute of, 24A Highbury Grove, London N5 2EA *tel* 071-359 7445 *fax* 071-354 0202. To provide language qualifications; to encourage

Government and industry to develop the use of modern languages and encourage recognition of the status of professonal linguists in all occupations; to promote the exchange and dissemination of information on matters of concern to linguists.

Literary Societies, Alliance of. *Secretary:* H.W. Woodward, c/o Birmingham and Midland Institute, Margaret Street, Birmingham B3 3BS *tel* 021-236 3591. Alliance of a number of Literary Societies formed to give mutual help in preserving particularly properties with literary associations. List of member societies available on payment of £2.00 from Philip Fisher, Assistant Secretary. Newsletter (*Chapter One*) published annually.

Little Presses, Association of (1966), 89ʌ Petherton Road, London N5 2QT *tel* 071-226 2657. *Co-ordinator:* Bob Cobbing. A loosely knit association of individuals running little presses who have grouped together for mutual self-help, while retaining their right to operate autonomously. Publications include: *Poetry and Little Press Information, Catalogue of Little Press Books in Print, Getting Your Poetry Published, Publishing Yourself. Membership fee:* £10.00 p.a.

Little Theatre Guild of Great Britain. *Secretary:* Ann Mattey, Flat 6, 34 Broad-water Down, Tunbridge Wells, Kent KT1 5NX *tel* (0892) 34710. To promote close co-operation between Little Theatres, to maintain and further the highest standards in the art of theatre. Membership is confined to independent play producing organisations which control their own established theatres.

The Arthur Machen Society (1986), 19 Cross Street, Caerleon, Gwent NP6 1AF *tel* (0633) 422520. *President:* Barry Humphries; *secretary:* Rita Tait. To honour the life and work of Arthur Machen. Provides a forum for the exchange of ideas and information and aims to bring Machen's work before a new generation of readers. Publishes twice-yearly journal *Avallaunius* and biannual newsletter *The Silurist.* Also publishes hardback books, by and about Machen and his circle, and an audio-cassette tape, under its Green Round Press imprint. *Annual subscription:* £12.00; £18.00 libraries; overseas, please enquire.

Master Photographers Association, Hallmark House, 97 East Street, Epsom, Surrey KT17 1EA *tel* (0372) 726123. To promote and protect professional photographers. Members can qualify for awards of Licentiateship, Associ-ateship and Fellowship. *Subscription:* £68.91 p.a.

Mechanical-Copyright Protection Society Ltd (MCPS), Elgar House, 41 Streatham High Road, London SW16 1ER *tel* 081-769 4400 *telex* 946792 MCPS G *fax* 081-769 8792. *Chief executive:* Frans De Wit. See article in **Copyright** section.

The Media Society (1973). *Secretary:* Rodney Bennett-England, Church Cottage, East Rudham, Norfolk PE31 8QZ *tel* (0485) 528664 *fax* (0485) 528155. To promote and encourage independent research into the standards, perfor-mance, organisation and economics of the media and hold regular discussions, debates, etc. on subjects of topical interest and concern to print and broadcast journalists. *Subscriptions:* £15.00 p.a.

Medical Journalists Association (1966), 14 Hovendens, Sissinghurst, Kent TN17 2LA *tel* (0580) 713920. *Chairman:* Alan Massam; *hon. secretary:* Tony Thistlethwaite. Formed by doctor-writers and journalist/broadcasters specialising in medicine and the health services. Aims to improve the quality and practice of medical journalism. Administers major awards for medical journalism and broadcasting. *Membership fee:* £20.00 p.a.

Medical Writers Group, 84 Drayton Gardens, London SW10 9SB *tel* 071-373 6642. *Secretary:* Jacqueline Granger-Taylor. Specialist unit within the membership of the Society of Authors.

Miniaturists, The Hilliard Society of (1982), Mrs S.M. Burton, 15 Union Street, Wells, Somerset BA5 2PU *tel* (0749) 674472. International membership. Founded to increase knowledge and promote the art of miniature painting. Annual Exhibition and lunch held in May at The Bishops Palace, Wells. Encourages Patron membership to keep collectors in touch with artists. Newsletter which includes information from other miniature societies around the world.

Miniaturists, Society of (1895), *Director:* Leslie Simpson, FRSA, Ralston House, 41 Lister Street, Riverside Gardens, Ilkley, West Yorkshire LS29 9ET *tel* (0943) 609075. The oldest miniature society in existence. Membership by selection.

William Morris Society (1955), Kelmscott House, 26 Upper Mall, London W6 9TA *tel* 081-741 3735. *Secretary:* John Purkis. To spread knowledge of the life, work and ideas of William Morris. Publishes a *Newsletter* (Q.), and a *Journal* (2 p.a.). Library and collections open to the public Thu and Sat, 2-5 pm.

Motoring Writers, The Guild of. General Secretary, 30 The Cravens, Smallfield, Surrey RH6 9QS *tel* (034 284) 3294. To raise the standard of motoring journalism. For writers, broadcasters, photographers on matters of motoring, but who are not connected with the motor industry.

Music Publishers Association Ltd (1881), 7th Floor, Kingsway House, 103 Kingsway, London WC2B 6QX *tel* 071-831 7591 *fax* 071-242 0612. *Secretary:* P.J. Dadswell. The only trade organisation representing the UK music publishing industry; protects and promotes its members' interests in copyright, trade and related matters. A number of sub-committees and groups deal with particular interests. Details of subscriptions available on written request.

Musicians, Incorporated Society of, 10 Stratford Place, London W1N 9AE *tel* 071-629 4413. *President:* 1991: Sir John Mandnell, CBE; *chief executive:* Neil Hoyle. Professional association for musicians. *Aims:* promoting the art of music; maintaining the interests of the musical profession; representing all professional musicians. *Subscription:* £59.50 p.a.

Name Studies in Great Britain and Ireland, Council for. *Chairman:* R.A. McKinley; *hon. secretary:* Miss Jennifer Scherr, 21 Caledonia Place, Bristol BS8 4DL. The advancement, promotion and support of research into the place-names and personal names of Great Britain and Ireland and related regions in respect of, i) the collection, documentation, and interpretation of such names, ii) the publication of the material and the results of such research, iii) the exchange of information between the various regions. Acts as a consultative body on Name Studies. Membership consists of representatives from relevant British and Irish organisations and a number of individual scholars elected by Council and usually domiciled in one of the relevant countries. Membership is by invitation, and members pay a small annual subscription. Publishes an annual newsletter, *Nomina,* which includes news of research in progress, publications, courses in name studies, reviews, short articles, notes and queries; edited by Dr Alexander Rumble, Dept. of Palaeography, University of Manchester, Oxford Road, Manchester M13 9PL.

National Graphical Association—see **NGA.**

National Poetry Foundation (1981), 27 Mill Road, Fareham, Hants PO16 0TH *tel* (0329) 822218. Aims to provide a truly national poetry organisation which in turn provides a worthwhile appraisal system, advice and information, magazine and discussion documents, all for a single low-cost fee, and to help poets have a book of their own poetry published at no additional cost, once they have sufficient poetry of a high enough standard. The Foundation also gives grants to deserving causes directly related to poetry.

National Society of Painters, Sculptors & Printmakers (1930). *Hon. secretary:* Gwen Spencer, 122 Copse Hill, Wimbledon, London SW20 0NL; *president:* Denis Baxter. An annual exhibition in London representing all aspects of art for artists of every creed and outlook.

National Union of Journalists. Head Office: Acorn House, 314 Gray's Inn Road, London WC1X 8DP   *tel* 071-278 7916   *telex* 892384   *fax* 071-837 8143. Trade union for working journalists with 27,893 members and 165 branches throughout the UK and the Republic of Ireland, and in Paris, Brussels and Geneva. Its wages and conditions agreements cover the newspaper press, news agencies and broadcasting, the major part of periodical and book publishing, and a number of public relations departments and consultancies, information services and Prestel-Viewdata services. Administers disputes, unemployment, benevolent, and provident benefits. Official publications: *The Journalist, Freelance Directory, Freelance Fees Guide* and policy pamphlets.

New English Art Club, 17 Carlton House Terrace, London SW1Y 5BD   *tel* 071-930 6844   *fax* 071-839 7830. *Hon. secretary:* William Bowyer, RA, RWS, RP. For persons interested in the art of painting, and the promotion of fine arts. Open Annual Exhibition at Mall Galleries.

New Zealand, Book Publishers Association of, Inc., Box 44146, Point Chevalier, Auckland 2, New Zealand   *tel* (09) 302 2473   *fax* (09) 302 2474. *President:* John Seymour.

New Zealand Copyright Council Inc., PO Box 5028, Wellington, New Zealand   *tel* (04) 724430   *fax* (04) 710765. *Chairman:* Bernard Darby; *secretary:* Tony Chance.

Newspaper Press Fund, Dickens House, 35 Wathen Road, Dorking, Surrey RH4 1JY   *tel* (0306) 887511. *Secretary:* P.W. Evans. For the relief of hardship amongst member journalists, their widows, and dependants. Limited help is available for non-member journalists and their dependants. Financial assistance and retirement housing are provided.

The Newspaper Publishers Association Ltd, 34 Southwark Bridge Road, London SE1 9EU   *tel* 071-928 6928   *fax* 071-401 2428.

Newspaper Society, Bloomsbury House, Bloomsbury Square, 74-77 Great Russell Street, London WC1B 3DA   *tel* 071-636 7014   *fax* 071-631 5119. *Director:* Dugal Nisbet-Smith; *deputy director:* Norman Walker.

NGA, National Graphical Association, Graphic House, 63-67 Bromham Road, Bedford MK40 2AG   *tel* (0234) 351521   *fax* (0234) 270580.

Outdoor Writers' Guild (1980). *Hon. secretary:* Hugh Westacott, 86 Burford Gardens, London N13 4LP   *tel* 081-886 1957. Aims to promote a high professional standard among writers who specialise in outdoor activities; represents members' interests to representative bodies in the outdoor leisure industry; circulates members with news of media opportunities; provides a forum for members to meet colleagues and others in the outdoor leisure industry. *Membership:* £10.00 p.a.

Painters in Oils, Pastels and Acrylics, British Society of (1988), Ralston House, 41 Lister Street, Riverside Gardens, Ilkley, West Yorkshire LS29 9ET   *tel*

(0943) 609075. *Director:* Leslie Simpson, FRSA. Promotes interest and encourages high quality in the work of painters in these media. Exhibitions open to all artists. *Membership:* £25.

The Pastel Society (1899), 17 Carlton House Terrace, London SW1Y 5BD   *tel* 071-930 6844   *fax* 071-839 7830. *President:* John Blockley. Membership open to all. Pastel and drawings in pencil or chalk. Annual Exhibition open to all artists working in dry media.

The Mervyn Peake Society (1975). *Hon. president:* Sebastian Peake; *chairman:* John Watney; *secretary:* Frank Surry, 2 Mount Park Road, Ealing, London W5 2RP. Devoted to recording the life and works of Mervyn Peake. Publishes a journal and news letter. *Annual subscription:* £10 (UK and Europe): £8 students; £12 all other countries.

P.E.N., International. A world association of writers. *International president:* György Konrád; *international secretary:* Alexander Blokh, 9/10 Charterhouse Buildings, Goswell Road, London EC1M 7AT   *tel* 071-253 4308   *telegrams/cables* Lonpenclub London EC1   *fax* 071-253 5711; *president of English Centre:* Ronald Harwood. *general secretary of English Centre:* Josephine Pullein-Thompson, MBE, 7 Dilke Street, London SW3 4JE   *tel* 071-352 6303.

P.E.N. was founded in 1921 by C.A. Dawson Scott under the presidency of John Galsworthy, to promote friendship and understanding between writers and defend freedom of expression within and between all nations. The initials P.E.N. stand for Poets, Playwrights, Editors, Essayists, Novelists – but membership is open to all writers of standing (including translators), whether men or women, without distinction of creed or race, who subscribe to these fundamental principles. P.E.N. takes no part in state or party politics; it has given care to, and raised funds for, refugee writers, and also administers the P.E.N. Writers In Prison Committee which works on behalf of writers imprisoned for exercising their right to freedom of expression, a right implicit in the P.E.N. Charter to which all members subscribe. The Translations Committee strives to promote the translations of works by writers in the lesser-known languages. International Congresses are held most years. The 54th Congress was held in Toronto and Quebec in September 1989 and the 55th in Madeira in May 1990.

Membership of the English Centre is £20.00 p.a. for country and overseas members, £25.00 for London members. Associate membership is available for writers not yet eligible for full membership and persons connected with literature. Membership of any one Centre implies membership of all Centres; at present 101 autonomous Centres exist throughout the world. The English Centre has a programme of literary lectures, discussion, dinners and parties. A yearly *Writers' Day* is open to the public.

Publications: P.E.N. International (bi-lingual, Fr.-Eng., reviews of books in languages of limited currency; sponsored by UNESCO); *The Survival and Encouragement of Literature in Present Day Society* (Archive Press) 1979; News Bulletins published by various Centres; English Centre edited a series of annual anthologies of contemporary poetry; *New Poems* – 1952-62; from 1965 the volume appeared biennially and from 1972 to 1977 annually. From 1978 to 1983 P.E.N. and the Arts Council and Hutchinson combined to publish *New Poetry* and *New Stories* annually. From 1984 to 1988, in partnership with Quartet Books, the English Centre published prose and poetry anthologies, *P.E.N. New Fiction* and *P.E.N. New Poetry*, in alternate years.

The Penman Club, 175 Pall Mall, Leigh-on-Sea, Essex SS9 1RE   *tel* (0702) 74438. *President:* Trevor J. Douglas; *general secretary:* Leonard G. Stubbs,

FRSA. Literary Society for writers throughout the world, published and unpublished. Members in almost every country. Benefits of membership include criticism of all MSS without additional charge, marketing and general literary advice, also use of large writers' library. *Subscription:* £8.25 p.a. plus £3.00 entry fee: first year only. Stamp for Prospectus from the General Secretary.

Performing Right Society Ltd (1914), 29-33 Berners Street, London W1P 4AA   *tel* 071-580 5544   *fax* 071-631 4138. See article on page 418.

Periodical Publishers Association, Imperial House, 15-19 Kingsway, London WC2B 6UN   *tel* 071-379 6268   *fax* 071-379 5661. *Chief executive:* Ian Locks.

The Personal Managers' Association, Ltd, *Liaison secretary:* Angela Adler, 1 Summer Road, East Molesey, Surrey KT8 9LX   *tel/fax* 081-398 9796. Association of personal managers in the theatre, film and entertainment world generally.

Player-Playwrights (1948), St Augustine's Church Hall, Queen's Gate, London SW1. *Secretary:* Peter Thompson, 9 Hillfield Park, London N10 3QT   *tel* 081-883 0371. The society reads, performs and discusses plays and scripts submitted by members, with a view to assisting the writers in improving and marketing their work. There are six competition evenings a year. *Annual membership:* £5.00 (and £1.00 per attendance).

The Playwrights' Co-operative (1978). *Administrator:* Vivienne Cottrell, 117 Waterloo Road, London SE1 8UL   *tel* 071-633 9811. Supports and encourages playwrights who, having already written at least one script, want to move forward but need professional advice and contact. Offers story conferences, workshops, rehearsed readings and criticism; publishes plays. *Membership:* £15.00 p.a.

Playwrights Trust, New, Whitechapel Library, 77 Whitechapel High Street, London E1 7OX   *tel* 071-377 5429. *Director:* Polly Thomas; *administrator:* Ben Payne. Support and development organisation for playwrights and aspiring playwrights, and those interested in developing and producing new work. Services include script-reading. Workshops, writer/company Link Service. Issues *Newsletter* monthly. *Subscriptions:* £15.00 (waged), £9.00 (part-waged), £6.00 (unwaged), £14.00 (EEC), £15.00 (Europe), £20.00 (other); *company membership:* £15.00 (unfunded/community group), £30.00 (funded/commercial group).

Playwrights Workshop (1949). A meeting place where those people in the Manchester area interested in drama can meet to discuss playwriting in general and their own plays in particular. Details of places and times of meetings from *Hon. secretary:* Robert Coupland, 22 Brown Street, Altrincham, Cheshire WA14 2EU   *tel* 061-928 3095. Plays read privately by experienced playwright and detailed assessments made. Details from above with sae.

The Poetry Society (1909) Incorporated, 21 Earls Court Square, London SW5 9DE   *tel* 071-373 7861/2551. *Chairman:* Sebastian Barker; *director/general secretary:* Chris Green; *treasurer:* Michael Ivens, CBE. National body entirely devoted to the encouragement of the art. It publishes *Poetry Review* quarterly, runs poetry readings all over Britain with a special London programme, children's events, verse-speaking examinations and administers various prizes and competitions.

Beatrix Potter Society (1980), *Chairman:* Judy Taylor; *secretary:* Brian Riddle, 24 Warren Road, Wanstead, London E11 2NA. Promotes the study and appreciation of the life and works of Beatrix Potter as author, artist, diarist, farmer and conservationist. *Subscription:* UK £7.00, overseas £12.00.

The Press Complaints Commission (1953), Independent. *Chairman:* Lord McGregor of Durris; *director:* Kenneth Morgan, OBE, 1 Salisbury Square, London EC4Y 8AE *tel* 071-353 1248 *fax* 071-353 8355.

Private Libraries Association (1956), Ravelston, South View Road, Pinner, Middlesex HA5 3YD. *President:* Peter Eaton; *hon. editor:* David Chambers; *hon. secretary:* Frank Broomhead. International society of book collectors and private libraries. Publications include the quarterly *Private Library*, annual *Private Press Books*, and other books on book collecting. *Subscription:* £20.00 p.a.

The Producers Association, Paramount House, 162-170 Wardour Street, London W1V 4LA *tel* 071-437 7700 *fax* 071-734 4564. *Chief executive:* John Woodward; *chair:* Charles Denton. To encourage film, video and television production, as well as stimulate finance, distribution and exhibition within the UK and overseas. TPA currently has 860 members, the majority of whom are independent film and/or television producers. Facilities available to members include direct information service, feature film, television and technical producer courses, seminars, lectures, budgeting consultancies, legal surgeries, workshops, producer magazine and a variety of media publications.

Publishers Association, 19 Bedford Square, London WC1B 3HJ. Established 1896 *tel* 071-580 6321/5 and 7761; 323 1548 *telex* 267160 Pubass G *fax* 071-636 5375. *Chief executive:* Clive Bradley; *director of administration:* Philip Flamank; *director of Book Development Council:* Ian Taylor; *director of educational and professional publishing:* John Davies. Association of British publishers whose overall membership represents some 200 members (embracing 600 companies, starred in the list of British Publishers given earlier in this book).

Publishers Licensing Society Limited (1981), 90 Tottenham Court Road, London W1P 9HE *tel* 071-436 5931 *fax* 071-436 3986. *Chairman:* Charles Clark; *Secretary:* Gervase E. Muller. Aims to exercise and enforce on behalf of publishers the rights of copyright and other rights of a similar nature, to authorise the granting of licences for, *inter alia*, the making of reprographic copies of copyright works, and to receive and distribute to the relevant publisher copyright proprietors the sums accruing from such licensed use.

The Radclyffe International Philosophical Association (1955), BM-RIPhA, Old Gloucester Street, London WC1N 3XX. *President:* William Mann, FRIPhA; *secretary general:* John Khasseyan, FRIPhA. *Objects:* To dignify those achievements which might otherwise escape formal recognition; to promote the interests and talent of its members; to encourage their good fellowship and to form a medium of exchange of ideas between members. *Entrance fee:* £10.00. *Subscription:* £15.00 (Fellows, Members and Associates). Published authors and artists usually enter at Fellowship level.

Railway Artists, Guild of (1979). *Hon. administrator:* F.P. Hodges, 45 Dickins Road, Warwick CV34 5NS *tel* (0926) 499246. Aims to forge a link between artists depicting railway subjects and to give members a corporate identity; also stages railway art exhibitions and members' meetings.

Regional Arts Boards. RABs are funded by the Arts Council, British Film Institute, Crafts Council and their constituent local authorities, as well as educational and priv *e sources. They exist to promote and develop the arts in their regions.

With their grasp of regional needs and demands they are well equipped to provide a service of information, help and guidance to all kinds of arts organisations in their area, and in many cases can provide financial assistance.

They can take the initiative in promoting activities themselves and in planning and co-ordinating regional tours.

Representatives of all the associations meet as the Council of Regional Arts Associations (CORAA), 5 City Road, Winchester, Hants SO23 8SD   *tel* (0962) 851063   *fax* (0962) 842033.

The subsidy responsibility for many activities in England and Wales has been transferred from the Arts Council of Great Britain to the Regional Arts Boards. The Arts Council retains as direct beneficiaries a number of the larger organisations, including certain regional theatre companies and major festivals, but these are scheduled for devolution by 1993/94.

Consequent upon the Minister for the Arts' statement to the House of Commons on 13 March 1990, a restructuring of the arts support system is proceeding. This redefines roles between the Arts Council and the regions, the latter to be strengthened and given more authority. They are being transformed into ten Regional Arts *Boards* taking the place of the original twelve RAAs in England with effect from 1 October 1991.

Annual Subscriptions for Full Membership (Organisations) and Associate Membership (Individuals) vary between the Boards and details may be obtained from the addresses listed below. Membership entitles one to the periodicals and broadsheets and to other benefits.

There are no regional arts boards in Scotland and all enquiries should be addressed to The Scottish Arts Council, 12 Manor Place, Edinburgh EH3 7DD   *tel* 031-226 6051.

East Midlands Arts (1969), Mountfields House, Forest Road, Loughborough, Leics. LE11 3HU   *tel* (0509) 218292   *fax* (0509) 262214. *Director:* John Buston. *Literature officer:* Debbie Hicks. Derbyshire (excluding High Peak District), Leicestershire, Northamptonshire and Nottinghamshire.

Eastern Arts (1971), Cherry Hinton Hall, Cherry Hinton Road, Cambridge CB1 4DW   *tel* (0223) 215355. *Director:* Jeremy Newton. Specialist officers for each art form. Bedfordshire, Cambridgeshire, Essex, Hertfordshire, Lincolnshire, Norfolk and Suffolk.

London Arts Board (1966), Coriander Building, 20 Gainsford Street, London SE1 2NE   *tel* 071-403 9013. *Director:* Timothy Mason. The area of the 32 London Boroughs and the City of London.

North Wales Arts (1967), 10 Wellfield House, Bangor, Gwynedd LL57 1ER   *tel* (0248) 353248   *fax* (0248) 351077. *Director:* D. Llion Williams. Clwyd, Gwynedd and District of Montgomery in the County of Powys.

Arts Board: North West (1966), 12 Harter Street, Manchester M1 6HY   *tel* 061-228 3062   *fax* 061-236 5361. *Director:* David B. Pirnie. Greater Manchester, Merseyside, High Peak District of Derbyshire, Lancashire and Cheshire.

Northern Arts (1961), 9-10 Osborne Terrace, Newcastle upon Tyne NE2 1NZ   *tel* 091-281 6334   *fax* 091-281 3276. *Director:* Peter Stark; *literature officer:* Don Watson. Cumbria, Cleveland, Tyne and Wear, Northumberland and Durham.

South East Arts (1973), 10 Mount Ephraim, Tunbridge Wells, Kent TN4 8AS   *tel* (0892) 515210. *Director:* Christopher Cooper. Covers Kent, East and West Sussex and Surrey. Publishes arts magazine *Event* 10 times a year, as well as 'Support for the Arts' information pack for artists and arts organisations.

South-East Wales Arts (1973), Victoria Street, Cwmbran, Gwent NP44 3YT   *tel* (0633) 875075   *fax* (0633) 875389. *Director:* Michael Trickey. South

Glamorgan, Mid-Glamorgan, Gwent, Districts of Radnor and Brecknock in the County of Powys, and the City of Cardiff.

South West Arts (1956), Bradninch Place, Gandy Street, Exeter, Devon EX4 3LS   *tel* (0392) 218188   *fax* (0392) 413554. Avon, Cornwall, Devon, Dorset (except Districts of Bournemouth, Christchurch and Poole), Gloucestershire, Somerset.

Southern Arts (1968), 13 St Clement Street, Winchester, Hants SO23 9DQ   *tel* (0962) 855099. *Director:* Bill Dufton; *literature officer:* Jane Spiers. The arts development agency for Berkshire, Buckinghamshire, Hampshire, Isle of Wight, Oxfordshire, Wiltshire, and Bournemouth, Christchurch and Poole, Districts of Dorset.

West Midlands Arts (1971), 82 Granville Street, Birmingham B1 2LH   *tel* 021-631 3121   *fax* 021 643 7239. *Director:* Michael Elliott. County of Hereford and Worcester, West Midlands Metropolitan Area, Shropshire, Staffordshire, Warwickshire.

West Wales Arts (1971), Red Street, Carmarthen, Dyfed SA31 1QL   *tel* (0267) 234248   *fax* (0267) 233084. *Director:* Carwyn Rogers. Dyfed and West Glamorgan.

Yorkshire and Humberside Arts (1969), Glyde House, Glydegate, Bradford, West Yorkshire BD5 0BQ   *tel* (0274) 723051   *fax* (0274) 394919. North, South and West Yorkshire and Humberside. Funds schemes and projects for the promotion of contemporary literature and writing activities. Provides grants for festivals, events, courses, residencies, publishing. Offers advice and information on various aspects of literature. Priorities change annually; preliminary enquiry advised.

Ridley Art Society (1889), 69 Sterndale Road, London W14 0HU   *tel* 071-603 4371. *President:* Carel Weight, CBE. RA; *chairman:* Hermione Thornton-Lofthouse. Represents a wide variety of attitudes towards the making of art. In recent years has sought to encourage young artists. At least one central London exhibition annually.

The Romantic Novelists' Association. *Chairman:* Marina Oliver, Half Hidden, West Lane, Bledow, Princes Risborough, Bucks. HP17 9PF   *tel* (08444) 5973; *hon. secretary:* Marie Murray, 9 Hillside Road, Southport, Merseyside PR8 4QB. To raise the prestige of Romantic Authorship. Open to romantic and historical novelists. See also under **Literary Awards.**

Royal Academy of Arts, Piccadilly, London W1V 0DS   *tel* 071-439 7438. *President:* Roger de Grey, PRA; *keeper:* Norman Adams, RA; *treasurer:* Sir Philip Powell, RA; *secretary:* Piers Rodgers. Academicians (RA) and Associates (ARA) are elected from the most distinguished artists in the United Kingdom. Major loan exhibitions throughout the year with the Annual Summer Exhibition, June to August. Also runs art schools for 60 post-graduate students in painting and sculpture.

Royal Birmingham Society of Artists, 69A New Street, Birmingham B2 4DU   *tel* 021-643 3768. *President:* C.A. Sawbridge; *hon. secretary:* Victor Kelly, RBSA. The Society has its own galleries and rooms prominently placed in the city centre. Members (RBSA) and Associates (ARBSA) are elected annually. There are two annual Spring Exhibitions open to all artists and an Autumn Exhibition of Members' and Associates' works. *Annual Subscription* (Friends of the RBSA): £8.00 entitles subscribers to attend painting days, criticisms and lectures organised by the Society and to submit work for the Annual Friends' Exhibition in February and July. Further details from the Hon. Secretary.

Royal Institute of Oil Painters, 17 Carlton House Terrace, London SW1Y 5BD *tel* 071-930 6844 *fax* 071-839 7830. *President:* Brian Bennett. Promotes and encourages the art of painting in oils. Open Annual Exhibition.

Royal Institute of Painters in Water Colours (1831), 17 Carlton House Terrace, London SW1Y 5BD *tel* 071-930 6844 *fax* 071-839 7830. *President:* Ronald Maddox. The Institute promotes the appreciation of watercolour painting in its traditional and contemporary forms, primarily by means of an annual exhibition at the Mall Galleries, London SW1 of members' and non-members' work and also by members' exhibitions at selected venues in Britain and abroad. Members elected from approved candidates' list.

The Royal Literary Fund, 144 Temple Chambers, Temple Avenue, London EC4Y 0DT *tel* 071-353 7150. *President:* Arthur Crook; *secretary:* Fiona Clark. Founded in 1790, the Fund is the oldest and largest charity serving literature. The object of the Fund is to help writers and their families who face hardship. It does not offer grants to writers who can earn their living in other ways, nor does it provide financial support for writing projects. But it sustains authors who have for one reason or another fallen on hard times – illness, family misfortune, or sheer loss of writing form, all of which can afflict established authors and deprive them of that peace of mind so necessary for work.

    Applicants must have published work of approved literary merit, which may include important contributions to periodicals. The literary claim of every new applicant must be accepted by the General Committee before the question of need can be considered.

    The Fund has never received a subsidy from the Government nor has the Welfare State replaced its function. It is supported by the investment of legacies, subscriptions and donations. The principal contributors are authors themselves, publishers and others in the book trade.

The Royal Musical Association, Peter Owens, 135 Purves Road, London NW10 5TH *tel* 081-960 5239.

The Royal Photographic Society (1853), The Octagon, Milsom Street, Bath BA1 1DN *tel* (0225) 462841. Aims to promote the general advancement of photography and its applications. Publish *The Photographic Journal* monthly, £50.00 p.a., overseas £55.00 p.a. and *The Journal of Photographic Science,* bi-monthly £80.00 p.a., overseas £90.00.

Royal Scottish Academy (1826), Princes Street, Edinburgh EH2 2EL *tel* 031-225 6671. *President:* William J.L. Baillie, PRSA; *secretary:* Jack Knox, RSA; *treasurer:* Ian McKenzie Smith, RSA; *administrative secretary:* W. T. Meikle. Academicians (RSA) and Associates (ARSA) and non-members may exhibit in the Annual Exhibition of Painting, Sculpture and Architecture, held approximately mid April to August; Festival Exhibition August/September. Other artists' societies' annual exhibitions, normally between October and January. Royal Scottish Academy Student Competition held in March.

The Royal Society (1660), 6 Carlton House Terrace, London SW1Y 5AG *tel* 071-839 5561 *telex* 917876 *fax* 071-930 2170. *President:* Sir Michael Atiyah; *treasurer:* Sir Robert Honeycombe, *secretaries:* Professor B.K. Follett, Sir Francis Graham-Smith; *foreign secretary:* Sir Anthony Epstein, CBE; *executive secretary:* Dr P.T. Warren. Promotion of the natural sciences (pure and applied).

Royal Society for Asian Affairs, (1901), 2 Belgrave Square, London SW1X 8PJ *tel* 071-235 5122. *President:* The Lord Denman, CBE. MC. TD; *chairman of council:* Sir Michael Wilford, GCMG; *secretary:* Miss M. FitzSimons. For the study of all Asia past and present. Fortnightly lectures, etc. Library. Publishes *Asian Affairs*, 3 p.a., free to members. *Editor:* R.A. Longmire. *Subscription:* £32.00 London members, £25 members more than 60 miles from London, £22.00 overseas members, £5.00 junior (under 21), £50 affiliated.

Royal Society of British Artists, 17 Carlton House Terrace, London SW1Y 5BD *tel* 071-930 6844 *fax* 071-839 7830. *President:* Tom Coates, ROI, RWS, RP, NEAC, PS; *keeper:* Leslie Worth, VPRWS. Incorporated by Royal Charter for the purpose of encouraging the study and practice of the arts of painting, sculpture and architectural designs. Annual Open Exhibition at the Mall Galleries, The Mall, London SW1.

Royal Society of British Sculptors (1904), 108 Old Brompton Road, London SW7 3RA *tel* 071-373 5554. *President:* Philomena Davidson Davis; *vice-president:* Philip Jackson; *hon. treasurer:* Maurice Blik; *administrator:* Dr Simon Hincks. Established 'to Promote and advance the art and practice of Sculpture'. The Society offers advice and services to sculptors; advice on commissions to corporations, developers and individuals; organises a number of national bursaries and competitions in the field of sculpture.

Royal Society for the encouragement of Arts, Manufactures and Commerce (RSA) (1754), 8 John Adam Street, London WC2N 6EZ *tel* 071-930 5115 *fax* 071-839 5805. *Chairman of council:* Professor John Tomlinson, CBE, MA; *secretary and chief executive:* Christopher Lucas. Annual lecture programme and projects on a wide range of subjects, monthly journal, library. Closely linked is the RSA Examinations Board, now a separate company, based at Coventry. The RSA's current work is indicated by its main committees: Arts, Manufactures and Commerce, Design, Education, Environment.

Royal Society of Literature (1823), 1 Hyde Park Gardens, London W2 2LT *tel* 071-723 5104. Fellows and Members. Men and women. *Chairman of council:* John Mortimer, CBE, QC, FRSL; *secretary:* Mrs P.M. Schute. For the advancement of literature by the holding of lectures, discussions, readings, and by publications. Administrators of the Dr Richards' Fund and the Royal Society of Literature Award, under the W.H. Heinemann Bequest and the Winifred Holtby Memorial Prize.

Royal Society of Marine Artists, 17 Carlton House Terrace, London SW1Y 5BD *tel* 071-930 6844 *fax* 071-839 7830. *President:* Terence Storey. To promote and encourage marine painting. Open Annual Exhibition.

Royal Society of Miniature Painters, Sculptors and Gravers (1895). *President:* Suzanne Lucas, FLS, PRMS, FPSBA; *treasurer:* Alastair MacDonald; *hon. secretary:* Pauline Gyles. Membership is by selection and standard of work over a period of years (ARMS associate, RMS full member). Annual Exhibition in November in London. Open to non-members. Hand-in Sept/Oct, schedules available in July (send sae). Applications and enquiries to the *executive secretary:* Mrs S.M. Burton, 15 Union Street, Wells, Somerset BA5 2PU *tel* (0749) 674472.

Royal Society of Painter-Printmakers (1880), Bankside Gallery, 48 Hopton Street, London SE1 9JH *tel* 071-928 7521. *President:* Joseph Winkelman; *secretary:* Michael Spender. Membership (RE) open to British and overseas artists. An election of Associates is held annually, and applications for the necesssary forms and particulars should be addressed to the Secretary. Open exhibition held in early spring. One members' exhibition per year. Friends of the RE open to all those interested in artists' original printmaking.

Royal Society of Portrait Painters (1891), 17 Carlton House Terrace, London SW1Y 5BD *tel* 071-930 6844 *fax* 071-839 7830. *President:* David Poole.

Annual Exhibition when work may be submitted by non-members with a view to exhibition.

Royal Television Society (1927), Tavistock House East, Tavistock Square, London WC1 9HR   *tel* 071-387 1970   *fax* 071-387 0358. *Membership services manager:* Deborah Halls. The society promotes the arts and sciences of television and runs lectures, conferences and training courses to this end. *Annual membership:* £40.00.

Royal Watercolour Society (founded 1804), Bankside Gallery, 48 Hopton Street, London SE1 9JH   *tel* 071-928 7521. *President:* Charles Bartlett; *secretary:* Michael Spender. Membership (RWS) open to British and overseas artists. An election of Associates is held annually, and applications for the necessary forms and particulars should be addressed to the Secretary. Open Exhibition held in summer. Exhibitions: spring and autumn. Friends of the RWS open to all those interested in watercolour painting.

Royal West of England Academy (1844), Queens Road, Clifton, Bristol BS8 1PX   *tel/fax* (0272) 735129. *President:* Leonard Manasseh, OBE, RA, PRWA, AA(Dipl), FRIBA, FCSD; *Academy secretary:* Jean McKinney. Aims to further the interests of practising painters and sculptors. Holds art exhibitions and is a meeting place for artists and their work.

The Ruskin Society of London (1985). *Hon. secretary:* Miss O. E. Madden, 351 Woodstock Road, Oxford OX2 7NX   *tel* (0865) 310987. To promote literary and biographical interest in John Ruskin and his contemporaries. *Annual subscription:* £7.50.

The Dorothy L. Sayers Society (1976). *Chairman:* Dr Barbara Reynolds; *secretary:* Christopher J. Dean, Rose Cottage, Malthouse Lane, Hurstpierpoint, W. Sussex BN6 9JY   *tel* (0273) 833444. To promote and encourage the study of the works of Dorothy L. Sayers; to collect relics and reminiscences about her and make them available to students and biographers, to hold an annual seminar, to publish proceedings and pamphlets and a bi-monthly bulletin. *Annual subscription:* £6.00.

Scientific and Technical Authors' Group, 84 Drayton Gardens, London SW10 9SB   *tel* 071-373 6642. Specialist unit within the framework of the Society of Authors, concerned with the interests of non-fiction authors in all areas of specialisation.

Scientific and Technical Communicators, The Institute of (1972), PO Box 479, Luton, Beds. LU1 4QR   *tel* (0582) 400316. *President:* Ray Green, FISTC; *executive secretary:* A. Gavin, FISTC. Professional body for those engaged in the communication of scientific and technical information. *Objects:* to establish and maintain professional standards, to encourage and co-operate in professional training and to provide a source of information on, and to encourage research and development in, all aspects of scientific and technical communication. *The Communicator* is the official journal of the Institute, and is published 4 times per year.

Scottish Arts, 24 Rutland Square, Edinburgh EH1 2BW   *tel* 031-229 1076. *Hon. secretary:* W.B. Logan   *tel* 031-229 8157. *Subs.:* Full £220.00, but various reductions. Art, literature, music.

Scottish Arts Council, 12 Manor Place, Edinburgh EH3 7DD   *tel* 031-226 6051. *Chairman:* Sir Alan Peacock; *Director:* Seona Reid. Principal channel for government funding of the arts in Scotland, the Scottish Arts Council forms part of the Arts Council of Great Britain. It aims to develop and improve the knowledge, understanding and practice of the arts, and to increase their accessibility throughout Scotland. It offers about 850 grants a year to professional artists and arts organisations concerned with the visual arts, drama, dance and mime, literature, music, festivals, traditional and ethnic arts and community arts.

Scottish History Society (1886), Department of Scottish History, St Salvator's College, University of St Andrews, Fife KY16 9AJ. *Hon. secretary:* Norman Macdougall, PhD. The Society exists to publish documents illustrating the history of Scotland.

Scottish Newspaper Publishers' Association, 48 Palmerston Place, Edinburgh EH12 5DE *tel* 031-220 4353 *fax* 031-220 4344. *President:* Iain W. Bell; *director:* J.B. Raeburn, FCIS. To promote and represent newspaper interests.

Scottish Publishers Association (1974), 1st Floor, Fountainbridge Library, 137 Dundee Street, Edinburgh EH11 1BG *tel* 031-225 5795 *fax* 031-220 0377. *Director:* Lorraine Fannin. *Publicist:* Anna Fenge. To assist Scottish trade publishers primarily in the publicity, promotion and marketing of their books.

Screenwriters Workshop, London (1983), House of St Barnabas, 1 Greek Street, London W1V 6NQ *tel* 081-551 5570. Formed by a group of film and television writers to serve as a forum for contact, discussion and practical criticism. Membership open to anyone interested in writing for film and television, and to anyone working in these and related media. *Annual subscription:* £15. Send large sae for further details.

SCRIBO (1971), K. Sylvester, Flat 1, 31 Hamilton Road, Boscombe, Bournemouth BH1 4EQ. SCRIBO is a friendly and informal postal forum for novelists. Its aim is to bring together and encourage novelists, to provide information, criticism, advice and friendly discussion of anything of interest to novelists: research, agents and indvidual problems.

Shakespearean Authorship Trust. *Hon. secretary:* Dr D.W. Thomson Vessey, 26 Ouse Walk, Huntingdon, Cambs. PE18 6QL; *hon. treasurer:* John Silberrad, Dryads' Hall, Woodbury Hill, Loughton, Essex IG10 1JB. *Aims:* The advancement of learning with particular reference to the social, political and literary history of England in the sixteenth century and the authorship of the plays and poems commonly attributed to William Shakespeare. *Annual Subscription:* £10.00. Subscribers receive copies of the Trust's publications, and are entitled to use its library.

The Shaw Society, 6 Stanstead Grove, Catford, London SE6 4UD *tel* 081-690 2325. *Secretary:* Barbara Smoker. Improvement and diffusion of knowledge of the life and works of Bernard Shaw and his circle. Meetings in London, annual festival at Ayot St Lawrence; publication: *The Shavian.*

Singapore Book Publishers Association, PO Box 846, Raffles City Post Office, Singapore 9117. *President:* Charles Cher; *hon. secretary:* N.T.S. Chopra.

SLADE—Society of Lithographic Artists, Designers, Engravers & Process Workers—see NGA.

Society of Authors—see **Authors, The Society of.**

Songwriters, Composers and Authors, British Academy of, (1947), 34 Hanway Street, London W1P 9DE *tel* 071-436 2261. *General secretary:* Eileen Stow. To give advice and guidance to its songwriter members and look after their interests within the industry.

South African Publishers Association, PO Box 5197, Cape Town 8000, South Africa *tel* (021) 418-2050 *fax* (021) 25-1256.

SPREd – Society of Picture Researchers and Editors, BM Box 259, London WC1N 3XX *tel* 071-404 5011. Professional organisation of picture researchers and picture editors. Operates a freelance register service – details from Miranda Smith *tel* 081-539 6758. See article on page 321.

Strip Illustration, Society of, 7 Dilke Street, Chelsea, London SW3 4JE. Founded in 1977 by a group of professionals, the Society is open to artists, writers, editors, and anyone professionally concerned with comics, newspaper strips and strip illustration. Monthly Newsletter, monthly meetings, and other events.

Sussex Playwrights' Club. Founded in 1935. Members' plays are read by local actors before an audience of Club members. The Club from time to time sponsors productions of members' plays by local drama companies. Non-writing members welcome. Details: Hon. Secretary, Sussex Playwrights' Club, 2 Princes Avenue, Hove, East Sussex BN3 4GD.

Syndicat de Conseils Littéraires Français, c/o Agence Hoffman, 77 bd Saint-Michel, 75005 Paris, France *tel* (1) 43-26-56-94 *telex* 203605 Aghoff *fax* (1) 43-26-34-07.

Theatre Research, The Society for. *Hon. secretaries:* Mrs Eileen Cottis and Miss Frances Dann, c/o The Theatre Museum, 1E Tavistock Street, London WC2E 7PA. Publishes annual volumes and journal, *Theatre Notebook,* holds lectures, runs enquiry service and makes research grants annually.

Theatre Writers' Union. Contact: Actors Centre, 4 Chenies Street, London WC1E 7EP *tel* 071-631 3619. Formed in the mid 1970s. Specialises in the concerns of all who write for live performance. Responsible for the very first standard agreements on minimum pay and conditions for playwrights in British theatre. Actively seeks a membership which reflects the rich cultural diversity of playwriting today. Has national branch network. Membership open to every playwright who has written a play, whether performed or not performed. Members receive legal and professional advice, copies of standard contracts and regular newsletters. *Annual subscription* is related to income from playwriting.

The Edward Thomas Fellowship (1980), 3 South Court, Halswell House, Goathurst, Nr Bridgwater, Somerset TA5 2DH *tel* (0278) 662856. *Hon. secretary:* Richard N. Emeny. To perpetuate the memory of Edward Thomas, foster an interest in his life and work, to assist in the preservation of places associated with him and to arrange events which extend fellowship amongst his admirers. *Annual subscription:* £5.00.

The Francis Thompson Society, now incorporated in **The Eighteen Nineties Society,** *qv.*

The Tolkien Society (1969), *Secretary:* Debi Haigh-Hutchinson, Flat 2, 42 Frankland Place, Leeds, W. Yorks LS7 4DG; *membership secretary:* C.D. Oakey, Flat 5, 357 High Street, Cheltenham, Glos. GL50 3HT *tel* (0242) 577232. Dedicated to promoting research into and educating the public in the life and works of Professor J.R.R. Tolkien. *Subscription:* UK £15.00; surface (outside Europe) £15.50, Europe letter rate (including Eire) £16.50; airmail zone B (US) £17.00, zone C (Australia) £18.00.

Translation & Interpreting, The Institute of, 318a Finchley Road, London NW3 5HT *tel* 071-794 9931 *fax* 071-435 2105. All correspondence to be addressed to the *Secretary.* Professional association for translators and interpreters which restricts its qualified entry to those who have either passed translation or interpreting examinations in technical, scientific, commercial or social science fields, or can provide evidence of a similar degree of competence and experience gained by other specified means. Subscriber membership (non-qualified) and student membership are also possible. Details of members capable of handling particular language and subject combinations are available from the Institute office.

The Translators Association (1958), 84 Drayton Gardens, London SW10 9SB *tel* 071-373 6642. *Secretary:* Kate Pool. Specialist unit within the membership of the Society of Authors, exclusively concerned with the interests and special problems of writers who translate foreign literary or dramatic work into English for publication or performance in Great Britain or English-speaking countries overseas. Members are entitled to general and legal advice on all questions connected with the marketing of their work, such as rates of remuneration, contractual arrangements with publishers, editors, broadcasting organisations, etc. The annual subscription is £45 by direct debit, £50 by cheque and includes membership of the Society of Authors. Full particulars may be obtained from the offices of the Association.

Travel Writers, The British Guild of. *Hon. secretary:* Penny Visman, Bolts Cross Cottage, Peppard, Henley-on-Thames, Oxon RG9 5LG *tel* (04917) 411 *fax* (04917) 669. Arranges meetings, discussions and visits for its members (who are all professional travel writers) to help them encourage the public's interest in travel.

The Trollope Society (1987), 9A North Street, London SW4 0HN *tel* 071-720 6789. *Chairman:* John Letts. Aims to produce the first ever complete edition of the novels of Anthony Trollope. *Membership fee:* ordinary (one year) £12.00, life £120.

The Turner Society (1975), BCM Box Turner, London WC1N 3XX. *Chairman:* Eric Shanes. To foster a wider appreciation of all facets of Turner's work; to encourage exhibitions of his paintings, drawings and engravings. Publishes: *Turner Society News. Subscriptions:* £5; overseas: £5 (surface mail), £10 (airmail); corporate: £10.

Typographic Designers, Society of. *President:* Colin Banks, FSTD, FCSD; *chair:* John Harrison, FSTD, FCSD; *hon. secretary:* Mike Seaton, MSTD, 21-27 Seagrave Road, London SW6 1RP. Founded in 1928, the Society has been recognised as the authoritative organisation for the typographic profession in the UK. It advises and acts on matters of professional practice, provides a better understanding of the craft and the rapidly changing technology in the graphic industries by lectures, discussions and through the journal *Typographic* and the Newsletter. Typographic students are encouraged to first gain Licentiateship of the Society as the accepted yard stick by employers by an annual assessment of submitted work to a sponsored professional brief. The STD is a full member of The International Council of Graphic Design Associations, ICOGRADA, which brings professionals together for a General Assembly, Congress and exhibition of work, every three years.

United Society for Christian Literature (1799), Robertson House, Leas Road, Guildford, Surrey GU1 4QW *tel* (0483) 577877 *fax* (0483) 301387. *President:* Lord Luke; *chairman:* Alan Brown; *general secretary:* Revd Alec Gilmore, MA, BD. To aid Christian literature principally in the Third World and Eastern Europe.

United Society of Artists, 4 Frogmore Cottage, High Street, Watford, Herts. WD1 2HX. *President:* Robert Hill, ROI, NEAC. Membership by election on application. Annual exhibition open to all non-members.

University, College and Professional Publishers Council—see **Publishers Association.**

Voice of the Listener (1983), 101 King's Drive, Gravesend, Kent DA12 5BQ *tel* (0474) 564676. *Chairman:* Jocelyn Hay; *administrative secretary:* Ann Leek. Independent association working to ensure the maintenance of high standards in broadcasting in the UK. Membership open to all concerned about the future of public service broadcasting.

Edgar Wallace Society (1969), 7 Devonshire Close, Amersham, Bucks. HP6 5JG *tel* (0494) 72 5398. *Organiser:* John A. Hogan. To promote an interest in the life and work of Edgar Wallace through the *Crimson Circle* magazine (Q.). *Subscription:* £8.00 p.a.

The Walmsley Society (1985), Sherbrook, Newlands Drive, Leominster, Hereford and Worcester HR6 8PR *tel* (0568) 611733. *Secretary:* Jack L.W. Hazell; *treasurer and membership secretary:* Miss Jane Ellis, 152 Osmondthorpe Lane, Leeds, West Yorkshire LS9 9EG. Aims to promote and encourage an appreciation of the literary and artistic heritage left to us by Leo and J. Ulric Walmsley. Affiliated to the Alliance of Literary Societies.

Watercolour Society, British (1830), *Director:* Leslie Simpson, Ralston House, 41 Lister Street, Riverside Gardens, Ilkley, West Yorkshire LS29 9ET *tel* (0943) 609075.

Mary Webb Society (1972). *Secretaries:* Mrs H.M. Dormer, 6 Ragleth Road, Church Stretton, Shropshire SY6 7BN *tel* (0694) 722755 and Mrs A. Parry, 4 Lythwood Road, Bayston Hill, Shrewsbury SY3 0LU *tel* Bayston Hill (074 372) 2766. To further an interest in the life and works of Mary Webb by meetings, lectures and excursions. Affiliated to the Alliance of Literary Societies.

The H.G. Wells Society (1960), Hon. General Secretary, English Department, Nene College, Moulton Park, Northampton NN2 7AL *tel* (0604) 715000 *fax* (0604) 720636. *Secretary:* Sylvia Hardy. Promotion of an active interest in and encouragement of an appreciation of the life, work and thought of H.G. Wells. Publishes *The Wellsian* (annually) and *The Newsletter* (bi-annually). *Subscription:* £6.50 p.a., corporate £10.00 p.a.

Welsh Arts Council, Museum Place, Cardiff CF1 3NX *tel* (0222) 394711 *fax* (0222) 221447. *Chairman:* Mathew Prichard; *director:* T.A. Owen. An autonomous committee of the Arts Council of Great Britain, the Welsh Arts Council shares that body's aims and has responsibility for implementation of the council's policies in Wales. Its seven departments are Music, Art, Literature, Drama, Craft, Film and Dance. It also runs the Oriel Bookshop and Gallery in Cardiff.

Welsh Books Council/Cyngor Llyfrau Cymraeg, Castell Brychan, Aberystwyth, Dyfed SY23 2JB *tel* (0970) 624151 *fax* (0970) 625385. *Director:* Gwerfyl Pierce Jones. Founded in 1961 to encourage and increase the interest of the public in Welsh literature and to support authors of popular books in the Welsh language. With the establishment of Editorial, Design, Marketing Children's Books and Wholesale Distribution Departments, the Council promotes all aspects of book production in Wales and provides a service for Welsh-language books and English-language books of Welsh interest. Also distributes the government grant for Welsh-language publications.

The West Country Writers' Association. *President:* Christopher Fry, FRSL; *chair:* Dorothy Stiffe; *hon. secretary:* Anne Double, Malvern View, Garway Hill, Orcop, Hereford HR2 8EZ *tel* (09818) 495. Founded in 1951 by Waveney Girvan for the purpose of fostering the love of literature in the West Country and to give authors an opportunity of meeting to exchange news and views. An Annual Weekend Congress is held in a West Country town and there are Regional Meetings. Newsletter (2 p.a.). Membership is open to published authors. *Annual Subscription:* £5.

Wildlife Artists, Society of, 17 Carlton House Terrace, London SW1Y 5BD *tel* 071-930 6844 *fax* 071-839 7830. *President:* Robert Gillmor. To promote and encourage the art of wildlife painting and sculpture. Open Annual Exhibition.

Charles Williams Society (1975), 26 Village Road, Finchley, London N3 1TL *Secretary:* Mrs Gillian Lunn. To promote interest in Charles Williams' life and work and to make his writings more easily available.

The Henry Williamson Society (1980), *Secretary:* John L. Homan. All correspondence to *membership secretary:* P.F. Murphy, 16 Doran Drive, Redhill, Surrey RH1 6AX *tel* (0737) 763228. Aims to encourage a wider readership and greater understanding of the literary heritage left by Henry Williamson. Two meetings annually; also weekend activities. Publishes journal twice yearly. *Annual subscriptions:* £8.00; family, student and overseas rates available.

Women Artists, Society of (1855), Westminster Gallery, Westminster Central Hall, Storey's Gate, London SW1H 9NU. *President:* Barbara Tate. Annual Exhibition of painting, sculpture, etc. Open to all women.

Women in Publishing (1977), c/o J. Whitaker, 12 Dyott Street, London WC1A 1DF. Promotes the status of women within publishing; encourages networking and mutual support among women; provides a forum for the discussion of ideas, trends and subjects to women in the trade; offers practical training for career and personal development; supports and publicises women's achievements and successes. *Subscription:* £15.00 p.a.

Women Writers and Journalists, Society of (1894). *Secretary:* Jean Hawkes, 110 Whitehall Road, Chingford, London E4 6DW *tel* 081-529 0886. For women writers and artists. Lectures, monthly lunch-time meetings. Free literary advice for members. *The Woman Journalist* (3 p.a.) *Subscription:* Town £18.00; Country £15.00; Overseas £10.00.

Women Writers Network (1985), c/o Susan Kerr (Vicechair), 55 Burlington Lane, London W4 3ET *tel* 081-994 0598; *membership secretary:* Cathy Smith, 23 Prospect Road, London NW2 2JU *tel* 071-794 5861. The network provides a forum for the exchange of information, support and career and networking opportunities for working women writers. WWN serves both salaried and independent women writers from all disciplines. *Annual membership:* £20.00.

Worshipful Company of Musicians (1500), 1 The Sanctuary, Westminster, London SW1P 3JT *tel* 071-222 5381. *Clerk:* M.J.G. Fletcher.

Worshipful Company of Stationers and Newspaper Makers (1557), Stationers' Hall, London EC4M 7DD *tel* 071-248 2934. *Master:* W.C. Young, MA, FIOP; *clerk:* Captain P. Hames, RN. One of the Livery Companies of the City of London. Connected with the printing, publishing, bookselling, newspaper and allied trades.

Writers' Circles. The *Directory of Writers' Circles*, containing addresses and telephone numbers of several hundred writers' circles, guilds, workshops and literary clubs through the UK, is published regularly by Laurence Pollinger Ltd. It is available from compiler/editor Jill Dick (£3.00 post free) at Oldacre, Horderns Park Road, Chapel-en-le-Frith, Derbyshire SK12 6SY.

Writers' Guild of America, East (1954). *Executive director:* Mona Mangan, 555 West 57 Street, Suite 1230, New York, NY 10019, USA *tel* 212-245-6180.

Represents writers in screen and television for collective bargaining. It oversees member services (pension and health) as well as educational and professional activities. *Membership:* 1¾% of covered earnings p.a.

Writers' Guild of America, West (1933). *Executive director:* Brian Walton, 8955 Beverly Boulevard, West Hollywood, CA 90048, USA *tel* 213-550-1000 *fax* 213-550-8185. Union representing writers in film and broadcast industries for purposes of collective bargaining. *Membership:* initiation $1500, quarterly $25, annually 1½% of income.

The Writers' Guild of Great Britain, 430 Edgware Road, London W2 1EH *tel* 071-723 8074-5-6. See also article on page 556.

Yachting Journalists' Association, (1973). *Secretary:* Steve Ancsell, The Glider Centre, Bishop's Waltham, Hants SO3 1DH *tel* (0489) 896311 *fax* (0489) 892416. To further the interests of yachting journalists and boating and administer the Yachtsman of the Year Award. *Subscription:* £15.00 p.a.

The Yorkshire Dialect Society (1897). *Hon. secretary:* Stanley Ellis, Farfields, Weeton, Leeds LS17 0AN. The aims of the Society are to encourage interest in: (1) dialect speech; (2) the writing of dialect verse, prose and drama; (3) the publication and circulation of dialect literature and the performance of dialect plays; (4) the study of the origins and the history of dialect and kindred subjects – all dialects, not only of Yorkshire origin. *Annual subscription (1991):* £5. *Meetings:* the Society organises a number of meetings during the year – details from the Hon. Secretary. *Annual Publications: Transactions* and *The Summer Bulletin* free to members, list of other publications on request.

Young Publishers, Society of (1949). The Secretary, 12 Dyott Street, London WC1A 1DF *tel* 071-836 8911. Provides a lively forum for discussion on subjects relevant to its members in publishing. Membership open to anyone under 35 years of age employed in publishing, printing, bookselling or allied trades. Meetings held monthly at the Publishers Association, on the last Wednesday of the month at 6.30 p.m.

Francis Brett Young Society (1979). *Secretary:* Mrs J. Pritchard, 52 Park Road, Hagley, Stourbridge, West Midlands DY9 0QF *tel* (0562) 882973. To provide opportunities for members to meet, correspond, and to share the enjoyment of the author's works. Journal published twice yearly. *Annual subscription:* £3.00, organisations/overseas £5.00, life membership £45.00.

The Society of Authors

The Society of Authors is an independent trade union, representing writers' interests in all aspects of the writing profession, including publishing, broadcasting, TV and films, theatre and translation. Founded over a hundred years ago by Walter Besant, the Society now has more than 5000 members. It has a professional staff, responsible to a Management Committee of 12 authors and a Council (an advisory body meeting twice a year) consisting of 60 eminent writers. There are specialist groups within the Society to serve the particular needs of broadcasters, literary translators, educational writers, medical writers, children's writers, and scientific and technical writers. There are also regional groups representing Scotland, the North of Engand, and the Isle of Man.

WHAT THE SOCIETY DOES FOR MEMBERS

Through its permanent staff (including a solicitor), the Society is able to give its members a comprehensive personal and professional service covering the business aspects of authorship, including:

providing information about agents, publishers, and others concerned with the book trade, journalism, broadcasting and the performing arts;

advising on negotiations, including the individual vetting of contracts, clause by clause, and assessing their terms both financial and otherwise;

taking up complaints on behalf of members on any issue concerned with the business of authorship;

pursuing legal actions in respect of breach of contract, copyright infringement, and the non-payment of royalties and fees, when the risk and cost preclude individual action by a member and issues of general concern to the profession are at stake;

holding weekend conferences, seminars, meetings and social occasions;

producing a comprehensive range of publications, free of charge to members, including the Society's quarterly journal, *The Author*, and *Quick Guides* covering many aspects of the profession such as: copyright, publishing contracts, libel, income tax, VAT, authors' agents, permissions and the protection of titles. The Society also publishes a model book contract, a model translator/publisher agreement, *Guidelines for Educational Writers, Guidelines for Medical Writers* and *Sell Your Writing*. Members concerned with radio and television receive *Broadcasting* regularly, and translators are sent *Translators News*. *STAG*, the journal of the Scientific and Technical Authors Group, is circulated to scientific, technical and educational writers.

Members have access to:

the Retirement Benefit Scheme,

Group Medical Insurance Schemes with both BUPA and the Bristol Contributory Welfare Association,

the Pension Fund (which offers discretionary pensions to a number of members),

the Contingency Fund (which provides financial relief for authors or their dependents in sudden financial difficulties),

automatic free membership of the Authors' Licensing and Collecting Society,

books and stationery at special rates,

membership of the Royal Over-Seas League at a discount,
use of the Society's photocopying machine at special rates.

The Society frequently secures improved conditions and better returns for
members. It is common for members to report that, through the help and
facilities offered, they have saved more, and sometimes substantially more, than
their annual subscriptions (which are an allowable expense against income tax).

WHAT THE SOCIETY DOES FOR AUTHORS IN GENERAL

The Society lobbies Members of Parliament, Ministers and Government Departments on all issues of concern to writers. Recent issues have included the
establishment and funding of Public Lending Right, the threat of VAT on books
and changes to copyright legislation. Concessions have also been obtained under
various Finance Acts.

The Society litigates in matters of importance to authors. For example, the
Society backed Andrew Boyle when he won his appeal against the Inland
Revenue's attempt to tax the Whitbread Award. It backed a number of members
in proceedings against the BBC and Desmond Wilcox in connection with the
publication of a book, *The Explorers*, and also in a High Court action over
copyright infringment by *Coles Notes*.

The Society campaigns for better terms for writers. With the Writers' Guild,
it has negotiated agreements with BBC Books, Faber and Faber, Century
Hutchinson, Bloomsbury, Headline, Hodder & Stoughton, Methuen London,
Chapmans, Sinclair-Stevenson and Penguin. Other publishers are now being
approached, and the campaign is active. The translators' section of the Society
has also drawn up a minimum terms agreement for translators which has been
adopted by Faber and Faber, and has been used on an individual basis by a
number of other publishers.

The Society is recognised by the BBC for the purpose of negotiating rates for
writers' contributions to radio drama, talks and features, as well as for the
broadcasting of published material. It was instrumental in setting up the Authors'
Licensing and Collecting Society (ALCS), which collects and distributes fees
from reprography and other methods whereby copyright material is exploited
without direct payment to the originators.

The Society keeps in close touch with the Arts Council of Great Britain,
the Association of Authors' Agents, the British Council, the Broadcasting,
Entertainment and Cinematograph Technicians' Union, the Institute of Translation and Interpreting, the Minister for the Arts, the National Union of
Journalists, the Publishers Association and the Writers' Guild of Great Britain.

The Society is a member of the European Writers Congress, the British
Copyright Council, the National Book Committee, the Radio and Television
Safeguards Committee and the International Confederation of Societies of
Authors and Composers (CISAC).

AWARDS ADMINISTERED BY THE SOCIETY

Two travel awards – The Somerset Maugham Awards and the Travelling
Scholarships.

Three prizes for novels – The Betty Trask Awards, the McKitterick Prize and
the Sagittarius Prize.

Two poetry awards – The Eric Gregory Awards and the Cholmondeley
Award.

The Tom-Gallon Award for short story writers.

The Crompton Bequest for aiding financially the publication of selected original work.

The Authors' Foundation and Kathleen Blundell Trust, which are endowed with wide powers to support literary and artistic effort and research.

The Margaret Rhondda Award for women journalists.

The Scott Moncrieff Prize for translations from French.

The Schlegel-Tieck Prize for translations from German books published in Germany.

The John Florio Prize for translations from Italian.

The Francis Head Bequest for assisting authors who, through physical mishap, are temporarily unable to maintain themselves or their families.

HOW TO JOIN

There are two categories of membership (admission to each being at the discretion of the Committee of Management):

Full Membership – those authors who have had a full-length work published, broadcast or performed commercially in the UK or have an established reputation in another medium.

Associate Membership – those authors who have had a full-length work accepted for publication, but not yet published; and those authors who have had occasional items broadcast or performed, or translations, articles, illustrations or short stories published.

Associate members pay the same annual subscription and are entitled to the same benefits as full members. The owner or administrator of a deceased author's copyrights can become a member on behalf of the author's estate.

The Annual Subscription (which is tax deductible under Schedule D) for full or associate membership of the Society is £65 (£60 by direct debit after the first year), and there are special joint membership terms for husband and wife. Authors under 35, who are not yet earning a significant income from their writing, may apply for membership at a lower subscription of £47.

Further information from The Society of Authors, 84 Drayton Gardens, London SW10 9SB   *tel* 071-373 6642.

IN CONCLUSION

'When we begin working, we are so poor and so busy that we have neither the time nor the means to defend ourselves against the commercial organisations which exploit us. When we become famous, we become famous suddenly, passing at one bound from the state in which we are, as I have said, too poor to fight our own battles, to a state in which our time is so valuable that it is not worth our while wasting any of it on lawsuits and bad debts. We all, eminent and obscure alike, need the Authors' Society. We all owe it a share of our time, our means, our influence': *Bernard Shaw*

The Writers' Guild of Great Britain

The Writers' Guild of Great Britain is the writers' trade union, affiliated to the TUC, and representing writers' interests in film, radio, television, theatre and publishing. Formed in 1959 as the Screenwriters' Guild, the union gradually extended into all areas of freelance writing activity and copyright protection. In 1974 when book authors and stage dramatists became eligible for membership substantial numbers joined, and their interests are now strongly represented on the Executive Council. Apart from necessary dealings with Government and policies on legislative matters affecting writers, the Guild is, by constitution, non-political, has no involvement with any political party, and pays no political levy. The Guild employs a permanent secretariat and staff and is administered by an Executive Council of 29 members. There are also Regional Committees representing Scotland, Wales, the North and West of England.

The Guild comprises practising professional writers in all media, united in common concern for one another and regulating the conditions under which they work.

WHAT IT DOES

The Guild gives help and advice to individual members on any aspect of their business life, including contracts, agents, publishers, television companies and fees. Also in:

Television

The Guild has national agreements with the BBC and the commercial companies regulating minimum fees and going rates, copyright licence, credit terms and conditions for television plays, series and serials, dramatisations and adaptations. One of the most important achievements in recent years has been the establishment of pension rights for Guild members only. Both the BBC and the Independent Television Association pay an additional 7.5% of the going rate on the understanding that the Guild member pays 5% of his or her fee. The Guild Pension Fund amounts to well over £1 million at present.

In 1985, a comprehensive agreement was negotiated with the BBC to cover cable sales. In addition, a special agreement was negotiated to cover the very successful twice-weekly serial *EastEnders*.

In 1991, the first every Light Entertainment Agreement was signed with the BBC.

Most children's and educational drama has been similarly protected within the above industrial agreements.

Film

On 11 March 1985, an important agreement was signed with the two producer organisations: The Producers Association and the Independent Programme Producers Association. For the first time, there exists an industrial agreement which covers both independent television productions and independent film productions. Pension fund contributions have been negotiated for Guild members in the same way as for the BBC and the ITV. The Agreement was comprehensively re-negotiated and a new Agreement signed in 1991. The areas of participation have been improved and the money paid upfront is considerably more than it was in the past.

Radio

The Guild has fought for and obtained a standard agreement with the BBC, establishing a fee structure which is annually reviewed. The current agreement includes a Code of Practice which is important for establishing good working conditions for the writer working for the BBC. In December 1985 the BBC agreed to extend the pension scheme already established for television writers to include radio writers. It was also agreed that all radio writers would be entitled to at least one attendance payment as of right. Again this brings the radio agreements more into line with the television agreements. In 1991 a comprehensive revision of the Agreement has been undertaken.

In 1990/91 small independent radio companies have arisen producing drama for the networks. Agreements have been concluded with the Guild and the Society of Authors to cover these new ventures. Both unions will be watching the development in the independent radio field with interest. In the past there has been little opportunity for dramatic writing in the independent sector.

Books

The Guild fought long, hard and successfully for the loans-based Public Lending Right to re-imburse authors for books lent in libraries. This is now law and the Guild is constantly in touch with the Registrar of the scheme which is administered from offices in Stockton-on-Tees.

The Guild together with its sister union, the Society of Authors, has drawn up a draft Minimum Terms Book Agreement which has been widely circulated amongst publishers. In 1984, the unions achieved a significant breakthrough by signing agreements with two major publishers; negotiations were also opened with other publishers. The publishing agreements will, it is hoped, improve the relationship between writer and publisher and help to clarify what the writer might reasonably expect from the exploitation of copyright in works written by him or her.

Agreements have now been signed with Hamish Hamilton, W.H. Allen, The Journeyman Press, BBC Books, Faber and Faber, Century Hutchinson, Headline Book Publishing, Bloomsbury Publishing, Hodder & Stoughton, Methuen London, Sinclair-Stevenson and Penguin Books. Negotiations are currently taking place with other leading publishers.

Theatre

In 1979, the Guild with its fellow union, the Theatre Writers' Union, negotiated the first ever industrial agreement for theatre writers. The Theatre National Committee Agreement covers the Royal Shakespeare Company, the National Theatre Company and the English Stage Company. A major revision of the Agreement has been undertaken, and it is hoped that negotiations will be concluded, with new rates and improved conditions.

On 2 June 1986, a new Agreement was signed with the Theatrical Management Association. That agreement covers some 95 provincial theatres. In 1991 a comprehensive revision of the Agreement has been undertaken.

In 1991, after many years of negotiation, an Agreement was concluded between the Guild and Theatre Writers' Union, and the Independent Theatre Council, which represents some 200 of the smaller and fringe theatres as well as educational, touring companies. The Agreement breaks new ground.

Only the West End is not covered by a union agreement.

Miscellaneous

The Guild is in constant touch with Government and national institutions wherever and whenever the interests of writers are in question or are being discussed. In 1988, the Guild hosted a lunch at the House of Lords, under the auspices of its Honorary Life President, Lord Willis of Chislehurst, with a view to achieving a lobby which will represent writers' interests. A similar cross-party lobby involving also the Guild's fellow arts unions, Equity and the Musicians Union, was held in the House of Commons in January 1989. The Guild and its fellow unions believe that it is important to keep in constant touch with all parties to ensure that the various arts forms they represent are properly cared for.

Amongst matters dealt with recently are the Gerald Howarth Private Member's Bill which proposed changes in the law on obscenity. Effectively, the Bill as it stood would have been a straitjacket on the writing professions, including as it did draconian measures for censuring the work of writers. The Guild had worked with other organisations to deal with a similar Bill which had been introduced by Winston Churchill in 1985. As one Bill disappears, so another takes its place. The Guild was very much involved in trying to have the dreadful Clause 28 of the Local Government Bill deleted. Unfortunately, the campaign to rid the Bill of the clause was unsuccessful, but the Guild, along with other institutions, continues to fight for freedom of expression.

Proposals for changes in the law on copyright were published in a draft Bill in August 1987. The Guild along with other organisations made important submissions on behalf of the Guild and writers in general. The new Bill was published in 1989. Moral rights have been granted to writers for the first time.

Working with federations of other unions, that is the Federation of Film Unions, the Federation of Theatre Unions and the Federation of Broadcasting Unions, the Guild makes its views known to Government bodies on a broader basis. It is constantly in touch with the Arts Council of Great Britain, the Library Campaign and other national bodies.

Perhaps one of the closest working relationships the Guild has established is with its fellow arts unions, Equity and the Musicians Union. The three unions have agreed to work much more closely together where they share a common interest. Representatives of the three governing bodies meet on a quarterly basis. Other meetings are held if thought necessary.

Regular craft meetings are held by all the Guild's specialist committees. Each section (television and film, radio, theatre, books and women's) holds some four craft meetings per annum. This gives Guild members the opportunity of meeting those who control, work within, or affect the sphere of writing within which they work. Through its craft meetings the Guild has established a new relationship with the British Academy of Film and Television Arts.

Internationally, the Guild plays a leading role in the International Affiliation of Writers' Guilds, which includes the American Guilds East and West, the Canadian Guilds (French and English) and the Australian and New Zealand Guilds. When it is possible to make common cause, then the Guilds act accordingly. The Writers' Guild of Great Britain was responsible for establishing an association between the Affiliation and the Banff Television Festival in 1986. The writers' contribution was such a great success that the Banff Television Festival have asked the British Guild to continue its association with the event.

The Guild takes a leading role in the European Writers' Congress. In 1987, the conference was held in Segovia in Spain. There a paper, jointly prepared by the Writers' Guild of Great Britain and the Swedish Writers Union, on the question of Public Lending Right, was adopted as the official policy of European countries from Iceland to Greece. The Writers' Guild also took a leading role in the discussion of minimum terms publishing agreements. In 1989, the conference was held in Fribourg in Switzerland. In 1991, a conference was held in Germany. The Writers' Guild was very much involved in helping to organise the agenda, and the general structure of recent conferences. The General Secretary of the Writers' Guild of Great Britain is Treasurer to the EWC.

The Guild in its day to day work takes up problems on behalf of individual members, gives advice on contracts, and helps with any problems which affect the lives of its members as professional writers. A 'From the Office' newsletter gives general advice and information of opportunities for Guild members on a regular basis.

A Newsletter, published bi-monthly and edited by Patrick Campbell, keeps members in touch with current matters of debate. The magazine carries articles, letters and reports written by members and the General Secretary.

MEMBERSHIP

Membership is by a points system. One major piece of work (a full-length book, an hour-long television or radio play, a feature film, etc.) entitles the author to Full Membership; lesser work helps to accumulate enough points for Full Membership, while Temporary Membership may be enjoyed in the meantime. Importantly, previously unpublished, broadcast or performed writers can apply for membership when he or she receives his or her first contract. The Guild's advice before signature can often be vital. Affiliate Membership is enjoyed by agents and publishers.

The minimum subscription is £50 plus 1% of that part of an author's income earned from professional writing sources in the previous calendar year.

Temporary members can join the Guild during their first year for a minimum subscription of £30. In succeeding years, at current rates, it is £50.

IN CONCLUSION

The writer is an isolated individual in a world in which individual voices are not always heard. The Guild brings together those individual writers in order to make common cause in respect of those many vitally important matters which are susceptible to influence only from the position of collective strength which the Guild enjoys. The writer properly cherishes his or her individuality; it will not be lost within a union run by other writers.

The Writers' Guild of Great Britain, 430 Edgware Road, London W2 1EH *tel* 071-723 8074. *General secretary:* Walter J. Jeffrey.

Literary Prizes and Awards

The following list provides details of many British awards, prizes and competitions, as well as details of major international prizes. In the UK, details of awards for novels, short stories and works of non-fiction, as they are offered, will be found in such journals as *The Author*. Book Trust (*q.v.*) publish a useful *Guide to Literary Prizes, Grants and Awards* (£3.75 inc. postage).

J.R. Ackerley Prize for Autobiography
This £2000 prize, first awarded in 1982, is given annually for an outstanding work of literary autobiography written in English and published during the previous year by an author of British nationality. Books are nominated by the judges. Information from P.E.N., 7 Dilke Street, Chelsea, London SW3 4JE   *tel* 071-352 6303   *fax* 071-351 0220.

The Age Book of the Year Award
Founded in 1974, this annual award gives two prizes of $3000 each, one to a work of imaginative writing, the other to a non-fiction work. Authors must be Australian by birth or naturalisation. Publishers only must submit books (maximum two works of imaginative writing and/or three works of non-fiction). Details from the Literary Editor, *The Age*, 250 Spencer Street, Melbourne, Victoria, Australia 3000.

Air Canada Award
Given annually to a Canadian writer, in any genre, who is younger than 30 and shows promise. Nominations by governing executive of any CAA Branch or other writers' organisation. Administered by the Canadian Authors Association. Award is two tickets to any destination served by the airline. Further details from the CAA, 121 Avenue Road, Suite 104, Toronto, Ontario M5R 2G3, Canada   *tel* 416-926-8084.

The Alexander Prize
Candidates for the Alexander Prize, who must either be under the age of 35 or be registered for a higher degree, may choose their own subject for an Essay, but they must submit their choice for approval to the Literary Director, Royal Historical Society, University College London, Gower Street, London WC1E 6BT   *tel* 071-387 7532.

The Hans Christian Andersen Medals
The Hans Christian Andersen Medals are awarded every two years to an author and an illustrator who by the outstanding value of their work are judged to have made a lasting contribution to literature for children and young people. Details from International Board on Books for Young People, British Section, Book Trust, Book House, 45 East Hill, London SW18 2QZ   *tel* 081-870 9055.

Angel Literary Award
Prizes of £1000 and £500 are awarded annually to writers living and working in East Anglia. One prize is given for a work of fiction and one for non-fiction. Further details from Caroline Gough, Angel Hotel, Angel Hill, Bury St Edmunds, Suffolk IP33 1LT   *tel* (0284) 753926   *fax* (0284) 750092.

Arts Council of Great Britain
Writers' Bursaries
The Arts Council gives annual bursaries to writers whose work is of outstanding quality. In 1991-92 there will be twelve such awards. They will be

offered only to already published authors who are writing works of poetry, fiction, autobiography or biography. The value of each bursary is £6000. The closing date for applications is 30 September each year. Details are available from July onwards from the Literature Department, Arts Council of Great Britain, 14 Great Peter Street, London SW1P 3NQ *tel* 071-333 0100.

Translation Fund
The Arts Council has created a fund to support the publication of translated work. Any text suggested for support should already have secured a publisher by whom nominations should be made. Grants may be given for specimen chapters of a work in progress. The budget for 1991-92 stands at £72,000 which includes £10,000 from the British Council and there are two deadline dates each year. Further information may be obtained from Dr Alastair Niven, Director of Literature, Arts Council of Great Britain, 14 Great Peter Street, London SW1P 3NQ *tel* 071-333 0100.

The Arts Council/An Chomhairle Ealaíon, Ireland
Bursaries for Creative Writers
In 1991 awards totalling IR£50,000 were offered to creative writers of poetry, fiction and drama to enable them to concentrate on or complete writing projects. At least the same amount will be distributed in 1992.
Denis Devlin Memorial Award for Poetry
This award, value approximately IR£1500, is made triennially for the best book of poetry in the English language by an Irish citizen published in the preceding three years. The next award will be made in 1993.
Macaulay Fellowship
Fellowships, value IR£3500, are awarded once every three years to writers under 30 years of age (or in exceptional circumstances under 35 years) in order to help them to further their liberal education and careers. The cycle of awards is: Music (1992), Literature (1993), Visual Arts (1994).
The Marten Toonder Award
This award is given to an artist of recognised and established achievement on a rotating cycle as follows: Literature (1992), Visual Arts (1993), Music (1994). Candidates must be Irish-born (Northern Ireland is included). Value IR£3500.
Prize for Poetry in Irish
This is Ireland's major award to Irish-language poetry; it is given triennially for the best book of Irish-language poetry published in the preceding three years. The next award will be made in 1993. Value IR£1500.
Travel Grants
Creative artists (including writers) may apply at any time of the year for assistance with travel grants to attend seminars, conferences, workshops, etc. Applications are assessed four times each year.
Please note that these literary awards are available only to Irish citizens, or to those who have been resident in Ireland for the previous five years. Further details may be obtained from The Arts Council (An Chomhairle Ealaíon), 70 Merrion Square, Dublin 2, Republic of Ireland *tel* (01) 611840 *fax* (01) 761302.

Arvon Foundation International Poetry Competition
This competition, founded in 1980, is awarded biennially for previously unpublished poems written in English. First prize £5000 plus other cash prizes. Full details from Arvon Foundation Poetry Competition, Kilnhurst, Kilnhurst Road, Todmorden, Lancs. OL14 6AX *tel* (0706) 816582 *fax* (0706) 816359.

Authors' Club First Novel Award
The award was instituted in 1954 by Lawrence Meynell and is made to the author of the most promising first novel published in the UK during each

year. The award takes the form of a silver mounted and inscribed quill plus £500 and is presented to the winner at a dinner held in the Club at 40 Dover Street, London W1X 3RB. Entries for the award (one from each publisher) are accepted during October and November and must be full length novels – short stories are not eligible.

Authors' Club Sir Banister Fletcher Award
The late Sir Banister Fletcher, who was President of the Authors' Club for many years, left the Authors' Club a sum of money to be held upon trust: 'to apply the income thereof in or towards the provision of an annual prize for the book on architecture or the arts most deserving.' The Committee of the Club present a prize of £500 at a dinner held in the Club. Details from the Authors' Club, 40 Dover Street, London W1X 3RB.

Authors' Club Marsh Christian Trust
Introduced for the years 1985-86, this major national biography prize of £3000 plus a trophy is presented every two years. Entries must be serious biographies written by British authors and published in the UK. Details from the Authors' Club, 40 Dover Street, London W1X 3RB.

The Authors' Foundation
The Foundation, which was founded in 1984 to mark the centenary of the Society of Authors, provides grants to authors for specific projects which have been commissioned by a British publisher. The aim is to provide funding (in addition to a proper advance) for research, travel or other necessary expenditure. Grants are available to novelists as well as writers of non-fiction. Application should be in the form of a letter sent to the Authors' Foundation at the Society of Authors, giving reasons for the application (including information about the basic terms of the publishing contract). The closing date for applications is 30 June.
The Phoenix Trust has been merged with the Foundation, which hopes to provide grants totalling at least £35,000 in 1992, helped by support from the Arts Council and Mrs Isobel Dalziel.

Verity Bargate Award
This award, founded in 1983, is given annually to a new play suitable for production in a studio theatre. The winning play will be published by Methuen and the writer will receive a prize of £1000. The play may also receive a production by the Soho Theatre Company. Details from Soho Theatre Company, 24 Goodge Street, London W1P 1FG   *tel* 071-580 6982   *fax* 071-436 3594. Please send sae for details.

H.E. Bates Short Story Competition
This annual prize is awarded for a short story – maximum length 2000 words – to anyone resident in Great Britain. The first prize is for £100, other prizes to a total value of £150. Further details from the Leisure Office, Leisure & Recreation Department, Cliftonville House, Bedford Road, Northampton NN4 0NW   *tel* (0604) 34734 ext 4243.

BBC Wildlife Magazine Award for Nature Writing
BBC Wildlife Magazine awards prizes annually with the aim of reviving the art of nature writing, discovering and encouraging new essayists and focusing attention on those writers whose skills might otherwise be neglected. Entries may be from professional or amateur writers and there are prizes of £1000, £400 for the best essay by an amateur and £200 and £100 for writers aged 17 and under. Further information may be obtained from BBC Wildlife Magazine, Broadcasting House, Whiteladies Road, Bristol BS8 2LR.

The Samuel Beckett Award

Founded in 1983, this award is open to residents of the UK and the Republic of Ireland. Two prizes of £1500 each are awarded annually, one for a stage play and one for a television play. Plays entered must be the first full-length work by the entrant professionally performed in the UK or the Republic of Ireland, and adaptations or translations are not eligible. Two non-returnable typed scripts must be submitted. The judges, who change yearly, reserve the right to call in entries at their own discretion, to vary these provisions in ways consistent with the aims of the award and to withhold the award. Further information available from Editorial Department, Faber and Faber, 3 Queen Square, London WC1N 3AU tel 071-278 6881.

The David Berry Prize

Candidates for the David Berry Prize may select any subject dealing with Scottish History within the reigns of James I to James VI inclusive, provided such subject has been previously submitted to and approved by the Council of the Royal Historical Society, University College London, Gower Street, London WC1E 6BT tel 071-387 7532.

The James Tait Black Memorial Prizes

The James Tait Black Memorial Prizes, founded in memory of a partner in the publishing house of A. & C. Black, were instituted in 1918 and since 1979 have been supplemented by the Scottish Arts Council. Two prizes, of £1500 each, are awarded annually: one for the best biography or work of that nature, the other for the best novel, published during the calendar year. The prize winners are announced normally in the February following the year of the awards. The adjudicator is the Professor of English Literature in the University of Edinburgh.

Publishers are invited to submit a copy of any biography, or work of fiction, that in their judgement may merit consideration for the award. Copies should be sent to the Department of English Literature, David Hume Tower, George Square, Edinburgh EH8 9JX, marked 'James Tait Black Prize'. They should be submitted as early as possible, deadline for submission is 30 November, with a note of the exact date of publication. Co-operation on this point is essential to the work of the adjudicator.

By the terms of the bequest, and by tradition, eligible novels and biographies are those written in English, originating with a British publisher, and first published in Britain in the year of the award; but technical publication elsewhere, simultaneously or even a little earlier, does not disqualify. Both prizes may go to the same author; but neither to the same author a second time.

The Kathleen Blundell Trust

Miss Kathleen Blundell (who died in 1985) generously left the bulk of her estate to establish a charitable trust for the benefit and encouragement of young writers. The Trust, established in 1987, provides awards to writers under the age of 40 to assist them with their next book. Applications should be in the form of a letter sent to the Kathleen Blundell Trust at the Society of Authors, giving reasons for the application (including information about the basic terms of the publishing contract). The application must be accompanied by a copy of the author's latest book and the author's work must 'contribute to the greater understanding of existing social and economic organisation'. The closing date for applications is 30 June.

The Boardman Tasker Prize

This annual prize of £1000, founded in 1983, is given for a work of fiction, non-fiction or poetry, the central theme of which is concerned with the mountain environment. Authors of any nationality are eligible but the work must be published or distributed in the UK. Further details from Mrs Dorothy Boardman, 14 Pine Lodge, Dairyground Road, Bramhall, Stockport, Cheshire SK7 2HS.

Book of the Year
Founded in 1990, an annual award (1st IR£1500 + 3 at IR£500) to a writer or illustrator of children's books, born or currently living in Ireland. Details from: Irish Children's Book Trust, Dublin Writers Museum, 18-20 Parnell Square, Dublin 1, Republic of Ireland   *tel* (01) 726282.

The Booker Prize
This annual prize for fiction of £20,000 is sponsored by Booker plc, and administered by Book Trust. The prize is awarded to the best novel in the opinion of the judges, published each year. The Prize is open to novels written in English by citizens of the British Commonwealth, Republic of Ireland and South Africa and published for the first time in the UK by a British publisher. Entries are to be submitted only by UK publishers who may each submit not more than three novels with scheduled publication dates between 1 October of the previous year and 30 September of the current year, but the judges may also ask for other eligible novels to be submitted to them. In addition, publishers may submit eligible titles by authors who are previous Booker Prize winners. Entry forms and further information are available from the Publicity Officer, Book Trust, Book House, 45 East Hill, London SW18 2QZ   *tel* 081-870 9055.

Books for a Change—Green Book of the Year Award
Founded in 1990, a £500 award is given annually to a 'green' book, either fiction or non-fiction, published in the previous 12 months, which makes a contribution to the awareness of environmental threat. Details from: Books for a Change, 52 Charing Cross Road, London WC2H 0BB   *tel* 071-836 2315   *fax* 071-497 1036.

Katharine Briggs Folklore Award
An award of £50 and an engraved goblet is given annually for a book in English, having its first, original and initial publication in the UK, which has made the most distinguished contribution to folklore studies. The term folklore studies is interpreted broadly to include all aspects of traditional and popular culture, narrative, belief, customs and folk arts. Details from the Convenor, The Folklore Society, University College London, Gower Street, London WC1E 6BT   *tel* 071-387 5894.

The British Academy Research Awards
These are made annually (in the case of Learned Societies or group research applications) and quarterly (in the case of individual applications) to scholars conducting advanced academic research in the humanities and normally resident in the UK. The main headings under which an application would be eligible are: (a) Travel and maintenance expenses in connection with an approved programme of research; (b) Archaeology fieldwork; (c) Costs of preparation of research for publication; (d) In special cases, aid to the publication of research. Details and application forms from The British Academy, 20-21 Cornwall Terrace, London NW1 4QP   *tel* 071-487 5966.

British Book Awards
These awards, founded in 1989, are presented annually. Major categories include Author of the Year, Publisher of the Year, Bookseller of the Year, Children's Author and Illustrator of the Year, Book Promotion of the Year and Travel Book of the Year. Further information from Mike Beattie, British

Book Awards, Publishing News, 43 Museum Street, London WC1A 1LY *tel* 071-404 0304 *fax* 071-242 0762.

The British Film Institute Michael Powell British Book Award
The Award highlights the importance of film and television literature and is presented for books published in the UK dealing with film and television by a UK author. Details from Wayne Drew, Press Officer, British Film Institute, 21 Stephen Street, London W1P 1PL *tel* 071-255 1444.

Canadian Authors Association Literary Awards
The awards consist of a silver medal and $5000 and apply in (a) fiction, (b) non-fiction, (c) poetry, (d) drama (for any medium). These annual awards are to honour writing that achieves literary excellence without sacrificing popular appeal and are given to works by Canadian authors (citizens or landed immigrants). Further details from the Canadian Authors Association, 121 Avenue Road, Suite 104, Toronto, Ontario M5R 2G3, Canada *tel* 416-926-8084.

Children's Book Award
Founded in 1980 by The Federation of Children's Book Groups, this award is given annually to authors of works of fiction for children published in the United Kingdom. Children participate in the judging of the award. 'Pick of the Year' booklist is published in conjunction with the award. Details from Jenny Blanch, 30 Senneleys Park Road, Northfield, Birmingham B31 1AL *tel* 021-427 4860.

Children's Book of the Year Awards
The Children's Book Council of Australia makes annual awards in three sections: (1) Book of the Year: Older Readers (for literary merit, quality of production and appeal to readers over 10 years of age); (2) Book of the Year: Younger Readers (criteria as above, plus appeal to newly independent readers, approxiamtely 7-10 years of age); (3) Picture Book of the Year (for readers of any age, with special consideration of the quality and unity of text and illustration). The Council may select up to one winner and two honour books in each category. In all three categories, winners receive a cash award of $6000 and a Book Council Medal while honour book nominees receive $2000 and a certificate. Prize money is donated by the council's major sponsor, Myer/Grace Brothers (Australia). Information from Children's Book Council of Australia (Inc.), PO Box 202, Sandy Bay, Tasmania 7005.

Cholmondeley Awards
In 1965, the Dowager Marchioness of Cholmondeley established these non-competitive awards, for which submissions are not required, for the benefit and encouragement of poets of any age, sex or nationality. In 1991 the total value of the awards was £8000. The scheme is administered by the Society of Authors.

Collins Biennial Religious Book Award
This £5000 prize was founded in 1969 to commemorate the 150th Anniversary of the founding of Wm. Collins Sons & Co. Ltd. It is given biennially to a living citizen of the UK, the Commonwealth, the Republic of Ireland, and South Africa for a book which in the judges' opinion has made the most distinguished contribution to the relevance of Christianity in the modern world. Details from Lesley Walmsley, HarperCollins Publishers, 77-85 Fulham Palace Road, London W6 8JB *tel* 081-741 7070.

Commonwealth Writers Prize
Funded by the Commonwealth Foundation, this annual award is for the best work of fiction in English by a citizen of the Commonwealth published in the

year prior to the award. A prize of £10,000 is awarded for best entry and a prize of £2000 for best first published book, selected from eight regional winners who each receive prizes of £500. The award is currently administered in Canada. Details and entry form available from Commonwealth Foundation, Marlborough House, Pall Mall, London SW1Y 5HY   *tel* 071-930 3783   *fax* 071-839 8157.

The Constable Trophy
A biennial competition supported by the three Northern-based Regional Arts Boards for fiction writers living in the North of England (Northern Arts, Arts Board: North West, Yorkshire and Humberside Arts), for a previously unpublished novel. The winning entry will receive a prize of £2000 and will be considered for publication by Constable & Co. Ltd, as may up to two runners-up. The winning novel may also receive an advance of £1000 against royalties on publication; next award to be presented in 1992. Full details from The Publicity Officer, Book Trust, Book House, 45 East Hill, London SW18 2QZ   *tel* 081-870 9055.

Thomas Cook Travel Book Awards
Awards are given annually in three categories to encourage the art of travel writing; (a) Travel Books award: value £7500; (b) Guide Books, £2500; (c) Best Illustrated Travel Book, £1000. Books written in English and published in the current year are eligible. Details may be obtained from the Thomas Cook Travel Book Awards, The Thomas Cook Group Ltd, 45 Berkeley Street, London W1A 1EB   *tel* 071-499 4000.

The Duff Cooper Memorial Prize
Friends and admirers of Duff Cooper, first Viscount Norwich (1890-1954), contributed a sum of money which has been invested in a Trust Fund. The interest is devoted to an annual prize for a literary work in the field of biography, history, politics or poetry published in English or French by a recognised publisher during the previous twenty-four months. There are two permanent judges (the present Lord Norwich, and the Warden of New College, Oxford) and three others who change every five years. All communications should be sent to the Viscount Norwich, 24 Blomfield Road, London W9 1AD.

Cosmopolitan Short Story Award
Annual short story competition, offered in conjunction with a different sponsor each year. Entries should not exceed 3000 words, and should not have been submitted elsewhere. Winner receives £5000; £1000 awarded to the best story by an unpublished writer under 35 years of age. All entries should be accompanied by a special coupon from the November or December issue of the magazine. Closing date for entries is January each year.

The Rose Mary Crawshay Prizes
One or more Rose Mary Crawshay prizes are awarded each year. The Prizes, which were originally founded by Rose Mary Crawshay in 1888, are awarded to women of any nationality who, in the judgement of the Council of the British Academy, have written or published within three calendar years next preceding the date of the award an historical or critical work of sufficient value on any subject connected with English literature, preference being given to a work regarding Byron, Shelley or Keats.

CWA Cartier Diamond Dagger Award
This award was first given in 1986 and is for outstanding contribution to the genre. Nominations not required. It is sponsored by Cartier in conjunction with the Crime Writers' Association, PO Box 172, Tring, Herts. HP23 5LP.

CWA John Creasey Memorial Award
The award was founded in 1973 following the death of John Creasey, to commemorate his foundation of the Crime Writers' Association. It is given annually, for the best crime novel by a previously unpublished author, by the Crime Writers' Association. Nominations by publishers only. PO Box 172, Tring, Herts. HP23 5LP.

CWA Gold Dagger Award and Silver Dagger Award
Founded in 1955 and awarded annually for a crime novel published in the United Kingdom. Nominations by publishers only. The panel of five judges are reviewers of crime fiction. Given by the Crime Writers' Association, PO Box 172, Tring, Herts. HP23 5LP.

CWA Gold Dagger Award for Non-Fiction
Founded in 1977 and awarded annually for a non-fiction crime book to an author published in the UK. Nominations by publishers only. Chosen by four judges of different professions. Given by the Crime Writers' Association, PO Box 172, Tring, Herts. HP23 5LP.

CWA Last Laugh Award
Founded in 1989 and awarded annually for the most amusing crime novel of the year. Nominations by publishers only. The judges are reviewers of crime fiction.

CWA '92 Award
Founded in 1990, this prize will be awarded annually for three years to 1992 for a crime novel set mainly or entirely in Continental Europe. Nominations by publishers only. The judges are reviewers of crime fiction.

CWA Rumpole Award
Sponsored by *New Law Journal* and founded in 1990, this award will be given biennially for the crime novel which best portrays legal procedure. Nominations by publishers only, for novels published between 1 October 1990 and 30 September 1992, to 9-12 Bell Yard, Temple Bar, London WC2 *tel* 071-405 6900.

CWA Silver Dagger Award—for details see under **CWA Gold Dagger Award.**

The Deo Gloria Award
An annual award for a full-length novel written from the standpoint of a positive Christian world view by an author of British nationality. Authors must be under 50 years old, unless the entry is a first novel. The £5000 award is given by the Deo Gloria Trust, and the closing date for entries is 1 June. Entry forms are available from Book Trust, Book House, 45 East Hill, London SW18 2QZ.

The Isaac Deutscher Memorial Prize
This prize of £100 was founded in 1968 and is awarded each year to the author of an essay or full-scale work, published or in manuscript, in recognition of outstanding research and writing in the Marxist tradition of Isaac Deutscher. Material should be submitted before 1 May of the current year to The Isaac Deutscher Memorial Prize, c/o Gerhard Wilke, 75 St Gabriel's Road, London NW2 4DU *tel* 081-450 0469.

The Earthworm Award
The Earthworm Award was set up by Friends of the Earth to promote and reward environmental awareness and sensitivity in literature for children of all ages. The award is given in the summer each year for children's books, both fact and fiction, published in the UK in the twelve months preceding the award. There is a first prize of £2000 and prizes of £250 each for three runners-up. The Earthworm Award has been sponsored by the Save and Prosper

Educational Trust. Applications to The Arts for the Earth, Friends of the Earth, 26-28 Underwood Street, London N1 7JQ   *tel* 071-253 3553/071-490 2380.

Encore Award
This annual award of £7500 is for the best second novel of the year. The work submitted must be (a) a novel by one author who has had one (and only one) novel published previously, and (b) in the English language, first published in the UK. Closing date: 30 November. The Society of Authors, 84 Drayton Gardens, London SW10 9SB   *tel* 071-373 6642.

The European Poetry Translation Prize
Founded in 1983 a prize of £500 is given every two years for a published volume of poetry which has been translated into English from a European language. It is part-funded by the British Council and administered by the Poetry Society, 21 Earls Court Square, London SW5 9DE.

Christopher Ewart-Biggs Memorial Prize
This Prize of £4000 is awarded once every two years to the writer, of any nationality, whose work contributes most, in the opinion of the judges, to peace and understanding in Ireland; to closer ties between the peoples of Britain and Ireland; or to co-operation between the partners of the European Community. Eligible works must be published during the two years to 31 December 1992. Entry forms are available from Secretary, Memorial Prize, Flat 3, 149 Hamilton Terrace, London NW8 9QS   *tel* 071-624 1863.

The Geoffrey Faber Memorial Prize
As a memorial to the founder and first Chairman of the firm, Faber and Faber Ltd established in 1963 the Geoffrey Faber Memorial Prize.

An annual prize of £1000, awarded in alternate years for a volume of verse and for a volume of prose fiction. It is given to that volume of verse or prose fiction first published originally in this country during the two years preceding the year in which the award is given which is, in the opinion of the judges, of the greatest literary merit.

To be eligible for the prize the volume of verse or prose fiction must be by a writer who is: (a) not more than 40 years old at the date of publication of the book; (b) a citizen of the UK and Colonies, of any other Commonwealth state, of the Republic of Ireland or of the Republic of South Africa.

There are three judges who are reviewers of poetry or of fiction as the case may be; and they are nominated each year by the editors or literary editors of newspapers and magazines which regularly publish such reviews.

Faber and Faber invite nominations from such editors and literary editors. No submissions for the prize are to be made.

The Eleanor Farjeon Award
In 1965 the Children's Book Circle instituted an annual award to be given for distinguished services to children's books and to be known as the Eleanor Farjeon Award in memory of the much-loved children's writer. A prize of (minimum) £750 may be given to a librarian, teacher, author, artist, publisher, reviewer, television producer or any other person working with or for children through books. The award is sponsored by Books for Children.

Prudence Farmer Poetry Prize
This poetry prize was founded in 1974 and is awarded annually for the best poem printed during the previous year in the *New Statesman & Society*, Foundation House, Perseverance Works, 38 Kingsland Road, London E2 8DQ   *tel* 071-739 3211   *telex* 28449   *fax* 071-739 9307.

FAW Awards (Victoria Fellowship of Australian Writers)

(FAW) Australian Natives Association Literature Award
Founded in 1978, this $1000 award is given for a book of sustained quality and distinction with an Australian theme.

FAW C.J. Dennis Award
Founded in 1976, and chosen on literary merit, this $1000 award is given annually for a book on Australian natural history.

FAW Barbara Ramsden Award
Founded by public subscription in 1971 to honour Barbara Ramsden, MBE, a publisher's editor of distinction. This major Australian award for quality published writing is given each year for literary merit to both author and then, in symbolic recognition of the importance of the publishing process, to the publisher's editor. The winners are each presented with a plaque specially designed by Andor Meszaros. There is no restriction of category and more than one work may be submitted. The award is administered by the Victorian Fellowship of Victorian Writers, of which Barbara Ramsden was a treasurer of long standing, as well as an editor for Melbourne University Press.

Details of these awards and other national awards (all of which open in October each year and close 31 December), organised by the administrator of the largest group of literary awards in Australia, from The Secretary, Victorian Fellowship of Australian Writers, 1/317 Barkers Road, Kew, Victoria 3101, Australia *tel* (03) 817 5243.

The Fawcett Book Prize
This annual award of £500, which was founded in 1982, is given to 'the book which does most to illuminate women's position in society'. The prize, which is given for fiction and non-fiction books in alternate years, is awarded in June, and the deadline for applications is 31 December. Books published in Great Britain and the Commonwealth during the previous two years are eligible. Details from the General Secretary, The Fawcett Society, 46 Harleyford Road, London SE11 5AY *tel* 071-587 1287.

The Kathleen Fidler Award
An annual award of £1000 is given to an author of any age or nationality for an unpublished novel for the 8-12 age range, which must be the author's first attempt for this age range. Details from Book Trust Scotland, 15a Lynedoch Street, Glasgow G3 6EF *tel* 041-332 0391.

The John Florio Prize
This prize was established in 1963 for the best translation into English of a twentieth-century Italian work of literary merit and general interest published by a British publisher during the preceding two years. It is awarded under the auspices of the Italian Institute and the British-Italian Society, and named after John Florio. Details from the Secretary, The Translators Association, 84 Drayton Gardens, London SW10 9SB.

E.M. Forster Award
The distinguished English author, E.M. Forster, bequeathed the American publication rights and royalties of his posthumous novel *Maurice* to Christopher Isherwood, who transferred them to the American Academy and Institute of Arts and Letters (633 West 155th Street, New York, NY 10032, USA), for the establishment of an E.M. Forster Award, currently $12,500, to be given from time to time to an English writer for a stay in the United States. Applications for this award are not accepted.

Glaxo Prize for Medical Writing and Illustration
Thanks to the generosity of Glaxo Laboratories Ltd, the Medical Writers

Group of the Society of Authors is offering two prizes of £1000 each for an illustrated book and for a textbook. The closing date for entries, which must be submitted by publishers, is 30 June. Details from the Secretary, MWG, 84 Drayton Gardens, London SW10 9SB.

Goodman Fielder Wattie Book Award

This annual award, sponsored by the Goodman Fielder Wattie Group since 1967, is run by the Book Publishers Association of New Zealand, and is given for the best book taking into account writing and illustration, design and production, and impact on the community. Authors must be New Zealanders or resident in New Zealand. It is New Zealand's major literary award; 1st prize $20,000, 2nd $10,000, 3rd $5000. Details from Goodman Fielder Wattie Award, Box 44146, Auckland 2, New Zealand.

GPA Book Award

This prize, to the value of IR£50,000, is awarded every three years for a work of fiction or poetry or a general work (autobiography, biography, history, essays, belles lettres and criticism) by an author born on the island of Ireland or, if born elsewhere, resident on the Island of Ireland since October 1989. Seven copies of eligible books to be submitted to: Award Administrator, GPA House, Shannon, Co. Clare, Republic of Ireland   *tel* (061) 360000.

E.C. Gregory Trust Fund

A number of substantial awards are made annually from this Fund for the encouragement of young poets who can show that they are likely to benefit from an opportunity to give more time to writing. A candidate for an Award must: (a) be a British subject by birth but *not* a national of Eire or any of the British dominions or colonies and be ordinarily resident in the UK or Northern Ireland; (b) be under the age of thirty at 31 March in the year of the Award (i.e. the year following submission); (c) submit for the consideration of the Judges a published or unpublished work of belles-lettres, poetry or drama poems (not more than 30 poems). Entries for the Award should be sent not later than 31 October to the Society of Authors, 84 Drayton Gardens, London SW10 9SB.

Guardian Award for Children's Fiction

The *Guardian*'s annual prize of £500 for an outstanding work of fiction for children by a British or Commonwealth writer, instituted in 1967. Further details from Stephanie Nettell, 24 Weymouth Street, London W1N 3FA   *tel* 071-580 3479.

The Guardian Fiction Prize

The *Guardian*'s annual prize of £1000 for a work of fiction showing originality and promise published by a British or Commonwealth writer. The winning book will be chosen by the Literary Editor in conjunction with the *Guardian*'s regular reviewers of new fiction.

The Hawthornden Prize

The Hawthornden Prize, for which books do not have to be specially submitted, is awarded annually to the author of what, in the opinion of the Committee, is the best work of imaginative literature published during the preceding calendar year by a British author. It was founded by the late Miss Alice Warrender in 1919 and is administered by Hawthornden Castle International Retreat for Writers, Hawthornden Castle, Lasswade, Midlothian, Scotland EH18 1EG.

The Felicia Hemans Prize for Lyrical Poetry

The Felicia Hemans Prize of books or money is awarded annually for a lyrical poem, the subject of which may be chosen by the competitor. Open to past and present members and students of the University of Liverpool only. The prize shall not be awarded more than once to the same competitor. Poems, endorsed 'Hemans Prize', must be sent in to the Registrar, The University of Liverpool, PO Box 147, Liverpool L69 3BX   (*tel* 051-794 2458   *fax* 051-708 6502), on or before 1 May. Competitors may submit either published or unpublished verse, but no competitor may submit more than one poem.

David Higham Prize for Fiction
This prize of £1000 which was founded in 1975 is awarded annually to a citizen of the British Commonwealth, Republic of Ireland, South Africa or Pakistan for a first novel or book of short stories written in English and published during the current year. Publishers only may submit books. Entry forms are available from Book Trust, Book House, 45 East Hill, London SW18 2QZ   *tel* 081-870 9055.

Historical Novel Prize
The prize, value £5000, was founded in 1977 in memory of Georgette Heyer and is awarded annually for an outstanding full-length previously unpublished historical novel. Details from: The Bodley Head, Random Century House, 20 Vauxhall Bridge Road, London SW1V 2SA.

The Calvin and Rose G. Hoffman Memorial Prize for Distinguished Publication on Christopher Marlowe
This annual prize of not less than £7500 is awarded to the best unpublished work that examines the life and works of Christopher Marlowe and the relationship between the works of Marlowe and Shakespeare. The adjudicator is Professor E.A.J. Honigmann, formerly of Newcastle upon Tyne University. The closing date for entries is 1 September, and the competition is open to all. Applications to The Headmaster, The King's School, Canterbury, Kent CT1 2ES   *tel* (0227) 475501.

Winifred Holtby Memorial Prize
The prize will be for the best regional novel of the year written in the English language. The writer must be of British or Irish nationality, or a citizen of the Commonwealth. Translations, unless made by the author himself of his own work, are not eligible for consideration. If in any year it is considered that no regional novel is of sufficient merit the prize may be awarded to an author, qualified as aforesaid, of a literary work of non-fiction or poetry, concerning a regional subject.
Publishers may submit novels published during the current year to The Royal Society of Literature, 1 Hyde Park Gardens, London W2 2LT. Entries must be submitted by 31 October.

The Independent Foreign Fiction Award
Any full-length novel or collection of short stories translated into English from another language, and published in the UK in the year preceding the award. Any book must have been published in its original language not more than 15 years preceding entry. Monthly winners shortlisted for annual prize of £10,000. Details from: *The Independent*, 40 City Road, London EC1Y 2DB   *tel* 071-956 1657.

International Poetry Competition
Prizes totalling £1000 are awarded biennially for the best four poems. Open to anyone over 16 writing in English. Details from the Greenwich Festival, 151 Powis Street, London SE18 6JL   *tel* 081-317 8687   *fax* 081-316 5009.

Irish Times–Aer Lingus Literary Prizes
Founded in 1989, these prizes are awarded by the Governors of the Prizes from nominations submitted by literary editors and critics. Irish Literature Prize – IR£10,000 for a non-fiction work (history, biography, autobiography,

criticism, politics, sociological interest, travel and current affairs) in English or Irish; IR£10,000 for a first book of creative literature (novel, collection of short stories or a volume of poetry) in English or Irish. International Fiction Prize – IR£25,000 for a work of fiction, in English or Irish, published in Ireland, the UK or the USA.

Sir Peter Kent Conservation Book Prize
Established in 1987, the European Year of the Environment, for the best book on an environmental or conservation issue published in the UK in the year ending 31 December. Two awards – £5000 for an adult book and £2000 for a children's book – are sponsored by BP Exploration. Details and entry form from Book Trust, Book House, 45 East Hill, London SW18 2QZ   *tel* 081-870 9055.

King George's Fund for Sailors Book of the Sea Award
This £1000 award goes annually to the best non-fiction book which contributes most to the knowledge and/or enjoyment of those who love the sea. A second award of £250 may be given at the discretion of the judges and a similar prize for presentation. Books must have been published in, or have first gone on sale in, the UK, during the year in question. Five copies of entries should be sent to KGFS, 1 Chesham Street, London SW1X 8NF   *tel* 071-235 2884.

The Martin Luther King Memorial Prize
A prize of £100 is awarded for a literary work reflecting the ideals to which Dr Martin Luther King dedicated his life: viz. a novel or non-fiction book, poetry collection, essay, play, TV, radio or motion picture script, first published or performed in the UK during the calendar year preceding the date of the award. Details from John Brunner, c/o NatWest Bank, 7 Fore Street, Chard, Somerset TA20 1PJ. No enquiries answered without sae.

The Library Association Besterman Medal
The Library Association Besterman Medal is awarded annually for an outstanding bibliography or guide to the literature first published in the UK during the preceding year either in print or in electronic form. Recommendations for the award are invited from members of the Library Association, who are asked to submit a preliminary list of not more than three titles. The following are among the criteria which will be taken into consideration in making the award: (1) the authority of the work and the quality and kind of the articles or entries; (2) the accessibility and arrangement of the information; (3) the scope and coverage; (4) the quality of the indexing; (5) the adequacy of the references; (6) the up-to-dateness of the information; (7) the physical presentation; (8) the originality of the work.

The Library Association Carnegie Medal
The Library Association Carnegie Medal is awarded annually for an outstanding book for children written in English and first published in the UK during the preceding year or co-published elsewhere within a three-month time lapse. Recommendations for the award are invited from members of the Library Association, who are asked to submit a preliminary list of not more than three titles, accompanied by a 50-word appraisal justifying the recommendation of each book. The following criteria may act as a general guide: *fiction:* choice to be based upon consideration of: (1) plot; (2) style; (3) characterization; *information books:* choice to be based upon consideration of: (1) accuracy; (2) method of presentation; (3) style. Format should also be taken into account. The award is sponsored by Peters Library Service and selected by the Youth Libraries Group of the Library Association.

The Library Association Kate Greenaway Medal
The Library Association Kate Greenaway Medal is awarded annually for an

outstanding illustrated book for children first published in the UK during the preceding year or co-published elsewhere within a three-month time lapse. Recommendations for the award are invited from members of the Library Association, who are asked to submit a preliminary list of not more than three titles, accompanied by a 50-word appraisal justifying the recommendation of each book. Books intended for older as well as younger children are included, and reproduction will be taken into account. The award is sponsored by Peters Library Service and selected by the Youth Libraries Group of the Library Association.

The Library Association McColvin Medal
The Library Association McColvin Medal is awarded annually for an outstanding reference work either in print or in electronic form first published in the UK during the preceding year. The following types of work are eligible for consideration: (1) encyclopedias, general and special; (2) dictionaries, general and special; (3) biographical dictionaries; (4) annuals, yearbooks and directories; (5) handbooks and compendia of data; (6) atlases. Recommendations for the award are invited from members of the Library Association, who are asked to submit a preliminary list of not more than three titles. The following are among criteria which will be taken into consideration in making an award; (1) the authority of the work and the quality and kind of the articles or entries; (2) the accessibility and arrangement of the information; (3) the scope and coverage; (4) the style; (5) the relevance and quality of the illustrations; (6) the quality of the indexing; (7) the adequacy of the bibliographies and references; (8) the up-to-dateness of the information; (9) the physical presentation; (10) the originality of the work.

The Library Association Wheatley Medal
The Library Association Wheatley Medal is awarded annually for an outstanding index published during the preceding three years. Printed indexes to any type of publication may be submitted for consideration, providing that the whole work, including the index, or the index alone has originated in the UK. Recommendations for the award are invited from members of the LA and the Society of Indexers, publishers and others. The final selection is made by a committee consisting of representatives of the LA Cataloguing and Indexing Group and the Society of Indexers, with power to co-opt.

The Sir William Lyons Award
The Lyons Award of £500 is to encourage young people in automotive journalism, including broadcasting, and to foster interest in motoring and the motor industry through these media. It is awarded to any person of British nationality resident in the UK under the age of 22 and consists of writing two essays and an interview with the Award Committee. Further details from the Gen. Secretary, 30 The Cravens, Smallfield, Crawley, Surrey RH6 9QS.

The McKitterick Prize
This annual award of £5000 was endowed by the late Tom McKitterick for first novels by authors over the age of 40. The closing date for entries is 21 December and the award is open to first published novels and unpublished typescripts. Full details from The Society of Authors, 84 Drayton Gardens, London SW10 9SB.

The Enid McLeod Literary Prize
This annual prize of £100 is given for a full-length work of literature which contributes most to Franco-British understanding. It must be written in English by a citizen of the UK, British Commonwealth, the Republic of Ireland, Pakistan, Bangladesh or South Africa, and first published in the UK. Further

details from the Secretary, Franco-British Society, Room 636, Linen Hall, 162-168 Regent Street, London W1R 5TB   *tel* 071-734 0815.

The Macmillan Prize for a Children's Picture Book
Three prizes of £750 (1st), £400 (2nd) and £150 (3rd) are awarded annually for children's book illustrations by art students in higher education establishments in the UK. Applications to Publicity Manager, Macmillan Children's Books, 18-21 Cavaye Place, London SW10 9PG   *tel* 071-373 6070   *fax* 071-370 0746.

Macmillan Silver Pen Award for Fiction
This award of £500 founded in 1969 and sponsored by Macmillan since 1986 is given annually for an outstanding collection of short stories written in English and published during the previous year by an author of British nationality. Books are nominated by members of the P.E.N. Executive Committee. Information from P.E.N., 7 Dilke Street, Chelsea, London SW3 4JE   *tel* 071-352 6303   *fax* 071-351 0220.

The McVitie's Prize for Scottish Writer of the Year
This prize of £5000 is awarded annually. Submissions can include novels, volumes of short stories, poetry, biography, autobiography, journalism, science fiction and children's books as well as theatre, cinema, radio and television scripts. The award is open to writers who were born in Scotland, who have Scottish parents, who have been resident in Scotland or who take Scotland as their inspiration. The closing date is 30 August for work first published, performed, filmed or transmitted during the previous twelve months. Ms Deborah Watson, The McVitie's Prize, Michael Kelly Associates, 95 Bothwell Street, Glasgow G2 7HY   *tel* 041-204 2580   *fax* 041-204 0245.

The Mail on Sunday-John Llewellyn Rhys Prize
The prize, increased to £5000 in 1989 when *The Mail on Sunday* became the sponsor, was inaugurated by the late Mrs Rhys in memory of her husband who was killed in action in 1940 and is offered annually to the author of the most promising literary work of any kind published for the first time during the current year. The author must be a citizen of this country or the Commonwealth, and not have passed his or her 35th birthday by the date of publication of the work submitted. Publishers only may submit books. Entry forms and further information are available from The Mail on Sunday-John Llewellyn Rhys Prize, c/o Book Trust, Book House, 45 East Hill, London SW18 2QZ   *tel* 081-870 9055.

Arthur Markham Memorial Prize
A prize for a short story, essay, poems, one-act play or first chapter of novel on a given subject is offered annually as a memorial to the late Sir Arthur Markham. Candidates must be manual workers in or about a coal mine, or have previously worked as miners. Full details can be obtained from The Academic Registrar's Office, PO Box 594, Firth Court, University of Sheffield, Sheffield S10 2UH.

Kurt Maschler/Emil Award
An annual prize of £1000 was founded in 1982 and is given to a British author/artist or an author/artist who has been resident in Britain for more than ten years. It is given for a children's book in which text and illustrations are of excellence and enhance and balance each other. Details from Book Trust, Book House, 45 East Hill, London SW18 2QZ   *tel* 081-870 9055.

The Somerset Maugham Trust Fund
The purpose of these annual awards, totalling about £15,000, is to encourage young writers to travel, to acquaint themselves with the manners and customs

of foreign countries and, by widening their own experience, to extend both
the basis and the influence of contemporary English literature. Mr Maugham
urged that in the selection of prize-winners, originality and promise should
be the touchstones: he did not wish the judges to 'play for safety' in their
choice.

A candidate for the award must be a British subject by birth and ordinarily
resident in the UK or Northern Ireland. He or she must, at the time of the
award, be under thirty-five years of age, and must submit a published literary
work in volume form in the English language, of which he or she is the sole
author. The term 'literary work' includes poetry, fiction, criticism, history and
biography, belles-lettres or philosophy, but does not include a dramatic work.
A candidate who wins an award must undertake to spend not less than three
months outside Great Britain and Ireland, and to devote the prize to the
expenses of this sojourn.

Any questions relating to the terms of the award should be addressed to The
Society of Authors, 84 Drayton Gardens, London SW10 9SB, to which
candidates (or publishers) should send the literary work they wish to submit
for an award. Four copies of one published work (which are non-returnable)
should be submitted by a candidate, and it must be accompanied by a
statement of his or her age, place of birth, and other published works.

The closing date for the submission of books to be considered is 31 December.

The Vicky Metcalf Awards for Short-Fiction and a Body of Work
These awards are given annually to Canadian writers to stimulate writing for
children. $10,000 for a Body of Work; $3000 for a Short story; $1000 to the
responsible editor if published in a Canadian journal or anthology. Details
from Canadian Authors Association, 121 Avenue Road, Suite 104, Toronto,
Ontario M5R 2G3, Canada   *tel* 416-926-8084.

MIND Book of the Year—the Allen Lane Award
This £1000 award, inaugurated in memory of Sir Allen Lane in 1981, is given
to the author of any book – fiction or non-fiction – published in the current
year which outstandingly furthers public understanding of the prevention,
causes, treatment or experience of mental health problems. Entries by 31
December. The award is administered by MIND, the National Association
for Mental Health. Further details from Anny Brackx, MIND, 22 Harley
Street, London W1N 2ED   *tel* 071-637 0741.

The Mother Goose Award
The award, sponsored by Books for Children, is open to all artists having
published a first major book for children during the previous year. Only books
first published in Britain will be considered and this includes co-productions
where the illustration originated in Britain. The award is presented annually
at Easter and is in the form of a bronze egg together with a cheque for £1000.
Recommendations for the award are invited from publishers and should be
sent to each panel member. Full details and names and addresses of the panel
members from Sally Grindley, Books for Children, Whiteway Court, The
Whiteway, Cirencester, Glos. GL7 7BA.

Shiva Naipaul Memorial Prize
This annual prize of £1000 was founded in 1985, and is given to an English
language writer of any nationality under the age of 35 for an essay of not
more than 4000 words describing a visit to a foreign place or people. Details
from *The Spectator*, 56 Doughty Street, London WC1N 2LL.

National Book Awards
Books written by US citizens and published by US publishers are eligible for
this annual prize of $10,000 in each of three categories: fiction, non-fiction

and poetry. Runners-up in each category will receive $1000. Books are entered by publishers by 15 July each year. Details from the National Book Foundation, Inc., 260 Fifth Avenue, Room 904, New York, NY 10001, USA.

National Book Council Awards for Australian Literature
Banjo Awards
Named after Australia's best-loved folk poet, A.B. (Banjo) Paterson, these awards are given for books of the highest literary merit and which make an outstanding contribution to Australian literature. There are two equal awards ($15,000) – one for fiction, the other for non-fiction.

Turnbull Fox Phillips Poetry Prize
Founded in 1990, this $5000 prize is given for a published work of poetry by a single author.

Lysbeth Cohen Memorial Award
Annual prize of $2500, awarded in alternate years for a historical biography by an Australian writer, and for contributions made by Jewish individuals or organisations to the Australian way of life. The 1992 award is for the former.

National Book Council/Qantas New Writers Award
One Qantas return airfare awarded annually to a writer under the age of 35 or for the first published book of a writer of any age.

Details from The Secretary, National Book Council, Suite 3, 21 Drummond Place, Carlton, Victoria 3053, Australia   *tel* (03) 663 8655   *fax* (03) 663 8658.

National Poetry Competition
Now established as the major annual poetry competition in Britain. Prizes of £2000, £1000, £500, five of £100, ten of £50. Entry fees of £4 for first poem and £3 each for subsequent entries, maximum entry of 15 poems, length of each poem not to exceed 40 lines. Details and entry forms from National Poetry Competition, National Poetry Centre, 21 Earls Court Square, London SW5 9DE.

Natural World Book of the Year Award
This £500 prize is awarded annually to the best book on British wildlife or the countryside by *Natural World*, the magazine of RSNC The Wildlife Trusts Partnership. Submissions must be made by 1 September, and books must have been published between 1 October of the previous year and 30 September of the year of the award. Details from Natural World Book of the Year Award, 20 Upper Ground, London SE1 9PF   *tel* 071-928 2111   *fax* 071-620 1594.

The NCR Book Award for Non Fiction
An annual award founded in 1987 and sponsored by NCR Limited to stimulate more interest in non-fiction writing and publishing in the UK. The award carries a prize of £25,000, currently the highest award available in the UK. Additionally, £1500 goes to the other three shortlisted authors. Applications welcomed from publishers. Details from The Administrator, NCR Book Award, 206 Marylebone Road, London NW1 6LY   *tel* 071-725 8271   *telex* 263931   *fax* 071-724 6519.

John Newbery Medal
This annual prize which was founded in 1922 is given for children's literature to a citizen or resident of the USA. The judges are 15 members of the Association for Library Service to Children (ALSC), a division of the American Library Association (committee members change annually) and the prize is given to the author of the most distinguished contribution to American literature for children published in the US during the preceding year. Further

details from ALSC, The American Library Association, 50 East Huron Street, Chicago, IL 60611, USA *tel* 312-280-2613   *fax* 312-280-3257.

The Nobel Prize
The Nobel Prize in Literature is one of the awards stipulated in the will of the late Alfred Nobel, the Swedish scientist who invented dynamite. The awarding authority is the Swedish Academy, Box 2118, S-10313 Stockholm, Sweden *tel* (08) 10-65-24   *fax* (08) 24-42-25. No direct application for a prize will, however, be taken into consideration. For authors writing in English it was bestowed upon Rudyard Kipling in 1907, W.B. Yeats in 1923, George Bernard Shaw in 1925, Sinclair Lewis in 1930, John Galsworthy in 1932, Eugene O'Neill in 1936, Pearl Buck in 1938, T.S. Eliot in 1948, William Faulkner in 1949, Bertrand Russell in 1950, Sir Winston Churchill in 1953, Ernest Hemingway in 1954, John Steinbeck in 1962, Samuel Beckett in 1969, Patrick White in 1973, Saul Bellow in 1976, William Golding in 1983, Wole Soyinka in 1986 and Joseph Brodsky in 1987. The Nobel Prizes are understood to be worth about £550,000 each. They number five: Physics, Chemistry, Physiology or Medicine, Literature, and Promotion of Peace.

The Noma Award for Publishing in Africa
Established in 1979, this annual book prize of $5000 is available to African writers and scholars whose work is published in Africa. The principal aim of the Award is to encourage publication of works by African writers and scholars in Africa. The prize is given to the author of an outstanding new book published (during the preceding twelve months) by a publisher domiciled on the African continent or its offshore islands, in any of these three categories: (1) scholarly or academic, (2) books for children, (3) literature and creative writing, including fiction, drama and poetry. Any original work in any of the indigenous or official languages of Africa is eligible for consideration. Full details from The African Book Publishing Record, PO Box 56, Oxford OX1 2SJ *tel* (0865) 511428 *telex* 94012872 Zell G   *fax* (0865) 793298.

Odd Fellows (Manchester Unity) Social Concern Annual Book Award
A prize worth £2000 is awarded for the book, or pamphlet of not less than 10,000 words, in an area of social concern (to be specified each year). Entries must be published in the current year; must be written by citizens of Britain, the Commonwealth, Republic of Ireland or South Africa; and must first have appeared in English. Entry forms are available from Book Trust, Book House, 45 East Hill, London SW18 2QZ *tel* 081-870 9055.

Oppenheim-John Downes Memorial Trust
Awards, varying from £50 to £1500 depending on need, from this Trust Fund are given each December to deserving artists of any kind including writers, musicians, artists who are unable through poverty to pursue their vocation effectively. Applicants must be over 30 years of age and of British birth. Full details and Application for an Award form from the Trust, c/o 36 Whitefriars Street, London EC4Y 8BH, enclosing sae.

Catherine Pakenham Memorial Award
Young women journalists (over 18 and under 25 years of age), resident in Britain, are eligible for this award which was founded in 1970 in memory of Lady Catherine Pakenham. The award of £1000 is given for a non-fiction article or TV or radio script, between 750 and 2000 words long. Entry forms, after 1 September, from: Jo Henwood, Marketing Dept, The Sunday Telegraph, 181 Marsh Wall, London E14 9SR *tel* 071-538 6966 *fax* 071-538 0366.

Peterloo Poets Open Poetry Competition
Founded in 1986 this annual competition sponsored by Marks & Spencer

offers for 1992 a first prize of £1000 and five other prizes totalling £1600. Closing date for entries is 1 February 1992. Full details and rules of entry from Peterloo Poets, 2 Kelly Gardens, Calstock, Cornwall PL18 9SA.

The Portico Prize
Founded in 1985, this annual prize of £1500 is awarded for a work of general interest and literary merit set wholly or mainly in the North West of England (Lancashire, Manchester, Liverpool, High Peak of Derbyshire, Cheshire and Cumbria). Information from the Portico Library, 57 Mosley Street, Manchester M2 3HY　*tel* 061-236 6785.

Radio Times Drama Awards
Founded in 1973 and now given biennially, these Awards, totalling at present £15,000, are given for an original play for radio and also for television. Last awarded 1990. Full details in *Radio Times* early 1992.

Radio Times Radio Comedy Awards
Founded in 1985 and now given biennially, these Awards, totalling at present £5000, are given for an original 30 minute radio comedy script with the potential to become a series. Last awarded 1991. Full details in *Radio Times* early 1993.

Trevor Reese Memorial Prize
Founded in 1979, a prize of £1000 is given every two years for an historical monograph on Imperial or Commonwealth history. Details from The Director, Institute of Commonwealth Studies, 27-28 Russell Square, London WC1B 5DS.

Rhyme International Annual Poetry Competition
The only international competition exclusively devoted to rhymed poetry, it was founded as Rhyme Revival in collaboration with Coventry Chamber of Commerce in 1981. Annual prizes average over £1000, divided into two classes, 'formal' and 'open'. Entry fee: £2.50 per poem; closing date: 30 September each year. Adjudication takes place during a special workshop weekend open to the public. Full details and entry forms from *Orbis Literary Magazine*, 199 The Long Shoot, Nuneaton, Warks. CV11 6JQ　*tel* (0203) 327440.

The Margaret Rhondda Award
This award, first made in July 1968 on the tenth anniversary of Lady Rhondda's death, and afterwards every three years, is given to a woman writer as a grant-in-aid towards the expenses of a research project in journalism. It is given to women journalists in recognition of the service which they give to the public through journalism. Closing date for next award 31 December 1992. Further details from The Society of Authors, 84 Drayton Gardens, London SW10 9SB.

The Rogers Prize
This prize of the value of £250 will be offered by the Senate, for an essay or dissertation on the subject of Advance in Surgery or Medicine. The Prize is open to all persons whose names appear on the Medical Register of the UK. The essay or dissertation must be submitted to the Secretary to the Scholarships Committee, University of London, Senate House, London WC1E 7HU (from whom further particulars may be obtained) not later than 30 June.

Romantic Novelists' Association Award
The annual award of £5000 (sponsored by Boots Company plc) for the best romantic novel of the year is open to non-members as well as members of the Romantic Novelists' Association. Novels must be published between 1 January and 31 December of year of entry. Three copies of the novel are required. The Netta Muskett Award is for unpublished writers in the romantic

novel field who must join the Association as probationary members. MSS entered for this award must be specially written for it. No Award will be made unless a MS is accepted for publication through the Association. Details from the Hon. Secretary, Marie Murray, 9 Hillside Road, Southport, Merseyside PR8 4QB   *tel* (0704) 60945.

The Rooney Prize for Irish Literature
The Rooney Prize was set up in 1976 to encourage young Irish writing talent. The sum of IR£3500 is awarded annually to a different individual, who must be Irish, published in either Irish or English and under 40 years of age. The prize is non-competitive and there is no application procedure or entry form. Information from J.A. Sherwin, Strathin, Templecarrig, Delgany, Co. Wicklow, Republic of Ireland   *tel* (01) 287 4769.

The Royal Society of Literature Award under the W.H. Heinemann Bequest
The purpose of this foundation is to encourage the production of literary works of real worth. The prize shall be deemed a reward for actual achievement. Works in any branch of literature may be submitted by their publishers to the verdict of the Royal Society of Literature which shall be final and without appeal. Prose fiction shall not be excluded from competition, but the Testator's intention is primarily to reward less remunerative classes of literature: poetry, criticism, biography, history, etc. Any work originally written in the English language shall be eligible. The recipient of a Prize shall not again be eligible for five years. Entries must be submitted by 31 October.

Runciman Award
Established in 1985 by the Anglo-Hellenic League for a literary work wholly, or mainly, about Greece. The £1000 prize is sponsored by the Onassis Foundation and to be eligible a work must be published in its first English edition in the UK. Details from c/o Nan White-Gaze, Flat 35, 67 Elm Park Gardens, London SW10 9QE.

The Ian St James Awards
These awards, founded in 1989, are made annually to twelve previously unpublished authors for short stories of between 5000 and 10,000 words (excluding children's stories). The fifty best writers will each receive a Parker Pen. The writers of the twelve best stories each receive £1000 and then the three best (announced in September) win an additional £1000 (3rd), £4000 (2nd) and £11,000 (1st). To be eligible writers must be 18 or over and resident in Great Britain or Ireland and must not have had fiction previously published in Great Britain or Ireland in book form. Entry forms are available only in all good bookshops between October and January. Further information from the Ian St James Awards, PO Box 1371, London W5 2PN.

The Schlegel-Tieck Prize
This prize was established in 1964 under the auspices of the Society of Authors and its Translators Association to be awarded annually for the best translation published by a British publisher during the previous year. Only translations of German twentieth-century works of literary merit and general interest will be considered. The work should be entered by the publisher and not the individual translator. Details may be obtained from the Secretary, The Translators Association, 84 Drayton Gardens, London SW10 9SB.

The Science Book Prizes
These prizes, established in 1987 by COPUS and the Science Museum and sponsored by Rhône-Poulenc Ltd, are awarded annually to the authors of popular, non-fiction, science and technology books written in English and published in the UK during the previous year that are judged to contribute most to the public understanding of science. The Rhône-Poulenc prize

(£10,000) is awarded for books with a general readership; the COPUS/ Science Museum prize (£10,000), also sponsored by Rhône-Poulenc, is divided between books for the under-14s, under-8s and other categories at the judges' discretion (e.g. for illustrations); publishers may enter up to five books for each prize. Entries may cover any aspect of science and technology, including biography and history, but books published as educational textbooks or for professional or specialist audiences are not eligible. The author of a prize-winning book will be ineligible for another Science Book Prize for three years following the Award. Details from COPUS, c/o The Royal Society, 6 Carlton House Terrace, London SW1Y 5AG   *tel* 071-839 5561   *fax* 071-930 2170.

The Scott Moncrieff Prize
This prize was established in 1964 under the auspices of the Society of Authors and its Translators Association to be awarded annually for the best translation published by a British publisher during the previous year. Only translations of French twentieth-century works of literary merit and general interest will be considered. The work should be entered by the publisher and not the individual translator. Details from the Secretary, The Translators Association, 84 Drayton Gardens, London SW10 9SB.

Scottish Arts Council Awards
A limited number of Book Awards, value £750 each, are made each year by the Scottish Arts Council to published books of literary merit written by Scots or writers resident in Scotland. These awards are for new writing as well as for work by established authors (applications from publishers). Writers' bursaries are awarded twice a year to writers resident in Scotland who display professional standing and a record of publication. Applications from writers should be supported by an appropriate reference. Details of both schemes from the Literature Department. The Scottish Arts Council, 12 Manor Place, Edinburgh EH3 7DD   *tel* 031-226 6051.

Shell Young Poet of the Year
An annual prize administered by The Poetry Society. It is open to writers up to and including 18 years of age for an unpublished collection of poetry; the prize for writers over 13 is £250 and for those under 13 £150. Entry details from The Poetry Society, 21 Earls Court Square, London SW5 9DE.

The Signal Poetry for Children Award
A prize of £100 is given annually for an outstanding book of poetry published for children in Britain and the Commonwealth during the previous year, whether single poet or anthology and regardless of country of original publication. Articles about the winning book are published in *Signal* each May. Not open to unpublished work. Further details from The Thimble Press, Lockwood, Station Road, South Woodchester, Stroud, Glos. GL5 5EQ.

The André Simon Memorial Fund Book Awards
Two prizes of £2000 each have been awarded annually since 1977 to the authors of a book on food and a book on drink respectively. Applications to Tessa Hayward, 61 Church Street, Isleworth, Middlesex TW7 6BE   *tel* 081-560 6662   *fax* 081-847 0660.

Smarties Prize
Established in 1985 to encourage high standards and stimulate interest in books for children of primary school age. Prizes of £1000 are awarded to each of three category winners, with a further £8000 to the overall winner. Eligible books must be published in the 12 months ending 31 October of the year of presentation and be written in English by a citizen of the UK, or an author resident in the UK, and published in the UK. The prize is sponsored by

Rowntree Mackintosh. Details from Book Trust, Book House, 45 East Hill, London SW18 2QZ   *tel* 081-870 9055.

The W.H. Smith Annual Literary Award

A prize of £10,000 is awarded annually to a Commonwealth author (including a citizen of the UK) whose book, written in English and published in the UK, within 12 months ending on 31 December preceding the date of the Award, in the opinion of the judges makes the most outstanding contribution to literature. Submissions are not accepted; the judges make their decision independently. Further details are available from W.H. Smith Group, Strand House, 7 Holbein Place, London SW1W 8NR   *tel* 071-730 1200 ext 5458.

W.H. Smith Illustration Awards

These annual awards are given to practising book and magazine illustrators, for work first published in Great Britain in the 12 months preceding the judging of the award. Book covers, illustrations of a purely technical nature and photographs together with works produced as limited editions are excluded. Cover illustrations to magazines are eligible. Enquiries to The National Art Library, Victoria and Albert Museum, South Kensington, London SW7 2RL, or Book Trust, Book House, 45 East Hill, Wandsworth, London SW18 2QZ   *tel* 081-870 9055.

South London Playwrights Festival

Established in 1985, an annual competition for full-length plays and/or playwrights with a South London connection. Entries by 31 July; winner given a professionally directed and acted rehearsed reading (many winners have been given a full production). Details from: Warehouse Theatre, Dingwall Road, Croydon, Surrey CR0 2NF   *tel* 081-681 1257.

Southern Arts Literature Prize

The £1000 prize is awarded annually on a rotating basis for a published novel, poetry collection, or work of literary non-fiction to writers living within the Southern Arts region. The 1992 award is for literary non-fiction. Closing date: end September. Details from The Literature Department, Southern Arts, 13 St Clements Street, Winchester, Hants SO23 9DQ   *tel* (0962) 855099.

Stand Magazine Short Story Competition

Founded in 1980, this biennial short story competition – prizes to the value of £2250 – is open to any writer for an original, untranslated story in English, not longer than 8000 words, not previously published, broadcast or under consideration elsewhere. Entry forms available only on receipt of an sae or International Reply Coupons. Further details from Stand Magazine, 179 Wingrove Road, Newcastle upon Tyne NE4 9DA   *tel* 091-273 3280.

Winifred Mary Stanford Prize

The prize was founded in 1977 by Mr Leonard Cutts in memory of his wife who died in 1976. The prize of £1000 is awarded biennially and is open to any book published in the UK in the English language which has been inspired in some way by the Christian faith, written by a man or woman 50 years of age or under at the date of publication. The subject of the book may be from a wide range, including poetry, fiction, biography, autobiography, biblical exposition, religious experience and witness. Books must have been published in the two years prior to the award which is made at Easter. Literary merit will be a prime factor in selection. Submission by publishers only to the Secretary to the Judges, Winifred Mary Stanford Prize, c/o Hodder & Stoughton, 47 Bedford Square, London WC1B 3DP   *tel* 071-636 9851.

Sunday Express Book of the Year Award

A prize of £20,000 is awarded annually to the author of an outstanding, new work of fiction, including short stories, which is first published in English in Britain. No entries are accepted from authors or publishers. Nominations are made by a panel. Details from the *Sunday Express*, 245 Blackfriars Road, London SE1 9UX.

E. Reginald Taylor Essay Competition

A prize of £100, in memory of E. Reginald Taylor, FSA, is awarded biennially for the best unpublished essay submitted during the year. The essay, not exceeding 7500 words, should show *original research* on a subject of archaeological, art-historical or antiquarian interest within the period from the Roman era to AD 1830. The successful competitor may be invited to read the essay before the Association and the essay may be published in the *Journal* of the Association if approved by the Editorial Committee.

Competitors are advised to notify the Hon. Editor in advance of the intended subject of their work. The next award will be made in May 1993 and the essay should be submitted not later than 31 October 1992 to the Hon. Editor, Dr Martin Henig, British Archaeological Association, Institute of Archaeology, 36 Beaumont Street, Oxford OX1 2PG.

Anne Tibble Poetry Competition

This annual prize is awarded for a poem, maximum length 20 lines, to anyone resident in Great Britain. The first prize is for £100; other prizes to a total value of £200. Further details from the Leisure Office, Leisure & Recreation Department, Cliftonville House, Bedford Road, Northampton NN4 0NW *tel* (0604) 34734 ext 4243.

Time-Life Silver Pen Award for Non-Fiction

This award of £1000 founded in 1969 and sponsored by *Time-Life* since 1986 is given annually for an outstanding work of non-fiction written in English and published during the previous year by an author of British nationality. Books are nominated by members of the P.E.N. Executive Committee. Information from P.E.N., 7 Dilke Street, Chelsea, London SW3 4JE   *tel* 071-352 6303   *fax* 071-351 0220.

The Times Educational Supplement Information Book Awards

There are two annual awards of £500 to the authors of the best information books – one for children up to the age of 9, the other for children aged 10-16. The books must be published in Britain or the Commonwealth. Details from the Times Educational Supplement, Priory House, St John's Lane, London EC1M 4BX   *tel* 071-253 3000   *fax* 071-608 1599.

The Times Educational Supplement Schoolbook Award

£500 is given for the best school textbook. The age range and subject area vary from year to year. Details from the Times Educational Supplement, Priory House, St John's Lane, London EC1M 4BX   *tel* 071-253 3000   *fax* 071-608 1599.

Tir Na N-og Awards

Three annual awards to children's authors and illustrators, founded in 1976. (1) Best Welsh fiction, including short stories and picture books; (2) best Welsh non-fiction book of the year; (3) best English book with an authentic Welsh background. Total value of prize £500. Details from: Welsh Books Council, Castell Brychan, Aberystwyth, Dyfed SY23 2JB   *tel* (0970) 624151 *fax* (0970) 625385.

The Tom-Gallon Trust

This Trust was founded by the late Miss Nellie Tom-Gallon and is administered by the Society of Authors. An award is made biennially from this Fund to fiction writers of limited means who have had at least one short story accepted for publication. An award of £500 will be made in 1991. Authors wishing to enter should send to the Secretary, Society of Authors, 84 Drayton Gardens, SW10 9SB: (1) a list of their already published fiction, giving the name of the publisher or periodical in each case and the approximate date of publication; (2) one published short story; (3) a brief statement of their financial position; (4) an undertaking that they intend to devote a substantial amount of time to the writing of fiction as soon as they are financially able to do so; (5) a stamped addressed envelope for the return of the work submitted. Closing date for next award 20 September 1992.

The Betty Trask Awards
The Betty Trask Awards are for the benefit of young authors under 35 and are given on the strength of a first novel (published or unpublished) of a romantic or traditional, rather than experimental, nature. They stem from a generous bequest by Miss Betty Trask (who died in 1983) and are administered by the Society of Authors. It is expected that prizes totalling at least £25,000 will be presented each year. The winners are required to use the money for a period or periods of foreign travel. Full details of the conditions of entry can be obtained from the Society of Authors, 84 Drayton Gardens, London SW10 9SB.

The Travelling Scholarship
This is a non-competitive award, for which submissions are not required (see article: **The Society of Authors**).

The Dorothy Tutin Award
This award of a suitably inscribed carriage clock was founded in 1980, and is given to the person who it is felt has done the most to encourage the writing and love of poetry throughout the UK each year. Details from The National Poetry Foundation, 27 Mill Road, Fareham, Hants PO16 0TH   *tel* (0329) 822218.

UEA Writing Fellowship
Funded by the University and by Eastern Arts, this Fellowship is offered annually, to be held in the School of English and American Studies at the University of East Anglia for the Summer Term.
The duties of the Fellowship will be discussed at interview. It will be assumed that one activity will be the pursuit of the Fellow's own writing. In addition, the Fellow will be expected to take part in some of the following activities: (a) contributing to the teaching of a formal course in creative writing; (b) running a regular writers' workshop on an informal extra-curricular basis; (c) being available for a specified period each week to advise individual students engaged in writing; (d) giving an introductory lecture or reading at the beginning of the Fellowship; (e) organising one or two literary events involving other writers invited from outside the University; (f) making some contribution to the cultural and artistic life of the region (by, for instance, a public lecture or reading). The salary for the Fellowship will be £2500 plus free flat. Applications for the Fellowship should be lodged with the Administrative Secretary, University of East Anglia, Norwich NR4 7TJ by 1 October of each year.

'Charles Veillon' European Essay Prize
Launched in 1975, a prize of 20,000 Swiss francs is awarded annually to a European writer or essayist for essays offering a critical look at modern society's way of life and ideology. Details from: The Secretary, Charles Veillon Foundation, CH 1017 Lausanne, Switzerland   *tel* (021) 702 29 11.

Wandsworth London Writers Competition
The competition is open to writers of 16 years and over who live, work or

study in the Greater London Area. Awards are made annually in three classes, Poetry, Short Story and Play, the prizes totalling £775 in each class. Entries must be previously unpublished work. The award is sponsored by London Arts Board, and the judging is under the chairmanship of Martyn Goff, former Chief Executive of Book Trust. Further details from Assistant Director of Leisure and Amenity Services (Libraries, Museum and Arts), Wandsworth Town Hall, High Street, London SW18 2PU   *tel* 081-871 7037.

The David Watt Memorial Prize
This £2000 prize, introduced in 1988 and organised, funded and administered by Rio Tinto Zinc, is awarded for outstanding written contributions towards the greater understanding of international and political issues. Those eligible for the prize are writers actively engaged in writing for newspapers and journals in the English language. Entries should comprise an article in English of not more than 10,000 words. The closing date for entries and nominations is mid-March each year. Full details and entry forms are available from The Administrator, The David Watt Memorial Prize, RTZ Limited, 6 St James's Square, London SW1Y 4LD.

The Welsh Arts Council's Awards to Writers
Prizes of £1000 each are awarded to the authors of books published during the previous calendar year which, in the Literature Committee's opinion, are of exceptional literary merit. Bursaries totalling £43,000 are awarded annually to authors writing in both Welsh and English. The Council also organises competitions from time to time. For further details of the Welsh Arts Council's policies, write to the Literature Department, Welsh Arts Council, Museum Place, Cardiff CF1 3NX   *tel* (0222) 394711   *fax* (0222) 221447.

The Wheatland Translation Fund
Established in 1987 by Ann Getty and George Weidenfeld, the Wheatland Translation Fund promotes international literary exchange through grants for the translation of works of literature. Grants are given to American and English publishers to help defray the costs of translating works of fiction or in the humanities from any language into English; grants generally range from $1000 to $3000. Priority is given to works of fiction and poetry by contemporary authors. Applications must be submitted by publishers. The Wheatland Foundation, 841 Broadway, New York, NY 10003-4793, USA   *tel* 212-614-7900.

Whitbread Literary Awards
Awards to be judged in two stages and offering a total of £30,500 prize money open to five categories: Novel, First Novel, Children's Novel, Biography/Autobiography, Poetry. The winner in each category will receive a Whitbread Nomination Award of £2000. The five nominations will go forward to be judged for the Whitbread Book of the Year. The overall winner receives £22,000 (£20,500 plus £2000 Nomination Award). Writers must have lived in Great Britain and Ireland for three or more years. Submissions only from publishers. Closing date for entries: 26 July. Further details may be obtained from The Booksellers Association, Minster House, 272 Vauxhall Bridge Road, London SW1V 1BA   *tel* 071-834 5477.

The Whitfield Prize
The Whitfield Prize (value £1000) is announced in July each year for the best work on a subject within a field of British history. It must be its author's first solely-written history book, an original and scholarly work of historical research and have been published in the UK in the preceding calendar year. Three non-returnable copies of a book eligible for the competition should be submitted by the author or the publisher before 31 December to the Executive

Secretary, Royal Historical Society, University College London, Gower Street, London WC1E 6BT   *tel* 071-387 7532.

John Whiting Award
Founded in 1965, this prize of £4000 is given annually. Eligible to apply are any writers who have received during the previous two calendar years an award through the Arts Council new theatre writing schemes, or who have had a premier production by a theatre company in receipt of an annual subsidy. Details from the Drama Director, Arts Council of Great Britain, 14 Great Peter Street, London SW1P 3NQ   *tel* 071-333 0100.

Wolfson Literary Awards for History
The awards were established in 1972 to pay tribute to a lifetime's contributions to the study of history and also to encourage the writing of scholarly history for the general public. No application is necessary, but further details from M. Paisner, Messrs. Paisner & Co., Bouverie House, 154 Fleet Street, London EC4 2DQ.

Yorkshire Post Literary Awards
A prize of £1200 is awarded for the Book of the Year and a prize of £1000 for the Best First Work each year. Also annual awards of £1000 each are made for works which in the opinion of the Panel of Judges have made the greatest contribution to the understanding and appreciation of Music and Art. Nominations are only accepted from publishers and should arrive (together with one copy of the book) by 15 December in the case of main prizes, by 16 January in the case of the Art and Music Awards. Correspondence to Secretary of the Book Awards, Yorkshire Post Newspapers Ltd, PO Box 168, Wellington Street, Leeds LS1 1RF   *tel* (0532) 432701 ext 1512.

Index

paperbacks, fastsellers 213-19
Password Distribution Service 237
payment for contributions 3-4, 233, 259-60
Payne, Margaret
  on books, research and reference sources 438-44
P.E.N. International 539
pension contributions 368-9
pensions 386-8
  from Society of Authors 553
  from Writers' Guild 556
Performing Right Society 323, 418, 540
philately magazines 116
philosophy magazines 117
photocopying 238, 426
  Copyright Licensing Agency 427-30
photographers, freelance 288-92, 313-14
photographic agencies and picture libraries 293-312
photographs
  copyright of 319
  loss or damage of 289, 292, 319
  markets for 313-14
  presentation of 288-92
photography, markets for 313-14
photography magazines 116
picture libraries 288-90, 293-312, 315-20
  how to run 289-90
picture research 315-22
Picture Researchers and Editors, Society of 321-2, 548
plays
  agents 276
  for films 248, 274-5, 463-5
  manuscript preparation 463-5
  marketing 246-56
  publishers of 255-6
  radio 248, 258, 259
  for television 248, 258, 259, 466-8
playwrights' contracts 246-9, 259-60
Poems on the Underground 241
poetry
  competitions 240-1, 576
  how to submit 232-4
  magazines 232-5
  markets for 231-45, 284-7

poetry (continued)
  prizes see literary prizes and awards
  publishing today 231-45
  workshops 242
Poetry Book Society 243
Poetry Ireland 244
Poetry Library 234, 237, 242, 243
Poetry Review 233, 236
Poetry Society, The 234, 236, 240, 241, 244, 540
police magazines 114
political magazines 116
Portugal
  literary agents 356
postage 4, 102, 103, 128, 233-4, 459
PostScript 479
preparation of typescript 233, 457-62, 463-5, 467, 480-90
press agencies 121-7
press-cutting agencies
  overseas 505-6
  UK 505
  USA 506
presses, small 128, 227, 229, 234, 236
print, photographs for 290-2
printing and publishing magazines 111
prizes and awards, literary 560-85
production services 491-502
profit sharing and commission agreements 432
proof correcting 461, 480-90
proofs, stages of 461
provincial theatres 252-4
Public Lending Right 419-26, 504, 537
  Act 419
  authorship 420
  illustrators and 420
  ISBNs 420, 429, 436-7
  payments 419, 423
  sampling 419-20, 422
  Writers' Guild and 105, 557
public libraries
  most borrowed authors 423-4
  services of 439, 441
Public Order Act 1986 415
public services, Government offices and 507-14